HUMAN ARRANGEMENTS

AN INTRODUCTION TO SOCIOLOGY ▣ THIRD EDITION

HUMAN ARRANGEMENTS

AN INTRODUCTION TO SOCIOLOGY ◧ THIRD EDITION

Allan G. Johnson

Under the General Editorship of
Robert K. Merton
Columbia University

HARCOURT BRACE JOVANOVICH COLLEGE PUBLISHERS
Fort Worth • Philadelphia • San Diego • New York • Orlando • Austin • San Antonio
Toronto • Montreal • London • Sydney • Tokyo

Acquisitions Editor: Rick Roehrich
Manuscript Editor: David Watt
Production Editor: Judi McClellan
Designer: Don Fujimoto
Art Editor: Rebecca Lytle
Production Manager: Diane Southworth

Requests for permission to make copies of any part of the
work should be mailed to: Permissions Department, Harcourt
Brace Jovanovich, Inc., 8th Floor, Orlando, Florida 32887.

ISBN: 0-15-539777-X

Library of Congress Catalog Card Number: 91-70585

Printed in the United States of America

PREFACE

TO STUDENTS

Like many others, I spent much of my undergraduate career trying to discover what I wanted to do with my life. Although I changed majors several times, I always knew that whatever field I entered would have to appeal to several important sides of me. It would have to be challenging and interesting; it would have to stimulate and increase my ability to understand how things work, to see the ways in which things that appear unconnected are in fact connected and affect one another. Perhaps most important, it would have to touch my desire to understand not only my own life, but the lives of other people in relation to one another. As a sociologist, I have been able to do all of these things, not simply to make a living, but to live with far more awareness and understanding than I would have otherwise had.

As a writer, I hope you will enjoy what you read, that the care with which I have tried to shape ideas and experience will come across clearly and draw you in as an active reader; and I hope that the examples and analyses of social life will give you reason to stop and reflect on your own life and the circumstances in which you live it.

As a teacher, I hope you will *use* this book as well as read and enjoy it, that you will learn from it and thereby acquire some of the ability to use sociology that has made it such a satisfying part of my life and the lives of other sociologists. This textbook is intended to be worked with, studied, pondered, and, at times, struggled with. It will challenge you to look at the world from what will probably be a very new perspective; to turn the world upside down at times if for no other reason than to get a clearer understanding of what right side up is all about.

Several features of the book were designed to make it more useful to you. Each chapter begins with a detailed chapter outline and ends with a summary of major points, a list of key terms, and recommended readings. I suggest you begin each chapter by studying the outline and the summary in order to gain an overall sense of what the chapter is about and how it is put together. Each of the key terms is followed by a page number indicating where the term was first introduced and discussed. Together, the chapter outline, summary, and list of terms provide an approach to organizing study and review. Also note that at the end of each chapter there is "Looking Elsewhere," a reference to related discussions in other chapters of *Human Arrangements*. As you will learn, social life is so inherently complex that it is impossible to discuss one area without touching on others. These cross-references will help you to get a clearer grasp of the interconnectedness of different areas of sociological analysis.

You may find several sections at the end of the book useful. The glossary, like the lists of key terms, refers you to the page where each term was first introduced and discussed. The glossary will be particularly helpful when, in later chapters, you encounter key terms first introduced early in the book. Use the glossary to refresh your understanding and, if necessary, use the page reference to go back for a fuller explanation. If a term paper is part of the requirements for your course, be sure to read Appendix A.

If your copy of *Human Arrangements* came with the pamphlet, *Getting the Most from Human Arrangements*, by Professor Patti Said I urge you to pay careful attention to it. I have noticed that my students who follow Professor Said's advice greatly improve both the quality of their learning experience and their performance on exams and papers. Like any new way of doing things, it will take some time to get used to it; but once you get the hang of it, this approach lets you make far more efficient use of your time. It works!

One final note. I wrote this book for you, and I would like to hear from you, especially if you have suggestions for making this book more useful. Please feel free to write to me at Harcourt Brace Jovanovich, Inc., 301 Commerce Street, Ft. Worth, TX 76102. I will be pleased to respond.

TO INSTRUCTORS

At the first meeting of an undergraduate sociology course, I once asked students to write a short paragraph describing sociology as a discipline. Most of them had completed more than an introductory course, and I wanted some idea of who I would be working with. I was startled to discover that none could produce a short, workable definition.

I suspect many students leave introductory courses with a lot of facts and terms but with a fuzzy understanding of what it means to observe, explain, and understand anything in a sociological way. They lack a clear sense that no matter what we look at, there is a clear framework for identifying what makes an issue sociological. Without that sense, there is little hope that students will ever grasp the importance of sociological thinking.

To resolve this problem I have tried to write a book that makes sense on every level—from phrase and sentence to the ordering of chapters—and that represents sociology as a coherent, integrated conceptual and theoretical framework. I begin with a conceptual framework—culture, social structure, population, and ecology—which I then weave through the book. Within this conceptual framework there are, of course, many theoretical elements—from the conflict, functional, and interactionist perspectives to such specific theories as political process theory in the study of social movements, exchange theory in the study of social interaction, labeling theory in the study of deviance, and world systems theory in the study of international stratification. All of these, however, touch in some way on basic core concepts that provide a common sociological ground.

The inclusion of population and ecology in the conceptual framework rather than relegating them to the end of the book where they are often found is unusual in sociology texts, but it serves an important purpose. Because even the smallest and simplest so-

cial system has population and ecological characteristics, a textbook should at least provide the option of integrating these concepts into the field's conceptual core. It is something you can forgo. Some instructors skip Chapter 4 and address students' questions about the population/ecology sections of later chapters as they occur without much trouble. Others use only selected portions of Chapter 4 (skipping, for example, discussions of birth, mortality, migration, and the demographic transition) and focus on the general concepts of population and ecology as they relate to social systems, including various types of societies (horticultural, agrarian, industrial, and so on). In short, *Human Arrangements* encourages but does not require extensive discussion of population and ecological characteristics of social systems.

The book is divided into six parts; Part One introduces the basic conceptual framework of culture, social structure, population, and ecology. Part Two focuses on theory and theoretical perspectives and research methods. (For more on the theory chapter, see the next section, "What's New in the Third Edition.") The remaining parts apply the sociological perspective systematically to increasingly large levels of analysis. Part Three, for example, moves from relatively small-scale, simple processes such as socialization to more complex, large-scale phenomena such as communities. Parts Four and Five focus on social inequality and social institutions; and Part Six contains discussions of collective behavior and social change. Instructors should probably begin with Part One, but beyond that, the remaining chapters can be assigned in any order that best fits the classroom needs.

It is in the internal organization of chapters that my approach to sociology is most apparent. Many chapters are organized around the central sociological concepts introduced in Part One and around the major theoretical perspectives so that students can develop a sense of sociology as a coherent framework applicable to any aspect of social life. The core of these chapters is devoted to culture and social structure, with less extensive discussions of population and ecology.

There are a number of features in this book that have been designed to make the introductory course both more rewarding and easier for teachers and students. There is extensive use of data in figures and tables, for example, including "One Step Further" boxes that expand upon points raised in the text.

Most of these draw on recent General Social Survey data and all use nothing more sophisticated than percentages and straightforward graphics. I intend them to be engaging but unintimidating ways of bringing students closer to the kinds of data sociologists use.

A glossary includes page references to major discussions of each entry, and an author index allows students to locate each citation of an author's work. There are two appendices, one dealing with student research projects and another offering a simple guide to the logic behind statistical inference. Each chapter ends with a summary, a list of recommended readings, key terms with page references, and a "Looking Elsewhere" section that provides cross-references to related discussions in other chapters. All of this helps underscore the interrelatedness of the phenomena sociologists study.

A thoroughly revised *Study Guide* will accompany this edition, as will a *Testbook* and an *Instructor's Manual*. The *Testbook* (available in print and on disk) has been prepared by William Snizek, an experienced test question author from Virginia Polytechnic Institute and State University. The *Instructor's Manual* by William Sweeney of Modesto Junior College includes chapter overviews and outlines, suggested student projects, and current audio-visual sources, as well as the most recent Data Set tables and graphs. All of the ancillaries have been completely revised for this edition.

WHAT'S NEW IN THE THIRD EDITION

The Third Edition brings a major change that, when it first occurred to me, seemed so obvious that I could only wonder why I had not seen it long ago. Instead of the daunting prospect of understanding sociological theory right away in Chapter 1 followed immediately by the equally daunting subject of research methods in Chapter 2, I have written a new chapter on theory and grouped it with the research methods chapter *after* Part One. This eases students into sociology in a more appealing way and gives theory the attention it deserves, especially when trying to make it comprehensible to undergraduates who may never have encountered sociology before. This change will smooth the flow from the first chapter into the sociological framework and, for instructors who want to cover theory, provide a much richer resource.

In this edition I also rely more heavily on the social system as a unit of analysis. Although the concept of social systems has been associated with the functional perspective, its use here does not indicate a functional approach to sociology—as anyone who reads the chapters on stratification, race and ethnicity, gender, and economic institutions will see. In previous editions I used the idea of a social environment; I now believe that the concept of a social system provides a clearer, more precise focus. I think your students will find—as mine have—that giving social systems a central place in sociological thinking is very useful, regardless of which theoretical perspective we use.

Like its predecessor, this edition has been thoroughly updated and revised in light of comments from instructors and students. This is especially true of Chapters 1 and 3. Chapter 1 has expanded sections on the concept of a social system and the kinds of questions sociologists ask about social behavior and social life. In Chapter 3, ("Social Structure"), technical material has been cut considerably and, where appropriate, relocated to later chapters. The result is a cleaner, more manageable introduction to this crucial concept.

You will also notice that the interactionist perspective has a more visible and prominent place in the new organization of chapters, providing a better balance with the conflict and functional approaches. In addition, I have reorganized the closing pair of chapters by devoting an entire chapter to collective behavior and integrating social movements into the social change chapter.

Throughout the writing and revision of *Human Arrangements* I have worked from a long-standing conviction as a teacher that instructors should not have to choose between being understood by our students on the one hand and exposing them to the richness of sociological thinking on the other. I have tried to write a book that gives students both sociological literacy and a critical sense of sociological ideas and analysis—the heart of sociology. This is, then, more than anything a book to help students observe and think about the world. To do that, of course, students need to know something about the technical language we use to label what we observe. From this perspective, I have tried to give instructors and students the best of both worlds—a clear text that is relatively easy to teach and learn from, and a book that students actually will want to read.

ACKNOWLEDGMENTS

One of the attractions of revising *Human Arrangements* is that it gives me another opportunity to work with the fine editorial and production staff at Harcourt Brace Jovanovich. As advisory editor for sociology, Robert K. Merton played a crucial role in my working through the many drafts that resulted in the new theory chapter. My manuscript editor, David Watt, has been, once again, a delight to work with, lending to the task his sharp ear for clear and effective prose, his wit and good humor, and his steady attention to the mountain of details that would overwhelm a lesser being.

My thanks also go to Judi McClellan, production editor, and Diane Southworth, production manager, for overseeing with such effectiveness the difficult process of guiding the book into print; to Rebecca Lytle for one of the best collections of photos I have ever seen in a textbook; to Don Fujimoto for his bold, sophisticated design; to Florence Kawahara for her ability to transform data into clear and appealing graphics; and to Barry Age whose clean, balanced page layouts smoothly integrate the text with all the diverse elements that go with it.

Many of my colleagues have helped by sharing their critical insights as reviewers for all three editions (their names appear in the separate acknowledgments list). I appreciate their many suggestions that have gone into this work. I also want to express appreciation to James A. Davis and Tom W. Smith—co-principal investigators of the University of Chicago's National Opinion Research Center—whose General Social Survey continues to provide sociologists with high quality data at minimal expense. My appreciation also goes to the Roper Public Opinion Center, Storrs, Connecticut, for their assistance in providing codebooks and other information relevant to the General Social Survey. All tables using these data were created with MicroCase software produced by Cognitive Development, Inc., Seattle, Washington.

Every three years, the writing of the closing sentences of the preface to this book has become an occasion to remind me of where my work as a sociologist and writer has brought me and of the people whose importance in my life inevitably affects that work. I am especially mindful these days of my students at Hartford College for Women, whose dedication to the struggles of learning and growing have both challenged me as a teacher and writer and touched me deeply as a human being; my friend, Brent Harold, who shares a love of language, writing, and ideas; my parents, who did more than they will ever know to plant and nurture the seeds of the thinker and writer I was to become; my children, who through the seven-day workweeks of producing a new edition remind me from time to time of what's really important; and my partner and deepest friend, Nora Jamieson, who has done so much to make this a life I would trade for none other, a life from which this book continues to flow.

ALLAN G. JOHNSON

ACKNOWLEDGMENTS

John W. Bardo, Southwest Texas State University

Julie Brown, University of North Carolina, Greensboro

Diane M. Bush, Colorado State University

Craign Calhoun, University of North Carolina, Chapel Hill

Henry Camp, Kansas State University

J. Stephen Cleghorn, Emory University

Mary Ruth Clowdsley, Tidewater Community College

Albin J. Cofone, Suffolk Community College

Henry Comby, Tulsa Junior College

Nick Costa, Greater Hartford Community College

John Crowley, Manchester Community College

Clark A. Davis, California State University, Chico

Carolyn Ellis, University of South Florida

Charles F. Emmons, Gettysburg College

Robert Freymeyer, Presbyterian College

T. Neal Garland, University of Akron

Avrama Gingold, Intermarket Research, Inc. and The Academic Factor

Vaughn Grisham, University of Mississippi

Leon Grunberg, The University of Puget Sound

Gerard Grzyb, University of Wisconsin, Oshkosh

B. G. Gunter, University of South Florida

Patricia Gwartney-Gibbs, University of Oregon

Harry Hale, Jr., Northeast Louisiana University

Kelley Hancock, Portland State University

Allen C. Haney, University of Houston

Jeremy Hein, University of Wisconsin—Eau Clare

Charles Henderson, Memphis State University

Donald W. Hinrichs, Gettysburg College

Walter Hirsch, Purdue University

Eric O. Hoiberg, Iowa State University

Joan Huber, Ohio State University

Rose Jensen, Lander College

Sidney J. Kaplan, University of Toledo

Will C. Kennedy, San Diego State University

Sally B. Kilgore, Emory University

Thomas Koenig, Northeastern University

Joel Lapin, Cantonsville Community College

Charles Levenstein, University of Lowell

Robert C. Liebman, Portland State University

George Lowe, Texas Tech University

Gary Madsen, Utah State University

John Markoff, University of Pittsburgh

Stephen L. Markson, University of Hartford

Anselyn Marshall, San Antonio College

Joseph A. McFalls, Temple University

Robert McLaren, Portland Community College

Scott G. McNall, University of Kansas

Bernard N. Meltzer, Central Michigan University

Eleanor M. Miller, University of Wisconsin, Milwaukee

Harvey Molotch, University of California, Santa Barbara

Harlan L. Mueller, College of DuPage

Charles Nam, Florida State University

Pamela Oliver, University of Wisconsin, Madison

Fernando Parra, California State Polytechnic University, Pomona

Anne K. Peters, California State University, Dominguez Hills

Donald R. Ploch, University of Tennessee, Knoxville

Jeffrey P. Rosenfeld, Nassau Community College

Martin Scheffer, Boise State University

Eugen Schoenfeld, Georgia State University

Arnold R. Silverman, Nassau Community College

Randall Stokes, University of Massachusetts

Ann Sundgren, Tacoma Community College

Joseph B. Tamney, Ball State University
Edgar Webster, Oklahoma State University
Blane Weller, Baker College
Ronald T. Wohlstein, Eastern Illinois University
Charlotte Wolf, Memphis State University
Gary Wyatt, Emporia State University
Thomas J. Yacovone, Los Angeles Valley College
John Zipp, University of Wisconsin, Milwaukee

CONTENTS

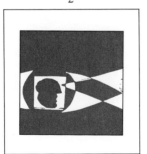

PART TWO

SOCIOLOGICAL WORK: THEORY AND RESEARCH

90

PART THREE
SOCIAL ORGANIZATION
132

PART FOUR
SOCIAL STRATIFICATION
264

14

GENDER INEQUALITY

15

AGE STRATIFICATION

PART FIVE
SOCIAL INSTITUTIONS
382

18

SCIENCE, TECHNOLOGY, AND MEDICINE 442

19

ECONOMIC ARRANGEMENTS 468

20

POLITICAL INSTITUTIONS 500

21

RELIGIOUS INSTITUTIONS

PART SIX

SOCIAL CHANGE
552

PART ONE

WHAT SOCIOLOGY
IS ALL ABOUT:
A CONCEPTUAL FRAMEWORK

We are surrounded by all kinds of arrangements. Wherever you happen to be sitting right now, look around you and you will find that everything can be looked at in terms of its relation to other things. The room you are sitting in differs from other rooms, not only by what is in it, but by how things are arranged (try moving about with your eyes closed and you will see what I mean). This book is at its simplest a collection of electrons, atoms, and molecules that are arranged in such a way as to produce paper, ink, and color. The most important arrangement in this book, however, consists of words arranged into sentences, and the most important thing about them is that you understand them and they are thus the link in the arrangement between you the reader and me the author.

Sociologists, physicists, biologists, psychologists, economists, historians, literary scholars—all are interested in arrangements, whether it be the meter and rhyme in a poem, the structure of an atom, or what goes on among human beings. This book is about sociology, the study of the arrangements through which people know, share, and affect one another's lives.

Sociologists focus on three basic types of arrangements: the arrangement of words and ideas (culture) that we use to make sense of one another and our surroundings; the arrangement of social relationships (social structure) such as those that link authors and readers, parents and children, lovers, enemies, rich and poor, powerful and weak; and the arrangement of people in physical space (ecology), from how the placement of furniture can affect who emerges as a group's leader to the differences between life in large, populous cities and life in small, rural villages.

Part One introduces you to sociology as a perspective from which we look at the world and ask questions about it.

1
A FIRST LOOK AT SOCIOLOGY

 This is not an easy world to live in, much less to understand. There probably has never been a time in human history with such widespread day-to-day awareness of the crises and problems that arise from social life. From the news to films to life in our neighborhoods there is no escaping at least some sense that the world is huge and interconnected and a place of much trouble. In the U.S. alone, we have seen homelessness of unprecedented proportions, a full-fledged AIDS epidemic, the increasing poisoning of ground, air, and water with garbage and toxic wastes, mismanagement and criminal misconduct in the savings and loan industry that will cost generations of taxpayers hundreds of billions of dollars, a worsening economy, a widening gap between rich and poor, and continuing evidence that there has been little progress towards racial or gender equality in spite of decades of social activism. To these we must add problems that extend beyond our borders, from the international drug trade, apartheid in South Africa, and the brutal crushing of the pro-democracy movement in China to a world economy destabilized. Most recently, following quickly on the heels of the breathtaking shifts towards democracy in Central Europe and the reunification of Germany, much of the industrialized world was plunged into panic by Iraq's invasion of Kuwait, and the ensuing war between Iraq and the U.S. and its allies.

In the face of all this, it is understandable that many people do not even try to make sense of it. It is a world that was already here when we were born into it; a world we did not make, and, which we often think, we cannot change. The world is enormously complex and seems to change faster than we can grasp a piece of it. For all our collective awareness of the events and problems of our times, we really do not know what to do with it, except, perhaps, to attribute the problems in some vague way to society or the flawed personalities of people in general or our leaders in particular. In the end, it often seems easier if we do not read the newspapers, if we turn off the news, and try to go about our personal lives.

Our personal lives, though, are no less complicated. In the midst of all the world's problems we wrestle with what we tend to think of as personal troubles—of how we appear to other people, of being accepted, liked, and loved; of having our sexuality without giving up safety; of figuring out who we are and reconciling that with who we want to be; of getting along with (and without) our parents; of earning a living, of deciding whether to marry, to have children, or to divorce.

What we tend to miss is the fact that our personal lives are not truly personal. We are not alone in our troubles, which is precisely the point of this book: everything *is* connected to everything else, and we are inevitably a part of that. We all participate in a social environment that presents us with both the troubles we must struggle with and the resources that are available to us. Each of us has characteristics of gender, race, age, religion, ethnicity, and social class in a society in which these matter a great deal in what happens to us. Our emotional needs are strongly influenced by the social relationships we participate in. The conditions under which we can earn a living depend on the fact that we live in an industrial capitalist society. The food we eat, the water we drink, the clothes we wear, the books we read, the toxic chemicals that make their way into our bodies—all depend on the social environment we live in. Virtually every aspect of our lives connects us to a larger world that most of us barely begin to understand.

Although none of us made this world, as participants in it, we do affect it. The social world is not frozen; it is a process of continual making and remaking in which we take part; and we choose to participate in that process with as much awareness and understanding of it as we can achieve. At the very least it makes life more interesting and meaningful, for by appreciating the complexity of the world and our connections to it, we also appreciate the richness of our own lives. At the most, this commitment can help change the world itself, including the terms by which we live.

The purpose of this book is quite simple: to offer you the sociological framework as a set of tools for making sense of the social world and understanding your own life by seeing more clearly its connection with the lives of others in a shared social environment.

SOCIOLOGY AND SOCIAL SYSTEMS

Sociology is the systematic study of social life and behavior, especially in relation to social systems—how they work, how they change, the consequences they produce, and their complex relation to people's lives. The concept of a system is widely used in the physical and social sciences as well as in such diverse fields as philosophy and linguistics. In general, a system is a set of elements or parts related to one another through some kind of interdependency, and can be thought of as a whole. Biologists, for example, think in terms of living organisms as systems consisting of interrelated parts, such as the circulatory, nervous, and digestive systems. Philosophers speak of systems of thought, and linguists speak of language as a system whose elements—words—are linked by rules of syntax and grammar.

A **social system** is also a set of relationships that can be thought of as a whole. It can be as large and complex as a society or as small and relatively simple as a married couple. The parts that comprise social systems are of many different types. They include the positions that people occupy in social relationships: in many societies, for example, a marriage consists of a wife and husband, while in others it may include multiple husbands or wives. On a larger scale, an army's elements range from the positions soldiers occupy with their different ranks and duties to collections of soldiers such as platoons and battalions. Elements larger than individuals—such as companies—can be thought of as social systems connected to still larger units such as divisions of multilevel corporations.

Social systems also include elements as varied as language, beliefs, values, laws, and other rules of behavior; music, art, dance, poetry, drama, literature, and other forms of knowledge; and physical products such as houses, computers, and the paper on which these words are printed. As a social system, for example, a university includes teachers, students, and administrators. It also includes, however, less tangible elements, such as ideas about the value of higher education, the different ways of discovering truth, and the right of people to express unpopular opinions. It includes physical elements such as libraries, laboratories, dorms, classrooms, theaters, and athletic facilities. All of these are part of what we think of as a university.

There is much more to a social system than a collection of parts, however, for the parts are connected to one another through interdependency. In the simplest sense, for example, the social positions we occupy are interdependent—each exists only in relation to the other. There is no mother without a child, just as there is no teacher without a student. In a more complex sense, positions within social systems are related through the expectations and ideas attached to them. The expectation that spouses will have sex only with each other, for example, is not simply an idea shared by two people. Sociologically it is part of what connects wife and husband as positions in the social system known as marriage.

The basic characteristics of social systems apply no matter how large or small, simple or complex, the system is. The world economy, for example, is about as unlike a marriage as one can imagine, but it too is a social system whose elements include corporations, nations, and international arrangements such as the European Community. These in turn are connected to one another through relationships involving trade, investment, political cooperation and conflict, and inequalities of wealth and power. At the heart of these relationships are expectations such as those embodied in international law and trade agreements, as well as ideas about what a contract is and the rights to own property and make a profit.

In using the concept of a social system, remember that social life takes place in a far less rigid, organized, and predictable way than the word "system" might imply. Social systems, for example, are not like biological organisms whose parts work together smoothly and harmoniously in the interests of furthering the life of the organism as a whole. Although there is a degree of harmony, cooperation, and common purpose in social systems, there also can be conflict among the various parts. Exploitation and oppression, war, revolution, jealousy, greed, revenge, fear, and competition are easy to find in social systems; but there is nothing that corresponds to these in other kinds of systems, such as the human body, the internal combustion engine, or a language.

Nonetheless, the concept of social system makes it easier to describe, understand, and explain social life by framing the larger contexts in which it takes place. If we note, for example, that people in the U.S. tend to base marriage on romantic love, we might conclude that this is simply human nature. If we look beyond the contemporary U.S., however, we find that, historically, romantic love is a relatively unimportant basis for marriage in most societies. In other words, the idea that romantic love is the primary legitimate basis for marriage is a characteristic of the U.S. as a social system. Like all social behavior, choosing spouses cannot be understood fully unless we see its relation to larger contexts that account for it as a social phenomenon. "Social system" is a general term, then, that refers to the elements and relationships that make up those contexts.

Perhaps the most important aspect of social systems is that they are more than the sum of their parts (see Durkheim [1895] 1938). A human body is more than a collection of cells and organs; it is the particular *arrangement* of cells and organs in relation to one another that distinguishes humans from other species. In the same way, a group or society is more than a collection of specific people; it is a particular arrangement of individuals in relation to one another. If you were asked to define a volleyball team, it would not be enough to simply list the names of the people on a particular team. Instead, you would have to describe the relationships and expectations that bind people together in particular ways that distinguish a volleyball team from a group of office workers (both of which might include the same individuals).

The traditional folk costumes worn by these Norwegian dancers reflect a cultural homogeneity that sharply distinguishes Norway from more heterogeneous societies, such as the Soviet Union and the United States.

Groups and Societies

Perhaps no two words are more often associated with sociology than "group" and "society." There is good reason for this, for although sociologists are interested in many social systems that are neither groups nor societies, these two are nonetheless central.

A **group** is a particular kind of social system in which people interact in regular patterned ways and share a sense of being identified as members of the group. Groups are a basic unit of sociological analysis because we spend so much of our lives in them and they are important sources of both social control and social conflict. In addition, the characteristics of groups affect not only individuals, but the entire social systems of which they are parts. Relationships within families, for example, affect not only the health and welfare of their members, but the ability of societies to teach their children how to participate in social life.

It is important not to confuse groups with social categories. A **social category** is a collection of people who have a social characteristic in common, such as being married or unemployed or female. (To a sociologist, what is commonly referred to as an "ethnic group" is in fact an "ethnic category," a collection of people who share a common ethnicity.) Social categories are particularly important in sociological thinking because people who have similar social characteristics also tend to have similar life experiences, perspectives, and resources.

A **society** is a social system that shares a geographical territory, a common culture, and way of life. It is held together by a shared identity, and is relatively independent and self-sufficient. Because of their central place in social life, sociology has a great deal to say about how societies are put together and how they operate—as you will see in the chapters to come.

Societies differ greatly from one another. They may differ in how homogeneous they are. In Iceland, for example, most people trace their heritage back hundreds of years to common roots in Norway. In contrast, the republics that comprise the Soviet Union include scores of languages, and a diversity of races and ethnicities that are often at odds with the white, Russian-speaking central government. In some ways, the U.S. is similar, for, although we have English as a common language, our population includes many ethnic and racial categories that often go to great lengths to preserve their language, values, and distinctive clothing, food, and customs. As we will see, this heterogeneity is a source of rich diversity but also of prejudice, discrimination, and social conflict.

Societies also differ in their degree of independence and self-sufficiency, especially in a world in which international trade and politics are as important as they are now. Japan is an independent nation free from political control of other countries. By comparison, Tibet has a distinct way of life and territory, but is under the military and political control of China. In other cases, dependence takes more subtle forms. Countries such as South Korea, El Salvador, the Philippines, and Panama have been so dependent on military and economic aid from the United States that the U.S. has been able to exert considerable pressure on the internal affairs of these countries, including the invasion of Panama in 1989. Until recently, similar relations, although in a more extreme form, existed between the Soviet Union and most of Eastern Europe.

Societies can be very large (the territory of the Soviet Union is more than twice that of the U.S., and the people of China make up a fifth of the entire world population) or very small (Iceland's population amounts to barely 300,000 people). They vary enormously in their complexity, from modern industrial societies in which many aspects of life are affected by huge bureaucracies to relatively simple societies with no schools, government, military, corporations, banks, or churches.

Perhaps the most important difference among societies centers on their ability to obtain material needs—how they arrange themselves to produce goods, to grow food, and meet other physical needs. At one extreme, gatherer-hunters grow none of their own food and have few possessions, while at the other extreme, industrial societies grow all of their own food and place a high value on accumulating possessions. Many important aspects of life in a society are affected by these productive arrangements, from the existence of inequality and social oppression to various forms of religious beliefs.

A SOCIOLOGICAL VIEW OF FAMILIAR WORLDS

Sociology helps us see the human arrangements of shared ideas and relationships that connect our otherwise separate lives, just as astronomy helps us see constellations where before we saw only a sea of indi-

Just as there are patterns among stars, so too are there patterns in relationships among people. In the photo of people on a patio, few tables have an odd number of people. How would you explain this simple pattern? What does it say about life in our society?

vidual stars. The stars were there all the time, but to see Orion's Belt or the Big Dipper, we have to look for patterns; and to see the constellations of relationships that characterize social life, we have to pay attention to the patterns that exist among individuals, groups, and societies, and other kinds of social systems.

In the remainder of this chapter we will use a series of examples to introduce some of the major concepts that organize sociological thinking as a way of looking at the world and trying to make sense of it.

Social Expectations: How Do We Know Who People Really Are?

Perhaps it was just this morning that you entered your first class of the new term, most likely a large room with rows of chairs which may be bolted to the floor, forcing you to face the front of the room. As students talk among themselves, a person—perhaps it was a woman—entered the room, walked to the front, and stood behind the lectern. Everyone in the room stopped talking soon after she arrived—except for her. When she wanted to talk, she just talked; when others wanted to talk, they raised a hand and

waited for her permission. Students asked questions; she made statements. She did not write down what you said, but you wrote down what she said.

This scene repeats itself so often in college classrooms that it may never have occurred to you how remarkable it is. What is remarkable is that no one ever asks those people behind lecterns if they are who we think they are. Without any personal knowledge of the professor in the scene just described, students pay attention to her and enter into relationships in which she has power over them and controls rewards they value highly.

Students do "know" something about her, however, knowledge which they substitute for details of her personal identity. They know that according to the catalogue the course was supposed to meet in that room at that time, that every student was expected to read the catalogue and be guided by it. They went to the room at the designated time and found other people there. Some asked, "Is this Intro Soc.?," were told "yes," and believed what they heard. The woman entered the room and took the position at the front. Anyone could have stood there, but only she did. This is important, for if anyone had

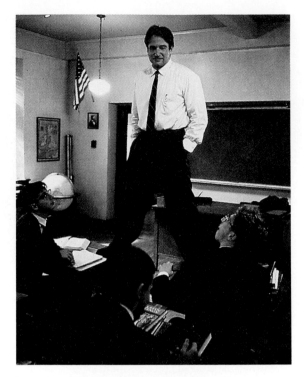

In most social situations we are unaware of how many expectations we have until someone violates them, as Robin Williams' character, Mr. Keating, does so effectively in the film *Dead Poet's Society*.

challenged her for that spot, your knowledge of who she was would have been shaken. No one challenged her, however, because someone was *expected* to occupy that position, someone who looked as though she was supposed to be there.

You expected her to be older than you, to dress in a certain way, to speak English, and behave appropriately. So long as people's appearance and behavior fit our expectations, we treat them accordingly even though their "real" selves may not be what they appear to be. The acceptance of a teacher's authority in a classroom does not depend only on the personalities of individuals but also on expectations that students and teachers share about one another as students and teachers, not as unique individuals.

One point of this is that we often enter into relationships with people without any direct personal knowledge of who they are. We take our clothes off in front of people we believe to be physicians and may even allow them to perform surgery on us. We allow dentists to drill our teeth and airline pilots and bus drivers to take our lives in their hands. Rarely, if ever, do we ask doctors for their credentials or demand assurance that a pilot really knows how to fly a plane.

What we know of one another consists primarily of expectations about people's positions in social relationships (professor, doctor, bus driver) and about ourselves in relation to them (student, patient, passenger). The power of those expectations comes in part from the fact that we share them with one another and in part from our general lack of awareness of them as characteristics of a social system. Rarely are we conscious of the complex relationships that tie us to one another, and, as a result, we often try to understand who we and others are solely by focusing on characteristics such as personality.

Social Relationships: Mothers and Children

Our positions in social relationships affect not only how we perceive one another, but how we behave. While most of us experience our mothers as unique individuals, for example, from a sociological perspective "mother" is a social position that profoundly affects how those unique individuals behave.

We enter the world knowing not a single soul. Our knowledge of others is largely sensory, consisting of smells and tastes, touch and sound. We soon learn something very useful, however: the magic of words through which things and people can be named. "Mother" is, when we first learn it, the name we give to a particular woman. The word "mother" tells us who that woman is, and so we tend to think that this is who she is to everyone.

Enter confusion: other people do not call our own mother "mother." Also confusing is the fact that many women are called "mother"; and every mother has a mother, so she is both "mother" and "daughter." What is hard for small children to understand is that the word "mother" is not like "tree" or "rock," for "mother" describes a *position* in a particular *social relationship* with another person. It need not be the woman who bore the child; it can be any woman who occupies the social position "mother" in relation to someone who occupies the social position "son" or "daughter."

Most of us do not have shared ideas about any particular mother, but we do share ideas about mothers in general, about what they are like, their behavior, what is important in their lives, and how they are supposed to feel in relation to their children. To the extent that a mother shares these ideas, they influence what she thinks, feels, and does. To understand a woman's behavior as a mother, we cannot pay attention only to her mental and emotional life. "Mother" represents more than biological fact: it represents a complex set of ideas that she and others use to decide who she is, what her children and she may expect of one another, and how she should choose between conflicting alternatives. While she may act and feel contrary to those ideas, she does not have the power to remove them from her social environment.

In a social sense, who we are depends on the positions we occupy in relation to other people and the shared ideas attached to us as a result. To ignore the social component of our selves is like trying to explain why apples fall from trees by examining only the characteristics of apples without taking into account their relationship to the earth's gravitational pull. This attention to the relationship between individuals and social systems is at the core of sociology as a perspective.

Perspectives: How Did They Come to Die?

Sociologists pay attention not only to relationships between individuals, but also to the larger social systems in which those relationships exist. More than anything else, it is this focus that distinguishes sociology as a point of view, as we will see in the case of four New Jersey teenagers.

On a spring evening in 1987, Thomas Olton, a Bergenfield, N.J. 18-year-old, left home in his Chevy Camaro and picked up his three best friends—Thomas Rizzo, 19, Cheryl Burress, 17, and her sister Lisa, 16. They drove around town for most of the night, stopping at a gas station at 3 A.M. to buy $3 worth of gas and to try, unsuccessfully, to steal the long rubber hose attached to the gas station's vacuum cleaner. Sometime between 4:00 and 5:30 that morning, they parked the car in the garage of a garden apartment complex in this small middle-class suburb of New York City, closed the garage door, and sat together with the car's engine running and windows open. Several hours later, a man on his way to work found them dead from carbon monoxide poisoning.

Figuring out how and why these four young people committed suicide is not simple. Since we can look at things from different points of view, or per-

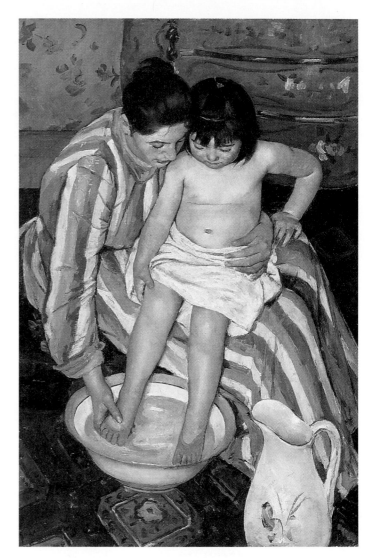

Mary Cassatt's painting, *The Bath* (1891/1892), reflects the nurturing and caring that are so often associated with the social position of motherhood.

spectives, we can ask various questions about the same thing and arrive at different explanations. Perspectives influence what we look at and what we make of what we observe (see Chapter 5). It is fairly simple to explain these deaths from the perspectives of biology, chemistry, and physics—the points of view coroners use to determine the cause of death. These perspectives raise questions about what happens when gasoline is burned in internal combustion engines, how carbon monoxide accumulates in a closed space, and how it combines with hemoglobin

In 1987, four New Jersey teenagers committed suicide by locking themselves in a garage and sitting in a car with the engine running. As the facial expressions on these teenage mourners show, making sense of why someone close to us might commit suicide is a haunting and difficult thing. For sociology, the problem is less personal but no less compelling: why would rates of suicide for young people increase in a society? What social forces are at work, and what can be done to change them?

in the blood to deprive the brain and other vital organs of oxygen.

While these disciplines explain how the deaths occurred, other perspectives produce new questions. The psychological perspective raises questions about human choice and the emotional and mental processes that influence what we choose. But the explanations of physical science cannot solve the psychological puzzle: *why* did these young people choose to kill themselves?

According to family, friends, and school officials, the four had been deeply despondent over the deaths of several friends during the previous year, had troubles with school and work, and had many family problems, including divorced parents, poor relations with step-parents, and, for two of them, fathers who had died in tragic circumstances—one shot himself

and the other overdosed on drugs. Rizzo and Olton both had drinking problems and were drunk at the time of their deaths. All four had taken cocaine.

Many concluded afterwards that their mental states matched those known to make people susceptible to suicide—feelings of depression, despair, helplessness, and hopelessness, and an inability to cope with life, to which we can add the disinhibiting effects of cocaine and alcohol (see Lester 1983). Many people have such feelings, however, without committing suicide, which means that such an explanation is not a full solution to the psychological puzzle. We would still want to know why some people in such states kill themselves while others do not.

Even a complete physical and psychological explanation falls short, for it looks at them only in terms of individuals' processes and characteristics.

They made their choices within a social system, and to understand their deaths from a sociological point of view, we must understand that system.

From suicide rates in the United States, we know that young people—15 to 24 years old—are 10 percent more likely to commit suicide than the population as a whole (USDHHS 1990). This general comparison, however, needs qualification in two important ways. First, it was not always so: in 1950 the young adult suicide rate was less than half that of the general population. Since then, however, the 15–24 year-old suicide rate has almost tripled while the rate for the population as a whole has remained virtually unchanged. This means that while the suicide rate among the young has grown rapidly, the rate for older people has actually declined.

Secondly, while the overall suicide rate for 15- to 24-year-olds is higher than the national rate, this is due primarily to the much higher rate among white males and, to a much lesser degree, black males. Compared with others of the same age, young white males are almost twice as likely as black males to kill themselves, five times more likely than white females, and nine times more likely than black females. As a form of behavior, then, suicide is strongly connected with being white and male.

These four suicides, then, are part of a behavior pattern that varies not only among different social characteristics such as age, race, and gender, but also historically (see One Step Further 1-1). To understand what these four people did that morning, it is not enough to know their state of mind; we also have to know how that state of mind was linked to a social environment. While suicide rates tell us only about categories of people and not about individuals, they do give us clues about the pressures exerted on people who occupy similar social positions and have similar social characterstics and the resulting patterns of behavior. Over the past forty years, the United States has changed in ways that make young people dramatically more likely to commit suicide, and from a sociological perspective, only by understanding such changes in social systems will we fully understand the different kinds of choices that individuals tend to make.

If we accept the psychological explanation that people are more likely to kill themselves when they feel helpless and hopeless and alone, then we have to ask how social systems either promote or discourage such factors. Helplessness and hopelessness, attachment and alienation, meaning and meaninglessness all have to do primarily with our involvement with other people—in other words, with social systems. A society in which people have little effect on what happens to them, lack socially valued roles to perform, and in which their major connection to others are weak and unstable is, sociologically, a social system which contributes to a relatively high suicide rate.

In this light, it is easier to see why increasing numbers of young adults choose suicide in response to personal troubles. Families tend to be unstable because of high divorce rates, the tensions that come when both parents must work, and the difficulties of forming new families when divorced parents remarry. Teenagers have few socially valued roles to perform and, as such, lack a valued place in their communities. They confront intense competition in school and must look forward to an unstable economy in which the ability to earn a living seems difficult for any but the most privileged to control. They live in a society in which pain and suffering are not accepted as parts of life, but are viewed as intolerable conditions that must be relieved at all costs, especially through the use of drugs, alcohol, and consumerism—from buying cars, clothes, and stereos to going out to the movies. Add to all of this that most young people have not yet developed fully the personal resources to deal effectively with uncertainty and stress, and suicide is easier to understand.

In his classic study of suicide, the great French sociologist Émile Durkheim ([1897] 1951) argued that suicide is most likely when the social ties that bind people to one another are too weak or, in the case of sacrificing ourselves in the interests of the group, too strong. The strength of such bonds is not an aspect of our personalities; it is an aspect of social systems and our *relationship* to them. *How* we respond depends on the options that social systems make available to us. The use of drugs, for example, is an accepted and widely promoted response to personal pain.

Clearly, the four New Jersey teenagers were not just isolated organisms that thought, felt, and acted. They participated in a social system which constructed their world and they made choices from what they saw as their alternatives. Had they lived in some other society, their circumstances and choices would have been quite different.

When we pay attention to patterns of behavior in relation to social systems and people's positions in them, we gain insights that other perspectives overlook. As valuable as it is to identify the psychological aspects of

ONE STEP FURTHER 1-1

Age, Gender, Suicide, and a Little Bit of History

This is the first of the One Step Further boxes that you will find throughout *Human Arrangements*. Each takes a point made in the text and explores it in more detail with the kinds of data sociologists use to test ideas about social life. If you feel uncomfortable with charts, graphs, and tables, just take your time and read along with the explanation that accompanies each box. There is nothing here that requires any statistical sophistication.

In October 1929, the U.S. stock market crashed, plunging this country and much of the world into a decade of severe economic depression. Thousands of people had been speculating in the market in the hope of making a quick fortune, and many lost everything in the crash. To illustrate how people's social characteristics affect their response to such events, consider the following information about variations in suicide rates during this difficult period in history.

The graph in Figure B-1-1 shows how suicide rates changed between the years 1925 and 1939, a period that included the stock market crash. The years are marked off along the horizontal axis, and the suicide rates

are marked off along the vertical axis. There are seven lines, each one showing the experiences of categories of white people who differ by gender or age. Each line is marked with a description at the right and a Roman numeral at the left. The top line (VII) shows suicide rates for 65–74-year-old white men; the bottom line (I) shows suicide rates for 25–34 year-old white women. Stop for a moment and make sure you see everything described above in the graph.

Beginning at the bottom (line I), you can see that suicide rates for younger white women changed barely at all from 1925 to 1939—the line is almost straight across. The same is true for white women 55–64 (line II). In addition, notice that the lines for older

FIGURE B-1-1   Rate of Suicides for White Males and Females by Age Group, 1925 to 1939, in the U.S.

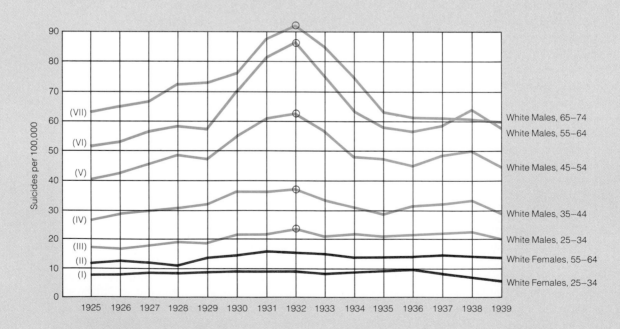

Source: National Office of Vital Statistics, 1956.

and younger women are quite close to each other, showing that older women were not much more likely to kill themselves than were younger women.

The situation for white men, however, is dramatically different. First notice that for each year, with each older age group, there is a large jump in the suicide rate, which you can see from the fact that the lines for older age groups are located quite a ways above the lines for younger age groups. In 1932 the suicide rate for white men was 23 per 100,000 for those 25–34, 36 for those 35–44, 62 for those 45–54, 86 for those 55–64, and 92 for those 65–74 (see the small circles on each line). This is a pattern that still holds in the U.S. Why should older men be so much more likely to kill themselves? Is it because they have a more difficult time adjusting to the inevitable disappointments that occur as we age? What do you think?

Now notice how the shape of the lines changes as we move from younger men to older men. The suicide rate for the youngest men (line III) increased only slightly by 1932, but as we move upward to each older age group, the jump is more and more pronounced. For the oldest men (line VII), the rate jumped from 63 per 100,000 in 1925 to 92 in 1932 and then fell back down to its previous level over the next three or four years. Notice also how different the line for 55–64-year-old men (line VI) is from the line for 55–64-year-old women (line II).

Stop for a moment and make sure you see these patterns.

Differences in gender and age go along with sharply different tendencies to commit suicide. Why these patterns exist is still an unsolved puzzle, but they raise intriguing questions about age and gender as social characteristics that affect our behavior.

PUZZLE

ARE YOU WHO YOU THINK YOU ARE?

Before reading any further, write down ten words or phrases that, for you, answer the question, "Who am I?" Then, as you read the following section, look again at your answers and think about what this says about "who you are."

suicide, we also need to appreciate the social circumstances affecting the emotional and mental processes through which people make choices. These four acts of suicide tell us things about these four people; but they also mirror characteristics of our social systems. Their act is connected to a collective process unfolding through history, and by locating them in that process we come to a fuller sociological understanding of their individual circumstances, experience, and behavior.

Each of the preceding examples shows in its own way that who we are and what we do is affected by our positions in social systems. This is true in even the simplest, most informal situation, such as when we meet someone for the first time.

Social Identities: Who Do You Think You Are?

Suppose that you live by yourself in an apartment, and to make ends meet, you decide to advertise for a roommate. In response to your ad, someone writes to you: "Most people think I'm intelligent and have a good sense of humor. I'm neat, keep regular hours, don't play music too loudly, pay my bills on time. I enjoy most sports, a good book, lively conversation, and meeting new people."

Would this be enough information for you? Would you like to know if this person is male or female, homosexual or heterosexual, 16 years old or 55 years old with two grandchildren? Would it matter to you if this person is an illegal alien, a child of the president of the United States, is unemployed, or works as a police officer, a journalist, a farm worker, a computer programmer, a taxi driver, or a restaurant cook? Would you like to know if this person is black,

Hispanic, white, or Asian, is fabulously wealthy or desperately poor, went to a posh prep school in Boston or a run-down high school on the south side of Chicago, grew up on a farm or in the Bronx or on a native American reservation? Does it matter if your roommate is Catholic, Protestant, Jewish, or Muslim, or grew up in a tribe of cannibals on New Guinea?

More than likely, most or all of these things would interest you to some degree, although none tells us about the individual you are thinking of living with. They do tell us about people's positions in social systems, and this gives us clues about their beliefs, values, and expectations in relation to others. It is such characteristics that we use in shaping our initial knowledge of people.

Most people never know our private selves. They know our *social* selves—our positions in social systems—and know us through the ideas attached to those selves. Similarly, our social selves are an important source of ideas about who *we* think we are.

WHAT SOCIOLOGY IS ALL ABOUT

The examples given earlier in this chapter stressed the importance of our positions in social relationships; but most people find it hard to grasp the idea that relationships exist independently of the individuals who participate in them. The relationship between children and parents is defined by shared ideas about children and parents, their behavior, goals, feelings, and expectations in relation to one another. Those ideas, and the relationships they define, exist apart from you and your parents.

Without individuals acting in those relationships, however, the relationships would not exist, and there is the crux of it: all of us participate in something we did not create, and yet through our involvement we give those relationships life; we stamp them with our own interpretations and thereby participate in changing or maintaining them as parts of social systems.

The examples in this chapter center on vital aspects of social systems that are at the core of sociology. We use shared ideas to make sense of the world, one another, and ourselves; we spend our lives in webs of relationships with other people, relationships that affect not only how we behave, but who we think we are; and social life is itself affected by physical conditions, including the ways in which societies produce goods. These key aspects of social life correspond to three major concepts that define

sociology as a perspective and describe the basic characteristics of social systems: culture, social structure, and population and ecology. As you read the brief introduction to these concepts in the remaining sections of this chapter, try not to be too concerned with technical definitions of new terms such as culture or ecology—there will be plenty of time for that in Chapters 2–4, where each is covered in detail. Instead, concentrate on the overall idea of a sociological perspective that focuses on different aspects of social systems.

Culture

At the core of every social system is a **culture** consisting primarily of shared ideas that guide what people perceive, think, feel, and do. What goes on in college classrooms, for example, is affected by a variety of shared beliefs—that teachers know more than students; that a college education will enable graduates to get better jobs; and that papers, exams, and grades are valid ways of measuring knowledge and intellectual ability. Some of these ideas take the form of rules about how people are supposed to appear and behave—students who cheat should expect to be punished if they are caught, as should teachers who sexually harass students, accept bribes in return for high grades, or come to class under the influence of alcohol or drugs. Everyone is expected to conform to certain standards of dress, to use the same language, to arrive on time, and to refrain from behavior that is defined as inappropriate, from laughing at something not generally thought to be funny to throwing frisbees, taking off one's clothes, or shouting down people because we dislike their ideas.

Those who participate in social systems also share ideas about what is important or trivial, good or bad, desirable or undesirable. Colleges place a high value on education itself, for example, as well as what it takes to become educated—including taking intellectual risks, speaking up in class, being honest, striving to achieve, and being creative. In many cases, such ideas have emotions attached to them, such as the respect that students may feel for their professors (reflected in the practice of addressing them by formal titles such as "professor," "sir," or "Doctor") or the feelings of intense loyalty that students often feel towards their school as well as hostility towards rival schools. These kinds of ideas also include racial prejudice and the feelings that go with it that are surfacing at increasing numbers of U.S. colleges and universities.

While ideas constitute the major part of culture, societies have also developed material objects that both extend human abilities and limit choices. The material culture of college classrooms, for example, is rich and varied, from the physical classroom itself to blackboards, chalk, erasers, desks, pens, pencils, books, paper, computers, microscopes, maps, slide projectors, and test tubes. The scale and intensity of higher education in the U.S. and other industrial societies would be impossible without the physical resources contained in their material culture. Material culture affects virtually every aspect of social life, from how and what people eat to how they communicate, plan their communities, and resolve conflict.

In both its material and nonmaterial forms, culture is an enormously important part of social systems because it is largely through culture that humans create the world they live in. Culture provides the means for creating a sense of what is real and enables human communities to adapt to and affect one another and their surroundings. It is the ultimate source of all the ways of thinking about and making sense of the world, from the simplest uses of language to describe something to the theorizing of science to the depths of religious belief. In its physical forms, it is literally the stuff of which humans make their material world, from books and eating utensils to homes and highways to weapons of war. In order to understand how social systems operate, then, it is essential that we understand their cultures.

Social Structure

The concept of **social structure** is used to describe social systems in two different ways. In the first sense, structure refers to the relationships that connect different parts of the system to one another, from individual human beings to groups to entire societies or groups of societies (such as political alliances). On the micro—or small-scale—level of social life, structure refers to the arrangement of people in relation to one another and the patterns of expectation attached to each position in those relationships. When we identify ourselves as children in relation to our mothers and fathers, for example, we define an important part of the structure of family systems. On the macro—or large-scale—level, groups, organizations, and societies interact with one another through patterns of shared expectations. Universities have structured relationships with their communities, with other universities, with government agencies, and, often, with corporations

Cultural beliefs are used to construct basic ideas about reality, especially aspects we cannot observe, such as what happens after death. Bosch's 16th century vision of hell is a cultural attempt to grasp the unknown.

Population and ecology are concepts that focus on differences such as those between rural Japanese who cultivate rice largely by hand and urban Japanese who live in crowded cities dominated by the mass production of modern industry. Just as

they relate to their physical environments in radically different ways, so too do they relate to one another in different ways—from the structure of family life to politics, religion, education, and social inequality.

(through research contracts) and the military (through research and military training programs such as R.O.T.C.).

The concept of social structure also refers to the ways in which people are *distributed* among various social positions as well as how major rewards of social life—in particular, wealth, power, and prestige—are distributed among members of a group or society. The medical profession in the United States is structured so that women rarely occupy the prestigious social position surgeon and, as a result, are denied the high income and prestige and influence that accompany that specialty.

The concept of social structure describes how we are arranged in relation to one another, from personal interactions to society as a whole. As a concept, it is extremely useful, because it draws our attention to the distributions and patterns of expectation that characterize social life.

As important as culture and structure are, we cannot overlook the fact that social systems exist in *physical* environments that include both the physical world and the biological facts of life on this planet. This brings us to the third major area in the sociological perspective—population and ecology.

Population and Ecology

Population and ecology focus on human beings as organisms who live in relation to physical environments. In sociology, a **population** is any collection of people who share a physical environment. It can be as small as a single person living on a desert island or as large as the population of the world, which numbered in excess of 5 billion people in 1991.

Ecology focuses on the characteristics of physical environments and the relation of populations to them. The characteristics of physical environments include the availability of resources such as fertile land, water, and fuel; access to transportation routes such as rivers; and isolation by mountains, deserts, or other barriers. The relation of populations to physical environments includes such factors as how large populations are, how rapidly they grow or shrink, and how they are distributed in physical space. This relation also includes cultural technology, a population's ability to make use of natural resources. Plows, electric generators, printing presses, crop irrigation systems, and computers all represent ways in which human beings make use of the physical environment. Population and ecology are important parts of the sociological perspective because the physical conditions of human life have important effects on how social systems develop, and social systems can profoundly affect their physical environments.

The development of large industrial societies depends on more than culture and social structure, for it also results from rapid population growth, the concentration of workers in large cities, and the successful application of technology to problems of production. In turn, the ability to produce more than people need to survive allows some people to accumulate wealth and power at the expense of others.

While the concepts of culture and structure define the social environment, population and ecology focus on humanity as a species of life, whose numbers shrink and swell, distribute themselves geographically, and learn to use their physical environments—all of which affects social life.

The Personal and the Social

A crucial element of sociological thinking is the distinction between the individual and the social. A behavior or experience may be common to many individuals and yet not be social; or be rare and yet profoundly social.

Everyone inevitably experiences death, but by itself, the universality of this experience does not make it social. How people respond to us when they know we are dying, however, as well as how we respond to them and to our own condition are *social*, because these are affected by cultural ideas about death; also, our age at death and the cause of our death are strongly affected by our positions in social systems.

I sit alone in my office writing a book about sociology—a rare activity in any society, but nonetheless a highly social one. To explain this activity only in terms of my motivation and ability ignores the social and material world within which I act. This book is socially possible because humans invented paper, ink, and printing presses, and developed language and the idea that writing books is socially valuable, allowing me to do it in exchange for a share of what other people produce—food, shelter, clothing. I am also writing this book because humans developed a particular way of thinking about social life (sociology), just as they developed ways of thinking about physical life (biology), matter and energy (physics), mental and emotional processes (psychology), the unknown (religion), beauty (art), sound (music), and other cultures (anthropology).

If I belonged to one of many other societies around the world, I would not be writing this book, because in those environments there would be no paper, presses, or audience of college students trying to understand the social world in a systematic way. So, what I do at this moment cannot be explained solely by my motives and thoughts; I must also understand my position in the social system within which I act as a human being, a context I did not create.

Sociology provides us with a window on the world and a mirror of our participation in it. To use it, however, is difficult, for we actively participate in the very thing we are trying to understand; the intellectual tools, themselves, are part of culture. In addition, sociology often challenges us to raise uncomfortable questions about the connection between ourselves and social problems.

We could look at many suicides as personal solutions to personal problems. When, however, we see that some people are far more likely to kill themselves than others, we can no longer regard such behavior as purely personal. The patterns reflected in suicide rates for people in different positions indicate that something is going on in the variety of social systems in which people find themselves, something that makes people in some positions more likely than others to kill themselves. Like all behavior, suicide reflects both personal troubles and social problems.

As we begin to understand the social causes of personal troubles, we must acknowledge that as participants in social life we are connected in some way to them. Racism, sexism, and ageism are not problems for only those individuals who happen to have a particular skin color, sex, or age. We are understandably reluctant to connect ourselves with other

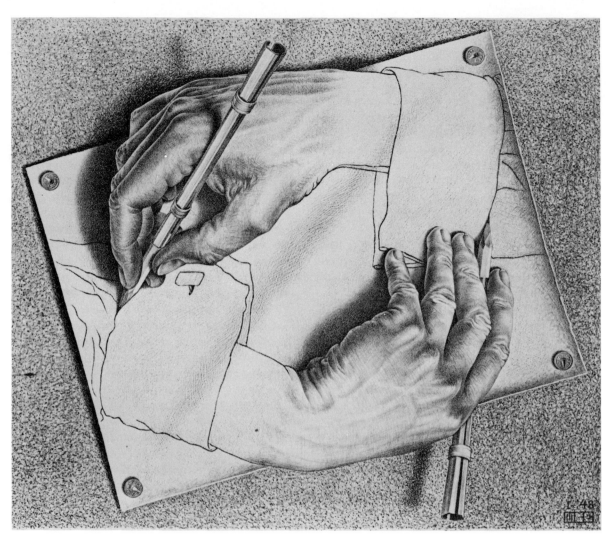

A fundamental challenge of sociology is to understand the connection between individuals and their social environments, to explain social life and participate in it at the same time. Our relationship to society is complex, reciprocal, and difficult to unravel, much like M. C. Escher's famous drawing of two hands drawing each other.

Drawing Hands, 1948, M. C. Escher, 1898–1972, National Gallery of Art, Washington, D.C., Cornelius Van S. Roosevelt Collection.

people's troubles, and we resist giving up comfortable beliefs in order to see the world in a new way. As Berger (1963) wrote, a society

> provides us with warm, reasonably comfortable caves, in which we can huddle with our fellows, beating on the drums that drown out the howling hyenas of the surrounding darkness. "Ecstasy" is the act of stepping outside the caves, alone, to face the night. (p. 150)

To "step outside" is to adopt a kind of consciousness that Mills (1959) called "the sociological imagination," the engaging in a particular kind of thinking about the social contexts in which collective and individual human life unfolds. It is to make sense of the ways in which social systems operate and the ways in which people participate in them. It is to learn to think in a sociological way.

What Do We Want to Know?

We have said that sociology is about social life and behavior, especially in relation to social systems—but what is it about all of this that we want to know?

As you will see in the chapters ahead, sociological thinking poses four basic questions: How is social life organized? What consequences does this produce? How does it change? And what does it have to do with the lives of individuals?

Social Life and Its Consequences   As the study of marriage and the family makes clear, social systems can be organized in many different ways. Depending on the society, for example, people have varying degrees of freedom to choose their own spouses, and marry for reasons ranging from romantic love to economic or political gain. Families also vary in how responsibilities and power are distributed, in the number of wives or husbands people may have, and the rules that govern how family members may treat one another and how marriages may be dissolved.

We need to understand how social life is organized because it produces an astounding variety of consequences—from how people feel about their parents to whether nations go to war, from poverty and wealth to art and rock music, from religion to revolution, from air pollution to designer jeans, from democracy to slavery. In the simplest sense, the organization of social life promotes patterns of thought, feeling, appearance, and behavior. Families, for example, have patterns of interaction through which people express deep feelings and involve themselves in almost every aspect of one another's lives. Paradoxically, this may also include abuse and violence, forms of behavior that seem out of place in the family, which we tend to think of as a source of safety and caring. In search of a sociological understanding of this, we find among other things that violence is more likely in families with an unequal distribution of power, especially when husbands dominate. Looking deeper, however, we also find that the characteristics of families that contribute to the intimacy and emotional support we value so highly—such as privacy, being together a lot, depending on one another, and being heavily involved in one another's lives—can also create the potential for violence and abuse. This is particularly true when external conditions related to family life—such as high unemployment rates—increase stress and strain, and, with it, the likelihood that people will strike out violently at those nearest to them (see Gartner 1990).

One of the most important things to understand about the consequences of social life is that they affect people differently depending on their social characteristics. This is especially true of social inequalities in the distribution of wealth, income, and power. A tiny percentage of U.S. families, for example, controls the vast majority of income and wealth; black and Hispanic families have far less wealth than whites and are far more likely to live in poverty; women earn far less than men; and children are more likely to be poor than other age categories. On a world scale, a small elite of industrial nations controls the vast majority of the world's wealth, technology, and military power. The consequences of social inequality are varied, profound, and deeply felt, ranging from inadequate health care and high infant mortality among poor people to international warfare over control of natural resources such as oil.

Social Change   In addition to understanding how social life is organized and the consequences it produces, we also need to understand forces that promote change and those that keep things the way they are. As a process, social change involves many factors, from social movements and new technology to changes in the natural environment or population size. Although we know generally what promotes social change, a more difficult problem is understanding how and under what conditions different changes occur, from political revolution to the emergence of new forms of music or art. Why, for example, did the prodemocracy movements in Eastern Europe and China arise and why did they succeed in the former but fail in the latter? How did the Industrial Revolution affect family life in the United States? What will it take for impoverished Third World nations to become industrialized?

In some ways we can look at social systems as always being in the process of changing—sometimes rapidly, as in the case of revolution and the invention of new technology, but often more slowly, as in the transition from European feudalism to capitalism in the seventeenth, eighteenth, and nineteenth centuries or the long-term decline in the influence of organized religion. In this sense, every understanding of how social life works also involves attention to how it is changing. For this reason, although Chapter 23 focuses on theories of change, the subject of change is raised throughout this book.

Individuals and Society   While a great deal of sociological thinking focuses on larger questions about organization, consequences, and change, we also have to pay attention to the simple fact that the core of social life consists of what individual people experience and do in relation to one another. To understand how this happens we have to question how people perceive and interpret themselves and others. How do we use language, appearance, and behavior to participate in social life, to present ourselves to other people, create impressions, and perform roles? How do we develop a stable and acceptable sense of who we are as people, and how does this depend on relationships with others—in other words, on our participation in social life?

These, then, are major kinds of questions that define themes underlying the rich diversity of sociolog-ical thinking—the organization of social life and the consequences it produces on every level from the intimacy of marriage to relations among nations; the dynamics of change and stability; and the complex ways people shape and live their lives in relation to one another and their environments. To ask such questions and to develop the ability to think sociologically, we must begin with the basic concepts that define the sociological perspective—culture, social structure, population, and ecology. For these we turn to the following three chapters that complete Part One.

SUMMARY

1. Sociology is the study of social life and behavior, especially in relation to social systems and how they affect and are affected by the people who participate in them. One of the most difficult things to understand about social systems is that they are more than a sum of their parts.

2. Groups and societies are the two most important types of social systems. They are often confused with social categories.

3. What we know about one another consists largely of ideas we share about the social positions that people occupy. As individuals we participate in social systems in many ways; but sociology focuses primarily on patterns of appearance and behavior that are more likely in some social systems or positions than others. Thus, all personal choices are to some degree reflections of the limitations on social life imposed by social systems.

4. Social systems have cultural characteristics which consist primarily of ideas and material products. In both its material and nonmaterial forms, culture is the major medium through which humans create and shape their world.

5. Social systems have two kinds of structural characteristics: the patterns of expectation that govern relationships involving individuals as well as entire social systems such as groups or societies; and the distribution of people among social positions and the distribution of valued rewards and resources such as wealth, power, and prestige.

6. Social systems and their physical environments have often complex relationships through which they affect each other, especially through the size and distribution of a social system's population and how it makes use of its environment.

7. Sociological thinking involves questions of how social life is organized, the consequences it produces, how social systems change, and how individuals and social systems are related to each other.

KEY TERMS

culture 16	population 18	social system 6
ecology 18	social category 8	society 8
group 8	social structure 17	sociology 6

LOOKING ELSEWHERE

Although Chapter 1 is an introductory chapter whose themes form the basic structure of the book, having studied it you might want to look at related discussions in *Human Arrangements*, several of which expand on examples used here, such as

- interaction in college classrooms (Chapter 8, p. 174–76; Chapter 17, pp. 425–27)

- suicide as deviance (Chapter 11, p. 236)
- gender roles and health (Chapter 14, pp. 346–47)
- perspectives: theoretical perspectives in sociology (Chapter 5, pp. 96–108)

RECOMMENDED READINGS

Berger, P. 1963. *Invitation to sociology*. New York: Doubleday (available in paperback). An elegant, personal, and sometimes passionate introduction to the sociological perspective and the dilemmas posed by living as an individual in the social world.

Mills, C. W. 1959. *The sociological imagination*. New York: Oxford University Press. This brief paperback is a passionate view of sociology as both a point of view and as a profession. Pay particular attention to Chapter 1 ("The Promise"), which ranks as the classic statement about the relationship between the "personal" and the "social," and to Chapter 8 ("The Uses of History"), in which Mills urges an attention to history as a vital part of sociological thinking.

2
CULTURE

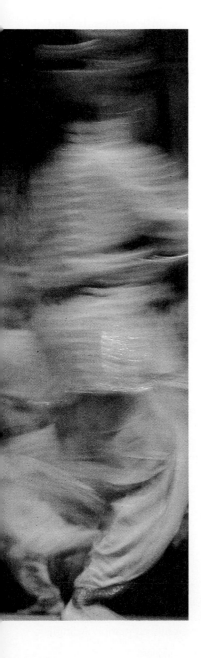

 **Culture** is the accumulated sum of symbols, ideas, and material products associated with a social system. It is a dynamic medium through which societies create a collective way of life reflected in such things as beliefs, values, music, literature, art, dance, science, religious ritual, and technology. In this sense, it is literally the source from which we create most of what we experience as reality, and as such its place in human life is enormously important.

Although it includes both material and nonmaterial aspects, the essence of culture consists of ideas. These depend on the human ability to use symbols in order to attach meaning to experience and perceptions and thereby think about the world (Geertz 1973). Therefore, it is with symbols that we begin.

NONMATERIAL CULTURE: SYMBOLS, LANGUAGE, AND IDEAS

Take a moment to look at Figure 2-1 (see p. 26). What is it? On a piece of paper make a list of all the answers you can think of. Do not read any further until you have at least four items on your list.

What is Figure 2-1 a picture of? "A bunch of dots?" "Two lines of dots, one shorter than the other, joined at a right angle two-thirds of the way up the longer line?" "X- and y-axes used to plot data?" "Two roads intersecting?" "A cross?" While the first two answers are a mere physical description, the remaining three go beyond what the lines look like to say what they *are*. They transform the lines into *symbols* by attaching *meaning* to them; and it is meaning that is at the heart of **nonmaterial culture**.

FIGURE 2-1   What Is It?

In the United States, the burning cross has become a powerful symbol of bigotry and intolerance. How do you think you might feel to find one in your community?

A **symbol** is anything that represents more than itself. In many cultures a cross—whether made of two sticks or lines on a piece of paper—is more than what our eyes see: people pay great attention to it, carry it around their necks, and hang it in their homes. Members of the Ku Klux Klan gather around large ones and watch them burn in the night. In many places, however, and during many periods of history, people would see nothing more than a pair of sticks held together or two lines joined at right angles.

There are four kinds of symbols, which include, first, symbolic *objects*—flags representing nations and money representing labor and goods; second, symbolic *characteristics* of objects—such as black for mourning, yellow for cowardice, white for purity. The third type of symbol is the **gesture**, an action that has meaning: a smile or a wink, a raised right

hand in oath taking, a shrug of the shoulders, a frustrated snap of the fingers—all of these actions have meaning in a particular cultural context (Malandro and Barker 1983; Patterson 1983). The fourth type of symbol is the vast range of *spoken and written words* that make up *language*, which is so important that it deserves a separate discussion. Language is the most important set of symbols in any culture, for it embodies the symbolic building blocks used to construct ideas.

In a culture, then, objects, the characteristics of objects, gestures, and words are more than our senses perceive them to be; they *are* what they *mean*. Suppose you walk down a street on a summer day and come upon an auction in the front yard of an old house. You spy an empty seat in the shade and, being hot and tired, you sit down to watch. On the auction block is a large ornate desk, and the bidding is high. "Two thousand dollars," the auctioneer barks. "Do I hear twenty-one hundred? Going once. Going twice . . ." Suddenly, your nose itches and you scratch it with your index finger. Just as suddenly, the auctioneer points a finger at you and shouts, "Twenty-one hundred! Going once! Going twice! Sold!" You have just bought yourself a $2,100 desk.

Strictly speaking, you only scratched your nose, and you did so just to relieve an itch. You had no intention of bidding for a desk. How do you get out of it? "I didn't *mean* anything by it," you say. "I just scratched my nose." Had you been sitting across from the auctioneer on a subway and scratched your nose in just the same way, the outcome would have been very different.

You got into trouble because in the social system of an auction it is agreed that a nose scratch is more than a physical act; it is a gesture, a symbolic act that represents more than itself: a nose scratch at an auction is a positive response to the auctioneer's call for bids. Thus, there is no necessary connection between the cultural meaning of a nose scratch (or any other action) and an individual's reason for performing it.

Symbol systems tell their users how to mark and categorize perceptions depending on the circumstances; hence, the auctioneer categorizes a nose scratch as a bid at certain points in the auction (but not at others) and never does so outside of auctions. Depending on the situation, the simple act of touching your nose can have many meanings: when con artists are about to "sting" a victim, a finger on the side of the nose means "all is ready"; or a thumb drawn across the nose can signify contempt. A single action can be transformed into many different meaningful gestures, depending on the cultural context.

This example illustrates a vital aspect of symbols: *we respond to them just as we respond to what they represent*. While the word "fire" represents something that can hurt us, the word itself cannot; yet the word "fire" can make us run just as readily as the sight or heat of fire itself. Without the word, we can experience fire only with our senses, by seeing its color, hearing its crackle, feeling its heat. With the word, on the other hand, fire exists as an *idea* even when there is no fire: it exists in our minds, and when we share the symbol with other people, it exists among us. We can think about it, teach each other about it and its uses. We can attach the idea of "fire" to things that have no concrete relation to it, as "the fiery anger in her eyes." Symbols, themselves, then, are *real* to us; and as W. I. Thomas (1931) pointed out, what we define as real has real consequences.

Symbols are created, which means we can create symbols to which we respond just as we do to physical objects and forces. There is nothing inherent in any symbol that gives it power over us; its power lies in what it signifies to those who share its meaning. If children learn the meaning of "danger" by touching a hot stove and hearing the word from an adult, the word "danger" can be used to keep them away from all kinds of things that may not be dangerous at all. Similarly, the symbol "immoral" can be attached to virtually any behavior. This explains why the meaning of a behavior is often more important to us than its objective characteristics or consequences.

Culture provides a framework of ideas that we use to interpret what we perceive, and people's appearance and behavior are fully understandable only if we pay attention to their cultural context. If we feed our guests roast chicken and after the meal tell them they just consumed the flesh of a dog, their reaction depends only in part on what they actually ate or think they ate. To predict their response, we must know the system of meaning they use to interpret what they did—some Asians might thank us for the delicacy, while most Europeans would look disgusted.

Language

There would be no culture without **language**, which includes both the collection of symbols (words) and rules for their use with which we think and communicate with one another. Without culture, humans would be hard-pressed to survive. We are not born knowing what kinds of berries to eat and which are poisonous, or how to catch and eat a wild animal, but we do have the ability to use symbols. Because "edible" and "inedible" are important distinctions for us, we have symbols for them; we can categorize objects and, most important, we can teach those categories to one another.

Every language has two elements: a collection of words and a set of rules—syntax and grammar—that governs the arrangement of words to express thoughts. Some words—such as "telephone"—have fixed meanings, while many depend on their relation to other words. The phrase "he threw up" means one thing followed by "his lunch," but quite another in the poem, "A Visit From St. Nicholas," in which the father "ran to the window and threw up the sash."

The words and their meanings contained in a language represent the distinctions that its users tend to make as they perceive and mark their world. To Alaska's Inuit, a detailed understanding of different kinds of snow is vital for survival. Inuit languages typically include as many as 20 different words for "snow"—snow that is good for making igloo blocks, hard and crusty snow, dry snow drifted by the wind, and so on—while English has only one. Argentine cowboys ("gauchos") have over 200 separate words that describe the color of horses. English, on the other hand, has an enormous number of words used in making precise scientific measurements. A nanosecond (one billionth of a second) is a unit of time that exists only in computer operations and is otherwise beyond human experience (see Rifkin 1987).

The second element of language—the rules of syntax and grammar—tells us how to arrange words in order to express ourselves. Different arrangements of the same words convey very different meanings, as in "The whale swallowed Jonah" or "Jonah swallowed the whale," or convey nothing at all, as in "Whale Jonah the swallowed."

The Marx Brothers were famous for manipulating language as a source of humor. In the film *The Coconuts* (1929), Groucho owns a hotel, and his bellboys want to be paid. "Oh," Groucho says, "you want your *money*?" "Yes," they reply. "So, you want *my* money," Groucho says, as he changes the meaning by changing the pronoun. "Is that fair? Do I want *your* money? No, my friends, no. Money will never make you happy. And happy will never make you money."

Meaning also depends on the cultural context. The subtlety of such variations is painfully obvious to those who learn a language as adults and thereby often know only literal meanings. A foreign dinner guest who hears "Oh, you *must* try some of this stew" may interpret the statement as an order, not as friendly encouragement. The social relationship between the speaker and the hearer can also be important in determining meanings: "I love you" spoken by a child to a parent has a different meaning than when spoken between two unrelated adults.

The complexity of language reflects the complexity of culture as a system for representing and interpreting the world. As Farb (1973) pointed out, even the simplest statements are impressively complex.

> Children who unravel a simple statement like "The chair broke" must do more than decode a grammatical utterance. They must first master the subtle category of things that *break*, like *chairs* and also *machines* and *windowpanes*. Then they must distinguish the category of things that *break* from things that *tear*, like *paper* and *bedsheets*, or things that *smash*, like *vases* and *cars*. They must next interpret the influence on the chair of the verb *broke* out of all the possibilities that verb implies, such as that the breaking of a chair is conceptually different from breaking the bank at Monte Carlo or from waves breaking on a beach. To achieve all this, children unconsciously unravel the sentence into parts that can be analyzed, and then put the elements together again in a meaningful fashion. (pp. 262–63)

The language of words is not the only type of language found in cultures. Mathematics is a language used to represent the quantitative aspects of reality: it is a set of symbols (such as "2," "3," "+," "×," "=") with specific rules that define their relationships to each other ("2 + 3 = 5" or "2 × 3 = 6"). Musical notation is also a language, symbols on paper representing sounds.

Language develops from the interactions of group life, and those who share a culture use its language to represent reality (Berger and Luckman 1967). The fact that the words "wizard," "bachelor," and "Indian brave" have more positive connotations than "witch," "spinster," and "Indian squaw" reflects long-standing patterns of discrimination against women. To grow up with these categories of meaning affects the way people think about women and men, and thus, as patterns of living foster certain views of reality, those views in turn help to sustain and reproduce those same patterns of social life.

The limitations of language are clearest when we look at their ambiguities and internal contradictions. Many slang expressions do not mean what they literally say: "it blew my mind," "a heavy idea," "I'll catch you later," "he spilled his guts," "she picked his brain," and "he shot his mouth off" all illustrate the flexibility with which language can be used to describe reality.

The Uses of Language

Language is the foundation of culture because language is what we use to represent what we perceive, feel, think, and do. We use it to label and describe the world, and in doing so, we create what most of us experience as reality. When Iraq invaded Kuwait in 1990, for example, and threw much of the industrialized world into a panic about threats to oil supplies and the possibility of war, most people—including national leaders—became aware of what was happening not by being there or seeing pictures, but by listening to what reporters, politicians, and others wrote and said. What most people treated as real about those events was based entirely on words used to represent them. In turn, what we take to be real is critically important as we decide how to respond to what we believe is happening.

On a smaller scale, we use language to represent ourselves to others, to describe ourselves, to reflect our inner feelings, thoughts, and expectations, and to create and sustain impressions in people's minds about who we are. This also applies to how we see ourselves, for language is the medium that we use to think about ourselves and, often, to reflect on the difference between who we think we are and who we think we ought to be.

On both levels, language is a profoundly important resource that lies at the heart of social life as a creative, dynamic process. This is true not only in the limited literal sense of creating works of poetry, drama, and literature, but in terms of creating all of the kinds of knowledge that we experience as reality itself.

In addition to its uses to represent reality, language fulfills four other social functions (Farb 1973). First, language allows us to assume that those who share it with us (our **speech community**) know what we mean when we talk or write. It is precisely our expectation that strangers will understand us when we speak that makes a language social; a "personal" language is not a language at all, for its meanings are not shared. Because there is practically no one who speaks Latin in an existing social environment, for example, it is described as a "dead" language.

Second, the common language of a speech community allows its members to distinguish themselves from outsiders, helping to maintain group boundaries and solidarity (see Edwards 1984; Stevens and Swicegood 1987). In Shaw's play *Pygmalion* (and later on Broadway as the musical *My Fair Lady*), Eliza Doolittle's cockney accent immediately identifies her social class to Professor Higgins. When blacks in the U.S. leave urban ghettos to attend college, they often find on their return that subtle changes in their use of language alienate them from friends who now see them as outsiders to their speech community.

Children in school create special languages such as pig Latin or use little-known languages such as American Sign Language as ways of forming exclusive groups. Many occupations use special vocabularies (jargon) to distinguish themselves from others. Each generation of college students has its own set of slang terms for students who study a lot or who party a lot, for hard courses and easy ones—terms that have different meanings (or none at all) for those outside the college speech community. Ethnic and racial groups have derogatory terms that label the members of other groups; there are more than a thousand such terms in English alone (Allen 1983).

If immigrants do not learn their new society's language, they must restrict themselves to small groups that contain their speech community. When the children of immigrants learn the new language while their parents cling to the old, a distance often results between family members who participate in different speech communities and, in many respects, different cultures.

When Africans were brought to the U.S. as slaves, they were forbidden to speak their native languages and were given new names. Wars have been fought over which language would dominate in a culture (see McRae 1984, 1986). The struggle between French and English Canadians in Quebec is reflected in the French Canadians' insistence that French have the same importance as English, that bank tellers be able to speak French (Giniger 1981; La Ponce 1987). In similar ways, there has been great controversy in the United States about the idea of adopting English as the "official" language. Although mainstream social life is certainly carried on in English, some fear that to include other languages—most notably Spanish—in schools and public affairs undermines the sense of social solidarity and national identity that rest on sharing a common language. As of 1990, laws declaring English to be the official language had passed in seventeen states and were pending in nine others.

Language exists as a part of social environments only when it is shared. As this elderly teacher in Ethiopia passes on his language to his student, with it follows the gateway to a common culture and way of life.

The third social function of language is that it often serves as a kind of nonphysical contact: we "keep in touch" by telephone, letter, and small talk that often appears to be meaningless. When we meet someone and ask, "How are you?" we rarely expect more than a short reply such as "fine" or "OK." Many people look upon such exchanges as phony or trivial, but they allow us to briefly "touch" one another. It is as if we say, "I see you; do you see me?" and thereby make contact, reaffirming our existence in the eyes of others (the importance of which is painfully evident when people ignore us). We also use language as a symbolic substitute for physical violence and yell at each other just as some birds angrily spread their tail feathers or elk toss their antlers.

Fourth, some utterances, known as **performative language**, constitute meaningful actions simply by being spoken. To say "I promise" *is* to make a promise, just as "I do" seals a marriage. When a friend

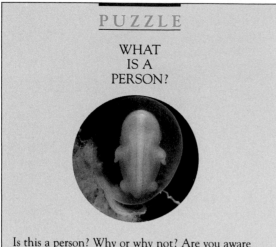

Is this a person? Why or why not? Are you aware of people who would answer these questions differently? What is the basis of the difference? How does this question differ from "Is the earth round?"

On both sides of the abortion controversy, sincere people argue about not when life literally begins, but at what point a fetus becomes a person in a social sense, subject to the protections of its community. As you can see in the section on beliefs, such arguments persist because they have less to do with objective scientific fact than with the beliefs that make up a basic part of culture.

looks you in the eyes and says "I love you" for the first time, it is often more than an expression of feeling. It is an invitation to enter into a relationship with particular expectations; that it is an offer is painfully clear if you fail to reciprocate with "I love you, too." If you do reciprocate, you, too, may have done more than express feelings. The general terms of your new relationship are established simply by uttering such phrases, and they can be undone only with other performative utterances such as, "I don't love you any more." What makes such language performative is its specialized culturally recognized authority to change existing relationships or create new ones.

Perhaps the most marvelous aspect of language, aside from its sheer complexity and seemingly endless variations, is that we are able to participate in it with little or no conscious effort. It is so familiar to us, so close to our everyday lives, that we are likely to think of it as an inherent part of each human being. Language, however, does not arise from the iso-

lated psychological experience of individuals, even though each of us possesses the biological and psychological characteristics that make language possible. The creation of a single word is complete only when two or more people share its meaning. While a single mind can create a sound, until it has a shared meaning it is only a noise, not a word. The development of separate languages—English, French, Swahili, Chinese, Hebrew, Arabic, or the thousands of others—does not rest on differences in physiology or psychology, but on the endless variations produced by social interactions extending across many generations.

As a collection of symbols and rules, language is the basis of all beliefs, values, norms, and attitudes. The following sections describe in detail each of these components of nonmaterial culture.

Beliefs: The Real and the Unreal

Beliefs are symbolic statements about what is real, such as "The earth is flat," "There is a God," "There are 100 centimeters in a meter," and "The way to get ahead in the world is to obey the rules and work hard." All of these are beliefs because they try to describe some aspect of reality. Whether or not we accept them as true, they are nonetheless beliefs.

Not all statements about what is real are *cultural* beliefs. An individual cannot create or change cultural beliefs by waking up one morning and saying, "The earth is a cube." A belief is cultural only if the ultimate authority for its validity lies outside of individuals—in our assumptions that others share in the particular belief. When the astronomer Copernicus observed the heavens and concluded that the earth was not the center of the universe, his sole authority rested in his own observations, and his belief—at least initially—was strictly a personal one. Copernicus and, later, Galileo were persecuted not because their beliefs were objectively incorrect, but because they contradicted those of the surrounding culture and struck at the heart of an entire system of religious beliefs about the relationship between God and humanity.

Beliefs furnish us with the "obvious" facts of our existence: it is "obvious" to anyone reading this book that the earth is round. But it was equally obvious to some living in fifteenth-century Europe that the earth was flat and anyone sailing far enough from land would surely fall off the edge. No thing, then, in itself, is either obvious or obscure. What we call "obvious" is that which we do not question, and whether or not we question it is often more a matter of culture than objective reality. Just as beliefs provide us with categories for sorting perceptions and experiences, so they limit our awareness to those things that have a place in our cultural framework.

Values: Shoulds and Shouldn'ts

Whereas beliefs define what is real, cultural **values** define goals by ranking forms of behavior and social arrangements in terms of their relative desirability (see One Step Further 2-1, p. 32). "Honesty is better than dishonesty," "Competition is better than cooperation," and "People should not engage in premarital sex" are all statements about what we believe *should* be rather than about what *is*. Notice that in everyday speech people often use the word "belief" to refer to what is in fact a value. "I believe people

should be honest" is a cultural value statement, since it describes what *ought* to be, not what is. "I believe that most people *are* basically honest," however, is a belief since it refers to what is rather than to what should be.

We are born preferring some states of being over others. Infants prefer warmth to extreme cold or heat, satiation to hunger or thirst, comfort to pain, and contact to isolation. There are no ideas involved in such preferences, for infants have no symbols with which to construct ideas. Values, however, are abstract ideas about goals. Many readers of this book attend college, even if it involves considerable hardship, because they share the value that education, as an end in itself, is inherently desirable. It is "good" to be educated, and more education is better than less. Many also share the value that being able to use our brains well is more desirable than being able to use our hands well, and that high-prestige, high-paying jobs are more desirable than lower-prestige,

One of the hallmarks of nonindustrial societies is the need for cooperation for survival. This 1854 picture of a quilting party in Virginia shows not only a common effort towards producing basic household goods, but also a sense of community. Both are more difficult to find in modern industrial societies where independence and competition have become more important than cooperation.

ONE STEP FURTHER 2-1

Is Premarital Sex Wrong?

Only a minority (36%) of U.S. adults hold the value that premarital sex is always or almost always wrong (Davis and Smith 1990), but like most values in complex societies, the positions people take on this issue depend strongly on their social characteristics. The figures in Table B-2-1 show differences by education, region of the country, family income, age, race, gender, and ethnicity in the percentage of adults saying that premarital sex is always or almost always wrong. If you have not yet studied Chapter 6, you might want to look at "How to Read a Table" on p. 115 before going on.

Notice how strongly some social characteristics affect the tendency to disapprove of premarital sex:

The more education people have, the less likely they are to disapprove.

Southerners are most likely to disapprove, least likely in the Northeast.

The higher the family income is, the less likely adults are to disapprove.

The elderly are three times more likely to disapprove than younger people (63% vs. 20%).

Protestants disapprove more than Catholics (42% vs. 30%) and "others" (which include Jews and those with no religious preference) are a distant third (21%).

Whites and nonwhites are equally likely to disapprove.

Women are more likely than men to disapprove (40% vs. 30%).

There has been a steady decline in disapproval of premarital sex, from 46% in 1972 to only 36% in 1990.

It is important, as you study these figures, to begin to acquire an appreciation for the idea of *variation*, that elements of culture such as beliefs and values change over time and differ from one social grouping to another, something which is a source of diversity and conflict.

TABLE B-2-1   Percent Who Say Premarital Sex Is Always or Almost Always Wrong by Selected Social Characteristics, United States

SOCIAL CHARACTERISTICS	PERCENT WHO DISAPPROVE OF PREMARITAL SEX	SOCIAL CHARACTERISTICS	PERCENT WHO DISAPPROVE OF PREMARITAL SEX
Education		*Age*	
Less than high school graduate	42	18–25	20
High school graduate	38	26–39	25
Some college	32	40–59	31
College degree	35	60 and older	63
Graduate education	23	*Religion*	
Region		Protestant	42
Northeast	24	Catholic	30
Midwest	36	Other	21
South	44	*Race*	
West	33	White	36
Family Income		Nonwhite	34
Less than $10,000	45	*Gender*	
$10,000 to $20,000	40	Female	40
$20,000 to $30,000	31	Male	30
$30,000 to $40,000	34		
$40,000 to $60,000	33		
$60,000 or more	30		

Source: Computed from 1990 General Social Survey data.

lower-paying ones. The cultural desirability of education is reflected in individual choices, but as an idea it exists independently of individuals, just as do cultural beliefs.

Also, like beliefs, values are quite different from personal tastes and preferences. If you say, "I like mayonnaise," no one can say "you shouldn't like it," for it expresses a preference whose sole authority is you as an individual. A value judgment, on the other hand, rests on sources of authority outside the individual. "You should not eat mayonnaise because the cholesterol in it is bad for your health" is a judgment that rests on the value we place on good health and long life (and the belief that cholesterol contributes to heart disease).

If you reply, "I don't care if I get heart disease," the response will likely be one of shock (except in a subculture that values eating whatever you like more than health), and the shocked person will know that others share that negative judgment. As a value, health is not more important than self-indulgence because you say it is; its relative "goodness" is part of a culture in which some ends rank higher than others.

Because we share such ideas with others in our culture, they influence our choices. They not only predispose us to strive in competition, to be honest and loyal, but they may also be used to manipulate our decisions. The advertising industry, for example, regularly uses established values to sell merchandise. The interior of a car may be described as sexy; spark plugs may be displayed next to a picture of a beautiful woman. In both cases, the masculine values placed on attracting, possessing, or having power over a woman are paired with the idea of buying something that has no inherent connection to them. If men accept the pairing, they are more likely to buy the product, not because they value it but because they value the goals the advertisement associates with it.

While we may pursue what we want, values powerfully influence what it is we want in the first place. As the German philosopher Schopenhauer put it, "We want what we will, but we don't will what we want." We may *think* that we freely choose to compete with others rather than cooperate, but we are largely unaware that in a different culture we would place different values on such behavior and make very different choices. The Zuni Indians of the U.S. Southwest, for example, value cooperation more than competition:

Personal authority is perhaps the most vigorously disparaged trait in Zuni. A man who thirsts for power or

knowledge, who wishes to be as they scornfully phrase it, "a leader of his people," receives nothing but censure and will very likely be persecuted for sorcery. . . . The ideal man in Zuni is a person of dignity and affability who has never tried to lead, and who has never called forth comment from his neighbors. . . . Even in contests of skill like their foot races, if a man wins habitually he is debarred from running. They are interested in a game that a number can play with even chances, and an outstanding runner spoils the game: they will have none of him (Benedict 1934, p. 95).

The value systems of most societies are complex, changing, and often contradictory. Williams (1970), for example, identified fifteen core values that he believed have an enduring place in U.S. culture. Americans, he pointed out, tend to value achievement and success; competition and hard work; doing what is morally right; looking out for the underdog and those less fortunate; being efficient and practical; facing the future optimistically; having material comforts; equal opportunity and treating everyone as equals; freedom; conformity; solving problems rationally and scientifically; being proud of the "American way of life"; guaranteeing democratic rights; individual autonomy, responsibility, and self-respect; and the use of characteristics such as race, ethnicity, gender, and age to value some people more than others.

As with any complex society, these values are not shared equally by everyone and vary in their authority from one social situation to another. In addition, they are often a source of contradiction and conflict: the value placed on being white, for example, conflicts with the value of equal treatment and opportunity, just as the value of conformity conflicts with the value of individualism. Although such conflicts are important on the level of entire societies—as ongoing struggles such as the civil rights movement make clear—they also exist on the individual level as each of us tries to resolve value conflicts.

When Values Conflict   We often hold values that, in a particular situation, produce conflict. Suppose you see a friend cheating on an exam. On the one hand, you value truth and honesty, for these are among the most fundamental values in a university. On the other hand, you value loyalty to friends. No matter what you choose to do—to tell on your friend or not—you will violate a value.

Values produce conflict because they make up a loose "grammar" of thought about the importance of different alternatives, and because we occupy many

As you will see in the section on norms, both lying and telling the truth are forms of social behavior and whether or not we are expected to do one or the other depends very much on the social situation.

Norms: Dos and Don'ts

While values provide us with general guidelines for behavior, norms are specific rules. A **norm** defines punishments or rewards (called **sanctions**) for various forms of behavior or appearance according to people's positions in social relationships. While all actions have objective consequences, norms specify *social* consequences for the person performing the action.

If I kill a man, he dies; if I smack my lips at the dinner table, a noise results. The death and the noise are objective consequences. If I kill a man identified as the enemy in a war, however, his death is not the only consequence, for I might be rewarded with a medal. If I kill a man because I do not like the color of his eyes or disagree with his politics, on the other hand, I will be punished. If I smack my lips over dinner in the United States, people may show disapproval by frowning, but if I smack them in India, people are more likely to smile at me. If I am caught stealing a traveler's suitcase in the United States, I might be sent to jail; in the Sudan, however, the penalty for one unfortunate thief was to have his right hand cut off in a public ceremony.

In each case, the link between the act and the consequences for the actor is artificial; it is not inherent in the act itself. The statements "If you kill an enemy, you will get a medal" and "If you kill a man because you don't like him you will be punished" are norms that link specific acts to social consequences that we can expect from other people who share our culture. When we are punished for violating a norm (or rewarded for conforming to one), it is not because of what we did, it is because of the *rule*; if the rule changes, the same behavior no longer brings with it the same sanctions (Durkheim [1924] 1974).

There are several types of norms; the most important are *folkways* and *mores* (pronounced "morayz"), each of which can take the form of a *law.*

Folkways In a classic work, William Graham Sumner (1906) defined a society's **folkways** as the set of manners and customary acts that characterize everyday life in a society. As a set of norms, folkways regulate behavior whose consequences are relatively trivial and in which the resulting sanctions tend to be correspondingly mild. We are not supposed to stare at people or stand too close when talking with them. We are expected to face front in elevators, replace

---

PUZZLE

IS HONESTY ALWAYS THE BEST POLICY?

How do you know when to lie and when to tell the truth? Have you ever been in a situation in which you were expected to lie and would be punished if you told the truth?

As you will see in the section on norms, both lying and telling the truth are forms of social behavior and whether or not we are expected to do one or the other depends very much on the social situation.

---

social positions in different social systems, each with its own values. The values of "respect for the law" and "loyalty to one's friends" are *general* guidelines that do not tell us what to do in specific situations.

By presenting them with a series of dilemmas, Kohlberg (1963) studied how children choose among conflicting values. In one, a man's wife is desperately ill and can be saved only with a new drug invented by a local pharmacist. The pharmacist demands an exorbitant price, far beyond the man's ability to pay. The husband later breaks into the pharmacy and steals the drug. Was he wrong? The answer depends on which value we consider to be more important.

To Kohlberg, we learn to apply values in the same way we learn grammatical rules that allow us to construct and interpret sentences we have never encountered before. We learn only general rules—such as "It's wrong to steal" and "Put family first"—which we then apply to specific situations. Just as no one ever taught you the meaning of the preceding sentence, no one teaches us what to do if someone in our family needs a medicine that we cannot afford to buy. To solve such dilemmas, then, we participate in a system of values, interpreting and choosing in search of what Roger Brown (1965) called "some reasonable consistency among judgment, feeling, and action" (p. 414). In doing so, we also learn to interpret and apply the abstract principles contained in values in light of our concern and caring for the actual human consequences that may result from choosing one alternative or another (see Gilligan 1982).

Folkways include customs that govern how people greet each other when they meet. Soviet Premier Mikhail Gorbachev would never greet George Bush as he would one of his own countrymen.

caps on toothpaste tubes, return library books on time, and not refer to our parents by their first name.

Folkways are a particularly fluid form of norm, subject to rapid change, inconsistent application, and enormous variation among the world's cultures. It was not very long ago that men were expected to open doors for women, but now expectations have changed considerably, and the simple act of passing through a doorway can be an occasion for substantial negotiation and uncertainty (Walum 1974).

As with all norms, the application of folkways, depends on the situation (see Edgerton 1985). Staring at a stranger on a bus violates a folkway, for example, but we are expected to stare at performers in a theater. Folkways also vary enormously from one culture to another. In Latin cultures people are expected to stand close to each other when talking; to North Americans and Europeans this proximity would feel uncomfortable. Compared with the British up-

per class, Americans are more likely to assume familiarity by calling people by their first name. The Japanese remove their shoes whenever they enter a house and many Icelanders consider it impolite to leave a party before three or four o'clock in the morning.

A society's folkways describe the fine texture of everyday life, the manners and customs that its members take for granted as "the way we do things." Only when we encounter the folkways of different cultures do we become aware of ours as peculiar rather than as the natural way of going about life.

Mores and Morality   **Mores** are norms that reflect deeply held cultural ideals about how people should behave (Sumner 1906). While folkways distinguish between relatively unimportant categories—polite and impolite, clean and dirty, sophisticated and vulgar—mores make more important distinctions, such as those between good and bad, virtuous

and sinful, laudable and repugnant. A society's
mores define standards of behavior that are more serious than those defined by folkways, and punishment for their violation tends to be both more certain and more severe.

There is a story about two children, the first of
whom has two apples, one large and the other small,
and offers to share them. When the second child
takes the large apple, the first protests, "Hey, why'd
you take the big one?"

"Which one would you have taken?" asks the second child.

"The small one."

"Then you got what you wanted, didn't you?"

The first child is outraged because the second ignored an important moral principle: When one person offers something to another, the recipient is expected to reciprocate—to return the favor—by not
taking full advantage of the choice. There is actually
an exchange going on in this interaction—an apple
in exchange for restraint and moderation—and the
second child's failure to reciprocate violates important cultural ideas about fairness and reciprocity
(Gouldner 1960; see also Fisher, Nadler, and De-
Paulo 1983).

Mores focus on what most of us think of as morality, and several social characteristics distinguish
moral acts from immoral ones. First, moral acts
never have the actor's self-interest as their only goal.
This is what distinguishes Robin Hood's acts of steal-

ing from similar acts by someone who steals for personal gain. This does not imply that an act is immoral if done purely for personal reasons: to run into
a burning house to save people's lives is a moral act,
but to stay outside out of concern for our own lives
usually will be excused. A moral act thus differs from
other acts in that it is performed in the interests of
other people.

The second social characteristic of moral acts is
that they have a quality of command. We do them
because we are supposed to, out of a sense of duty and
obligation not simply to another individual, but to
the values embodied in the act (the value of honesty
or of a human life). We refrain from some acts simply
because they are forbidden in our culture. If a cashier
in a store gives us too much change and we knowingly take it, we do not simply hurt the cashier or the
company; we violate one of the terms of our participation in social life. If we return the money, we
affirm our place in society and feel the pleasure of
belonging.

Third, moral acts have an element of social desirability. They are "good," just as immoral acts are
"bad," and we feel genuine pleasure simply from doing "the right thing" (or guilt from doing "the wrong
thing"), whether or not we tell other people and
bask in the glow of their approval.

Finally, ideas about morality are sacred. Because
they reflect the deepest collective feelings about who
we are and should be, we attach strong feelings to
them. While specific laws may allow some people to
do things forbidden to others, the idea that "no one
is above the law" is a moral one that applies to us all,
even, as Richard Nixon discovered, someone who is
the president of the United States.

As with folkways, the application of mores often
depends on the situation. While dishonesty violates
general cultural mores, there are situations in which
it is permitted or expected. As Bok (1979) pointed
out, mores permit us to lie in order to save a life or
mislead an enemy during wartime. Scientists may
deceive and lie to subjects about the aims of their
research, parents lie to their children about everything from the existence of Santa Claus to the details
of sexual behavior, and physicians may lie about the
true condition of terminally ill patients.

There is also considerable cross-cultural variation
in the definition of moral behavior. Cannibal tribes
in Oceania do not consider it immoral to eat human
flesh, and the Nayar of India do not define adultery
as immoral. Eating pork violates the mores of Ortho-

dox Jews, but in other cultures the consumption of pork is part of an annual celebration of great importance (Harris 1974). In addition, while the mores of all known cultures prohibit murder, there is considerable variation in its definition. In Western cultures, killing for personal revenge is defined and punished as murder, but in some other cultures killing to avenge the murder of a relative is expected.

Mores extend beyond the rightness or wrongness of certain acts to the most profound ideas of what life

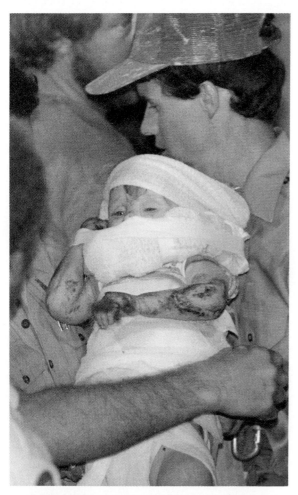

In Midland, Texas, rescuers worked feverishly for 58 hours—some at the risk of their lives—to rescue Jessica McClure, a small child who had fallen down a well. Several months later, two different groups of rescuers organized to compete for financially lucrative contracts for movie rights to their stories. From a social point of view, how does this development affect the moral standing of their heroism?

in a society is supposed to be about. Mores have been used throughout history to justify everything from self-sacrifice and charity to outrageous cruelty. The murder of over eleven million people, including 6 million Jews during the Holocaust was seen by the Nazis as "the final solution" to the "Jewish problem" that, they believed, stood between them and the realization of the "supremacy of the Aryan race." To many Nazis, the execution of millions of men, women, and children was part of a crusade for racial "purity," full of moral self-righteousness; while, to those who did not share their vision, the Holocaust was a crime of unimaginable immorality and horror (see Dawidowicz 1975).

Laws   As norms, both folkways and mores involve sanctions which can be either informal or formal. **Informal sanctions** are not clearly defined and anyone has the right to impose them. If we belch loudly in the company of others, anyone has the right to impose a variety of sanctions ranging from the slightest frown to an angry outburst.

Formal sanctions, on the other hand, are clearly defined and people in specialized social positions have the power and responsibility to impose them. If I steal your radio, it is not up to you to enforce the sanctions attached to the norm prohibiting theft. The sanctions as well as the procedures for deciding if and how to apply them are clearly specified; and specific people are authorized to apprehend me, determine my guilt or innocence, and impose punishment. Norms with formal sanctions are called **laws**.

Criminal law links specific acts with punishments (expulsion from school for cheating; imprisonment for stealing; fines for reckless driving). To violate such a law is not simply an act against an individual, for it represents an act against society itself. When someone commits murder, we may feel outrage regardless of our relationship to the victim, and it is the state that prosecutes the case, not the victim's friends and family.

Civil law regulates social relationships and, when possible, undoes the negative effects of a particular act. Civil law regulates relationships among producers, buyers, and sellers (commercial law); the functioning of courts and their officers (procedural law); the relationship between citizens and their government (constitutional law); and the relationships among family members (family law), determining, for example, which parent gets custody of children in case of divorce. In addition, if you slip on a

In some cultures, as in France, dogs are cherished as pets who, when they die, are accorded the kind of treatment usually reserved for humans. In others, such as China, dogs are valued in quite a different way. How do these pictures make you feel, and how do you explain your feelings?

skateboard on my front porch and break your leg, the state will not prosecute me under criminal law; but you might sue me in order to pay for your hospital bills and compensate you for the results of my negligence.

One of the most basic cultural ideas in civil law is that of the *contract*, which is an agreement between two parties to exchange one thing for another; such as, I will give you $5,000 if you will paint my house. The idea of a contract clearly illustrates the fact that norms exist apart from individuals, for the power behind the agreement extends beyond the people who are directly involved. If I refuse to pay you when you fulfill your part of the bargain, society itself supports your claim—*not* out of concern for you as an individual, but to preserve the culturally valued idea of a contract. Society is an "interested party" in all contracts (Durkheim [1893] 1933).

Formal and informal sanctions are used to enforce both folkways and mores. While mores usually involve formal sanctions (as in the case of murder), in some cases (such as lying to a friend) the sanctions are informal. Spitting on a sidewalk violates a folkway, but the sanctions are formal (it is against the law); but if we spit on the floor at a party, the sanctions are informal (the host cannot have us arrested). Note, however, that while specific laws may or may not have a moral content (double-parking is not immoral, but murder is), the *idea* of "the law" is a profoundly moral one.

Keep in mind that although folkways and mores may be the most sociologically significant types of norms, there are many norms that fall into neither category. Much of what we include under the general term of ethics, for example, concerns behavior that is serious but not immoral. The same can be said of behaviors that violate a variety of laws—such as those against speeding while driving a car or cheating on income taxes: each is far more serious than failing to display proper table manners, but neither is generally considered to be immoral, either.

Attitudes: Evaluation and Feeling

Unlike beliefs, values, and norms, attitudes focus on emotions. **Attitudes** are positive or negative evaluations of objects, people, or situations that predispose us to feel and behave toward them in positive or negative ways (Allport 1935; Hill 1981; Kiecolt 1988). Although they involve beliefs and values, what sets attitudes apart are the feelings that are connected to these ideas, feelings such as hatred, reverence, awe, disgust, affection, contempt, and pity. This means that the key to identifying an attitude is to see the emotions that it involves.

We have the ability to experience and display many emotions, but to understand their ebb and flow, we must go beyond the psychology of individual motives to the cultures that produce patterns of thought, feeling, and behavior (see Thoits 1989). The shared love of a country—patriotism—is an at-titude that encompasses beliefs ("our country is the best there is") and emotions (pride, excitement, love), and makes us more likely to behave aggressively toward anyone who threatens our positive national image. In many respects, popular U.S. sports such as hockey and football show many of the characteristics of warfare, complete with injuries and hatred of the "enemy." From a cultural point of view, hockey players (and their fans) are not violent because of an aggressive human nature; rather, they are aggressive because they play hockey and share in its subcultural attitudes.

Guilt, pride, shame, sympathy, love, and gratitude are attitudes that exist only in a social context (Clark 1987; Gordon 1981; Kemper 1987). Without culture, there is no occasion for such emotions, for they rest on beliefs and values used to interpret and judge behavior. Fear exists as a primary emotion in many animal species, but only in a cultural context

As a cultural attitude, racial prejudice often includes deep feelings of contempt, hostility, and fear. In this Pulitzer Prize winning picture, whites, who have just recited the pledge of allegiance, attack a black businessman as he walks near a rally against a court-ordered busing plan to integrate schools. The incident took place during the bicentennial year in Boston, a city considered by many to be the "cradle of liberty."

do we find the concept of cowardice and the shame that goes with it.

All attitudes are connected to beliefs, but people may share an attitude without sharing a particular belief, just as they may share a belief without sharing a related attitude. Attitudes of racial hatred are often justified by a variety of beliefs such as a belief in the genetic inferiority of a hated group. Others, however, might feel just as strongly but justify their attitude with a different belief—such as "they're cruel and dirty."

Cultural ideas influence what we think, feel, and do. Just as gravity pulls our bodies toward the center of the earth, cultural ideas "pull" us toward centers of meaning, value, and expectation. We resist—even defy—gravity in many ways; in the simplest act of standing up an individual resists gravity's pull. We also resist, and sometimes defy, the constraining force of culture as when we play with language or violate norms. In this sense, culture does not determine who we are, what we feel and think, or what we do. Nor do we act in a vacuum, free of the limitations imposed by social environments. The character of our lives and our relationships with one another are, rather, the result of an *interaction* between ourselves and our environments.

Cultural Relativism, Subcultures, and Ethnocentrism

Some aspects of culture—such as dancing, games, and language—are found in every known society and are thus referred to as **cultural universals** (see Table 2-1). In general, however, symbols and ideas vary enormously among societies: What is regarded as truth in one may be unrecognized or regarded as nonsense in others. Ideas that exist in one culture may not exist in others or, if they do, they may be considered less important. This phenomenon is called **cultural relativism**. The belief that the deliberate killing of a child is murder does not exist in all cultures, for in some—such as Brazil's Tenetehara tribe—the killing of infants is a culturally legitimate practice. Most westerners experience kissing as a very pleasurable activity, but when the Thonga of Africa first encountered the practice among visiting Europeans, they were horrified by what they regarded as "eating each other's saliva and dirt" (Hyde 1979, p. 18).

Ideas also vary within cultures. A **subculture** is a distinctive set of cultural ideas that sets a group of people apart from the culture of its surrounding community or society. While U.S. culture generally defines marijuana as a dangerous substance, many knowingly share the belief that it is harmless, and such beliefs support and encourage its use among those who share in that subculture. This is especially true in the criminal subculture of smugglers and dealers who live the "fast lane" life of the drug trade (Adler 1985).

Because cultural ideas define reality for us, we often judge the ideas of other cultures as incorrect, if not inferior—an attitude called **ethnocentrism** (Sumner 1906). Most societies have, at one time or another, regarded outsiders as "barbarians" whose cultures were "uncivilized" or "stupid" simply because they were different. "How could they live that way?" we may ask. The essence of ethnocentrism is that we rarely realize that people in other cultures might ask the same question of us.

In our own culture many of us believe that romantic love is essential for marriage, and if ours is the only culture we have ever known, we might believe that this reflects human nature rather than cultural beliefs and values. If we study history, we find that in

TABLE 2-1   Some Aspects of Culture Found in All Known Societies

Beliefs about death	Inheritance rules
Bodily adornment	Interpretation of dreams
Calendar	Joking
Cleanliness training	Language
Cooking	Law
Cosmology	Magic
Courtship	Medicine
Dance	Mourning
Decorative art	Numerals
Divination	Personal names
Education	Population policy
Ethics	Property rights
Etiquette	Puberty customs
Faith healing	Religious ritual
Feasting	Sexual restrictions
Fire making	Soul concepts
Folklore	Sports
Games	Superstition
Gift giving	Surgery
Hair styles	Toolmaking
Hospitality	Trade
Hygiene	Weaning
Incest taboos	Weather control

Source: Murdock 1943.

Western cultures the idea of romantic love is quite recent, dating back only to the fourteenth century, and in our own time there are many cultures, such as China's, in which the importance of romantic love in marriage is considerably less than in our own.

Ethnocentrism distorts our perceptions by encouraging us to think of the world only from our own point of view. People of European ancestry like to think that explorers, such as Columbus, "discovered" the "Dark Continent" of Africa and the "New World" of North and South America. This would come as a great surprise to the peoples of many cultures who lived and thrived throughout those areas for centuries before any European set sail. To these peoples, what were mysteries to the Europeans were simply part of their everyday environment. It is only through the narrow eye of ethnocentrism that we in the U.S. can believe that before whites set foot in North America it was an "undiscovered" place (see Braudel 1981).

The opposite of ethnocentrism is **xenocentrism**, or the tendency to see aspects of other cultures as superior to our own. People in the United States, for example, often assume that goods made in Europe are better or more desirable than the same goods made at home, even though they actually might be of inferior quality. We may tend to assume that French and German wines or European cheeses are superior to those produced in the U.S., for example, or that a product whose name is simply in a foreign language is more exotic and, hence, valuable—even if it is in fact made here. Like ethnocentrism, xenocentrism is a common cultural phenomenon—many people in Third World countries assume that Western cultures are superior and may devalue their own as a result. In the Philippines, for example, most popular music is derived from U.S. rock and not traditional Philippine musical forms. Even folk festivals may exclude the rich Filipino folk heritage.

MATERIAL CULTURE

The production of material goods lies at the core of human existence, and the development of **material culture** takes place only through a web of social relationships. We produce not only to satisfy our needs, but also because "free, conscious activity" and "productive life" are important aspects of what makes us human (Marx, in Schaff 1970, p. 125).

Through the course of history, people have developed an astonishing variety of objects that affect human life. The invention of the plow and wheel,

Computer technology has revolutionized warfare by making it possible to fight devastating wars without ever seeing the enemy. This picture of the Pentagon War Room in Washington, D.C., shows how remote from the realities of war modern decision-makers can be.

around 6,000 years ago, revolutionized the ability to travel, produce food, and conduct trade. The development of printing, first by the Chinese in the fifth century A.D. and then with Gutenberg's invention of movable type in the fifteenth century, stimulated a rapid spread of literacy and new ideas. The Industrial Revolution began in the middle of the eighteenth century with the invention of machines such as textile looms and the use of new sources of power such as steam. The application of the steam engine to transportation in the mid-1800s vastly expanded the markets for goods and hence stimulated their production. The last hundred years have seen the rapid development of mass production, the automobile, light and durable plastics, and revolutions in communications and computer technology.

Such objects are cultural in that they arise from the human ability to think in symbolic terms, to share the resulting knowledge, and to build on previous inventions in the creation of others. They also reflect values and beliefs: the rapid development of industrial technology, for example, reflects not only possessions as a value, but, in capitalist societies, the value of profit, which is increased by mechanization and more efficient production.

The development of material culture is often a social response to the pressures of population and ecological conditions. Growing populations require new methods for satisfying subsistence needs. Those methods, in turn, often create the need for further innovation. When coal was first used as a source of power in the United States it was easy to obtain: in Pennsylvania, it lay on the surface of the earth. As we consumed it in greater and greater quantities, it became necessary to go underground, and this required more sophisticated machines to drill and haul the coal.

Material culture, however, is not merely a way of adapting to a changing physical environment, for as we will see in Chapter 4 and elsewhere, it is also a major way for social systems to affect their environments, sometimes with disastrous consequences. Many of the most pressing social problems of the 1990s, such as pollution, hazardous waste, acid rain, and the shortage of cheap, clean energy are closely connected with material culture. Without the technology that made industrialization possible, for example, there would be no voracious demand for oil, nuclear power, and other forms of nonrenewable energy; nor would there be the mountains of waste that outstrip our ability to dispose of it.

Material culture affects not only the physical environment, but social systems as well. Without the medical technology to extend life, for example, we would not be struggling with questions of whether a family has the right to withdraw life-support systems when there seems to be no hope of recovery. Technology has transformed the experience of dying—both for those who die and for those involved with them—and in the process has raised profoundly troubling social and moral issues. In similar ways, reproductive technology has created dilemmas that were unforeseen when they were developed. The ability to identify the sex of a fetus, for example, has been used in some countries to choose abortion as a method of sex selection by parents. In India, this has already resulted in a decline in female births due to the cultural bias in favor of male infants (see Corea et al. 1987).

Material culture affects social systems in countless other ways that shape everyday life. From the kinds of dwellings we live in to the food we eat and the clothes we wear, from how we learn about events in the world to how we travel about, from the conduct of warfare to saving an endangered life—material culture plays a prominent role. The automobile, for example, did more than allow increased mobility; it also contributed to the growth of cities and rush hours with all their tensions. It became a place for young people to be alone, beyond the watchful eyes of parents; and, for many, it provided an instrument for aggression, self-expression, and displays of wealth and individuality. In similar ways, the development of reliable contraceptive technology has also had widespread and varied consequences. Not only has it contributed to dramatic declines in birth rates (see Chapter 4), but it has given women unprecedented control over their bodies and has for the first time in history made in possible to separate human sexual expression from reproduction.

The relationship between material and nonmaterial culture is both complex and reciprocal. The explosive growth in electronics and computer technology, for example, raises new threats to rights of privacy. There is now a growing alarm over the relative ease with which the operators of home computers can gain access to records stored in computers in hospitals, universities, banks, military research laboratories, and other institutions. When this was first discovered, there were no laws that defined it as a crime, because the spread of computer technology had been so rapid that such invasions had not come up as a serious possibility. As new laws are passed in order to protect the security of computers and the right to privacy, new technology must be invented to secure computers against unauthorized access.

An even more important aspect of material culture is that objects, once created, become independent parts of their creators' culture. Computers do only what programmers and operators tell them to do, and yet we often blame computers for everything from errors on telephone bills to the junk mail we would rather not receive. With the blame often goes the belief that computers somehow have power to control our lives, power beyond what their human creators and operators choose to do with them. As machines and other products of material culture assume greater and greater importance, we may "begin to feel ourselves as things that are parts of the surrounding world of things" (Schaff 1970, p. 106).

THE PRODUCTION OF CULTURE

By definition, material culture is produced by people; but this is also true of nonmaterial culture even though we may not think of it that way. Mainstream sociology typically views culture as a set of symbols and ideas that underlie social life, and exists as taken-for-granted assumptions that shape how we perceive, feel, think, interpret, and act. A growing number of sociologists, however, also pay attention to culture as something actively produced by social systems—books and magazines, music, art, architectural styles, plays, radio and television programs, comic books, stories, legends and fables, political propaganda, science, technical knowledge, religious ritual. These sociologists raise questions about both how culture is produced in social systems and how its content affects social life (see Becker 1982; Peterson 1990; Powell 1985; Wuthnow 1987; Wuthnow and Witten 1988).

Art, for example, is a cultural product that emerges from complex relationships between artists, gallery owners, private and public funding agencies, museums, and audiences. The controversial exhibit of the late artist Robert Maplethorpe's homoerotic photographs provoked such a storm of outrage that some Congressional leaders tried to pressure the National Endowment for the Arts to withhold support from any artist who refused to promise not to produce "offensive" works. This raised deep concerns within the artistic community since many artists depend on financial support from government and corporate sponsors and yet regard their freedom to create as fundamental to the work that they do. The debate that followed raised questions about the social importance of free artistic expression, the place of art in community life, and whether artists have a right to some share of public resources in order to produce art (see Pankratz and Morris 1990; Wyszomirski 1988). The related issue of censorship in music was raised in 1990 when two members of the rap group 2 Live Crew were arrested in Florida for performing songs that local authorities, later backed up by a federal judge, had declared obscene.

If we look at culture as something that is produced, then, rather than take it for granted as part of the social environment, we can ask questions about the social conditions from which it emerges. To what degree, for example, are scientists objective in their research, and to what degree does research result from a social process governed by values and methods that have relatively little to do with science (see Chapter 18)? How do families as social systems produce elements of their culture such as shared stories about childhood or special ways of celebrating holidays? How do subcultures emerge in corporations? How do political ideologies develop, such as the prochoice and pro-life sides of the abortion controversy, positions so polarized that there is no shared common ground on which they can meet to communicate (see Luker 1984; Wuthnow and Witten 1988)?

In Jasper Johns's painting By the Sea (1961) he uses culturally symbolic images to question ideas about color and language. What does this tell you about the social system in which it was produced? © Jasper Johns/VAGA, New York 1991.

This approach to cultural analysis is important because it reminds us that culture is not a static background in social systems but is always in the process of being produced, shaped, and changed.

The concepts of material and nonmaterial culture are tools that make up a major part of the sociological perspective. Social systems, however, are more than a vast collection of ideas and objects swirling about us like a thick soup. They are organized around social relationships that produce patterns of expectation and behavior. These patterns are part of the second major sociological concept, social structure, the subject of Chapter 3.

SUMMARY

1. Although culture consists of both material and nonmaterial products, the essence of culture is nonmaterial and is made up of abstract beliefs, values, attitudes, and norms. These are expressed through symbols: objects, characteristics of objects, gestures, or words that represent more than themselves. Language is a collection of symbols and rules for their use shared by those who make up a speech community.

2. Language is a creative medium through which we construct knowledge and what we experience as reality. In addition, it serves four social functions. It allows people to express experience, to store records of it, and to assume that others know what they mean when they write or talk; it allows members of a speech community to distinguish between themselves and outsiders; and it often substitutes for physical contact. In addition, performative language is a meaningful action that alters people's positions in social relationships.

3. Beliefs are statements about reality, and are cultural only if their authority lies outside of individuals in the shared assumption that other people support them. Values rank behavior and social arrangements in terms of relative desirability. Values often conflict because they are loose guidelines for making choices and because we occupy positions in many different relationships, each governed by its own set of values.

4. Norms are rules that prescribe sanctions—punishments or rewards—for appearance and behavior according to positions in social relationships. Sanctions may be either informal—loosely defined with no specific people authorized to impose them—or formal—clearly defined with specific people empowered to deliver them.

5. There are three kinds of norms. Folkways are norms (such as table manners) that regulate relatively trivial behaviors in everyday social interactions. Mores, however, reflect deeply held ideas about how people should behave. Norms with formal sanctions are called laws. Criminal law links specific acts with punishments, while civil law regulates social relationships (such as marriage and divorce), deals with contracts, and undoes the effects of an action (as when someone sues someone else to pay for damaged property).

6. Attitudes are predispositions to feel positive or negative emotions toward people and to behave toward them in positive or negative ways. Attitudes also include the feelings people have toward themselves, such as guilt, pride, or shame.

7. Cultural relativism refers to the fact that the importance of a particular cultural product varies from one social environment to another. Ethnocentrism describes the tendency of people to regard other cultures or subcultures as inferior to their own. The concepts of cultural relativism and ethnocentrism can also apply within a society in relation to subcultures, which set a group apart from a surrounding community or society.

8. Material culture consists of objects people make as they interact with each other and the physical world. The relationship between material and nonmaterial culture is complex and reciprocal. Ideas often lead to the creation of objects, but objects can become so important a part of the environment that they affect the cultural ideas that regulate social interaction.

KEY TERMS

attitude 39	gesture 26	performative language 29
belief 30	informal sanction 37	sanction 34
cultural relativism 40	language 27	speech community 28
cultural universals 40	law 37	subculture 40
culture 25	material culture 41	symbol 26
ethnocentrism 40	mores 35	value 31
folkways 34	nonmaterial culture 25	xenocentrism 41
formal sanction 37	norm 34	

LOOKING ELSEWHERE

Although you will be reading about culture throughout *Human Arrangements*, having studied this chapter you may want to look at some discussions with a particularly strong cultural focus, which include

■ the importance of language in socialization (Chapter 7, pp. 140–41)

■ language and gender roles (Chapter 14, pp. 329–31)

■ the controversy over English as the official language of the U.S. (Chapter 13, p. 303)

■ technology and material culture (Chapter 4, pp. 82–85; Chapter 18, pp. 452–58)

RECOMMENDED READINGS

Barlow, W. B. 1989. *"Looking up at down": The emergence of blues culture.* Philadelphia: Temple University Press. An insightful history of the blues as a musical form, from its rural beginnings to its development in major U.S. cities.

Benedict, R. [1934] 1960. *Patterns of culture.* New York: New American Library (paperback). A classic analysis of cultural relativism with a special emphasis on native American tribes.

Harris, M. 1985. *Good to eat: Riddles of food and culture.* New York: Simon and Schuster. Anthropologist Marvin Harris offers a rich and fascinating look at the cultural basis of what people like (and don't like) to eat.

Kephart, W. M., and Zellner, W. W. 1990. *Extraordinary groups: An examination of unconventional life-styles* (4th ed.). New York: St. Martin's Press. A fascinating analysis of past and present subcultures in the U.S., including the Amish, Oneida, Shakers, Mormons, and Jehovah's Witnesses.

Slater, P. 1976. *The pursuit of loneliness* (rev. ed.). Boston: Beacon Press. A passionate and articulate analysis in which a sociologist shows how cultural values can promote social isolation and loneliness.

Zborowski, M. 1953. Cultural components in responses to pain. *Journal of Social Issues*, 8, 16–31. A fascinating exploration into ethnic differences in the ways people experience and respond to pain in a hospital setting.

3
SOCIAL STRUCTURE

 Social structure is the second major concept that defines the sociological perspective. It describes the relationships we participate in during our lives, the limits they impose on our choices, and the conflicts that inevitably result; and it describes the place of each relationship in a complex web of patterns that give form to social life. As this chapter will make clear, understanding social structure is important in two ways—first, because through social structure we perform roles that connect us as individuals to other people and to social systems; and second, because a social system's structural characteristics profoundly affect what goes on in it and the consequences it produces.

THE CONCEPT OF SOCIAL STRUCTURE

One night an insurance agent named George feels ill and goes to the hospital emergency room. A doctor named Mary takes his case, and they talk in a small room. They have never met before, yet they share some expectations: he will call her "Doctor," not "Mary"; he will answer her questions as accurately as he can; he will follow her advice; and he will pay for her services. They also share the expectations that she knows what she is doing, that she will confine herself to questions that are relevant to his illness, and that she will keep his answers in strict confidence. While both are capable of a vast array of acts, they limit themselves to a very narrow range: they do not go to sleep or read aloud from the Bible; she does not undress (although he might), and he does not try to sell her an insurance policy.

George and Mary would behave differently when relaxing at home with their families, eating dinner in a restaurant, or meeting in the office of his insurance agency. Moreover, if the physician were Harry and the patient were Susan, the expectations would be the same. The behavior of physicians and patients is limited by shared expectations about what is and is not supposed to take place. These expectations form a pattern that we recognize, and the pattern imposes limits on both participants regardless of who they are as individuals.

The Two Aspects of Social Structure

The concept of **social structure** includes two characteristics of social systems: relationships and distributions. The former rests on the idea that "a whole is more than the sum of its parts." A human face is not simply a collection of parts—two eyes, a nose and mouth, cheeks, lips, chin, and forehead. What makes it recognizable as a human face is the *arrangement* of those parts in relation to one another. Similarly, the behavior of physicians and patients cannot be understood solely in terms of their individual characteristics. It is their arrangement in relation to each other, and their orientations to that arrangement that produce the unique interactions of doctor and patient.

In this sense, structure refers to the relationships that connect the different "parts" of social systems to one another, whether they are individuals, groups, communities, or entire societies. The structure of health care systems includes not only the relationships among doctors, patients, and other medical staff, but also the complex relationships that connect hospitals, insurance companies, state regulatory agencies, drug manufacturers and so on. To describe the structure of a social system, then, it is necessary to identify the participants and the patterned expectations that connect them to one another as parts of a system (see Bates and Peacock 1989).

The second aspect of social structure is *the distribution of people among various social positions* (there are many more patients than physicians) *as well as the distribution of various kinds of rewards, the most sociologically important of which are wealth, power, and prestige* (doctors earn far higher incomes than do most people). The fact that there are relatively few brain surgeons means that brain surgeons are always in demand; as a result, they can charge very high fees for their work.

In both of its aspects, the concept of social structure refers to the arrangement of people and groups in relation to one another.

Social Statuses and Status Sets

The positions that we occupy in social systems are called **social statuses** (not to be confused with the common use of "status" to refer to prestige) (Linton 1936). To say "He is a doctor's patient" describes one of George's statuses. As well, the definition of a baseball team centers on a set of statuses—outfielder, pitcher, catcher, shortstop, and so on—that makes up its structure. A status exists only in relation to other statuses: the status "college student" has no meaning except in relation to other positions such as "college teacher" or "college administrator." But not all characteristics are statuses. Being left- or right-handed is not a position in a social relationship, for it does not carry with it patterned expectations. Being blind, deaf, or mentally handicapped, however, can be a social status if the condition affects people's expectations.

The most enduring statuses are **ascribed** to us at birth. These include age, race, ethnicity, and gender. Others are **achieved**, such as marital status,

As this picture of John Kennedy as both president and father illustrates, all of us occupy different statuses that make up our status sets.

educational attainment, and occupation. The word achieved can be misleading if taken to mean that effort is required to occupy an achieved status, for this is not always true. A person may be taken hostage by terrorists, for example, without doing anything to bring it about, except, perhaps, being in the wrong place at the wrong time.

Unlike achieved statuses, it is very difficult if not impossible to change an ascribed status. (It is true that some people undergo sex-change surgery, and we all change our age status—but only in one direction.) We can, however, control with greater success how others *perceive* our ascribed statuses. People often alter various aspects of their appearance—with hairstyles, clothing, cosmetics, and even plastic surgery—to affect others' perception of their age.

The third type is **temporary statuses**, and these can be either *situational* or *transitional*. A **situational status** is a position that we occupy only while we are in a particular situation. While ascribed and achieved statuses such as gender and occupation are statuses that we carry with us everywhere we go, situational statuses are not. When we walk into a store, we enter the status of "customer," and when we walk out, we leave that status and enter others such as "pedestrian" or "bus passenger." Some states of being are also temporary statuses: when a person believes another to be asleep or sick their expectations of each other are different from those they might have when both are awake or well.

A **transitional status** is one that is socially structured to be occupied for a limited time as a bridge between statuses (Coser 1966). The status "engaged to be married" is a transition from "single person" to "spouse," just as "probation" is a status designed to link "nonemployee" with "permanent employee." Note that a transitional status is not simply one that we occupy between two other statuses in the sense that having an occupation, for example, comes between never having worked and being unemployed. A transitional status is *solely* a stepping stone from one status to another. The status of "engaged" exists for no other reason than to get people from the status of single to the status of married.

It is important to be aware that what makes situational and transitional statuses temporary is *not* the length of time people occupy them. Marital status, for example, is an achieved status whether you are married for twenty years or twenty minutes. If a status is neither situational nor transitional, then it cannot be regarded as a temporary status: it is either achieved or ascribed.

Since statuses are *positions* in social systems, they exist independently of the individuals who occupy them. Even though no one in a given year might occupy the status of "presidential candidate" the position still exists. This distinction is crucial, for it draws our attention to the limitations of a particular position over and above the personal characteristics of whoever occupies it. A psychologist, for example,

The Marx brothers make us laugh because they turn the world upside down by violating expectations of how people are supposed to perform their roles. In this scene from A *Night at the Opera*, people have crowded into a ship's stateroom to perform a task or take care of a problem created by the person who entered before.

FIGURE 3-1   Mary's Partial Status Set

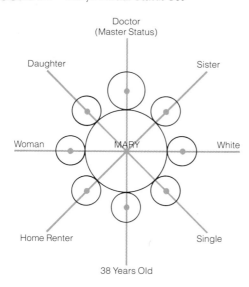

FIGURE 3-2   Partial Role Set for Status of Doctor

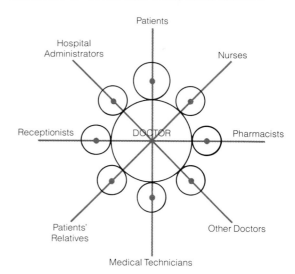

might be interested in President *Bush*; but a sociologist would be interested in *President* Bush.

We all occupy a wide variety of statuses. The most socially important are called **master statuses** because they affect almost every aspect of our lives. In racially segregated South Africa, for example, race is a master status. In most countries, occupation is usually treated as a master status.

If you made a list of all the statuses you occupy, the result would be your **status set** (Merton 1968). Figure 3-1 shows a portion of the status set for Mary, the doctor in our opening example.

Roles and Role Sets

The importance of social structure for understanding behavior lies in the patterned expectations of those who occupy statuses. Attached to each status is a **role**, a set of beliefs, values, attitudes, and norms that define expectations shared by status occupants in their relationships with the occupants of other statuses (Linton 1936; see also Heiss 1981). Mary and George, for instance, play the roles of doctor and patient in relation to each other.

Roles are collections of ideas about the thoughts, feelings, and behavior of status occupants, and **role performance** is behavior that results from our orientation to those ideas. Infants who cry because they are hungry are not performing a role, because they are not orienting themselves to a set of cultural expecta-

tions attached to the statuses of infant and parent. Doctors and patients, however, are limited by cultural ideas such as the value placed on health and the belief that doctors know more about medicine than do patients.

Notice, however, that when doctors interact with one another, the expectations change, even though they still occupy the status of "doctor." They are more likely to treat one another as equals, less likely to tell one another what to do. Why does the role change?

The answer is that the content of a particular role depends on the other statuses involved in the relationship. When Mary performs the role of doctor in relation to George the patient, George is Mary's **role partner**, and Mary is George's role partner. A status occupant may have relationships with several different role partners, and each relationship involves different expectations. Doctors have role relationships with patients, patients' relatives, nurses, hospital administrators, receptionists, and other doctors. In other words, "doctor," by virtue of being a doctor, has a *set* of roles (called a **role set**) with the occupants of various other statuses (Merton 1968). Figure 3-2 shows the role set for Mary's master status "doctor."

The structure of social life—which we take for granted most of the time—is complex. We all occupy many different statuses (making up our status set), and for each status, we play a variety of roles (a role set). In addition, we are often influenced by sev-

ONE STEP FURTHER 3-1

Role Conflict and Changes in Women's Status Sets

As status sets become more complicated, the potential for role conflict increases. For women this has been particularly true as they become more likely to combine marriage, motherhood, and paid employment. In Figure B-3-1, the top line shows changes in the percentage of U.S. women who combine two of these statuses—married and working—since 1890. In 1890 only 2.5% of all women were both working and married. By 1988, however, the percentage was twelve times as large—30%— indicating that close to one out of every three women had to deal with the conflicting demands of marriage and work outside the home.

Just as dramatic are more recent increases in the percentage of women

combining all three statuses (bottom line). Since 1948, the percentage who are married working mothers has almost tripled from 5.7% to 16.3%. Although the line shows that the rate

of increase in this role conflict "Triple-Threat" slowed somewhat during the 1970s it is accelerating again in the 1990s as more and more women try to combine work and family life.

FIGURE B-3-1

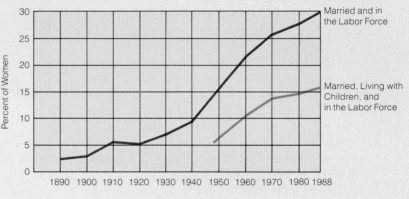

Source: Computed from USCB 1975a, 1990a.

---

eral roles at one time. To see the inherent complexity of status and role sets helps us appreciate the inevitability of conflict, ambivalence, and ambiguity as we try to satisfy conflicting expectations.

Role Conflict

Because we occupy many statuses, each with its own role set, we frequently experience **role conflict**— the difficulty in satisfying role requirements (Merton 1968).

In the U. S., 59 percent of working women are married, and 34 percent live with children under the age of 18 (USCB 1990a). As an employee, a woman is expected to devote her days to her work, while as a mother she is expected to care for her children—to stay home with them when they are sick and respond to emergencies at school. As a wife, she is expected to keep house and be supportive of her husband's work. The three statuses—employee, mother, and wife—carry roles whose expectations can often produce conflict within the status set (see One Step Further 3-1).

Not all role conflict is so clear-cut, for we are often unaware of statuses that produce it. People's expectations of police officers, for example, differ according to the officer's gender. When officers are on duty, "police officer" is their **manifest status** because that is the status that defines their role set. Like everyone else, however, police officers occupy other statuses—such as male, female, father, mother, husband, wife—that make up their status sets. When these statuses are socially defined as irrelevant in a situation, they are called **latent statuses**. They are important because although they are defined as irrelevant, they often affect performance in a manifest status. As a latent status, gender often influences people's expectations. Women police officers may be barred from hazardous duty (and thus denied an avenue toward promotion). In some occupations, a latent status is considered to be important enough to be incorporated into the manifest status, creating such statuses as "policewoman," "chairwoman," and "congresswoman."

Conflict also occurs within a role set, for when we occupy a status we must orient ourselves to a variety

Doctors, like those portrayed in "M*A*S*H" who act in an unprofessional manner, may do so as a way of using role distance to protect their ability to be effective physicians during the horrors of war.

of role partners. The professor's students expect her to pay attention to them, to give them her time and energy; at the same time, other professors expect her to conduct research, serve on committees, and write books and articles. The result is conflict that may be resolved in several ways.

Resolving Role Conflict   There are many ways of responding to role conflict (Merton 1968). We are often more committed to one role than to another and act accordingly. In the case of the role conflict previously mentioned, the professor may choose to comply with the expectations that carry the more severe punishment if violated (losing a job is more serious than making students angry). We can also minimize conflict by choosing statuses whose roles do not conflict with one another, as students do when they enroll in easy courses to balance their demanding ones. What can we do, however, when we cannot avoid conflicting roles?

The most drastic response to conflict is to abandon a role relationship altogether. Quitting a job, divorcing a spouse, dropping a course, and leaving school are frequent responses to conflicting role demands. Another tactic is to make our behavior in one of the roles less visible so that we can violate its expectations in greater safety. National politicians, who must satisfy several conflicting constituencies, may express different opinions before different audiences, hoping that one will not hear about the message delivered to the other. For this to work, the actors must *insulate* their behavior from certain audiences. A third approach is to **segregate** statuses and roles so that specific individuals are not role partners for more than one of our roles (Goffman 1961b). Surgeons do not perform operations on their own children—in other words, those who are role partners in family relationships are never role partners in surgical relationships. In this way, surgeons avoid the strain of making life-and-death decisions about the people closest to them.

There are other sources of strain in role behavior in addition to role conflict. To perform a role, we must know what the expectations are and have the ability and motivation to meet them. Few experiences are as anxiety-producing as entering a status and not knowing what is expected of us. First-time parents are rarely prepared for the demands of child care and often spend a great deal of time and energy worrying about whether or not they are doing what they should.

Even when we meet the requirements for role performance, we may find the performance itself to be unbearably disagreeable. In combat zones, army doctors are exposed to a steady stream of mutilated bodies day after day, and often use humor or other irrelevant talk to distract themselves from what they are doing (as beautifully portrayed in the television show *M*A*S*H*). Occupational jargon often serves a similar purpose—referring to the death of a patient as a "negative patient outcome" rather than simply, and more directly, as a death. Corporate executives also use occupational jargon to insulate themselves from the unpleasantness of laying off workers by, for example, referring to layoffs as "outplacements," "involuntary terminations," or "downsizing." These are examples of **role distance**—the disassociation from a role—which helps people endure the strain inherent in the performance of difficult roles (Goffman 1961b; Snow and Anderson 1987).

These examples illustrate some of the ways in which we move from one role relationship to another, trying to achieve a sense of harmony and continuity among the roles we are expected to play. In a sense, much of our lives consists of this delicate juggling of expectations and choices, and how we go about it is a major concern of sociological analysis.

STRUCTURAL CHARACTERISTICS OF SOCIAL SYSTEMS

Whether we are looking at a corporation or two people meeting on a street, we can describe social systems in terms of eight basic structural characteristics. The first six describe relationships in social systems in terms of boundaries, time, roles, affection, power and prestige, and communication. The last two describe the distribution of valued resources and rewards and the distribution of people among social statuses.

Boundaries: Insiders and Outsiders

The **boundaries** of a social system specify who may occupy statuses within it. Structural boundaries differ in their clarity—how easily we can tell who occupies which statuses—and their openness—how easily people can occupy or leave statuses. Table 3-1 shows how these two characteristics combine to describe social situations.

The Clarity of Boundaries   The clarity of boundaries plays an important part in social life. Military combat units must be able to tell the difference between friend and foe at every moment, and maintain clarity by wearing uniforms and using passwords. One of the most serious violations of the rules of war is to impersonate enemy soldiers. During the Battle of the Bulge in World War II, some German soldiers dressed in U.S. uniforms, carefully copied speech patterns, and even memorized facts about U.S. cities and baseball teams. As the clarity of group boundaries broke down, U.S. soldiers did not know whom they could trust, and the result was confusion and fear (Goolrich and Tanner 1980).

Some groups deliberately draw vague boundaries in order to avoid offending potential members. Political parties use positions on issues to define their boundaries. The candidates of these parties may try to be all things to all people by never taking a clear position on controversial issues. The vagueness of their boundaries can allow people with very different political opinions to vote for them.

The boundaries of social relationships are not fixed walls that never change; and they depend on the situation. In relation to civilians, soldiers define the boundary of their group as military vs. civilian; but in relation to one another, they draw different lines, separating officers from enlisted men and women, short-timers from career soldiers, or military academy graduates from reserve officers.

The Openness of Boundaries   The clarity of boundaries is related to their degree of openness. While almost anyone can enter the status of pedestrian at any time, for example, only a relative few can enroll in prestigious universities.

Closed boundaries lie at the heart of discrimination based on such characteristics as race, ethnicity, religion, gender, and age. Many whites exclude nonwhites from neighborhoods and workplaces in the name of supporting group values. Racism, therefore, is a matter both of culture *and* social structure. The forced integration of workplaces and schools is an attempt to open previously closed boundaries, in the hope that by altering the structure of race relations,

---

TABLE 3-1
The structural boundaries of social situations differ in their degree of openness and clarity and can best be described in terms of the combination of these two characteristics.

	OPEN BOUNDARY	CLOSED BOUNDARY
CLEAR BOUNDARY	A sidewalk	Prison wall Football team during a game
UNCLEAR BOUNDARY	Mobs during riots	The population of U.S. citizens College student Terrorist group

"Coming out" parties—called debutante balls—at which daughters of prominent families are "presented" to high society have long been used to maintain the exclusiveness of upper-middle- and upper-class membership.

the increased interaction that results will remove negative beliefs and attitudes.

Some groups close their boundaries to preserve their *idea* of themselves as a group. The "high society" of wealthy families strictly limits entry into their social circles. An elite position is an essential part of their social identity, and if "high society" is easily entered, it is, by definition, no longer elite.

Structuring Time

Within the boundaries that regulate entry into statuses, a number of structural characteristics affect social systems. One is **time structure**, or the way that what goes on is organized in relation to clocks and calendars as well as more subjective measures of time. In his novel *The Magic Mountain* (1924), Thomas Mann wrote:

Time has no divisions to mark its passage, there is never a thunder-storm or blare of trumpets to announce the beginning of a new month or year. Even when a new century begins, it is only we mortals who ring bells and fire off pistols.

The way we think of and therefore experience time is affected by culture (see Young 1988). The 7-day week is a unit of time that is a human creation, for unlike days, months, and years, it does not correspond to any natural cycles such as the seasons or the phases of the moon (see Zerubavel 1985). Yet, no unit of time so profoundly affects our lives, from terrible Monday mornings to "Thank God it's Friday"

and the relief of weekends. Depending on the culture, the week has included as many as twenty days and as few as five. For ten years after the French Revolution in 1792, the French experimented with a 10-day week (and also divided days into 10 hours of 100 minutes, each of which was broken down into 100 seconds).

We "don't have time," we "make" time, "lose" time, and "waste" it as if it were an object. We eat not when we are hungry but when it is "time" for it. We go to bed at "bedtime" and whether or not we are tired may be irrelevant. The demands of work and school in many industrial societies lead people to overrule their natural body rhythms that call for mid-afternoon naps, although the cultures of Mexico, Spain, and Italy among others still allow for them. In the U.S., we are famous as sticklers for precise schedules; consequently, we often feel "pressed" for time, while Latin Americans are comparatively loose about time, and do not consider being half an hour late for an appointment to be worthy of comment. We routinely orient ourselves to the future, while many Arabs view anyone who tries to see into the future as slightly crazy (Hall 1959, 1969).

As an element of social structure, time has important effects on social life (Lauer 1981; Maines 1987; Merton 1984b; Sorokin and Merton 1937; Zerubavel 1981). We tend to make weaker commitments to relationships we expect to last a short time. We may feel we can afford to be rude to a waitress we will never see again; and it is often difficult to arouse the interest of students in the long-term futures of their universities. In prisons, however, the most dangerous inmates are those with life sentences, for without hope of parole, they feel they have nothing to lose: there is no more time in the outside world to take away from them.

Like most aspects of social life, time structures are something we are unaware of until they are disrupted. When students go on long vacations, they often find themselves feeling lost without a schedule

The marking of time—from workers punching in on the job to New Year's celebrations, such as this one in San Francisco's Chinatown—is an integral part of the structure of social systems.

to adhere to, and the unemployed, accustomed to years of knowing what they will do in relation to a clock, often feel that one day drifts into the next. Our social sense of time is a vital aspect of the shaping of our lives.

Role Structures: Who's Who

In social systems, people take on different roles that, together, form a **role structure**. Role structures describe divisions of labor in relationships, and differ in both content and complexity—the number of statuses recognized in a system and the degree to which they are interconnected. When two people play tennis, the structure of the game is simple not only in the number of people involved, but in the number of statuses as well. Each occupies the status of player, and one occupies the status of server while the other is receiver. When four people play doubles, however, there are more people and more statuses. In addition to those above, we now have the status of partner, which significantly increases the structural complexity of the game. The pattern of expectations be-

comes far more complex as partners orient themselves to each other as well as to their opponents.

While large systems are usually more complex than small ones, this is not always so. A college lecture may include hundreds of people, but since all except one of them occupy the same status (student), it has a simple role structure. A baseball team, however, has nine different positions and a complex role structure whose rules define each status' relationships with all the others. Successful players are not simply those with the strongest arms or the sharpest eyes. They are the ones who can quickly and accurately read a situation in relation to the structure of the game and their position in it (a good outfielder does not stand there trying to figure out who to throw the ball to).

We can also use the concept of role structure to describe entire societies. Societies that existed some 10,000 years ago fed themselves by gathering food and hunting small game; they therefore tended to be very small. Their division of labor was simple and few people were specialists capable of performing only one particular job. In the 1990s, by contrast, there are cities with over 20 million people and production depends on complex relationships among growers, makers, and marketers. The division of labor is complex and specialized: skills that were shared broadly within smaller, simpler communities are now possessed by a relative few. One ironic result of this specialization is that we are more vulnerable as individuals.

> Specialization . . . involves doing many things badly or not at all in order to do other things well. . . . We live in the most powerful societies in the world, but as individuals we are babes in arms compared to members of the most primitive societies, all of whom, unlike us, are generally capable of maintaining their own independent existence. We are utterly dependent on others in a way that they are not. (Barnes 1985, p. 25)

Sociometric Structure: Patterns of Affection

While role structures connect people in webs of shared expectations that vary in content and complexity, participants in social systems also vary in how much they like one another, and this difference affects the way they play their roles. If you watch people discussing a problem, you may notice that some tend to stick together, supporting one another's views and whispering quietly to one another. Sociologists have long noted the importance of these patterns of affection, which can profoundly affect social systems. How can we identify the existence of such patterns?

In 1943 J. L. Moreno developed a method called **sociometry**. Asking members of test groups how

much they liked or disliked each other, he mapped their answers in a diagram or **sociogram** that revealed the existence of patterns of affection. If we apply his technique to six students working together on a project, what might the sociometric structure look like, and why would it be important? The sociograms in Figure 3-3 show two possibilities. In this figure, a single arrow represents one member's affection for another, while an arrow pointing in both directions represents mutual liking between two members.

In *(a)*, all the members like one another, so they will tend to be highly committed to the group and will try to avoid disagreement with one another in order to maintain unity and consensus. In *(b)*, the group has two subgroups, so there will be a greater possibility for conflict to split the members. (Which member do you think is most likely to smooth relations between the subgroups?) Opinions will be more varied since members run lower risks of feeling excluded; expressions of frustration and anger are more likely, and decisions may be harder to reach. Sociograms are useful for understanding why groups operate in different ways, for they reveal that members frequently value subgroups more than the group.

In addition to their different structures of roles and affection, social systems also differ in their distribution of power among the occupants of different statuses.

Power and Prestige Structures

Social **power** may be defined as *the potential to have an effect on ourselves, others, or our environment even when there is opposition* (see Weber [1925] 1947;

FIGURE 3-3   Sociograms of a Student Project Group

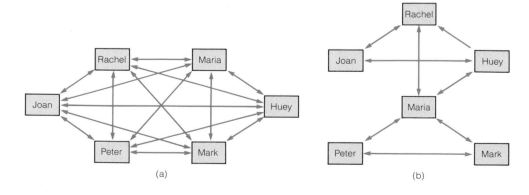

(a)   (b)

As the British royal family illustrates, people may be very high in wealth and prestige and yet have relatively little power.

Wrong 1980). This can take the form of controlling other people or resources such as land and factories, but it can also consist of freedom from control by others. The ability to express unpopular opinions is as much an example of social power as the ability to control what others say. Sociology focuses on how power is distributed in social systems and how this affects social interaction.

Power assigned according to norms is called **authority**. Corporations, military units, and governments all have power structures based on authority. It is important to note that power and authority are not always the same, for authority represents power supported by norms and generally accepted by those subject to it. Power, however, can result from a person's expertise, persuasiveness, control over resources, or physical ability to coerce others. Hijackers who threaten to blow up an airplane unless their demands are met, for example, have a great deal of power but no authority. While having power

is sometimes a personal characteristic, being a leader is always a status under group control. For this reason, authority tends to be more stable over time than personal power, and is one of the most enduring characteristics of social systems (see Ridgeway and Berger 1986; Zelditch and Walker 1984).

Some systems have two power structures: a leadership structure defined by norms, and informal structures reflecting the power of individuals and subgroups. An army combat platoon's leadership structure is defined by regulations that assign a lieutenant as the leader; but sergeants are often more experienced and command greater loyalty and trust from combat soldiers. Lieutenants may allow sergeants to overrule their decisions, giving them greater power than the leadership structure calls for. In extreme cases, when lieutenants refuse to share authority with more competent subordinates, soldiers have murdered the leaders rather than suffer from their mistakes in combat. When lieutenants

TABLE 3-2
As these examples show, power and prestige often go together, but not always.

	RELATIVELY HIGH PRESTIGE	RELATIVELY LOW PRESTIGE
RELATIVELY HIGH POWER	President of the United States Army general	Blackmailer Airplane hijacker Unpopular dictator
RELATIVELY LOW POWER	College professor Minister Honorary degree recipient Nobel Prize winner	Someone on welfare Assembly-line worker A child

do share power, of course, they remain responsible for the actions of their soldiers in combat, so the relationship between lieutenants and sergeants is delicate, and requires them to use the informal power structure in order to survive without threatening the formal leadership structure.

Related to the distribution of power is the distribution of rewards such as wealth and prestige which, because they have similar bases, generally go together (Markovsky, Smith, and Berger 1984). Jury members who have more highly respected occupations, for example, tend not only to exercise more power but to receive higher levels of respect—to be given more opportunities to talk and to have their opinions taken more seriously (Strodtbeck, James, and Hawkins 1957). Nonetheless, people can be respected highly without having correspondingly high power (Table 3-2). This is true of former U.S. presidents and members of the British royal family. The Queen of England, although certainly the most respected person in all of Britain, is expected to make no open attempts to influence the official policies of her government. There was once an uproar over rumors that the queen was preparing to openly disagree with her government's refusal to support sanctions against South Africa. Many Britains were shocked that she would even consider expressing her views in public.

The concept of social structure describes how roles, affection, power, and prestige are arranged in social systems. These structural aspects of social life are reflected in **communication structures** that consist of how frequently and extensively the occupants of different statuses interact with one another.

Communication Structures

When four roommates sit down to decide how to arrange furniture, an important characteristic of their interaction is that each person is able to talk with all the others. The pattern resembles a circle in which each person is connected to everyone else. But when they meet with a dean to resolve a dispute among them, the pattern changes: comments are directed mostly to the dean, who acts like the hub of a wheel, holding the four spokes together and coordinating their interaction. In armies, the patterns—called a chain of command—are dramatically different: generals talk only with high-level officers, and enlisted personnel rarely interact with anyone other than comrades or immediate superiors. Such patterns of communication affect the performance of groups and the lives of their members (Bavelas 1950).

In a classic experiment, Leavitt (1951) gave five-man groups a simple problem to solve: each man had a card with a list of symbols, only some of which were on every card. The task was to find out which symbols were held in common by all members of the group. The men sat around a table, separated from each other by partitions, and communicated by passing written notes through slots in the partitions. By using different arrangements of partitions, Leavitt created four different structures of communication (Figure 3-4).

Leavitt found that the wheel structure produced correct answers more quickly than any other, whereas the circle was the least efficient. People who occupied central positions (Bill in the Y and the wheel, and Mike in the chain) tended to emerge as leaders and enjoyed the task the most. He also found that the most efficient groups were the least enjoyed by their members. Another researcher (Shaw 1954) repeated the experiment using different kinds of tasks and found that for complex problems with more than one solution the group efficiency ranks were reversed, with the circle reaching a consensus faster than the others and the wheel finishing last.

Students find that lectures (wheels) are boring but efficient ways to pass on a lot of information, whereas discussion groups (circles) are more enjoyable but often frustratingly inefficient ("We never get anywhere"). Complex issues are difficult to discuss in wheel structures, while brainstorming to solve a mathematical problem is fast and efficient.

Authoritarian governments are structured as wheels, enabling them to make decisions more efficiently than more democratic circles such as the U.S. Congress, whose decisions depend on consensus and whose members are pressured by lobbyists. The slow pace of legislation in the U.S. is due to more than the personalities of legislators: the structure itself is inefficient.

The preceding sections describe structural characteristics of social systems that influence everyday interactions, from the simple building blocks of status and role to groups and their boundaries; and the structures of roles, power, prestige, friendship, and communication. The structure of social systems, however, also involves the important concept of distributions.

Structural Distributions

The concept of social structure refers to two different kinds of distributions in social systems, the first of which—the distribution of valued resources such as power and prestige—was discussed earlier. The structural characteristics of social systems also include the pattern of distribution of people among the different statuses—such as the number of corporate managers relative to the number of workers, the number of women relative to the number of men, or the number of whites relative to the number of blacks.

The example that begins this chapter, for example, illustrates the fact that most cultures distinguish between healers and patients and regulate their interactions through social roles. This role relationship, however, exists in a larger structural context. Small societies might have only one healer, whose monopoly on a vital status brings with it great power (you could not afford to be on the wrong side of the tribal healer). In more developed countries, however, there are thousands of doctors; if you dislike one, you can always find another. The power associated with the status "doctor" depends in part on how many doctors are competing with one another. It also depends on the number of patients relative to the number of doctors: the fewer patients there are, the more eager doctors will be to please. The number of status occupants is an important element of large-scale (macro) social structures that affects relationships among individuals in the small-scale (micro) structures of everyday life.

The distribution of people by age is also important (see Table 3-3). In 1850 only 2 percent of the people in the U.S. were 65 or older, whereas 35 percent were in the more economically productive age group of 20 to 64. There were roughly 17 workers to support each elderly citizen in 1850. By 1990, however, the percentage who were 65 or older had increased by six times to 13 percent, but the percentage of those 20 to 64 years old had increased only to 59 percent. In 1990, then, there were fewer than *five* workers to support each elderly person.

FIGURE 3-4 Leavitt's Four Group Structures

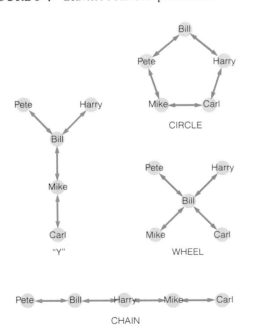

TABLE 3-3 Distribution of the U.S. Population by Age and the Number of People 20–64 Years Old for Each Person 65 or Older (1850 to 1990 with projection to 2010)

YEAR	LESS THAN 15	20–64	65 AND OVER	RATIO OF THOSE 20–64 TO THOSE 65 OR OVER
1850	42%	35%	2%	17:1
1900	34%	50%	4%	12:1
1940	25%	59%	7%	8:1
1960	31%	52%	9%	6:1
1980	23%	57%	11%	5:1
1990	22%	59%	13%	4.5:1
2010	20%	61%	14%	4.4:1

Sources: For 1850, 1900, 1940, and 1960: U.S. Census Bureau 1975a. Otherwise U.S. Census Bureau 1990a.

There have been dramatic changes at the lower end of the age scale as well: the percentage under the age of 15 dropped from 42 percent in 1850 to 25 percent in 1940 and, with the post–World War II baby boom, jumped to 31 percent in 1960. By 1990 it had declined to only 22 percent of the population.

The effects of such changes have been clear in recent years. The Social Security system has been in serious long-term trouble because an ever-larger number of people are depending on the labor of an ever smaller number of workers. The elderly, worried over their declining security, have organized politically (see Chapter 15). In addition, the baby boom that followed World War II resulted in the construction of thousands of public schools and an enormous increase in the demand for teachers; and the subsequent decline in the school-age population closed hundreds of schools (some of which, ironically, are now used as social centers for the elderly) and produced massive unemployment among teachers. Such long-term structural shifts illustrate the ever-changing, fluid nature of social systems. They also illustrate that although social structure is a major source of cohesion in social life, it can produce disruptive change and conflict as well.

Institutions

As we have seen, the structural characteristics of social systems strongly influence the way we experience our lives and the bonds we feel with our work and other people. As we will see in the chapters that compose Part Five, in some cases a social system is so important to a group or society that it is preserved as an enduring pattern of expectations—in other words, it becomes an *institution*. An **institution** can be defined as an enduring set of ideas and relationships organized around important goals. When a social arrangement has a relatively permanent place in a group or society, it has been institutionalized.

All societies, for example, rely on the institution of the family to produce, socialize, protect, and care for new members, and in many societies, schools provide additional training. Economic institutions produce and distribute goods and services; science provides a systematic method for increasing our understanding of the material world; political institutions distribute and apply collective power; and religious institutions help people grapple with important questions about morality, the unknown, and the meaning of life.

It is important to point out that, unlike families or schools, institutions do not always correspond to groups. U.S. political institutions include not only groups such as the Senate budget committee, but also ways of doing things that have an enduring place in the political system. No one has the right to prevent voters from casting their ballots, or to observe voters to see whom they are voting for. These procedures clearly define social relationships in a political system, and are as much a part of political institutions as the White House staff, the House of Representatives, the Cabinet, or a town council.

Institutions are designed to accomplish goals defined as important and continuing; each existed long before our births and will persist long after we die. While their cultural and structural characteristics change and vary from one society to another, institutions themselves exist as long as the needs they meet persist. The family exists in all known societies while schools are peculiar to those societies that require (and can afford) prolonged training for their members.

Just as individuals make a variety of choices within the general limitations of social systems, however, individual families vary from the general institutional guidelines laid down by society. As each of us participates in family life, we do so in relation to models that indicate how family relationships should be structured and what goals families should pursue. Institutions are social blueprints that describe how to accomplish important goals.

The importance of institutions lies in their relative permanence. Whereas friends can change their expectations of one another and bureaucrats can alter their rigid rules at the stroke of a pen, an institution is far more difficult to change, for it represents deeply imbedded ideas about how goals ought to be achieved. Bureaucrats might explain a particular rule as most efficient; but, if we are asked why U.S. families usually consist of a mother, father, and their children, we would tend to reply, "Because that's what a family *is*."

The permanence of institutions places them at the heart of what makes one society different from another. Macrostructural blueprints define the broad course of political, economic, religious, and family life, and in doing so they affect virtually every aspect of human existence, from the most intimate to the most public. It is impossible to understand social life today without also understanding the historical transformations that have taken place in major social institutions—the dominance of world capitalism and the emergence and decline of socialism and communism in response to it (Chapter 19); the decline of organized religion and the growing power of the state (Chapters 20 and 21); the bureaucratization of so many aspects of social life, from business to schools to the making of war (Chapters 9 and 17); the enormous influence of science and technology as ways of making sense of and manipulating ourselves and our environments (Chapters 4, 18, and 23); and the transformation of the family in response to a rapidly changing world (Chapter 16). In order to understand even our intimate lives as individuals, we must place ourselves in the larger context of the major institutional structures that define and dominate societies (see Tilly 1985).

SUMMARY

1. The concept of social structure draws attention to the recurring patterns of relationships through which people live their lives and perform roles as occupants of social statuses. Whether referring to expectations between lovers, relationships among groups, or the distribution of income, power, and prestige in a society, social structure describes patterns that are more than a sum of their parts and that exist independently of us as individuals even though we participate in them.

2. Statuses and their associated roles are at the heart of any social system. Status sets include statuses that are ascribed, achieved, or temporary (situational or transitional), and for each status, we are expected to perform a variety of roles (the role set) in relation to different role partners. In each case we must define the situation in order to know which role we are expected to perform.

3. Statuses and roles often subject us to role conflict when we have difficulty satisfying the demands associated with two or more roles. The roles we are expected to perform in a situation are manifest, whereas those defined as irrelevant are latent, and conflict often occurs between manifest and latent statuses. A master status is the most important status in a status set.

4. There are a variety of ways to reduce role conflict. We may insulate our role behavior from those whose expectations we fail to live up to, or make sure that we do not perform different roles in relation to the same person. When role performance is unpleasant, we may use role distance to avoid being aware of what we are doing.

5. The structural patterns that make up social systems have many characteristics that affect what goes on within them. Boundaries differ in clarity and openness. Time structures affect both

how long relationships last and how we feel and behave in them.

6. Role structures differ in their content and their complexity. Large systems are usually but not always more complex than small ones, and in complex structures it is particularly important for everyone involved to have a clear idea of what is supposed to happen.

7. Sociometry uses sociograms to map the ties of affection among participants in a system. These ties are often the basis for subgroups, which may be sources of conflict.

8. Systems distribute a number of important rewards and resources. The most sociologically important of these are power, prestige, and wealth. Unlike personal power, which is based on individual characteristics, authority is power assigned according to norms.

9. Communication structures describe who interacts with whom and have important effects on behavior and experience and the effectiveness of systems themselves.

10. A key structural characteristic is the relative numbers of people who occupy particular statuses. The distribution of people by age or occupation, for example, is an important aspect of a society's structure.

11. Institutions are enduring social systems organized to accomplish important goals. They include arrangements such as the family as well as those that focus on education, economics, politics, and religion.

KEY TERMS

achieved status   48
ascribed status   48
authority   57
boundary   53
communication structure   58
institution   60
latent status   51
manifest status   51
master status   50
power   56

role   50
role conflict   51
role distance   52
role partner   50
role performance   50
role segregation   52
role set   50
role structure   55
situational status   49
social status   48

social structure   48
sociogram   56
sociometry   56
status segregation   52
status set   50
temporary status   49
time structure   54
transitional status   49

LOOKING ELSEWHERE

Although the concept of social structure is fundamental to every chapter in the rest of the text, some of the examples in this chapter are also discussed elsewhere, such as

■ gender and status/role conflict (Chapter 14, pp. 334–36)

■ relationships between doctors and patients (Chapter 18, pp. 460–62)

■ the importance of age structure (Chapter 4, pp. 78–80 and Chapter 15, pp. 366–74)

RECOMMENDED READINGS

Biddle, B. J., and Thomas, E. J. (Eds.). 1979. *Role theory: Concepts and research.* New York: Wiley. A rich collection of articles dealing with many aspects of social structure including statuses, roles, and conflict.

Blau, P. M. (Ed.). 1975. *Approaches to the study of social structure.* New York: Free Press. A demanding but highly informative set of articles on various aspects of social structure, written by leading sociologists.

Coser, L. A. (Ed.). 1975. *The idea of social structure: Papers in honor of Robert K. Merton.* New York: Harcourt Brace Jovanovich. A collection of essays that explore the concept of social structure, from the complexity of roles and the uses of power to the status of functional theory in sociology.

Goffman, E. 1961. *Encounters*. Indianapolis: Bobbs-Merrill. A pair of essays, the second of which focuses on role distance as a means of resolving role conflict, especially in high-stress situations such as hospital operating rooms.

Lauer, R. H. 1981. *Temporal man: The meaning and uses of social time*. New York: Praeger. A look at an aspect of social structure that we rarely think of as social at all.

Merton, R. K. 1968. *Social theory and social structure* (revised and enlarged edition). New York: Free Press. Perhaps the classic statement on the importance of social structure as a concept in sociology.

Zurcher, L. A. 1983. *Social roles: Conformity, conflict, and creativity*. Beverly Hills, CA: Sage Publications. An entertaining book at the creative ways in which we perform roles while trying to maintain some sense of personal autonomy.

4
POPULATION AND ECOLOGY

 In 1839 Fanny Calderon de la Barca traveled to Mexico City, and as her coach came within view of the Valley of Mexico, she remembered lines from Robert Southey's long romantic tribute to the city:

> Thou art beautiful.
> Queen of the valley! Thou art beautiful!
> Thy walls, like silver, sparkle in the sun.

Later that night, she wrote to a friend:

> At length we arrived at the heights on which we look down upon the superb Valley of Mexico, celebrated in all parts of the world, with its framework of magnificent mountains, its snow-capped volcanoes, great lakes, and fertile plains. (Both quotations in Fisher and Fisher 1966, p. 87)

Robert Southey and Fanny Calderon would hardly recognize Mexico City now. It is rapidly becoming not only the largest but the city with the most poverty in the world. In 1991, more than 20 million people were living in Mexico City, and by the year 2000 an estimated 31 million—more than the number found in many *nations*—will be living there. Half of its adults have no jobs, there is not enough water to drink, and most residents live in slums. Rush-hour traffic lasts from 6 A.M. to 10 P.M.; the air is so polluted with dust, smoke from industry and burning garbage, and automobile exhaust that rarely can one see the beautiful mountains that surround the city; and schoolchildren draw the sky gray, not blue.

> Old Mexicans still remember spending afternoons in nearby fields and rivers within view of Popocatepetl, the snow-capped volcano. Many of today's schoolchildren must play in dusty streets or open sewers, and they learn about Popocatepetl from books. (Riding 1983, p. 12)

To understand how Mexico City, a city celebrated for its beauty, was transformed into a polluted "blueprint for hell," we have to pay attention to its population and ecology.

What happened to transform the "Queen of the Valley" into a congested, polluted center of poverty that one Mexico City doctor described as a "blueprint for hell"?

To answer this question about Mexico City—and similar questions about other cities around the world—we have to understand population and ecology, which focus on how societies adapt to physical environments and the consequences these adaptations produce. This chapter describes four key concepts that define this perspective and illustrates some of the ways in which population and ecology help to explain how societies change and why so many are in a state of crisis in the late twentieth century.

POET

Every social system is affected not only by its cultural and structural characteristics (including its use of cultural technology), but also by the size and characteristics of its population and the nature of its physical environment. The ecological perspective combines all of these with four concepts that can best be remembered with the acronym POET, which stands for *population, organization, environment, and technology* (Duncan 1961; Duncan and Schnore 1959).

The most common definition of a **population** in sociology is a collection of people who share a geographic territory. The concept is also useful, however, for referring to a collection of people who participate in a social system—such as an extended family or a corporation—even though this may not involve a common territory. **Demography** is the study of the size, growth, composition, and distribution of human populations: why birth and death rates rise and fall, why populations are distributed over the land in particular ways, and why people migrate from one place to another. The inhabitants of Mexico City are a population, and we cannot understand their problems without understanding how so many people came to live in one place. A major part of this involves understanding the society of which Mexico City is a part.

Ecology is the study of how populations—and societies, in particular—adapt to and act upon physical environments: climate, the shape of the land, and the availability of natural resources (see Buttel 1987; Hawley 1986; Micklin and Choldin 1984). This is accomplished in two ways. First, populations *organize* themselves culturally and structurally in different ways. Gatherer-hunter societies have relatively simple divisions of labor based on gender and age and do not grow their own food. Industrial societies have complex divisions of labor and produce goods on a massive scale. Second, societies use **technology**—the accumulated knowledge of how to use physical environments. The wheel, the horse-drawn plow, computers, automobiles, electricity, telephones, and nuclear energy are all part of cultural adaptations to physical environments:

It is important to remember that societies not only adapt to their physical environments, but in making use of them, they act upon and affect them in often profound ways. No species on earth comes remotely close to the human capacity for changing—or damaging—the earth.

The four concepts summed up in POET are useful for understanding all kinds of social systems, from families, school classes, and work groups, to cities, countries, and the world.

POPULATION AND DEMOGRAPHY

Why have conditions in Mexico City deteriorated so much since Fanny Calderon's visit in 1839? From a population perspective, the problems of Mexico, Mexico City, and much of the world are caused by the size, rate of growth, age characteristics, and physical distribution of populations. The following sections deal with the central questions of demography: what causes rates of birth, death, and migration to rise and fall?

Births

To survive, every social system must acquire new participants. Unlike most social systems (such as factories and colleges), societies depend directly on the process of reproduction, the *rate* of which varies enormously. The **crude birth rate** is the number of babies born each year per 1,000 people in the population. For example, the crude birth rate in Mexico (30 births per 1,000 people) is twice that in the U.S. (PRB 1990). On a larger scale, birth rates in Africa are roughly three times as high as those in North America and Europe, and rates in Latin America and Asia are about twice as high (Table 4-1). Birth rates also vary within societies. In the U.S., people with high education, occupation, and income tend to have fewer children than those who occupy lower positions. Whites generally have fewer children than nonwhites, and birth rates tend to be higher in rural areas than in cities (USCB 1979, 1986a). From a sociological perspective, such variations occur because like any other behavior, having babies is affected by the ideas and relationships that make up social environments (Davis and Blake 1956; Mosher 1988; Tilly 1978b).

Birth rates are much higher in Mexico than in the U.S. for several reasons that include culture and social structure. Mexican women are expected to marry and marry young (see Merrick 1986). If women marry young and quickly remarry after the death of a husband, they are more likely to become pregnant than if they remain single or marry at older ages. Mexican parents prefer male children, in part because the family line is traced through men (see Williamson 1976). This value encourages higher birth rates, for in order to be sure of having a son, parents whose first children are girls must keep trying. Like people in many less developed countries, Mexicans also value large families, in part because

TABLE 4-1 Crude Birth Rates in Major World Regions

Crude birth rates range from their highest levels in Africa to their lowest levels in Europe. What is perhaps most troublesome is that most of the world's population lives in those areas that not only have the highest birth rates but also have the most impoverished conditions. Those countries that can least afford rapid population growth are precisely those with the highest birth rates. How would you explain this?

REGION	CRUDE BIRTH RATE[1]
Europe	13
North America	16
Soviet Union	19
Oceania	20
Asia	27
Latin America	28
Africa	44
World	27

[1]Births per 1,000 people.

Source: PRB 1990.

societies that rely heavily on manual labor use children to help produce goods. In addition, when parents become too old to work, they often rely on their children for support, an arrangement that encourages having many children (Vos 1984). In industrial societies, however, children perform few productive tasks and are more likely to be economic liabilities. As we will see, industrialization has brought with it lower birth rates in many countries, including the U.S.

Mexicans have more children not only because they want more, but also because their children have a smaller chance of surviving. The **infant mortality rate** is the number of infants under the age of 1 who die each year for every 1,000 births. The infant mortality rate in Mexico is five times that in the U.S. (PRB 1990). If Mexican parents want to have four children and expect some to die during childhood, they may compensate by having five or six.

Birth rates are also affected by social policies that encourage or discourage childbearing. During this century, Germany, Japan, France, Brazil, Argentina, Rumania, and the Soviet Union have used rewards ranging from medals to cash payments to encourage parents to have large families. Norms have also been used to restrict or prohibit the use of contraceptives in many of these countries—as well as

China has gone to great lengths to promote one-child families as a cultural ideal to slow the birth rate.

among Catholics in many societies, whose norms forbid the use of contraceptives. As U.S. Catholics have increasingly violated those norms, their birth rates have become more similar to those of non-Catholics (Westoff and Jones 1979; Mosher and Hendershot 1984).

On the other hand, the governments of China and India have deliberately promoted low birth rates for over a decade. India uses massive advertising campaigns and financial incentives to encourage couples to limit their families to two children—but such programs have had little measurable effect on birth rates. China has laws limiting each family to one child. Women who become pregnant with their second child are expected to have abortions, and couples who already have had more than one child are expected to undergo sterilization. In spite of considerable control, however, the Chinese government's policy has lost its iron grip on the country's more than one billion people. As in most less developed societies, children have economic value in China, particularly in rural farm areas where birth rates tend to be relatively high. There is some evidence, however, that among younger Chinese the social pressures and economic benefits of fewer children are leading to smaller families (Kristof 1990).

While pressures to marry and have children are weaker in the U.S. than countries such as Mexico, they do exist. Griffith (1973) asked a national sample of adults 18 to 39 years old to imagine how they would feel and how people would treat them if they never had children. Most believed that family and friends would urge them to have children, and almost half said they would feel out of place among other married people and would be accused of selfishness. Most also believed that having only one child was undesirable (see Polit and Falbo 1987), that friends and parents would urge them to have more, and that it would probably be bad for the child. More recent evidence suggests a decline in the judgment that voluntary childlessness is selfish. Huber and Spitze (1983) found that only a quarter of a national sample of adults made such a judgment about a hypothetical couple that chose not to have children.

An important structural aspect of social systems is the number of people who occupy different statuses, and birth rates are strongly affected by the relative number of women in a population who are of child-bearing age. Figure 4-1 shows changes since 1950 in the average number of children born to each woman of childbearing age (the bars) and the total number of children born each year (the shaded area above the bars). As you can see, the average woman has had fewer children, but at the same time the number of babies born has increased substantially. This is because the large number of babies born during the baby boom years are reaching childbearing age, and this great increase in the number of potential parents produces an increased number of children. In short, we have smaller families but many more of them.

Mortality, Morbidity, and Health

In addition to the birth rate, a social system's population size also depends on how high or low death rates are. The **crude death rate** is the number of deaths in a given year for every 1,000 people in a population. A common way of expressing the death rate in a population is the concept of **life expectancy**, which is the average number of years people of a given age can expect to live if current death rates remain unchanged throughout their lifetime. **Morbidity** refers to disease and illness in a population, which is important in demography because it is the major cause of mortality (Kammeyer and Ginn 1986).

Like birth rates, death rates, life expectancy, and morbidity vary enormously among and within societies (Table 4-2); and once again, social factors help explain why. Causes of death are frequently divided into five categories: infectious, parasitic, and respiratory diseases; circulatory diseases (such as heart disease and strokes); cancer; violence (suicide, homicide, and accidents); and other causes (such as starvation, diabetes, and birth injury). These distinctions are sociologically important because different causes are related to characteristics of physical and social environments.

Infectious diseases such as tuberculosis and diphtheria are more common among poorly nourished people who live in unsanitary conditions. Prior to the discovery of vaccines and an understanding of the importance of sanitation and nutrition, infectious disease accounted for the major portion of deaths in most societies. The incidence of infectious disease depends heavily on material living conditions; it accounts for a much higher percentage of deaths in developing countries such as Colombia

FIGURE 4-1   Smaller Families, but More of Them
Changes since 1950 in the average number of children born to women 15–44 years old (bars) and the total births per year (shaded area above the bars), United States. White area (scale at left) shows total births each year. Bars (scale at right) show children per woman of childbearing age (15 to 44).
Source: USCB
The New York Times/Oct. 31, 1989, p. A18

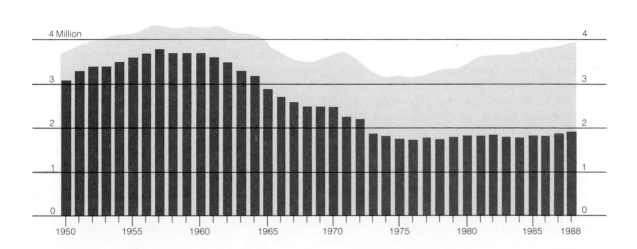

TABLE 4-2   Crude Death Rates and Infant Mortality Rates for Selected Countries

Looking down each column, there is enormous variation around the world in health and mortality, especially in the first year of life. Notice, however, that differences in infant mortality rates are much more dramatic (ranging from a low of 5 to a high of almost 200) than differences in crude death rates. As you will see, this has more to do with differences in age structure than with differences in health.

COUNTRY	CRUDE DEATH RATE[1]	INFANT MORTALITY RATE[2]
Japan	6	5
Mexico	7	50
China	7	37
Brazil	8	63
United States	9	10
France	9	8
Soviet Union	10	29
United Kingdom	12	10
Germany[3]	11	8
Czechoslovakia	14	12
India	11	95
Iran	10	91
Bangladesh	14	120
Afghanistan	22	182
World	10	73

[1]Deaths each year per 1,000 people.
[2]Deaths of infants less than one year old for every 1,000 births in a population.
[3]Figures pool East and West.

Source: PRB 1990.

than in industrial societies such as the U.S. In contrast, cancer and circulatory disease are the most frequent causes of death in industrial societies. In part this difference occurs because wealthy countries have already conquered infectious diseases, and—since people are mortal—they must die from something. However, the difference is also due to factors associated with industrialization such as exposure to cancer-causing agents. Coal miners suffer from blacklung disease, and workers in cotton mills often develop brownlung disease from continually breathing cotton dust. Other workers are exposed to dangerous pesticides and cancer-causing substances such as asbestos. Cultural factors also contribute to differences among industrialized countries. Heart disease is more common in the U.S. than in Japan in part because of differences in diet (people in the U.S.

consume far more red meat), personal habits such as cigarette smoking, and levels of stress.

If you look at crude death rates for different countries, you may be surprised to find that the crude death rate is *lower* in relatively poor countries than it is in the U.S. Before concluding that people are healthier in impoverished Mexico than they are in affluent countries, you need to understand what it is about crude death rates that makes them "crude."

Specifically, the population of Mexico has a very high proportion of children. If you walk through a Mexican community on a Sunday afternoon, almost *half* (42 percent) of all the people you see will be under the age of 15. In the U.S., only 22 percent of the population is under 15, and the percentage of elderly people is increasing rapidly (PRB 1990). How does this affect crude death rates? Children are less likely to die than people at any other age, and a population with a large percentage of children will, as a result, experience relatively few deaths. Although health conditions are certainly worse in Mexico than they are in the United States, the large percentage of children in Mexico—and the correspondingly low percentage of elderly people—pushes the crude death rate down below that of the U.S.

Levels of morbidity and mortality vary not only between societies, but within them, as well. Females generally have lower death rates than males in industrial societies, although in many underdeveloped societies it is males who fare better. This is largely because the resources needed for survival are scarce in underdeveloped societies and the higher value placed on being male is often a matter of life and death.

Social inequality also plays an important part in creating differences in morbidity and mortality (see Williams 1990). In the U.S., death rates are higher among blacks than whites, and higher among lower and working classes than among the middle and upper classes (see Kammeyer and Ginn 1986). In comparison with those with an income of $35,000 or more, those earning less than $10,000 are twice as likely to be hospitalized, and when they are disabled by disease or injury, the average length of the disability is much longer. Poorer people are three times more likely to have heart disease, anemia, and arthritis, and almost four times more likely to suffer from diabetes (DHHS 1990; USCB 1980b, 1983c). In comparison with white infants, black infants are more than twice as likely to die during their first year, and overall life expectancy among blacks is six years

TABLE 4-3   Percent Who Say They Are in Excellent Health, and Percent Who Say They Are in Fair or Poor Health, by Race, Family Income, Education, and Occupational Prestige, United States

Looking down the first column, you see that higher income, education, occupational prestige, and being white go along with a greater tendency to report being in excellent health. The second column shows how the likelihood of being in poor health has the opposite pattern.

CHARACTERISTICS	EXCELLENT HEALTH	FAIR OR POOR HEALTH
Family Income		
Less than $10,000	16%	45%
$10,000–$19,999	24%	26%
$20,000–$29,999	34%	16%
$30,000–$39,999	43%	16%
$40,000–$59,999	40%	14%
$60,000 or more	42%	13%
Education		
Less than high school graduate	17%	45%
High school graduate	29%	18%
Some college or more	39%	15%
Occupational Prestige		
Low	23%	34%
Medium	32%	20%
High	51%	14%
Race		
Black	27%	31%
White	31%	22%

Source: Computed from 1990 General Social Survey data.

shorter than among whites (NCHS 1990). As Table 4-3 shows, whites and people with a higher income, education, and occupational prestige are more likely to say that they are in excellent health and much less likely to say they are in only fair or poor health than are those lower in the stratification system (see also Farley and Allen 1987; Polednak 1989).

Explanations of such differences draw on many factors, including limited access to medical care (see Chapter 18), poor diet, unsanitary living conditions, and dangerous occupations. Average black workers are in occupations that are between 37 and 52 percent more likely to produce serious illness or accidents (J. Robinson 1984). As the cost of medical care has risen dramatically, health has become a commodity to be bought and sold in markets limited to those who can afford it. This is especially true in the U.S., which is still the only industrial society without a national system of health insurance guaranteeing basic medical care for all.

Epidemiology and AIDS

Epidemiology is the study of where diseases come from, how they are distributed geographically and socially, and how they are transmitted from one place or person to another. Epidemiology is of particular interest to those who work in fields related to public health, but because of the connections between health and mortality and social life, it is also important to demographers and, increasingly, to sociologists.

Epidemiologists distinguish between diseases that are normally found in a population (an **endemic** disease such as measles or the common cold in the U.S.) and those that are not (an **epidemic** disease such as the Hong Kong flu) but which, from time to time, spread rapidly through a population and then die out. Of the two, epidemic diseases are the most serious because when they are introduced to populations that have not built up resistance to them, they can have devastating effects. When European explorers and conquerors first came to the Americas, for example, they brought with them diseases such as smallpox, which, although endemic to Europe, were, to the Native American populations, epidemics that decimated local populations (Thornton 1987).

A **pandemic** disease is an epidemic that spreads across several different populations, even to include the entire world. In the past decade, the newest and certainly most important pandemic disease has been AIDS—acquired immune deficiency syndrome—whose discovery represents a classic case of epidemiological research (see Altman 1986; Nichols 1986; Shilts 1987). First detected by U.S. physicians in 1981, the human immune virus (HIV) can destroy the body's immune system, leaving people vulnerable to death from a variety of diseases, especially rare cancers and pneumonia. Infection does not automatically result in an active case of the disease, but it is believed that most who are infected will eventually develop symptoms.

The vital questions of where AIDS came from and how it spreads were answered by studying the social characteristics and behaviors of those infected. Most infected people share one or more of these three characteristics—sexually active bisexual or

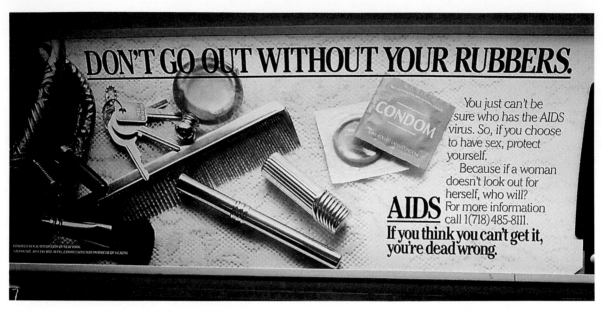

A visible sign of the social impact of the AIDS pandemic has been the unprecedented willingness— and need—of schools, the media, and health officials to discuss publicly and graphically the usage of condoms, and the relative safety of different sexual practices.

homosexual men, drug users who share needles, and hemophiliacs who must undergo frequent blood transfusions. Others include the children of infected mothers and those who receive blood transfusions. From these patterns, researchers discovered that AIDS is transmitted through bodily fluids—most notably blood and semen.

Epidemiologists believe that AIDS originated in central Africa, perhaps through human contact with green monkeys who were infected with a related virus. The virus was probably spread to the Western Hemisphere by Haitians who had worked in Zaire, and to Europe by travelers from Africa. AIDS spread rapidly, expanding to more than 160,000 cases in the U.S. by 1991 and upwards of 400,000 worldwide, just nine years after it was discovered (WHO 1991). Since it is possible to be infected with the AIDS virus without actually developing the disease, these estimates are only a fraction of some 1 million in the U.S. and 8 to 10 million people worldwide who are believed to be already infected, a figure expected to grow to 15 to 20 million by the year 2000 (WHO 1990). Although in the U.S. few people with AIDS (called PWAs) are women or heterosexuals who do not use drugs, this does not mean that heterosexuality per se provides some protection from the disease. In central Africa most PWAs are heterosexual men and women.

AIDS powerfully illustrates the importance of social factors in patterns of disease in a population. The rapid spread of AIDS depended on the movement of infected people over great distances—something quite difficult to accomplish only a few centuries ago and which makes pandemics an increasingly common occurrence. Transmission was also facilitated by the existence of a large drug subculture using such modern technology as syringes, and by widespread tolerance for the sexually active, especially male homosexuals in large cities.

Of even greater sociological significance are the dramatic effects that the AIDS pandemic has had on social life. Many PWAs have been excluded from schools, workplaces, and housing, and discrimination against homosexuals has intensified in housing, employment, and medical care. The minority status of gays was also apparent in the slowness with which government and health officials responded to the early signs of the epidemic (see Shilts 1987). The gay communities of major cities such as New York and San Francisco have been devastated as the death toll has mounted. Sexual activity among both homosexuals and heterosexuals has been greatly curbed as a result of the fear of AIDS. The practice of dentistry and medicine has changed dramatically as health care providers have tried to insulate themselves from their patients: rubber gloves, gowns, and masks have become commonplace in settings in which they were rarely seen before. Some doctors, nurses, dentists, and dental hygienists have refused to treat AIDS patients, prompting the American Medical Association to declare to its members in 1987 that this was unacceptable behavior for a health care professional. Health officials project staggering costs for caring for hundreds of thousands of AIDS patients.

The AIDS pandemic has also raised issues about threats to the civil rights of patients posed by efforts to stop the spread of the disease. The right to privacy has become a key issue as government and health officials have wrestled with the idea of identifying those infected with the virus in order to slow its spread. There is considerable controversy over whether massive screening programs would be of any use, and even greater concern that attempts to identify those carrying the AIDS virus could lead to segregation and massive discrimination. In the hysteria that often accompanies epidemics and pandemics, however, it is difficult to weigh such issues objectively and, as a result, those who already suffer the most are the most likely to suffer the additional damaging effects of a frightened population trying to protect itself.

The Rate of Natural Increase

The rate of population growth is determined primarily by the **rate of natural increase**, which is simply the birth rate minus the death rate. The U.S. population increases at a rate of 0.7 percent: the birth rate is 16 births per 1,000 people (1.6 percent) and the death rate is 9 deaths per 1,000 people (0.9 percent). The difference between the two is 0.7 percent (PRB 1990).

An easy way to see the consequence of a given rate of natural increase is to divide it into 70. The result—100 for the United States—is roughly the number of years it will take for the population to double in size if its current rate of natural increase continues. Rates of natural increase vary widely among the world's societies. As Table 4-4 shows, the lowest rate of natural increase in the world today is found in Germany, where deaths match births. Britain's rate of natural increase is only 0.2 percent, and

TABLE 4-4   Population Statistics for Selected Countries

Crude birth and death rates vary greatly among societies, as does the rate of natural increase. Notice that the rate of increase depends on *both* birth and death rates, which means that high birth rates result in rapid population growth only when death rates are relatively low. India has a higher birth rate than Mexico, but a lower rate of natural increase.

COUNTRY	CRUDE BIRTH RATE	CRUDE DEATH RATE	RATE OF NATURAL INCREASE	YEARS TO DOUBLE[1]
Germany[2]	10	11	0.0%	—
United Kingdom	14	12	0.2%	350
Czechoslovakia	15	14	0.1%	700
France	14	9	0.5%	140
United States	16	9	0.7%	100
Japan	10	6	0.4%	175
Soviet Union	19	10	0.9%	78
China	21	7	1.4%	50
India	32	11	2.1%	33
Afghanistan	48	22	2.6%	27
Brazil	27	8	1.9%	37
Mexico	30	7	2.3%	30
Bangladesh	39	14	2.5%	28
Iran	45	10	3.5%	20
World	27	10	1.7%	41

[1]The number of years it would take for the population to double in size if its current rate of growth continues.
[2]Pooled figures for East and West.

Source: PRB 1990.

at this rate, its population will take 350 years to double. The population of Mexico, on the other hand, is growing at a rate of 2.3 percent per year (3.0 percent minus 0.7 percent). At this rate of natural increase, the population of Mexico will double every 30 years.

The rate of population growth in Mexico and most nonindustrial countries is high because birth rates are far higher than death rates. In the U.S. and Europe growth rates are low because both birth and death rates are roughly equal. The rate of natural increase is almost negative in Germany, and Westoff (1978) estimates that negative population growth rates are likely to occur soon in Australia, Great Britain, Luxembourg, Belgium, Sweden, Norway, Denmark, Greece, Italy, and Switzerland; in the Netherlands and France by 2000; and in the United States by 2040 (USCB 1989a; see also Westoff 1983). In most of Europe, from Italy to Norway, there is concern that a declining population will bring a decline in national prosperity and power (K. Davis et al. 1987; Teitelbaum and Winter 1985). In 1984, Rumania launched a national program to encourage larger families by limiting the availability of contraceptives, banning abortion, and giving financial incentives (van de Kaa 1987).

Why would fertility decline far enough to cause a negative rate of growth? There are several answers. The percentage of people who have never married continues to rise, as so does the cost of raising children especially when the cost of college education is included (Espenshade 1984). As women become more heavily involved in the work force, the indirect cost of raising children—measured by the income women forego when they leave work to care for children—also increases. The dependency of elderly parents on their adult children is lessening as the financial security of the elderly increases (Duncan and Smith 1989). In short, "the costs of childbearing are increasing while the rewards are decreasing" (Huber and Spitze 1983, p. 38; see also van de Kaa 1987).

The Demographic Transition and the Economics of Childbearing

As we have seen, the sharp differences in growth rates of nonindustrialized and industrialized societies reflect, in part, changing historical circumstances (see Harris and Ross 1987). One attempt to describe these long-term shifts is the theory of the **demographic transition**, which describes a three-stage pattern of population growth that has occurred in most societies that are now industrialized. In the first stage of the transition both birth and death rates are high, and the rate of natural increase is therefore low. In early societies, when food was plentiful, death rates dropped for a while and populations increased; and when food was scarce or epidemics struck, death rates jumped and populations leveled off or shrank.

Although available information is at best sketchy, most demographers agree that the world population was quite stable until around 7000 B.C. when people first started to grow their own food (Weinstein 1976). Although higher food production probably lowered death rates by improving nutrition, the rate of natural increase was probably very low. Over the next 9,000 years—roughly up to the mid-1600s—growth rates around the world were low and uneven—going up in some years and down in others. Infectious diseases kept death rates high in most years. During the fourteenth century the Black Plague killed more than one-third of the population of Europe (Tuchman 1978).

From the seventeenth century on, however, growth rates shot up dramatically in most of the world and especially in Europe. Although the population of the world took roughly 1,600 years to double (to A.D. 1600), it took only 200 years (from 1600 to 1800) to double again. Improved sanitation and inexpensive cures for infectious diseases resulted in a redoubling of the world population by 1930, and by 1980—only 50 years later—the population of the world had doubled yet again. The population of the world is now growing at a rate of 1.7 percent, which may seem like a small figure until it is applied to a base of 5.3 billion people, producing 95 million additional people every year (PRB 1990). (Question: At this rate, in how many years will the population of the world double to 10.6 billion?)

Declining death rates in the eighteenth century triggered the second stage of the demographic transition, during which birth rates stayed high while death rates fell, producing higher rates of natural increase. As nutrition and sanitation improved in industrializing Europe, death rates continued to fall and the population of Europe doubled between 1800 and 1850. During this period, however, Europe (and, a bit later, the U.S.) entered the third stage of the demographic transition as birth rates also fell and approached the level of death rates, producing very low rates of natural increase.

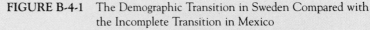

ONE STEP FURTHER 4-1

Sweden, Mexico, and the Demographic Transition

Figure B-4-1 shows how Sweden reached the third stage of the demographic transition in the early 1900s, while Mexico remains in the second stage. In the first figure (for Sweden), notice how death rates began to fall in the early 1800s, widening the gap with birth rates (and, therefore, the rate of natural increase). In the later years of the 1800s, the birth rate fell, too, eventually catching up to the death rate in the 1970s. The second figure shows how Mexico's death rate fell sharply in the early 1900s, but the birth rate remains high in spite of declines since 1970. The combination of the two results in a high rate of natural increase.

FIGURE B-4-1 The Demographic Transition in Sweden Compared with the Incomplete Transition in Mexico

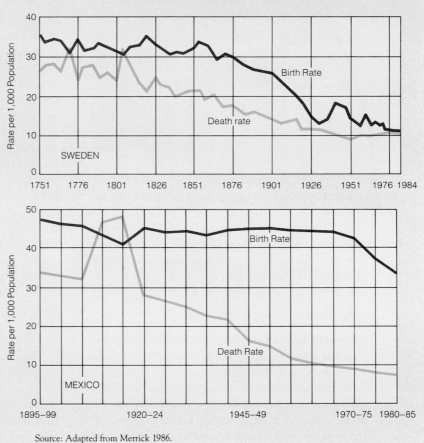

Source: Adapted from Merrick 1986.

The populations of most nonindustrial societies such as Mexico continue to grow rapidly, for although death rates have fallen sharply through the use of medical technology, birth rates are still high (see One Step Further 4-1). These countries appear, in short, to be taking a long time to get through the second stage of the demographic transition. Why?

You might think that if high birth rates make life so hard, people would have fewer children. Historical evidence suggests, however, that it is the prosperity brought by industrialization that causes families to control their fertility. Birth rates in Europe and the U.S. did not begin to fall until the Industrial Revolution took hold at the beginning of the nineteenth century. Japan experienced a similar decline when it industrialized in the twentieth century. Industrialization not only raises hopes for prosperity, but also converts children from an asset to a liability. Parents who want to exploit expanding opportunities simply have an easier time if they have small families. The desire for upward mobility raises parents' aspirations for their children, and if they have small families, they maximize the resources they can devote to each child's development (see Harris and Ross 1987; Kristof 1990; Rindfuss, Bumpass, and St. John 1980).

At the heart of the ecological problems of most less developed nations are rates of natural increase that add people faster than jobs and goods can be produced. Natural increase is the most important

As the sun goes down, a Mexican family begins their illegal attempt to cross the border, leaving Tijuana, Mexico, behind.

component of population growth, but migration also plays an important part in the growth of many societies and in the distribution of people within them. The populations of Mexico City and cities in other less developed societies are exploding only in part because fertility is high.

Migration: Gains and Losses

Migration is the movement of people from one population to another. **Immigrants** are people who enter a population, and **emigrants** are those who leave (someone who moves from Mexico to the U.S. emigrates *from* Mexico and immigrates *to* the U.S.). The causes of migration can be divided into "push" factors—such as poverty or oppression—that drive people away from an area and "pull" factors—such as the promise of higher income or greater freedom—that attract them to a new area (see Bouvier and Gardner 1986).

For centuries people have migrated to escape poor conditions. Hundreds of thousands of Irish immigrated to the U.S. after the potato famine of 1846. The westward expansion that took place in the U.S. in the nineteenth century resulted as much from crowded living conditions and limited opportunities in East Coast cities as from the lure of exploiting new territories (Limerick 1987). When the farmers of the Midwest were ruined by years of drought during the Great Depression of the 1930s, hundreds of thousands packed up all they could carry and migrated to what they thought would be better conditions in California (a desperate story powerfully portrayed in John Steinbeck's novel *The Grapes of Wrath*, published in 1939).

Since the 1930s, migration has involved millions of people moving within a short time and under intense pressure. Tens of millions of European civilians were uprooted by World War II and Nazi persecution, and in 1948 thousands of Palestinians fled from the territory that is now Israel (Bouvier, Shryock, and Henderson 1977). Across the world, roughly 50 million people left their homelands between 1946 and 1955 alone (Cook 1957), and in the 1970s political and economic upheavals created tens of millions of refugees in Southeast Asia. When Iraq invaded Kuwait in 1990, thousands of refugees fled from those two countries into neighboring Jordan. Many countries, including Mexico and Haiti, still look upon the U.S. as a place for people who cannot be supported by their economies at home. Illegal immigration of Mexicans into the U.S. is so massive that no one really knows just how many cross the 1,900-mile border each year (see Massey 1981a; Massey et al. 1987). An estimated 1.7 to 2.3 million people are in the U.S. illegally (INS 1989).

Migration is a major cause of population growth especially in low fertility countries such as the U.S. (Bouvier and Gardner 1986). Between 1840 and 1930, roughly 52 million people emigrated from Europe, mostly to the U.S. (Davis 1974). From 1651 to the abolition of slavery in the nineteenth century, between 9 and 11 million Africans were forcibly brought to the United States (Curtin 1969). These migrations rapidly expanded the populations of receiving countries and substantially redistributed a sizable portion of the world's people. By 1930 one-third of the world's whites lived outside of Europe, and one-fifth of all blacks lived outside of Africa (Davis 1974).

Migration is the primary cause of the growth of cities. Although birth rates are generally lower in cities than in rural areas, urban populations have increased while rural ones have declined. The populations of many cities such as Mexico City, however, are exploding under the pressures of migration from rural areas. Like many less developed countries, Mexico is trying to industrialize rapidly, and is therefore investing far more in industry than in agriculture. Mexico City acts like a magnet that pulls thousands of poor, unskilled rural workers who are motivated by the hope that life in the city will be better (see Bradshaw 1987; Grindle 1988; London 1987). The flood of migrants, however, only makes life in the city worse.

As in Mexico, migration affects the distribution of people within the U.S. Almost 20 percent of the population moves to a new house each year (USCB 1990a). During the nineteenth century, migration flows were from east to west and south to north; but since 1970, the northerly flow has reversed as northerners leave home in search of jobs, and the South and West account for most population gains through migration (USCB, 1989b).

Patterns of migration often have important social consequences. As people move from the North and East to the West and South the "receiver" areas gain political power in Congress, because representation is based on population. Migration also causes problems for receiver areas, however. Massive migration of unemployed workers severely strains states whose job markets, schools, public services, and natural resources (water) cannot keep up with a rapidly expanding population (Weller and Bouvier 1981).

Migration is also a major source of change in the social composition of populations (Bouvier and Gardner 1986) (Figure 4-2). The Detroit area now has

FIGURE 4-2 Legal Immigrants to the U.S., by Region of Origin, 1820–1988

Change in the flow of immigrants from different parts of the world has an enormous potential to affect the ethnic composition of the United States. In 1820–1860, virtually all immigrants were from Europe; but by 1961–1970, less than half were from Europe, and by the early 1980s, almost half were from Asia and more than a third were from Latin America.
Source: Bouvier and Gardner 1986, Figure 2; USCB 1990a.

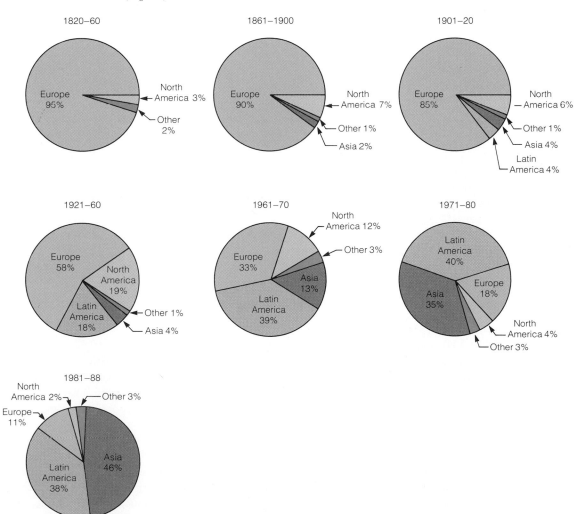

ONE STEP FURTHER 4-2

"Give Me Your Tired, Your Poor . . ."?

Although the U.S. has long prided itself on being a nation of immigrants, it has also had long periods during which immigration was sharply curtailed and newcomers were greeted with something far short of open arms. Today, there are many countries that have a larger proportion of foreign-born than the U.S., including France, Canada, and Australia, and annual immigration into the U.S. constitutes a small portion of the annual population growth.

Still, the perception of many is that the U.S. is being inundated by a flood of legal and illegal immigrants. As of mid-1986, just under half of the adult population favored decreasing the number of immigrants, but, as with all values, opposition to immigration has some revealing social patterns, as the data in Table B-4-2 show.

Groups with the most recent immigrant experience are least in favor of decreasing immigration—whites are most in favor, followed by blacks and Hispanics in that order. Those who trace their U.S. ancestry to pre-Revolutionary days are far more likely to be in favor of decreasing immigration than are those who arrived more recently.

The last two sets of percentages shed some light on the social reasons behind opposition to immigration. Those with less income and education tend to be more in favor of decreased immigration than are those with higher income and education. Why do you think this would be true?

TABLE B-4-2

SOCIAL CHARACTERISTICS	PERCENT WHO BELIEVE IMMIGRATION LEVEL SHOULD BE DECREASED
Race	
White	52
Black	39
Hispanic	31
Ancestry	
First arrived before 1776	50
Born abroad or from family arriving after 1941	29
Income	
Under $12,500	55
$12,500 to $24,999	53
$25,000 to $34,999	51
$35,000 or more	42
Education	
Less than high school graduate	55
High school graduate	51
Some college	49
College graduate	35

Source: *New York Times*/CBS News Poll, *New York Times*, July 1, 1986, p. A21.

the largest concentration of Arab-speaking people outside of the Middle East, and, according to at least one estimate, Spanish-speaking people will constitute a majority of California's population by the year 2000 (*New York Times*, June 30, 1986). These changes have prompted strong opposition to immigration and hostility towards immigrants (see One Step Further 4-2).

Birth, death, natural increase, migration, and population growth are basic processes that define the study of populations by determining a population's *age structure*, *size*, and *distribution*.

Age Structure

The **age structure** of a population is the distribution of people according to age. Age structures are usually represented by "pyramids," which give a revealing picture of one of a population's most important characteristics.

Figure 4-3 shows age structures for the U.S., Mexico, and Sweden. They are all broader at the bottom than at the top, because people die as they grow older. Here, however, the similarities end: the age structure of Mexico is much broader at the bottom

FIGURE 4-3   Age Structures
Source: UN 1985.

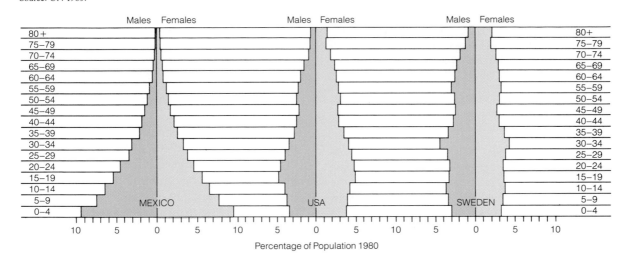

than those of Sweden and the U.S., and Sweden's is tall and thin. Why do they have such different shapes?

In general, age structures reflect the history of births, deaths, and migration in a population; but of these factors, birth rates are by far the most important (Coale 1964). Mexico has a history of high birth rates, whereas birth rates in Sweden have remained low. This is why Mexico has such a large proportion of children and Sweden has a large proportion of elderly people. The U.S. age structure, on the other hand, has a bulge that primarily reflects changing birth rates. Prior to World War II, U.S. birth rates had declined steadily for over a century, so that each new generation was smaller than the one that preceded it. Between 1945 and the early 1960s, the United States experienced a "baby boom"; then a drop in birth rates resulted in a "baby bust" in the 1970s. The "bulge" contains maturing "boom babies" and the relatively narrow base contains the "bust babies" born in the 1970s.

Age structures have important effects on both societies and individuals. An "old" population such as Sweden's must devote a relatively large share of its resources to the elderly, whereas Mexico is burdened with a disproportionately large number of children who produce less than they consume. A large proportion of children in a population poses problems for economic development, particularly in poor societies that are trying to industrialize. Pakistan, for example, can put little toward industrialization because the huge numbers of dependent children require a great deal just to survive. Rather than in-

vesting in higher standards of living, such countries must use much of what they produce simply to maintain their already poor living conditions; and in order to industrialize, they must go into debt by borrowing money from wealthier countries.

Unlike "old" countries such as Sweden and "young" ones such as Mexico, the U.S. is aging and must make a difficult transition between meeting the needs of a young population (building more schools for the "boom babies") and meeting those of an aging one (providing medical care and retirement benefits).

Birth Cohorts   Age is an important social status in all societies, but our experiences and opportunities at different ages depend strongly on the period in history in which we reach each age and the relative numbers of people who are younger or older than we are.

A birth cohort consists of all people who are born at roughly the same time, and the cohort we belong to has important effects on our lives (Riley 1987; Ryder 1965). If you had been born in the 1930s your cohort would have been smaller than those born before 1930, because the economic hardship of the depression discouraged childbearing. As a member of the depression cohort, you would have enjoyed a relatively rich supply of jobs and educational opportunities, because *the relatively large cohorts that preceded you created more opportunities than your cohort required.* For this reason, Harter (1977) called the 1930s cohort the "Good Times Cohort":

By virtue of their smaller number, the thirties cohort, upon encountering each important life cycle event, have experienced relative abundance. . . . In all their important life cycle events, the 1930s cohort has "had it made." . . . Insofar as the number of high school classrooms, glee clubs, athletic teams . . . had not diminished, then the 1950 fifteen-year-old had a greater chance than did the 1940 fifteen-year-old of being in a smaller class, of being a class officer . . . and when the 1930s cohort was 21–30, they required fewer new jobs and housing units than did their predecessors ten years earlier. (pp. 3–4)

As a member of a baby boom cohort, however, you would encounter enormous competition in the job market for the relatively few jobs created by the smaller cohorts that preceded yours. If you were born after the late 1960s (a bust baby) your relatively small cohort will have the greater opportunities enjoyed by those that preceded the baby boom (assuming, of course, that other factors do not change for the worse).

Population Size and Distribution

Along with age structure, population *size* and *distribution* are important both for societies and individuals. In comparison with large, densely settled societies, small, sparsely settled ones, such as the Kung Bushmen of Africa, require fewer resources, find it easier to move to more supportive environments, tend to have less complex divisions of labor, and tend to be less urban. By comparison, the populations of industrial societies are in the tens and hundreds of millions. Such large populations are a continuing source of diversity and innovation because they allow individuals to specialize in specific tasks. Large societies are vulnerable, however, for they demand enormous natural resources and cannot simply move in order to meet their needs.

While large, densely settled populations have greater potential for innovative technology and complex divisions of labor (Bosrup, 1981), their sheer size need not have this result. Many of the poorest countries of the world—Bangladesh, China, India, and El Salvador—have among the largest and most densely settled populations. If the United States were as densely settled as Bangladesh, its population would exceed the current population of the entire world by 40 percent (PRB 1990).

In part, the poverty of many large, dense populations is due to high birth rates that result in relatively large numbers of children who produce less than

they consume. A full explanation, however, involves the characteristics of physical environments and the ways in which human populations organize themselves and use natural resources.

PHYSICAL ENVIRONMENTS

The social characteristics of a society often reflect the problems of adapting to a physical environment—from the isolation imposed by mountains to the splitting of an urban neighborhood by a new highway (Buttel 1987). For this reason sociologists have paid increasing attention to the relationship between social and physical environments, which include nonliving elements such as land, water, and air as well as other species of life.

Land, Water, and Air

Mountains, deserts, oceans, and seas are barriers to easy movement from one place to another; as a result, they isolate and protect societies from one another. Rivers and seas also allow people to travel and trade over distances that would be difficult if not impossible to cover over land; and landlocked societies without access to major rivers rarely prosper. It is no accident that most of the world's great cities—New York, Los Angeles, Chicago, Rio de Janeiro, London, Paris, Rome, Moscow, Bombay, Calcutta, Shanghai, and Tokyo—lie on seacoasts or major rivers.

The physical characteristics of land profoundly affect the way communities develop. Los Angeles lies in what was once a desert, and the long valley extending from the sea to San Bernardino encouraged the development of a sprawling city with relatively low-rising buildings. The vastness of Los Angeles now makes it difficult to use bus and subway transportation efficiently, and so the city has developed into a place in which cars are a necessity (see Bottles 1987). The air pollution generated by cars, in turn, is held and concentrated by the hills that line the valley and intensified by sunlight. The famous smog of Los Angeles results from both geography and the development of the city.

Varieties of Life

Each species of life lives in relation to other species, and ecology focuses on the place of human beings in such relationships (Hawley 1968, 1986; Park and

Much of the prosperity enjoyed by the United States results from the richness of its farmland—an ecological condition quite unlike that found in famine-stricken African countries, including Ethiopia, Chad, and Sudan, where, despite international relief efforts, hungry people have been driven to scavenging grains of cattle feed. The suffering, starvation, and death of tens of thousands have been caused, in part, by deforestation, extensive monoculture (cultivation of a single kind of crop, usually for export rather than to sustain those who grow it), and widespread droughts, making agriculture all but impossible and creating new deserts.

Burgess 1921). To survive, each form of life continually exchanges one thing for another. We take oxygen from the air and give back carbon dioxide (whereas plants do just the opposite); we take coal and oil from the ground and give back heat and pollution as we burn them; cows transform grass into milk, which we then transform into teeth, bones, muscle, fat, heat (energy), and wastes (which bacteria thrive on).

Forms of life often benefit from one another's behavior. As bees gather nectar, they unwittingly pollinate flowers and allow them to reproduce; as worms dig tunnels, they loosen the soil and allow it to absorb air and water more easily, making it more supportive of plants and, in turn, of humans and others who eat the plants.

Just as living things benefit one another, so can they harm one another—and themselves. People cut down forests in order to build homes, make paper, and keep warm; but, although this benefits us in the short run, it destroys forests that thousands of animals depend on for their survival; in the long run, it also deprives us of vital oxygen that green plants add to the air.

ORGANIZATION: ECOSYSTEMS AND NICHES

An **ecosystem** consists of all forms of life that live in relation to one another and a shared physical environment (the word "ecology" refers to the study of such systems). The limits of a particular ecosystem depend on how we define a "shared physical environment"; a vacant lot in a city, a small pond, or the world might all be defined as ecosystems, so long as what goes on in one part of that environment affects life in other parts.

Within ecosystems, species of life survive through relationships with other species and the physical environment, and their positions in such relationships are called **niches**. While a status refers to a position in a social system, a niche refers to the position of an

PUZZLE

WHY ARE COWS SACRED IN INDIA BUT RAISED FOR SLAUGHTER IN THE U.S.?

A simple answer is that the Hindu religion of India forbids the eating of beef, but this sidesteps the question of why this ever became a part of the Hindu religion. Anthropologist Marvin Harris argues that the holy status enjoyed by cattle in India came about in response to ecological and population conditions. India's recurring droughts and resulting crop failures made it tempting for farmers to use their cattle for food. Farmers who did this, however, faced starvation when the rains returned because they had eaten the only animal that could pull their plows. While eating cows may have made sense in the short run, it was ecologically disastrous in the long run. Making the cow sacred was a way to ensure that even in the most severe crisis, the precious work animals would be preserved. This is one of many examples of the ways in which ecology and population affect human culture in unexpected ways (Harris 1977).

entire population in its physical environment. Wheat draws nutrients and water from the soil and carbon dioxide from the air. As it grows it gives off oxygen, and when it dies it decomposes, providing food for bacteria and fertilizer to be used by other plants. Much of the carbon dioxide it needs to survive comes from animals (such as ourselves) who extract oxygen from the air and exhale carbon dioxide. What is waste to plant life—oxygen—is vital to animals, and what is waste to animals—carbon dioxide—is vital to plants.

Human niches in ecosystems are unique because they are extremely complex and can be altered deliberately. Human beings do not dominate the earth because they are bigger, faster, or stronger than other creatures. It is through culture and structure that we organize our activities and vastly extend our otherwise modest biological endowment. Whereas most species must adapt through slow biological evolution, we can quickly adapt to an extraordinary range of environmental conditions.

We have an enormous ability to alter the physical environment itself: we can pollute the waters and clean them, plant trees and cut them down, and

build roads and buildings on land that would otherwise sprout vegetation (which would in turn produce oxygen). We can plow the land in such a way that rains wash away the topsoil, ruining it for further cultivation, or we can carefully terrace the land and protect it from erosion.

Most species occupy narrowly defined niches, but the relationship of societies to ecosystems is far more complex. Tiny fish eat plants and microorganisms, then are eaten by bigger fish, which in turn provide food for still larger fish. Humans, however, eat all manner of plants and animals and have the ability to exterminate almost any animal species; we mine the earth and send a vast range of radio waves and chemicals into the air. Whereas most species have biological predispositions to slow their consumption before the food supply becomes too scarce, humans have no such inborn checks.

A major point of all this is that societies can deliberately alter and create ecological conditions within which people and other forms of life must survive. The populations that make up societies grow, shrink, distribute themselves over physical environments, and survive by organizing their relationships with one another and the natural environment and its many species of life.

TECHNOLOGY

For humans, a major element of our organization for survival is cultural technology. The number of people who can survive in a physical environment depends on natural resources and the ability to use them, and when a growing population has too few resources, the range of adaptations is limited. The simplest responses are to move the society to a more supportive physical environment or to intensify the use of existing technologies—by increasing kills of wild game, farming more land, or drilling for more oil. These adaptations have limited value, however, for the emigration of an entire society is impractical, and any technology ultimately reaches the limits of its usefulness.

In such circumstances, a society has only four options: to change social systems and technology in ways that increase production, to shrink its population through migration, to control reproduction and death, or to wait for nature to take its toll. Throughout history, societies have relied on the first option—social and technological change—in order to support larger populations. The results have produced four major types of societies—gatherer-hunter, horticultural, agrarian, and industrial.

Preindustrial Societies

In the earliest societies—existing between roughly 35,000 and 7000 B.C.—people survived by gathering vegetation and by hunting animals. They lived in small, autonomous communities, their division of labor was simple (there were few if any full-time specialists), and wealth, power, and prestige were distributed fairly equally. Because they did not produce their own food, they had to move whenever they exhausted the supply, although archeological evidence suggests some communities stayed in one place for most of each year (Price and Brown 1985). Their technology was primitive, but appropriate to their way of life. They domesticated sheep and dogs, developed basketry and fishing, and invented spears, bows and arrows, lamps, combs, spoons, shovels, fish traps, hooks, and nets; they had no knowledge of how to fabricate metals, however, and the human body was their only source of energy for work.

Horticultural Societies   Around 7000 B.C., people in Asia Minor discovered how to cultivate plants, and for the first time in history people produced some of their own food. They planted crops with hoes and digging sticks, and after the harvest they burned the stubble (which eventually provided fertilizer) and started again. Although the technology of these horticultural societies was crude and they often exhausted the soil's fertility, these simple innovations were enormously important, for as food supplies grew, so did populations.

Because people could produce more than they needed for themselves, others could specialize in work that was not necessary for survival, such as pottery and weaving. Plant cultivation provided a more stable food supply, and settlements were more permanent. With a greater variety of goods, people accumulated possessions and built larger dwellings. Although these early communities were still relatively autonomous, trade began, which made it possible to support larger populations since they could acquire goods they did not produce themselves.

Advanced horticultural societies were more permanent, more complex, and larger than their predecessors, averaging just under 300 people. For the first time, they were linked to multicommunity societies

---

PUZZLE

WHICH CAME FIRST, THE KING OR THE PLOW?

If it were not for the invention of the plow, there might never have been kings, queens, emperors, or popes. Why?

The answer is that without the plow societies might never have had the ability to produce a surplus, and as you will see in Chapter 12, without a surplus societies rarely develop social inequalities of wealth and power.

---

with average populations of more than 5,000. Work was more specialized: whereas metal and leather working, boat and house building, pottery making, and weaving were specialties in only 2 percent of the early horticultural societies, they were specialties in almost 30 percent of advanced horticultural societies (Murdock 1967).

Agrarian Societies   What historians refer to as "the dawn of civilization" began around 3000 B.C. Although this period saw the development of the wheel, alphabetic writing, numbers, and the calendar, the most important innovation was the plow. The plow helped solve the problems of weeds and the exhaustion of the soil's fertility by digging deeply as it turned over the soil. For the first time, plants could be cultivated in large fields rather than in small gardens, and animal and wind power—useless in a technology dependent on sticks and hoes—were harnessed.

The agrarian age coincided with the development of the first real cities, some with populations exceeding 100,000. Cities came into being because technology enabled a relatively small portion of a population to produce the entire food supply, allowing people to live in densely settled communities that did not produce their own food. Permanent settlements were now the rule, and larger crops produced greater surpluses, which in turn supported still more complex divisions of labor.

Industrial Societies

The Industrial Revolution began in Great Britain between 1760 and 1830 with the development of

The development of agriculture, through the invention of the plow in ancient societies such as Egypt made it possible to produce a surplus. This, in turn, supported emerging elite classes and their followers. Even with slavery, the millions of workers who built astonishing monuments—the Great Sphinx and Pyramids—would never have been available without ecological conditions that enabled part of the population to produce enough goods to meet the needs of themselves as well as others.

more efficient machinery for making textiles (Mathais 1983). With a flying shuttle, one worker could weave as much as two could before, and the resulting demand for yarn prompted the invention of spinning jennies, which could spin not one but 120 threads at once. This led to such a large supply of yarn that the weavers could not keep up; so Britain, lacking a large network of rivers and streams to provide water power, had to find a new source of energy to power looms that wove yarn into fabric.

The idea of using steam to generate power was not new. Hero of Alexandria—a Greek scientist—invented the steam turbine in the first century A.D. Like Leonardo da Vinci's helicopter, however, it was an idea whose time came only after centuries of social development had produced societies such as Britain (in which someone like James Watt could invent a workable steam engine to provide power for enormous looms). By the early 1800s England depended more on manufacturing than on agriculture, and was, therefore, the world's first industrial society. Iron and coal production grew rapidly, and machines capable of manufacturing interchangeable, precisely tooled metal parts were developed, paving the way for greater, more efficient production.

Most societies continue to rely on technology to cope with the demands of population growth. Scientists are now using discoveries in genetics to create new varieties of food plants that are resistant to disease and produce higher yields, and the Chinese are increasing their supplies of energy by converting human wastes into flammable methane gas on a massive scale.

In comparison with biological evolution, cultural technology allows societies to alter their relationship with physical environments at lightning speed. The daily expenditure of energy in large industrial societies is estimated to be 50 *million* times greater than that in the gatherer-hunter societies of only 10,000 years ago (Harris 1979). (Ten thousand years may seem like a long time, but it shrinks in the context of some 2 million years of human history.) World population is estimated to be 880 times greater now than it was at the dawn of horticultural societies around 8000 B.C. The current population constitutes 9 percent of all the people who ever lived (Westing 1981), and its density has increased from roughly one person per square mile in 8000 B.C. to more than 65.

While technological innovation often improves the ability to survive, it also may have unanticipated consequences that create serious problems. Chemical pesticides have dramatically improved usable crop yields by protecting them against insects; but a negative consequence is the chronic introduction of dangerous substances into food supplies—such as the discovery of ethylenedibromide (also known as EDB) in grains and fruits in 1983 and 1984 (see Chapter 18). The technology utilizing carbon-based fuels such as coal, oil, and gasoline contributed to the Industrial Revolution and the material wealth that has come with it. But the resulting air pollution may cause a warming of the global climate through the "greenhouse effect." This effect is compounded by the steady destruction of the South American rain forest to clear land for farming and other development (World Resources Institute 1990). Scientists predict that this may disrupt global weather patterns and have negative effects on crops as well as some melting of the polar ice caps and consequent flooding in coastal cities. Human societies face an accelerating race to understand and respond to the effects of technological change before it is too late to avoid natural—and social—disaster.

The relationship between social systems and ecosystems raises fundamental conflicts in cultural values. On one hand the unbridled exploitation of the environment has been making the earth a less supportive environment for many species, including our own. On the other hand, powerful values underlie that exploitation, including the value placed on corporate profit, private property rights, military power, economic well-being, and the idea that the needs and desires of human beings have primary importance in relation to the rest of the earth, its millions of species, and its complex ecosystems. It is a value conflict that has brought together dedicated and articulate adversaries, including environmental movements in many parts of the world that are challenging the presumed right of humans to do as they wish with their physical environment regardless of the consequences.

TOO MANY PEOPLE?

Historically, population size has been limited by high death rates from infectious disease, but inexpensive medical technology has sharply lowered death rates without also lowering birth rates. Less developed countries such as Mexico are growing at an unprecedented rate, and their young, rapidly expanding populations severely strain their resources. Rapid increases in the size of populations and projections into the future have generated widespread concern about overpopulation (see Johnson and Lee 1986).

World population has grown dramatically since 1750, from just under a billion to more than 8 billion projected for the year 2025. Of these people, 82 percent will live in less developed countries. Figure 4-4 (p. 86) shows the changing excess of births over deaths (natural increase) in more developed and less developed countries between 1925 and 2025. As the pair of short "walls" show, the number of births will remain stable in more developed countries while the death rate will rise slightly as the population age structure gets older. The difference between the height of the two "walls" (the amount of natural increase) is small. For less developed countries the number of deaths each year is much higher (the taller "walls") than in more developed countries, but the number of births is so huge that by the year 2000 there will be 60 million more births than deaths each year.

Many social scientists argue that rapid population growth—particularly in underdeveloped societies—makes economic progress all but impossible and continued widespread poverty, poor health, and starvation inevitable (UN 1987). High-fertility societies tend to have young populations, and if economies cannot expand fast enough to employ them, they are likely to be a source of social unrest and political instability. In addition, larger populations use up natural resources at faster rates and strain the physical environment's ability to absorb growing amounts of waste and pollution (Worldwatch Institute 1987).

In 1798 an English clergyman named Thomas Malthus published the first serious discussion of the problem of population size and growth. He used simple reasoning to arrive at a dramatic conclusion: populations grow exponentially (doubling and redoubling as in 2, 4, 8, 16, 32), whereas food supplies grow arithmetically (as in 1, 2, 3, 4) as new land is cultivated. Malthus argued that unless birth rates are controlled, the size of a population will inevitably be controlled through higher death rates caused by starvation, disease, or war.

Although it is obvious that there are upper limits on the number of people who can survive on a planet with finite space and resources, determining how many people constitute "too many" is complicated. Survival and the quality of life depend on ecological factors such as the size and distribution of populations, the characteristics of physical environments, and technology. Bosrup (1981) argues that the development of new technology, in turn, has depended

FIGURE 4-4   Population Growth, Births and Deaths in More Developed and Less Developed Countries, 1925–2025

Source: United Nations Fund for Population Activities, *Population Images*, 2 ed., 1987.

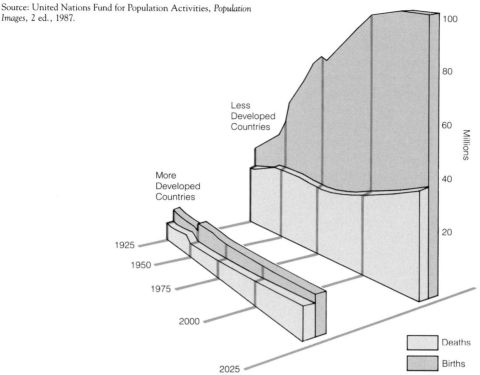

historically on the pressures of expanding populations: rather than face starvation, expanding populations *had* to come up with innovative ways to produce food and other necessities.

Survival also depends, however, on how societies organize production and distribute what they produce. Until recently, Mexico had a rapidly expanding economy, but little of its prosperity has been shared with its large peasant population (Gonzalez Casanova 1980). From one point of view, a population is too large when its social and ecological arrangements are unable to support its members, suggesting that the answer is either to alter those arrangements in order to increase production or to slow—if not reverse—the rate of population growth.

As we saw earlier, many societies with rapidly growing populations have tried to lower birth rates by promoting the use of contraceptives, but historical evidence suggests that people generally do not lower their fertility in order to improve their standard of living. From this perspective, the connection between population size and poverty is reciprocal: countries are poor because their populations are too large, and their populations are too large because they are poor. All of this suggests that an important answer to the problem of overpopulation is to change social and ecological conditions in ways that will both increase production and raise standards of living—and thereby motivate individuals to have fewer children (see Merrick 1986).

From another perspective, however, those who control societies are unlikely to choose this solution. As we will see in Chapter 12, many sociologists argue that the poverty found in rapidly growing societies is due both to overpopulation and to social relationships through which an elite exploits workers and hoards wealth (see Hernandez 1985; Mamdani 1981). Marx ([1867] 1975) argued that capitalist societies in particular depend on a "surplus" population to provide a supply of "readily exploitable manpower" (pp. 596–97; see also Whitaker 1989).

This does not mean that population size and

growth do not by themselves help perpetuate poverty. It does suggest, however, that slowing the growth of populations by controlling births may not by itself do much to improve living conditions. It also suggests that the causes and consequences of and the cures for problems of overpopulation depend not only on ecological factors such as technology, but on the organization of social life as well.

SUMMARY

1. Each species survives through a complex set of relationships with other species and with its physical surroundings. Ecology is the study of such relationships, and focuses on four basic concepts: population, organization, environment, and technology (POET). Demography is the study of the size, growth, composition, and distribution of populations.

2. The crude birth rate is the number of children born each year for every 1,000 members of a population, and birth rates vary among and within societies. The number of births depends on culture and social structure as well as on the proportion of women of childbearing age.

3. The crude death rate is the number of people who die in a given year for every 1,000 people. The infant mortality rate is the number of children under the age of 1 who die each year for every 1,000 births. Death rates differ among societies primarily because of differences in culture (medical knowledge) and material conditions (sanitation and nutrition). They vary within societies because of differences in the quality of living conditions and access to medical care and knowledge.

4. The epidemiological study of morbidity is of interest to demographers and sociologists because endemic, epidemic, and pandemic diseases affect not only death rates, but the quality of social life as well. As the example of AIDS shows, disease is social both in its causes and in its consequences.

5. The rate of natural increase is the birth rate minus the death rate. The theory of demographic transition is a three-stage pattern of population growth that has occurred in industrialized societies. In the first stage the growth rate is low because the birth and death rates are high. In the second stage the death rate falls while the birth rate remains high, producing a high rate of natural increase. In the third stage the birth rate falls and levels off close to the death rate, producing a low rate of natural increase.

6. Migration is the movement of people within societies or between them. People who leave an area are called emigrants, and those who enter are called immigrants. Migration is primarily responsible for the growth of cities, often contributes to population growth, and has important social consequences for both receiving and sending areas.

7. The age structure of a population is the relative number of people of each age. Prolonged high birth rates tend to produce a young population, whereas low birth rates produce an old one. Young populations have a relatively high proportion of children who consume more than they produce, whereas old populations must devote a relatively large share of what they produce to the support of the elderly. A birth cohort consists of people born in the same year, and a cohort's experiences and opportunities depend on when in history they reach each age as well as the relative numbers of people who are older and younger.

8. In comparison with small, sparse populations, large, dense ones require more resources, find it harder to move to more supportive environments, tend to have more complex divisions of labor, and tend to be more urban.

9. The survival of a species depends on its relationships with its physical surroundings and other living things. An ecosystem consists of all forms of life that live in relation to one another and a physical environment. A niche is the position a species occupies in an ecosystem. Human niches are unique because they are very complex and can be altered with relative ease.

10. Technology is the major way in which humans adapt to physical conditions. Gatherer-hunter societies rely on wild game and vegetation to meet subsistence needs; and in horticultural societies people cultivate small gardens with digging sticks and hoes. In most agrarian societies the use of plows allows people to cultivate large fields and produce a surplus of food. The Industrial

Revolution introduced new sources of energy such as steam and electricity, machinery that multiplied the amount of labor one worker could do, and centralized production in factories.

11. Although technology often has beneficial results, it can also have unanticipated consequences that create serious problems such as pollution.

12. Survival and the quality of human life depend on population size and distribution, the charac-

teristics of natural environments, technology, how societies organize production, and how they distribute what is produced. Malthus was one of the first to pay serious attention to the limited ability of physical environments to support large human populations. Although the resources of the earth are certainly finite, overpopulation is a complex problem.

KEY TERMS

age structure   78
birth cohort   79
crude birth rate   67
crude death rate   69
demographic transition   74
demography   66
ecology   66
ecosystem   81

emigrants   76
endemic disease   71
epidemic disease   71
epidemiology   71
immigrants   76
infant mortality rate   67
life expectancy   69

migration   76
morbidity   69
niche   81
pandemic disease   71
population   66
rate of natural increase   73
technology   66

LOOKING ELSEWHERE

Having studied Chapter 4, you might want to look at related discussions in *Human Arrangements*, which include

- additional major discussion of technology (Chapter 18, pp. 452–58)
- age structure, birth cohorts, and social inequality (Chapter 15, pp. 366–74)
- age structure and unemployment (Chapter 19, p. 490)
- cohorts as a source of social change (Chapter 23, pp. 575–76)
- fertility, mortality, and family life (Chapter 16, pp. 396–98)
- the effects of greater longevity on family life (Chapter 18, p. 465)
- the effect of technology on family life (Chapter 16, pp. 398–99)

- technology, production, and the development of capitalism (Chapter 19, pp. 469–76)
- automation and work (Chapter 19, pp. 489–90)
- postindustrial society (Chapter 19, p. 486)
- technology and varieties of religious belief (Chapter 21, pp. 541–43)
- inequality, health, and health care (Chapter 18, pp. 462–64)
- how ecosystems change (Chapter 23, p. 573)
- technology as a source of social change (Chapter 23, pp. 576–78)
- the importance of geography for political power (Chapter 20, p. 517)
- race, ethnicity, and hostility toward immigrants (Chapter 13, pp. 302–303, 314–17)

RECOMMENDED READINGS

Bogue, D. J. 1985. *The population of the United States: Historical trends and future projections.* New York: Free Press. A useful reference on population dynamics in the U.S., including trends in population growth and composition, with a special emphasis on change since 1960.

Coale, A. J. 1964. How a population ages or grows younger. In R. Freedman (Ed.), *Population: The vital revolution.* New York: Doubleday/Anchor (paperback). A readable and classic analysis of how birth and death rates affect the age structure of populations.

Ehrlich, P. R., et al. 1977. *Ecoscience: Population, resources, environment.* San Francisco: Freeman. An excellent introduction to the ecological perspective.

Harris, M. 1974. *Cows, pigs, wars, and witches.* (1977). *Cannibals and kings.* Both New York: Random House. Harris is now famous for his entertaining and provocative uses of the ecological perspective in search of the origins of a marvelous collection of cultural practices.

Jones, L. Y. 1980. *Great expectations: America and the baby boom generations.* New York: Coward, McCann, and Geoghegan. An interesting look at cohort effects, with an emphasis on the Baby Boom and post-Baby Boom generations.

Lenski, G. E., and Lenski, J. 1987. *Human societies* (5th ed.). New York: McGraw-Hill. An excellent description and analysis of the historical development of technology and its effects on human societies.

Papademetriou, D. G., and Miller, M. J. (Eds.). 1984. *The unavoidable issue: U.S. immigration policy in the 1980s.* Philadelphia: Institute for the Study of Human Issues. A thorough, readable, multidisciplinary introduction to the complex issues and debates surrounding immigration to the United States.

Weeks, J. P. 1986. *Population: An introduction to concepts and issues.* Belmont, CA: Wadsworth. A clear introduction to the science of demography.

Weinstein, J. A. 1976. *Demographic transition and social change.* Morristown, NJ: General Learning Press (paperback). A brief and clear description of demographic transition theory with a critical look at its usefulness when applied to nonindustrial and industrializing societies.

Whitaker, J. S. 1989. *How can Africa survive?* New York: Harper & Row. A disturbing analysis of the ecological crisis confronting the continent of Africa.

PART TWO

SOCIOLOGICAL WORK:
THEORY AND RESEARCH

In Part One, you encountered the basic concepts that define what sociologists pay attention to. Part Two focuses on sociological thinking and the questions it poses about social systems, and on the variety of research methods that sociologists draw upon to answer these questions.

In Chapter 5 you will encounter several major views of how the social world works. As you read about them, try to avoid choosing a favorite among them and focus instead on how they can work together to provide a rich perspective on social life. In Chapter 6 you will learn about the methods—scientific and otherwise—that sociologists use to test ideas. A careful study of them might prompt you to examine more closely the kinds of evidence and reasoning that you use to test and support your own theories about the world.

5

THINKING SOCIOLOGICALLY: THEORY AND THEORETICAL PERSPECTIVES

 As you probably discovered in Part One, exploring a new discipline involves learning a great deal of new vocabulary. This is because each discipline stakes out and labels a particular intellectual territory that defines its basic subject matter. In an introductory biology course, for example, one of the first things you learn is how biologists distinguish between what is "living" and "not living," since biology, as a discipline, focuses on those things that have the quality of being alive.

In Part One we defined sociology by its attention to social life and behavior, especially in relation to social systems and their cultural, structural, population, and ecological characteristics. It is impossible to think sociologically without including one or more of these concepts. By now, for example, you may be more aware that your family can be thought of as a social system with its own characteristics—values and norms, role and power structures, size, or how it uses physical space. Like the concept of living things to a biologist, concepts such as "value" and "role" are important because they make us more aware of sociological aspects of reality, focusing our attention in a new way and providing the foundation for a new way of thinking.

This is only the beginning, however, for a simple awareness of various aspects of social life is not enough. The whole point of *observing* the world in a new way is to *think* about it in a new way to understand more about how social life works (see Collins 1989). Once we learn how to observe families and describe their characteristics, for example, we can ask basic questions about them such as the questions outlined at the end of Chapter 1. How are families organized? What are the kinds of consequences they produce? How do they change? What is the relationship between families as social systems and the people who participate in them?

Whatever questions we ask about social life, the answers must include explanations. For this we must understand something about sociological theory and the perspectives that underlie them.

THEORY AND THE PROBLEM OF KNOWING

A **theory** is a set of interrelated ideas used to explain how things work. As we will see in Chapter 13, for example, theories of racism include ideas about how prejudice develops between people in different racial

This engraving illustrates a riot against Chinese immigrants, who were perceived by many low-status whites as unfair competitors for jobs. Racial stereotypes and scapegoating often serve as "justifications" for abuse of minorities.

or ethnic categories. First, when people compete for resources such as jobs or land, they tend to develop prejudiced ideas about one another. Secondly, when one group dominates and exploits another, it tends to develop prejudices about the subordinate group to justify what would otherwise be perceived as injustice. Many slaveholders in the South, for example, saw themselves as Christians and had to reconcile the oppression of blacks with their Christian beliefs and values. Today, whites still must reconcile values about fairness and justice with the privileges and advantages they have over blacks, Hispanics, and native Americans.

Third, the less experience we have with different kinds of people, the more likely we are to rely on stereotypes about them, including those that make up racial and ethnic prejudice (see Case, Greeley, and Fuchs 1989). Residential and school segregation, for example, contribute to racism by preventing direct exposure to racial and cultural diversity. Integration, on the other hand, tends to decrease prejudice by increasing people's knowledge based on actual experience of individuals rather than stereotypes about the social categories to which they belong. This helps explain stereotyping and prejudice within societies—as between whites and native Americans—and from one society to another. Most Japanese have no direct experience with blacks, for example, just as most people in the U.S. have no experience with Iraqis or Russians or, for that matter, Japanese. As a result, people rely on stereotypes about such outsider groups with whom they have little experience.

People often perceive theoretical thinking as a lofty activity engaged in only by philosophers or social and physical scientists. In fact, however, everyone who has ideas about how things work is thinking theoretically. If you ask people why minorities are so much worse off than other groups, for example, most people will offer some kind of explanation. There are, of course, important differences between the informal theorizing that most people engage in and formulating sociological theory. First, as we will see in the next chapter, sociologists try to construct theories that can be tested to see if they are supported by evidence—something most people do not bother with. Second, sociologists tend to pay more critical attention to whether a theory is constructed in a logical way. Third, we examine the assumptions and values that underlie our theories.

The early influence of science is reflected in this sixteenth-century painting, *The French Ambassadors*—a globe and scientific instruments serve as symbols of education and status.

Assumptions, Values, and Theoretical Thinking

Everyone makes assumptions about the world in order to think about it. In the simplest sense, we assume that what we see, hear, smell, taste, and feel is real and that we understand what people mean when they talk to us. We also may make assumptions about human nature and social life—that people are basically bad or good, that the distribution of wealth is fair or unfair, or that people are or are not basically responsible for what happens to them. These kinds of ideas are assumptions in that we rarely if ever test them to find out if they are true. They are important because they greatly influence what we pay attention to and how we interpret what we observe. If we assume that people are basically bad, for example, we tend to overlook or discount evidence of their goodness. Or if we assume that the state exists to maintain social harmony and serve the best interests of everyone, we might not ask how the power of the state can be used to further the interests of the wealthy at the expense of everyone else.

Values are important because they influence what we try to understand. If we choose to research the effects of pornography on the level of violence against women, for example, rather than research the causes of poverty or how leaders emerge in urban gangs or why divorce rates go up or down, we are making a value decision about what we think is interesting or important. Everyone does this in deciding how to use limited time and attention to understand ourselves and the world around us.

Since assumptions and values are ideas, and since ideas are part of culture, it follows that how we pay attention to the world and try to explain it are affected by culture (see One Step Further 5-1). But our thinking is also affected by the social conditions and historical framework in which we live. Eigh-

teenth-century scientists, for example, never pondered the dangers of nuclear power plants, not because of their values or assumptions but because nuclear power plants did not exist. Explaining rapid social change was not a theoretical problem for medieval scholars because the pace of change was not rapid at all. If today many sociologists are drawn to questions about racism, urban living, poverty, war and peace, and rapid technological change, it is in large part because these phenomena exist in a way that they did not in other societies at other times.

Theoretical thinking, then, is profoundly affected by the kinds of social systems in which people live, and sociological theory is no exception.

How Sociology Developed as a Way of Thinking

We can trace the roots of sociology to Europe at the turn of the nineteenth century when its development was spurred by three major social forces and conditions. The first was a general philosophy that emerged in Europe in the eighteenth century. It assumes that understanding based on reason and experience would make it possible to solve social problems and improve society, in the process promoting

The Industrial Revolution rapidly expanded pollution and slum living conditions, creating unprecedented social problems and challenging traditional values.

human rights and freedom from oppression. A major part of this view was a preference for science over religion as a way of explaining reality. Science offered new methods of observation and explanation and rested on the idea that the physical world could be controlled and improved. In applying the scientific approach to societies, the French philosopher Auguste Comte (1798–1857) argued that social life was governed by laws that could be discovered by a new science that he was the first to call sociology (Comte [1854] 1898).

A second factor contributing to the emergence of sociological thinking was the existence of widespread social upheaval throughout most of Europe. The French Revolution toppled the monarchy in 1789 and Napoléon Bonaparte plunged the Continent into war in an unsuccessful attempt to conquer Europe. At the same time, capitalism was growing rapidly as the Industrial Revolution brought unprecedented productivity and technological change, but also rapidly growing and congested cities, high unemployment, increased poverty, miserable living conditions for great masses of people, and political instability. In short, these rapid social changes

prompted some to search for new ways of understanding social life.

Comte responded to this by searching for clear scientific principles that might explain what was going on in terms of some logical course of development and change. Other early major sociologists such as Karl Marx, Émile Durkheim, and Max Weber relied less heavily on the belief in scientific laws of social life, but also wrestled with fundamental questions about a world that seemed to be moving in a dangerous direction. How were order, social cohesion, and morality possible in human societies? What were the causes of social oppression, injustice, and inequality, especially in the new capitalist system? How was the distribution of power changing and how would this affect both the way societies were organized and the degree of control people had over their lives?

A third factor in the emergence of sociology was utilitarianism, a popular way of thinking that early sociologists reacted against. Utilitarianism is based on the assumption that humans behave rationally and that social life results solely from the rational choices made by individuals. From this perspective, social systems result from the calculated decisions of individuals, and nothing of importance exists beyond the limits of the individual psyche. By rejecting this view as too narrow, sociology developed as a way of understanding social life as more than a collection of individual lives. Instead, individual lives are seen as taking place in relation to social systems. This view is based on the belief that societies are more than the sum of their parts; they are entities in themselves whose characteristics must be included in any full understanding of social life.

From its beginnings in the nineteenth century to today, sociological thinking has been influenced by the social conditions in which sociologists have lived and worked. To understand this is to understand how assumptions and values influence the choices sociologists have made about what kinds of questions to ask and how to go about answering them.

THEORETICAL PERSPECTIVES

Because assumptions and values have such a great influence on the theories people come up with, it is important not to let them stay in the background to be discovered by accident, if at all. Sociologists try to do just the opposite by creating explicit frameworks of assumptions called **theoretical perspectives**.

ONE STEP FURTHER 5-1

Assumptions, Values, and Research on Social Inequality

One of the most important ways assumptions and values affect how we think is by influencing the kinds of questions we ask. In trying to understand social inequality, for example, sociologists ask some kinds of questions more than others. As Table B-5-1 shows, between 1965 and 1975 most research articles in mainstream sociological journals focused on individual characteristics of the poor (59 percent) and poverty programs (28 percent), while a small portion focused on the economic and political causes of poverty (10 percent) or the extent of poverty (2 percent). Notice, also, that studies of individual characteristics and poverty programs received 94 percent (55 percent plus 39 percent) of all government funding on poverty research.

By asking how the characteristics of poor people cause and perpetuate poverty, we ignore the characteristics of social systems and how these promote poverty and wealth. This tendency reflects the cultural assumption that individuals and not social systems are the primary cause of social problems. In doing so, it helps to perpetuate the status quo by directing critical attention away from underlying social conditions.

TABLE B-5-1   Research Articles on Poverty, by Focus and by Extent of Government Funding

ARTICLE'S FOCUS*	PERCENT OF ALL POVERTY ARTICLES	PERCENT OF GOVERNMENT FUNDING
Amount of poverty	2	0
Individual characteristics of poor people	59	55
Political or economic causes of poverty	10	6
Poverty programs	28	39
Other	1	0
TOTAL	100%	100%

*Articles published between 1965 and 1975 in *American Sociological Review, American Journal of Sociology, Social Problems, Social Forces,* and *Sociological Quarterly.*

Source: Kerbo 1991, Table 10-3

These help to spell out what we are paying attention to, what kinds of things we intend to explain, and how we are going to go about it. By doing this, we clarify our thinking and sharpen our observational skills. But by stating from the outset what our point of view is, we can also minimize the bias created when people are unaware of the assumptions and values that underlie their thinking. Being human, of course, we can never be completely aware of such things; but we can get considerably closer than is usually the case in people's everyday experience.

To understand anything effectively, we have to have a theoretical perspective that defines our point of view. Unlike theories, theoretical perspectives do not explain; rather, they contain assumptions about what we are trying to explain. In Chapter 1, for example, we encountered the problem of trying to explain the suicide of four teenagers. Biologists, physicists, chemists, psychologists, and sociologists pose different kinds of questions about suicide because they approach problems from different points of view. This is also often true *within* disciplines: just as sociology and biology differ, sociology includes perspectives that draw attention to and emphasize different aspects of the same social phenomenon. All sociologists consider some aspects of social systems and people's relation to them in trying to understand suicide; but what aspects they try to explain and how they go about that will vary according to the theoretical perspective they use.

In the following sections we will look at the three most important theoretical perspectives in sociology—functional, conflict, and interactionist. Each reflects not only different assumptions about social life, but different choices about which aspects of it are most important to pay attention to and understand. As Markson (1990) puts it, each is like a flashlight in a darkened room, whose beam illuminates some aspects of social life while leaving others still unrevealed.

PUZZLE

IS WAR ALL HELL?

"War is hell," declared the U.S. Civil War Union general William Tecumseh Sherman. Everyone can think of lots of bad consequences of war, but we may be less aware of how war produces consequences that are valued in social systems. War often stimulates economic production, for example, and creates jobs in the process. In addition, it tends to increase feelings of pride, unity, and solidarity among citizens.

As we will see later in this chapter, understanding these kinds of unanticipated consequences of social life is an important focus of sociological thinking.

The Functional Perspective

The great French sociologist Émile Durkheim (1858–1917) objected to the utilitarian idea that a society can be understood simply by paying attention to individuals' characteristics, motives, and behavior. He was reacting in part to the growing influence of psychological thinking. In developing what became the **functional perspective**, Durkheim argued that social systems are entities in and of themselves that can be understood as more than the sum of the various parts that make them up, including the people who participate in them.

Like Comte, he borrowed from the rapidly emerging field of biology, in particular the concept of an organism whose various parts are related in ways that enable it to function. Like a biological organism, he argued, societies are wholes whose parts have little significance *except in relation to one another and the whole* (Durkheim [1893] 1933). As an organism, a human being is not simply a collection of parts—muscle tissue, organs, and bones—but of parts that are functionally *related* to one another in particular ways. It is this set of relationships and not merely the collection of parts that makes humans what they are. In addition, like organisms, social systems have certain requirements—they need to adapt to a changing environment, to have a certain level of stability and cohesion among their parts, to establish and achieve various goals, and so on (see Parsons 1951).

(Today, sociologists no longer use the organism model because in too many ways it does not fit reality. Unlike organisms, for example, societies often

include diverse interests and oppression and conflict among their various parts. This does not, however, detract from Durkheim's basic insight into social life, for unlike some of his contemporaries he used the organic analogy only in a limited sense.)

Sociologists who use the functional perspective emphasize the importance of (1) how social systems operate (or "function"), (2) how they change and remain stable, (3) how they produce consequences, and (4) how consequences support or interfere with system requirements or cultural values. A consequence is **functional** if it contributes to one or more requirements or values, and is **dysfunctional** if it interferes (Merton 1968). In school, for example, academic competition is functional if it promotes hard work and high achievement, both of which are valued. Competition, however, can also be dysfunctional when it encourages students to earn high grades by interfering with the work of other students, by cheating, or when it discourages students from learning how to cooperate and work together in teams.

In the U.S. legal system, people accused of crimes are protected by rights designed to make it difficult to convict and punish people unjustly, such as rights to legal counsel, trial by jury, and rules of evidence that prohibit practices such as torturing people in order to force confessions. These help to protect people from abuse and are functional for a system designed, in part, to promote the value of justice. However, they also make it easier for guilty people to go free, as when murderers are released because arresting officers fail to inform them of their legal rights or seize evidence without a proper search warrant. These norms, then, have both functional and dysfunctional consequences for the criminal justice system and the society of which it is a part.

When functional or dysfunctional consequences are intended, they are **manifest**; and when they are unintended, they are **latent** (Merton 1968). The norms that protect accused criminals have the manifest consequence of upholding civil rights; but they can also have the latent consequence of interfering with the effective prosecution of criminals. In constructing such protection, no one intended to make it easier for criminals to go free, and yet this is a real consequence produced by the criminal justice system.

Durkheim was particularly interested in latent consequences. People of his time (as well as today), for example, typically viewed crime as something abnormal caused primarily by personality defects. Durkheim ([1895] 1938), however, saw it as a normal

The expression of community support and cohesion that typically appears following the murder of police officers is a latent functional consequence of crime.

part of social life. When a society defines behavior such as child abuse as criminal, it helps define its structural boundaries by distinguishing between insiders who obey the law and outsiders who do not. As a result, those who obey the law will tend to feel closer to one another *simply because they abide by common laws* in contrast to those who do not. Since these kinds of feelings help to hold communities together, the act of defining certain behaviors as crimes has a latent functional consequence of increasing social cohesion. Crime can also be functional by bringing about needed social change. Rioting and civil disobedience in the U.S. during the 1960s, for example, heightened national awareness of racism and accelerated the civil rights movement (see Kerner Commission 1968; McAdam 1982).

Using the Functional Perspective Perhaps the most important contribution of the functional perspective is that it encourages us to ask questions about social systems as systems and to understand the relationship between their characteristics and the social consequences they produce (see Durkheim

[1895] 1938, [1924] 1974). If, for example, a society has the technology to produce an abundance of goods, and if its culture includes the idea that people can and should own and accumulate private property, this increases the likelihood that social inequality and oppression will emerge. In this sense, although it is individuals who are either poor or wealthy, it is societies that produce social conditions in which these extremes are possible and encouraged by being defined as legitimate if not desirable. Without norms and values that support the ideas of private property and inheritance, great wealth—and, therefore, great poverty—would be far less likely to occur.

The functional perspective also helps to explain why it is so difficult to alleviate social problems such as poverty in spite of the many negative effects they have on human life. As Gans (1971, 1987) argued, poverty persists in part because it contributes to the operation of many societies as social systems—in other words, because of its functional consequences. The existence of poverty is one way to ensure that the "dirty work" that no one wants to do will indeed get done, from the backbreaking labor of picking vegetables by hand to cleaning public toilets. It ensures this by providing a large number of people whose circumstances are so desperate that they cannot afford to turn down a job simply because the work is unappealing or degrading or poorly paid or dangerous. Without poverty, for example, it would be much more difficult to maintain an all-volunteer army, because recruits are drawn heavily from those with poor job prospects in the civilian labor market.

Poverty also creates thousands of jobs that regulate and serve the needs of the poor, from social workers and police to pawnbrokers and manufacturers of cheap goods that no one else will buy. It reinforces key cultural values about hard work and thrift by providing a category of people who can be held up as contemptible examples of laziness and irresponsibility—even though these are largely stereotypes that do not describe real differences between the poor and everyone else. Poverty even contributes to innovations in medicine: because poor people cannot afford private medical care, they often seek low-cost or free care in teaching and research hospitals associated with medical schools where they are more likely to be used as subjects in medical experiments that may lead to new treatments.

It is important to remember that the concepts of functional and dysfunctional are not simply formal ways of saying "good" and "bad" in a moral or ethical sense. How we judge the consequences produced by a social system is of course important; but it is a separate issue from determining whether something has functional or dysfunctional consequences for that system. Slavery, for example, was functional for the plantation system of the South prior to the Civil War, but this hardly means that slavery was either desirable or necessary. As well, war often has functional consequences in addition to all of its destruction and horror. World War II, for example, played an important part in the U.S. economic recovery from the Great Depression of the 1930s because it required a resurgence of industrial production and put Americans back to work. Wars also tend to greatly increase social cohesion because otherwise conflicting groups join together in a common cause. Noting these effects, however, does not imply that war is good and desirable.

Gans makes similar points about the functional consequences of poverty. That poverty is associated with a variety of functional consequences for social systems does not imply that poverty should or must exist. As he argues, there are alternative ways of achieving the same goals, such as by paying people enough so that they would be willing to perform disagreeable jobs. These alternatives are resisted because they would require other changes such as raising the cost of getting this work done. In other words, the fact that poverty is associated with functional as well as dysfunctional consequences makes it all the more difficult to eradicate.

The basic insight of the functional perspective is that a complete understanding of any aspect of social life must include its relation to social systems and their characteristics. In this sense, poverty as a social problem involves far more than the distribution of income and wealth among individuals or the many factors in people's individual lives that affect it, such as education, motivation, or luck. It is also a *social* problem produced by social systems.

The Conflict Perspective

Like the functional perspective, the **conflict perspective** focuses on how social systems operate, but it emphasizes how they promote division, inequality, and struggle between different categories of people. It is based on the insight that control over social systems is usually distributed unevenly and those who have greater control can use it to benefit themselves at the expense of others. As such, the conflict perspective is concerned primarily not with social systems as a whole, but with how the consequences of social life are distributed unevenly among the people who participate in them. As in most industrial societies, for example, a small percentage of people in the U.S. owns most of the wealth and has far more political authority and influence than the average person. Whites are generally more powerful and wealthy than nonwhites, and men are more powerful and wealthy than women. Those who own or control factories and other means of production are more wealthy and powerful than the vast majority of the population who work for wages.

The conflict perspective asks questions about how division, inequality, and struggle arise, from relationships between husbands and wives to those between rich and poor nations. What are the consequences of inequality for the quality of people's lives, for their material, emotional, and spiritual well-being and health, for their life satisfaction and happiness? How are the family, religion, schools, the mass media, and the state used to control subordinate groups and keep them in their place? How is it

The conflict perspective draws attention to the causes and consequences of divisions between and within societies, especially those that center on social inequality. The struggle between Arabs and Israelis in the Middle East is a complex conflict that involves ethnic, economic, political, and religious differences which, in 1987 and 1988, erupted in violence between Israeli authorities and Palestinians in the Israeli-occupied West Bank territory. In this picture, an Arab woman is trying to stop an Israeli soldier from searching her house in Gaza.

possible to lessen the degree of inequality and end social oppression?

Origins of the Conflict Perspective   The conflict perspective originated primarily in the work of Karl Marx (1818–1883) and Max Weber (1864–1920), who felt compelled to understand a world that was not only changing rapidly, but raising serious threats to social justice and the quality of life. After the defeat of Napoléon Bonaparte, for example, Marx and many other Germans anticipated a new era of freedom but soon found themselves in a police state that was worse than life under Napoléon. Political meetings were banned, universities were tightly controlled, and there was no representative government, trial by jury, or right of free speech. Widespread expectations of liberty were frustrated by the power of an elite to oppress and exploit the masses of people.

Unable to find a position in universities, Marx spent the early part of his working life as a journalist in Germany and France. His critical analyses of the plight of the lower classes made him unpopular with the authorities and he eventually moved to England. Here the Industrial Revolution was in full swing and the lot of workers was growing steadily worse as control over production became increasingly concentrated in the hands of a capitalist elite. Marx spent

the rest of his life studying economic history and theory, and writing about industrial capitalism and its effects on the human condition. In his work, he developed the view that the production of goods is the most important thing humans do, and the way a society organizes and controls productive work affects every aspect of social life.

In capitalist societies, the means of production—such as machines and factories—can be privately owned by people who hire others to produce goods in return for wages. Marx ([1867] 1975) argued that these simple aspects of the productive process—wage labor and private ownership of capital—affect virtually every area of social life. In particular, they create class divisions between people who own property and those who work for wages, because employers will try to increase their profits by paying workers as little as possible. This kind of system creates class conflict that, Marx believed, eventually would lead to revolutionary social change (see Marx and Engels [1846] 1976, [1848] 1932).

Marx also argued that such divisions are reflected in major social institutions whose survival depends on adapting themselves to the prevailing economic system. The state, for example, supports a society's basic economic values. It will defend private property rights in capitalist societies or, in the case of state socialism in China, defend the state's right to decide economic policy and enforce laws that subordinate the interests of individuals to the larger goals of the nation as a whole. Other institutions — schools, the media, religion, and so on—fall in line by avoiding criticism of the economic system and, if only by their silence, promote the idea that it is legitimate and not in need of fundamental change.

George Tooker's *Government Bureau* powerfully evokes a nightmarish vision of life in a society ruled by anonymous, faceless bureaucrats.

Marx approached these kinds of problems in a sociological way, for he looked not at the private motivations of individuals, but how social systems make people more likely to behave in some ways than others (see Marx [1859] 1970). Capitalists, for example, often make decisions—such as to close a factory or lay off workers—that have cruel consequences for workers and their families. Marx argued that the cause of such behavior is not that employers are cruel, but that they participate in a social system that makes it difficult for them to do otherwise and still maintain their elite position. In a capitalist system, firms must compete successfully to survive, and a major factor in this is the ability to maximize profit by minimizing costs, including the cost of labor. This means that in order to succeed, employers must to some degree exploit their workers—by paying them as little as possible, by laying them off in order to protect company profits, or by moving operations to other regions or countries where workers will work for less. The problem, argued Marx, is not employers but capitalism itself as an economic system.

Using the Conflict Perspective The conflict perspective is not limited to Marx's analysis of social inequality, although this has been the most influential and widely used example. Like Marx, Max Weber was also concerned with social change that accompanied industrial capitalism, but his approach was broader than Marx's. Weber believed that inequality and conflict have a much broader social basis than economic relationships and control over production, including people's ideas about prestige and the distribution of power and authority in organizations such as corporations and government. He saw bureaucracy as a pervasive form of social organization that is ideally suited to enforcing ever greater degrees of inequality and oppression. He believed it also threatens to make social life increasingly impersonal and subject to external control and manipulation (Weber [1922] 1958). Social life is becoming rationalized in that decisions are made on the basis of what will accomplish certain goals in the most efficient way, with less attention to their human costs.

Since the early work of Marx and Weber, the conflict perspective has developed a general concern with the ways in which division, inequality, and struggle develop in all kinds of social systems (see Collins 1975; Dahrendorf 1959; Mills 1956). Wallerstein's world systems theory, for example, uses a conflict approach to explain relations among rich and poor nations and the inability of Third World countries to improve their standards of living (Wallerstein 1976a, 1980, 1989). He focuses on the fact that the world economic system is dominated by wealthy industrial nations such as the U.S., Japan, and Germany who control most wealth, productive technology, and military power. He argues that wealthy nations can exploit other nations by preventing them from developing an independent industrial base and making them politically and economically dependent. World systems theory raises many questions about how this happens, about why poor nations grow poorer while wealthy nations grow wealthier, about who benefits most from foreign investment in poor nations, and about whose interests are served by political oppression in Third World countries.

Together, the conflict and functional perspectives focus on how social systems operate and the kinds of consequences they produce. Both, however, tend not to deal with what engages people most directly—how we participate in social life and how this affects our experience and behavior. For this we must turn to the interactionist perspective.

The Interactionist Perspective

The **interactionist** perspective focuses on people's actual experience and behavior in everyday life and the relation of these to how they perceive, interpret, and feel about themselves and others (see Adler, Adler, and Fontana 1987). In contrast to the conflict and functional perspectives, the interactionist focus is quite small-scale because it is less concerned with the relatively large-scale characteristics and consequences of social systems than with individual people acting in relation to one another. Although the scale of analysis is small, however, the importance of the questions it raises is not.

The interactionist perspective began with the work of the German sociologist Georg Simmel (1858–1918) and most importantly the American social philosopher, George Herbert Mead (1863–1931). Mead focused on the relationship between individuals and societies and the importance of symbols in it (for this reason, many interactionists who followed in Mead's tradition refer to their approach with the more specific term, **symbolic interactionism**) (see Blumer 1969; Mead 1934). The reality of something—including our perception of and ideas about ourselves—is primarily a matter of how we *think* about it, and thinking is largely done with language. As a cultural medium through which we think, language is what we use to create much of what we experience as reality itself. As we will see in

A symbolic interactionist sitting in on the Iran-*contra* hearings in 1987 would have paid careful attention to the ways in which witnesses, such as Lt. Colonel Oliver North, used language, dress, and gestures to create and sustain a favorable impression. Notice his facial expressions, how he uses his hands, and his wearing of his marine uniform. What impression do these pictures convey?

Chapter 7, Mead argued that we use language to interact with and become aware of other people when we establish and maintain relationships with them. In doing this, we also develop a sense of self.

From an interactionist perspective, we cannot understand social life without paying attention to how people attach meaning to their experience and behavior. To do this, we rely on symbols, our primary source of meaning. To explain why people behave as they do, we must have some idea of what they believe and value, and what they think others expect of them—and these will vary from one social situation to another. When we enter a new situation we must identify the **definition of the situation**, which is to say, we have to figure out which statuses and roles apply (McHugh 1968). We do this by interpreting people's appearance, behavior, and, most of all, what they say. When we visit a doctor for the first time, for example, we define the situation by observing and interpreting all kinds of clues, from the physical appearance of the waiting room to the clothing worn by the doctor and nurse, to the language they use when asking us questions about our health. If the doctor begins by asking how wealthy you are or whether you have ever belonged to the Communist party or whether you would mind lending your car for the weekend, you would most likely question just what kind of doctor this was.

In some ways, social life is like a game in which we are players who follow rules in pursuit of various goals (Mead 1934). Unlike most games, however, the rules and understandings of social life are open to negotiation and interpretation, and symbols play an important part in that process. A date, for example, is a situation that tends to follow patterns in a particular culture, but people can appear and behave in many ways, each of which can have more than one interpretation. When a man opens a door for a woman or insists on driving the car or paying the check, his behavior can be interpreted as politeness and a show of respect or as an assertion of dominance based on the belief that men are strong and women are weak and need protection. When someone acts friendly on a date, this may or may not mean he or she is interested in having sex. Gutek (1985) shows that, among heterosexuals, how such behavior is interpreted depends on whether the person acting friendly is a man or a woman. Men more than women tend to interpret friendly gestures as having sexual significance and intentions (see also Abbey

1987). Similarly, when women say "no" to sex, it is more likely to be interpreted by men as "maybe" or even "yes" than when men say "no" to women. The symbolic interaction perspective identifies such details of social life that we encounter as we move through the world in a continuing process of using, interpreting, and responding to symbols.

Life as Theater   To sociologist Erving Goffman, there is something very theatrical about all of this (which is why his approach to symbolic interaction is often referred to as the **dramaturgical perspective**. See Goffman 1959, 1967, 1981). As William Shakespeare wrote in *As You Like It,*

> All the world's a stage,
> And all the men and women merely players;
> They have their exits and their entrances,
> And one man in his time plays many parts . . .
> (2.7.139–42)

As actors and actresses, we present images of ourselves to audiences and construct images of others by watching their performances. To Goffman, we are always acting, trying to create favorable impressions from one stage and audience to the next as we perform various roles. We may be confident and aggressive while playing a sport, but meek when a police officer hands us a traffic ticket; wild and crazy at a party, but serious and calm at a funeral. None of this is faking; there is no "real self" deceiving the world. From Goffman's point of view, this is just the way it is: *We are who we present ourselves to be.* The masks do not hide us; they are all parts of us and reveal different aspects of who we are to different people in different situations. The members of each audience, in turn, are also actors who use *us* as an audience, and so each performance is tied to and dependent on the performances of others, and in this way our otherwise separate lives overlap with and touch one another.

That all of this takes place within social systems raises a key question in the interactionist perspective: how do we view the relationship between social systems and individuals (see Lyman and Vidich 1988; Meltzer and Petras 1970)?

Individuals and Social Systems   Some interactionists, such as Manford Kuhn, argue that social systems and social life consist primarily of networks of statuses and roles (see Biddle 1979; Kuhn 1964).

The widespread use of ritual masks in most cultures dramatizes how we use our faces to present ourselves in different ways to the world sometimes, but usually not with conscious intent, as in this turtle shell mask from New Guinea.

These are external to individuals and produce patterns of thought, feeling, experience, and behavior. A basketball team, for example, can be thought of as a network of players, coaches, and managers, and the roles they are expected to perform. When people join a team, they perceive the team as something external to them, larger than themselves and to which they belong. They are affected by the characteristics of that system—such as the distribution of power that makes coaches more powerful than players—and this produces patterns of behavior associated with the system known as a basketball team.

Interactionists such as Simmel ([1902] 1950) and Herbert Blumer (1969) offer a very different view. They argue that social systems are just abstractions that do not exist as something external to the people who participate in them. "Society," wrote Simmel, "is merely the name for a number of individuals, connected by interaction" ([1902] 1950, p. 10).

From this perspective, social systems exist in a concrete way only when people actually *do* something. We can think of a college classroom as a social system, for example, but it is just an idea in our minds until the students and professor go into a classroom and begin to talk and interact. At that moment they literally recreate the system known as a college classroom. As they proceed, that social system continues to exist through their behavior until they leave and go on to recreate *other* social systems—a dining hall, family gathering, workplace, library reserve room, and so on.

Blumer argues that a great deal of what people do in social life cannot be predicted merely by knowing which roles are involved. Much of our behavior is not defined as a clear role expectation, and even when we do conform to the general expectations associated with a particular role, we often do a great deal of improvising as we go along. There are patterns of behavior that we can expect to see in any college classroom, for example, but there is a lot of variation around it. The language people actually use during any given class, their gestures, how they respond to one another, whether they laugh at particular moments or express anger—all of these details are improvised and made up by the participants. By acknowledging this, Blumer is saying that we must not underestimate the importance of individual decisions and creativity in social interaction, that it is not social systems that make individuals, but the other way around.

As with many arguments, the most useful position combines the best elements of the two extremes. Social systems certainly would not exist without people to participate in them. It is also true, however, that we do tend to experience social systems as separate from us, with role expectations that have an authority that can override our individual wants, needs, and preferences. The actual words, tone of voice, facial expressions, and other gestures that students might use to answer a professor's question, for example, can take on any number of forms; but in a college classroom, behavior is unlikely to include profanity, physical assault, shouting, undressing, sex, or topics defined as irrelevant. We do a great deal of improvising in social life, but we generally do not feel free to do whatever we want. That feeling of being limited by role expectations is rooted in our perception of social systems as something real and external to us as individuals.

Ethnomethodology   Since people will not feel limited by a social system unless they are aware on some level that it exists, there must be ways of reminding them of the situation they are in and the role expectations that go with it. What distinguishes a classroom from a basketball game is the particular patterns of expectation about how people are supposed to appear and behave. In order for that system to operate, however, people have to share among themselves the idea that it—the classroom—exists at that moment. If two students begin tossing a basketball back and forth in class and taking shots at an imaginary basket on the wall, they may be reminded of what this situation is and is not. This can be accomplished in many ways, from people clearing their throats or staring in a pointed manner to someone yelling, "Hey, cut it out!" Whatever the actual method, what is being accomplished is the reconstruction of a shared sense of what is going on.

Based on the work of the sociologist Harold Garfinkel, this approach to interaction is called **ethnomethodology**, which refers, literally, to the study of the methods that people ("ethno") use in everyday life (see Garfinkel 1967; Heritage 1984; Livingston 1987). We use various methods to help us sustain a shared sense that the social relationships in which we participate are real. Conversations, for example, depend on various kinds of gestures to keep going. While one person is talking the other typically nods and maintains eye contact and says things like "uh huh" every once in awhile as a way of sustaining the shared belief that a conversation is in fact taking place. Without the use of such methods, a conversation can rapidly fall apart ("Are you listening to me?").

Ritual has similar uses. With religious ritual people can come together and remind one another that they exist as a community of believers. When spouses kiss each other good-night before going to sleep or good-bye when leaving for work in the morning, they are using ritual in subtle ways to reinforce a shared sense that their connection as spouses is real and enduring. Families have many such rituals, from how they celebrate holidays to eating meals together, that reinforce the social reality that they are, in fact, a family.

Such methods come into play even in situations that we might not at first think of as part of social systems. When people enter an elevator and one person faces the rear rather than the front, people are likely to react with a funny look, for example, or a smirk or a comment. All of these indicate that there is a social reality here with role expectations that are not being adhered to. Most people do not think of being in an elevator as a social situation with a specific set of expectations; elevators are, instead, what people use to ride from one situation to another. It is most likely only when someone violates the expectations that we become aware of the social reality of elevator rides. It is people's reactions that are the "methods" that ethnomethodologists study, for it is these that help to sustain an ongoing sense of social reality.

Putting It All Together

The functional, conflict, and interactionist perspectives touch on the most important aspects of sociological thinking, from the consequences of social systems to the intricacies of social behavior. Although many sociologists prefer one perspective over the others, it is both possible and desirable to draw upon all three in a way that makes us more aware of the richness and complexity of social life.

Consider, for example, the social system known as a school. As recently as a century ago, schooling was not part of most people's lives, and yet now it is enormously important in industrial societies and, to a lesser but significant degree, in nonindustrial societies. How do we describe and explain what goes on in this kind of system? What kinds of questions do the different theoretical perspectives raise?

The functional perspective emphasizes the operation of schools as social systems that produce various kinds of consequences. Schools play an important part in the socialization process, from instilling a sense of patriotism to teaching basic skills to preparing advanced students for professional occupations. They provide a place for children to be while parents are at work, and keep millions of young people out of the labor market and, therefore, out of competition for jobs with adults. How well schools perform these functions has major effects on society, from the degree to which citizens are aware of world geography and the history of their own country or the cultures of other societies to how well workers are prepared for an increasingly demanding and technologically sophisticated occupational market. The functional perspective raises questions about how schools produce consequences not only for schools but for other social systems to which they are connected, such as the family, economy, and political institutions.

The conflict perspective shifts the emphasis to issues about social inequality, division, and struggle. Since schools play a major role in socialization, including giving young people a sense of what they are most suited for in life, we must raise issues about the effect of schools on social inequality. In addition to producing educated adults able to perform adult roles, for example, schools also prepare people to accept and support basic aspects of their society, including an unequal distribution of wealth, power, and prestige.

Bowles and Gintis (1976) argue, for example, that the organization of U.S. high schools reflects the industrial capitalist economic system and helps reproduce the class system by preparing students from different social classes to know and accept their "place." Schools are arranged as rigid hierarchies that encourage students to accept the idea of others having authority over them. Like most workers, students have little control over their work, but rather are told by someone in authority what to do as well as how and when to do it. Schools foster the belief that rewards are distributed according to merit and hard work, which legitimates stratification in society at large by encouraging students to blame themselves if they do not succeed as adults. In this way, argue Bowles and Gintis, schools play an important part in maintaining a system of social classes.

In contrast to the functional and conflict perspectives, the interactionist perspective focuses on the relationship between individuals and social systems and how people appear and behave in relation to one another. This raises related but very different types of sociological questions about schools. How do the effects of race, class, and gender inequality appear in classrooms through the language, appearance, and behavior of students, teachers, and administrators? How are teachers' expectations of students affected by differences of race, class, and gender? Observations of classroom interaction find, for example, patterns that contribute to male dominance (see Sadker and Sadker 1985). Boys tend to receive more attention than girls, are allowed to dominate discussions, and are more likely to assert themselves by calling out answers while girls wait to be called upon by teachers. When girls speak in class, teachers are less likely to show support for their efforts by looking at them, nodding, or verbally reinforcing what they are saying ("Yes, that's interesting," or even just an "uh huh"). Instead, they are more likely to not respond at all or to cut the student's response short and move

on to another. These kinds of interactions are crucial because it is through them that we develop our sense of what we can do and who we are.

Social interaction in schools also reinforces class differences. Bowles and Gintis (1976) argue, for example, that teachers reward working- and lower-class students for behaviors that will make them "good workers" as adults, such as punctuality, neatness, and obedience to authority. At the same time, middle- and upper-class students are rewarded for being independent, creative, and learning to exercise authority over others. In this way, patterns of interaction in schools help to reproduce the class system by shaping the personalities and expectations of students from different class backgrounds.

Although these three theoretical perspectives require attention to different aspects of social life, they are all closely related to one another. Conversations between teachers and students are more than simple, isolated instances of symbolic interaction, for they are also major ways in which social inequality is reinforced in schools and affect how they operate as social systems. In this sense, there is no question asked from one theoretical perspective that does not have the potential to involve the other two. The differences among the perspectives are those of emphasis, and the best sociological thinking is informed by an appreciation of all three. In fact, once you understand them, you may find the distinctions among

Table 5-1   Major Theoretical Perspectives: A Summary

Functional Perspective

1. Emphasis on social systems, how they operate as a whole, and balance tendencies towards change and stability (Durkheim).
2. Evaluation of various consequences produced by social systems as functional or dysfunctional in relation to system adaptation, maintenance, and values.

Conflict Perspective

1. Emphasis on inequality, division, and struggle as products of social systems (Marx, Weber).

Interactionist Perspective

1. Emphasis on the use of symbols and gestures to represent, interpret, construct social reality, including the ideas of self and other (Mead, Goffman, Garfinkel).
2. Relationship between individuals and social systems (Kuhn, Blumer).

them starting to fade in your mind as you blend basic elements of functional, conflict, and interactionist thinking.

We can see how this happens by returning to the problem of understanding racism. In the U.S., racism is a set of cultural ideas that benefit whites by justifying the oppression and exploitation of blacks. Negative stereotypes about blacks, beliefs that white advantages result from superior personal characteristics, such as intelligence, white hostility to the idea of integrated schools and neighborhoods—all of these are part of a pervasive ideology that helps keep the majority of blacks in a disadvantaged position.

Because racism plays an important part in how people see themselves and others, it also affects how they treat one another. A great deal of racism, for example, is acted out through language and gestures—from verbal insults to body postures, looks, and gestures that show deference or that assert contempt or superiority. These are used to control how people present themselves to others. A social system that includes racial oppression, in short, is made visible and real through the racist behavior of people in everyday life.

Racism also has consequences for social systems as a whole. In slave societies such as the South prior to the Civil War, it was a key part of a labor-intensive agrarian economic system. From this perspective, giving up racism would have made it extremely difficult to sustain crucial aspects of Southern society. The challenge to slavery posed by the Civil War threatened not only the self-image and self-interest of slaveholders but what many Southerners perceived as their entire way of life (see McPherson 1988). Today racism continues to have economic consequences by, for example, providing a pool of poor, unemployed workers who are available to perform disagreeable jobs for low wages (see Reich 1981, 1986).

If you study the last few paragraphs carefully, you can identify how the functional, conflict, and interactionist perspectives contribute to thinking about racism as a social phenomenon. In essence, the three major perspectives are simply ways of shedding light on the same thing from different angles. It is in developing this ability to draw upon different perspectives that the full potential richness of sociological thinking lies.

SUMMARY

1. Although basic sociological concepts draw our attention to social life, theory is necessary to interpret and explain what we observe.

2. The most basic theoretical problems focus on understanding how social systems are organized, how they produce and distribute consequences, how they change, and how they are related to the lives of individuals.

3. Theories are specific explanations of how things work. Theoretical perspectives are general points of view whose assumptions define how to observe something, ask questions, and pursue answers.

4. Sociology emerged as a discipline in the nineteenth century. Contributing factors were the rise of modern science, uncertain and chaotic social conditions in Europe, and utilitarian thinking, to which sociology was in part a critical response.

5. The functional perspective is concerned primarily with how social systems operate as a whole and how their various characteristics produce consequences that interfere with or contribute to their ongoing existence as systems and the values on which they are based. These consequences may be functional or dysfunctional, manifest or latent.

6. The conflict perspective focuses on division, struggle, and inequality in social systems, how they develop and change, and how they affect social life, particularly by benefiting some at the expense of others.

7. The interactionist perspective focuses on the use of symbols, gestures, and behavior among people who participate in social systems. It includes questions about the use of language and interaction to create and sustain a sense of reality, including who we are in relation to others; the playing of roles; and the relationship between social systems as something external to individuals and the behavior of individuals as what makes social systems real.

8. Different theoretical perspectives generate different kinds of questions, and yet the fact that they are all fundamentally sociological means that the best sociological thinking depends on all three.

KEY TERMS

conflict perspective   100
definition of the situation   104
dramaturgical perspective   104
dysfunctional consequence   98
ethnomethodology   106

functional consequence   98
functional perspective   98
interactionist perspective   103
latent consequence   98

manifest consequence   98
symbolic interactionism   103
theoretical perspective   96
theory   94

LOOKING ELSEWHERE

Although you will encounter the basic sociological questions and the three major theoretical perspectives throughout *Human Arrangements*, many of the issues used to illustrate them are discussed in greater detail elsewhere. You might want to use the guide below to pursue some of these in greater depth. See, for example,

■ how different disciplines might approach the problem of explaining suicide (Chapter 1, pp. 11–15)

■ bureaucracy (Chapter 9, pp. 193–96)

■ the family as a social system (Chapter 16)

■ social inequality (Chapters 12–15)

■ how schools, religion, and the state are used to perpetuate inequality (Chapter 17, pp. 433–36; Chapter 20, pp. 518–21; Chapter 21, pp. 544–45)

■ the world economic system and international inequality (Chapter 12, pp. 287–91; Chapter 19, pp. 492–95)

■ social movements and theories of social change (Chapter 23)

■ individuals and groups (Chapter 9, pp. 204–206)

■ social interaction (Chapter 8)

■ how we use language to create our idea of ourselves (Chapter 7, pp. 140–41)

■ the emergence of science (Chapter 18, pp. 445–47)

■ how the legal system works (Chapter 11, pp. 247–50)

■ capitalism (Chapter 12; Chapter 19, pp. 470–90, 495–97)

■ schools as social institutions (Chapter 17)

■ interaction in college classrooms (Chapter 17, pp. 425–27)

RECOMMENDED READINGS

Coser, L. A. 1977. *Masters of sociological thought: Ideas in historical and social context* (2nd ed.). New York: Harcourt Brace Jovanovich. A particularly clear and interesting look at the major thinkers who laid the theoretical groundwork for sociology. Especially well done is the placement of each thinker in the historical circumstances that gave rise to various approaches to understanding social life.

Hewitt, J. 1988. *Self and society: A symbolic interactionist social psychology* (4th ed.). Needham Heights, MA: Allyn and Bacon. A rich source of examples of how interactionists make sense of the complexities of everyday life.

Livingston, E. 1987. *Making sense of ethnomethodology.* London: Routledge & Kegan Paul. An authoritative text that helps make sense of what can be a difficult area of sociological thinking.

Merton, R. K. 1968. *Social theory and social structure* (enlarged ed.). New York: Free Press. Perhaps the classic statement of the fundamentals of functional analysis.

Turner, J. H. 1991. *The structure of sociological theory* (5th ed.). Chicago: Dorsey Press. A comprehensive critical overview of a wide variety of theoretical approaches in sociology.

6
RESEARCH METHODS

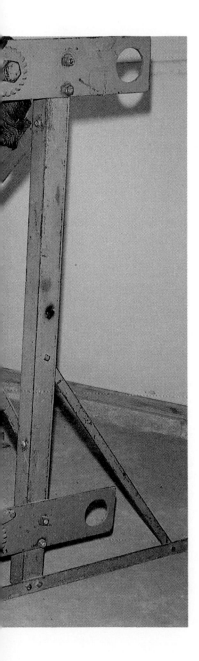

 Chapters 1 through 5 introduced major concepts and theoretical perspectives that lie at the heart of most sociological questions. This chapter takes a detailed look at how sociologists use research methods to answer such questions. We begin by looking at the scientific method and its importance in sociology; then we follow the research process from deciding what you want to know to designing research, interpreting results, and wrestling with some of the difficulties of studying human beings and their social world.

ASKING SOCIOLOGICAL QUESTIONS

Among full-time, year-round workers, why do men earn almost two-thirds more money than women? In the simplest sense, we can answer this or any question by sitting back and thinking about it; but, how can we know whether or not such personal explanations are correct? If you ask enough people, you will get a variety of answers to the above question, ranging from the effects of genes and hormones to cultural prejudice. How do we decide where the truth lies?

As we will see in this chapter, one response to this problem is the **scientific method** which tries to establish objective standards for gathering and interpreting evidence. Unlike personal explanations, scientific results are more likely to rest on *observable, unambiguous facts that lead everyone to the same conclusion.* Scientists try to avoid relying on subjective perceptions and judgments by confining themselves to questions about observable facts. Did God intend

111

Athough science can answer many questions, there are many it cannot. The story of Adam and Eve—shown in Michelangelo's portrayal on the ceiling of the Sistine Chapel in Rome—is regarded by tens of millions of Christians as a sacred and true account of the origins of the human race, an account that they would never judge on the basis of scientific standards of evidence and truth.

that men should be more powerful than women? Science can do nothing with this kind of question, because there are no observable facts that provide an answer. Other questions, however, can be answered scientifically because relevant facts can be observed: Are women discriminated against in the workplace? Are women as capable as men? Do men have advantages in the labor market? How would economic equality between men and women affect other aspects of social life?

Durkheim's study of suicide ([1897] 1951) was one of the first sociological attempts to use the scientific method. If suicide is a purely individual act unaffected by social systems, then the *rate* of suicide (the relative number of people who kill themselves each year) should be the same for every group regardless of culture and social structure. Yet when Durkheim examined death records, he found that Protestants were more likely to kill themselves than were Catholics and that Jews had the lowest suicide rate of all. Single people were more likely to commit suicide than married people and soldiers had higher rates than civilians. Durkheim reasoned that such differences reflect forces beyond individual personalities and troubles, forces that affect choices according to positions in social systems.

Durkheim considered purely cultural factors—shared ideas about suicide—that might explain differences in suicide rates, but logic and evidence led him to discard that explanation. There is no reason to believe that married people disapprove of suicide more than single people do, and while Catholicism views suicide more seriously than does Judaism (regarding it as a mortal sin), Catholics have higher rates of suicide than Jews.

Durkheim turned to social structure for an explanation. In particular, he was interested in the degree of *social cohesion* found among people in different social categories. Protestants stress independence and individualism, while Catholics and Jews stress active involvement with other members of their religious communities. In a similar way, married people tend to have stronger ties than single people. This is reflected in Durkheim's theory of suicide: when social bonds are weak, people are more likely to kill themselves.

Durkheim also noticed, however, that suicide rates tend to be relatively high in groups with very high levels of cohesion. Professional soldiers, for example, are more likely than draftees to take fatal risks in battle. In such cases, people are more likely to commit suicide because they value the group more than their individual lives. Consequently, Durkheim's theory of suicide predicts that suicide rates will be relatively high when social cohesion is either very low or very high.

This first attempt to apply scientific methods to sociological questions was understandably flawed. Durkheim used official records that were often distorted to conceal suicides, and while his theory fit the facts, other explanations might fit them as well. Nevertheless, his attempt to find connections between people's behavior and the observable characteristics of social systems established a model of sociological research that continues to be one of Durkheim's most important contributions. (For a more recent test of Durkheim's ideas about suicide, see Breault 1986; Pescosolido and Georgianna 1989).

Sociological research centers on three basic tasks. First, in order to identify the effects of social structure, culture, population, and ecology, we must be able to *describe* them. What beliefs prevail in a society? How are families, schools, governments, and economies structured? How are rewards such as power, wealth, and prestige distributed?

Second, how do we *explain* what we describe—such as variations in people's behavior? How do we explain the recent rise in teenage suicides? How is social inequality maintained, and what are the consequences for those involved? How do we explain why societies differ and why they change?

Third, how can we make *predictions* about the future? Will our cultural emphasis on individuality and mobility weaken our bonds with our families and communities, and will this cause a rise in suicide rates? How many children will be born in the next five years? Will there be enough jobs for them when they become adults?

The remaining chapters in this book are filled with the results of sociological research. To prepare you for them, this chapter focuses on the research process that produces such results. Any research project involves four basic phases:

1. Deciding what we want to know.
2. Deciding how we are going to find out.
3. Gathering information.
4. Interpreting our results.

Understanding how research is done will enable you not only to ask critical questions about scientific results, it will also help you do your own research when you write term papers (see Appendix A). In addition, many of the research skills described below are used in a variety of occupations.

WHAT DO WE WANT TO KNOW?

If you have ever gotten bogged down trying to write a term paper, it was probably because you did not have a clear idea of just what it was you wanted to know. For undergraduates and research scientists alike, deciding what we want to know is the first and often the most difficult part of any research project. Are we interested in learning about such behavior as lying or telling the truth, stealing, marrying and divorcing, having children or remaining childless, voting or not voting, cheating on college exams or telling on someone who does? Do we want to know about people's beliefs, values, and attitudes and how these ideas are reflected in their behavior? Or are we interested in a society's distribution of wealth, power, and prestige? In short, what aspects of social life do we want to understand?

Our interest in trying to understand the income gap between men and women, for instance, might well lead us to study women's liberation. Before we can begin, we have to define "women's liberation" and what, in particular, we want to know about it. "Women's liberation" can have many meanings. It can mean "equalizing rewards such as wealth, power, and prestige," "changing the structure of family life so that fathers are equally responsible for child care," or "changing cultural ideas that define women as inferior." It can also refer to the women's movement— how it began and how different segments of it try to achieve different goals.

Suppose we focus on "removing inequalities." Because that problem has many different aspects, we have to narrow it down and ask questions that can be answered by observing measurable phenomena. To show how the research process works, let us ask the following question: Do most people in the U.S. favor equality for women? Favoring or opposing women's equality are values, and before we can do a study, we have to decide how we are going to *measure* them.

Variables

Because favoring women's equality is a characteristic that varies from one person to another; it is called a **variable**. Variables can be events, behaviors, or any measurable characteristic of individuals or social systems. Group size, unemployment rates, believing in God, personal income, criminal behavior, and educational attainment are all variables.

Just as we must use a thermometer to measure heat, we need some way to observe and sort people according to their level of support for equality. One simple possibility is to ask people if they favor the Equal Rights Amendment, which states: "Equality of rights under the law shall not be denied or abridged by the United States or by any State on account of sex." We could then interpret a "yes" answer as favoring equality and a "no" as opposition. This kind of procedure is a **measurement instrument**, because it clearly classifies people according to some characteristic.

Measurement, Meaning, and Validity

A measurement instrument has **validity** if it measures only what we intend it to measure. In 1982 a national sample was asked, "Do you strongly favor, somewhat favor, somewhat oppose, or strongly oppose the Equal Rights Amendment?" The result: 39 percent expressed opposition (Davis and Smith 1984). Does this mean that 39 percent of U.S. adults oppose women's equality? Is opposition to the ERA a valid measure of opposition to equality?

Opposition to the ERA reflects a general value about women's rights, while equality for women involves a variety of specific goals that have direct and immediate implications for people's lives. It is possible for people to oppose the ERA generally and actually support equality for women in terms of specific issues. (Before reading on, you might want to take a look at the box, "How to Read a Table".)

For example, Table 6-1 summarizes responses to a series of specific questions about men and women, *among respondents who expressed opposition to the ERA in 1982.* Among ERA opponents, 64 percent disagree that women should stay home and leave running the country to men; 67 percent disagree that married women whose husbands can support them should not have jobs themselves; and almost three-quarters say they would vote for a qualified female presidential candidate. A majority disagree with the idea that men are better suited emotionally for politics than women, and almost 40 percent believe married women should have the right to legal abortions if they are too poor to afford additional children.

While opposition to the ERA may be a valid measure of opposition to the ERA, this evidence suggests that it is an invalid measure of opposition to specific aspects of social life that must be changed in order to bring about equality. In a similar way, people may oppose specific aspects of women's liberation and yet support the ERA as a general idea. Consequently, "opposition to equality" is too complex to be measured with one instrument. When we hear a statement such as "A majority of adults favor equality for women," we have to ask a critical question: What does "favoring women's equality" *mean*? In other words, did the researcher use a valid instrument to measure this concept?

Reliability   Measurement instruments must not only be valid; they must have **reliabilty**: they must produce the same results no matter who uses them. In addition, if the characteristic they measure remains constant, then the results must remain constant as well.

One way to measure the incidence of crime, for example, is to count the number of crimes reported to police each year. The problem with this is that most crimes are never reported to police. The incidence of crime might go down from one year to the next, but the *measure* of crime might show an increase if people become more willing to report crimes to police.

Official crime statistics are *unreliable* because they may indicate change even when what they try to measure does not. Their lack of reliability also makes them invalid because they reflect two things at once: the incidence of crime *and* the willingness of people to report it. Whether the official rates go up, down, or remain the same, we cannot be sure about what is happening.

Measurement Problems   Measurement poses difficult problems for social scientists (Schuman and Presser 1981). Much of what we try to measure is difficult to observe directly. We cannot measure attitudes in the same way that we can measure the weight of an object. We must rely on what people tell us or what they reveal through their actions, and all of this requires interpretation. This problem occurs in all sciences. Astronomers rely on what little they can observe in order to construct theories about what they cannot observe—such as the origin of the

HOW TO READ A TABLE

Most research results begin as a set of observations of the characteristics of anything from people to entire societies. Researchers face the problem of organizing and summarizing masses of information in order to answer questions. As a reader, your problem is to understand what researchers present to you. We start with information, such as people's answers to the question, "Are you in favor of the Equal Rights Amendment?" A total of 453 adults answered "no" in a 1982 national study.

Any arrangement of numbers in columns and rows is called a *table*, and there are several things we can learn from one such as Table 6-1. It shows how opponents of the ERA answered some other questions about men and women. Here is how to go about reading it:

1. Read the title, for it tells you what the table is about. Look at the column and row headings to be sure what each number means. Are the numbers percentages or are they frequencies or averages? The first column contains a list of questions the respondents were asked, and the second and third columns give the percentages who answered "Agree" and "Disagree." The last column totals the percentages in the row (100%) and indicates the number of people—453—who answered each question, sometimes represented by the letter "N").

A good way to make sure you know what the numbers represent is to use one in a sentence. For example, 36 is the first number in the "Agree" column: Thirty-six percent of the people who oppose the ERA agree that "It is more important for a wife to help her husband's career than to have one of her own."

2. Next, look to see if there are any footnotes. These often provide important information, including when the information was gathered and by whom as well as the meaning of key words ("adult" might be defined in terms of age).

3. Now you are ready to learn something from the table. This is a relatively simple table because it gives only the percentage breakdown for each variable without comparing the responses of different kinds of people (such as people of different ages); and yet it has some interesting findings. In spite of the fact that everyone in the table expressed opposition to the ERA, substantial percentages nonetheless take quite different positions on more specific questions about men's and women's roles. As the text points out, this table raises questions about the meaning of opposition to the ERA, since many of those who say they oppose the ERA seem to support equality in some more specific areas of social life.

TABLE 6-1   Values about Men and Women among Adults Who Oppose the ERA

VALUE STATEMENT	AGREE	DISAGREE	TOTAL (N)
1. Women should take care of running their homes and leave running the country to men.	36%	64%	100% (453)
2. A married woman should not earn money in business or industry if she has a husband capable of supporting her.	33%	67%	100% (453)
3. If your party nominated a woman for president, would you vote for her if she were qualified for the job?	73%	27%	100% (453)
4. Most men are better suited emotionally for politics than are most women.	47%	53%	100% (453)
5. It should be possible for a pregnant woman to obtain a legal abortion if the family has a very low income and they cannot afford any more children.	38%	62%	100% (453)

Source: Computed from 1982 General Social Survey data.

Scientists observed this supernova in 1987, and from it derived theories about what they will never be able to observe—the origins of the universe.

universe. Atomic physicists developed nuclear reactors long before they could actually see atoms with electron microscopes, and even now the image they see is not the atom itself, but its shadow.

While in some ways the need for interpretation may be seen as a liability in social research, Max Weber (1949) pointed out that when we study human beings, subjective interpretation of behavior is essential. A falling object has no motives or desires that affect its rate of fall. People are far more complicated, however, and we cannot understand the effects of social environments on our behavior simply by observing people as if they were objects. Research in the social sciences requires a delicate balance of objectivity and subjectivity: we must put ourselves in another's place while at the same time standing apart and trying to observe with objectivity.

An additional problem is that while the characteristics of objects tend to remain the same over time, people are far less constant. Social research relies heavily on how people present themselves, and information about them can easily be distorted. People sometimes lie about themselves in order to make a good impression, or answer questions they do not understand rather than appear to be ignorant. There is evidence that highly educated people tend to give what they believe are socially acceptable responses when they report their views and behavior (Crowne and Marlowe 1980).

Sociological research is also difficult because the act of gathering information about people is itself a social process (see Mishler 1986). When people know they are being observed, their behavior is affected by the social situation and the characteristics of the observer. Most of the interviewers who asked the question about support for the ERA, for example, were women, and it is reasonable to assume that people are less willing to express opposition to the ERA to a woman than they are to a man.

Other studies find similar effects by race. Blacks, for example, are more likely to express warmth and closeness towards whites when they are interviewed by whites rather than by blacks (Anderson et al. 1987). Such effects can seriously distort research findings. Between 1976 and 1984, national studies found a declining percentage of blacks who said they felt close to other blacks. As Anderson et al. (1987) discovered, however, this was due not to a shift in feelings among blacks but to changes in the racial composition of interviewer staffs of national surveys. As the percentage of blacks who were interviewed by whites increased, the reported feelings of closeness to other blacks decreased.

HOW TO FIND OUT: DESIGNING RESEARCH

Once we decide what we want to know and how we are going to measure it, we have to decide how we are actually going to *use* our measurement instruments.

Because all approaches have shortcomings, sociologists use a variety of research methods. Some, such as in-depth interviews, allow us to examine social interaction in great detail, but restrict us to small numbers of people who may represent no one but themselves. Other methods, such as surveys, allow us to study large representative samples of a population, but limit us to more superficial kinds of information. While all methods have their advantages and disadvantages, together they can produce results that are detailed and broadly representative.

Populations

In scientific research, a **population** is any precisely defined set of people, groups, or societies (notice that this definition differs slightly from that used in the study of population and ecology in Chapters 1 and 4). Once we decide what we want to know, we define the population, which may be as small as a group of two people or as large as the entire human race. "Currently married people in Ohio," "Japanese corporations," and "countries that use the death penalty" can all be defined as populations.

If we want to find the percentage of U.S. adults who support women's equality, we have to decide *whose* support or opposition we want to measure. "U.S. adults" is not a precisely defined population for scientific research, because it does not clearly indicate who is included. What age groups are considered "adult," and will we include citizens who currently live outside the U. S.? Will we include people living in Alaska and Hawaii? Will we include people who live in the U. S. but are not citizens—illegal aliens and college exchange students? One solution to the problem is to define our hypothetical population as "U.S. citizens over 18 years old living in the continental United States at the time of the study."

Censuses versus Samples With small populations, it is possible to conduct a **census** by gathering information about all of its members. With large populations, however, the expense and time involved make it difficult if not impossible to observe each member. The U.S. Census Bureau does this every ten years at a cost of tens of millions of dollars (see Mitroff, Mason, and Barabba 1983) and, as you will see throughout this book, it provides a rich source of information about social life (see Anderson 1988).

If we want to know if members of a small labor union support women's equality, we could ask all of them; but if we want to pose this question to our population of all adult U.S. citizens (more than 186 million people), we face an enormous task out of all proportion to what we stand to gain from it. (You only need stop a moment and try to imagine the

number of different studies we might want to do on the U.S. population and then realize that each would cost tens of millions of dollars.) In such cases, practical necessity forces researchers to select a subgroup—called a **sample**—and use it to represent the population.

The necessary use of samples raises important questions about all scientific research: Are some samples better than others? How do we tell? Can a sample accurately represent a large population? How, for example, can the Gallup Poll use 1,500 people to accurately describe the beliefs, values, and attitudes of tens of millions?

Good Samples and Bad Samples Any set of observations selected from a population constitutes a sample, and there is virtually no way to be certain that a sample accurately represents the population it came from. How, then, can we use samples with confidence?

The answer to this question lies in the way samples are selected. Suppose there are 10,000 students in your college and you want to find out how strongly they support women's equality. You stand at the library door during the evening and question students as they enter. After you question 200 students, you stop. Do their answers accurately represent the student body?

While your sample *may* represent the student population, you have no reason to believe this, because you failed to consider the students who never use the library at night (or who never go there at all); and their views may differ from those of students who spend their evenings in the library. This haphazard sample is likely to be *biased* because you did not actually select the sample; rather, students selected themselves.

What if you used a different procedure, putting each of the 10,000 students' names into a big bowl and then picking 200 names? You would have good reason to feel confident in this sample *because every member of the population had an equal chance to be included*. Samples selected in this way are called **random samples**. Many sampling methods use the principle of randomness (Kalton 1984). To save time, you might select at random one of the first 50 names on the list of 10,000 students and use that as a starting point to select every 50th name on the list (a systematic sample). Or if you wanted to gather information on all U.S. college students, you might first select a sample of colleges and then randomly select students in each one (a multistage sample). What all of these procedures have in common is that each member of the population has a known chance of being selected, and this is a crucial characteristic that distinguishes good samples from bad ones.

You might be saying to yourself at this point, "I still don't see how they can use a sample to describe millions of people. So what if it's random?" The answer involves some mathematical reasoning that we will not go into here; but if you are curious, take a look at Appendix B.

Surveys

In most **surveys**, information is gathered either in **interviews**, in which respondents interact with someone who asks questions, or in **questionnaires** which respondents fill out in private. In the simplest sense, we use surveys to find out "what's going on out there" by asking people to tell us (see Alreck and Settle 1985; Schuman and Presser 1981).

Surveys are useful because they allow researchers to gather large amounts of information. Surveys can be used to describe prevailing cultural values, beliefs, and attitudes as in Table 6-1. They also allow us to describe broad aspects of social structure—the number of people who are unemployed, the extent and distribution of poverty, or how income, prestige, power, jobs, and education are distributed in a population.

When surveys focus on specific problems, they often go beyond mere description and shed light on the social processes through which structure and culture affect individuals' lives. One survey, for example, sheds light on the process of discrimination in medicine, the highest-paid profession in the U.S. A sample of male physicians was asked to rank different medical specialties in terms of prestige, and their replies placed surgery at the top and pediatrics and psychiatry at the bottom (Quadagno 1976). Women physicians are overwhelmingly concentrated in low-paying, low-prestige specialties such as pediatrics (AAMC 1987). How does this happen? When Quadagno asked a sample of female physicians to explain their choice of specialty, two reasons were always given: male surgeons treated them with hostility, and they received far more encouragement from superiors to pursue "feminine" specialties.

Their awareness of negative attitudes toward them in certain areas combined with positive reinforcement in others led them to avoid situations where conflict might occur. Rather than confront possible rejection, women selected specialties in which they felt comfortable and welcome. (p. 450)

Case Studies   While most surveys try to represent entire populations, sociologists often begin by studying samples that may not represent the full population they are interested in. These are called **case studies**, and they allow researchers to explore and clarify problems and perfect measurement instruments before mounting an expensive survey.

W. F. Whyte (1981), for example, was interested in the intimate details of life in an urban slum; Helen and Robert Lynd (1929) spent years studying social relationships in a small U.S. city; and Erving Goffman (1961a) observed life in a mental institution for many months. In each of these studies, detailed descriptions of social life required enormous amounts of time and would have been impossible if researchers had focused on large samples of slum neighborhoods, small cities, or asylums. Instead, they used case studies to focus on a single instance that was carefully chosen to make it as representative as possible. In effect, they based their conclusions on samples that contained only one case.

While a study of a mental hospital cannot be used to describe mental hospitals in general, it can provide insights that can then be tested with more representative samples. In addition, case studies can provide a depth of understanding that is impossible in surveys. While a case study rarely describes a population, the accumulated findings of many case studies often can. If Goffman's observations of a single hospital are added to other studies, the regular patterns that emerge can tell us much about how people behave in those environments.

In-depth Interviews   Like surveys, **in-depth interviews** gather information by asking questions and recording answers. Unlike most surveys, in-depth interviews can last for many hours during which respondents and interviewers can develop a rapport that enables them to explore issues whose subtlety and personal nature are beyond the scope of most surveys. Researchers are able to explore the reasons that underlie people's behavior and to record intimate details of their lives.

Rubin (1976), for example, studied life in working-class marriages by interviewing each husband and wife in 50 couples. Some of the interviews lasted as long as ten hours and required repeated visits.

Wives and husbands talked about their marriages, their early hopes and dreams, how their families and relationships grew and changed over the years, their disappointments when the reality of married life collided with their dreams, and how they adapted within the limitations and financial hardships of working-class life. Rubin's result is a set of richly textured portraits that reveal, among other things, how husbands and wives often experience their relationship with each other in strikingly different ways.

In-depth studies like Rubin's are limited in several ways. We cannot know if the families in her sample represent anyone other than themselves; and the closeness of her relationship with them carries the danger that her results are distorted because respondents may tell her what they think she wants to hear. In spite of these limitations, in-depth interviews can yield a wealth of detail about social relationships and human experience. They remind us that sociological research concerns the lives of people who are trying to come to terms not only with themselves, but with the cultural, structural, and ecological conditions of their lives.

As longitudinal studies show, time works many effects on the human being.

Limitations of Survey Research   Surveys do have limitations. First, they rely on what people report on questionnaires or to interviewers, and people may either misperceive the question or, for a variety of reasons, give inaccurate reports. If we ask someone, "Why do you oppose the ERA?" the answer may have little to do with actual causes. Some surveys directly observe behavior; but most measure what people *say* about their behavior. The problem is not that verbal behavior is less "real" than other behavior, for we are quite capable of deceiving others through our actions. Rather, surveys limit us to a relatively narrow range of behavior (what people say), which may or may not correspond to their actions.

Surveys are also limited in time. A survey is like a still photograph, whereas social life is a continuing process. While surveys measure the results of social processes (gender differences in occupation and income, for example), they are not very effective for discovering how those results come about. One solution is a **longitudinal survey**, in which a sample of people is interviewed at regular intervals and tracked over time to record changes in their social positions, behavior, beliefs, values, and attitudes (see, for example, Gottfried and Gottfried 1988). The problem with longitudinal surveys is that keeping track of sev-

eral thousand people over a period of many years is difficult and expensive.

A more practical approach is to use a series of surveys that gather information from *different* samples selected from the *same* population. To find out if support for women's equality changes as people age, we could interview a national sample of 20-year-olds in 1995 and then interview a sample of 30-year-olds in 2005. In both cases, the samples represent the same population: people who were born in 1975.

Because single surveys are "still photographs," however, their results cannot be used to test conclusively ideas about cause and effect, and this is their most serious limitation (see, however, Blalock 1964, 1985). A scientist cannot answer the question "Does heat make balloons expand?" simply by gathering a sample of balloons and measuring their temperatures and their volumes. Why not? Because other factors—such as the initial size of the balloons—may account for some of the observed differences.

The only way to answer this question is to take a group of balloons of the same size, heat them to different temperatures, and then record differences in volume. In other words, every factor other than heat must be controlled by holding it constant, and then the suspected *cause* (heat) must be manipulated to see how it, and it alone, produces an *effect* (increased volume). This is the experimental method, and it requires time and controlled conditions, both of which are beyond the capability of single surveys.

Experiments

An interest in finding out why men earn much more money than women might lead us to explore the ways in which women are discriminated against. Do people tend to assume that women are less capable than men and evaluate men more favorably than women even when their performances are of equal quality? Assuming they are even aware of it, people would be reluctant to admit such a bias in survey interviews, and even if they did admit it, we could not use a survey to see if women are actually discriminated against simply because they are women.

To see if gender, by itself, affects people's evaluations of ability and performance, we have to *hold constant all other factors that might affect evaluations*—that is, we must use an **experiment**. In experiments, groups are exposed to conditions that are exactly alike in all ways but one. If people's behavior differs from one group to another, then those differences must be due to the different conditions they were exposed to, since the groups are alike in all other ways.

Etaugh and Kasley (1981) used the experimental method when they randomly selected samples of male and female college undergraduates at a midwestern university (see also Paludi and Strayer 1985). Each was given a packet of written materials including a sample newspaper article) which supposedly represented a job application submitted by someone who had recently been hired to write for a local newspaper. Each application was identical except that the applicant was identified as female in one half of the cases and as male in the other half. The experimental subjects were asked to fill out forms in which they assigned letter grades (ranging from "A" for superior to "F" for inferior) in eight areas, including the applicant's overall competence, status in the field, future job success, and the quality of the article itself.

For all eight areas, applicants identified as male consistently received higher evaluations than did those identified as female. Male applicants were seen as more competent professionally, as having a higher chance for success in their profession, and as having a higher professional status. The articles themselves were rated higher in every respect when subjects thought the author was male.

Because the students were randomly assigned to male and female applicants, students were, as subjects, similar in all important respects. They read and evaluated the same articles in the same social situation; thus, any pattern of differences in their evaluations can be due to only one factor—their perception of the author's gender. Experiments allow researchers to control all factors that might account for different responses and to manipulate the one factor they are interested in. In this way, they are able to identify cause-and-effect relationships between variables.

Limitations of Experiments   Like all methods, experiments have limitations. When people know they are participating in an experiment their behavior may be affected in ways that distort the results. Experimental subjects who know that their behavior is observed are aware that what they do matters. The experimental setting itself may exert an uncontrolled influence on subjects' behavior.

A classic study of factory workers suggested that people's behavior in experiments is affected simply because they get more attention than they are accustomed to. Researchers studied workers at the Hawthorne plant of the Western Electric Company to discover how working conditions affect productivity (Roethlisberger and Dickson 1939). They varied such factors as the amount of lighting and the frequency and duration of coffee breaks and found, to their surprise, that no matter what they did, productivity increased.

They eventually concluded that merely by participating in the experiment, workers received more attention than they were used to, and their feelings of being special resulted in higher productivity. Distortions caused by experimental situations came to be known as the "Hawthorne effect" and are a serious problem for experimenters. Had the researchers been aware of this effect, they might have used a **control group** of workers who were told they were experimental subjects but were *not* exposed to different working conditions. The researchers might then have found that their productivity increased just as the other workers' had.

While the Hawthorne effect made researchers more aware of experimental conditions as sources of error, subsequent studies consistently failed to duplicate these findings in a variety of settings (Parsons 1982). This illustrates an important principle in all scientific research: we run a considerable risk of error if we accept the findings of a single study as conclusive proof of any proposition. Science depends on **replication**—repeating studies in different settings to see if the initial findings hold true.

The "Real World" as Laboratory The experimental method is also limited by the artificial nature of laboratory research settings. The students in Etaugh and Kasley's study knew that their evaluations would not affect the job applicants ("It's just an experiment") and it is impossible to estimate how such settings affect people. If these same students were personnel managers whose decisions affected people's lives, would they still discriminate against women? Laboratory experiments cannot answer such questions, and for this reason researchers often conduct **field experiments** outside the laboratory.

Fidell (1970) sent fake applications for faculty positions to 238 university psychology departments. The résumés that accompanied the applications were the same in each case, but half of the applicants were identified as males ("Patricks") and the other half as females ("Patricias"). The heads of departments were asked to give a "current appraisal of the applicant's chances of getting a full-time position." The results showed that Patricks were judged to be suitable for more appointments and at higher levels than were Patricias, even though their experience and qualifications were identical; and only Patricks were considered to be qualified for full professorships.

Field experiments allow us to control and manipulate key variables in "real world" settings; to do this we must focus on a narrow problem involving only a few variables. This illustrates an important trade-off among research methods: those that allow a large scope (surveys) make it difficult to test ideas under carefully controlled conditions; however, those that permit such controls (experiments) restrict us to simple problems, when in fact behavior is caused by many related factors. When the findings produced by different methods are combined, it is possible to piece together richer, more complex explanations.

Participant Observation

While surveys ask people to describe their social situations, behavior, and experience, and experiments allow researchers to observe behavior in controlled laboratory conditions, with **participant observation** we can directly observe behavior outside of laboratories (Jorgensen 1989). Many sociologists use this technique to gain insights into social behavior. W. F. Whyte (1981), for example, lived for several years in a lower-class neighborhood of Boston and observed urban gangs by participating in their activities. The trust that developed between researcher and subjects allowed Whyte to observe the lives of these gang members in ways that would otherwise be impossible.

Goffman (1961a) observed life in a mental hospital and identified ways in which depersonalization and humiliation aggravate mental problems. Festinger, Riecken, and Schachter (1956) joined a religious cult whose members believed the world would soon be destroyed and that only they would be saved by aliens from outer space. The researchers were able to observe firsthand when cult members reacted to the failure of their prophecy.

Limitations of Participant Observation Participant observation allows us to explore aspects of behavior that individuals are often unaware of, to witness daily life as it occurs. While this method has clear advantages over surveys, it also has limitations. One of the most serious drawbacks is that it requires enormous amounts of time—sometimes as long as several years. More serious is that since researchers participate in the social systems they study, there is always the danger that their presence will affect people's behavior and that the observers may identify so closely with their subjects that their own objectivity is impaired. They may develop positive and negative feelings toward their subjects that lead them to unconsciously select and interpret observations in biased ways.

In the 1920s, for example, anthropologist Margaret Mead lived for several years on the island of Samoa. Her classic book, *Coming of Age in Samoa* ([1928] 1953), described Samoans as a graceful and gentle people among whom adolescence was a trouble-free time of life. Mead's book was particularly important because it was written at a time of great concern about the "adolescent crises" so common in U.S. society; her discovery of a society in which such crises did not occur supported the view that culture is more important than biology in determining behavior.

More recently another anthropologist, Derek Freeman (1983), attacked Mead's study. He argued that Mead went to Samoa looking for evidence of the importance of culture, and her observations and interpretations were determined by what she wanted to see. A storm of controversy followed, and while Mead's research did have its methodological flaws, it appears that her interpretation of Samoan society in the 1920s was nonetheless basically accurate (see Holmes 1986).

Winslow Homer's 1866 painting, *The Morning Bell*, shows a young woman going to work in a factory, whose schedule was probably similar to that shown to the right.

As Marcus (1983) wrote in his comments on this controversy, the outcome is not the most important lesson we can draw from it. More important is the fact that two observers can arrive at "radically different interpretations from fieldwork in the same culture" (Marcus, p. 22). Like all case studies, the results of participant observation must be interpreted in comparison with the findings of other observers, an important principle in all scientific research.

Secondary Analysis: Using What Is Already There

Surveys, case studies, experiments, participant observation, and in-depth interviews are methods used to gather fresh evidence that sheds light on sociological problems; but a great deal of information already exists in historical documents, government statistics, and published studies. When researchers apply information gathered by someone else to their own questions, they are using **secondary analysis**. When Durkheim studied suicide, for example, he found a new use for information that already existed—death certificates.

One of the richest sources of sociological information is the U.S. Census, conducted every ten years by the Census Bureau, which gathers detailed information about every citizen. Additional information is gathered several times a year through the Current Population Survey. Other government agencies gather a wealth of information on births, deaths, marriages, divorces, crime, health, work, education, and various indications of the quality of life. In addition, organizations such as corporations, military units, universities, public school systems, hospitals, and police departments regularly gather information about their activities. When we add to this the thousands of social science research projects conducted over the last half century, we have a rich store of information that can be applied to a variety of research questions never anticipated by those who originally gathered the information.

Because data gathering is expensive and time-consuming, sociologists are increasingly using secondary analysis. In her study of a corporation, for example, Kanter (1977a) examined forms used to evaluate employee performance. The forms existed for the purpose of making personnel decisions, but Kanter found a new use for them as she looked to see which aspects of men's and women's performances

Time Table of the Holyoke Mills,

To take effect on and after Jan. 3d, 1853.

The standard being that of the Western Rail Road, which is the Meridian time at Cambridge.

MORNING BELLS.

First Bell ring 4.40, A.M. Second Bell ring is at 5, A.M.

YARD GATES

Will be opened at ringing of Morning Bells, of Meal Bells, and of Evening Bells, and kept open ten minutes.

WORK COMMENCES

At ten minutes after last Morning Bell, and ten minutes after Bell which "rings in" from Meals.

BREAKFAST BELLS.

October 1st, to March 31st, inclusive, ring out at 7, A.M.; ring in at 7.30, A.M.
April 1st, to Sept. 30th, inclusive, ring out at 6.30, A.M.; ring in at 7, A.M.

DINNER BELLS.

Ring out at 12.30, P.M.; ring in at 1, P.M.

EVENING BELLS.

Ring out at 6.30,* P.M.

*Excepting on Saturdays when the Sun sets previous to 6.30. At such times, ring out at sunset.

In all cases, the first stroke of the Bell is considered as marking the time.

Historical documents, such as this 1853 factory worker timetable, tell much about the social conditions in which people lived. Notice at what time people were expected to come to work, how little time was allowed to arrive and to eat, how long the work day and the work week were, and how precisely regimented the day was. No mention is made of breaks from work other than for meals. In what ways do you think work has changed, and in what ways are conditions similar?

led to high ratings. Kanter found that secretaries were evaluated according to two main characteristics: "initiative and enthusiasm" and "ability to anticipate and take care of their bosses' personal needs." Secretaries were rewarded on the basis of personal relationships with superiors, while men were rewarded more on the basis of professional skills and performance.

Content Analysis   The methods discussed thus far focus primarily on what people do and what they say. **Content analysis** is an additional method that examines not *what* people communicate, but *how* they communicate it, and this often reveals messages that are conveyed when people write or talk. Content analysis is widely used to investigate how the mass media transmit cultural ideas and images that reinforce the subordinate position of women in society. How is it done?

Suppose you want to find out if school textbooks portray males and females in different ways. You could do this by assembling a collection of textbooks and perhaps counting the number of characters used in stories or examples and determining what percentage of them are male. Content analyses of school texts find that most adult characters are male, as are most important people. Working women are portrayed less often than working men, and when they are, their jobs tend to be lower in prestige and pay—secretaries, nurses, and school teachers (Pur-

cell and Stewart 1990; St. Peter 1979; Women on Words and Images 1975a).

Content analyses of television shows reveal similar biases. Whether the shows are aimed at children or adults, the vast majority of leading characters are male, and successful working women are rarely portrayed (Cantor and Pingree 1983). In commercials, women are often portrayed as consumers whose most important concern is clean laundry, and the "voice of authority" is male 90 percent of the time (Bretland and Cantor 1988; Women on Words and Images 1975b).

While books, television shows, commercials, and movies serve a variety of intended purposes for their creators (education, entertainment, selling products), their contents reveal important aspects of the culture in which they are created, and such messages affect our ideas of who we are and should be as men and women.

Historical Research   Historical documents are an additional valuable source of information for secondary analysis, for they shed light on the ways in which societies develop and change. What light does history shed on the current standing of women in society?

Historical research methods, by definition, focus on what has already occurred. We cannot, therefore, scientifically observe or experimentally manipulate history. We can learn a great deal, however, from records that reflect the social environments in which people once lived. Perhaps the most important lessons to be learned from historical research are that societies are always changing, and that the social arrangements we live in today developed over long periods of time. This may be the only world we have ever known, but it is not the only world that has ever been known or that ever will be.

Baxandall, Gordon, and Reverby (1976) wanted to understand how capitalism and the Industrial Revolution affected working-class women in the U.S. between the early seventeenth century and 1975. How did they do it? Their biggest problem was that most working-class women had neither the time nor the ability to leave written records of their experiences, and even when they did, they often did not consider their lives to be important enough to write about.

By systematically scouring libraries and archives for documents, the researchers found union records, diaries, short stories, poems, songs, letters, advertisements, social worker reports, factory rules and regulations, petitions, newspaper and magazine articles, government reports, and statistical studies. They found that colonial families met most of their needs through their own labor. While men and women performed different tasks in general, women still played a full role in economic production—weaving fabric, making soap and candles, and trading in the marketplace. It was not uncommon for women to be blacksmiths, tailors, printers, and shopkeepers; and widows often assumed full managerial control of family businesses.

The Industrial Revolution and the rise of capitalism physically separated the family from economic activity, and people no longer worked in the same place they lived. Life was divided into the private sphere of unpaid housework and the public sphere of paid employment. Because most work done at home was unpaid, it gradually lost its cultural value, and the self-esteem of women suffered as a result. Although many women worked outside the home, they were restricted to low-paying jobs, and census takers routinely ignored wives' earnings when they recorded family income. Because paid work was socially defined as a secondary role for women, they were expected to be temporary workers who could be paid little and laid off when it suited their employers' interests. Women played an important part in the labor movement's long struggle for better working conditions, and many rebelled against the domination of their husbands.

The most serious limitation of historical studies is that we cannot use them to demonstrate cause-and-effect relationships between variables. We cannot manipulate history in order to see what would have happened without an Industrial Revolution and without capitalism.

Cross-cultural studies, which compare different societies, are a partial solution to this problem. By comparing Samoa with the United States, Mead ([1928] 1953) concluded that "adolescent crisis" is not an inevitable part of growing up. Studies of the Native American Hopi Indians show that families are headed by women, not men, and "women's work"—such as making pottery and baskets—is valued just as highly as men's (Leavitt 1971). Such studies are important because they provide clues to the mystery of why societies develop in so many ways.

The preceding sections show how the complexity of social life requires sociologists to draw upon a wide range of research designs as they gather data. What happens, however, after the data are gathered? How are thousands of bits of information used to answer the questions we ask?

INTERPRETATION: USING INFORMATION TO ANSWER QUESTIONS

Of all research tasks, the interpretation of data is the most fascinating, for it is here that we must exercise a detective's skills in order to discover the clues and patterns that solve puzzles such as the income gap between men and women. At this stage, statistics are particularly useful.

Some Useful Statistics

Variables that have a small number of categories (such as the "Agree" and "Disagree" in Table 6-1) are easily summarized with percentages, allowing us to compare different groups. Variables such as income, however, present a more difficult problem, for there are thousands of different numbers that represent people's earnings. Each year the Census Bureau interviews almost 60,000 adults and records annual incomes for full-time, year-round workers (USCB 1989d). How can we use this massive set of facts to describe and compare the incomes of women and men?

We could simplify the information by sorting people into a small set of income categories (Table 6-2). We could then compare women and men by seeing which categories they are most likely to be in.

TABLE 6-2   Annual Income of Year-Round, Full-Time Workers by Gender (United States)

INCOME	WOMEN (%)	MEN (%)
Less than $5,000	12	8
$5,000 to $9,999	15	9
$10,000 to $14,999	21	12
$15,000 to $19,999	18	13
$20,000 to $29,999	22	22
$30,000 to $49,999	11	25
$50,000 to $74,999	1	7
$75,000 or more	*	4
TOTAL	100	100

*Less than 0.5 percent

Source: USCB 1989d.

Women are more clustered in the lower income brackets than men. For men, the *most frequent* income category (the **mode**) is between $30,000 and $49,999, while the mode for women is $20,000 to $29,999. Although these descriptions show that men are better off than women, they are crude, for they do not allow us to gauge how *much* better off men are.

A second approach to this problem is to add up all the money earned by men and divide the total by the number of men, giving us the average earnings *per man*. This statistic is what most people think of as an average and is called the **mean**. When we calculate means, we find that men earned an average of $27,600—61 percent more than the average of $17,100 earned by full-time women workers.

As a description of groups, however, the mean has its disadvantages, for a few people who make a great deal of money "pump up" the mean and inflate the group's income. For example, suppose we have five people with the following incomes:

Vincent	$9,000
Joe	$15,000
Teresa	$15,500
Barbara	$17,000
John	$1,000,000
TOTAL	$1,056,500

If we want to summarize the incomes of the people in this group with a single number, would the mean give an accurate picture? Four of the five people have in-comes between $9,000 and $17,000, and yet the mean income for the group is $211,300 (or $1,056,500/5). Certainly the mean is not a good indicator of the income of the people in this group. Clearly, whenever a few members of a group have extreme characteristics, the mean is not an effective way to describe the group. The mean does accurately tell us that men *as a group* earn 61 percent more than women, but it may give a distorted picture of how *most* men compare with *most* women.

This brings us to a third important statistic—the **median**—which is simply the middle number in any group of numbers that is ranked from high to low or from low to high. In the group above, Teresa's income, $15,500, is the median. The median income for full-time women workers is $15,400, while the median for men is $23,400 (USCB 1989d). This indicates that half of all women made more than $15,400 and half made less. Because the median is unaffected by extremely large or small incomes, it is a better summary description.

All these measures describe groups imperfectly, but they are useful because they allow us to summarize thousands of observations of individuals and use them to compare different groups. We can use means to see that while in 1955 full-time working women made 64¢ for every dollar earned by men, women have actually fallen behind still further and earn only 62¢ for every dollar earned by men (USCB 1983b, 1989d).

Note that such statements do not tell us anything about individual men and women. While there are certainly some women who earn more money than most men and some men who earn less than most women, the focus of sociological research is not on individuals per se. Rather, it is on the characteristics of social systems in which individuals live.

Causal Relationships between Variables

If men and women were equally likely to fall in each income bracket, we would say that the variables "gender" and "income" are *independent* of each other. As we saw in the previous section, however, if you are a woman, you tend to have a lower income than if you are a man, and in this sense, the variable "income" *depends on* the variable "gender."

There is, in other words, a relationship between gender and income. In this relationship, gender is an **independent variable**, because we consider it to affect income. Because income depends to some

TABLE 6-3   Occupation by Gender (United States)

OCCUPATION[1]	WOMEN (%)	MEN (%)
Upper white-collar	28	25
Upper blue-collar	4	33
Lower white-collar	46	19
Lower blue-collar	10	15
Farm and service	12	8
TOTAL	100	100

[1]Ranked by average income for full-time wage and salary workers. Excludes self-employed.

Source: U.S. Census Bureau 1990a.

degree on a person's gender, it is a **dependent variable**. Note that for one variable to affect another, it must occur before the dependent variable. In other words, it would be silly to suggest that income determines whether a person is male or female.

How do we explain the relationship between gender and income? That is the function of a **hypothesis**, a statement that predicts a relationship between variables. The first step is to consider other variables—such as educational attainment and occupation—that we know affect people's income, and with these generate possible hypotheses.

Our first hypothesis is that women work at poorer-paying jobs. In the first column in Table 6-3 we find that only 32 percent of working women are in better-paying white-collar or blue-collar jobs. Fifty-six percent are in white-collar jobs (such as secretaries) or blue-collar jobs (such as assembly-line workers) that are lower-paid, and an additional 12 percent are in farm, service, and private household jobs that are the least well-paid. By comparison, the second column of Table 6-3 shows that 58 percent of all male workers are in upper white-collar or upper blue-collar occupations. The data support the first hypothesis.

Although part of the relationship between gender and income is due to the concentration of women in poorly paid jobs, we have to consider a second hypothesis: women are paid less than men even when they work at the same job. To test this hypothesis, we compare the average incomes of men and women who have similar jobs, trying to see if men still earn more money. By looking at men and women who have the same kind of job, we are, in a sense, holding occupation "constant"; and when we do this, we are using occupation as a **control variable**.

The result is in Table 6-4, which shows the mean incomes of men and women according to their occupations. As we saw before, women in general earn 62¢ for every dollar earned by men. For some occupations, however, the gap is smaller: women scien-

TABLE 6-4   Mean Earnings of Wage and Salary Workers by Occupation and Gender (United States)

OCCUPATION	MEAN EARNINGS		FOR EACH DOLLAR MEN EARN, WOMEN EARN
	WOMEN	MEN	
Executive and managerial	$24,900	$41,800	60¢
Professional specialty	$25,600	$41,500	62¢
Accountants	$23,900	$40,100	60¢
Engineers	$32,700	$41,200	79¢
Scientists and Mathematicians	$32,300	$39,600	82¢
Teachers (postsecondary)	$29,500	$40,300	73¢
Lawyers and judges	$39,400	$61,500	64¢
Public officials and administrators	$27,600	$37,400	74¢
Sales representatives (retail)	$12,700	$21,200	60¢
Office supervisors	$22,200	$32,400	69¢
Service workers	$11,800	$19,700	60¢
Farm and forestry	$7,100	$15,700	45¢
Computer operators	$17,500	$24,400	72¢
Janitors and cleaners	$12,000	$16,900	71¢

Source: USCB 1989e.

TABLE 6-5 Occupation by Education and Gender (United States)

	HIGHEST DEGREE					
	College Graduate		High School Graduate		Less than High School	
	Women	Men	Women	Men	Women	Men
OCCUPATION	(%)	(%)	(%)	(%)	(%)	(%)
Upper white-collar	68	67	18	17	6	6
Upper blue-collar	1	4	3	26	5	29
Lower white-collar	26	22	53	22	21	8
Lower blue-collar	1	3	9	22	28	38
Farm and service	4	4	17	13	40	19
TOTAL	100	100	100	100	100	100

Source: USCB 1990a.

tists and mathematicians earn 82¢ for each dollar earned by men. Thus, *some* of the difference in earnings is due to different occupations; but notice that in almost *no* occupation do women earn as much as men, and in most jobs, women earn far less. (Notice how each new explanation generates more questions: why is the gender gap in income smaller among computer operators than among lawyers and judges?)

By testing our first two hypotheses we found that women have poorer-paying jobs and are paid less for doing the same work. Why are they concentrated at the low end of the job market and paid less for the same work? These questions lead to our third hypothesis, which focuses on education: women hold poorer-paying jobs and are paid less for the same work because they have lower average levels of education.

To test the third hypothesis, we control for the variable "education," *by comparing the jobs of men and women who are alike on that characteristic.* Do men and women with similar education hold similar jobs? Table 6-5 provides an answer (this is a multicolumn table, so go through it slowly, one column at a time). The first two columns describe the occupations of men and women who have at least a college degree, and show quite similar distributions.

When we look at the occupations of less-educated workers, strong gender differences emerge. Among workers with high school diplomas (the second pair of columns), men are more likely to have upper blue-collar jobs, and women are concentrated in lower white-collar and service occupations. Among the least-educated workers (the last two columns), only 11 percent of women have upper white-collar or up-

per blue-collar jobs compared with 35 percent of comparably educated men. (Pause for a few minutes and verify these statements by examining the table carefully.)

Table 6-5 clearly suggests that education benefits men more than women in the job market (see also Spenner, Otto, and Call 1982); but how does education affect income? Do women and men with the same education have the same income? As Table 6-6 shows, controlling for education does not explain the relationship between gender and income, for at each level of education, the median income for men is much higher than that for women. In fact, women with college degrees averaged $1,200 less than men who never went beyond high school ($23,500 versus $24,700), and women high school graduates make $2,700 less on the average than men who never went beyond elementary school ($16,200 versus $18,900).

This analysis reveals some aspects of the relationship between income and gender. Women earn less than men because they hold poorer-paying jobs regardless of their education, and even when they have similar jobs, they are paid less. While a complete explanation involves other variables (see Marini 1989), these findings strongly suggest that women are discriminated against on the basis of gender, both in getting jobs and being rewarded for their work (see Bergmann 1986; Duncan et al. 1984; England et al. 1988a).

This analysis describes a series of patterns—occupation, gender, education, and income—and examines the *relationships* among them. In this way, we can see how social characteristics, such as gender, are related to others, such as occupation, education,

TABLE 6-6   Mean Income by Years of Education and Gender for Year-Round, Full-Time Workers (United States)

YEARS OF SCHOOL COMPLETED	MEAN INCOME		FOR EACH DOLLAR MEN EARN, WOMEN EARN
	WOMEN	MEN	
Elementary			
0 to 7 Years	$10,200	$16,900	60¢
8 Years	$12,700	$18,900	67¢
High School			
1 to 3 Years	$13,100	$21,300	62¢
4 Years	$16,200	$24,700	66¢
College			
1 to 3 Years	$19,300	$29,300	66¢
4 Years	$23,500	$38,800	61¢
5 Years or more	$30,300	$47,900	63¢

Source: USCB 1990a.

and income, that have important effects on people's lives. This kind of analysis lies at the heart of sociological research, for it illuminates the complex effects of social systems on human life.

Correlation   Percentages, medians, means, and modes enable us to describe groups in terms of single variables, but we also need to describe relationships between variables.

A perfect statistical **correlation** is one in which two variables overlap completely. In parts *a* and *b* of Figure 6-1, if we know someone's education, we also know his or her income. In *a*, the correlation is *positive*, because the higher education is, the higher income is. In *b*, the correlation is *negative* because the higher education is, the *lower* income is. In *c*, the variables are *independent* of each other, because the chances of having high or low income are the same regardless of education: education does not make a difference.

Most relationships between variables are neither perfect nor independent; rather, they are somewhere in between.

SOME DIFFICULTIES IN SOCIOLOGICAL RESEARCH

The study of people and the characteristics of their social environments poses a number of scientific and ethical problems for sociological researchers.

Complexity and Objectivity

The forces that influence human behavior and cause changes in social environments are enormously complex. The position of women in society cannot be described or explained by a few variables; rather, it flows from many aspects of culture and social structure that are related to each other in complex ways.

In addition, as sociologists study social systems they cannot be immune from the effects of those systems on their own activity as scientists. Survey researchers may ask loaded questions ("You aren't a racist, are you?"); the biases of participant observers may influence what they notice as well as how they interpret their observations; and experimental conditions may themselves produce their own effects. In comparison with most other scientific disciplines, the demands of objectivity are particularly difficult for sociologists to meet. It is for this reason that they so carefully scrutinize their measures and methods

FIGURE 6-1   Income by Education (Hypothetical)

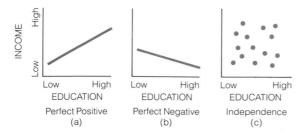

Perfect Positive (a)   Perfect Negative (b)   Independence (c)

in order to be aware of any possible sources of distorting bias.

As Max Weber argued, however, complete objectivity is not only difficult to achieve, it is also undesirable. Unlike rocks, beams of light, and barnyard animals, humans behave according to complex perceptions and interpretations, and all of these are influenced by social environments. To understand how the Grand Canyon was formed, we do not have to imagine what it would be like to *be* the Grand Canyon; but we cannot understand people in the same way.

Ethics, Research, and People's Lives

Another difficulty in sociological research involves ethical questions (Reynolds 1982). While the experimental manipulation of objects is culturally acceptable, scientists must take far greater care with people. Researchers may not explore the effects of child abuse on emotional development by systematically abusing a sample of children and comparing them with a control group of unabused children. In many cases, however, the ethical issues are less clear-cut.

Humphreys (1970), for example, wanted to learn more about men who have homosexual encounters in public rest rooms. To gather information, he served as a lookout, and as an observer he was able to gather detailed data about these interactions. To gather further information, he kept a record of automobile license plates, which he used to locate the subjects a year later. He then presented himself as a survey researcher gathering information having nothing to do with homosexuality, and he found, among other things, that most of these men were married.

In spite of the fact that his study dispelled many myths about homosexual behavior, Humphreys was criticized on ethical grounds because he lied about his identity and, although he safeguarded subjects' identities, he risked exposing them and their actions. He later agreed that he had improperly invaded the privacy of his subjects and unnecessarily endangered them (Humphreys 1975). For all scientists, but for social scientists in particular, his methods raise a troubling question: Do the research ends justify the research means?

Ethical questions involve not only research methods, but the possible *uses* of research findings. Scientists are bound by professional norms that require careful interpretation of findings ("the differences are small and apply only to men and women in gen-

Relatively little research has been done on homosexuals in the United States, in part because as a minority they are reluctant to be identified and, in part, because of ethical issues. To what degree do social scientists have the right to invade people's privacy in order to do research, even if their findings might bring about positive social change?

eral"); but parents, teachers, potential employers, and government policymakers are not. There is a danger that scientific findings will be used sloppily or indiscriminately to reinforce damaging cultural stereotypes and social inequality or injustice.

In the 1960s, for example, the U.S. Army provided funds for the study of the social conditions likely to cause or prevent revolutions in Latin American countries. From a scientific point of view, Project Camelot (as it was known) was simply one more set of questions to be answered, but from the Latin American perspective, it involved information that would enable the U.S. government to interfere in the domestic affairs of their countries (Horowitz 1965). When news of Project Camelot reached Chile, a public furor erupted, the program was canceled, and the researchers confronted ethical issues they had previously ignored. To a scientist, one bit of knowledge is no better or worse than any other, subject only to rigid standards for determining truth. Outside the scientific community, however, knowledge often represents power that can be used destructively as well as constructively.

In spite of the difficulties inherent in their research, most sociologists are committed to the scientific method. By limiting themselves to aspects of reality that can be observed and measured, sociologists necessarily limit the kinds of questions they can investigate. For this reason, few would suggest that scientific research alone is sufficient to solve the many puzzles of social life; but through systematic observation sociologists obtain the information needed to test a wide range of ideas that contribute to our overall understanding of the human condition.

SUMMARY

1. The scientific method involves careful and exacting procedures for gathering and interpreting objective evidence that helps sociologists accomplish the three major tasks of research: description, explanation, and prediction.

2. Research begins with the problem of deciding what it is that we want to know, which variables are involved, and how best to measure them in a valid and reliable way. Measurement is particularly difficult in sociology because much of what is measured is invisible, changes over time, and depends on how people present themselves.

3. The complexity of social life calls for many methods for gathering and interpreting information, and each has its own strengths and weaknesses. Research design begins with the definition of the population to be studied and the decision to study all its members (a census), a representative sample, or carefully selected cases.

4. Interview and questionnaire surveys allow researchers to gather large amounts of information, but are limited by time and their dependence on the accuracy of people's reports about themselves. In-depth interviews yield greater detail, but must compromise by focusing on a smaller number of people who are less likely to represent a population scientifically.

5. Laboratory and field experiments allow us to discover cause-and-effect relationships by carefully controlling the conditions in which variables are measured. Participant observation allows us to observe directly the behavior of subjects, but our involvement makes it more difficult to be objective.

6. Content analysis and historical research are types of secondary analysis in which existing information is applied to new research problems. Cross-cultural comparisons of different societies help researchers discover how social environments change.

7. Regardless of methods, sociologists often use statistics to summarize and condense large amounts of detailed information and to discover and explain relationships between variables.

8. Sociological research is difficult in several ways. We must pay attention not only to the biases that threaten any scientist's objectivity, but also to the risks that research may pose for the people we study. Ethical issues are enormously important in sociology, both in relation to the process of gathering information and to the ways in which that information is eventually used.

KEY TERMS

case study   118
census   117
content analysis   123
control group   120
control variable   126
correlation   128
cross-cultural study   124
dependent variable   126
experiment   120
field experiment   121
hypothesis   126

independent variable   125
in-depth interview   118
interview   118
longitudinal survey   119
mean   125
measurement instrument   114
median   125
mode   125
participant observation   121
population   117

questionnaire   118
random sample   117
reliability   114
replication   121
sample   117
scientific method   111
secondary analysis   122
survey   118
validity   114
variable   113

LOOKING ELSEWHERE

Having studied Chapter 6, you might want to look at related discussions in *Human Arrangements*, which include

- science and the scientific method (Chapter 18, pp. 443–52)
- gender inequality (Chapter 14)

RECOMMENDED READINGS

Cole, S. 1976. *The sociological method* (2nd ed.). Chicago: Rand McNally (paperback). A clearly written, lively introduction to the logic of sociological research and the many uses of statistical techniques. Full of interesting examples.

Converse, J. M. 1988. *Survey research in the United States: Roots and emergence.* Berkeley: University of California Press. A fascinating history of the development of one of the most important research tools used by sociologists today.

Glazer, M. 1972. *The research adventure.* New York: Random House. A series of accounts of sociological research projects, the practical problems the researchers encountered, and how they solved them.

Hunt, M. 1986. *Profiles of social research: The scientific study of human interactions.* New York: Russell Sage. A clear and engaging look at different ways of designing sociological research. Hunt truly manages to convey what it is like to do research.

Katzer, J., Cook, K., and Crouch, W. 1978. *Evaluating information: A guide for users of social science research.* Reading, MA: Addison-Wesley (paperback). A book for consumers of research reports. It is lively and clearly written and focuses on basic problems that confront anyone trying to make sense of scientific research and trying to decide which findings to accept and which to reject.

Reynolds, P.D. 1982. *Ethics and social science research.* Englewood Cliffs, NJ: Prentice-Hall. A recent examination of the ethical problems encountered by social researchers and some of the ways of dealing with them.

Rossi, A. S. 1982. *Feminists in politics: A panel analysis of the first national women's conference.* New York: Academic Press. A fascinating account of the process of designing and carrying out a large survey.

Whyte, W. F. 1981. *Street corner society* (3rd ed.). Chicago: University of Chicago Press. In what has become a sociological classic, pay particular attention to the Appendix, "On the Evolution of Street Corner Society." It is a rare and profound look into the problems and promises of participant observation research.

PART THREE
SOCIAL ORGANIZATION

Having read Parts One and Two you should now have a solid introduction to the major sociological concepts and theoretical perspectives. In Part Three we begin a task that will occupy us throughout the remainder of the book: to use these to focus attention on the world in a new way. Along the way we will introduce you to still more concepts and theories that apply to particular areas of social life.

We begin Part Three with Chapter 7, a look at what is perhaps the most important of all social processes, socialization, through which each generation learns the fundamentals of its culture and how to perform the roles that go along with the many statuses we occupy. Chapter 8 is the first of a series of three chapters that look at social life as it operates on three levels: the individual, the group, and the community. We close Part Three with an in-depth examination of deviance and conformity, phenomena that exist in all kinds of social systems.

As you work your way through these chapters, keep in mind that the framework we are using rests on the basic concepts of social system, culture, social structure, and population/ecology, as well as other key ideas introduced earlier. If you feel uncertain when you encounter them again (or encounter some that you do not remember seeing before) be sure to use the glossary at the end of the book.

7
SOCIALIZATION

 On any given day, almost 200,000 babies are born in the world (PRB 1990). They vary enormously in their coloring, their weight and length, and in how often they cry or smile. With relatively few exceptions they can all see, hear, smell, touch, taste, eat, move, babble, sleep, play, grimace, smack their lips, and chew their fingers. They can follow a moving light with their eyes, grasp a small object, move toward and suck a nipple, and distinguish light and dark as well as different colors. Most important, babies are all dependent on others to take care of them (Fischer and Lazerson 1984).

In time they will learn to sit, walk, talk, make choices, think, and feel in relation to themselves and the world. They will acquire ideas and feelings about who they are, ought to be, and might be. They will, in short, become social actors through **socialization**, the process through which people learn to behave, think, and feel as individuals in relation to their environments (see Bush and Simmons 1981; Featherman and Lerner 1985). What these babies learn and how they learn it depend on their social and physical environments. If we could gather them together and try to predict something as basic as the language they will speak as adults, we would be wrong much of the time. Even if we knew which infants had Chinese parents it would still be hard to predict, for those who live in San Francisco's Chinatown will probably never learn to speak Chinese.

If we consider babies who grow up in a particular society—such as the U.S.—we can make more accurate predictions. Most will speak English, believe in Christianity or Judaism, aspire to a college education, value scientific thinking, drive cars, and spend more than 15,000 hours in front of television sets by

their eighteenth birthday (Liebert et al. 1982). The similarities that reflect a common social environment will be matched by differences, however, for some will be poor and others will be rich; some will raise children but others will not. Within any given society there is uniformity and variation in how we develop. The sociologist's task is to explain how the socialization process enables us to participate in social systems and yet also leads us along divergent paths as we become social actors. Many children play cops and robbers, but only some grow up to be cops, and some to be robbers—and most grow up to be neither.

Social life is a continuing process of interpreting perceptions and making choices in relation to other people. Babies cannot use symbols to order their world in terms of ideas, nor do they have a sense of themselves and their rights and obligations in relation to others. All of this must be learned by interacting with people who share their environments.

What and how we learn is what socialization is all about; and to see how this happens, we begin by critically examining a long-standing debate about human development and then explore theories about how people learn. This leads to a discussion of what

it takes to become a social being, and we end the chapter with a detailed look at the systems in which socialization occurs and how socialization continues throughout the life course.

GENES AND THE FALSE DEBATE OF "NATURE VERSUS NURTURE"

The development of a human embryo is guided by 46 chromosomes, which have roughly 100,000 parts (genes) whose arrangement provides information—just as the arrangement of dots and dashes of Morse code, representing letters of the alphabet, provides information. The genetic code determines characteristics such as the color of hair, as well as a variety of disorders—such as mental retardation—that interfere with learning (Suzuki, Griffiths, and Lewontin 1981). Genes also seem to affect IQ scores (Munsinger 1975), some personality traits (Wilson and Harpring 1972), and mental disorders such as schizophrenia (Vandenberg et al. 1986).

The most important effect of genes is not on *who* people become, but on *how* they develop. The noted linguist Noam Chomsky (1966), for example, believes that we are born with a "mechanism" that enables us to construct rules from the sentences we hear. When we begin to talk, we use these rules to create grammatically correct sentences. Genes also give us a voracious appetite for new information and experience. From infancy, we absorb knowledge like sponges, and yet—unlike sponges—we do not passively wait for something new to come along. We seem to be innately eager to interact with our environment, to sense as much as we can, and to act in ways that produce movement and change in our surroundings.

When scientists first raised questions about human development, they tended to take one of two extreme positions. Some believed that "nature" controlled every aspect of development—that behavior, feelings, and personality were dictated solely by genes (McDougall [1908] 1950). Others believed the opposite—that when exposed to the correct environment, infants could be molded through "nurture" to become any kind of person (Watson 1928). During the last 25 years, research in biology, psychology, and sociology has made it clear that both explanations are naive and that the "nature versus nurture" debate rests on the false assumption that nature and nurture operate independently of each other (see Reynolds 1980).

How, for example, do we explain the fact that dogs can see? The "nature" explanation is that they see because they have genes that result in eyes. But if we take a healthy puppy and raise it in total darkness, it will be utterly blind when full grown. The dog's genes gave it perfectly good eyes, but now it cannot see. If eyes are not exposed to light, they become useless. Is sight, then, simply a matter of the right genes? Apparently not. Is it simply a matter of environment? No again, for all the light in the world will not enable an eyeless dog to see. The answer lies in neither genes nor the environment, but in the *combination* of the two.

Most scientists no longer consider the issue of nature versus nurture to be a real debate (see Bleier 1984), but its importance extends far beyond science. As we will see in Chapters 13–15, the belief that biological factors cause social differences by race, gender, and age is often used to justify prejudice and discrimination. If, however, the subordinate position of groups, such as blacks, women, and the elderly, is produced by social systems, then prejudice and discrimination are *not* inevitable.

THE IMPORTANCE OF HUMAN CONTACT

Like the puppy, we cannot develop unless we are stimulated to use our abilities. Just as the eye needs light, infants require the stimulation of interaction with their surroundings in order to take shape as social beings. How often and in what ways people interact with us are characteristics of social relationships, in which contact plays an important part.

Although the skin is the largest human organ, it is only since the 1940s that scientists have begun to understand the importance of touch to human development (Montagu 1971). Touch, the most fundamental kind of contact, constitutes our earliest interaction with other people. In some cases, touch is the *only* way to communicate (recall the famous story of Helen Keller, who was born deaf and blind).

As important as physical contact is, it is language that lies at the heart of social life, and without interaction with others we cannot possibly acquire it. The more often children are spoken to and played with, the more rapidly they develop their mental abilities (Yarrow, Rubenstein, and Pedersen 1975). The importance of such contact is illustrated by documented cases of infants raised in isolation. In one case, a 6-year-old girl named Isabelle was discovered

Gestures and language enable us to reveal ourselves and discover others. The intensity and joy on this child's face reflect the importance of this interaction not only to socialization and social life, but to the lives of the participants.

in an attic in Ohio (Davis 1940, 1947). From birth her only human contact had been with her deaf and mute mother. When she was found, she could not talk; she could only make a croaking sound. Her performance on intelligence tests was so poor that researchers believed she would never be able to develop normally. After only a week of care and training, however, she began to talk, and within two years her speech was as fully developed as that of any normal 8-year-old.

In another case, a group of children were orphaned after the Nazis killed their parents during World War II. Hidden in attics and basements and moved every night, they had only one another for companions. When they were rescued at the end of the war, they were poorly developed mentally and physically, and their grasp of language was minimal (Freud and Dann 1951). As they became attached to their adult teachers, however, their language skills grew rapidly.

Itard ([1801] 1962) recorded some cases of children who were abandoned by parents and apparently grew up in the wild. The physical development of such feral children had usually progressed normally, but their behavior resembled that of a different species altogether: they showed no interest in what went on around them and sat in corners and rocked themselves back and forth, not unlike some zoo animals deprived of normal interaction with their kind (Benedict 1934).

The importance of interaction goes beyond normal physical and mental development, however, for in order to participate in social relationships we must feel open to contact with other people. Research suggests that the development of trust and responsiveness and, therefore, our attraction and responsiveness to other people, depend on the amount of nurturing contact we receive as infants. When the children who were hidden from the Nazis during World War II were rescued, they feared and resisted any contact with adults. Only later did they learn to trust and form attachments with teachers, explore their surroundings, and participate in relationships with new people.

SOME THEORIES ABOUT LEARNING

We are born with vast potential for experiencing ourselves and our surroundings, for using language and ideas to negotiate a complex world. Without social interaction, however, we are like the puppy raised in the dark or the child raised in the attic. It is through contact that we learn; but how? This section includes several answers to this question.

The Behavioral Approach

The **behaviorists'** approach to learning focuses on the observable things that people do, rather than on such unobservable things as what we think about what we do.

The psychologist B. F. Skinner (1938) put rats in cages equipped with a lever that, when pressed, released a small pellet of food. In their wanderings about the cage, the rats happened to press the bar and received a bit of food. Soon they pressed the bar as fast as they could eat the food. A simple principle emerged from such experiments: we tend to repeat behaviors that are rewarded. A related principle is that we tend to avoid behaviors that are punished.

The behavioral approach focuses on the effects of conditioning on behavior and attaches no importance to what people feel or think about what they do (Skinner 1981). Certainly no one would deny that the effects of reward and punishment are important. Students may pick courses they do not like (but that offer an easy A) or avoid courses that interest them (in fear of doing badly). We may avoid trying to make new friends because we have been punished with rejection in the past. If we grow up with parents who demand perfection in return for love, we may struggle to be perfect, believing that only then will people reward us with love.

However, the belief that all behavior is shaped by conditioning is not supported by the evidence of science or everyday experience (see Zuriff 1985). The complex behavior of 250 million people in the U.S. is certainly not due to monitoring of behavior and the delivery of rewards and punishments. Although punishment is effective with young children, its effectiveness among older children and adults is very limited (Kagan and Havemann 1980). There is still considerable disagreement about the effectiveness of capital punishment as a deterrent to crime, for example, and punishing older children or adults often results in rebellion, not obedience. If punishment is often ineffective among adults, then reward is the only explanation offered by the behavioral perspective; yet much of our behavior is never rewarded by others.

In addition, behaviorism cannot explain our ability to make choices based on abstract ideas such as moral codes. A bomber pilot who disobeys an order to destroy a village because he believes it contains only innocent civilians can expect to be punished. Unless we assume that the pilot experiences punishment as a reward, it is difficult to explain his decision from a behavioral point of view.

Much of our behavior is learned without reward or punishment. Children often copy the behavior of people they admire even when they are told not to. In short, we often imitate **models**.

Models and Social Learning

The realization that much learning takes place in the absence of rewards and punishments led to the development of the **social learning perspective**, which focuses on the way we select models whom we then imitate (Bandura 1977). Children, for example, often use sexual words years before they have any no-

Our need to feel we belong to the social world is so strong that we will identify with and imitate behavior long before we are able to understand it fully. These boys in war-torn Beirut, Lebanon, are learning through play a way of life that they may very well help perpetuate as adults.

tion of what the words mean. In the same way, they may imitate parents who use racial or ethnic slurs long before they understand what they are saying.

Most studies conclude that we choose models who are "attractive"; and, during early childhood, attractiveness appears to be mostly a matter of power. We imitate those who appear to control events and other people: young girls and boys tend to imitate the parent who dominates the family, regardless of that parent's gender (Williams 1987).

Neither the behavioral nor the social learning perspectives includes people's thoughts and feelings in explanations of behavior; and neither can explain behavior that appears when there is no model present. The bomber pilot had no disobedient model to imitate. He made a difficult moral decision, weighing what others expected of him against his own moral values about duty and the sanctity of life.

If 3-year-old children were confronted with a moral dilemma, however, they would have little idea of what to do, for moral values mean little if anything to them. At that age, moreover, they are incapable of learning how to make such judgments, regardless of the availability of models or the influence of punishments or rewards.

How is it, then, that adults can make complex judgments and children cannot, regardless of learning opportunities? One answer comes from the **cognitive development perspective**, which focuses on the growth of our mental abilities to make complex judgments about ourselves as well as our environments.

Learning to Think

A one-year-old girl sits on the floor next to her father, who holds out a toy. As she reaches for it, he slowly hides it behind his back, letting her see exactly where he puts it. She wants the toy, but shows no sign that she knows where it is. Even though she saw where he hid it, she acts as though it no longer exists.

A 5-year-old boy sits in front of two sets of ten coins spread out on a table. If asked, "Which group has more coins?" he will reply, "They're the same." If we then stack one group into a column, he will probably say that the stacked group has more coins than the one still spread out on the table. By the age of 8, however, most children will know that the number of coins in each group remains the same no matter how we arrange them.

These kinds of observations led the Swiss psychologist Jean Piaget to argue that children's mental development passes through stages, each bringing with it greater abilities to process information and make judgments. The ages that define each stage are approximate, and children often progress from one stage to another at differing rates (Piaget and Inhelder 1969).

Between the ages of 2 and 7, for example, they can use symbols to label things ("this is a jelly bean"), but they cannot use concepts to express the relation of one thing to another. If I hold up a bag of jelly beans and say to a 4-year-old boy, "There are ten jelly beans in this bag"; then hold up a second bag and say, "This one has just as many beans as the first"; then a third bag, saying "This one has just as many as the second bag," he will not know how many beans are in the third bag, because he cannot yet think in terms of the relationship among the bags.

It is not until about age 12 that children begin to develop the ability to use rules to solve abstract problems. If we play the game Twenty Questions, and I say, "I'm thinking of an animal," a child in this stage is likely to make an immediate random guess—"A cow!"—whereas an adolescent will approach the problem more efficiently and systematically, asking, for example, "Does it have four legs?"

Like the behavioral and social learning perspectives, the cognitive point of view tends to ignore the fact that the decisions and judgments made by people depend on the ideas they acquire about themselves and others. Learning to be a social actor involves more than seeking reward, avoiding punishment, or copying those around us; and it involves more than the ability to think. The disobedient pilot was not imitating a model or seeking rewards; nor did he make his decision simply because his level of cognitive development enabled him to make a moral decision. He oriented himself to a third source of motivation and guidance: his ideas about himself and his relationships with other people. As a social process, socialization depends on the social contexts in which we learn, develop, and behave over the course of our lives.

BECOMING SOCIAL ACTORS

The seventeenth-century philosopher John Locke believed that infants come into the world knowing nothing at all: their minds are a *tabula rasa*, or "blank slate" on which others "write" the sum total of children's knowledge as they mature. Recent research, however, suggests that infants know more than we might think they do. In one study, 3-month-old infants watched videotapes of a woman reciting nursery rhymes. In the first tape she read the rhyme normally, but in succeeding tapes the voice did not match the movement of her lips. In the distorted versions, infants were more easily distracted and lost interest in the rhymes. By 3 months of age, infants are already aware of the relationship between the human voice and face. As one of the researchers concluded, the research of the last two decades "shows that the infant, instead of being a blooming mass of confusion . . . is a very complex creature who is capa-

ble of thinking, feeling, and processing enormous amounts of information about the world" (Michael Lewis, in Rubin 1982).

Locke's view that infants' minds are a blank slate is correct in a very important sociological sense, however, for they cannot use symbols. They do not have to be taught to withdraw their fingers from a hot flame and cry in pain, but they do have to learn the idea of "hot" so that if someone says, "Don't touch that; it's hot!" they can avoid being burned. Although we are born with some basic drives and reflexes, we are unable to make a connection between abstract ideas and actual experience.

Locke was also correct in the sense that infants have no idea of social relationships and the expectations that govern them. They certainly experience themselves and others—feeling their own hunger and the smell, touch, and taste of their mother's breast—but without words they cannot have an *idea* of themselves or of others. They cannot think about what ought to happen or what they ought to do, about what is "right" and what is "wrong," about which goals are worthy and desirable and which are not. They may love to play with their food, but only later will they learn if this is defined as bad manners in their culture. In short, infants are unaware of social systems. Their awareness grows, however, at an astonishing rate, and the key to this process is language.

Language

A one-year-old girl sits on a kitchen floor and watches her father put the groceries away. He reaches into a box of cookies and holds one out to her. Her face lights up and she reaches for it, but he holds it back. "Cookie," he says, and she reaches harder. "*Cookie*," he says again, and then gives it to her. Later he gives her another, but only after getting her attention and repeating the word "cookie." Later still, while he sits and reads, a seemingly small event occurs. She crawls to his chair, hauls herself up, tilts her head to get his attention, and says, "cookie!"

This event is in fact tremendous, for it marks the beginning of a revolution in the child's relationship to the social world. The cookie is no longer simply an object: it is represented by a symbol that she can use to affect other people. No longer does she have to cry until an adult figures out what it is she wants: now she can *tell* them. The word is a bridge between her desire and its satisfaction, and in the words of the sociologist Charles Horton Cooley ([1902] 1974), she has "tasted the joy of being a cause, of exerting social power."

Just as she uses symbols to affect others, so can others use them to affect her, and once the meaning of a word is shared between them, life will never be the same. Consider another scene: she stands next to a flower pot, rocking it back and forth on the table. Suddenly she is startled by her father: "No," he says. She turns to the sound and sees a stern look on his face. She looks at him for a moment, then rocks the pot one more time, and it falls to the floor and crashes in a heap. Suddenly she feels a painful spank on her behind and hears that sound again—"No!"

The word "no" is no longer simply a sound; it is a sound the child associates with anger, fear, and pain. If she stops what she is doing, no anger or pain follows; if she continues, the unpleasant experience is repeated. From this she learns that the word is related to both her behavior and the speaker's; *it is a bridge of meaning between them.*

One word begets others, and words are the building blocks of cultural ideas which are part of social systems. Just as the little girl learns the names of objects, so too does she learn to name herself and others. This is of enormous importance, for the act of naming is more than mere pointing: "to tell what a thing is, you place it in terms of something else. . . . To *define* a thing is to mark its boundaries" (Burke 1945). Language ties us to a world of meaning and social expectations, boundaries that both require and enable us to participate in social life.

Cultural Ideas

With language, children acquire beliefs ("There is a God"; "Santa Claus comes at Christmas"; "What goes up must come down") and use them to interpret the world. We allow young children to believe in magic, ghosts, and goblins, but require older children to give up such beliefs. Adults cannot prove that goblins do not exist; they can only assert the belief with words. In order to belong to the adult world around them, children must literally change their beliefs about what is real.

Language is also the medium through which children learn values, norms, and attitudes. The value that "it is better to give than to receive" flies in the face of infantile desires to take in as much as they can and hold on tightly to what they have; they literally must learn to give, and they must learn to support

such acts as "good." There is nothing "natural" about eating with silverware (fingers are often more efficient) or defecating and urinating in a toilet, and yet children in Western societies learn that adults expect such behavior. There is also nothing inherent in skin color that would lead children to despise people of different races, nor anything inherent in age that would cause them to despise and fear or to revere the elderly. Like other cultural ideas, attitudes are social creations that are expressed and learned through the use of symbols.

It is important to emphasize that socialization is not a uniform experience for everyone. Although a culture may contain ideas about what everyone should become—honest, for example—it also includes ideas that make distinctions among people who occupy different statuses. When Bem and Bem (1976) asked adults to predict what a newborn boy would be doing as an adult, it was difficult for respondents to answer the question, because they could imagine many possibilities for him. When asked the same question about a girl, however, respondents tended to predict readily that she would be a wife and mother and that these would be her most important roles in life.

Variations also occur because in most societies children are exposed only to portions of the surrounding culture. In a small Vermont town, children might never encounter a black or Asian person, and might have little sense of what racism is. The children of professional parents are unlikely to consider coal mining as an occupation, whereas the children of coal miners may imagine nothing else. Because our statuses are points of view from which we perceive society, they influence our exposure to its cultural and structural characteristics.

It is inaccurate to think of complex societies as having a single, universal culture. Although some cultural ideas apply to everyone—laws and a common language—many exist only in subcultures. Russian is the official language of the Soviet Union, but that country includes many different peoples speaking scores of languages that reflect sharp cultural differences. Similarly, walking through Chinatown in San Francisco, a Mexican neighborhood in San Antonio, New York City's Harlem, or the Italian section of Boston makes it clear that although all are located in the U.S., they represent subcultures that foster striking differences in social life.

Whatever culture or subculture we are exposed to, one aspect of socialization is universal: children

In large complex societies, socialization cannot be a uniform experience. Among the Amish in Lancaster County, Pennsylvania, children are raised to reject most of what people take for granted in the surrounding society—from politics, science, and electricity to colorful clothing, rock music, cars, alcohol, and movies.

learn that their bodies and experiences do not belong solely to themselves, that there is an expanding world of others who express active interest in what they feel, think, and do. Awareness of other people is perhaps the most fundamental element of socialization, for it underlies the discovery of ourselves and others as participants in social life.

Socialization, Social Structure, and the Self

At the heart of socialization is the growing awareness that the social world involves more than our own experiences, desires, and needs. Infants are totally absorbed in themselves and their needs experienced through their senses, through hunger and thirst, pain and comfort, cold and warmth, loneliness and contact; but society is more than individuals who act, feel, and think. The core of social life is a complex set of relationships among individual selves, and before children can participate fully they must acquire an awareness of themselves in relation to others.

To the symbolic interactionist sociologist George Herbert Mead (1934) socialization depends more than anything else on the process through which we use *symbols* to discover both other people and ourselves and thereby learn to participate in the social world.

"I," "Me," "Others," and "Mind"   As an illustration of Mead's point of view consider anger, which as an emotion is invisible to others. We may feel enraged, and yet present ourselves to other people as contented and calm. We may even hide the truth of our anger from ourselves. When we make an angry face, shake our fist, and say, "Damn it, I'm mad!" we are using gestures and language to communicate otherwise invisible feelings.

Children fear adult anger and may learn to avoid provoking it, but cats and dogs are fully capable of the same kind of learning. It is when children learn to *label* another's feelings, expectations, and actions that they take a crucial step toward full participation in social life. Angry words represent feelings; behind the angry words are selves who think, feel, and act both in relation to themselves and to others. Without symbols, however, infants cannot know that people have points of view; that they think, feel, and make decisions. This is of enormous importance, for "being unaware of other points of view, they are necessarily unaware of their own—as a point of view. It simply is the way things are" (Brown 1965, p. 220).

When infants are punished, they learn to use the word "angry" to label a person's response. The label marks an important transition because they can apply it to their own feelings as well. Now when someone says, "I'm angry," children know how the speaker feels. Something familiar to them is going on behind the words, in another person. To understand such statements, children must look at their own behavior from another person's point of view. In this way, *they discover themselves through their discovery of others*.

Mead (1934) developed the sociological concept of **mind** to describe this ability to "put ourselves in another's place," to take the role of another person and imagine different possible responses. Mind is the ability to use symbols in order to be aware of other people's feelings, thoughts, and expectations, and we develop mind by using language. Children begin their lives without this awareness, for without symbols they experience the world directly through their senses: things are what they appear to be, not what they mean. Mead identified this "self"—this direct experience of ourselves and others—as "**I**." "I" is that part of us that feels hunger, satiation, pain, frustration, joy, ecstasy, and desire.

As children acquire language, they learn that they live in a social system in which people share ideas about themselves, the world, and their relationships with one another. In this way, Mead believed, children learn to look upon themselves as others look upon them, to view themselves and their behavior from other people's points of view. This transition can be seen in small children when they respond to themselves just as their parents respond to them. When children learn "no," for example, they often apply it to themselves: it is not uncommon to hear them say "no" to themselves as they are about to do something they should not, or to scold themselves after the fact ("bad boy"). Who are these "selves" who scold and say "no" to themselves?

To Mead, the impulse to "knock that thing over and see what happens," comes from the "I"; but the interior voice that says "no" is enormously important to their social development, because it shows that *they have a point of view on their own behavior*. Language enables us to talk to ourselves, to conduct internal conversations in which one part of us looks at "I," interpreting its desires, needs, feelings, and behavior in terms of cultural ideas. Mead identified this voice as the "**me**."

Although we are all born with an "I," our "me" arises *only* from social interaction, for the "me" is that part of ourselves capable of viewing ourselves and our behavior as if we were another person. Without language, Mead asserts, the "me" cannot develop, for it is the medium through which we share our different points of view with one another.

Mead uses the example of a game to demonstrate his concepts of "I," "me," and "mind." When several infants play in the same room, they pay very little attention to one another. They may struggle over possession of a toy, but they do not orient themselves to one another's expectations, for without symbols and ideas they can have no expectations. They are "parallel playing"—alongside one another but not *with* one another.

The first step away from parallel play comes when children use language to pay attention to the expectations of particular people, such as a parent. When a little girl's "I" is tempted to grab every toy in the room, her "me" may say, "I'd better share them with my brother, because if I don't, mommy will get angry." In this case, she is orienting herself to the expectations of what psychiatrist Harry Stack Sullivan called a **significant other**—a particular person whose expectations we pay attention to. She is not yet playing a role, because she has no awareness that she occupies the status of "playmate" and that sharing toys is an expectation of playmates in her culture.

To learn a game such as baseball, she must orient herself not to the expectations of significant others, but to an abstract set of rules that describe the relationships among the players, telling them who does what in each situation. If she fields a hit while George is playing first base and the bases are empty, she does not base her decision to throw the ball to him on her personal knowledge of what he wants her to do. She throws it to him because that is what someone occupying the status "fielder" does in that situation regardless of who is playing each position. The person playing first base may be a stranger to her, yet she still knows when to throw the ball to first and when not to.

In a game, players orient themselves less to the expectations of significant others than to what they believe are the expectations shared by players in general. They orient themselves to what Mead (1934) called the **generalized other**, which is our perception of the social environment itself, including both the

statuses and roles that make up social systems in which we participate. The generalized other is important because it is our only source of knowledge about a social system in which we have no specific knowledge of the people who are involved. When we travel in a bus, buy something in a store, or go to the movies, we have no personal knowledge of what other individuals in the crowd expect of us. Instead, we rely on social knowledge of what people *in general* expect of people who occupy such statuses; and our perception of these expectations *is* the generalized other.

When children learn to orient themselves to the generalized other in a game, they take a crucial step toward fully social behavior, for in order to know what to do in each situation, players must put themselves in the place of anyone playing each of the other positions. They must, in short, learn to play roles in relation to role partners in social relationships.

Statuses and Roles   As children develop an awareness of themselves and others, they learn that their experience and behavior take place in the social context of statuses and roles that affect people's expectations, including their own. The adults who take care of them are mothers or fathers, wives or husbands, employees or bosses. As children begin to understand their positions in a family, they discover that siblings, mothers, and fathers have expectations and obligations that differ from those of casual playmates, aunts, uncles, grandparents, and total strangers. Although their parents have the legal right to

hit them, other adults do not; and even parents do not have the right to physically injure them. When children are told never to go anywhere with a stranger, they learn to make distinctions among people according to their social relationship with them. They learn that their alternatives depend on the situation, not merely on their impulses (such as to accept candy offered by a stranger). They are learning about the structural basics of social life, to choose among alternatives according to the statuses they occupy.

As early as the fourth year, children in the U.S. become aware of racial differences (Ambron 1978); and they can identify their own gender by age 3. As children label themselves and others in terms of statuses such as gender, race, ethnicity, social class, age, and family position, they learn to categorize people just as they learn to distinguish rocks from plants and night from day. There is much more involved, however, for cultures attach ideas to each status and its occupant. By locating themselves structurally in social systems, children learn "who they are" in the eyes of those who share their culture, how they are valued, how people feel about them, and what their rights and obligations are in relation to others. They are developing ideas about themselves that will become major parts of their *social* selves.

Self-Concepts and Self-Esteem

We experience the world largely through our senses until we learn to use language. With language we construct ideas, and just as we have ideas about ob-

In the pictures on the opposite page, the children differ in their shared focus of activity and in their taking of roles in relation to one another. In which situation are the children being affected by a generalized other? How can you tell?

jects outside us, so we have ideas about ourselves. Taken together, they form a **self-concept**, the sum total of our beliefs and feelings about ourselves (Gecas 1982; Rosenberg 1979, 1981; Rosenberg and Kaplan 1982).

Self-concepts are a curious phenomenon. When I describe myself, the object of my attention is "me"—myself. If I say, "I am a good dancer," I describe myself just as I might describe someone else. We use symbols to split ourselves into subject and object (Aboulafia 1986; Mead 1934), to feel love and hate, respect and contempt, tenderness and rage for ourselves, and to hold beliefs about ourselves that may or may not be true—that we are God or Wonder Woman, or that we cannot possibly understand calculus. Unlike ideas we have about objects outside ourselves, the self-concept is important to everyone because we bring it to almost every experience.

Self-concepts are rarely simple or objective, for they include evaluations of who we are, and emotions such as pride, contentment, and shame. Self-concepts are also difficult to confirm as true. We may believe that we are intelligent and place a great deal of importance on that image of ourselves, but we are continually vulnerable to evidence to the contrary. Self-concepts are fragile, and given their importance to us, they can produce considerable anxiety.

The Self in Social Mirrors Where do self-concepts come from? Imagine Victor meeting Teresa on their first date. In such a situation, Cooley (1927) argued, we have:

1. The real Victor, known to no one.
2. Victor's idea of himself, such as "I look terrific in this new shirt."
3. Victor's idea of Teresa's idea of him, such as "She thinks I look great."
4. Victor's idea of what Teresa thinks he thinks of himself, such as "Teresa thinks I think I look terrific."

5. Teresa's idea of what Victor thinks of himself, such as "Victor thinks he's something else."
6. What Teresa really thinks about how Victor looks, such as "That's the worst shirt I ever saw."

And of course six analogous phrases that apply to Teresa.

In the simplest interaction, we use each other as mirrors, both casting another's reflection and looking for our own. Like the Queen in "Snow White," who chants "Mirror, mirror on the wall, who is fairest of us all?" we look to others for confirmation of who we think we are. Social relationships are "an interweaving and interworking of mental selves" (Cooley [1902] 1964): Victor imagines Teresa's mind, especially what she thinks about him. Unlike a mirror, however, we do not simply reflect each other; we evaluate and judge the selves we encounter, and those judgments are part of the reflection.

We all have ideas about how good-looking we are, for example, and they do not come simply from looking in a mirror on the wall. If we think others see us as plain, we tend to think of ourselves as plain (until, perhaps, we meet someone who thinks we are beautiful). Whether or not others consider us beautiful depends in part on our culture, for each culture has its own standards for beauty. Like beauty, many aspects of ourselves exist in the eye of the beholder, and each beholder is influenced by culture. Because we depend on other people's perceptions of us in order to see and evaluate ourselves, we tend to perceive ourselves as we believe others perceive and define us (Mead 1934; Shrauger and Schoeneman 1979).

When we imagine how others perceive and feel about us, we are constructing what Cooley (1927) called the **looking-glass self**. The looking-glass self is not who we actually are; nor is it how other people actually perceive us. Rather, it is our perception of how other people see us. A few studies show that we tend to see ourselves as others actually see us (Rosenberg 1979), but most show relatively little correspondence between our self-concepts and how we are perceived by others (Gecas 1982). The strongest relationship is between how we see ourselves and our *perception* of how others see us—our looking-glass self.

In many cases, we form a looking-glass self by using significant others as mirrors; but we also use perceptions of how the generalized other portrays us according to our statuses. Presidents are expected to be "presidential"—decisive, courageous, and "in charge" of the nation's affairs. Vice-presidents, on

Which of these women from Sweden, Taiwan, and Kenya is most beautiful to you? Which is least beautiful? How do you explain your preferences?

What standards do you use to judge how you see? Where do they come from, and how do they affect how you feel about yourself?

the other hand, are generally invisible—little if any real leadership is expected of them and they take a "back seat." When vice-presidents suddenly become presidents—as Harry Truman and Lyndon Johnson did when Presidents Roosevelt and Kennedy died—they often surprise the public by "rising to the occasion" and displaying leadership abilities that no one thought they had. In many cases, rising to the occasion is a matter of looking at ourselves in a different mirror. When Harry Truman succeeded to the presidency, he was suddenly seen by other people as the president, and so he *became* the president.

Social Identities   From a sociological point of view, the most important parts of a self-concept are those that reflect our status sets. As we develop a generalized other and learn the cultural ideas associated with statuses, we use those ideas to describe ourselves not only to other people, but to ourselves as well (see Thoits 1985). This social component of the self-concept is our **social identity** (Rosenberg 1979; Stryker 1981).

All cultures include categories that make distinctions such as "living" and "dead," "animal" and "mineral," "good" and "bad"; and at the moment of birth, children enter a variety of such categories. In Western societies, infants are described in terms of gender, race, age, nationality, and social class. Al-

though such statuses have no meaning to infants, they do influence how others perceive them. A male Irish Catholic newborn living in Belfast, Northern Ireland, cannot know that members of society will tend to have differing expectations of him, his sister, and a male Irish Protestant newborn living across town, but as he matures and participates in the life of his society, he is likely to use such external ideas about him as he forms his own ideas about himself.

Children expand their social identities by joining groups formed around shared interests or beliefs. Religious beliefs or interest in sports take on new meaning as children define themselves in terms of group membership. "I play baseball" becomes "I'm a Yankee in the Little League"; "I go to school" becomes "I'm a third-grader"; "I believe in Muhammad" becomes "I am a Muslim."

Social identities are also based on behavior. A child who steals may be labeled a "thief," a girl who is obedient and kind a "good girl," a boy who likes poetry a "sissy," a brilliant student a "genius," and a struggling one a "dummy." Thus, what we do may become an important part of who we think we are, and this, in turn, will influence our behavior and feelings. A child who accepts the label of "dummy" may give up in school, whereas a "genius" may feel the pressure to live up to extraordinary, if not impossible, expectations.

In forming identities we also draw upon an enormous number of psychological traits such as "generous," "aggressive," or "shy"—just a few examples of the more than 12,000 English words and phrases that describe such characteristics (Gordon 1976). Although we tend to think of such traits as personal, they often come from the roles attached to statuses. "Nurturant" mothers, "serious" bankers, and "scholarly" professors tend to be seen according to the expectations attached to their roles, often regardless of behavior and feelings to the contrary.

Although statuses, behavior, and psychological traits refer directly to individual characteristics, culture often extends the boundaries of social identities to include possessions and other people (Cooley [1902] 1964). When people talk about the things they own, they often reveal that these form an important part of their sense of who they are (Csikszentmihalyi and Rochberg-Halton 1981). Some people value expensive cars because they believe others will see them as rich and sophisticated. This principle also extends to people: when children taunt one another by saying, "Your mother has a mustache," it is clear to all involved that the attack is on the child, not the mother.

The most stable parts of our identities are those that other people will confirm, and for this reason, when we describe ourselves, we tend to focus on our status sets. When Kuhn and McPartland (1954) asked people to answer the question, "Who am I?" with 20 words or phrases, their first answers most often referred to their social identities: "Mary Callahan, woman, graduate student, daughter, sister." Only after exhausting social categories did they describe themselves in terms of *personality*—the complex patterns of thought, feeling, and behavior that make each of us unique. Thus, in important ways, we know ourselves as we are known by others, and the vast majority of people know us only through our positions in relationships with them. If someone points to your sister and asks, "Who is she?" your first response will be, "She is my sister," indicating not what makes her a unique self, but her structural position in relation to you.

The last part of our social identity that distinguishes us as unique individuals is our name and, in complex societies, our numbers: social security, driver's license, credit cards. Although it may seem strange—if not offensive—to suggest that names and numbers are all that socially define us as individuals, it is important to remember that other people cannot possibly know the combination of characteristics (many of which are invisible) that presumably make each of our selves unique. I could describe a man's personality in the most minute detail, and yet you could not be certain that you knew him until I told you his name.

Social identities are powerful because we have little control over them. We can hide some statuses (if we lie about our education on a job application), but in many cases we cannot. Race, age, and gender are visible statuses, and we are severely limited in how much personal control we can exert over how other people perceive and respond to us as "white," "black," "woman," or "man."

By giving us a sense of who we are, social identities are like anchors that hold us in the world by connecting us to other people. This is never more apparent than when social identities are disturbed, especially when people do not confirm that we are who we think we are. When we lose important parts of our identities—by being expelled from school, fired from a job, or losing a spouse—we often feel a sense of nonexistence, as if we had been cut loose and were drifting aimlessly through the world, and in a social sense this is true. We still are who we are as individuals, but our social ties have been severely damaged, and until they are replaced or repaired, there is a feeling of loss, sadness, and disorientation.

Social identities, then, are the basis of our participation in social systems, our feelings of belonging and being known by others. There is more to self-concepts, however, for identities indicate not only who we are, but who we *ought* to be as well. (In light of what you have now learned about social identities, look back at Chapter 1, pp. 15–16, and make a new self-survey of who you are.)

Ideals, Self-Esteem, and Reference Groups

When children are asked, "What do you want to be when you grow up?" their first answers tend to follow individual interests—to ride fire engines or dance in the ballet; but they soon learn that there is more involved than what appeals to them. In the U.S., we share the value that it is better to be a lawyer, doctor, engineer, or business executive than to be a firefighter, coal miner, or carpenter, and children draw upon such values to construct an **ideal self**.

In an important sense, culture is "the stuff that dreams are made of," dreams that become parts of self-concepts: "I am not only a little girl who writes stories; I am a girl who will someday be a great writer." Such images are important not only as descriptions of ourselves that we use as maps to guide our way into adulthood, but also as sources of **self-esteem**—the positive and negative feelings we have about ourselves (Rosenberg 1979). Feelings such as pride and shame, or confidence and insecurity all reflect different levels of self-esteem.

As children identify their places in social systems, they learn that cultural values rank some statuses higher than others. In the U.S., they may learn that white is valued above nonwhite; male above female; intellectual labor above manual labor; and young above old. We rarely describe anything without passing judgment on it: "kind," "intelligent," and "beautiful" are not simply different from "cruel," "stupid," and "ugly"; they are culturally ranked as better. When self-concepts correspond to culturally valued identities, we tend to feel good about ourselves, and if they do not, our self-esteem suffers, sometimes to the point of being stigmatized by negative labels such as "alcoholic," "mental patient," "thief," or "bum" (Goffman 1963b; Snow and Anderson 1987).

Through socialization, we use values to create an ideal self and to make judgments about ourselves. We also compare ourselves to **reference individuals** and **reference groups**, which we use as models of desirable or undesirable appearance or behavior (Hyman and Singer 1968; Singer 1981). Some research suggests that when political and entertainment celebrities commit suicide, extensive media coverage leads to higher suicide rates in the population at large. That celebrities who kill themselves may act as reference individuals can be seen in the fact that with extensive coverage of a *foreign* celebrity—with whom people are less likely to identify—suicide has no effect on domestic suicide rates (Stack 1987).

We select reference individuals because we want to be like them or because we want to be *un*like them. Children often say they want to be like their mothers or fathers when they grow up, and evaluate themselves according to their parents' values. As adolescents, however, they often select new reference individuals—from professional athletes and rock musicians to teachers and famous writers—and this may involve a rejection of parental values. In this sense, a punk-rock musician replaces a parent as a positive reference individual, and parents become negative reference individuals.

We also use reference groups to evaluate ourselves. Students who are at the top of their high school senior class often find that they are no longer

As the great popularity of the cartoon character, Bart Simpson shows, young people sometimes choose reference individuals who openly violate the standards set by parents, teachers, and other adults.

at the top in college, and may as a result feel they are not as capable as they thought they were. Their self-concept may change not because they have changed, but because they have adopted a new reference group.

We do not actually have to belong to a reference group in order to use it to evaluate ourselves. For many people the Ku Klux Klan is an example of racism at its worst, and, as a negative reference group, it gives them a point of comparison for favorably evaluating their own racial attitudes. That we can use reference groups without being members is important for four reasons. First, it explains why we so often differ from the groups to which we do belong. The children of immigrant families may never learn their native language, because—as they aspire to become members of the surrounding society—they choose a reference group whose language differs from that of their parents.

Second, because we do not need to belong to reference groups, we can have more than one, and this contributes to conflicting self-evaluations. Lesbians may feel good about themselves when they use other lesbians as a reference group, but feel bad about themselves if they use coworkers who disapprove of homosexuality.

Third, the concept of reference groups helps explain why people begin to change their attitudes *in anticipation* of joining a group. This is called **anticipatory socialization** (Merton and Rossi 1968), and it plays an important part in learning roles. When children try to act grown up, they are using adults as a reference group long before they become adults themselves. Graduate students typically evaluate themselves in terms of the professional group they are preparing to join. A great deal of socialization, both among children and adults, is anticipatory, because we are learning about roles we do not yet perform.

Finally, reference groups affect which parts of our identities we are most aware of and care the most about. Most characteristics have meaning only in comparison with other characteristics: the idea of "female," for example, has no meaning without the idea of "male." To identify ourselves as "female," "black," or "heterosexual," we must have some point of comparison—such as those who are male, white, or homosexual. Without an awareness of people with contrasting characteristics, we have no reason to attach any special significance to our own.

This can be seen in the results of a study in which 500 high school students were asked to spend five minutes talking about themselves, saying anything that came to mind. Only one percent of the white students mentioned their race, whereas 17 percent of the blacks and 14 percent of the Hispanics mentioned theirs. Why the difference? The study was conducted in a school in which 83 percent of the students were English-speaking whites; only 9 percent were black and 8 percent were Hispanic. As far as racial identity was concerned, dominant whites compared themselves with students of their own race, whereas many of the visible minority of non-white students compared themselves with members of the dominant group and were thus more likely to be aware of their racial status (McGuire et al. 1978).

If we are unhappy with how we compare with reference individuals or groups, we can change our identities by acquiring new statuses that have higher cultural value—getting a better job or going to college—or by concealing characteristics that lower our self-esteem. We can also choose (or create) new reference groups. When lesbians or blacks separate themselves from society, they are trying to create reference groups in which "lesbian" and "black" are highly valued characteristics.

Another way to narrow the gap between who we think we are and who we want to be is to lower our commitment to various parts of our ideal self. This changes not the content of our self-concept, but its structure, rearranging characteristics in terms of their importance to us. We all have fantasies about who we might be, and so long as they are mere fantasies they do not threaten our self-esteem. Most of us spend our lives performing quite ordinary roles, and we protect ourselves when we say, "Sure, I'd like to be rich and famous, but I can live without it."

The most radical social solution to low self-esteem is not to change from one reference group to another, but to change the reference group itself. This is a major goal of many social movements such as the women's, civil rights, gay rights, and senior citizen movements. When blacks proclaim to a white-dominated society that "black is beautiful" or when feminist artists write song lyrics that celebrate being female, they are supporting their own self-esteem and sending a message to the surrounding society, exerting pressure for change in the prevailing value system. The goal is to create a culture in which people can participate fully and openly and have high self-esteem.

SOCIALIZATION AND THE LIFE COURSE

The fact that we adopt many different reference groups during our lives highlights an important fact about socialization: childhood may be the most intense learning period of our lives, but socialization does not end when we reach adulthood. Socialization takes place over the course of our entire lives, and is affected by major social institutions including the family, schools, the mass media, and the economy (see Part Five). We repeatedly discard old roles and learn new ones, and as our reference groups change, so do our perceptions and evaluations of who we are (Bush and Simmons 1981; Gecas 1981).

Rites of Passage

Because people's rights and responsibilities depend not on who they are apart from their social identities, control of the statuses people claim to occupy is important in all societies. In order to legitimately assume the status of "college graduate" or "married," for example, we must participate in cultural ceremonies that mark our movement from one status to another. These **rites of passage** are a form of social control over the boundaries of social statuses (Van Gennep [1909] 1960).

The passage from childhood to adulthood is perhaps the most universally important transition, for

PUZZLE

ARE YOU
A
CHILD OR
AN ADULT?

How do you know that you are one and not the other? What about other people—do they always agree that you are what you think you are? If not, why?

As you will see in this chapter and again in Chapter 15, age is more than a matter of time. It is one of the most significant and universally recognized of all social statuses. That is why it is so important that we know which age group we are in and why being unsure can generate so much anxiety.

adulthood brings with it social power. In all societies people are children until they are culturally defined as adults, and this may take place long after they are physically mature. In some societies the rite of passage from childhood to adulthood is well defined, involving, for example, a ceremony in which the child's genitals are mutilated (Van Gennep [1909] 1960). Among the Masai of Kenya, young males must live in isolation in the bush country and wrestle with and kill lions in order to demonstrate the bravery necessary to attain full adult male standing. In others, such as the U.S., the rites are more ambiguous: in most states young men and women are allowed to marry and have children before they are old enough to vote or purchase liquor. Although the law defines adulthood in terms of age, simply reaching the age of 18 or 21 does not necessarily lead others to treat us as adults. The important thing in the social world is not so much who we really are, but who other people think we are.

Socialization in Families

One of the primary functions of the family as an institution is to socialize children. How children are socialized as family members depends on the reference groups and individuals that parents orient themselves to (such as their own parents, their social class, or their ethnic subculture), and the structure of family relationships.

As they raise their children, lower-class parents generally value obedience to authority, neatness, cleanliness, and staying out of trouble more than middle-class parents do. Middle-class parents in a variety of societies are more likely to stress creativity, self-discipline, ambition, independence, curiosity, and self-direction (Ellis et al. 1978; Kohn 1977; Slomczynski et al. 1981). Although lower-class parents tend to evaluate their children's behavior primarily in terms of its positive or negative consequences, middle-class parents tend to pay more attention to their children's intentions (Wright and Wright 1976). Class differences in family values produce differences in the methods parents use to socialize children. Lower-class parents who value obedience are more likely than middle-class parents to use physical punishment. Middle-class parents rely more on reasoning, guilt, and threatened loss of love to control their children (Maccoby and Martin 1983; Wright and Wright 1976).

Class differences in child-rearing values do not occur simply by accident. Lower-class children can eventually expect to depend on the kinds of jobs that require them to follow orders rather than make independent judgments, and they are much less likely to have advanced educations that lead to higher responsibilities within a given occupation. Middle-class children, on the other hand, are more likely to become professionals, managers, and administrators when they join the work force. Parents tend to pass on to their children the outlooks that are suited to their own experience in the world. A study of 122 cultures found, for example, that the more parents are supervised in their lives the more they tend to stress obedience and conformity in their children (Ellis et al. 1978).

While one might think that being born into the upper class would make for easy childhoods, the truth is sometimes quite different (see Cookson and Persell 1986). Unlike other classes, the upper class has a strong class identity organized around protecting its privileged status, and the family is a key institution used to maintain that position. Because of this the socialization of upper-class children often involves greater restrictions than are applied to children in the middle, working, and lower classes. Children are often sent away from home to private boarding schools that are typically sex-segregated. Here they acquire not only academic knowledge, but a sense of themselves as members of a privileged elite (Cookson and Persell 1985). Their daily schedules

ONE STEP FURTHER 7-1

Social Class, Race, and Who We Want Our Children to Be

The percentages in Table B-7-1 give a detailed picture of how child-rearing values vary among adults with different social statuses related to class and race. Each column represents a value measured by asking, "Which *three* qualities listed on this card would you say are the *most desirable* for a child to have?" The columns show the percentage of adults in each category—income, education, occupation, and race—who named each quality as one of the three most important.

There are a lot of numbers here, but if you follow them carefully it should all become clear. Column I shows percentages who mentioned "has good sense and sound judgment" as an important quality. If you look down the first column, you will see that the percentage increases as we go from lower to higher income, education, and occupational prestige, and from nonwhites to whites. The same is true for being "considerate" and "intellectually curious" (columns III and IV). Stop and find these patterns in the numbers. Take your time.

The opposite pattern, however, holds for obedience to parents (II) and being a good student (V). Whites and adults with more income, education, or occupational prestige are *less* likely

to value these qualities most highly. Equally as important are the qualities of children for which there are *no* class or racial differences (not shown here): having good manners, being neat and clean, being honest, having self-control, trying hard to succeed, conforming to gender roles, getting along well with other children, and being responsible.

From what you have read in the text, how do you explain these findings?

TABLE B-7-1 Percentage of U.S. Adults Who Mention This Quality as One of Three Most Desirable for a Child to Have

ADULT'S SOCIAL STATUS	QUALITY				
	(I) Good Sense	(II) Obeys Parents	(III) Considerate	(IV) Intellectually Curious	(V) Good Student
Income					
Less than $4,000	19	49	29	19	32
$4,000–$13,999	32	45	35	24	22
$14,000–$34,999	49	35	40	22	14
$35,000 and over	49	25	37	26	15
Education					
Less than high school	28	54	29	15	28
High school graduate	43	36	38	23	18
Some college	45	28	40	23	9
College degree	46	26	45	37	11
More than college	58	21	45	42	17
Occupational Prestige					
Low	27	49	27	14	22
Lower-middle	41	37	39	23	18
Upper-middle	43	35	36	25	16
Upper	46	23	48	35	11
Race					
Nonwhite	22	56	29	21	32
White	44	34	39	24	16

Source: Computed from raw 1986 General Social Survey data.

are more regimented and tightly controlled than those of most public school students, in part to give them the discipline they will need to assume positions of authority as adults. Thus, although an upper-class upbringing brings with it many advantages, it is not accomplished easily or without cost.

Class differences in child-rearing values thus play an important part in the reproduction of classes. When working-class parents raise their children to be "good workers" who obey authorities, they unwittingly prepare them to participate in social systems that will give them an unequal share of wealth, power, and prestige in the adult world. In similar ways, when upper-middle- and upper-class parents see to it that their children have the best educations, they, too, play a part in the reproduction of class relations (R. V. Robinson 1984) (see One Step Further 7-1.)

Socialization in Schools

Like the family, the school is an institution whose major function is socialization. What most students learn in school consists primarily of formal studies—math, history, languages, and science—but perhaps the most important contribution of schools to socialization lies in their hidden curricula—lessons imparted in the process of learning formal subjects.

Students in U.S. schools, for example, learn that they are expected to be punctual, neat, obedient, and polite. What they want to do is no longer important, and activities are rigidly scheduled. They learn that individual competition and success are more valued than working together in groups. For many middle-class students, the cultural messages in the hidden curriculum are an extension of socialization in their families; but for many others—such as students from the lower and working classes—the middle-class values of most schools differ sharply from those they experience at home. In fact, one of the major functions of early public schools in the U.S. was to weaken the ability of immigrant families to socialize their children according to their ethnic subcultures, so that their children would grow up sharing the dominant white, Anglo-Saxon culture (Lasch 1977).

Because they help prepare children for adult life, schools play a major role in anticipatory socialization by shaping children's social identities, including their visions of which statuses they can occupy as adults. Lower-class students generally receive less encouragement to go on to college than do middle- and upper-class students; and they are more likely to be placed in slow tracks in school, regardless of their test scores. Children from upper-middle and upper-class families, by contrast, are more likely to attend private prep schools where teachers assume their students will attend prestigious colleges and occupy high positions in business, government, or the professions (see Cookson and Persell 1985).

In comparison with boys, girls receive less encouragement to pursue careers, especially in science and the professions (Marini and Brinton 1984). As early as nursery school, boys generally receive more attention on academic work and more encouragement to work independently. Girls, on the other hand, are rewarded for showing dependency on the teacher and are more likely to have a teacher offer assistance whether or not they need it (Sadker and Sadker 1985).

The hidden curriculum of most U.S. schools sends different messages to students of different genders, races, and social classes. In comparison with students who are nonwhite, female, or poor, those who are white, male, and middle- or upper-class generally receive more encouragement to perceive themselves as people who will one day occupy responsible positions that will bring them a disproportionately large share of wealth, power, and prestige. They are more likely to see themselves as people who will go to college and get good jobs, and in anticipation of this, they are more likely to do what they have to do in order to prepare themselves (Smith 1981).

Peer Groups   The concept of **peer group** refers to people who have a similar level of social standing, especially in terms of age. Schools compete with families for influence in the socialization process, but adolescent peer groups compete with both families and schools. Students often worry about pleasing friends as often as they worry about pleasing parents, and whereas teachers generally place their highest values on academic performance, student peer groups often do not; rather, they may value athletic ability and popularity more highly.

Peer groups are particularly powerful in industrial societies because young people are excluded from adult statuses and their success as adults does not depend on family ties. In small village societies, however, the entire village is regarded as a single family, and adult statuses are distributed according to people's positions in the village. Eisenstadt (1956) believes that adolescents in industrial societies turn to one another because they feel isolated from adult society. As they struggle toward adulthood, they are therefore likely to feel that other adolescents are the only ones who really understand what they are going through. The distinctive music, language, and dress of adolescent subcultures exist not in order to set them apart from adults, but as a reflection of the fact that society has already set them apart. It is not surprising that pressure from peers is a frequent motivation for adolescents to engage in behaviors—such as sex and the use of alcohol, cigarettes, and drugs—that violate the restrictions placed on them by adults.

The Importance of the Media

The mass media—television, radio, movies, books, newspapers, and magazines—produce a stream of cultural images. Rock music videos often portray ste-

In industrial societies, the exclusion of young people from important adult statuses elevates the importance—and therefore the power—of peer groups.

reotyped views of women and men (Hansen and Hansen 1988). To sell products, advertisers tell us how we should look, smell, and behave as well as what we ought to own in order to be attractive to others. Cigarettes are associated with beautiful women who have "come a long way"; cars are described as "sexy" and offered as a way to show how "free-spirited," "independent," or "intelligent" their owners are. Expensive liquor is offered as a sign that those who drink it have succeeded in the world.

Like schools, the media often transmit hidden messages. Advertisements rarely portray women as the equals of men: women rarely instruct men and television voice-overs are almost always male (Bretl and Cantor 1988; Courtney and Whipple 1983). Advertisements for products designed to make men and women sexually attractive never use men and women of different races in the same situation, implying that interracial attraction does not or should not exist.

For many of us, the images portrayed in various media are like mirrors in which we look for reflections of ourselves as well as information about other people. "Is *my* breath bad? Is *this* what it's like to be in love? Is this what whites (or Hispanics or Chinese) are *really* like?" The media attempt to portray most aspects of social life, from the way police officers perform their jobs to family and work relationships, personal hygiene, and life in different social classes. In *All in the Family*, and, later, *Archie Bunker's Place*, Archie Bunker reinforced the stereotype that working-class people are ignorant racists (which

draws attention away from racism among middle- and upper-class people) (Gans 1980). The general absence of nonwhites in leading roles in television and films (to which Bill Cosby is a notable exception) reinforces the stereotype that only whites have dramatic lives and are capable of heroic action (Withey and Abeles 1980).

The power of the media lies primarily in the fact that they portray what is beyond the experience of many viewers; and, thus, images of social life can replace experience as our source of knowledge about the social environment (van Dijk 1987). Most people in the U.S. are strongly anti-communist, for example, and yet have never read Marx and have no experience of communism except through the images presented in the mass media. The media consistently emphasize the problems of countries such as the Soviet Union and China, which they usually attribute to failings of communism itself as a social system. Rarely, however, do they raise critical questions about the fundamental problems of capitalism as a system (MacDonald 1985). Similarly, the mass media of communist countries present their citizens with biased views of capitalism, emphasizing problems such as poverty, racial inequality, and paying less attention to such benefits as political freedom.

When images are oversimplified and distorted, they support stereotypes, but they also encourage us to experience life at such a distance that we do not feel the consequences of behavior. Many war movies focus on glory and heroics, not pain and suffering, and the thousands of fictional murders portrayed on television can turn violence into a meaningless event for all but those who are directly involved. The mass media also have the power to educate and to challenge stereotypes. Movies such as *Platoon, Glory, Born on the 4th of July, Dances with Wolves* and *Do the Right Thing*, for example, may have done much to make people more aware of racism and the human consequences of war.

Just how much influence the media have over us is still unclear. Whether or not watching violent behavior on television stimulates aggressive behavior in children is still debated (Freedman 1984, 1986; Friedrich-Cofer and Huston 1986). Although some critics take the view that the media are a major socializing agent, it has yet to be demonstrated scientifically that they are any more than one piece of an intricate web of social factors.

It Never Ends: Adult Socialization

The idea that we can ever "grow up" reflects an important and false belief that socialization is confined primarily to children, for we acquire new roles, drop old ones, and change current ones as we age (see Riley 1987). Socialization continues throughout our lives, and often takes the form of *re*socialization as we adapt to changing circumstances (Gecas 1981).

Paper Chases and Professional Training   In *The Paper Chase*, John J. Osborn's book about life at Harvard Law School, Professor Kingsfield gives his first-year law students a crisp and clear statement about professional training: "You come in here with a head full of mush, and if you survive, you'll go out thinking like a lawyer." Notice that he does not say "knowing the law," but "*thinking* like a lawyer." "You will teach *yourselves* the law," he tells them, "but *I* will teach you how to *think*."

Like most people who undergo training for an occupation, many graduate students believe they are in school only to acquire skills or a degree; but they are often unaware that they are learning more than medicine, law, business management techniques, or sociology: they are also learning to *be* doctors, lawyers, business executives, and sociologists. They are, in short, learning to perform roles that require far more than technical knowledge and skills (see Jack and Jack 1990).

Physicians, for example, are noted for paying less attention to patients as people than as cases that offer opportunities to diagnose and treat conditions. A common explanation is that doctors practice role distance in order to protect themselves from repeated exposures to suffering and death. Becker and Geer (1958), however, offer another explanation based on participant observation in a medical school (see also Mizrahi 1986). First-year students, they found, enter medical school full of idealism based on sincerely held values and, in some cases, with a desire to disprove the common belief that doctors are greedy and self-serving. They are eager to help people, to heal the sick, and relieve suffering; but in

their first two years, they rarely see—much less actually treat—patients. Instead, they study subjects such as chemistry and anatomy, taught by Ph.D.s who are not physicians. They soon learn that they cannot possibly learn everything there is to know about medicine, and quickly adjust to medical school as a place in which students learn to please their professors and pay as much attention to passing exams as they do to learning skills that will enable them to put their ideals into practice.

It is not until their third and fourth years that they see patients; but even then, they are constantly quizzed about technical knowledge:

> The student becomes preoccupied with the technical aspects of the cases with which he deals because the faculty requires him to do so. He is questioned about so many technical details that he must spend most of his time learning them. (Becker and Geer 1958, p. 53)

There is good reason to believe that physicians who treat patients as cases rather than as people do so in part because they were socialized to think of patients in this way. As Becker and Geer note, however, many medical students become more concerned with human factors in medical practice as they near graduation, showing that in even the most intense socialization, people may hold on to their values until they are in a position to put them into action.

Starting Out: The Twenties   Between the ages of 20 and 30, a majority of U.S. adults begin their first jobs, marry, and have children. In spite of the fact that most grow up with married parents, there are limits on how well anticipatory socialization can prepare anyone for marital roles, for emotional intimacy is one of the most difficult challenges adults face, and we tend to place heavy emotional demands on marriage. Young married people must also struggle with change in the roles of women and men. It is no longer taken for granted that wives will stay at home while husbands devote themselves to paid work outside the home. For many couples, the families they grew up in do not serve as models, and husbands and wives must create their own roles to a considerable degree.

The birth of a first child brings with it serious readjustments. A new and demanding member is added to the family, and spouses acquire the new statuses of mother and father. In addition to learning how to parent, both must adjust to the loss of the continuous intimacy and free access they had to each other when they were first married (Heaton 1990; Mac-Dermid et al. 1990; McLanahan and Adams 1987).

Those who remain single must also adjust to new roles as they make their way in a society dominated by married couples. In their early twenties, most of their friends are also single, but as they approach 30, many are married and interact primarily with other married couples. Single people nearing 30 must learn how to satisfy their emotional needs outside of marriage, and find themselves having to consider whether or not they will ever marry at all (Staples 1981; Stein 1981).

Married or not, most people in their twenties are employed, and because occupational roles occupy a large portion of people's time, they are important sources of socialization. Lawyers learn to focus more on legally relevant facts and winning arguments than their consequences for people; advertisers learn to value selling a product more than conveying accurate information about it. Teachers become disciplinarians and guides for their students, and office workers often adapt to bureaucratic settings by becoming rule-minded and rigid themselves.

Because we frequently change jobs during our lives, occupational socialization is a common experience. We start our first jobs as the "new kid on the block," and after a period of probation and possible disappointment and confusion, earn our places as work-group members. When we change jobs, however, we must in some ways start all over again.

Although the twenties typically have been a time for moving out into the world, recent evidence suggests that young people are taking longer and longer to make that transition. Young adults are leaving home to live on their own at earlier ages than before, but they are also returning to their parents' homes in record numbers. Since 1974, for example, the percentage of 20- to 24-year-old single men still living with their parents has increased from 40 to 50 percent, and the percentage for 25- to 29-year-old men has doubled from 10 to 20 percent (Figure 7-1). The reasons are complex, and include greater difficulty finding jobs that pay enough to support them on their own, a reluctance to assume full adult responsibilities, and the stretching out of cultural ideas about what constitutes youth.

Decision Time: The Thirties   The twenties are generally an exciting and challenging period of trying new roles, and our youth makes us unaware that our life spans are limited. By comparison, the thirties are often a time of serious reflection about our lives. Parents must learn to give up control over their children who now approach adolescence. Many couples divorce during their thirties, and must adjust to the disruption of family life and the demands of living alone or raising children by themselves—often in poverty (Gordon 1981; Rosenthal and Keshet 1978).

Unmarried people must deal with the difficult question of whether or not to marry at all; and childless women in particular—whether married or not—must cope with the biological fact that their years of potential childbearing are limited. Whether or not to include motherhood as a part of their lives is a difficult and irrevocable decision, because childbearing is limited by biological aging.

The thirties also are a time of intense reflection about occupations. The excitement over a first job in the twenties is often replaced by a disturbing question in the thirties: "Is this what I want to do for the rest of my life?" For many people—especially those in the working class—such questions are a luxury, for they have relatively little control over how they earn a living. For middle- and upper-class people, however, the choice is real—between the security of a job they do not like and the risks involved in cutting loose and looking for a better one.

FIGURE 7-1   Percent of Single Young Adults Living with their Parents, by Age and by Sex, U.S.

Sources: Alan Schnaiberg; Census Bureau
The New York Times/March 12, 1989, p. 30.

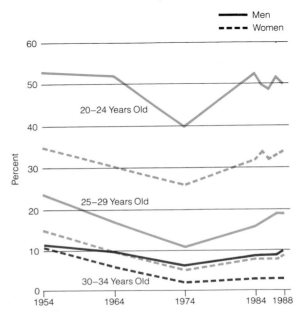

The thirties appear to be a time for making important decisions about major roles. This period is, for many, like a pivot on which the rest of their lives will turn.

Mid-Life Crises: The Forties and Fifties

At midlife, we begin to adjust to the consequences of all the decisions we have made, and it is often a time of reconciling dreams with reality (see Karp 1989).

Marriage and parenthood are not the bliss that many thought they would be. Children leave home, and even parents who breathe a sigh of relief must adjust to their shrinking roles and loss of responsibilities. For childless women, time has run out, for childbearing becomes riskier after 40 and by age 55, most women have experienced menopause. By this time, many have also discovered that dreams of success are unlikely to come true, and they must be content with what they have. With fresh generations of workers entering the labor force each year, older workers are less able to take occupational risks, because the chances of successfully competing for new jobs are relatively slim.

Perhaps the most difficult adjustment of midlife involves the realization that we are not immortal, especially in societies in which death before old age is rare. For younger people, death often seems only a remote idea; but in midlife, the "end of the tunnel" comes into view, and as we adjust to the failure of many dreams, we must also confront the reality of our eventual deaths.

Learning to Grow Old

Old age is a time of major readjustments in status and role sets. Retirement ends occupational roles, which—until old age—occupy most of people's daily lives. Aging can also mean the death of one's spouse and friends. Elderly men who become widowers and who do not remarry have death rates significantly above those for other men of their age (Helsing and Szklo 1981); but Hyman (1983) found no massive short- or long-term negative effects on elderly women who become widows.

In industrial societies, many of those who retire after working their entire lives must adjust to the lower prestige of people who no longer earn a living. For many, old age also causes sharp declines in income: 75 percent of those over the age of 64 have incomes of less than $15,000, compared with only 41 percent of those between the ages of 35 and 44 (USCB 1990a). Because women generally outlive men, a substantial proportion of older people are widows who live in poverty because Social Security is their only source of income. Elderly women are also more likely to live by themselves: 41 percent live alone compared with only 16 percent of elderly men (USCB 1990a).

Perhaps of most importance is the fact that the elderly must fully confront the reality of death, because for the first time in their lives many people of their own age are dying (Kübler-Ross 1969,1975). Time is literally running out at a rapid pace, and for many old age is a time of serious reflection about the meaning of their lives.

Stereotyped views of old age often portray it as a negative stage in life in which people are socialized to accept loss of loved ones and important roles and, ultimately, of life itself. It is important to emphasize, however, that for many elderly people old age is a very positive experience. The loss of roles is also an end to responsibilities—to children, spouses, and employers—and for many, old age is a time in which they have more freedom to run their own lives than ever before (see White and Edwards 1990). There is also evidence that the older we get the more comfortable we tend to feel with ourselves and the more meaning and satisfaction we tend to find in life (Gove, Ortega, and Style 1989).

SOCIALIZATION AND FREEDOM

As a lifelong process, socialization brings with it countless changes in the roles we play and raises some important issues about the nature of social life. Infants sometimes wake in the night and cry until someone picks them up and holds them for a while. They often have more difficulty falling asleep on a large bed than in a crib whose size is closer to their own. They seem to need boundaries, solid contact with people and things that give them a sense of where, if not who, they are. We are not unlike infants in this way: when we are left without limits we can feel lost, floating in a void, and we reach out for familiar things and people in order to reorient ourselves. We are social animals who need one another, and yet our relationships are regulated by ideas we draw from a shared culture. As the studies of isolated children show, we cannot survive as autonomous, lone individuals, and so to satisfy our need for one another we must forego some portion of individual freedom.

In Nazi Germany, to be a good German was to be a good Nazi. What does it mean to be a good American?

Socialization is more than a process that prepares individuals for social life, however, for it is also a means by which societies are perpetuated. There is more at stake than what we become as individuals and how we adjust to expectations. Also at stake is the kind of society we adjust to and the part we play in changing or perpetuating it. It is ironic that if we are socialized effectively, adjusting perfectly to our surroundings, we may at the same time perpetuate injustice and cruelty. For children who grew up in Nazi Germany during the 1930s, hating Jews and Poles was part of being a "good German," and their acceptance of this ultimately led to World War II,

the Holocaust, and the eventual destruction of Nazi Germany (see Peukert 1987).

In similar ways, girls who learn to be "feminine women" and boys who learn to be "masculine men" are not merely acquiring roles and identities that allow them to operate in a sexist society. As we will see in Chapter 14, they are also learning to participate in the dominance of women by men. Girls who adopt traditional roles learn to accept a subordinate position, whereas boys learn to use the power that comes with their gender. While we learn to be masculine or feminine in a sexist society, we also help to perpetuate sexism.

This raises a crucial point about socialization and the relationship between individuals and societies. All of us are socialized in the sense of becoming social beings. In every society, almost everyone forms an identity and learns to interact with other people and to perform roles. This does *not* mean, however, that each of us is molded according to a uniform cultural model—that we all become no more than a mirror image of our environment (Wrong 1961). Like individuals, societies constantly change, and how they change depends strongly on the choices individuals make. Without society the individual does not exist; it is also true, however, that without individuals there can be no society (see Giddens 1984). Because we are social beings, our dependence on others makes us vulnerable; and yet we have the power to resist the limitations imposed by social systems, to define and redefine the terms by which we live.

SUMMARY

1. Socialization involves both what we learn and how we learn as we become social beings; these, in turn, depend on culture and social structure. We learn to orient ourselves to cultural ideas according to our statuses, and through this we acquire an awareness of ourselves and of others and develop self-concepts and self-esteem. Although our ability to be socialized is rooted in biological development, the process itself cannot unfold without interaction and language.

2. The behavioral, social learning, and cognitive perspectives are three principal theories about how people learn. (1) According to the behavioral approach, our behavior results from the application of punishment and reward in classical and operant conditioning. (2) The social learning perspective pays attention to models whom we imitate. (3) Cognitive development theory focuses on developing the ability to make complex judgments. Although all three perspectives

are useful, they do not take into account the crucial effects of social systems.

3. Socialization begins with language, the basis for connecting our experience with the experience of others; through this, we develop mind, the ability to use symbols to put ourselves in the place of another person.

4. The "I" consists of direct experience of ourselves and others, and the "me" is that part of us that looks upon the "I" as an object. Significant others are particular people we orient ourselves to, and the generalized other is our perception of statuses and what is expected of those who occupy them. Through significant others we are able to discover ourselves as selves. Our self-concept is the total of our beliefs and feelings about ourselves; it is strongly influenced by our looking-glass self, our perception of how other people perceive and evaluate us.

5. As we develop, we enlarge our status and role sets. The cultural ideas people share about the occupants of statuses are, in turn, used to form a social identity, an ideal self, and self-esteem. An important part of this process is the use of reference groups and individuals for comparison.

This is particularly important for anticipatory socialization.

6. The family, schools, and the mass media are three major agents of socialization. Past childhood, we continue to adapt to new social circumstances throughout the life course. Rites of passage mark the transition from one status to another; and we adjust to change in work and family, modifying relationships as we grow into adulthood and old age. In many ways, we learn to play new roles and to reformulate our ideas and feelings about others and ourselves.

7. As we mature, the socialization process confers on us the power of selfhood, the ability to make choices which at times may conflict with the same society in which we were socialized. We are not simply limited by social systems; we are part of them, and so long as we participate in them we cannot help but punish and reward others and provide them with models. We are born into a world not of our own making, but as we are socialized and participate in social life, we become the makers who help fashion social systems in which future generations will be born and become social beings.

KEY TERMS

anticipatory socialization 148	looking-glass self 145	rite of passage 149
behaviorist perspective 138	me 143	self-concept 145
cognitive development	mind 143	self-esteem 148
perspective 139	model 138	significant other 143
generalized other 143	peer group 152	social identity 146
I 143	reference group 148	social learning perspective 138
ideal self 147	reference individual 148	socialization 135

LOOKING ELSEWHERE

Having studied Chapter 7, you might want to look at related discussions in *Human Arrangements*, which include

- age and rites of passage (Ch. 15, pp. 366–68).

- maintaining an authentic self (Chapter 8, pp. 180–81)

- race, ethnicity, social identity, and self-esteem (Chapter 13, pp. 308–310)

- gender, self, and self-esteem (Chapter 14, pp. 331–32, 334–35)

- learning gender roles (Ch. 14, pp. 342–45)

- deviant social identities (Ch. 11, pp. 256–57)

- socialization and deviance (Chapter 11, pp. 251–53, 254–55)

- biology, society, and race (Chapter 13, pp. 297–98)

- biology and gender roles (Ch. 14, pp. 327–29)

- biology and age roles (Ch. 15, pp. 361–62)

- the effects of rewards on learning in school (Chapter 17, p. 421)

- schools and the hidden curriculum (Chapter 17, pp. 421–22)

- social inequality, schools, and the hidden curriculum (Chapter 17, pp. 433–36)

- medicine as a profession (Ch. 18, pp. 460–62)

RECOMMENDED READINGS

Ariès, P. 1962. *Centuries of childhood: A social history of family life.* New York: Knopf. A fascinating look at how the definition of childhood has changed over the centuries, with a special emphasis on the ways in which this has affected the treatment of children.

Becker, H. S., et al. 1976. *Boys in white: Student culture in medical school* (rev. ed.). New Brunswick, NJ: Transaction Books. The classic study of the socialization process that turns college graduates into doctors.

Brim, O. G., Jr., and Wheeler, S. 1966. *Socialization after childhood: Two essays.* New York: Wiley. Two classic essays that show that socialization only *begins* in childhood.

Brown, R. 1965. *Social psychology.* New York: Free Press. In this classic text, chapters on the acquisition of language and morality are both extremely well written and full of ideas and information.

Davis, K. 1947. Final note on a case of extreme isolation. *American Journal of Sociology, 50,* 432–37. One of the few existing studies of a documented case of a child raised in isolation, Davis' article makes for fascinating reading.

Freud, S. 1961. *Civilization and its discontents.* New York: Norton. Freud's classic theory about the tension between the demands of society and inborn human drives. (Original work published 1930)

Gracey, H. L. 1972. Learning the student role: Kindergarten as academic boot camp. In D. H. Wrong (Ed.), *Readings in introductory sociology* (2nd ed.) (pp. 243–54). New York: Macmillan. This widely reprinted article shows how early training begins with amusing and sometimes disturbing insights into the world of kindergarten.

Jack, R., and Jack, D. J. 1990. *Moral vision and professional decisions: The changing values of women and men lawyers.* New York: Cambridge University Press. How law schools train their students to think, feel, and behave as lawyers.

Kübler-Ross, E. 1975. *Death, the final stage of growth.* Englewood Cliffs, NJ: Prentice-Hall. Kübler-Ross has been a pioneer in the study of death as a human experience. As the title of this book suggests, she views death and dying as another stage of life that has its own lessons to be learned.

McCarl, R. 1985. *The District of Columbia fire fighters' project: A case study in occupational folklife.* Washington, D.C.: Smithsonian Institution Press. An unusual and fascinating look at the process through which fire fighters are socialized into their occupational subculture.

Montagu, A. 1971. *Touching: The human significance of the skin.* New York: Columbia University Press. A fascinating look at the importance of touching in human development with a special emphasis on cross-cultural variation in how people touch each other.

Raphael, R. 1989. *The men from the boys: Rites of passage in male America.* Lincoln: University of Nebraska Press. An insightful and often compelling look at the problems created among American men by the absence of clear rites of passage marking the transition from boyhood to adulthood.

Rosenberg, M. 1979. *Conceiving the self.* New York: Basic Books. A thorough, thoughtful, and well-written look at key concepts in the sociological study of socialization.

Wrong, D. H. 1961. The oversocialized conception of man in modern sociology. *American Sociological Review, 26* (April), 183–93. An important statement of the problems of viewing socialization as a process that is determined either by society or by forces within the individual. Wrong argues effectively for a more balanced view.

8
SOCIAL INTERACTION

 Everyday life is a complex process through which we organize and interpret our perceptions and expectations of people and situations; present ourselves to others; and try to understand who people are, what they are doing, and why. As a result, we *act* in relation to others, which is to say, we participate in **social interaction**. How we do it and the effects it produces have long been important subjects in sociology.

ACTION AND INTERACTION

Writing in the *New York Times*, columnist A. M. Rosenthal (1987) expressed his troubled feelings about how to react when passing by a homeless person lying on a sidewalk, or when encountering those who mutter or scream to themselves while walking the streets of many large U.S. cities these days. What, he wondered, were his responsibilities in such situations? Should he summon medical help? The police? Should he inquire if the person is all right?

In thinking about his dilemma he was reminded of an incident that occurred late one night in March 1964 when a woman named Kitty Genovese was murdered outside her apartment in a middle-class neighborhood of New York City. Thirty-nine people watched from their apartments as she screamed in agony and terror while her attacker stabbed her repeatedly in a struggle that lasted for more than 30 minutes. He left her bleeding, but alive, only to return later and attack her again. Not one of the witnesses did anything to help her; no one even called the police until the final fatal wound had been inflicted.

The witnesses violated important norms and values against which we might judge their behavior as outrageously immoral and unfeeling. In the public shock that followed, the question was raised repeatedly: How could people behave that way? For each one who raised that question, there was probably an underlying statement: "*I would have done something.*"

If we think of the witnesses' behavior as simple actions carried out by individuals, our explanations will tend to be psychological: they were perhaps too insensitive, immoral, or frightened to pick up a telephone and call for help. Sociologists, however, are reluctant to settle for that kind of explanation, for it ignores the fact that when we act, we act in *relation* to one another and social systems.

Latané and Darley (1970) tried to answer the question "How could people behave that way?" and to test the common assumption that most people would have behaved differently (see also Dantin and Carver 1982; Latané and Nida 1981). As a participant in their experiment, you would have been invited to a small group discussion about personal problems. You are told that there are six of you, and to help you be more open about yourselves, each of you will sit in your own room from which you cannot see one another. Each person has two minutes to talk through an intercom system, and during that time, no one else can communicate with other members of the group. After everyone has spoken, each member may speak for an additional two minutes. You will go last.

The first person to talk mentions that he sometimes has violent seizures, especially when he is under strain. After you and other members talk about your lives and problems, the first person speaks again. Suddenly he says:

> I-er-if somebody could help me out it would—it would er-er s-s-sure be—sure be good . . . because er-the-er-er-a cause I-er-I-uh I've got a-a one of the-er-seiz . . . er-er-things coming on and-and-and I could really-er-use some help so uh-er-er-er-er c-could somebody er-er-help er-uh-uh-uh—(choking sounds) . . . I'm gonna die er-er-I'm . . . gonna die erer-seizure-er (choking sound again; then quiet).

What would you do? Immediately leave the room and look for help? Or sit and wonder if you should do anything? (At the end of the experiment, by the way, you learn that all the voices you heard were recorded.)

Latané and Darley wanted to explain why some subjects respond faster than others and why some fail to respond at all, and they focused not on personality differences but on how population characteristics of the situation affected the subjects' responses. In particular, they wanted to know how the number of people in a group affects interaction.

Their results were dramatic. Of those who believed they were in a six-person group, only 30 percent went for help, whereas 62 percent of those who believed they were in a three-person group responded to the plea. Of those who believed they and the victim were the only group members, fully 85 percent went for help. Although individual characteristics may explain why some people in six-person groups went for help and others did not, they cannot explain why those in larger groups were less likely to act than those in smaller groups.

A sociological explanation of why people may not help others combines social and population factors. First, the more bystanders there are, the more likely we are to assume that someone else will help; we spread responsibility over the entire group, and the larger the group is, the more thinly we can spread responsibility, leaving less for ourselves (Berkowitz 1978).

Second, we are always in danger of misinterpreting situations and making fools of ourselves (being an alarmist), and the larger the number of people present, the more potential witnesses there are to ridicule us. Third, we are often unsure of our perceptions and interpretations, and we look to other people for confirmation: if no one else responds, it reinforces the interpretation that action is not called for. This is a classic "Catch-22" (Heller [1955] 1961): we wait for someone else to act first; hence, no one acts, because each potential "someone else" is also waiting for someone else to do something.

Such findings suggest that Kitty Genovese's neighbors were not cruel or callous, but that each felt their responsibility spread out over many others. Ironically, each may have refrained from helping because they could not imagine that *no* one would help. Had they seen someone go to her aid, they might well have called the police; or if each believed he or she was the only witness, they would have been far more likely to respond.

The sociology of interaction focuses on the way our awareness of ourselves, one another, and social environments influences our behavior. Basic to all interaction are these two questions: Who are you? and Who am I?

Visibility: Seeing and Being Seen

Few things are more important to us than to be seen by other people. To be ignored for even a few minutes can make us feel shy and uninteresting, and to be shunned is one of the worst things that can happen.

In the prologue to Ralph Ellison's great novel *Invisible Man* (1952), a black man accidentally collides with a stranger on a dark street. The stranger insults him, and the black man violently attacks him:

> And in my outrage I got out my knife and prepared to slit his throat . . . when it occurred to me that the man had not *seen* me, actually; that he, as far as he knew, was in the midst of a walking nightmare! . . . I ran away into the dark. . . . Poor blind fool, I thought with sincere compassion, mugged by an invisible man!

The black man feels that his low social standing makes him invisible to others, treated with so little regard by white society that he might as well not exist at all. The importance of this for social interaction is clear in his thoughts:

> Irresponsibility is part of my invisibility; any way you face it, it is a denial. But to whom can I be responsible, and why should I be, when you refuse to see me? Responsibility rests on recognition, and recognition is a form of agreement.

Our statuses affect whether or not people see us and how they see us; and these influence the terms by which we interact with one another, the often unspoken, unconscious agreements that structure social life.

Culture, Social Structure, and Perception

Since we cannot pay attention to everything at once, we necessarily select what we perceive. To remember and communicate, we must simplify and organize information. When we describe someone as "intelligent" we select a few observations from many, and simplify, organize, and interpret them in terms of an abstract category. Culture is a framework of ideas that we use in this process, and our statuses influence which parts of that framework we use and how we use them.

Perceptions of others depend on two kinds of information. The first consists of *impressions* of personal characteristics such as "kindness" or "cruelty," "beauty" or "ugliness." First impressions are particularly important because they foster expectations that influence our subsequent perceptions, feelings, and behavior. In a classic experiment, college students read a description of a guest instructor just before he arrived (Kelley 1950). The descriptions gave identical information about his academic background and experience, but differed in one detail: half read, "People who know him consider him to be

The simple feeling that people can see us lies at the heart of our connection to social life. American artist Edward Hopper is known for his paintings that capture the sense of social isolation and loneliness—hallmarks of life in modern industrial societies.

a rather cold person, industrious, critical, practical, and determined," but in the other half, the words "very warm" were substituted for "cold."

The guest led the group discussion for twenty minutes—during which the researcher observed and recorded student participation—and after he left, students anonymously evaluated him. The single piece of information—"very warm" or "cold"—strikingly affected how students interacted with and evaluated him. Among students who were told he was very warm, 56 percent participated in the discussion, whereas only 32 percent of those who were told he was cold took part. When asked to evaluate his performance, students who were told he was cold thought that he seemed more self-centered, formal, unsociable, unpopular, irritable, humorless, and ruthless than did students who were told he was very warm.

Many social psychologists argue that perceptions of physical attractiveness are particularly important in forming first impressions (see Patzer 1985). People we see as attractive, we also tend to see as having other positive features as well, such as being intelligent and likable. This can then become a **self-fulfilling prophecy**, a belief that comes true because people think and act as if it were, in fact, already true. Our beliefs about people lead us to treat them in particular ways; and our treatment, in turn, leads them to fulfill the prophecy contained in our beliefs (Merton 1968). We treat those we see as unattractive as if they are also unlikable and this, in turn, makes it more likely that they will behave in ways that we will see as unlikable.

We use first impressions to form expectations around which we organize perceptions and judgments that strongly influence our behavior. From a sociological perspective, however, our expectations depend even more importantly on a second type of information: our perceptions of people's social identities, their status sets.

Stereotypes Cultures contain many beliefs about the occupants of various statuses. Although it is impossible to avoid using statuses as a source of information about people, they often lead to errors. When we select certain characteristics and make inferences from them, we not only lose the informa-

tion we choose to ignore, but often add misinformation as well. These cultural sketches of people in different statuses sometimes take the form of **stereotypes**—rigid, oversimplified beliefs that are applied to all members of a social category. We all depend on stereotypes to some degree when we interact with other people. In fact, without them we could not predict other people's behavior in role relationships.

When stereotypes are our only source of information, however, they cause several problems. First, they oversimplify. We forget that people we regard as heroes are human beings who dream, have fears, and make mistakes just like the rest of us. Second, stereotypes tend to be much more rigid than people. When we identify people as former mental patients, we tend to interpret their behavior as a reflection of mental instability, and expect them to continue to be "crazy" regardless of their actual behavior.

Third, although some characteristics are more common among those in one status than another, it is often a mistake to apply status characteristics to individuals. Men are far more likely than women to commit violent crimes; but this does not mean that every man you meet is likely to be a criminal.

Fourth, when we define people in terms of a social status, we often mistakenly assume that they represent all occupants of that status. A native American college student may be called upon in class to give "the native American point of view" on a particular issue, a request that ignores the enormous variation among native Americans.

Finally, stereotyping can have the effect of a self-fulfilling prophecy by encouraging people to conform to cultural beliefs about them. People often mistakenly assume, for example, that hearing-impaired people are mentally retarded because they express themselves with difficulty and in unusual ways. If, based on this stereotyped view, we deny hearing-impaired children regular schooling, they may in fact grow up with limited intellectual abilities.

For many decades prior to the civil rights movement, the image of "Aunt Jemima" was a pervasive stereotype of black women as jolly cooks, maids, and caretakers of white children. In startling contrast, black artist Joe Overstreet's 1964 alternative depicts a proud, angry "New Jemima" wielding a machine gun. Courtesy of the Menil Collection, Houston, Texas.

Social interaction, then, is based on the perception of people's social characteristics, from which we identify "who they are." We do not encounter them in a vacuum, however, for interaction occurs in social systems whose characteristics affect both how we perceive others and how we and they define our expectations.

The Definition of the Situation

To interact we must identify the statuses and roles that define expectations. The result is called the **definition of the situation** (McHugh 1968). How people define the situation is enormously important, for if we "define situations as real, they are real in their consequences" (Thomas and Thomas 1928, p. 572). In his movie *Take the Money and Run*, for example, Woody Allen wants to rob a bank, and he hands a teller a note that reads, "I have a gun. Give me all your cash." The teller, however, is puzzled because he reads, "I have a gub."

"No, it's '*gun*,'" Allen says.

"Looks like 'gub' to me," the teller says, then asks another teller to help read the note, then another, and finally everyone is arguing over what the note means. Allen does not succeed in robbing the bank, because he is the only one who defines the situation as a robbery (see Watzlawick 1976).

We continually activate and deactivate statuses in our daily lives, and as we do, we perform roles through which we express different aspects of our identities. One minute we are riders on a bus, then pedestrians, then restaurant customers, employees, or college students in class. When someone gives us a gift, it immediately activates the status of recipient and a role that includes gratitude and some obligation to return the favor (see Fisher, Nadler, and DePaulo 1983).

The statement "I'm in love with you" is more than an expression of feeling; it is an attempt to define a relationship, and the response "I love you, too" invokes a complex set of expectations. In the same sense, the statement "I don't love you any more" is as much an attempt to redefine a situation as it is an expression of feeling.

When someone approaches us with a definition of a situation—such as "This is a holdup" or "We're lovers"—we must decide whether or not to adopt it, for once we do, we feel bound to perform the role implied. Doctors, for example, may lie to terminally ill patients about the seriousness of their conditions and justify their dishonesty in the name of protecting the patient from a horrible truth. From a sociological perspective, however, the deceivers also protect themselves, because once a patient is socially defined as dying, other people must activate their own status of attendant to a dying person and face all of the sadness, frustration, and other difficult feelings that go with it.

Our ability to define social relationships gives us considerable creative power. We can be taken care of as though we were children even when we reach adulthood, so long as there is someone willing to play the role of adult in relation to us as child. Or we can be strong and domineering if someone is willing to be weak and submissive in relation to us. In many ways, we seek people who share our definitions of the situation, because they, in effect, allow us to be who we want to be.

The definition of the situation is important not only in the activation of statuses and roles, but also in the way people interpret one another. Studies in the sociology of sexuality, for example, have found that men who work with women tend to define business lunches as dates, while women do not. They also find that men are much more likely than women to interpret friendliness as sexual (see Gutek 1985). Given that a smile or any other gesture can indicate many different emotions—from pleasure to embarrassment—how we define the situation in which it occurs has an enormous impact on what we think it means and, therefore, how we act.

From a sociological perspective, interaction is based on a complex process of perception and interpretation of people and the situations in which we encounter one another, activate selected parts of our social selves, and, in responding to one another, interact. In some ways, interaction is like an elaborate dance in which we move in relation to one another, each creating variations on the themes contained in roles. If you observe department store clerks and customers, for example, you will soon discover that although most of the interactions are between complete strangers, the patterns are astonishingly consistent throughout the day.

Interaction is a vital activity in any society, for it is literally the means through which social life takes place. It is in interaction that social structure and culture become more than ideas, for here they are reflected in what people actually do in relation to one another.

Social Attribution

When we interact with people, we often use the definition of the situation to explain their behavior. This process of interpretation is called **social attribution** (Bierhoff 1989). Suppose a man picks your pocket and gets away with a week's pay, and the police catch him after he has spent your money. How severely would you want him punished? If you learned that he is a professional thief who drives a fancy car, you would feel quite differently than if you learned that he is desperately poor, was laid off from his job through no fault of his own, and used the money to buy fuel oil for his family during a bitterly cold winter. He is a thief in both cases, but your response to him depends on how you explain his behavior.

We cannot explain the thief's behavior simply by observing his actions—we need two basic types of additional information. First, we need to know the **internal causes** of the thief's behavior: personal motives, abilities, and emotional states. Was he desperate or just greedy? Or was he mentally ill and unaware of the seriousness of his behavior? Second, we

For what kind of crime would you guess this person has been arrested? On what do you base your attribution?

need to know the **external causes** to be able to explain behavior in any situation. If the thief is unemployed, poor, married, and the father of small children, his family roles require him to earn a living, but his statuses of poor and unemployed deprive him of socially legitimate ways to do so. In this way we use people's statuses and roles to explain their behavior.

Several studies show, for example, that explanations of behavior can vary according to the actor's gender. When asked to explain the success of a "Dr. Mark Greer" or a "Dr. Marcia Greer," people tend to attribute the man's success to his abilities and the woman's success to luck, hard work, or a less demanding job (Feldman-Summers and Kiesler 1974). They also tend to explain a man's failure as a case of bad luck, while explaining similar failures of women as due to a lack of ability (Deaux 1972; Erkut 1984).

We generally use internal causes to explain other people's behavior, but rely on external causes to explain our own (Davis and Stephan 1980; Monson and Hesley 1982; Reeder and Spores 1983). When college students try to explain why their work is late, they are unlikely to offer laziness, lack of motivation, or incompetence as causes. They are more likely to refer to the demands of other roles ("I have four papers due this week") or circumstances beyond their personal control ("My dog ate my paper").

We add the demands of latent statuses (student in another course; dog owner) to our definition of the situation in order to explain our failure in a manifest status (notice also, in the "Dr. Greer" example above, how people used the latent statuses male and female to explain performance in the manifest status of doctor). Professors, on the other hand, are more likely to attribute student performance to internal causes and regard external factors as a poor excuse.

Why should this difference occur? Jones and Nisbett (1971) argued that as actors we look outward on the world and are therefore highly aware of the circumstances that affect our behavior. But, as Tetlock (1981) pointed out, we also want to appear in the best possible light and therefore tend to present ourselves to others as victims of circumstances we cannot control. As observers of other people, however, we tend to focus on individuals, not on their situations. All we see is them and what they do, and we therefore tend to believe that the causes of their behavior rest solely within themselves.

Social interaction is more than a dance between partners who share a rhythm and listen to the same music, for every act directed at someone else crosses a boundary that separates and protects that person from others. To interact is to act *upon* one another. It is important to examine the nature of those boundaries, how we cross them, and with what effects.

Social Boundaries

> Some thirty inches from my nose
> The frontier of my Person goes. . .
> Stranger, unless with bedroom eyes
> I beckon you to fraternize,
> Beware of rudely crossing it;
> I have no gun, but I can spit.
>   —W. H. Auden

Physical contact is closely regulated in social life. While our skin separates and protects us from others, the cultural ideas that regulate human contact form an invisible boundary around us, and only those who occupy certain statuses in relation to us have the right to cross it, and even then only under certain circumstances. Clothes insulate us in public and shield us from other people's eyes, and only under special circumstances do we allow someone to reach the skin beneath. Strangers may shake our hands, but only those close to us may touch our faces. We allow dentists to work in our mouths and physicians to penetrate our skins, but they may do so only within the strict limits of their roles.

The right to forcibly move us from one place to another is also limited to a narrow range of statuses, such as that of police officer (but only when arresting us) or parent (but only while we are still children). In general, people do not have the right to shoot, stab, or hit us; and yet, under culturally defined circumstances—such as self-defense or war—they may.

Our skin is a last line of defense, for the limits of our personal boundaries extend beyond it to include culturally prescribed limits to our selves. Hall (1959, 1969), for example, suggests that each culture contains ideas about appropriate physical distances between people for each situation. If you are sitting on a park bench and a stranger sits down right next to you, how do you feel? Chances are you feel less comfortable, as if there were no longer enough room for you, even though in a strict physical sense there is. In the U.S. the "zone of intimacy" extends to a distance of about 18 inches and is reserved for intimate acquaintances, whereas those who are close friends—but not intimate—must stay at a "personal distance" of 18 inches to 4 feet. Impersonal interactions—those among workers—take place at a distance of

The close proximity in which these men in La Paz, Bolivia, sit reflects cultural norms about personal distance.

from 4 to 12 feet; and the "public zone" of 12 feet or more is appropriate among strangers.

The use of physical space is an important ecological factor in social interaction. In the U.S., people use automobiles to insulate themselves from others (although some interaction may result from aggression and competition) and prefer the stresses of rush hour traffic to the forced intimacy of buses and trains. Many Europeans (the French, in particular) and Latin-Americans, on the other hand, prefer being close to other passengers (Hall 1969).

Each culture specifies the limits of physical zones. Personal distance in Latin cultures resembles the zone of intimacy in the U.S., and non-Latins often feel uncomfortable among Latins who seem to stand "too close." What we experience as natural boundaries are in fact social boundaries whose use depends on how we define the situation in a cultural context (see LaFrance and Mayo 1978). In an experiment about the use of physical zones, a researcher sat down six inches from people sitting alone on park benches (Sommer 1969). He then recorded how long the other person stayed, and compared this with observations of people who were left alone. Almost 50 percent of those whose social boundary was crossed left within five minutes, compared with only 10 percent of those who were left alone (see also Ruback 1987).

Norms do more than regulate physical contact, however, for they also specify expectations in role relationships. We may look at strangers, but folkways do not allow staring; even close friends may experience staring as an invasion of privacy, especially when directed at their eyes, which have been described as "the windows of the soul." There are many ways to shield ourselves from other people. As children we tend to reveal ourselves openly and directly in social interactions, but as we are socialized, we learn subtlety and concealment (Cooley [1902] 1964). Because we rely on gestures to express our feelings and thoughts to others, we can use them as screens that withhold or distort information about ourselves.

Many roles allow us to maintain contact with others without revealing ourselves. "Hello, how are you?" someone asks, to which we reply, "Fine, how are you?" On one level, such interactions are dishonest, for we rarely want to know how someone really feels when we pass them on the street, and "fine" is often an inaccurate description. Indeed, to describe feelings in great detail violates the expectations attached to the role of "acquaintances."

As meaningless as such exchanges appear to be, they play an important part in social life, for without them we feel invisible and uncomfortable ("Why didn't you say 'hello'?"). Although the apparent question is "How are you?" the underlying question is often "How am I?" as we look for our reflection in other people's recognition of us. Without such roles, we would have to choose between extensive, revealing interactions or none at all. Few people are above the small talk that allows us to keep in touch with other people without revealing more of ourselves than we want to.

It is ironic that although social boundaries must be crossed if friendship is to occur, the likelihood of forming a friendship is diminished, not enhanced, when boundaries are unclear or too easily crossed. In one experiment, for example, sailors volunteered to be isolated in pairs for ten days in a small chamber equipped with cots, tables, and toilet and eating facilities, as well as a video camera that recorded their interactions (Altman et al. 1971). Some became friends, but others did not get along. The researchers noticed that friendship was more likely when the men established clear boundaries at the start of their stay: who would sleep where, what parts of the chamber were reserved for each man, how and when furniture was to be used. Those who failed to establish clear boundaries were far less likely to get along.

Interaction involves a complex balance among boundaries; and, as the definition of the situation changes, boundaries swell and contract. Among in-

PUZZLE

WHEN IS RAPE NOT A CRIME?

When can a man force a woman to have sexual intercourse with him and not be charged with rape even if he confesses?

In most states of the United States, the answer is: when he is her husband and the couple is not legally separated. (A notable "exception that proves the rule" is a 1984 case in Florida in which a husband was tried and convicted of sexually assaulting his wife.) Power is often an important part of social interaction, and as explained in this chapter and in Chapter 14, the statuses of husband and wife have built-in power inequalities that allow husbands to behave toward their wives in ways that are prohibited in relation to other women.

timate friends we draw boundaries close to ourselves and allow others to cross them with relative ease, but among strangers, boundaries expand and become increasingly difficult for people to cross.

Power and Social Interaction

We maintain some control over the extent and strength of our boundaries, but the ability to control contact and interaction with others is often limited by differences in power. As we saw in Chapter 3, power can take many forms, but most depend more on roles and the definition of the situation than on individual personality characteristics.

Most states, for example, define rape as sexual contact gained through the use of force or the threat of force. In rape, the victim's body as well as his or her right to control it are violated. As a member of society, a victim may call upon the legal system to support her right to be protected from assault (Brownmiller 1975; LaFree 1989). If the attacker happens to be her husband, however, laws in many states define his behavior as "assault," not rape. In these states, "sexual contact gained through the use of force" simply cannot happen between spouses (see Russell 1982). Why not?

Criminal laws exist to protect us from other people. Laws that forbid rape, murder, assault, robbery, and harassing telephone calls, or that limit a government's power to record our telephone calls, open our mail, or arrest us without good cause, all specify boundaries that people may not cross without risking punishment.

In many states, rape laws grant husbands the right to behave toward their wives in ways that would be criminal in relation to other women. Such laws are based on the seventeenth century writings of the English jurist Matthew Hale who argued that husbands cannot be held guilty of raping their wives, because upon marriage a wife is assumed to give unconditional consent to her husband's sexual desires, a consent which she cannot retract (Hale 1847). This reflects the historical subjugation of women—in which they have been viewed as property, belonging first to their fathers, then "given" to their husbands in marriage. In every sexual interaction between spouses, the law grants a husband the right to cross his wife's personal boundaries at will, and although he may choose not to exercise that right, it is always nonetheless available (see Finkelhor and Yllo 1985).

In the simplest sense, we all have personal power. Even small children have power in relation to adults: they can refuse to do what they are told, throw embarrassing tantrums in public places, or obey, but slowly and reluctantly. Sociologists, however, focus primarily on authority which differs from other forms of power in that it is socially supported, and rests on the belief that those who possess it have a right to it, and those who do not have a duty to obey. Our statuses determine who has the authority to invade our boundaries, to act upon us regardless of what we want. The statuses of child, mental patient, and "under arrest," for example, have roles that include little authority, and people in those statuses must rely on personal power to control what happens with more powerful role partners.

Sociologically, authority is a particularly important source of power, because people with authority can exercise power that is vastly beyond their resources and abilities. They act not in their own names, but in the name of an entire social system. Because society grants some status occupants power they would otherwise never have, authority is particularly subject to abuse (Sennett 1981).

In a classic experiment (Haney, Banks, and Zimbardo 1973; Zimbardo 1971), male college students volunteered to play the roles of prisoners and guards in a laboratory designed to resemble a prison. The students were paid to participate, and the "guards" were given complete control over the daily lives of their "prisoners." The experiment began with the handcuffing and arrest of the prisoners who were then transported to mock prison cells in a university building. The guards stripped and searched them, sprayed them with delousing fluid, took their pictures, and ordered them to remain silent in their cells. The researchers were testing the common belief that the brutality of guards in real prisons is caused by cruel personalities. Is it possible that the situation itself, in which some people have complete power over others, fosters abusive behavior?

As the days passed, the prisoners became increasingly depressed, sometimes crying or showing signs of rage and acute anxiety. Almost half had to be released before a week had passed, and the rest said they would gladly forfeit their pay in exchange for an early release. The guards readily used their authority to abuse the prisoners. They rarely spoke to them except to deliver commands, frequently denied them privileges, and in one case locked a prisoner in the solitary confinement of a small closet all night. They concealed much of their abusive behavior from the experimenters, who they believed were "too soft" on the prisoners. Guards appeared to enjoy their work,

The Zimbardo experiment suggests that extreme power inequality is conducive to abuse. In few situations is this potential more dramatic than when we must remove our clothes in front of someone who has power over us—as do these Texas prison guards searching inmates. Can you imagine how you might feel in each of the social positions in this situation?

volunteered to work overtime without pay, and were disappointed when the experiment ended prematurely. As one of the experimenters recalled:

> At the end of only six days we had to close down our mock prison because what we saw was frightening. It was no longer apparent to us or most of the subjects where they ended and their roles began. The majority had indeed become "prisoners" or "guards," no longer able to clearly differentiate between role-playing and self. There were dramatic changes in virtually every aspect of their behavior, thinking, and feeling. . . . We were horrified because we saw some boys ("guards") treat other boys as if they were despicable animals, taking pleasure in cruelty, while other boys ("prisoners") became servile, dehumanized robots who thought only of escape, of their own individual survival, and of their mounting hatred of the guards. (Zimbardo 1971, p. 3)

These apparently decent young men gave support to Lord Acton's famous statement that "power tends to corrupt and absolute power corrupts absolutely" (see Kauffman 1988). Why should power have this effect? Kipnis (1972) suggested that high levels of power lead to abuse for three reasons.

> 1. Status occupants will use as much power as is available to them. When we have only the power of persuasion, that is what we will use; if our roles allow us to punish and reward others, however, we will rely less on persuasion than on the more powerful means available to us.
> 2. Power allows people to control other people's behavior. In turn, those who have power may come to believe they are superior to those they control. Power may in fact lead to such a boost in self-esteem that the powerful believe they are exempt from usual standards of moral behavior, and they may feel contempt for those they are able to control.
> 3. Contempt for others and an exalted self-image cause people to distance themselves from those they control, to shield themselves from an awareness of how their actions affect others. Under such circumstances, abuse is more likely.

Although authority certainly provides the potential for abuse, there is no reason to expect that everyone will take advantage of it. Masculinity, for example, places a high value on the ability to control and dominate others, while femininity does not. Given this, it would be interesting to see if the Zimbardo experiment would yield similar results if repeated with female prisoners and guards.

The corrupting potential of power is great, but research suggests that powerlessness can have equally corrupting effects. We all need to feel that we can affect other people. In one study, students visited elderly people living in homes for the aged. Half of the elderly people controlled the timing and length of visits, whereas the other half had no control and were visited at random (Schulz 1976). At the end of two months, independent evaluators rated the health of the subjects, and the differences were dramatic. Those who controlled this small segment of their lives were judged to be healthier, more active, and more optimistic about life than those who did not (see also Rodin 1986; Timko and Moos 1989). In addition, other studies find that elderly people who *believe* they control their situations live longer than those who do not believe it, even when the actual levels of control are the same (Rodin and Langer 1977; see also Deci 1980; Schulz and Hanusa 1980).

The importance of power is evident in what often seem to be the most insignificant behaviors and situations (see Molotch and Boden 1985). When we interact with more powerful role partners, for example, we tend to restrict our movements and sit erect with our legs uncrossed and our hands hanging at our sides or clasped in our laps; whereas more powerful people assume relaxed postures that indicate their relative invulnerability to how we judge them (Mehrabian 1972). More powerful people are also more likely to look at people they are speaking and listening to and hold eye contact longer when first meeting someone (Ridgeway, Burger, and Smith 1985). The more powerful are also more likely to cross the boundaries of the less powerful by touching them, staring at them, initiating conversations, or interrupting during conversations (Smith-Lovin and Brody 1989; West 1982). Observations of men and women show that men are more likely to touch women than women are to touch men (Henley 1977; Major et al. 1990), a tendency that is especially evident in the workplace, where men usually occupy more powerful positions than women (Gutek 1985; National Law Journal 1989; Radecki and Walstedt 1980).

Power, perception, definitions of the situation, and attribution are basic elements in all interaction. Like all aspects of social life, however, interaction takes place in physical circumstances that affect what happens.

Microecology

As we saw in Chapter 4, ecology is primarily the study of the relationship between physical environments and societies. The following sections describe **microecology**, which focuses on the ways in which the concepts of population and ecology help explain what goes on in social life on a smaller scale. How does the size of a group affect relationships among its members? How does the physical design of buildings affect interactions among those who live or work in them? How do individuals use physical distance to regulate the intimacy of their contact with other people?

Numbers Count   The old saying "Two's company, three's a crowd" is a statement about one of the simplest aspects of human population, the number of people involved in a social system. How many people, for example, does it take to have a party? Two friends sitting around talking and laughing would hardly say, "What a wonderful party!" but 20 certainly might. Why do numbers matter?

Simmel ([1908] 1965) pointed out that the key to a party is in the number of people. When two friends share dinner, a single mood dominates; but a party is dotted with small subgroups that display different moods and do different things, from dancing and joking to serious conversation. We enjoy parties precisely because they allow us to move freely and find a subgroup in which we feel comfortable regardless of our mood. A party therefore requires enough people to allow subgroups to form.

The smallest group (a dyad) has two members, and we can see some of the effects of size by comparing dyads with three-person groups (triads). As Simmel ([1908] 1965) noted, dyads have the unique property that both members control the relationship's survival, for if either leaves it no longer exists. So long as each partner is free to leave, a dyad depends on consensus, giving each person considerable control over the other and motivating both to resolve conflicts through compromise. In addition, each member of a dyad is highly visible, and any violation of norms is easily noticed.

With three people, one person can lose control over relationships with the other two as their behavior becomes less visible and they form closer ties, or **coalitions** (Caplow 1968; Gamson 1968a; Simmel 1908). Two siblings, for example, may gang up on a third; or when a child is born, one parent may become jealous of the child's bond with the other parent. There is more involved in jealousy than human emotion, for such feelings come about when we perceive a threatening change in our relationships with other people.

As the number of people in a system increases beyond 3, the patterns of interaction tend to change.

TABLE 8-1

The number of possible combinations of members increases much faster than the size of a group. With two people, only one conversation is possible, but that number quadruples with the addition of a third member and almost triples with the addition of a fourth.

GROUP MEMBERS	POSSIBLE COMBINATIONS OF MEMBERS
Anthony Barbara	Anthony-Barbara
Anthony Barbara Peter	Anthony-Barbara Anthony-Peter Barbara-Peter Anthony-Barbara-Peter
Anthony Barbara Peter Gloria	Anthony-Barbara Anthony-Peter Anthony-Gloria Barbara-Peter Barbara-Gloria Peter-Gloria Anthony-Barbara-Peter Anthony-Barbara-Gloria Anthony-Peter-Gloria Barbara-Peter-Gloria Anthony-Barbara-Peter-Gloria

---

We have all experienced the effect that class size has on classroom discussions. With 2 people, only 1 conversation is possible; with 3 people, 4 are possible; and with 4 people, 11 are possible (see Table 8-1). As the numbers increase, the number of possible combinations of group members rises dramatically. With only 7 people there are 120 possible subgroups involving anywhere from 2 to 7 people at a time. With only 25 people (small by current classroom standards), there are 33,554,406!

In even relatively small groups—say 10 people—we find that those who are designated as leaders tend to take over more and more of the interaction (group discussions may be little more than conversations between the professor and one or two students). Other group members tend to feel stifled in their ability to express themselves (and guilty about taking up the group's time). Something as simple as shyness, then, has its roots not only in personality, but in the ecology of groups.

As a characteristic of social systems, the number of people who are involved is neither cultural nor structural, and yet it clearly affects social interactions. It is a *physical* aspect of social systems within which individuals act and experience both themselves and other people.

Coalitions Since Simmel's ([1902] 1950) observations about the tendencies of two people to combine forces against a third member of a triad, two theories have emerged to explain why people form coalitions. Caplow (1956, 1968) suggested that we form coalitions to maximize our control over others and minimize the control others have over us. Gamson (1961, 1964), however, argued that power is not the only motivation—that people also try to maximize their rewards. They realize that if they form a coalition with others, their share of any rewards may depend on the size of their contribution. From this perspective, coalitions form when (1) there is a decision to be made and people want to maximize their own gains from it; (2) no alternative will maximize everyone's gain; (3) no one has the power to make decisions alone; and (4) no one has veto power.

The two theories lead to similar predictions except in the case of a weak person who contemplates joining with a strong one when there are substantial rewards at stake. To see how these theories predict coalition formation, let us apply them to three different situations.

In the first there are three roommates—Sam, Bill, and Mark—who have equal amounts of power. Three coalitions are possible: Sam-Bill, Sam-Mark, and Bill-Mark. Both theories predict that all three coalitions are equally likely: Sam's power increases no more by joining with Bill than with Mark; nor does his share of rewards depend on whom he chooses for a partner.

The second case is a family consisting of Ann and her parents, both of whom have equal power. Ann increases her power regardless of which parent she joins with, and in both coalitions her partner has more power than Ann does. The parents will tend not to form a coalition between them, because each already has more power than Ann. On the other hand, a parent who forms a coalition with Ann gains increased control over the other parent. The most likely coalition is between Ann and one of her parents.

The third case is a gang, one of whose members is more powerful than any of the others and yet is *less* powerful than all of the others combined. Which coalitions would you predict? In this third situation, Caplow and Gamson make different predictions. Caplow's theory predicts that weak gang members will join with the strong in order to increase their

power in relation to other weak members. The strong one would welcome such a coalition because it increases his or her power while still controlling the partners. Gamson however, would predict a coalition that combines the weaker members against the strongest. Why? Weak members increase their power by combining with the stronger one, but when it comes time to divide any rewards, they cannot prevent their more powerful partner from taking the lion's share. By combining only with each other, weak members can both control a stronger one *and* share equally in the rewards, since their partners are equally powerful.

The study of coalitions is important because it shows how members of groups combine to change distributions of power even when there is no formal leadership structure. Weak members of groups and societies can use coalitions to end domination and exploitation by other groups. As individuals, for example, black members of Congress have no more influence than white representatives, but as a coalition, they have considerable influence over legislation.

Space and Social Interaction Physical space affects social interaction in a variety of ways. Intimate distances allow us to see facial details and detect body heat and odors, and make it difficult to be unaware of another's feelings. At moderate distances, we experience people more as objects, which is why we prefer such distances for conducting business or talking with casual acquaintances. Great distances allow us to act without an awareness of others; thus, long-range weapons such as guns and missiles enable us to kill one another with minimal awareness of the harm we do.

Physical arrangements are often used to reinforce the structure of social systems (Sommer 1969). Waiting areas in airports are usually so large that people have little difficulty avoiding contact with one another. In Britain's House of Commons, members of opposition parties are seated across from one another and at close quarters, which encourages heated debate. By contrast, seating in the U.S. House of Representatives is comparatively spacious, resembling a large college lecture hall, and debate involving several members at once is rare.

Physical space is also used to reinforce differences in authority and is an important tool for social control. Judges in courtrooms and clergy in pulpits have physically elevated positions that reinforce their authority. The desks of senior corporate executives are

Notice how the seating in the U.S. House of Representatives is arranged similarly to a theater or large lecture hall. Attention is always focused on the front of the room. Compare this with the British House of Commons. Opponents sit directly across from each other and at close distance, an arrangement that is far more conducive to intense interaction.

often placed far from office doorways, requiring visitors to cross a long expanse while their superiors can sit and examine them. The ability to limit people's access to physical spaces also reinforces power inequality. In many corporations, for example, the offices of lower-level personnel may differ from those of their superiors by not having doors or windows.

People often use space to insulate themselves from others. Privacy and secrecy depend on people not being able to observe behavior. When we vote, our behavior is concealed by booths; houses insulate their occupants from observation by others. Having a room of your own is an important ecological aspect of family life, for it allows individuals a protected place.

When students write take-home exams, their role behavior is invisible to their professors, an ecological problem that is often dealt with through complex norms and values such as honor codes. With in-class exams, however, student behavior is visible both to the professor and other students, making cheating less likely to occur. In both situations, the norms and values concerning cheating are the same, but the physical arrangements in which role performances take place are quite different.

One consequence of all this is that we often misperceive reality when we cannot observe what is happening. The president of the United States is unable to directly observe the actions of most people in the executive branch. This not only makes it impossible to control the everyday workings of government, but also makes the president almost completely dependent on others to act as eyes and ears, a fact that greatly increases the opportunities for misinformation and poor decisions. Almost every president enters office with plans to bring the government under stricter control, but soon learns the ecological fact that it is almost impossible to control people whose behavior cannot be observed.

Microecology adds an important dimension to an understanding of social interaction, but interaction is more than the sum of such factors, for they are but pieces of a larger process. There are several models of interaction, and we will examine three of them.

THE DRAMATURGICAL APPROACH: INTERACTION AS THEATER

Interaction involves people who have ideas about who they are, who present themselves to one another in a variety of ways in order to achieve different effects or simply to act out their ideas of who they are (Tedeschi and Riess 1981). Officials who act "official" and students who act "studious" are creating and maintaining impressions of themselves in the minds of others, just as actors perform before an audience; and, in this sense, all interaction is *dramaturgical* in that it includes an element of theater (Goffman 1959, 1981).

Teachers, for example, often present themselves to students as knowledgeable and capable, thoroughly in command of their subject, and able to answer any question. Students may support this image by blaming themselves when they do not understand what a teacher says, by assuming they have nothing to teach the teacher, or by refraining from asking challenging questions. With colleagues, however, teachers may reveal a very different side of themselves: one that includes feelings of inadequacy, doubts about knowing what they are doing in class, fear of being unable to answer a question, or hostility toward students. Are professors capable, confident, and knowledgeable? Or are they insecure, doubting, and afraid? The most likely answer is that teachers (and everyone else) feel all of these emotions at one time or another, but control how they reveal themselves to others depending on the social situation.

In *The Presentation of Self in Everyday Life* (1959), Erving Goffman described the **dramaturgical approach** to the analysis of social interaction as a continuing performance of actors before audiences. As we saw earlier, we approach people with an awareness that their behavior is affected by their impressions of us and their definition of the situation. We thus have an interest in presenting ourselves to others in ways that produce the results we want (Sagatun and Knudsen 1982). More important, we have an interest in working together to keep the "play" going, for it is only in this way that we can sustain the definition of the situation in which we perform our roles.

To Goffman, we are actors who interact with other actors who are our audience (Goffman's term for role partners). Our performances take place in physical settings, and are guided by the roles we play—the expected behaviors and feelings that we associate with our status in each situation. Together, the roles we play make up a **social script**. When we approach others, we present them with a **front**—our physical appearance, behavior, and definition of the situation—which audiences use to help define the situation for themselves. We rely on various cues to define situations, orient ourselves to the appropriate script, and align our behavior to fit the role we choose to perform. Like theater, interaction has a **frontstage** on which roles are performed before an audience, and a **backstage** where players are freed from the requirements of their role. Just as players are careful not to let the frontstage audience see what they do while backstage, so do social actors **segregate** their audiences.

We can see the sociological usefulness of the dramaturgical approach by seeing how it works in the college classroom. Both students and professors are actors who use one another as audiences for their performances. Before the professor arrives, students sit among themselves and play a variety of frontstage roles appropriate to the pre-class situation, such as "casual acquaintance," "close friend," "stranger," "fellow athlete," and "self-absorbed and not wanting to be bothered." During this frontstage performance students often talk about the professor and the course, as if they are discussing the performance that is about to begin. In this sense, frontstage performances are often at the same time backstage performances in relation to another role.

The professor's entrance is the first of several cues that redefine the situation. On the first day of class the professor's front is a particularly important set of cues for students, for if the professor arrives dressed in dirty jeans and sweatshirt and sits in the back of the room, students lack signals to shift their attention from other students to the professor. Students present fronts of their own that help professors define the situation for themselves. College professors expect to see a room full of young people dressed for the occasion, and if they found a group of people dressed in gym shorts and sporting tennis rackets, they would think they had walked into the wrong "theater."

When the professor stops shuffling papers and looks at the class, the redefinition of the situation is complete. Students then perform **aligning actions** (part of their front) to signal their acceptance of the new definition: they sit quietly, look at the professor, and perhaps take out pencils and open notebooks. Frontstage is now the performance of students and

 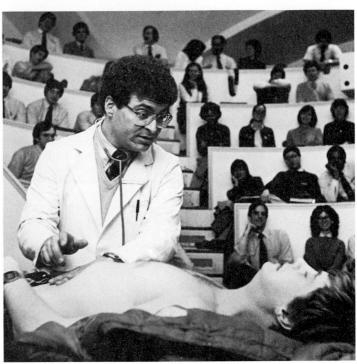

Interaction is this medical school classroom, among students before class and with the professor once the class begins, shows—according to the dramaturgical approach—how students and professors perform as actors and audiences for one another.

professor in relation to one another, and the informal interactions among students that once took place frontstage now take place only backstage. Once actors and their audiences signal agreement on the script, the performance begins.

Professors play their role, controlling who talks and when, and speak with confidence. Students also play their role, taking notes, looking at the professor, and talking only after being recognized. Students are often reluctant to participate in class discussions because they risk making a bad impression on professors and other students. Yet, their role requires that they be there in mind as well as body, and they can indicate their involvement only through behavior.

To protect themselves, many students create an appearance of enough commitment to satisfy their role requirements without exposing themselves to unnecessary risks. They engage in civil attention—by nodding their heads or laughing at appropriate moments, taking notes, refraining from talking among themselves—and they participate when there are low-risk opportunities (Karp and Yoels 1979). Civil attention allows people to play such roles while min-

imizing the risks associated with them (Goffman 1961b, 1963a).

Occasionally students go backstage for a moment to talk among themselves, but they must conceal such behavior from their audience, the professor. Not only does such backstage behavior threaten their own performance, but it also threatens the professor's by redefining the situation and making the professor's script inappropriate. As the center of attention, however, professors have no immediately available backstage in which to escape the pressures of their role.

Throughout the performance, students and professors try to manage the impressions that others have of them, and this process lies at the heart of interaction as theater. In drama, it is not who we really are that matters; rather, it is who we *appear* to be that is central to our performance. Both students and professors try to appear confident and intelligent while concealing ignorance and feelings of insecurity from their respective audiences. They try to maintain the impression that they are seriously committed to the play (lest they appear to be cynical or insincere) and avoid behaviors that are out of character.

Actors defend their performances in a variety of ways. They depend on the loyalty of those who share their status (a student does not reveal to the professor that another student did not do the assigned reading); they try to choose their audiences carefully (professors may prefer young students, who are less likely to challenge them); and they control their faces, bodies, and voices, keeping them "in character." If they fail in their role performance, they often feel embarrassment and are quick to align themselves once again to the situation and its script. Goffman (1956–1957) pointed out that embarrassment actually plays an important part in maintaining the integrity of the play and the actor's part in it. When we make foolish mistakes our embarrassed reaction is a way of signaling to everyone that we know what we were supposed to have done and implies that we will do better from now on. Embarrassment thus expresses a commitment to the script that ties the actors together.

Audiences also feel obliged to help protect an actor's performance. If a professor makes a foolish mistake or stumbles and falls, for example, students may also feel embarrassed and support the professor's performance by acting as if they are unaware of what happened. Such tactful inattention protects both the performer and the audience by maintaining the integrity of the play in which all participate. In this sense, social interaction is unlike the theater, for participants are simultaneously audience and actors.

When professors give the appropriate cues, students know that the performance is over and all actors may retreat to backstage areas—faculty lounges, student dorms, coffee shops, or campus grounds—in which they are free to relax, drop their classroom fronts, and openly discuss what happened on the frontstage. Because the safety of backstage areas depends on controlling who enters them, both professors and students are careful to stay away from each other's respective backstages. (It is important to note that although college dorms and faculty lounges are backstage relative to the classroom, they are themselves frontstages, each with its own particular script.)

In many interactions the definition of a situation is unclear, and actors negotiate about the scripts they will follow. If a woman and man go out on a first date, for example, their cues are often ambiguous, and they explore ways to arrive at a mutually agreeable definition of the situation. The cues each gives off are invitations—such as an invitation to perform the role of friend. Having agreed on a definition, one or both may later try to redefine the situation with a **realigning action**. Such actions constitute a new invitation (or demand), and require them to renegotiate the script.

The negotiation of scripts defines relationships by activating one or more statuses in a person's status set, and the struggle over definitions involves a conflict over which statuses will be defined as latent and which will be defined as manifest in a particular situation. In universities, male professors sometimes try to define a female student's manifest statuses as "female" and "sex object," while she struggles to define those statuses as latent, and defines "student" as her manifest status (see Dziech and Weiner 1984).

Goffman's dramaturgical approach is useful because it focuses on the social mechanisms through which people create and maintain impressions of themselves, choose and control audiences, and rely on one another for the successful performance of roles and confirmation of self-images. Only in the theater of social interaction can we perform before others and find out if they see us as we see ourselves.

When audiences accept a performance, they are in effect saying, "We believe in you." By accepting our presentation of ourselves, they also accept parts of us *as* selves. When audiences reject performances, however, we are likely to feel embarrassment, if not shame, and may then defend ourselves by disowning our performances: "I'm not myself today."

FUNCTIONS AND CONFLICT: INTERACTION AS EXCHANGE

Exchange Theory

On one level, the Golden Rule—"Do unto others as you would have them do unto you"—is a norm that commands us to treat others well. We soon learn, however, that it can also be a strategy for getting what we want: If we are kind to others, then they will more likely be kind to us. Because our behavior affects other people just as theirs affects us, interaction can be seen as a process of *exchange*.

Social **exchange theory** rests on four assumptions about human behavior:

1. We are motivated primarily to avoid pain and gain pleasure.

2. Other people's behavior is a source both of pleasure and pain for us.

3. Because human behavior is performed in relation to others, we can use our own behavior to influence what other people do in relation to us.

4. We try to gain pleasure and avoid cost: we try to make the best deal we can in order to get what we want from others (Blau 1964; R. M. Emerson 1981a).

While we may believe that we love someone "just because," exchange theory suggests that loving is in part a strategy for gaining love for ourselves. In fact, Homans (1974) suggested that we behave according to an emotional "profit motive," by which we judge relationships according to how much we have to invest in them relative to what we gain from them (but see McClelland 1986, for a different view). Caplow (1982) suggested from his study of families that the giving of Christmas gifts is often directed toward those whose relationships are both important to us and not secure enough to take for granted.

The importance of exchange in social life is made clear by the fact that all cultures have norms about what constitutes a fair exchange. Norms about fairness, justice, and reciprocity are vital to the well-being of any social system and apply across the entire spectrum of behavior, from large questions of justice and equality to everyday interactions in which we expect others to do unto us as we have done unto them.

Competition, Cooperation, and Exploitation: The "Prisoner's Dilemma"

As a process of exchange, interaction gives rise to competition and exploitation as well as cooperation. Few studies illustrate the difficult choice between these possibilities more dramatically than the classic "prisoner's dilemma" (Luce and Raiffa 1957).

Imagine a situation in which two criminals are arrested. The police are certain that these two committed the crime, but without a confession they have insufficient evidence to get a conviction. So the police put each in a separate room and present the following alternatives: "(1) If neither of you confesses, you'll be convicted on a minor, trumped-up charge and spend six months in jail; (2) If you both confess, the district attorney will recommend less than the maximum punishment, say four years; (3) If only one of you confesses, the one who does will go free while the other will receive the maximum sentence, ten years." As one of the prisoners, what would you do?

From one point of view, it is best to remain silent, for if neither confesses, both will suffer minimally. The problem with this cooperative strategy is that if you remain silent while your partner confesses, you suffer the maximum penalty while your partner goes free. Hence, there is a dilemma between cooperation and exploitation.

When Luce and Raiffa presented volunteers with this dilemma, they found that prisoners generally do not make cooperative choices: they usually confess, hoping that the other will not, and thus try to gain their own freedom at their partner's expense. Such dilemmas occur frequently in social interaction. When two people consider intimacy, for example, each may feel reluctant to make a commitment, for those who fully commit themselves risk being abandoned or exploited by others. If neither makes a commitment, however, the relationship cannot be truly intimate (Table 8-2).

On a larger scale, the choice between cooperation and exploitation occurs frequently in economic behavior. Economic recessions sometimes confront workers with two alternatives: some lose their jobs so that others may keep theirs at their current rate of

---

TABLE 8-2   The Prisoner's Dilemma Often Occurs in Social Relationships

Consider two people, Arthur and Valerie, who love each other but are unaware of each other's feelings. They can reveal themselves or not, and each option has its risks.

VALERIE'S OPTIONS	ARTHUR'S OPTIONS	
	Reveal Himself	*Not Reveal Himself*
Reveal Herself	They might have a love affair.	Valerie may feel like a fool if Arthur doesn't love her too.
Not Reveal Herself	Arthur may feel like a fool if Valerie doesn't love him too.	They may miss out on the love of a lifetime.

pay, or everyone's pay is cut so that no jobs are lost. The first choice is exploitative, for some workers gain only at the expense of others, while the second is cooperative. The prisoner's dilemma experiments suggest that people will exploit in such circumstances, but other evidence suggests that personal gain is not our only motive. In negotiations between auto workers and manufacturers, unions agreed to lower benefits in exchange for greater job security for all their members, a clear instance of cooperative behavior. Thus, although people rarely cooperate in prisoner's dilemmas in the laboratory, there are many systems whose structure compels us to run the risks inherent in cooperation. In many cases we cannot get what we want without it. When two people want intimacy or when nations want to reduce the risk of war, both parties must make a commitment.

The likelihood of cooperation or exploitation depends partly on the structural aspects of interactions, especially, visibility, communication patterns, and the degree of interdependence (see Axelrod 1984). In the prisoner's dilemma experiment, prisoners could not communicate with each other to share intentions, desires, and needs; nor was a long-term relationship involved. Similar structures can also be found outside the laboratory: when people hear rumors of a bank failure they may rush to withdraw their funds before others do, saving themselves at the expense of others. Or, when goods such as food seem to be in short supply, people may buy up more than they need, thereby depriving others of having any.

Social structures also specify how rewards and costs are distributed in social systems. In a race there is only one winner, and the prize can be had only at the expense of others. Such "zero-sum" games (Von Neumann and Morgenstern 1964; Zagare 1984) exist in many colleges: when grading is done on a curve that limits the number of students who can receive A's (and guarantees that a certain number at the bottom of the curve will fail), competition and exploitation are likely results, with students possibly refusing to help one another. In other situations—such as among combat soldiers in the field or police officers on patrol—the team is no stronger than its weakest member. Each depends on the success of the others to survive. When systems are structured in this way, competition and exploitation threaten the welfare of everyone.

Although social interaction almost always include elements of exchange, it certainly is not the only motivation in social life, as we will now see.

INTERACTION AS A BALANCING ACT

Why are we attracted to some people, but not to others? Why do we sometimes choose as friends people who treat us badly? Why do we feel uncomfortable when two of our friends do not like each other? From an exchange theory perspective, we are attracted to people who give us what we want and want what we have to give, but this does not explain problems such as why we prefer to have our friends like one another. In all these cases, *balance theory* is a useful theoretical point of view (Alessio 1990; Heider 1946).

According to **balance theory**, we organize perceptions of people and objects into units, and we strive for consistency in the positive and negative feelings among them. Consider a paper you write for a college course. You work hard and feel good about it. You also respect and like your professor. In terms of balance theory, you, your paper, and your professor are a unit that involves three relationships—each of which can be positive or negative. Balance theory can be stated in a generalized form: *if we multiply the positive and negative relationships together and the result is positive, then the unit is balanced; if it is*

PUZZLE

FACING THE PRISONER'S DILEMMA

Suppose that during an exam you and a friend help each other. Immediately afterward the professor asks your friend to wait in the classroom alone while she talks to you in her office. She tells you that she thinks the two of you cheated. "If neither of you confesses to me now," she tells you, "I'll find a way to give you both a D for the exam. If you both confess, you'll both flunk the course. If one of you confesses and the other doesn't, however, I'll let the one who confesses go unpunished while the one who doesn't will flunk the course and be reported to the dean's office, which could lead to expulsion from school." What would you do? Why?

This is a classic situation in the study of cooperation, exchange, and exploitation in social interaction.

negative, the unit is unbalanced. Your professor reads, grades, and returns your paper to you. Look at Figure 8-1 and think about how you would feel in each situation.

In (a) the system is balanced and you would feel just fine, but in (b) it is not, and to balance the relationships, you must change your feelings toward your paper ("It must not have been good after all") or toward your professor ("What a creep"). If, however, you did not like your professor to begin with, a low grade will not create an unbalanced situation, whereas a *good* grade will. In the latter situation, you will tend to change your feelings toward the professor ("Not so bad after all") or toward your paper ("If *that* professor liked it, it must not be so hot").

Balance theory also describes what happens when we view ourselves or our behavior as objects in a set of relationships. People with low self-esteem are more likely to associate with people who treat them badly than are people with high self-esteem. Balance theory thus explains Groucho Marx's famous statement, "I wouldn't want to join any club that would accept me as a member" (Figure 8-2). If the club likes Groucho (a "+") but Groucho does not like Groucho (a "−"), then Groucho can balance the relationships only by rejecting the club (a "−") or by liking the club *and* himself.

By the same token, if you and I like each other (two "+'s"), but you dislike yourself (a "−"), the relationships will be unbalanced, and I might try to balance them by getting you to like yourself or by changing my feelings toward you. You also might try to balance the relationships by doing things to show me how dislikable you are.

Balance theory suggests that we are attracted to people who share our values, beliefs, and attitudes, for then the relationships are balanced ("I like you, and we both oppose sexism"). Newcomb (1961) invited college students to live in a house for a semester, and asked them during their stay to complete questionnaires about who they liked and disliked. He found that pairs of students were more likely to become friends if they agreed about themselves, other members of the house, and their values, beliefs, and attitudes. More important, Newcomb predicted friendships with some accuracy using students' views measured *before* they ever met.

What, however, of the belief that "opposites attract"? Does this contradict balance theory? Newcomb (1956) suggested that in many cases differences between people reflect an underlying agree-

FIGURE 8-1 Balance Theory and Students, Professors and Papers.

In (b), the system is unbalanced, and (a) represents one way of balancing it. How else might the imbalance be resolved? With what effects on you or your professor?

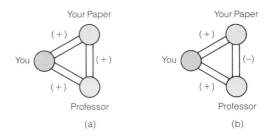

Each positive relationship is marked by a " + " sign, and each negative relationship is marked by a " − " sign.

FIGURE 8-2

Groucho: "I wouldn't want to join any club that would accept me as a member."

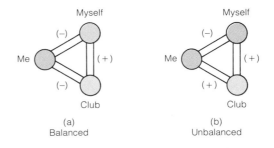

ment on important values. Dominant and submissive people may be attracted to each other not simply because they are opposites, but because they both value dominant-submissive relationships.

Balance theory predicts not only that we tend to like people who are similar to us, but also that we tend to agree with people we like. When friends disagree, there are strong pressures to reduce the imbalance by finding a way to agree. Married couples often adopt similar views in order to balance their relationships (Berger and Kellner 1964; Mirowsky and Ross 1987); and if we are strongly attracted to someone, we may try to change some of our feelings for the sake of balance.

The complexity of social interaction raises many problems for us. We often find ourselves expected to perform according to several different roles at once (resulting in role conflict), or we may confront several possible definitions of a situation. Role playing also raises disturbing questions about authenticity: Are there real selves behind "exchangers," "balancers," and "theatrical performers"?

PERSONAL IDENTITY: AUTHENTICITY AND CONSISTENCY

To see how changes in social status affect people's beliefs, values, and attitudes, Lieberman (1956) asked 2,354 U.S. rank-and-file factory workers questions about unions and management. A year later, he asked the questions again and compared the responses of those who had been promoted to management with two other groups of workers: those who had been promoted to union shop stewards and those who remained rank-and-file workers.

He found that after a year, workers who became supervisors adopted promanagement, antiunion ideas, whereas those who became union shop stewards became more prounion and antimanagement. Before changing statuses, almost none of the workers believed that management really cared about them. After a few years in their new statuses, however, 67 percent of the new supervisors believed management really cared about workers, whereas none of those who became union shop stewards shared this positive view. By comparison, workers who had no change in status showed little change in their perceptions or feelings about unions and management. When Lie-

berman returned to the factory three years later, he found that the supervisors who had been demoted to rank-and-file status tended to return to the attitudes they had held prior to their promotions. How do we explain such shifts?

Exchange theory suggests that workers who become supervisors adopt promanagement ideas because it is in their best interests. Balance theory, however, suggests that when we change statuses, we adopt new reference groups, and our positive feelings toward a new group produce a strain of imbalance if we continue to hold ideas associated with our former status and its reference group. In short, it is difficult to maintain positive feelings toward two reference groups that have a negative view of each other (see Figure 8-3).

From a dramaturgical point of view, new supervisors adopt roles whose scripts call for promanagement ideas and behaviors. Their supervisor status becomes part of their social identity, and they can be true to their new self only by feeling, thinking, and acting accordingly. As Goffman (1961b) wrote, "A self virtually awaits the individual entering a position; he need only conform to the pressures on him and he will find a *me* ready-made for him." As we follow a new script, our behavior reinforces the new role. In Kenneth Burke's words, "doing is being."

Social life is full of such transformations: the radical political activist is elected to Congress and becomes "one of the boys," and although former friends may use exchange theory to explain the change as

FIGURE 8-3 Social Status, Attitudes, and Reference Groups

New supervisors who identify with management, but who continue to share negative attitudes toward management find themselves in an unbalanced situation (a) which can be resolved by adopting positive attitudes. How else might the imbalance be resolved?

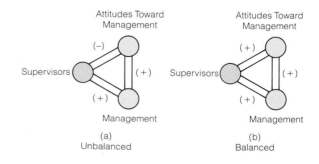

"selling out," the full explanation is undoubtedly more complicated than this, involving both problems of balance and changing identities (Gecas 1981). Graduate students are among the severest critics of faculties, yet as professors they often become more profaculty and antistudent.

Because we play many roles, we may feel as though we have many different selves that we juggle as we shift from one situation to another (Alexander and Wiley 1981; Goffman 1961b). For many people, the dramaturgical perspective in particular paints a disturbing picture of people adopting one "mask" after another, "playing at" being different people in different situations. As Robert Park ([1939] 1950) wrote,

> It is probably no historical accident that the word "person," in its first meaning, is a "mask." It is a recognition of the fact that everyone is always and everywhere, more or less consciously, playing a role. . . . It is in these roles that we know each other; it is in these roles that we know ourselves. (p. 249)

Goffman, however, was careful to point out that role playing does not necessarily involve insincerity or falseness. When we play a role, we reveal some aspects of ourselves while concealing others. We often put on a "mask" only to the extent that we select which parts of ourselves to reveal, and when we perform a role, we integrate one segment of who we are with selected segments of other people (Goffman 1961b). In one situation, we display our "intelligent, competent, independent" self, in another, our "insecure, confused, dependent" self. We do not have to decide which is the "real me," for both are merely different parts of extraordinarily complex creatures.

Although we reveal different aspects of ourselves in different situations, our self-images are relatively stable, and we strive for consistency in our presentations of ourselves (Burke and Reitzes 1981; Mortimer, Finch, and Kumka 1981). The desire to maintain a self-image and the self-esteem that goes with it can be as powerful a motivation as the desire to gain through exchange, to balance relationships, or to act according to expectations inherent in social scripts (Rosenberg 1979).

We are, of course, perfectly capable of faking performances, of donning masks that represent no segment of ourselves (except, perhaps, our desire for approval and other rewards). When capable, intelligent women act dumb and helpless in the presence of men, or when men who need emotional support act tough and self-sufficient, both misrepresent themselves by pretending to be what they are not. With time, others will expect such false performances (accepting and depending on them as real) and the contradictions between who we are and how we appear to others may cause an identity crisis.

In this sense, we struggle not only for balance in our relationships with others, but for an internal balance between what we do and who we think we are. If Goffman is correct that "we are who we present ourselves to be," then self-images will have powerful effects on how we present ourselves to others. This, then, is a central problem for individuals in social interaction: to satisfy our needs and respond to the demands of social life while maintaining a consistent, stable sense of who we are. Because our identities are heavily anchored in statuses whose roles often conflict, the problem of maintaining an "authentic self" can be formidable.

SUMMARY

1. Social interaction is the process through which people act in relation to one another. It depends on a complex process through which we organize and interpret our perceptions of people and situations.

2. How we perceive one another often rests on first impressions that rely heavily on stereotypes. When we act as though stereotypes were true, we may help bring about self-fulfilling prophecies.

3. The definition of the situation identifies which statuses and roles are relevant in a given situation. We often use such definitions in social attribution, which focuses on internal causes such as emotional states and external causes such as role requirements.

4. All cultures include norms about the physical distance between role partners, ranging from the zone of intimacy to personal, impersonal, and public zones. Social boundaries also regulate access to information about ourselves as well as behavior that may not involve physical contact.

5. Power is a factor in most social interaction. Sociologists are less interested in personal power than in authority, for authority is purely social in its origins. Extremes of both power and powerlessness can lead people to do things they would otherwise never consider themselves capable of.

6. Microecology focuses on the ways in which the number of people involved in a situation and physical arrangements affect social interaction. One difference between a dyad and a triad is that in a triad two people can gang up on the third by forming a coalition.

7. The dramaturgical approach to interaction focuses on individuals as actors who are also audiences for each other as they perform parts of a social script. Like the theater, there is a frontstage and a backstage, and audiences and actors use various techniques to protect performances and ensure the continuation of the "play." Realigning actions introduce new definitions of the situation, and aligning actions signal acceptance of them.

8. Exchange theory looks on interaction as a process in which we give to others in exchange for what we want. It assumes that we want to avoid pain and gain pleasure and that these are accomplished primarily in relation to other people. It also assumes that we try to maximize our gains while minimizing our costs. This can be accomplished in ways that, depending on the situation, may involve cooperation, competition, or exploitation.

9. Balance theory suggests that we organize our perceptions of people and objects into units, and that we strive for some consistency in the positive and negative feelings among them. Balance theory helps predict not only how we will feel toward others, but also how we may feel toward ourselves in a particular set of relationships.

10. A major problem for us is to satisfy our needs and respond to social demands while maintaining a consistent, stable sense of who we are.

KEY TERMS

aligning action   174
audience segregation   174
backstage   174
balance theory   178
coalition   171
definition of the situation   165
dramaturgical approach   174

exchange theory   176
external causes   166
front   174
frontstage   174
internal causes   166
microecology   170

realigning action   176
self-fulfilling prophecy   163
social attribution   166
social interaction   161
social script   174
stereotype   164

LOOKING ELSEWHERE

Having studied Chapter 8, you might want to look at related discussions in *Human Arrangements*, which include

■ interaction in college classrooms (Chapter 1, p. 9; Chapter 17, pp. 425–27)

■ interaction in families (Chapter 15, pp. 367–68; Chapter 16, pp. 401–402)

■ group size and social interaction (Chapter 9, pp. 196–97)

■ spatial relationships and interaction in groups (Chapter 9, p. 197)

■ the interactionist perspective (Chapter 5, pp. 103–106)

■ coalitions in politics (Chapter 20, p. 516)

■ racial stereotyping (Chapter 13, pp. 300–301)

■ racial differences in explanations of racial inequality (Chapter 13, p. 302)

■ interaction between men and women (Chapter 14, pp. 349–51)

■ sexual harassment and violence (Chapter 14, pp. 349–50)

■ when doctors lie to their patients (Chapter 15, p. 377)

RECOMMENDED READINGS

Bailey, F. G. 1983. *The tactical uses of passion: An essay on power, reason, and reality*. Ithaca, NY: Cornell University Press. Evoking feelings of recognition often brought up by reading Erving Goffman's work, a social anthropologist looks at the ways in which we use emotion and reason in conflict talk.

Goffman, E. 1959. *The presentation of self in everyday life*. New York: Doubleday. Goffman's classic introduction to his dramaturgical perspective. See also *Forms of talk* (1981). Philadelphia: University of Pennsylvania Press. A collection of essays that focus on the importance of how we talk to each other.

Hall, E. T. 1969. *The hidden dimension*. New York: Doubleday. An anthropological look at how the human uses of physical space affect social interaction.

Sommer, R. 1969. *Personal space: The behavioral analysis of design*. Englewood Cliffs, NJ: Prentice-Hall. An important book that explores the effects of architecture and interior design on social interaction.

9
GROUPS AND FORMAL ORGANIZATIONS

 The group is a basic unit of sociological analysis for several reasons. We orient most of our lives to groups, from the intimacy of romantic couples to the overwhelming complexity of bureaucracies. We experience our most intense desires to "belong" in relation to groups, our greatest fears of rejection, and our deepest conflicts as we perform roles in exchange for the privileges of membership. Some groups are like tiny islands—havens in which we are known and accepted, or prisons from which there is no escape—whereas others are so large and complex that we feel lost and insignificant in them.

Groups meet many of our needs, including those for approval, acceptance, protection, safety, and support for values. We use reference groups to define important parts of who we are and to establish and maintain self-esteem. We grow up in groups, learn, earn livings, and practice religion in them. It is through them that societies govern and defend themselves, distribute justice, heal the sick, distribute rewards, and inflict punishments. Groups are also a source of social conflict and problems: persecution, discrimination, oppression, and warfare are often based on relationships between groups.

The characteristics of groups affect the way they achieve their goals as well as their success in doing so. Social life centers on groups, and by understanding how they work, we can better understand ourselves as participants. We can also understand how groups affect the welfare of society itself: the ability of families to raise children, of governments to govern, of criminal justice systems to control crime, of hospitals to provide health care—all are vitally important.

185

PUZZLE

WHAT KEPT THE WEHRMACHT GOING?

During World War II, units of the German Army often kept fighting even when things looked hopeless, and long after most U.S. units in similar circumstances would have stopped fighting. Why did the German soldiers hang on so long?

Many observers at the time thought (as you might) that perseverance among the German soldiers came from their dedication to their country and the Nazi cause, but as explained in this chapter, the social organization of military units in an army has more to do with the behavior of individual soldiers than any amount of ideology.

The sociological study of groups centers on several kinds of questions, which this chapter examines in some detail. How can we describe groups in ways that allow us to see the cultural, structural, population, and ecological differences among them? How do they distribute power and assign roles to their members? How do group structures and cultures affect what goes on in them? How do groups survive, manage conflict, and maintain the loyalty and obedience of their members? How are individuals affected by groups? How do groups affect our freedom and the quality of our lives?

GROUP CULTURE

All groups are based on shared cultural ideas. Stein and his colleagues argue, for example, that whites often exclude nonwhites from groups not only because of race, but because they assume that nonwhites do not share their values and beliefs (Stein, Hardyck, and Smith 1965). Researchers asked white high school students to answer questions about their values—the desirability of having school spirit, being intelligent, neat, and attractive, or being concerned about other people. They used these responses to create for each student descriptions of two pairs of fictitious teenagers. One pair of teenagers shared the respondent's values, whereas the second did not. In each pair, one of the teenagers was black, and the other was white.

Respondents were then asked how interested they would be in different kinds of contact with the teen-

agers, such as inviting them home to dinner, going to a party together, attending the same school, belonging to the same group, living in the same building, or working together on the same committee. Although the willingness for close contact was negatively affected by race, a wide range of contact was not. What did make a difference in these cases was the respondents' perception of shared values.

Group Norms

The power of group norms is illustrated by a classic study of workers who built telephone switchboards at the Hawthorne plant of Western Electric (Roethlisberger and Dickson 1939). In trying to find how to increase productivity, researchers were surprised to discover that workers often violated company norms (by trading jobs) and seemed unaffected by company rewards for increased production. They worked quickly in the mornings, but slowly in the afternoons, and never reported fellow workers who failed on the job. Men who worked too hard were labeled "rate busters," whereas those who worked too slowly were "slackers."

By working together, these men formed a subgroup with its own subculture that affected their behavior more strongly than the company's norms and values. That this subculture supported violations of company rules stems in part from sharing a common position in relation to the company and society as a whole. As members of the working class, they shared a long-standing tradition of resistance against the attempts of management to extract as much work from them as possible (see also Jones 1990).

The common circumstances of these workers help explain the formation of their subgroup and the conformity of members to its norms; but in many groups, individuals conform even when they do not want to. What conditions allow groups to exert such power over their members?

Pressures to Conform   Pressures to conform in groups have several sources. First, by defining reality and expectations, group culture specifies requirements for membership. Whether we value a group for itself or as a means for achieving personal goals, conformity is the surest way to remain members: we conform to keep our jobs, to stay in school, to keep the love and respect of family members, to maintain a sense of pride and avoid feelings of shame (see Scheff 1988).

Second, we conform to the cultural ideas of reference groups whether or not we are members. Our admiration and affection for the members of a close-knit work group will lead us to use them as models, and when such models are part of our social identity, conformity to the ideas that make up their culture is important if we are to maintain a stable sense of who we are. When we have "heroes and heroines" we often adopt their standards of behavior as our own.

Third, we depend on one another to support our perceptions of reality. If you sit with friends and suddenly smell gas, you are most likely to turn to other people for confirmation: "Do you smell gas?" If they do not support us, we are likely to conclude that our perceptions are faulty; but if they *do* support us, we are far more likely to act on our perceptions as if they were accurate.

The pressures to conform are illustrated by a classic experiment in which eight-member groups were shown a series of sets of four lines for which they were asked to judge which of three lines was the same length as a fourth "standard" line (Asch 1952; see also Perrin and Spencer 1980). Look at Figure 9-1 and imagine that you participated. Each member makes a judgment out loud, and you go last. With the first two sets of lines everyone agrees on which line is the same length as the "standard," but, with the third set, you hear the first person match the standard line with line 1, which is obviously not the same length. As you think about what a big mistake that was, you hear the second member make the same error, then the third, the fourth, and all the rest. Now it is your turn. Do you agree with the group's unanimous judgment or insist on your own?

Asch found that chances are quite good that you would agree with the majority even though their judgments are clearly wrong. Faced with overwhelming opposition, only 20 percent of Asch's subjects openly disagreed with the group. Those who conformed reported afterward that they feared ridicule ("Every time I disagreed I was beginning to wonder if I looked funny") and doubted their own perceptions ("Maybe where I'm sitting is making me see the lines wrong").

Fear of ridicule and rejection are especially important, as Asch (1952) found in a later experiment (see also Noelle-Neumann 1984). This time, only one of the eight people was employed by Asch and instructed to make errors. As the lone confederate made wrong judgments, the other subjects laughed and expressed sarcastic disbelief. As one subject

FIGURE 9-1 Lines Presented to Subjects in Asch's Experiment

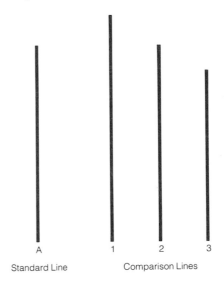

Subjects were asked which of the three lines on the right matched the length of the standard line on the left.
Source: Asch 1952.

said later, "I felt the person was attempting a stupid joke. . . . Then I felt sorry for a person with such poor eyesight." Other studies found similar effects of group pressure (Deutsch and Gerard 1955; Sherif 1936; but see also Perrin and Spencer 1980).

Groups exert strong pressures to conform, especially on people who are attracted to them. Such pressures are particularly important for moral questions that rest less on fact than on values and abstract principles of right and wrong. These studies help us appreciate how extraordinary it is for individuals to defy majority judgments, and how difficult it is to maintain a sense of who we are and what we know in groups.

THE STRUCTURE OF GROUPS

As we saw in Chapter 3, social systems have many structural characteristics that affect what goes on in them. Groups differ in the boundaries that define membership, and in the number and content of the roles members are expected to perform. They have patterns of affection that may bind some members more closely to one another than to the group as a whole. Groups differ in the amount of power they have in relation to other groups and the ways in which power and prestige are distributed among members. Patterns of communication describe which members interact, with whom, how often and for what length of time.

Groups such as families and friendship groups exist for their own sake, endure through time, and involve members in many aspects of one another's lives. Others—such as work groups—are limited to specific goals that, once reached, usually end a member's involvement in the group. Groups may be informal, relying on folkways to control behavior; or they may be formal, with specific rules that rigidly define and control role relationships.

Boundaries

All groups have boundaries that distinguish nonmembers from members. Norms not only define who is eligible for membership, but also distinguish between different kinds of nonmembers: some are eligible to belong whereas others are not, and some want to belong more than others (Merton 1968). A large pool of eligible members who refuse to join a group can harm it by raising questions about its attractiveness. In this sense, groups have relationships not only among their members, but with nonmembers as well.

Time, Space, and Boundaries   Time is often used to define group boundaries. Whereas some groups exist only briefly, others survive across many generations. Individual membership also varies in duration from a few hours to a lifetime. Some groups literally use time to define themselves, such as "the college class of 1996."

If you listed the members of your family, you would probably include only living relatives. A family tree, however, spans hundreds of years and includes both living and deceased members. We expect membership in a family to endure for a lifetime, and the family itself to endure long after we die. Such expansive time boundaries give us a sense of permanence, continuity, and stability, and make the family the most important group in our lives (Back 1981). In contrast, work groups are defined primarily by strict limitations of time and place; and, although the groups may survive indefinitely, their members generally do not stay very long, which makes it difficult to maintain a strong commitment of members to the group.

During the Vietnam War, for example, U.S. troops were trained in one group, then transferred to others

for one-year tours of duty. Because membership was clearly limited in time, soldiers cared less about the goals of their unit or the army than they did about the safety of themselves and their friends (George 1971; Moskos 1969). Their attitude toward replacements tended to be, "I've done my time; let the others do theirs."

> The end of the war is marked by the date a man leaves Vietnam, and not by its eventual outcome—whether victory, defeat, or stalemate. Even discussion of broader military strategy and the progress of the war . . . appears irrelevant to the combat soldier: "My war is over when I go home." (Moskos 1969, p. 16)

Clarity and Openness   Group boundaries sometimes restrict membership in subtle ways (Simmel [1902] 1950). In her study of corporations, Kanter (1977b) found that since women almost always constitute a small minority at middle and upper job levels, men try to "heighten" group boundaries to exclude women. The men were more likely to make sexual remarks in front of women than in front of other men. At meetings, they sometimes apologized for an off-color expression they were about to use and then went ahead and used it anyway. This simple act singles women out as outsiders who interfere with what is defined as the normal functioning of the group. By making the presence of "token" women more visible, men increased their solidarity with one another by heightening their own visibility as members of a dominant social category.

Voluntary and Involuntary Membership   People often join groups because they value the group as an end in itself. Many people are church members because they enjoy the ritual of the services and the contact with other people who share their faith. Similarly, many people attend college because they enjoy learning, or work because they find it satisfying. In other cases, individuals join groups as a means to an end. Some people attend church to avoid damnation, to make business contacts, or to impress their neighbors. Students often attend college not to satisfy a desire to learn, but to earn the degrees required for good jobs.

Whereas membership in some groups is voluntary, in others—mental hospitals, prisons, and elementary schools—it is not. In such cases, membership is a means to someone *else's* end. Involuntary membership not only ensures a group's survival, but also gives it more control over its members who are deprived of the right to make many decisions and are

Groups use a variety of ways to define boundaries. For this urban gang in Los Angeles, use of a hand sign is one way to distinguish the in-group from out-groups.

vulnerable to abuse and exploitation by those whose ends their membership serves.

The draft illustrates the importance of involuntary membership for the survival of groups, for many argue that the military needs it to get enough members to achieve its goals. While ensuring a sufficiently large membership, however, the draft is dysfunctional for social cohesion: people who are forced to join have a low commitment to the organization, which can have disastrous consequences in combat. The draft also raises important questions about individual rights, as it forces young men to kill and risk their lives for goals they do not choose.

In-Groups and Out-Groups William Graham Sumner (1906) believed that groups become **in-groups** by developing a strong sense of "we-ness" and hostile attitudes toward **out-groups**. "Loyalty to the group, sacrifice for it, hatred and contempt for outsiders . . . all grow together, products of the same situation" (p. 13). There are many examples of this: the hostility of students toward "arch rival" schools, intense hatreds between nations, and the hostility that underlies the use of hundreds of slurs and epithets that different racial and ethnic groups apply to one another (Allen 1983).

In the late 1970s a religious cult called the People's Temple formed around a single man, the Reverend Jim Jones, and settled in the South American country of Guyana (see Hall 1987). While the cult gave many downtrodden people a sense of purpose, it maintained its boundaries by requiring such intense in-group loyalty that members had to cut their ties with all outsiders, fearing out-groups as "the enemy," and labeling criticism from the outside as lies. When a congressman, journalists, and concerned relatives visited the colony, Jones convinced his followers that the visitors wanted to destroy the cult. Not only were several of the visitors murdered, but over 900 members obeyed Jones' command to commit suicide, accepting his belief that the only alternative was the destruction of their colony.

Although there is ample evidence that groups develop a strong sense of in-group loyalty and a hostile, superior attitude toward nonmembers, such attitudes are by no means inevitable (Merton 1968). Many groups, for example, are subgroups of larger groups: members of college athletic teams may have a strong sense of group loyalty, but they are also members of other groups—dorms, fraternities, sororities, and classes—on whom they depend for support.

Power and Leadership

Who controls groups, and why are some groups more powerful than others? Groups distribute power in distinct ways, and sociologists are interested how this affects groups and their members. Power differences between groups are also important, for groups are often a source of social conflict.

Members who are able to define a group's culture have considerable control over group life. In Jonestown, Jones had the power to define all nonmembers as "enemies," and his control over group beliefs and values resulted in mass obedience to his command to commit suicide. Individuals also derive power from their ability to control resources: when children play baseball, it is not unusual for the one who supplies the bat and ball to have a disproportionate share of power to decide which rules to play by. Control over patterns of communication is an additional source of power: committee chairpersons decide who talks during meetings, and can use their power to stifle dissenting points of view. Those who perform roles that are important to a group or organization—and who perform them well—also tend to have a relatively large share of power (Pfeffer 1981).

In groups with leadership structures, leaders perform a variety of roles, such as coping with external and internal threats, maintaining unity and order, managing anxiety and conflict among members, and motivating them to participate. **Expressive leaders**, for example, concern themselves with maintaining group harmony, soothing frustrated or angry members, breaking tension with humor, or being a scapegoat who takes the blame for group failures. **Instrumental leaders** are oriented toward group tasks, from deciding who will do what in order to accomplish a goal to being a critic who observes and comments on how well the group is working. As Whyte (1981) observed in his study of urban gangs, some groups depend on leaders for their very identity as a group:

> The leader is the focal point for the organization of his group. In his absence, members of the gang are divided into a number of small groups. There is no common activity or general conversation. When the leader appears . . . the small units form into one large group. . . . The leader becomes the focal point in the discussion. A follower starts to say something, pauses when he notices that the leader is not listening, and

begins again when he has the leader's attention. When the leader leaves the group, unity gives way to the divisions that existed before his appearance. (p. 258)

When power is distributed evenly, the power structure is **democratic** (or egalitarian), and as power is increasingly concentrated in the hands of a few people, the structure becomes more **authoritarian**. Most fall between these two extremes, with some people having more power than others but no one having complete control. Some groups have a **pluralistic** structure in which authority is divided among specialists. Families in which spouses divide task and expressive roles are typical of groups that rely on pluralistic leadership. Groups that exist to accomplish specific goals, however, such as a jury, usually have a single leader.

Many groups do not have leaders, but even in those that do, authority is not necessarily concentrated in a few hands. This is particularly true in complex organizations. The presidents of corporations, for example, are clearly the most powerful leaders; and yet their effectiveness depends on hundreds if not thousands of employees organized into small work groups. Leaders depend on their followers to perform their roles and keep them informed of what is happening in the organization. The ability of followers to withhold or distort information gives them considerable power in spite of their low position in leadership structures (Weber [1925] 1947).

When Are Leaders Necessary? Although people are generally reluctant to surrender individual freedom by giving power to a leader, several social conditions prompt the emergence of leaders. First, members often give power to leaders in order to achieve valued goals. A group of friends, for example, usually lacks specific goals, and, therefore, has no leader; but people adrift in a lifeboat share a deep commitment to survival and are far more likely to appoint one.

Second, the more complex a group's role structure is, the more it needs a leader to coordinate the different roles its members perform. Students working on a project may not need a leader until they divide tasks. Third, regardless of complexity, large groups are more likely to have leaders than small ones are. Studies of groups of varying sizes reveal that regardless of members' personalities, as size increases, a few members tend to dominate group interaction (Reynolds 1971).

Finally, leaders tend to emerge when a crisis threatens the group. Many nations and organizations have given enormous power to leaders during crises: Robespierre during the French Revolution, Adolph Hitler in Germany, Stalin after the Russian Revolution, Franklin Roosevelt during the Great Depression, and Lech Walesa during the labor crises in Poland in the 1980s. For this reason, times of crisis are particularly dangerous for groups, because leaders are in a position to abuse the power given to them by their members.

Where Do Leaders Come From?   Crises, group size and complexity, and a commitment to common goals help explain why some groups have leaders, but how do members decide who will lead them? Professors are not hired by the students they teach; nor do workers appoint managers. In such cases, the selection of leaders depends on norms, and from a sociological point of view, such processes are straightforward and of relatively little interest. A more interesting case is the emergence of leaders in groups that initially lack a leadership structure. How are they selected?

During the 1930s and 1940s, researchers tried to identify personality characteristics shared by leaders, including self-confidence, intelligence, dominance, empathy, and an outgoing personality. Their research methods were so varied and ambiguous, however, that later research found many contradictions: traits that were related to leadership in one study were unrelated in others. Although personality certainly makes a difference (shy, retiring people are unlikely to become leaders), the personality approach was abandoned in the 1950s as researchers focused on behavior in groups.

One factor that affects the rise of individuals to leadership is their *rate of participation in group interactions*: the more members talk, the more influence they tend to have. Even shy people can become leaders if they are encouraged to participate. In an experiment, Hastorf (1965) asked small groups to discuss case studies; during the first session, he identified individuals whose participation was next to the lowest. In the second phase, members were separated by panels equipped with green and red lights. Participants were told that experts on group interaction controlled the lights, that "green" encouraged talk, while "red" advised silence.

During this phase, the lights were used to encourage the previously silent members to talk, and their contributions jumped by 50 percent. In the third phase, discussion continued without the lights, yet these members continued to talk the most; and in members' final ratings of one another's contributions, the initially silent member moved from third to second place.

Apparently, under the right circumstances, anyone has the potential to play a leadership role. People who cannot imagine themselves as leaders may find that merely by speaking up, they acquire surprising levels of power. This underscores the fact that leadership is a social status, that leaders are those whom group members *identify* as leaders (see Zelditch and Walker 1984). From this perspective, it is easier to see how "unlikely people"—Presidents Harry Truman and Lyndon Johnson—who are thrust into leadership positions during crises can perform very well. It is also easier to understand how people who are unfit for leadership nonetheless attain positions of authority through frequent, highly visible participation in group activities.

A second factor in leader selection is *latent statuses* that have no recognized role in group activities (Markovsky, Smith, and Berger 1984; Ridgeway 1981; Ridgeway and Berger 1986; Smith-Lovin and Brody 1989). In newly formed groups, members lack specific information about one another and therefore tend to rely on their general expectations and judgments of other, nongroup statuses such as race, gender, occupation, and age. On juries, for example, men and those with high-prestige occupations tend to be given greater credibility and have more influence than women and those with lower-prestige occupations.

Conformity to norms is a third factor in the selection of leaders, especially in a group's early stages. Hollander (1960) planted confederates in problem-solving groups and supplied them with the correct answers to the problem. The groups established norms, which the confederates violated (by speaking out of turn) at different stages of the meeting. Although the confederates always offered the correct solution to the problem, when they spoke out of turn at the beginning of the session they were generally ignored; when they obeyed the rules until mid-ways in the meeting, the confederates' influence was greater; and when they conformed until the meeting was nearly over, their influence reached a maximum. Members initially identified as nonconformists are unlikely to become leaders regardless of their contributions.

Ridgeway (1981) used a similar experiment and found that the effect of conformity may not be as simple as Hollander suggests. She found that non-conformity can increase influence by attracting the attention of other members, but that this can be tricky since nonconformists may be seen as caring more about themselves than the group. Nonconformity was particularly dangerous for members who occupy latent statuses that are relatively low in prestige. Ridgeway concluded that the most important factors in determining influence are other people's perceptions of a member's motivation and competence in performing group tasks and, as we saw above, latent statuses such as gender and occupation.

Communication Structures

One of the most important aspects of a group's structure is its *communication structure*. Figure 9-2 shows several family communication structures. In (a), family members interact with one another a great deal, whereas in (b), the father interacts heavily with the mother, but little with his children. In (c), which represents many families with divorced parents, the father is "absent," interacting minimally with other family members, and in (d), the heaviest interaction takes place between the children, as might occur when both parents are employed.

Such differences are important in several ways. First, observations of small groups show that frequent interaction strengthens attachments to the group and tends to make them happier. Thus, group cohesion and member satisfaction will tend to decrease as we go from (a) to (c). Second, members must communicate in order to know about each other and get feedback about their behavior. In

(b), the father and children depend largely on the mother for information about each other, while in (c), they are isolated from each other. In comparison with (a), then, the structures in (b) and (c) are likely to result in considerably more misunderstanding and conflict between the father and his children.

Third, because interaction strengthens ties between group members, communication structures affect the formation of subgroups. The tendency to form subgroups will be least in (a), while in (b) three distinct subgroups are likely: mother-father, mother-son-daughter, and son-daughter. In (c), the father is a peripheral member and may be excluded by the mother-son-daughter subgroup, and in (d) the children may develop a bond that strongly influences family decisions.

Primary and Secondary Groups

Primary groups are based on relationships in which the welfare of individuals is more important than the achievement of goals. Primary relationships are valued for their own sake, they endure even when circumstances change, and involve many aspects of people's lives. Primary ties are based on affection and involve frequent face-to-face interaction (Cooley [1909] 1962). We do not expect to gain from such relationships: we would not say, "She's my sister because she lends me money." It would be more accurate to say, "She lends me money because she's my sister."

Relationships in **secondary groups** focus on goals that are valued more highly than the welfare of individuals. They involve only the parts of mem-

FIGURE 9-2   Family Patterns of Communication

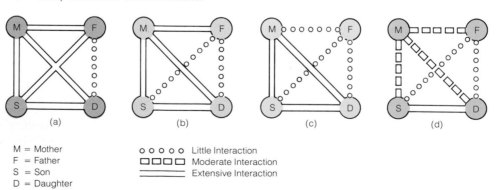

M = Mother
F = Father
S = Son
D = Daughter

○ ○ ○ ○ ○   Little Interaction
▢▢▢▢   Moderate Interaction
———   Extensive Interaction

Each diagram represents the lines of communication that connect members of a family. Which is closest to your own family? How would life in your family change if the pattern changed to one of the others?

bers' lives that are related to achieving those goals, are based on rational considerations of self-interest rather than feelings of affection, and are relatively short-lived. Interaction is limited to specific times and places and is often impersonal. This is the kind of relationship found most often in complex societies such as our own—buyers with sellers, teachers with students, bosses with employees, judges with lawyers, nurses with patients. Most groups include relationships that contain both primary and secondary characteristics—police officers, for example, work together not only to achieve specific, limited goals (such as earning a living and enforcing the law) but, often, because they like one another.

The distinction between primary groups such as families and small groups of close friends and secondary groups such as those found in school classrooms and most work settings, is important to individuals and groups. Primary groups are at the heart of social life, for it is within them that we are valued and protected simply because we are members of the group. They give our lives a sense of continuity and stability and provide the only opportunities for affection and being known by others as complex individuals.

Secondary groups cannot give us a sense of stability and continuity, of belonging and worth, for they value group goals more than the welfare of individual members. We can lose our places in them quite easily, and the groups themselves can dissolve quickly. When individuals heavily invest themselves in secondary groups—such as at work—they often find that their world "falls apart" if they suddenly lose their jobs. Secondary groups, however, offer us greater control over our participation, including the aspects of ourselves we reveal to others (for this reason many people use workplaces as a refuge from the revealing intimacy of family life).

It is generally more difficult for a secondary group to control its members, since their loyalty is usually limited to specific goals and activities. It is difficult for employers to have much control over what workers do outside of working hours. Secondary groups, on the other hand, are more likely to survive across generations, because they can replace their members more easily. They can also coordinate large numbers of people to accomplish complex goals. It would be impossible, for example, to organize a university or an army solely around primary relationships.

Primary groups are often regarded as superior to secondary groups because they help meet human needs such as those for intimacy and emotional support. However, they also can be sources of considerable problems for their members. We lose a great deal if we "quit" a family and such ties are difficult to replace. By exposing many aspects of our personal lives in them, we make ourselves vulnerable to exploitation, humiliation, and abuse. Many emotional problems that plague us as adults have their roots in our experiences in the family, and studies of family violence identify the family as one of the most dangerous of all groups (see Chapter 16).

Formal Organizations and Bureaucracy

By definition, primary groups have an informal structure in which relationships are flexible and norms are rarely stated explicitly. Although this is true of some secondary groups (social clubs), most have a formal structure that clearly defines role relationships. In groups with specific goals, it is difficult to coordinate people's behavior in predictable ways. Especially when groups have many members who specialize in a variety of tasks, they cannot depend on members to negotiate the terms of their relationships as they go along. A response to this problem is the **formal organization**, in which relationships are regulated by clearly stated, rigid norms oriented to the achievement of specific goals.

The most complex type of formal organization is **bureaucracy**, a set of secondary relationships rationally organized to achieve specific goals. People specialize in roles that are narrowly and rigidly defined. Power is distributed in a hierarchy, and administrators oversee other people's role behavior to ensure that everything works as it is supposed to (Weber 1922a, 1922b). Bureaucracies value the organization and its goals most highly, and place a premium on technical efficiency, rationality, precision, speed, reliability, strict obedience, and the highest possible production at the lowest possible cost. Bureaucracies also rest on beliefs that the best decisions are made by experts (without regard for feelings) and that efficiency is highest when leaders are authoritarian and members are motivated by the desire to maximize their own rewards, rather than by ties of love and affection. A bureaucracy is a particularly passionless organization that tries to rely exclusively on rationality, impersonal relationships, inequality, specialization, and loyalty based on calculations of individual self-interest.

Bureaucracies are unique in the norms that structure relationships among their members. As an ideal type, bureaucracy rests solely on norms that clearly

Every college and university student knows that higher education has become increasingly bureaucratic, as this all-too-familiar scene of college registration suggests.

specify how roles are assigned, how power and rewards are distributed, and how decisions are made. Such norms specify what members should do in every situation and forbid the use of personal feelings and individual discretion: decisions are made "by the book," not on a case-by-case basis. In contrast, expectations are loose in informal groups, and each member has some power over group interactions ("You can't do that." "Who says?"). In a bureaucracy, however, even the most powerful member is limited by clear norms that anyone can refer to ("According to the bylaws, you can't do that").

While bureaucracies are relatively efficient producers and distributors of goods and services, their higher efficiency comes at a price. People tend to feel lost and invisible, participating in something so complex that they easily are kept from understanding how it works. College students often feel as though they are known more by numbers than by names; workers are easily laid off by people they have never met—and then replaced by other workers who

are equally unknown as individuals with names and faces. The productive work of the office and the assembly line is split into increasingly specialized tasks performed in efficient, yet impersonal settings. Walk through the offices of any large corporation, and you will see endless rows of desks that, save for a small picture or a flower, look exactly the same.

Bureaucratic norms require people to respond to others as "cases"—not as people with individual needs, desires, and circumstances—and this both solves and creates problems. On the one hand, formal relationships allow us to disclaim personal responsibility for the consequences of our behavior, so long as we adhere strictly to the rules. This, however, requires us to distance ourselves from other people in a way that may make us feel more like machines than human beings.

Consider the example of Clare, who applies for unemployment compensation and is told by the claims processor, Julio, that due to a technicality, she does not qualify for benefits. "If it were up to me," he says, "I'd give you the benefits, but the rule is clear. I haven't got a choice. It's nothing personal; I'm just doing my job."

Clare tries to make eye contact with him, to arouse feelings of sympathy and make it a personal matter between the two of them. Julio, however, sticks to the rules, acting not as a feeling individual but as a status occupant who has no personal control over his clearly and rigidly defined role. Clare wants him to treat her as an individual with feelings, to relate to her on a personal level that calls upon his human capacity for empathy and compassion. Julio, on the other hand, uses his status and its role requirements as a shield against personal involvement; yet he cannot help feeling some responsibility.

In a bureaucracy, individual members are easily replaced, for unlike informal groups, bureaucracies do not depend on particular individuals for their survival. Whereas a family is a group of specific *individuals*, a bureaucracy is a collection of social *statuses* whose relationships are structured not to benefit individuals, but to achieve goals within a rigid, stable set of mutual expectations among members. The bureaucratic ideal represents a complete submersion of individuals in a social organization and the resulting irrelevance of individual feelings and needs.

The Birth of a Bureaucracy Whyte's (1950) study of restaurants shows how bureaucracies emerge as groups grow larger and more complex. Suppose two people decide to open a small restaurant. In its early stages, the structure is informal and may have some of the characteristics of a primary group. Everyone is identified as an individual; shares specific tasks such as cooking and serving food, paying bills, and ordering supplies; and handles crises as they arise. Because they interact continually with each other, they can negotiate responsibilities as they go along.

Business booms and they add several employees to cook and serve the food. The owners now have to coordinate the work of several different people, which might lead to the creation of formal expectations about work hours, dress, and conduct on the job. If their business is very successful, they might open several restaurants, or perhaps expand into a chain extending across many states. Now they must hire managers to direct each restaurant, accountants to keep the books, and, if they sell stock in their company, a board of directors to oversee the entire operation. What began as a small informal group grows into a bureaucracy in which relationships are

formally defined. The company tends to become more important than its members, any of whom can be replaced with relative ease. Although the original members had equal levels of power, this more complex, formal organization has a clearly defined hierarchy, with directors at the top and dishwashers at the bottom.

The structural complexity of bureaucracy is rooted in the development of more complex societies over the last 1,000 years. Murdock's data on preindustrial societies (1967) show that only 29 percent of villages in advanced horticultural societies were autonomous, free of dominating governments above them, whereas in simple horticultural societies, fully 79 percent were governed solely at the local level. The establishment of central governments spawned increasingly complex societies with formal legal codes, standing armies, and thousands of administrators (Lenski and Lenski 1987).

The Industrial Revolution gave the growth of bureaucracy an enormous boost by bringing together large numbers of people with specialized roles. The increased scale and the complexity of production changed the organization of society itself as governments, schools, hospitals, and other organizations adopted the bureaucratic model (Zucker 1983). In the 1800s, schools in the U.S. had only one teacher who was responsible for everything from deciding what and how to teach to disciplining students. There were no principals, vice-principals, secretaries, or heads of departments. By comparison, the twentieth-century public school has all of the hallmarks of a bureaucracy. Teachers no longer decide what they will teach or, in many schools, *how* they will teach. Jobs once performed by a single teacher are now divided among many specialists, from the lowest clerk to the most powerful principal. Students are required by law to attend school and cannot graduate unless they fulfill specific academic requirements. Teachers must be certified by the state in order to work, and the conditions under which they are promoted or fired are clearly spelled out. Power is distributed in a hierarchy from the principal at the top to students at the bottom. Written records are kept on every aspect of school life, from test scores to school budgets and teacher performance; and specialists—administrators—do nothing but manage the complex relationships and ensure that everything works as it is supposed to.

The bureaucratic ideal has even influenced criminals, for although organized crime once revolved

FIGURE 9-3   Organizational Chart for the Benguerra Crime "Family"

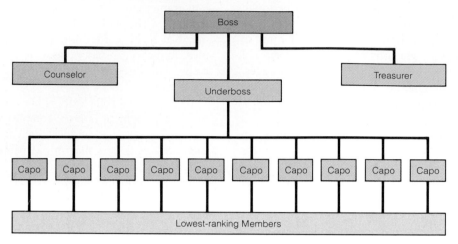

As you can see, bureaucracy has extended into areas of life where you would not expect to find it. The lines show directions of authority (who is answerable to whom). An underboss sees to it that the orders of the boss are carried out and is like a vice-president who takes over in the absence of the president. The counselor and treasurer are answerable only to the boss and have no authority of their own. There are ten "capos"—leaders of subgroups that control particular areas (such as neighborhoods) or operations (such as numbers, drugs, bookmaking, loansharking, or prostitution)— and below each capo are the lowest-ranking group members who carry out the work of a subgroup (such as collecting bets, enforcing loans, bribing public officials, and murder).

Source: Anderson 1979.

around primary family ties, it now operates much like large corporations (see Figure 9-3).

POPULATION, ECOLOGY, AND GROUPS

The size of a social system's population is an important part of the rise of bureaucracy, and the ecological perspective draws attention to both group size and the spatial arrangement of its members, two important factors that affect the cultural and structural characteristics of social systems.

Group Size

Although the smallest group has only two members, it is difficult to establish the upper limit on possible group size. At some point, however, a group ceases to be a group and becomes a **collectivity**, in which people identify themselves as members but do not interact with one another. The American Civil Liberties Union, for example, began with only a few members who, together, made up a group; but it now has tens of thousands of members and hundreds of chapters across the country. Since many of its members never interact with other members (they join simply by making a donation), the ACLU is no longer a group.

As group size increases beyond three, members tend to specialize in different tasks, and the group may become more formal in order to control a more complex role structure. In addition, members of large groups are less visible than those in smaller ones and can violate group norms with less chance of being detected. A large group allows its members to "hide," which lowers their sense of responsibility to the group. As a result, large groups generally have less cohesion than smaller ones, and individuals tend to feel less valued. Some students prefer small group discussions for this reason—they feel more involved, important, and visible—whereas others avoid such classes for the same reason (see Sale 1980).

A large group is also more likely to include members with unusual characteristics. If only 10 percent of a student body are political radicals, a four-member student judiciary board is unlikely to have a radical member. A 100-member student senate, on the other hand, can expect to have at least ten radicals

(10% of 100) simply by chance. Larger groups are more likely to be heterogeneous, which increases the chances for internal conflict.

The power of groups in relation to other groups is also affected by size. Although small groups are generally weaker than large ones, the relationship between size and power depends both on a group's *absolute* size and its *relative* size (Merton 1968; Simmel [1902] 1950). Three hundred blacks fighting for their civil rights have far less power in a city of a million whites than in a small town with 500 residents.

Group power also depends on the *completeness* of membership—the proportion of eligible members who are actual members (Simmel [1902] 1950). Seventeen million U.S. workers belong to labor unions; but 84 million workers do *not* belong, even though many of them could if they wanted to (USCB 1990a). While the absolute and relative size of the labor movement gives it considerable power, it is undermined by the visible pool of eligible workers who do not join.

Space and Social Structure

Spatial relationships affect the structure of groups in many ways. Family members interact frequently simply because they share the same dwelling; and while children are young, frequent interaction supports family unity and allows members to exert considerable control over one another. When children mature and leave home, interaction declines, sometimes causing shocks to parental power and the family's sense of itself as a group. Members may lose touch with one another, and no longer share important events such as holidays. At best, they may feel they no longer know one another; at worst, they may feel they no longer have a family at all.

The spatial arrangement of people within groups also affects patterns of interaction. When discussion groups are arranged in a circle people tend to talk with those across from them more than the ones next to them. At rectangular tables, the people sitting at each end tend to interact more frequently and, as we saw earlier, those who interact the most in groups are the most likely to emerge as leaders.

The military often uses spatial relationships to build cohesion in small units such as platoons. In the U.S., recruits enter the military with a variety of backgrounds and personal characteristics that distinguish them from one another. During training, they are housed in open barracks that give them no privacy and force them to live in the same conditions.

No personal articles—such as pictures—may be displayed. The physical environment of basic training is designed to submerge the recruits' sense of themselves as unique individuals in order to foster a new, common identity as platoon members. As we will see later, such ties are vitally important for the performance of groups and individuals. When prisoners of war are isolated from one another, for example, the resulting lack of interaction seriously damages group cohesion and the support that each member receives.

Spatial relationships are also used to reinforce distributions of power and prestige in groups. In his study of restaurants, Whyte (1950) observed that cooks often avoid face-to-face interaction with waitresses, because they dislike "taking orders" from workers who are ranked below them in prestige. In most restaurants, cooks and waitresses are separated by physical barriers; and in larger ones, orders are written and then passed to the cooks without any direct contact between cooks and waitresses.

The preceding descriptions and analyses of how groups vary in culture, structure, size, and spatial arrangements may give the false impression that groups consist of rigid relationships that lead their members to behave in predictable ways all of the time. What members *do*, however, often changes group structures and cultures.

SOCIAL INTERACTION: GROUP PROCESS

Group process—what people actually do in groups—is important because it causes groups to change in response to new circumstances and to the behavior of their members.

A major problem in the study of group process is that of accurately observing what goes on. After participating in a small group discussion, for example, you might have many impressions of what happened, such as "So-and-so talked a lot," "We got nowhere," or "Things went well." Although such impressions help us make sense of what happens, they are not a scientific description. You might describe one member's contributions as "stupid," but someone else might describe that same person as "daring and constructive." In short, you most likely do not use an objective point of view that would yield similar results no matter who did the observing. Your impressions also tend to be highly selective. You may pay little attention to the remarks of people you do not like or miss large chunks of the meeting while you are thinking about what you are going to do afterwards.

The problem of inaccuracy in observing group process is especially great when it blinds us to systematic patterns that underlie important social differences. In their study of sexism in schools, for example, Sadker and Sadker (1985) showed a film of a classroom discussion to teachers and administrators and then asked them who talked more, the boys or the girls. The educators reported overwhelmingly that the girls talked more; but trained observers who counted each act of talking found that boys talked more than three times as much as girls. The dominance of boys in the classroom was apparently masked by the cultural stereotype that girls are more talkative than boys.

In response to such problems, Bales (1950) and his colleagues developed a method for observing and recording interaction in small groups. They developed a set of categories (Table 9-1) to measure who does what in relation to whom, how and when they do it, under what conditions, and with what effects on other members and the group as a whole. To use this method, observers must record everything members say and do in the appropriate category. The result is a record of (1) the total number of each type of act; (2) each member's total participation, overall and for each category; and (3) the patterns of interaction—who did what in relation to whom. Such records create a "map" of group interactions.

TABLE 9-1   Bales' Group Process Categories

TYPE OF ACT	EXAMPLE
Shows Solidarity	"I think we've done well."
Shows Anger	"You stink."
Agrees	"I'll vote for that."
Disagrees	"That's not how it happened."
Shows Tension	Taps a pencil on the table.
Releases Tension	"I'll drink to that!" (laughs)
Makes a Suggestion	"Let's take a vote."
Asks for Suggestion	"Any ideas?"
Gives an Opinion	"I don't think it'll work."
Asks for Opinion	"Will it work?"
Gives Orientation	"We're running out of time."
Asks for Orientation	"What was the assignment?"

In solving problems, groups tend to pass through a series of stages that can be charted using Bales' categories. Groups begin with pleasantries—saying hello, making jokes—that heighten feelings of group solidarity and lower tension. When the group gets down to work, behavior shifts to asking for and giving orientation as members try to see clearly what they are to accomplish. Then opinions and suggestions increase, followed by disagreement and, sometimes tension and anger. Tension marks a critical phase, for groups can bog down if they cannot release tensions and regain a sense of solidarity. Acts that increase solidarity ("I think we can work this out if we stop fighting"), release tension (jokes), or orient the group ("I think we've lost sight of the problem") are very important, for, as groups thrash their way toward a solution, they can tear themselves apart with anger, disagreement, and frustration. If the group passes through this difficult phase, interaction shifts to releasing tension and repairing any damage to group solidarity.

Getting the Job Done: Explaining Group Effectiveness

Groups confront a variety of tasks. Factory workers produce goods, and universities produce graduates and research. Groups of scientists solve problems involved in sending a rocket to a distant planet, and families figure out how to balance their budgets and keep everyone happy. Research teams judge the effectiveness of new drugs and juries judge the guilt or innocence of defendants in criminal trials. Most group work involves one or more of these areas: balancing a family budget requires judgment (estimates of future needs and income) and problem solving (how to raise income or cut spending). Regardless of the mix of tasks involved, all groups must cope with the problems of keeping their members satisfied and committed to the group.

The sociological study of group performance grew out of the Industrial Revolution and the concentration of production in larger and more complex groups. Although early research focused on finding ways to increase productivity (and profits), the study of group performance now includes schools, government bureaucracies, the military, and scientific research laboratories. The settings vary, but the sociological question is the same: How do the cultural, structural, population, and ecological characteristics of groups influence their performance? Before de-

Roger Boisjoly was the engineer who first warned of the flaws in the Challenger's O-rings. After the disaster, he was treated so badly by coworkers that he resigned. He has been awarded the Prize for Scientific Freedom and Responsibility from the American Association for the Advancement of Science.

scribing the importance of some of these characteristics, we first examine a basic question: Do groups perform better than individuals?

Individual versus Group Effectiveness "Two heads are better than one," the poet John Heywood wrote, and most research comparing the performance of individuals and groups bears him out. Individuals usually learn better and faster in the presence of others, and groups solve puzzles more quickly than individuals do (Hill 1982; Laughlin 1980). When Warnick and Sanders (1980) asked groups and individuals to recall details of a videotape portraying a crime, the groups produced more accurate and more detailed accounts.

Although two heads are often better than one, are they *twice* as good? Research suggests they are not, because individuals tend to reduce their effort as a group grows in size (Harkins 1981; Harkins, Latané and Williams 1980). In one experiment, Moede (1927) asked men to pull as hard as they could on a rope attached to a machine that, unknown to them, measured their pull. By themselves, men pulled twice as hard as they did in groups of eight.

Although groups are generally more effective than individuals, they do have their disadvantages, especially when they are small and members want to maintain group harmony at all costs. When the desire for unity is strong, individuals are less likely to object to poor decisions and suggest alternatives. Groups, in other words, are vulnerable to what Irving Janis (1968, 1982) called **groupthink**, in which the desire for consensus overpowers group members' better judgment.

The events leading up to the destruction of the U.S. space shuttle Challenger and its crew illustrate how disastrous groupthink can be. Years before, many engineers who worked for NASA and the company responsible for building the Challenger (Morton Thiokol) were convinced that the shuttle was unsafe, but pressure both within NASA and Thiokol to keep the project on schedule silenced many of those who would have objected. As one member of the presidential investigative commission put it, "No one wanted to be the one who raised a show-stopping problem. No one had the guts to stand up and say, 'This thing is falling apart'" (*New York Times*, June 29, 1986, sec. 3, p. 1).

In an experiment illustrating the effects of group think, Hall and Watson (1970) asked groups of management trainees to decide what equipment would be needed in order to live on the moon. "Consensus groups" were instructed to reach a collective solution, whereas "conflict groups" were told to avoid changing views simply for the sake of harmony, to view differences of opinion as healthy and constructive, and to *not* use majority votes to reduce conflict. Both individuals and groups submitted solutions, which were compared to those prepared by experts. Not only did conflict groups produce better solutions, but 75 percent of the conflict groups produced better solutions than their most capable member. By comparison, only 25 percent of the consensus groups performed better than their most capable member.

Groups and individuals differ not only in effectiveness, but in willingness to take risks as well. When stakes are high, groups tend to be more cautious than individuals (Knox and Safford 1976). When the Soviet Union placed nuclear missiles in Cuba in 1964, for example, most of President Kennedy's advisers initially urged an extreme response: the invasion of Cuba. Kennedy, however, insisted that his advisers reach a consensus. As a result, they made a "conservative shift" to a more moderate solution: a naval blockade around Cuba.

In less dangerous cases, groups make riskier decisions than individuals do. In one study, groups were asked to consider the following situation (Stoner 1961):

> A man with a severe heart ailment must seriously curtail his customary way of life if he does not undergo a delicate medical operation that might cure him completely or might prove fatal. What would you advise? (p. 58)

Members were asked to consider the problem alone first and then as a group, and the results showed that group decisions were consistently more risky than those reached by individuals. In a group, individuals made a "risky shift."

Such findings raise disturbing questions: Do governments make group decisions that are riskier than those individuals would reach? Is group decision making more conducive to recklessness? Were decisions such as those to drop the atomic bomb on Japan or to seize the U.S. Embassy in Iran caused by risky shifts in groups? Why do such shifts occur? In some cases, groups value risk taking as a sign that the group is "tough" and unafraid, and members increase their prestige by suggesting and supporting risky alternatives. Also, people tend to feel less individual responsibility when they are in groups and may feel less responsible for any failure that results from a risky decision. Finally, as Simmel ([1902] 1950) noted,

groups tend to release the inhibitions of their members: we often feel freer to act out wild impulses at a large party than we do in a small group.

Groups tend to be more effective than individuals in achieving goals, but the results depend on the task and the size of the risks involved. Groups differ not only from individuals, however, but from one another, and such differences strongly influence their effectiveness.

Effectiveness and Group Culture Although norms are supposed to help groups achieve their goals, they sometimes have just the opposite effect. Bureaucratic norms cannot anticipate all possible situations, for example, and yet members are expected to obey the rules no matter what. Soldiers are required by law to obey the orders of their commanders, no matter how foolish those orders may appear to be. Bureaucratic norms often become ends in themselves, obeyed not because they help accomplish group goals, but because "a rule is a rule." Procedures that work in one situation, however, may be totally inappropriate in another. In such cases, highly disciplined training becomes what Veblen called a "trained incapacity." During the Japanese attack on Pearl Harbor in 1941, some U.S. officers refused to issue weapons to soldiers without "proper written authorization" from the commander, even though they were being shot at by enemy planes.

In some cases, the content of norms affects group performance. In bureaucracies members are supposed to ignore feelings as they make decisions, to deal with each person as a "case," not as an individual. This often causes the arrogance, abruptness, and coldness so often associated with "bureaucrats," and creates hostile attitudes between bureaucracies and those they serve.

Effectiveness and Group Size Ever since Simmel, sociologists have been interested in the effects of group size. Larger groups tend to perform better than smaller ones when problems require a large number of skills or have a single solution. Small groups, however, tend to be more stable, and their members can communicate more easily. Small groups perform better when tasks require a limited range of skills and more creative solutions. Small groups also appear to be better at satisfying their members, but this can be deceiving. Slater (1958) gave problems to 24 groups ranging in size from two to seven members and after-

TABLE 9-2   Issues on Which Large-Group Members Agreed More Often Than Small-Group Members[1]

1. The time available to solve the problem is insufficient.
2. This group doesn't make the best use of its time.
3. This group needs somebody to keep it on track.
4. Some people in this group talk too much.
5. Some people in this group are crowded out of the discussion.
6. Some people in this group should participate more.
7. There are considerable differences of ability and competence between members of this group.
8. There is too much competition among members in this group.
9. This group is not accomplishing as much as it could.

[1]Small groups have 2, 3, or 4 members, large groups 5, 6, or 7.
Source: Slater 1958.

ward asked if members thought their group was too small or too large. The proportion responding "too small" decreased steadily with greater size, whereas the proportion of "too large" responses increased. Only in groups of five members did no one feel the group was either too large or too small. In addition, members of large groups were more likely to complain about the group and its members (Table 9-2), whereas those in the smallest groups expressed no complaints at all. Why should size have this effect?

One might argue that in small groups we feel more important and freer to speak our minds. Yet, when Bales and Borgatta (1955) examined Slater's data, they found that in smaller groups members rarely showed tension or anger, whereas in larger groups anger and disagreement were common. Bales and Borgatta explained these findings by suggesting that as groups increase in size, some problems are diminished while new ones emerge. The smallest groups depend on agreement and harmony for their survival (Simmel [1902] 1950), and although they may lack the resources they need to accomplish a task, members are likely to conceal disagreement and anger and give a rosy picture of group life. Large groups, however, have more resources and do not need the agreement of all their members in order to survive or reach a decision. Members feel freer to disagree and show anger because this poses a less serious threat to

the group and their standing in it. This suggests that whereas *physical* freedom (to talk) is greater in small groups, *psychological* freedom (to express unpopular opinions) is greater in large groups (Mullen 1983).

This contradicts the common belief that small groups are the only places where we can truly be ourselves. Large groups limit our participation, but small ones limit expression of feelings and outrageous impulses. Whereas large groups tend to make us feel insignificant and lost, small groups tend to inhibit us by making us feel highly visible.

Effectiveness, Roles, and Leadership   As we saw earlier, the more complex a group is, the better it can accomplish complicated tasks that require a wide range of skills. Complex groups, however, also find it more difficult to coordinate and control their members' behavior.

Group complexity also creates problems when it becomes an end in itself. The essence of a bureaucracy is the management of some members by others. In order to demonstrate their importance, bureaucrats often create work that requires assistants, which results in more paperwork as assistants report to their bosses. More assistants are then added, and the organization continues to grow, using more and more resources to manage its mushrooming staff.

Other problems arise from the ways in which groups decide who plays which roles. Bureaucracies, for example, try to secure the loyal, devoted service of their members by offering them job security and clear lines of promotion so long as they obey the rules. This causes three kinds of problems.

First, members may use their security to do no more than what norms require. College professors are sometimes criticized for working less after achieving the security of tenure. Second, because advancement in bureaucracies requires obedience to norms, people may become afraid to show initiative for fear of ruining chances for promotion (Merton 1968). Third, in bureaucracies people tend to be promoted to higher positions on the basis of performance in *lower* positions. Inevitably, members reach positions that are beyond their abilities and there they stay, unable to perform well enough to reach the next rung on the ladder.

Peter and Hull (1969) called this phenomenon the Peter Principle: "In a hierarchy each employee tends to rise to his level of *incompetence*; every post tends to be occupied by an employee incompetent to execute its duties." They suggested that the only reason top positions are sometimes occupied by competent people is that "there are not enough ranks for them to have reached their level of incompetence: in other words, *in that hierarchy* there is no task beyond their abilities." Although complex role structures increase group effectiveness in many ways, they also produce unanticipated negative consequences that affect their members and interfere with group performance.

Social situations affect not only the emergence and selection of leaders in groups, but their effectiveness as well. Task leaders are most effective in extreme situations—when groups verge on falling apart during disasters or when they are cohesive and strong. Expressive leaders, however, are more effective than task leaders in less extreme circumstances, when members have less need of a task leader and are in a stronger position to question a leader's authority (Fiedler, Chemers, and Mahan 1976). A leader who improves group performance in one situation may damage it in another.

Effectiveness and Communication   We saw in Chapter 3 that communication patterns affect both success at different tasks and member satisfaction. When members can interact freely with one another (a "circle"), groups have more difficulty solving puzzles with single solutions than they do with tasks having many workable solutions. In addition, although groups that channel communication through a single member (a "wheel") are efficient problem solvers, their members are less satisfied.

From this point of view, it is easier to see why large numbers of people with free and open communication structures (such as street mobs) are inefficient at solving problems. It is also easier to see why bureaucracies have so much trouble satisfying their members and performing efficiently. Their communication structures often leave members feeling insignificant and powerless. They also make it difficult for one part of the organization to know what other parts are doing, for each piece of information must pass through many hands before reaching its ultimate destination.

We have seen, then, that the ability of groups to achieve goals depends on their cultural and structural characteristics. No group, however, can perform well or even survive if it cannot maintain its members' loyalty. All groups must continually cope with the problem of social cohesion.

Staying Together, Falling Apart: Cohesion and Conflict

A central problem in the study of social systems is understanding the forces that affect **social cohesion**, the degree to which participants feel committed to the system and to one another. What makes groups stay together? When membership is involuntary as in junior high schools, social cohesion is maintained by the power of authority; but in voluntary groups, the attraction of members is more difficult to maintain. In the simplest sense, a group cannot exist unless people are motivated to interact with one another, and a group survives only if the forces keeping it together are stronger than those that would tear it apart.

In many groups and subgroups of larger organizations, members are joined by primary ties. In the last days of World War II, for example, the German army maintained its effectiveness even though it was badly

The caring shown by these two U.S. soldiers during the Korean War illustrates the importance of primary relations in holding small combat units together. In other respects, the units are merely specialized task groups in an enormously complex organization.

outnumbered, undersupplied, and had to rely on damaged and inferior equipment. Some analysts believed that the German army continued to function as a cohesive unit because its soldiers strongly believed in their cause; but in a postwar study, Shils and Janowitz (1948) found that German soldiers were generally indifferent to Nazi ideology. What, then, held them together? Shils and Janowitz concluded that it was the loyalty that each soldier felt toward the members of his small combat squad or platoon (see also Van Creveld 1982). The German soldier, they wrote,

> was likely to go on fighting, provided he had the necessary weapons, so long as the group possessed leadership with which he could identify himself, and so long as he gave affection to and received affection from the other members of his squad or platoon. . . . As long as he felt himself to be a member of his primary group and therefore bound by the expectations and demands of its other members, his soldierly achievement was likely to be good. (p. 284)

Studies of U.S. soldiers during World War II also showed that primary ties were vital sources of group cohesion in small combat units (Stouffer et al. 1949). A study of soldiers in Vietnam, however, suggests that although primary ties were important, they arose in part from the fact that soldiers could not survive on their own.

> The fact is that if the individual soldier is realistically to improve his survival chances, he must *necessarily* develop and take part in primary relationships. Under the grim conditions of ground warfare, an individual's survival is directly dependent upon the support . . . he can expect from his fellows. He gets such support to the degree that he reciprocates to the others in his unit. In other words, primary relations are at their core mutually pragmatic efforts to minimize personal risk. (Moskos 1969, p. 18)

In contrast, the communist Vietcong, against whom the U.S. fought, were organized in small "cells" of 3–5 soldiers each, an arrangement that promoted strong primary ties of loyalty more than ideological fervor (Karnow 1983).

Primary ties are often based on common experience and a shared culture; but the example of the war in Vietnam introduces a second major source of cohesion: the degree to which the structure of a social system requires members to depend on one another. One of the most recognizable examples of this is the bureaucracy. While small combat units are held together by primary ties, the larger organizations of

The German bombing of British cities during World War II only strengthened the refusal of Britain to give up. Here, Prime Minister Winston Churchill tours London streets after a German raid, inspects damage and, as is plain to see, bolsters morale.

which they are a part—battalions, divisions, and armies—cannot function unless each unit does its specialized job. A small unit that delivers food, ammunition, and other supplies, or one that specializes in communications can stay together as a unit based on the primary ties among its members. An army, however, stays together only insofar as its various units function effectively as parts of the whole.

Social structure affects group cohesion by defining not only relationships within groups, but among them as well. As Thomas Jefferson and Winston Churchill noted, groups that conflict during peacetime suddenly pull together during wartime in the face of a common enemy, burying their differences and sacrificing individual interests for the common good. When the external threat is removed, old differences resurface, unity breaks down, and group conflicts resume (Coser 1964). During World War II, for example, German leaders believed that continuous bombing of Britain's cities would beat its population into submission; but the bombings had the opposite effect, for they aroused a sense of solidarity and defiance in the British people. Later in the war, Allied commanders failed to learn from the German mistake, and researchers discovered after the war that saturation bombing of German cities only increased resistance and prolonged the war (Janis 1951). Nor did the U.S. heed this lesson thirty years later during the Vietnam War when it tried unsuccessfully to break communist resistance through massive bombing of North Vietnam (Karnow 1983; Neustadt and May 1986).

When social cohesion is low, leaders may increase solidarity by convincing members that other groups threaten their survival (Markides and Cohen 1982). During its revolution, for example, Iran was torn by power struggles and disagreements about how the country should be run, and its leaders frequently unified their followers by directing attention to "foreign devils"—the U.S.—who, the leaders claimed, wanted to destroy them. Libya's leader, Mohamar Khadafi, has used similar tactics to calm discontent at home.

In groups, we interact, work toward goals, and try to maintain a sense of cohesion. These are the basic elements of group life, but what are the implications for group members? How do the characteristics of groups affect the quality of our lives?

INDIVIDUALS, FREEDOM, AND LIFE IN GROUPS

The social characteristics of groups affect societies and their people. Groups are capable both of supporting and protecting their members and of corrupting and harming them. Through groups, human beings have accomplished stunning and wonderful things, but groups are also the source of our most astonishing cruelty and destruction. How do groups and organizations affect us?

Culture, Groups, and Individuals

Perhaps one of the most significant cultural changes during the last 2,000 years has been the enormous increase in the social value of individuals and their freedom in relation to groups. Durkheim ([1893] 1933) went so far as to suggest that in the simplest tribal societies with their uncomplicated divisions of labor, the idea of an individual simply did not exist. The group, he argued, was everything, and it never may

have occurred to people to stand apart from it as unique individuals.

From Durkheim's point of view, individuality cannot exist without supporting cultural beliefs (that such a thing is possible), values (the individual is important), and norms (individuals have rights in relation to groups); and these ideas are relatively new in history. In this sense, if sociology had existed thousands of years ago, it would not even have identified the effects of groups on individuals as a problem.

The social value of individuals seems to have reached its highest point in industrial societies. As societies raise the value of individuals, people are less vulnerable to being "buried" in the group, to having no right to stand apart and celebrate their uniqueness. This, however, creates the danger of being *isolated* from groups. In industrial societies, we spend increasingly large portions of our lives in groups and organizations that value efficiency, precision, speed, control, production, and obedience more than they value the happiness and satisfaction of their members. In addition, Slater (1971) argued that an extreme emphasis on individuals and their uniqueness creates a cultural environment that frustrates basic human needs to trust and cooperate with others, to deal directly with interpersonal problems, and to share responsibility for the conduct of our lives.

In short, Slater argued that modern cultures not only raise the social value of individuals to new heights, but also create unprecedented levels of isolation and loneliness. "Who am I?" is perhaps the most common and disturbing question individuals face in modern cultures, because simple group membership no longer provides a solid basis for existence. Whereas ties between individuals and groups may have been too strong in pre-industrial societies, in industrial societies they are in danger of being too weak (Durkheim [1897] 1951).

Such cultural changes, however, do not simply "happen" by accident; they are often responses to structural changes in social systems. Weber (1946) and Durkheim ([1893] 1933) saw in the Industrial Revolution a threat to human welfare. What structural changes did they see and why were they so concerned?

Social Structure, Groups, and Individuals

Preindustrial societies are held together by a common culture, and groups tend to be small, informal, and primary. Work, family, and religion form a unified whole. Those who share in the culture and obey its norms have a secure place in the social world. The Industrial Revolution, however, accelerated a long-term change in which social relationships became increasingly rational, secondary, and formal in societies based less on shared culture than on rational calculations of individual self-interest (Weber [1922] 1958). This change resulted from the rise of bureaucracy as a model of social organization.

In complex industrial societies, we are known as individuals, and as individuals, we are known primarily by the statuses we occupy. Children no longer grow up confident of their place in society, knowing exactly what is expected of them, what roles they will play as adults. To survive in modern societies, each of us must achieve a place for ourselves somewhere in the complex division of labor.

Nowhere are the consequences of these structures clearer than in bureaucracies with their formal rules, rigidly defined relationships, and inattention to individual feelings and needs. Argyris (1957) suggested that bureaucracies actually interfere with the needs of healthy people. Maturity includes the ability to act and make judgments independently, to think abstractly and in terms of long-term consequences of behavior. Bureaucracies, however, encourage dependency and timidity, short-term thinking, and ignorance of long-term consequences. Argyris concluded, "Formal organizations are willing to pay high wages and provide adequate seniority if mature adults will, for eight hours a day, behave in a less mature manner." As a result, we often feel frustrated and helpless because we have little control over our environment, goals, or behavior, and the lack of control creates anxiety and uncertainty. Karl Marx described the resulting feelings of being lost and insignificant as *alienation*—a feeling of helplessness and detachment in relation to work and its results.

Unlike primary groups, bureaucracies do not derive their security from the welfare of their members. We may be fired when it is no longer in an employer's "best interests" to keep us, regardless of our abilities. Middle-aged executives often lose jobs because they are *too* experienced and *too* capable and therefore command higher salaries than younger employees. Some people defend themselves by leaving the system (a risky choice), or by achieving more powerful positions within it. Others, however, who can neither advance nor afford to leave, may retreat into apathy and daydreams, or create informal groups that support feelings of alienation.

The rational basis of bureaucracy leads many to participate in order to achieve personal—not orga-nizational—goals, the most important of which is earning a living. We can work in a bureaucracy without valuing its goals or liking our jobs or other workers. This often minimizes feelings of loyalty to large organizations and encourages members to exploit every opportunity for personal gain—whether on the large scale of criminal embezzlement or the small scale of stealing office supplies and equipment, padding expense accounts, or using company cars for personal trips.

As bureaucracy spreads, we find ourselves with fewer and fewer groups in which we are known and valued as individuals. We spend increasing portions of our lives in secondary groups that involve limited parts of ourselves, and our lives are divided into separate spheres of family, work, friendships, and religion that have little if any connection to one another. In such environments, it is difficult to maintain a sense of "wholeness" about our lives; rather, we tend to feel split in many directions at once as we divide our time, energy, and loyalty between family, friends, and the formal demands of work.

The structures of complex industrial societies create feelings of insignificance and rootlessness in their members, yet how do they differ from Durkheim's vision of tribal societies in which individuals are indistinguishable from their groups? Is it not true that individuals have little significance in both simple societies and the bureaucracies of modern societies?

Although individuals tend to be "lost" in both types of societies, there is an enormously important difference between the two. In the societies Durkheim referred to, individuals had no need to stand apart from their groups, because groups and their members depended on each other for survival. There was a close connection between the welfare of groups and the welfare of their members. In a bureaucracy, however, people are used as a means for achieving goals that they neither determine nor control, and may not even share. In a bureaucratic society, individuals cannot afford to place their welfare in the hands of organizations that can and often do quickly dispense with them. It is no accident of history that as social systems become increasingly bureaucratic, concern for the rights and welfare of individuals grows stronger. As groups become more exploitative, members must establish new sources of protection and security, and aside from the family, the individual is the last line of defense.

The increased size, complexity, and formality of social systems also affect the welfare of entire societies, for although bureaucracies support efficiency, control, and complex divisions of labor, they also oppose the strong emotional ties that are the basis of human morality, compassion, and empathy. In bureaucracies we are supposed to simply do our jobs and leave the establishment of goals to our leaders. This gives bureaucracies what Sabini and Silver (1982) have called "a genius for organizing evil" (see also Kelman and Hamilton 1989). Nazi Germany was a model of bureaucratic efficiency, and prided itself on the strict formal organization of its society. When Adolph Eichmann managed the railway systems that transported millions of people to their deaths in concentration camps, he behaved as a model bureaucrat, carrying out his orders quickly, efficiently, and without question. In the final chaotic months of World War II, when Germany was defending itself on three fronts, Eichmann's proudest achievement was his astonishing ability to keep the trains running on time.

Marx believed that bureaucracy turns individuals into cogs in machines and that as we are more alienated from our work and its results, we are also more alienated from one another and from ourselves. In bureaucratic societies, in which organizations and their rules assume primary importance, it is not surprising that we are often motivated by rational self-interest ("What's in it for *me?*") and insensitive to the fate of others.

Groups will always be a part of human life, and it is for this reason that decisions about their characteristics are so important for they set the terms on which we live our lives in relation to other people.

SUMMARY

1. The group is an important sociological concept because individuals perform their most important roles in them; groups meet many human needs and are an important source of social conflict; and the performance of groups strongly affects the achievement of important social goals.

2. All groups rest on a shared culture to which members are expected to conform. In most cases, it is very difficult for us to defy the majority opinion in a group to which we belong.

3. Group structures differ in many ways, defining their existence in terms of time and space, and drawing boundaries that differ in their clarity and openness. Membership in some groups is voluntary, whereas in others it is compulsory. Group members may think of themselves as members of superior in-groups and express hostile attitudes toward out-groups.

4. Groups distribute power in a variety of ways, and while many groups have leaders, many do not. Expressive and instrumental leaders emerge under a variety of conditions as groups struggle to stay together and achieve goals. Some groups have no leadership structure, whereas others have more than one.

5. Communication structures affect many aspects of group life, including levels of cohesion, the amount of misunderstanding and conflict, and the formation of subgroups.

6. The growth of bureaucracy as a type of formal organization is one of the most significant transformations of the past two centuries. It was given an enormous boost by the Industrial Revolution.

7. Absolute and relative size are important factors in the power of groups and the complexity of their structures.

8. Spatial relationships affect the frequency and duration of interaction in groups, which in turn affects the level of cohesion. Spatial relationships also serve to reinforce power structures.

9. Group process refers to what members actually do, regardless of the expectations attached to roles. Bales' techniques for recording group process are useful in identifying critical stages in the life of a group.

10. Many factors affect group effectiveness, depending on the goals involved. Factors include group size, the formality of norms, the complexity of role and communication structures, and the presence of leaders.

11. Group cohesion depends on the degree to which members share a common base of culture and experience and the degree to which members depend on one another.

12. The characteristics of groups profoundly affect the experience and behavior of their members, their levels of self-esteem, their feelings of belonging and security, their ability to determine and pursue their own goals, and their power to control others and protect themselves.

KEY TERMS

authoritarian structure   190
bureaucracy   193
collectivity   196
democratic structure   190
expressive leader   190

formal organization   193
group process   197
groupthink   199
in-group   189
instrumental leader   190

out-group   189
pluralistic structure   190
primary group   192
secondary group   192
social cohesion   202

LOOKING ELSEWHERE

Having studied Chapter 9, you might want to look at related discussions in *Human Arrangements*, which include

■ power structures in small army units (Chapter 3, pp. 56–58)

■ the political power of interest groups (Chapter 20, p. 515)

■ the school as bureaucracy (Chapter 17, pp. 423–24)

■ the effects of physical space on social interaction (Chapter 8, pp. 172–73)

■ conformity in groups as a cause of deviance (Chapter 11, pp. 252–54)

■ organizations as a source of crime (Chapter 11, p. 246)

■ alienation in the workplace (Chapter 19, pp. 486–88)

RECOMMENDED READINGS

Chackerian, R., and Abcarian, G. 1984. *Bureaucratic power in society*. Chicago: Nelson-Hall. A compelling critique of bureaucracy with a special emphasis on the connection between schools and the economy. An excellent source for students who want to deepen their understanding of bureaucracy.

Janis, I. 1982. *Victims of groupthink*. Boston: Houghton Mifflin. A look at the sometimes disastrous effects of groupthink on decision making, focusing on U.S. foreign policy.

Kanter, R., and Stein, B. A. (Eds.). 1979. *Life in organizations*. New York: Basic Books. A collection of essays about work experiences in formal organizations.

Olmstead, M. S., and Hare, A. P. 1978. *The small group* (2nd ed.). New York: Random House. A well-written summary of important research on small groups. See also Paulus, P. B. 1983. *Basic group processes*. New York: Springer-Verlag.

Slater, P. E. 1971. *The pursuit of loneliness*. Boston: Beacon Press. Slater's compelling analysis of a central tension in group life between independence, freedom, and a sense of belonging and commitment is one of those books that many people read more than once.

Weber, M. 1946. *From Max Weber: Essays in sociology*. Edited and translated by H. H. Gerth and C. Wright Mills. New York: Oxford University Press. One of the best and most accessible sources of Weber's ideas on bureaucracy.

Whyte, W. F. 1981. *Street corner society* (3rd ed.). Chicago: University of Chicago Press. Whyte's classic participation observation study of groups in an Italian slum in Boston.

10
CITY, TOWN, AND VILLAGE: COMMUNITIES

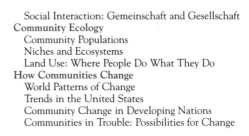

 What does the word "community" make you think of? Friends, family, home town, neighborhood, politics, school, church, work, "a place where I belong," busy streets, quiet country lanes, burglar alarms, doors locked only at night? Whatever the association, community refers to one of the most important aspects of our lives—where we live; and where we live affects *how* we live, for it is in communities that we are born, attend school, make and lose friends, find and lose jobs, raise families, grow old, and die. Communities may be sources of attachment that make us feel rooted in the world; they may be like prisons from which we see little chance of escape; or they may be no more than stopovers on the way to someplace else (see Bellah et al. 1985).

As social systems, **communities** are unique in several respects. First and most important, their identity is bound up with a sense of place, of geography. There are, of course, exceptions to this, such as nomadic tribes that regularly move from one place to another; but for the most part, a community has a geographical identity. Second, communities are places where people live, work, and carry out the other basic activities of life. Communities often correspond to political boundaries, such as those that define towns and cities, but they can also have less formal identities, as in the case of neighborhoods. As communities become larger and more complex, we also find communities existing within communities—such as Chinatown in San Francisco.

The study of communities as social systems occupies an important place in the development of sociology in the U.S. At the University of Chicago, sociologists Robert Park (1864–1944), Ernest Burgess (1886–1966), W. I. Thomas (1863–1947), and

Florian Znaniecki (1882–1938), combined a commitment to social reform with an intense curiosity about urban life. They were particularly interested in ecological studies of social problems created by rapid industrialization and urbanization, and massive immigration. Chicago abounded with a variety of human adaptations to the dizzying pace of urban life, and these members of what came to be known as the Chicago School used the city as a natural laboratory for the study of everything from urban gangs, slums, dance halls, and racism to life among the wealthy (Blumer 1984; Coser 1977).

We begin by describing basic types of communities, and then see how their characteristics as social systems affect the lives of the people who live in them and cause communities to change.

SOME BASIC TYPES OF COMMUNITIES

There are many ways to describe differences among communities, but perhaps the two most important sociological distinctions are *rural* or *urban* and *traditional* or *modern*.

The Rural-Urban Continuum

Rural communities consist of small, homogeneous, sparsely settled populations, whereas **urban communities** are large, heterogeneous, and densely settled (Wirth 1938). How large and densely settled must a population be in order to be urban? Any limit is somewhat arbitrary, but most sociologists use the Census Bureau definition of 2,500 or more people. Although this figure has the practical advantage of being clear and precise, the concepts of urban and rural are most useful if we think of them as two extremes of a continuum. At one end are tiny, isolated villages such as early North American settlements. The larger and more densely settled a population is, the more urban it is. An **urbanized area** is a city and the densely settled territory around it (its **suburbs**) that together contain 50,000 or more people. On a larger scale, a **metropolitan area** is either a city with 50,000 or more inhabitants or an urbanized area that is socially and economically linked with surrounding counties that bring its total population to 100,000 or more (USCB 1990a). The specific definitions of urbanized and metropolitan areas are less important, however, than the basic concept behind them: they are large, densely settled population centers whose economic and social activities are closely linked with those of surrounding communities.

New York City contains over 7 million people, and activities in the city are tied to the populations of surrounding counties in New York, New Jersey, and Connecticut. Many residents of these counties work and shop in New York City, making the city and its adjacent counties an integrated unit with more than 16 million people (USCB 1990a).

Urban communities are divided into neighborhoods which often serve as communities for their

The obvious difference of sheer size that distinguishes tiny Topsham, Vermont and New York City is only a starting point for a sociological understanding of the variety and complexity of communities. In what ways would you expect life in these communities to differ, and why?

Hasidic Jews, like the Amish, maintain their traditional beliefs, customs, and manner of dress, even while living within modern communities such as New York.

residents (Gans 1982; Hallman, 1984). Neighborhoods are where people carry out most of the small details of everyday life: they are where children play and where adults shop for groceries, have shoes repaired and clothing cleaned. Neighborhoods are communities in which we are most aware of and affected by other people's behavior and where, therefore, conformity is most highly valued.

Traditional and Modern Communities

In addition to the urban/rural distinction, communities also differ in the degree to which they are *traditional* or *modern* (Inkeles and Smith 1974). The Amish in the U.S., for example, live in **traditional communities** that are culturally isolated from the rest of society (Kephart and Zellner 1990). Their religious beliefs preclude the use of scientific technology, and they reject most aspects of the modern society that surrounds them—including electricity, indoor toilets, jewelry, machinery, politics, watches, life insurance, loans, and social security. Their style and color of dress—simple and black—is the same as it was 250 years ago.

In comparison with traditional communities, **modern communities** tend to have more complex divisions of labor, more sophisticated technology, more highly developed mass media, and higher levels of education and literacy. Residents are more likely to accept new ideas, and social relationships tend to be more secondary and formal than primary and informal. Urban communities are not necessarily modern, nor are rural communities necessarily traditional. Many cities in less developed countries—particularly in Africa and Asia—are traditional, while many rural communities in Europe and North America are, in relative terms, quite modern.

The concepts of urban, rural, traditional, and modern describe communities only in very general terms. In the rest of this chapter, we will focus on the detailed cultural, structural, population, and ecological characteristics of communities, and how they affect the lives of the people who live in them.

COMMUNITY CULTURE

Like groups, communities are characterized by a culture which, in some cases, lies at the core of a community's existence: the early Puritan settlements in New England, for example, came into being because their members wanted religious freedom. Throughout history, groups such as communes have been based on decisions to live according to cultural ideas considered deviant in the surrounding society (Kanter 1972; Kephart and Zellner 1990; Zablocki 1980). The Twin Oaks commune in Louisa, Virginia, was inspired by the community described in B. F. Skinner's novel *Walden Two*. At Twin Oaks, cooperation is valued more than competition for individual advantage, and decisions based on consensus are valued more than leadership by a few. With the exception of private belongings, which members must keep in their rooms, all property is held in common and all that is earned or produced is contributed to the group (Cordes 1984).

A major focus in sociological analysis has been on cultural differences between rural and urban communities. As politicians need to remember, most rural communities rest on traditional values, and their members tend to be less open to change and less tolerant of strange life-styles than their urban counterparts. In the U.S., rural dwellers are more likely to be religious fundamentalists and political conservatives: major opposition to the Equal Rights Amendment, for example, has come mostly from sparsely settled rural states.

In comparison with urban dwellers, people in rural communities generally place less value on literacy, formal education, the arts and mass media, the use of sophisticated technology, and individual advancement through competition (Inkeles and Smith 1974). They tend to share a common set of cultural ideas and to place higher values on large families, traditional roles for men and women, conformity, cooperation, and loyalty to the community.

City populations include far greater cultural diversity (diversity was, in fact, a major part of Wirth's 1938 definition of cities as communities). Cities contain a vast array of people in different occupations, social classes, and racial and ethnic groups. Cities are more likely to have substantial numbers of artists and musicians, judges and college professors, political radicals, the very wealthy and the very poor, as well as criminals and their victims. The mix of people from different cultural backgrounds is also far greater in cities: there are more Poles in Chicago than in Warsaw, the capital of Poland, and the Detroit area has the largest concentration of Arabic-speaking people outside of the Middle East.

One result of such diversity is a generally higher level of tolerance for nonconformity, although this level has fallen somewhat in recent years (Abrahamson and Carter 1986). Stephan and McMullin (1982) found that people who live in the largest cities report far more tolerance for homosexuality, pornography, and extramarital and premarital sex than do people living in smaller cities and towns. They found even greater differences in attitudes toward sexual nonconformity when they compared people in terms of the size of the communities they lived in as adolescents (see also Wilson 1985, 1991).

Why should such cultural differences occur between small, sparsely settled communities and large, densely populated ones? Early sociologists such as Simmel ([1908] 1965) and Wirth (1938) attributed urban-rural differences to the physical characteristics of the communities themselves—the number of people who occupy a given area. Large populations are bound to be more heterogeneous than small ones, and conformity will be valued more highly in small communities where people cannot escape awareness of one another's behavior. When we are surrounded by large numbers of people, we protect our privacy, Simmel believed, by being aloof and superficial toward others.

Simmel's approach is purely ecological, because it suggests that physical differences between urban and rural communities (population size and density) cause cultural differences among their inhabitants. The ecological approach, however, ignores the effects of culture on the formation of communities. In other words, as more recent urban sociologists argue, it is culture that created the city—not the other way around (Castells 1977; Gans 1962; Jaret 1983).

Since the beginning of the Industrial Revolution in the eighteenth century, the most important characteristic of urban areas has not been their size and density; rather, it is their *industrial and commercial activity* that has affected community culture and structure. Industrial and commercial communities require large pools of workers in a complex occupational structure; to advance, individuals must compete for jobs and be willing to move to different neighborhoods or communities in search of better opportunities. These two facts help explain why industrial communities attract large numbers of people with a variety of cultural backgrounds.

People also choose to live in cities because cities foster a variety of subcultures, communities-within-communities in which shared interests draw people together. People with unusual interests or beliefs often feel isolated in small towns, but city populations are so large that people have a variety of supportive subcultures to choose from (Fischer 1975, 1982, 1984; Wilson 1986).

The cultural differences between urban and rural communities are not caused simply by the population characteristics that define communities as urban or rural. Nowhere has this misperception been more evident than in early sociological studies of suburbia.

The Myth of Suburban Culture

Although suburbs existed in the U.S. as early as 1815, they did not emerge as a major community form until the turn of this century (Binford 1985; Stilgoe 1989). Suburbs were inhabited by people who could afford country homes from which they commuted by train and streetcar to work in cities (see Jackson 1986). In the 1920s, suburbs grew rapidly with the mass production of cars and paved roads, and after World War II they were built on a massive scale for returning veterans and their families (Long 1981; Muller 1981).

Suburbia received considerable attention from sociologists because it appeared to represent a new kind of community with a distinctive culture that em-

In contrast to the diversity and complex organic solidarity of industrial societies, tribes such as this one in South Africa are held together primarily by the mechanical solidarity that results from a relatively homogeneous culture.

phasized family life, home ownership, security and safety, active community involvement, and close, friendly relations among residents—all the things that made for "the good life." It was also seen as a social environment in which conformity and "keeping up with the Joneses" were valued more than anything else. Wives were prisoners in their homes, and husbands could not escape the deadening daily commute to the city. With the help of movies (such as *Rebel Without a Cause*) and literature (such as John Cheever's short stories), suburbia was identified as a culturally unique form of community life.

In the last 20 years, however, sociologists have challenged the idea that a suburban culture exists at all. Rather, they argue that the cultures found in suburban communities depend on the statuses of their residents, such as their social class, occupation, age, marital status, and race. Berger's 1960 study of a working-class suburb in California, for example, reveals a social life that contradicts the suburban ideal, with little participation in local affairs, limited involvement with neighbors, and an almost exclusive concentration on the family, home, and television. Other studies report a variety of cultures in different suburban communities (see Bell 1969; Gans 1962, 1982). Knowing that someone lives in a suburb or city tells us far less than do statuses such as occupation, ethnicity, race, income, education, age, and marital status.

Norms and Community Life

Like all norms, those that regulate life in communities differ in their formality, the strictness with which they are applied, and their content.

The small populations and relatively simple division of labor in traditional communities, such as the Amish, allow them to control their members with informal sanctions that are strictly applied. Individual behavior and appearance are highly visible in such communities: any member of an Amish community who violates prohibitions on smoking cigarettes or who dresses inappropriately will quickly be noticed. Because most residents know one another and interact on a regular basis, there is little need for formal mechanisms—police departments, courts, and correctional systems—for enforcing norms.

In cities, however, it is impossible to regulate people's behavior through informal mechanisms. Populations are large and culturally heterogeneous, which makes it relatively easy for people to conceal their behavior. In cities, therefore, norms tend to be formal, enforced through a complex division of labor designed to discover, prosecute, and punish those who violate them. Urban neighborhoods, however, can be small communities themselves and often rely on the informal mechanisms used by traditional communities. Because cities offer residents a variety of neighborhood environments and a relatively high degree of anonymity, norms cannot be applied strictly, especially if they apply to personal choices such as sexual preference and clothing.

Urban and rural communities differ not only in the formality of norms and how strictly they are enforced, but in their content as well. This fact, too, results from the cultural and structural complexity of industrial and commercial communities. In his classic book *The Division of Labor in Society* ([1893] 1933), Durkheim identified differences in the *content* of norms that hold communities together by regulating the behavior of their members (see also Lukes and Scull 1983). He described two types of social solidarity that correspond to the content of community norms: mechanical and organic.

The concept of **mechanical solidarity** refers to social cohesion based on a relatively simple division of labor and a common culture—conditions found most often in small, traditional communities. In communities held together in this way, most norms take the form of criminal laws that prohibit specific behaviors because they are considered "wrong." **Organic solidarity**, however, is based not on how alike people are, but on how different they are. City residents are connected to one another not so much by a shared culture as by their dependency on one another. Each resident performs a specialized task— food store manager, doctor, police officer, trash collector, department store clerk, electrician—in a complex division of labor. Because each person specializes in a narrow portion of the activities required to meet people's needs, city dwellers depend on people with whom they often have very little in common.

In communities that depend on organic solidarity—most of which are urban—only a relatively small proportion of the norms focus on forbidden behaviors. Instead, most norms are civil laws that regulate relationships involving groups and individuals who may never be more than strangers to one another. Commercial law, procedural law, constitutional law, contract law, and tort law, for example, regulate social relationships rather than prohibit specific behaviors. To Durkheim, such differences in norms reflect differences in how communities stay together. The Industrial Revolution brought with it communities of such complexity and diversity that a vast body of civil law was needed to regulate a web of social relationships involving enormous numbers of people.

The concepts of organic and mechanical solidarity represent what Max Weber ([1922] 1958) called **ideal types**; that is to say, social cohesion in communities is rarely based purely on one or the other. Mexican villages and small African tribes are examples of communities held together primarily by mechanical solidarity, but many small, rural communities combine the two. Farming communities in most industrial societies, for example, have close relationships with urban and international markets.

As this discussion illustrates, it is impossible to fully understand cultural differences between communities without paying attention to the way social systems are structured. As we will see below, this includes many structural aspects of communities, including boundaries, time, and power.

THE STRUCTURE OF COMMUNITY LIFE

Like every social system, communities have structural characteristics that affect what goes in them as well as their relationships with other systems. These include not only relationships involving individuals, groups, and organizations, but also distributions of power, prestige, and other resources and rewards. We begin this discussion at the outskirts of community life—community boundaries.

Community Boundaries and Xenophobia

Although all social systems have boundaries, community boundaries also have a physical dimension, for a shared physical space is part of what defines a community. Physical boundaries may be actual barriers, such as the walls that protected ancient cities (see Braudel 1981). They may also be geographic boundaries that are drawn politically (the city limits). Political boundaries are important because they define the area within which officials have jurisdiction and, thereby limit their authority. One of the most important aspects of communities, however, is that they provide people with a sense of belonging. Crossing physical boundaries does not necessarily mean that newcomers will be accepted as members of the community; it is here that the clarity and openness of a community's social boundaries are important.

In small communities, the clarity of boundaries depends on the simple fact that residents know one another. In some cases—resort communities and university towns—the massive influx of outsiders blurs community boundaries and leads permanent residents to adopt new ways of maintaining their sense of community, including hostile attitudes toward the perceived invaders. For example, each summer in Nantucket, a small island community just off the Massachusetts coast, tourists outnumber the permanent residents. Some residents spend most of their time at home in order to avoid feeling that they have lost their community to strangers; others display bumper stickers that read "Native."

Particularly in urban neighborhoods, people often draw symbolic boundaries that define the area with which they identify (Suttles 1972). These may not correspond to physical or political boundaries and may include a variety of ethnicities, races, and social classes. Harlem and Greenwich Village in

For decades the Berlin Wall—now torn down—divided Germans from one another, a stark and visible boundary separating two ways of life.

New York, the Back Bay and Beacon Hill sections of Boston, and the Nob Hill and Haight-Ashbury sections of San Francisco are all well known neighborhoods whose residents tend to think of them as their real home.

Boundaries are sometimes drawn in ways that select residents on the basis of statuses: the exclusion of blacks, Jews, and various ethnic minorities is a long-standing practice in U.S. communities. Until recently, the only true national urban policy centered on the value of "culturally homogeneous neighborhoods"—a thinly disguised way of saying that non-white and poor families should be excluded from white, middle-class neighborhoods. During the housing construction boom that followed World War II, the National Association of Real Estate Boards' code of ethics discouraged realtors from selling housing to members of "incompatible"—that is, black—groups. This deliberate policy of segregated housing was supported by the Federal Housing Administration, whose official guidelines for realtors and banks (which provided mortgages) virtually forbade integration (Muller 1981; Stahura 1986).

In many cases, attempts to maintain closed community boundaries are based on **xenophobia**—the fear of strangers (see Bennett 1989). The United States is a nation of immigrants (with the exception of native Americans), but this has not prevented people from claiming their communities as their own. The Protestant English who inhabited the early colonies attempted to exclude Jews and Catholics, and in the seventeenth century, Mary Dyer was hanged in the Massachusetts Bay Colony for preaching Quaker religious doctrine. The Pennsylvania Quakers, on the other hand, opposed the influx of German Protestants in the 1750s, and Benjamin Franklin ([1751] 1974) was among those who believed that America should be reserved for Anglo-Saxon whites.

Throughout the nineteenth century, cities such as New York, Boston, and Philadelphia experienced widespread fear over the influx of Catholic immigrants, most of whom were Irish and German. The late 1800s was a period of bewildering social change in the rapidly industrializing Northeast, and residents found a convenient explanation for crime and corruption in the expanding population of "foreigners." Numerous groups—such as the Oriental Exclusion League, the Native American Party, and the Immigration Restriction League—tried to limit immigration into the U.S. In California the excluded became the excluders as Irish workers formed the Workingmen's Party in 1877 and urged exclusion of Chinese immigrants who competed with them for jobs (see Boswell 1986). In 1915 the Ku Klux Klan expanded its list of enemies to include Jews and Catholics.

Xenophobia and exclusion have not ended in the U.S.; what has changed are the statuses used to define community membership. Now Mexican-Americans, Puerto Ricans, and Asian refugees are perceived by many as a threat to jobs held by "natives," a burden on public welfare systems, and a source of crime. Whites continue to exclude blacks from their neighborhoods and, if unsuccessful, are likely to move because they consider their neighborhoods to be less desirable (Farley et al. 1979).

To some degree, it is inevitable that communities will accept some newcomers more readily than others, for a boundary that anyone can cross is no longer a boundary. When cities become wide open, the residents may lose their sense of community and then create smaller communities within the city (Gans 1982). The ethnic neighborhoods of large cities attest to the human desire to maintain physical spaces within which life goes on according to predictable social arrangements. A continuing problem with closed boundaries, however, is that some communities and neighborhoods offer better schools, housing, health care, and jobs than others do. In this sense, boundaries not only maintain cultural homogeneity, but also perpetuate social inequality.

The Importance of Time

Time is an important aspect of community structure because communities and neighborhoods differ in age, and residents stay for varying lengths of time. In the simplest sense, the age of communities and neighborhoods is important because as communities age, their buildings, roads, sewer and water systems deteriorate. It takes a considerable amount of time to transform a neighborhood of large, stately homes into an urban slum that is falling apart.

Because communities differ widely in age, it is often difficult to compare them. The first U.S. suburbs were primarily bedroom communities in which people lived but did not work, and were, therefore, strikingly different from cities. In more recent years, however, businesses—including factories—have be-

gun to move from central cities to the suburbs. As a result, suburbs may in time resemble cities with all their problems of overcrowding, pollution, and physical decay.

Time is also important because the longer we live in a community, the more likely we are to make the status of resident a part of our social identity ("I'm a Chicagoan"), and this motivates us to conform to the community culture. We are also more likely to care about a community if we believe we will live there a long time. If we are short-timers, we have less stake in a community, because however bad it may be, we expect its effect on us to be temporary.

In highly mobile societies—in which job changes usually involve a change of residence—it is difficult for communities to foster loyalty and involvement among residents. College towns, vacation resorts, and communities near military bases, for example, are heavily populated with temporary residents whose home towns are far away. In such cases the problems of community loyalty and unity can be particularly acute.

The Social Composition of Communities

Our status sets tell a great deal about our probable beliefs, values, attitudes, and expectations. Similarly, the mix of statuses in a community can tell a great deal about its social life. Retirement commu-

Differences in social composition—an extremely affluent, primarily white population in Beverly Hills, California, contrasted with the poverty and ethnic and racial diversity found in New York City—create different problems and needs from health care and education to recreation and crime control.

TABLE 10-1   Type of Community by Various Characteristics, United States

| CHARACTERISTICS | TYPE OF COMMUNITY | | |
| | Metropolitan Areas | | |
	Central Cities	Suburbs	Nonmetropolitan Areas
Race			
% White	73	90	88
% Black	23	7	9
% Hispanic*	14	7	3
Median Family Income			
Whites	$32,000	$39,100	$27,000
Blacks	$18,700	$25,000	$14,600
Spanish origin	$19,500	$26,200	$17,200
% Below poverty level	15	6	13
% Above $50,000	13	27	7

*Includes people of all races.
Source: USCB 1987g, 1989d, 1989e.

nities face different problems than do small suburbs with large numbers of young children; and wealthy suburbs offer a social environment very different from that of a working-class suburb or an inner-city neighborhood in which most residents live in poverty.

Many of the differences between communities are caused by the mix of statuses found in their populations. In comparison with suburban populations, central-city residents in the U.S. tend to be nonwhite, elderly, female, single, unemployed, and poor. Non-metropolitan communities (most are rural) have a racial composition similar to that of suburbs, but tend to be poorer than central cities (Table 10-1). Central cities and suburbs, however, are equally likely to include well-off families. In other words, central cities have a wider *mix* of incomes, with relatively high proportions of both the very poor and the well-to-do. Bloomfield, Michigan (the home of many auto executives), is homogeneously prosperous, whereas Manhattan contains both the wealthy residents of Park Avenue and the poorest ghetto dwellers. Central cities tend to be poor and nonwhite because for centuries they have been a receiving area for impoverished migrants seeking industrial jobs. The heaviest concentrations of blacks in the U.S., for example, are in industrial cities such as Atlanta, Detroit, Newark, and Gary, Indiana.

Until the 1970s, blue-collar workers were heavily represented in urban labor forces, but as many manufacturers have moved to suburbs, the mix of occu-

pations in cities has become more concentrated in white-collar jobs: professionals, administrators, clerks, and secretaries. Blue-collar jobs, however, have long been the major source of employment for poor migrants; and because they cannot afford to follow manufacturing jobs to the suburbs, many of them are trapped in central cities. This helps explain why unemployment rates in central cities are 50 percent higher than those in suburban communities (USDL 1990).

Because white-collar workers are increasingly likely to live in suburbs and work in central cities, those who *work* in cities tend to be in white-collar occupations, but those who *live* in cities are more likely to have blue-collar job skills. Unlike rural and suburban communities, then, the urban population during the day differs substantially from the nighttime population (see Melbin 1978).

In cities, women outnumber men, whereas rural communities usually have more men than women. The reason is the relative scarcity of opportunities for women in rural areas compared with the relative abundance of jobs elsewhere. Cities are also more likely to include single people and childless couples because people tend to prefer the physical and social conditions in suburbs for raising children (Frey 1983).

Such differences are not found in all societies or in all U.S. cities. In many developing countries, for example, poverty is worse in rural areas than in cities, and men are more likely than women to migrate to cities. Mexico City's poor neighborhoods are on its fringe, not at its center, primarily because the city lies in a bowl between mountains and the most desirable land is in the middle. There are, in other words, few green suburbs to which the wealthy can flee. One of the wealthiest sections of Boston, too, is Beacon Hill, located in the middle of the city. Although wealthy families left Beacon Hill for the nearby Back Bay neighborhood at the turn of the century, the poor people who moved in were eventually displaced by affluent Bostonians whose sentimental attachment to Beacon Hill prompted them to buy and restore its stately homes (Abrahamson 1980).

In spite of such exceptions, the social composition of U.S. central cities differs sharply from suburban and rural areas. Such differences are important because the mix of statuses found in communities affects the cultural orientation of their inhabitants. The values people place on personal advancement, music and the arts, material possessions, conformity, and family life are determined more by their social class than whether their community is urban, suburban, or rural. Communities with young populations have different values than those with larger proportions of the middle-aged and elderly. Ann Arbor, Michigan, and Berkeley, California, are sites of major universities, and have been the birthplaces of radical social movements.

Community Power Structures

In communities the occupancy of important statuses and control of resources such as land, wealth, and jobs are two main sources of power. Some statuses are recognized by residents as legitimate authorities whose roles require them to make decisions about the community. Mayors, city managers, and councils pass laws and ordinances and decide how to spend tax revenues; police officers decide when to enforce particular laws; school boards decide which books students will read and how many teachers to hire. Such statuses also include that of "voter"; and, when organized, voters can exert considerable power. In many small towns voters have the power to approve (or reject) local budgets and to override the decisions of elected officials. In cities, neighbors often form associations that, because they represent relatively large numbers of voters, vastly multiply the power of individual residents.

A more subtle source of power lies in the functional importance of a particular status. Trash collectors are not thought of as powerful by most people,

but if they go on strike their power is revealed as residents watch garbage pile up on the sidewalks. Statuses also give power to their occupants by allowing easy access to local officials. Business leaders and local politicians often belong to the same clubs, and in locker rooms and private dining rooms they have far greater access to one another than do other citizens.

In addition to social statuses, power also comes to those who control valued resources. Landowners can tear down low-rent tenements to build office buildings or luxury condominiums. Affluent residents can affect local government decisions by giving or withholding contributions to political campaigns. Bankers decide how to invest the money that residents put into savings, and their decisions can have important effects on community life. Communities may also be victimized by the practice of redlining, in which bankers decide that some neighborhoods are poor investment risks and refuse to give home improvement loans in those neighborhoods. This often provokes an outraged response from residents who see their money being used to improve other neighborhoods at the expense of their own.

The shape of community power structures also depends on the degree to which social life is organized around social systems of varying degrees of size and complexity. Life in small, rural villages is often organized on a small scale in that relationships among individuals are more important than those among groups or organizations. In the cities of industrial societies, however, formal organizations are more important and tend to hold a large share of wealth and power. In a few small New England towns, decisions are still made at town meetings in which residents have an opportunity to present their views and cast their votes. In larger communities, power is primarily concentrated in labor unions, government agencies, businesses, political parties, and neighborhood associations.

The large scale of city life makes it difficult for individuals to participate directly in community decisions. At best, city residents are heard only through groups that represent them; and those who do not belong to influential groups are virtually powerless.

Control over jobs, on the other hand, can give businesses considerable power. Companies may threaten to move and take hundreds if not thousands of jobs with them unless they receive special treatment (such as tax breaks or exemption from antipollution laws) from local governments. This affects not only workers and their families, but the financial health of the entire community: businesses are major sources of tax revenues, both directly through the taxes they pay and indirectly through the taxable income of their employees; and local businesses cannot survive if residents have little money to spend (Bluestone and Harrison 1982; Raines, Berson, and Gracie 1982). This is especially true in communities whose economies are dominated by a single company that shuts down (Buss and Redburn 1983).

Given these basic sources of power, a major focus of sociological research has been to understand how they fit together to produce power structures. How is power distributed, and who influences which kinds of decisions?

Who Rules? Since sociologists began to study community power structures some 50 years ago, two major views have emerged. The first argues that power in communities is concentrated in the hands of a **power elite** whose members dominate all important areas of community life. A second and more recent view is **pluralism**, which holds that power is distributed among a wide variety of groups and individuals who influence decisions in different areas of community life.

The power-elite view first appeared in Robert and Helen Lynd's monumental Middletown studies (1929, 1937), in which they tried to identify a community's most influential individuals. They did this by living in the community for many months, interviewing residents, examining newspaper articles and official records, and acquainting themselves with the community's historical background. From this emerged the conclusion that an elite group of upper-class residents dominated community life in their own interests.

Floyd Hunter (1953, 1980) studied Atlanta, Georgia, and reached similar conclusions with the more efficient "reputational" method. Hunter located people he believed to be knowledgeable about various aspects of community life and asked them to compile a list of influential people. A panel of judges then used these lists to compile a final list of people whose names were mentioned most often, and these people were then interviewed and asked such questions as: "Which ten people on this list would you choose to make a decision about the community?" and "Who is the biggest man in town?"

The problem with these studies and their findings is that they focus not on who actually *makes* decisions about school expenditures, taxes, zoning, housing, or attracting businesses, but on who people *believe* make decisions or have the greatest potential to make decisions. More recent studies try to solve this problem by focusing on events rather than individuals: Who makes actual decisions, and what does this reveal about a community's power structure?

Dahl (1961) studied decisions made in New Haven, Connecticut, and Banfield (1965) conducted similar research in Chicago. Both studies (as well as many others) suggest that decisions in urban communities are influenced by a broad range of groups and individuals; that is, power is pluralistic, rather than concentrated among a single elite. Although specific decisions—how to zone a particular area or whether to build a new school—are usually controlled by small segments of a community, elite groups are not unified into a single, integrated whole that dominates community life, and they often have competing interests (Weissberg 1981). Insurance companies, police departments, and groups of citizens may favor raising the legal drinking age in a community, for example, but liquor companies and bar owners may oppose it.

Dahl found that few business leaders influenced community decisions, and then only in the area of urban redevelopment. None participated in decisions affecting education, and only a few were involved in political parties. The mayor and school officials made most decisions about education, and political party regulars were most influential in nominating candidates.

As Mintz and Schwartz (1985) argue, however, the close connections that tie most business communities together can often overwhelm conflicts of interest to produce a powerful united front on important community issues (see also Domhoff 1983).

This and other recent work argues that neither the elite nor the pluralist models are accurate. According to the **structuralist** approach, cities are dominated by fairly stable coalitions—including politicians, political parties, corporate leadership, labor unions, and other interest groups—whose resources enable them to shape city politics to suit their interests (see Manley 1983; Mollenkopf 1989). Politicians generally protect corporate interests, for example, because corporate allies are important in supporting and furthering political careers. In turn, corporations have an interest in supporting politicians because government can help shape conditions in which corporations do business.

The structuralist argument is not that a cohesive, unified social elite makes decisions as the Lynds found in the Middletown studies, but that dominant coalitions tend to support a status quo that, in spite of conflict over specific issues, in the long run serves the interests of their various members. In general, the larger and more diverse a community is, the more diverse the membership of the dominant coalition.

Whichever view of community power structures we adopt, the fact remains that in most communities power is unequally distributed. Immigrants and the poor generally have little influence over community decisions, and in cities, residents are governed by representatives who have far more power than those they represent. The distribution of power in communities is an enduring source of conflict and an important area of sociological analysis.

Social Interaction: Gemeinschaft and Gesellschaft

To sociologists such as Simmel, Weber, and Tönnies, industrialization and urbanization caused a disturbing shift in social relationships. Small, intimate communities gave way to large cities and the complex divisions of labor characteristic of mass production and bureaucracy. Weber ([1922] 1954) was disturbed by the increasing importance of rationality in social life, the rise of the specialist, and impersonal bureaucratic models. To Simmel, city populations were so large and diverse that individuals protected themselves from overstimulation by becoming distant and aloof from other people.

Tönnies ([1887] 1963) used a pair of concepts—*gemeinschaft* and *gesellschaft*—to describe this shift in social relationships. **Gemeinschaft** refers to a "'community of feeling' . . . that results from likeness and from shared life-experience" (Miner 1968). A **gesellschaft** relationship is held together less by a common culture than by rational considerations of self-interest and role structures that make people depend on one another. The city dweller who manufactures farm equipment and the farmer who uses it live sharply different lives, but each depends on the other in order to survive. Whereas gemeinschaft rests on shared values and interpersonal liking, the secondary relations of gesellschaft do not. Lawyers in small towns, for example, might refuse to defend an innocent man for fear of alienating a community certain the defendant is guilty, while city lawyers may represent clients they personally dislike and believe to be guilty.

If these concepts seem familiar to you, it is probably because they are similar to Durkheim's ([1893] 1933) concepts of mechanical and organic solidarity discussed earlier in this chapter. Both pairs of concepts are ideal types that are useful for comparing the general character of relationships in different communities or in the same community over time. Since the colonial period, for example, social relationships in the U.S. have dramatically shifted from gemeinschaft toward gesellschaft. In colonial America, people who grew food and exchanged it for products such as candles knew those they were dealing with. Today, however, the structures through which goods are produced and exchanged are far more complex and impersonal. The lettuce eaten by someone in Kansas City was probably grown in California, picked by migrant farm workers from Mexico, sold to a wholesaler and then to a retailer, transported by truckers, and ultimately sold to an individual in a supermarket for money earned, perhaps, by working in a candle factory. Our relationship with lettuce growers is now based less on a shared culture than on a complex structure through which we exchange goods and services and thereby satisfy our needs and desires.

With such changes came a decline in cooperation and an increase in competition. Prior to industrialization, for example, U.S. farm communities often gathered together for cooperative work, from corn huskings and quilting bees to barn raisings. With the growth of the cash market economy, however, these practices were soon regarded as economically inefficient and died out, along with the strong community ties that went with them (see Larkin 1988).

The first urban sociologists were as pessimistic about cities as they were optimistic and romantic about life in gemeinschaft communities. To Wirth (1938), rural communities were cozy and intimate: people knew one another well, actively participated in community life, and could turn to others for comfort and support in times of trouble. Cities, however, were seen as cold and impersonal places in which people disappeared in anonymous and superficial relationships and rarely participated in community affairs, because they were "just passing through." As Tönnies ([1887] 1963) wrote, in gesellschaft communities,

Everybody is by himself and isolated, and there exists a condition of tension against all others . . . intrusions are regarded as hostile acts . . . nobody wants to grant and produce anything for another individual . . . (p. 65)

Sociological research, however, suggests that neither the Chicago School's pessimism about urban life nor its romanticism about what anthropologist Rob-

The gemeinschaft ties reflected in George Luks's painting of the predominantly Jewish Hester Street neighborhood of Manhattan's Lower East Side in the early 1900s enabled immigrants to come to the United States and immediately establish a sense of familiarity and belonging.

ert Redfield (1947) called the "folk society" represents reality (see Gulick 1989). When Kasarda and Janowitz (1974) interviewed residents of urban and rural communities in Britain, they found little difference in the satisfaction people reported about their social lives. In fact, urban residents tended to report more friendships than their rural counterparts. In two U.S. studies, Fischer (1982, 1984) found that urban dwellers reported no more isolation than rural residents, no less involvement with their families, and, in some cases, higher levels of social support. Fischer found no evidence that urban and rural dwellers differ in the amount or the quality of their social relationships.

People who live in cities are no more likely than others to report feeling always rushed in their daily lives. Nor are they more likely to report dissatisfaction with community conditions such as schools and police protection. Indeed, they are *less* likely to re-

port dissatisfaction with health care, transportation, and annoyances such as street noise or poor street lighting or repair (USCB 1980b; FHA 1987). The larger the community, however, the more likely people are to feel afraid to walk alone in their neighborhoods at night (see One Step Further 10-1).

How do people maintain social ties in cities? One explanation is that when confronted with astounding numbers of people and a dizzying cultural diversity, people tend to form communities within cities. Whereas Simmel believed that urban dwellers orient themselves to the entirety of a city and its population, Gans (1982) argued that the neighborhood is their primary focus. The size and diversity of city populations foster and sustain the strong subcultures found in many urban neighborhoods, and it is within them that people often meet their needs for a sense of belonging and involvement in what Robert Park ([1925] 1967) called "little worlds that touch, but do

ONE STEP FURTHER 10-1

Feeling Safe: The Social Distribution of Fear

Feeling secure in our neighborhoods is a product of social life and, not surprisingly, how much of a secure feeling we have depends on our communities and our positions in them. The numbers in Table B-10-1 are the percentages of U.S. adults who say that they are afraid to walk alone at night within a mile of their homes. There is a column for each of three community sizes ranging from less than 100,000 to a half-million or more inhabitants.

There is a lot to see in this table. The top row shows that fear rises dramatically with community size, from 34% to 65%. The rows below it show how fear is affected by community size within a variety of social categories. The second and third rows, for example, show how fear rises among women (from 49% to 77%) and men (from only 14% to 41%). Look at each row and you can see that community size increases fear regardless of age, race or income. Stop for a moment and check for yourself.

Notice also that *regardless of community size* feeling afraid in our communities depends to some degree on social statuses. Look down the first column and you will see that in communities of less than 100,000 people, women are more afraid than men, nonwhites are more afraid than whites, old and young people are more afraid than those middle-aged, and those with less income are more afraid than those with more. Do these patterns hold in larger communities as well (second and third columns)?

Why should fear be distributed in these ways? What do you think?

TABLE B-10-1

	SIZE OF COMMUNITY		
	Less than 100,000	100,000 to 500,000	500,000 or More
Percent who report being afraid to walk alone at night.	34%	52%	65%
SOCIAL CHARACTERISTICS			
Sex			
Female	49%	71%	77%
Male	14%	27%	41%
Race			
Nonwhite	47%	49%	63%
White	33%	53%	66%
Age			
18–25	38%	38%	•
26–39	30%	52%	50%
40–59	28%	47%	60%
60 and older	43%	65%	77%
Family Income			
$0–$20,000	39%	58%	62%
$20,000–$40,000	37%	50%	56%
$40,000 or more	29%	46%	67%

*Too few cases to percentage.
Source: Computed from 1989 General Social Survey data.

not interpenetrate" (p. 40) (see also Popenoe 1985).

Even those who appear to be isolated—such as elderly people living alone—often form "telephone communities" through which they maintain contact with one another (NCHS 1986). Whereas Simmel and Wirth believed that the size of cities caused isolation and weak social ties, Fischer's analysis suggests just the opposite: although city dwellers may avoid interaction with *most* people, they have such a wide range of subcultures to choose from that their ties to other people are often stronger than they might be in small communities.

Although cities certainly have their share of serious problems—higher crime rates and higher percentages of poor people—they are free from the stifling pressures to conform found in small communities where "everyone knows your business." Life in gesellschaft communities can be as overstimulating as Simmel suggests, but it is no less true that the homogeneity and closeness of a gemeinschaft community can be very boring.

Beyond weighing the relative merits of urban and rural life lie the concerns of sociologists who see a general longing among people in the United States for the sense of belonging and rootedness that we often associate with the idea of community. In their book *Habits of the Heart* Robert Bellah and his colleagues argue that the strong emphasis that U.S. culture places on individualism, self-sufficiency, success, and mobility has created a society in which people feel isolated from one another and long for a sense of attachment to other people and a sense of place (Bellah et al. 1985).

COMMUNITY ECOLOGY

Whereas the concepts of culture and social structure draw our attention to the social environments that distinguish one community from another, ecology focuses on characteristics of populations and their physical environments. Communities differ in the size and density of their populations as well as in how rapidly they grow or shrink. In addition, they find themselves in a variety of physical settings to which they adapt by organizing activity and using technology.

Community Populations

The size and density of a community's population are sociologically important in several ways. In comparison with small, sparsely settled communities, for example, those that are large and densely settled can support a more complex division of labor—a greater variety of people performing specialized tasks. They tend to be culturally more heterogeneous, including people with a greater diversity of backgrounds. Because they cannot grow their own food, they are more dependent on technology—both in agriculture (so that farmers can grow enough to feed themselves as well as the urban population) and in industry (to provide employment for city residents). By current standards, the earliest cities hardly qualified as cities at all, for their populations rarely exceeded 20,000. In comparison, New York City has 7 million inhabitants and Mexico City has over 16 million. Such large populations allow a division of labor whose complexity dwarfs that of previous cities. Tax records for fourteenth-century Paris list 157 occupations (Russell 1972), but the number of different jobs found in Los Angeles or Atlanta is in the thousands.

Much has been written about the negative effects of living in cities. In comparison with small rural communities, for example, cities are more vulnerable to social disruption: their division of labor is complex, they are highly dependent on energy such as electricity, and they are far less self-sufficient. An electrical blackout in a city brings economic activity to a halt, and if transportation from rural areas is disrupted by a strike, no food can reach the city. Evidence on the supposed negative effects of crowded living conditions on human health and behavior, however, is far from conclusive (Baldassare 1983; Simmel [1902] 1950; Wirth 1938). Simmel and Wirth argued that urban crowding causes social relationships to be superficial and transitory; and others argue that crowding causes deviant behavior, mental illness, and poor physical health.

Most arguments linking high population density to deviant behavior and poor health are based on animal studies (such as Calhoun 1962) and have yet to be demonstrated conclusively among humans (Hawley 1981). International comparisons also raise questions about the effects of population density on human behavior (see Jain 1989). The density of Japan's population is 12 times greater than that of the U.S. and individual housing units are twice as crowded. Yet, in comparison with Japan, infant mortality rates in the United States are twice as high, and homicide rates are 9 times higher (USCB 1990a).

It cannot be denied, however, that social life is affected by the size and density of the community populations in the diversity of cultures found among residents and the ways in which communities organize activity in relation to physical environments.

Niches and Ecosystems

Each community participates in an ecosystem—a physical environment that includes both natural resources and other species of life—and survives through its relationships with it and other communities. The ways in which a population participates in an ecosystem comprise its ecological niche, and communities differ both in the kinds of ecosystems they inhabit and how they interact within them.

Communities that survive by hunting game and gathering wild food can support only small, sparsely settled populations with minimal divisions of labor. The earliest cities were made possible by revolutionary advances in technology—such as the plow—that enabled people to produce more food than they needed for their own survival; this surplus, in turn, supported cities, whose residents did not grow their own food.

The greatest leap in world urbanization resulted from the Industrial Revolution, which rested on innovative technology and changing values. When machines were introduced on farms, the resulting increase in efficiency created a labor surplus in rural communities. At the same time new machinery, sources of energy, and ways of organizing factories allowed factory owners to vastly increase production and profits.

These changes affected urban communities. Masses of people who could no longer find work in rural communities—here and in Europe—migrated to urban areas in search of factory jobs (the enormous influx of Irish immigrants to U.S. cities in the middle of the nineteenth century was caused in large part by the Irish Potato Famine of 1846). Figure 10-1 shows how profound this change was in the U.S. Since 1820 the percentage of people employed in nonagricultural occupations has increased from a low of 21 percent to a current high of 98 percent. At the same time the percentage of people living in urban areas increased from around 10 percent to 77 percent. Work became increasingly specialized and this fostered diversity by attracting migrants with a vast range of backgrounds.

The phenomenal growth of cities during the last two centuries did not just happen and then create cultural differences between rural and urban communities. The size and density of city populations were

FIGURE 10-1 Percentage of U.S. Population Living in Urban Areas and Percentage of Workers Outside Agriculture and Fishing, 1820–1989
Sources: USCB 1975, 1990a.

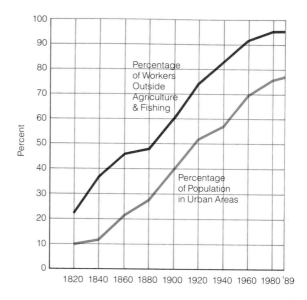

caused by changes in both culture and social structure—in technology, the values of profit and mass production, and the increasingly complex divisions of labor that resulted.

The Industrial Revolution transformed community life by creating cities whose survival depended on increasingly complex technology, vast amounts of energy, and expanding markets in which to sell manufactured products. This change in the ecological niche of communities altered societies and relations among them. The colonial expansion of urbanizing European nations during the eighteenth and nineteenth centuries was the direct result of industrial needs for raw materials and markets in which to sell finished goods. In the late twentieth century, the phenomenal growth of cities across the world has created an enormous demand for energy that dominates international politics. As recent events have made clear, industrial nations such as the United States, Japan, and most of Europe, for example, depend heavily on the stability of oil-producing countries in the Middle East, because without a steady supply of oil, the industries and cities that dominate these countries cannot survive.

The ecological shift from communities based on agriculture to industrial cities dependent on technology, huge supplies of energy, and vast markets brought with it increased interdependency among communities and nations and, therefore, increased vulnerability to economic disruption and international conflict. A drop in the demand for oil in 1982, for example, brought the economy of Mexico to the edge of bankruptcy, and in 1991 the war in the Persian Gulf created panic in the global economy.

The shift to industrial communities also increases damage to the physical environment by producing enormous amounts of waste and pollution. Until quite recently, death rates in cities were higher than in rural areas, largely because human waste was thrown into the streets or into rivers that were also used as water supplies. As recently as the nineteenth century the Thames River in London was an open sewer, and London streets were littered with horse manure (see Wohl 1983). As Larkin (1988) describes urban living conditions in U.S. cities in the early nineteenth century,

> City streets were thickly covered with horse manure and few neighborhoods were free from the spreading stench of tanneries and slaughterhouses. New York City's accumulation of refuse was so great that it was generally believed that the actual surfaces of many streets had not been seen for decades. . . . In most cities, hundreds or even thousands of free-roaming pigs scavenged the garbage; one exception was Charleston, whose streets were patrolled by buzzards (p. 158).

In the 1990s Mexico City is in serious danger of depleting its supplies of drinkable water, and many U.S. cities produce more waste than they can dispose of without threatening the natural environment.

Land Use: Where People Do What They Do

Within any community, people and their activities are distributed spatially, and the larger a community is, the more complex these arrangements are. With the boom in urban growth during the last century, ecologists and urban sociologists have tried to describe how the uses of space give communities their physical shape (Figure 10-2).

Early in this century Park, Burgess, and McKenzie (1925) theorized that cities develop in *concentric zones* or rings of activity around a core devoted to business and entertainment. As commercial activity spills into the next ring, residents move outward, leaving behind a mixture of commercial activity and relatively impoverished residential neighborhoods, including ethnic neighborhoods such as Chinatown and Little Italy. The next ring consists mostly of the homes of blue-collar workers, and as we move farther from the core, neighborhoods rise in social class, with the upper-middle and upper classes living in the outermost rings.

The **concentric-zone** model of city growth assumes that business activities are concentrated in a

FIGURE 10-2   Models of Urban Growth
Source: Adapted from Chauncy D. Harris and Edward L. Ullman, "The Nature of Cities," *Annals of the American Academy of Political and Social Science*, 242 (November 1945).

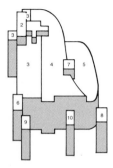

Concentric-Zone Theory
1. Central business district
2. Wholesale; light manufacturing
3. Low-class residential

Multiple-Nuclei Theory
4. Middle-class residential
5. High-class residential
6. Heavy manufacturing
7. Outlying business district

Sector Theory
8. Residential suburb
9. Industrial suburb
10. Commuters' zone

single core, and that rings develop as people compete for land away from industrial activity and poor neighborhoods. Although this model fit Chicago early in this century, city development is generally more irregular than a smooth set of concentric rings. Paris, for example, has no single business district.

Hoyt's (1939) variation on the concentric zone model takes into account the effects of transportation on patterns of land use. Like the zone model, Hoyt's **sector** model suggests that cities develop outward from a core. Instead of a ring pattern, however, cities grow along transportation lines that go out from the center like pieces of a pie. According to Hoyt, upper-class neighborhoods are not necessarily clustered in an outer ring, but can be found at varying distances from the center of the city along transportation lines.

Harris and Ullman (1945) suggested the **multiple-nuclei** model, which de-emphasizes central business districts and suggests that cities have centers for different kinds of activities—finance, theater, restaurants, clothing, and industry.

What do we make of these models, none of which accounts for the variety of spatial arrangements? Perhaps their greatest usefulness lies in what they have in common: they acknowledge that the intensity of land use for different purposes varies from one part of a community to another, which affects not only what people do, but how communities change.

HOW COMMUNITIES CHANGE

The process of community change involves a combination of cultural, structural, population, and ecological factors. Although large cities have existed for many centuries, the rapid urbanization of the world was created by the Industrial Revolution, which represented a shift in values and technology and a change in structure toward increasingly complex divisions of labor. These social changes, however, produced cities only in combination with population factors such as massive immigration of workers. The poverty of U.S. cities results not simply from inequality in the distribution of wealth, but also from the migration of businesses and middle- and upper-class families away from central cities. Community change is a complicated process, and finding solutions to community problems continues to be particularly difficult.

World Patterns of Change

Across the world there are some clear patterns of change in communities. There is a general trend toward modernism—seen in the acceptance of change, the increased use of technology, and the spread of mass media such as newspapers and television. The most dramatic trends, however, are ecological and structural, for the world's population is increasingly concentrated in urban areas. Only about 3 percent of the world's population lived in urban communities in 1800, but by the year 2025, cities will contain an estimated 60 percent (Table 10-2). As industrialization attracts migrants, city populations mushroom and include an astounding diversity of races, ethnic groups, occupations, and social classes.

Increasingly complex divisions of labor cause community relationships to shift from gemeinschaft to gesellschaft. The organization of community life around family ties, cooperation, and local economies gives way to mass markets, competition, and rational, contractual relationships. As the scale of communities grows larger, power is increasingly concentrated in formal organizations such as governments and corporations, and as this happens, individuals are further removed from the decision-making process.

The rise of the city as the dominant form of community also affects rural communities. The increased use of agricultural technology, for example, makes farm communities less autonomous and less isolated. Rural villages are increasingly oriented to distant urban markets on which they depend for cash income as well as for bank loans to finance investments in machinery, seed, pesticides, and irrigation. The growing orientation to distant markets—rather than

TABLE 10-2 Degree of World Urbanization, 1800–2025	
YEAR	PERCENTAGE LIVING IN URBAN AREAS
1800	3
1900	14
1950	25
1975	41
2000	55
2025	60

Source: PRB 1990.

to local subsistence needs—encourages farmers to specialize in only a few crops, many of which (such as coffee) cannot be used as food. This specialization, in turn, makes them still more dependent on urban markets, for they can no longer survive by consuming what they produce themselves. Rural farm populations such as those in El Salvador—who spend their lives growing food—often find themselves in the ironic position of starving when the prices offered for their cash crops decline in urban markets.

Trends in the United States

Although the world trends described above also apply to the U.S., since 1970 urban areas have experienced significant changes that are not typical of the world as a whole. Between 1970 and 1988 the combined population of U.S. central cities grew by only 4 percent while the suburban population grew by 37 percent, a rate of increase almost double the national average (USCB 1983c; 1989d). While the *size* of central-city populations remained almost the same, however, their social *composition* changed dramatically (Frey 1983).

The number of blacks living in central cities has grown one-third faster than the number of whites (USCB 1983c; 1989d). According to one estimate, nonwhites constitute majorities of the residents of many large cities including New York, Baltimore, Chicago, Detroit, and Cleveland (Kasarda 1986). Because those who left central cities generally had higher incomes than those who stayed behind and those who moved in, the poverty rate increased in central cities by 38 percent, but poverty in suburban communities remained unchanged at 8 percent (USCB 1983c; 1989d).

What caused these shifts in the composition of central-city populations? To some extent, the flight of middle- and upper-class whites from central cities is due to racism. The answer is not this simple, however, for affluent blacks have also been leaving central cities at an accelerated rate (Long and De Are 1981). An additional piece of the explanation lies in the relocation of many businesses to suburban communities, due in part to the attraction of less congested environments, but also to the fact that as central cities become poorer, governments must increase tax rates in order to maintain essential services such as sanitation, fire and police protection, and welfare programs. It is here that cities find themselves in a vicious circle, for as businesses and their middle- and upper-middle-class employees move to the suburbs, living conditions in cities (including tax levels) become worse, precipitating still more flight (Bradbury, Downs, and Small 1982). Many cities find themselves in a downward spiral toward greater poverty and on the edge of financial collapse.

The problems of central cities are bound up with changes taking place in the suburbs. Although most suburbs have been little more than "bedroom-community" appendages to nearby cities a new form of community—called **outer cities**—is emerging as suburbs become more densely settled and dominated by business and manufacturing that have moved from central cities (see Hartshorn and Muller 1987). Industrial and office parks, shopping malls, major hotels and restaurants, and growing downtown centers of some suburban communities are, in some cases, competing successfully with major cities as centers of economic life.

Community change in the U.S. has not been confined to urban areas, for in the last half-century the use of sophisticated agricultural technology has caused

Athough America's "War on Poverty" began nearly three decades ago, this rural Appalachian family remains relatively untouched. Without indoor plumbing, they are left to use wells and streams often contaminated by nearby mining companies.

the decline of small family farms, which have been replaced by huge corporations. Since 1930 the number of farms has dropped from 6.5 million to 2.2 million, and the average size of farms tripled. This, coupled with the migration to cities, has dramatically lowered the populations of rural communities: since 1930 the number living on farms has dropped from 30 million to just under 5 million (USCB 1990a).

Migration from rural areas, however, has been selective: those who leave tend to be young adults, leaving rural communities with relatively high percentages of children and the elderly—people who produce less than they consume—which helps explain why poverty is most common in rural areas (USCB 1987a).

Community Change in Developing Nations

Many early urban sociologists and ecologists shared the belief that urbanization took the same form in all societies (Wirth 1938). The experience of the past 20 years, however, suggests that in developing countries it is quite different from the urban growth in Europe and the U.S. that accompanied the Industrial Revolution (see Bradshaw 1987; Hawley 1981; London 1987). Whether or not these different lines of development will ultimately converge and produce cities like those of industrial societies is still an open question.

Urbanization in developing countries is unique in four ways. First, urbanization in Europe and the United States was a response to the needs of rapidly expanding industry. By comparison, the world's most rapid urbanization now takes place in poor, nonindustrial countries.

Second, the Industrial Revolution prompted a decline in birth and death rates in Europe and the U.S. Together, expanding industry and falling birth rates allowed these countries to keep industrial production ahead of population growth. In developing countries, however, birth rates remain high while death rates have fallen sharply through the use of health technology. In rapidly urbanizing poor countries, populations increase faster than production, and urban economies cannot absorb enormous numbers of migrants from rural areas (see Bradshaw 1987).

A third unique aspect of urbanization in developing countries is the spatial distribution of residents (Peattie and Aldrete-Haas 1981). In most U.S. cities the social class of residents increases with distance from the center of the city (although many city centers attract a small elite of wealthy residents). Urban growth in most developing countries, however, reverses this pattern, with poor immigrants settling at the outskirts of cities (Berry and Kasarda 1977).

Fourth, special changes predicted by early sociologists have not occurred in many developing countries. Tönnies, for example, believed that the shift from gemeinschaft to gesellschaft relationships was inevitable—that all cities would be dominated by formal, secondary relationships in which the individuals' primary loyalties are to themselves, rational thought is most highly valued, and people are rewarded strictly according to their performance. These early predictions, however, were based on a U.S. model of city life that may not apply in the social context of many nonindustrial societies. The cultures of developing societies are more likely to value spiritual life, tradition, extended family ties, and religion—none of which match the "rational" model of Western bureaucracy. Although urbanization in Europe and the U.S. was synonymous with industrialization in a modern cultural context, this is often not the case in developing countries.

The most important consequence of this difference lies in the social relationships among urban dwellers. In Africa, urban and rural culture are often similar because migrants to the cities bring their village culture with them. One writer describes the "gusto," "camaraderie," and "casual ease with which relations are established" in many African cities, and attributes this to the fact that "the African who comes to town rarely arrives as a complete stranger" (Epstein 1967, p. 206). This pattern is repeated throughout the world in squatter settlements outside cities in countries such as India, Turkey, Mexico, Egypt, and Kenya, where traditions are grounded in family and tribal ties and do not give way to the rational, secondary relationships found in the cities of industrial nations.

Despite the variety of their forms and patterns of growth, however, the world's cities have one thing in common: as communities, they find it increasingly difficult to feed, house, and employ their residents, and still preserve their physical environments.

Communities in Trouble: Possibilities for Change

The most serious problems facing urban communities are overcrowding, poverty, unemployment, and

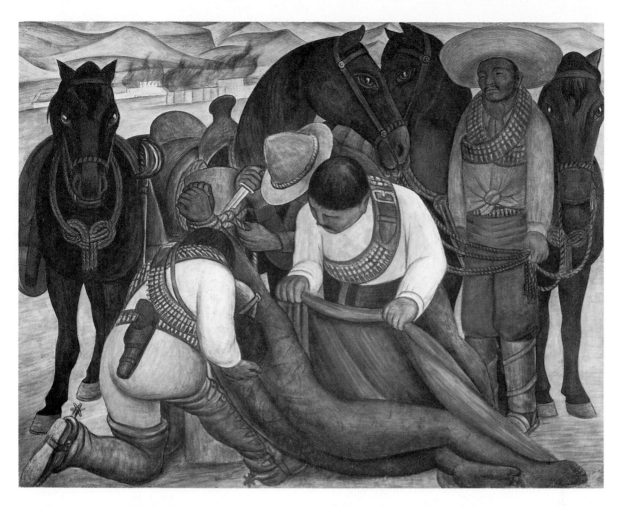

The prevalence of social inequality and conflict in rural areas is dramatically reflected in the work of Mexican artist Diego Rivera. His *Liberation* *of the Peon* shows revolutionary soldiers untying a peasant who has been beaten by a wealthy landowner.

a deteriorating physical environment. It is important to remember that all but the first of these are not unique to cities. Some of the worst poverty is found in rural areas (see Lichter 1989) as are some of the most dangerous environmental conditions, such as land erosion and drought. Revolutions in developing countries such as El Salvador often focus on rural communities where the best land is owned by wealthy families who use it to grow cash crops for export while the least productive land is owned by the poorest families (Barry 1987; Weller and Guggenheim 1982).

Most of the world's population, however, will soon live in urban areas; and for this reason, poverty, overcrowding, and deteriorating physical conditions are most visible and serious in cities. What are some possible solutions? In the simplest sense, the answers are obvious: redistribute populations in order to alleviate overcrowding, provide jobs for community residents, rebuild cities. *How* to accomplish these goals, however, is another matter, and it is here that we find three major approaches to solving community problems: government planning, private enterprise, and social movements among community residents.

Government Planning   The most notable examples of government planning are found in Britain, the Soviet Union, Israel, and China. In the early years of this century, the British government decided to build a series of "New Towns" near urban centers such as London. They were designed as self-contained communities—not suburbs—in which people would live and work. The planners seem to have achieved most of their goals: most residents work in their local areas, and physical conditions are better than those in crowded cities (Berry and Kasarda 1977).

After the Russian Revolution in 1917, the Soviet government began long-term planning to organize cities according to the number of workers needed for local industries and to ensure socialist ideals of equality and eradication of social class differences. The result in many Soviet cities (and in those of some Eastern European communist countries that used the Soviet Union as a model) has been massive construction of cheap, uniformly designed apartment houses forming neighborhoods whose residents represent a broad mix of occupations. Although physical conditions in the Soviet Union are harsh by Western standards, Soviet urban planners appear to have achieved some of their goals (Berry and Kasarda 1977).

In Israel the construction of planned communities, or *kibbutzim*, continues to be a major part of nation building. In a kibbutz, property ownership and decision making are shared among residents, and the community as a whole provides care for children and the elderly (Bettelheim 1969; Spiro 1956). There is some dissatisfaction among members—primarily among younger people who strain under the pressures to conform to community norms and values—but in general, community planning has resulted in high production, emotional support for residents, and a high degree of social cohesion and loyalty.

China has tried to stem the flood of migrants from rural areas in order to combat enormous overcrowding in its cities. Migration is tightly controlled by the government, and it is illegal to change residence without permission. China has also made major investments in rural areas in an attempt to make rural life more attractive.

In developing countries such as Egypt, urban planners try to increase urban employment through industrialization and lure migrants back to rural communities. This planning, however, has been unsuccessful. Their populations grow so rapidly that industrial development cannot meet the demand for jobs; and rural poverty is so extreme that migrants are reluctant to leave the cities that, however unpleasant, provide better conditions than rural areas (see London 1987).

Alternatives to Government Planning   Although many countries have developed planning strategies for community development, in the U.S. there has been strong resistance to government participation in community planning, leaving the fate of communities largely in private hands. The piecemeal planning that has taken place has often ignored the needs of residents and the social factors that brought cities to their current crises in the first place. The problems of U.S. cities result in part from uncoordinated decisions of business owners and families over the past 200 years. City populations grew rapidly in the nineteenth century because immigrants were attracted to factory jobs. Because cities have been like lightning rods—attracting the poor who seek a better life—they have for two centuries been the home of large populations of poor people crowded into substandard housing.

In many neighborhoods, low-income families have been forced to leave even substandard housing through a process called **gentrification**, in which real-estate developers buy up old, deteriorating housing largely inhabited by poor people who pay low rents. They then remodel the buildings and either live in them or rerent or sell them at rates far beyond the means of their original tenants (Laska et al. 1982; Zukin 1987). Although gentrification restores old neighborhoods, increases property values (and city tax revenues), and makes large profits for developers, it also displaces low- and middle-income residents who have no choice but to move to less desirable neighborhoods (Besser 1979).

For many who have no place to move, the result is homelessness (Rossi 1989; Wright 1989). Wright (1989) estimates that about three million Americans are homeless at some time during each year, a number that exceeds the entire population of Chicago and is just under that of Los Angeles. Homelessness has many social causes, including the rapid increase in the market value of homes and apartments, an economy that does not provide enough jobs that pay enough, declining public assistance to the poor and near-poor, and new fiscal policies resulting in the release of many mental patients from state institutions. As a result, while the homeless population once consisted primarily of single men, it now increasingly includes women, children, and entire families.

The scattered efforts to improve life among poor urban populations have failed because planners have assumed that the social aspects of community life depend primarily on ecology—the size and density of populations and the quality of buildings. They have largely ignored cultural and structural factors that affect life in communities—such as the inequalities produced by race and social class (Gans 1982; Gottdiener 1985).

In the last few decades, conditions in older U.S. cities have grown worse as businesses leave and take with them thousands of jobs. As cities become poorer, taxes increase, and to save money, landlords let their buildings deteriorate. This, in turn, makes cities increasingly unattractive places to live in, and middle-class families move to the suburbs. The development of communities has thus depended primarily on what businesses and middle- and upperclass families consider to be in their own best interests, *not* on the overall needs of communities. What substitutes for a national urban policy

> is a complex set of uncoordinated, often contradictory . . . random public policies and programs provided in the wake of strong economic forces which set the agenda for urban growth. Thus, if in the past urbanization has been governed by any conscious public objectives at all, these have been, on the one hand, to encourage growth, apparently for its own sake; and on the other hand, to provide public works and public-welfare programs to support piecemeal, spontaneous development impelled primarily by private initiative. (Berry and Kasarda 1977, p. 371)

The populations of U.S. cities are increasingly poor, elderly, and nonwhite; and yet these groups have little power over the economic and political decisions that affect community development. So long as U.S. culture values the right of organizations such as banks and corporations to act only in their self-interest—without regard for the fate of communities—how can conditions in cities improve (see Gottdiener 1985)?

One answer lies in the ability of community residents to organize and influence business and government (Fisher 1984; Van Til 1980). Neighborhood groups have successfully opposed the building of highways that threatened to split neighborhoods; tenants have successfully opposed the demolition of apartment houses or their conversion into luxury condominiums they cannot afford to buy. When companies that provide most of a community's jobs move out, residents sometimes pool their resources and become owners as well as workers, saving both themselves and their community.

Examples of residents organizing to fight for their communities are increasingly common, especially in less developed countries. In their extreme form, local efforts such as these are part of social movements that are sometimes revolutionary in scope. El Salvador and Mexico are vivid examples of citizen-initiated revolutions based in large part on the desire to improve economic and social conditions in communities.

SUMMARY

1. A community is a population that lives and works together in a shared geographic territory. Rural communities are small, homogeneous, and sparsely settled; urban communities—or cities—are large, heterogeneous, and densely settled. Suburbs are communities around a city.

2. In comparison with modern communities, traditional communities tend to resist change, have relatively simple divisions of labor, use unsophisticated technology, have less highly developed mass media, and rely more on informal relationships than on secondary, formal relationships.

3. Community cultures differ in content and the homogeneity of community residents. There are no distinct urban, suburban, and rural cultures.

4. Community norms vary in their formality and strictness of application. They also differ in their content, and this corresponds to different sources of social cohesion. Mechanical solidarity refers to communities held together primarily by criminal laws; organic solidarity refers to communities held together by civil laws that regulate relationships in complex divisions of labor.

5. Communities differ in the clarity and openness of their physical and social boundaries. Closed boundaries are often based on xenophobia, the fear of strangers and outsiders.

6. Community structures also differ in age and how long residents stay; in social composition and the importance of groups and formal organizations; in distributions of power; and in the social relationships through which residents know and interact with one another.

7. Power in communities depends on authority and control of valued resources. Power-elite theory argues that an elite group dominates decision making; pluralist theory maintains that power is spread out among various interest groups.

8. Gemeinschaft communities are held together by primary relationships based on likeness and shared life experiences; gesellschaft communities are held together by secondary relationships based on rationality and interdependence.

9. Communities differ in population size and density, and this affects the complexity of the division of labor. The Industrial Revolution caused a major change in the human niche by concentrating both production and people in relatively small areas (cities).

10. According to concentric-zone theory, cities develop in rings around a core of business activity. Outer rings are higher in social class than inner rings. The sector model states that cities grow in pie-shaped segments going out of a central business core. The multiple-nuclei theory maintains that cities have many different cores of activity. According to all three theories, the intensity of land use for different purposes varies from one part of a community to another, and residential neighborhoods tend to be segregated according to important social statuses.

11. Communities change through a complex process involving social and ecological factors. The world population is becoming increasingly urban and modern. In the United States, suburbs are growing faster than central cities, and some are becoming outer cities that rival the economic and political power of central cities. At the same time, city populations are becoming poorer and racially more nonwhite, while suburbs are becoming wealthier and racially more white. Urbanization is not the same in developing countries that lag behind in industrial growth.

12. The major approaches to solving community problems are government planning, private enterprise, and social movements among residents, and these can both solve and create problems.

KEY TERMS

community   209
concentric-zone theory   225
gemeinschaft   220
gentrification   230
gesellschaft   220
ideal type   220
mechanical solidarity   214
metropolitan area   210

modern community   211
multiple-nuclei   226
organic solidarity   214
outer city   227
pluralistic theory   219
power-elite theory   219
rural community   210

sector model   226
structuralist theory   219
suburb   210
traditional community   211
urban community   210
urbanized area   210
xenophobia   215

LOOKING ELSEWHERE

Having studied Chapter 10, you might want to look at related discussions in *Human Arrangements*, which include

■ population and the crisis of large cities (Chapter 4, pp. 65–66, 76–77)

■ gemeinschaft and gesellschaft ties in groups (Chapter 9, pp. 202–204)

■ mechanical and organic solidarity in groups (Chapter 9, pp. 202–204)

■ urban-rural differences in crime (Chapter 11, p. 245)

■ the distribution of national political power (Chapter 20, pp. 510–12)

■ racial segregation (Chapter 13, pp. 311–13)

RECOMMENDED READINGS

Boggs, V., Handel, G., and Fava, S. F. Eds. 1984. *The apple sliced: Sociological studies of New York City.* New York: Praeger. Drawing on the classical approach of the Chicago School, these 19 articles provide a richly entertaining and informative look at life in New York City.

Buss, D. M., and Redburn, F. S. 1983. *Shutdown at Youngstown: Public policy for mass unemployment.* Albany, NY: State University of New York Press. An examination of what happens when a "one-factory town" loses its factory.

Fischer, C. S. 1984. *The urban experience* (2nd ed.). San Diego: Harcourt Brace Jovanovich. A critical appraisal of urban research with a particular emphasis on subcultures.

Friedrichs, J. (Ed.). 1988. *Affordable housing and the homeless.* Berlin and New York: Walter de Gruyter. An international examination of the problem of homelessness including discussions of Europe, the U.S., Australia, and New Zealand.

Gans, H. 1982. *The urban villagers* (2nd ed.). New York: Free Press. The second edition of an important study of tight-knit ethnic communities that struggle to maintain themselves in the midst of modern urban decay.

Jacobs, J. 1961. *The death and life of great American cities.* New York: Random House. Although more than 25 years old, Jacobs' observations about the problems of urban planning, urban renewal, and life in American cities are still of great value and make for interesting reading.

Roberts, B. 1979. *Cities of peasants.* Beverly Hills, CA: Sage. A look at the unique problems of cities in newly industrializing countries, with an emphasis on Latin America.

Stilgoe, J. R. 1989. *Borderland: Origins of the American Suburb.* (New Haven: Yale University Press). A richly detailed history of the suburb as a form of community, relying heavily on first-hand accounts.

White, M. J. 1988. *American neighborhoods and residential differentiation.* New York: Russell Sage Foundation. A comprehensive ecological analysis of trends and patterns in the neighborhoods of twenty-one metropolitan areas in the United States.

11
DEVIANCE AND CONFORMITY

 Any behavior or appearance that violates a norm is **deviance**, while **conformity** is behavior consistent with norms. Everyone violates norms at one time or another—such as overparking, telling "little white lies," failing to offer a bus seat to an elderly passenger, or keeping library books past their due date—while a smaller number of people violate more serious norms, such as lying habitually, cheating on exams, or committing crimes such as robbery, sexual assault, or murder. Since norms are elements of social systems, the sociological importance of deviance and conformity lies in their relationship to them. All societies have ways of controlling the amount of deviance that occurs; but we can also look to the characteristics of societies for explanations of why deviance occurs in the first place. Competition and grades, for example, are important parts of schools as social systems, and their mere existence creates social pressures for students to cheat.

This chapter focuses on three kinds of sociological questions about norms, deviance, and conformity. First, how do social systems use norms to draw structural boundaries, and what are the resulting varieties of deviance? Second, how do the characteristics of social systems contribute to patterns of deviance—why, for example, is murder more common in the United States than in Europe? Third, how do conformity and deviance affect social systems—what are their positive and negative consequences?

To begin, we return to a familiar and central concept, the norm.

235

NORMS AND "THE NORM"

In any society, people behave in many different ways. Some behaviors are unusual—never eating meat, for example, but their rarity in itself does not make them socially unacceptable. Most people in the U.S. eat meat, and such common behaviors are often referred to as "the norm"; but the mere fact that individuals behave in ways that are statistically rare does not necessarily mean they are committing deviant acts. Performing heart transplant operations, for example, is an extraordinarily rare behavior in any society.

What, however, of someone who eats people? Cannibalism is not simply unusual; it also violates norms that define the moral acceptability of behaviors. In our culture there are thousands of different acceptable foods, but individuals who cross the cultural boundary and eat people are classified as *abnormal* and, to put it mildly, risk their standing as members of society (see Farb and Armelagos 1980).

Norms are not merely ideas used to control individuals; they also establish social boundaries of acceptable and unacceptable behavior. This is clear in social responses to what is defined as immoral behavior: "You are not one of us, and must either become one of us or leave." People who are identified as criminals or insane are either rehabilitated so they can once again fit within culturally defined limits of normality, or are excluded from society, through isolation in prisons and mental hospitals or—in more extreme cases—through death or exile.

Suicide clearly illustrates the connection between deviant behavior and social boundaries. By definition, it is an act in which the offender and the victim are one and the same (although other people certainly are affected). Even the most isolated individual, however, is legally forbidden to commit suicide. In England suicide was once viewed as so grave an act that the penalty for attempted suicide was a cruel death. How can we explain so extreme a response?

An obvious answer is that antisuicide laws support values about the importance of human life, but it is not this simple. Perhaps the clearest social boundary is the one that separates life from death. Life is difficult, and it is not uncommon for people to contemplate leaving society by ending their lives. In its simplest sense, the will to live is a basic prerequisite for the existence not only of individuals, but of social systems. A society that allows suicide undermines its most fundamental hold on its members: "If you don't think life is worth living, why should anyone else?" Each time we prevent a suicide, we both save the potential victim's life and reaffirm the belief that even the most unhappy life is worth preserving.

What of societies in which suicide is sometimes permitted or expected? In feudal Japan, for example, suicide was expected of those who had dishonored their families or their emperor. The key to such exceptions is that suicide is not seen as rejection of life itself or of society; rather it affirms important values. When Japanese pilots committed suicide during World War II by crashing their planes into U.S. ships, they strengthened social boundaries by reaffirming the value that the emperor was more important than any citizen.

Although deviant behavior is by definition forbidden by norms, it is nonetheless common in many cases. Eighty percent of U.S. adults support laws pro-

As much as we value our individuality, there are social risks associated with nonconformity. Which hat would you feel most comfortable wearing in this picture, and why?

hibiting marijuana use (Davis and Smith 1990); yet by their mid-20s, 80 percent of young adults have tried an illegal drug, and by age 27 roughly 40 percent have tried cocaine (L. D. Johnson 1988).

The line between acceptable and deviant behavior varies both among and within cultures. Ancient Greeks, for example, considered homosexuality a higher form of love than heterosexuality, and male homosexuality is an important part of rituals among Melanesian tribes (Greenberg 1989; Herdt 1984). Most societies, however, have persecuted homosexuals (including the murder of thousands in Nazi concentration camps). In seventeenth-century colonial America, adultery carried the death penalty (D'Emilio and Freedman 1988). Although 90 percent of adults in the U.S. profess the belief that adultery is wrong (Davis and Smith 1990), adulterers today are far less likely to be shunned and are no longer punished under the law.

Prior to 1914 there were no legal controls on the use of addicting drugs such as opium and heroin in the United States. Cocaine, in fact, was an early ingredient in Coca Cola, and heroin and morphine were publicly advertised as over-the-counter drugs. In 1914 the federal government passed the Harrison Act, prohibiting the sale and use of opiates. In 1937 marijuana was added to the list, as were LSD and other psychedelic drugs in the 1960s. More recently, tobacco smoking has been increasingly restricted by laws forbidding it in offices, airplanes, and public places, a movement through which what was once a staple of U.S. culture may eventually be transformed into a deviant behavior. Although considerably weaker, there are similar trends regarding the use of alcohol (Gallup Poll 1991; NIDA 1991).

Boundaries that define deviant behavior, then, are cultural creations, which means that deviance itself is a cultural creation (Durkheim [1895] 1938). Because merely passing a law defining drug use as a crime creates hundreds of thousands of criminals, statements such as "marijuana use is deviant" describe not the individual user, but the *cultures* that define certain behaviors as deviant.

SOCIAL CONTROL AND SOCIAL CONFLICT

From a functional perspective, deviance and conformity can be understood in terms of their connection to social systems—the ways in which systems pro-

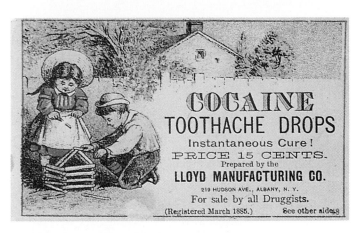

In 1885, cocaine was widely available in the U.S. as a pain remedy—much as aspirin or ibuprofen are today—advertised with pictures of children at play. Sigmund Freud believed that cocaine was a miracle drug that would cure a variety of physical and emotional ailments. In the century that followed, cocaine came to be regarded as a dangerous drug.

duce them and the consequences they have for systems. Since every social system has norms, it is inevitable that some people will conform to them and some will violate them, which means that in the simplest sense, both deviance and conformity are normal consequences in any social system (Durkheim [1895] 1938; see also Cohen and Machalek 1988). The consequences of deviance and conformity, however, can also be evaluated in terms of their effects on social systems. Erikson (1966), for example, argued from his study of Puritans in colonial America that laws reflect an underlying moral consensus in a system—what Durkheim ([1924] 1974) referred to as a **collective conscience**. When moral codes are violated, the outraged response that usually follows has the functional consequence of increasing social cohesion by reinforcing the sense of shared commitment to a common set of standards and principles.

The conflict perspective adds the important insight that since control over social systems and their norms may be distributed quite unequally, norms may reflect the interests of dominant groups more than those of the system as a whole (Turk 1979). In the eighteenth- and nineteenth-century U.S., for example, blacks were not allowed to learn to read, nor were others allowed to teach them. They could not sue in courts of law or testify against whites.

Members of dominant groups—such as the owners of this Tacoma, Washington paper mill—are often able to influence the legal process in their own best interests. They can block laws that would force industry to control air and water pollution at the expense of higher profits.

They could not vote or sit on juries, and the law specified harsher penalties for blacks than for whites convicted of the same crime. We can explain such laws as reflecting a moral consensus only if we ignore the glaring omission of blacks and abolitionist whites from that consensus. From a conflict perspective, acts may be defined as criminal because it serves the interests of those who dominate a system. Members of dominant groups may be allowed to violate laws, whereas others are punished (Chambliss 1973). As Quinney (1972) wrote,

> The established authority is thus able to use the law in the attempt to maintain control over the people. Furthermore, those in power are able to justify their actions through law. And most critically, they can pursue *their own* criminal activities without being defined as criminal. The police are seldom charged and convicted of crimes when they murder, violate constitutional rights, assault, and so on. The government itself, when engaging in an illegal policy, is not prosecuted as criminal. All of this is understandable . . . *since those in power, those who control the legal system, are not likely to prosecute themselves and define their official policies as criminal.* (p. 29, italics mine)

Dominant groups use the law to maintain their power by controlling which acts are defined as serious crimes. When people call for "law and order," they usually refer not to tax evasion, corporate fraud, or violations of civil rights by police and government agencies; rather, they refer to acts such as burglary and theft, which are committed more frequently among middle- and lower-class people (Clinard and Yeager 1980). Dominant groups also create laws that favor their members. Housing codes favor landlords over tenants, credit laws favor lenders over borrowers, and tax laws favor the rich over the middle and lower classes.

Dominant groups benefit in several ways from their control over cultural definitions of deviance. First, they do not *need* to resort to burglary or larceny, so that laws prohibiting such acts do not threaten them. Laws often are changed only when they threaten members of dominant groups. As long as drug use was confined to the poor, there were no strong public pressures to legalize it. When it began to spread to children of upper-middle- and upper-class families in the 1960s, however, there was sudden public pressure to remove criminal penalties.

Second, dominant groups perpetuate inequality by using laws to limit poor people's options, forcing them to choose between the risks of criminal prosecution and the likelihood that they will never escape their social class by socially legitimate means. After blacks were granted the right to vote following the Civil War, many Southern states enacted literacy laws and poll taxes that denied the vote to anyone who could not read from the Constitution or who was too poor to pay a tax. These laws diluted blacks' newly won political freedom and power, thereby protecting the privileged position of whites.

Third, by limiting cultural definitions of deviance, members of dominant groups draw public attention away from their own criminal methods, thus protecting themselves and their elite positions.

Thus, although norms often reflect a moral consensus in society, they can also be used to exploit others and maintain inequality. We have to keep in mind that deviance is a cultural category, and that people differ in their power to control such categories in their own interests.

VARIETIES OF DEVIANCE

Sociologists make three basic distinctions concerning deviance. First, although all deviance violates norms, violators may or may not accept the values enforced by those norms (a murderer may or may not value human life). Second, although deviance is usually defined in terms of behavior, it also includes personal characteristics (such as having AIDS) and statuses (such as religion) that may be regarded as deviant (Goffman 1963b). Third, the social response to deviance (sanctions) may be informal or formal.

Values, Norms, and Deviance

All norms are related in some way to underlying values. Folkways governing table manners, for example, support values about such things as politeness, regard for others' feelings, and health. Norms also specify legitimate means for achieving valued ends. There are many norms, for example, that identify legitimate and illegitimate ways to acquire wealth, such as those that prohibit theft or require employers to pay their employees for their work.

Although all deviant acts violate norms, social responses to them depend on how people perceive the connection between norm violations and the violator's support of cultural values. To illustrate, consider the deviant behavior of three college students. The first deeply believes that grades and exams destroy the learning process by turning students into "machines" who care about nothing but grades. She believes this so strongly that she steals the exam and the answer sheet beforehand, distributes copies to students, and publicly announces her action as a protest against grades and examinations.

The second student, in desperation, steals the exam and answer sheet and secretly uses them to prepare for the test. The third student is so frustrated with college work that he abandons all attempts to get good grades. He spends most of his time under the influence of drugs, rarely studies, and fails to appear for the exam at all. Merton (1968, 1976a) describes these relationships between deviance and norms and values in terms of several different types of deviance. The first student is a **rebel**, someone who openly violates a norm in order to challenge and change both the norm and the values it supports. Her actions are also **nonconformist**, for she committed them openly and without consideration for personal gain. When faced with punishment, she may defend herself by appealing to other values shared by her community (such as the importance of learning) that she believes are more important than the norm she violated.

The second student's actions are **innovations**, for although he accepts the value of good grades, he rejects culturally legitimate means for achieving them. His behavior is also **aberrant** because he had stolen the exam answers secretly and for personal gain. He is concerned not with challenging university norms, but with escaping their sanctions. If caught, he will defend himself not by appealing to higher values served by his behavior, but to circumstances that explain his actions ("I was desperate; I was overloaded with work this term").

The third student's behavior represents **retreatism**, a stance that rejects both norms and values without any interest in changing them. Like the rebel, he refuses to accept the university's norms and its values; but the retreatist offers nothing as a replacement. He has simply dropped out by refusing to participate. The retreatist's behavior is also aberrant, for it represents not an active concern with university culture, but a self-serving, apathetic rejection of the community itself.

Innovative behavior may be either aberrant (as in the case of the second student) or nonconformist. A student might share the cultural value of academic success and yet believe that exams are the wrong *means* for measuring accomplishment. Openly stealing the exam answers would then be an innovative, nonconforming act designed to protest norms while supporting cultural values.

These distinctions (shown in the box "Types of Deviant Behavior") are important because social responses to deviant behavior depend on the type of deviance the act represents. Nonconforming rebels and innovators act in the name of important values and without consideration of personal gain, so other people are more likely to support them. In addition, nonconformity often leads to positive social change. When blacks refused to sit in the back of buses or be turned away from "Whites Only" restaurants in the 1960s, they did so in order to promote social change. There can be little doubt that without such civil disobedience, the black civil rights movement would never have achieved as much as it has (see Chapter 23).

Aberrant behavior, however, provokes harsher punishment because it is done for personal gain. Unlike nonconformists, people who commit aberrant acts such as theft cannot say to society, "I did this for our own good." The behavior of nonconformists reflects a concern for values that connects them with the society that considers punishing them, whereas

Types of Deviant Behavior

NONCONFORMING BEHAVIOR   Done openly in the name of positive social change, not for personal gain; appeals to higher values.

Rebellion   Openly rejects *both* norms and the values they support, and offers alternatives.
Example: Revolutionary.

Innovation   Openly rejects norms and offers alternatives; supports values that rejected norms enforce.
Example: Publicly burning a military draft card while calling for a volunteer army to meet defense needs.

ABERRANT BEHAVIOR   Done secretly for personal gain; concerned more with avoiding punishment than with positive change.

Retreatism   Rejects *both* norms and the values they support, but does not offer alternatives. Uses illegitimate means to achieve culturally illegitimate goals. "Dropping out."
Example: Skid row drug addict.

Innovation   Rejects norms, but accepts the values they support. Uses illegitimate means to achieve culturally legitimate goals.
Example: Robbing banks.

Source: Adapted from Merton 1968, 1976a.

aberrant and retreatist behavior identifies individuals as outsiders.

The severity of punishment for aberrant behavior depends on the values involved. A starving man who steals in order to feed himself violates a norm while conforming to important values about the preservation of human life. If he steals in order to feed starving children, he conforms to even more powerful values—helping others and caring for children. A woman who steals simply because she wants to possess a luxury she cannot afford, however, acts only in her self-interest and conforms to a less-valued goal—accumulating possessions—and is therefore more likely to be punished harshly.

The social response to deviance also depends on the actors' orientations to values and norms as re-

vealed by how they present themselves and their behavior to others. For this reason, people who describe themselves as political terrorists have something to gain by defending their behavior with appeals to "higher values" rather than personal gain (Rappoport and Alexander 1982). In this way, they try to define killing as something other than murder, and abduction as something other than kidnapping, hoping to thereby escape punishment.

Stigma: When Who We Are Is Against the Rules

Stigmas, Goffman (1963b) wrote, are characteristics that render people not quite human in the eyes of others, who reduce them in their minds from a whole and usual person to a tainted, discounted one. Bernard Pomerance's play (and, later, movie) *The Elephant Man* tells the true story of an Englishman who was horribly disfigured by a disease. Like many disfigured people, he was regarded as a freak and accepted only by a sympathetic physician and a rare few who were willing to seek out the witty, charming, and intelligent human being who lived within the deformed body. The 1985 movie *Mask* tells a similar story of someone whose departure from cultural standards of beauty is treated as a form of deviance (see Beuf 1990).

Most recently, people diagnosed as having AIDS have found themselves often treated as outcasts. There are numerous cases of landlords who refuse to rent to AIDS patients, of employers who refuse to hire them, and of health professionals—including physicians—who refuse to provide them with medical care. Children afflicted with AIDS have been excluded from schools, and in one Florida case the family's home was firebombed.

Stigmas are also attached to personality characteristics such as dishonesty or mental instability. Former convicts and mental patients may be treated as outcasts even when they "go straight" (or "go sane") (see Link et al. 1987). The mentally retarded may be subjected to humiliation even by those responsible for taking care of them (Dudley 1983).

Stigmatized people are treated as deviants not for what they do, but because of who they *are* or are thought to be; and who they are or are thought to be is, as we have seen, a matter of social definition based on cultural beliefs and values about people's characteristics. It is perhaps the most damaging form

The television show, "Life Goes On," broke new ground not only by portraying the life of someone with Downe's syndrome, but by casting an actor with Downe's syndrome in the starring role.

Although the actor was more functional than most others with his condition, he challenged many stigmatizing stereotypes.

of deviance, for while we can control our behavior, it is all but impossible to change our bodies or our pasts, no matter how much we may want to do so. Stigmas have the power to condemn people to lives of shame and isolation over which they have little if any control.

Formal and Informal Sanctions

In most cases, telling lies violates folkways that have informal sanctions such as expressions of anger. If we lie habitually, however, people may refuse to trust or associate with us, and as informal as such sanctions are, they can be powerful reasons to tell the truth.

Informal sanctions, however, are not strong enough to compel people to tell the truth in court. People often have powerful personal reasons for lying, and such behavior (perjury) can have serious consequences. In many cases, therefore, the norms take the form of *laws* with formal sanctions and spe-

cialists such as police officers, judges, and prison officials to enforce them. In general, *crime* is deviant behavior that violates the law, and the social causes of criminal behavior are a major focus of sociological research.

CRIME, CRIMINALS, AND VICTIMS

Although **crime** technically includes all acts that violate laws, it is important to note at the outset that many violations of law are not socially defined as crimes, and some crimes are not defined as deviant. Few people consider speeding on the highway a criminal act; and although restaurant waiters who fail to report all their tip income to the Internal Revenue Service are committing a crime, most people—including restaurant owners—do not treat such people as deviants.

"There is no society that is not confronted with the problem of criminality," wrote Durkheim ([1895]

FIGURE 11-1   Homicide Rates for 15–24
Year-old Males, Selected Countries
Source: Fingerhut and Kleinman 1990, Figure 1.

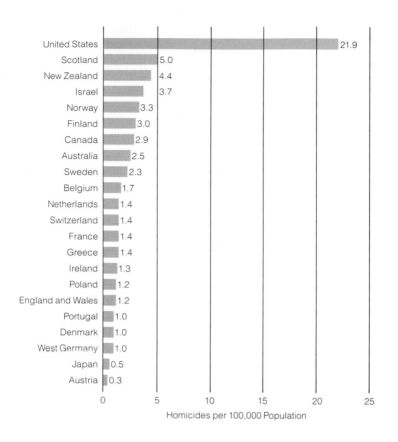

Homicides per 100,000 Population

1938), and the United States is a prime example. A murder is reported to police every 29 minutes, a sexual assault every 6 minutes, an assault every 7 seconds, and a theft every 4 seconds (USCB 1990a). In comparison with other modern industrial societies, the United States is the undisputed "murder capital of the world" (Figure 11-1) in no small part because of the much greater availability and ownership of handguns and cultural support for the right of individuals to use them (see Wright, Rossi and Daly 1983). Among teenage boys, deaths from gunshots exceed those from all natural causes combined; and among young black males, homicide is the leading cause of death, involving firearms 88 percent of the time (NCHS 1991).

The crime rate increased sharply during the last two decades. Since 1960 the U.S. population has grown by 39 percent, whereas the rate of reported crime has grown by 500 percent—in spite of tripled public spending for law enforcement (USCB 1975a,

1990a). In 1973 about 16 percent of adults had had the experience of being shot at or threatened with a gun, but by 1990 the figure had risen to 20 percent (Davis and Smith 1990).

We must remember that these statistics include only crimes reported to the police, and as people become more or less willing to report crimes, trends in *official* crime rates may not accurately reflect trends in *actual* rates. In the 1970s the U.S. Department of Justice began a series of national surveys to measure the incidence of crime (see Gottfredson and Hindelang 1981). By comparing the results with police statistics, the researchers found that crime often goes unreported to the police (USDJ 1980). The victimization studies found that the incidence of violent crimes was almost five times higher than that recorded by police (USCB 1986a).

Like most behavior, crime is influenced by social environments. Criminals are more likely to occupy some statuses than others, as are their victims, and criminals have relationships with one another. In addition, criminals, their victims, and those charged with law enforcement are related in ways that affect not only themselves, but the capacity of society to prevent crime as well.

Who Are the Criminals?

From a sociological point of view, criminal behavior is partly due to social structure, in that criminals as a social category differ from noncriminals in their likelihood of occupying important statuses such as gender, age, race, and social class.

Gender   More than 10 million people are arrested each year, and 86 percent of them are male (USCB 1990a). The gender difference in known criminal behavior has existed in virtually all societies, communities, and age groups as long as statistics on crime have been gathered. Prostitution is the only crime committed primarily (although not exclusively) by females.

In recent years the gender difference in crime has narrowed slightly in the U.S., particularly among nonwhites and for relatively minor crimes. Smith and Visher (1980) suggest that as males and females increasingly come to occupy similar positions, such as occupation, their behavior—including deviance—should become more similar as well (see also Hagan et al. 1985, 1987). Gora's 1982 study of arrest rate trends, however, found no support for the common belief that increases in female criminal activity have been caused by the women's movement and a redefinition of women's roles.

Age   Some crimes are defined literally by the age of the criminal. *Juvenile delinquency* refers to illegal acts committed by people under 16 years of age. Prior to the nineteenth century, child criminals were either shielded from the law or treated as adults, but during the last 100 years Western societies have created a separate legal category for youthful offenders, with its own set of procedures (Sutton 1983).

Age is also important because it affects the likelihood of criminal behavior (see Hirschi and Gottfredson 1983; Steffensmeier et al. 1989). A third of those arrested for theft in 1988 were under the age of 18, as were 43 percent of those arrested for arson (USCB 1990a). Adults are more likely to be arrested for violent crimes such as homicide and for crimes

PUZZLE

WHO CONSTITUTES THE CRIMINAL CLASS?

Who is most likely to break the law—someone from the lower class, the middle class, or the upper class?

If you answered, "the lower class," you might be right; and you might also be wrong. Popular stereotypes portray members of the lower class as particularly prone to criminal behavior, but, as this chapter shows, a long history of scientific research challenges this view amid a continuing debate among sociologists.

that require expertise (counterfeiting), money (drug smuggling), or special opportunities (embezzling bank funds).

The high rate of arrests for teenage arsonists underscores the problem of estimates of crime based on arrests. Arrest information does not measure the *frequency* of crime, for it misses all unreported crimes as well as those reported crimes for which police do not make arrests. That teenagers are more likely to be arrested for arson may indicate not a greater likelihood of committing arson, but a lack of adult skills needed to get away with it.

Race and Social Class   The inadequacy of official statistics is particularly apparent when we try to estimate racial and class differences in criminal behavior. Blacks make up 12 percent of the U.S. population, but account for 31 percent of all arrests (USDJ 1990). The criminologists Wolfgang, Figlio, and Sellin (1972) kept track of almost 10,000 boys throughout adolescence and found that lower-class boys were twice as likely to be arrested as middle- and upper-class boys.

Do such findings indicate that nonwhites and the poor are more likely to commit crimes or that they are simply more likely to be singled out by police? Many studies that rely on private interviews suggest that official records are biased against nonwhites and people from the lower class. Hindelang (1978) reviewed studies based on reports from victims and concluded that whites and nonwhites have very similar overall rates of criminal behavior; and review of 35 studies of crime and social class concluded

TABLE 11-1   Violent Crimes and Property Crimes by Size of Place, United States, 1970 and 1988 (Rates per 100,000 Population)

	VIOLENT CRIMES			PROPERTY CRIMES		
SIZE OF PLACE	1970	1988	% CHANGE	1970	1988	% CHANGE
Large metropolitan	458	752	+ 64	4389	5676	+ 29
Smaller cities	182	371	+ 104	2727	4550	+ 67
Rural	121	180	+ 49	1233	1759	+ 43

Source: USCB 1990.

that class has no effect on the likelihood of committing criminal acts (Tittle, Villemez, and Smith 1978). Although nonwhites living in inner cities are more likely to commit theft and violent crimes, the overall criminal tendencies of youths at all class levels are strikingly similar (Elliott and Ageton 1980; R. E. Johnson 1980).

The criminal acts of middle- and upper-class adults often go unrecorded because they tend to be **white-collar crimes**, crimes that people are able to commit because of the social statuses—usually occupations—that they occupy (Mars 1983; Reiss and Biderman 1980; Sutherland 1983). Now that computers are used so heavily in business, for example, employees have new opportunities to steal. One computer operator with access to payroll records modified the computer program so that each employee's paycheck was rounded down to the nearest ten cents, with each small reduction transferred to the thief's own paycheck. With 3,500 employees this amounted to an additional $300 a week for the computer operator, whose real weekly salary was only $120 (*New York Times*, January 29, 1984).

White-collar crimes may be committed by individuals or by groups. Factories that violate worker safety laws may cause the injury or death of employees. More people are killed each year because of unsafe working conditions than are murdered (see Hagan and Palloni 1986; Hills 1987). Companies that fix prices, violate patent and copyright laws, engage in fraud, or evade taxes cause far more economic loss than thieves and vandals. Although such acts violate laws, they often go undetected; and, even when discovered, they are rarely considered true crimes.

Even when companies are found guilty of crimes, the individuals involved are often not prosecuted; rather, the company itself is punished (usually a fine). Douglas and Waksler (1982) suggested that social ambivalence toward white-collar criminals reflects a deep underlying value conflict. On the one hand, we value honesty; but on the other hand, we also value making the best deal and "looking out for Number 1." W. C. Fields was not speaking only for himself when he said, "Never give a sucker an even break."

Shapiro (1990), however, argues that what distinguishes white-collar crime from others is that those who commit them are in positions of trust which their crimes violate. That white-collar crimes are more likely to go undetected and unpunished may reflect not so much a class bias as the conditions of trust under which white-collar criminals work, making it difficult to identify and successfully prosecute them. Because they are on the "inside," they can conceal their activities and destroy or alter incriminating evidence.

Because official statistics miss most white-collar crime, some researchers suggest that middle- and upper-class people may actually be *more* prone to criminal activity than people from lower classes (Reckless 1973). Tittle and Villemez (1977), for example, interviewed a large sample of adults and found no evidence of greater criminality in lower classes. Petty theft, gambling, and tax evasion were more commonly reported by upper- and upper-middle-class respondents. There is, of course, reason to be suspicious of any study that relies on people to report their own criminal behavior. What is important to note here, however, is that these data do not support the common belief that lower-class people are more prone to criminal behavior than everyone else. The debate continues (see, for example, Braithwaite 1981) and, so long as problems of measurement are as difficult to solve as they appear to be, it may be some time before the issue of social class and deviance can be resolved.

Urban, Rural, and In-between   The likelihood that people will commit crimes depends not only on statuses such as gender, age, race, and class, but also on their ecological (or spatial) relation to one another. People who live in large cities are more likely to commit crimes than those who live in small cities or rural areas (Table 11-1). In some cities the annual rate of violent crime is extraordinarily high: the overall reported rate of violent crime is 752 in large metropolitan areas, but the rate is over 2,000 in New York, Dallas, Detroit, St. Louis, Boston, and Portland, and over 3,000 in Denver, Atlanta, and Newark, N.J. (USCB 1990a).

Historically, large cities have experienced more criminal behavior than smaller communities, but as Table 11-1 shows, small cities and rural communities are rapidly catching up. Since 1970, violent crime has risen by 64 percent in the largest cities, but by 104 percent in small cities. Small cities and rural areas also had higher rates of increase for property crimes.

As we found earlier with age and social class, the effect that the size of a community has on crime rates depends on the type of crime. Reported rates of violent crime are twice as high in large cities as in smaller ones, but rates of violent death among young people are highest not in cities, but in the sparsely settled wide open spaces of the Far West where population density is less than six people per square mile. According to Popper et al. (1987), the frontier still exists, complete with risk-taking and violent solutions to personal quarrels. Rates of death among whites in frontier areas are even higher than those for blacks in high crime rate cities. The answer to the question "Who are the criminals?" depends, then, on which crimes are involved.

The fact that crime involves both criminals and their victims brings us to a second question: What social characteristics distinguish victims from nonvictims?

Who Are the Victims?

Just as social statuses influence the likelihood of committing criminal acts, they also affect the likelihood of being victimized, and this too depends on the type of crime. Table 11-2 shows that for major

TABLE 11-2   Who Are the Victims? Violence and Theft by Victim's Gender, Race, Age, and Income in the United States, (Rates per Year per 1,000 Population)

VICTIM'S RACE AND GENDER	TYPE OF CRIME		
	Violence	*Murder*	*Theft*
White males	35	9	73
White females	20	3	64
Nonwhite males	49	51	71
Nonwhite females	32	11	56

VICTIM'S AGE	*All Violent Crimes*	*Theft*
12–15	57	112
16–19	72	121
20–24	59	123
25–34	35	82
35–49	22	65
50–64	10	39
65 and older	4	18

HOUSEHOLD INCOME	*All Violent Crimes*	*Theft*
Less than $7,500	50	74
$7,500 to $9,999	45	65
$10,000 to $14,999	31	59
$15,000 to $24,999	29	64
$25,000 to $29,999	27	73
$30,000 to $49,999	22	72
$50,000 or more	21	83

Source: USDJ 1989, 1990.

crime categories, men are more likely than women to be victimized. In the case of sexual violence, however, almost all victims are women (USDJ 1987). We can also see that nonwhites are more likely than whites to be victims. The murder of black men is astoundingly frequent, occurring at a rate almost six times greater than among white men. The data in Table 11-2 also show that victims of violent crime are heavily concentrated in younger age groups. In the case of sexual violence, most victims are young women between the ages of 16 and 24 (USDJ 1987).

The effect of social class on victimization also depends on the type of crime. Lower-income people are more likely to be victims of violence (USDJ 1990b) and burglary. Higher-income people, however, are somewhat more likely to suffer theft.

Although men are more likely than women to be victims of violence, women are six times more likely than men to suffer violence at the hands of those intimate with them, such as family members.

The most important thing these findings tell us about crime is that for *non-white-collar* crime, the statuses most likely to produce criminals are also those most likely to produce victims. For many types of crime, people who are young, nonwhite, poor, or city dwellers are more likely to be involved in crime either as offenders or as victims than are those who are older, white, with higher income, or living in smaller communities.

As we will see later in this chapter, the social characteristics of criminals and victims provide some of the basis for sociological explanations of criminal behavior. Before considering the causes of deviance, however, we must first examine criminal activity as a structured set of social relationships among criminals and between criminals and their victims.

Structures of Crime

The simplest element of crime's structure is how complex it is, ranging from individuals to large organizations. Crimes may be committed by a small adolescent street gang, a large crime syndicate, or a major corporation. In the same way, victims may be either groups or individuals. Social relationships among criminals also vary in their complexity, from the simplicity of a pair of bank robbers to the bureaucratic complexity of organized crime. We need,

then, to take a closer look at two kinds of relationships—those among criminals and those between criminals and their victims—in order to describe crime as social behavior.

Relationships among Criminals   Although violent crimes tend to have simple structures involving single offenders, crimes such as theft, prostitution, and drug smuggling involve more complex relationships. Thieves, for example, rely on "fences" to buy what they steal, and fences, in turn, rely on people who are willing to buy stolen property (which is itself a crime) (Steffensmeier 1986). A fence may sell a truckload of stolen stereos to legitimate dealers who then sell them to an unsuspecting public.

Just as industrialization made most institutions more bureaucratic, it also changed the organization of crime. **Syndicated crime** is highly bureaucratic, with rigid authority structures controlling complex divisions of labor (Abadinsky 1983; Block and Chambliss 1981). The smuggling and distribution of illegal drugs such as heroin and cocaine require large amounts of cash and precise coordination among overseas buyers, smugglers, and distributors, from the wholesaler to the lowliest pusher (see Adler 1985; Posner 1988).

Syndicated crime may be organized in a variety of ways, from a rigid military model of bureaucratic efficiency complete with salaried employees, to a tight-knit family business. In some cases, syndicates operate as franchises (like fast-food chains), providing capital and expertise to local operators who then share their profits with the parent company (Anderson 1979; Ianni 1972), often making the structures of crime and legitimate business quite similar.

Criminals and Victims   Crime involves social interaction in which criminals victimize groups or individuals (Table 11-3). Most violent crimes involve people who are of the same race (O'Brien

1987) and who know each other: a majority of murders, sexual and other assaults involve family members or acquaintances (USDJ 1980). White-collar crimes, however, tend to victimize groups, as do crimes that systematically victimize people on the basis of statuses such as race, ethnicity, age, or gender (illegal job discrimination).

In some cases, the distinction between individual and group victims is unclear. If a black man is lynched by the Ku Klux Klan as an example to blacks in general, the effects ripple beyond the immediate victim to those who share his racial status. Brownmiller (1975) made a similar point about sexual assault: the fact that some women are assaulted provokes fear of assault in many women.

Although most crimes involve an individual or group as victim, in **victimless crimes** there either is no victim or the criminal and the victim are one and the same. Most states define prostitution, some types of gambling, and the use of certain drugs as illegal, but who are the victims? If one argues that drug addiction victimizes the abuser, this means society punishes those who victimize themselves. Schur (1965) argues that norms defining victimless crime exist not to protect people from victimization, but to prohibit behavior that is culturally defined as immoral. Because victimless crimes involve voluntary interactions, laws that prohibit them are difficult to enforce, for legal authorities are the only complainants.

The connection between victimless crime and morality helps explain why the response to such crimes is so severe even though individuals are not victimized. A society's mores reflect deeply held ideas about right and wrong and are an important part of the boundaries that define membership. In the case of prostitution, society itself is defined as the victim, and the punishment does more to maintain clear social boundaries than to protect individuals.

Structures of Justice and Injustice

Police, courts, and prisons constitute a **criminal justice system**, which carries out three basic social processes: identifying and arresting criminals, determining guilt and innocence, and deciding how to treat those who are convicted. How do culture and social structure affect who is arrested, prosecuted, and convicted? How effectively does the criminal justice system control crime?

Arrest   Arrest is a social process through which people enter the criminal justice system. Police face the impossible task of enforcing thousands of laws, and therefore have considerable discretion in deciding when to arrest someone. Police responses to criminal behavior depend on cultural definitions of the situation and the social statuses of those involved. Until recently, for example, our culture has defined wife beating as a family matter, not a crime, so police have been reluctant to arrest men who abuse their wives, and usually persuaded the victim not to press criminal charges. As well, enforcement agencies tend to ignore white-collar crime because our culture defines it as a less serious offense.

Blacks are far more likely than whites to perceive the police and courts as being unfair (Hagan and Abonnetti 1982). Although the evidence on racial discrimination is mixed, it is clear that poor people are frequently singled out for arrest. The better off a neighborhood, the fewer contacts there are between police and young people regardless of the amount of crime. Among young people who are arrested, the higher their socioeconomic status, the less likely they are to be prosecuted, regardless of their prior court records (Sampson 1986). Smith (1987) found that the likelihood that a contact between police and criminal suspects will result in an arrest declines as the status of the neighborhood increases, and this occurs regardless of such factors as race, the type of crime, and how suspects behave towards police.

TABLE 11-3   Individuals and Groups as Criminals and Victims

CRIMINAL	VICTIM	
	Individual	*Group*
Individual	Assault Mugging Auto theft Sexual assault	Treason Tax evasion Bank robbery Embezzlement
Group	Gang burglarizes a home	Job discrimination
	Mob collects "protection money" from merchant	Mob bribes government officials
	Ku Klux Klan lynches a black man	Nazi group bombs Jewish synagogue

In a now-classic study, Chambliss (1973) studied the Saints and the Roughnecks—two gangs in the same town—and found that Saints committed more criminal acts than Roughnecks, caused more property damage, and often endangered other people's lives with their stunts and practical jokes. Saints, however, were never arrested during Chambliss' two-year study, whereas Roughnecks regularly found themselves in trouble with the law. Why? The Saints belonged to middle-class families, drove new cars, spoke politely to teachers, police, and others in positions of authority, and had parents whom the police knew might cause trouble if their children were arrested. Middle- and upper-class parents have resources to shield their children (and themselves) from arrest—resources that are unavailable to poor people. They are more aware of their legal rights, and their relatively high prestige gives them credibility when they guarantee their children's future good behavior. Most residents looked upon the Saints as no more than a group of good boys who were having a good time. Roughnecks, however, were from the lower class and were assumed by residents to be bad characters.

Police officers' perceptions influence their decisions to arrest individuals, and such perceptions are affected by cultural beliefs attached to social statuses. Most evidence shows that such factors continue to influence the criminal justice system after arrests are made.

Prosecution   From the moment of arrest, legal procedures discriminate against the poor (Forer 1984). Middle- and upper-class defendants can afford to hire their own lawyers rather than depend on overworked public defenders. This is especially true of white-collar criminals, who often can afford skilled lawyers who succeed in keeping damaging evidence from the prosecution (Mann 1985; see also Shapiro 1990). Poor people are also more likely to stay in jail while awaiting trial, for the bail system allows the wealthy to buy their freedom.

Trial verdicts may depend more on stereotypes about defendants and victims than on factual evidence. Under the law the only issues in a rape trial, for example, are the fact of sexual contact and whether or not the victim consented at the moment the act took place. People in the U.S., however, often blame the victim and treat her as if she were the actual defendant (Holmstrom and Burgess 1983; Medea and Thompson 1974). Judges are obliged to decide cases on strict legal grounds, but juries are allowed to take extralegal factors into account, including stereotypes about women. Even when victims have been brutally beaten, their attackers may go free if the woman appears to be of "poor character" (typically, unmarried and sexually active). Juries often believe that such women "ask for it" and "deserve what they get." In so doing, they ignore the fact that a crime took place (see LaFree 1989).

Defendants have the right to choose to be tried by a jury or by a judge alone, and Kalven and Zeisel's classic study, *The American Jury* (1966), shows why accused rapists prefer jury trials. Kalven and Zeisel examined 106 jury trials for aggravated rape (with physical evidence of brutality) and simple rape (when the victim was threatened with a weapon but not visibly beaten), and compared jury verdicts with those favored by the judge. In aggravated rape cases in which judges favored conviction on the basis of the evidence, juries acquitted defendants 14 percent of the time; but in simple rape cases in which judges favored conviction, *juries found defendants not guilty 95 percent of the time.*

In cases of simple rape, therefore, juries often ignore legal evidence, and judge the victim rather than the defendant. Judges favored conviction 52 percent of the time, whereas juries found defendants guilty in only 7 percent of such cases. By choosing a jury trial in which stereotypes about women can overshadow the facts of the crime, defendants are seven times more likely to go free.

Punishment   Once convicted, a defendant's statuses significantly affect the sentencing process. White-collar criminals usually receive lower sentences than other criminals, and nonwhite adults typically receive stiffer sentences than whites who commit the same crime, especially if the victim is white (LaFree 1980). In a study of 2,484 murders in Georgia, Baldus (1987) found that blacks who murdered whites were 22 times more likely to be sentenced to death than were blacks who murdered other blacks; and whites who murdered other whites were three times more likely to receive a death sentence than were whites who murdered blacks (see also Nakell and Hardy 1987). Sociological documentation of such unequal treatment in fact formed the basis for the Supreme Court's 1968 decision to ban the death penalty (Zeisel 1981).

Criminologists have long maintained that the severity of punishment depends on the defendant's

DOONESBURY

by Garry Trudeau

race and social class (Chambliss 1969; Thornberry 1973); but more recent evidence suggests that such discrimination may have declined (Hagan and Bumiller 1983). Sentences *do* depend on the culturally defined severity of the offense, however, and here there is a clear bias in favor of white-collar criminals (see Hagan and Parker 1985).

In spite of the little evidence that criminal behavior is more likely among nonwhites and poor people than among whites and the middle and upper classes, the U.S. prison population is disproportionately black and poor. In 1989, for example, the jail population was 14 percent Hispanic and 47 percent black, even though Hispanics make up only 8 percent of the total U.S. population and blacks make up only 12 percent (USCB 1990a, USDJ 1990a). Taken as a whole, the social processes of arrest, prosecution, and sentencing clearly discriminate against people in these social categories.

Does the System Work? The criminal justice system is organized around a variety of goals, the most important of which are prevention, deterrence, and punishment. How effective is the system, and how is this related to its characteristics?

Criminal justice systems combat crime by increasing the size of police forces and, therefore, the ability to observe criminal acts; by imprisoning and thereby isolating criminals from potential victims; by imposing harsh penalties; and by attempting to alter the

personalities of people who commit crimes. The evidence is clear that none of these methods has been very effective.

Since 1960, per capita expenditures for police protection in the U.S. have more than doubled (after adjusting for inflation); but the rate of reported crime has grown by 500 percent (USCB 1980b, 1990a). Between 1985 and 1988, federal spending for antidrug programs tripled, and yet the number of cocaine-related hospital emergencies quadrupled, the number of frequent cocaine users increased by a third, and the purity of cocaine sold on the streets doubled (Vacon 1990). A greatly increased investment in crime prevention did not cut crime rates; instead, crime far outran efforts to prevent it. (It is of course possible that crime rates would have increased even more if expenditures had not increased.)

Most people who commit crimes are never caught, much less imprisoned. In 1985 the Justice Department's victim survey conservatively estimated a total of 22 million serious crimes. Of these, only half were reported to police and only 10 percent resulted in an arrest (USCB 1986a). More than 90 percent of serious criminal offenses never result in an arrest, much less in prosecution, conviction, and punishment. Since the vast majority of criminals are never caught and convicted, the threat of punishment is too low to effectively discourage criminal behavior.

In 1990, 82 percent of U.S. adults believed that courts do not treat criminals harshly enough (Davis

There is a great deal of debate over how the severity of punishment and the certainty of punishment affect rates of crime. This poster from Malaysia seems to reflect both approaches by warning potential drug traffickers of a certain and severe punishment if caught.

and Smith 1990), but dozens of studies show that long prison sentences are no more effective than short ones in preventing crime (Babst et al. 1976) and there is a great deal of controversy about whether capital punishment helps to deter crime (see Archer and Gartner 1984; Zeisel 1977). What does make a difference is the *certainty* of punishment (Chapman 1976; Silverman 1976). In the United States, for example, over 90 percent of kidnappers are caught, convicted, and severely punished, and as a result, kidnapping is quite rare. When public perception of the certainty of punishment for drunken driving increases, the incidence of drunken driving tends to decline (see Ross 1984).

Finally, efforts to rehabilitate criminals by altering their personalities through therapy or by providing them with occupational skills have had, at best, mixed results (Lipton, Martinson, and Wilks 1975; Martinson 1974). A sociological point of view suggests several reasons for this failure.

Prison is what Goffman (1961a) called a **total institution**—in which inmates' lives are almost completely controlled. They are isolated from society, deprived of meaningful work and heterosexual contact, and can make few decisions for themselves. On entering prison, inmates experience **degradation ceremonies** (Garfinkel 1956), in which they are stripped, searched, and labeled as inferior human beings. The physical and social organization of prisons is designed primarily to prevent escape, a goal that has little effect on crime rates since, as we have seen, few criminals are ever imprisoned. With prison in-

mates learning to adapt to and function in a social environment that bears little resemblance to the outside world it should come as no surprise that 63 percent are arrested for new crimes within three years of their release (USDJ 1990a).

A second reason for the failure of the U.S. criminal justice system lies in its assumptions about the *causes* of deviance. In particular, it assumes that fear of punishment is the most important factor in preventing deviance and that the causes of deviance have relatively little to do with the pressures and limitations imposed by social systems. We know, however, that fear of punishment has relatively little effect on behavior, including deviance (Piliavin et al. 1986), and there is no reason to believe that deviant behavior is any less affected by social systems than any other form of behavior.

All of this points strongly to the importance of sociological explanations. How do the characteristics of social systems increase the chances that people will commit crimes?

WHAT CAUSES DEVIANCE?

Researchers have long tried to identify biological and psychological causes of deviant behavior (see Kamin 1986; Wilson and Herrnstein 1985). Lombroso (1911) argued that crime results from "animalistic body types"; but Goring (1913) later discovered that the physical appearance of criminals differs little from that of noncriminals. Sheldon (1949) found that delinquents tend to have sturdy, muscular bodies. The problem with such findings is that they ignore the ways in which people's social responses to physical appearances affect behavior. Muscular boys are more likely to be chosen as members of gangs that regularly engage in fighting, but this is a far cry from concluding that muscularity in itself causes deviance.

Sociologically, choices between conformity and deviance depend a great deal on the social systems we participate in. This does not mean that sociological explanations of deviance relieve individuals of personal responsibility; rather, they help identify social factors that encourage people to make deviant choices. To the extent that society itself fosters deviance, all the individual therapy in the world will only treat the symptoms of deviance, not its causes. Deviant behavior is an enormously complex puzzle, and researchers in all disciplines are far from identifying all its pieces, and even farther from putting them together. The following sections identify some of the pieces revealed by sociological analysis and research.

Deviance and Culture

In the simplest sense, culture contributes to deviance by creating norms that define some behaviors as deviant. As Durkheim ([1895] 1938) asserted, deviance is an inevitable consequence of social life, for societies use categories of deviant behavior to draw their boundaries and maintain social cohesion.

The U.S., for example, could reduce the annual number of arrests by more than 2 million if the law no longer defined public drunkenness, drug use, liquor sales to minors, prostitution, gambling, and vagrancy as crimes (USCB 1990a). When drugs such as marijuana and cocaine are outlawed, their price skyrockets because they can be obtained only at greater risk. For many addicts, crime is the only way to support an expensive habit. Schur (1965) argues that the criminal justice system would in fact be far more effective if certain behaviors, especially victimless crimes, were no longer defined as crimes.

Since deviance is inevitable in all societies, however, we are confronted with the problem of explaining why some people deviate from norms and others do not. Two sociological theories help explain the role of culture.

Deviance and Anomie According to the first of these theories, we tend to conform to norms only insofar as we identify ourselves as members of a social system and feel an attachment to its values. Norms regulate social relationships, and if we feel cut off and isolated from systems, their norms will have little effect on us. In a related sense, if there is wide disagreement and confusion about which behaviors are acceptable, we lack clear guidelines and are more

Jasper Johns' painting, *Target with Four Faces* (1955), evokes the sense of social isolation, disconnection, and normlessness characteristic of anomic social systems.

likely to create new ones which may include innovative deviance.

Durkheim ([1897] 1951) believed that human desire has no natural limits, and that if it were not for the pressure of norms and values, social systems would be unable to control destructive behavior. When norms break down and people no longer feel a solid connection between themselves and society, the result is a condition in social systems that Durkheim called **anomie**. During civil wars, for example, people often feel that "anything goes," and commit acts they would never consider in less chaotic conditions.

As Durkheim ([1897] 1951) noted in his study of suicide, anomie is a dangerous social condition, for it "deceives us into believing that we depend on ourselves only." As Hirschi (1969) found in his comparisons of delinquents and nondelinquents, feelings of isolation are associated with deviant behavior. Typical delinquents are weakly attached to friends and family, and lack the close relationships and values that motivate most people to obey the law. Wiatrowski, Griswold, and Roberts (1981) supported Hirschi's findings and emphasized the particularly strong effects of adolescent attachments to parents and school as inhibitors of delinquent behavior (see also Liska and Reed 1985).

In some cases, the connection between groups and society is so weak that they deviate by retreating, creating their own communities. In 1875, a religious group called the Hutterites rejected the capitalist, competitive way of life in the U.S., and forbade marriage between their members and outsiders. Early in the same century, another religious group—called the Oneida Community—rejected ideas of marriage, the family, and private property. Sexual relations were unrestricted, and children were raised not by parents, but by the entire adult community. In more recent years, there have been numerous attempts in the U.S. to form communes that reject values and norms in the dominant culture (Kephart and Zellner 1990; Zablocki 1980).

Deviance and Subcultures   A second cultural perspective raises the paradoxical idea that deviance may represent conformity. Even when there is gen-eral agreement about which behaviors are deviant and how serious each is, the larger and more complex a social system is, the more likely subgroups are to form, and their subcultures may include ideas that conflict with those of the rest of the system.

In the U.S., for example, drug use, vandalism, theft, and teenage drinking and sex are defined as deviant behaviors; but adolescent friendship groups are powerful reference groups that may support such behavior. Not yet recognized as adults with important roles to play, adolescents must find other ways to feel rooted in society, and when they turn to peer groups to satisfy their desire to belong, they encounter strong pressures to conform to adolescent subcultures.

In defiance of an adult society that refuses to grant them full membership, adolescent subcultures often include norms that require *non*conformity to norms and values in the surrounding culture (Coleman 1961; Douvan and Adelson 1966). Adolescents who refuse sex, drugs, and alcohol may be treated as deviants by their peers, excluded and ridiculed. Society defines car theft as criminal, but a street gang's subculture may define it as conformity. Reporting crime to the police conforms to legal norms, but criminal

The value placed on masculine toughness is not restricted to the lower class.

subcultures define it as deviant ("ratting," "snitching," and "finking"). For this reason, gang members who act as police informants occupy an insecure position between two cultures, neither of which may be willing to support or protect them.

The pressures to conform in small groups are often rooted in larger subcultures. Miller (1958) spent three years observing lower-class gangs, and concluded that the high value they place on toughness (being brave, daring, and strong), autonomy ("No one tells me what to do"), smartness (ability to con others), excitement (risk and danger), and fate (luck), reflected not the subculture of the gang itself, but elements of lower-class culture as a whole.

Miller did not suggest that lower-class subculture values criminal behavior; rather he suggested that values prevalent in that subculture increase the likelihood of behaviors defined as deviant by middle- and upper-class authorities. We should also note that the lower class has no monopoly on values such as toughness and machismo. Many U.S. presidents have been motivated by the desire to maintain a tough and manly image (Halberstam, 1972) (see One Step Further 11-1).

ONE STEP FURTHER 11-1

Violence and Social Class

It is a commonly held belief that physical violence is largely a phenomenon of the lower and working classes, but a variety of evidence suggests otherwise in terms of experience and values. In Table B-11-1 the first column of percentages shows that the more income or education people have, the *more* likely they are to ever have been punched or beaten. This is true, also, for nonwhites in comparison with whites. The second column shows few clear differences in the likelihood of having been shot at or threatened with a gun.

The third column focuses on values about violence rather than actual experience, and here the differences are even more striking. When people were asked if they could think of situations in which they would approve of a man hitting an adult male stranger, the percentage who could is considerably higher among those with more income or education and among whites. Such findings raise questions not only about the kind of public violence most often associated with crime, but also with more hidden violence such as child and spouse abuse (see Chapters 14 and 16).

TABLE B-11-1

SOCIAL CHARACTERISTICS	PERCENT WHO HAVE EVER BEEN		Approve of Hitting?[1]
	Punched or Beaten	Shot At or Threatened with a Gun	
Family Income			
Less than $10,000	37%	23%	51%
$10,000–$19,999	36%	16%	63%
$20,000–$39,999	39%	20%	64%
$40,000 or more	35%	19%	73%
Education			
Less than high school graduate	36%	21%	42%
High school graduate	35%	19%	64%
Some college	39%	22%	69%
College degree	36%	16%	72%
More than college	39%	18%	81%
Race			
Nonwhite	42%	25%	46%
White	35%	19%	66%

[1]"Can you imagine a situation in which you would approve of a man punching an adult male stranger?" Percent answering "yes."
Source: Computed from 1990 General Social Survey data.

From this perspective, deviant behaviors are often *learned* through socialization. Toughness and defiance are learned through the same process as politeness and respect for the law. Prostitutes learn their craft just as plumbers, lawyers, and accountants learn theirs (Heyl 1977). Why, however, are some people socialized into deviance, but others are not?

Differential Association   According to Sutherland's theory of **differential association**, complex social systems offer many beliefs, values, and attitudes, including both respect and disrespect for various norms (Matsueda 1982; Sutherland and Cressey 1978). Which ideas we adopt depends on the intensity of our exposure to competing alternatives. Since the intensity of our exposure to different norms and the values they support depends on many things—from the kinds of role models we are exposed to, to how different kinds of behavior are portrayed in the media—we should expect to find a great deal of variation in how people are socialized. In addition, complex cultures contain a variety of conflicting standards; and differences in exposure to competing alternatives during socialization produce different definitions of acceptable behavior.

Many cultures, for example, contain a variety of beliefs, values, and attitudes about women, some of which promote crimes of aggression and hostility (see Brownmiller 1975; Dijkstra 1987; Russell 1984). On the one hand are images of women as pure, innocent, and good, as embodied in ideals of motherhood or, for Christians, in the Virgin Mary. On the other hand are images of women as a source of evil and corruption, as sex objects, as wanting domination and control by men, and so on. From Sutherland's perspective, whether men grow up to commit crimes against women will depend to some degree on how they are exposed to such diverse and often contradictory elements of a complex culture.

Although cultural explanations reveal that deviant behaviors are often learned and transmitted from one generation to the next, they do not explain where such patterns come from in the first place. Why would anyone choose crime as an occupation? Why do some groups require members to conform to norms and values that society defines as deviant? A sociological response to such questions involves a second major concept in the sociological perspective—social structure.

Deviance and Social Structure

If we focus on how statuses and roles limit people's choices, three structural theories help explain deviant behavior. First, people may violate norms from a sense of *duty*—because they believe that the legitimate demands of their roles require it. Second,

Pham Thic Trinh was nine years old when her entire family and the population of My Lai was massacred. She played dead by crawling beneath the bodies of her parents. Here she stands in 1988 in front of a memorial in My Lai. William Calley, the lieutenant who was held primarily responsible for the killings, was placed under house arrest for three years. More than twenty years later, Trinh tends the monument and lives with her nightmares.

societies can create deviant roles by *labeling* people as deviants and expecting them to violate norms. Third, people may find themselves in situations in which they can achieve legitimate goals only by violating norms—in other words, situations in which legitimate means will not work. The following section discusses each of these theories in turn.

Deviance as Duty According to the Uniform Code of Military Justice, U.S. soldiers are required to obey the orders of their superiors; during wartime, the penalty for disobedience is death. This raises a serious dilemma: What happens when a commander orders troops to commit illegal acts?

In Vietnam a platoon of U.S. soldiers, demoralized and frustrated by ambushes, booby traps, and an elusive enemy, wandered into the village of My Lai (Hersch 1970). Most of the residents were women, children, and old men, and there was no reason to believe they threatened the soldiers in any way. Yet, within minutes, the GIs had killed several Vietnamese, and shortly thereafter both the platoon leader and the company commander ordered the soldiers to kill everyone in the village.

By day's end, between 450 and 500 civilians had been murdered in spite of their cries and pleas for mercy. They were stabbed, thrown down wells, pushed into ditches and shot, or forced into huts and then blown up with grenades.

> One further incident stood out in many GIs' minds: seconds after the shooting stopped, a bloodied but unhurt two-year-old boy miraculously crawled out of the ditch, crying. He began running toward the hamlet. Someone hollered, "There's a kid." There was a long pause. Then Calley ran back, grabbed the child, threw him back in the ditch and shot him. (Hersch, 1970, p. 74)

How could people do this? Although their state of mind helps explain their behavior, one thing is clear: had their leaders not ordered them to fire, or had they ordered them *not* to fire, the massacre never would have happened.

From a sociological point of view, the soldiers did their duty by obeying orders. As Hersch noted, those who did not like what was happening "kept their thoughts to themselves," for disobeying orders during wartime is a serious crime. It seems incredible to most people that anyone would obey such orders, and yet, as Milgram discovered in his classic experiments, we tend to violate norms when an authority we define as legitimate tells us to.

PUZZLE

AT WHAT POINT WOULD YOU STOP OBEYING LEGITIMATE ORDERS?

If the president of the United States ordered you to push a button that would execute a stranger for no good reason that you could see, would you do it?

If your answer is "no," pay particular attention to the following discussion of the Milgram experiment, for it suggests that you may not know yourself as well as you think you do.

Milgram (1965) conducted a controversial and now-famous experiment in which people volunteered to assist in a "learning experiment" at a prestigious university. Each subject (who was paid to participate) was told by a man dressed in an official-looking white lab coat that researchers were interested in the effects of punishment on learning. The subjects stood in a small room equipped with a large electronic panel with a series of 30 buttons, each of which, they were told, delivered increasingly severe shocks to a man strapped to a chair in the next room. The lowest shock level (15 volts) was labeled "SLIGHT SHOCK," the third highest (420 volts) was labeled "DANGER: SEVERE SHOCK," and the last two switches (435 and 450 volts) had the ominous label "XXX." Subjects were told to read a list of words to the "learner" in the next room, and to punish him with shocks when he failed to recite the list correctly. (In fact, the "learner" worked for Milgram and there were no actual shocks.) A window allowed each "teacher" to see the "learner."

The learner consistently failed, and each time the experimenter told the teacher to increase the shock by 15 volts. At 75 volts, the learner grunted, and by 150 volts, he banged on the walls and begged to be released. When subjects protested to the experimenter, they were told, "The experiment requires you to continue" or "You have no other choice; you must go on." The learner said he had a weak heart, and after 330 volts was reached, he no longer responded at all. How do you think these ordinary people behaved? Did they refuse to endanger a person's life in the name of scientific research?

Milgram expected few subjects to deliver what they believed to be dangerous shocks, and a sample of 40 psychiatrists predicted that most would stop at the 150-volt level and that only a rare neurotic individual would deliver the maximum shock (Milgram 1974). In fact, however, almost *two-thirds* of the subjects were fully obedient and went all the way to the most dangerous level. In doing so, they showed a great deal of anxiety—verbally attacking the experimenter, twitching or laughing nervously—but, nonetheless, most did as they were told.

Milgram's experiment dramatically illustrates the ability of authorities to force people to violate norms (see also Haritos-Fatouros 1988; Kelman and Hamilton 1989). When presidents order illegal wiretaps or the assassination of foreign leaders, or when business executives order subordinates to fire an employee without good reason, they are likely to be obeyed by people who define obedience to legitimate authority as part of their role obligations.

In the simplest sense, then, social structure often encourages deviance by giving some people the authority to demand deviant behavior from subordinates as a requirement for successful role performance (see Clinard 1983). Deviant behavior is also encouraged, however, when societies label deviance as a social status whose role includes the violation of norms.

The Power of Labels

When people steal, they are usually punished if discovered; but the social response to deviance often goes beyond mere punishment. In some cases, both the actor *and* the behavior are labeled as deviant: the person who steals is labeled a thief, or the student who cheats is labeled a cheater. According to the **social labeling** perspective, societies often reinforce their boundaries by labeling *people* as deviants as well as their behavior. In this sense, behaviors such as theft, cheating, or drug use are transformed into statuses that people may make part of their social identities (Becker 1964, 1973).

Deviant acts that are performed before any labels are applied are called **primary deviance**. Primary deviance may be committed for any number of reasons—from peer pressure to use drugs to the desire to become wealthy—but what they all have in common is that the people who commit the acts do not yet think of themselves as deviant *people*. In some cases the person might not even consider the behavior itself to be truly deviant, as is the case with many victimless crimes. Once caught, however, and referred to and treated as a junkie or a criminal, they might find that the label itself fosters further deviance—called **secondary deviance** (Lemert 1951). If people who shun drug use also shun users once the label of junkie is applied, then users are more likely to seek the company of others who are also labeled as junkies; and at this point they might be on their way to a career of deviance and repeated arrests. Secondary deviance, then, may have nothing to do with the original cause of the primary deviance—since it is a way of responding to or defending against the labeling and punishment that occur when primary deviance is discovered.

As the case of the Saints and the Roughnecks showed, high school students are often labeled as troublemakers or good students. When a student is labeled a troublemaker, it alters people's expectations and interpretations of behavior: if teachers catch a troublemaker outside of class without a pass, they are likely to assume the student is doing something wrong. Finding a good student under the same circumstances, however, teachers are more likely to assume the student is there for a good reason.

Although students who get into trouble may not initially define themselves as deviant people, cultural labels are sticky, and make it difficult for people to resist seeing themselves as others see them—the looking-glass self (see Link 1987; Thoits 1985). As Hawthorne wrote in *The Scarlet Letter*, his novel about a colonial woman labeled an adulteress by her community,

> No man, for any considerable period, can wear one face to himself, and another to the multitude, without finally getting bewildered as to which may be the true.

In some cases, a deviant status becomes a master status. Others use stereotypes attached to the deviant master status to form expectations, interpret the deviant's behavior, and decide how to respond. When former convicts apply for jobs they often find that their status as "ex-cons" overshadows all others in the eyes of potential employers. Thus, latent statuses may become the most important part of a person's current status set, a fact that can lead to secondary deviance whether or not stigmatized people actually accept the label as part of their social identities. If the thief or drug addict label excludes them from jobs, they may then have to steal in order to survive. Whether or not individuals accept the deviant label, secondary deviance is an example of a self-fulfilling prophecy: people are treated in ways that increase the chances that they will violate norms, and they do.

In a dramatic illustration of the power of cultural labels, Rosenhan (1973) planted volunteer "patients" in 12 different mental hospitals. Each reported a sim-

Jack Nicholson, in the movie version of *One Flew Over the Cuckoo's Nest*, portrayed an inmate of a mental institution who heroically resisted the labeling and the consequent dehumanization imposed upon him and the other patients by the staff.

ple symptom—hearing a voice that said "empty," "hollow," and "thud." All were admitted with diagnoses of schizophrenia, and all *stopped reporting symptoms immediately after being admitted as patients.* They openly made written observations of ward activity, and when asked how they felt, replied that they felt fine and no longer heard voices.

Despite their public show of sanity, the pseudopatients were never detected by the hospital staff. They were hospitalized for an average of 19 days (some as long as 52 days) and all were discharged with diagnoses of schizophrenia in remission. Once the mentally ill label was applied, the staff used it to interpret patients' behavior. Note taking was described as "behavior indicative of psychological disturbance." When a "patient" paced up and down a corridor, a nurse asked, "Are you nervous?" "No. Bored," he replied. When a psychiatrist saw a group of patients sitting outside the lunchroom half an hour before mealtime, he remarked to other staff members that this was a compulsive behavior typical of schizophrenics, ignoring the fact that meals are one of the few events that interrupt the boredom of hospital life.

Rosenhan's study clearly shows the power of labels such as "crazy" and "schizophrenic":

> Once the impression has been formed that the patient is schizophrenic, the expectation is that he will continue to be schizophrenic. When a sufficient amount of time has passed, during which the patient has done nothing bizarre, he is considered to be in remission and available for discharge. But the label endures beyond discharge. . . . Such labels, conferred by mental health professionals, are as influential on the patient as they are on his relatives and friends, and it should not surprise anyone that the diagnosis acts on all of them as a self-fulfilling prophecy. Eventually, the patient himself accepts the diagnosis, with all of its surplus meanings and expectations, and behaves accordingly. (pp. 253–254)

Some authors use the labeling perspective to argue that mental illness is as much a social role that is forced upon people as it is an illness (Scheff 1975, 1984; Szasz 1987). Others note, however, that although such labels have devastating effects on people, they cannot account for the years of serious emotional disturbance that precede most mental hospital admissions. As Clausen (1976) wrote:

> It is probably true that in the past we launched many acutely disturbed persons on careers of chronic mental illness by keeping them in mental hospitals until every spark of motivation and zest for life had been snuffed out. But mental illness existed long before psychiatry and mental hospitals, and it simply will not do to blame psychosis on labeling. (p. 127)

More recently, Link et al. (1989) have argued that even if labeling did not produce mental illness directly, it would have a variety of related negative consequences. When people identify themselves as mental patients, for example, they are affected by the belief that people tend to reject mental patients, and in response to this may tend to withdraw from contact with people with all kinds of harmful effects for their self-esteem and social support networks (see also Thoits 1985).

Deviance and Social Inequality Although labeling limits people's access to legitimate ways of achieving goals, such limitations also exist on a broader level. A major structural characteristic of social systems is the distribution of opportunities to attain rewards such as wealth. Roles include values that define goals, but they also include norms that define appropriate *means* for achieving goals. From a structural perspective, the likelihood of deviance depends on our access to legitimate means for achieving goals, the *adequacy* of legitimate means, and our access to illegitimate means. In other words, we are more likely to commit deviant acts if we cannot achieve goals in legitimate ways and if we can achieve them in illegitimate ways.

Earlier, we saw how social responses to deviance depend in part on the relationship between deviant acts and cultural values. "Innovators" support values, but reject norms by using deviant methods to achieve them. This approach helps explain the *causes* of deviance as well as social responses to it.

Merton (1938) expanded Durkheim's concept of anomie to pose a fundamental question about structural causes of deviance: What happens when we share important values but, because of our statuses, are denied access to legitimate ways of achieving them? Many poor people share the value of financial success and yet find themselves hopelessly cut off from well-paying jobs. They tend to have few marketable skills, are chronically unemployed, and have poor schooling opportunities. How then are they to share in the American dream of prosperity and security?

Merton argued that we often conform to norms when we do not *need* to break laws in order to get what we want, and we may violate norms when our statuses leave us no alternative but to change our values and abandon our goals. People who are limited in this way are more likely to find new ways to achieve goals, and these are often defined as deviant by elites who *do* have access to legitimate means. Cultures that emphasize that everyone can and should succeed ("*Any* one can become president") exert strong pressures on disadvantaged people to resort to crime.

Merton's theory is important because it shows how an aspect of social systems—the **opportunity structure**—distributes legitimate opportunities among the occupants of different statuses and makes deviance more common when legitimate means for achieving important values are unequally distributed. In his study of crime rates in large U.S. metropolitan areas, for example, Jacobs (1981) found that levels of property crime—burglary and larceny—tended to be higher in areas in which income inequality was the greatest. Property crime rates were *not* related, however, to the absolute levels of poverty—only to the size of the gap between the rich, the poor, and those in the middle (see also Farnworth and Leiber 1989). In another study, Williams (1989) found that although teenage drug gangs in New York's Spanish Harlem support many main-stream values about the work ethic and the American dream, they resort to innovative deviance such as theft and drug dealing because legitimate means for achieving those goals are not available to them. Gartner (1990) argues that the level of inequality also affects rates of homicide, especially among adults.

Conflict theory also explains deviance as a response to political and economic conditions. Industrial societies—capitalist societies in particular—depend on consumers to buy the products produced by the system, most of them luxuries not necessary for survival. Capitalism also depends on workers who are willing to spend their lives at dull, tedious, unrewarding jobs; and in order to motivate them, capitalists depend on large pools of impoverished people who stand ready to take the jobs of dissatisfied workers (Bottomore and Rubel 1965; Marx [1867] 1975; Marx and Engels [1846] 1976).

Industrial societies create "both the desire to consume *and*—for a large mass of people—an inability to earn the money necessary to purchase items they have been taught to want" (Chambliss 1978, p. 192). Many crimes are committed because the opportunity structure limits opportunities *without* limiting goals. Crime is not caused simply by deviant subcultures that create and support criminal personalities and disrespect for the law. It also depends on values and the structural distribution of opportunities for achieving them.

Illegitimate Opportunities   Societies distribute not only legitimate opportunities but illegitimate ones as well (Cloward and Ohlin 1960). Government officials occupy statuses that allow them to do favors for others in exchange for bribes; computer programmers in banks are in an ideal position to embezzle funds by altering records; police officers who use their discretion in making arrests or responding to calls for help can demand various kinds of payoffs ranging from bribes from criminals to free services from local merchants who want to ensure adequate protection. Regardless of individual motives and personalities, social systems create opportunities and temptations that increase the likelihood of certain types of deviance.

Inadequate Means   Social systems also contribute to deviance when culturally defined ways of achieving goals are *available*, but *inadequate*. For example, the most important goals of police officers are to prevent crime and apprehend criminals; and,

AMERICA'S FINEST?

BENCH AD 1-800-234-5460

Police are sometimes criticized for using more force than necessary—in violation of the law—to perform their jobs. In San Diego, a group of artists protested by renting bus stop benches to display signs with silhouette targets showing what some victims wielded when shot by police: a garden trowel, a baseball bat, and nothing at all.

on every level, they are rewarded only when they produce results. An officer's role also includes norms that define legitimate means for controlling crime. In the U.S., they are not allowed to torture prisoners, to wiretap telephones without a court order, to arrest people without informing them of their rights, or to search people's homes without due cause.

The best efforts of police to control crime, however, are largely unsuccessful. If you were a police officer, what would you do in the face of repeated failures to achieve the goals that define your job? Many officers believe that their roles limit them so severely that it is impossible for them to control crime. Public pressures on police provide incentives for them to *break laws in the name of enforcing the law.* (As recent news stories make clear, police officers in many societies are not as restrained as they are in the U.S. Torture has been widely used by authorities in many countries.)

Maximizing business profits is a value in our culture, in pursuit of which executives may bribe public officials, misrepresent income to tax collectors, falsely advertise products, or dispose of hazardous wastes in economical but dangerous ways (see Coleman 1987). Many corporations contend that if they obeyed all antipollution laws, they could not survive the intense competition of capitalism and many jobs would be lost. Faced with bankruptcy, some business owners hire arsonists to burn their buildings so that they can collect insurance payments. Similarly, government agencies have been known to illegally wiretap telephones or break into homes or offices in search of information—all in the name of national security.

The inadequacy of legitimate means is also a problem at the lower end of the class system. There are many full-time jobs in the United States, for example, that do not pay enough to support a single person, much less an entire family. This means that although many people have access to legitimate means for earning a living—a full-time job—this is not enough to meet their needs.

Another response to the inadequacy of legitimate means is **ritualism**—which results when people, convinced they cannot achieve their goals, "go through the motions" by conforming to norms without fully supporting the values those norms support (Merton 1938, 1968). Office workers who see no hope for promotion may simply show up each day and do no more than their roles require of them. College students who believe their grades will be mediocre no matter how hard they work may also "give up" by lowering their aspirations and working only enough to get passing grades. Although ritualism is often not viewed as true deviance (since norms are obeyed), it clearly poses a problem for social systems.

A sociological approach to deviance would not be complete without considering the population and ecological characteristics of social systems. How do these affect rates of deviant behavior?

Population, Ecology, and Deviance

Rates of crime vary according to population characteristics such as age structure, urbanization, complexity, diversity, and equality. Since 1960, crime rates in the U.S. have tripled. During this same period, the population became younger as the percentage of people 15 to 24 years old increased, and 22 percent more urban (USCB 1990a). Some of the increase in crime may be the result of an increasingly young, urban population (Cohen and Land 1987).

Population characteristics also help explain variations in crime rates among social categories. Because birth rates are higher among blacks than among whites, for example, the black population has a higher percentage of young people (USCB 1990a). Since blacks are also more likely to live in cities, the distribution of blacks by age and residence contributes to higher rates of deviance. (Remember, however, that these statements do *not* include white-collar crime, most of which is committed by adults and rarely included in official crime statistics.)

Differences in age structures and urbanization also suggest a partial explanation for cross-cultural differences in crime. Crime rates in Europe, for example, are generally lower than in the U.S. Only one-fifth of the people of Europe live in large cities, compared with more than a third in the U.S. (Goldstein and Sly 1977; USCB 1986a). Decades of low birth rates have also made European populations considerably older than the U.S. population.

Durkheim's theory of anomie suggests that deviance is more likely when social cohesion is low, and this implies that large, complex societies with many subcultures will have higher rates of deviance. It also suggests that highly *mobile* societies, in which people frequently move, will have more deviance because people will have weaker ties to communities and their norms. The U.S. has one of the most heterogeneous and mobile populations in the world, as well as one of the highest crime rates. More than one-third of the U.S. population changes residence every three years, producing an average of 13 moves in each person's lifetime (Long and Boertlein 1976).

Iceland provides a particularly interesting comparison, for its population is homogeneous and stationary (the vast majority of its 300,000 inhabitants are native born and share a common heritage). There is only one jail in the entire country, and it is rarely used (Markham 1982). Iceland's low crime rate is not due simply to a small, homogeneous population, however, for the opportunity structure is far more egalitarian than that of the U.S. The Icelandic standard of living is considerably higher, and prosperity is distributed far more evenly. Literacy is universal and unemployment is virtually nonexistent. These cultural and structural differences offer a partial explanation for Iceland's relatively low rate of crime.

It is important to emphasize the *tentative* nature of such explanations: evidence from so few comparisons is not conclusive, and the effects of population and ecology are complex. Japan is more urban than the U.S. but its crime rates are lower, not higher. Why? One explanation is that the Japanese population is more culturally homogeneous, resulting in greater social cohesion. No single factor operates alone: the high rate of crime in the U.S. is produced, in part, by a *combination* of social, population, and ecological factors.

SOCIAL CONSEQUENCES OF DEVIANCE

Most of this chapter has focused on descriptions and explanations of deviance (for a summary, see the box on p. 261). We come now to a final question: What are the social consequences of deviance?

Much deviant behavior exacts enormous costs from individuals and social systems. Each year in the

Causes of Deviance: A Summary

Cultural Explanations

Anomie (Durkheim)
Confusion, disagreement, ambiguity
Weak social ties of individuals or groups
to society

Deviance as conformity
Socialization in subcultures (Miller)
Differential association in complex cultures
(Sutherland)

Social Structural Explanations

Deviance and role behavior
When legitimate roles require deviant
behavior
Social creation of "deviant roles"—labeling
(Becker)
   Primary and secondary deviance

Deviance and opportunity structures
Unequal access to legitimate means (Merton)
Unequal access to illegitimate means
(Cloward and Ohlin)
Inadequacy of legitimate means

Population and Ecological Explanations

Age of population
Urbanization
Diversity of population
Size, complexity, and formation of subcultures
Mobility and social cohesion

U.S., some 20,000 people are murdered and 5 million assaulted—including 141,000 sexual assaults (USCB 1990a). In 1990, 41 percent of adults said they were afraid to walk alone at night within a mile of their homes (Davis and Smith 1990; see also Gordon and Riger 1989).

Crime not only causes suffering and fear; it results in enormous economic losses. Tens of millions of people are robbed and assaulted each year with direct losses to victims amounting to some $15 billion (USDJ 1989). The cost of drug and alcohol abuse to the U.S. economy is estimated to amount to almost $200 billion each year (*New York Times*, December 12, 1988). The profits of syndicated crime amount to

tens of billions of dollars a year. Conservative estimates put annual losses from white-collar crimes such as embezzlement and tax evasion at more than $250 million a *day* (Meier and Short 1982).

The costs of deviance are not this simple, however, for the line between victim and offender is often unclear. Criminal behavior results in the labeling and punishing of thousands of lower-class, nonwhite people; and thousands of people labeled as mentally ill are forcibly committed to mental institutions. Homosexuals are regularly discriminated against in housing and jobs—32 percent of U.S. adults believe homosexuals should be denied teaching jobs in colleges and universities. Forty-four percent would also bar communists and atheists from college faculties (Davis and Smith 1990). Those labelled deviant are often victims not only of social inequality, but of cultural stereotypes and stigmas as well.

Many people benefit from deviance. Tens of thousands of jobs depend on crime, for without it there would be no need for police officers, criminal lawyers, judges, prison guards, probation officers, locksmiths, and the thousands of people who record and report criminal activity. Although it is in the interests of some of these people to diminish crime (if only to justify keeping their jobs), it is not in their interests to eradicate it completely.

Furthermore, behaviors that some regard as problems are regarded by others as *solutions* to problems (Merton 1976a). Homosexuality, adultery, divorce, drug use, alcoholism, prostitution, and tax evasion are culturally defined as deviant behaviors that constitute social problems. Yet, divorce is a common solution to the problem of unsatisfying and destructive marriages, homosexuality allows millions of people to express themselves sexually, and families and businesses often rely on tax evasion in order to survive.

Conformity is important because it gives social life a sense of predictability, continuity, and stability. As important as these manifest functions of conformity are, however, there are also latent dysfunctional consequences. Too much conformity tends to stifle creativity and constructive criticism. Conformity can also be disastrous when values and norms are destructive as in the case of racism. Deviance also has unanticipated consequences, some of which are functional. Nonconformity stimulates social change by challenging the status quo (Janeway 1987). The well-being of social systems and their members, then, depends on a delicate balance between deviance and conformity.

SUMMARY

1. Deviance is any appearance or behavior that violates a norm; conformity is obedience to norms. What most people actually do is "the norm," but the rarity of a behavior does not make it deviant. Because deviance is a cultural creation, the classification of behaviors as deviant varies historically and between cultures.

2. The functional perspective views deviant acts as violations of a moral consensus, and outraged responses of citizens as beneficial for social cohesion. The conflict perspective argues that deviance reflects social inequality, and that the law protects the interests of the powerful rather than a moral consensus.

3. Nonconformists openly violate norms in order to bring about change. Nonconformists may be either rebels who challenge norms and values, or innovators who accept values but reject norms that define legitimate means for achieving them. Aberrance is the secret violation of norms for personal gain. It may be either retreatist, in which a person withdraws from social life by rejecting values and norms without offering alternatives, or innovative, in which a person secretly uses illegitimate means to attain goals.

4. A stigma is a personal characteristic that others treat as deviant.

5. Some violations of law are not defined as crimes or as deviance; many forms of deviance are not defined as crimes; and an act defined as criminal may be regarded as normal in a subculture.

6. Males are more likely than females to commit crimes. Young people are more likely to commit many traditional crimes such as burglary, but older people are more likely to commit white-collar crimes. Nonwhites and the poor are more likely than whites and the nonpoor to be arrested; but most evidence shows that class and race differences in crime influence the kinds of crime committed, not the amount. Crime is more common in urban areas than in suburban or rural areas, but the difference is greater for violent crimes than for those against property, and has been shrinking.

7. Men are more likely than women to be victimized by crime, except in the case of sexual assault. Nonwhites are more likely to be victimized than whites, and young people are more vulnerable than older people.

8. Relationships among criminals vary in complexity. Both criminals and victims may be either individuals or groups, and most victims of violence know their assailant. Some crimes—such as prostitution—are victimless, representing an offense against society.

9. Social class and race affect the likelihood of being arrested, prosecuted, and convicted of a crime, as well as the length of sentence. At all stages, the criminal justice system discriminates against blacks and lower-class people.

10. The criminal justice system responds to crime with punishment, rehabilitation, and isolation of criminals from society. Most evidence indicates that these do not control crime very well.

11. Culture contributes to deviance in several ways, the most basic of which is the definition of deviant acts. When norms are unclear or disputed, or when individuals are weakly attached to their society—anomie—deviance is more likely to occur. Deviance may also be conformity to subcultural values and norms that support behavior regarded as deviant in the surrounding society. In complex cultures, people are exposed to competing standards, and differential association helps explain why some adopt cultural ideas that are defined as deviant in society at large.

12. Social structure also contributes to deviance. Deviance is sometimes required in the performance of legitimate roles.

13. Primary deviance is behavior that is done without the person being labeled as deviant. Secondary deviance occurs when people are labeled and treated as deviant, and deviant becomes a part of their identity. This encourages secondary deviance, which conforms to people's expectations of those labeled deviant.

14. Structure also causes deviance by unequally distributing legitimate opportunities for achieving goals; by creating illegitimate opportunities for some status occupants; and by providing inadequate means for achieving goals.

15. In general, deviance is more likely in populations that are large, diverse, young, and urban.

16. Deviance results in negative consequences, including injury, fear, and economic loss. Widespread deviance weakens group boundaries and lowers social cohesion. Deviance also damages groups and individuals identified as deviant. Despite the costs of deviance, some benefit from it by holding jobs designed to record and control it.

KEY TERMS

aberrance 239
anomie 251
collective conscience 237
conformity 235
crime 241
criminal justice system 247
degradation ceremony 250
deviance 235

differential association 254
innovation 239
nonconformity 239
opportunity structure 258
primary deviance 256
rebellion 239
retreatism 239
ritualism 260

secondary deviance 256
social labeling 256
stigma 240
syndicated crime 246
total institution 250
victimless crime 247
white-collar crime 244

LOOKING ELSEWHERE

Having studied Chapter 11, you might want to look at related discussions in *Human Arrangements*, which include

■ the scientific validity of crime statistics as measures of criminal activity (Ch. 6, p. 114)

■ pressures to conform in groups (Chapter 9, pp. 180–81)

■ conformity as a source of power in groups (Chapter 9, p. 191)

■ rites of passage and deviance among the young (Chapter 15, pp. 366–67, 371–72)

■ peer pressure and deviance (Chapter 7, p. 152)

■ family violence (Chapter 16, pp. 405–406)

■ deviance among scientists (Chapter 18, pp. 448–49)

■ civil disobedience and democracy (Chapter 20, pp. 506–507)

■ deviance as a source of religious change (Chapter 21, pp. 537–39)

RECOMMENDED READINGS

Bowers, W. J. 1984. *Legal homicide: Death as punishment in America, 1964–1982*. Boston: Northeastern University Press. A passionate and unusually thorough discussion of the uses and effects of the death penalty.

Goffman, E. 1963. *Stigma: Notes on the management of a spoiled identity*. Englewood Cliffs, NJ: Prentice-Hall.

Gussow, Z. 1989. *Leprosy, racism, and public health: Social policy in chronic disease control*. Boulder: Westview Press. A historical analysis of leprosy, one of the oldest sources of stigma and yet also one of the least studied by social scientists.

Hagan, J. 1989. *Structural criminology*. New Brunswick, NJ: Rutgers University Press. A wide-ranging, insightful analysis of the importance of incorporating the structural aspects of social systems into any explanation of patterns of crime.

Kadish, S. H. 1983. *Encyclopedia of crime and justice* (3 Vols.). New York: Free Press. An extraordinarily comprehensive, interdisciplinary summary of what is known about criminal behavior and social responses to it.

Reasons, C. E., and Rich, R. M. Eds. (1978). *The sociology of law: A conflict perspective*. Toronto: Butterworths. A provocative set of articles that examine the ways in which the law and definitions of deviance help maintain social inequality and oppression.

Rutter, M. and Giller, H. 1984. *Juvenile delinquency: Trends and perspectives*. New York: Guilford Press. An excellent survey of the causes and consequences of juvenile delinquency.

PART FOUR

SOCIAL STRATIFICATION

F ew areas of social life provoke as much strong feeling and conflict as social inequality. The gulf that separates rich and poor, the damage to individuals, families, communities, and societies caused by prejudice and discrimination—all touch deeply held values about justice and fairness. The problem is far from simple, however, for in many societies, including the United States, the issue of how rewards such as wealth, power, and prestige are distributed also touches deeply held values about individualism, hard work, self-reliance, and the importance of merit. In short, while there is widespread support for justice and fairness, there is also strong support for social arrangements that produce inequality, in spite of the damage it inflicts on millions of people's lives.

We begin in Chapter 12 with a detailed examination of the general problem of social stratification—the process through which wealth, power, and prestige are distributed. We will look at the nature and extent of inequality both within societies and between them and consider major theories that try to explain why inequality exists at all. We will also look at the social processes through which some people gain a greater share of wealth, power, and prestige than others. In the remaining three chapters of Part Four we look at prejudice, discrimination, and social inequality based on the ascribed statuses of race, ethnicity, gender, and age.

12

SOCIAL STRATIFICATION: WHO GETS WHAT, AND WHY?

 All social systems produce rewards that are valued in their culture. Some are possessions such as land, automobiles, or buildings; money represents the power to buy possessions and services. Other rewards, such as respect, are nonmaterial, but are nonetheless important. The concept of **social stratification** refers to the social structures through which rewards are distributed unequally among the occupants of different statuses.

STRATIFICATION, INEQUALITY, AND SOCIAL CLASS

The definition of stratification has three aspects that you should understand. First, stratification is a social *process*, even though the word calls up images of layers of rock. Societies continually sort people into different statuses and distribute rewards among them. Second, a society is stratified only if wealth, power, and prestige are distributed unequally according to people's social statuses—age, gender, education, occupation, and ethnicity. If we took all the income produced in a society during each year and distributed it through a lottery that gave more to some than others, the distribution of income would be unequal but *not* stratified. The difference is that in a stratified society rewards are distributed *systematically* according to social status, not randomly. Third, *what* is distributed in a society varies according to cultural values. In a poor village society, food and clothing may be the major rewards, while in wealthier, more complex societies, political power, leisure time, health care, and luxuries are also distributed.

The most important concept in the study of stratification is *social class*, an idea that was developed

267

It is workers who produce wealth, but the means of producing it as well as the wealth itself belong to their employers.

most notably by Karl Marx and Max Weber. Their perspectives differ in important ways, however, and lead to different views of stratification.

Marx: Class, Production, and Social Systems

To Marx, the most basic human activity is the production of necessities such as food, clothing, and shelter, and he focused on two key questions about that process: How do societies produce goods and services and how does the relationship between people and the ways in which goods are produced affect their lives?

Because Marx ([1867] 1965) was primarily interested in how societies produce goods, he defined **social class** as a category of people who occupy similar positions in relation to the production process. Although he identified several classes, the most important are the **capitalists** (or **bourgeoisie**), who own the **means of production** such as machines, tools, and factories, and the **workers** (or **proletariat**), who survive by selling their *labor power* to capitalists.

The distinction between labor and labor power is important in Marx's theories. **Labor** refers to the production of products and services that can either be used (shoes to wear, food to eat) or exchanged for something else (one farmer may trade surplus wheat for another's surplus milk, or farmers sell crops or milk in the marketplace). Farm workers, however, who spend their days picking lettuce that grows in someone else's fields are not selling their labor. It is not as if they pick the lettuce and sell it to the farmers, who then sell it on the market. The workers

FIGURE 12-1 The American Class Structure
from a Marxist Perspective
Source: Adapted from Wright et al. 1982.

Social Class

 Bourgeoisie (capitalists): Own means of production; ten or more employees (the owners of a factory; the controlling stockholders of a major corporation) — 2%

 Small employers: Own means of production; two to nine employees (an electrical contractor with three employees) — 6%

 Petite bourgeoisie (small capitalists): Own means of production; no more than one employee (people who knit sweaters at home and sell them through stores) — 7%

 Managers and supervisors: Do not own means of production; moderate to high levels of autonomy and authority (office supervisor; personnel manager; military officer) — 30%

 Semiautonomous wage earners: Do not own means of production; low to moderate levels of autonomy and authority (journalist; teacher) — 10%

 Proletariat (workers): Do not own means of production; little autonomy; no authority (assembly-line worker; secretary; telephone operator) — 45%

Percentage of All Workers

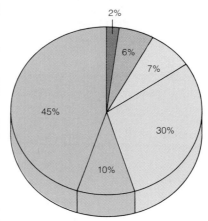

do not own the lettuce, the fields, or the machinery. What, then, *do* they sell? They sell their *time* in exchange for *wages*. They control neither what they do with that time nor what becomes of the products. Workers sell their **labor power**—so many dollars for each day's work—and not their labor. Unlike labor, labor power represents only the *potential* to produce something, not production itself.

In any society, Marx argued, the way production is organized determines social relationships, and to understand social life we must pay attention to people's positions in those relationships. Those who control the means of production also control jobs, while workers must sell their labor power for whatever wages they can get—or not work at all. When the means of production are privately owned, the capitalist class is in a position to exploit workers and accumulate wealth and power.

The complexity of modern societies makes it difficult to categorize everyone as either owners or workers. Professionals, such as physicians and lawyers, for example, cannot easily be categorized as capitalists or workers, nor can managers and administrators in government and business (Gagliani 1981). For this reason, it makes more sense to define classes according to *control* over production, which may or may not take the form of ownership. Wright et al. (1982) use

this perspective to divide the labor force into six class categories based on the amount of control workers have over the means of production, other workers, and their own work (Figure 12-1) (see also Wright 1985). Using data from a national survey, they estimated that roughly 45 percent of all workers are in Marx's working class, 2 percent are capitalists (the bourgeoisie), and 7 percent are small capitalists, or what Marx called the petite bourgeoisie. The remainder are in gray areas of social class: 30 percent are managers or supervisors, 6 percent are small employers, and 10 percent are semiautonomous wage earners such as college professors.

Weber: Class, Prestige, and Power

Whereas Marx focused on how the production process causes inequality, Weber (1946) paid more attention to the levels of wealth, power, and prestige people actually have than to how they come to have it. From Weber's perspective, stratification has three major dimensions—wealth, power, and prestige—and to identify social classes, we must first decide which one we are referring to.

Weber used **social class** to describe the ability of people to get what they want in the market—their life chances. A highly paid lawyer, or someone who inherits income-producing property such as land or stocks, is in a higher class than a secretary or factory worker because the lawyer has greater access to the goods and services that are bought and sold in the marketplace (see One Step Further 12-1).

Weber referred to **power** as "party," a term that is important because it reflects the fact that most social power in modern societies is held by large organizations and bureaucracies, and the power of individ-uals depends very much on their position in such organizations. For prestige, Weber used the term **status** (unlike our earlier usage of this term to stand for a social position).

Unlike Marx's approach, Weber's leads us to rank people from upper to lower in terms of these three different dimensions, and people who rank high on one dimension usually rank high on the other two. It takes a great deal of money to be elected to powerful,

---

ONE STEP FURTHER 12-1

Social Class and the Distribution of Happiness and Unhappiness

Weber described class differences in terms of our life chances to get what we want and need in the marketplace. This has obvious effects on well-being when it involves the necessities of life such as food and shelter; but in a society that places much importance on the ability to consume luxuries, class position can strike at the heart of happiness itself.

The figures in Table B-12-1 show the percentage of people with different class characteristics who describe themselves as generally "very happy" (first column) or "not too happy" (second column). At the top of the first column, 30 percent of those with less than high school diplomas describe themselves as very happy. At the top of the second, 13 percent of this same group report being not too happy.

If you look down the first column, you can see that in general, the more highly placed people are, the more likely they are to say they are very happy. People who say they belong to the lower class are less than half as likely to say they are very happy as are those who put themselves in the upper class (21 percent as opposed to 53 percent).

The second column shows that class differences in being not too happy are even more striking. People in the lowest class categories are two to four times more likely to say they

are not too happy than those in the highest class categories.

Notice that education and occupational prestige make less of a difference than the other variables. Why do you think this is so?

TABLE B-12-1

SOCIAL CHARACTERISTICS	PERCENT WHO SAY THEY ARE	
	Very Happy	*Not too Happy*
Education		
Less than high school graduate	30	13
High school graduate	32	7
Some college	31	10
College graduate	43	4
More than college	38	8
Family Income		
Less than $10,000	22	13
$10,000–$19,999	29	12
$20,000–$29,999	31	12
$30,000–$39,999	39	6
$40,000–$59,999	40	5
$60,000 +	46	3
Social Class[1]		
Lower	21	21
Working	29	11
Middle	37	6
Upper	53	5
Occupational Prestige		
Lower	28	10
Lower-middle	33	8
Upper-middle	37	8
Upper	43	6

[1]The class people place themselves in.
Source: Computed from raw 1990 General Social Survey data.

prestigious political offices in the United States, for example, and the winners tend to be those who spend the most money in their campaigns (USCB 1986a).

The tendency of wealth, power, and prestige to go together leads many sociologists to classify people according to **socioeconomic status**, a concept that combines wealth, occupational prestige, and educational attainment into an average rank, usually expressed in terms of upper class, middle class, and lower class (see Powers 1982). There are many exceptions, however, that make it difficult to assign people an overall rank. Successful criminals may rank high on wealth and power, but low on prestige; college professors and religious leaders rank high on prestige, but relatively low on wealth and power. Which of these has the highest overall rank in the stratification system and which has the lowest?

Some sociologists (such as Parsons 1964) believe that prestige is valued more highly than wealth and power. Even if we confine ourselves to this single reward, however, ranking individuals is difficult because each of us occupies a variety of statuses whose levels of prestige may be inconsistent with each other (a phenomenon called **status inconsistency**). Physicians rank higher on prestige than do factory workers, and heterosexuals rank higher than homosexuals. Who, then, will be treated with greater respect in a heterosexual society—homosexual physicians or heterosexual factory workers?

One way to identify who is in which social class is simply to *ask* people which class they think they belong to. In 1990, 4 percent of U.S. adults placed themselves in the lower class, 46 percent in the working class, 47 percent in the middle class, and 3 percent in the upper class (Davis and Smith 1990). This is a useful measure insofar as self-perceptions of class position affect our expectations and behavior, but it is misleading insofar as *actual* positions in a stratification system are more important than *perceived* positions. For example, 4 percent placed themselves in the lower class in 1990, while 13 percent had incomes below the poverty level (Davis and Smith 1990; USCB 1990a). It is doubtful that *thinking* we are not poor is enough to undo the effects of poverty.

In addition, sociologists commonly make a distinction between **blue-collar workers**—workers whose jobs involve manual labor—and **white-collar workers**—professionals, business executives, and secretaries whose jobs are more mental than manual. One of the problems with the blue-collar/white-collar

distinction is that it leads to many inconsistencies. Some skilled blue-collar workers, for example, make more use of mental skills than some unskilled white-collar workers such as file clerks or cashiers. In addition, although white-collar jobs are often seen as having greater prestige, some blue-collar occupations have higher levels of income, power, and autonomy. Since many different occupations are typically included in each of these broad categories, it is unclear just what it means when we make comparisons between them.

In their analysis of perceptions of class in the U.S., Vanneman and Cannon (1987) found that the class category that people identify with depends on a variety of factors and characteristics. Among white men, for example, having authority over others is more closely associated with seeing themselves as members of the middle class than it is among women or nonwhites. For white women, however, the blue-collar/white-collar distinction between manual and mental labor is a more important determinant of middle-class membership than is power. Regardless of gender or race, the manual/mental labor distinction is a more powerful predictor of identifying with the middle class than income, occupational prestige, or educational attainment.

Neither Marx's nor Weber's approach allows us to unambiguously assign everyone to clearly defined categories, but we do not need to do this in order to understand how societies distribute resources and rewards. Marx draws attention to how the means by which goods and services are produced affect social relationships; Weber focuses on the *results* of the distribution process in a stratified society: sets of people with similar levels of rewards and resources. By concentrating on different aspects of a complex social process, Marx and Weber lead us to pay attention to fundamentally different aspects of stratification and its effects on people's lives.

Comparing Marx and Weber: The Case of Carol, Susan, and George

Carol is a self-employed plumber in a small city. She owns her own tools, employs an apprentice, and, after paying all her expenses, earns $25,000 a year. She rents a modest apartment, drives an old Ford pickup truck, rarely takes vacations, and usually dresses in jeans and sneakers. She never attended college, is divorced, and her daughter attends a community college.

Susan works on an assembly line in an automobile plant. She earns $30,000 a year, drives a three-year-old car, takes a week off every year, rents a large apartment, and wears jeans and work boots to work. She earned a college degree by taking night courses at a community college. She is married and has three teenage children.

George is a design engineer at Susan's plant. He earns $60,000 a year (plus a bonus in good years), supervises ten employees, owns his own home, drives a new car, takes a three-week vacation each summer, and wears tailored suits. He has a graduate degree in engineering, and his only child attends an Ivy League college.

How would we compare these three people in terms of their relative standing in the U.S. stratification system? From Weber's perspective, George ranks highest because he has more wealth, a graduate degree, a more powerful and prestigious job, enjoys long vacations, and can point with pride to his child's Ivy League education. Susan is a distant second and Carol a close third, because although Susan has a higher income and a college degree, most would rank Carol's occupation higher in prestige (Hodge, Siegel, and Rossi 1964). (See Table 12-3 on p. 282).

Marx would look at these people very differently, however, for while Carol sells her labor and owns some capital—her plumbing equipment—George and Susan neither own nor control any means of production and must sell their labor power to whoever will pay them for it. From Marx's perspective, Carol is a small capitalist (a petit bourgeois) and George and Susan are workers; and there may be reasons to prefer Carol's class position to George's and Susan's.

Susan and George have little control over their jobs and, therefore, little control over the rewards they receive by performing them. In the early 1980s, for example, the U.S. automobile industry experienced a deep slump in sales, and unemployment in Detroit was the highest in the nation. While George's position as an engineer is better protected than Susan's, if a company closes an entire plant, virtually everyone except top managers is likely to be laid off. Carol's position has an important advantage, for, as she might put it, "People always say, 'you can never find a plumber when you need one'—and that's me. I can always get work."

Marx and Weber emphasize different aspects of people's positions in stratification systems. Weber focuses more on the rewards and resources people have, while Marx concentrates more on how the pro-

duction process fosters social relationships through which rewards are distributed. Because our positions in social systems determine our rights and obligations, Marx's perspective gives greater importance to the important fact that whatever our class position may be now, our security depends on our control over the social systems that keep us there.

The two perspectives are, of course, related. Those who control the means of production will tend to have greater power, wealth, income, and prestige than those who do not. Corporations, for example, represent major concentrations of economic power, and the more managerial control people have over them, the higher their income will tend to be (Spaeth 1985). In a similar way, those who have a great deal of wealth and income are in a position to buy the means of production by purchasing stock and, in this way, they can turn wealth into a source of considerable power. By looking at these kinds of interrelationships among Marx's and Weber's categories of class, status, and power we can construct a comprehensive framework within which to understand social inequality.

EXPLAINING INEQUALITY

Sociologists use the functional, conflict, and interactionist perspectives to understand stratification. There are many ways in which these perspectives generate different explanations of inequality, but they are most useful if we think of them as revealing different aspects of a complex puzzle.

The Functional View: Social Structure and Cultural Values

Kingsley Davis and Wilbert Moore's (1945) functional theory of stratification focuses on two functions of inequality: first, differences in the level of rewards are necessary to motivate people to perform important roles; second, a complex division of labor requires unequal distributions of power, because some must coordinate the activities of everyone else.

Davis and Moore pointed out that each culture values some activities more than others, in part because not all activities contribute equally to the well-being of society. They then argued that the most important tasks require abilities that few people possess, and that to prepare themselves, people must undergo rigorous training that often requires considerable self-sacrifice. Given these requirements, social systems inevitably confront the major problem

One way to measure the functional importance of a job is to see what happens to the quality of life when people stop doing it. From this perspective, who would you say makes a greater contribution: lower-paid, lower-prestige garbage collectors or higher-paid, higher-prestige advertisers?

of motivating people to play important, demanding roles. How do we motivate people to endure the long years of study required to become physicians? How do we motivate people to run businesses, command armies, or govern societies?

Davis and Moore answer that to ensure that the most important roles are adequately performed, systems must offer high levels of prestige and wealth to those who are able and willing to perform them. Conversely, jobs which rank lower on cultural scales of values—washing dishes, driving trucks, or assembling cars—will carry lower levels of reward, because it is relatively easy to find people who can and will adequately perform them and there is, therefore, no need to offer special rewards in order to make sure such jobs are performed.

If the Davis-Moore theory is correct, we should find that the most highly trained people receive the highest levels of reward. This is generally true for formal education (Table 6-6, p. 128): for both men and women, more years of schooling mean higher average incomes. Studies of occupational prestige in the U.S. and elsewhere are also consistent with the Davis-Moore argument. Hodge, Siegel, and Rossi (1964) analyzed national survey data in which adults rated 91 occupations from excellent to poor in terms

of how much respondents "look up to them." The most important finding is that the relative prestige of these occupations has remained essentially unchanged since the first study was done in 1925. The stability of occupational prestige rankings could be interpreted as a reflection of stable cultural evaluations of jobs and their importance to society.

In an international study, Hodge, Treiman, and Rossi (1966) compared prestige ratings of occupations in 31 countries that varied considerably in culture and level of industrialization. In general, there was strong agreement across societies about which occupations are most prestigious, which, the authors suggest, supports the idea that some occupations are more important than others regardless of the society (see also Lin and Xie 1988):

> Specialized institutions to carry out political, religious, and economic functions, and to provide for the health, education, and welfare of the population, exist in one form or another in all national societies. Considering the importance of these functions to the maintenance of complex social systems, it is not surprising that occupations at the top of these institutional structures should be highly regarded. (p. 310)

The functional explanation also emphasizes that complex divisions of labor require some individuals to have authority to make decisions about what people do and how resources are distributed and used. To Parsons (1964, 1971), equality of power is simply impossible in any society with a complex division of labor.

While Davis and Moore's theory identifies some important functional consequences of inequality, it has been criticized on six major grounds (Tumin 1953). First, motivation to perform roles competently is a problem for *all* jobs—if garbage collectors fail to perform, life rapidly becomes intolerable for everyone. That a culture values engineers or business managers more than garbage collectors has less to do with maintaining society than with maintaining the privileged position of managers and engineers.

Second, Tumin challenged the belief that those who occupy highly rewarded positions have made sacrifices for which they must be compensated with a lifetime of privilege. The costs of professional education are often borne by families and government, not the trainees themselves. Even when they bear a considerable portion of the cost, they quickly earn it back with higher-than-average incomes and then go on to 20 or 30 years of relatively high prestige and income. In addition, while trainees are in professional schools, they enjoy a higher level of prestige than many who work in low-level jobs, and they have greater opportunities for leisure.

Third, Tumin questioned the belief that wealth and prestige are necessary to motivate people to perform important roles. Davis and Moore minimized the importance of the satisfactions that come with important roles: the challenges, creative opportunities, high levels of control over work conditions, and the chance to make an important contribution to one's community and society.

Fourth, the Davis-Moore theory cannot explain why some people in some statuses—women and blacks—receive fewer rewards regardless of their training. Table 6-6 (p. 128) shows that the average income of women with graduate training is only slightly more than that of men who never finished college, and women college graduates average $1,200 less than men who never went beyond high school. Nor can their explanation account for wide variations in income among people who work at the same or similar jobs and have the same levels of education, skill, and experience.

Fifth, Tumin criticized Davis and Moore for not making full use of the functional perspective, which focuses on *dysfunctions* as well as functions. The tal-

ent of those at the "bottom of the heap" is less likely to be discovered, encouraged, and developed; and, as a result, society is denied the full range of its population's abilities. Inequality encourages hostility, suspicion, and distrust between those at the top and those at the bottom; and those who must go through life with little prestige and little hope of a better life are less likely to be loyal to a society that deprives them.

Finally, while Davis and Moore argued that people receive high incomes because their jobs are perceived as being more important, some sociologists argue just the opposite—that we tend to perceive those who make a lot of money as being more important than the rest of us *because* of their high incomes and not because their jobs make a more important contribution to society (Jenkins 1981a).

While Davis and Moore's approach has many problems, the functional perspective is useful in several respects. First, although great inequalities of wealth and prestige may be as dysfunctional for social systems as they are functional, some inequality of authority may be necessary to coordinate activities in a complex system. Second, the functional perspective also suggests that when the organization of a social system includes pervasive inequality, it may be difficult to lessen the degree of inequality without changing the larger system as well—a problem we will return to later in the chapter.

The Conflict Perspective: To Each According to the Ability to Take

When societies can produce a surplus of goods, it is inevitable that some people will be in a position to take more than their share; and, as they accumulate wealth and power, they will use their dominant position to create and sustain a social system that perpetuates their privilege (Marx and Engels [1846] 1976). Marx explained stratification as the result of conflict over resources and of the ability of those who dominate society to maintain their privileged position by exploiting those below them.

Lenski (1966) supported Marx's view by tracing the development of societies and showing that stratification exists only in those that produce a surplus. (He does not say that there is no inequality in societies that barely survive; only that inequality is not determined by social statuses.) Gatherer-hunter societies such as the Kung Bushmen of Africa do not

The Duke and Duchess of Devonshire, England, have a 175-room house and 170 personal servants. An enormous amount of surplus production and the labor of many people is needed to support two people in such lavish style, as well as a social system that permits large concentration of wealth.

produce their own food, and they move from place to place in order to find it. This way of life discourages the production of surpluses and the accumulation of private property. As technology created greater surpluses, settlements became more permanent, elite groups accumulated wealth and power, and eventually stratification became an enduring characteristic of societies.

If inequality is imposed by the powerful on the weak, why do the lower classes stand for it? The first response is, "They often don't." Throughout the last thousand years, people have been drawn to the idea of equality. During the Middle Ages, European peasants often joined bands of robbers and revolted against landowners. The story of Robin Hood, who "stole from the rich to give to the poor," has found a place in the folk histories of many societies (Hobsbawm 1971). Peasant revolts were common in England, France, and other European countries (Froissart 1961; Genicut 1966).

Why, then, does stratification persist? A large part of the answer lies in the ability of elite classes to use force to take what they want and keep what they have—by controlling police, armies, governments, and other institutions (Vanneman and Cannon 1987). But since stratification is an enduring characteristic of most societies, few of which resemble a police state, the rest of the answer lies deeper, in the *acceptance* of inequality by members of *all* social classes.

Controlling Culture   In the *Manifesto of the Communist Party*, Marx and Engels ([1848] 1932) argued that members of dominant classes use their privileged positions to influence the cultural ideas that affect people's perceptions of reality, aspirations, feelings, and expectations. The wealthy tend to be among the best-educated members of society and occupy positions of authority—in government, university boards of trustees, the mass media, and legal systems (see Freire 1985; Parenti 1986; Peschek 1987). They provide financial support for political candidates and universities. They are in a position to foster beliefs, values, attitudes, and norms that keep those in lower classes "in their place."

Norms are an important tool through which the wealthy perpetuate privilege. Norms that protect private property, for example, favor the wealthy over the poor, and most inheritance laws allow families to accumulate wealth over many generations. By extreme contrast, in some Native American tribes, no one is allowed to own land. An individual may lease land for a lifetime, but when he or she dies, the land becomes community property once again, to be leased to someone else (Matthiessen 1984).

U.S. income tax laws were once designed to tax the wealthy at substantially higher rates than everyone else. This policy was based on several principles: the wealthy are more able to pay and therefore should pay more; they have more to gain from a healthy society and therefore should contribute more; and they receive a disproportionately large

TABLE 12-1   Distribution of Before-Tax and After-Tax Household Income (United States)

INCOME GROUP	SHARE OF BEFORE-TAX INCOME (Percentage)	SHARE OF AFTER-TAX INCOME (Percentage)
Lowest Fifth	3.7	4.4
2nd Fifth	9.7	10.9
3rd Fifth	16.2	17.2
4th Fifth	24.3	24.8
Top Fifth	46.1	42.7
	100.0	100.0

Source: USCB 1988a.

share of income, and therefore the burden of supporting society should fall more heavily on them.

In practice, however, income tax laws always allowed many of the wealthy to avoid paying taxes on much of their income (Devine 1983). Deductions sometimes enable millionaires to pay no tax at all, and few wealthy individuals pay the full rate. Because wealthy people have considerable influence over the passage of laws, they are often able to bring about laws that serve their best interests (such as lowering the 70 percent rate to 50 percent in 1982 and then to only 31 percent in 1991). The effects of this are clear in Table 12-1, which shows the effect of income taxes on the distribution of income. In terms of before-tax income, the poorest 20 percent of the population received less than 4 percent of all income, while the richest 20 percent received 46 percent. The second column shows the distribution of after-tax income, and you can see that it differs very little from the distribution of before-tax income.

The tax structure thus has little effect on the distribution of income (see also Pechman 1984). In addition, however, the Congressional Budget Office (1987) estimates that the drastic tax law changes enacted during the Reagan administration have actually shifted some of the tax burden from the highest to the lowest income families. In 1988, the poorest tenth of people in the U.S. paid 20 percent *more* in total federal taxes than they did in 1977, while the richest one percent paid 20 percent *less*.

Culture and the Uses of Ideology   When Marx ([1843] 1967) described organized religion as "the opiate of the masses," he was not attacking religion itself; rather, he was arguing that religion can

function as a distraction for workers. The more attention they pay to heaven, hell, and the hereafter, he argued, the less attention they pay to social relations on earth through which they are exploited.

Religious beliefs often cloud awareness of classes and their relationships with one another, especially in societies whose workers are poorly educated. Religion focuses attention on individuals, and this, too, draws attention away from social factors that affect living conditions, experience, and behavior. Marx called this lack of awareness of the true extent and causes of social inequality **false consciousness**. It is an important concept that shows how social conditions persist when we misperceive important aspects of reality.

Religion is not the only potential source of false consciousness. We commonly believe, for example, that the U.S. is a land of equal opportunity, and value the right of individuals to own property. In 1990, 65 percent of adults in the U.S. reported the belief that hard work is the most important factor in getting ahead (Davis and Smith 1990), and most believe that success and failure are due primarily to individual, not social, causes (Kluegel and Smith 1982, 1986). A major part of the American Dream is to "make it big" and share in the affluence of the upper class.

Such aspects of culture support stratification by legitimating the social arrangements that produce it and by explaining success or failure in purely individual terms. The belief in the importance of hard work helps maintain the privilege of dominant classes by keeping the lower classes hard at work and in a state of false consciousness without threatening members of the upper class, most of whom depend on inheritance (rather than hard work) for their wealth (Projector and Weiss 1966). Instead, it legitimizes their privilege (if they are wealthy, they must have worked hard). When lower-class people fail to get ahead, they tend to blame themselves rather than a stratification system that severely limits their opportunities no matter how hard they work. After all, the U.S. was founded on the idea that "All men are created equal" (a constitutional ideal that still excludes women). By blaming themselves, members of lower classes tend to ignore the fact that while higher-class people may work no harder than they, they still receive far greater rewards.

When cultural ideas are used to justify a social system, they constitute an **ideology** (see Swidler 1986; Turner 1986). In the late eighteenth and early nineteenth centuries, for example, England enjoyed an

TABLE 12-2   Perceptions of Class Inequality, by Family Income, United States

PERCENT WHO AGREE THAT	FAMILY INCOME						ALL
	$0–$4,999	$5,000–$14,999	$15,000–$24,999	$25,000–$34,999	$35,000–$49,999	$50,000 or more	
The U.S. has an open society and what one achieves in life no longer depends on family background, but on the abilities one has and the education one acquires.	78%	84%	88%	86%	89%	85%	86%
Everyone in this country has an opportunity to obtain an education corresponding to their abilities and talents.	72%	72%	71%	69%	74%	62%	71%
Differences in social standing between people are acceptable because they basically reflect what people made out of the opportunities they had.	72%	76%	75%	75%	71%	75%	74%
All in all, social differences in this country are justified.	54%	51%	54%	55%	52%	66%	54%

Source: Computed from 1984 General Social Survey data.

unprecedented period of prosperity which included virtual technological and economic dominance of most of the Western world (see Adas 1989). In that social environment, it is not surprising that the English philosopher and sociologist Herbert Spencer developed a theory that Britain's dominance and prosperity were justified by the superiority of the British society and culture. Spencer's theory tried to apply Charles Darwin's theory of evolution to social inequality by arguing that the wealth, privilege, and power of some, and the deprivation and misery of others, was a natural and inevitable result of some people being more fit than others (see Jones 1980). According to this theory, which became known as **social Darwinism**, the most capable people will and should gain more in the struggle for survival than the less capable.

Spencer's ideas found an enthusiastic audience in the U.S. which was then experiencing an orgy of economic speculation, the building of vast personal fortunes, and increasingly dismal living and working conditions (Hofstadter 1955). In his book, *What Social Classes Owe to Each Other* (1883), sociologist William Graham Sumner applauded Spencer's ideas and argued that the upper classes deserve their privi-

lege because the mere fact of *having* it demonstrated their greater fitness. The main problem with this argument is that it is circular and thereby true by definition: If we accept the idea that wealth is a valid measure of fitness, then by definition the wealthy must be more fit than everyone else.

In general, those who benefit most from an ideology tend to be its strongest supporters (see Rytina, Form, and Pease 1970; Kluegel and Smith 1986). As Marx argues, however, dominant classes tend to use their influence to shape culture in their own interests, including promoting widespread acceptance and support for the status quo (see Peschek 1987). Rarely, for example, do the U.S. mass media criticize capitalism as an economic system. Problems such as high unemployment, poverty and homelessness, or the 1987 crash of the stock market tend to be attributed to factors such as poor worker training, technical problems, unfair foreign competition, or investor panic—not to inherent flaws in the system. As a result, there is a high level of consensus in the U.S. that the stratification system functions fairly, that inequality is based primarily on personal attributes and talent, and that educational opportunity is available to all (last column of Table 12-2). This holds regardless of family income: looking across each row in Table 12-2, you see that the percentages are quite similar from one income category to another. Such findings illustrate Marx's view that culture is used to support the privileged position of the dominant class.

The Interactionist Perspective: The Social Construction of Inequality

While the functional and conflict perspectives are useful for drawing attention to the causes and consequences of stratification on a macrolevel, it is also important to be aware of the central insight provided by the interactionist perspective—that through social interaction we identify ourselves and others as members of different classes. In doing so we recreate the human reality of class distinctions in everyday life.

This process begins with symbolic indicators of class position, such as the way people talk and carry themselves, the cars they drive, and the clothes they wear. Extending from this are the ways in which social interaction is used to act out and reinforce class

inequality, from the gestures of deference servants show toward their employers to the ways in which people are told they may not eat in certain restaurants unless they are "properly attired." If a man approaches people on the street and asks them to give him some change for bus fare because his wallet has been stolen, they are likely to respond differently if he is dressed in a three-piece suit and carries a briefcase than if his clothes are ragged and torn.

One of the most important parts played by interaction in the maintenance of class systems occurs in the major institutions through which people acquire their social identities. As we will see in Chapter 17, for example, students in working-class schools tend to have expectations reinforced that they will have jobs where others control what they do. They are generally not trusted to make decisions for themselves or to move about without written permission, and are rarely accorded the kind of dignity and respect that support the development of an independent, autonomous adult. In upper-class schools, by contrast, the behavior of teachers towards students tends to reflect an underlying assumption that these are special young people who are destined to lead independent lives with important responsibilities and privileges. They are encouraged to develop self-reliance and a deep sense of their own worth and identification with the major social institutions through which their privilege is exercised.

The effects of social class on social interaction are also found in families which, as institutions, play a major role in reproducing class distinctions. In the upper class, for example, a primary responsibility of family members is to maintain the social position of the family and its lineage. Because of this, family interactions tend to be more formal than in other classes, as children are encouraged to acquire a sense of obligation to their lineage and the self-discipline, and adult outlooks, skills, and manners that will define their indentities as members and supporters of upper-class values and privileges. In the middle class, by contrast, families exist less to perpetuate the privileges of a particular lineage than to support

The sense of confidence and entitlement to privilege instilled by elite private schools is apparent in the faces and postures of these New England prep school students.

the striving for upward mobility. As such, interaction tends to be less formal than in the upper class and emphasizes independence and autonomy rather than a sense of obligation to the family. Children are encouraged to make lives for themselves rather than remain dependent on the family (see Leslie and Korman 1988).

As we negotiate our way through social life, there are few factors whose effects are as pervasive and profound as our perceptions and interpretations of social class differences, for through them we create and sustain major portions of our sense of who we and others are, and in doing this, we participate in the recreation of class systems that the functional and conflict theorists try to explain on a larger level.

The preceding sections introduce the major perspectives we use to understand stratification, and those that follow apply these perspectives to the U.S. and less developed societies.

SOCIAL STRATIFICATION IN THE UNITED STATES

Because the United States was founded, in part, as a reaction against the aristocracies of Europe with their rigid divisions between nobility and commoners, we like to think of our society as classless. We may locate ourselves in the "lower class," "middle class," or "upper class," but we tend to believe that people who work hard can go as far as they want. But is this true?

From Marx's Perspective

To Marx, a classless society is one in which the means of production are collectively owned and controlled by everyone, and in which no one has the power to deny someone the right to earn a living. No industrial society has achieved Marx's ideal; but we can use his perspective to describe our class structure by answering two questions: (1) How likely are we to work for ourselves rather than for someone else? and (2) How concentrated is the ownership of the means of production?

In the early 1800s around 80 percent of working people were self-employed, mostly as farmers. By 1840, this had dropped to two thirds, and to only a third by the 1870s, when the Industrial Revolution was in full swing. Today the figure is under 9 percent (Larkin 1988; USCB 1990a; see also Steinmetz and

Wright 1989). While we began as a country in which most people owned and controlled some means of production, the vast majority of contemporary workers work for someone else. While this suggests the existence of capitalist and worker classes in the U.S., we have to remember that ownership and control of the means of production is not as simple now as it was in the 1800s when most businesses were family-owned. Most businesses are now owned by stockholders, and anyone who has money to spare can own a "piece of the action" by purchasing stocks and bonds.

This brings us to the second question: How *concentrated* is ownership of business? The wealthiest 10 percent of the population owns 90 percent of all bonds and corporate stock; the wealthiest *one* percent owns 50 percent of all bonds and 60 percent of all stocks; and 80 percent own *no* stocks or bonds at all (JEC 1986a; USCB 1986a).

This, when added to the findings shown in Figure 12-1, shows that from Marx's perspective, the U.S. is divided into classes defined by their relationship to the means of production. The dominant class is a small minority who are either self-employed professionals, own means of production, or occupy top management positions. Most people are in the working class; for whether they are professors, engineers, fire fighters, or clerks, they cannot work unless those who control jobs are willing to buy their labor power.

The importance of Marx's concept of class is painfully evident to millions of workers who lose their jobs during the economic recessions that seem to be recurring phenomena in industrial capitalist societies. In 1982, for example, almost 20 percent of those who wanted to work were either out of work and still looking for jobs or had given up the effort. Many of the newly unemployed had occupied well-paid positions, lived in mortgaged houses, and had children in college; they were shocked to suddenly find themselves without a way to earn a living. By drawing attention to the importance of owning and controlling the means of production, Marx reveals that whatever the level of rewards may be today, in a class society, what workers earn may be gone tomorrow no matter how hard they work or how competent they may be.

It is no accident that late in the twentieth century labor unions are shifting their focus from the rewards of work—pay, benefits, and vacation time—to control over working conditions. Some unions now demand membership on corporate boards of directors, so that workers can have some control over the organizations on which they depend for a living. While pay was the issue of the 1960s and 1970s, job security is the issue of the 1990s, and this inevitably involves a struggle over control of the means of production.

Through Weber's Eyes: Dimensions of Inequality

Unlike Marx, Weber divided societies according to the distribution of wealth, power, and prestige. How evenly are these distributed?

Wealth and Income It is important at the outset to distinguish between wealth and income. **Wealth** refers to valued possessions, including cash, property, stocks and bonds, buildings, jewels, and cars. **Income** refers to money that we receive each year. Wealth is what we *have*, while income is what we take in. The distinction is important because wealth is often a source of income, such as interest on investments, rent payments from tenants, or profits from a business or the sale of property that has increased in market value.

A small minority owns most of the wealth in the U.S. For example, the richest 10 percent of the population holds 67 percent of all the wealth, including 87 percent of all cash assets, 49 percent of all real estate, 94 percent of all business assets, and 90 percent of all stocks and bonds (JEC 1986a).

Like wealth, the distribution of income is also unequal. The wealthiest 5 percent of families receives 17 percent of all income—more than three times what they would receive if everyone got equal shares; and, the wealthiest 20 percent receives 44 percent of all income. Meanwhile, the lower 60 percent receives only 32 percent; the poorest 20 percent receives under 5 percent—less than a quarter of what they would have received if income were distributed equally; and the income of one out of every ten families falls below the poverty level (USCB 1990a).

It is important to note that income figures based on tax returns understate the true extent of inequality, for much of the income of wealthy families and individuals is never reported to the Internal Revenue Service. Top executives, for example, enjoy large expense accounts that pay for travel and entertainment, and are often given the opportunity to buy stock at a cost far below its actual value. The most lucrative tax-free investments are typically beyond the reach of all but the wealthy.

Power C. Wright Mills (1956) argued that power is concentrated in the hands of an elite, that business, political, and military leaders share common backgrounds, values, and attitudes, and cooperate with each other in order to maintain their dominance. Business leaders are often appointed to top positions in government agencies designed to regulate business; or, those in charge of government agencies that regulate business may later work for corporations, using their special knowledge to help businesses avoid government regulations. From Mills' point of view, elite individuals move from one powerful position to another—whether economic, political, or military—and because these people know each other well and share values and experiences, they are in a position to exercise considerable control over important decisions.

Domhoff (1967, 1971) compiled a list of the upper class—those at the highest levels of wealth and education—and found that while its members may belong to different political parties, they are closely related through intermarriage, attendance at the same elite schools, and club memberships (see also Cookson and Persell 1985). Most important, they strongly value capitalism and the rights to accumulate private property and make profits, and are far more likely to occupy powerful positions in business and government than are those in the classes below them. A majority of U.S. presidents have had upper-middle or upper-class origins (Pessen 1984), and the highest reaches of the corporate world are generally reserved for members of the upper class (Useem and Karabel 1986; see also Domhoff 1983; Useem 1984). In addition, the upper class is in a position to influ-

---

PUZZLE

IS EDUCATION THE ANSWER?

In the last twenty years, the educational attainment and level of training in the population in the U.S. has grown dramatically. As a result, has the distribution of income become less unequal, more unequal, or stayed just about the same?

The answer is that the distribution of income has become *more* unequal in the last ten years. This chapter explains why.

In the late 1800s, the upper class attempted to enhance its prestige by flaunting its wealth—conspicuous consumption. The marble "summer cottages," such as this mansion built for William K. Vanderbilt, were used for only two months of each year; otherwise, they were occupied only by the servants.

ence political institutions both by contributing to the campaigns of candidates who support their interests and by supporting think tanks and other policy-making organizations that do much to shape public thinking about social problems (Allen and Broyles 1989; Peschek 1987).

Riesman (1961), on the other hand, argued that Mills overstated the power of elites. To Riesman, the distribution of power is *pluralistic*, concentrated in a wide variety of interest groups such as: labor unions, professional organizations, consumer action groups, political parties, the National Association for the Advancement of Colored People (NAACP), the Civil Liberties Union, the Urban League, and the National Organization for Women.

Both views are correct to a degree. The upper class clearly has more control over economic and political decisions than do people in any other class. The power of the upper class is by no means absolute, however. While no group controls the U.S., it is also true that most citizens have good reason to feel powerless unless they are represented by an interest group.

Prestige Unlike power and wealth, the distribution of prestige depends heavily on cultural values. Parsons (1964) argued that prestige depends on how a culture values *possessions, qualities* (such as natural talent or ascribed statuses such as race, gender, and parents' social class), and *performance* (including achieved statuses such as education, marital status, and occupation).

If a culture values possessions, such as cars and stereos, prestige tends to go to those who own them regardless of their power. For this reason, people often buy things (such as designer clothes) not simply to use or enjoy them, but to indicate to others that they have achieved an important cultural value.

This is what Thorstein Veblen (1934) called **conspicuous consumption**—owning objects in order to enhance or affirm prestige.

Conspicuous consumption has not always brought with it higher levels of prestige. Harris (1974) argued that historical shifts in the *basis* for distributing prestige have helped perpetuate stratification in industrial societies. In the early stages of capitalism, prestige went to those who were frugal. When the privileged position of the rich became more secure, they engaged in conspicuous consumption—building enormous estates and spending their wealth openly and freely as a symbolic expression of their power and privilege.

As production increased and capitalists needed people to buy their goods, conspicuous consumption became associated with prestige among the middle and lower classes. Most recently, as the gap between rich and poor has become a source of social conflict, the old rich protect their high prestige by regarding conspicuous consumption as vulgar. This shift lowers their visibility and changes the rules of the game, once again reserving the highest levels of prestige for themselves.

TABLE 12-3   Prestige Ratings[1] of Occupations in the United States

OCCUPATION	RATING	OCCUPATION	RATING	OCCUPATION	RATING	OCCUPATION	RATING
Physician	82	Social worker	52	Mail carrier	42	Hairdresser	33
College teacher	78	Athlete	51	Tool and die		Plasterer	33
Judge	76	Computer		maker	42	Shoe repair	33
Lawyer	76	programmer	51	Practical nurse	42	Stone cutter	33
Dentist	74	Editor or reporter	51	Farmer	41	Bus/truck driver	32
Bank officer	72	Optician	51	Plumber	41	Cashier	31
Architect	71	Radio or TV		Railroad		File clerk	30
Airplane pilot	70	announcer	51	conductor	41	Painter	30
Chemist	69	Bank teller	50	Tailor	41	Precision machine	
Minister	69	Buyer, Wholesale	50	Carpenter	40	operator	29
Biologist	68	Office manager	50	Telephone		Sales clerk	29
Civil engineer	68	Sales manager	50	operator	40	Shipping clerk	29
Sociologist	66	Electrician	49	Receptionist	39	Assembly line	
High school		Aircraft mechanic	48	Restaurant/bar		worker	27
teacher	63	Bookkeeper	48	manager	39	Mine worker	26
Registered nurse	62	Dental assistant	48	Telephone		Childcare worker	25
Dental hygienist	61	Machinist	48	installer/repair	39	Garage worker	22
Pharmacist	61	Police officer	48	Barber	38	Guard	22
Public official/		Insurance agent	47	Dancer	38	Taxi driver	22
administrator	61	Science		Building		Bartender	20
School		technician	47	superintendent	38	Waiter	20
administrator	60	Musician or		Auto mechanic	37	Household maid	18
Author	60	composer	46	Jeweler/		Peddler	18
Elementary school		Secretary	46	Watchmaker	37	Garbage collector	17
teacher	60	Office machine		Airline stewardess	36	Laborer	17
Accountant	57	operator	45	Brickmason	36	Fast-food worker	15
Actor	55	Firefighter	44	Radio/TV repair	35	Janitor/cleaner	15
Librarian	55	Real estate agent	44	Baker	34	Shoe shiner	9
Funeral director	52	Postal clerk	43				

[1]Rated on a scale of 1 to 100.
Source: Davis and Smith 1990, Appendix F.

Prestige is also distributed according to ascribed statuses such as race, gender, and ethnicity—characteristics people are powerless to change. When people are asked to rank the prestige of occupations, for example, they tend to rank them lower if they are presented with a hypothetical person holding the job who is a woman, or if they perceive the job as being held more often by women than by men (Bose 1985). The prestige of occupations, in short, depends in part on the gender of those who hold them.

Prestige is also affected by cultural values attached to achieved statuses. Since 1947, several studies have measured the amount of prestige attached to different occupations by asking respondents to rate occupations as excellent, good, average, somewhat below average, or poor (see Table 12-3). Each occupation is

given an average rank (Hodge, Treiman, and Rossi 1966; North and Hatt 1947; Treiman 1977). The most prestigious occupations either require extensive formal education or involve high levels of responsibility and power—professionals and technical workers, business owners and managers, and high public officials. At the bottom are jobs that depend mainly on manual work, require relatively little training, and involve little or no power.

Roughly 30 percent of U.S. workers hold jobs whose prestige is rated good or excellent—professionals and technical workers, managers, and administrators (USCB 1990a). Like wealth, income, and power, the distribution of prestige is highly unequal; and, as Studs Terkel (1974) found when he interviewed people in many different occupations,

Although related to wealth and power, the prestige of an occupation has less to do with either of these than the simple regard that one human being has—or does not have—for the life and work of another.

the high prestige of those at the top is paid for by those at the bottom. As a washroom attendant in a large Chicago hotel put it:

> I'm not particularly proud of what I'm doing. . . . I don't go around saying I'm a washroom attendant. . . . Outside of my immediate family, very few people know what I do. . . . This man shining shoes, he's had several offers . . . where he could make more money. But he wouldn't take 'em because the jobs were too open. He didn't want to be *seen* shining shoes. . . . No, I'm not proud of this work. (p. 108)

Whether we view stratification from Weber's point of view or Marx's, the United States is, like every complex society, clearly divided into social classes. The degree of inequality is only one aspect of stratification systems, however, for societies also differ in how *rigidly* they are stratified. In other words, societies differ in how easily individuals can change their social class or their standing within a class. Such changes can be positive or negative, for people can move down as well as up. Together, the movement of individuals within and between classes is called **social mobility**.

The following sections look at mobility in terms of Weber's and Marx's concepts of class. As you might guess, the resulting picture of mobility depends on which concept we use.

SOCIAL MOBILITY: GOING UP AND GOING DOWN

There are two types of mobility. We can think of *lifetime* mobility—a woman begins as a researcher in a publishing company and retires as a senior editor; or, she becomes an editor at age 36, loses her job when the company goes bankrupt, and ends her work life as a waitress. Or, we can compare people's class position with that of their parents in order to detect *intergenerational* mobility.

In a closed stratification system, the major groupings are **castes**, not classes. Unlike classes, caste membership is based on ascribed statuses such as ethnicity and race, and because it is assigned at birth, it cannot be changed. While individuals can improve their position within a caste, it is impossible to change their caste. Before the abolition of slavery in the U.S., caste was an important aspect of race relations, and in some respects it still is (Frederickson 1981). Housing, for example, is highly segregated by race.

In an open stratification system, individuals may freely compete for wealth, power, and prestige regardless of their ascribed statuses. In the U.S., as in most of the world's societies, the system allows some mobility from positions of lower power, wealth, or prestige to higher ones. Most people believe that whatever their class position is today, with hard work, education, and a little luck, there are few limits on what they can achieve. Sociological research suggests that such perceptions are accurate in the sense that we often do improve our positions; but it also shows that how *far* we can move is, for most of us, very limited.

The next three sections try to answer three basic questions about social mobility. First, what characteristics of societies determine how much mobility there is in their populations? Second, which social characteristics allow some individuals to be more mobile than others? Third, does mobility lead to less inequality in society as a whole?

How Much Mobility?

The extent of upward mobility in a society depends on two basic aspects of its structure. People can move up to better positions if there are enough openings;

As one of India's "untouchables," the lowest among the caste of laborers, the woman holding a broom she uses to clean toilets was assigned her status (and even her occupational specialization) at birth. The teacher is a member of a higher caste, but her status, too, was ascribed, based on her parents' caste. This traditional closed stratification system has been undergoing changes since India achieved its independence.

and in order to occupy higher positions, they must have the characteristics and abilities required for entry into those statuses. Feudal societies, for example, were divided into two classes—the land-owning nobility and the peasants—and mobility was severely limited (Rossides 1990). There were very few positions available, and since only the eldest son could inherit his father's estate, the younger sons had few options other than a religious career. The daughters of nobility could marry a nobleman, spend their life in their father's house, or enter a convent. It was almost impossible for peasants to move upward, since the only higher status in the system was the usually ascribed status of "noble."

Industrialization accounts for the relatively high rates of mobility found in the U.S. and other modern societies in part by causing a vast expansion of educational opportunities. Of people 18 to 24 years old, the percentage in college in the U.S. increased from 1 percent in 1870 to 29 percent today, and since 1918 the number of people in vocational training programs has increased from under 100,000 to more than 16 million (USCB 1980b, 1990a).

By creating thousands of different jobs, industrialization also created mobility by dividing the distance between the highest and lowest occupations into a series of small steps. Whereas in feudal societies the ladder of success had only two rungs— with the top rung hopelessly beyond the reach of those on the bottom—the ladder in industrial societies has thousands. While the poor still have almost no chance of reaching the upper rungs, they can experience some progress and may eventually make it to the middle class.

Kahl (1961), for example, found that between 1920 and 1950, 67 percent of sons were in higher-ranked occupations than their fathers. In their path-breaking study, Blau and Duncan (1967) compared the educations and occupations of fathers and sons and found that 37 percent of men with white-collar jobs had fathers who worked in blue-collar jobs. Both studies, however, find that the *degree* of movement from one generation to the next is quite small. The vast majority of those who occupy high statuses in government and business come from upper-class families, and a study of professionals in the 1960s found that 40 percent had fathers who were professionals as well (Jackson and Crockett 1964; Lipset and Bendix 1959). In general, the lowest levels of mobility are found in the highest and lowest classes and the highest amount of mobility occurs among farmers and those in the middle of the class system (see Featherman and Hauser 1978; Kurz and Muller 1987).

PUZZLE

MOBILITY AND AFFLUENCE— REAL AND APPARENT

Average family income in the United States has risen in the last decade, as has the number of possessions such as washers, dryers, televisions, and home computers that people have in their homes. Given this progress, why do most people report that the "lot of the average man" is growing worse?

The answer, as this chapter explains, has less to do with what people have than with how they come to have it.

As the structure of the job market—the kinds of jobs available—changes, it causes both upward and downward **structural mobility**. In the 1990s the job market is expanding in industries that require technical training—computer programming—and service occupations such as veterinarians, legal assistants, tax preparers, and employment interviewers. There are not enough children of upper- and middle-class parents to fill these jobs since fertility is lower in the middle and upper classes than in the lower and working classes. Thus structural changes in the economy and relatively low birth rates in the middle and upper classes have created opportunities for the children of lower-class parents to move into the middle class.

Technological advances that create thousands of jobs for those with technical training, however, also can spell disaster for millions of manual workers. The automobile industry will increasingly replace workers with robots on assembly lines, and while this creates jobs for engineers and technicians, it causes severe downward mobility for many skilled and unskilled blue-collar workers. Some can go back to school, but this is a long-term solution that ignores short-term effects of downward mobility. Bills—including medical bills and those for college tuition and home mortgages—must be paid now, not later. In many cases, the shock of downward mobility is so severe that families never recover (see Newman 1988).

Who Goes Up and Who Goes Down?

Sociologists identify several statuses that affect who moves up and who moves down in the stratification system, the most important of which are education, social class of parents, race, gender, occupation, and age.

People in the U.S. generally agree that education is the most important factor in upward mobility, a view that is generally supported by research (see Table 12-4). The beneficial effects of education are not guaranteed, however. In 1987, 40 percent of college-educated workers had lower incomes than the average worker with only a high school diploma; and 10 percent of workers with high school diplomas had *higher* incomes than the average college-educated worker (USCB 1989e). As Thurow (1975), Jencks et al. (1972), and Bane and Jencks (1972) concluded, training and skill cannot explain why some people have more income than others. Bane and Jencks went so far as to suggest that "luck" is the single most important factor. If we compare the incomes of brothers who have similar IQ scores and similar educations, they differ by an average of $5,300. If we choose pairs of men at *random*, however, the average difference between their incomes is only slightly higher— $6,200. As explained by Bane and Jencks:

> These estimates mean that people who start off equal end up almost as unequal as everyone else. Inequality is not mostly inherited: It is re-created anew in each generation. . . . Adult success must depend on a lot of things besides family background, schooling, and the cognitive skills measured by standardized tests. (p. 39)

The positive effects of education also depend on ascribed statuses such as race and gender. In Table 6-6, we saw that while education increases women's incomes, they still lag far behind men with far less formal education.

TABLE 12-4   Income by Educational Attainment, United States

EDUCATIONAL ATTAINMENT	AVERAGE INCOME
Professional degree	$46,500
Doctorate	$39,200
Master's degree	$27,500
Bachelor's degree	$22,100
Associate's degree	$16,200
High school diploma	$12,300
Less than high school diploma	$ 8,300

Source: USCB 1987f.

"If debt is a measure of consumer confidence,
we have become very confident indeed."
Drawing by Lorenz © 1983, The New Yorker
Magazine, Inc.

Although education has long been viewed as a great equalizer, this depends on the belief that everyone has an equal chance to go to college; but this is far from true. In 1988, 61 percent of 18–24 year-olds with family incomes of $50,000 or more attended college; but in families making less than $20,000, only 27 percent were enrolled (USCB 1990b). While education promotes mobility regardless of parents' class, *access* to education strongly depends on parents' resources (see Jencks et al. 1979). Even when children begin schooling with equal IQ and grow up to have equal education, class background strongly affects adult income. Bowles and Nelson (1974), for example, found that among white males 35 to 44 years old, children from families in the top tenth of the population were three times as likely to wind up in the top fifth as children from families in the poorest tenth.

Studies of mobility in the U.S., then, give us a mixed picture. People often enjoy higher incomes and more prestigious occupations than their parents, but in general the differences are small. Achieved statuses, such as education, are important, but they offer no guarantee of success and their effects are often limited by ascribed statuses such as race and gender. The number and variety of jobs available are a structural characteristic of society itself and are beyond the control of individual workers. As that structure changes, it inevitably produces opportunities for some and hardship for others.

We come now to our third question about social mobility: What effect does it have on stratification? Does mobility lead to a less stratified society?

Is Mobility an Illusion?

Upward mobility would seem to be a common occurrence in the United States, and if one were to judge by the quantity of consumer goods found in the average household, it would seem that people are generally better off each year than they were the year before. The median income of intact husband-wife families, for example, has increased by almost 50 percent since 1960 and the worth of household possessions such as appliances and cars has more than doubled (USCB 1986a, 1990a). Such appearances, however, mask deeper realities about social mobility and the class system.

First, the increased levels of family income and household wealth have come about primarily because people are working harder and taking on substantial debt. Since 1960, for example, the percentage of intact husband-wife families depending on the earnings of both spouses has risen from 43 to 73 percent and the number of unmarried people holding two or more jobs has doubled. At the same time, the amount of consumer debt has almost doubled and now amounts to roughly $3,000 for every child, woman, and man in the country (see Ellwood 1988; USCB 1981, 1990a). This means that a substantial portion of the increase in household possessions is owned by banks and loan companies that allow people to buy on credit.

Second, while income and wealth have increased in the population in general, they have risen so much faster among the wealthy that the degree of class inequality has increased. In the last ten years, for example, income going to families in the top fifth of the population has grown at a rate three times that of families in the middle fifth, while income going to the lower two-fifths has actually declined (see Figure 12-2; see also Levy 1988). At the same time, the distribution of wealth has become far more lopsided, with the share owned by the richest 0.5 percent rising from 25 to 35 percent and the share owned by the bottom 90 percent falling from 35 to 28 percent.

Third, in spite of all the moving around within classes, the class structure itself remains intact—except for those in the poorest class, movement of people to a higher position is uncommon. Since 1964, for example, people's perceptions of which social

FIGURE 12-2 The Poor Are Getting Poorer
Percent change of adjusted family income from 1979 to 1987. Figures are weighted for number of people and are figured from constant 1987 dollars.
Source: House Ways and Means Committee.

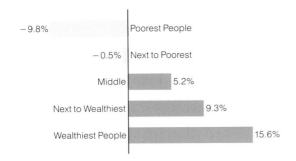

class they belong to have shifted downward. In 1964, 61 percent of adults placed themselves in the middle class, and 35 percent in the working class (Hodge and Treiman 1968). By 1990, however, only 47 percent placed themselves in the middle class and the working class had swollen to 46 percent (Davis and Smith 1990; see also Blackburn and Bloom 1985; Kuttner 1984).

It is certainly true that many individuals improve their levels of income, wealth, and prestige, both during their own lifetimes and in comparison with their parents; but the gap between those who control the means of production and those who do not is virtually unaffected by such individual progress. For the vast majority, upward mobility is strictly limited by the stratification system. Most people spend their work lives inching up a short ladder with many rungs, and even when they reach the top of it, they are not very high and do not have much of a view (see Duncan et al. 1984).

Marx: Mobility as an Uninteresting Problem

The tendency to focus on social mobility and competition for rewards *within* a stratified society leads us to ignore the stratification system itself (see Mach and Wesolowski 1986). From Marx's perspective, so long as the upper class controls the means of production and the working class must sell its labor power, mobility from one income or occupational level to the next is largely a case of those at the lower levels fighting to keep from being on the bottom. After all, if

everyone made it to the middle class, the middle class would no longer be "middle"—it would be the lower class in comparison with everyone else.

To Marx, the key to understanding how rewards are distributed lies in how goods are produced and whether or not the means of production are owned by workers. The self-employed, for example, who by definition control their own means of production, are more than twice as likely to be in the top income brackets as are those who work for someone else (GSS 1990; USCB 1981).

To Marx, social mobility as we often view it is largely irrelevant and only contributes to false consciousness. More important, Marx's concept of social class focuses on the considerable *downward* mobility that most studies ignore. As we saw earlier, the percentage of people who are self-employed dropped from around 80 percent in the early 1800s to under 9 percent today. In addition, the *control* of the means of production remains concentrated in a relatively small portion of the population. Since 1900, the percentage of employed people who were managers, administrators, or officials only increased from 6 percent to 12 percent (USCB 1980b, 1990a). If we define "upward mobility" as movement from less control over the means of production to more control, then Americans have been *downwardly* mobile for almost two centuries, and only a small percentage have risen to positions that afford any real control over the means of production (see Steinmetz and Wright 1989).

What of societies other than the U.S.? How does stratification differ among societies, and why are some wealthier than others?

INTERNATIONAL STRATIFICATION

Countries differ in the degree of inequality and the amount of mobility they allow. In addition, there is enormous inequality between countries. International stratification is particularly important, for the amount of wealth available for distribution *within* a society often depends on relationships among societies.

Varieties of Inequality Within Societies

In general, inequality is less severe in industrial countries than in agrarian societies that are just beginning to industrialize (Kerbo 1991; Weede 1980).

The disparity between rich and poor is nowhere more apparent than in the large cities of countries in the early stages of industrialization.

In this picture of Bombay, India, the shacks of the poor are built adjacent to luxury high-rise apartments.

Mexico is typical of industrializing countries: when the economy grows, the rich get richer and the poor get poorer because increased production is used not to better the living and working conditions of the entire population but to satisfy the urban elite's desire for luxuries (London and Smith 1988). Increased production in less developed countries is also used to protect the privileged position of the elite class. Countries such as Argentina, Chile, Indonesia, the Dominican Republic, and South Korea invest heavily in military and police units whose primary function is to control the local population and prevent revolutions that would threaten the privileged upper class.

In socialist countries such as the Soviet Union and China, wealth, power, and prestige are also unequally distributed, just as they are throughout most of the world (see Szelenyi 1983). Party leaders are wealthier, live in better housing, and have access to a variety of luxury goods beyond the reach of most people. While the means of production are not owned by the elite, they have, until very recently, been tightly controlled by a relative few.

While the vast family fortunes of the Rockefellers and Hunts have no parallel in socialist countries, socialist and capitalist societies are similar in an important way. In socialist societies surpluses are appropriated by the state and controlled by the party elite. In capitalist societies surpluses are appropriated by capitalists who can then use them for their own benefit. In neither type of society do the workers have the power to control and dispose of what they produce.

Social Mobility   Nineteenth-century India was divided into four castes: priests and scholars at the top, then nobles and warriors, merchants and skilled workers, and common laborers. Below all of these were the outcasts, or "untouchables," with whom physical contact was avoided at all costs by members of castes. In 1949 the caste system was officially abolished. Its importance has declined in urban areas, but caste remains an important force in traditional rural areas.

South Africa is one of the few remaining caste societies. Although whites make up only 17 percent of the population, they have dominated many aspects of social life through a rigid racial policy called **apartheid**. Blacks are not allowed to vote in national elections and are forced to live in impoverished areas. All skilled and the better unskilled jobs are reserved for whites, blacks are forbidden by law from striking, and the average black worker's income is a small fraction of that of the average white.

In comparison with caste societies, class systems are relatively open, allowing varying degrees of mobility from lower to higher positions and using a variety of criteria to determine who is most likely to move. Does the U.S. offer more or less opportunity for mobility than other industrial societies? Most recent studies conclude that overall mobility chances and equality of opportunity in the United States are quite similar to conditions in other advanced capitalist societies, although towards the bottom of the class system opportunities appear to be fewer in the U.S. than elsewhere (see Kerbo 1991).

Inequality is a pervasive feature of the world's societies. Perhaps the most striking levels of inequality in the world, however, are found *between* societies, not within them.

Inequality Between Societies

In 1988, *per capita income* (what each person would receive if income were distributed evenly) in industrialized societies ranged from a high of $27,300 in Switzerland to a low of $12,800 in Great Britain. In most countries, per capita income was startlingly low: $330 in China, $650 in Egypt, $330 in India, and $120 in Ethiopia (PRB 1990).

These differences are even more striking if we remember that per capita income is the amount of money each person would receive *if* income were distributed equally *within* countries. While under conditions of equality each person in India would receive $330 a year, for example, the vast majority of Indians must actually live on far less. Even if income were distributed equally within countries, the people of the wealthiest countries would receive more income each *week* than most of the world's inhabitants would receive each *year*.

The effects of world stratification extend to every aspect of living conditions. Almost half of the people in Africa and Asia can neither read nor write. The U.S. contains less than 5 percent of the world's people, and yet uses 24 percent of the energy consumed each year, including 40 percent of all gasoline. China, however, contains roughly 21 percent

of all the people in the world, and yet its annual share of energy is only 8 percent. In industrial societies, less than 2 percent of all infants die during their first year of life; but in many nonindustrial societies, between 15 and 20 percent die. The average person in Japan can expect to live 76 years, but in Ethiopia life expectancy is only 41 years (PRB 1990; USCB 1990a). In industrial societies, death among children is rare; but millions of children in Third World nations die each year due to the effects of poverty (UNICEF 1988). Many die from diseases for which cheap and effective cures exist (WHO 1990).

Part of the explanation of such inequality is ecological. The U.S. is rich in natural resources, and industrialization both here and in Europe took place when populations were relatively small. In most of today's poor countries, however, populations already outstrip food supplies and are growing faster than the ability to provide jobs and basic necessities.

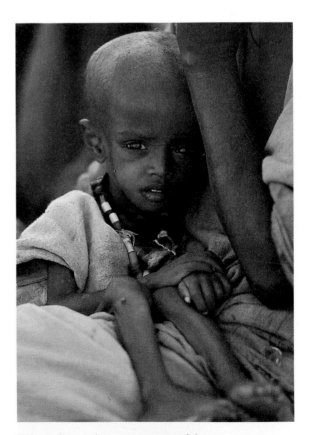

Perhaps the cruelest consequence of the impoverished status of much of the world's population is the millions of starving children.

The answer, however, is not this simple, for the poverty of most of the world is linked with the prosperity of the rest. The Industrial Revolution in Europe, for example, depended on **colonialism**, when one country controls and dominates another. England's colonies provided raw materials for its industry, and England then sold the finished goods to its colonies. Because England controlled its colonies, it would not allow them to trade with any other country or develop industries of their own, which guaranteed England a source of raw materials and a captive market in which to sell manufactured goods. This arrangement enriched colonial powers; but for the colonies themselves it was an exploitative relationship that left them poorer (see Wallerstein 1989).

Although the colonialism of the seventeenth, eighteenth, and nineteenth centuries no longer exists today, the relationships between rich and poor countries still contain elements of it. Many of the industries in less developed countries, for example, are owned and operated by U.S., European, or Japanese corporations, and while many people believe that poor countries should be grateful to wealthy

foreigners who build businesses and provide jobs, this ignores some important facts (Barnet and Muller 1974). When a U.S. corporation builds a factory abroad, for example, if often uses little of its own money. Instead, it borrows from banks in the host country that prefer to risk their money on established U.S. corporations. Many new industries in less developed countries do not represent a flow of resources (capital) from the wealthy countries to the poor. In addition, although less developed countries provide most of the financing for new industry, they receive a small share of the profits.

Such relationships resemble colonialism. Poor countries are less likely to develop industries owned and controlled by local inhabitants, and become dependent on the dominant country. Most important, they stay relatively poor, partly because profits are not reinvested in their own economies. In many respects international stratification enables wealthy nations to dominate and exploit other countries (Evans 1981; Evans and Timberlake 1980). Why do the people in less developed countries tolerate such exploitation? In many cases, the exploitation of poor nations by rich ones is supported by the poor countries' elites, who grow richer while the majority of the population stays poor. They often maintain stability (and their privileged position) with large numbers of soldiers and police, often financed with generous contributions from wealthy industrial nations.

Mobility among Nations   For the world, estimated per capita income increased by 15 percent between 1970 and 1987, over and above the increase caused by inflation. While all but a handful of small countries shared in this, some took a much larger share than others. In the poorest 15 countries, per capita income rose to about $360; but in the wealthiest countries, the *increase* in per capita income was many times larger than *total* per capita income in the poorest countries. What makes these figures even

Children are often the victims of the exploitation of poor nations by wealthy ones. Their poverty and homelessness provoke them to crisis survival—they may beg, steal, or even sell themselves to survive.

more disturbing is the fact that the 15 poorest countries contain almost half of the world's population and income is distributed very unequally within them. This means that most of the world's people receive a very small share of what is *already* a very small share of all income (USCB 1990a).

While most countries improved their incomes during the 1980s, the gap between the wealthiest and the poorest has widened, with the wealthiest 13 percent of the world's population now receiving around 74 percent of all income. In many Third World countries, per capita income has actually fallen since 1980, especially in parts of Africa (USCB 1990a). In many respects, stratification among societies is similar to stratification within them. Like upper-class elites, the wealthy maintain the gap between themselves and those who have less. Although individual countries make progress, the international pecking order remains largely intact, just as the relative positions of social classes remain unchanged. It is a dismal picture and raises important questions about prospects for change and the social and ecological conditions under which equality is most likely to come about, both within societies and between them.

PROSPECTS FOR CHANGE

Debate over stratification centers on two kinds of change: equality of *opportunity* in the form of increased mobility, and equality of *outcomes*—an end to stratification itself.

Mobility and Equal Opportunity

In the early 1830s Alexis de Tocqueville visited the U.S. and recorded his impressions of the new country. In *Democracy in America* ([1835] 1954) he wrote:

> I know of no country . . . where the love of money has taken stronger hold on the affections of men and where a profounder contempt is expressed for the theory of the permanent equality of property.

Tocqueville's observation remains largely true today. In their study of Boston and Kansas City, for example, Coleman and Rainwater (1978) found that most people did not favor an end to stratification. In explaining their positions, people mentioned beliefs that this is a land of opportunity, that inequality is an important source of motivation for hard work, and that the possibility of mobility gives people a feeling that their lives are going somewhere. One of the major suggestions for change was to increase mobility by making higher education available to all and ending discrimination based on ascribed statuses such as race, ethnicity, and gender.

Coleman and Rainwater's study also revealed several important misperceptions of the U.S. stratification system. People commonly reported the belief that the gap between the upper class and those below is closing, although most evidence shows that it is widening. They used a definition of social class that narrowly defines a class society as one organized around rigid castes. They also reported a great deal of faith in education as a route to upward mobility. Evidence suggests, however, that while higher education aids upward mobility more than any other factor, it is no guarantee of success, and its impact will weaken as college degrees become more common (Freeman 1976; Jencks et al. 1979; Thurow 1975). The more plentiful the supply of college graduates, the more likely employers will raise educational standards for job applicants even if higher levels of education are not necessary to perform the job. College graduates are increasingly likely to have occupations previously associated with a high school education, such as bakers, clerks, and supervisors in factories; and high school graduates are increasingly likely to have no job at all. As a result, the economic value of both college and high school degrees has fallen and the income gap between the two educational levels has widened dramatically (CSAWF 1990).

Perhaps most important, people generally thought of stratification in individualistic terms. The responses of many are summarized by one answer: "We're still a competitive society; *people are still trying to get ahead of the next person*, and if that ever changes, it won't be America anymore" (Coleman and Rainwater 1978, p. 294). This kind of response suggests that people tend to accept stratification because they believe that mobility will allow them to escape being at the bottom of the distribution system. In effect, they are saying, "Inequality is acceptable so long as I can feel that I'm doing better than someone else."

This, however, ignores the *structure* of stratified societies. So long as an elite controls most wealth and income, a stratification system can become open only to a very limited degree, whether the society is capitalist or socialist. However freely people may move from the lower to the middle class, 80 percent will still be competing with one another for the relatively small portion of wealth and income that remains after the wealthiest 20 percent takes its "share."

Herman (1975) argued that a significant shift toward equality will occur only when the lower 80 percent focus not on competition among themselves, but on the share of wealth and income left to them by the top 20 percent:

> Change, if it comes, will likely arise out of a continued series of shocks and a failure of the system to "deliver," not only to the bottom 20 percent, but to the lower 80 percent. Only substantial material blows are apparently capable of breaking through false consciousness. (p. 117)

Equality and Classlessness

To Weber, a classless society is one in which everyone receives an equal share of wealth, power, and prestige. Marx defined a classless society as one in which the distinction between owners and workers is removed and no one has the power to control opportunities to earn an equal share of what a society produces. Weber's view tells us little about how to achieve a classless society, because it pays little attention to the ways in which classes are created and perpetuated. Marx, however, was primarily interested in change, and suggested how it might come about.

Davis and Moore (1945) held that inequality is functional, but they were uncertain about its inevitability (Davis 1953). Marx believed that inequality will persist until societies are able to produce an abundance of goods without depending heavily on physical labor. He saw capitalism as a necessary step in a long historical process toward the utopian goal of equality, because capitalism dramatically increases production. Marx believed that *all* forms of inequality will disappear in advanced societies—for which he reserved the term "communist"—and capitalism will no longer be necessary. Indeed, Marx (in Marx and Engels [1846] 1976) contended that the division of labor itself will disappear:

> In a communist society, where nobody has one exclusive sphere of activity, but each can become accomplished in any branch he wishes, society . . . makes it possible for me to do one thing today and another tomorrow, to hunt in the morning, fish in the afternoon, rear cattle in the evening, and criticize after dinner. (p. 22)

This vision is clearly utopian, and even Marx's colleague, Engels, believed that the most advanced societies will depend on complex divisions of labor that require some inequality of authority (see also Dahrendorf 1959). Some functional theorists also see inequalities of prestige as inevitable, for high prestige is, by definition, always in short supply: There is no such thing as high prestige except in relation to those who have lower prestige. What is unclear, however, is whether inequality of prestige requires that some receive levels of respect so low that it damages their self-esteem.

The industrial nations appear to have the ability to produce the abundance that Marx believed is necessary for equality. If all U.S. income for 1987 were distributed evenly among families, for example, each would receive $36,600. In fact, however, 48 percent of all families had incomes more than $6,000 below this amount, and 40 percent had incomes more than $10,000 below. In order for family income to be equally distributed (20 percent going to each fifth of the population), 28 percent of all income would have to be redistributed from the top 40 percent of the population to the lower 60 percent (USCB 1989e).

While the United States clearly produces enough to provide well for all its people, the actual distribution is far from this goal. Efforts to redistribute income—by taxing the rich at higher rates and supplementing poor people's incomes with welfare payments, food stamps, and free medical care—have only slightly increased the share of income going to the poorest class. At the same time, they have lowered the share received by the middle class (Beeghley 1983; USCB 1987a) and done nothing to weaken the dominance of the upper class (Devine 1983; Page 1983).

In addition, by defining the problem of inequality primarily in terms of poverty, we ignore the fact that even if poverty were eradicated entirely, the enormous gulf separating the wealthiest 20 percent from everyone else would remain. In many ways, a single-minded concentration on poverty as *the* problem maintains inequality by distracting both lower- and middle-class people from the fact that they have far more in common with each other than either has with the classes above them.

Why does stratification persist, even in societies that produce a huge surplus?

Class Consciousness and Social Change

Marx believed that classes will disappear only when members of the working class achieve **class consciousness**—when they become aware of the true extent of inequality as well as its social causes. Without this, classes are little more than social categories—collections of people who have a status in common.

With class consciousness, however, common interests become a basis for organizing social movements.

Why have the middle and lower classes not achieved class consciousness and demanded change? As we saw earlier in this chapter, strong cultural ideologies support stratification; but, there is more involved than simple ideology. Life for many *has* improved within the existing class system, and each small step upward reinforces the belief that it is possible to go still higher. This belief, in turn, supports competition as a way of life, and when people are competing with each other, they are unlikely to come together and recognize their common interests.

An additional piece of the answer lies in the concept of **alienation**—a social condition in which people feel disconnected from other people or their own behavior (Marx [1884] 1961). When we work for someone else rather than for ourselves, we lose control over the conditions under which we live and work. The resulting lack of autonomy and self-control causes us to feel less than fully human, for as we lose control over work, we feel separated from it— alienated—and because work is such an important part of our lives, alienation from it produces feelings of alienation from one other. The alienation produced by a class society, then, makes it less likely that members of the working class will critically examine the true nature of their condition.

C. Wright Mills (1951) suggested that an important part of alienation is fear. Because those who control the means of production control people's ability to make a living, workers tend to live in a constant state of anxiety over the future. If they fear what employers may decide to do with them, they are less likely to threaten them and more likely to turn their anxieties on those who have less power over them—on other workers. In socialist countries fear is directed at the state, which, like employers in capitalist societies, controls people's ability to earn a living.

This explains why to many white male workers in the U.S., for example, the enemy is not the upper class, but nonwhites and women who compete with them for jobs; and to many nonwhites and women the enemy is the white male worker who stands in the way of their upward mobility by trying to maintain control over skilled jobs. As a result, members of different racial, gender, and ethnic categories fail to see what they have in common—membership in the working class. Instead, they tend to explain their circumstances in terms of *one another*, rather than as

The work of Mexican muralist Clemente Orozco reflects powerful ideas about the causes and consequences of social inequality and the use of violence to bring about change as well as maintain the status quo.

the inevitable consequence of the stratification system itself (see also Vanneman and Cannon 1987).

While inequality within societies is likely to cause severe strains in the coming years, inequality between nations is an increasingly serious source of international tension and conflict. Countries that once supplied industrial nations with raw materials such as rare metals and oil are becoming more militant and demanding an end to relationships through which wealthy nations prosper at the expense of poorer ones. Less developed countries, for example, realizing that industrial nations depend on them for raw materials, are using this awareness to exact higher prices for their goods.

Although the future is uncertain, one thing is not: Change toward a more equitable and just system for distributing wealth, power, and prestige requires a full understanding of the structures and cultural ideas that produce and sustain stratification. The lot of individuals will improve little until we appreciate that everyone participates in social systems that affect their lives.

SUMMARY

1. Social stratification refers to the process through which the products of social life—including wealth, power, and prestige—are distributed unequally.

2. One of the most important concepts in the study of stratification is social class. To Marx, class position depends on a person's relationship to the means of production. Capitalists own or control the means of production, while workers sell their labor power to capitalists.

3. To Weber, class position depends on the *outcomes* of stratification; in other words, on how much power, prestige, or wealth a person has.

4. Davis and Moore's functional theory of stratification argues that inequality exists because some tasks are more important than others and it is necessary to offer higher rewards in order to motivate individuals to acquire the training to perform them. Complex divisions of labor also require that some people have authority over others.

5. Conflict theorists argue that inequality benefits only those who are in dominant positions and that culture often serves the interests of the elite and constitutes an ideology that supports the status quo. False consciousness exists when people misperceive the true nature and causes of the inequalities in their lives.

6. From an interactionist perspective, class differences are created and perpetuated through social interaction, how people perceive, interpret, appear, and act in relation to one another.

7. From the perspectives of both Marx and Weber, almost all societies are stratified. In the United States, the control of the means of production is concentrated in the hands of a small minority and the distributions of wealth, power, and prestige are very unequal.

8. Social mobility is the movement of people within or between social classes. In closed systems class position is based on ascribed statuses (or castes) and no movement between them is allowed. There is a moderate amount of mobility in the United States and other industrial societies, but most upward moves are quite small.

9. The most important factors in mobility are education, social class of parents, race, gender, occupation, and age. Mobility has little effect on the relative positions of social classes. Family mobility often requires that both spouses work and that the family go into considerable debt. Job ladders often foster the illusion of mobility by dividing a short distance into many small steps.

10. Societies differ in the degree of inequality and there is great inequality among societies. Inequality is more severe in poor and newly industrializing societies than in industrial countries. While socialist countries do not base inequality on ownership of the means of production, they still have considerable inequality.

11. The gap between rich and poor nations is stable, in part because wealthy nations are in a position to exploit poorer ones.

12. Debate about change in stratification focuses on two issues: an end to inequality and social classes, and equality of opportunity within stratified societies.

13. Marx's communist utopia, in which social classes would disappear, is unlikely to ever come to pass. Both conflict and functional theorists believe that inequality of authority will always be necessary, and some functional theorists also believe that inequality of prestige is inevitable.

14. Efforts to redistribute income in the U.S. have slightly improved conditions among the poor but have had no effect on the upper class.

KEY TERMS

alienation   293
apartheid   289
blue-collar worker   271
capitalist (bourgeois)   268
caste   283
class consciousness   292

colonialism   290
conspicuous consumption   281
false consciousness   276
ideology   276
income   280
labor   268

labor power   269
means of production   268
power (party)   270
social class (Marx)   268
social class (Weber)   269
social Darwinism   277

LOOKING ELSEWHERE

Having studied Chapter 12, you might want to look at related discussions in *Human Arrangements*, which include

- poverty in communities (Chapter 10, pp. 216–18, 227–31)
- how criminal law benefits dominant groups (Chapter 11, pp. 237–38)
- social class, crime, and punishment (Chapter 11, pp. 243–45, 247–49)
- deviance and inequality of opportunity (Chapter 11, pp. 257–60)
- the distribution of political power (Chapter 20, pp. 506–516)
- the distribution of power in communities (Chapter 10, pp. 218–20)
- socialism as a political system (Chapter 20, pp. 519–21)
- capitalism and socialism as economic systems (Chapter 19, pp. 473–82, 490–92, 495–97)
- how capitalists control labor (Chapter 19, pp. 476–78, 483–84)

- alienation in the workplace (Chapter 19, pp. 486–88)
- the world economy and international stratification (Chapter 19, pp. 492–95)
- class and age inequality (Chapter 15, p. 368)
- class and family life (Chapter 16, pp. 400–402)
- schools and the perpetuation of social classes (Chapter 17, pp. 421–22, 431–32, 433–36, 439–40)
- education and opportunity (Chapter 17, pp. 436, 439–40)
- religion, false consciousness, and the class system (Chapter 21, pp. 531, 544–46)
- class conflict and social change (Chapter 23, pp. 585–88, 589–93)
- science, technology, and social inequality (Chapter 18, pp. 456–58)
- inequality, health, and health care (Chapter 4, pp. 69–71; Chapter 18, pp. 463–64)

RECOMMENDED READINGS

Adas, M. 1989. *Machines as the Measure of Men: Science, Technology, and Ideologies of Western Dominance*. Ithaca, NY: Cornell University Press. A historical look at the ways in which European colonial powers used their technological superiority to justify their exploitation of colonial peoples.

Beeghley, L. 1983. *Living poor in America*. New York: Praeger. An important book that challenges many common beliefs about welfare and the causes of poverty.

Bendix, R., and Lipset, S. M., eds. (1966). *Class, status, and power* (2nd ed.). New York: Free Press. A comprehensive collection of classic articles about social stratification.

Bowles, S., and Gintis, H. 1976. *Schooling in capitalist America: Educational reform and the contradictions of economic life*. New York: Basic Books. An important book about the ways in which schooling reproduces social classes and inequality in the United States.

Kerbo, H. R. 1991. *Social stratification and inequality*. (2nd ed.) New York: McGraw-Hill. A clear, interesting, and thorough text.

Lenski, G. 1966. *Power and privilege*. New York: McGraw-Hill. A fascinating look at the relationship between historical changes in the mode of production and the emergence of social inequality. The early chapters are particularly useful as overviews of the general problem of social stratification.

Marx, K. 1964. *Selected writings in sociology and social philosophy*. Edited by T. Bottomore and M. Rubel. Baltimore, MD: Penguin. A highly accessible introduction to Marx's major ideas on social stratification.

Sennett, R., and Cobb, J. 1972. *The hidden injuries of class*. New York: Vintage. A thought-provoking look at the ways in which social class differences affect how working-class people feel about themselves and one another.

13
RACE AND ETHNICITY

 Whereas Chapter 12 focused primarily on the importance of achieved statuses such as occupation in stratification systems, in this and the next two chapters we look at the importance of ascribed statuses such as race and ethnicity, gender, and age. We begin with some basic concepts—race, ethnicity, minority group, and social oppression—and then examine cultural, structural, population, and ecological aspects of inequality based on race and ethnicity. Then we use different theoretical perspectives to explain how and why societies have for centuries used ascribed statuses as bases for inequality. Finally, we explore what it might take to end social oppression.

RACE AND ETHNICITY

Imagine that you apply for a copy of your birth certificate one day, and when you receive it, you discover that it lists your "race" as something other than what you and everyone else always considered it to be. You are black, and the certificate says you are white; or you are Asian, and it says you are black. How would you feel?

This is exactly what happened to Susie Guillory Phipps—a New Orleans resident who had always been white to herself and to everyone who encountered her. She had twice married white men, and her family album was filled with pictures of blue-eyed, white ancestors. The state of Louisiana, however, defined her as "colored." When she protested to state authorities, they carefully traced her ancestry back 222 years and found that although her great-great-great-great grandfather was white, her great-great-great-great grandmother was black. Under Louisiana

What differences does race make? In some U.S. theaters this question is receiving an interesting response as plays are cast with nontraditional racial combinations. Not only are characters usually played by actors of one race now played by other races, but in extreme cases parents and children may be portrayed by actors of different races. Here, Denzel Washington plays the title role in Shakespeare's *Richard III*.

law, anyone whose ancestry was at least 3 percent black was considered black. Even with an ancestry 97 percent white, the state defined her as black (Jaynes 1982). Susie Phipps spent $20,000 to force Louisiana to change her birth certificate, and Louisiana eventually repealed the law.

Why would a state have a formula for officially deciding what each person's race is? Why would a tiny percentage of black ancestry cause her to be considered black, while an overwhelmingly white ancestry would not mean she is white? The key lies in the word "mean" in the previous sentence, for as we have seen, what things objectively *are* is often less significant to people than what things *mean* culturally. As a biological concept, **race** refers to people who share a genetic heritage that results in distinct physical features, such as the color of skin, eyes, and hair, or the shape of the eyes. The biological concept, however, is useful only if different races remain separate from one another and do not combine their genes in reproduction. Most scientists agree that the genes that determine biological race have become so mixed that the vast majority of people have a mixed racial heritage. From a biological point of view, the concept of race has lost its usefulness (Sutton 1988).

Most cultures, however, define race as an ascribed status which has important consequences for the occupants of different racial statuses. A biologist would have to say that Susie Phipps is certainly more white than black, but her dilemma has little to do with bi-

ology and everything to do with a culture in which, once she is defined as black, she is perceived, evaluated, and treated as black.

The cultural meaning of race is far more important than biological distinctions. Although Adolph Hitler's claim that there exists a distinct Aryan race of tall, blond, blue-eyed people is scientifically incorrect, for example, his error (as well as the fact that he was short and dark-haired) did not prevent him and his followers from identifying Jews, Gypsies, Poles, and others as members of inferior races. Nor did it prevent them from exterminating millions of people who fell into the "wrong" racial category.

Unlike race, **ethnicity** refers to a shared cultural heritage. An ethnic group is a collection of people who identify with a common culture, share a common heritage of food and styles of dress, music and literature, and look back upon a history that reflects the collective experience of "their people." Jews, Italians, Egyptians, white Anglo-Saxon protestants (WASPs), Irish, Ugandans, native Americans, and Mexicans all constitute distinct ethnic groups whose members identify with a particular cultural and historical heritage.

The U.S. population includes an extraordinary variety of ethnic backgrounds (see Lieberson and Waters 1988). In 1980, 10 percent of all those 5 to 17 years old spoke a language other than English at home, and 14 percent spoke English only with difficulty. Fifty-four percent of adults trace their origins to single ethnicities—the largest of which are German, English, Irish, Italian, Spanish, and Polish— and 46 percent report multiple origins (USCB 1982).

Race and ethnicity are often a major basis for feelings of pride and solidarity among people, but they also have been used for centuries as a basis for distributing wealth, power, and prestige, as well as for systematic violence, exploitation, and oppression.

PUZZLE

WHEN IS 80 PERCENT OF A POPULATION NOT A MAJORITY?

When they are blacks living in South Africa. It is also true that women do not dominate any known societies even though they are a numerical majority in virtually all of them.

Minorities and Social Oppression

Everyone in the U.S. traces their origins to ethnic groups that constitute relatively small percentages of the U.S. population. The largest set of people who cite only one ethnic origin are German, but they make up only 10 percent of the population. In terms of *numbers*, everyone belongs to ethnic minorities. Sociologists, however, are less concerned with relative numbers than with the social consequences of ethnic and racial distinctions. From this point of view, a **minority** is a category of people

> who, because of their physical or cultural characteristics, are singled out from the others in the society in which they live for differential and unequal treatment. (Wirth 1945, p. 351)

A minority is defined not by relative numbers of people with certain characteristics, but by how they are treated as a result of such characteristics. In South Africa, blacks are a minority because they are singled out for unequal treatment in spite of the fact that numerically they make up the vast *majority* of the population. Regardless of their relative numbers, South African blacks would not be a minority in a society that treated whites and blacks in the same way. What all minorities have in common is that they are the objects of socially supported mistreatment, injustice, and exploitation that are the essence of **social oppression**.

It is important to understand that individuals may be abused or exploited without being oppressed. The concept of oppression describes relationships in which minorities are defined as inferior by dominant groups. Individuals are mistreated simply because they are members, regardless of their behavior or personal characteristics. When a man is beaten and robbed because his attacker wants his money, he is not being oppressed; but, if he is beaten and robbed because his attacker hates him as a member of a minority, then he is a victim of oppression.

Moreover, a group may be defined as a minority even though some members are not oppressed; and a group may be socially dominant even though some members do not personally oppress minority people. Oppression is a social phenomenon based on the belief that some groups are superior to others and should benefit from the exploitation and mistreatment of those defined as inferior to them.

Whether or not we behave as victims or victimizers, the oppressive relationships between groups nonetheless exist. A white man in the U.S. may not personally oppress blacks; but this does not wipe away the fact that blacks as a group occupy an oppressed position, and he, as a white man, may benefit from their oppression whether he wants to or not.

What are the social bases of oppression? What forms does it take and what are the consequences? As with other social phenomena, the sociological perspective focuses on several basic aspects of oppression—culture, structure, population, and ecology.

In South Africa, blacks are treated as a social minority even though they are an overwhelming numerical majority comprising more than 80 percent of the population. The extreme poverty they are forced to endure vividly underscores the fact that relative numbers have nothing to do with minority standing.

CULTURE, RACE, AND ETHNICITY

Culture plays an important part in the mistreatment of minorities. How people perceive and evaluate others, as well as how they feel and behave toward them, is strongly affected by beliefs that describe them, values that rank them, attitudes that direct positive and negative feelings toward them, and norms that restrict people as participants in social systems.

Racial and Ethnic Prejudice

Prejudice is an attitude based on stereotypes about members of a group or social category (Allport 1954; see also Seeman 1981). Like all attitudes, prejudice includes beliefs that describe different kinds of people as well as values that rank their relative worth. Prejudice based on race is **racism**; and prejudice based on ethnicity is **ethnicism**. Prejudice may be either positive or negative: the belief that Hindus are superior to Muslims, for example, is just as prejudiced in favor of Hindus as it is against Muslims.

Whether positive or negative, prejudice has four characteristics that make it an important part of social oppression (Memmi 1964). First, it is based on real or imagined differences between groups. Prejudice against blacks includes the belief that they are lazy, stupid, happy-go-lucky, dirty, musical, and oversexed—descriptions that have also been applied to European Gypsies and poor people in southern Italy. With the notable exception of Bill Cosby, family life among nonwhites is rarely portrayed and when it is, it does not reflect the experience of most blacks (Steenland 1989). Nonwhites rarely have lead roles in television shows, and when they do, they are usually cast in comic, servile roles (Unger 1983; Withey and Abeles 1980). Say the words "organized crime" and people may think of Italians. Many people think of Jews as ambitious, sly, and dishonest, and of white Anglo-Saxon Protestants (WASPs) as snobs who only attend Ivy League schools.

Historically, blacks in the U.S. have been confined to the most menial occupations, such as washing and ironing clothes. This status has been based on prejudiced beliefs that blacks are capable of little else.

Second, prejudice attaches values to differences in ways that benefit dominant groups at the expense of minorities. To many Irish Protestants—who dominate Northern Ireland—"Protestant" is good and "Catholic" is bad. The drive to feel superior then leads people in the dominant group to *maximize* the perceived difference between themselves and minorities, for "the smaller he makes his victim, the bigger he becomes" (Memmi 1964, p. 189).

Third, prejudice is generalized to all members of a target group—in other words, each individual's self is summarized by stereotypes (Lieberson 1982). Stereotypes often do have a grain of truth—the average black score on school achievement tests is lower than the white average; the Italian word "Mafia" does describe *some* criminal organizations; and WASPs are more likely than others to occupy top positions in large corporations. Stereotypes, however, ignore enormous differences among individuals who share social characteristics: many blacks, for example, are more intelligent than most whites; most Italians are not criminals; and the vast majority of white Anglo-Saxons are neither executives nor professionals and do not attend Ivy League colleges.

Fourth, in order to ensure their superior position, members of dominant groups support the belief that the inferior position of those in a minority is absolute and inevitable because it results merely from membership in the group. This is often extended back in time and into the future: "Jews have always been greedy and blacks have always been inferior; therefore, they always *will* be." In the case of racism, biology is often used to explain the disadvantaged position of minorities, a form of racism that is enormously powerful because, once accepted, it defines differences as absolute and, therefore, unchangeable. As Memmi (1964) put it:

> biological racism . . . penetrates the flesh, the blood and the genes of the victim. It is transformed into fate, destiny, heredity. From then on, the victim's very *being* is contaminated, and likewise *every manifestation of that being:* behavior, body, and soul. (p. 190)

For centuries, some have tried to prove that members of minorities are biologically inferior. Jensen (1969), for example, argued that most of the difference between the average IQ scores of blacks and whites is due to genetic factors. The crux of his position is that racial differences in IQ persist even among people who have similar social class backgrounds. From this he argued that since racial differences persist even when social environments are similar, then genetics must be the cause. He concluded that blacks as a group will always be intellectually inferior to whites, regardless of educational efforts.

There are several problems with Jensen's argument. First, IQ tests measure a set of mental skills that are developed in and reflect a particular cultural context—that is, the world of the white middle class. Many black children do relatively poorly on IQ tests, not because they are less intelligent, but because the examples and language used in test questions reflect white middle-class culture and experience. The tests used to measure IQ are to some degree *culturally biased* in favor of whites.

Second, a genetic explanation of racial differences rests on the false assumption that blacks and whites represent pure racial types. The most serious criticism of Jensen, however, is that he misinterpreted his own evidence. Specifically, Jensen assumed that when he compared the IQs of blacks and whites who came from the same social classes, he was comparing people whose social environments were the same. As we have seen in earlier chapters, however, the measurement of social class is, at best, quite crude. To conclude that people whose parents had similar educations and occupations are alike on all the known and unknown social factors that affect the development of intelligence is simply unjustified. In other words, we do not *know* how social environments affect intelligence, and controlling for social class does not eliminate the social causes of IQ differences.

Racism and ethnicism therefore rest on negative stereotypes about minorities and positive stereotypes about dominant groups. They are more than simple sets of ideas, however, for they play a vital part in justifying and perpetuating the interests of those who benefit from social oppression. Racism and ethnicism, in other words, are used as *ideologies*.

Ideology and Oppression

In the simplest sense, racism and ethnicism support oppression by denying the existence of oppression itself. This is accomplished primarily by blaming the negative consequences of oppression on its victims. Many people in the U.S., for example, believe that theirs is a land of opportunity in which ability and motivation largely determine success and failure. Such a belief can be used to mask the oppression of

---

ONE STEP FURTHER 13-1

Race and Perceptions of Inequality

Blacks and whites disagree not only about the extent of inequality, but about its causes. The figures in Table B-13-1 show the percentage of blacks and whites who attribute inequality in jobs, income, and housing to various causes.

There are two interesting patterns here. First, Row (A) shows that both blacks and whites express relatively little support for the belief that blacks have less in-born ability to learn.

Second, blacks are far more likely than whites to attribute inequality to discrimination (B), more likely to attribute it to lack of educational opportunity (C), and far *less* likely

to attribute it to a lack of will power or motivation (D).

How would you explain these patterns?

TABLE B-13-1

On the average, blacks have worse jobs, income, and housing than white people. Do you think these differences exist mainly because of:

EXPLANATION	BLACKS	WHITES
(A) Blacks have less in-born ability to learn	18%	12%
(B) Discrimination	67%	35%
(C) Blacks lack educational opportunities	67%	50%
(D) Blacks lack motivation or will power to pull themselves out of poverty	37%	60%

Source: Computed from 1990 General Social Survey data.

---

minorities, however: "the U.S. is a land of equal opportunity; if you have failed, you must be at fault." Not surprisingly, whites are far more likely than blacks to believe that blacks have equal opportunity, for such a belief effectively blames blacks for their disadvantaged position (see One Step Further 13-1).

Within the framework of prejudiced ideologies, members of minorities are not perceived as varied and complex individuals who have many of the same feelings, goals, and needs as other people. This view makes it easier to perceive them as faceless objects, and, therefore, easier to treat them in ways that members of dominant groups would never accept for themselves. During the Vietnam War, for example, Asians were labeled "gooks" and were stereotyped as people to whom "life is cheap." This made it easier to kill large numbers of Vietnamese civilians since, after all, the U.S. military was not taking away something of much importance to *them*. Members of minorities may of course also have ideologies of their own that justify violence toward members of dominant groups.

The Destruction of Culture

Minority groups only exist in societies whose populations include people from different racial or ethnic

backgrounds, which raises the question of how racial and ethnic groupings come together in different ways. Mexico is a good example of **amalgamation**, which occurs when diverse cultures merge into a single new culture. Modern Mexico is a mixture of Indian and Spanish culture. (This is what Zangwill ([1909] 1933) meant when he mistakenly described the U.S. as a "melting pot." **Assimilation** occurs when people from different backgrounds conform to the dominant culture; and **pluralism** occurs when people of different ethnicity live side-by-side and maintain their cultural diversity.

Assimilation best describes cultures in most heterogeneous societies, including the U.S. In spite of immigrants' varied backgrounds, the most important elements of U.S. culture are Anglo-Saxon. English is its language, its legal system is based on English Common Law, and basic cultural ideas about liberty and the rights of individuals are based on the English Magna Carta.

Assimilation often requires ethnic minorities to abandon their cultures in order to escape minority status and participate fully in the life of a society. The first U.S. public schools, for example, were designed to enforce Anglo-conformity among immigrants, and immigrant children still find that their native language and customs are unacceptable in white schools that regard non-Anglo-Saxon cultures as inferior. The children of immigrants typically do not learn the language of their parents, and it is not uncommon for children to have difficulty understanding their own grandparents. As a result, entire cultural traditions may eventually be lost (see Conklin and Lourie 1983; Stevens 1985).

The decline of non-English languages in the U.S. is not uniform, however. While native speakers of European languages such as French have declined, Spanish and Portuguese language groups have grown, fostering a strong Latino ethnic identity (see Stevens and Swicegood 1987). In some states, especially those with large Spanish-speaking populations such as California, Texas, and New York, this has prompted controversial proposals to make English the "official" language by, for example, no longer printing voting ballots in both Spanish and English. Supporters of such bills argue that widespread use of languages other than English undercuts a sense of national cultural unity, while opponents see such laws as an attempt to destroy ethnic subcultures in the interest of enforcing uniformity and the dominance of the Anglo culture.

Contrary to the pressures toward assimilation, immigrants may go to great lengths to preserve their cultural heritage while outwardly conforming to their adopted society. Some immigrants from South Asia, for example, continue their religious practices while eliminating ceremonies that might be offensive in the wider community—such as the animal sacrifices used by some Muslims and Hindus. In this way a kind of American Hinduism takes the place of their original religion (Williams 1988).

By devaluing ethnic and racial differences, racism and ethnicism can destroy cultural diversity (Blauner 1972). When blacks were brought to America as slaves, for example, their African cultures were systematically destroyed by their white owners. They were forced to take new names, and family members were separated from one another. They were not allowed to govern themselves, to administer justice, or practice their religions. African-Americans found themselves in the midst of a white culture that excluded them in every way except as slaves (Frederickson 1981).

Native Americans also experienced systematic efforts by whites to destroy their cultures. For centuries, they had been free peoples who effectively governed themselves and administered justice. Since their conquest by whites, however, they have been forced to adopt a uniform type of government mod-

The devastation of native American societies by white conquest is reflected in many ways, including lowering native American culture to the point of selling it as a commodity to tourists, most of whom are white.

eled after Anglo-Saxon institutions: constitutionally elected tribal officers, tribal courts, and legislatures. Most power, however, is vested in a federal agency—the Bureau of Indian Affairs—not in the tribes (Barsh and Henderson 1980).

With autonomy and self-government went many beliefs and values. Some tribes, for example, valued cooperation more than competition, group success more than personal ambition, the careful management of nature more than its conquest and exploitation. People were seen as an integral part of the natural world, not separate from it, and had neither the need nor the right to dominate it. Such values were unacceptable in the Judeo-Christian tradition of whites, a tradition that included centuries of individualism, political domination, economic development, and exploitation of the natural environment. Native Americans and their cultures stood in the way of white "progress," and so the dominant whites forced them to choose between adopting white culture and being annihilated (Josephy 1973).

The destruction of cultural diversity often takes more subtle forms. It is common, for example, to use a single term, "Hispanic," to refer to people with enormously varied backgrounds—Mexicans, Puerto Ricans, Cubans, Brazilians, Colombians, Chileans, Argentinians, Salvadorcans, and Nicaraguans (see Bean and Tienda 1988; Portes and Truelove 1987).

TABLE 13-1   Distribution of Wealth, by Race, United States

WEALTH	WHITES	BLACKS	HISPANIC
Median net worth[1] of households	$43,300	$4,200	$5,500
Percent with			
zero or negative net worth	9%	29%	24%
$100,000 or more	29%	5%	12%
Percent who own homes	68%	44%	40%

[1]Net worth is the sum of assets minus debts and other liabilities.
Source: USCB 1991.

In each of these countries, people distinguish themselves from other Latin American peoples; but in the U.S., Hispanic is used by the white majority to conveniently label many nonwhites who are not black. In the same way, Africans are referred to as if they were culturally homogeneous, when in fact there are hundreds of different languages and cultures on the African continent.

RACE, ETHNICITY, AND THE STRUCTURE OF INEQUALITY

As we will see later in this chapter, the importance of race in social systems is most visible in the everyday interactions through which stereotyping, exploitation, abuse, and injustice occur. We will look first, however, at how the distribution of wealth, power, and prestige depends on racial and ethnic categories.

Wealth, Income, and Life Chances

Race exerts a powerful effect on the distribution of income and wealth in the U.S. White households accumulate an average of ten times the net wealth of black households, and almost a third of all black households have no wealth at all (see Table 13-1).

The 1988 median income of white households was $28,800, but it was only $20,400 for Hispanics and $16,400 for blacks. Black households constituted 12 percent of the population and yet received only 7 percent of all income, 60 percent of what they would receive if income were distributed equally. Only 10 percent of black and Hispanic households had incomes of $50,000 or more, compared with 22 percent of whites. Blacks and Hispanics were almost three times more likely than whites to have incomes below the poverty level (USCB 1990a).

Why do whites make so much more money than nonwhites? Education appears to explain some of the difference, for whites are 6 percent more likely than blacks to have high school diplomas and almost twice as likely to have college degrees. There are three problems with education as an explanation, however.

First, average education is slightly higher among blacks than among Hispanics, but average income is lower. Second, when we compare families whose adults have similar educational levels, the racial difference remains: in families with a college-educated householder, median income in 1987 was $51,000 for whites, $43,000 for Hispanics, and $36,000 for blacks. Third, unemployment is more likely among nonwhites regardless of education: in 1988, blacks with four or more years of college were more than twice as likely to be unemployed as similarly educated whites (USCB 1990a).

What about occupation? Do whites have higher incomes because they have better jobs? Here the evidence is more convincing: whites are twice as likely to hold upper-level white-collar jobs and 20 percent more likely to have lower-level white-collar jobs. Blacks, on the other hand, are 73 percent more likely than whites to have low-paying, unskilled jobs (Table 13-2). Take a moment to study Table 13-2. Check the jobs you would like to have, and then see which columns they are in to determine the chances of having that job if you are black.

Racial differences in income are affected not only by the kinds of jobs people have but also by whether or not they have jobs at all. In 1988 the unemployment rate among blacks was 10 percent—more than twice as high as the rates for whites and 25 percent higher than the rate for Hispanics (USCB 1990a). It is generally true that unemployment levels whites experience as a recession—6 or 7 percent—represent relative prosperity for nonwhites. If whites ex-

TABLE 13-2   Representation of Blacks in Various Occupations (United States)

OCCUPATIONS IN WHICH BLACKS ARE UNDERREPRESENTED, BY DEGREE

Severe[1]	Substantial[2]	Slight[3]	Overrepresented
Architect	Accountant	Public official	Social worker
Engineer	Social scientist	Mail carrier	Elementary teacher
Lawyer	Computer programmer	High school teacher	Military, enlisted grade
Judge	Electronic technician	Shipping clerk	Vocational counselor
Librarian	Personnel worker	Nurse	Police officer
Dentist	Military officer	Science technician	File clerk
College teacher	Health technician	Stock clerk	Clerical supervisor
Scientist	Drafter	Bank teller	Recreation worker
Pharmacist	Restaurant or bar manager	Storekeeper	Computer operator
Physician	Secretary	Health administrator	Mail clerk
Journalist	Counter clerk	Public administrator	Stenographer
Writer	Cashier	Painter	Telephone operator
Artist	Receptionist	Hairdresser	Crane operator
Entertainer	Carpenter	Punch and stamp	Typist
Editor, Reporter	Plumber	press operator	Insurance adjustor
Financial manager	Machinist	Child care worker	Factory assembler
Sales representative	Auto mechanic	Welder	Seamstress
Bookkeeper	Butcher	Stock handler	Laundry worker
Electrician	Blue-collar supervisor	Telephone installer	Food service worker
Sheet metal worker	Aircraft mechanic	Electric line worker	Machine operator
Tool and die maker	Baker	Printing press operator	Barber
Radio and TV repair	Business manager	School administrator	Meat or produce packer
Type compositor	Economist	Psychologist	Textile factory worker
Typesetter	Actor, Director	Librarian	Chauffeur
Mine worker	Dispatcher	Clergy	Truck, bus, taxi driver
Farmer or farm manager	Mechanic	Musician, Composer	Freight handler
Waiter		Legal assistant	Construction laborer
Therapist		Sales worker	Cook
Dental hygienist		Firefighter	Practical nurse
Airline pilot		Farm worker	Nurse's aide
Real estate sales			Gardener
Bartender			Cleaning worker
			Guard
			Hospital orderly
			House servant
			Dietician
			Athlete
			Lab technician
			Cashier

[1]Percentage less than half the percentage of blacks in the labor force.
[2]Percentage between half and three-fourths of blacks percentage in the labor force.
[3]Percentage just under blacks percentage in the labor force.
Source: USCB 1990a.

perienced the unemployment risks that are usual for blacks, they would consider themselves in the midst of a deep economic depression.

Whites are not only more likely than nonwhites to have *a* job, but are also more likely to be working at two or more jobs. What is most interesting, however, is that the reasons for working at more than one job vary by race. Blacks are more likely than whites to have extra jobs in order to pay regular bills, pay off debts, or save for future needs. Whites, on the other

Although the civil rights movement has enabled a small minority of blacks to make it to the middle and upper-middle classes, the vast majority of blacks are no closer to equality with whites than they were 30 years ago. Nowhere are these effects more widespread or compelling than among black children, almost half of whom live in poverty.

hand, are more likely to work at extra jobs in order to gain new work experiences or to make "special" purchases (USCB 1982). Even though whites are more likely to have two or more jobs, they are less likely to have them because they *must*.

While blacks generally have poorer jobs and less education than whites, these differences do not fully explain why the income of black families is so much lower. Nor do education and occupation fully explain the income gap between blacks and other nonwhites and their greater likelihood of being unemployed. What is left is racial discrimination: the cost of being black includes being systematically paid less than whites for jobs that require comparable levels of skill and training (NCPE 1987). One study concludes that even among blacks the relative lightness or darkness of skin affects educational, occupational, and income level. Dark-skinned blacks, for example, earn an average of only 70 cents for every dollar earned by light-skinned blacks and are only half as likely to have professional or managerial occupations. These differences hold even after controlling for differences in parents' status (Hughes and Hertel 1990).

Although discrimination plays a major part in perpetuating the minority standing of blacks, William J. Wilson (1978) and Hout (1984) have argued that race, itself, is slowly losing its importance. Until recently, blacks were discriminated against universally simply because they were black; but, during the last few decades, some blacks have entered the middle and upper-middle classes. While the historical legacy of racism still affects *all* blacks, Wilson argued that the disadvantaged position of most blacks is now caused more by social *class* than by race. Many blacks are poor not because of *current* racial discrimination, but because a history of systematic racism and discrimination has concentrated them in the lower class, thereby confining them to unemployment and jobs that offer little hope of advancing into the middle class.

Wilson was criticized by Willie (1978, 1979) who maintained that race was becoming *more* significant, not less, and was having an increasingly damaging effect on the quality of life among blacks. Thomas and Hughes (1986) took Willie's position a step further by focusing on measures of psychological harm taken between 1972 and 1985 and found that "blacks have lower life satisfaction, less trust in people, less general happiness, less marital happiness, more anomie, and lower self-rated physical health than whites regardless of social class, marital status, age, or year" (p. 839) (see also Farley and Allen 1987).

Although blacks are the largest racial minority in the U.S., native Americans are in the worst position of all. Many of the roughly 1.5 million native Americans live on impoverished reservations where unemployment is six to seven times the national average, family income is far below even that of blacks, and alcohol abuse and suicide are major problems, especially among adolescents and young adults. The native American population as a whole, however, which includes those living outside of reservations, have average levels of educational attainment, unemployment, family income and poverty similar to those for blacks (Rose 1981; Snipp 1989; USCB 1990a).

Ethnic Differences   Clearly, race is an ascribed status that affects class membership. Nonwhites are heavily overrepresented in the lower class and virtually absent from the upper class. Ethnicity also affects class membership, although to a lesser degree than race. White Anglo-Saxon Protestants and Jews, for example, have higher average incomes, better jobs, and more education than do most other ethnic groups (see Farley and Neidert 1984).

Ethnicity played its strongest role in social stratification during the nineteenth and early twentieth centuries. Successive waves of immigrants were confined to the worst jobs and living conditions in urban ghettos. Mexicans were perceived as "aborigines" who were inferior to white Anglo-Saxons. Each new wave of immigrants, however, brought a fresh supply of poor people to occupy the bottom rung of the stratification ladder, and those who had come before were able to move upward, although only with considerable effort. Those whose culture was most similar to that of the dominant Anglo-Saxons—Germans and Scandinavians—were able to move upward with greater ease than those who were culturally more different, such as Catholic Irish, Poles, and other East Europeans.

Since then, ethnicity has become a relatively minor determinant of social class among whites (see Lieberson and Waters 1988; Neidert and Farley 1985). Nonwhite ethnics, however, continue to lag behind whites in average income. Among college graduates, average income among native Americans, Chinese, and Filipinos amount to only two-thirds of the average income for all college graduates; and Hispanic and Japanese earnings amount to roughly 85 percent of the national college-graduate average (Jencks 1983a; see also Farley and Neidert 1984).

In contrast with ethnicity, the legacy of racial prejudice and oppression persists largely because race is more visible, but also because nonwhites have a unique history in the U.S. Whites killed native Americans in vast numbers as they seized their land, and African-Americans were property to be bought and sold and used in any way their owners saw fit. As oppressed as ethnic minorities such as the Irish once were, they were never slaves, were never systematically slaughtered, and were never forced to abandon their cultural heritage. In addition, European minorities were able to improve themselves in part through the protections offered by government. Laws that protected the rights of workers, for example, were important aids to upward mobility that were largely denied to blacks until quite recently (see Smith 1987).

What prejudice there has been against European immigrants has been softened by the fact that it has been largely sporadic—there were many places where the Irish were not treated as a minority, for example—but prejudice against African-Americans and native Americans was universal and has lasted for generations.

> Discrimination only poses a serious barrier to economic success if it is almost universal, or if its existence transforms the victims' behavior in self-defeating ways. Discrimination against European minorities was common but never anything like universal. The descendants of European immigrants have almost all had the option of shedding their ethnic identity and "passing" as just plain "Americans." Physical differences, combined with extreme social sensitivity to the significance of these differences, made this much more difficult for most blacks and somewhat more difficult for Asians, American Indians, and even Latin Americans. (Jencks 1983a, p. 34)

As an ethnic group, Jews are an exception to these generalizations (see Johnson 1987). For centuries, they were not allowed to own land, were regarded by Christians as the embodiment of evil, and were periodically murdered in large numbers, culminating in the World War II Holocaust during which an estimated 6 million were murdered. A few, however, were allowed such financial pursuits as banking and

Jews in Nazi Germany and countries under Nazi control were regularly subjected to humiliation. In this rare 1933 photograph, a Jewish boy is forced to cut off his father's beard while German soldiers look on with contempt. As the Holocaust proceeded, Jews were forcibly segregated and deported by the millions, usually to their deaths by disease, starvation, torture, and mass execution by machine gun or in gas chambers.

tax collecting, for when banking first came into being, it was regarded as immoral, and tax collectors
were far from popular. Some Jews were middlemen
between the upper and lower classes. This allowed
the upper class to profit while avoiding the resentment of people in the lower class.

Through this, many Jews developed important
skills, and when banking and business became more
culturally respectable, they flourished. Because they
made the best of what was left to them, Jews have,
for centuries, been despised and envied. Their somewhat unique position is duplicated by some racial
and ethnic minorities in other societies, such as
Chinese merchants in Indonesia and Malaysia, and
Muslim merchants in eastern and southern Africa.

It is important to remember, however, that while
Jews have relatively high *average* education and income, most are in the middle and working classes.
The popular image of Jews as bankers is nothing more
than a stereotype. Jews are rarely found on the boards
of large corporations, including commercial banks
(Domhoff and Zweigenhaft 1983; Korman 1988).

Power

In caste societies such as South Africa and, until recently, India, power is sharply divided according to
race. The Indian constitution specified which castes
were eligible for benefits such as college scholarships,
welfare, and government jobs. South African blacks
are denied the vote in national elections and representation in the national parliament. They have not
been able to travel freely, conduct strikes against employers, or, until very recently, choose where they
will eat, work, live, or educate their children. Almost every aspect of life in South Africa was segregated by race—including public transportation, restaurants, beaches, residential neighborhoods, and
schools.

For much of their history in the U.S., the situation of blacks has been as bad as or worse than that of
today's South African blacks (Frederickson 1981).
Slavery flourished for 200 years before the Civil War,
and even "free Negroes" were denied the rights to
vote, testify in court, own land, or make contracts.
In spite of federal efforts after the Civil War, the late
1800s and early 1900s were a period in which African-Americans had little power to participate in
their society or to live in safety. In southern states,
Jim Crow laws restricted African-Americans in every
conceivable aspect of their lives. Literacy tests and
poll taxes prevented many from using newly won

voting rights, and they were "kept in their place" by
the terror of lynchings and church burnings.

In the last 20 years blacks have greatly increased
their collective power, largely by using the federal
courts to fight discrimination, registering as voters,
running for public office, and staging mass demonstrations. After the passage of the 1965 Voting Rights
Act, the registration of black voters in the South
more than doubled, and the percentages of whites
and blacks registered are now nearly equal. Between
1970 and 1989 the number of political offices held by
blacks increased from 1,479 to 7,190. Blacks have
become mayors of 300 cities including New York,
Philadelphia, Los Angeles, Atlanta, Washington,
D.C., Detroit, Cleveland, Baltimore, Seattle, and
New Orleans. Between 1962 and 1981 the number of
black federal and state legislators almost tripled
(USCB 1990a), and in 1988, Jesse Jackson became
the first black to come within striking distance of
being a major party's nominee for national office.

While such gains are important, power is still
disproportionately concentrated in the hands of
whites. Blacks comprise 12 percent of the U.S. population but hold only 1 percent of all public offices.
As of 1991, there were no blacks in the U.S. Senate,
and blacks made up only 6 percent of the House of
Representatives.

Nowhere is inequality of power between whites
and blacks more evident than in the criminal justice
system. Because blacks are more likely than whites
to be poor, they are more often unable to use bail in
order to stay out of jail during their trials; and numerous studies show that accused criminals are more
likely to be convicted if they are imprisoned during
their trials (Wice 1973). Once convicted, blacks
receive harsher sentences than whites—those who
murder whites, for example, receive far more severe
sentences than do those who murder blacks (Baldus 1987).

As with differences in income, ethnicity plays a
less important part than race in the distribution of
power. Major corporations and government bodies
such as the U.S. Congress are still dominated by
whites of Anglo-Saxon descent, but the ethnic lines
that once clearly defined elite groups are becoming
increasingly blurred (see Alba and Moore 1982).

Prestige and Self-Esteem

When we find ourselves in an achieved status, such
as occupation, that brings little respect from others,
we may suffer; but we may be able to increase our

standing by achieving a higher-level status. With ascribed statuses such as race and ethnicity, however, it is, by definition, impossible to change our status, unless we misrepresent ourselves.

Racism and ethnicism involve strong cultural values, attributing superior qualities to members of dominant groups and inferior qualities to those subordinate to them. Just as the relative ranking of occupations has remained quite constant, so, too, has the ranking of different ethnicities and races. Generations of whites have defined nonwhites as undesirable and inferior: light skin is better than black, yellow, brown, or red skin; wavy and straight hair is better than "wooly" hair. Generations of white Anglo-Saxon Protestants have defined those who do not speak English or who are non-Protestant as inferior and undesirable. The world, they believed, was reserved for those of "superior" ethnicity and race—for those like them (Hofstadter 1955).

Inevitably, the low value placed on minority groups is attached to individuals who must confront a fundamental problem: How do I perceive and value *myself* in a culture that thinks so little of me? If my life is bad, does that mean *I* am bad? As we grow up, we acquire social identities that define who we are in relation to other people, and an important part of our identities is self-esteem. We cannot define and evaluate ourselves without taking into account how we think others see and evaluate us—our looking-glass self. Culture provides mirrors in which we see images of ourselves that are difficult to reject. Minority status can be a stigma that carries with it the danger of leaving individuals with "spoiled identities" (Goffman 1963b). As Kenneth Clark (1965) wrote:

> Human beings . . . whose daily experience tells them that almost nowhere in society are they respected and granted the ordinary dignity and courtesy accorded to others, will, as a matter of course, begin to doubt their self-worth. . . . These doubts become the seeds of pernicious self- and group-hatred. (p. 64)

When Robert Coles (1968) observed the first black children to attend integrated schools in the South, he found that the hatred directed toward them and their families strongly affected how they saw themselves. When one black girl—Ruby—drew pictures,

> she drew white people large and more lifelike. Negroes were smaller, their bodies less intact. A white girl we both knew to be her own size appeared several times taller. While Ruby's own face lacked an eye in one drawing, an ear in another, the white girl never lacked any features. (p. 47)

More recent studies suggest that the negative effects of racial stereotypes on self-esteem have grown weaker since the civil rights movement of the 1960s, during which many blacks participated in a collective reevaluation of blackness (see Hughes and Demo 1989). For centuries, blacks had been named by others—niggers, coloreds, and then Negroes; but in the 1960s, blacks aggressively insisted on naming themselves and establishing their own value as people. When they adopted the label "black," they intended to create a cultural category free of associations with slavery and oppression. Many blacks now argue that "African-American" is preferable to "black" because by focusing on cultural background more than race it promotes a stronger sense of social identity and, with it, greater self-esteem.

Black gains in self-esteem have been won in *spite* of a culture that still often places a relatively low value on them. Unlike whites, blacks and other minorities must continually maintain levels of pride and self-esteem that are contrary to the evaluation of

In the 1988 U.S. presidential race, Jesse Jackson stunned political experts with his ability to win not only the overwhelming support of black voters, but an unprecedented number of white voters as well. He is the first black in U.S. history to emerge as a serious contender for the nomination of a major party.

those who dominate their society. What whites can take for granted—the relatively high standing of their race—is, for blacks, a daily struggle against a waning, but still formidable, tide of prejudice.

Minorities and Social Mobility

As we saw in Chapter 12, social mobility is very limited for most people in the U.S. Many ethnic groups have shared in this limited progress (Farley and Neidert 1984; Neidert and Farley 1985) as well as racial groups such as Asian-Americans (Duleep 1988), but until quite recently, nonwhite minorities have not.

Since 1959 the percentage of blacks living below the poverty level has dropped from 55 to 32 percent, and the average income of black families (taking inflation into account) has increased by 60 percent. The percentage of blacks working in professional and technical jobs has tripled, and the percentage in managerial positions has doubled (USCB 1980b, 1986a, 1990a). What these numbers miss is the fact that the position of blacks *relative* to whites has not improved greatly, especially since 1970. This is primarily because while black standards of living have risen, so have those for whites. In 1959 blacks were three times more likely than whites to live in poverty. By 1988—26 years later—blacks were still three times as likely to live in poverty (USCB 1980b, 1990a).

By many measures, the relative position of blacks has scarcely improved (see Farley and Allen 1987; Landry 1987; National Research Council 1989). In 1970 blacks received a share of national income equal to 57 percent of what they would receive if income were distributed equally; by 1988 they received 61 percent. The average black family's income in 1950 was 54 percent of the white average, and by 1988 it had only risen to 57 percent (USCB 1981b, 1990a). Undoubtedly, some blacks have made impressive gains; but, after more than 20 years of mass protest and federal programs to remove the disadvantages of race, the vast majority of blacks have barely improved their relative standing. Why is mobility so much more difficult for blacks, and why does it have so little effect on the distribution of income?

Harrington (1963) maintained that blacks stay poor because

> they made the mistake of being born to the wrong parents. . . . Poverty breeds poverty. . . . Poor parents cannot give their children the opportunities for better

health and education needed to improve their lot. Lack of motivation, hope, and incentive is a more subtle but not less powerful barrier than lack of financial means. Thus the cruel legacy of poverty is passed from parents to children. (p. 21)

In other words, blacks inherit the disadvantages of *poverty* from their parents. Duncan (1969) and others (Blau and Duncan 1967; Jencks et al. 1972) have argued, however, that the inheritance of *race* is the crucial factor that distinguishes blacks from others (see also Pomer 1986). Even when we compare blacks and whites whose fathers had similar occupations, educations, and who came from the families of the same size, blacks have jobs considerably below those of whites. Even blacks who enter the same occupations as whites, with equal education levels, have incomes that average only 63 percent of white incomes (Jencks et al. 1972; see also NCPE 1987).

In some ways, the slow progress of blacks in the U.S. illustrates the power of prejudice to act as a self-fulfilling prophecy, for the position of minorities is often exactly what cultural stereotypes predict. For centuries, the dominant white culture has defined blacks as childlike, inferior beings with no use for education. The prophecies inherent in racism came true for many blacks because, as a result of racism, they were denied access to education and decent jobs. They were not allowed to vote and were excluded from juries. Perhaps most important, generations of blacks were taught by experience that, regardless of ability, ambition, or effort, they were unlikely to escape poverty and the stigma of their race.

The social oppression of minorities rests on cultural beliefs, values, norms, and attitudes that, in turn, are reflected in relationships among groups and individuals. Oppression, however, depends not only on the characteristics of social environments, but also on *ecology*—the relationship between populations and their physical environments.

THE SOCIAL ECOLOGY OF OPPRESSION

Social oppression is often connected to the nature of physical environments and the ways in which societies make use of them to produce goods. Slavery, for example, is relatively rare in gatherer-hunter and horticultural societies in part because without the technological ability to produce a surplus, there is little to be gained by the use of forced labor (see Lenski and Lenski 1987). Slaves were first brought to America in response to a labor shortage. Slavery was most profitable in colonies that had warm climates and fertile land—Maryland, Virginia, and South Carolina—and was, therefore, uncommon in New England. In the early 1800s, aided by Eli Whitney's cotton gin, cotton production jumped enormously, as did the demand for slaves, whose numbers rose from fewer than 1 million in 1800 to almost 4 million by 1860 (USCB 1918). The Industrial Revolution mechanized agriculture and created masses of unemployed farmers and farm workers, while at the same time creating an enormous demand for cheap industrial labor. This led to exploitation of European immigrants from Ireland, Germany, and Poland.

While technology often facilitates social oppression, it can also have the opposite effect. When agriculture in the South was mechanized early in this century, the demand for farm labor dropped sharply and blacks migrated to cities in great numbers. The conditions blacks found in the North were in many ways little better than those they left behind, with low wages, too few jobs, and poor working and living conditions (Marks 1989). What progress blacks have made since then, however, is probably due largely to their migration from rural to urban areas, for it was in cities that they eventually found new opportunities for employment in industry and a less-racist social environment.

Segregation: The Social Uses of Physical Space

Most U.S. cities are **segregated** in that people who differ in occupation, education, race, ethnicity, and income tend to live in different neighborhoods. In general, the farther apart people are in racial status or social class, the greater is the physical separation of their homes. This simple ecological observation has profound social implications. Physical segregation heightens awareness of status differences by associating social characteristics with specific communities or neighborhoods. This, in turn, reinforces stereotypes by making it unlikely that members of different groups will experience each other directly. The physical segregation of minorities also reinforces their disadvantaged social and economic position, especially for blacks (Massey and Denton 1985; Massey and Eggers 1990). Massey (1990), for example, shows that when poverty increases among minority

populations in cities, poverty becomes more concentrated in the form of increased neighborhood segregation. This, in turn, leads to further deterioration of living conditions in minority neighborhoods and the growth of a black underclass.

Next to native Americans, blacks are the most highly segregated minority in the U.S., particularly in the large urban areas in which most blacks now live (Massey and Denton 1988, 1989). In 1980, the most segregated cities were Chicago, Cleveland, and St. Louis, in which *90 percent* or more of all residents would have to move in order for each neighborhood to reflect the racial composition of the cities as a whole. In most other major cities, at least 75 percent would have to move in order to achieve integration (Taeuber in Farley 1984, p. 35; see also Massey and Denton 1987). In general, Asian and Hispanic Americans are far less segregated from whites—with the exception of Puerto Ricans, whose rates of segregation are similar to those of blacks (Massey 1981b). Hispanics of Caribbean origin, however, are segregated both by race and ethnicity. Hispanics whose racial characteristics fall somewhere between black and white, for example, are not highly segregated from white Hispanics, but are highly segregated from both black Hispanics and non-Hispanic blacks, as well as from non-Hispanic whites (Denton and Massey 1989).

In general, the degree of segregation falls as socioeconomic status increases for all white ethnic groups as well as for Asian-Americans and most Hispanics. For blacks, however, segregation remains at a high level regardless of socioeconomic status (Denton and Massey 1988).

What Causes Neighborhood Segregation? As Farley and his colleagues (1978) suggest, many cities are well on their way to becoming what a popular song described as "chocolate cities with vanilla suburbs" (Malbix/Ricks Music, BMI 1976). How do we explain this trend?

The most common explanations are that blacks cannot afford to live in white neighborhoods and prefer all-black neighborhoods, and that whites resist the entry of blacks into their neighborhoods, move out when blacks move in, and will not move to integrated neighborhoods. Numerous studies (summarized in Farley et al. 1978) show, however, that residential segregation increased in Detroit in spite of black economic gains; and in national studies, blacks increasingly express a preference for integrated neighborhoods. In Farley's Detroit study, 83 percent of blacks preferred integrated neighborhoods.

What of white resistance to integration? Most studies ask whites if they would be upset if blacks of similar economic status moved into their neighborhoods, and most whites in national samples say they would not be upset. What, then, is going on?

Farley and his co-researchers tested two additional explanations of segregation in Detroit. First, they tested the hypothesis that blacks overestimate the cost of housing in white neighborhoods or differ from whites in their evaluation of the relative attractiveness of different neighborhoods. Second, they used a new measure of attitudes toward integration, for they suspected that the "black on your block" question was too general because it failed to confront whites with specific residential possibilities. Their findings show clearly that whites and blacks accurately perceive the cost of housing in different areas and share views of which areas are the most attractive to live in. In addition, while blacks report a strong preference for integrated neighborhoods, whites generally believe that blacks want to "stick to their own kind." In other words, whites seriously underestimate blacks' preference for integration.

Apparently, this misperception reinforces the reluctance of whites to share neighborhoods with blacks, for Farley's most important finding is that whites do not want to live in integrated neighborhoods. Rather than ask whites if they would mind living near a black family of similar economic status, Farley presented them with diagrams that showed different neighborhood mixes of black and white families. The diagrams showed 15 houses colored white or black with the center house labeled "your house." Hypothetical neighborhoods ranged from all white to just over half black (8 out of 15 houses).

Whereas in most surveys a majority of whites say they would not mind living near blacks, Farley's results tell a very different story (Table 13-3). As the hypothetical neighborhoods become increasingly black, the reported discomfort of whites, their desire to move out, and their reluctance to move in all rise sharply (see also Schuman and Bob 1988).

If Detroit is typical of U.S. cities, Farley's results offer little hope that segregation in housing will ease in the near future. Blacks will continue to find themselves excluded from many neighborhoods by real estate renters, sellers, and agents (National Research Council 1989). While better-educated whites tend

TABLE 13-3   White Responses to Racial Integration Possibilities (Detroit)

PROPORTION OF WHITE RESPONDENTS WHO WOULD:	HYPOTHETICAL NEIGHBORHOODS: PERCENTAGE OF FAMILIES THAT ARE BLACK			
	14	20	33	53
Feel uncomfortable in the neighborhood	24	42	57	72
Try to move out of the neighborhood	7	24	41	64
Would not move into such a neighborhood	27	50	73	84

Source: Farley et al. 1978, Figure 7.

to be more tolerant of integration, the differences between the least and most educated are small. Higher-*income* whites, however, are *less* tolerant of racial integration than are lower-income whites, while higher-income blacks are *more* likely to accept integrated neighborhoods than are lower-income blacks (Farley et al. 1978). Racially segregated housing, complete with its negative effects on black people, is likely to remain for some time to come (see Farley and Allen 1987).

Segregated Schools and Living with Contradictions   There are two basic causes of school segregation. ***De jure*** segregation is required by law, a type of segregation found in southern states until the 1954 Supreme Court decision outlawed separate schools. ***De facto*** segregation results from other causes—from whites refusing to move into nonwhite neighborhoods, for example, or refusing to sell or rent their houses to nonwhites. De facto school segregation is caused by residential segregation: children live in segregated neighborhoods and, since they attend neighborhood schools, their schools are segregated, as well. Roughly half of all public school students would have to change schools in order to make the racial composition of schools match that of the entire U.S. population. In Chicago, 90 percent would have to move, and in most other major cities the percentages amount to two-thirds or more (Farley 1984).

School segregation denies white and black children the opportunity to know one another and negatively affects the educational careers of black children. Blacks who attend segregated schools are less likely to finish high school, attend college, and secure white-collar jobs than are blacks who attend integrated schools (Crain 1975). Racial segregation also affects whites, for those who attend integrated schools are least likely to prefer all-white classes and all-white friends (Coleman et al. 1966; see also Hallinan and Williams 1989). White adults who attend integrated schools are also more willing to live in integrated neighborhoods, have their children attend integrated schools, and have black friends (U.S. Commission on Civil Rights 1967).

Residential and school segregation illustrate a basic contradiction in U.S. culture, for while most whites say they do not object to living in integrated neighborhoods, most reverse their position when they are presented with specific integration possibilities. A similar reversal occurs with school segregation. Eighty-one percent of whites say they would not object to their children attending a school whose student body was half black; and yet, 61 percent oppose the busing of black and white students from one school district to another and 40 percent support the right of whites to deliberately exclude blacks from their neighborhoods by refusing to sell their houses to them (GSS 1990).

These contradictions illustrate that individuals may support general cultural values and yet violate them when they believe their interests are threatened. Many people are what Merton (1948) called "Fair-Weather Liberals," who support the "American creed" until it threatens them personally. We value equality and fairness, but we also live with a centuries-old legacy of racism and value the right of individuals to control basic aspects of their lives, including who will live near them and where their children will go to school. These are deep contradictions that will not be resolved easily or quickly.

Population and Minorities

In the simplest sense, superior numbers make it easier for one group to oppress another. In the late 1800s and early 1900s, for example, many prominent people in the U.S. worried that relatively high rates of population growth among nonwhite peoples of the world (including the U.S.) would soon make it difficult for whites to maintain their dominant position (Hofstadter 1955). As we near the twenty-first cen-

tury, Census Bureau projections suggest that this is becoming an ever more likely reality. By 2040, for example, whites will constitute an estimated 62 percent of the U.S. population, down from 76 percent in 1990. At the same time, the black population is expected to increase to 15 percent, and the Asian, Pacific Islander, and native Americans population is expected to increase to 8 percent (USCB 1989a, 1991a).

In some cases, those who dominate a society try to control the size and growth of minority populations. The most extreme form of this is **genocide**, the deliberate attempt to annihilate an entire racial or ethnic group (see Kuper 1977, 1982, 1985, 1989). The most brutal was the Nazi Holocaust during World War II (see Dawidowicz 1975; Gilbert 1986), but there are other examples. The early Hebrews tried unsuccessfully to exterminate the Canaanites; entire tribes of native Americans were all but annihilated during the nineteenth century; between 1917 and 1919, Turks massacred over a million Armenians (Dadrian 1971); and massacres have plagued many newly independent African states (Kuper 1977). In a single attack in 1983, 600 Moslems were slain by Hindus in the rural area of Assam, India (Hazarika 1983).

A less extreme form of population control is **expulsion**—forcing an entire racial or ethnic population to move. In 1830, the Indian Removal Act forced thousands of native Americans of different

Robert Lidneux's painting, *Trail of Tears*, portrays the brutal 1838 forced migration of some 16,000 Cherokee Indians, during which more than 4,000 died.

tribes in the Southeast to move west of the Mississippi, primarily to allow whites to seize their tribal lands. During their long forced marches—often covering thousands of miles—some tribes lost as many as 40 percent of their people to disease and starvation (Larkin 1988).

After the Japanese attacked Pearl Harbor in 1941, 77 thousand U.S. citizens of Japanese descent were confined to relocation camps for the duration of the war. They were loyal citizens, many of whose sons fought in Europe as members of an all-Japanese unit that earned more battle decorations than any other in the U.S. Army. Nonetheless, they were removed from their homes and effectively imprisoned simply because of their ancestry, while U.S. citizens of German and Italian descent—culturally and racially more similar to the dominant Anglo-Saxons—retained their full rights as citizens. It was not until 1983 that U.S. courts awarded financial compensation to those who were interned (Irons 1983).

We come now to the central problem in understanding oppression and prejudice—why do they exist at all?

UNDERSTANDING SOCIAL OPPRESSION

The conflict, functional, and interactionist perspectives can be used to understand the mistreatment of minorities. A conflict perspective focuses on competition and the ability of some groups to exploit others, while a functional view identifies the consequences of oppression for social systems. An interactionist perspective focuses on oppression as it is acted out in everyday life.

A Conflict Perspective

There is historical evidence that prejudice and discrimination are most likely to occur when there is intense competition over scarce resources and rewards. In Hawaii and on the U.S. West Coast, for example, there was little open prejudice against Japanese until whites and Japanese competed for the same jobs; and the economic success of Chinese in Southeast Asia preceded sharp rises in prejudice against them. In the 1990s, many countries in Western Europe depend heavily on foreign workers and have larger foreign-born populations than the U.S. In France, West Germany, Britain, and the Netherlands there have been increasing pressures to expel foreign workers in order to decrease competition for jobs.

In the U.S., lower-class whites are more likely to express racist attitudes than are higher-class whites, which is consistent with a competition explanation of discrimination. Until recently, many white-dominated labor unions resisted increases in black membership, in part because unemployment was already a problem for white members. Large unions—the AFL-CIO—however, are now among the most integrated of all organizations.

The openness of large labor unions to minorities suggests that prejudice is not simply a result of competition, for we need to remember that competition among the lower classes is caused in large part by the fact that the upper classes take a disproportionately large share of wealth and income. The scarcity of rewards in the lower classes is, itself, a product of a class system.

To Marx, the most important aspect of capitalist societies is the division between those who own the means of production and those who do not. From this perspective, racial and ethnic prejudice benefit the capitalist class (Reich 1981). The existence of minorities provides a continuing source of cheap labor, for "inferior" people cannot demand high wages. Prejudice against minorities also divides the working class by setting workers of different ethnicity and race against one another. This perpetuates inequality through false consciousness and interfering with solidarity within the working class: rather than blame the upper class or the class system itself, lower-class groups blame each other. As Lipset and Bendix (1959) put it:

> A real social and economic cleavage is created by widespread discrimination against minority groups, and this diminishes the chances for the development of solidarity along class lines. . . . This continued splintering of the working class is a major element in the preservation and the stability of the class structure. (pp. 105–106)

During the first third of this century, few blacks belonged to unions, and white employers actively recruited blacks as strikebreakers to take the place of striking union workers (Griffin et al. 1986). This intensified racism among working-class whites and, until blacks were actively recruited as union members, divided the working class along racial lines.

To Marx, prejudice and exploitation are inevitable in class societies—whether the targets are defined by race, ethnicity, or gender. Oppression main-

In 1987, hundreds of KKK members gathered in Forsyth County, Georgia, to harass protestors objecting to the exclusion of blacks in a white community. Membership in the KKK is overwhelmingly lower and working class.

tains upper-class privilege and the class system. It also encourages members of lower classes to vent their anger and frustration on relatively safe—and undeserving—targets by using minorities as scapegoats.

In the ancient Roman Empire, Christians were "thrown to the lions" whenever disaster struck. When Christianity became the dominant religion, Jews replaced Christians as scapegoats, and when plagues ravaged Europe during the fourteenth century, Jews were blamed and hundreds of their communities were wiped out. The ruling class often used Jews as tax collectors, making them convenient targets for the dissatisfaction of those whose taxes supported the wealthy. During the Great Depression of the 1930s, Hitler used Jews and Communists as scapegoats on which Germans could blame all their political and economic troubles (Dawidowicz 1975; Johnson 1987). Similarly, as revolutionary movements spread throughout the socialist countries of Central Europe in 1989, Romanian officials were quick to blame the nation's troubles on a "plague" of gypsies described as parasites and anarchists. As a result, many gypsies were attacked, denied the right to vote, and driven from their communities.

In nineteenth-century America, Irish immigrants were blamed for crime, poverty, and political corruption. When they became established, prejudice was turned against other ethnic and racial groups—Germans, Polish Catholics, Chinese, and Japanese. During the Depression in the 1930s, anti-Semitism grew sharply (Strong 1941). After World War II, veterans who felt they had received bad breaks in the

army were more likely than others to report anti-Semitic attitudes (Bettelheim and Janowitz 1950). Campbell (1947) found that people who report themselves as being dissatisfied with economic and political conditions are almost three times more likely than satisfied people to express dislike for Jews, avoid them, or show hostility toward them. Whites who are dissatisfied with community services and local government are more likely than others to express hostile attitudes toward blacks (Campbell 1971). Hispanics, blacks, and Asian refugees are the current scapegoats on which many blame urban decay, the increasing burden of welfare demands, unemployment, disorder in schools, and crime.

Social oppression is connected to both competition for scarce rewards and class inequality, and from this perspective it is easier to understand why prejudice is more often expressed by lower-class people (Adorno et al. 1950; Selznick and Steinberg 1969). The upper class can *afford* to appear liberal and unprejudiced because minority gains pose no threat to them (Kerbo 1991). In the lower class, however, people are more vulnerable to unemployment and a loss of prestige and income; and, because they depend on the upper class for their jobs, they are more likely to vent their anger and frustration on people who are less powerful than they.

A Functionalist Perspective

A functionalist perspective draws attention to the ways in which social oppression is made an integrated part of social systems, producing both functional and dysfunctional consequences. In the simplest sense, for example, racial and ethnic distinctions are used to define social boundaries and establish cultural identities with or without accompanying feelings of superiority. In eighteenth- and nineteenth-century America, stereotypes about immigrants contributed to social cohesion among Anglo-Saxons by heightening awareness of ethnic differences and devaluing non-Anglo-Saxons. Similar patterns may be found in many social systems in which "foreigners" and other "outsiders" serve as reminders of the distinctive qualities attributed to being "natives" and "insiders."

The various aspects of social oppression are integrated into social systems in other ways as well. Slavery, for example, has played an important economic part in numerous societies, as has the exploitation of cheap immigrant workers. Oppression ensures that undesirable jobs will get done by providing a continuing supply of people who are so downtrodden that they may have few alternatives to performing tasks that are poorly rewarded in every respect. Without the effects of social oppression, however, the prices of many consumer goods—from fruits and vegetables to ready-made clothing—would be considerably higher than they are.

Of paramount importance in any functional analysis of social oppression, of course, are the dysfunctional consequences it produces both for social systems and the people who participate in them. Oppression condemns millions of people to lives of deprivation, frustration, fear, and injury. It contributes to resentment, hostility, and suspicion. It denies people the opportunity to develop fully and use their abilities, not only depriving social systems of the full range of talents available in their populations, but also contributing to a wide range of social problems, from violence and community decay to drug abuse and growing welfare roles.

The functional perspective is important because it makes it easier to understand why social oppression is so difficult to end, for it is not ethnic and racial groups that are the problem. The problem is their exploitation and mistreatment that have become an enduring part of social systems. This means that the elimination of prejudice, discrimination, and oppression involves more than changes in attitudes and behavior, for these problems are deeply embedded in the arrangements that make up social life.

An Interactionist Perspective

Functionalist and conflict understandings of the causes and consequences of prejudice and discrimination are incomplete without an awareness of the ways in which relations among and between minority and dominant groups are played out through the social interactions of everyday life. It is, after all, individuals who feel and act upon prejudiced attitudes and feel their effects, and in so doing create the human reality of social oppression. It is individuals who use cultural definitions to identify racial differences between themselves and others, or who, upon hearing the way someone speaks, make assumptions about them based on ethnic stereotypes.

Whereas prejudice is an attitude, **discrimination** refers to unequal *treatment* of people based on stereotypes. Expectations and feelings during interactions depend on how people define social situations, and this, in turn, depends on how they perceive other people. When we see people dressed in police uniforms, we immediately act and feel as though we have significant information about them. In the same way, when we identify people's race or ethnicity, we draw upon cultural ideas that identify how we should behave, what we should expect of them, and how we feel toward them.

Discrimination can take obvious forms, such as denying someone a job, promotion, or equal pay, shouting racial or ethnic slurs, or physically assaulting someone. Discrimination can also take more subtle forms, especially among those higher up in the social class system where outward expressions of prejudice are more likely to meet with social disapproval. When middle-class blacks go to restaurants or shopping malls, for example, they often feel the effects of racism by people's behavior—when they are seated at noisy tables next to the kitchen door, for example, or are followed around stores as though they were about to steal merchandise. On the street, black men are often avoided by whites as if all black men are dangerous. In all such cases, whites are often unaware that they are behaving in a discriminatory way, and yet the effects on blacks are damaging nonetheless (see Feagin 1991).

Prejudice differs from discrimination in the same way that our beliefs about people differ from what we *do* in relation to them. In this sense, our behavior and attitudes may often contradict each other. Some members of dominant groups are not prejudiced and do not discriminate against minorities, while other unprejudiced people may nonetheless discriminate against minorities when it is expedient or profitable to do so. Prejudice does not necessarily result in discriminatory behavior. Our culture strongly values equality for all, and both prejudice and discrimination are against the "American creed." Prejudiced people are under pressure to conceal their prejudice, and for this reason some people are what Merton (1948) called "timid bigots."

Regardless of our attitudes, whether or not we *act* on them depends strongly on the social situation. It is far easier for people to discriminate over a telephone or through the mail than it is when they are face-to-face with the person who will be hurt by discriminatory behavior. It is also easier to discriminate in secondary relationships ("It's nothing personal"), because people can then claim that they are simply following rules formulated and enforced by others. In this way, they are able to conceal their own motives, which may or may not rest on prejudiced attitudes.

Social interaction is an important arena in which the attitudes of racism and ethnicism are played out to the benefit of dominant groups and at the expense of minorities. It is here, on the smallest level, that cultural ideas about race and ethnicity become visible in social relationships.

SOCIAL CHANGE: ENDING PREJUDICE AND OPPRESSION

As we have seen, oppression has three major sociological aspects: prejudice (culture), discrimination and inequality (social structure), and population control and segregation (ecology). What are the prospects for change in each of these areas?

Cultural Change: Reducing Prejudice

One way to reduce prejudice is by attacking its cultural legitimacy. Racial and ethnic prejudice run deep in U.S. culture; and yet, at the same time, there are strong values on equality, fairness, equal opportunity, and freedom from oppression. It is a culture that pulls us in opposite directions; and as Myrdal (1945) wrote in his classic analysis, *An American Dilemma*, the resulting strain would make social change inevitable.

One of the major accomplishments of the U.S. civil rights movement of the 1960s, for example, was that it forced many people to confront serious cultural contradictions. As Myrdal predicted, Martin Luther King, Jr., and other civil rights activists used one part of U.S. culture—beliefs and values about equality—to attack another—racial prejudice. This is a particularly effective method of bringing about

Much of the progress made by blacks has been due to the willingness of civil rights supporters to risk their lives in order to confront the white power structure. In 1965, when 600 marchers left Selma, Alabama as part of a drive to increase black voter registration, they were attacked by police using dogs and tear gas. When the march resumed, it was joined by volunteers from around the country; and by the time it reached Montgomery, the state capitol, its ranks had swelled to an estimated 25,000 people.

Bloom County / By BERKE BREATHED

© 1989, Washington Post Writers Group. Reprinted with permission.

social change, for it makes people confront uncomfortable contradictions between what they envision as their *ideal* culture and the cultural ideas they actually live by.

As prejudice is exposed and becomes unacceptable, however, people often respond merely by withholding expressions of prejudice or by expressing it in less visible ways (see Wilson 1987). Surveys show a steady decline in outward expressions of racial and ethnic prejudice in the U.S., especially in the South (Firebaugh and Davis 1988). This does not prove, however, that prejudice itself is declining (Dovidio and Gaertner 1986). Recent evidence suggests that while most people favor equality in principle, for example, they do not support concrete changes and programs that might actually do something to bring it about (Schuman, Steeh, and Bob 1985). This is an important distinction, because if prejudice remains strong while its outward expression declines under social pressure, it can quickly reemerge under less restrained conditions. This may help to explain why in the last several years there has been a dramatic increase in the number of racial incidents on more than 100 U.S. college campuses, ranging from top private schools such as Brown and Stanford to major public universities such as Michigan, Wisconsin, and Arizona State (see Carnegie 1990).

A second approach to reducing prejudice is to change people's perceptions of minorities, which involves the destruction of stereotypes as bases for people's knowledge about one another.

Changing Perceptions of Minority Groups
Because prejudice focuses on differences between groups, one solution is for minorities to assimilate—to change their culture so they conform to the dominant culture. When Hispanics or Asians adopt English as their primary language, for example, or when Jews change their names, they may become more acceptable and less visible as members of a minority (my great grandfather emigrated from Norway to the U.S. and changed his name from Mokestaad to Johnson in order to fit in). Many immigrants avoid prejudice by replacing ethnic customs, styles of dress, and modes of speech with those favored by dominant ethnic groups.

The problem with this solution is that it requires minorities to surrender unique cultural identities, which can be yet another form of oppression. In addition, while assimilation can reduce ethnic prejudice, it is largely ineffective for reducing racism, since race is much more difficult to conceal. How, then, can minorities keep their unique cultural identities and free themselves from negative stereotypes and prejudice?

We use stereotypes as substitutes for direct experience and knowledge of people. They distort reality by leading us to overestimate differences between groups, to underestimate the amount of variation within them, and to apply general descriptions of entire groups or social categories to all individuals within them (see One Step Further 13-2). It is easiest to maintain stereotypes if we avoid evidence that contradicts them. One way to do this is to avoid interacting with people of different races or ethnicities, so there is no opportunity to compare stereotypes with the actual people those stereotypes describe. So long as we are isolated from one another, we can make up our own explanations for people's behavior without ever taking their point of view into account.

ONE STEP FURTHER 13-2

Perceptions of Race, Ethnicity, and Religion

Cultures include beliefs about categories of people who differ on characteristics such as race, ethnicity, and religion. Table B-13-2 shows percentages of U.S. white and nonwhite adults who attribute various characteristics and experiences to whites, Jews, blacks, Asian-Americans, and Hispanics. The top row, for example, shows how white respondents view wealth and poverty in these groups: 37 percent believe that whites tend to be more rich than poor; 62 percent believe Jews tend to be more rich than poor; only 4 percent believe blacks tend to be more rich than poor, and so on. The second row gives comparable figures for nonwhite respondents.

As you study this table, ask yourself some critical questions: Which of these perceptions do you share and which do you not share, and why? What is the basis for such beliefs? How are they connected to one another? How do they affect the standing of these various groups in the stratification system? How would you explain racial differences in perceptions?

TABLE B-13-2   Perceptions of Whites, Jews, Blacks, Asian-Americans, and Hispanics, by Respondent's Race

Percent who believe people in these groups tend to	WHITES	JEWS	BLACKS	ASIAN-AMERICANS	HISPANICS
Be more rich than poor					
Whites	37	62	4	22	6
Nonwhites	53	58	6	24	9
Be more hard-working than lazy					
Whites	55	66	17	47	24
Nonwhites	42	59	33	42	27
Be more violent than nonviolent					
Whites	16	10	51	17	38
Nonwhites	28	15	43	25	39
Be more intelligent than unintelligent					
Whites	55	59	20	37	18
Nonwhites	53	53	37	43	35
Be more self-supporting than dependent on welfare					
Whites	71	76	13	41	18
Nonwhites	62	69	16	36	22
Be more patriotic than unpatriotic					
Whites	72	54	40	33	39
Nonwhites	68	46	41	36	36
Have too little political influence					
Whites	6	12	42	35	42
Nonwhites	2	17	68	44	57
Be hurt a lot by job discrimination					
Whites	*	*	25	10	19
Nonwhites	*	*	48	15	35
Be hurt a lot by housing discrimination					
Whites	*	*	31	11	16
Nonwhites	*	*	44	12	30

*Questions not asked in reference to whites and Jews.

Source: Computed from 1990 General Social Survey data.

This suggests that we can reduce prejudice by structuring social systems so that people have more opportunities to experience and learn about diverse cultures and see others as unique individuals rather than through the distorting lens of stereotypes. Many studies support the idea that increased interaction and an increase in knowledge of cultural diversity reduce prejudice (Case, Greeley, and Fuchs 1989; Miller and Brewer 1984). A simple increase in interaction does not guarantee an end to prejudice, however (blacks and whites interacted with each other for several hundred years in the American South without decreasing the level of racism). Interaction is most likely to reduce prejudice when people: (1) occupy the same status (such as co-workers); (2) share common goals (as in problem-solving groups); (3) can achieve their goals only by working together (as in athletic teams and military units); and (4) have the support of authorities (Allport 1954; Gaertner 1989).

The reduction of prejudice through interaction illustrates how cultural, structural, and ecological factors affect one another. New ecological arrangements (such as integration of schools, workplaces, or neighborhoods) produce structural change (more interaction) that, in turn, often reduces prejudice (a cultural attitude). The 1954 Supreme Court decision to integrate public schools attacked racism by creating ecological arrangements and patterns of interaction that made it more difficult to maintain stereotypes. Other structural changes—putting people of different races or ethnicities in similar statuses in which they must depend on one another for the achievement of common goals—also affect how people value, feel and think about, and behave toward others.

Structural Change: Reducing Inequality

Over the last several decades, expressions of racial and ethnic prejudice seem to have declined in the U.S., and many whites infer from this that blacks are no longer oppressed. In 1977, roughly 60 percent of whites reported the belief that blacks receive equal treatment when applying for housing and white-collar jobs, or when dealing with police; and 68 percent reported the belief that blacks are treated equally when they apply for skilled-labor jobs. Blacks, however, reported very different perceptions. Less than a quarter said they receive equal treatment in the economy, housing, and by police (Harris 1977). In more recent studies, blacks are far more likely than whites to perceive the police and courts as unfair (Hagan and Abonnetti 1982) and to see blacks as victims of job and housing discrimination (see One Step Further 13-2). In short, whites are far more likely than blacks to believe that race is no longer an important factor in social stratification.

There is little question that some segments of the black population have made considerable gains over the last 20 years, especially those who are young, married, and well educated; but, in general, the relative standing of blacks has improved very little, and there is considerable evidence that a large black underclass is being left behind in conditions of desperate poverty, especially in large cities (Farley 1980; National Research Council 1989; Wilson 1987). During the 1970s, the earnings gap between white and black *workers* decreased slightly. The gap between white and black *families*, however, did not change at all, and actually increased in the 1980s (Commission on Minority Participation 1988; USCB 1990a). How could this happen?

Part of the answer is that for blacks and whites single-parent families headed by women became increasingly common during the 1970s and 1980s, and such families have lower average incomes than two-parent families. Because this trend was stronger among blacks than among whites, black gains in the labor market were offset by changes in family structure (Farley 1980, 1984). Wilson (1987) argues that the strong trend toward single-parent families among blacks is itself due in part to the terrible job prospects for young black males.

In spite of black gains in occupational status, an enormous racial gap remains, and while employed blacks have made some progress, even they are vulnerable, for when unemployment increases, blacks are among the first to be laid off. Each year since 1947, unemployment rates have been twice as great among nonwhites as among whites. Compared with whites, unemployment rates are twice as high among blacks and Hispanics (USCB 1990a). In the late 1980s, corporate mergers and acquisitions resulted in the loss of many managerial positions. Blacks were far more likely than whites to be affected, therefore undoing many of the gains of the 1970s and early 1980s (*New York Times*, January 4, 1987, Section 3).

It is important to point out that the progress made by blacks came about only with the assistance of the federal government and a decade of mass protests and riots in cities such as Los Angeles, Detroit, and

Washington, D.C. (McAdam 1982). R. B. Freeman (1975) showed the close relationship between black progress and antidiscrimination activities of federal agencies such as the Equal Employment Opportunity Commission. The likelihood that companies would hire blacks was directly related to the amount of pressure applied by the federal government, as were changes in discriminatory hiring, firing, and promotion practices.

The most controversial attempt to eliminate economic inequality is affirmative action, the practice of giving minorities preferential treatment when they apply for jobs or college. Opponents argue that it is "reverse discrimination"—progress for minorities at the expense of others. Our culture, they argue, values ability as the main consideration in distributing resources and rewards, and affirmative action violates this important value.

Supporters of affirmative action point out that variations in individual ability have relatively little to do with patterns of social inequality (see Chapter 12). In addition, the ability argument ignores the cumulative effect of centuries of oppression, because it assumes that blacks and whites are now in equally strong positions to compete. It is not enough to say, "From now on, everyone has an equal chance," when history has left blacks with relatively low levels of education, training, and job experience.

While affirmative action programs have helped some blacks who are highly skilled, well educated, or who have long, steady work histories, in some ways it has hurt blacks by reinforcing prejudice: the mere existence of a double standard reinforces the belief that blacks are inferior to whites. As Jencks (1983b) points out, when colleges recruit blacks whose average preparation for college is weaker than the average white's, it reinforces perceptions that "blacks just aren't very bright":

> The logic is precisely the same as the logic that convinces students and faculty that athletes, who are also admitted even if they are academically unpromising, aren't very bright. The difference is that encouraging the nation's future professional and managerial elite to think athletes are nitwits does no serious social harm, whereas encouraging the belief that blacks are nitwits does incalculable harm. (Jencks 1983b, p. 14)

Racial oppression is strongly linked with class systems, with both upper- and middle-class whites benefiting from the exploitation of nonwhites. Many whites have relatively little to lose by giving up racist ideas; but unequal distributions of wealth, income, and power will be with us for a long time to come, for they have been deeply embedded in our economic, social, and political fabric for centuries. As Farley (1980) wrote:

> We are a long way from the segregated society of 1950, but we are still far from the dream of Martin Luther King. If the next generation of blacks is not to remain a generation behind whites, society has a long road ahead. (p. 16)

Violence and Social Change   Just as dominant groups often use violence to oppress minorities, so, too, do minorities sometimes resort to violence as the only way to end prejudice and discrimination.

Gandhi and his followers freed India from Britain's colonial rule largely without the use of violence, and Martin Luther King, Jr., used Gandhi as a model. There can be little doubt, however, that the U.S. did not pay serious attention to civil rights until blacks asserted their willingness to engage in violence. The riots in Detroit, Los Angeles, and other cities during the 1960s, for example, prompted the

In 1963, police dogs were used against unarmed, nonviolent black demonstrators in Birmingham, Alabama. The willingness of blacks and whites to violate the law to call attention to racism and to endure the often violent efforts of police to stop them, appealed to deeply held American values about courage in the face of injustice.

appointment of a national commission whose conclusions focused on the frustrations of blacks in a racist society.

More recently, many black South Africans have concluded that peaceful, legal action will not bring about an end to their oppressed minority status. Denied any effective voice in government and forbidden to protest by breaking even the most minor laws, many blacks believe that their government will only allow opposition that it knows will be ineffective; this leads them to the conclusion that "the only language the government understands is force" (Slambrouck 1983, p. 13).

Similarly, in 1990, a Milwaukee, Wisconsin black alderman announced the formation of a militia whose purpose would be to wage war against the city if the city failed to improve the living conditions of the poorest black neighborhoods within five years. "We've done things the nonviolent way, and it hasn't gotten us anywhere," he said in an interview. "The only way to get respect is to be willing to use violence. We either stand there with our backs to the wall or fight our way out" (*New York Times*, April 6, 1990, p. A12). Although many would argue that the alderman's point of view is too extreme, Gamson's study of 53 social movements in U.S. history supports the idea that the more "unruly" social movements are, the more likely they are to achieve their goals (Gamson 1974, 1975; see also Haines 1988; McAdam 1982). As Gamson concluded, "The meek don't make it."

Ecological Change

One of the most important ecological aspects of social oppression is physical segregation. Paradoxically, both more and less segregation have been proposed as responses to the oppression of minorities in the United States and elsewhere.

For years, for example, many French Canadians in the province of Quebec have urged a separation of Quebec from the rest of Canada and the establishment of an independent state in which "French Canadian" is treated as a dominant status. Israel is the only country in the world in which "Jew" is not a minority status. During the 1920s Marcus Garvey proposed seizing European colonies in Africa and transforming them into a free United Black Africa populated by U.S. blacks and sympathetic Africans. More recently, the Republic of New Africa move-

ment suggested taking over several southern states for an independent black nation, an idea that is also supported by Nation of Islam leader Louis Farrakhan. All of these efforts to preserve cultural diversity and escape exploitation and mistreatment involve separatism, which calls for greater segregation, not less, and rests on the belief that separation is the only way people can control the social and ecological conditions in which they live.

In contrast to separatists are those who advocate greater integration, and their efforts have focused on two major areas—housing and schools.

Desegregation and Resegregation   In 1954 the Supreme Court decided that separate schools for whites and blacks are "inherently unequal," and ordered an end to segregated schools. As we saw earlier, however, segregation persists.

When measuring change in the distribution of blacks and whites, it is important to distinguish between racial **integration** and racial **isolation**. Within school districts, schools are integrated if whites and blacks are evenly distributed among schools. In other words, if the population is 10 percent black and 90 percent white, full integration exists only if every school has that racial composition.

Racial isolation, however, refers to comparisons *between* school districts. Suppose one district's population is entirely white and another's is entirely black; *within* each district, schools are integrated, because the racial composition of the schools matches the racial composition of the communities they serve. Black and white students, however, are isolated from each other, because they live in different school districts (see One Step Further 13-3).

Although segregation has decreased, it remains high in many large cities such as Chicago, Cleveland, and Newark. In fact, segregation in these and other cities actually increased in the 1970s (Wurdock 1979; Wurdock and Farley 1979; Farley 1984). This occurred primarily because *residential* segregation *within* school districts increased: whites moved from integrated neighborhoods to all white neighborhoods in the same school district. Thus, de facto *re*-segregation is slowly undoing much of the desegregation achieved between 1954 and 1967.

Racial isolation fell between 1967 and 1976, but as whites have left central cities in increasing numbers, the separation of white and black students has not declined since (Orfield and Montford 1988).

ONE STEP FURTHER 13-3

What Racial Isolation Looks Like

The map of Connecticut, Figure B-13-3, provides a vivid example of how isolated black and white students are from one another in the United States. Although nonwhite children make up 22 percent of the student population, notice that in the vast majority of school districts the nonwhite share falls below 5 percent (white areas). Most nonwhites are concentrated in larger cities such as Hartford, New Haven, Bridgeport, Waterbury, and Stamford, where they make up as much as 90 percent of the student population. Even if Connecticut schools were perfectly integrated *within* school districts, racial isolation would guarantee that most students would still have relatively little contact with students of other races.

FIGURE B-13-3   Percentage of Minority Students by School District

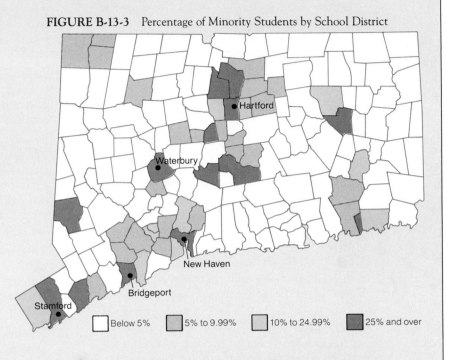

Below 5%   5% to 9.99%   10% to 24.99%   25% and over

Only two of the nation's 20 largest cities—Phoenix and San Jose—have school districts in which whites outnumber nonwhites; and whites make up only 4 percent of enrolled students in Washington, D.C., 18 percent in Detroit, and 25 percent in Chicago (Wurdock and Farley 1979). Increased interaction between blacks and whites made possible by desegregation is likely to be undone by increased racial isolation caused by changing racial compositions of communities (see also Farley 1984; Massey and Denton 1988, 1989).

Coleman, Kelly, and Moore (1975) argued that desegregation in many communities has actually caused increased racial isolation, because white parents leave rather than send their children to integrated schools. Farley, Richards, and Wurdock (1980) showed, however, that the migration of whites away from cities has been going on continuously for several decades, and when such communities desegregate their schools, white migration increases only for

the following year and then settles back to its former rate. In other words, school desegregation has a relatively small and temporary effect on the "flight" of white families from communities.

Migration is only one factor in school segregation, however, for in the last decade the number of private schools has grown rapidly while the number of public schools has decreased (USCB 1987a). Many of these schools exclude blacks—some of them on supposedly religious grounds—and this introduces a major new way for whites to separate their children from blacks.

If the goal of integration is to reduce prejudice and discrimination by improving educational opportunities for blacks and by increasing contact between students of different races, we clearly have a long way to go. In fact, there is reason to believe that we are retreating from the goal of a society in which people from different ethnic and racial backgrounds can share the same neighborhoods and schools.

SUMMARY

1. Biological races are collections of people whose distinct physical characteristics are passed on through reproduction. Social race is a status defined in physical terms. An ethnic group is a collection of people with a common cultural heritage.

2. A minority is a group of people who are singled out for unequal treatment. Social oppression is the systematic, socially supported abuse or exploitation of one group by another.

3. Prejudice is a positive or negative attitude directed toward members of a group. Prejudice is based on real or imagined differences between groups, attaches values to group differences, is generalized to all members of a target group, and usually includes the belief that group differences are absolute and inevitable.

4. Prejudice functions as an ideology by denying the existence of oppression and by blaming minorities for the effects of oppression.

5. Cultural differences within societies are dealt with in several ways. Amalgamation occurs when several cultures mix to become a new culture; assimilation occurs when ethnic groups conform to the culture of a single group; and pluralism occurs when diverse ethnic groups maintain their differences within a society.

6. Discrimination is unequal treatment of people because they belong to certain groups. Whether or not our treatment of each other is consistent with our attitudes depends on the situation.

7. Race strongly affects the distribution of wealth, occupation, education, income, prestige, employment, power, health, and living conditions. Ethnicity has weaker effects because it is less visible and has weaker prejudices attached to it.

8. Upward mobility among blacks has been slow and has barely affected the distribution of wealth, income, power, and prestige. Blacks are handicapped not only by poorer education and occupation, but by the stigma of race itself. Prejudice often creates self-fulfilling prophecies.

9. Ecology often affects the creation and perpetuation of minorities. Discrimination and prejudice often are encouraged by economic arrangements.

10. Segregation reinforces the disadvantaged position of minorities. Residential segregation is the norm in the U.S. and results mostly from the refusal of whites to live near blacks. *De jure* segregation is required by law; *de facto* segregation is a latent consequence of other social or ecological arrangements. Most children attend segregated schools because they live in segregated neighborhoods.

11. Genocide is the systematic killing of members of a group. Expulsion is a form of oppression in which minorities are forced to leave their community or society.

12. Conflict theorists focus on the ways in which prejudice and discrimination arise out of competition for scarce resources in which some groups exploit others. Prejudice serves the interests of dominant groups and contributes to false consciousness among subordinate groups that often use minorities as scapegoats.

13. The functional perspective shows that, in spite of their negative consequences both for minorities and societies, prejudice and discrimination are often integrated into basic social institutions and are, therefore, very difficult to change.

14. The interactionist perspective identifies the ways in which the various aspects of social oppression are acted out in everyday life, from the recognition of racial and ethnic distinctions to discriminatory behavior.

15. Prejudice may be reduced by attacking its social legitimacy or by reducing perceived differences between minorities and dominant groups. Increased interaction often lowers prejudice when people occupy the same statuses and share common goals that can be achieved only through cooperation. Affirmative action programs—preferential treatment given to minorities—have generally had little effect on the disadvantaged position of minorities in the U.S.

16. Separatism is a belief in increased segregation as a way of preserving minority culture and ending discrimination.

17. Racial integration of schools exists when the racial composition of schools matches the composition of their communities. Racial isolation refers to comparisons between school districts and communities and the degree of contact between people of different races. U.S. schools have become more racially integrated and less isolated since 1954, but in many large cities the trend toward less isolation is reversing as whites move out of integrated neighborhoods.

KEY TERMS

amalgamation   302
assimilation   302
de facto segregation   312
de jure segregation   312
discrimination   316
ethnicism   300

ethnicity   298
expulsion   313
genocide   313
integration   322
isolation   322
minority   299

pluralism   302
prejudice   300
race   298
racism   300
segregation   311
social oppression   299

LOOKING ELSEWHERE

Having studied Chapter 13, you might want to look at related discussions in *Human Arrangements*, which include

■ racism, ethnicism, and xenophobia (the fear of outsiders) in communities (Chapter 10, pp. 214–16)

■ race, crime, and punishment (Chapter 11, pp. 243–45, 247–49)

■ South Africa as a caste system (Chapter 12, pp. 288–89)

■ learning and school segregation (Chapter 17, pp. 428–29)

■ race and I.Q. (Chapter 17, pp. 417–18)

■ how minorities are treated in schools (Chapter 17, pp. 422, 435, 436, 440)

■ women as a unique minority (Chapter 14, p. 357)

■ origins of the civil rights movement (Chapter 22, pp. 586–87, 589–92)

■ race and health (Chapter 4, p. 71)

RECOMMENDED READINGS

Allport, G. 1958. *The nature of prejudice*. Cambridge, MA: Addison-Wesley. A classic exploration of the nature of prejudice, including a look at the ways in which minorities often respond.

Blauner, R. 1989. *Black lives, whites lives: Three decades of race relations in America*. Berkeley: University of California Press. Using oral histories gathered from both blacks and whites, Blauner offers a compelling view of what has—and has not—happened to race relations since 1960.

Conklin, N. F., and Lourie, M. A. 1983. *A host of tongues: Language communities in the United States*. New York: Free Press. A study of linguistic assimilation through which the diverse cultural origins of the American people are dominated by a single language.

Cornell, S. 1988. *The return of the native: American Indian political resurgence*. New York: Oxford University Press. An insightful examination of the ways in which American Indians have been treated by the United States and the political movements that have emerged as a result.

Dunbar, L. W. (Ed.). 1984. *Minority report: What has happened to blacks, Hispanics, American Indians, and other American minorities in the eighties*. New York: Pantheon. Seven civil rights activists argue that while many cultural aspects of racial and ethnic inequality have changed, economic discrimination continues and will continue without government intervention.

Farley, R., and Allen, W. R. 1987. *The color line and the quality of life in America*. New York: Russell Sage Foundation. An exhaustive and definitive summary of the historical trends in the conditions of blacks in the United States.

Fernandez, J. P. 1981. *Racism and sexism in corporate life*. Lexington, MA: D. C. Heath. A study of attitudes among managers toward existing company-sponsored affirmative action programs. One major finding is that the more highly placed executives are, the more racist and sexist their personal attitudes tend to be.

Meredith, M. 1989. *In the name of apartheid: South Africa in the postwar period*. New York: Harper and Row. A revealing historical portrait of the evolution of apartheid in South Africa and its effects on blacks and whites.

Simpson, G. E., and Yinger, J. M. 1985. *Racial and cultural minorities: An analysis of prejudice and discrimination* (5th ed.). New York: Plenum. The latest edition of an important source book on discrimination and prejudice, which pays attention to both theory and research.

Wilson, W. J. 1978. *The declining significance of race*. Chicago: University of Chicago Press. A provocative book that argues that class, not race, is the most important impediment to progress for American blacks. See, also, his more recent book—(1987). *The truly disadvantaged*. Chicago: University of Chicago Press—about public policy and the black underclass.

14
GENDER INEQUALITY

 In the fall of 1990, the United States sent hundreds of thousands of troops to Saudi Arabia in response to the invasion of Kuwait by Iraq. In addition to the harsh desert conditions, the U.S. forces had to adjust to some striking cultural differences between themselves and their Arab allies. One of the most difficult involved the presence of female U.S. soldiers whose regular on-the-job behavior offended their Saudi hosts. Female soldiers drove vehicles, for example, and worked side-by-side with their male counterparts; and in temperatures that typically exceeded 120 degrees, they may—like their male counterparts—have stripped down to their undershirts while doing maintenance work on aircraft and other machinery. As well, female officers gave orders to both male and female soldiers under their command. The Saudis were shocked by such behavior, for under Saudi civil law, women are not allowed to drive vehicles, to attend public events such as movies with men, or to give men orders, and are required to cover most of their faces and all torso skin above the waist when in public.

As liberal as the Americans must have felt next to the Saudis, U.S. culture also makes sharp distinctions by gender. After all, only a small minority of U.S. troops are women, few ever reach the highest ranks, none are allowed in combat, and most experience various forms of harassment from men (Moskos 1990). Although the patterns associated with gender differ, virtually every known society makes social distinctions among people based upon biological sex. In most of these, sex plays a part in social stratification, and in many, it is the basis for prejudice and discrimination; that is, females are treated as members of a social minority. Unlike most minorities, females are

Among the Navajo pictured here, women are the weavers; but among the Hopi, who share the same territory, it is the men who weave. Only social factors can account for such differences.

a numerical majority in all societies, which makes their minority standing all the more compelling.

How have culture, social structure, and ecological arrangements been used to transform a numerical majority into a social minority? We begin by looking at the difference between sex as a biological characteristic and gender as a social status. From there we analyze the bases for gender inequality and the socialization process through which people learn to take their place as males and females and play the roles associated with them. The rest of the chapter uses the functional, conflict, and interactionist perspectives to understand how and why gender is used as a basis for inequality, and closely examines the myths and realities of change in contemporary society.

BIOLOGY, CULTURE, AND SOCIAL STRUCTURE

Biological sex is a crucial and relatively simple human characteristic, for it takes two types of people to create new people. All fetuses initially look the same, but after the first few months, males develop testicles and penises and females develop vaginas, clitorises, ovaries, wombs, and fallopian tubes. These differences occur because males have an "X" and "Y" pair of chromosomes and females have two "X" chromosomes. Males and females also differ in body chemistry, for while both have the same hormones, females generally have more estrogen and males more testosterone, and this difference plays an important part in physical development (determining, among other things, the size of people's bodies, amounts of body hair, potential for muscle development, and the size of breasts and hips).

Sociologically, however, there is more to being male or female than chemistry, physiology, and the parts played in reproduction, for these *physical* differences have been culturally transformed into two **genders**, which are distinguished by different social characteristics. Cultural beliefs define the basic nature of males and females in different ways, for exam-

ple; values rank males higher than females; norms support male privilege; and females are the object of both positive and negative attitudes—from the adoration of the Virgin Mary to the contempt for women expressed in pornography.

Most societies also assign males and females to different statuses and, on this basis, distribute wealth, power, and prestige unequally. In industrial societies, women are usually the ones who care for the children, whereas most men spend their time producing goods. Even among people who work outside the home, there are sharp differences in what men and women do: all but a few women follow instructions given by men; men are far more likely to make decisions and supervise other people. Women are also more likely than men to live in poverty, and to have no paid work at all.

People differ by gender not only in what they do, but in how they do it, for in most societies, male and female patterns of response to other people differ in many ways. In Western societies, men tend to display more aggressiveness and self-confidence, whereas women display more tenderness, vulnerability, and emotion.

Because all societies make important social distinctions between females and males, it is tempting to conclude that such distinctions are biologically determined and are, therefore, inevitable and natural. Edward O. Wilson (1975) revived this point of view in his study of sociobiology and the genetic basis of social behavior among humans and other species. Females, he asserted, are nurturant toward children because the species needs such behavior in order to successfully reproduce itself. There is, he contended, a nurturant gene, and biological differences between males and females explain important differences we observe in what men and women do and how they do it.

This conclusion, however, fails to pay enough attention to the crucial fact that cultures distinguish between males and females in different ways, and the distinctions made within cultures often change over time. As Wilson (1977) later acknowledged, "The evidence is strong that almost but probably not quite all differences among cultures are based on learning and socialization rather than on genes" (p. 133) (see also Benderly 1987; Boyd and Richerson 1985; Epstein 1989).

Biological determinism also ignores the fact that aside from the roles males and females play in reproduction, there is little scientific evidence that other differences are biologically caused; and those differences that may have biological influences are relatively few in number. Studies that attempt to document biologically-based gender differences have often produced contradictory results. In addition, many of the differences that are consistently found do not appear until later in childhood or during adolescence, making it virtually impossible to conclude that such differences are biological rather than social in origin (Fausto-Sterling 1985; Maccoby and Jacklin 1974; Renzetti and Curran 1989).

The absence of scientific support for biological determinism does not mean that there is no connection between sex and gender (Rossi 1984). For example, the fact that, until recently, only women could feed infants, by nursing, certainly affected the division of labor in most nonindustrial societies by making it difficult for women to engage in work—such as hunting—that requires extensive travel. Such differences, however, do not constitute a biological basis for the complex gender division of labor found in most contemporary societies. Even more important is the lack of a biological basis for gender inequality and the treatment of women as a minority in *any* society.

In short, sex does not determine gender (see Bleier 1984; Fausto-Sterling 1985). From a sociological perspective, the position of women as a minority depends on the characteristics of social systems, each of which is connected to the others in often complex ways.

GENDER, CULTURE, AND THE IDEOLOGY OF SEXISM

Male and female are ascribed statuses, attached to which are **gender roles**—sets of ideas about how males and females should appear and behave. As you read the following sections, keep in mind that although females are treated as a minority in most societies today, this has not always been the case. In most gatherer-hunter and some horticultural societies the division of labor was based on gender, but women were not treated as inferior. In fact, in many societies they were highly revered (Eisler 1987; Etienne and Leacock 1980; Lerner 1986).

In social interaction, we first define the situation. We decide who other people are in relation to us. Culture is the source of such definitions, providing us with the categories through which we "know" and evaluate people, decide what to expect of them as well as what they will expect of us. At the heart of definitions is language, which makes important distinctions between females and males.

Language and Gender

Language is more than a tool for communication, for the use of a particular language focuses attention on some aspects of reality more than others. We are less likely to focus on women's adult strengths, for example, if we think of them as girls rather than women.

Language reinforces the minority status of females in four ways (Richardson 1981; Smith 1985). First, in many languages, females do not exist independently of males. In English, "man" and masculine pronouns such as "he" are commonly used to refer to both males and females (as in "Peace on earth and good will toward men"). When women marry, they usually replace their last name with their husband's,

---

P U Z Z L E

WHAT
WORD MEANS
"HATRED OF MALES"?

There is no such word. This chapter explains why this is so, even though we have the word misogyny, which means "hatred of females."

surrendering a unique part of their social identity. In general, men are referred to as "Mr."—a title that reveals nothing about their marital status—while women are known either as "Miss" or "Mrs."—in other words, according to their relationship with men. In French, the word "femme" means both "woman" and "wife," but "husband" and "man" are distinct words—"mari" and "homme." A French man can be referred to independently of his relationships with women, whereas a French woman's identity as "woman" is synonymous with her relationship to a man (see Henley, Hamilton, and Thorne 1985).

Some argue that it's only semantics and everyone knows that "man" and "he" refer to both males and females; but both common experience and research suggest otherwise. When the word "man" is used, it is more likely to evoke male images than female ones, so the idea that women can be congressmen often puzzles children (see Wolfe, Struckman-Johnson, and Flanagin 1986). Scheider and Hacker (1973),

for example, asked college students to submit photographs for a new textbook. Half the students were given chapter titles such as "Urban Life" and "Political Behavior," and the other half received titles such as "Urban Man" and "Political Man." The second group produced far more pictures of men than of women, reflecting the subtle but powerful influence of cultural imagery (see also Hamilton 1988; Martyna 1980).

Second, we tend to associate masculine and feminine pronouns with specific statuses. We refer to telephone operators and elementary school teachers as "she," but use "he" to refer to college professors, engineers, and physicians. When men or women hold jobs dominated by the other gender, we draw attention to the exception by using titles such as "male nurse" and "policewoman." In both cases, language reflects beliefs about who occupies each status, rather than the objective fact that both men and women do (see Kramer and Freed 1991). We also use masculine and feminine pronouns to label nonhuman objects in ways that reflect the subordinate social position of females. Things that men build and control (or try to)—airplanes, ships, and nature—are "she," while forces that are too powerful for men to control—the Devil and God—are "he."

Third, we use language in ways that portray women as weak, incompetent, and undesirable, and men as strong, competent, and socially valued. Women are often called "girls," but men are rarely called "boys" unless they occupy inferior statuses such as "busboy," or, in some cases, "black." Unmarried older men are called "bachelors," a far more flattering label than comparable words for women—"old maid" and "spinster." Most sexual slang that is applied to women describes their desirability to men ("fox," "chick," and "broad"), whereas slang that applies to men refers to power over women ("stud"). Many people are familiar with the word for "excessive sexual desire in a female" (nymphomania), but few have ever heard the word for comparable males (satyriasis). In addition, although English includes words for the hatred of females (**misogyny**) and the hatred of all people (misanthropy), few dictionaries list a word for the hatred of males.

Japanese contains two vocabularies and grammars—one of which expresses ideas more directly and assertively than the other—and females are expected to use the less assertive form (Shibamoto 1985; see also Cherry 1988). American speech produces parallel examples: women are more likely than men to smile and to use words such as "lovely," "cute," and "precious," and less likely to use strong profanity or make direct, powerful statements (Lakoff 1975; Kemper 1984; Selnow 1985). Not only do males and females tend to use different vocabularies, but in some cases people assign different meanings to words depending on the speaker's gender. Many people, for example, support the belief that when a woman says "no," she really means "yes."

Language reinforces the minority status of women in a fourth way: there is a clear historical trend through which words used to describe women acquire negative meanings. "Madam" and "mistress" went from respectful forms of address to "keeper of a whorehouse" and "lover kept by a man." "Hussy" once meant "housewife"; "tart" and "biddy" were affectionate names; "whore" once meant "lover of either sex"; "nymph" meant "beautiful young woman"; and "broad" meant "young woman," with no negative connotations. Words that describe men, however, have not been degraded in this way. In fact, favorite insults directed toward men are often derived from words that describe women—as in "sissy" (from "sister"), "pussy," and "son of a bitch" (which attacks men by insulting their mothers). Interestingly, "bitch" was originally a term of great reverence for the pre-Christian Goddess of the hunt, Artemis-Diana, and "son of a bitch" referred to a spiritual son of the Goddess (Walker 1983).

Language does not cause women to occupy inferior positions, but it plays an important part because we use it to think about ourselves and other people (see Hamilton 1988). The fact that there is no English word for "the hatred of males" does not mean that no one hates males; it does mean, however, that systematic, socially supported negative attitudes toward males are unlikely to be a part of a society whose culture includes no such word. In the same way, the existence of the word "misogyny" does not mean that everyone will hate females, but it reflects a cultural idea that lends legitimacy to prejudice and discrimination against them.

Beliefs: Feminine and Masculine

At the heart of cultures are beliefs that define reality, and these include gender stereotypes: men are smarter than women; women cannot take pressure like men can; men are less emotional than women and are only interested in sex; women make better parents and housekeepers than men; aggressive men

are "go-getters" and aggressive women are "pushy"; women's talk is all chatter and women only think about clothes; women want to be raped; menstruation makes women unreliable. These are only a few of the beliefs that have been used to distinguish between males and females. Together, they purport to portray a vision of the true nature of females and males, and in our culture these "natures" are summarized by the concepts of feminine and masculine.

Regardless of gender, race, age, or social class, and across a variety of cultures, there is general agreement that **masculinity** describes people who are aggressive, rational, strong, independent, competitive, self-confident, dominant, active, tough, emotionally insensitive, and reluctant to show their feelings. **Femininity** describes people who are intuitive, emotionally excitable, weak, vulnerable, dependent, insecure, submissive, noncompetitive, passive, tender, sensitive, and quick to show their emotions (Edwards and Williams 1980; Williams and Best 1982).

Like all stereotypes, the concepts of masculinity and femininity describe people in oversimplified terms that bear little relation to what individual men and women are really like. No one is aggressive or passive all the time, for example, and we all have moments of intelligence and moments of stupidity. Gender stereotypes also ignore the enormous variation *among* women and *among* men: there are many men who come closer to the feminine ideal than many women do. Perhaps most important, stereotypes about gender are strongly linked to cultural values.

Values: Vive la Différence?

To many people, beliefs that distinguish females and males do no more than just that: the two genders differ from each other, and what is the harm in that? The harm lies in the fact that most cultures also generally value males more than females, and different criteria are used to evaluate men and women.

Schur (1984) goes so far as to suggest that the status of female is treated in many ways as a deviant, stigmatizing characteristic. Several studies reveal a preference for male children among parents in most societies (Williamson 1976; see also Corea et al. 1987; Hammer and McFerran 1988). In parts of rural India, infanticide—the killing of infants—is relatively common and is more likely to be inflicted on female children (Korbin 1983). As many as 25 percent of girls born in India die before reaching the age of 15, largely because of neglect and infanticide. This does not include those who are never born because of the use of selective abortion aided by medical testing that enables parents to know the sex of their unborn child (UNICEF 1990).

Not only is maleness a preferred characteristic, but traits associated with masculinity tend to be valued more highly than those associated with femininity. Broverman et al. (1970) asked male and female mental health professionals to use lists of personality traits to describe the "mature, healthy, competent" male, female, and human being. Although they described the ideal male and ideal human being in similar terms, they described the ideal female in sharply different terms. Females who fulfill their cultural ideals are valued less than men who conform to theirs (see also Showalter 1985).

The higher value placed on maleness leads to different perceptions and evaluations of men's and women's behavior. In an experiment, Paludi and Strayer (1985) asked 300 women and men to evaluate articles identified with names that suggested the authors' gender, or left gender unclear. The articles also varied by field, from stereotypically masculine (politics) to stereotypically feminine (psychology of women). The experimenters found that even in stereotypically feminine fields, articles perceived as written by men were judged to be more persuasive, insightful, and higher in overall quality. These results are echoed in nonexperimental research findings that wages in an occupation tend to go down as the percentage of women in an occupation increases regardless of the actual skills required for the job (England and Dunn 1988; Strober and Arnold 1987).

It is significant that cultures commonly value maleness and masculinity more highly than femaleness and femininity; but they also tend to evaluate men and women according to different criteria. An important basis for evaluating women, for example, is their physical attractiveness to men, and women often go to great lengths to force their bodies to conform to male values about how they should look (see Lakoff and Scherr 1984). As Chernin (1981) describes in her powerful analysis of values about female slenderness, dieting and being thin are a national obsession among U.S. females as young as 7 years old (Feldman et al. 1988; see also Hesse-Biber 1989; Simmons and Blyth 1986).

Slenderness is far from a natural or universal criterion for female beauty. In Western Samoa most women gain weight with each pregnancy and are, by U.S. standards, "fat" by the time they reach middle age. Rather than suffering shame, they are widely admired and perform "humorous, almost lascivious" dances on public occasions (MacKenzie 1980). In the U.S., however, as married couples age, changes in the wife's physical appearance have a much greater negative effect on how attractive they are to their husbands than physical changes in husbands have on how attractive they are to their wives (Margolin 1987).

In some cultures, the values against which women are judged have prompted extreme measures. For example, each year almost 100,000 U.S. women have surgery in order to increase the size of their breasts (ASPRS 1985). The Chinese once practiced footbinding, the distortion of women's feet that made it painful and almost impossible for them to walk (Dworkin 1974). Tiny feet were culturally valued as delicate, beautiful, and feminine, and feet of normal size were considered ugly. Footbinding was accomplished by bending all toes except the big one under a girl's foot and into the soles of her feet. The result—in addition to excruciating pain, chronic bleeding, and frequent infection—was a woman who could barely do more than shuffle. Although footbinding is a far cry from chronic dieting, it is hard to escape the parallel, for in each case women's bodies are subjected to distortion and pain in order to conform to cultural values.

Although physical attractiveness is not unimportant among men, the primary criteria for evaluating them are power, wealth, and prestige. As with women, there are costs associated with these values. As we will see later in this chapter, the continual striving by men to prove their manhood and masculinity encourages them to take risks such as working too much and devoting too little to developing close and supportive friendships, or risking physical injury and death by driving cars recklessly or getting into fights. Unlike the case with women, however, the risks associated with manhood and masculinity generally enhance men's social standing and increase their independence and autonomy. For women, living up to feminine ideals generally results in greater dependence on men and a loss of social power.

Attitudes

Several authors argue that beneath beliefs and values that define females as inferior are negative attitudes. Pornography, for example, portrays women as objects that exist to please men, and women are often

The practice of footbinding shows how class and gender can have extreme effects. The peasant woman oaring her boat has healthy feet that were considered crude and ugly. The maidservant must carry her aristocratic employer everywhere because footbinding has tortured her feet into "perfect" but useless stumps.

the victims of verbal and physical abuse (Lederer 1980; Malamuth and Donnerstein 1984).

Chernin's (1981) analysis of values about female beauty shows their relationship with negative attitudes. U.S. women, she observes, are often dissatisfied with their bodies and regard them as enemies that refuse to conform to cultural ideals of slenderness. The desire to live in a different body reflects

> a bitter contempt for the feminine nature of my own body. The sense of fullness and swelling, of curves and softness, the awareness of plentitude and abundance, which filled me with disgust and alarm, were actually the qualities of a woman's body. (p. 18)

The dislike that many women feel for their bodies reflects negative cultural attitudes toward the natural physical characteristics of female bodies (Chernin, p. 22), just as the Chinese belief that normal female feet were crude and unattractive reflected attitudes of that culture.

Negative attitudes toward females are common throughout the histories of many societies (see Dijkstra 1987). Ancient Greeks believed women were evil, and misogyny was a recurring theme in literature that portrayed women as the cause of all human problems (Pomeroy 1975). The Greek philosopher

and mathematician Pythagoras wrote, "There is a good principle which created order, light, and man, and an evil principle which created chaos, darkness, and woman." Among the ancient Celts in Ireland, women were regarded as "'senseless,' like slaves, prisoners, and drunks" (Anderson and Zinsser 1988, p. 27). In the 15 centuries after the death of Christ, women and sexuality were increasingly associated with evil in many cultures, and negative attitudes peaked in Europe during the Middle Ages when millions were persecuted as witches, in part because their power and authority as healers threatened male dominance (Ben-Yehuda 1980; Christ 1983; Dworkin 1974).

Norms

Laws limit the rights of females in most societies. Until quite recently, for example, women could not vote in the U.S., own property, dispose of their earnings, or enter into contracts. A majority of states still do not include a husband's use of force to have sex with his wife as a legal definition of rape (Finkelhor and Yllo 1985). In 1982 the Equal Rights Amendment to the Constitution was defeated, and as a result women still do not enjoy equal standing and protection under the law.

The effects of the folkways and mores on the everyday lives of men and women are no less important than the effects of law. Women are expected to marry and, once married, to have and raise children, leaving the job of breadwinning to men. In 1990, 39 percent of U.S. adults agreed that, "It is much better for everyone involved if the man is the achiever outside the home and the woman takes care of home and family" (Davis and Smith 1990). Even when women do work outside the home, they are expected to put family obligations before their jobs (Hochschild 1989).

When they interact with men, women are expected to conceal their intelligence and strength. When a man is sexually aroused, many women feel an obligation to do something to satisfy him. Many men still feel they should open doors for women, defend them if another man offends them, and pay the check when they go out with them. On a superficial level, these may appear to be no more than harmless courtesies that make life more pleasant. On a deeper level, however, they reinforce the minority status of women by expecting them to pretend they are inferior when they are not, to subjugate their own feelings to men's desires, and to pretend that they are incapable of providing for, taking care of, and defending themselves.

Because we use culture to make sense of the world, we are often unaware that it is a human creation until we look at cultures other than our own. In her classic study of New Guinea tribes, Margaret Mead ([1935] 1963) found startling departures from Western ideas about gender. Among the Arapesh, both men and women conformed to our ideas about femininity: both took care of children, aggressive behavior was discouraged for both genders, and gentleness and warmth were valued. Among Mundugamoors, however, the opposite prevailed: both men and women were aggressive and violent, and men and women attacked each other with equal ferocity. The third tribe—the Tchambuli—distinguished between men and women, but the behavior of women corresponded to our ideas of masculinity, whereas the men conformed to our ideas of femininity.

Culture is a framework that we use to make sense of ourselves and others. Ideas that apply to males and females, however, go beyond the task of making sense of the world, for they also help justify and perpetuate social systems in which females are treated as

a minority and men struggle to maintain dominance. Most cultures are **sexist** because they support prejudice against females; and because sexism is used to justify inequality, it is an *ideology*. What do these structures of inequality look like, and how do they affect people's lives?

GENDER AND SOCIAL STRUCTURE

The structures of most contemporary societies place women in a minority status; but, as we saw earlier, gender-based inequality is by no means universal. In most gatherer-hunter and in some horticultural societies, women and men have shared equally in wealth, power, and prestige, in spite of their different positions in divisions of labor (Eisler 1987; Etienne and Leacock 1980; Sanday 1981).

Gender Roles, Status Sets, and Social Identity

Gender roles define expectations for males and females. When we interact with people of different genders, we use beliefs to identify and describe them as male or female, values to determine their rank in relation to us, attitudes to direct positive and negative feelings and behavior toward them, and norms to form expectations of them and ourselves.

We do not have to think, evaluate, feel, and behave according to roles, but we have strong reasons to do so. Roles have coercive power over us because reward and punishment depend on them and because we use roles to orient ourselves to other people. If we deviate from a gender role, we risk punishment or lost rewards. At the very least, we may lose our sense that we know who we are and who other people are in relation to us.

In our culture, gender roles correspond to masculinity and femininity. Females who conform to their gender role define physical beauty as slenderness; value the ability to be attractive to and supportive of men more than they value independence; admire and look up to men; and behave in ways that perpetuate their subordinate position (letting men interrupt them, asking men to do things for them that they could do themselves, or allowing men to dominate them sexually). Men who conform to their gender role believe they are more intelligent than women; value wealth, power, and prestige more than intimate relationships; feel hostility toward women; and behave in ways that reinforce their dominance (controlling conversations, "defending" women without asking them if they want to be defended, or being sexually aggressive regardless of women's feelings).

As important as gender roles are, however, they are only the "tip of the iceberg," *because gender is a status that affects which other statuses are included in our status sets.* Men dominate society not simply because they are masculine, but because they have greater access to powerful achieved statuses. They control legislatures, governments, courts, labor unions, corporations, religious organizations, schools, universities, and important professions such as law and medicine. Similarly, women's inferior position rests on more than the demands of femininity, for women are confined to relatively powerless statuses. As wives or mothers, they have little power outside the home, and those who do not work for pay must depend on men for their security. In families, they enjoy few legal protections from abuse by their husbands. In the workplace, most hold the lowest paying, least powerful jobs.

Gender roles have an enormous impact on status sets and, with them, social identities. In the U.S., a successful woman is not simply feminine: she is also traditionally a supportive wife and devoted mother who values her children's happiness and her husband's occupational success more than her own. She is expected to be content with poorly paid or part-time jobs. In the same way, a successful man is not simply masculine. He has a beautiful wife, a highly paid, prestigious job, his own home, and a new car. In this sense, gender roles are not single, unified roles. Rather, they are the core of clusters of statuses and roles that make up much of people's identities as women and men.

Role Conflict: Binds and Double-Binds   The variety of statuses people occupy and the complexity of their role sets often produce conflicting expectations that cause role conflict. Working mothers, for example, experience conflict because they are expected to stay home to care for a sick child and go to work (see Barnett and Baruch 1983). Added to this is the widespread belief that children's development suffers if women work (Davis and Smith 1990)—a belief that consistently finds no support in scientific research (Gottfried and Gottfried 1988; Hayes and Kamerman 1983). Men experience conflict when other men (and many women) expect them to be

Women who want to work outside the home and have children face role conflict that men have been able to avoid. What are the different ways in which such conflict might be resolved? What changes would they require?

strong and domineering, and yet many women expect them to behave with tenderness and treat them as equals.

Although everyone experiences conflict because of gender, a society that treats women as a minority generally produces more strain for them than for men (see Michelson 1985). In industrial societies, women who cannot hire someone to care for their children have a difficult time combining marriage, motherhood, and full-time work. Men are in less of a bind, for there are relatively fewer demands placed on husbands and fathers, enabling men to have both families and commit themselves to occupations. Men are able to separate their different roles from one another in time and space. Women who marry and have children, however, cannot separate family and nonfamily roles so easily (Hochschild 1990). The result is considerable strain for many women who want to work or who must work (because their husbands cannot support their families or because they are divorced and are the sole source of support). One result of this is that marriage disrupts the educational progress of women but not that of men (Alexander and Reilly 1981; Teachman and Polonko 1988).

Divisions of Labor: Ecology and Social Structure

Divisions of labor in most societies use gender as a basis for sorting people into adult statuses, but only a few statuses such as mother and father are directly tied to biological sex. Historically, however, mother and father have been statuses of enormous importance in creating and perpetuating gender inequality.

In early gatherer-hunter societies, for example, the dependence of children on their mothers confined women to tasks that allowed them to remain in one place for long periods. Although women participated in hunting, men were in the best position to be hunters who left their villages for days at a time. Some anthropologists argue that hunting provided the most important source of food for these societies, and biological roles allowed men to monopolize the most culturally valued social roles (Friedl 1975; Huber 1990).

Harris (1977) argued that different reproductive roles also created inequality by allowing men to dominate warfare:

Warfare required the organization of communities around a resident core of fathers, brothers, and their sons. This led to the control over resources by pater-

nal-fraternal interest groups and the exchange of sisters and daughters between such groups . . . to the allotment of women as a reward for male aggressiveness. . . . The assignment of drudge work to women and their ritual subordination and devaluation follows automatically from the need to reward males at the expense of females. (p. 86)

This line of reasoning suggests that early ecological arrangements enabled men to monopolize important tasks and laid the groundwork for cultural values that rank males higher than females.

Others maintain that the gender division of labor did not result in inequality in hunter-gatherer societies or in most horticultural societies. In all societies, adult standing depends on performing socially productive labor (Huber and Spitze 1983). In the earliest societies, all labor contributed to the community. The domestic work of women was no less socially productive than the hunting and warfare conducted by males, and even when women were less powerful than men, they were treated as full adults. There is considerable evidence that the importance of hunting in many of these societies is much less than previously believed and that, in fact, women provided most of the food in a diet that was largely vegetarian. In addition, women's control over childbearing, before the male role in reproduction became known, gave them a highly revered place, long before the development of patriarchal ideas about male deities who created life (see Eisler 1987; Fisher, 1980; Lerner 1986).

Among the Hopi Indians, for example, families were headed by women, not men; Hopi women did not depend on marriage for their security; and privilege based on gender did not exist. Although men were primarily responsible for hunting, herding, and farming, these tasks were not more highly valued than women's work—making pottery, baskets, and clothing. It is revealing to note that Hopi society differs sharply from our own in another crucial way: child care was the responsibility of the entire community, not of women alone (Leavitt 1971).

Engels ([1891] 1972), Sacks (1974), Goody (1976), and others argue that it was when technology enabled societies to produce surpluses that the position of women dropped dramatically. The ability to produce surpluses created two distinct types of production: goods that were consumed and goods that were traded. Here the concept of "private property" emerged, and while men monopolized the production of surplus goods, women were confined to producing goods for immediate consumption. This dis-

tinction is crucial because surplus goods are wealth that is a basis for exchange and social power. The family emerged as a social unit separate from the community; production was for the family, not the community; and because domestic work no longer contributed to the community, women lost adult standing and were viewed as little more than the wives and daughters of men (Etienne and Leacock 1980).

As divisions of labor became more complex, gender distinctions went beyond childbearing, child care, hunting, and warfare to include a wide range of occupations. In colonial America, families produced most of what they consumed, and although men and women usually did different things, women performed important productive roles—weaving cloth, making products such as soap and candles, and trading in the marketplace. Some women worked as blacksmiths, tailors, printers, and shopkeepers, and when husbands died, wives often assumed full control of family businesses (Baxandall et al. 1976; Demos 1970; Larkin 1988).

In colonial times, family life and production of goods were usually carried on in the same place, but this ecological arrangement changed with the Industrial Revolution (Cherlin 1983; Tilly and Scott 1978). With the introduction of factories, home became a private sphere, separated and isolated from the public sphere of paid work. Ecological changes made it increasingly difficult for women to occupy the statuses of wife and mother and perform more highly valued and powerful roles outside the family (Sachs 1983). This, in turn, affected the division of labor in families.

It is important to be aware that while these patterns are true for women in general, there are important exceptions. The Industrial Revolution, for example, affected whites and blacks quite differently. For most black women in the United States, there has never been a period in which they were confined solely to domestic tasks. The impoverished condition of most blacks has always required women to both care for children and earn a living. In this sense, the split between the private and public spheres has been a largely white phenomenon.

Divisions of Labor in Families   In most U.S. families, husbands tend to have more power than wives. However, women who work outside the home, and who have more education than their husbands, tend to have more power within their families than women who do not (Hood 1983).

In most families, women still do most of the housework. In families with two working parents, husbands generally do a small fraction of the domestic work that their wives do, mostly shopping or doing dishes (Hochschild 1989; Huber and Spitze 1983). Fathers, as a whole, spend an average of only 12 minutes a day alone with their children (Tavris and Wade 1984), time more likely spent in play than in caretaking (Rossi 1984). Among women who work full time, roughly 90 percent do most or all of the family cooking and shopping (*New York Times*, February 24, 1988, p. 1).

Women are not only expected to devote themselves to family life, but must live with a cultural contradiction: they are expected to value family roles above all, yet those roles have a relatively low cultural value. We tend to value people who work for pay more than we value those who do not, and family roles are not defined as productive work. The U.S. Census Bureau does not count homemakers in the labor force, and if you ask a full-time homemaker, "Do you work?" she will most likely say, "No, I'm a housewife."

The relatively low value placed on family roles puts women in an insecure position in which they receive little outside support. Few businesses provide day-care facilities for employees; the demands of child care make it difficult for women to establish themselves in secure, well-paying jobs; and the status of "homemaker" has little financial security, lasting only as long as the marriage.

The division of labor within families affects the position of women in society. The domestic responsibilities of women are not only the historical root of gender inequality, but a major aspect of social structure that continues to deny women equality.

Gender and the "Public" World   In all societies, most women are part of the labor force. In 1988, 78 percent of single women in the U.S. were in the labor force, as were 56 percent of married women, including 57 percent of those with preschool children and 72 percent of those with children of school age. Among divorced women, 76 percent were in the labor force, including 70 percent of those with young children and fully 84 percent of those with school-age children (USCB 1990a).

The persisting ideal that a "woman's place is in the home" clearly does not describe most societies and is, in fact, a historically curious idea. Yet, while most women work, they are still less likely than men to be considered part of the labor force. In 1988, 79 percent of males over the age of 15 were in the labor force, compared with 56 percent of females. Women are also more likely than men to work at part-time jobs: in 1988 only 10 percent of male workers were part-time, compared with 26 percent of women (USCB 1990a).

Even among full-time workers, however, the labor force is highly segregated by gender. In fact, for women and men to have the same occupational distribution, an estimated half of all workers would have to change their occupations (Jacobs 1989). Women, however, do not just work at different jobs; they are also concentrated in occupations with the lowest levels of prestige, power, autonomy, and income. Look, for example, at Table 14-1. Each column shows occupations according to how well women are represented in them, *relative to their representation in the entire employed labor force.* Women make up 45 percent of the employed labor force. If women had an equal share of all jobs, they would comprise 45 percent of every occupation, but they make up only 7 percent of engineers and 19 percent of lawyers (top of first two columns), whereas 85 percent of all librarians (top of last column) are women.

The table reveals three patterns that describe the position of women in the labor force. First, they are overrepresented in jobs that involve taking care of other people's needs (nurses, secretaries, elementary school teachers, and child-care workers), few of which include authority over other adults, and all of which carry low pay and prestige. Second, women are severely or substantially underrepresented in the best white-collar jobs (engineer, lawyer, physician) as well as blue-collar jobs that are highly skilled or represented by unions (plumbers and electricians, machinists, truck drivers, and police officers). Only 13 percent of employed women belong to unions, compared with 20 percent of working men (USCB 1990a). Third, in virtually all jobs in which women are heavily overrepresented, they are supervised by men.

Women not only occupy inferior positions *among* occupations, but within them. In medicine, women are rarely surgeons (the highest paid specialty) and

TABLE 14-1 Representation of Women in Selected Occupations, United States

UNDERREPRESENTED			OVERREPRESENTED	
Severely[1]	Substantially[2]	Slightly[3]	Moderately[4]	Heavily[5]
Engineer	Lawyer	Social scientist	Accountant	Librarian
Dentist	Athlete	College teacher	Psychologist	Nurse
Senator or representative	Judge	Artist	High school teacher	Therapist
Carpenter	Natural scientist	Entertainer	Personnel worker	Health technician
Plumber	Computer programmer	Bank officer	Vocational counselor	Social worker
Electrician	Chemist	Restaurant manager	Editor	Elementary/ kindergarten teacher
Firefighter	Physician	Typesetter	Buyer	Bank teller
Construction worker	Pharmacist	Cleaning worker	Health administrator	Office manager
Metalcraft worker	Science technician	Sales representative	Building manager	Insurance adjustor
Machinist	Sales manager	Baker	Real estate agent	Computer operator
Mechanic	Insurance agent	Public official	School administrator	Clerk
Police officer	Stockbroker	Machine operator	Assembly-line worker	Cashier
Heavy equipment operator	Mail carrier	Religious worker	Bus driver	Bookkeeper
Meat cutter and butcher	Telephone installer	Economist	Postal clerk	Secretary
Mine operative	Storekeeper	Biologist	Commercial cook	Telephone operator
Welder	Farm supervisor	Actor	Author	Clerk supervisor
Taxi and truck driver	Security guard		Office supervisor	Stenographer
Clergy	Salesworker (except clerks)		Bartender	Typist
Airline pilot	Blue-collar supervisor			Receptionist
	Precision machine operator			Textile worker
	Farmer or farm manager			Laundry worker
	Purchasing manager			Dressmaker
	Architect			Waiter
	Musician/composer			Child-care worker
	Photographer			Household servant
				Dietician
				Lab technician
				Dental hygienist
				Legal assistant

[1]Equal to less than ¼ of women's share of the employed labor force.
[2]Equal to between ¼ and ¾ of women's share of the employed labor force.
[3]Equal to between ¾ and all of women's share of the employed labor force.
[4]Less than ⅓ more than women's share of the employed labor force.
[5]More than ⅓ more than women's share of the employed labor force.
Source: USCB 1990a.

are more likely than men to be psychiatrists, pediatricians, or internists, all of which are at the bottom of the medical hierarchy (AAMC 1987). Women with Ph.Ds in science and engineering are more likely than comparable men to be unemployed, earn lower salaries, and work for less prestigious institutions regardless of the quality of their graduate department or their professional experience (Haas and Perrucci 1984). In writing for movies and television, males get more jobs than women, with better pay and higher prestige (Writers Guild of America 1987),

and few women make it to top posts in the media (Wilson 1988). In college faculties, women are less likely than men to have tenure or full professorships, and women in the military rarely reach the rank of general. Among lawyers, women are more likely than men to work in government agencies, whereas men more often work in higher-paying private law firms. Women who manage to make it into large private firms are overrepresented among associates but severely underrepresented among partners (Epstein 1983; Hagan 1990; *National Law Review* 1984).

Over the course of their lives, women tend to be somewhat downwardly mobile, whereas men tend to move upward (Marini 1980; Sewell et al. 1980). Even when men and women have equal education, the greater opportunities for men mean that over the course of their working lives, the educational payoff in terms of occupation prestige, complexity, and skill is nearly three times as great as it is for women (Spenner et al. 1982).

Divisions of labor that place women in inferior positions are found throughout the world. Rural Uganda is typical of many agrarian Third World countries in which women do most of the physical labor, and yet are dominated by men, including the custom of being married at about age 14 in exchange for a dowry of cattle. In socialist industrial countries such as the Soviet Union, women are far less likely than men to occupy positions of high income, prestige, or power (see Holland 1985). The Chinese family is heavily dominated by men (Johnson 1983; Stacey 1983); and although roughly three-quarters of all Soviet physicians are female, they have less prestige than U.S. physicians and earn less than skilled Soviet workers (Lapidus 1983).

Wealth and Income

Men are far more likely than women to be among the top wealthholders under 50 years of age in the U.S. Among older top wealthholders, women fare better, but this is largely because women outlive men and therefore outnumber them at the older ages (USCB 1986d, 1990a).

Among full-time workers, women received only 68¢ for every dollar received by men; and families headed by unmarried women are more than twice as likely to live in poverty than were those headed by unmarried men (USCB 1990a; see also Zopf 1989). Divorce is perhaps the leading cause of the impoverishment of women. In California, divorce causes an average drop of 73 percent in the standard of living of divorced women and their children, but brings a 42 percent *increase* in the average standard of living of divorced men (Weitzman 1985). There are more than 20 million married women in the U.S. who are not in the labor force and are therefore dependent on their husbands' earnings and vulnerable to becoming impoverished in the event of divorce (NDHN 1990).

As we saw in Chapter 6 (pp. 125–28), women earn less than men in part because they have relatively low-paying jobs regardless of their qualifica-

tions, and even when they work at the same jobs or jobs requiring comparable skills, they tend to be paid less (England and Dunn 1988; England et al. 1988; Hartmann 1985; Remick 1984). The segregation of women into inferior occupations accounts for as much as 40 percent of the gender gap in earnings (Treiman and Hartmann 1981). As the percentage of women in an occupation increases, the relative earnings of that occupation tends to decline (Baron and Newman 1989). Duncan et al. (1984) conclude that at least two-thirds of the gender gap in wages is undeserved in that it cannot be accounted for by differences in education, work experience, work continuity, and differences in socialization and on-the-job training (see also Marini 1989).

Income inequality between men and women exists regardless of race, but it is more severe among whites than among nonwhites. This is largely because nonwhites are crowded into a narrow range of low incomes, and so the potential for large gender differences in income *among* nonwhites is small.

Although inequality of income is common throughout the industrialized world, there are notable exceptions to the rule. In 1968, for example, Sweden began an aggressive program designed to eliminate gender inequality. As a result, average earnings for Swedish women have risen to 87 percent of those of men, with percentages as high as 91 percent among blue-collar workers (Intons-Peterson 1988). Although in many important respects Sweden has yet to achieve gender equality (Gelb 1989; Moen 1989), it provides a vivid contrast to the rate of progress in the U.S.

Power, Patriarchy, and Matriarchy

Patriarchy and matriarchy describe the distribution of power by gender in a society. A **patriarchy** is a society in which men in general and fathers in particular dominate women, children, and major social institutions, and a **matriarchy** is a society dominated by women and mothers. So far as we know, there has never been a truly matriarchal society, although there have been numerous societies in which women were highly regarded and held major institutional power (Bamberger 1974; Lerner 1986).

Strictly speaking, industrial societies are no longer patriarchies even though they are male-dominated. This is because the center of power in patriarchal societies is the father, and the father's major source of power is his control over production, especially through his control over land. The industrial revolution changed all of that, however, by transferring production from the family to the factory and depriving men of their patriarchal basis of power in both their families and society at large. Few men in the United States are now patriarchs even though they generally have more power than women.

It would probably be more accurate to describe the power structure of contemporary industrial societies as **androcratic**—meaning "ruled by men"—rather than patriarchal (Eisler 1987). Men control business and banking, government, religious organizations, the mass media (including most magazines written for women), schools and universities, legal and correctional systems, prestigious professions such as law, medicine, and science, the military, and most of the nation's wealth (Epstein and Coser 1981). As of 1991, women held only 5 percent of the seats in the U.S. Congress, and only 20 percent of those in state legislatures (CAWP 1991). In some Scandinavian countries, such as Norway, women have more political power than in the U.S., but, as in the U.S., women's power is more likely to be focused on traditionally female concerns such as child care than on male-dominated areas such as economic policy (Haavio-Mannila et al. 1985). Iceland is a notable exception. In 1987 a feminist political party won 10 percent of the seats in the national parliament, enough to make it a pivotal force in national politics (*Los Angeles Times*, August 19, 1987, p. 1).

On a smaller scale Goldberg (1973) has argued that women have great power, because their feminine qualities and child-rearing role make them "the directors of societies' emotional resources" (p. 140; see also Kranichfeld 1987). Because most of women's power is over children, however, it is short-lived and ironic in its consequences, for insofar as women raise their children to conform to gender roles, they are, like the Chinese mothers who bound their daughters' feet, perpetuating a society in which females are treated as a minority.

Women *do* have some power in relation to men; but as Hacker (1951), Janeway (1971), and others point out, it is the peculiar kind of power wielded by subordinate groups. Few would argue that small children are powerful, and yet they often control their parents with astonishing effectiveness. Like children, women are often stereotyped as "manipulative," *but their social status gives them few other sources of power.*

As part of her traditional role, it is only in intimate situations that she can use power and feel its rewards. The more she is precluded from acting for herself in man's world and limited to managing emotions . . . the likelier it becomes that her need for autonomy, her search for identity . . . and the unused energies she possesses will come to expression in private because they can't be put to work in public. The negative role of bitches is almost built into a woman's role and it surfaces at the heart of the duality of marriage *if this is to be the only place where she has a chance to exercise power* [italics mine]. (Janeway 1971, p. 205)

Women also derive power from their unique position as a minority, for while virtually all other minorities are segregated from those who dominate them, intimate relationships between men and women lie at the heart of the most universal of all social institutions, marriage and the family. Although women are a minority, most women also live in relationships in which they depend on men and men depend on them.

Women, Virginia Woolf (1929) noted, serve as "looking-glasses possessing the magic and delicious power of reflecting the figure of man at twice its natural size" (p. 35). She then described how men depend on women to play this role in order for men to feel powerful:

Without that power, the earth would still be swamp and jungle. The glories of all our wars would be unknown. . . . mirrors are essential to all violent and heroic action. That is why Napoleon and Mussolini both insist so emphatically upon the inferiority of women, *for if they were not inferior, they would cease to enlarge. That serves to explain the necessity that women so often are to men. And it serves to explain how restless they are under her criticism;* how impossible it is for her to say to them that this book is bad, this picture is feeble, or whatever it may be. . . . For if she begins to tell the truth, the figure in the looking-glass shrinks; his fitness for life is diminished. How is he to go on giving judgement, civilizing natives, making laws, writing books . . . unless he can see himself at breakfast and at dinner at least twice the size he really is? (italics mine) (pp. 35–36)

As Janeway (1971) put it, the paradox is that "women are weak because they can be strong only through giving. They are strong because what they give is needed" (p. 57). Social systems distribute power unequally between women and men in complex ways. Men dominate, but the unique interdependency between men and women gives women power unavailable to most other minorities.

Prestige

In most societies, males generally have more prestige than women, because they are male and because the roles they perform are valued more highly (see Bose 1985). When men conform to their role by committing themselves more heavily to work than to family, they increase their prestige. Women who fulfill their role through femininity, marriage, motherhood, and working at low-level jobs, however, automatically place themselves in low-prestige positions.

The generally low prestige of women is powerfully reflected in everyday experience. Women office workers are often treated as servants who are incapable of making independent decisions. Many domestic tasks that women are regularly expected to perform involve chores—washing floors, changing soiled diapers, and cleaning bathrooms—that, as occupations, rank at the bottom of the prestige scale (Oakley 1974). Women's work, therefore, is work that men avoid because it detracts from their prestige (Polatnick 1973).

The preceding sections give a detailed look at cultural and structural factors that perpetuate gender inequality. Male and female are social positions, and just as people learn to play the roles associated with statuses such as teacher or lawyer, so, too, do they learn to play gender roles as their culture defines them.

In almost all societies—from nonindustrial to high tech—it is women who take care of the personal needs of other people, including washing dirty clothes.

SOCIALIZATION: LEARNING TO BE FEMALE OR MALE

Most socialization centers on roles people are currently trying to play, as when children learn to play a game or adults learn to perform in a job. Anticipatory socialization, however, involves preparation for roles to be performed later. Gender roles involve both types of socialization, for as people learn to be feminine or masculine, they also prepare themselves for adult statuses that are defined as appropriate for them. In this process, people locate themselves in relation to their families, and then in a continually widening scope of relations in the larger social world.

Gender Roles and the Family

The interactionist perspective is very useful for understanding the ways in which the socialization process is used to construct each person's idea of his or her gender. Most studies show few gender differences in the behavior of infants, but many show that parents tend to treat infant girls and boys differently and to have different expectations of them. Parents generally give boys and girls different toys, and discourage aggressive behavior in girls, but not in boys. They also tend to give sons less help than they give to daughters. When parents are asked if they treat sons and daughters differently, however, they generally report no awareness of the differences observed by researchers (Fagot et al. 1985; Fischer and Lazerson 1984). These patterns vary somewhat by race. Some evidence suggests, for example, that black girls are encouraged to be more independent and self-reliant than white girls, and black boys may be more pressured than white boys to be strong and unemotional (see Barwell, Cochran, and Walker 1986; Hale-Benson 1987).

The expectations adults have of male and female children also tend to lead them to perceive the behavior of children differently. In one study, parents watched videotapes of infants at play, and when they were told the infant was a boy, men tended to describe "his" behavior in terms of independence, aggressiveness, activity level, and alertness. When the infant was identified as a girl, on the other hand, men described "her" behavior in terms of passivity, delicacy, and dependency. Although women made distinctions, men paid more attention to gender-appropriate behavior than women did (Meyer and

Sobieszek 1972; see also Stern and Karracker 1989). Johnson (1988) argues that the greater tendency of fathers to treat children differently by gender is especially important in relation to daughters, whom fathers prepare to assume the role of a "good wife" who pleases her husband, first by learning to please her father.

Both social learning and developmental theory have been proposed as explanations of gender-role socialization in childhood. Social learning theorists argue that children learn gender roles through a combination of conditioning—reward and punishment—and imitation of adults of their own gender. Most studies, however, show that conditioning and imitation explain only part of the process. Both boys and girls imitate adults who display warmth, dominance, and power, regardless of the adult's gender (Bussey and Bandura 1984); and most studies find no consistent evidence that children imitate adults of one gender more than the other (Maccoby and Jacklin 1974; Raskin and Isreal 1981).

Developmental theorists focus on the way children think about gender. In the first stage of development, children discover that there are two sexes and learn to identify people as male or female. At first they use physical characteristics such as hair length to distinguish males and females, but by age seven their idea of gender is more stable and they begin to identify which behaviors are appropriate for each. In the second stage, children develop a sense of value about their gender and begin to imitate people of their own gender as they strive for acceptance as males or females. In the third stage, children develop deep emotional bonds with their same-sex parent, bonds that generally assure gender-role socialization.

Developmental theory is more comprehensive than social learning theory, but does not explain how children select behaviors from the many that are defined as appropriate for their gender. In addition, both perspectives ignore the fact that the particular abilities children develop depend on the activities they are encouraged or allowed to perform. In families, sons and daughters tend to be assigned domestic tasks that conform to gender roles such as cooking and cleaning for girls and lawn mowing for boys (White and Brinkerhoff 1981). Less self-confidence among women reflects more than conformity to roles or imitation of models. It also rests on the fact that girls tend to be excluded from activities such as sports, through which children develop self-confidence.

In addition to being models of masculine and feminine behavior, adults offer children a preview of the statuses they can expect to occupy. Most research on occupational mobility uses only the father's occupation to predict mobility among sons and daughters. More recent research, however, shows that whether or not a mother works, as well as the kind of job she holds, affects career plans and mobility among both daughters and sons (Stephan and Corder 1985) as well as daughters' attitudes towards gender roles (Kiecolt and Acock 1988). Working mothers provide role models of mothers who work outside the home; and fathers in such families can provide role models of men who work outside the home and share domestic responsibilities.

Schools and Gender Roles

Children begin school with a clear idea of their own gender, but know relatively little about adult gender roles. In schools, children learn about gender roles from what they are taught and from the structure of the school itself, which serves as a mirror of the adult world.

Although there has been considerable change in recent years, textbooks continue to reinforce gender roles (Best 1983; Purcell and Stewart 1990). Girls are now portrayed as often as boys, but among adult characters, men still are found more often than women. For female characters, the range of occupations is narrower than for men, and although girls are less passive than they were, they are still often portrayed as needing help or rescue from boys.

The structure of schools also reinforces gender roles (Apple 1986). In elementary grades, when school work has little prestige in the outside world, most teachers are female. Their role is similar to a mother's, and much of the day is spent in play, nurturing, and discipline. Most principals, however, are male. In high school and college, work is more demanding and more prestigious, and most teachers are male. In this way, the structure of schools reinforces cultural expectations that women take care of others and men are authorities with serious roles in the world outside the home.

There is considerable evidence that teachers treat girls and boys differently. In their study of fourth-, sixth-, and eighth-grade classes in the U.S., Sadker and Sadker (1985) found that boys received more attention, dominated classroom discussions, and were allowed to be more academically assertive (by calling out answers rather than waiting to be called upon). In higher grades, girls are often discouraged from participating in serious athletic competition and advanced courses in math and science, while on the other hand boys are encouraged to study science and math but are discouraged from developing their skills in less marketable areas such as language, home economics, and literature (Marini and Brinton 1984).

As children strive for stable identities as males or females, schools play an important role—by presenting cultural images of men and women, by mirroring adult gender roles, and by selectively encouraging boys and girls to engage in activities that develop different skills.

Gender Roles and the Media

Television, radio, films, literature, and journalism provide us with streams of images in words, pictures, and sound. Such images do more than represent the world as it is; they also reflect ideas about how the world ought to be. On television shows most leading characters are male and both men and women are portrayed in stereotypical ways. Women are usually shown in family settings, for example, and most educated professional characters are male (McArthur 1982; WIFP 1986). In newspapers, women are far less likely than men to be covered in text or pictures (Luebke 1989; Russman 1989). In his analysis of the use of gender in advertising, Goffman (1976) identified ways in which men and women are presented that contribute to gender inequality (see also Barthel 1988; Bretl and Cantor 1988; Courtney and Whipple 1983; Lovdal 1989). In most ads, there are clear patterns:

1. Women are taller than men only when men are their social inferiors.

2. Women's hands are rarely portrayed as holding anything firmly—only touching it lightly.

3. Women never instruct men; even among children, the boy is the one who instructs the girl.

4. Men are rarely shown lying down; it is usually a woman or child who is in this vulnerable pose.

This advertisement is typical in portraying men in a physically dominant position over women. How would the impression change if their positions were reversed?

5. The eyes of men focus only on important people; the eyes of women focus on men.

6. Women are often portrayed as "dreamlike" and physically close to a man, as if they did not need to be aware of their surroundings so long as there was a man present to look out for them.

7. Women are more likely than men to be shown in a state of shock or surprise.

Particularly in commercial advertising, images of women and men do more than sell products. As Gornick (1979) wrote, they also

> serve the social purpose of convincing us that this is how men and women are, or want to be, or should be, not only in relation to themselves, but in relation to each other. . . . That orientation accomplishes the task a society has of maintaining . . . order, an undisturbed on-goingness, *regardless of the actual experience of the participants* [italics mine]. (p. vii)

The media often seem to be an independent force in society, but it is important to remember that the images they present are designed to fit the expectations of their audience. As such, the media often

function as cultural mirrors in which people look for familiar reflections, both of themselves and the world they live in.

Gender and Adult Socialization

Learning gender roles involves more than masculinity and femininity, for the place of men and women in society depends on their entire status sets. For this reason, socialization extends throughout the life course as people learn to perform roles associated with adult statuses considered appropriate for their gender.

It is often not until after people marry that they learn how their new status limits their rights in relation to spouses. For many women, childbearing confronts them with the fact that they no longer control their own bodies. As Rich (1976, p. 28) wrote, "The new life of my third child was a kind of turning point for me. I had learned that my body was not under my control; I had not intended to bear a third child."

At work, men learn that most women are there to serve them, and that their success as men is measured by the size of their paycheck and their ability to compete. Women learn that they are expected to occupy subordinate, inferior positions. Even in the professions, they are often excluded from informal interactions through which vital professional knowledge is passed (Schur 1984). They are less likely to be made assistants to those in powerful positions, and are thus more likely to find their upward mobility blocked (Speizer 1981).

When their children reach adulthood, most mothers must adjust to the fact that their major activity in life is now a low-level job that offers few rewards. Although men escape this, they face their own crisis when retirement forces them to surrender their most important status and live at a diminished standard of living. Among the elderly, women must learn to live as widows (Lopata 1979): among people 65 years old and older who live alone, there are more than three times as many women as there are men (USCB 1990a). This is due in part to the fact that women generally live longer than men do. It is also due, however, to the tendency of men to marry women who are younger than they, giving elderly women relatively few potential husbands who are their age or older.

Socialization is a lifelong process through which people learn to participate in societies that treat men as a privileged class and women as a minority. All of this, however, begs the most important question of all: Why are women a minority in the first place?

UNDERSTANDING INEQUALITY

The functional, conflict and interactionist perspectives contribute important pieces to the puzzle of stratification based on gender.

The Functional View: Are Gender Roles Necessary?

The functional perspective raises a basic question: In what ways are gender inequality and the division of labor between men and women functional, and in what ways are they dysfunctional?

As we saw earlier in this chapter, it is reasonable to conclude that in nonindustrial societies a division of labor that places women in charge of childrearing produces functional consequences for social systems. This is primarily due to the dependence of small children on their mothers for breastfeeding as well as the pattern of frequent pregnancies that are characteristic of those societies. Conditions in industrial societies, however, are quite different. Bottled formulas free women from having to remain close to children in order to feed them; contraceptives allow women to limit childbearing to relatively small periods of their lives; women live much longer now and have many years to live after their children have grown; and people no longer range far from home in search of food (Rossi 1984). What functional consequences, then, do inequality and the gender division of labor have now?

Parsons and Bales (1953) argued that because people now live and work in different places, the most efficient division of labor is one in which parents split paid and domestic work. If we accept the belief that women are better suited for child care than men are, then the gender division of labor is functional for reproduction and socialization and making sure that economic, political, and other public roles are performed properly.

We certainly *believe* that "child care" and "mother" are two terms that mean the same thing. Most interpret the verb "to mother" as meaning "to care for," but attach very different meaning to the verb "to father" (to impregnate a woman). Although our association between women and child care is strong, there is considerable evidence that it is based more

There is every reason to believe that men have the potential to provide infants with the physical and emotional comfort, contact, and care that are necessary for healthy development. What is less clear is what it will take for men to feel responsible for such care.

in myth than fact. In his famous experiments, Harlow (1958; see also Harlow and Harlow 1969) raised monkeys with nonliving "mother substitutes" (wire cages shaped like adults) and found that providing food is not the most important part of "mothering"; rather, warmth, cuddling, and physical comfort make the most difference in the healthy development of infant monkeys. "The American male," he concluded, "is physically endowed with all the really essential equipment to compete with the American female on equal terms in . . . the rearing of infants" (Harlow 1958, p. 685).

People, of course, are not monkeys, but Harlow's evidence challenges the notion that only women can give infants what they need. To this we must add the fact that some women dislike children and show little inclination to take care of them, and many men care for children very well. An experiment in Washington, D.C. (Herzig and Mali 1980), found that ten-year-old boys welcomed the opportunity to take care of babies and eagerly learned how to take care of them (their first response on entering the nursery was characterized by the title of Herzig and Mali's book—*Oh, Boy! Babies!*). In their exhaustive review of the research literature, Maccoby and Jacklin (1974)

concluded that whether or not people are "positively nurturant or indifferent" toward children "depends in large measure on how much contact they have with children and how much responsibility they have for child care" (p. 372) (see also Bielby and Bielby 1989; Risman 1987).

Even if we believe that females are better suited than males for child care, a functional analysis shows that discrimination against women is unjustified. A large number of women never marry or have children. As many as one out of every five women born after 1950 may not have any children at all, and for white women the figure could approach one of every three (Bloom 1982; USCB 1989f). Even women who marry and have children have, on the average, two children, who by the age of six begin to spend their days in school.

As we saw in chapter 12, Davis and Moore (1945) argued that social inequality is functional for ensuring that the most qualified people perform the most important roles, but evidence strongly suggests that discrimination against women does not serve this end. As Table 14-2 shows, women college graduates have lower average incomes than men who only finished high school. Discrimination against women appears to have little to do with ensuring that the most capable, highly trained people perform the most important roles (Treiman and Roos 1983).

A functional analysis also reveals ways in which the exclusion of women from important nonfamily statuses is *dys*functional, for it excludes more than half of the population from contributing their talents and abilities to important roles in business, government, education, and other institutions. There is also evidence that gender roles are dysfunctional for women's health (see Golding 1990; Franks and Rothblum 1983). For every category of mental illness, married women have higher rates than single women, whereas married men have lower rates than single men (Gove and Tudor 1973; see also Litwak and Messeri 1989; Mirowsky and Ross 1989). Weiss (1981) found that female graduate students who were divorced or separated were more productive and self-confident than those who were married, but that the effect was just the opposite among men. Women are twice as likely as men to suffer from depression, a difference that recent reports attribute to the standing of women in society (Task Force on Women and Depression 1990).

The pressures men experience appear to be dysfunctional for their health, as well. Their heavy in-

TABLE 14-2   Mean Income by Years of Education and Gender for Year-Round, Full-Time Workers (United States)

YEARS OF SCHOOL COMPLETED	MEAN INCOME WOMEN	MEN	FOR EACH DOLLAR MEN EARN, WOMEN EARN:
Elementary			
0 to 7 years	$10,200	$16,900	60¢
8 Years	$12,700	$18,900	67¢
High School			
1 to 3 Years	$13,100	$21,300	62¢
4 Years	$16,200	$24,700	66¢
College			
1 to 3 Years	$19,300	$29,300	66¢
4 Years	$23,500	$38,800	61¢
5 Years or More	$30,300	$47,900	63¢

Source: USCB, 1990a.

vestment in work makes them particularly prone to depression when they lose their jobs or retire (Schaffer 1981), and weak family ties often leave them without emotional support during personal crises. The strains of the male role may be reflected in suicide rates, for men are almost three times more likely than women to kill themselves, and among older men—who face retirement and the end of their work lives—suicide rates are four to thirteen times higher than for women of the same age (see Table 14-3).

The masculine ideal of toughness may also be dysfunctional for men's health. Men are four times more likely than women to be murdered and almost three times more likely to die in motor vehicle accidents (USCB 1990a). Men are more likely than women to be treated for psychotic disorders involving drug and alcohol abuse and violence toward others (Dohrenwend and Dohrenwend 1976). They are also more likely to smoke cigarettes and less likely to seek medical attention when they are sick or to reach out for emotional support in times of stress (see Verbrugge and Wingard 1987).

A functional analysis makes it clear that a division of labor based on the demands of child care, and the inequalities between men and women that result, are not socially necessary. Many women never become wives or mothers, and those who do spend a small portion of their lives with small children; and men, with proper socialization, can perform most child-care tasks. The gender-based division of labor and its resulting inequalities also appear to produce many dysfunctional consequences for both society and the health of men and women. How, then, do we explain the persistent and pervasive position of women as a minority? One approach to this question is to rephrase it from a conflict perspective: Whose interests does gender inequality serve?

The Conflict Perspective: Perpetuating Patriarchy

The conflict perspective focuses on the struggle over the distribution of wealth, power, and prestige. From this perspective the gender division of labor benefits males at the expense of females. Child care is a key to women's inferior position. As long as women are responsible for child rearing and men are not, women will be unable to securely establish themselves

TABLE 14-3   Suicide Rates by Age, Race, and Gender (United States)

Age	WHITES Males	Females	BLACKS Males	Females
15–24	23	5	12	2
25–34	26	6	20	4
35–44	24	8	18	3
45–54	26	10	13	3
55–64	29	9	10	4
65–74	38	8	16	3
75–84	59	8	16	3
85 and older	66	5	18	2

Source: USCB 1990a.

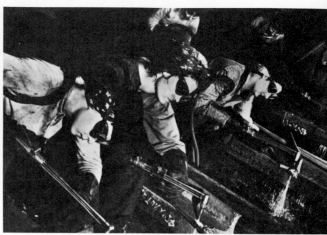

Women's labor has been exploited for well over a century in the United States, from providing cheap labor in nineteenth-century factories to performing vital industrial jobs during World War I and World War II, only to be replaced by returning veterans at war's end.

outside the family, and it is such work that primarily determines shares of wealth, power, and prestige in industrial societies (see Bergmann 1986). Why do women accept child-care responsibility and why do men avoid it?

Polatnick (1973) and others argue that women accept child-rearing responsibilities because existing societies are dominated by men and offer women few socially supported alternatives. Most men, on the other hand, avoid child-rearing responsibilities because their gender role does not require them to take care of children, and because taking care of children does nothing to improve or maintain their dominant position in society.

Although women have long been treated as a minority, Marxian analysis argues that industrialization—and capitalism in particular—sharply lowered the social standing of women. Engels ([1891] 1972) argued that when the family became the private sphere in industrializing nations, women were denied full and equal participation in production, and their resulting dependency on men rendered them little more than domestic slaves (see also Laslett and Brenner 1989).

Capitalists have been quick to exploit women, using them as cheap labor and quickly dispensing with them when they are no longer needed (Smith 1981). Married women contribute domestic labor each year that, by market standards, amounts to billions of dollars; and yet, they do so in return for only a share of their husbands' earnings over which they have only partial control. Domestic labor, however, includes socializing future workers, and thus the domestic exploitation of women also serves the interests of capitalism (Laslett and Brenner 1989; Sacks 1974).

Gender, like ethnicity and race, is also part of a larger system of classes that share unequally in the control over the means of production and the distribution of rewards. The treatment of women as a minority does not result simply from conflict between men and women, but is also tied to larger structures that maintain general inequality in societies. It is here that the functional and conflict perspectives come together.

Unlike other minorities, the subordinate position of women results from more than their relationship to the means of production, for in male-dominated societies, *that* relationship is directly tied to women's roles in social reproduction—the bearing and raising of children (Huber 1989; Mitchell 1966). *Within* each social class, women have unequal standing, just as do the members of other minorities. From this perspective it is easier to understand why lower-class men are more likely to oppose equality for women, for gender divides the working class in the same way that race and ethnicity do. Working-class men are already at the bottom of the stratification system and are likely to experience women's equality as a threat to their already deprived conditions (explaining, in part, why some labor unions exclude women). Black women in particular find themselves doubly discriminated against because they occupy two minority statuses that they cannot change.

Just as the most highly placed black person is, in some ways, culturally defined as inferior to lower-class whites, so, too, is the most wealthy woman culturally defined as inferior in some ways to lower-class men. The parts of our culture that degrade women and define masculinity and femininity apply to males and females of all social classes.

Both the functional and conflict perspectives make it clear that gender inequality is deeply rooted in cultural, structural, and ecological characteristics of societies. These produce many conflicts and dilemmas in the interactions of everyday life.

The Interactionist Perspective

From an interactionist perspective, gender roles and inequality are social realities that are sustained through what people actually do in relation to each other, especially through their use of language. We saw earlier that men and women tend to use language differently in ways that contribute to the inferior social position of women. Observations of interactions between men and women reveal inequality of power in other ways as well, most notably in the control men tend to exercise over conversations (see Kollock, Blumstein, and Schwartz 1985). Women tend to say less than men and more often abandon topics they introduce in favor of what men want to talk about. In mixed-gender couples, men are usually the ones who interrupt; but, when men and women talk with people of their own gender, interruptions are more evenly distributed (Smith-Lovin and Brody 1989; Tannen 1984). When women interact with men, they often appear to be "a class of speakers . . . whose rights to speak are casually infringed upon by males" (p. 117). As a female student wrote in her journal, "he assumes that *whatever* I'm doing is interruptible; that I will be ready to do what he wants to do when he wants to do it" (in Richardson 1977, p. 29).

Men and women differ not only in control over conversations, but in the content of what they say. It is generally true, for example, that people of higher status are not required to reveal as much of themselves as are people of lower status (Goffman 1967), and this appears to be true for women and men. Masculine men are expected to hide emotion and weakness, while feminine women are expected to be open and vulnerable (Henley 1973; Friedman, Riggio, and Segall 1980).

Language is only one of the tools we use in social interaction, and in many cases our bodies send nonverbal messages that are more important than what we say. Women tend to smile more often than men regardless of how they are feeling (Halberstadt et al. 1988). They tend to remember people's faces more accurately than males, a difference that has been detected in children as young as 4 years old; females also are more willing to make eye contact with others and to hold it for longer durations (see Haviland and Malatesta 1981). A substantial body of research shows that women are more sensitive than men to nonverbal expressions of how people are feeling (see Eagly 1987).

Men are more likely to touch women than to be touched by them (Major, Schmidlin, and Williams 1990; Mayo and Henley 1981); and, as Goffman (1967) reminds us, if we are more powerful than others, we feel greater freedom to touch them when we want to (teachers touch students more than students touch teachers). In public we are more likely to see a man's arm around a woman's shoulders than the other way around, and even when holding hands, men tend to hold the back of their hand facing forward, as if leading a child. Men and women also tend to touch in different ways. When a man cuddles a woman in his arms, his position is a controlling one, for her arms are confined by his. Men, however, are less likely to allow themselves to be cuddled, especially in public, because this threatens to reduce them to a childlike status (Henley 1973).

Gender roles create for women a variety of difficulties in their interactions at work. Men generally prefer to have male supervisors and resent women who are placed above them (Frank 1988; Dubnos 1985; Kanter 1976). When competent women have jobs that match their abilities, male co-workers tend to dislike them and exclude them from informal activities such as meeting for lunch or coffee—all of which are important in being accepted as co-workers (Hagen and Kahn 1975; Schur 1984).

In corporations, highly placed women may be the only women in their workplace. Such tokens are pressured to conform to stereotypes that have nothing to do with their jobs (see Zimmer 1988). Executive women may be expected to "mother" male executives—by preparing coffee or providing emotional support. They may be looked upon as sexual objects that men compete for, or as "office pets" who play the role of a "younger sister" who adds humor and does not threaten men (Kanter 1977b). In 1983, for

In Cairo, Egypt, sexual harassment has become so pervasive that the first car on public trains is now reserved for women.

example, one of Atlanta's leading law firms sponsored a swimsuit contest for female law interns (Morello 1986).

Gender roles affect interactions among women and among men, as well as between them. Except for handshaking and contact during sports, for example, men are reluctant to touch each other, for to do so may threaten the power of the man who is touched. Women, however, have less power to lose through touching, and are more likely than men to touch people of their own gender (Rands and Levinger 1979). In one experiment, experimenters stood very close to men and women on a street and found that men moved away from men but not from women. Women, however, were more tolerant of such "invasions" of space, regardless of the "invader's" gender (Dobbs 1972; see also Berman and Smith 1984; Sussman and Rosenfeld 1982).

Gender roles affect not only inequalities of power, but also the kinds of relationships people have. Friendships among women tend to be more intense than among men, tend to last longer, and involve more emotional support (Aukett et al. 1988; Barth and Kinder 1988; Williams 1985). The evidence suggests that men pay a price for dominance—fewer enduring, self-revealing, personal ties that provide emotional support (Fox et al. 1985).

Sexual Harassment and Violence   Among all the pressures and conflicting expectations women face in their interactions with men, one of the most serious is sexual harassment—repeated and unwanted sexual comments, looks, propositions, and physical contact (Gutek 1985). Whether at work, on the street, or on campus, women often experience a violation of their social boundaries, including "those mysterious hands that suddenly appear from under attaché cases, coats, or simply out of nowhere"—what Medea and Thompson (1974) call "little rapes." One study estimates that 75 percent of working women have experienced sexual harassment at work (Kolson 1979; see also Russell 1984). Among U.S. government employees, 42 percent of women report being sexually harassed (Merit Systems Protection Board 1988), and among women in the military, the figure rises to two-thirds (USDD 1990). In a study that included many of the largest U.S. law firms, 60 percent of female lawyers reported unwanted sexual attention on the job (*National Law Journal* 1989). Sexual harassment is common not only in the workplace, but on college campuses. Studies estimate that sexual harassment touches the lives of 20 to 49 percent of female faculty as well as 20 to 30 percent of students (Paludi 1990; Reilly et al. 1986; Sandler and Hall 1986). That men so often assume that women enjoy such experiences reflects a culturally supported lack of regard for women's right to choose the circumstances under which they will interact with others (see Beauvais 1986; Gutek 1985).

Minorities are commonly the victims of violations of social boundaries, which often extend to physical violence. Although men are more likely than women to be victims of violence, women are six times more likely to be assaulted by someone with whom they are intimate (BJS 1991). This is especially true of sexual violence. Using data from the National Victimization Studies, Johnson (1980) estimates that as many as one-third of U.S. females will experience an attempted or completed criminal sexual assault in their lifetime (see also Russell 1984; Russell and Howell 1983). A nationwide study of college women conservatively estimated that 15 percent had been raped since the age of 14 and an additional 12 percent had been victims of attempted rape (Koss et al. 1987; see also Martin and Hummer 1989). Virtually all rape is committed by males against females and damages the victim's life in serious and often irreparable ways (Brownmiller 1975; Holmstrom and Burgess 1983; Russell 1984). In some ways, women are victimized by sexual violence in that the fear of violence seriously limits women's freedom of movement and peace of mind.

The three major sociological perspectives can tell us much about gender inequality from its historical origins to the way it operates in contemporary social systems. What, however, of its future?

GENDER ROLES AND SOCIAL CHANGE

To understand how gender roles and inequality might change, we need to appreciate how we got to where we are now. Most families in frontier America lived in isolated farm communities. Families were large, and women were valued primarily as domestic laborers. Children were valued as economic assets, for the cost of raising them was relatively low and they began to share the load of farm work at an early age.

Urbanization and the Industrial Revolution caused major shifts in the social positions of men and women. Children became less valuable as producers—and, therefore, more costly to raise—and the only way that women could participate in paid labor was to limit child-care responsibilities by limiting their fertility. From 1800 on, the average number of children born by each woman in the U.S. and Europe steadily declined.

As nineteenth-century women became increasingly aware that wealth, power, and prestige were distributed according to statuses outside the family, dissatisfaction over their confinement to family roles formed the basis for the early stages of the women's movement, which sought, among other goals, the rights to vote, own property, and enter into contracts, as well as equal access to higher education and the professions. The first Equal Rights Amendment was proposed in the 1920s but received little support (see Cott 1987).

Women made slow progress in education and employment until World War II created a massive demand for industrial workers. At the war's end, however, women workers were displaced by returning veterans (Milkman 1987); as the postwar economy

A significant cultural change is a growing awareness of the invisibility of women's lives in school curricula, from history and literature to science and mathematics. This prompted one Columbia University student to unfurl this 140-foot banner bearing the names of great women writers over the facade of a university library and its inscribed names of male scholars.

boomed, women returned to traditional domestic labor in the newly emerging suburbs, and the long downward trend in fertility reversed itself in the baby boom that followed.

After 1950 women's participation in the labor force increased dramatically (Bergmann 1986), in part because as the economy expanded, so, too, did the demand for low-level service workers such as secretaries and waitresses. In the 1960s the Baby Boom ended and the costs of raising children increased as more and more young people attended college. As women devoted less time to child care, they once again looked outside the family for roles that would redefine their social identity and increase their share of social rewards. In 1963 Betty Friedan published *The Feminine Mystique* in which she urged women to reevaluate their traditional roles and demand the opportunity to fully develop their abilities; and in 1966 Friedan and others formed the National Organization for Women and rejuvenated the women's movement.

Pressures for social change, therefore, did not occur simply because people began to change their ideas about men and women. Rather, changes in economic production coupled with a decline in the birth rate provided new opportunities for women and pressures for change. As women took advantage of them by dramatically increasing their participation in the labor force, their social position as a minority became increasingly obvious as they were systematically excluded from all but the most low-level occupations. Changes in population and the economy created ideal social conditions for a new and pervasive "consciousness-raising" among women, and many began a concentrated attack on the inferiority of their social statuses *and* on the cultural ideas that underlie them.

New Ideologies and Cultural Change

Just as cultural ideas about gender have been used as an ideology supporting male dominance, the women's movement is based on **feminism**. Feminism is a complex collection of theoretical approaches to understanding how gender affects social life; but it is also an ideology that directly opposes sexism by supporting gender equality and portraying women and men as social equals.

The women's movement is too diverse to be guided by a single perspective, and, in fact, there are at least three approaches (see Ferree and Hess 1985;

Kahn-Hut et al. 1982). **Liberal feminism** defines gender inequality as the result of arbitrary arrangements such as child care, and argues that women and men can have the same opportunities for work and child care to the benefit of both. Its focus is primarily on achieving equal rights and economic opportunities for women without challenging the basic masculine values on which male-dominated societies are based and by which rewards are distributed.

Socialist feminism argues that the causes and cures of gender inequality run much deeper, that women cannot achieve equality without challenging the capitalist system that profits from their exploitation (see Chapter 19). The economic system has made the subjugation of women an integral part of its functioning, and the fact that equality may enrich the lives of both men and women is not enough to bring it about.

Radical feminism goes even further than socialists by arguing that in a male-dominated society, women and men have fundamentally different interests, and equality will require sacrifices of power, wealth, and prestige that men will be unwilling to make (see MacKinnon 1987). Even if the exploitative arrangements of capitalism were overthrown, for example, men would still benefit from the oppression of women, just as they do in most socialist societies, although to a somewhat lesser degree.

Culturally, the women's movement has focused on masculinity and femininity by publicly challenging the definition of females as inferior, and by promoting **androgyny**, a concept that combines masculinity and femininity. Androgynous people are neither masculine nor feminine. Rather, they choose their behaviors without regard to gender. Androgynous men, for example, would not avoid child care simply because they feared others might consider them "feminine." In the same way, androgynous women base their decisions about bearing and caring for children on their personal preferences, not to protect an image as "feminine" women.

Lott (1981) criticized the concept of androgyny on the grounds that it depends on and therefore supports the practice of thinking of people in terms of the masculine and feminine stereotypes. Masculinity and femininity, she argues, are artificial concepts that arbitrarily divide the wide range of human traits into sets associated with each gender. To talk of combining these two sets of traits still treats them as if they are real. A different approach would be to end *all* references to gender when discussing behavior

FIGURE 14-1 Change in Beliefs and Values about Gender in the U.S., 1977 and 1990
Source: Davis and Smith 1982, 1990.

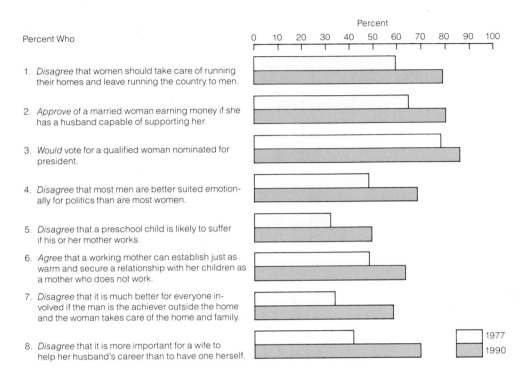

Percent Who

1. *Disagree* that women should take care of running their homes and leave running the country to men.

2. *Approve* of a married woman earning money if she has a husband capable of supporting her.

3. *Would* vote for a qualified woman nominated for president.

4. *Disagree* that most men are better suited emotionally for politics than are most women.

5. *Disagree* that a preschool child is likely to suffer if his or her mother works.

6. *Agree* that a working mother can establish just as warm and secure a relationship with her children as a mother who does not work.

7. *Disagree* that it is much better for everyone involved if the man is the achiever outside the home and the woman takes care of the home and family.

8. *Disagree* that it is more important for a wife to help her husband's career than to have one herself.

1977
1990

and personality, a position that argues against the use of androgyny as much as it does against the concepts of masculinity and femininity.

The women's movement also focuses on norms that perpetuate their subordination. Working through legislatures and courts, women have struck down many discriminatory laws (such as those excluding women from military service academies) and have lobbied successfully for new laws that equalize opportunity (such as those forbidding discrimination against women in pay, hiring, and promotion).

The more subtle norms found in folkways are also the target of the women's movement. Women's insistence that they pay their own way on social occasions, that they be referred to as "Ms.," that men stop rushing to open doors for them, that women be respected when they say "no" in sexual situations, or that they no longer be expected to clean up after men—all reflect a growing awareness that an end to male dominance depends on more than what happens in courts, legislatures, and boardrooms of large corporations. It also depends on what happens in the interactions of everyday life—on the street, in offices, classrooms, kitchens, and bedrooms.

We often feel surrounded by rapid social change, and there are many who believe that most aspects of sexism have been eliminated in our society. As Figure 14-1 shows, it is certainly true that there have been significant changes in values and beliefs about gender. In the thirteen years between 1977 and 1990, increasing percentages of adults support the political and economic rights of women in general and wives and mothers in particular. It is also true, however, that the Equal Rights Amendment was defeated in 1982. Even now fewer than half of all adults disagree with the erroneous belief that preschool children suffer when their mothers work (item 5 in Figure 14-1).

Perhaps most serious is the enduring appeal of the masculine ideal. As Roszak and Roszak (1969, p. viii) wrote, "the world belongs to what . . . masculinity has become"—we value rationality more highly than intuition, control of emotions more highly than their open and free expression, toughness more than vulnerability, the conquest of nature more than respect for it, independence more than dependence, being perceived as right more than admitting we are wrong. For many, then, the liberation of women merely allows them to participate in a male-dominated society according to the cultural ideas associated with masculinity. In this sense, the liberation of women implies the *negation* of women and the cultural ideas associated with them.

On a deeper level, some segments of the women's movement seek to change a male-dominated culture to one based on the full range of human potential. This is a radical goal that would affect not only the positions of men and women, but basic assumptions about how people in general ought to think, feel, and behave.

Social Change and Social Structure

A second major focus of the women's movement is on women's access to statuses that offer higher levels of wealth, power, and prestige. This includes access to higher education and occupations previously monopolized by men; but on a deeper level it extends to the family, for a division of labor that leaves child care to women lies at the heart of their minority status.

It is true that women "have come a long way" since the earliest women's movement. They are more likely now to be in the labor force than at any time since the Industrial Revolution, and they occupy many positions previously reserved for men. They work in coal mines and in police and fire departments; they drive trucks, work on construction crews, manage businesses, and teach in universities. In art, music, and literature, there has been a virtual explosion in new works created by women. Since 1960, the number of women's studies programs at U.S. colleges and universities has grown from almost none to more than 500 in 1989, including more than 30,000 undergraduate- and graduate-level courses (National Women's Studies Association 1989).

The 1980s saw the first woman appointed to the Supreme Court and an increasing number of women lawyers, judges, and physicians. The first U.S. woman astronaut flew as a space shuttle crew member. The number of women in the military more than doubled to 11 percent, and women played active roles in both the U.S. invasion of Panama and the war with Iraq. By 1990, one of every seven West Point cadets was a woman and it was no longer uncommon for women to graduate as top-ranked students in their military academy classes (Moskos 1990). The 1980s also saw Geraldine Ferraro became the first woman nominated by a major political party as a candidate for vice-president of the United States. In 1987, major civic organizations such as the Lions and

Women have managed to break into many occupations once reserved exclusively for men. In 1985, Lynette Woodward made sports history by becoming the first woman to play for the Harlem Globetrotters.

Kiwanis Clubs voted to admit women for the first time, and the Rotary Club was ordered to do so by the Supreme Court. In 1988, the Boy Scouts allowed women to serve as scout masters for the first time.

In families, there is evidence that some men are making greater commitments to child care, most notably in seeking custody of their children during divorce proceedings (Greif 1985). During recent years, there has been a dramatic increase in research examining the importance of fathers for child development (Cath, Gurwitt, and Ross 1982; Furstenberg et al. 1987) and the ways in which married couples can adjust to the demands of work and family. There are also signs that wives who seek careers are increasingly likely to have the support of their husbands, although most research shows that working women are still held primarily responsible for domestic work even when they work full time (Hochschild 1989; Michelson 1985; Pleck 1985).

Such gains sound impressive—especially when highly publicized—but the vast majority of women are still heavily concentrated in low-level, poorly paid occupations (see One Step Further 14-1). Relative to men, working women were less well off financially in 1988 than they were in 1955, in spite of the fact that

ONE STEP FURTHER 14-1

Who Supports the Women's Movement?

As we saw in Chapter 12, those who stand to benefit most from an ideology tend to be among its strongest supporters. Thus far, progress for women has occurred primarily among those with relatively high education and class background—especially those who aspire to careers in business and the professions. Are these social categories also the most likely to take feminist positions on issues related to women's equality?

As a partial answer, Table B-14-1 shows responses to the traditional idea that a woman's place is in the home. If you look down each column, you can see that, for both women and men, higher income, education, or occupational prestige goes along with greater opposition to the idea that a woman's place is in the home (a pattern that holds for several other similar questions as well). Notice also that the answers of blacks and whites are almost identical.

How would you explain the similarity of blacks' and whites' responses? What are the implications of the other patterns for the women's movement?

TABLE B-14-1

It is much better for everyone involved if the man is the achiever outside the home and the woman takes care of the home and family.

	PERCENT WHO DISAGREE AMONG		
SOCIAL CHARACTERISTICS	Women	Men	All
Education			
Less than high school graduate	39	42	40
High school graduate	60	49	55
Some college	69	54	66
College graduate	63	58	61
Some graduate training	81	75	78
Family Income			
Less than $10,000	45	46	45
$10,000–$19,999	50	60	54
$20,000–$39,999	60	55	59
$40,000 or more	73	58	66
Occupational Prestige[*]			
Low	50	49	51
Lower middle	59	53	56
Upper middle	70	64	67
Upper	82	57	66
Race			
Black	56	51	54
White	60	56	58

[*]Pooled from 1989 and 1990 data.
Source: Computed from 1990 General Social Survey data.

women have outnumbered men among college students since 1979 (USCB 1986a; 1990a). Men still rarely involve themselves in the care of infants, and the high divorce rate means that the overall child-care burden still falls overwhelmingly on women (Hochschild 1989; Rossi 1984).

Why Is Change So Difficult and Slow?

It will be difficult for women to free themselves of their minority standing because their position in the public world is strongly tied to their roles in the family; they are a minority in all classes, including within other minorities; and gender is one of the most important bases for the identities of both men and women.

Social Structure   Even if women were not discriminated against, so long as men avoid the responsibilities of child care they will have a huge advantage in the marketplace. Coverman (1983), for example, found that among married, white, employed men and women, the more time people spend on domestic tasks, the lower their income tends to be, especially if they are working-class men or middle- to upper-class women (see also Shelton and Firestone 1989). Coltrane (1988) studied 90 societies and found that the less involved fathers are in

Whether societies are rural or urban, modern or developing, the responsibility of childcare almost always rests on the shoulders of women, leaving them at an economic disadvantage.

child care, the less likely women are to be involved in community politics and to occupy positions of authority. This leads many feminists to look upon the right to choose abortion as critical for women's liberation, for without it they cannot control their commitment to child care (Luker 1984). Even in socialist countries that proclaim equality for women as a major goal, gender equality does not include bringing large numbers of men into child care (Huber and Spitze 1983; Intons-Peterson 1988).

Industrial societies are structured in ways that make it convenient to hold women responsible for child care—"If women are allowed to have careers, who will take care of children?" It is vital to remember, however, that such a question is relevant only in societies that isolate the family from other social institutions by separating production from reproduction; and if the family is isolated, women are isolated with it.

Since most societies are male-dominated, it serves men's interests if societies are structured so that it is difficult for women to gain equal standing. It is true that the liberation of women would destabilize societies to some degree, requiring massive change in social institutions such as the family, government, and the economy. The other side of this, however, is that in order to perpetuate male dominance, domestic labor must continue to be defined as nonwork; and, therefore, females must continue to be treated as a minority.

Changing the division of labor in families may be the last and most difficult goal of the women's movement, for as long as rewards are distributed according to performance in the public world rather than in the family, most men will resist substantial commitments to domestic labor (Coverman 1983; Polatnick 1973).

There is also recent evidence that married men do not like their wives to work full time, especially when wives earn more than their husbands, as they do in one out of five two-earner marriages (USCB 1986e). In a national study of white married couples, Kessler and McRae (1982) found that although em-

FIGURE 14-2   Percentage of Women Who Are Single (Never-Married) by Age, 1890 to 1989, in the U.S.
Source: USCB, 1975, 1987h, 1990a.

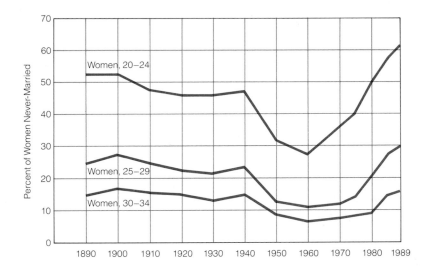

ployment lowered the incidence of depression, poor self-esteem, and psychological distress symptoms (such as insomnia) among wives, it increased such problems among husbands. Nothing indicated that the increased problems of husbands resulted from demands such as a greater contribution to domestic work. The problem, concluded the authors, seemed to be largely a matter of men having a difficult time accepting new definitions of the roles of husbands and wives (see also Michelson 1985).

Faced with the choice between child care and careers, women are increasingly choosing to remain single, at least during their twenties (see Goldscheider and Waite 1986). Since 1970 the number of unmarried couples in the U.S. has more than quadrupled, and the number of young adults living alone has more than doubled. The percentage of women who have never married has risen from 36 to 61 percent among women from 20 to 24 years old, and from 14 to 30 percent among women from 25 to 29 years old (USCB 1990a) (see Figure 14-2).

Women as a Unique Minority   The fact that the formation of families requires women to join with members of the social category that dominates them means that they are at the bottom of whatever other minority they belong to. This means that men will dominate social movements that promote an end to inequality based on social class, race, and ethnicity. Historically, women have made enormous contributions to movements for social justice (including the movement to abolish slavery in the early nineteenth century and the labor union movement in the late nineteenth and early twentieth centuries); but their own cause has been, for the most part, ignored (Kessler-Harris 1982).

This is due, in part, to the fact that women's liberation threatens the social standing of all men regardless of their minority status. During the 1960s, for example, the United States experienced violent social movements protesting injustice against blacks and the poor; and yet women were often treated as a minority *within* these movements.

Identity and the Power of Social Mythology
Janeway (1971) observed that many cultural ideas about men and women are myths—beliefs rooted more in emotion than in factual evidence. Such mythology is "illogical—or, at least, pre-logical" and rarely describes real men or women accurately; but *this has nothing to do with its importance to us*, for "from this very fact, it gains a certain strength: logic may disprove it, but it will not kill it" (p. 27).

Myths are important because regardless of their accuracy, they are beliefs that provide a feeling that the world makes sense and always will. We also value them because as social beings, we locate ourselves within them and depend on them for a stable sense of who we are. From this point of view, it is easier to understand why many women resist their liberation, for they can free themselves only by shattering myths that define important parts of their social identities. It is often easier to hang on to social arrangements that are familiar and yet oppressive than it is to give them up in favor of new ones that are both alien and only potentially better.

As the philosopher Langer (1962, p. 147) wrote, "We live in a web of ideas, a fabric of our own making." However necessary it may be to tear the web that holds us tightly in a world of meaning and social relationships, once we do, we experience the chaos of not knowing who we are, until we create a new social environment in which to live.

SUMMARY

1. Women are a minority in most societies in spite of the fact that they are a numerical majority. Sex refers to the physical characteristics that distinguish males and females; gender refers to social distinctions between them.

2. There is little scientific evidence that biological factors cause more than a very few gender differences in behavior or ability.

3. As part of culture, language reinforces gender inequality by always connecting the status of women with men, by associating male and female pronouns with social statuses, by portraying men and women in different terms, and by degrading the words used to describe women.

4. Masculinity and femininity are sets of beliefs about men and women that make up gender roles.

5. Cultural values both rank maleness above femaleness and evaluate men and women according to different criteria.

6. Historically, cultural attitudes have long reflected hostility toward females.

7. Both laws and folkways are used to reinforce the subordinate position of females.

8. In most societies, adult standing depends on productive labor, and as production has become separated from the home, the standing of women has steadily declined.

9. In families, women still perform the majority of domestic work. Outside the home, women are concentrated in the poorest paying, least prestigious jobs with the lowest chance of advancement.

10. The concept of patriarchy refers to dominance by men, fathers in particular, and the concept of matriarchy refers to formal dominance by women, especially mothers. There is some debate over whether there has ever been a matriarchal society. Androcracies are societies dominated by men, but not through control over families.

11. Gender role socialization takes place primarily through the family, schools, and the media. It depends on portrayals of what males and females are supposed to be like and on how they are treated depending on their gender. Socialization continues throughout adulthood as we occupy marital, parental, and occupational statuses.

12. Functional analysis shows that gender inequality has few functional consequences in an industrial society and many dysfunctional consequences.

13. Conflict analysis shows that women are a minority in all classes and that the gender division of labor serves the interests of men as a group and rests primarily on the ability of men to avoid domestic work.

14. Gender roles define expectations for people according to sex. Gender roles cause considerable status and role strain for both men and women and result in many different patterns of interaction that reflect the subordinate status of females.

15. Pressures for change have grown in recent decades as women have entered the labor force in greater numbers and birth rates have declined.

16. The passage of the Equal Rights Amendment and the elimination of sexism are major cultural goals of the women's movement. Major structural goals include access to better occupations and a full sharing of domestic responsibilities with men.

17. Change toward gender equality is slow because women are a unique minority, because many ideas about gender are deeply rooted in cultural mythology, and because gender inequality is rooted in the structure of important institutions such as the family and the economy.

KEY TERMS

androcracy   341
androgyny   352
femininity   331
feminism   352
gender   328

gender role   329
liberal feminism   352
masculinity   331
matriarchy   340
misogyny   330

patriarchy   340
radical feminism   352
sexism   334
socialist feminism   352

LOOKING ELSEWHERE

Having studied Chapter 14, you might want to look at related discussions in *Human Arrangements*, which include gender and

- suicide (Chapter 1, pp. 11–15)
- income inequality (Chapter 6, pp. 125–28)
- poverty among the elderly (Chapter 15, pp. 369–70)
- role conflict (Chapter 3, pp. 51–52)
- power on juries (Chapter 9, p. 191)
- preference for male children (Chapter 4, p. 67)
- choosing role models (Chapter 7, p. 139)
- social identity (Chapter 7, pp. 142, 144–45, 146–47)
- rites of passage to adulthood (Chapter 7, p. 150; Chapter 15, pp. 366–67)
- attributions of success and failure (Chapter 8, p. 166)

- sexual violence as social interaction (Chapter 8, pp. 168–69)
- group boundaries that exclude women (Chapter 9, p. 188)
- crime (Chapter 11, pp. 243, 245)
- kinship systems (Chapter 16, pp. 387–88)
- sexual values (Chapter 16, pp. 388–89)
- marriage rules (Chapter 16, pp. 390–92)
- family divisions of labor (Chapter 16, p. 393–95)
- distributions of power in families (Chapter 16, p. 395)
- family violence (Chapter 16, pp. 405–406)
- the defeat of the ERA (Chapter 20, p. 517)
- religion (Chapter 21, p. 535)
- abortion (Chapter 23, p. 580)

RECOMMENDED READINGS

Benderly, B. L. 1987. *The myth of two minds: What gender means and doesn't mean.* Garden City, NY: Doubleday. An absorbing and enjoyable discussion of how science in general and sociobiology in particular have been used as part of the social construction of gender.

Berk, S. F. 1985. *The gender factory: The apportionment of work in American households.* New York: Plenum. A recent study of the gender division of labor in families and how this affects family life and gender stratification.

Cook, A. G., Lorwin, V. R., and Daniels, A. K. 1984. *Women and trade unions in eleven industrial countries.* Philadelphia: Temple University Press. A collection of articles that compare the status of women in unions and labor markets in Denmark, West Germany, Finland, France, Great Britain, Ireland, Italy, Japan, Norway, the United States, and Sweden.

Epstein, C. F. 1983. *Women in law.* New York: Anchor Press/Doubleday. An insightful study of what women encounter as they try to enter, survive, and succeed in the male-dominated legal profession.

Etienne, M., and Leacock, E. (Eds.). 1980. *Women and colonization: Anthropological perspectives.* New York: Praeger. A collection of articles on non-Western societies that focus on the sources of gender inequality.

Rollins, J. 1985. *Between women: Domestics and their employers.* Philadelphia: Temple University Press. An important book that, by focusing on black female domestics and their white female employers, explores the complex relationship between gender, race, and social class.

Saywell, S. 1985. *Women in war.* New York: Viking. Portraits of twenty-five women that illustrate the many roles played by women in combat, from World War II to El Salvador.

In recent years there have been an increasing number of publications in the area of "men's studies." See, for example, Franklin, C. W. (1988). *Men and society.* Chicago: Nelson-Hall; Kimmel, M.S. (Ed.) 1987. *Changing men: New directions in research on men and masculinity.* Newbury Park, CA: Sage; and Kimmel, M. S. and Messner, M. A. (Eds.) 1989. *Men's lives.* New York: Macmillan.

15
AGE STRATIFICATION

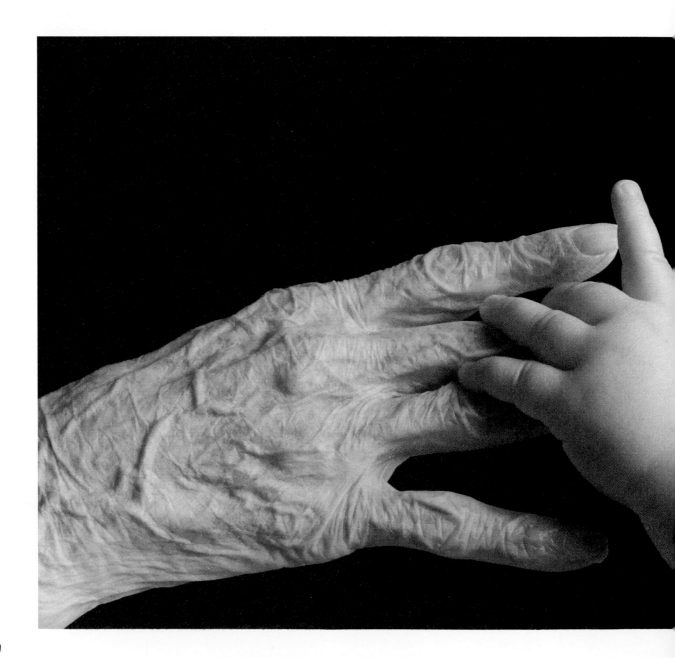

 How old are you? Are you a child, adolescent, adult, middle-aged, elderly? If your answer is "adult," how would you feel if people thought of you as an adolescent or a child? Or, if your answer is "adolescent," how would you feel if people thought of you as an adult?

As your feelings about these questions may tell you, the importance of age goes far beyond the passage of time, and the physical process of development, gradual deterioration, and death. Age and aging are socially important because cultures divide the human life span into age categories and apply different beliefs, values, attitudes, and norms to each. Age is a social status that affects our relationships with people who are younger, older, or the same age as we are; and aging is a continuous transition from one status to another.

We begin by comparing biological and sociological approaches to age and aging, and then see how age inequality is reflected in cultural, structural, and ecological arrangements. We then use the functional, conflict, and interactionist perspectives to help understand age stratification; and we close by considering the possibility of change towards age equality.

SOME DIFFERENT VIEWS OF AGE AND AGING

As a status, age is unique in three ways. First, it is always a temporary, transitional status, for we inevitably move from one age status toward another. Second, unlike other statuses, age provides a cultural map of our entire lives. All cultures include ideas

Age is always a temporary, transitional status placing all of us, at one time or another, in both dominant and subordinate age groups.

that describe the **life course**—the normal set of passages from one age to another (Clausen 1986; Eisenstadt 1956). Each map tells people where they are expected to be and what they are expected to be doing. In industrial societies, the life course usually involves being in school as children, at work in our early twenties, married and raising families by the thirties, and at a peak of wealth, prestige, and power by the fifties. When we are defined as elderly, we are expected to stop working, lose interest in sex, and become less active, less intelligent, and more rigid and conservative in our thinking.

As individuals we can deviate from cultural expectations tied to stages in the life course; but like all deviants, we risk being treated as outsiders and losing our sense of who and where we are. Age is more than a set of statuses whose roles influence our thoughts, feelings, and behavior in a given time and place, for it also defines our futures. Age describes where we are going as much as where we are and where we have been.

Third, more than any other social characteristic, age affects which statuses we achieve. It determines when we go to school, how we are treated when we break the law, when we can get a driver's license, free ourselves from parental authority, vote, be drafted into the military, marry and have children, work, or run for public office. For this reason, it is often viewed by others as a master status.

Of all the statuses that affect people's lives, few are as obvious as age. "Everyone knows" the differ-

ences between children, adults, and the elderly; but as we will see, age affects us in many ways of which we are often unaware. We will also see that what people take to be obvious facts about age and aging in one culture are quite different in others, have changed considerably over the last several centuries, and often have little to do with the biology of aging.

Age Stratification and Minorities

The structure of all societies includes age stratification in which some age groups are more wealthy, powerful, and privileged than others (see Foner 1984). The unique aspects of age as a status, however, make age minorities equally unique, for people of different ages do not stand apart from the rest of society in the same way that other minorities do.

Blacks do not spend part of their lives as whites and women do not spend part of their lives as men; but no one can control the aging process. This means that *we all belong to subordinate and dominant age groups at one time or another in our lives.* The most powerful adult was once a powerless child and has the potential to one day be defined as "old" and, in the U.S., suffer a loss of prestige, power, and wealth. Subordinate age groups are only "quasi-minorities" (Birren 1968), for while we cannot change our race, gender, or ethnicity, age is unique because we cannot *stop* it from changing so long as we live.

The uniqueness of age as a status also produces ironic twists and turns in social relationships as each generation moves through the life course. Middle-aged adults who treat the elderly as a minority perpetuate inequalities that will eventually work against their interests. Similarly, the children parents raise will someday be middle-aged adults in a position to treat *them* as a minority.

How do we make sense of the part that age plays in social systems? The answer should, by now, be a familiar one: the social position of different age categories depends on cultural ideas about age and aging, on social structures that define role relationships and distribute wealth, power, and prestige, and on ecological conditions under which populations grow and use the physical environment.

CULTURE, AGE, AGING, AND AGEISM

Cultures abound with ideas about different ages, and these affect our experience and behavior in social

As Arthur Fiedler, conductor of the Boston Pops Orchestra, illustrates, cultural beliefs about the incompetence of the elderly are based more on stereotypes than reality.

systems. In addition, cultural ideas about age often take the form of **ageism**—prejudice based on age—and ageism, in turn, is related to unequal distributions of wealth, power, and prestige.

Beliefs: "Funny, You Don't Look Old"

The most basic beliefs about age define it as a status, not just a numerical label. In some African societies individuals do not know their exact age, for it is not culturally significant. In China, the age of infants who have lived for 1.5 years is "two"—which means they are in their second year of life. In the U.S., however, age is defined as the number of years we have *already* lived, and those same infants are only one year old.

Cultures also differ in the number of age groups that divide up the life course. The Nupe of Nigeria have 3—children, young people, and the old—while the Nandi of Kenya have 28 (Eisenstadt 1956). In the United States there are 6 age groups: infancy, childhood, adolescence, young adulthood, middle age, and old age.

Beliefs not only define age groups, but also describe people who belong to them. We tend to think of elderly people as asexual, and this often causes younger people to ignore gender distinctions among them, in spite of the fact that gender is one of the most important parts of our social identities. As Burnside (1975) wrote:

> I once asked a class to draw two pictures, one of an old man and one of an old woman. One student said, "What's the difference?" (p. 31)

Beliefs also portray the elderly as mentally and physically slow, inactive, and unproductive. Television frequently portrays the elderly as "doddering old fools who cause problems for their relatives or as wise old ancients who are always ready with a pithy saying or a piece of warm gingerbread" (Jones 1977, pp. 89–93). Physicians often deny medical care to elderly patients on the mistaken belief that the elderly do not have long to live—regardless of their actual health (Wilkes and Shuchman 1989).

Most of these beliefs, however, are stereotypes that do not accurately describe most elderly people (Clausen 1986; Cox 1990). Sexuality is an important part of people's lives well into old age (Cox 1990). Many artists and scholars are most productive after the age of 50; workers' accuracy, steadiness, and reliability decline only slightly with age; and with moderately good health, "individuals can expect high levels of mental competence beyond the age of 80" (Birren 1968, p. 19).

None of this means that biological age does not affect abilities. Infants are far less capable physically and mentally than older children and adults. Among the elderly, aging has many negative effects: slower physical reactions, poorer hearing and eyesight, and less physical strength and agility. In 1988, 37 percent of people 65 and older had chronic medical conditions that limited major activities, compared with only 22 percent of those 45 to 64 years old and 8 percent of those under 45 (DHHS 1990).

Like most stereotypes, beliefs about age often have some basis in fact; but they are often exaggerated, and even when they accurately describe age differences, they oversimplify and distort reality by ignoring substantial variation within them. People over 65 years old, for example, are *generally* weaker physically than those under 65, but there are many elderly people who are considerably stronger than many who are much younger than they. It is also important to remember that, as with all stereotypes, beliefs about age can promote self-fulfilling prophecies. Elderly people may suppress and deny sexual needs and desires because they share the belief that they do not even *have* them. The negative effects of self-fulfilling prophecies can extend to virtually all the roles we perform:

> For all age strata, barriers in the social structure can destroy the motivation to perform in accustomed roles. And once motivation is lost, a vicious circle sets in: Skills and capacities deteriorate through disuse, and the disuse fosters actual physical and mental incompetence. As incompetence becomes apparent, social stereotyping . . . follows, and this stereotyping in turn further undermines motivation to perform. (Riley and Waring 1976, p. 373)

Beliefs about age often have little to do with biologically determined differences, and this fact is clearest when we look at different cultures, as well as historical change within cultures. Beliefs about children have changed dramatically over the last several hundred years. In the U.S., we think of children as distinct kinds of people: innocent, helpless, and un-

As this 1656 painting by Diego Velazquez shows, for centuries children were depicted as small adults without the distinctive styles of dress found in today's societies. To some degree, this may have reflected actual adult views of what children were like as people.

able to perform adult roles. Ariès' (1962) careful study of diaries, clothes, tapestries, and paintings from the last 10 centuries, however, suggests that until the twelfth century, children were portrayed as no more than short adults. In one miniature painting, for example,

> the subject is the scene in the Gospels in which Jesus asks that little children be allowed to come to Him. . . . Yet the miniaturist has grouped around Jesus what are obviously eight men, without any of the characteristics of childhood; they have simply been depicted on a smaller scale. (p. 33)

As recently as the eighteenth century, children and adults wore identical clothes and children were often treated as "small adults." It was not until the Industrial Revolution that cultural beliefs began to describe childhood as a special and unique stage of life (see also Pollock 1984).

Like all cultural ideas, beliefs about age and aging are important ingredients in our construction of reality, including our perceptions of other people and ourselves.

Values: "Why Jack Benny Died So Young"

One of the longest-standing jokes in show business was the late Jack Benny's insistence that he was only 39 years old, even though he was well into his seventies when he died. The joke became funnier the older he got, but beneath its humor lay the unpleasant reality that to be defined as old in the U.S. is something most people want to avoid, because it diminishes their social value.

Children and adolescents understandably want others to perceive them as older than their years, and they often overstate their ages, especially when they approach ages that substantially increase their legal rights. Middle-aged people, however, often understate their ages in an effort to put off the devaluation that comes with retirement and the status "old." Elderly people often protect themselves from this by believing that they are not really old: those over 65 years old tend to believe that old age starts at an older age than younger people do (Riley and Foner 1968). In addition, the older people are, the older their definition of middle age tends to be (ABFP 1990).

Age understatement is common among women, perhaps because age devalues them more than it does men. Adults are 1.5 times more likely to attach the label "old" to a woman under the age of 60 than to a

man (Riley and Foner 1968). This may reflect the fact that men and women are evaluated according to different values—physical attractiveness for women and wealth, power, and prestige for men (Chernin 1981; Margolin and White 1987). As a result, men in their fifties are generally at their peak of wealth and power, while women are losing the feminine beauty that influences how other people evaluate them.

In the U.S., the cultural value of people usually increases as they move from childhood, through adolescence, into adulthood, but then declines in old age. In many societies, however—among the Andaman Islanders, the Soviet Georgians, and the Chinese—the elderly are valued most highly (Davis-Friedmann 1983; Ishii-Kuntz and Lee 1987; Radcliffe-Brown 1948).

Attitudes: "Never Trust Anyone Over 30"

Our culture has many attitudes toward people of different ages. Insults such as "old bag," "old biddy," and "old as the hills" reflect negative attitudes toward the elderly, just as compliments such as "venerable," "dignified," "stately," "statesmanlike," and "wise old woman" and "wise old man" reflect positive ones. Negative attitudes toward the elderly are particularly important because, although everyone can grow beyond the devalued statuses of child and adolescent, death is the only escape from old age. Not only is old age devalued in the U.S. it also signals the approaching end of life, and beneath the contempt often expressed toward the elderly is a cultural attitude of fear. As Mary Gordon (1978) wrote in her novel, *Final Payments*,

> "The old are the invisible minority," she said. "They have no power; they're worse than blacks or women."
>
> "But they do have the power to menace us with our own inevitable futures. White people aren't afraid of becoming black or men of becoming women. Many people act as they do to old people because they're afraid of being like them." (p. 137)

One rare example of negative attitudes toward the middle-aged appeared in the 1960s with the phrase, "Never trust anyone over 30"; but this hostile attitude was limited to a subculture of young people who were actively involved in social movements such as the anti-Vietnam War and civil rights movements. Ironically—and inevitably—those people are now

---

PUZZLE

FINANCIALLY, BEING ELDERLY MAKES ONE BETTER OFF AND WORSE OFF AT THE SAME TIME. HOW IS THIS POSSIBLE?

As you will see later in this chapter, the answer lies in the difference between the effects of aging and the differences between cohorts. On the one hand, it is true that today's elderly are much better off than previous generations. It is also true, however, that if we compare the financial condition of today's elderly cohorts with their own financial condition when *they* were younger, they are considerably *worse* off.

If we compare different *cohorts* of elderly, those today are better off; but if we look at changes in financial conditions *within* cohorts, we find that growing older means substantial downward mobility.

---

over 30 years old and most likely do not define themselves as untrustworthy. This illustrates one of the unique aspects of age as a social status. Young radicals can afford to rebel against adult society, because, as members of an excluded age category, they have relatively little to lose. As they approach middle age, however, opportunities for wealth, power, and prestige increase and the price of expressing contempt toward adult society rises with each passing year.

Norms: "Act Your Age"

All societies use norms to assign rights and responsibilities to people of different ages. In the U.S., laws confine children to schools and generally exclude them from most jobs until they are 16 years old. They control the age at which young people can drive cars, leave home, sign leases and other contracts, join the military, and marry. In some states, age also determines whether a pregnant teenager can obtain an abortion without the consent of her parents. The law sometimes allows adults to have elderly parents declared legally incompetent, deprived of control over their money and assets, and committed to institutions against their will.

Although many laws enhance the power of middle-aged adults at the expense of children and the elderly, some protect those groups from exploitation

and abuse. Parents, for example, can lose custody of their children if they abuse or neglect them. Children and elderly people who commit crimes are treated less harshly than others; boys under the age of 18 are protected from the draft; and the law generally prohibits employers from discriminating against employees on the basis of age.

The folkways that regulate everyday interactions also distinguish between ages in ways that reinforce differences in power. Children are expected to respect their elders and to "be seen and not heard." Adults may call children by their first names, but children generally use more formal titles such as "Mr." and "Mrs." when they speak to adults. Elderly people are not expected to show interest in sex or interfere in the lives of their adult children.

Norms define appropriate behavior for people in each stage of the life course. "Act your age" applies to everyone—from children to the elderly—and reflects the importance of norms in relationships between and within age groups. In a stratified society, such relationships are also important because they result in social inequality.

AGE, SOCIAL STRUCTURE, AND INEQUALITY

On the microlevel of role relationships, age affects the statuses we occupy, the roles we perform, and the resulting patterns of interaction among role partners. On the macrolevel, age affects the distribution of people among statuses, the relative numbers of children, middle-aged adults, and elderly people who are full-time workers. Age also affects the distribution of wealth, power, and prestige. Structurally, few statuses are as important as age, and because of this, the ability to clearly define membership in age categories is particularly important.

Rites of Passage and Age Boundaries

Like all statuses, age categories have boundaries that determine who occupies each age status, and clarity is one important characteristic. I once asked some first-year college students if they considered themselves to be adults or adolescents, and I was surprised to see how many of them were unsure. What does this tell us about our society and why is it important?

Many societies practice rites of passage that mark the transition from one status to another and allow

members to know their social standing in terms of age (Van Gennep [1909] 1960). In such cultures, different age categories have clear rights and obligations and often dress in distinctive ways. Among the Masai of Africa, "learning warriors" help protect the community, carry messages, repair fences, and water the stock. They may not marry or eat meat in public, and wear clothes and hair styles that clearly identify their age group (Gulliver 1968). Young men must spend time living in isolation with older men in the bush and proving their bravery through such feats as wrestling with lions.

By comparison, rites of passage between age categories in the U.S. are rare and provide few clear guidelines that distinguish one from another. Adolescence generally begins at puberty; but, when does it end? How many of us can identify the day on which we become adults? What events tell us when a

Tribal societies often use formal rites of passage to mark a permanent transition to adulthood. In this ceremony for young Mandingo boys in Gambia, an adult man dresses in a frightening costume and makes threatening gestures toward the boys with a knife. When the rite is complete, the boys know they will always be considered men by their tribe.

girl becomes a woman, a boy becomes a man, or a middle-aged adult becomes old? We do not agree on the age that defines "elderly": 38 percent of adults believe that men are "old" before they reach the age of 65 but 21 percent say old age starts at 70, and an additional 14 percent say 75 or older (Riley and Foner 1968).

This lack of clarity about age groups has a number of consequences, the most important of which is the awkwardness and anxiety that afflict people in the "gray area" between age groups. Adolescents are given few clear signs by adult society that they have passed into adulthood (except, perhaps, for the ceremony of Bar Mitzvah for Jewish boys or Bas Mitzvah for Jewish girls) and yet "man," "woman," and "adult" are enormously important statuses. Nor are there rites that mark the entry of people into old age and give broad recognition and support for a major change of status. As Pauline Bart (1971) wrote of aging women, "There is no Bar Mitzvah for menopause."

The absence of rites of passage raises a number of questions that are worth thinking about. Is there a connection between the lack of clarity about manhood and the fact that older adolescence is the most violent and aggressive period in the lives of males in the U.S.? Does this reflect the continuing effort of young males to prove their manhood in the absence of clear rites of passage? Do high rates of sexual behavior and pregnancy among adolescent girls reflect a desire to be regarded and treated as adults, even though such behavior violates norms? Is the "identity crisis" that seems to be so common among adolescents caused by cultural ambiguity about the passage from adolescence to adulthood? (See Raphael 1989).

As we saw in Chapter 6, Margaret Mead's ([1928] 1953) study of life in Samoa during the 1930s suggests that the answer to these questions is "yes." Samoan adolescents, she observed, were fully integrated into adult life: they participated in production, observed sexual behavior among adults, and freely experimented with sexuality. They were not confined to a vaguely defined area between childhood and adulthood, and they showed little of the awkwardness and anxiety so common among adolescents in the U.S.

By telling us who we are in relation to other people, social identities are like anchors that hold us firmly in social systems. We may know how many years we have lived, but it is our social age that really matters. The clarity of the boundaries that distinguish one age category from another is enormously

important, for without it we may find ourselves feeling lost, as if we do not know where we are in social space. This, in turn, makes it difficult for us to clearly define social situations, including our expectations of ourselves and others.

Cohorts, Peer Groups, and Subcultures

One of the most important concepts in the sociological study of age is the birth cohort. Strictly speaking, a birth cohort is an aggregate of people born in the same year, but sociologists often use a wider range of time—usually 5 years—to define them. We could, for example, define those born between 1930 and 1935 and those born between 1960 and 1965 as two different cohorts.

The birth cohort is an important concept because it defines peer groups on the basis of age and because it shows how different populations of people experience the stages of the life course during various historical periods. Each cohort, for example, tends to identify with its own unique history, especially events occurring during adolescence and young adulthood (Schuman and Scott 1989). My cohort reached adulthood during the 1960s, and many of us identify with the trauma of Vietnam, the civil rights movement, and the protest music created by people such as Bob Dylan. Today's elderly are drawn together by the shared experience of the Great Depression and World War II. Cohorts born in the late 1960s and early 1970s have grown up in a society in which nuclear annihilation has been an everyday possibility, and have borne the brunt of the Persian Gulf war. Because of AIDS, they are perhaps the first cohorts for whom sexual coming of age involves risks not only of unwanted pregnancy and venereal disease, but of death.

Such shared experiences can create subcultures that isolate cohorts from one other; but many aspects of social systems—such as primary family ties—encourage interaction among members of different cohorts. Almost 75 percent of people in the U.S. over age 65 have living children, for example, and 25 percent live with them. The percentage of adults who think it is a good idea for elderly parents to live with their children increased from 31 percent in 1973 to 44 percent in 1990; and those who thought it was a bad idea dropped from 58 percent to 37 (Davis and Smith 1990).

Parents and adult children interact quite frequently in the United States. In 1990, 28 percent of adults with living parents reported spending social evenings with them at least once a week, and 44 percent did so at least several times a month (Davis and Smith 1990). In addition, most people—regardless of age—say they *prefer* to spend their time with people of different ages rather than only with peers (National Council on Aging 1975).

There are social forces that both encourage and discourage interaction among age categories. We benefit by interacting with people who are younger or older than we are, for it gives us a continuing sense of where we are in the life course by reminding us of where we have been and where we are going. Yet, the unique experience of each cohort as it moves along the life course encourages us to limit ourselves to our peers, and the more isolated we are from people of other ages, the less aware we are of the effects of ageism, age discrimination, and age inequality on our relationships with other people.

Status Sets and Divisions of Labor

All societies use age as a basis for assigning roles, and the resulting divisions of labor affect the distribution of wealth, power, and prestige by age. Work and family roles depend strongly on cultural ideas about age—both in terms of when we can start performing them and when we are expected to stop.

Throughout history, age stratification has resulted from the confinement of children and the elderly to low-level occupations and, most recently, the exclusion of children and the elderly from productive work itself. Prior to the nineteenth century, production centered on the family, and children were trained for work from an early age. Children were a source of cheap labor in agrarian societies, and by the time they reached adolescence they were full-grown workers.

The Industrial Revolution separated production from the family, and during the eighteenth and nineteenth centuries lower-class children as young as 4 or 5 often worked 14-hour days in dark, filthy, and dangerous mills, mines, and factories. These conditions are powerfully described in Charles Dickens' novels—*Oliver Twist* and *Hard Times*—as well as Engels' 1845 study, *Conditions of the Working Class in England in 1844* (see also Smelser 1959). As the Industrial Revolution advanced in the late nineteenth and early twentieth centuries, however, and machines steadily replaced human labor, new laws prohibited the employment of children and confined them to schools.

As long as it was profitable, industrialists exploited child labor even though children were three times more likely than adults to be injured on the job. Working 10 hours a day, 6 days a week, boys often were used as "breakers" to sort coal; girls were more often used to tend machines in textile mills. Between the dust in coal mines and the cotton lint that hung in the stale, humid air of mills, children often fell victim to lung ailments, and grew old long before their time.

TABLE 15-1   Average (Mean) Money Income by Age, Gender, and Race (United States)

AGE GROUP	TOTAL POPULATION	GENDER		RACE	
		MEN	WOMEN	WHITES	BLACKS
15–19	$1,900	$1,900	$1,900	$1,900	$1,800
20–24	$8,000	$9,500	$6,900	$8,500	$5,300
25–34	$15,400	$20,100	$11,000	$16,000	$11,300
35–44	$19,100	$26,800	$12,000	$19,900	$14,500
45–54	$18,700	$27,900	$11,200	$19,600	$13,400
55–64	$13,100	$21,900	$7,400	$13,900	$8,700
65–69	$8,600	$13,800	$6,800	$10,200	$5,800
70 and older	$8,000	$10,900	$6,700	$8,400	$4,900

Source: USCB 1989e.

Although these laws reflected humanitarian concern for children, they also reflected the fact that child labor was becoming less profitable for employers. In the process, they transformed children from productive workers into full-time students. Since 1850 the percentage of children 5 to 17 years old enrolled in school has climbed from 47 to 97 percent (USCB 1975, 1990a). During the same period, the percentage of those 10 to 15 years old who are employed has dropped from 18 percent (25 percent among boys) to virtually zero. Even though a substantial percentage of older adolescents are now in the labor force, they are far more likely than older workers to be unemployed (Riley and Waring 1976; USCB 1990a).

The elderly have experienced a similar transition. Since 1890, the percentage of men over the age of 65 who are in the labor force has dropped from 68 to 16 (USCB 1975, 1990a). Mandatory retirement laws created room at the top for upwardly mobile younger workers. In 1967, however, the Age Discrimination Act protected workers between the ages of 40 and 65, and by 1987 the act had been amended to eventually forbid forced retirement even at age 70.

It is important to note that the exclusion of children and the elderly from productive work occurs primarily in industrial societies. The elderly in Soviet Georgia, as well as those in many other less developed societies, continue to work as long as they are able, in part because they own their own land. In industrial societies, however, both the youngest and the oldest age groups have been virtually excluded from the productive work through which wealth, power, and prestige are distributed.

Wealth and Income

Children and the elderly are among the poorest age groups in the U.S., with incomes generally being highest among people 35 to 54 years old (Table 15-1). Children are 50 percent more likely to live in poverty than the population as a whole. For the elderly, economic well-being has increased dramatically during the last few decades—due largely to increases in Social Security payments (Duncan and Smith 1989). However, they are still 20 percent more likely to be poor than are other adults, and their average income is lower than that of every age group except for children and young adults.

The degree of poverty among children varies by race; among the elderly, poverty varies by both race and gender. Poverty-level living conditions are found among almost half of all black children, almost 40 percent of Hispanic children, almost a third of elderly blacks, and just under a quarter of elderly Hispanics. Households headed by elderly women are twice as likely to live in poverty as those headed by elderly men (USCB 1990a; see also Applewhite 1988).

The poor position of elderly women illustrates how cultural, structural, and ecological factors combine to produce inequality. Cultural values rank elderly women relatively low, but this alone does not explain their high rates of poverty. Their position as women excludes them from good jobs for most of their adult lives, which, in turn, makes them dependent on their husbands. In addition, women live longer than men, which means that widowhood is far more common among women. Almost half of all women over the age of 64 are widows, compared

TABLE 15-2   Average (Mean) Money Income by Age, Education, and Gender (United States)

EDUCATION		45–54 YEARS OLD		55–64 YEARS OLD		65 AND OLDER	
		(I) Men	(II) Women	(III) Men	(IV) Women	(V) Men	(VI) Women
Elementary	0–8	$11,100	$5,100	$9,800	$4,600	$7,600	$4,700
	8	$15,600	$5,600	$14,800	$5,300	$9,100	$5,600
High school	1–3	$20,100	$6,800	$17,100	$5,700	$10,600	$6,200
	4	$26,200	$10,800	$21,800	$7,700	$13,400	$7,500
College	1–3	$33,200	$14,300	$28,200	$10,000	$17,100	$9,800
	4	$39,900	$19,100	$33,200	$13,300	$20,300	$12,800
	5 or More	$45,400	$26,600	$41,600	$23,200	$29,300	$16,900
Highest-Lowest Income Gap[1]		$34,300	$21,500	$31,800	$18,600	$22,300	$12,200

[1]Equals highest income minus lowest for each age-sex group.

Source: USCB 1989e.

with only 14 percent of elderly men (USCB 1990a).

Widows are also more common than widowers because elderly men are more likely to remarry. Cultural values encourage men to marry younger women, while elderly women are expected to look for husbands among men who are *older* than they. Widowed elderly men have a larger pool of prospective mates than do elderly women: among people 65 years or older, there are only 27 unmarried men for every 100 unmarried women (USCB 1990a).

Unlike income, the distribution of wealth favors the elderly because the longer we live, the more wealth we can accumulate. In 1976, for example, 55 percent of the wealthiest individuals were more than 49 years old, even though this age group made up only 24 percent of the population. Among the wealthy, at least, age generally favors women, because they tend to outlive their husbands and become wealthy through inheritance. The majority of wealthy women are over the age of 50; the majority of wealthy men are less than 50 years of age (USCB 1983c).

Although poverty has declined among the elderly, the incidence of poverty is only one way of comparing the incomes of people in different social categories and ignores the fact that age generally acts as an income leveler because most people are downwardly mobile after the age of 65. This is especially true for women and those who spend their adult lives in the middle class (Tissue 1979).

Table 15-2 shows the negative effects of aging on mobility, particularly among women (take your time

as you study this table). Columns I and II show incomes for men and women 45 to 54 years old with different educations. As you can see, higher education brings higher income, and the income difference between the highest and lowest education groups is $34,300 for men and $21,500 for women. The picture is much the same among those 55 to 64 years old (columns III and IV); but look at what happens after age 65 (columns V and VI). The income difference between the most and least educated men drops by almost a third (from $31,800 to $22,300) and the corresponding difference for women is cut by a third (from $18,600 to $12,200). While the elderly are only slightly worse off than everyone else, most of them are considerably worse off than they were as younger adults, especially if they are women (see Riley 1987).

Power, Prestige, and Self-Esteem

A **gerontocracy** is a society ruled by an elderly elite, and this describes the governments of most societies. The most powerful members of the U.S. Congress are those who have been there the longest and whose seniority puts them in control of important committees. Presidents, top leaders in business, the military, universities, and religion all tend to be elderly. Ronald Reagan was 78 in the last year of his presidency. This pattern repeats itself in many societies—from China, the Soviet Union, and Japan to the Andaman Islands. In 1985, 73-year-old Konstantin Chernenko died while serving as president of the Soviet Union and was replaced by 54-year-old Mikhail Gorbachev, who, in comparison with most of his predecessors, was regarded by many as a "youth."

Although many top leaders are elderly—usually because they were chosen over younger candidates with less experience—such high positions are relatively rare, and in most societies the elderly as a whole are neither powerful nor prestigious. The U.S., for example, is ruled primarily by elderly leaders. Ironically, Uhlenberg (1988) finds that as the population age structure in the United States has grown older, the age of stucture of political and occupational leadership has in fact grown younger. Most people experience a sharp decline in power and prestige when they enter old age, primarily because they lose important work and family statuses. The majority of elderly people live on fixed retirement incomes; they can no longer take good health for granted; most no longer work, in a society that values workers more than nonworkers; and they are expected to depend on others to take care of them, to enjoy depending on other people for a change (Barton, Baltes, and Orzech 1980).

All of these social factors add up to a general loss of control by many elderly over important parts of their private lives and their environments. Elderly residents of nursing homes, for example, often have little power over the most fundamental aspects of their daily lives—when they will eat or sleep, or when they can see visitors—and this loss of control often damages their health and lowers their level of activity and enthusiasm for life (Rodin 1986; Timko and Moos 1989). Whether in families or nursing homes, the dependency of the elderly on others also makes them vulnerable to neglect and abuse which affect an estimated 1.5 million elderly people each year in the United States (House Select Committee on Aging 1990). In nursing homes this is compounded by the frequent use of powerful drugs, not to improve the health of elderly residents but to make it easier for staff to control them (Avorn 1988).

The cultural devaluation of the elderly suggests that the U.S. is a youth-oriented society, but the high value that adults place on delaying the loss of their *own* youth does not mean that a culture values young *people*. As a characteristic, a youthful appearance may enhance the power and prestige of older adults, but it diminishes the power and prestige of the young. Children have little if any power, either over other people or their own lives. Throughout history, fathers in many societies have had the power to kill children who displeased them. Even in industrial societies, children are highly vulnerable to physical abuse by parents (see Chapter 16).

As noted earlier, it would be difficult to argue convincingly that children are an oppressed minority in the same sense that nonwhites and women are, for children eventually become adults, and the powerlessness of children results in part from biological limitations. Many 13-year-old boys and girls are biologically capable of having children, but they certainly are unable to care for them or earn a living in industrial societies. In many industrial societies, however, childhood is extended to include older adolescents and even those in their early twenties; and while adolescents are also not an oppressed minority, their levels of power and prestige are greatly out of line with their abilities. Denied power and prestige in the adult world, many adolescents compensate by expressing power among their peers—especially through the use of violence—and often direct their frustration toward adults by rebelling against parental and legal authority.

The low standing of adolescents may help explain their unusually high levels of deviance (Steffensmeier et al. 1989). Those 15 to 17 years old make up 4 percent of the U.S. population, but account for 10 percent of all arrests for rape, 17 percent of arrests for robbery and larceny, 30 percent of arrests for car

The rebelliousness common among the teenagers in industrial societies may be caused by the relatively useless social statuses young people are forced to occupy and the resulting difficulty they have defining themselves as socially important.

theft, 15 percent of arrests for arson, and 20 percent of arrests for vandalism. Overall, they accounted for 17 percent of all arrests for serious crimes—a share four times larger than their share of the population (USCB 1990a).

Exclusion from adult statuses contributes to lowered levels of power, prestige, and self-esteem among children and the elderly, who are more likely than those in other age groups to feel useless, trivial, and socially invisible. Children who grew up during the Great Depression of the 1930s often made important contributions to the survival of their families and had good reason to feel that they were needed and valued (Elder 1974). By comparison, the primary role of many of today's children is that of consumer, and they often have good reason to feel superfluous, as if their dependent emotional attachment to their families is their only meaningful connection to adult society (see Zelizer 1985).

In other ways, however, historical changes have increased the relative power of adolescents. When the family was the center of production, adolescents had few alternatives to working under the authority of their parents. As the Industrial Revolution shifted productive work away from the family, however, the availability of paid employment outside the family gave adolescents a way to get out on their own (see Frey and Kobrin 1982).

POPULATION, ECOLOGY, AND AGE STRATIFICATION

The ecological perspective reveals two key aspects of age stratification. First, it focuses on the relationship between population *age structures* and *role structures* through which societies produce goods and services. Second, it draws attention to the fact that each cohort experiences stages of the life course at different times in a society's history and, therefore, in different circumstances. Such differences, in turn, affect levels of social inequality.

Age Structures, Role Structures, and Inequality

As we saw in Chapter 4, the age structure of a society is the relative number of people who are of each age. Primarily due to declining birth rates, populations in Europe and North America have been growing older

for over a hundred years. Since 1870, the percentage of the U.S. population under the age of 15 has fallen from 39 percent to 23, while the percentage over the age of 64 has quadrupled from 3 percent to 13 (PRB 1990a; USCB 1975a) (see Figure 15-1).

The role structure of a society has three aspects: the *number of different roles*, the *number of openings* that exist for each role, and the *requirements for role performance*. Role structures depend on the level of technology and how labor is organized in relation to it. Gatherer-hunter societies use simple technologies and have simple role structures; but industrial societies use sophisticated technologies and divide labor into thousands of different jobs, some of which employ far more people than do others. For example, there are some four million secretaries in the U.S., but only 143,000 architects, 100 U.S. senators, and one president (USCB 1990a).

On the one hand, all societies have role structures that determine the kind and number of roles that are available for people to perform, and age is an important characteristic used to assign people to those roles. On the other hand, populations have age structures that determine the relative numbers of people available to perform roles that are culturally defined as appropriate for each age group. If we consider age and role structures simultaneously, we can see that *age structures and role structures always have the potential to be out of balance with each other*, a condition which Riley et al. (1988) call **structural lag** (see also Riley 1976, 1987). Productive work in agrarian societies requires relatively little sophisticated training, and children and the elderly can perform many productive roles. In agrarian economies—where machines do little of the work—the more workers there are, the higher production will be. In agrarian societies, age structures are rarely out of balance with the opportunities provided by role structures.

Industrial societies, however, have less use for unskilled workers and rely heavily on machines to replace human labor; and this provides few work opportunities for children. The relative scarcity of jobs also creates pressures to exclude the elderly in order to make room for young adult and middle-aged workers. The more numerous children and the elderly are in industrial societies, the more likely they are to be excluded from the labor force.

This means, however, that "young" and "old" age structures—those with large percentages of children or the elderly—create more strains in industrial soci-

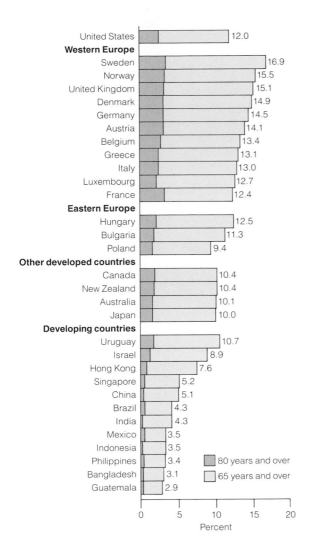

FIGURE 15-1 Percentage of the Population that is 65 Years and over or 80 Years and over for Selected Countries. Notice how much older the populations of industrialized countries are in comparison with less-developed societies. Why is this so?
Source: Cockerham 1991, p. 38

People's ability to compete successfully in industrial societies depends on two cohort effects. First, trends in birth and death rates produce cohorts of different sizes. Between 1800 and the late 1940s, for example, birth rates fell steadily in the U.S. and Europe, and this meant that each new cohort was smaller than the next older cohort. In addition, the Industrial Revolution rapidly expanded the demand for workers. Together, these changes meant that an economy that had enough jobs for one generation of workers could easily absorb the smaller generations that followed.

From the late 1940s through 1960, however, the post–World War II baby boom temporarily reversed the fertility decline, and adults who are now in their thirties are far more numerous than were older generations. The result is a role structure whose opportunities are out of balance with the population age structure: the number of jobs being vacated by the relatively small generations of people who are now in their fifties and sixties is insufficient for the larger baby boom generation. It is, in part, for this reason that there is so much pressure on older workers to retire in order to make room for younger workers.

A second cohort effect arises from the fact that each cohort experiences stages in the life course under different social conditions, and this produces differences in characteristics, such as educational attainment, that strongly affect our share of wealth, power, and prestige. The cohorts born between 1915 and 1920, for example, are among today's elderly. They experienced childhood in the Roaring Twenties, adolescence during the Great Depression when educational opportunities were very limited, young adulthood during and after World War II when the job market exploded with new opportunities, and middle age during the turbulent 1960s. By comparison, the 1945–1950 cohort experienced childhood during the relatively prosperous 1950s, adolescence during the 1960s that saw an explosion of educational opportunities, and young adulthood during the economic recession of the 1970s. In the 1990s,

eties than in agrarian ones, because the role structure provides relatively few positions for large portions of the population. Thus, *the relationship between age and role structures* determines their effect on age inequality: the more out of balance with each other they are, the greater age inequality will tend to be.

Cohorts and the Importance of Generations

At any one time, a population includes people from a series of cohorts, each of which may pass through important stages of the life course under different social circumstances that produce what are called **cohort effects** (Riley 1987; Riley and Foner 1972; Ryder 1965).

this cohort approaches middle age in an economy with limited opportunities, and they must compete for upper-level jobs with a rapidly expanding older population.

Differences in cohort histories produce sharp differences in their ability to compete: only 9 percent of people over the age of 65 have four or more years of college, compared with 26 percent of those 30 to 44 years old (USCB 1990a). As new, more sophisticated technology redefines requirements for successful role performance in the job market, members of older cohorts inevitably find themselves at a competitive disadvantage. Computer technology is one of the most rapidly expanding segments of the labor market, and the relatively low education of older workers poorly equips them to compete for these jobs.

As each new cohort benefits from expanded educational opportunities, it enlarges its advantage in relation to older cohorts, but eventually *loses* ground in relation to *younger* cohorts. While older workers are less likely than younger workers to *lose* their jobs, if they do, it is much harder for them to find new ones.

UNDERSTANDING AGE STRATIFICATION

Age stratification can have both functional and dysfunctional consequences, and these often depend on population and ecological characteristics of social systems. Age stratification also reflects the ability of some age categories to dominate others in the competition for wealth, power, and prestige. The functional and conflict perspectives help answer a question that can be stated far more simply than it can be answered: Why does age stratification exist at all? From the interactionist perspective comes insight into how age affects relationships in everyday life.

Functions and Dysfunctions of Age Stratification

Age stratification produces a variety of functional consequences (Eisenstadt 1956). Young children, for example, are physically, emotionally, and mentally incapable of performing adult roles in industrial societies that rely on skilled labor and sophisticated technology. Continuity from one generation to the next requires that children be socialized so that they will be able to perform adult roles when they grow

up. This requires training, and adults can train their children only if they have power over them.

Successful performance of any role requires motivation as well as ability, and all societies use inequality between adults and children to encourage children to strive for adult standing. Because adults are wealthier, more prestigious, and more powerful than children, children are motivated to learn what they have to in order to escape the limitations and disadvantages of childhood.

Although age stratification has some functional consequences, as we have seen before, aspects of social systems may be functional in some ways and dysfunctional in others. Forced retirement is functional for creating opportunities for younger workers, but is dysfunctional for keeping the most experienced workers in the labor force. This creates a growing class of older people who must be supported by younger adults who are already feeling the strain of trying to provide for their own growing families. Excluding adolescents from the labor force is functional for lessening competition for jobs; but it also creates a large number of people who produce far less than they consume, feel disconnected from society, and often express their resulting frustration in destructive ways.

Age and Social Conflict

The conflict perspective identifies relationships between age stratification and the conditions that create and maintain social classes. Beliefs that portray adolescents as incapable of performing adult roles and that define the elderly as senile arose in part from class conflict. Nineteenth-century laws that prohibited child labor were strongly supported by labor unions that wanted to reduce competition for jobs. Mandatory retirement for older workers increased in popularity during the 1930s—the years of the Great Depression—when jobs were scarce and labor unions were becoming more powerful (Atchley 1982).

The low standing of the elderly in the U.S. is also related to class conflict, because competition between age groups is produced by the concentration of wealth and income in the upper class. Retirement benefits the capitalist class by lowering costs and increasing business profits. Employers can replace experienced—and more expensive—older workers with younger workers who, although they are generally better educated, are willing to work for lower wages because they are inexperienced (Haber 1983). Pension plans serve the interests of capitalists by helping to remove older workers (Williamson et al. 1985).

As the age structure of the population becomes older, the potential for conflict increases. When Social Security was enacted in 1935, for example, it was designed as a self-supporting fund that would provide supplementary benefits for all elderly people who contributed to the fund during their working years. Workers and employers would contribute, and when workers retired they would draw from the fund. By design, then, each cohort contributed to a "safety net" that would protect those who survived to old age from living in poverty.

In practice, the system has worked quite differently. In 1956, disabled workers under age 65 became eligible for benefits; in 1961, workers retiring before age 65 also became eligible; and in 1965, hospital insurance under the Medicare plan was added to the list of benefits. Because the elderly population was still relatively small in the early 1970s, the fund had a huge surplus, and Congress decided to adjust social security payments according to the level of inflation.

In the 1970s, however, the cost of living—as measured by inflation—was rising *faster* than the income of workers. Between 1970 and 1981 average real family income actually *dropped* by almost one percent, but social security benefits increased by 40 percent. At the same time, the age structure of the population was becoming older at a rapid rate. Together, these two factors meant that for the first time money was flowing *out* of the fund faster than it was coming *in*, and by 1983 the social security system was losing money at the rate of $20,000 each *minute*.

As benefits rose rapidly, retired workers were drawing far more from the social security fund than they and their employers had contributed. The average person who retired in 1980 had, together with his or her employer, contributed $24,000 to the system; but those retirees could expect to draw $125,000 in benefits. The result is a growing burden on the young and middle-aged working population, whose contribution to social security is now used immediately to pay *current* benefits to those who are already retired (Figure 15-2). In 1960 there were five workers to provide benefits for each retired person. The elderly population is now much larger relative to the working population that pays social security taxes, and there are only 3 workers to support each retired person. The Social Security Administration (1988) estimates that by 2035, this ratio will drop to 1.9.

FIGURE 15-2   Number of Workers per Beneficiary, with Projections
Source: Social Security Administration 1988.

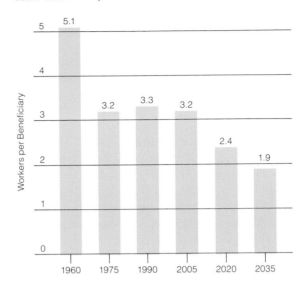

The social security problem is not simply a matter of changing age structures and rising retirement benefits, for it also reflects the U.S. economic structure. The large population of retired people is produced in part by an economy that cannot provide jobs for everyone who wants to work, and from this perspective, retirement programs benefit capitalists as well as (if not more than) middle- and lower-class workers. Without such programs, workers would either insist on remaining in the labor force well into old age or would demand wages high enough to provide for retirement (Smith 1981). In this way, retirement programs operate as "a kind of insurance for capitalists and corporations" (O'Connor 1973, p. 138).

Age and Social Interaction

Like all statuses, age affects our choice of role partners, and the roles attached to age affect our perceptions, evaluations, feelings, and expectations of ourselves and other people. This, in turn, produces patterns of interaction that vary according to the ages of those involved.

Each age status has a role set. Young adults orient themselves to different sets of expectations when they interact with children, adolescents, peers, middle-aged adults, and the elderly. We readily call a boy by his first name, for example, but would wait for permission to call a 70-year-old woman by hers.

Role sets change as people move from one age category to another. In the U.S., children have few responsibilities or rights, and their roles consist more of what they should *not* do than what they should do. They are surrounded by an adult world whose statuses are forbidden to them, and aside from attending school and doing what they are told, they live with relatively few important expectations from their society.

Rights and responsibilities increase in adolescence and adulthood, especially in relation to people of a younger age. As adolescents, for example, we feel obliged to help a lost child or an ailing elderly person in ways that rarely occurred to us as children. The older we become, the more responsible we tend to feel for other people and the groups and communities to which we belong. In the U.S., however, old age reverses the upward trend of rights and responsibilities. The social position of the elderly reverts in many ways to that of children, which consists more of what they should not do than what they should.

Like members of minorities, children and the elderly are often treated by young and middle-aged adults as if they were socially invisible, and this reflects and perpetuates their subordinate social position. Adults frequently discuss children's problems with other adults even when the children are present and often refer to them in the third person, as if they were not there. The elderly also find themselves treated in this way, because younger people may assume they are senile and unable to hear what is said or to understand what they hear.

There is a deeper reason for treating the elderly as if they were invisible, however. Especially in industrial societies, the death of young people is rare, so most awareness of death is associated with the elderly, who remind people that death is inevitable. In the U.S., people over the age of 75 constitute 5 percent of the population but account for 48 percent of all deaths (USCB 1990a).

> Although the old have always died, the dying have not always been old. It is only in very recent decades that death has become primarily the province of the elderly, rather than an event scattered erratically across the life span. . . . Because of the close association between old age and death in modern industrial societies, the individual and social issues relating to death are in many ways individual and social issues of aging. . . . One of the significant reasons that the old are avoided and isolated is their proximity to death. (Kalish 1976, p. 494)

The fear of death affects interactions with the elderly when they are identified as terminally ill. Dying is a social event as well as a biological one, and it involves relationships among people who occupy different statuses and perform different roles (Brown 1990; Sudnow 1967). Most elderly people die in hos-

Unlike most elderly people in the U.S., the grandfather in this family died at home under the care of his wife, his grandson, and his grandson's family. This arrangement brings out many of the roles involved in dying as a social event, including saying goodbye.

pitals or nursing homes, for example, and they are often treated in ways that protect other people's feelings more than their own. Terminally ill patients are often treated as though they were already dead: autopsies are arranged, relatives are asked to approve donation of vital organs after death, and patients may find themselves isolated and shut away in back hallways. Doctors, nurses, and family members may pretend that terminally ill patients are not dying (Benoliel 1973), and they may justify this as a way to avoid upsetting the patient. A number of studies show, however, that most patients would rather know the truth (Glaser and Strauss 1965). How, then, do we explain such deception?

One answer is that people deceive dying patients in order to control the definition of the situation, which, in turn, determines the roles they must play. By lying about patients' true conditions, doctors, nurses, and family members promote a definition of the situation that prevents dying patients from expressing the grief, rage, and need for emotional support that often accompany awareness of impending death (Kübler-Ross 1969, 1975). Such pretenses enable people to avoid performing painful roles. Doctors and nurses can avoid the frustration of being unable to keep an elderly person alive, and family members can postpone their grief and avoid feelings of helplessness and rage. While this protects the feelings of doctors, nurses, and family members, however, it denies dying patients the emotional support of other people and the opportunity to prepare themselves emotionally for death.

Concern for the needs of dying patients has recently prompted the development of alternative social institutions. Unlike most hospitals and nursing homes, a **hospice** is designed specifically for the terminally ill; it supports patterns of interaction that differ sharply from those found in most hospitals and nursing homes. Hospices are designed to be as home-like as possible and allow frequent contact between patients and other people. Awareness of death is openly shared, and this calls upon family, friends, and health professionals to perform roles in which they confront their own feelings and support patients during their final transition to death (Mor 1987; Munley 1983).

This example illustrates an important dilemma in social interactions involving dying patients. The hospice movement is based on the value judgment that it is preferable for dying patients to be fully aware of what is happening to them. The deliberate avoidance of such awareness is based on the judgment that awareness of dying unnecessarily adds fear and anxiety to what is already probably the most difficult experience in the life course. It is a difficult value judgment to make, for those who make it are not themselves approaching death and yet have a great deal of power and responsibility to define the social situations in which people die.

Apparently the medical profession has moved rapidly toward greater openness with dying patients. A 1961 study of U.S. physicians found that only 10 percent favored telling terminal cancer patients the truth about their conditions; but a similar study in 1979 found that the percentage had risen to 90 percent (reported in J. Riley 1983).

The position of the elderly can be understood from functional, conflict, and interactionist perspectives. It is also closely tied to changing age and role structures and to biological aspects of age and aging. The uniqueness of age as a social status produces both barriers to change and pressures for change.

AGE STRATIFICATION AND SOCIAL CHANGE

Pressures toward age equality come from organized social movements, the unique characteristics of age as a social status, changing age structures of populations, and the changing characteristics of age cohorts.

In the U.S., the elderly have greatly increased their political power in the last decade. They are not only more numerous than ever before but are more likely to vote than any other age group (USCB 1990a). The American Association of Retired Persons has 28 million members, and the Gray Panther organization has tens of thousands who actively challenge stereotypes while promoting equal rights for the elderly. Says Maggie Kuhn, the 81-year-old founder of the Gray Panthers:

> We have used street theater, we have marched, we have demonstrated, we have picketed. . . . But more than that, we have brought together a group of people who have first-class minds and who read a lot, who have the ability to think and who have a creative social analysis. (*Hartford Advocate*, July 28, 1982, p. 6)

The Gray Panthers is an intergenerational organization that attracts people of all ages. In part, its attractiveness rests on the uniqueness of age as a

social status, for we all face the time when we will be culturally defined as "old." Whites can ignore the oppression of blacks; men can ignore the oppression of women; and adults can ignore the disadvantaged position of children. Few can ignore the fate of the elderly, however, without also ignoring the inevitability of old age itself.

Perhaps the most important pressure for change results from long-term shifts in the age structure of populations and the flow of generations through the life course. The long-term decline of birth rates in Europe and North America has caused major shifts in population age structures. By the year 2030, an estimated 22 percent of the U.S. population will be over the age of 64, compared with 13 percent in 1990 and only 4 percent in 1890 (USCB 1975, 1990a). From 1980 to the year 2000, the number of centenarians—people 100 or more years old—is expected to jump by seven times, from 15,000 to more than 100,000 (USCB 1987i). Throughout Europe, populations are expected to be even older than in the U.S. (OECD 1987).

The resulting "graying" of the U.S. age structure will increase the political power of the elderly and pressure decision makers to devote larger portions of national resources to elderly people's needs, such as health care and retirement income and housing. Opposition to mandatory retirement laws will grow along with the size of the elderly population, and this will put pressure on a job market that excludes the elderly in order to provide jobs for young and middle-aged adults.

Such changes are particularly important in southern parts of the U.S. whose populations have swelled with elderly migrants attracted by warm climates and low costs of living. People over the age of 64 make up 13 percent of the U.S. population but 18 percent of Florida's (USCB 1990a). Many communities in Florida and other Sun Belt states are being designed and built specifically to meet the needs of older residents, and the elderly increasingly dominate local and state politics.

Increased power among the elderly also results from the different social characteristics of cohorts. In 1988, 31 percent of those over the age of 64 had never gone beyond elementary school; only 11 percent had college degrees; and 20 percent were foreign-born and relatively unfamiliar with U.S. laws and the political process. By comparison, less than 10 percent of the elderly in 2010 will have never gone beyond elementary school; roughly 20 percent will have college degrees; and almost all will be native-born (USCB 1981, 1986a, 1990a). This, combined with an increasing consciousness of the importance of age as a social status, will probably result in considerable increases in the social power of the elderly.

Greater tension between age groups appears to be an inevitable consequence of changing age structures and the increased political power of each succeeding generation of elderly people. How might these tensions be resolved? Is equality a possible answer?

Is Equality Possible?

Age stratification results primarily from the use of age to determine which statuses people may occupy and, therefore, which roles they may perform in the division of labor. Equality among age groups implies that age would no longer limit people's access to statuses, especially jobs. This kind of arrangement, however, would inevitably result in renewed age stratification, because societies still have to allocate roles among their members, and the most likely criteria are strongly related to age (Riley and Waring 1976).

Suppose that work roles were allocated on the basis of skill and ability. Adolescents would be at a disadvantage, and the middle-aged and elderly would have to compete with healthy and vigorous younger cohorts fresh out of college where they have learned the latest technological skills. If work experience were the most important factor, young and middle-aged workers would lose their competitive edge over the elderly. If jobs went to those who needed them most—such as those with families—the middle-aged would benefit, because they are the most likely to have families with college age children.

This analysis suggests that age stratification among adolescents, adults, and the elderly is unavoidable, but it rests on an assumption that may not be. All of these hypothetical consequences of age equality would occur only in a society that cannot provide jobs for everyone, making it necessary to exclude some people from the labor market in order to employ everyone else. As we saw in Chapter 13, competition tends to breed prejudice, and prejudice is the cultural bulwark of discrimination.

To Marx, such conditions are main features of capitalist, industrial societies in which the means of production are privately owned, and competition among workers keeps wages low and profits high. Marx argued that these conditions would disappear in a technologically advanced communist society, and, with them, all forms of social inequality. From Marx's perspective, age inequality is directly related to the same social conditions that produce social classes.

Since Marx's view is utopian, we cannot know if the ideal society he envisions is possible. His perspective is useful, however, because it underscores the fact that social change is severely limited by the basic ways in which societies organize production and distribute wealth, power, and prestige. It is impossible to eliminate age stratification in industrial societies—including capitalist and socialist countries—without changing fundamental economic and political structures that perpetuate inequality. To see why this is true, consider the recommendations of two panels of scientists who studied the disadvantaged positions of the young and the elderly in the U.S. (Coleman et al. 1974; Riley 1974).

In industrial societies, education is confined primarily to children and adolescents who, in turn, spend most of their time in school. Similarly, young and middle-aged adults are confined to work, and the elderly are largely excluded from paid work. In spite of the fact that they focused on dramatically different age categories, the panels made similar recommendations: education, work, and leisure should not be rigidly distributed by age; rather, they should be distributed evenly throughout the life course (see Vaupel and Gowan 1986).

Under this arrangement, adolescents would split their time between school and on-the-job training. Young and middle-aged adults would work less in order to make room for continuing education and increased leisure. The elderly would continue to work—although perhaps at reduced levels—while enjoying increased amounts of leisure and education. These proposals rest on the idea that the total amount of time devoted to education, work, and leisure would remain the same in the population as a whole. What would change would be the distribution of these activities over the life course.

There is some evidence that this kind of shift has already begun. Adults, for example, are increasingly likely to change careers at least once and such changes often require a return to school for additional training: since 1960, the percentage of adults over the age of 29 who are enrolled in school has more than doubled (USCB 1990a). Unless total production and income increase, however, redistribution of education, work, and leisure across age groups will reduce inequality of income only if people in higher-income age groups are willing to lower their incomes. Raising the average income of elderly people to the national average would cost more than $100 billion, or $700 for every adult under the age of 65.

Where would this money come from? From the 60 percent of younger adults who *already* earl less than the national average? Or from the upper classes that not only control most of the nation's wealth and income but also heavily influence those who make laws? Will the upper class weaken itself in order to bring about equality for the elderly, especially given that old age does not threaten *them* with financial insecurity? Certainly this seems unlikely.

Inequality, whether based on gender, race, ethnicity, or age, is ultimately created by social conditions that produce and perpetuate social stratification itself. In capitalist socieites, an end to age stratification would require the redistribution of the enormous wealth, power, and prestige now concentrated in the upper classes. In sociality societies, the state and those who control it would have to surrender their power over the economy and the distribution of what is produced. So long as control over the means of production is unequally distributed, there will be scarcity and competition; and so long as people must compete for scarce rewards, privileged groups will use their advantages to maintain their position. In order for some groups to be privileged, others must pay the cost. Without substantial changes in industrial socieutes, the most important question is not, Will minorities continue to exist? but, Who will the minorities be?

SUMMARY

1. Societies divide the life span into age categories each of which is a social status within its own role set.

2. As a social status, age affects the distribution of wealth, power, and prestige. Age is unique in that it is always temporary, provides a map of the life course, and affects the content of status sets more than any other status. Because we all belong to subordinate and dominant age categories at one time or another, subordinate age categories are only quasi-minorities.

3. Relationships between age statuses are supported by a variety of beliefs, values, attitutdes, and norms; and in many societies, the prejudice of ageism perpetuates age stratification and creates self-fulfilling prophecies.

4. Like other statuses, age categories have boundaries, and in some societies rites of passage clearly indicate when people move from one age to another.

5. The birth cohort is an important concept because ti defines peer groups on the basis of age and because it reveals how different categories of people experience the stages of the life course during different historical periods.

6. Divisions of labor use age as a basis for assigning roles, and this, in turn, creates and supports social inequality. In the U.S., children and the elderly generally occupy lower positions than young and middle-aged adults, and while most elderly people are not poor, they are worse off than they were as younger adults, especially if they are women.

7. Age stratification is functional for the socialization and motivation of children to perform adult roles, and is also closely connected to ecological arrangements, population growth, and changing age distributions. Work and family roles are assigned according to age, and when structural lag causes the role structure in a society to be out of balance with the population age structure, opportunities increase for some age categories at the expense of others. Age stratification also has dysfunctional consequences. It creates large numbers of dependent people who consume more than they produce, and fosters feelings of alienation and frustration among young and old alike.

8. While age stratification has many functional consequences, it is also perpetuated by conflict among social classes. The exclusion of children and the elderly from employment lessens competition for jobs made scarce by a class society. It also contributes to false consciousness among young and middle-aged adult workers by focusing attention on competition between age groups rather than on the upper class whose privileged position creates the scarcities over which people compete.

9. In social interaction, the role sets attached to age statuses affect our perceptions, evaluations, feelings, and expectations. In many relationships age acts as a latent status that affects how we play other roles.

10. While social movements for age equality have benefited the elderly, the strongest pressures for change center on changing population age structures and characteristics of new generations. Each new cohort of elderly people is more numerous, educated, and politically aware than the last, which increases their political power.

KEY TERMS

ageism   363
cohort effect   373

gerontocracy   370
hospice   377

life course   362
structural lag   372

LOOKING ELSEWHERE

Having studied Chapter 15, you might want to look at related discussions in *Human Arrangements*, which include

- birth cohorts and age structures (Chapter 4, pp. 79–80)
- age structure and unemployment (Chapter 19, pp. 488–90)
- age and crime (Chapter 11, p. 243)

- socialization throughout the life course (Chapter 7, pp. 149–56)
- the abuse of children and the elderly (Chapter 16, p. 405)
- changing patterns of education and the life course (Chapter 17, p. 439)

RECOMMENDED READINGS

Fennell, G., Phillipson, C., and Evers, H. 1988. *The sociology of old age*. Philadelphia: Open University Press. A clearly written cross-cultural approach to the meaning and consequences of old age in Western societies.

Foner, N. 1984. *Ages in conflict: A cross-cultural perspective on inequalities between old and young*. New York: Columbia University Press. A richly detailed look at the varieties of age stratification and their effects on relations between age groups in traditional societies.

Hayes-Bautista, D. E., Schink, W. O., and Chapa, J. 1988. *The burden of support: Young Latinos in an aging society*. Stanford: Stanford University Press. An intriguing case study in California brings together several dimensions of inequality by examining the consequences of a population that is not only aging but, at the younger ages, becoming increasingly Hispanic. As a result, many of the elderly population's financial needs will depend on the earnings of its relatively poor ethnic minority young adult population.

McPherson, B. D. 1983. *Aging as a social process: An introduction to individual and population aging*. Toronto: Butterworths. An excellent introduction to aging as a social process, including the ways in which that process is affected by historical, gender, racial, social class, and cross-cultural factors.

Riley, M. W., Hess, B. B., and Bond, K. (Eds.). 1983. *Aging in society: Selected reviews of recent research*. Hillsdale, NJ: Lawrence Erlbaum Associates. An excellent collection of papers originally written for the 1981 White House Conference on Aging, and touching on topics such as aging and economics, the family, work, retirement, mortality, stress, learning and memory, health and mortality, nutrition, and geographic mobility.

Zelizer, V. A. 1985. *Pricing the priceless child: The changing social value of children*. New York: Basic Books. A fascinating analysis of how children in the U.S. became economically useless and emotionally "priceless" at the turn of the 20th century, and the relationship between these two transformations.

SOCIAL INSTITUTIONS

Parts One and Two provided a basic conceptual framework for sociological thinking—the organization of human life through cultural, structural, and ecological arrangements. Part Three applied this to basic aspects of social life: the socialization process, interaction, groups, formal organizations, communities, and the ways in which groups and societies try to control the behavior of their members. Part Four focused on the ways culture, social structure, and ecology produce and perpetuate inequality based on characteristics such as social class, race, ethnicity, gender, and age.

Part Five focuses on social *institutions*, the most enduring and important arrangements in any society. As we saw in Chapter 3, institutions are enduring sets of cultural ideas and social relationships organized to accomplish important social goals. All societies rely on some variation of the *family* to produce, socialize, protect, and care for new members. In many societies, *schools* provide additional education and skills; *economic institutions* produce and distribute goods and services; *political institutions* distribute and apply collective power; and *religious institutions* help members of society grapple with enduring questions about the meaning of life itself.

MARRIAGE AND
THE FAMILY

 Look through a Sunday newspaper and you will find announcements of engagements, weddings, births, and divorces. In the obituary columns you will find the names of people who "survive" those who die. On a residential street you will see houses and apartments, each with its own assortment of people living together. Think about your childhood, and more than anything else you will probably think of your family—a group that may include anyone from you and one parent to scores of people—parents, stepparents, sisters and brothers, grandparents, distant cousins, aunts, and uncles, some of whom are no longer alive.

On the surface, such aspects of marriages and families seem to involve no more than people's personal decisions about their lives, and we may think that each relationship is unique for the people who define themselves as a married couple or a family. Sociologically, however, marriages and families are systems that exist in environments that affect how they are formed, how they fall apart, and what goes on among their members; just as what goes on in families affects the nature of those environments. In spite of variations from one family to another, families tend to conform to predictable social and ecological patterns within societies. These patterns, and their importance to both society and to us as individuals, are what this chapter is all about.

We begin by looking at how culture and social structure characterize the family in different societies and how these are affected by ecology and population. We then use the functional, conflict, and interactionist perspectives to better understand families as social systems. The closing sections include a systematic analysis of family disorganization—divorce

PUZZLE

WHERE
ARE WE
SAFE?

If you wanted to avoid being physically assaulted, what common group would you avoid?
    As this chapter explains, the answer may surprise you.

and violence in particular—and the causes of change in the family as a social institution.

MARRIAGE AND THE FAMILY AS INSTITUTIONS

The definition of marriage is relatively simple, regardless of the society. **Marriage** is a socially supported union between individuals in what is intended to be a stable, enduring relationship that involves sexual interaction as one of its key elements. As such, the institution of marriage is the basis for the institution of the family.

If asked to define a "family," you would probably describe it as a group consisting of parents and their children. In an Israeli kibbutz, however, the entire community serves as a family, and all women take collective responsibility for child care (Lesser-Blumberg 1983); among India's Nayar, fathers have no role relationship with their children (Gough 1974); and Indonesia's Dani have no word for "family" at all (Heider 1972). Although these examples reveal cultural differences in the definition of the family, all three have one thing in common. In each case the family is a social institution that contributes to the achievement of social goals.

In most societies the **family** performs six basic social functions, and these define it as an institution. The family is responsible for regulating sexual behavior by specifying who may have sexual contact with whom; reproduction; nurturing and protecting children and providing emotional support for adults; socializing children; playing a part in the production and consumption of goods; and providing a source of ascribed social statuses—race, ethnicity, and social class—that affect people's life chances. Even among the Dani—who have no word for the family—the institution nonetheless exists in social relationships

that perpetuate Dani society. Since the essence of the family lies in *why* it is organized rather than *how*, we should not be surprised by the astounding variety found in the world, for the same goals can be achieved in many ways.

Your Family, My Family, and The Family

If we compared your family and mine, we would probably find many differences—in values, beliefs, and attitudes that we share; in norms that define our rights and responsibilities; and in the number of children, patterns of interaction and affection, and divisions of labor and power. Just as no two individuals are exactly alike, individual families also have their own idiosyncrasies and variations.

As an *institution*, however, the family is more than a collection of families, just as a group is more than the sum of its members. An institution is a social "blueprint" that defines how family relationships ought to be structured and what goals families and their members should pursue in order to make sure that important social goals are achieved. Each of us participates in family life in relation to cultural models that produce patterns of actual family relationships, and these patterns are at the heart of the family as an institution. In the United States, for example, fathers generally have more power than mothers; children have few legal rights until they reach 18 years of age; and most families have three or fewer children and do not have aunts, uncles, and grandparents living in the same dwelling.

Although some societies have a single model for the family, others—such as the U.S.—include several, each of which reflects a different subculture. In some ways all families in the U.S. are alike, but ethnic and racial subcultures often produce unique patterns of family relationships (see Stack 1974). It is therefore misleading to refer to the institution of "the American family" as if it has only one meaning.

This chapter focuses on several of the many questions about marriage and the family that interest sociologists: How does culture define marital and family relationships and regulate behavior within them? How are these relationships structured? How do ecological arrangements affect family life? What are the relationships between families and the rest of society? How do we explain the problems that threaten the well-being of marriages and families? How and why do the institutions of marriage and the family change?

All societies have families, but they vary greatly in cultural and structural forms—the relatively simple parent–child families found in most industrial societies; families that include several generations, such as those in Turkey; and families that include entire communities, such as the Yagua Indians of Brazil.

CULTURAL VARIATIONS

Marriages and families are affected by a variety of cultural ideas. Beliefs define who is related to whom; values motivate us to form families and guide our choices within them; attitudes affect our feelings toward family members and outsiders; and norms define family roles and govern how family relationships are established, maintained, and broken.

Beliefs and the Concept of Kinship

At the heart of all family institutions is the concept of **kinship**, which refers to social relationships based on common ancestry, adoption, or marriage. In all societies children and their mothers are defined as kin, but beyond this there are great differences among cultures.

In the U.S., for example, there are special terms for hundreds of relatives: such as spouses, parents, children, aunts, uncles, nieces, nephews, in-laws, and grandparents. To these we can add fictive kin, such as godparents and "honorary aunts and uncles," who are not formal members of a family but nonetheless may play important roles. The number of possible kin relationships is enormous, and for this reason virtually all societies simplify kinship by considering only some to be "true" relatives. In contrast, when Malinowski studied them in 1929, Trobriand Island-

ers were unaware of the biological tie between fathers and children, and although fathers were affectionate with their children, they were regarded as outsiders. Southern India's Nayar acknowledged the biological role of fathers; but, as in several other societies, the mother's eldest brother was responsible for her children (Gough 1974).

Kinship, therefore, depends more on cultural definitions than on biology, and if "fate makes our relatives," then part of that fate is the culture we happen to be born into (Sahlins 1976). For societies, kinship provides continuity from one generation to the next by establishing ties between those who carry a society's culture and those who learn to live by it. For individuals, kinship is important because it links each of us to the past, present, and future.

Unlike all other social relationships, those among kin have the power to transcend death itself. In most horticultural societies, people worship their ancestors, believing that if they do not appease them, their spirits might return to harm them (Shiels 1975). Even in societies that do not worship ancestors, people often refer to deceased relatives as living parts of their social identities.

Kinship is defined in one of three ways. In societies with **matrilineal descent**, ancestry is traced through mothers and their blood relatives, and children are not defined by their relation to their father's family. Matrilineal descent is relatively rare among known

The worship of ancestors among the Chinese includes annual meetings at burial grounds and offerings of food and incense to reinforce their sense of attachment with kin both living and dead.

societies, and is found most often in horticultural societies in which women produce most of the food (Murdock 1967). The situation is reversed in societies with **patrilineal descent**, in which children are related only to their father's blood relatives. In most societies, descent is either matrilineal or patrilineal; there are only a few with **bilateral descent**, tracing ancestry through both the mother's and father's families.

While kinship defines basic family ties, other beliefs affect relationships within families. Until not too long ago, for example, Americans believed that when men and women marry, they become "one," and the "one" is the husband. This belief affects family relationships by undermining a wife's standing as a separate individual with her own rights in relation to her husband and the rest of society. It is still evident in the tendency of most married women to adopt their husband's last name as their own. In contrast, in Sweden husbands and wives are free to choose their own last names, and if they choose no last name for a newborn child, after three months it automatically takes its *mother's* name.

Many people in the U.S. believe that marriage is better for women than it is for men, a belief reflected in jokes about women trapping men into marriage and about husbands continually trying to escape married life. Most research, however, shows just the opposite: single women report greater happiness and less psychological stress than married women of the same age, while married men report less psychological distress than single men (see Chapter 14).

Values

Cultural values strongly affect both the formation and dissolution of marriages and families and social interactions within them.

There are many reasons for marrying, and in the U.S., romantic love is generally considered to be the most important. Rural Greeks, however, arrange marriages as economic exchanges between the bride's family and the groom's, and spouses rarely know each other before they marry (Friedl 1962). Similar arrangements have been found among North America's Blackfeet Indians and the Swazi of southeast Africa (Kuper 1963; Wissler 1911). In northern Australia, the marriages of Tiwi girls are arranged before they are even born, and they grow up as members of their future husband's family (Hart and Pilling 1960). Many people would flinch at the idea of basing marriage on purely economic and political values; but this has its advantages. Romantic love thrives on rushes of excitement that come with exploring the mysteries of another person (as well as the mystery of why they find *us* so exciting). Married life, however, makes heavy, practical demands on spouses, from earning a living to cleaning house, caring for children, and managing relationships with in-laws.

Some societies also place a high value on virginity in brides and sexual fidelity in marriage, particularly on the part of women. In 1990, for example, 90 percent of U.S. adults considered extramarital affairs to be wrong, and in spite of rapidly changing values, 36 percent held similar values about premarital sex (Davis and Smith 1990). Values supporting virginity at marriage are rare in preindustrial tribal societies— Murdock (1949) estimated that premarital sex is prohibited in less than 5 percent of them. Virginity has no value among Samoans or Trobriand Islanders, and the Mentawei of Indonesia go so far as to require women to give birth before marriage in order to prove they are fertile (Malinowski 1929; Mead [1928] 1953; Murdock 1949). Women in Scandinavian countries increasingly choose to have children without marrying the father (Popenoe 1987), and Blake (1982) argues that similar trends may be occurring in the U.S. as disapproval of premarital sexual behavior declines and acceptance of children born out of wedlock increases. There are, for example, almost 3 million never-married women in the U.S. who have had children (USCB 1989g).

Values about adultery also differ among societies. Alaska's Inuit and Australian aborigines, for example, consider it to be good manners to share wives with visitors, and a Nayar wife is free to have sex with any man, so long as he belongs to her husband's caste (Gough 1974; Montagu 1971).

Although many societies place a lower value on virginity and marital fidelity than in the U.S., others value them much more highly. In Muslim societies, a family's honor depends on the virginity of its daughters (Pastner 1974), and although Trobriand Islanders do not value virginity, they strongly value fidelity between spouses. Virginity was a required condition for marriage among ancient Hebrews, and a bride who failed to show signs of virginity on her wedding night (such as spots of blood) was killed and her family was shamed (Brownmiller 1975). More recently, when thousands of single women in Bangladesh were raped by invading Pakistani soldiers, they lost all chance of marrying, even though they had no control over the loss of their virginity. It is important to note that in no society are virginity at marriage and marital fidelity valued more highly in men than in women, and this clearly reflects the subordinate position of women, especially in societies

The requirement that women wear veils in Saudi Arabia and some other Moslem countries underscores their status as closely guarded sexual property in patriarchal societies.

that regard them as actual property of their fathers or husbands.

Other values also play a part in family relationships. In the U.S. people tend to value the success of individuals more than loyalty to kin, and value marital ties more highly than those to the families in which they grow up. In contrast with children of traditional Japanese families, adult offspring in the U.S. are expected to control their own lives, even when they conflict with their parents' desires, and the independence of husbands, wives, and their children from the influence of parents-in-law is closely guarded.

Values also affect how many children parents have. The cultural value of small families, for example, tends to increase with industrialization. In the U.S. lower-class families generally have more children than those in the middle and upper classes, but this is due more to ineffective birth control than to differences in values. Income makes little difference in the number of children people say they want to have, only in the number they actually do have (Ryder and Westoff 1971).

Attitudes

In the U.S., attitudes toward marriage and the family are a curious blend of opposites. Regardless of social class, people tend to attach intense emotional needs to families and look upon the idea of the family with a great deal of reverence. They worry about whether or not the family is being destroyed by a rapidly changing industrial society; over 90 percent marry at some time in their lives and although roughly half will probably experience a divorce, around 65 percent of those who divorce remarry within five years (Grady 1980; Thornton and Rodgers 1983; USCB 1982). They celebrate Mother's Day and Father's Day and regard holidays such as Thanksgiving, Christmas, and Hanukkah as important family events.

Such positive attitudes, however, exist side by side with negative ones. Hostile jokes about mothers-in-law, hen-pecked husbands, and Jewish mothers are a staple ingredient of American humor, and comedians typically include hostile remarks about spouses in their routines. We often avoid revealing negative attitudes toward families—even to ourselves—in part because the cultural ideal of the happy family is so strong that we tend to bury feelings of disappointment, frustration, and bitterness that inevitably arise in intense primary relationships. Perhaps this is why hostile jokes about marriage and families are so popular, for they express negative feelings that we, ourselves, would rather not see or let others see in our own lives.

The importance of marriage and the family—as institutions and as basic aspects of human life—causes people to make heavy emotional investments in them. Individual needs and the perpetuation and stability of societies require their continued existence in one form or another. We cannot live without them, and we often find it difficult to live with them. From this point of view, the existence of ambivalent cultural attitudes about marriage and the family should not surprise us.

Norms

Cultural norms affect almost every aspect of social relationships in marriages and families, and generally fall into one of two categories: norms that regulate the formation and dissolution of marriages, and those that regulate role behavior among kin.

In a number of societies—including Japan—arranged marriage is still common, reflecting the fact that the authority and interests of the family are valued more highly than the personal desires of the couple.

Courtship and Marriage Rules In all cultures, **marriage rules** limit whom people may marry, when, and under what conditions. Incest rules prohibit marriage and sexual intercourse between people who are defined as close relatives. With the exception of a few ancient societies in Hawaii, Egypt, and Mexico, all societies include parents and their children, as well as brothers and sisters, in that category. Even in Hawaii and Egypt incest was regarded as a privilege reserved for royal families (see Rubin and Byerly 1983), although Lewis (1983) argues that in ancient Egypt brother-sister marriage was fairly common in the urban middle class as well.

In the United States, incest is becoming increasingly identified as a form of child abuse that involves various forms of sexual contact, not just intercourse. Russell (1984) estimated that more than a quarter of U.S. female children have been sexually abused by age 15 and a third by age 18. Of this, 29 percent takes the form of incest involving relatives, of which 40 percent takes place within nuclear families.

U.S. law prohibits marriages involving parents and their children, siblings, grandparents and grandchildren, aunts and nephews, and uncles and nieces, and 30 states prohibit marriages between first cousins. Shoshone Indians, however, do not distinguish between siblings and cousins, and therefore prohibit marriages that involve even the most distant cousins.

That incest taboos are universal suggests a biological basis for them, but cross-cultural differences in the definition of incest and illogical definitions within cultures show that incest rules are as much a matter of culture as biology (see Arens 1986). In some societies people commit incest if they marry a child of their mother's sister or father's brother; but they are often *expected* to marry a child of their mother's *brother* or father's *sister*. Biologically, the son of a mother's sister is no closer a relative than the son of a mother's brother, but the incest rule clearly defines marriage to the first as revolting and marriage to the second as socially desirable.

Incest taboos are not the only norms that regulate who marries whom. Norms of **endogamy** require people to marry those belonging to their own group. Nazi Germany forbade marriage between Jews and gentiles. Orthodox Jews may not marry gentiles, and a Balinese woman may not marry a man from a caste lower than her own (Mead 1968). Norms of **exogamy**, however, require marriage to someone who is culturally defined as an *outsider*.

In the U.S., marriage is generally endogamous in relation to race and religion. Less than 2 percent of married couples are interracial, and almost a fifth of all adults favor laws prohibiting interracial marriage (Davis and Smith 1990; USCB 1990). Marriage tends to be exogamous, however, in relation to ethnicity, especially among the young. It is most exogamous among European whites and much less so among Puerto Ricans and Mexicans (Lieberson and Waters 1988), although as the Spanish-speaking community becomes more firmly established in the U.S., the rate of exogamous marriage among different Spanish-speaking ethnicities is increasing (Stevens and Swicegood 1987). Marriage is also exogamous in relation to gender, for the law does not yet recognize marriage between people of the same gender. In contrast, East Africa's Nuer and Nandi tribes allow childless women to marry younger women and claim their children as heirs (Lévi-Strauss 1956; Obaler 1985).

Norms also specify how many people can be married to each other at one time. In his survey of 238 societies, Murdock (1949) found that 18 percent insist on **monogamy**—marriage to only one spouse at a time—while the remainder permit some form of multiple marriage, or **polygamy**. Men are allowed to have more than one wife (**polygyny**) in 80 percent of all societies, including the Swazi of Africa, the Tiwi of Australia, and, until 1896, U.S. Mormons. **Polyandry**—in which women marry more than one husband—is very rare, but has been found among the Toda of India, the South Pacific Marquesian Islanders, and Tibetans in northern Nepal (Goldstein

1987; Murdock 1949). Most societies that allow multiple spouses are small, preindustrial, and contain a small fraction of the world populations. This means that most people live in societies in which monogamy is the only legitimate alternative.

Once couples marry, norms also affect where they can live. In **matrilocal** family systems such as the American Hopi Indians, married couples live in or near the wife's mother's household. In **patrilocal** systems, such as Greek villages and Africa's Swazi, they live in or near the husband's father's household. In **bilocal** systems such as the Blackfeet Indians, couples may choose between the husband's and the wife's families (but they cannot choose neither). Couples may live wherever they want in **neolocal** systems, with couples starting new households. Murdock's (1949) survey of 238 societies shows that family systems are patrilocal in 73 percent, matrilocal in 18 percent, and neolocal in 9 percent.

These patterns describe residence rules in most but not all societies. Among western Africa's Ashanti, for example, husbands and wives do not live

A Bakhtiari man in Iran stands with his three wives and many children. Although polygyny is allowed in many societies, most men are monogamous since they cannot afford to pay the bride price often associated with marriage in such societies.

Although the percentage of interracial married couples has doubled during the last twenty years, it is still a rarity in the United States.

together at all—each lives with his or her own mother's relatives. Children may eat meals at their father's house and then return to their mother's house for the night (Fortes et al. 1947). In India, once a Nayar husband spent three nights with his wife, he left her, and the wife lived as a member of her mother's household (Gough 1974).

Together, values and norms affect who marries whom in other ways as well. In most societies, spouses tend to have similar social statuses. In the U.S., people generally marry people of similar ages (Leslie 1989) and rarely marry people of different races, although the rate of interracial marriage is highest in communities in which there is the least amount of racial inequality (South and Messner 1986). People also tend to marry people who are similar to them in educational attainment, social class, and religion. Eighty-four percent of Protestants, 88 percent of Jews, and 76 percent of Catholics marry people of their own religious faith (GSS 1990). As factors such as religion and ethnicity become less important in the choice of marriage partners, however, the rate of intermarriage will increase and the level of endogamy will decline (Stevens and Swicegood 1987).

Although marriage patterns—those of age, race, and religion—are largely due to culture, they are also affected by ways in which social systems limit people's interactions to people who have statuses in common with them. People live in neighborhoods that tend to be homogeneous with respect to social class, race, and ethnicity; college students are more likely to meet and fall in love with each other than with high school graduates who are already in the labor force. The relative frequency of intermarriage across ethnic, class, and religious boundaries is strongly affected by how homogeneous the population is, with intermarriage far more common in large heterogeneous cities than in small rural communities (Blau, Blum, and Schwartz 1982).

Just as norms regulate the conditions of marriage, so, too, do they regulate their dissolution. Until quite recently, most U.S. states permitted divorce only under a limited set of circumstances—adultery and desertion—and the Catholic Church does not recognize divorce as legitimate, although the practice of annulment is often used to accomplish the same end. Only in recent years have states adopted no-fault divorce laws under which spouses can divorce each other by nothing more than mutual consent.

Norms and Family Relationships   In addition to regulating the formation and dissolution of marriages, norms define roles within marriages and families. While most norms about sex set limits on it, marital norms define sexual access to spouses as a right, and refusal to have sex is grounds for divorce in most of the U.S. (Collins 1982). Although all societies define sex as a basic part of marriage, norms regulate sexual behavior in sharply different ways. In India and most Muslim countries, for example, husbands may not sexually approach wives who are menstruating or who have recently given birth. In the U.S., many states still have laws that specifically prohibit certain sexual behaviors—such as oral and anal sex—even between spouses.

Family norms differ sharply from those found in other groups in their informality and the way in which they are applied. In comparison with other groups, family norms are often applied in different ways to each member depending on his or her personal characteristics and needs. Because families are intimate primary groups, members are more likely to be treated as unique individuals, each with his or her own special needs, abilities, and limitations.

Much of the world outside the family, however, operates under formal norms that apply to everyone who occupies a particular social status. Relationships in school are secondary, and when children first attend school they are often jarred by the fact that they no longer receive the individual attention and special considerations that they enjoy as family members.

VARIETIES OF SOCIAL STRUCTURE

Sociologists study the institutions of marriage and the family on both the micro- and macrolevels of social structure, for what goes on in families is affected by the relationships between families and other social systems. It is no less true, however, that societies are affected by what goes on in their families. The following sections describe some basic family structures and then look at variations in their role structures, and distributions of wealth and power.

Basic Elements of Family Structure

Although kinship includes people who are related to us whether they live with us or not, family boundaries generally include only people who live together. From this point of view, family composition usually takes one of five forms.

A **nuclear family** consists of parents and their natural or adopted children, and this structure describes most families in industrial societies. **Extended families** include additional relatives such as grandparents, aunts, uncles, or cousins. The remaining three structures are variations on the nuclear family. **Single-parent families** are nuclear families with one parent absent. **Divorced families** are nuclear families in which children and one of two divorced parents live together and maintain a relationship with the absent parent. Divorced families are complex because the absent parent, although not physically present in the family, may still interact with both the former spouse and the children. The effects of this vary widely, from financial and emotional support to conflict and violence. In **compound families** the structure of a divorced family is

complicated still further by the introduction of a new spouse through the remarriage of one of the parents. The resulting family—parent, children, and stepparent—constitutes a compound family.

Even when they are relatively small, compound families can have very complicated structures. Both wife and husband may bring to their new family children from prior marriages and then have children together. Compound families have the potential to include a variety of complicated relationships in which children have closer family ties to one parent than the other and, in the most complicated cases, other children have equally strong family ties to both parents.

Although these four structures describe families in most societies, there are other variations as well. As we saw earlier, in the Israeli kibbutz child care is the responsibility of adult females as a group; and yet, nuclear family ties exist within the larger structure and parents spend time with their children at the end of each day. Among Indonesia's Dani the family as an isolated social group barely exists at all; the community as a whole is the major focus of social life. Spouses, parents, and children spend relatively little time together, and children live with other relatives by the time they are ten years old (Heider 1972).

Divisions of Labor and Role Structures

Biological reproduction, socialization, consumption, and the regulation of sexual behavior are the most important functions of families in most societies; and in nonindustrial societies, production is still a major family function. It is around such functions that family divisions of labor are organized.

In virtually all societies responsibility for child care falls almost exclusively on women; but women are also economically active in production. The cultural ideal division of labor in the U.S.—women are confined to housework and child care and men are solely responsible for breadwinning—has not been achieved in any society, including our own. In the U.S., 56 percent of married women are in the labor force, as are 57 percent of those with preschool children and 72 percent of those with school-age children. Divorced mothers have the highest rate—fully 84 percent of those with school-age children (USCB 1990a).

As a result, the traditional family consisting of parents and children supported solely by earnings of

FIGURE 16-1   The Changing Labor Force Patterns of
Families, 1940–1988

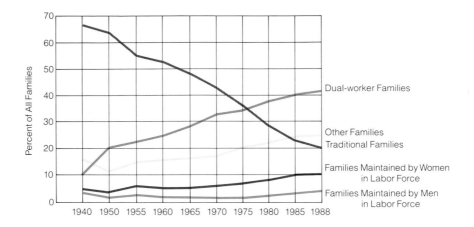

the husband has become something of a rarity in the United States (see Figure 16-1).

In all societies, then, women contribute heavily to important family functions—reproduction, socialization, and production—while in almost all societies fathers focus their attention primarily on production. This is true even in the Israeli kibbutzim, for while child-rearing tasks are not the responsibility of each individual mother, child care and other domestic work are still defined as women's work (Lesser-Blumberg 1983).

Within this basic structure, however, there is much variation. In industrial societies, for example, the higher a family's class position, the more likely it is that outsiders will be hired to perform housekeeping and child-rearing roles. In working-class families, mothers have primary responsibility for meeting children's emotional needs, while fathers generally play the role of punisher (LeMasters 1975). In middle-class families, both parents are expected to support their children emotionally. Regardless of social class, fathers rarely participate in child care before their children are 18 months old (Entwistle and Doering 1981); and while fathers are more likely to play with children than care for them, the pattern is the opposite for mothers (Hochschild 1989; Lamb and Goldberg 1982; Rossi 1984).

The responsibility for child care reflects only one aspect of the general responsibility that women have for taking care of people's personal needs. As the population age structures of industrialized societies grow older, for example, the number of elderly parents in need of care increases as well, and women are

three times more likely than men to be the ones who provide it (AARP 1989b). As birth rates continue to fall, increasing numbers of married couples find themselves with more parents than children to care for. "In 1989, a woman whose children are grown has completed, on average, less than half the care giving she will provide during her life. Far from being free of

Unlike parents in most social classes, the upper class has traditionally made use of hired help to take care of children, as does this "nanny" in Kensington, England. To some degree, day-care centers perform a similar function for upper-middle and some middle-class two-earner families in the U.S.

responsibility, in many cases her most difficult years lie ahead" (Older Women's League 1989).

Power, Matriarchy, and Patriarchy

Who rules the family? In a **patriarchy** fathers are culturally defined as the heads of major institutions, including the family; in a **matriarchy** women dominate; and in **egalitarian marriage** power is shared equally between husbands and wives. As we saw in Chapter 14, patriarchal is not the most accurate description of family power structures in most industrial societies because production, wealth, and power are no longer organized primarily around families. Thus, although virtually all societies are still organized around the principles of male dominance, it is the status of male, not the status of father, that lies at the heart of this dominance.

In spite of variations among families, almost all existing societies are male-dominated. Even in matrilineal societies such as the Trobriand Islanders which trace kinship through the mother's family, family power structures are male-dominated. There is, in fact, some debate over whether any society has ever been truly matriarchal (Bamberger 1974), but most archeological evidence suggests that for most of human history gender equality has been the rule. Patriarchy is barely five thousand years old, which is not as old as it may seem when we put it in the context of upwards of two *million* years of human history (see Eisler 1987; Fisher 1980; Lerner 1986).

Although family institutions in most societies are male-dominated, the distribution of power varies considerably. Egalitarianism tends to be stronger in the middle and upper classes than in the working and lower classes. This may be due in part to the fact the husbands in higher classes have more power outside the home than lower-class husbands do, and therefore have less need to use the family as a situation in which they can feel powerful. Although middle- and upper-class families tend to be more egalitarian, they are still male-dominated, and husbands generally control most important decisions, such as what kind of car to buy or where the family will live.

In most societies individuals' power depends in part on their contribution to production, and this holds between husbands and wives (Huber 1990). In the U.S., wives who work tend to have more power than wives who do not; and the higher a wife's education or income is, the more power she tends to have in family decision making (Hood 1983; see also Mirowsky 1985).

Residence rules also affect authority relations in families (Warner et al. 1986). In a matrilocal society, for example, a husband's authority is undermined by the fact that his wife's kin can "gang up" on him. In patrilocal societies, however, the dominance of men is increased enormously by the wife's isolation from her family, and her greatest source of power is to leave the marriage and return to her parents' house. From this point of view, matrilocal residence supports egalitarian marriage by giving the wife more authority. Societies that allow married couples to freely choose where they will live also support equality by separating husbands and wives from their families.

Keep in mind that the concepts of matriarchy, patriarchy, and egalitarianism refer to cultural models of the family and patterns of authority, and that although some women in societies may be in charge of families, this does not mean that matriarchy prevails. If we describe single-parent families headed by divorced women as matriarchal, we distort the basic meaning of matriarchy, for these women dominate by default, not because society defines women as the legitimate heads of families, including adult male members. This distinction is important because single-parent families are increasingly common in the U.S., particularly among blacks. Without this distinction, we might conclude that black families are more matriarchal than white families simply because they are more likely to be headed by women. In intact families, however, male dominance prevails among both blacks and whites.

The preceding sections describe basic structural characteristics of families and how they affect relationships and interaction within families. As groups, however, families occupy positions in relation to their surrounding societies, and one of the most important of these is their position in systems of social stratification.

Family Wealth and Power in Stratified Societies

In gatherer-hunter and horticultural societies community life is organized around kinship ties, and the family is the most powerful institution. Even in agrarian societies political authority rests largely in family units. Industrial societies, however, are too large and complex to be dominated by even the largest kin group, and authority lies in institutions outside the family—in schools, government, courts, corporations, churches, and the professions. Legal

TABLE 16-1   Median Family Income, by Race and Family Structure (United States)

FAMILY STRUCTURE	FAMILY INCOME			
	All Families	Whites	Blacks	Hispanics
Intact married couple	$36,400	$36,800	$30,400	$25,700
Wife works	$42,700	$43,200	$36,700	$31,900
Wife does not work	$27,200	$28,000	$18,500	$19,100
Male head—wife absent	$26,800	$28,900	$17,900	$21,900
Female head—husband absent	$15,300	$17,700	$10,700	$10,700

Source: USCB 1990a.

norms prohibit preferential treatment for relatives in occupations and the legal system. Families, in short, are not powerful groups in industrial societies.

This does not mean that all families have equal amounts of power. Inequality of wealth and income among families is common, and wealth is a source of power. Engels ([1891] 1972) went so far as to argue that the existence of family units in communities and societies is a basic cause of social stratification itself. It is only when families can accumulate wealth and have an interest in passing it on to their heirs that intense competition within societies comes into being.

The chapters in Part Four describe a variety of ascribed and achieved social statuses—race, ethnicity, gender, age, education, and occupation—that affect the distribution of income in stratified societies, and these characteristics affect inequality among families as much as they affect inequality among individuals. The structure of families, however, in addition to the statuses of their members, also affects the distribution of income. In the U.S., for example, family income is greatest in intact families (especially if both parents work) and single-parent families headed by men. Families with the lowest income are headed by unmarried women, a pattern that holds regardless of race (take a moment to study Table 16-1 carefully).

Clearly, families headed by unmarried women—whether divorced, single, or widowed—are in a poor economic position, especially if they are nonwhite. In comparison with intact families, families headed by white females are over four times as likely to live in poverty and over seven times as likely to depend on food stamps. These differences are less severe among blacks, primarily because they are crowded into a much narrower income range (USCB 1990a).

THE SOCIAL ECOLOGY OF FAMILY LIFE

The ecological perspective is basic to any study of marriage and family institutions since reproduction, production, and consumption are among their most important social functions.

Reproduction: Marriage, Family, and Society

In all societies, cultural and structural aspects of marriage and the family affect birth rates and population growth in several ways. The more common marriage is and the younger the age at marriage, for example, the higher birth rates tend to be. An estimated 44 percent of all African females 15 to 19 years old are married, and in countries of Western Africa the estimate is 70 percent. By comparison, less than 10 percent of U.S. and European females 15 to 19 years old are married (PRB 1980; USCB 1986a).

Birth rates also depend on the degree to which married couples limit childbearing. Contraception is practiced by 66 percent of married women in the U.S., resulting in longer periods between births and fewer births over the life cycle. Since 1955, the birth rate among married women 20 to 24 years old has dropped by more than 50 percent. The result has been a steady decline in the average size of families. Since 1967, the percentage of women 30 to 34 years old who expect to have two or fewer children has increased from 31 to 65 percent, and the percentage who expect to bear four or more children has dropped from 55 percent to 10 (PRB 1990; USCB 1990a).

While delayed marriage and childbearing are increasingly common in the U.S., men and women are also more likely than before to live together without marrying and to have children without marrying. Since 1960 the number of unmarried couples has increased from just over 100,000 to 2.6 million (Glick and Norton 1979; USCB 1990a). In the same period birth rates have increased by 48 percent among unmarried women and doubled among unmarried teenagers, the latter increase being due largely to increased sexual activity and a failure to use effective contraception (USCB 1981, 1990a; Zelnick and Kantner 1976, 1978). Although overall teenage pregnancy and birth rates began to drop in 1983, they began to rise again in 1988 (NCHS 1990). The rates for the U.S. are higher than in many industrial societies (see Table 16-2). This results in part from a loss of control by the institutions of marriage and the family over sexual behavior and reproduction, but it is also due to a failure to recognize how widespread teenage sexuality and the need for contraception and effective sex education are in the U.S. (see Guttmacher Institute 1987; Maciak 1987).

Changing values and norms about family life also affect birth rates (see Mason 1982). Hindus in India's West Bengal, for example, prohibit sexual intercourse between husbands and wives for almost 100 days out of every year, and in some societies intercourse is forbidden for two or three years after childbirth (Nag 1962, 1967). Before 1975, birth rates among American Catholics were higher than among non-Catholics primarily because Catholicism forbids the use of contraceptives and encourages childbearing. Since 1975, however, Catholics have increasingly ignored the ban on contraceptive use and abortion, and their birth rates are virtually equal to

those of other major religious groups (GSS 1987; Westoff and Jones 1979).

Finally, family size is strongly related to the nonfamily statuses that wives and mothers occupy. In nonindustrial and industrial societies women who work outside the home tend to have fewer children than women who do not, especially if their work is highly paid (GSS 1990; Weller and Bouvier 1981). In addition, the more highly educated women are, the fewer children they tend to have. Education lowers fertility not only by increasing the chances that women will work outside the home, but also by delaying the entry of women into marriage and increasing the chances that they will never marry (Kammeyer and Ginn 1986).

While the institutions of marriage and the family affect birth rates and population growth, changing birth rates, death rates, and age structures also have important effects on individual families and the institution of the family.

Birth Rates, Death Rates, and the Structure of Family Life

As birth and death rates fall and families grow smaller and people live longer, the structure of the family tends to change. In colonial America the average married-woman bore an estimated eight children during a lifetime that, by current standards, was short (Grabill, Kiser, and Whelpton 1959; Hawke 1988). Each woman could expect to have few years during which she was not pregnant or responsible for young children. By comparison, average lifetime fertility among married women is now just over two children, and life expectancy is far higher than it was in colonial times. This means that married women spend a relatively small portion of their lives bearing and caring for children. By the time most married women reach their early thirties, their children are in school, and these mothers have an average of 44 more years of life ahead of them (USCB 1990a).

These population changes encourage women to work outside the home, especially in career occupations that require years of training and involve steady advancement. This, in turn, breaks the monopoly that husbands have had over the breadwinner role ever since the Industrial Revolution separated the family—and mothers—from production. As women increase their share of earning power, they also tend to increase their prestige and power in marriages and families.

TABLE 16-2   Teenage Pregnancy and Birth Rates[1] in Selected Industrial Societies

COUNTRY	PREGNANCY RATE	BIRTH RATE
United States	96	53
England/Wales	45	29
Canada	44	26
France	43	23
Sweden	35	14
Netherlands	14	9

[1]Number of pregnancies and number of births per 1,000 females 15–19 years old.

Source: Guttmacher Institute 1987.

As recently as the turn of the century, there were many areas of the U.S. in which women spent much of their lives bearing children, as did this mother of nine in rural Tifton, Georgia in 1909.

Falling birth rates have had the additional effect of decreasing the number of relatives people have. As children, today's elderly had an average of 5 siblings, 20 uncles and aunts, and perhaps as many as 40 cousins. Children born in the last decade, however, have on the average less than half that number of relatives with whom they can form close ties (Bane 1976). As the number of kinship ties falls, so does the importance of extended kinship networks in everyday life.

The potential effects of declining birth rates on kinship systems is particularly startling in the case of China whose government, as we saw in Chapter 4, is trying to limit each family to just one child. If this plan were to succeed for many generations, the result would be a family system in which there literally would be no siblings, cousins, aunts, or uncles (Kertzer, in Riley 1987). Especially given the importance of family ties in traditional Chinese society, it is difficult to imagine how deeply such a change might affect the richness of family life.

Technology, Production, and Families

Social institutions change in response to changes in population and ecological arrangements. The family is certainly no exception, for it has changed dramatically over the last few centuries in response to indus-

trialization, population growth, and urbanization.

With small populations and a relatively simple division of labor, gatherer-hunter and horticultural societies organize social life almost exclusively around kinship ties. Production, education, religion, law, and government all revolve around kinship groups. The extended family is the source of individual rights, responsibilities, and social identities, and marriage is based more on economic and political considerations than on individual preferences. The larger and more complex agricultural societies, however, include a variety of kinship groups, none of which can dominate all aspects of social life. Even here, though, family membership is closely related to wealth and political power, for some families monopolize political offices that are inherited.

The Industrial Revolution rapidly accelerated a process that began centuries before: kinship ties were losing their importance as families lost control over societies. This ecological change affected families in important ways and continues to affect them in societies that are beginning to industrialize today. As production shifts to factories and relies on more sophisticated technology, child labor loses its value and large families become a liability. Birth rates began a steady decline in Europe in the early 1800s and somewhat later in the U.S.—well over a century before the invention of effective contraceptives. Thompson and Whelpton (1933) estimated that the U.S. birth rate was 55 births per 1,000 people at the end of the eighteenth century, but by 1900 it had fallen to 30 per 1,000 (Weller and Bouvier 1981).

Unlike gatherer-hunter and horticultural societies, industrial societies are dominated by secondary relationships and formal organizations and many of the functions once performed by the family have been transferred to other institutions. Responsibility for education shifts to schools, for example, and wealth and power depend more on individual performance and characteristics than on family ties. While discrimination in favor of relatives in politics and employment is expected in preindustrial societies, it is commonly outlawed (although not unknown) in industrial societies.

As vital social functions are transferred from the family to other institutions, the importance of economics and politics in the formation of marriages declines. This is one reason why romantic love is far more important in industrial than in preindustrial societies (Degler 1980; Goode 1959). As a basis for marriage, romantic love allows people to separate from the families they grew up in. Young people no longer have to wait to inherit the positions held by their elders, and can escape parental authority at a relatively early age (Cherlin 1981). Romantic love also promises to provide the emotional support once provided by extended families, and encourages people to marry in societies in which marriage is no longer required to preserve the power of kinship groups.

The extended family's loss of control over marriage increases the power of women. In agrarian societies, women were property to be exchanged by families for economic and political gain. In industrial societies, however, women are freer to choose their own husbands and have more bargaining power in the "marriage market."

Industrialization also creates social conditions in which the importance of nuclear families increases at the expense of extended families (Goode 1963). Industrial societies, for example, need workers who can move from one place to another as new industries are built, and the loose ties of nuclear families to kin increases geographic mobility. Industries also need people who are willing to be *socially* mobile— who will break away from the lower-class occupations of their parents and strive for middle-class jobs.

Finally, industrialization and the rise of the nuclear family affect the division of labor within families. Among the Inuit of Alaska and the Gusii of Kenya women work in or near their homes and strap their infants to their backs while they work (Montagu 1971; Whiting 1963). In industrial societies, however, the separation of production and the home makes it difficult for both parents to work (Cherlin 1983). As a result, child care and production are more specialized in industrial than in preindustrial societies: child care is almost the exclusive province of women, and men tend to be the primary breadwinners.

Over a period of many centuries, then, the family has been dramatically transformed from an extended kinship network that dominated social life to a relatively small primary group whose most important functions are to meet the emotional needs of its members, care for young children, and regulate sexual behavior. The powerful extended family of preindustrial societies has been largely replaced by a variety of social institutions. Families, however, are not isolated groups insulated from the outside world. They are a vital part of societies, responsible for reproducing that society in new generations. As such, they affect and are affected by surrounding social institutions.

THEORETICAL PERSPECTIVES ON MARRIAGE AND THE FAMILY

As institutions, marriage and the family are defined by the social functions they perform. This does not mean, however, that the characteristics of families always have functional consequences. Nor does it mean that conflict does not exist, both within families and between them and other institutions.

This carving of an Inuit woman and her baby portrays what was a universal aspect of family life for almost all of human history prior to industrialization. She carries a knife in one hand and a fish in another, showing that production and reproduction were not mutually exclusive activities.

Functions and Dysfunctions

While marriage and the family are defined in terms of major functions discussed earlier in this chapter, particular cultural and structural aspects of family life—incest taboos and marriage rules—can also be looked at from this perspective.

Incest taboos draw boundaries that distinguish close kin from everyone else and promote family stability by preventing hostility and jealousy among family members. They help keep family structures unambiguous and clear, and this minimizes status strain. If a mother and son had a daughter, the son would be the newborn's father and her brother. By forcing people to look outside the family for sexual partners, incest taboos also encourage social ties between families and the growth and solidarity of larger kinship networks and communities. Incest taboos are related to rules of exogamy that require people to marry outside their group, and exogamy performs an important function for communities. Among gatherer-hunters, for example, marriage between people of different communities helps establish cooperative political and economic ties (Service 1962).

Endogamous marriage can also be functional because by restricting marriage to group members outside the immediate family, it keeps group boundaries clear and helps maintain group solidarity. Endogamy among Orthodox Jews helps ensure the perpetuation of religious and cultural traditions and strengthens the in-group loyalties that support them against anti-Semitism. Ironically, Nazi Germany also imposed endogamous marriage to isolate Jews from the rest of German society.

The dysfunctional consequences of some family characteristics illustrate again the complexity of social systems. The nuclear family is by definition isolated from extended kinship networks, and this means that its members depend on relatively few people for emotional and material support. If a spouse dies in an extended family, other adults are available to assume important roles, but in nuclear families the loss of a spouse can cause a major crisis that threatens the survival of the family itself. Extreme interdependency among nuclear family members may create severe emotional strain. We spend most of our lives in secondary relationships and often rely on the family as our main source of emotional support. This makes nuclear families particularly vulnerable to emotional overload, and the intensity of family relationships may breed hostility and bitterness as well as love (Skolnick 1975).

The structure of the nuclear family—unlike that of the extended family—also excludes the elderly from meaningful roles, and this is dysfunctional for the well-being of the elderly and for society. Thousands of widowed, elderly parents spend their last years alone or in institutions, and even those who join their children's nuclear families often have no meaningful part to play in family life. In Japan, by contrast, the extended family is more common, and not only provides meaningful roles for the elderly, but also supports women working outside the home by providing child care (Morgan and Hirosima 1983).

In sum, although the nuclear family has many functional consequences in industrial societies, it brings with it social costs. Its structure contributes to family vulnerability, instability, and strain, and leaves elderly people in a "roleless" position. Like all aspects of social systems, it can produce both positive and negative consequences.

The Conflict Perspective

From a conflict perspective, social institutions like the family are arenas in which struggles for wealth, power, and prestige take place. Conflict takes place both within marriages and families and between them and society, and is related to the social characteristics of institutions in different societies and historical periods.

In lower- and middle-class families relationships among family members are strongly affected by the family's class position. In industrial societies workers have little control over work conditions that often have negative effects on family life. Many industries operate 24 hours a day, and although this increases industrial efficiency and profits, it creates severe strains on the families of workers (Lipset, Trow, and Coleman 1956; Rowbotham 1973; White and Keith 1990). Working spouses often must be away from their families during the night, and repeated changes in work shift assignments subject individuals to a variety of negative effects, such as insomnia and chronic fatigue. In the middle and upper-middle classes, managers and professionals are under intense pressure to care more about their jobs than their families, and because their jobs often take them away from home, they must choose between family life and the rewards of their occupations. Given the emotional needs that nuclear families are expected to satisfy, it is easy to see how industrial economies create strains within families by calling upon workers to neglect their families in the name of supporting them.

A more important effect of economic institutions on marriages and families comes from the structure of the economy itself. In industrial societies, families do not produce what they consume and must sell their labor power for money they can exchange for goods and services. Families, however, do not receive a substantial portion of what is produced by their members' labor power—a large percentage is kept as profit in capitalist societies or is appropriated by the state in socialist societies. The resulting strain on families is inevitable, for workers are paid less to make a product than it costs to buy it. One result of this is that most families have a hard time making ends meet and must depend on the earnings of both spouses. In 1890, only 14 percent of all women in the labor force were married. In 1988, 59 percent of women in the labor force were married, and 55 percent of these were mothers with children under the age of 18 (USCB 1975, 1990a).

Most of what is produced in industrial societies—food, clothing, appliances, housing, and medical care—is consumed by families. This means that the stress and strain that workers experience is inevitably reflected in the families that depend on their occupational success (Rubin 1976). It should not surprise us to find that marital and financial instability go together. Goode (1976) estimated, for example, that marriages involving service workers and laborers are twice as likely to be unstable as are those involving professional and technical workers, differences which are found in many industrial societies.

It is ironic that the family's most important function as an institution is to reproduce the very society that often has negative effects on families (Landes 1977–1978; see also Laslett and Brenner 1989). Whether they live in Manhattan or Moscow, parents who raise children to obey authorities and be good workers reproduce not only people, but the social relationships that create and sustain social inequality. In turn, they also help reproduce and perpetuate the stressful conditions under which their children will, themselves, marry and raise families. In this way, the victims of social inequality are expected by their society to perpetuate the social conditions that victimize them and their children.

The Interactionist Perspective

Like all groups, individual married couples and families develop their own patterns of interaction, but because each is part of a social institution, interactions in families often have similar patterns. In the

U.S., for example, nighttime is identified as the "appropriate" time for sex, in part because the structure of work in industrial society requires absence from the home during the day. This pattern may give rise to rigid expectations ("It's night; we're in bed; therefore we should make love") that can convert a natural pleasure into a burden.

In monogamous family systems, frequent interaction between spouses affects their perceptions, values, and attitudes. As Berger and Kellner (1964) suggest, when marriage involves intense and relatively exclusive relationships between wives and husbands, spouses tend to adopt similar views, even when they initially disagree. They may enter their marriage disagreeing about everything from politics to the likability of friends; but the longer they live together, the more similar they become (see also Mirowsky and Ross 1987).

This occurs for two reasons. First, we all depend on other people to confirm our perceptions of reality and support our values and attitudes, and we tend to depend on the people with whom we interact the most. In the U.S. in particular, when people marry they tend to focus more on each other than on friends they had before marrying. Friends often perceive a husband and wife as a couple—not as two individuals—and no longer feel free to spend time with one without including the other. It is difficult to invite a married woman to a dinner party, for example, without including her husband. Cultural ideas about married couples help produce exclusive and intense interactions between husbands and wives.

Second, the stability of intense and exclusive marital relationships depends in large part on the *perception* of a strong common bond between husbands and wives. Constant disagreement produces a strain in relationships, and this encourages the creation of a "common ground" on which spouses can live together in relative peace.

Marital interactions are also affected by major structural characteristics of families. In matrilocal systems the husband occupies the status of "outsider." This undermines his position in the family, contributes to his being left out of important interactions, and makes him vulnerable to coalitions formed against him by family "insiders." All these observations apply equally to wives in patrilocal societies.

Patterns of interaction in families are even more complex than between spouses. The presence of children makes married life far more complex and, in most cases, more difficult. Introducing children into a marriage tends to reduce interaction between spouses, increase the amount of conflict, tension, and nervousness, especially in relation to the division of labor within the family, and to decrease marital satisfaction (Glenn and McLanahan 1983; McLanahan and Adams 1987; Mirowsky and Ross 1989).

In nuclear families, where child care is usually the responsibility of the wife alone, children tend to interact far more with mothers than with fathers. In many cases mothers are children's only source of adult contact and, as a result, mothers frequently feel overloaded and children become heavily dependent on a single adult. This problem is especially acute in single-parent families—which make up 23 percent of all families with children under 18 — and affects both single mothers and single fathers (USCB 1990a).

Such patterns help explain why children often feel jealous of newborn babies with whom they must compete for the parent's attention. If the family structure includes more than one adult who is available to children, they are less likely to feel that the attention paid to newborns causes a loss of attention for them. In extended families the availability of several adults means that no one adult must bear the entire burden alone. This is also true of societies such as the Dani of Indonesia and the Israeli kibbutz in which entire communities share the responsibility of child care.

The structure of compound families can create very complex patterns of interaction and considerable stress and strain (Ihinger-Tallman 1988). Because children have a closer tie with a natural parent, for example, they may form coalitions against the stepparent and defy a stepparent's authority ("You aren't my *real* mother"). Stepparents may feel left out of family jokes, secrets, and memories that were created before they joined the family, and often feel in competition with the natural parent who no longer lives with the children. One result of such complexity is greater strain in compound families, especially when both spouses are remarried and have stepchildren. In these families, divorce is more likely, children tend to leave home at an earlier age, and spouses express less satisfaction with married life (White and Booth 1985).

A large body of research (summarized in Hess 1970) shows that family interactions vary a good deal among social classes. In general, for example, the higher a family's social class position, the more likely parents are to talk with their children, reason with them, use complex language in talking to them, express warmth and affection, and avoid physical punishment. At least one study, however, has found that working- and lower-class parents are less likely to have infants sleep in a separate room even if it is available (Tulkin 1989). The practice of parents not sharing a room or their bed with infants and toddlers is an interesting cultural approach to infant care that is rarely found outside of the industrialized world. Barry and Paxon (1989), for example, found that for 173 nonindustrial societies, mother and infant shared a bed in 44 percent, and in *all* of the societies infants slept in the same room as their parents. By contrast, at least one recent study suggests that most U.S. parents rarely take their infants into their bed (see Figure 16-2). When told of the U.S. practice, a Kung gatherer-hunter mother in Africa remarked, "Don't they understand that it's only a baby, and that's why it cries?" (Konner 1989, p. 40).

FAMILY DISORGANIZATION

A social system is organized if all its statuses are occupied by people who adequately perform their roles. A nuclear family, for example, is organized if it in-

FIGURE 16-2   Parent-Child Sleeping Arrangements

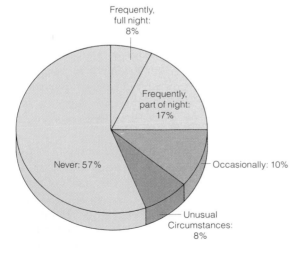

In contrast with nonindustrial societies, a study of white parents living in the Cleveland area finds that only 8 percent of parents frequently take their babies into their bed for the full night.

Source: Dr. Betsy Lozoff, Rainbow Babies and Childrens Hospital, Cleveland. Percentages Rounded Off.

In industrial societies, in which long lives are the rule rather than the exception, "'Til death do us part" is an increasingly difficult commitment to honor, although not, apparently, for this Swedish couple.

...cludes a mother and father and children, all of whom perform their roles. Family disorganization occurs when a status is unoccupied or when one or more members fail to perform their roles. It is of interest to sociologists because it affects a family's ability to perform important social functions and because it affects the lives of family members.

Structural incompleteness takes a variety of forms, the most common of which is separation of spouses through divorce. It also occurs, however, when women have children without marrying at all or when a spouse dies. Inadequate role performance also takes many forms—from mental or physical breakdowns or unemployment to an "empty shell" family in which members go through the motions of task roles while ignoring the emotional roles that make up the core of primary relationships (Goode 1976).

Divorce was outlawed in Catholic Europe during the Middle Ages and in Puritan New England, and most family disorganization was caused by the death of a spouse (Stephens 1963). In mid-eighteenth-century Sweden, roughly half of all marriages ended because a spouse died, as did approximately 60 percent of marriages in France and 70 percent in India (Lenski and Lenski 1987).

As death rates fell over the past century, divorce became the major form of family disorganization. Between 1860 and 1984 the divorce rate in the U.S. increased from 1.2 per 1,000 married couples to 23.1 per 1,000—a nineteen-fold increase—but has since begun to decline (Thornton and Freedman 1983; USCB 1975, 1990a). As of 1990, 36 percent of those who had ever been married had also experienced a divorce or legal separation (Davis and Smith 1990), and an estimated two-thirds of first marriages will end in divorce if current rates continue (Martin and Bumpass 1989).

Understanding Divorce

Sociological reseach has much to say about trends in divorce rates. Once again, explanations are related to the key sociological concepts of culture, social structure, population, and ecology.

Divorce and Culture   Just as cultural beliefs, values, norms, and attitudes affect the organization of marriages and families, so, too, do they affect their disorganization. As one would expect, divorce rates tend to be highest where norms restrict it the least and where values and attitudes place little stigma on divorced people. Socially legitimate grounds for divorce vary enormously among cultures. Stinginess and laziness are grounds among the Hopi Indians, for example, and the Iban of Borneo may divorce if they see a bad omen or have an ominous dream. In patrilocal societies the husband's parents can initiate divorce by sending his wife home if they do not like her. Divorce rates in nineteenth-century Japan were very high for this reason (Goode 1976).

In some societies—such as Afghanistan or the Navaho Indians—divorce involves no elaborate ceremonies (Das and Bardis 1978; Stephens 1963). In pre-Civil War New England, however, married couples could not divorce without a special act of the state legislature (Goode 1976). Divorce rates in the U.S. have risen, however, as the legal grounds for divorce have expanded and become less specific. In the nineteenth century the only grounds were desertion, adultery, and physical abuse, but since then "abuse" has been expanded to include mental cruelty, and the new grounds of incompatibility include virtually any behavior that one spouse dislikes in the other (Bane 1976). Almost half of all the states now have "no-fault" laws that allow couples to divorce without proving that either spouse was guilty of misbehavior.

Divorce has also been made easier by changing values about marriage, the family, and happiness. In societies that base marriage and the family primarily on economics and alliances between kinship groups, the fact that spouses are unhappy with each other is relatively unimportant. In the U.S., however, marriage is valued primarily as a relationship that satisfies emotional needs, and when these are not met divorce is seen as a legitimate solution (see Thornton and Freedman 1982).

As values and norms about divorce have changed, so, too, have attitudes. It was not that long ago that no divorced person could run for the office of president and win; but that changed with the election of Ronald Reagan. Until the 1960s most looked on divorce as a shameful admission of failure, and divorced women were assumed to be "loose," "wild," and promiscuous. These stigmas have since lost most of their importance.

Divorce and Social Structure   The structural causes of rising divorce rates take three forms: the changing relationship of married couples to kinship networks, the changing structure of families, and increased visibility of divorced people.

The more people a marriage involves, the greater the pressures are against divorce. Among the Subanum in the Philippines, for example, marriage is an economic exchange between two families, including a bride-price paid by the groom's family to the bride's. If couples divorce and the wife is found to be at fault, her family must repay up to twice the bride-price to the husband's family and turn over the children and most of the couple's property to them. Among the Navaho, marriage joins two kinship networks and divorce threatens to disrupt important social ties (Stephens 1963). In such cases extended families often oppose divorce because they stand to lose a great deal. By comparison, in industrial societies, extended families lose relatively little when couples divorce and so offer less opposition.

The isolation of nuclear families from extended kin also makes divorce more likely by increasing the emotional and financial insecurity of married couples. In prerevolutionary China, the relationship between spouses was less important than the contribution of each to the extended family, and spouses depended on a large set of family relationships to satisfy their needs (Goode 1976). Married couples in industrial societies, however, are both more independent and more isolated: spouses depend on each other to satisfy their needs, and in times of stress they can count on relatively little support from kinship networks.

Paradoxically, the increased importance of the nuclear family contributes to higher divorce rates in some societies and lower divorce rates in others. In Japan, divorce rates fell as parents-in-law lost the power to send their daughters-in-law home. In the U.S., where in-laws never had such power, the isolation of nuclear families has had just the opposite effect on divorce rates.

A second structural cause of rising divorce rates is the changing structure of the nuclear family and its relationship with the economy. In extended families production is shared among many adults, and divorce has little effect on either spouse's ability to survive. Each can simply return to the extended family from which they came. Divorce in nuclear families, however, threatens the financial security of both spouses (but particularly of wives). Divorce rates typically drop during economic depressions, because most couples cannot afford to separate.

Divorce rates increase as wives work outside the home more and become financially independent of their husbands (South 1985). When both spouses are heavily committed to demanding jobs, conflicts inevitably occur around the performance of domestic work, and although many couples succeed in creating marriages that are more egalitarian, it is difficult (see Kingston and Nock 1987). Husbands who earn less than their wives often feel threatened. If one spouse wants to take a job in a distant city, the other must choose whether to move at the expense of an existing job. In some cases, husbands and wives decide to live in different places—maintaining a "commuter marriage"—in order to keep their relationship intact while pursuing their occupational goals (Gerstel and Gross 1984). How the long-term stability of such marriages compares with that of other marriages is yet to be seen.

Family finances and economic relationships between husbands and wives help explain historical changes in social class differences in divorce rates. In the nineteenth century, when divorce was expensive and difficult to obtain, it was more common in the upper class than in the middle and lower classes (Bane 1976). Since that time, however, legal costs have dropped sharply and are within the reach of many more lower- and middle-class couples, and divorce is now more common among lower-class couples than among those in the upper class (Sweet and Bumpass 1987).

As divorce has become more accessible, other legal changes encourage upper-middle and upper-class couples to stay together. In particular, community property laws force divorcing couples to split property evenly, and wealthier couples often own valuable assets such as stock and real estate. This means that both spouses—but husbands in particular—have a great deal to lose in a divorce and may stay with an unhappy marriage.

A third structural change that helps explain rising divorce rates is the sheer increase in the number—and therefore the visibility—of divorced people. When divorce was rare, people who contemplated it believed correctly that divorce would place them in a small, deviant minority. Their only reference group consisted of married couples, and they got little support for the decision to end a marriage. As more and more people occupy the status of "divorced person," however, divorced people are increasingly visible to married people who contemplate divorce, and this provides unhappy spouses with a new reference group on which they can model their behavior and from which they can draw emotional support and social approval (see Thornton 1985).

Divorce, Population, and Ecology   Changes in population and ecology have contributed to rising divorce rates by making divorce easier and by making lifelong marriage harder.

When nuclear families produced most of what they needed, each spouse needed the other to perform important productive work. Prior to the late 1800s most U.S. families lived on farms, and it took at least two adults working together to produce enough to support them. People who divorced lost far more than a companion, for they also lost a producer of a variety of essential goods.

By shifting production out of the home, industrialization creates market economies in which people work for money that they use to buy what other people produce. This means, in turn, that wives and husbands can survive by their own labor, and this weakens the economic dependency of spouses on each other. As their dependency on each other lessens, so does the material cost of divorce.

Population trends also affect divorce rates by making lifelong marriage more difficult. In the eighteenth century, adult death rates were relatively high—especially among women of childbearing age—and people rarely spent their entire lives with a single spouse. High death rates contributed to relatively low divorce rates by ending marriages before the need for divorce ever arose. Death rates have fallen sharply over the last century, however, and this means that people who married in their early twenties could look forward to roughly 50 years of married life (USCB 1990a). This inevitably increases the chance that divorce will occur, because it is simply much harder to spend 50 years with one person than it is to live together for 10 or 20 years.

Population changes, therefore, have made "'Til death do us part" an increasingly difficult ideal to achieve.

Family Violence

One of the most important functions of families is to provide a safe haven for their members. For this reason family violence is particularly disturbing—and, ironically, difficult to control.

Straus, Gelles, and Steinmetz (1980) conservatively estimated that 8 million Americans are assaulted by family members each year. Violence occurs in one out of four marriages, and rape occurs in at least one out of ten. Battering is the most frequent cause of injury for women—more frequent than muggings, car accidents, and rape combined (JAMA 1990). Each year, at least half of all adolescents are victims of family violence and as many as 2.4 million younger children are "starved and abandoned, burned and severely beaten, raped and sodomized, berated and belittled," with several thousand dying as a result (DHHS 1990). As many as 2.5 million elderly family members are abused each year (Gelles and Cornell 1985; see also Straus and Gelles 1986; Pagelow 1984). Fifteen percent of all murder victims are killed by members of their own family (USDJ 1990).

These data paint a picture of family life that is a far cry from our cultural ideal of harmony and love. From a sociological perspective, however, the level of violence in families comes as no great surprise. Why?

Ecology and Family Violence   Interpersonal violence depends on people being physically close, and the nuclear family brings a small group of people into close and frequent interaction. Physical proximity is just as necessary for hitting another person as it is for hugging.

The chance of violence is increased by physical isolation of the nuclear family, since outsiders cannot see what goes on inside the home. The less publicly visible behavior is, the more likely people are to commit deviant acts.

Violence and Social Structure

Ironically, the very fact that the ideal nuclear family functions as a "haven in a heartless world" (Lasch 1977) increases the chances for violence. Most families, for example, have difficulty satisfying all their members' needs. The extreme emotional and material dependency of nuclear family members on one another inevitably creates some tension, anger, and bitterness because many family decisions—such as how to spend money—cannot satisfy everyone (Gelles 1972; Shupe et al. 1987).

Defining the family as a haven also supports violence because the family becomes the only place in which we feel free to "let off steam." You pay a much higher price if you punch your boss than you do if you punch your spouse, because your boss has far fewer reasons to tolerate such behavior. As Coser (1964) put it, the nuclear family is a "safety-valve institution," and this makes it conducive to violence. In general, the more stress a family undergoes—financial worry, trouble at work, legal problems, prolonged illness, or death of someone close—the more violence there is, especially towards children (Straus et al. 1980).

Because the family and its home are valued as private places, public officials are reluctant to intervene in what is culturally defined as a "family affair" (Berk and Loseke 1981; Pagelow 1984). This insulates family members from standards of behavior that prevail in the outside world and makes violence more likely to occur (Sherman and Berk 1984; Berk and Newton 1985).

Structural distributions of power in patriarchal families also contribute to violence by making women and children highly vulnerable (Dobash and Dobash 1979; Gartner 1990; Klein 1982). Children are generally powerless to leave abusive families, and wives often find themselves in the same position because they cannot support their children and themselves with their own earnings. (See One Step Further 16-1).

Culture and Family Violence

Although most cultures include disapproval of family violence, many also contain ideas that support it. In the U.S., one of the most important is the cultural support for the privacy of the individual home, an ideal that has consistently made it difficult to control family violence (Pleck 1987).

Culture also contributes to family violence by limiting the behaviors that are defined as violent. Most parents, for example, regard the physical punishment of children as both legitimate and necessary and rarely define it as violence. Norms often allow behavior within families that would not be tolerated among nonfamily members. Parents may slap children who refuse to eat their vegetables and the police will not intervene; but they risk punishment for criminal assault if they slap restaurant customers who do not eat their vegetables. The sanctions are quite different in these two situations, even though in both cases the violent behavior might be defended as "for the victim's own good."

In most of the U.S., a husband may force his wife to have sex with him by threatening violence if she refuses; but the same behavior toward any other woman is legally punishable as rape. How do we live with such contradictory norms? One way is to use cultural beliefs to define many physically violent acts as "nonviolent." In general, we do not define an injurious act as violent if the act is permitted or required by a role. A national study of U.S. men, for example, found that most do not define the killing of a criminal by police as violence (Blumenthal et al. 1972), and most parents do not define spanking a child as a violent act, because they regard it as a necessary part of their role (Gelles 1972). Almost 80 percent of U.S. adults, for example, agree that disciplining children sometimes requires "a good hard spanking" (Davis and Smith 1990). From this perspective, family violence is often neither defined nor treated by outsiders as such because family roles condone violence within limits that are always subject to interpretation.

Culture, social structure, and ecology help explain many aspects of family disorganization. As disorganization becomes more visible in families, however, we must confront issues about the future of the family that have disturbed many people for a number of years: Is the family as an institution in danger? Can it be destroyed?

FAMILIES AND SOCIAL CHANGE

Like all groups, families change in response to changes in their social and physical environments; but unlike most other groups, change is an inevitable part of family life. Membership in families spans the entire

ONE STEP FURTHER 16-1

Power, Dominance, and Family Violence

The tensions that inevitably arise in family life are most conducive to violence when power is unequally distributed between husbands and wives, especially in families in which the husband dominates. If we look at violence against wives in Figure B-16-1, the most violent homes are those in which husbands dominate (the right side of the graph), followed by those dominated by wives (the left side of the graph). The least violent homes are those in which husbands and wives share equally in power and neither dominates (the center of the graph). Child abuse is also more frequent in families with unequal distributions of power. Why do you suppose this would be true?

FIGURE B-16-1

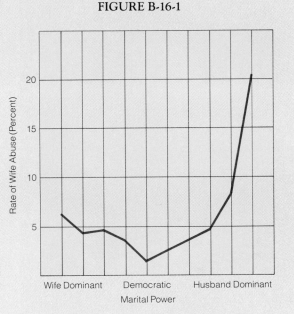

Source: Adapted from Straus, Gelles, and Steinmetz 1980.

life course, and as individuals inevitably age, their families must also change (Boss 1980).

In families with young children, for example, socialization, protection of the young, and children's obedience to their parents are highly valued, and family norms support those values. Interaction is frequent because they live in the same household, and power is unequally divided between parents and children and between husbands and wives. When children reach adulthood, however, family culture and structure change dramatically. Children are expected to make their own decisions, and parents lose much of their authority along with their socializing roles. Interaction drops sharply as children move away from home; and as parents enter old age, inequality between them lessens, particularly when the husband was once the primary breadwinner. By contrast, in many societies family changes over the life course are far less dramatic. In patrilocal and matrilocal societies newlyweds live with their in-laws, and adult children have far less autonomy.

Our concern in the following sections, however, is less with such internal changes than with changes in the family as an institution. What kinds of changes

are taking place in the cultural and structural characteristics of marriage and the family as social systems? What is the future of marriage and the family as institutions?

Cultural Change and the Family

Some of the most profound cultural changes during the last few decades focus on marriage and divorce. One of the most important social functions of marriage is the regulation of sexual behavior, and in the U.S. there is increasing support for values that promote sexual unions between unmarried people. Since 1960, for example, the percentage of adults who believe that premarital sex is always or almost always wrong has dropped from 80 to 36 percent (Davis and Smith 1977, 1990).

There is also increasing tolerance of interracial marriage. Since 1972 the percentage of adults who favor laws prohibiting interracial marriage has dropped from 38 to 18 percent. Disapproval of homosexual unions, however, has remained virtually unchanged, with roughly three-quarters of adults believing that homosexual relationships between adults are always

One of the more radical shifts taking place in family structures is the increasing number of lesbian and gay couples forming long-term, committed relationships that sometimes involve children. This couple and their son live in California.

or almost always wrong (Davis and Smith 1990). In spite of this, however, there are signs that homosexual unions are acquiring some legitimacy. In California and New York, for example, court decisions and changes in local government policies have led to increased recognition of gay couples as partnerships qualifying for treatment usually reserved for heterosexual marriages, such as being eligible for family health insurance coverage under city union contracts. In Denmark, gay couples may now officially marry, and although their unions are not called marriages, they have the same rights and responsibilities as married couples.

Values and norms about relationships within marriages and families are also changing. Marriage has always been a contract relationship—the moment people say "I do," they enter into a culturally defined set of rights, obligations, and expectations that are not explicitly stated in marriage ceremonies. Increasingly, however, couples are basing marriage on written contracts that specify the spouses' expectations of each other—sometimes including details about who does which domestic tasks (Weitzman 1981).

Both the surge of women into the labor force and the women's movement have contributed to a shift toward egalitarian values in some middle- and upper-class marriages. As wives become financially independent, the tendency toward equality is inevitable, and husbands have less and less choice about whether or not they will share in household tasks.

Values about adultery have remained stable since 1973; and in 1990, 90 percent of all adults disapproved of it. Perhaps in reaction to the fact that divorce has become easier to obtain and no longer carries the stigma it did 20 or 30 years ago, almost half believe that it should become *harder* to obtain (Davis and Smith 1990).

Changing values also affect the composition of families. Although the value of large families has declined sharply, other values have changed in ways that may increase the size of households. Since 1973, for example, the percentage of adults who believe that it is a good idea for elderly people to share a home with their grown children has increased from 31 to 44 percent (Davis and Smith 1990).

What do all these statistics tell us about the U.S. family? As a set, they seem to describe changes that go in more than one direction. There is greater tolerance of premarital sex, but not of adultery; divorce is easier to obtain, but a majority would make it harder. In an important sense, such patterns of change in this most important of social institutions are perhaps just what we should expect.

In a changing society, marriage and the family inevitably reflect those changes since they are the focal point of most people's lives. Nevertheless, because marriage and the family are so important to us as individuals, we tend to resist change in the interests of stability and continuity. When it comes to changing major institutions, in other words, we tend to be cautious, balancing a liberal attitude toward change in some areas with conservative attitudes toward change in others.

Shifting Structures

In the U.S., the composition of families is the most visible change in family structure. Adults are less likely to live in nuclear families and families are becoming smaller, less likely to be headed by a married couple, and more likely to include nonrelatives.

Since 1960 the percentage of people living in families has dropped from 93 to 72 percent. At the same time, the number of people living alone has tripled to 24 million and more than quadrupled to 6 million among those under 45 years old. In the last ten years, the number of households whose members are unrelated to one another—including unmarried couples—tripled, while the number of families rose by only 40 percent (USCB 1990a). Adult children are leaving home to set up their own households at younger ages than before, but without marrying and forming families. As a result, there may be some erosion in the rate at which families are formed as young adults—women in particular—experience living on their own in nonfamily situations (see Waite et al. 1986).

These numbers suggest massive experimenting with alternatives to the nuclear family. For many unmarried couples, for example, living together is a new form of courtship that may lead to formal marriage—a pattern that exists in a number of societies, including Poland and, especially, Sweden (Bumpass and Sweet 1989; Popenoe 1987; Tanfer 1987). It is possible, however, that a growing minority in the U.S. is reluctant to take on the burdens and restrictions of marriage and parenting, and although more than 90 percent of young people say they intend to marry, that figure may come down in the future (Sweet and Bumpass 1987; Thornton and Freedman 1982) (see Table 16-3).

What about the structure of families themselves? How are they changing? (Before you read on, take a moment to study Table 16-4 on p. 410 carefully.) Since 1960, average family size has dropped by 14 percent among whites and 20 percent among blacks. Although the nuclear family headed by a married couple is still the most common family structure, it has lost ground as the percentage of families headed by a divorced, separated, or single mother has increased by 44 percent among whites and 95 percent among blacks.

As a result, a growing percentage of children are living in single-parent families, and, therefore, in poverty (McLanahan 1985). The percentage of all children living with both parents has dropped from 89 to 75 percent, and to less than half among black children. Since 1970, single-parent families headed

TABLE 16-3 Nonmarital Cohabitation among Never-Married Women, 20–29 Years Old (United States)

As you can see, although there are no substantial racial differences in the percentage of women who are currently or have ever lived with a man, there are sharp differences by education and religion. Cohabitation is strongly related to lower levels of education and to expressing no religious preference (but note there is no difference between Catholics and non-Catholics).

SOCIAL CHARACTERISTICS	CURRENTLY COHABITATING OR EVER COHABITED	
	Current	Ever
Race		
Black	10%	29%
White	13%	30%
Education		
Less than high school graduate	23%	46%
High school graduate	15%	36%
More than high school	9%	22%
Religion		
Catholic	11%	29%
Non-Catholic	12%	28%
None	15%	48%

Source: Tanfer 1987, Table 1.

by women who have never married have also become more common. The percentage of all children living in such families was nine times greater in 1988 than in 1970, and among whites, more than ten times greater. Hofferth (1985) projects that 70 percent of white children and 94 percent of black children born in 1980 will spend at least part of their childhood with one parent.

The compound family is another structure that is becoming increasingly common in the U.S. In 1986, roughly half of all marriages were a remarriage for at least one of the spouses (USCB 1990a). A sixth of all children are living in compound families and there were 4.4 million households with stepchildren (Cherlin and McCarthy 1985; USCB 1989c).

TABLE 16-4   The Changing Composition of U.S. Families, by Race, 1960[1] to 1988

FAMILY STRUCTURE	ALL FAMILIES 1960	ALL FAMILIES 1988	WHITES 1960	WHITES 1988	BLACKS 1960	BLACKS 1988	HISPANICS 1985	HISPANICS 1988
Average family size	3.7	3.2	3.6	3.1	4.4	3.5	3.9	3.8
Percentage of Families with:								
Married couple	87	79	89	83	74	51	72	70
Female head	10	17	9	13	22	43	23	23
Percentage of All Children Who Live with:								
Both parents	89	75	92	81	69	42	72	69
Mother only	8	22	6	16	21	55	25	28
Percentage of All Children Who Live with:								
Single mothers[2]	0.8	7	0.2	3	4.4	28	6	9

[1]Except for Hispanics, who were not tabulated separately in earlier years.
[2]Single means never married, children are those under 18 years old, and figures are for 1970 and 1985.
Source: USCB 1990a.

The nuclear family is also changing by becoming more extended in some ways and less extended in others. A **subfamily** is a family that lives in the household of another family, and subfamilies can be either related or unrelated to the host family. Between 1960 and 1980, the number of related subfamilies dropped by 26 percent, indicating a decline in extended family networks. By 1989, however, the number of related subfamilies had doubled to its highest level since 1950. At the same time, the number of *unrelated* subfamilies more than doubled. In addition, the number of unrelated individuals in family households almost tripled (USCB 1990a). In addition to subfamilies, there has also been a recent trend towards single young adult children returning to live with their parents, often because of difficult times brought on by unemployment or divorce (see Glick and Lin 1986a).

The United States has never been a society in which most households included extended families (Demos 1986; Thornton and Freedman 1983), and although the importance of kinship seems to be declining as increasing numbers of adults live by themselves, families also seem to be expanding their households by including nonrelatives. This trend is paralleled by the increased number of nonfamily households in which unrelated adults live together and share expenses and housework. We seem, in short, to be trying out a number of ways of meeting our needs for companionship and financial and emotional security. The fact that we are less likely to live with extended kin does not mean that we have become a nation of "loners" and isolated nuclear families.

Families Come and Families Go, but The Family Is Here to Stay

Fear that the family is "falling apart" is nothing new in U.S. history (see Demos 1986). The historical durability of the family as an institution suggests that in spite of high divorce rates and a growing minority of young people who postpone marriage or forgo it altogether, the family will always be a part of society. We end marriages in record numbers, but we also remarry in record numbers (see Bumpass et al. 1990; Glick and Lin 1986b; Norton and Moorman 1987). Although many grow disillusioned with particular marriages, or delay marrying, there is little evidence that marriage itself is losing its appeal.

Both historical and cross-cultural variations in marriage and family life highlight the fact that social institutions are defined by the functions they perform, not by particular cultural and structural arrangements. From this perspective, institutions may change structurally or culturally; but they "die" only if other institutions take over their functions or the functions themselves lose their social importance. Many functions of the family have been taken over in part by other institutions such as schools, but there is no society in which the family does not exist in some form. Even the Soviet Union—which tried to replace the family with schools and day-care centers in the years after the 1918 Russian Revolution—returned to the family as the primary group in which children are cared for and socialized.

The family as we know it is changing and will most certainly continue to change; but primary groups in which people are born and grow up, and which meet their needs for emotional support and a sense of continuity in their lives are, as Bane (1976) put it, "here to stay."

SUMMARY

1. An institution is a social "blueprint" for groups. The family as an institution is not the same as your family or mine.

2. Marriage is a socially supported union between individuals in what is intended to be a stable, enduring relationship that involves sexual interaction. It is the basis for the family, an institution defined by six social functions: regulation of sexual behavior, reproduction, nurturance and protection of children, socialization, production and consumption, and the passing on of ascribed statuses such as race.

3. Marriage and the family rest on many beliefs, the most important of which is kinship. Matrilineal societies trace descent through the mother's blood relatives, whereas patrilineal societies trace descent through the father's. In bilateral societies descent is traced through the relatives of both parents.

4. Among the most important values and attitudes in marriage and the family are those focusing on the basis for marriage (such as love or economic exchange), sexual experience before and during marriage, and the relative importance of family ties and those with outsiders.

5. Marriage rules limit whom people may marry, when, and under what conditions. Incest rules prohibit sexual intercourse and marriage between kin; rules of exogamy require marriage outside the group; and rules of endogamy require marriage within it. Marriage rules define the acceptability of multiple spouses (polygamy), whether it be multiple wives (polygyny) or husbands (polyandry). In matrilocal societies married couples must live with the wife's family, whereas in patrilocal societies they live with the husband's. In bilocal societies couples must choose between the two. In neolocal societies, couples live wherever they want.

6. Families have a variety of structures, from the nuclear family consisting of parents and children, to extended families that include additional relatives, single-parent families, and compound families that include children from other marriages.

7. In all societies women are the primary caretakers of children, but they also participate in production. The more industrial a society is, the less likely women are to be economically active.

8. Most societies are patriarchies, and no known societies have been matriarchies. Egalitarian marriages are increasingly common in industrial societies.

9. The characteristics of families strongly affect birth rates. The younger the age at which people marry the higher birth rates tend to be. Changes in birth rates, in turn, affect family structure. Compared with colonial women, women today bear far fewer children and are more likely to work outside the home.

10. The way in which goods are produced in a society affects the power of family groups and the ways in which families are organized. In industrial societies, many of the functions once performed by the family have been transferred to other institutions.

11. The functional perspective identifies functional and dysfunctional consequences associated with different aspects of family organization. A conflict perspective shows how the interests of individual families and economic and political institutions clash.

12. Patterns of interaction in families depend on the structure of family institutions. The intensity of monogamy encourages couples to reach agreement on important views.

13. Family disorganization occurs when statuses are not occupied or roles are not performed. Divorce, death, and violence—themselves caused by social and ecological factors—are major causes of family disorganization.

14. As an institution, the U.S. family has undergone a variety of cultural and structural changes, particularly as families adjust to changes in the economy and the roles of men and women.

KEY TERMS

bilateral descent   388
bilocal marriage   391
compound family   393
divorced family   393
egalitarian family   395
endogamy   391
exogamy   391
extended family   393
family   386

kinship   387
marriage   386
marriage rules   390
matriarchy   395
matrilineal descent   387
matrilocal marriage   391
monogamy   391
neolocal marriage   391
nuclear family   393

patriarchy   395
patrilineal descent   388
patrilocal marriage   391
polyandry   391
polygamy   391
polygyny   391
single-parent family   393
subfamily   410

LOOKING ELSEWHERE

Having studied Chapter 16, you might want to look at related discussions in *Human Arrangements*, which include

- sexual values (Chapter 2, p. 32)
- socialization in families (Chapter 7, pp. 150–51)
- marital rape (Chapter 8, pp. 168–69)
- family divisions of labor and gender inequality (Chapter 14, pp. 338, 345–47, 351–52, 354–58)
- patriarchy, matriarchy, and gender inequality (Chapter 14, pp. 340–41)
- socialization, families, and gender roles (Chapter 14, pp. 342–43)

- learning to be spouses and parents (Chapter 7, pp. 154–55)
- age and changing patterns of family interaction (Chapter 15, pp. 376–77)
- social causes and consequences of fertility (Chapter 4, pp. 67–69)
- the effects of greater longevity on family life (Chapter 18, p. 465)
- conflict between families and schools (Chapter 17, pp. 430–31)

RECOMMENDED READINGS

Demos, J. 1986. *Past, present, and personal: The family and the life course in American history.* New York: Basic Books. A fascinating history that shows not only the changes that have taken place in family life, but the remarkable durability of this vital institution.

Emery, R. E. 1988. *Marriage, divorce, and children's adjustment.* Newbury Park, CA: Sage. A short but revealing review of what is known about the effects of divorce on the lives of children.

Gelles, R. V., and Cornell, C. P. 1985. *Intimate violence in families.* Beverly Hills, CA: Sage. A recent summary of what is known about violence in U.S. families.

Goode, W. J. 1976. Family disorganization. In R. K. Merton and R. Nisbet (Eds.), *Contemporary social problems.* New York: Harcourt Brace Jovanovich. A useful sociological overview of family disorganization.

Hood, J. C. 1983. *Becoming a two-job family.* New York: Praeger. An in-depth study of 16 married couples in which both spouses work. Hood sheds light on many issues, including the effects of a wife's work status and earnings on her power in the family and the ways in which spouses negotiate domestic responsibilities. See also Lein, L. 1984. *Families without villains: American families in an era of change.* Lexington, MA: D. C. Heath.

Journal of Marriage and the Family. Minneapolis, MN: National Council on Family Relations. The leading scholarly journal that focuses on marriage and the family.

Korbin, J. E. (Ed.). 1983. *Child abuse and neglect: Cross-cultural perspectives*. Berkeley: University of California Press. A collection of papers that includes a disturbing study that finds that behaviors such as child abuse are more common in "developed" societies than in what many people think of as "primitive" societies.

Simon, B. L. 1987. *Never married women*. Philadelphia: Temple University Press. In-depth interviews of fifty never-married women ranging in age from 60 to 101 provide an unusual outsider's view of the nuclear family.

Spiro, M., and Spiro, A. G. 1975. *Children of the kibbutz: A study in child training and personality*. Cambridge, MA: Harvard University Press. An analysis of the effects of a radically different approach to family life on the development of children.

Staines, G. L., and Pleck, J. H. 1983. *The impact of work schedules on the family*. Ann Arbor: University of Michigan Press. A clearly written, interesting study that shows how work schedules for both men and women affect the feelings and behavior of family members.

Sussman, M. B., and Steinmetz, S. K. (Eds.) 1987. *Handbook of marriage and the family*. New York: Plenum Press. An ambitious, encyclopedic book that provides a "state-of-the-art" overview of major sociological issues in the study of marriage and the family.

Sweet, J. A., and Bumpass, L. L. 1987. *American families and households*. New York: Russell Sage Foundation. A sweeping, beautifully documented analysis of changing patterns of leaving home, marriage, divorce, childbearing, family living arragements, and the varying economic conditions of U.S. households.

17
EDUCATION

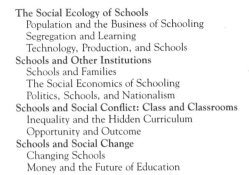 Students often describe everything outside of schools as the "real world." "School," they say, "isn't part of the real world. It's just a place I have to go if I want to get a decent job. *Real* life doesn't begin until after graduation." They could not be more mistaken. Few social institutions mirror societies as faithfully as schools do, and that so many students are unaware of this fact gives schools enormous power and influence in their lives.

What are schools and how do their characteristics define them as institutions? How are they related to other institutions, such as the family, religion, the economy, and the state? What kinds of consequences do they produce? What part do they play in social inequality? These are the kinds of questions this chapter will try to answer.

SCHOOL AS A SOCIAL INSTITUTION

All societies socialize people to perform adult roles. In gatherer-hunter and horticultural societies, children learn informally from the adults who happen to be around them. They learn the same way in agricultural societies, but because skills are more specialized and the division of labor is more complex, some children are apprenticed to adults—such as carpenters and blacksmiths—and also learn through on-the-job training (Larkin 1988).

Training in industrial societies, however, is too complex to be left to informal relationships, and families do not have the resources to prepare their children for adult roles. As a result, children spend large portions of their childhood in **schools**—formal organizations whose main purpose is to educate people. From this perspective, **education** is a special form of socialization, which involves the systematic, formal transmission of skills, knowledge, and other aspects of a society's culture.

A Short Social History of Schools

Schools have existed for centuries, but until the late nineteenth century they were restricted largely to the children of elite families. The ancient Chinese used schools to train government officials, just as medieval Europeans used them to train priests. In Victorian England, elite private schools trained future high-level government officials and business leaders, and this is still true today. In 1977, 86 percent of all senior officials in the Foreign Office (the British counterpart of the U.S. State Department) were graduates of just two elite colleges—Oxford and Cambridge (Sampson 1983). Similar patterns are found in the U.S. in relation to elite prep schools and Ivy League colleges (see Cookson and Persell 1985).

Education not only prepares the elite for prestigious and powerful occupations; it sets them apart symbolically from the classes below them. The ability to read and write, or to speak Latin and Greek, is for many a cultural indicator of high breeding and superiority. Schooling has been a major way for members of the upper class to prepare their children to be defined and treated as members of the upper class.

As the Industrial Revolution took hold in the nineteenth century, the upper class monopoly over formal schooling began to loosen. Social life became more bureaucratic and rational, and the demand for training in specialized skills—from typing and filing documents to operating telegraphs, engineering, and managing complex business organizations—grew rapidly. Examinations and grades were used to certify competence. Education as a symbol of "cultured," elite status was gradually replaced by education as a means for producing a large number of workers with a wide range of skills (Weber 1946).

In addition to a skilled work force, industrialists wanted good workers whose values and attitudes served the interests of employers and helped increase production (see Carnoy and Levin 1985). Horace Mann—one of the strongest early supporters of public education—won the support of manufacturers by promising that educated workers would be "docile and quick to apply themselves to work," disciplined, punctual, and loyal (Mann 1842).

By the 1850s every state supported public education. Between 1870 and 1900 the number of high schools grew from 160 to more than 6,000, and the percentage of young adults with high school diplomas more than tripled. Today, some 86 percent of those 25 to 29 years old are high school graduates (USCB 1975, 1990a). Colleges and graduate schools grew more slowly than public high schools, primarily because few families could afford to send their children to college, and higher education was widely perceived as a luxury until well into the twentieth century. In fact, around 1900, popular books giving advice on success generally told their readers that college was a waste of time for all but the wealthy, who did not have to worry about making a living (Huber 1971).

Although the dramatic rise of schooling resulted largely from the Industrial Revolution, other factors also played a part. Nations, for example, used schools to instill patriotism and national solidarity ("I pledge

In many societies, scholarly learning has been a key to high prestige. This was especially true in China where, as recently as the turn of this century, scholars commanded far greater respect than millionaires. In this detail from an eleventh-century scroll, a scholar composes a poem.

allegiance to the flag . . ."). In the late 1800s and early 1900s the U.S. was flooded with immigrants, and schools were used to assimilate them into the dominant Anglo culture (see Glenn 1988).

Over the last century education has also been perceived as the major source of upward mobility, an escape route leading out of poverty into the middle class. By the late 1970s—in sharp contrast to the early 1900s—79 percent of parents said they would like their children to go beyond high school, and 36 percent of all adults rated college education as "very important." Most significant, the perceived importance of college is highest among people who are at the *bottom* of the stratification system—nonwhites and those with relatively low incomes and educations (USCB 1975).

Whether or not such perceptions of education are accurate, one thing is certain: institutionalized learning affects not only societies, but the lives of millions of people. Given this, we need to understand how schools work—how cultural, structural, and ecological factors affect what goes on in them—as well as how schools affect and are affected by the social environments in which they exist. The next three sections analyze the characteristics of schools. Then, we take a broader perspective and examine the relationships between educational and other institutions and the effects of education on social inequality.

CULTURAL VARIATIONS

Like other institutions, schools rest on a cultural foundation. To understand what people do in schools, we first have to understand how people use culture to think about schools and about what goes on in them.

Beliefs

The most fundamental belief that underlies schooling in the U.S. is that in order to learn what we need to know as adults, someone must decide what it is that we need to know and then teach it to us. From the earliest grades, students and teachers generally share the belief that teachers know what is true and students do not. It is not surprising that college students seldom challenge their teachers—even when they believe their teachers are wrong.

A second important belief is that knowledge is a key to individual happiness and a solution to social problems. Jefferson argued that a healthy democracy depends on a well-educated public capable of making critical, independent decisions about social issues and government. Half of U.S. adults believe that blacks and other minorities are relatively poor because they "don't have the chance for the education it takes to rise out of poverty" (Davis and Smith 1990), a belief that, as we will see later in this chapter, is largely untrue.

A third belief underlying schooling is that tests and grades accurately measure intellectual ability and how much students learn. Most research shows, however, that this is at best only partly true. Standardized tests—such as IQ tests and college SATs—have come under heavy criticism for being biased in favor of white middle- and upper-class students. Tests depend on language and on examples that reflect cultural background and life experiences as much as—if not more than—mental ability.

Consider the following questions:

1. A "handkerchief head" is:
   (A) A bad dude, (B) A porter, (C) An Uncle Tom, (D) A preacher

2. Which word is most out of place here?
   (A) Bagel, (B) Lox, (C) Gefilte

Blacks have an edge with the first question ("C"—An Uncle Tom; do you know what that is?), and Jews have the advantage on the second ("A"—the other two are seafoods). The second question is designed to measure the ability to categorize objects on the basis of similar characteristics; but the correct answer depends on more than this. If you have never heard of gefilte fish and lox (foods popular among Jews), you might answer incorrectly regardless of your ability to distinguish between objects. You first have to know what the words mean, and that depends on your cultural background.

The validity of standardized tests is only part of the problem, however, for a large body of research suggests that teachers are very subjective when they grade papers and tests (Kirschenbaum et al. 1971). When teachers from many disciplines grade student papers, they vary enormously in the range of grades they assign to the same work. One teacher's "A" is often another's "C." This will surprise relatively few students and teachers, and this is, in itself, an important point. We suspect at some level that grades are invalid, and yet continue to act as if they were not. Since the school system hinges on the belief that grades are at least roughly valid, those who refuse to go along cannot succeed within it. Students who do not care about grades risk flunking out; and teachers who do not take grading seriously seldom escape criticism.

Values

As an institution, the school reflects important values, the most important of which is the value placed on socialization. U.S. students learn quickly that their teachers value obedience, punctuality, politeness, neatness, individual competition, and playing by the rules more highly than independent thought, rebelliousness, creativity, and group work. Whereas primary groups, such as families, value their members because they are members, secondary groups such as schools value students for their performance at standardized tasks; and for most students, schooling is their first experience of being ranked and graded in relation to other people.

Values also change. Standardized tests, grading, ranking, and individual competition were relatively unimportant in U.S. schools until the middle of this century, because the primary purpose of early schools was not to sort students on the basis of ability. The progressive education movement, which began late in the nineteenth century, favored learning through experience rather than through reading and rote learning, greater attention to the needs of each child than to the requirements of rigid curricula and the needs of society, cooperation rather than competition, schoolroom democracy rather than the unquestioned authority of teachers and administrators, and preparation for the everyday tasks of life rather than development of the intellect (Ravitch 1983).

From the 1920s through the late 1940s the progressive value system dominated much of public schooling; but in the early 1950s opponents attacked the progressive model, based on the belief that progressive values served a communist conspiracy aimed at undermining young people. Supporters of progressive education were unable to deny that the study of mathematics, literature, history, science, and foreign language had been severely curtailed in public education, and the following decade saw public education turn back to basics (Ravitch 1983).

In the late 1960s two important educational values clashed once again: Should schools exist for social purposes (to socialize the young) or should they exist to serve individuals (to provide them with resources controlled and used by them for their own benefit as they see it)? In the midst of antiwar and civil rights struggles that questioned the legitimacy of authority itself, many students demanded social and personal relevance in school courses and greater control over their own education. Like the earlier progressives, reformers in the 1960s advocated personal growth and autonomy for students, and many schools abolished grades and required courses. As requirements were loosened, students increasingly replaced courses in language, mathematics, and science with a range of electives—from driver education to home economics (National Commission on Excellence in Education 1983; Ravitch 1983). As unemployment soared in the early 1980s and parents became increasingly anxious about the job prospects of their children, support for a back-to-basics movement reappeared (see One Step Further 17-1; see also Shor 1986).

Value and Role Conflict   Cultural values also conflict within schools and often produce dilemmas for both students and teachers. College students, for example, are encouraged to value learning for its own sake, to think for themselves, critically examine ideas, and take challenging courses that force them to grow. They are also encouraged, however, to achieve high grades, and they know that their grades will affect their future once they leave school.

These two values often conflict with each other: students may feel they must choose between challenging courses that offer slim prospects of an "A" and easy ones whose chief benefit may be a high grade. If they read unassigned books, they may risk not having enough time to prepare for exams. If they challenge what their professors say in class, they may risk appearing to be foolish or disrespectful, and may fear (with some justification) that this will negatively affect their grades. Consequently, they often find themselves in what appears to be a "no-win"

ONE STEP FURTHER 17-1

From Meaning to Money: What Do College Students Want?

Since the late 1960s, national surveys of college freshmen have tracked changes in student values, and one of the most dramatic trends in values concerns the goals college students identify as most important to their educations. As Figure B-17-1 shows, in 1967, 83 percent ranked development of a "meaningful philosophy of life" as either "essential" or "very important," and just over 40 percent ranked being well off financially as essential or very important. Since then, however, the percentage placing a high value on developing a meaningful philosophy of life has dropped steadily to a new low of only 39 percent in 1987, while the percentage giving a high rank to being well off financially has risen just as steadily to a new high of 76 percent. Only in the past few years has this trend shown signs of reversing itself.

How would you have answered these questions if you had been included in this survey? How do you think your classmates would answer? How do you think such changes will affect life in our society? Why?

FIGURE B-17-1   Freshman Goals: Spiritual vs. Financial
Percent of freshmen who identified each goal as "essential" or "very important."

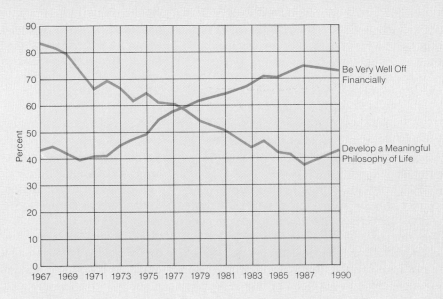

Source: The Higher Education Research Institute, University of California, Los Angeles. "The American Freshman and Follow-up Survey."

situation: "If I don't speak up in class, the professor may think I'm dumb; if I *do* speak up, the professor will *know* I'm dumb."

Teachers also face value conflicts in their roles. In helping students to learn, they often feel the need to be close to students, to know and care about them as individuals, to gain their trust so that they will openly reveal their doubts and weaknesses. As evaluators, however, who report student performance to schools and, eventually, to the outside world, they are expected to treat their students according to fixed standards, to ignore their unique characteristics, and to make decisions that may hurt the same students who trust and confide in them.

Schools are complex institutions that serve the interests of many constituencies and attempt to achieve a wide range of culturally valued goals. This makes value conflict inevitable, both within schools and between them and the outside world.

Norms

Values define goals; but norms define legitimate *means* for achieving those goals. Although people below the age of 16 are required by law to attend school, older adolescents and adults must satisfy specific requirements in order to attend. Teachers must be properly certified, and hiring, firing, and promotion are regulated by rules of seniority and specific procedures. Administrators oversee the performance of students and teachers. Written records of student performance are maintained, and access to them is restricted by law.

Of all school norms, those with the most immediate impact on students determine how rewards and punishments are distributed. "What do I have to do to get an 'A'?" is the number one topic of conversation among many college students at the beginning of a term. "How many papers and exams? How long should the papers be? How much does each exam and paper count? How much does classroom participation count? Does she want footnotes? Does he *really* want us to talk in class? Is she a hard grader? Does he expect us to actually read *all* of the reading list? Does she give extensions?" Such questions are even more important when grading is done on a curve that limits the number of high grades that can be assigned and requires a certain number of low grades. This is a classic example of a zero-sum game, one in which the success of one player requires the failure of another (Morgenstern 1968; von Neumann and Morgenstern 1964).

Forced to operate under these kinds of norms, it is not surprising that students often spend a great deal of time doing detective work in order to figure out the norms that actually determine success and failure. Listen carefully to what students ask professors in the early weeks of a term and you will notice that many questions are attempts to force the professor to reveal the rules of the game, which often vary considerably from one course to another. Students must often wait for several weeks for the professor to reveal the entire set of norms, and they are sometimes shocked to learn that they misperceived important norms or that norms have been changed. It is understandable that some students study the course as a social system as much as they do its subject.

The importance of grades lies at the heart of a fundamental dilemma in education. On the one hand, students learn more if they study because they are interested in the subject—in other words, if their primary rewards are intrinsic rewards they give to themselves: personal satisfaction, excitement, and growth. On the other hand, from early on, students learn that everything they do is connected to extrinsic rewards—a grade or expression of approval given

to them by someone else—and several studies suggest that interest in activities declines when outside rewards are introduced.

In one experiment, preschool children were offered an art project, and the experimenters identified those children who showed the greatest interest (Lepper, Greene, and Nisbett 1973). These children were then divided into three groups. In the first, children were told beforehand that they would receive a "good player" certificate if they took part. The second group unexpectedly received a certificate afterward; and the third group received no external reward. Two weeks later, the same children were again offered an art project—but with no promise of reward—and the children who were rewarded the first time spent the *least* amount of time working on the project. Even though all of these children had shown great interest in art work, external rewards apparently tended to replace internal rewards, for when external rewards were no longer offered, the children's motivation decreased. This effect has also been found among older children and adults (Deci 1975).

Attitudes

Value conflicts, compulsory schooling, and the ambiguity of classroom norms inevitably result in positive and negative attitudes between teachers and students. Perhaps the most common student attitude about school is that they do not like it—especially those who are unsuccessful in obtaining the reward of high grades. For many students—especially those whose social class or race severely limits their life chances—school is not a positive experience that will pay off someday with a good job. It is, instead, a place they have to be, a forced alternative to being on the street. For many students, school is like a prison, and the crime is being younger than 16 years old (Carnegie 1979, 1988).

Negative attitudes are common in schools, and rest on beliefs and values that affect perceptions. Teachers, for example, often assume that students value grades more than learning (which is not surprising given the normative structure of schools) and believe that students will cheat if they can get away with it. This not only supports negative attitudes toward students, but also toward teachers whom students openly like. Teachers commonly believe that since students value grades above everything else, popular teachers must be easy graders (and, therefore, bad teachers).

Values and norms also encourage students to become highly dependent on teachers, to wait anxiously for teachers to tell them exactly what to do, instead of using their own judgment. This, in turn, often makes teachers feel angry, resentful, and "overloaded" by demands from the long lines of students waiting anxiously outside their offices.

Students, however, often resent the power that teachers wield over their future, the arbitrary ways in which grades may be assigned, and teachers' reluctance to pay attention to students as individuals. They also tend to resent other students who are successful at the academic "game," especially those who "butter up" the teacher. This is due in part to the fact that schools are organized so that students and teachers are adversaries who strive for different and often conflicting goals. Students who try to "get in good" with the teacher are seen by many students as "going over to the other side" for their own personal gain. In contrast, successful athletes may be perceived as adding to the glory of the entire student body.

The Importance of Subcultures

As we have seen, although schools are regulated by an institutional culture, what goes on in them depends on subcultures that affect students and teachers. Student behavior is affected as much by the beliefs, values, attitudes, and expectations of other students as it is by the expectations of teachers and administrators. While teachers value academic achievement more than anything else, students often do not. Among males, athletes are most likely to belong to the leading crowd, followed by popular students, and, a distant third, by high academic achievers. Among girls, being considered good looking and popular may be valued more highly than academic success, and the best students may have the fewest friends.

College students belong to one or more of four distinct student subcultures (Clark and Trow 1966). The vocational subculture, because it defines college as a route to good jobs, values hard work for its pay off after graduation. The academic subculture also encourages hard work, but in the name of a different value—learning for its own sake—which is the classic liberal arts goal. The collegiate subculture values social activities—parties, football games, and drinking—while the nonconformist subculture values rebellion against authority and open deviation from the other three subcultures (and, of course, conformity to its own).

Teachers are also influenced by their subculture. Professors are often expected by their peers to value research and publishing more than any other goal, including teaching; and their peers are the ones who control their professional future. College students are often puzzled and frustrated by their teachers' apparent reluctance to spend time with them, to help them learn difficult materials. Few students realize that the values and norms that define student-teacher relationships compete with those that define relationships among teachers.

School culture is complex and riddled with competing values, attitudes, and norms. Far more is going on than simply the transmission of knowledge and skills. Merely by participating in the cultural environment of schools, students learn other lessons that make up what Jackson (1968) called the "hidden curriculum."

Cultural Lessons in the Hidden Curriculum

In many ways, the social process through which students learn formal subjects is a subject in itself—a **hidden curriculum**. Academic performance is measured by tests whose questions usually have only one correct answer. In addition to learning facts, such learning contains a hidden cultural lesson that all questions have a single correct answer, and that is what the teacher is looking for. Students are taught to *know* answers, not to search for them, and to value

What aspects of the hidden curriculum can you detect in this picture?

questions that have one correct answer. When students enter college, they are often disturbed when professors ask questions that have more than one correct answer ("How can nuclear war be prevented? What is the poet trying to say in this poem?"). All of us know the uneasy silence that sometimes comes over a class when this kind of question is asked, the fear of being called on, the frantic search for the right answer somewhere in the readings, and the wondering, "Will this be on the exam?"

The hidden curriculum contains many such lessons (Gracey 1972; Holt 1972). Even in kindergarten, children learn to value punctuality and being good. They learn to value themselves according to their performance and their ability to compete, and to value an expert's judgments more than their own. Whether they personally want to do something is no longer important.

The hidden curriculum teaches girls and boys a great deal about gender. As we saw in Chapter 14, the content of textbooks, the ways in which teachers treat male and female students differently, and the social organization of schools all send a variety of messages to students about who they are as boys and girls and the kinds of behavior and goals considered appropriate for them. Ethnic minority students often learn to devalue their own subculture and replace it with the culture of the white, middle-class. At home, for example, Puerto Rican children learn that it is impolite to look directly into an adult's eyes; but their middle-class, white teachers often interpret—and punish—such behavior as shifty and untrustworthy. Until the late 1960s, the Spanish language was forbidden by law in Texas schools, and Mexican-American children were often punished—sometimes by having to kneel and beg forgiveness—for saying a Spanish word (Silberman 1971).

School norms emphasize order, obedience, and uniformity; and one student's reward is usually gained at the expense of others. In elementary classrooms, when one student cannot answer a question, the others often hold their hands high in the air, straining for the teacher's attention (see Henry 1963). Students are also encouraged to adopt attitudes of cheerful, willing acceptance of authority—to do what they are told to do until they are told to stop, without complaining or questioning.

As we will see later in this chapter, the importance of such hidden cultural lessons extends far beyond schools, for they play a major part in the perpetuation of social inequality.

In Japan, competition for acceptance to universities is so fierce that many students offer prayers to a Shinto guardian of studies. If they are successful, they write a note of thanks and place it at a religious shrine, as this student is doing in Tokyo.

VARIETIES OF SOCIAL STRUCTURE

Like all social systems, schools have structural characteristics that affect what goes on in them.

Boundaries

The boundaries of social systems vary in their clarity and in how open they are. Of these two characteristics, the degree of openness is far more important, for schools control the distribution of knowledge and skills as well as the credentials for jobs. Prior to the mid-nineteenth century, virtually all schools were privately owned and reserved for the children—especially sons—of wealthy families. As recently as 1988, only 38 percent of all U.S. high school graduates went on to college (USCB 1990a). In most other societies, higher education is even more restricted. In Britain, Japan, Switzerland, and France, for example, competition for college entrance is especially fierce, and only an elite few go beyond secondary school (Eurich 1981).

Public education made elementary and secondary education available to most in the U.S., but white schools excluded blacks until the 1954 Supreme

Court decision outlawed separate schools for whites and blacks (Ravitch 1983). Until quite recently, women were largely excluded from professional education in law, medicine, business, engineering, and science.

Boundaries become more closed with each additional level beyond high school, owing primarily to competition for limited places and the high cost of college and professional education. This, in turn, affects the racial and class composition of college enrollments. As Table 17-1 shows, white male high school graduates are considerably more likely than comparable nonwhites to go to college, and enrollment increases steadily with each rise in family income (although the effect of income is less pronounced among blacks than among whites).

The exclusiveness of higher education has been lessened by the enormous growth of two-year junior colleges—especially the relatively inexpensive community colleges. Since 1970, the number of junior colleges has increased by two-thirds, enrollments have doubled, and the number of part-time college students has grown twice as fast as the number of full-time students (USCB 1990a).

Junior college students differ sharply from those in four-year colleges. They are more likely to be black, twice as likely to be married, are generally older, and most are employed. The rapid growth of alternatives to four-year colleges has opened up higher education for social categories that were generally excluded in the past, and almost half of all junior college graduates eventually transfer to four-year schools (AACJC 1977).

Complexity and Role Structures: The School as Bureaucracy

During this century, the size and complexity of U.S. schools have increased enormously, as their structure has been transformed from a simple role relationship between students and teachers to a large bureaucracy. In 1916 there were 200,000 schools with only one teacher; but now there are hardly any. During this same period the average size of schools increased by over seven times. Most important, while the number of public school students more than doubled and the number of teachers more than tripled, the number of principals and administrators increased more than sevenfold (USCB 1975, 1982, 1990a).

The transformation of schools closely paralleled a trend toward bureaucracy that was occurring through-

TABLE 17-1 College Enrollment among Those 14 to 24 Years Old, by Sex and Race and by Family Income (United States)

RACE AND SEX[1]	PERCENTAGE ENROLLED
White males	40
White females	37
Black males	25
Black females	31
Hispanic males	32
Hispanic females	30

RACE AND FAMILY INCOME[2]	
Whites	
Under $10,000	16
$10,000–$19,999	24
$20,000–$29,999	35
$30,000–$39,999	44
$40,000–$49,999	50
$50,000 or more	54
Blacks	
Under $10,000	12
$10,000–$19,999	24
$20,000–$29,999	23
$30,000–$39,999	38
$40,000–$49,999	39
$50,000 or more	*

[1]For sex and race, figures are percentages of high school graduates who are enrolled in college.
[2]Figures are percentages of all those 18 to 24 years old.
*Too few cases for accurate estimate.
Source: USCB 1986a; 1990a.

out the U.S. Business leaders dominated school boards and evaluated schools with the same standards of efficiency and productivity they applied to business: How many math problems do students solve per hour? How many students graduate each year, and what does it cost per student? As Callahan (1962) put it:

> They saw schools not as centers of learning, but as enterprises which were functionally efficient if the students went through without failing and received their diplomas on schedule and if the operations were handled economically. (p. 247)

The signs of bureaucracy are everywhere in schools. Teachers must be certified by state agencies. Formal records are kept not only on student behavior and performance but on teachers. Relationships between teachers, students, and administrators are

Winslow Homer's painting, *The Country School*, 1871, provides a striking contrast with today's large bureaucratic school systems.

clearly defined by school norms, as are those between administrators and outside authorities such as school boards, boards of trustees, and, in public institutions, state legislatures. Look at any college's student handbook and you will quickly see how many areas of student life are explicitly regulated by institutional norms. College students are assigned identification numbers, and in many classes enrollments are so high that teachers do not know which student names go with which faces. Students are judged by performance on tests that ignore individual needs and abilities, for attention to individuals is almost impossible under such circumstances. In many courses, students never meet their professors face-to-face, and when they need help, they turn to graduate students who run study sessions. Students have good reason to often feel lost in the crowd, because in today's bureaucratic schools, they often are.

In bureaucracies attention is on the organization as a whole rather than on individuals. The negative effect of this on educational goals is clear in the practice of social promotion, through which students who have not mastered the skills of the current grade are nevertheless sent to the next higher grade. Part of this is undoubtedly due to the desire of many teachers to spare students the humiliation of repeating a grade. We also have to remember, however,

that one function of schools is to produce graduates, and if large numbers of students are not promoted, the school's efficiency and productivity appear to decline.

The negative effects of social promotion are most glaring among minority students, many of whom graduate without having mastered basic math and verbal skills. While we may feel tempted to blame the students involved, such explanations ignore the fact that they were promoted in spite of the fact that they had not mastered basic skills.

It would be a gross oversimplification to suggest that bureaucratic structure is responsible for the decline of learning in U.S. schools. It is apparent, however, that the educational needs of many students have been ignored by an institution that serves several interests—including providing jobs for teachers and administrators—and that like all bureaucracies, schools may neglect individuals within them while perpetuating the organization itself (see Baldridge and Deal 1983).

Distributions of Power

Whether or not they are structured as bureaucracies, most schools rely on highly unequal distributions of power, with students placed at the bottom. Distributions of power vary substantially, however, from one level of schooling to another. In public elementary and secondary schools, administrators have power over teachers, teaching methods, and curriculum, and students have little power in relation to anyone but their peers. To some degree, however, the power of administrators over teachers is balanced by the fact that most public school teachers belong to labor unions that can use strikes to protect their interests.

In colleges and universities, the distribution of power is more complex. In many colleges, the administration controls the flow of money, which, in turn, allows it to affect the resources available to academic departments. Unlike public school teachers, college faculties generally control what goes on in classrooms—the kinds of courses that are taught and standards for grading—and play the most important role in deciding who will be hired, fired, or promoted.

In other ways, however, professors have less power than public school teachers. While most public school teachers belong to organized unions, professors often depend solely on the support of their own departments, which may consist of only a few members. Because faculty power generally lies in departments rather than the faculty as a whole, the administration can often overcome opposition because the faculty does not speak or act as an organized group.

The power of college faculties is also weakened by conflicting values and internal divisions of power.

Senior, tenured members have a great deal of power over the careers of junior members, for promotions and tenure depend primarily on their recommendations. Heads of academic departments are almost always tenured professors, and the interests of senior members often conflict with those of junior members. Tenured professors do not have to worry about job security and may value the long-term survival of their departments more than anything else. Junior members, however, often have young families and must worry about their individual futures. When a college administration suggests saving money by cutting the size of the faculty, junior members are the ones most likely to lose their jobs. Tenured members are less affected since the department can still survive, and it is through departments that they exercise much of their power.

Patterns of Interaction

Like other social systems, schools produce patterns of interaction. In most classrooms the teacher is the focus of all interaction. Students speak only when asked and are generally forbidden to communicate with one another. This pattern is reinforced by physical arrangements in which students sit in chairs facing the front of the room while teachers are free either to face the entire class or walk about and monitor student behavior. Some schools have open classrooms in which students are allowed to move about the room and interact with one another more freely (Silberman 1971). Open classrooms were introduced to encourage autonomy, initiative, and creativity, but they also tend to undermine the teacher's control over students and what they learn. Some critics of open classrooms suggest that autonomy and creativity are gained at the expense of basic skills such as reading, writing, and mathematics.

The complexity of today's schools is reflected in the many conflicting interests of the people involved—from parents, who argue about what should be taught, to teachers, who are among the lowest paid of all professionals.

DOONESBURY

by Garry Trudeau

Any pattern of interaction depends on how the participants define the situation, including the meaning of behavior, values, attitudes, and expectations. Karp and Yoels (1979) used this perspective to explore a simple question about college classrooms: Why do so many students remain silent during class discussions? They observed ten classes in a private northeastern university for an entire term and then asked students and teachers to complete questionnaires designed to measure perceptions of themselves and each other.

While most students and teachers said that large class size inhibits student participation, the number of students who actually participated was roughly the same, regardless of class size. Karp and Yoels concluded that early in each term students identify a few students who will take primary responsibility for class discussions. This is similar to Latané and Darley's (1970) findings about bystanders who do not help people in distress (see Chapter 8). Responsibility becomes diffused in groups of strangers so that most can remain passive. In classrooms, however, responsibility is consolidated in a few students, with the same effect. Professors also contribute to this. They are twice as likely as students to believe that the fear of looking foolish is an important cause of student silence, and they often protect students from embarrassment by not calling on them.

Although consolidation of responsibility protects students in some ways, it threatens them in others, because students who participate too much may raise the professor's expectations. Consolidation of responsibility in classrooms also encourages students to come to class unprepared, for they know that a few students will carry the load of interacting with the professor. It is not surprising, therefore, that students rate lack of preparation, ignorance of the subject, and a feeling that their ideas are not well formulated as the most important reasons for their silence; and this finding reveals the importance of students' and teachers' definitions of the social situation itself.

To many students, teachers are like banks that hold knowledge, and students make withdrawals, not deposits (Freire 1972). Their classroom role, then, is to absorb truth from the teacher, not to participate in a dialogue whose purpose is to determine what is true and what is not. Students frequently express reluctance to question the validity of what they read, much less to openly challenge what a professor says in class.

In performing their role, professors contribute to these perceptions by coming to class fully prepared—having hours to work out what they are going to say—and this makes it easy to see why students often feel intimidated. It is here, however, that students and professors rely on sharply different definitions of the situation, which often contribute to serious misunderstandings. From precollege experience, most students believe that giving the correct answer is the most important part of their role, and if they are unsure, the best strategy is to remain silent. To many professors, however, uncertainty is at the heart of intellectual work, truth is always open to question, and the most important thing that students can learn is how to think for themselves.

The result can be a vicious circle. Students feel put down when a professor challenges their ideas, for given their definition of the situation, an attack on their ideas is an attack on their role performance and, therefore, on their selves. This makes them still more reluctant to speak. Professors feel frustrated by student silence, and may wonder if their students *have* any ideas. The harder a professor pushes, the more students feel vulnerable and under attack; and the more defensive students become, the harder professors feel they have to push.

To protect themselves in what they perceive as a threatening situation, students often use what Goffman (1963a) called "civil attention." They maintain the *appearance* that they are involved in the classroom—by taking notes, nodding their heads, or laughing at appropriate moments—without becoming so involved that they risk exposing themselves to an attack from the professor. Many students become skilled at knowing when to look at the professor and when not to—if the professor is looking around the room as if searching for someone to call on, many students immediately look away, preferably to write some notes.

Perceptions and expectations play an important part in classroom interaction, and an intriguing experiment shows how teachers' expectations of students affect how well students perform. Rosenthal and Jacobson (1968) administered a test to elementary school students at the start of a school year and told teachers that the results would accurately predict which students would be "spurters"—that is, had high potential to achieve. In fact, however, the test was not intended to be valid, and students were randomly assigned to the spurter group. At the end of the year, students whose teachers *perceived* them as spurters increased their IQ scores by an average of 12 points, while the other students' scores increased by only 8 points. Among first and second graders, IQ gains by spurters were over twice as large as they were for other students. More recent studies find similar

effects of teacher expectations, although the effects are considerably more complex than originally believed (see Cooper and Good 1983).

This illustrates an important sociological insight: self-fulfilling prophecies are the rule, not the exception, in social life, because our expectations of other people affect how we behave toward them, and *their* behavior as well as their perceptions of themselves are affected by ours (Merton 1957a, 1968). All of us have experienced the rush of energy, excitement, and pride that comes when teachers tell us they think we are smart, or the crushing disappointment when they tell us that we are not; and when we feel intelligent, we are more likely to act intelligently. As we will see later, self-fulfilling prophecies are particularly important when cultural prejudice leads teachers to perceive entire social categories, such as nonwhites, the poor, or women as poor prospects.

THE SOCIAL ECOLOGY OF SCHOOLS

Schools exist primarily for socialization, and this means that the demand for schooling depends on the number of young people in a population. In addition, the existence of schools depends on material resources, for schools are expensive, and if children are in school, they are not available for productive work.

Population and the Business of Schooling

When birth rates increase in societies that use schools for education, so does the demand for

---

PUZZLE

IS EDUCATION THE GREAT EQUALIZER?

If every American had equal education, training, and intellectual ability, would the result be substantially less inequality of wealth, power, and prestige?

Probably not. This chapter helps explain why.

TABLE 17-2   Historical Trends in School Enrollment (1,000s) by Level of Schooling (United States)

YEAR	LEVEL OF SCHOOLING		
	ELEMENTARY	HIGH SCHOOL	COLLEGE
1990	33,549	12,563	13,213
1985	30,936	13,741	12,247
1980	31,666	14,652	12,097
1970	34,190	14,418	7,136
1960	30,119	9,600	3,126
1950	21,033	6,453	2,281
1940	20,466	7,130	1,494
1930	22,954	4,811	1,101

Source: USCB 1975, 1990a.

schooling. Before reading on, take a moment to study Table 17-2, which shows how enrollment at the elementary, high school, and college levels has changed.

Enrollment in elementary school was stable until the effects of the post–World War II Baby Boom were felt in the 1950s and enrollment jumped by almost 50 percent. In the next decade it rose by only 14 percent, because the Baby Boom was winding down; and in the first half of the last decade, enrollment actually declined as birth rates fell. High school enrollment jumped by almost 50 percent in the 1950s and by another 50 percent in the 1960s; but it barely grew at all in the 1970s, and began to fall in the 1980s. Notice that enrollment fell earlier in elementary schools than in high schools, because high school students are older, and it takes longer for falling birth rates to affect the number of teenagers.

College enrollment rose sharply in the late 1940s because government benefits under the GI Bill allowed many returning World War II veterans to afford a college education. As the economy boomed and a college degree became an important factor in the job market, enrollment continued to climb in the 1950s and 1960s, and as the Baby Boom generations reached college age, enrollment rose sharply through the 1970s and continued to rise in the 1980s, although more slowly.

In spite of the importance attached to a college degree, falling birth rates may cause a decline in future enrollment. This is not inevitable, however, because there is already some evidence that although

the number of people 18 to 23 years old is declining, the age structure of the college population is shifting upward. Since 1970, the percentage of college students who are 25 years old or older has increased from 28 to 42 (USCB 1990a). This is especially true in community colleges (see Cohen 1990). This includes large numbers of married women returning to school in order to improve their chances in the job market. Thus, while the age group traditionally served by colleges is shrinking, older students may make up the difference.

Why are these trends important? One answer is that education is the biggest business in the U.S. Over 5 million people earned a living by working in schools, and many more—from book publishers to construction workers—benefit from a large school population. The rapid increase in the student population over the last 30 years caused a dramatic increase in the number of teachers, and as the school population shrinks, thousands lose their jobs (USCB 1990a). College faculties more than doubled in size between 1960 and 1975, and tenure was relatively easy to achieve. After 1975, however, college faculties barely grew at all, but the percentage having tenure did—to 65 percent in 1988 (USCB 1990a). If the number of college professors remains stable, the percentage with tenure will remain high, and the prospects for those without tenure will be grim regardless of their qualifications. There is "no room at the top," and many professors have been forced to change careers or wander from one part-time job to another (Abel 1984). Ironically, as the heavily tenured faculties of U.S. colleges and universities reach retirement age in the late 1990s, the children of parents born in the baby boom will reach college age and the resulting surge in college enrollments may produce a severe shortage of qualified college faculty, especially in the humanities and social sciences (Bowen and Schuster 1986; Bowen and Sosa 1989).

Segregation and Learning

When public schools were first introduced in the U.S. on a massive scale at the end of the nineteenth century, blacks were largely excluded, either by law or because they had to work (Beale 1975). In the early 1900s public education was available to most blacks, but the distribution of funds clearly favored whites. In one Southern county, for example, expenditures per child in white schools were 33 times greater than in schools attended by blacks (Nasaw

1979). In 1954 the Supreme Court's landmark decision ruled that separate schools for blacks were inherently unequal, and the Court ordered an end to segregation "with all deliberate speed." More than 30 years later, blacks and whites still attend schools that are predominantly of one race. Full racial integration would require the reassignment of roughly half of all students (Farley 1984; Wurdock and Farley 1979).

In Chapter 13 we discussed the causes of racial segregation; but here we are concerned with its effects on students. It has long been noted that average scores on standardized tests are lower among blacks than among whites. Does segregation help explain this difference? Do blacks achieve higher scores in integrated schools?

At the request of the U.S. Civil Rights Commission, James Coleman and his colleagues conducted a survey of 570,000 students and 60,000 teachers in 4,000 public schools (Coleman et al. 1966). They expected to find lower quality in predominantly black schools than in predominantly white schools: older buildings, fewer library and science facilities, less qualified teachers, larger classes, fewer textbooks, and poorer funding. They were surprised, however, to find little difference between them. Average test scores for blacks were 15 points lower than for whites, and 84 percent of black students scored below the median score for whites; but Coleman also found that his measures of school quality explained little of the racial difference in achievement.

The factor that had the greatest impact on scores was social class. Regardless of race, students from middle-class families score higher than lower-class students. Most important, when students attend schools with students from a lower class than their own, their test scores suffer. When they attend schools with students primarily from higher social classes than their own, their scores tend to increase. Lower-class blacks who attend black schools whose students are mostly middle-class do better than lower-class blacks who go to school with other lower-class blacks. Coleman concluded that blacks generally score lower than whites because they are more likely to come from the lower class *and* attend school with other lower-class children.

The Colemen study generated a great deal of controversy, especially over how research methods affected the conclusions that were drawn. Bowles (1968), for example, reanalyzed Coleman's data and argued that improving school quality would improve

blacks' achievement twice as much as Coleman reported. Even Coleman noted that while improving school facilities has relatively little effect on white students, it would have a much greater effect on minorities.

Coleman's findings laid the groundwork for racial integration, and a number of later studies showed that, under the right circumstances, integration increases the average score of blacks by 2 to 3 points (Jencks 1972). Notice, however, that most of the racial difference remains. It is apparent from these studies that changing the racial mix of student populations has only a limited effect on racial differences in educational achievement. As we will see later, this has important implications for ending racial inequality in society as a whole.

Technology, Production, and Schools

In the U.S., 98 percent of those 5 to 17 years old are enrolled in school. In many countries, however, illiteracy is common and only a small fraction of young people attend school. More than half of the adult populations of Africa and South Asia are illiterate, and in Ethiopia, Afghanistan, Saudi Arabia, and other countries, over 80 percent are illiterate (USCB 1986a).

In countries such as India, the great expense of schooling means that the vast majority of the population is excluded from all but the most elementary form of training.

FIGURE 17-1   Secondary School Enrollment by Per Capita Income, Selected Countries

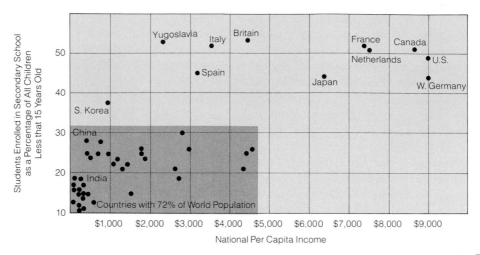

The wealthier a society is, the more likely it is to have a high proportion of young people enrolled in secondary school. There are no countries with low income and high enrollment (upper-left section) or with high income and low enrollment (lower-right section).

Source: Computed from USCB 1983c.

A major reason for such wide variations in education and literacy is that formal schooling is expensive. It not only takes an enormous investment in buildings, teachers, and equipment, but also requires that young people spend their time away from productive labor. Most societies simply cannot afford to formally educate their young on the scale found in the United States. If all the money spent on education in the U.S. in 1989 were equally distributed, it would amount to $1,320 for every woman, man, and child. For many countries, however, this level of spending would exhaust the entire national income: more than half of all the people in the world live in countries whose total per capita income is less than $500, a figure just under the U.S. per capita expenditure on higher education alone (USCB 1990a).

Take a moment to study Figure 17-1, which shows the relationship between per capita income and secondary school enrollment for a number of countries, each of which is represented by a dot. Note that most countries are clustered in the lower left-hand corner, with very low per capita income and secondary school enrollment. Most important is the fact that these countries contain almost three-quarters of the world's population, while the "educational elite" countries contain only 17 percent. The distribution of formal education among societies is just as unequal as the distribution of wealth and income.

The staggering expense of institutionalized learning raises serious questions about education and economic development in underdeveloped countries. Although universal literacy is relatively easy to achieve, it may be that the industrialized societies' model of education with its heavy emphasis on advanced training beyond the elementary school level will be beyond the means of most of the world's population for a long time to come.

SCHOOLS AND OTHER INSTITUTIONS

As an institution, the school does not exist in a vacuum. It is connected to other social systems—the economy, the family, and the state—in ways that produce a variety of social consequences.

Schools and Families

Latent consequences of compulsory schooling affect families in a variety of ways. By acting as "baby-sitters," schools make it easier for both parents to work outside the home. In their role as socializers, schools relieve parents of some of the burden of preparing their children for adult work roles. In many schools, the food provided is cheaper and better than what is available at home.

While transfers of family functions to schools make life easier for parents in many ways, they also create problems. As responsibility for socialization shifts to schools, for example, so does power over children. Before education became compulsory, families had greater control over socialization and could pass on subcultures to their children. Many advocates of public schooling, however, saw the family's influence as dysfunctional for social progress and wanted to use schools to break the family's hold on children, to replace "old-fashioned" ideas of many ethnic immigrants with the modern ideas of dominant groups (Lasch 1977).

In many ways, parents feel threatened by schools, not because schools have so much power, but because they separate children from the family and give parents less control over what their children do all day long. In his classic study of high schools, for example, Coleman (1961) found that students valued pleasing their friends almost as much as pleasing their parents. As we saw earlier, schools have played a major role in the creation of adolescent peer groups and subcultures, and it is in response to peer pressures that young people often have their first exposure to alcohol, drugs, cigarettes, and sex. As responsibility for children has shifted away from families, parents must compete with the formal and hidden curricula of schools and with the strong influence of student peer groups.

The Social Economics of Schooling

School and economy are related in several important ways. Because schools delay the entry of young people into the labor market, they help minimize competition for jobs. In 1988 there were 122 million people in the U.S. labor force, of whom over 6.7 million were unemployed. Almost 26 million people were enrolled in high schools and colleges (USCB 1990a). If all those students suddenly entered the labor force, the number of unemployed could almost quadruple.

Schools are also important to the economy in that they are primarily responsible for providing a supply of well-educated workers. In the 1990s there is growing concern that the cognitive skills of the work force are not keeping up with the changing job market in which mathematical and verbal abilities are becoming increasingly important. As Figure 17-2 shows, the current distribution of students' communication skills is considerably below the distribution of skills required in today's job labor force and is even

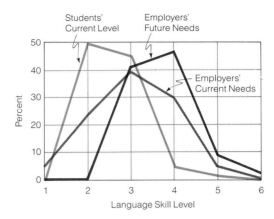

FIGURE 17-2   Job Skills: A Widening Gap
Percentage of students and jobs available at each level of verbal skill, ranked from 1 to 6.

The scale is prepared by the Labor Department. Level 6 signifies the ability to read technical journals. Rudimentary communication skills required in manual labor jobs fall into level 1. Level 3 is typical of retail salespeople or skilled construction workers.
Source: Labor Department
The New York Times, September 25, 1989

farther below the distribution of skills anticipated for the labor force of the future.

By evaluating and sorting students according to ability, schools also help determine which jobs students will qualify for as adults. As early as 1908, many educators shared the view of the president of Harvard who believed that schools "ought to sort the pupils and sort them by their evident or probable destinies" (in Nasaw 1979, p. 138). Many U.S. and European schools assign students to tracks. In Swiss schools, children are assigned to one of three tracks after four years of primary education. The lowest achievers finish primary school and then learn a manual trade; the middle group goes on to high school and trains for jobs in business and management. Only the highest track leads to college and graduate education and work in the professions, universities, and leadership in business and government.

Because schools do not produce a product that they sell in the market, they are not self-supporting. Public schools must depend on tax revenues, local school boards, and state and federal governments for funding. When the economy is in a slump, schools are often among the first institutions to feel the effects as teachers are laid off and programs are cut.

The dependence of schools on outside support makes them vulnerable, for if they displease their supporters, they may lose the funds they need to operate. During the 1960s the University of California had a running battle with then-Governor Ronald Reagan, who disapproved of student demonstrations against the war and student demands for greater control over the university. One of his major weapons in that struggle was his influence over the state budget.

Finally, schools are connected to the economy because they are *part* of it. Most public school teachers belong to unions whose interests may conflict with educational goals. The National Commission on Excellence in Education (1983) recommended merit pay for teachers and regular evaluation of teacher performance. The American Federation of Teachers, however, opposed merit pay because it would weaken the union's bargaining position; it also believed teacher evaluation would undermine job security.

Even college professors have unionized on some campuses in order to protect job security and pay levels—even though professors traditionally look upon unions as being inappropriate for middle-class professionals. The unionization of professors shows clearly that in spite of the fact that many people like to think of colleges as "Ivory Towers" that stand aside from the mundane affairs of society, colleges and universities are organizations in which people earn a living, and the economic interests of different groups often conflict.

Politics, Schools, and Nationalism

If an unfriendly foreign power had attempted to impose on America the mediocre educational performance that exists today, we might well have viewed it as an act of war. . . . We have in effect been committing an act of unthinking, unilateral educational disarmament. (National Commission on Excellence in Education 1983)

This startling conclusion about the current state of U.S. education reflects a strong belief in a connection between achievement in schools and the attainment of national goals. The Commission clearly defines education as a national armament that helps protect the nation.

The use of schools to promote national goals is not a new practice (see Freire 1985). The first public schools appeared in Germany at a time when Germans were trying to build a sense of national solidarity and patriotism, and in the 1930s the Nazis used children's literature to foster the image of Germans as a master race that would rule the world (Kamenetsky 1984). Students in U.S. schools pledge allegiance to the flag every day and sing the national anthem at sporting events. Courses in U.S. history tend to neglect the more unattractive aspects of the past—racism, imperialism, and atrocities committed during wars—while emphasizing accomplishments, praising the benefits of capitalism, and highlighting the shortcomings of socialism and communism.

Japanese textbooks have been criticized for ignoring atrocities committed by Japanese troops during World War II; and German textbooks pay little attention to the Nazis and the Holocaust. Lessons in Russian schools glorify socialism and communism, condemn capitalism, and, depending on the political climate, either attack or glorify various leaders of the past. Until as recently as the 1960s, the study of sociology was not allowed in China or the Soviet Union; and sociological work in the Soviet Union has only recently begun to raise issues and problems

Schools play an important part in instilling a sense of loyalty to nations and their governments. Here, for example, Asian-American immigrants in California pledge allegiance to the flag as part of their political socialization.

that challenge basic characteristics of its society (Greenfeld 1988; Shlapentokh 1987).

The tendency of the Soviet leadership to rewrite history is so pervasive that it has found its way into Russian jokes, one of which defines a Russian historian as "someone who can predict the past." More recently the new Soviet policy of *glasnost* (or "openness") has led them to adopt more accurate views of their history with a special emphasis on the problems of Soviet society. These revisions have been so extensive that in 1988 officials cancelled final secondary school exams in history while new texts were being written. There was, officials reasoned, no point in requiring students to continue learning a false history.

After World War II the U.S. and the Soviet Union engaged in a Cold War in which both sides struggled for economic and military superiority. In 1957 the Soviet Union launched the world's first space satellite—Sputnik I—and the U.S. reacted in fear to this startling technological advance. President Eisenhower argued that scientific education lay at the heart of self-defense and called for nationwide testing of high school students, incentives to pursue scientific careers, increased laboratory facilities, and better training for math and science teachers (Ravitch 1983).

Within a year of the launch of Sputnik I, Congress passed the National Defense Education Act, which provided federal funding for counseling programs designed to identify the most gifted students, training programs for science teachers, graduate fellowships, and undergraduate student loans. Schools were clearly being regarded as an instrument of national political policy. In the 1990s, schools are once again a focal point of national interests as concerns mount that the United States is losing its competitive edge in the world economy (see Apple 1986).

Changes in curriculum and funding were not the only educational consequences of the cold war. In the 1950s, for example, there was an anticommunist hysteria in the United States during which thousands of people lost their jobs because they were accused of being communists. A major focus of this movement was college and university faculties, and as Schrecker (1986) documents in her careful history of this period, many institutions not only failed to protect the intellectual freedom of their faculties, but actively participated in dismissing teachers solely on the basis of rumor and fear. Although often characterized as ivory towers removed from the pressures of everyday life, universities showed themselves to be deeply involved in and dependent on the political realities of their times, including financial dependency on government and fear of government intrusion.

On many levels, then, schools produce a variety of consequences—from socializing the young to advancing political goals. Because schools distribute skills and credentials, they have often been criticized as supporters of social inequality. Conflict theorists in particular focus on the ways in which characteristics of schools perpetuate inequality based on race, gender, and class.

SCHOOLS AND SOCIAL CONFLICT: CLASS AND CLASSROOMS

In the 1960s the civil rights movement targeted education as a major way of removing racial inequality. A basic assumption was that lower-class children could not escape poverty without the basic cognitive skills—the ability to read, write, and do arithmetic—required in the job market.

As explained below, the assumptions underlying this strategy are false, because cognitive skills do not explain why some people are rich and others are poor, and because there is little evidence that schools can substantially reduce class or racial differences in basic skills. Social characteristics of schools, however, do help perpetuate social inequality in other ways, for

> the real achievement of schools consists in their ability to train children to accept the prevailing class structure and their fate as workers within the industrial system. . . . What is learned in school . . . is rarely related to specific skills. . . . Rather students learn . . . to accommodate to the first requirement of industrial labor: respect for authority, the self-discipline needed to internalize the values of the labor process, and the place of the worker within the prevailing occupational hierarchies. (Aronowitz 1973, p. 74)

Inequality and the Hidden Curriculum

There is a New England town in which most of the residents are connected in some way to a local private, elite college. The public schools are relatively new and well staffed, and a large percentage of the students are the children of college professors and administrators. The neighboring town is inhabited primarily by working-class people, some of whom work at the college (Smith 1981).

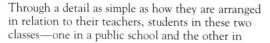

Through a detail as simple as how they are arranged in relation to their teachers, students in these two classes—one in a public school and the other in a private school—are receiving very different messages about who they are in the world and what is expected of them.

In both towns high school students study the same subjects, but the hidden curriculums are very different. The working-class students cannot leave classrooms without a hall pass; their behavior is watched closely; they have little choice over the courses they will take; and the subject of college is rarely brought up. In the college town, however, students are not required to have hall passes; they are allowed to make many decisions for themselves, including selection from a wide variety of elective courses; and their teachers often express confidence that most if not all of them will go on to college.

If they learn their lessons, students in these towns will graduate with quite different ideas about themselves and their place in society. Working-class students will learn that they are not to be trusted, that important decisions about their lives will rest in the hands of others. The middle- and upper-class students in the college town, however, will learn that they can be trusted to control their own lives and, most important, that they will become adults who will make decisions about *other* people's lives. The working-class students are being prepared to be workers under the authority of managers and professionals, while the middle- and upper-class students are learning to *be* managers and professionals (see Chackerian and Abcarian 1984). Such differences

are often reinforced by student subcultures in which middle-class students are supported and rewarded for college and occupational aspirations, while working-class students are encouraged to see school as an adversary (Eckert 1989).

Nowhere are class differences in the hidden curriculum more apparent than when we compare public high schools and elite private academies. As Cookson and Persell (1985) point out, in many ways student life in elite private schools is more tightly regulated than life in public schools. The harsher discipline in elite schools serves a very different purpose, however, for it serves as a rite of passage that prepares upper-middle- and upper-class students for prestigious and powerful adult statuses. The discipline found in middle- and working-class schools, by comparison, prepares students to obey authority, a very different consequence that reinforces class differences in power.

Such differences between schools intensify class differences among adults by transmitting different expectations to students. When Leacock (1969), for example, repeated the Rosenthal and Jacobson (1968) experiment in which teachers' expectations and behavior were affected by false reports of student potential, she found that the results were themselves affected by the school's social class. Teachers in schools whose students came primarily from the middle class treated students better if they were identified as bright and promising; but in lower-class schools, just the opposite occurred: "promising" students were often treated as "wise guys."

This raises a serious question about the study (Coleman et al. 1966), discussed earlier. Coleman found that measures of school quality did not explain the racial gap in academic achievement. Although these researchers did measure teacher qualifications, they did *not* measure the beliefs, values, attitudes, and expectations that affect teachers' perceptions and behavior in relation to students. This suggests that the relatively poor performance of students in lower-class schools—many of whom are black—may be in part a self-fulfilling prophecy: they achieve less because their teachers *expect* them to, regardless of the quality of schools and their teachers.

Tracking and Inequality

Tracking is used to divide students according to tests of academic ability. The manifest function of tracking is to allow slow students to get extra attention and to allow bright students to move at their own speed, rather than having to wait for the slow students to catch up. It often has other consequences, however.

Nonwhite and lower-class students are more likely than others to be assigned to slow tracks, regardless of their test scores (Edelman et al. 1985). Given what we know about the effects of expectations on student achievement, it is tempting to conclude that tracking helps explain racial and class differences in achievement (see Oakes 1985). The evidence of past research tends to support this conclusion. In general, higher-ability students do better when placed in homogeneous classes; but lower-ability students do worse and fall even further behind. Many studies also show that the gain by higher-ability students is less than the lost ground of lower-ability students, which suggests that for society as a whole the costs of tracking may outweigh the benefits (see Dar and Resh 1986; Oakes 1985; Rand Corporation 1990).

Tracking may also help perpetuate inequality in ways that have nothing to do with academic achievement. By affecting students' expectations, tracking may reinforce their acceptance of their position in society, whether it be high or low (see Hallinan and Sørensen 1987). In this sense, tracking may contribute to false consciousness and, therefore, to the perpetuation of inequality through self-fulfilling prophecy.

Grades, Ideology, and False Consciousness

Grades produce a number of functional consequences in schools. They reinforce the power of teachers, motivate students to work, and are fairly accurate predictors of future academic performance. Grades also have dysfunctional consequences, however. They are poor predictors of performance outside the school environment (McClelland 1973); they create tensions and anxieties that interfere with creativity and discourage close relationships between students and teachers; and they encourage students to manipulate teachers, to compete rather than cooperate with each other, and to avoid taking initiative and risks.

The finding that grades are inaccurate predictors of adult performance is important, because schools are often viewed as sorters of talent for the job market. If grades are poor predictors of which students will make the best lawyers, business managers, scientists, or teachers, then why are they still used to sort students? Part of the answer comes from the conflict perspective.

As we saw in Chapter 12, the perpetuation of social classes depends in part on people's acceptance of their class position. Part of the basis for this acceptance is the belief that the system through which rewards are distributed is fair, that everyone has an equal opportunity to achieve desirable jobs and relatively high standards of living. If individuals support the belief that the system is basically fair, then they have no one but themselves to blame if they are in the lower class, and no one but themselves to credit if they live a life of privilege.

Students generally enter college with unrealistic job aspirations, for there are not enough good jobs to go around (Guzzardi 1976). Grading dulls the aspirations of many students, but particularly those from the working and lower classes, for they are most likely to have below-average grades. Many students with low grades are advised to drop out of school altogether; but many others are encouraged to remain in school but to accept lower aspirations. This helps ensure that less desirable jobs will be performed; but, most important, it helps maintain the ideology of equal opportunity and, with it, the unequal distribution of rewards.

Trimberger (1971) and others claim that grading contributes to false consciousness among lower-class students by supporting the false belief that class position results more from individual abilities and performance than from the limitations imposed by a class society. Grading, however, also contributes to false consciousness among middle- and upper-class students, for it supports the equally false belief that their success is due entirely to their individual talent and effort.

You might be tempted to conclude from this analysis that if schools devised a grading system that did accurately predict adult performance, then actual ability would be the only basis for assigning people to adult roles, and the resulting distribution of rewards would be fairer. The problem with this solution, however, lies with the fact that the distribution of wealth, power, and prestige has relatively little to do with ability, however accurately it may be measured.

Opportunity and Outcome

From their earliest years, public schools were looked to as sources of economic prosperity, social equality, and upward mobility. A major part of the American dream is that individual ability and effort are the only limits on achievement, and equal opportunity for education is the key to equality of outcomes (see Hallinan 1988).

We saw earlier that lower class and minority members do not have equal access to higher education; but as many sociologists point out, even if there *were* equal educational opportunity, this would not eliminate social classes, because inequality is created by economic arrangements, not educational ones (Bane and Jencks 1972).

The educational attainment of the U.S. labor force rose sharply over the last three decades (see Table 17-3). Since 1960, the percentage of adults completing high school has increased by 85 percent, and among blacks the percentage has almost tripled. Among blacks and whites, the percentage with college degrees has more than doubled, with comparable gains for Hispanics. As we saw in Chapter 12, however, inequality between social classes has *increased*, which suggests that while education is certainly not irrelevant to economic success, other factors play an equal, if not more important, part.

Like all major structural characteristics of societies, inequality is not the result of any one aspect of social life. No institution has the power to remove the inequalities of race, gender, or social class. That schools have been looked to so often as a remedy for inequality may be due less to the actual power of schools than to the importance attached to the cultural values of equal opportunity and reward based solely on ability and effort.

SCHOOLS AND SOCIAL CHANGE

If you wanted to change a major aspect of society, where would you begin? When I pose this question to college students, more often than not they reply, "You have to start with kids." It is an obvious solution: it is easier to teach children new ideas than to change old ideas that are already deeply embedded in adults.

For this reason, schools have often been a battleground in struggles for social change. Racial integration increases interaction between children of different races before they firmly adopt the fundamentals of racism. A major focus of the women's movement has been on the images of males and females in school textbooks. Sex education is offered as a way to increase young people's understanding of their sexuality and decrease the likelihood of teenage pregnancy and AIDS.

Opponents of change focus on schools as sources of social opportunity and stability. Religious fundamentalists oppose the teaching of the theory of evolution, and 10 percent of U.S. adults are against sex education. Just under half would bar atheists, communists, or advocates of military rule from teaching

TABLE 17-3   Trends in Educational Attainment by Race and Sex (United States)

RACE AND SEX	HIGH SCHOOL GRADUATE		COLLEGE GRADUATE OR MORE	
	1960	1988	1960	1988
White males	22%	36%	10%	25%
White females	29%	43%	6%	17%
Black males	11%	37%	3%	11%
Black females	14%	37%	3%	11%
Hispanic males[1]	20%	27%	6%	12%
Hispanic females[1]	22%	29%	3%	8%

[1]Figures are for 1970 and 1988.
Source: USCB 1990a.

ONE STEP FURTHER 17-2

Schools and Resistance to Change

Because schools play such an important part in the socialization process, there are many pressures to control the kinds of ideas contained in what is taught there. Like most other social phenomena, however, how resistant people are to new or radical ideas in education depends on their own social characteristics.

In Table B-17-2, for example, opposition to letting an atheist teach in college declines steadily with education—61 percent of respondents with less than a high school education would not allow an atheist to teach in college compared with only 15 percent of those with more than a college degree. In general, the highest levels of resistance come from nonwhites, women, those living in the South, and the elderly. In addition, if you read across the rows, you will see that people tend to be more resistant towards some kinds of teachers than others. How might we explain such patterns?

TABLE B-17-2 Percent of U.S. Adults Who Would Not Allow Various Types of People to Teach in College, By Respondents' Education, Race, Gender, Region, and Age

Respondents' Education	PERCENT WHO WOULD NOT ALLOW SOMEONE TO TEACH IN COLLEGE IF SHE OR HE WAS				
	An Atheist	A Communist	A Homosexual	A Militarist[1]	A Racist[2]
Less than High School	61	59	50	67	54
High School Graduate	47	45	38	57	54
Some College	43	39	24	51	51
College Degree	27	21	18	37	35
More than College	15	23	12	24	35
Race					
White	43	40	32	51	47
Nonwhite	48	52	33	58	65
Gender					
Female	50	48	32	59	55
Male	37	34	33	44	42
Region					
Northeast	41	39	29	58	53
Midwest	40	41	31	48	43
South	53	50	40	58	55
West	38	38	21	52	50
Age					
18–25	35	35	28	44	55
26–39	34	32	23	43	44
40–59	41	46	26	52	50
60+	64	57	49	75	56

[1]Favors military rule.
[2]Believes blacks are genetically inferior.
Source: Computed from 1990 General Social Survey data.

in colleges or universities, and 32 percent would also bar homosexuals (Davis and Smith 1990) (see One Step Further 17-2).

Values also conflict in less specific areas. For many, schools exist in order to teach students to think for themselves, to solve problems, and to ask critical questions about their society—Thomas Jefferson's prescription for a healthy democracy. To others, however, the idea that any question can have more than one correct answer is unacceptable

This French student, injured in a 1986 confrontation with riot police in Paris, is one of the hundreds of thousands who protested government proposals to allow public universities to employ more selective admissions policies. In a matter of weeks, strikes shut down 50 of France's public universities. The government eventually backed down.

because it threatens the stability of predictable, orderly views of the world, especially those based on religion.

Schools embody a fundamental value conflict in social life: The freedom of people to think for themselves is highly valued in many cultures and is the major source of innovation and creativity; and yet, at the same time, free inquiry inevitably leads to critical questions about social life. The late Brazilian educator Paulo Freire (1972) was expelled from his country because he taught peasants to read. The dominant groups—especially the landowners who exploited the peasants—felt threatened because literacy helped the peasants understand their oppressed position in society.

Higher education, in particular, contributes to social change in ways that have nothing to do with what students learn. Many college students are free of work and family responsibilities, and this gives them time and energy to participate in social movements. The civil rights and anti-Vietnam War movements of the 1960s drew heavily on the support of students. In the 1970s university students in France succeeded in leading what became a paralyzing national strike, and the 1987 demonstrations by students in South Korea were powerful enough to force a change in that country's leadership and constitution.

Education has also fostered the growth of intellectuals as a category—people who are separated from production and are therefore free to analyze and criticize their society. The roots of sociology itself extend back to the turbulent 1800s in which scholars such as Durkheim, Weber, and particularly Marx, were motivated as much by a desire for positive social change as they were by intellectual curiosity. Most of the first U.S. sociologists saw themselves as social reformers, not detached intellectuals. (Bannister 1987). Many of today's sociologists believe that it is their responsibility to use their research and analytic skills to bring about positive change.

Writers, artists, scholars, and professionals such as Lenin, Leon Trotsky, Fidel Castro, and Che Guevara have played major roles in revolutions. For this reason, intellectuals are often viewed with considerable suspicion, if not hostility. When the Nazis seized power in Germany in the 1930s, university professors and other intellectuals were among their first targets as the Nazis tried to stifle criticism and dissent. In the U.S., college professors and other intellectuals have often been punished for views that were perceived as threats to the status quo. Tenure was instituted for the purpose of defending academic freedom from those who would try to suppress unpopular views.

As institutions, schools contribute to social change and conflict *and* to continuity and stability; but schools, themselves, have also been the objects of movements for social change.

Changing Schools

As we have seen, schools may be understood in terms of how they operate and their relationships with the rest of society. In order to understand changes in schools, therefore, we have to pay attention to both of these levels of analysis.

Because the functions of schools are so highly valued, criticism of schools and efforts to change them are almost as old as schools themselves. The practice of grading, for example, has a long and checkered history in U.S. education. Over the last hundred years, schools have adopted grading, dropped it, re-adopted it, and modified it with innovations such as pass-fail (Kirschenbaum et al. 1971). In the 1980s there was a renewed call for higher standards and stricter grading of student work (National Commission on Excellence in Education 1983). Such changes reflect competition between opposing beliefs and values. Opponents argue that grading inhibits creativity and independent thought, that it encourages students to care more about grades than learning. Supporters stress different values—the importance of motivating students to learn what they need to know whether they like it or not, and sorting out students of different ability levels.

Underlying these positions are beliefs about the nature of childhood and values about how much power children should have, and such differences have produced some radical alternatives to traditional schooling. At a British school called Summerhill, teachers exercise virtually no authority over their students, who run the school through democratic meetings and decide what they will learn and when they will learn it. The school's founder, A. S. Neill, maintained that the most important thing for young people to learn is how to live with others and make decisions for themselves. Subjects such as history and science can be learned later, when children decide they need them (Neill 1961).

Illich (1971) went so far as to advocate abolishing schools altogether and replacing them with "learning centers" in which people who want to learn get together with those who have something to teach. He objected to formal schooling not only because of his belief that it stifles the motivation to explore and learn about the world, but also because the hidden curriculum promotes control, obedience, and conformity more than enlightenment and independent thought. Illich and Neill were both embraced and ridiculed by experts in many fields, including education (see Gartner, Greer, and Riessman 1973; Hart 1970).

Beyond a few private experiments, it is unlikely that elementary and secondary schools will stray far from their current bureaucratic form in which power

is sharply divided between adults and children (see Shor 1986). In 1983 the National Commission on Excellence in Education urged that school days and years be lengthened, that student freedom to decide which subjects to study be severely limited, and that requirements for graduation be raised and strictly enforced.

There is evidence, however, that in higher education students are controlling their own education to an increasing degree. For the most part, this results from the fact that an increasing proportion of students are adults who are returning to school—especially community colleges— after spending several years in the labor force. It also results from the fact that many colleges are experiencing financial difficulties and shrinking enrollments, and they see the adult market as a new source of income.

This raises once again the economic reality that schools must have money in order to operate; and some of the most heated debates about schools focus on the issue of who will pay for them and how, and how this will affect the quality of education.

Money and the Future of Education

Many reformers would improve schools by forcing them to improve—by raising graduation standards and by requiring teachers to pass competency tests at regular intervals. Others, however, suggest that the best way to improve schools is to set them in economic competition with each other. If parents can send children to the school of their choice, then schools will have to compete in order to survive.

One suggestion is to take a community's school budget and distribute it among parents in the form of credits or vouchers. Parents could then redeem their vouchers in any way they wished, either by enrolling their children in a public school, or by seeking out private education. The best schools, of course, would get the most business, and this would encourage inferior schools to improve their performance. A second proposal would allow parents who send their children to private schools to pay less federal tax. By subsidizing private schools, supporters argue, this plan would increase healthy competition between public and private schools and give parents greater freedom of choice and control over their children's educations.

Critics—the NAACP, the American Civil Liberties Union, and professional educators—argue that both plans would make the distribution of education even more unequal than it is today. As additional family income, vouchers would enable middle-class parents to send their children to private schools, but would not be enough to give lower-class parents the same option. Tuition tax credits discriminate against lower-class families, who cannot afford private schools and already receive a relatively small share of educational resources. Critics fear that both proposals would further divide schooling into two separate and unequal systems: one well-financed, middle-class, and predominantly white, and the other poorly financed, lower-class, and predominantly nonwhite.

The characteristics of educational institutions seem forever tied to social conditions in society itself. Schools have been, are, and will continue to be important parts of the "real world."

SUMMMARY

1. Education is a form of socialization that involves systematic, formal transmission of skills, knowledge, and other aspects of culture. In many societies this takes place primarily in schools—formal organizations whose primary purpose is education.

2. Education was once restricted to the upper classes, but with the Industrial Revolution public schooling gradually included increasingly large segments of the population.

3. Like all institutions, schools are organized around cultural ideas such as a belief in the validity of grades, values of punctuality and competition, and norms such as those embodied in honor codes. Within this environment, there are subcultures such as those among students. While the manifest function of schools is to teach subjects such as math, they also teach a hidden curriculum that consists of values such as obedience to authority and the relative desirability of different social classes or of different ethnic backgrounds.

4. In general, the higher the level of schooling, the more likely school boundaries are to exclude students from disadvantaged backgrounds.

5. Like all social behavior, patterns of interaction in schools are affected by definitions of the situation and people's perceptions of each other. Teachers and students often feel frustrated with each other when students define their role as giving correct answers and teachers expect students to think independently.

6. Schools, like many institutions, have become bureaucratic. Some argue that this interferes with education by creating competing interests such as those of teachers and administrators.

7. Distributions of power differ sharply among schools, according to the level of schooling. For example, students generally gain power as they advance to college, and power structures are more complex in college than in elementary school.

8. Population affects schools primarily through changes in the birth rate, increasing or decreasing the number of potential students. This affects communities and professionals who make a living from the business of schooling.

9. Ecological factors, such as the use of space, also affect schools. Racial segregation and different models of classroom interaction, such as open classrooms, affect what and how much students learn. The mode of production in a society is also important, because schooling is expensive. Industrial societies are in a far better position to school their children than are nonindustrial countries.

10. Schools are related to other institutions in many ways. They have taken over many functions once reserved for families; compulsory schooling keeps young people out of the job market; and schools are often used to promote national political goals such as allegiance to the state.

11. Schools play an important part in social conflict. The hidden curriculum, tracking, and grades support social class differences by sorting and preparing students to accept their class position. While schooling has long been perceived as a solution for social inequality, most research shows that the causes of inequality are to be found primarily outside of schools.

12. Because they socialize the young, schools have been viewed as vehicles for social change. This has made them an ongoing scene of conflict as various interest groups vie to determine school policy and curriculum.

KEY TERMS

education   416   school   415   tracking   435
hidden curriculum   421

LOOKING ELSEWHERE

Having studied Chapter 17, you might want to look at related discussions in *Human Arrangements*, which include

- schools and socialization (Chapter 7, p. 152)
- socialization, schools, and gender roles (Chapter 14, pp. 343–44)
- interaction in college classrooms (Chapter 1, pp. 9–10; Chapter 8, pp. 174, 175)

- student cheating as deviance (Chapter 11, pp. 239–40)
- education and social mobility (Chapter 12, pp. 285–86)
- the causes of neighborhood segregation (Chapter 13, pp. 311–12)

RECOMMENDED READINGS

Barr, R., and Dreeban, R., with Wiratchai, N. 1983. *How schools work*. Chicago: University of Chicago Press. A study of how school systems work and their effects on education using a multilevel perspective ranging from political structures such as school boards to what goes on in classrooms.

Boocock, S. 1980. *Sociology of education: An introduction* (2nd ed.). Boston: Houghton-Mifflin. An excellent introduction to the field. See also Parelius, A. P., and Parelius, R. J. (1978). *The sociology of education*. Englewood Cliffs, NJ: Prentice-Hall.

Bowles, S., and Gintis, H. 1976. *Schooling in capitalist America: Educational reform and the contradictions of economic life*. New York: Basic Books. An important analysis of the ways in which schools and formal education help to reproduce social classes in America.

Illich, I. 1971. *Deschooling society*. New York: Harper and Row. A revolutionary plan to do away with schools as we know them. For an equally provocative collection of critical articles written in response to Illich's ideas, see A. Gartner, C. Greer, and F. Riessman (Eds.). 1973. *After deschooling, what?* New York: Harper and Row.

Jencks, C., et al. 1972. *Inequality*. An energetic challenge to the belief that education is the key to social mobility and reduction of social inequality.

Ravitch, D. 1983. *The troubled crusade: American education 1945–1980*. New York: Basic Books. A thoughtful, well-written analysis of 35 years of attempts at educational reform in the United States.

Rohlen, T. P. 1983. *Japan's high schools*. Berkeley: University of California Press. A highly recommended study that tries to explain how Japan's high schools produce levels of achievement unheard of in the United States. See also Cummings, W. K. 1980. *Education and equality in Japan*. Princeton, NJ: Princeton University Press.

18

SCIENCE, TECHNOLOGY, AND MEDICINE

 By definition, social institutions are conservative in that they try to preserve different aspects of social life. A major function of families and schools, for example, is to reproduce a culture by passing it from one generation to the next. It is in the nature of institutions to resist change, for they are designed to give social life a sense of continuity, regularity, and predictability.

As an institution, however, **science** is a unique case. Although it has enduring institutional characteristics as resistant to change as those of any institution, its major social function is to seek new knowledge, to test old assumptions, and approach what we think we know with a skeptical eye (see Barnes 1985). It is perhaps the only institution in history dedicated to change, and, as such, is a source of both unprecedented discovery and innovation and enormous conflict. From theories about the creation of the universe to an understanding of the social and biological aspects of race and gender differences, science continually tests a society's ability to make sense of itself and control its own affairs. While other institutions are designed to keep things as they are, the knowledge produced by science can change not only how we think about the world, but how we shape the physical and social world in which we live.

Unlike science, which consists solely of theories and knowledge, technology is the practical ability to manipulate and make use of the physical world. We are now able to splice genes and create forms of life, to transplant organs from one body to another, to enable one woman to bear a child for another; to use computers to store and retrieve detailed information on every citizen, and to destroy life on earth with nuclear weapons. However, we have barely begun to deal seriously with the profound moral, practical, and legal implications of such abilities.

443

In this chapter we take a detailed look at the social characteristics that make science a key institution in industrial societies, and at the dramatic and complex effects of science and technology on social life. We then turn to medicine, an institution that exists in virtually all known societies but which in industrial societies is increasingly dominated by technology and science.

SCIENCE AS A SOCIAL INSTITUTION

Science is a set of social arrangements whose major function is the seeking of new, largely reliable knowledge (see Merton 1973). As an institution, it provides a cultural blueprint that defines legitimate subjects for research, acceptable methods of seeking knowledge, and standards for evaluating and interpreting the results. The question of whether God exists falls beyond the realm of science because science concerns itself only with what can be observed and evaluated with objective evidence. Since the existence of God is a matter of faith rather than of observable evidence, it is not a legitimate question for scientific inquiry. The question, however, of whether a belief in the existence of God affects other aspects of our lives, such as happiness or tolerance for those who differ from us, can be answered scientifically, for it is possible to gather evidence about people's beliefs, their happiness, and their tolerance.

As an institution science is more than a set of ideas and symbols. It also involves social relationships through which knowledge is pursued by individuals and groups. Science, then, is a social process which itself can be understood in terms of how it operates and changes. It is not simply a source of change, for it is affected by its own findings and the social systems in which it operates (see Zuckerman 1988), producing both wondrous and disastrous results. We begin with the cultural and structural characteristics that define science as an institution, and then take a broader look at the complex relationship between science and society.

A Zen Buddhist sits and meditates on what he believes to be the undifferentiated wholeness of the natural world. Louis Pasteur, who discovered that germs cause disease, is typical of scientists who try to understand reality by taking it apart to see how it "works." These dramatically different approaches reflect not only different ways of understanding, but different ways of life.

THE CULTURE OF SCIENCE

Science is a cultural way of looking at the world, and, like all aspects of culture, it affects how we pay attention to it. Science, however, is unique in its dedication to understanding the world through the use of particular methods based on fundamental assumptions about the nature of reality.

Beliefs and Paradigms

At the heart of science as a cultural framework is the belief in science itself as a valid way of understanding the world. Most of us take this for granted, many going so far as to regard science as the ultimate authority determining what is true and what is not (Barnes 1985). What we tend to overlook is how ethnocentric this view is, that as members of other cultures we might look at the problem of truth very differently. To a Zen Buddhist, for example, all aspects of the observable and unobservable world form an integrated whole, to be accepted as it is, not understood by picking it apart and figuring things out in terms of their parts and the relationships that bind them. From this perspective, scientific efforts to explain the world by identifying how things work is at best a silly distraction, and at worst a futile and dangerous effort to control a world that is inherently neither understandable nor controllable in that way.

Within science, the most important beliefs take the form of **paradigms**—sets of guiding assumptions, theories, and methods that define a particular approach to scientific problems (see Kuhn 1970). A paradigm defines for scientists what they should pay attention to, how they should pay attention to it, and how they should interpret what they observe. As you might imagine, paradigms are enormously important in science because they have so much influence over what scientists do. Most scientists are socialized into the paradigms that dominate their fields and, as with any cultural belief system, they tend to hang on to them unless confronted with overwhelming evidence to the contrary.

The Ptolemaic view of the universe, for example, which places the earth rather than the sun at the center, was the dominant paradigm in astronomy for many centuries until it was finally upset by the Copernican view. The new paradigm, however, was fiercely resisted for centuries after it was first introduced in 1543. The old paradigm not only dominated astronomy, but was also an important part of religious views that placed humanity at the center of existence as God's most important creation. Both Copernicus and, a century later, one of his strongest advocates, Galileo, were persecuted, and Galileo was forced to recant his views under threat of torture and imprisonment. Historically, resistance to new paradigms has been the rule rather than the exception in science: Charles Darwin's theory of evolution, Louis Pasteur's theories of germs, Gregor Mendel's theory of genetics, and Sigmund Freud's theory of the subconscious—all represented dramatic shifts in paradigms, and all were greeted with enormous resistance.

The Making of Scientific Revolutions Because paradigms include basic assumptions that guide scientific work, they are the last element of any scientific field to change, and when they do, the result can be revolutionary.

As Kuhn (1970) describes this process in his classic book, *The Structure of Scientific Revolutions*, most scientists practice *normal* science, which means that they work within a particular paradigm without challenging its assumptions. A Ptolemaic astronomer would never try to measure the characteristics of the earth's orbit around the sun because according to the Ptolemaic paradigm the earth does not orbit around the sun. When a paradigm is wrong, however, its use will result in a growing number of findings that contradict the paradigm or make no sense. In the case of Ptolemy's view of the solar system, astronomers found that the planets were not where they expected them to be. Such findings that are inconsistent with a scientific paradigm are called **anomalies**, and as they accumulate, the position of the paradigm becomes increasingly insecure until a new paradigm is developed to account for the anomalies and replace the old one. It is this replacement of one paradigm with another that constitutes a **scientific revolution**.

One of the most intriguing new paradigms in science centers on the unpredictable side of nature found in the seeming chaos of everything from weather patterns to the irregular dripping of a leaky faucet. The principle of "chaos" is now being used to organize a revolutionary approach to understanding a wide range of natural and social phenomena that have, until now, had no place in existing scientific paradigms (see Gleick 1987). In this paradigm, what we tend to think of as so disorderly and unpredictable as to be beyond our understanding is as normal as the regularities produced by gravity. Consequently,

The Ptolemaic paradigm placed the earth at the center of the universe. Medieval thinkers also believed that the constant motion of the planets required some sort of "mover," which, in this fourteenth-century depiction, was provided by angels turning the wheels of the universe.

in this emerging paradigm, such phenomena have a place in the natural order of things and can be understood in a systematic, scientific way.

Conflict between competing paradigms is probably the most vital issue confronting a scientific discipline, for it is nothing less than a struggle over the fundamental assumptions and views that determine the research that will be done. In sociology, for example, the functional and conflict perspectives have been seen as direct opposites of each other, and advocates of each have argued their positions for years, often with some bitterness. The functional paradigm promoted by Talcott Parsons was based on the idea of society as a set of integrated social institutions, such as the family, economy, and law, supported by a general consensus on cultural norms and values. Each part of a social system can be understood in terms of its dependency on other parts and the ways in which it contributes to or interferes with the operation of the system. Within societies, individuals choose among culturally defined alternatives and are moti-

vated by norms and values to make choices that ultimately contribute to the maintenance of the system (Parsons 1937, 1951).

Particularly in the 1940s and 1950s, many sociologists accepted the functional paradigm's assumptions about societies and how they work and used it to approach research problems as diverse as social stratification, gender inequality, and the organization of the family (see Chapters 12, 14, and 16). To many other sociologists, however, there were too many aspects of social life that seemed to contradict the assumptions of the functional paradigm. As the anomalies of injustice and social unrest revealed by the civil rights and anti-Vietnam War movements in the 1960s mounted, the conflict paradigm became increasingly popular, especially from a Marxist perspective. Parsons' critics charged that his functional paradigm assumed a false picture of society as a harmonious, stable collection of social relationships and cultural values and norms (see Dahrendorf 1958; Gouldner 1970; Mills 1959). Societies, they argued, are not cohesive, unified wholes in which all work for common goals. Most societies are dominated by groups that use their power and privilege to shape society to serve their own ends, and it is impossible to understand societies with an approach that fails to take this into account. All societies experience continuing conflict and change, not stability and equilibrium; and each part of society contributes to that conflict and change. The basis of social order is not consensus, but the coercive use of power (Dahrendorf 1973).

Although the functional and conflict paradigms still have ardent advocates within sociology, as we have seen throughout this book, the result of this struggle has not been the replacement of one with the other. Instead, most sociologists have come to appreciate the paradigms as complementary parts of a larger sociological paradigm. The result here, then, has been one of integration, not revolution.

As we saw in Chapter 5, a similar debate over paradigms has taken place within the interactionist perspective about the nature of the relationship between individuals and social systems. According to what has been known as the "Chicago school" of symbolic interactionism, the structural characteristics of social systems are not external to individuals. In other words, a role is not something external to individuals that shapes their behavior. Instead, it is the behavior of individuals that creates the reality of a role and, with it, social systems themselves. From this perspective, social systems *are* what social actors *do*. By contrast, adherents to what has been called the "Iowa school" of symbolic interactionism argue that systems and their cultural and structural characteristics do have an independent existence that shapes the role behavior of individuals. As with the disagreement between functional and conflict theorists, this debate involves questions of emphasis that make it possible for the two approaches to exist together and complement each other.

The Values of Science

As with any institution, science is guided by a value system. Perhaps the highest scientific value is placed on verifiable knowledge itself, for this is the avowed goal of all scientific work. To a scientist, there is no good knowledge and bad knowledge, although there are certainly good and bad *uses* of knowledge.

The inability of scientists to control how knowledge is used raises a difficult value conflict: Should scientists seek knowledge that could be used for de-

"*We want you to do some pure disinterested fundamental research into something immensely profitable.*"
Copyright *New Scientist*, London.

structive purposes? If, for example, it were possible to demonstrate that members of a minority group tend to have a genetic makeup that results in lower *average* mental abilities, the high value placed by science on the pursuit of knowledge for its own sake might lead many scientists to go ahead. Other scientists, however, have a broader view of scientific values in the context of *other* cultural values such as the importance of social justice. These scientists would pay attention to how such findings might be used to reinforce negative cultural stereotypes and justify discrimination against individuals regardless of their abilities.

Such decisions cannot be made scientifically, for they force scientists to consider values that have nothing to do with science itself (see Fausto-Sterling 1985). A scientist's decision to search for a cure for AIDS or to develop a new plague that can be used against an enemy in war is not a scientific one. Nor is a biologist's decision to try to disprove the prejudiced belief that minorities are inferior to dominant groups. The mere act of choosing what questions to ask is, itself, profoundly influenced by a scientist's nonscientific values.

It is also important to remember that the individual scientist is not the only one whose values influence the choice of what knowledge to pursue. Scientific research today is so expensive that it requires the support of major social institutions such as universities, government, corporations, and private foundations, each of which has its own nonscientific reasons for preferring one line of research over another. Drug companies, for example, generally place a higher value on making a profit than on curing disease. They will often decide against pursuing cures for diseases that are devastating for their victims but which do not afflict enough people to result in a large profit for the company. Scientists often feel compelled to choose their research topics according to which kinds of problems are receiving a high priority from government agencies, corporations, and foundations that control research funds. For these, the choice may appear to be between doing research on what others consider to be important or not doing research at all.

The heart of the scientific value system focuses less on the selection of research problems than on the conduct of scientific work itself and the social relationships that bind the scientific community together. Scientific values define the difference between good science and bad science and establish the goals to which all scientists are expected to aspire. It is here that the norms of the scientific community become most important in regulating the behavior of scientists.

The Norms of Science

Merton (1968) identified four norms that govern scientific work. The norm of **universalism** requires scientists to use the same objective criteria for evaluating scientific findings regardless of their source. The anti-Semitic ideology of Nazi Germany, for example, led to a complete rejection of the results of "Jewish science"—including the fundamental work of Albert Einstein—a clear violation of this norm.

Until quite recently, science in the Soviet Union was dominated by a rigid communist ideology which rejected many of the assumptions which underlay Western (which is to say, capitalist) science, including many of the basic theories of genetic inheritance. The influence of political ideology on the interpretation of scientific evidence was so strong that it forced scientists to adopt the false view that acquired traits could be passed on genetically. According to Soviet genetic theory, if a crop of corn was particularly well-fertilized and watered and was therefore unusually productive, seed from that crop would also be highly productive. Since watering and fertilizing have no effect on the genetic makeup of corn or anything else, their effects cannot be passed on genetically. This fundamental error, dictated by the nonscientific standards of communist ideology, resulted in years of disastrous crops for Soviet farmers, and although the error was finally corrected in the 1960s, its long-term effects still keep the Soviet Union far behind the west in its ability to adequately feed its people.

The norm of **communism** (a term whose usage here has no connection with communism as a political system) requires scientists to share their findings freely with one another, based on the idea that knowledge is common, not private property that should be held in secret. This has produced conflict as scientific knowledge has become increasingly important in international power struggles between the United States and the Soviet Union. Scientists who do basic research for the U.S. Defense Department are often required not to share their findings with anyone outside the government for fear that it will be made available to the Soviets. This requirement has led many U.S. scientists to refuse to work for

their government rather than violate the norm of communism.

Since the scientific community does not regard ideas and knowledge as private property to be used to advance the interests of the individual scientist, the norm of **disinterestedness** requires scientists to act more for the benefit of science than themselves. In spite of the fact that original discoveries are the key to a scientist's professional success, such concerns are not supposed to influence how science is conducted. Scientists who falsify results in order to make names for themselves, for example, violate this norm by placing their own interests above those of science.

The fourth norm ensures that all evidence will be subjected to **organized skepticism**. No finding, argument, or theory should be accepted without first carefully weighing the evidence and critically evaluating the methods used to generate it. This norm has been institutionalized in the practice of publishing articles in scientific journals only after they have been carefully reviewed by other scientists, and of accepting published findings only after enough time has passed to allow the broader scientific community to comment on them. Scientists feel a sense of obligation to hold no idea, theory, or paradigm sacred, except, of course, the beliefs, norms, and values that underlie science itself.

The dangers of bypassing the procedures used to enforce the norm of organized skepticism were apparent in 1989 when two scientists at the University of Utah claimed to have discovered a way to produce cold fusion, a reaction using simple equipment operating at room temperature with the potential to produce virtually unlimited amounts of energy. Rather than submit their results to the usual process of peer review and, if successful, eventual publication in scientific journals, the scientists held a press conference at which they announced their spectacular claim. Although it brought them and their university instant worldwide attention, the result was months of confusion, claims, and counterclaims as scientists from around the world rushed to see if the revolutionary findings were valid—without success.

Conformity and Deviance in the Scientific Community   Because the focus of science is knowledge and truth, it depends on the ability of scientists to assume that other scientists are honest and forthcoming. Otherwise, scientists would be faced with the task of verifying independently every piece of research before accepting its results (see Zuckerman

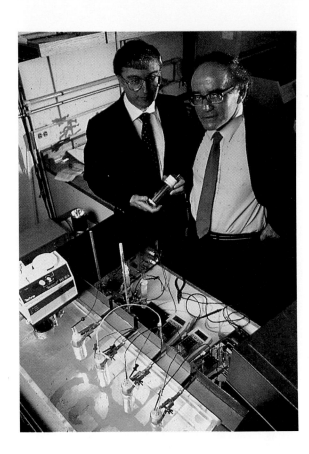

Stanley Pons and Martin Fleischmann violated the norm of organized skepticism when they claimed prematurely that their apparatus—shown here—could produce nuclear fusion at room temperature.

1988). This is impossible given that there are some 40,000 scientific journals in the world publishing upwards of a million articles each year (Broad 1988). "The institution of science involves an implicit social contract between scientists so that each can depend on the trustworthiness of the rest . . . the entire cognitive system of science is rooted in the moral integrity of individual scientists" (Zuckerman 1977, p. 113).

As with all values, however, those that underlie scientific norms are ideals that fallable humans will inevitably fail to achieve fully. As we have seen, it is impossible for scientists to ignore nonscientific values completely. In addition, scientific norms are difficult to enforce because violations of them are often invisible: no one may ever know of a finding that is kept secret, and scientists who reject the work of others because of their race, age, gender, or religion may do so without ever being discovered.

When norms are violated, the most severe sanction the scientific community can impose is to expel the scientist. Scientists found guilty of fraud may lose not only their jobs, but the respect of other scientists, their willingness to believe what they say and write. For a scientist, expulsion from the scientific community can amount to the virtual end of a scientific career.

Although known fraud is relatively rare in science in comparison with other spheres of social life, it does occur (see Broad and Wade 1983; Merton 1973). Jensen's (1969) argument in favor of a genetic explanation for racial differences in IQ, for example, drew heavily on the studies of twins reported by British psychologist Cyril Burt. As it turned out, Burt's studies were marred by numerous contradictions, inconsistencies, missing documentation, and questions as to whether some of his co-authors ever existed (see Kamin 1974; Wade 1976). More recently there has been a rash of fraud cases, some of which have taken place in prestigious Ivy League universities such as Harvard and Yale.

Why do scientists sometimes cheat? As with other forms of deviance, a sociological answer focuses on the pressures and opportunities to violate norms that are inherent in the social situations in which people find themselves (Merton 1957b, 1973). University scientists—especially graduate students or younger professors—cannot make a name for themselves (or achieve the security that goes with academic tenure) without making original discoveries, and the intense competition among scientists means there is always the danger that someone else will get there first. Scientists share the value of original discoveries, but they do not all have equal access to the opportunities to achieve them. Some have far greater access to research facilities, grant money, and support for time off to study and write. Ironically, it is those who are already established—and who, therefore, are least desperate in their need for recognition—who tend to have the greatest resources. The system itself, then, by making rewards depend so heavily on producing quick, new findings, and by distributing unequally the opportunities to achieve those rewards, encourages scientists to break the rules by placing their own self-interest above the goals of science (see Broad and Wade 1983; Merton 1984a).

THE STRUCTURE OF SCIENCE

As an institution, science has a structure in the form of social relationships through which scientists are trained and socialized, research is done, and knowledge is evaluated and shared within and beyond the scientific community. The structure of scientific work has changed dramatically over the last 300 years, especially in relation to the boundaries that define science as a profession and the complexity of social systems in which science is conducted.

Boundaries: Science as a Profession

The forerunners of scientists worked primarily alone and identified themselves as "natural philosophers." By comparison, today's scientists share a sharply defined subculture of symbols, language, paradigms, and role expectations that distinguish them from nonscientists and establish their right to determine what is considered to be valid knowledge about the natural and social world. Science has been transformed from an individual pastime and hobby into a profession whose members go to great lengths to define and defend its boundaries.

From this perspective, the recent controversy over the teaching of evolution and creation science in public schools is far more than a disagreement over competing versions of the truth, for it also involves the power of scientists to control their professional boundaries and a monopoly over what is identified as scientific knowledge (see Gieryn et al. 1985). Those who call themselves creation scientists claim that there is a scientific basis for a literal interpretation of the Biblical version of creation. In opposing them, scientists do not just argue that the Bible's version is a poor scientific theory that does not fit the facts; even more important, they argue that creation science is not science at all and its practitioners are not scientists because they do not support the scientific norm of organized skepticism. Creationists, they argue, practice religion, not science. The core of the scientific approach to the world is the quest for new knowledge based on an ongoing willingness to examine evidence showing that what we believe to be true is, in fact, not true. Religion, however, is grounded in the belief that the truth has already been revealed and is simply there to be accepted and lived by. Unlike science, what holds religion together is an unquestioning faith that the truth is already known, which is a far cry from organized skepticism.

The distinction between scientists and nonscientists is important because it reflects an ongoing struggle over the authority to determine what is true in a society. As we will see later, this can have important implications for the distribution of power in societies and the way in which they are governed.

The Structural Complexity of Science

It was not until 1662 that the Royal Society was founded in London as the first organization dedicated to the idea that it is important for scientists to talk with one another, to support one another's

This seventeenth-century painting by an unknown Flemish artist shows that the gentleman of the day was expected to be well versed in the arts, literature, music, and science. Science was not organized as a profession and discoveries depended primarily on the work of individuals who dabbled in science as a hobby.

work, and to discuss, evaluate, and share one another's theories and findings. Even here, however, science remained a relatively personal activity engaged in by amateurs who were wealthy enough to have the time to pursue it (Merton 1938).

In the more than 300 years since the founding of the Royal Society, science has been transformed from an informal activity carried out by isolated individuals to a formal profession that takes place mostly within large organizations. Today most scientists work as employees, not as independent thinkers, and earn their living by their scientific work. This change mirrors the transformation of science itself from something that could be done with a minimum of equipment and financial resources to an activity that is so expensive that few individuals can afford to do it on their own. We left what Price (1986) calls "Little Science" behind with World War II and entered the age of "Big Science." The lone genius has been replaced by teams working in formal organizations that provide the necessary expensive equipment. The self-sufficiency of the upper-class philosopher/scientist has been replaced by a dependency on massive funding from foundations, corporations, universities, and government agencies.

One consequence of this is that scientists have lost much of their independence and autonomy, for their dependence on outside support is so great that their choice of research problems becomes more a matter of organizational priorities than their own interests. The distribution of power, in short, has shifted from the individual scientist to the organizations on which scientists depend, a trend that, as we have seen in other chapters, has been repeated in many other institutions. This means that ultimately, the decision to conduct research on the causes of a disease such as AIDS is made not by research scientists but by leaders in business, government, and private foundations, many of whom are not scientists and do not feel bound by the norms or values of the scientific community. Shilts (1987) argues that research on AIDS was delayed not for scientific reasons, but because those who controlled research funds were slow to respond to the emerging crisis.

Against this, however, other social factors reinforce the autonomy of scientists. Perhaps the most important is the fact that the rewards that come from success in science depend more than anything on the recognition of other scientists (Barnes 1985; Merton 1973). For most people, successful job performance results in the payment of money which they use as

Science and politics have come together in the AIDS pandemic in a particularly dramatic way. Activists have charged the government and scientific community with failing to respond quickly enough or with adequate resources and have demonstrated and lobbied for more research and health expenditures.

currency to get what they want. In science, however, the currency is the recognition of other scientists, which is the basis for the major rewards scientists seek, from a better-paying job to landing a big research grant. Such recognition is controlled primarily by science as an institution, and this helps to insulate scientists from the potentially corrupting influences of organizations that offer money as a primary reward.

Another important consequence of the increased complexity of science is extreme specialization. As with most types of work, the scientific generalist who was familiar with a wide range of knowledge and theoretical perspectives is long gone. In part, this is due to the sheer magnitude of knowledge which is now so great that no one can master it all. The quantity of new findings generated each year is so vast that only a highly specialized network of specialists can sift through and evaluate it all in order to determine what should be accepted. Specialization also reflects, however, competition among scientists for scarce resources and the pressures on scientists to achieve the recognition of their peers. Zuckerman (1988) likens the process of specialization to mining for ore: As each area is exhausted, scientists try to identify and move on to new areas of ignorance in which to mine for new knowledge (see also Merton 1987). This kind of specialization is not unique to the physical sciences, for it has taken place in most areas of intellectual work, from philosophy to sociology (see Jacoby 1987).

The Structure of Scientific Work

The major values of science—the production and sharing of verifiable knowledge about the world—are achieved through the structure of scientific work in social systems. Consider the process through which findings are shared with and evaluated by the scientific community (see Barnes 1985). Most findings are reported in journals, which are typically edited by scientists. When authors prepare an article for possible publication, they must first orient themselves to a set of standards and conventions that govern such work. They know their work will be read and evaluated by other scientists who serve as referees, who will expect certain things, such as a review of previous research on the subject, a clear statement of how the research was conducted, and a discussion of how the new findings fit with what is already known. The specific people who serve as referees are anonymous to the author, which means that the author is guided by a general set of expectations associated with scientific work—the generalized other of the scientific community. This means that before a scientific report even reaches a journal it has already gone through a filtering process as authors make use of their knowledge of what other scientists expect of them.

The criticism provided by expert referees provides a second stage of filtering. Articles may be rejected or accepted outright or, more often, returned to the author for revision and resubmission. Once published, findings are then shared among scientists at large who then provide criticism or support of their own. Only after this has gone on for some time is a finding actually accepted as knowledge, and even then it is subject to continuing test in light of new evidence.

Although this complex process goes a long way toward ensuring the validity of scientific knowledge, in practice it is often less objective than it seems. How seriously a scientist's work is taken by other scientists, for example, depends in part on that scientist's reputation (just as, unfortunately, some professors feel they cannot assign a grade to a student's work without knowing who the student is). A paper written by a relative unknown might be judged by an editor to be nonsense; but that same paper might be seen in a far more positive light if the name of a famous scientist were attached to it. This means that a great deal of important scientific work may never come to light simply because of the unequal distribution of recognition and power within the scientific community.

Objectivity also depends on the ability and willingness of journal editors and referees to refrain from favoring research conclusions that support their own points of view. In a controversial 1988 experiment a social worker submitted to 140 journals two different versions of the same article. One version found that intervention by social workers in a particular situation was generally effective, while the other version concluded that it was ineffective. Overall, 53 percent of the journals accepted the favorable findings compared with only 14 percent that accepted the unfavorable findings (*New York Times*, September 27, 1988, p. C9).

All that this shows is that scientists are social beings like everyone else and that scientific knowledge, as with everything else we think we know about the world, is created through a social process that is inevitably affected by the characteristics of social systems (see Latour 1987; Zuckerman 1988). It is also true, however, that unlike other institutions, science is dedicated to identifying and minimizing the distorting effects of such social forces. That this value is, ultimately, unachievable is not surprising, since most major values that guide human life serve as ideals, not realistic goals.

TECHNOLOGY

Many scientists are dedicated simply to understanding the world in a clearer way regardless of what such understanding can be used for. It is usually through technology, however, that science affects social systems. Technological innovation touches virtually every area of social life, from the machines and robots of industry and the tools of mass warfare to the ability to communicate with loved ones who are far away, to prevent unwanted pregnancies or cause wanted ones, to alter genetic structures or make ourselves feel better when we have a cold. It is the source of some of the greatest improvements in the quality of human life and some of its deepest, most troubling problems. It has enabled a mere 1.3 percent of the U.S. population to produce enough food for the entire country with plenty to spare; and it

The technology that can keep people alive long after they would otherwise have died raises unprecedented ethical and moral issues. Who has the right to decide when to use such technology and when not to? Are we in danger of becoming so preoccupied with what we are able to do with sophisticated technology that we lose sight of the needs, rights, and interests of the people to whom the machines are attached?

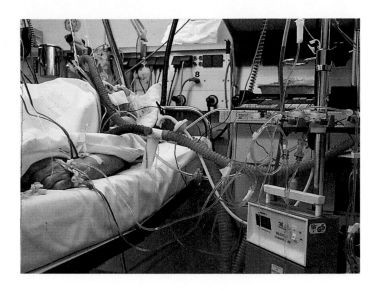

has, in varying degrees, contaminated much of the water we drink and the air we breathe.

Although people often think of science and technology as being the same, they are in fact quite different and the development of one need not involve the other. It is certainly true that science, especially today, often depends on technology. Without the invention of the telescope Galileo could not have made his observations that led him to support the Copernican view of the solar system. Without the ability to cool objects to hundreds of degrees below zero, we might never have discovered superconductivity—the capacity of a substance to allow electricity to pass through it with virtually no resistance and, therefore, with no loss of power or build-up of heat. The development of the space shuttle has made possible experiments that require a weightless environment, something that was unavailable before space travel.

It is equally true, however, that many scientific and technological breakthroughs occur independently of each other. Einstein's theory of relativity was not based on any real-world experiments. In fact, it was some decades after he developed his theory that science had the technology necessary to begin to test his ideas. New technology is often simply an improvement over existing technology that depends more on the skill and imagination of inventors and engineers than on the theoretical breakthroughs of science (Barnes 1985). This is especially true of technological growth before the rise of science as a social institution. Late in the horticultural period, for example, when societies had developed the simple technology required to grow their own food, people discovered the beginnings of metallurgy, first with copper in the Middle East and then with bronze—a harder alloy of copper and tin—in Southeast Asia and China. This was a major discovery, for people could now make harder, more durable tools as well as deadlier weapons. As we saw in Chapter 4,

the plow was one of the most revolutionary inventions of all time, and yet it came into being thousands of years before the advent of science around the seventeenth century.

The discovery of metallurgy illustrates how one development begets another: without the high temperatures of pottery ovens, it would not have been possible to extract metals from ores and melt, smelt, and mold them into different shapes. Next came the discovery of how to smelt iron and harden it into steel, and by the time of Jesus Christ the new technology had taken root throughout the Middle East, India, and China. In the next 1,000 years, it spread to Europe and Southeast Asia and then to the European colonies in the New World. Each technological advance produced still more inventions: gun powder, horseshoes and harnesses, screws, woodturning lathes, magnets, water- and wind-powered mills, the spinning wheel, printing, porcelain, wheelbarrows, and clocks. Still later, on the eve of the Industrial Revolution, the steam engine and power-driven tools were developed.

It is important to get some sense of the speed of technological innovation and its effects on industrial expansion during the early stages of the Industrial Revolution, for it shows how accumulated innovations and key inventions can bring about startling changes, even without scientific breakthroughs. The Industrial Revolution began in the mid-1700s, but by 1845, the production of textiles was five times greater than it was in 1760; iron production was 24 times greater; and coal mining was 9 times greater

The complexity and tightly-coupled structure of nuclear power technology raise profound questions about its safety. In 1987, a reactor at Chernobyl in the Soviet Union melted down and sent radiation over most of Europe. In this picture taken in the Alsace region of France, a woman uses a Geiger counter to check produce in a local market. The extensive amount of radiation made it necessary to plow under many crops and to dump great quantities of milk and other foods.

(Deane and Cole 1962). By contrast, it took horticultural societies the better part of 4,000 years to advance from hoes and digging sticks to the plow.

In the mid-1800s the use of steam power in transportation boosted industrialization by linking distant markets, lowering the cost of moving goods, and stimulating demand and production. Goodyear discovered how to make rubber hold up in extreme hot and cold, and the emerging chemical and petroleum industries added to the momentum of technological change. Farmers traded in horse-drawn plows for threshers, mowers, reapers, steam plows, and chemical fertilizers. In 1860, electric power became a reality with the invention of dynamos and transformers. In the twentieth century the pace of technological innovation has increased dramatically. Long-distance communications, nuclear power and weapons, transistors and micro-chips, lasers, organ transplants, genetic engineering, superconductors, and the widespread use of computers in everything from toys to industrial robots are only a few of the major innovations.

Over the last two centuries, then, both the sophistication and the quantity of technology have increased dramatically; but technology has also become more complex, which brings its own problems. In his book *Normal Accidents*, Perrow (1984) argues that such complex technologies as nuclear power plants are virtually certain to produce serious accidents regardless of how careful we are in running them or how many safety systems are involved. The key, Perrow shows, lies first in the complexity of such

systems, for the more connections there are between different parts of a system, the more things there are that can go wrong *in unpredictable ways*. If one small part in a complex system fails, it will affect several others which, in turn, will affect still others. The number of possible combinations of causes and effects quickly becomes so huge that it is impossible to anticipate them all.

The second key lies in how tightly coupled a system is. In a tightly coupled system, there is little flexibility, which means that when one part fails it has immediate effects on other parts, which leaves little room for error. Perrow argues that a system that is *both* complex *and* tightly coupled is bound to fail sooner or later. The only way to prevent accidents in these cases, he believes, is to not build such systems in the first place (see also Bogard 1989).

The problem of tightly-coupled, complex systems seems to have also played an important role in the 1987 stock market crash. Although the workings of the stock market are too complex to go into here, the crux of the problem is this: Increasingly, computers have been used to decide whether to buy or sell stock depending on how market conditions change from one moment to the next. The decisions are made automatically, with lightning speed, and involve transactions that can amount to hundreds of millions of dollars. Huge transactions can change the market conditions to which other computers react, stimulating—within a matter of seconds—equally huge transactions. The result can be chaotic conditions in the market with stock prices fluctuating so much that investors begin to lose confidence in their understanding of what is happening, precipitating the kind of panic of which stock market crashes are made.

As the above suggests, and as we will see in the following section, as technology becomes increasingly complex, so does its effects on social life.

SCIENCE, TECHNOLOGY, AND SOCIETY

As the functional and conflict perspectives make clear, science can be understood both in terms of its consequences for society and social life and in terms of the unequal distribution of its benefits.

Functions and Dysfunctions

In looking at science from a functional perspective, it is important to pay attention to the ways in which its own structure and culture produce functional and dysfunctional consequences. Intense competition among scientists and pressures to succeed are certainly functional for promoting rapid innovation, but they also encourage secrecy, distortion of research results, fraud, sabotage of competing projects, and the publication of results that, although trivial, add to a scientist's list of publications. Shilts (1987) reports that some scientists, in their rush to be the first to achieve a breakthrough on AIDS research, withheld information from one another, a violation of the norm of communism that improved their competitive advantage at the expense of AIDS victims.

There is a similar mixture of functions and dysfunctions in the complex division of labor in modern science. On the one hand, narrow specialization makes science more efficient in generating and evaluating enormous amounts of new information. On the other hand, it discourages scientists in different disciplines—or even in different specialties of the same discipline—from talking with one another. This kind of isolation interferes with the crucial process through which discoveries and insights in one area have unanticipated benefits for work in others (see Barnes 1985).

From a functional perspective, science and technology have a variety of functional consequences for society. Together, they have been responsible for unprecedented levels of agricultural and industrial production, revolutionary developments in communications, travel, energy, the storage and use of information (computers), and, as we will see shortly, enormous strides in health and longevity, from the virtual eradication of major infectious diseases to organ transplants and laser surgery.

As with most aspects of social life, however, science and technology also produce dysfunctional consequences. Control over infectious diseases saves millions of lives, especially those of small children;

The 1984 gas leak in Bhopal, India, killed thousands of people and injured many thousands more. Among them were many who were permanently blinded.

ironically, this has contributed to a population explosion, one of whose effects is to worsen already impoverished living conditions. Chemical pesticides have dramatically increased agricultural productivity around the world, and yet have also contaminated much of the natural environment. Although use of the lethal pesticide DDT has been banned in much of the world for some time, it was used so heavily that traces of it are now found everywhere, from the North Pole to mother's milk. At the same time that it enriches us, industry produces toxic wastes that poison water supplies and fall as acid rain on lakes and streams, defoliating trees and killing fish. In 1984, thousands of people were killed and hundreds of thousands injured by a leak of deadly gases from a U.S.-owned chemical plant in Bhopal, India. As we witnessed at Three Mile Island and, more recently, the Chernobyl accident in the Soviet Union, the benefits of nuclear power are offset by the continuing problem of disposing of nuclear wastes, and the danger of devastating accidents that affect people hundreds of miles away (see Perrow 1984).

Technology has also done much to make industrial production more efficient, but in the process it has produced unemployment and hardship for millions of workers by making their skills obsolete. Although innovations such as assembly-line robots and word processors create some jobs for those with higher levels of skill, it leaves behind the millions of poor people who do not have access to such skills.

As we have seen, the rise of science has been part of a general move towards the rationalization of social life, and science has become a dominant institutional approach to establishing truth in many societies. One problem with this is that as societies look to science as a source of truth, nonscientists—who include most citizens and politicians—are likely to lose confidence in themselves and implement decisions whose basis they do not fully understand. Habermas (1971) argues that the result can be a **technocracy** in which expertise is power and social problems are viewed in narrow and unrealistic terms as little more than technical issues of social management and maintaining and improving society as if it were only a machine (see also Barnes 1985).

Most people find it difficult to form a clear opinion on highly technical issues such as the safety of nuclear power or the feasibility of the Star Wars Defense Initiative because they hinge on knowledge that only specialists have. A 1988 study of Britain and the United States concluded that "at least nine out of ten citizens lack the scientific literacy to understand and participate in the formulation of public policy" on science and technology issues (Miller 1989). Given the enormous importance of such questions, the social boundaries that separate scientists and nonscientists take on added significance as an important part of the distribution of power in society.

As you may have gathered from these many functional and dysfunctional consequences, most flow not from science itself, but from technology. Science consists of nothing but knowledge and theories about how the world works, and there is nothing inherent in science that demands that it be used for anything. The knowledge of chemistry necessary to make plastics does not *have* to be used actually to make plastics, just as an understanding of atomic physics does not have to be used to make nuclear power plants or weapons. Such decisions usually rest with other institutions, which raises the critical issue of how different interests are served by science and technology.

Science, Technology, and Social Conflict

Although scientists are often seen as people who are insulated from the affairs of society, who carry out their work in the solitude of laboratories, the work of science is bound up with a wider social world. Nor does the high value science places on objectivity ensure that science will be simply a neutral vehicle for searching out truth regardless of whom it hurts or whose interests it serves. In increasingly complex ways, technology and scientific expertise are sources of power, and, as such, they play an important part in social conflict.

This is due, in part, to the dependence of "Big" science on the financial resources of large organizations, which often have goals that have little to do with objectivity or the pursuit of truth and much to do with social inequality. Many U.S. scientists, for example, do research that has military applications, which gives science a major role in political tensions, especially those involving the U.S. and the Soviet Union. This not only leads these scientists to engage in research projects that might otherwise have no appeal to them, but it can also lead them to make scientific judgments on political rather than scientific grounds. Such conflicts are even more apparent among engineers who design technology. The disastrous destruction of the space shuttle Challenger might never have happened were it not for the intense political and economic pressures being exerted on shuttle engineers to keep the launch program on schedule, pressures that led officials to ignore scientific judgments that the shuttle was unsafe.

Science and technology are also important in more general conflicts between wealthy and poor nations, for both military and economic power are more dependent than ever on scientific and technological abilities. A virtual monopoly over productive technology is one of the keys to the dominance of a relative few industrial nations over the world economy.

Within societies, science and technology also play an important part in the perpetuation of social inequality. Genetic technology may revolutionize agriculture by greatly increasing production, but as the Office of Technology Assessment (1986b) points out, this technology will be so expensive that only large farm corporations will be able to afford it. This, in turn, will make small and medium-size farms even less able to compete and will accelerate their demise and the increasing concentration of wealth and power in agriculture.

In industry, technology has been used increasingly to replace workers by making the production process more efficient. Strikes become less and less effective as employers are able to transfer work from one site to another (by sending computer files over

FIGURE 18-1   How One Global Office System Works

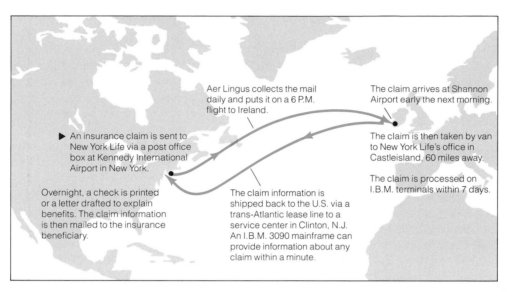

Aer Lingus collects the mail
daily and puts it on a 6 P.M.
flight to Ireland.

The claim arrives at Shannon
Airport early the next morning.

▶ An insurance claim is sent to
New York Life via a post office
box at Kennedy International
Airport in New York.

The claim is then taken by van
to New York Life's office in
Castleisland, 60 miles away.

The claim is processed on
I.B.M. terminals within 7 days.

Overnight, a check is printed
or a letter drafted to explain
benefits. The claim information
is then mailed to the insurance
beneficiary.

The claim information is
shipped back to the U.S. via a
trans-Atlantic lease line to a
service center in Clinton, N.J.
An I.B.M. 3090 mainframe can
provide information about any
claim within a minute.

Sophisticated communications and computer technology enable many corporations to shift work rapidly from one place to another. The system used by New York Life to process claims saves on labor costs by sending work from the U.S. to Ireland. Using overnight air freight and high-speed computer links, the company is processing insurance claims in Ireland, where wages and operating costs are low and there is an abundant supply of labor.

New York Life says it expects that processing costs will be about 25 percent lower than those in the United States. The same technology could be used, however, to circumvent a workers' strike in one country by simply sending the work they refuse to do to workers in another country—thereby depriving the strike and the workers of their major source of power.

Source: The New York Times, October 18, 1988

telephone lines, for example) or to get by with fewer workers through automation (see Figure 18-1). Computers are being used extensively in many offices to closely monitor worker behavior—effectively the same as having someone looking over your shoulder every second of the work day. Such developments strengthen the position of capitalists and weaken that of workers by making workers easier to replace and by making it less likely that highly skilled and less skilled workers will organize around common interests. As production becomes increasingly dependent on sophisticated technology and less dependent on relatively unskilled labor, the position of the working class becomes still more insecure (see Zuboff 1988).

Science also affects inequality when it is used to justify or explain it, or when it is used to refute prejudicial claims against minorities. On the one hand, scientific theory has often been looked upon as a source of support for prejudiced beliefs about nonwhites and women by giving prejudice the social legitimacy conferred by scientific objectivity (see V. J.

Williams 1989). This has been particularly true of the use of "nature" arguments to explain and justify the subordinate position of women on the grounds that the social arrangements around gender are dictated by biological differences. Science itself continues to be a largely male occupation dominated by strongly masculinist values, and it has only been recently that a feminist scholarship has emerged which systematically examines the impact of science on gender roles and inequality (see Bleier 1984; Fausto-Sterling 1985; Keller 1985).

On the other hand, what progress there has been toward racial and gender equality in the last thirty years owes much to the research of social and physical scientists which has sustained a vigorous and effective attack on the structures of inequality and the cultural stereotypes and mythology that underlie prejudice and discrimination. From the sociologists whose findings were instrumental in the landmark 1954 Supreme Court school desegregation decision to the scientists who have demonstrated that racial and gender differences have far more to do with social than biological factors, scientists have played a key role in the pursuit of social justice (see Katz and Taylor 1988).

Whether we use the conflict or the functional perspective, it is clear that the effects of science and technology on social life are increasingly pervasive and complex. Nowhere is this more visible than in the area of medical institutions and health care.

MEDICAL INSTITUTIONS

Human life is inherently frail—from the inevitability of dying to the ease with which new microorganisms, such as the AIDS virus, can devastate us. Beyond their effect on individuals, death and disease have profound social effects on everything from families to societies. In the fourteenth century, the Black Death killed one-third of the entire population of Europe (Gottfried 1983); in 1918 a worldwide influenza epidemic took some 20 million lives; and as we approach a new century, the true destructive potential of the AIDS pandemic looms as a frightening unknown. In the face of our fundamental vulnerability, it is no surprise that every known society has developed social arrangements around the issue of health.

Like other institutions, **medicine** is defined by basic social functions. The first two are to maintain health by preventing illness and injury, and to restore health by healing injury and curing sickness. Third, medicine often performs a social control function, by defining the difference between sanity and insanity, by certifying births and deaths, or by certifying that people's state of health relieves them of their role obligations. Fourth, medicine is responsible for maintaining a society's store of knowledge about health and illness. In societies with highly developed scientific institutions, medicine also performs a research function by continually challenging existing understandings of health and illness and searching for better ones.

Medicine has changed enormously over the last two or three thousand years, and perhaps the clearest way to see this is by looking at the cultural and structural characteristics that make up medical institutions.

The Culture of Medicine

At the heart of any medical institution is a belief and value system—what amounts to a paradigm (although not necessarily a scientific one)—that both defines and makes sense of health and illness. Each society has ways of identifying and explaining what is going on in a human body, distinguishes between what is considered healthy and what is considered pathological, and defines appropriate ways to maintain health and cure illness. In parts of nineteenth-century Europe, for example, open enjoyment of sexuality by women was taken as a sign of ill health, and some physicians went so far as to surgically remove the clitoris as a way to "cure" this "condition." Today, by comparison, it is considered unhealthy for women *not* to enjoy their sexuality.

The earliest known medical paradigm is traced to the Greek physician Hippocrates, who, some 2,500 years ago, developed the view that health and illness depend on the balance between different sorts of bodily fluids. The human body was likened to a furnace to which the lungs supply air and food supplies fuel. Hippocrates' approach was based on what amounted to the common sense of his culture, not on any scientifically verified knowledge of cause and effect.

This basic approach was influential throughout Europe for many centuries. As recently as the late eighteenth century in colonial America, typical treatments of disease included attempts to purify the body by drawing blood (a treatment that led to the death of George Washington, who had come down with nothing more than a bad cold); blistering (burning the skin in the belief that the resulting pus was a healthy vehicle for removing toxic substances); inducing massive vomiting or giving powerful laxatives; and prescribing medicines, some of which themselves contained potent poisons such as mercury.

It was not until the mid-1800s that Louis Pasteur discovered the causal connection between germs and disease and revolutionized beliefs about health and illness. Germ theory was an entirely new paradigm that explained a wealth of health problems such as the high mortality rate of mothers after childbirth (doctors often went from performing autopsies on corpses to delivering babies without washing their hands in between). Germ theory did more than revolutionize medical knowledge; it also was instrumental in making medicine a scientifically based profession of enormous power.

Sociologists draw a sharp distinction between the social and medical models of illness. According to the medical model, illness is an objective state of being—something goes wrong in the body and needs

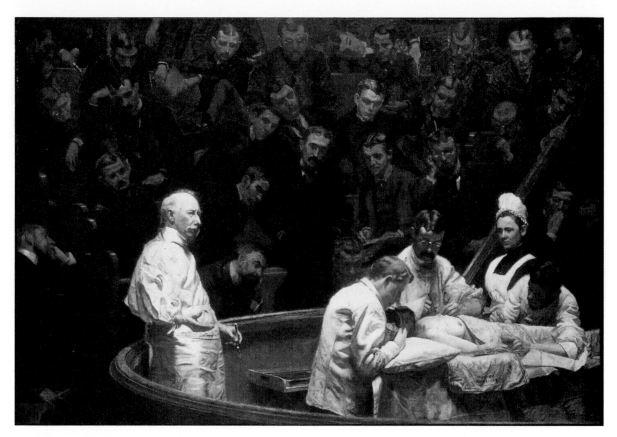

Hospitals were once very dangerous places, in large part because the importance of germs was not understood and surgery was typically carried out in highly unsanitary conditions (note the absence of gloves and masks as surgeons bend over and work on the open wound).

to be fixed through medical intervention. The social model, however, also considers that what may be defined as illness in one society may be looked upon as quite normal in another, and that social pressures and limitations can affect health. The American Psychiatric Association, for example, defined homosexuality as a mental illness until the 1970s when, partly in response to pressure from gay rights groups, it redefined homosexuality as nothing more than a nonpathological sexual preference.

Going in the opposite direction, what is initially defined as a nonmedical problem may come to be identified as an illness. Alcoholism and drug abuse, for example, have increasingly been defined less as moral failings than as treatable diseases. Alcoholism is an interesting case, for even if biological factors predispose some people to it, this is unlikely to be an explanation for differences in the rate of alcoholism among societies or subgroups within societies. To understand the causes of alcoholism, either in a spe-

cific individual or in society as a whole, it is necessary to pay attention not only to individual characteristics, but to the ways in which they interact with social environments. U.S. culture heavily promotes the use of alcohol, especially through advertising, and there are enormous pressures for people to drink at parties and other social occasions. A full understanding of something like alcoholism, then, depends on a combination of the medical and social models.

As with most social institutions, the culture of medicine varies not only historically, but from one society to another. Payer (1988) finds that in comparison with many Western European countries medical practice in the United States is considerably more aggressive and more likely to result in surgery or the use of antibiotics. She argues that this is due in part to the U.S. belief that the body is a machine that breaks down through the action of some external agent and, thus, requires fixing. By comparison,

Europeans are more likely to view illness as a result of weakened resistance which must then be reinforced through rest and other restorative therapies. In this sense, medical practice in the U.S. emphasizes the intervention—often dramatic—of physicians, resulting in some dramatic differences in the experience of patients. Some 20 percent of all children delivered in the U.S., for example, are delivered through caesarian section.

Values and Social Conflict   Because medicine deals with issues of life and death, values play a crucial role in medical practice and are often the source of deeply divisive social conflict. The central value of traditional medicine is to at least do no harm to patients if it is not possible to achieve the higher values of healing and curing. In the U.S., prevention and health maintenance generally have lower value since physicians tend to be more interested in helping those who are already in ill health, but this is not true of many alternative approaches to medicine such as holistic medicine (which emphasizes the importance of proper diet) (see Gevitz 1988).

The vital role played by physicians in life and death decisions often places them at the center of difficult moral dilemmas and bitter social conflicts. Is it preferable to live a long life plagued by chronic pain and dependence on machines or to live a shorter life with less pain and greater independence? Is it more important to save the life of an expectant mother or the life of her unborn child? Should badly deformed newborns or terminally ill patients be allowed to die? Should doctors and nurses have the right to refuse to treat patients who have dangerous infectious diseases such as AIDS? Should doctors have the right to force a pregnant woman to undergo surgery in order to ensure the safe delivery of her child even though she forbids it? Does the state have the right to participate in the relationship between doctors and their patients by forbidding abortion?

Given the close relationship between the growth of medicine and the growth of science and technology, it is not surprising that many of the moral dilemmas centering on health and illness are closely connected to technological innovations. The ability to detect birth defects in unborn children through the use of sound waves confronts parents and doctors with the option of aborting a badly deformed fetus, a choice that simply did not exist before technology made such knowledge of the fetus available. Technology that enables doctors to keep patients alive long after they would otherwise have been left to die raises profound questions about the meaning of life and death (when is someone dead?) and equally profound dilemmas for doctors and family members who must decide whether to terminate artificial life support. Similarly, the technological ability to transplant organs from one body to another can create pressures to give up on one patient perhaps prematurely in the rush to secure organs for donation to another. All of these and scores of other moral dilemmas simply would not occur without the appropriate technology.

As we would expect with values, there are no simple answers to these dilemmas, and yet they occur every day. Physicians, patients, family members, judges, and hospital administrators must decide one way or another. To solve many of them, physicians rely on the guidelines established by their profession, which raises the question of how medical institutions are structured.

The Structure of Medicine

On the simplest level, the structure of medical institutions revolves around the role relationship between patients and healers. The sick role defines what is expected of people who are identified as ill, including the requirement to do whatever they can to get well and resume their usual role obligations (see Parsons 1951; B. S. Turner 1987). Physicians are bound by norms such as the expectation that they will keep confidential whatever their patients reveal to them.

The explosive growth and increasing complexity of science and technology over the past century have gone hand-in-hand with similar changes in the structure of medicine. Gone is the simple relationship between doctor and patient, for the role set of the typical physician now includes not only patients, but complex bureaucracies such as hospitals, insurance companies, state licensing boards, and professional organizations that set standards and discipline their members. In many states, physicians are moving away from private practice and becoming employees of health care corporations known as Health Maintenance Organizations (or HMOs, for short).

Like science, the role structure of medicine includes an expanding number of specialties in which doctors concentrate not only on particular parts of the body (such as eyes, ears, nose, and throat), but on particular treatments (such as surgery or anesthe-

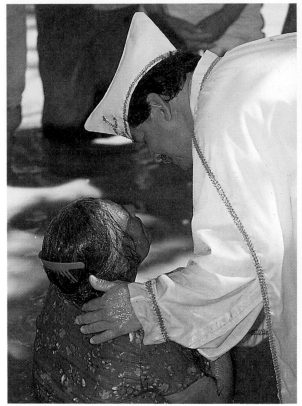

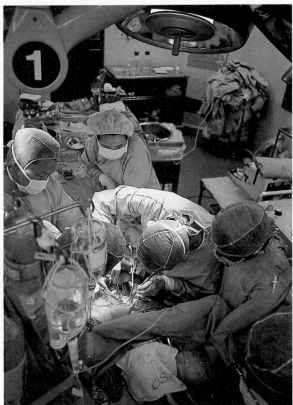

As a social activity, healing involves a variety of relationships, from faith healers and their followers, as shown here in Mexico, to doctors and patients in hospitals.

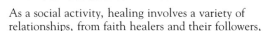

siology) or diseases (such as cancer) (see Cockerham 1986; Kurtz and Chalfant 1984). The most profound structural changes in medicine, however, involve the distribution of power and authority, both within the practice of medicine and in the relation of medical institutions to society as a whole.

Power and Authority From the perspective of the medical profession, one of the unanticipated effects of the development of germ theory and the emergence of scientific medicine is that physicians greatly increased their practical ability to cure and heal, to some degree by enabling them simply to avoid actually doing harm to their patients. Prior to the discovery of germs, hospitals were dangerous places that all but the poorest patients avoided (middle- and upper-class patients preferred to be treated at home). It was only when hospitals were perceived as doing more good than harm that they became popular, and this was due largely to an understanding of the role of germs in disease and death (see Rosenberg 1987).

In an important sense, the perception that doctors really knew what they were doing had an enormous impact on their authority over health care. Medicine rapidly became a highly skilled profession requiring rigorous training and certification, and granting its members almost complete autonomy, the highest level of prestige accorded any occupation, and a monopoly over what was accepted as valid knowledge and practice about health and illness (see Starr 1982). In 1846 physicians formed the American Medical Association (AMA) and soon persuaded state legislatures to grant them a legal monopoly over health care. Alternatives such as chiropractic medicine were denied legal standing, and midwives—who once delivered most babies—were gradually excluded from obstetrics (see Ehrenreich and English 1979; Sullivan and Weitz 1988). So deliberate and persistent were the efforts of the AMA

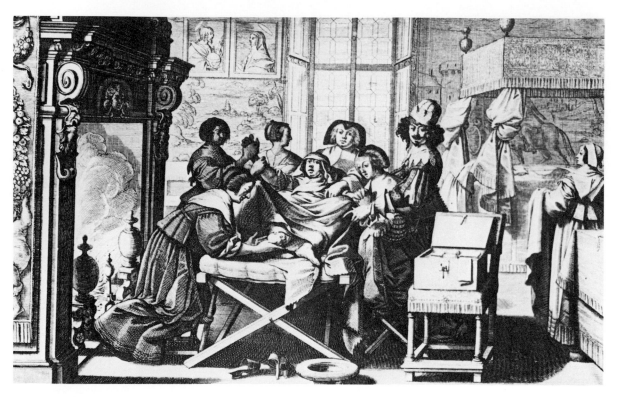

For most of history, child delivery has been exclusively in the hands of midwives. In this seventeenth-century engraving, midwives are shown with a special delivery table and obstetrical instruments. After more than a century of suppression by the medical profession, midwives are now making a comeback in many parts of the U.S.

to discredit chiropractors, that in 1987 a federal court found the AMA guilty of "systematic, long-term wrongdoing with the intent to destroy a licensed profession" (*New York Times*, August 31, 1987).

Today, gender continues to affect the authority structure of medicine as nurse-practitioners (most of whom are women) take over many of the functions traditionally performed by physicians, such as routine physical exams. Although many doctors resist such changes on the grounds that it lowers the quality of patient care, there are clearly other issues involved including a desire by physicians to maintain professional boundaries and the rewards and privileges that come with them.

Although medicine is still the most powerful and prestigious of all professions, recently many physicians have felt threatened as they have found themselves working as employees of large health maintenance organizations. Many physicians who work for HMOs believe their independence and autonomy to make medical judgments are being interfered with by corporations whose primary interest is in making a profit from medical care. In some cases—such as in Minneapolis—physicians have talked seriously of forming a union (*New York Times*, July 13, 1987). This is a dilemma similar to that faced by scientists, for science and medicine have become so dependent on expensive technology that it is difficult to practice either without accepting some measure of dependency on large organizations. The consequences of this include not only threats to the standing of individual doctors and the authority and autonomy of medicine as a profession, but also the people and society served by medical institutions (Hillman 1987).

Medicine and Society: A Functional Approach

From a functional perspective, one of the most dramatic changes that has occurred over the last century has been in the **medicalization** of industrial societies, a process through which medicine and the medical model have come to play a role in areas of life not usually associated with health and illness (see B. Turner 1987). This is seen most simply in the sheer growth of health care in industrialized societies. In 1940, total national expenditures for health care in the U.S. amounted to 4 percent of the gross national product (GNP—the value of all goods and services produced in that year). By 1987, however, the percentage of the GNP going to health care had tripled to 11 percent, or $1,987 for every woman, man, and child (USCB 1975; DHHS 1990). Even after taking inflation and the growth of the population into account, we spent almost eight times as much on health care in 1987 as in 1940 (Figure 18-2).

The medicalization of society also occurs through the growing influence of physicians and the medical perspective in many areas of life. The simple act of giving birth has been transformed from an event that rarely involved doctors and took place in the home to a highly medicalized procedure taking place in hospitals under the control of physicians. In an increasing number of cases, doctors, with authority granted them by the courts, have claimed the right to force expectant mothers to undergo surgery when they believe it is in the best interests of the fetus, even when the mother is opposed to it.

Many other life events have come to be viewed in medical terms, including hyperactivity in children, child and sexual abuse, alcoholism, drug abuse, obesity, mental disorders such as schizophrenia, insomnia, depression, and eating disorders such as anorexia (Brumberg 1988). In some cases the medical perspective plays a part in social control by redefining deviant behavior, such as by defining alcoholism and drug abuse not as moral failings but as diseases whose victims deserve help rather than blame and punishment. In criminal trials, the role played by psychiatrists in determining whether defendants are legally insane and therefore not legally responsible for their behavior has become increasingly controversial, especially since John Hinckley used the insanity defense to successfully avoid punishment for his attempted assassination of President Ronald Reagan in 1981.

As powerful as the medical profession is, public acceptance of its authority is far from absolute. Many argue against the use of psychiatry in courtrooms on the grounds that psychiatrists cannot accurately determine the state of mind of a defendant at the time a crime is committed and that the medicalization of crime is used inappropriately to relieve people of re-

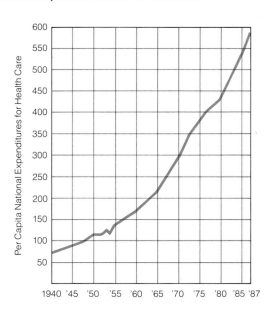

FIGURE 18-2   Trends in Per Capita National Expenditures for Health Care, in Constant (1967) Dollars, U.S.
Source: Computed from USCB 1975, 1986a; DHHS 1990.

sponsibility for their actions. In the health care system, patients have begun to organize and assert their rights in relation to physicians, from demanding access to their records and full disclosure of their medical conditions to resisting the authority of physicians to force unwanted surgery on them. Many doctors feel overwhelmed by the threat of malpractice suits and soaring malpractice insurance premiums, sometimes to the extent of refusing to treat patients with a history of suing their doctors, or of leaving medical specialties that involve risky treatments. These and other problems have resulted in a steady loss of morale among U.S. physicians. Recent studies find, for example, that 63 percent of physicians report declining control over the treatment of their patients and 39 percent say they would probably not become physicians if they could choose again (AMA 1990; see also Ritzer and Walczak 1988).

A Conflict Approach to Medicine

Health care is a product of social systems, and as with most valued products, access to it is often distributed unevenly. As we saw in Chapter 4, although Great Britain, Canada, and most of Europe have national health insurance plans that guarantee equal

ONE STEP FURTHER 18-1

Why Do So Many Babies Die in the U.S.?

In spite of the wealth and technological sophistication of the U.S., infants are more likely to die here than in almost any other industrial nation. Why? Part of the answer lies with our relatively large poor population, the inadequate prenatal health care they receive, and an unusually large rate of teenage pregnancy (also one of the highest among industrialized nations). Poor nutrition and the lack of good prenatal medical care are major causes of infant death. In addition, infants born to teenage mothers tend to be of low birth weight, which also makes infants vulnerable.

If you look at the percentages in the columns in Table B-18-1, you can see how the combination of these factors makes the health of expectant mothers and their babies especially vulnerable among blacks, who are far more likely than whites to be poor. In 1984, black babies were more than twice as likely as whites to be born to teenage mothers (24 percent vs. 11 percent) and 10 times more likely to be born to mothers under the age of 15 (1 percent vs. .1 percent). Black mothers were considerably less likely to begin prenatal care early (62 percent vs. 80 percent) and twice as likely to get little or no prenatal care at all (10 percent vs. 5 percent). As a result of these and other factors, black babies are twice as likely to have a low weight at birth (12 percent vs. 6 percent) and, as the infant mortality rates at the bottom show, twice as likely to die before their first birthday.

TABLE B-18-1

PERCENT OF ALL	WHITES	BLACKS
Births, 1984	80	16
Births to teenage mothers	11	24
Births to mothers under age 15	0.1	1
Births of babies with low birth weight	6	12
Babies born to mothers who began prenatal care in first three months of pregnancy	80	62
Babies born to mothers who began prenatal care in the last three months of pregnancy or not at all	5	10
Infant mortality rate	9	18

Source: National Center for Health Statistics, in the *New York Times*, June 26, 1987, p. A20.

access to health care, the United States is the only industrial country in which health care is marketed as a commodity whose availability depends on the ability to pay. A major consequence of this is that class position has a strong effect on health care, health, and, ultimately, mortality (NCHS 1990a). Blacks, native Americans, and the poor have poorer health than whites and the middle and upper classes. Infant mortality is considerably higher among blacks, largely because of poor prenatal care (see One Step Further 18-1) (see Farley and Allen 1987).

Similar inequalities exist among nations. The extreme poverty of much of the world's population, coupled with the inadequate distribution of readily available vaccines and other treatments, results in millions of premature deaths. An estimated 14.6 million children under the age of 5 die each year, more than half from diseases such as measles and tuberculosis that are relatively simple and inexpensive to prevent or cure. The poorest countries spend only $5 per person on health care, compared with $460 per person in Western Europe and almost $2,000 per person in the United States (WHO 1990).

The conflict approach reveals not only unequal access to medical care, but unequal treatment by medical institutions for those who seek care and the use of medical authority and expertise as a tool in social oppression. Involuntary surgery, for example, is far more likely to be forced on blacks and women—especially if they are poor—than on whites and others higher in the class system. One study found that elderly women are less likely than younger women to receive appropriate treatment for breast cancer even when they are otherwise in excellent health, a finding that may reflect discrimination based on both gender and age (Greenfield et al. 1987). Another study found that hospital patients who lack medical insurance not only enter hospitals in worse condition, but are several times more likely to die than are insured patients even when their initial conditions are similar. One of the reasons is that doctors are reluctant to order optional or expensive procedures for patients who cannot pay (Hadley 1991).

In authoritarian societies, such as the Soviet Union and, until recently, Argentina, medicine is often used as a means for controlling political dissidents, who may be diagnosed as schizophrenics and committed to mental hospitals as a form of punishment. Physicians in some countries have also lent their medical knowledge to the torture and abuse of political prisoners (Stover and Nightingale 1985).

This kind of abuse has a considerable history, especially when used to justify social oppression. In the pre-Civil War American South, for example, the authority of medical diagnosis was used to support the ownership and oppression of slaves. Blacks, it was believed, suffered from a condition known as drapetomania, which means "an insane desire to run away" (Proctor 1988). In perhaps no society did the medicalization of abuse and oppression reach the heights found in Nazi Germany. Under the guise of "racial hygiene" and medical research, physicians played a key role in the torture, abuse, and forced sterilization of hundreds of thousands, if not millions, of people (Lifton 1986; Proctor 1988).

Science, Technology, Medicine, and Social Change: The Social Effects of Longer Lives

As we have seen, science and technology are, by their very nature, sources of social change. This is particularly true of the ways in which they combine to produce dramatic changes in the structures of social systems.

Consider, for example, the simple fact that scientific findings on everything from germ theory to the causes of heart disease, combined with medical technology—such as the ability to maintain clean drinking water supplies or perform open heart surgery or organ transplants—have greatly increased human longevity, especially in industrial societies. In the nineteenth century, only two-thirds of all children ever became adults compared with 98 percent today. In the 1990s centenarians—those 100 years or older—are our fastest growing age group (USCB 1975, 1987i, 1990a).

The social consequences of the simple extension of the human life span are far-reaching and complex (see Riley 1987). As the population ages, there is a strain to shift resources from the needs of the young to those of the elderly, and this can cause friction between generations. Retirement—once a rarity—becomes commonplace and occupies up to a quarter of the life course. Perhaps most dramatic are the effects on family relationships, for they are the only ties that last a lifetime. Instead of having one parent die early in a child's adulthood (as was common less than a century ago), most children today can expect to have living parents long into their own old age. This not only makes the goal of having marriages last "till death do us part" more difficult, but raises challenges for changing relationships between children and parents. Longer life for our parents means many years of working out relationships as relative equals or, if parents become disabled late in their lives, as their caretakers as the direction of the dependency is reversed.

Greater longevity also changes family structures by making them more complex. A century ago less than half of middle-aged married couples in the U.S. had any surviving parents; but today half have two or more parents living (Uhlenberg 1980). One result is typical families whose living kin include at least four intact generations. When we combine this with high divorce and remarriage rates, the staggering complexity of kinship and step-kinship ties raises enormous challenges for family life. As Riley (1987) put it, "a new system of kinship is in the making" (p. 8).

Finally, as life is extended, often by technological means, the process of dying is itself being transformed (Riley 1983). A century ago most people died outside of hospitals, many of them at home. By comparison, in the late twentieth century most elderly people die in institutions—hospitals, hospices, or nursing homes—that, by comparison, confine death to sterile, medical settings devoid of familiar surroundings and dominated by a view that death is primarily a medical event. This not only changes the experience of dying but greatly increases the financial costs of caring for chronically ill patients, costs that are expected to increase dramatically over the next half century.

The technological ability to keep elderly people alive has also been linked to dramatic increases in suicide rates among the elderly during the 1980s. Several studies suggest that these trends are due to a combination of factors, including the simple desire to stop enduring continuing losses of friends, meaningful roles, and health as well as the enormous financial burden that life-prolonging medical technology places on families (AARP 1989a; McIntosh and Osgood 1989).

As with other changes associated with science and technology, none of these is inevitable, for they all depend on choices about how to use the knowledge and capabilities it makes possible. The enormous potential benefits as well as the dangers that go along with such choices guarantee that science, technology, and medicine will continue to confront societies with deep value conflicts and disturbing moral dilemmas. What they cannot provide, however, is a resolution of those conflicts or a way out of those dilemmas. For these we must look elsewhere in the institutional structure of societies.

SUMMARY

1. In its dedication to seeking new knowledge and testing old assumptions, science is unique among social institutions.

2. By providing assumptions and beliefs about the world, paradigms form the cultural core of science and are the most resistant to change. When the practice of normal science generates enough anomalies that do not fit prevailing paradigms, the result is a scientific revolution in which new paradigms replace the old. The functional, conflict, and interactionist perspectives are examples of three major paradigms in sociology.

3. It is important to be aware of the ways in which nonscientific values affect scientific work, especially those that guide the choice of research problems that can have important social implications.

4. Scientific work is guided by the norms of universalism, communism, disinterestedness, and organized skepticism. Deviance from scientific norms, especially in the form of fraud, is often caused by the same factors that explain deviance in other areas of social life, such as pressures to succeed without access to the means to succeed.

5. Historically, science has been transformed from a pastime engaged in primarily by well-to-do individuals to a highly skilled profession that carefully maintains its boundaries and its control over the determination of truth. At the same time, the structure of science has become far more complex as it has been taken over by large institutions and scientists have increasingly specialized their interests.

6. The institutionalization of science has greatly diminished the autonomy of scientists; but this is to some degree balanced by the fact that the reward scientists want most is the recognition of other scientists.

7. The relationship between technology and science is complex and often, although not always, reciprocal. Breakthroughs in each area are often made independently. The impact of technology on social life has accelerated greatly as technology has become increasingly sophisticated, complex, and tightly coupled.

8. The functional and conflict perspectives reveal important aspects not only of the workings of science itself, but of the effects of science and technology on society and social inequality. Most of these effects are due not to science and technology per se, but to the ways in which they are used in other institutional settings.

9. As an institution, medicine is defined by its social functions, which include prevention and healing, social control, maintaining the store of knowledge about health and illness, and, in some societies, by conducting medical research.

10. The culture of medicine rests on a medical model of health and illness which defines human conditions in terms of bodily functions that can be improved through medical intervention. This contrasts with the social model that also pays attention to the use of culture to define the difference between health and illness.

11. As with science, the structure of medicine has grown increasingly professionalized and complex, and the authority for medical decisions has begun to shift from individuals to large bureaucratic organizations. From a functional perspective, medicine has assumed increasing social importance, most notably in the medicalization of many aspects of social life.

12. Medicine also plays a part in social inequality. This is seen in inequality within the medical profession, unequal access to medical care, and inequalities in the ways in which patients are treated depending on their social statuses.

13. The far-reaching and complex social effects of science, technology, and medicine are illustrated by advances in human longevity, which have affected everything from schooling and the structure of marriage and the family to retirement and the meaning of death.

KEY TERMS

anomaly   445
medicalization   462
medicine   458
norm of communism   448

norm of disinterestedness   448
norm of organized skepticism   448
norm of universalism   448
paradigm   445

science   443
scientific revolution   445
technocracy   456

LOOKING ELSEWHERE

Having studied Chapter 18, you might want to look at related discussions in *Human Arrangements*, which include

- the use of scientific methods in sociological research (Chapter 6, pp. 111–13)
- the socialization of physicians (Chapter 7, p. 154)
- professions as occupations (Chapter 19, pp. 484–86)
- doctor-patient role relationships (Chapter 3, pp. 47–48, 50, 52)
- when doctors lie to dying patients (Chapter 15, p. 377)
- the hospice as a place to die (Chapter 15, p. 377)
- epidemiology—the study of how disease is distributed in populations (Chapter 4, pp. 71–73)

- technology and human ecology (Chapter 4, pp. 82–85)
- technology and social change (Chapter 23, pp. 576–78)
- technology and family life (Chapter 16, pp. 398–99)
- technology, automation, and work (Chapter 19, pp. 478–79)
- religion, science, and sociology (Chapter 21, pp. 540–41, 531–32)
- technology and varieties of religious belief (Chapter 21, pp. 541–43)

RECOMMENDED READINGS

Barnes, B. 1985. *About science.* New York: Basil Blackwell. A brief, clearly written, and provocative look at the problems confronting science as a social institution.

Fausto-Sterling, A. 1985. *Myths of gender: Biological theories about women and men.* New York: Basic Books. A biologist critically examines the uses and misuses of biological science in trying to understand gender differences.

Harrison, M. 1982. *A woman in residence: A doctor's personal and professional battles against an insensitive medical system.* New York: Penguin Books. A daily journal provides an inside look at the need for reform of the medical profession and what it will take to bring it about.

Katz, P. A., and Taylor, D. A. 1988. *Eliminating racism: Profiles in controversy.* New York: Plenum. A provocative set of essays that explore the role of the social sciences in the struggle against racism and segregation in the United States.

Kuhn, T. S. 1970. *The structure of scientific revolutions.* One of the most influential books ever written about the process through which scientific thought develops and changes.

Latour, B. 1987. *Science in action: How to follow scientists and engineers through society.* Cambridge, MA: Harvard University Press. A controversial look at the social production of scientific knowledge, including a challenging critique of the basic assumptions of both sociology and the sociology of science.

Merton, R. K. 1973. *The sociology of science.* Chicago: University of Chicago Press. A classic collection of articles by the leading figure in the sociology of science.

Perrow, C. 1984. *Normal accidents.* New York: Basic Books. A fascinating sociological analysis of the unavoidable risks inherent in the structure of technological systems such as nuclear power and air travel.

Starr, P. 1982. *The social transformation of American medicine.* New York: Basic Books. A Pulitzer prize went to this sociological analysis of the history of medicine in the United States. It is essential reading for anyone interested in the sociology of medicine.

Turner, B. S. 1987. *Medical power and social knowledge.* Beverly Hills, CA: Sage. A first-rate comprehensive introduction to the sociology of medicine.

19

ECONOMIC ARRANGEMENTS

 Stop for a moment and look at the characteristics of this book as an object: the print, pictures, cover, binding, use of color, and strings of words that communicate ideas. Now think about two questions: What did it take to bring this book into being, and how did it wind up in your hands?

In the simplest sense, this book has both material and nonmaterial origins: lumber and paper mills, photographic equipment, typewriters, word processors, artists' pens and brushes, typesetting machines, printing presses and ink, glue and binding machines, and the skill and knowledge of many people. In order to get to you, it had to be packed, shipped to a store, and then given to you in exchange for money. This book is also the result of energy—from electricity to human labor. Together, these constitute what Marx called the **forces of production**. As we saw in Chapter 12, one of the most important aspects of the forces of production are the *means of production*—the factories, machines, tools, and equipment used to transform raw materials into manufactured goods.

All this, however, is not the whole story of where this book came from, for the means of production were used by people who worked in relation to one another and to the means of production. The author, editors, administrators and managers, sociologists, clerks, secretaries, artists, designers, photographers, typesetters, bookbinders, market researchers, salespeople, bookstore owners—all these and many more participated in a set of social **relations of production** through which this book and thousands like it are produced and distributed. Together, the forces of production and the relations of production constitute the **mode of production** (see Edwards, Reich, and Weisskopf 1986).

Economic institutions are enduring sets of cultural ideas and social relationships through which goods and services are produced and distributed in societies. Cultural characteristics of economic institutions include values that define the goals of productive activity (to feed people, to make a profit, or both?). Structural characteristics of economic institutions refer to how people work in relation with one another and to the means of production: who owns and controls the means of production, who decides what will be produced and how, who controls what is done with the results, and the kinds of roles people play in the production process.

I, for example, work under contract with my publisher. I agree to produce a manuscript by a certain date, in return for which I am paid a share of the returns from selling the book. I work in my house and use a word processor that I own. No one checks to see if I am at work this morning. So long as I get the job done on time, *I* decide how and when I work.

Most of the others who helped produce this book, however (like most people in our society), work for employers who buy their time for wages and decide what they will do with that time. These employees do not get a percentage of the proceeds from selling what their labor power helps to produce; they do not decide how and when they will work; and, most important, they do not own any means of producing goods or services.

The characteristics of economic institutions determine how societies produce goods and services and how individuals participate in the production process. One way to see how economic institutions affect societies and their people is to look at how those institutions have changed over the course of history. Imagine that we can condense 35,000 years into a single life span, so that each of us can experience the changes that have occurred. Where do we begin, where do we end up, and how do we get from there to here? As you read the following sections, notice how the development of capitalism involves changes touching on every major aspect of the sociological perspective—the cultural, structural, population, and ecological aspects of social systems.

THE ROOTS OF CAPITALISM

We begin with small tribal societies whose members survive by gathering plants and hunting wild game. There are neighboring societies some distance away;

but we rarely encounter them except on long hunting expeditions, and generally have little to do with them. Virtually everyone except the smallest child produces something; we share what we produce with everyone else, for kinship is the most important tie that binds us together into a single society. Our division of labor is simple and based entirely on age and gender. Although each of us contributes to production in different ways, no one's contribution is valued so highly that it gives him or her a great advantage of prestige or power (see Lenski and Lenski 1987).

We consume everything that we produce, which means that the value of everything from meat to clothing is based solely on its **use value**. Control of the means of production is *collective*, and our economy is *communal*, much like that of the Melanesian tribes that Malinowski (1922) studied in the 1920s. We help one another as friends and family members—

The seemingly simple shift from producing food, such as tomatoes and peppers, for the purpose of eating to producing in order to buy and sell in markets, such as this one in Nigeria, brings with it a profound shift in economic and other values.

not for personal gain, but because we feel a social obligation to cooperate with and help one another.

Thousands of years pass (until roughly 7000 B.C.), and we discover how to grow food. We invent simple tools, and as our technology grows—especially with the invention of the plow—we are able to produce more than we need to survive. Our population grows because we can feed more people; but, most important, our ability to produce a surplus affects both the structure of our society and its relation to others.

Everyone no longer must produce food. Some can make clay pots, mats to sleep on, or fancy clothes to wear during celebrations. Whereas we once produced things only for their use value, we can now trade some of what we produce for goods that we do not make ourselves. We can trade some of our fancy clothes for things produced in other societies: arrows or medicinal herbs. Even food—if we produce a surplus—takes on **exchange value** in addition to use value.

When goods have exchange value, they are **commodities**. For the first time, we trade with each other—commodity for commodity—and our economy becomes a **market economy** in which the exchange value of goods determines what can be traded for what. I make fancy clothes but I do not grow food; you grow food but do not make fancy clothes; so we trade one for the other. This means that we have to deal continually with the problem of deciding what amount of clothing is worth what amount of food. The basic mechanism in bartering is the balance between how much labor it takes to make clothing and food and how much each of us wants or needs what the other produces.

As the number of different goods and services grows, we discover that bartering is a very inefficient way of getting what we need and want. Once you have all the clothes you want, or if you think the clothes I make are ugly, how do I get food from you? How, in short, can I get something that you produce when you do not want what I produce? The answer that developed around 2000 B.C. was money, and it profoundly affected market relationships (see Simmel [1907] 1978).

As a cultural yardstick for measuring wealth, money has taken many forms, including shells, furs, salt, cotton cloth, copper bracelets, bits of coral, dried fish, tobacco, sugar, cocoa, rice, and bitter almonds as well as precious metals such as gold and silver and, more recently, paper (Braudel 1981). Money is useful because it makes trading easier. Instead of trading commodities for commodities, we now use money. I trade my clothes for money and then trade my money for food. Exchanges now take the form of commodity-money-commodity, rather than the simpler form of commodity-commodity.

Although many aspects of our society—such as family life—do not operate like a market, a market economy significantly changes the culture and structure of our society. Getting a fair (if not the best) deal replaces sharing as our most important economic value, and the means of production are no longer collectively owned. Each of us owns and controls some means of production and uses it and what it produces to get what we need and want through market exchanges.

Feudalism: A Shift in Power

As the centuries pass (we are up to the early Middle Ages), populations grow more rapidly, divisions of labor are more complex, trade expands rapidly, and money is increasingly important as a medium of exchange. All of this supports an elite of nobles, kings, and queens, who maintain their positions by accumulating wealth in the form of money and land. The most significant aspect of this society, however, lies in the social relationships between producers and the elite.

The power of the nobility is based primarily on their military training and resources, and they use this power to both dominate the peasants who live in their feudal domains and to sustain their own privileges. The relationship between nobles and peasants is more complex than this, however, for in exchange for protection from *other* powerful nobles, peasants give some of what they produce to their nobles. Although peasants are bound to the land and live generally miserable lives, both they and free workers control the means of production. They use land or tools and decide how much to produce. Unlike slaves, then, feudal peasants control their own labor.

They, are not, however, allowed to dispose of what they produce as they choose. Even independent producers are regulated by craft guilds whose norms specify where and when they work, and what and how much they produce. Clearly, this new system—called **feudalism**—marks the beginning of a transformation that ultimately will affect almost every aspect of social life: *the control over the production process is shifting out of the hands of those who actually produce goods.*

Merchants, such as this man in his London office in 1532, were the prime movers in the breakdown of feudalism and the elevation of profit and control over markets and labor to the highest levels of economic value.

Buying, Selling, and the Rise of the Merchant Class

Around the eleventh century, towns develop outside the walls of feudal estates, and after some struggle people begin to free themselves from the dominance of the nobility. Producers can now produce what they want, make the best trades they can, and accumulate a surplus.

At about this time some of the more prosperous residents of towns make a discovery that will dramatically affect the development of societies: since economic exchange primarily involves money, why not use money to buy commodities and then sell them for still more money? These innovators—**merchants**—withdraw from the production process and make a radical transition from a commodity-money-commodity exchange to one that is money-commodity-money.

The new exchange is revolutionary because it changes the values that govern economic behavior. The purpose of exchange had been to get what we did not produce ourselves; and we were content to wind up with something whose value was comparable to what we gave. Merchants, however, want to end up with more money than they start with.

The early capitalists profit primarily through the use of trade. They buy commodities in one place and then take them to another market where the goods bring a higher price because, perhaps, they are not otherwise available there. Or they buy foodstuffs such as grains that store well and keep them until poor crops inflate the market price and then sell them at a profit.

As transportation improves and markets become more competitive, however, merchants cannot count on profiting from their ability to control or manipulate markets alone and begin to extend their control to the actual process of production. They do this not by producing goods themselves, but through a radically different social relationship with those who do. In this arrangement—which is at the heart of modern advanced capitalism—merchants profit by taking a share of what is produced through the labor of others by paying producers less than the value of their labor and keeping what is left over. "What is left over" is called **surplus value**, and it is created by the relationships among workers, means of production, and capitalists (Marx 1867; see also Braverman 1974). For the system to operate, workers must receive enough of the value of what they produce to maintain a standard of living that allows them to work (to buy enough food, shelter, clothing, and medical care to remain productive) and raise children who will become new workers. The surplus value consists of what is left over after taking out what is needed to maintain and reproduce workers.

It is important to understand that while surplus value is a form of profit, not all profit takes the form of surplus value. When merchants buy goods in one place and sell them in another for more than their cost, they make a profit; but this is not surplus value, because the merchants do not own the means of production used by workers to make the goods they buy and sell. Surplus value refers *only* to profit made by capitalists through their control over the means of production and, therefore, over workers.

Merchants increase profits by maximizing the difference between the value of goods and what it costs to produce that value—that is, by maximizing surplus value. Those who produce goods, however, can refuse to sell them to merchants if the offered price is too low, and consumers can refuse to buy if the price is too high. How, then, can merchants maximize their profits?

One answer is to increase control over those who produce goods and over the markets in which goods are sold—in other words, to change the structure of economic institutions. Before we see how this is accomplished, we have to understand the cultural and structural characteristics of *capitalism*—the economic arrangement toward which these changes are moving us.

Capitalism as an Economic Arrangement

As Adam Smith outlined in his influential book, *The Wealth of Nations* (1776), the values that underlie capitalism are those of private property, profit, rational self-interest, and free competition. The idea of private property does not refer to personal items such as clothing, but to the means of production. **Capitalism** is an economic system in which the means of production are not simply owned privately, but are *owned by people who pay someone else wages to use them to produce wealth*. When a means of production such as a machine is privately owned and used by others in exchange for wages, it is known as **capital**. In this sense, a woman who works for herself making pottery owns the means of production (wheels, clay-mixing machines, and kilns), but these are not capital because she does not pay someone else wages to produce pottery for her. If she hires a man to use her equipment to make pottery which she sells, however, then her equipment becomes capital and she becomes a capitalist (see Bottomore 1983). As we will see shortly, the full emergence of capitalism depends on the transformation of the means of production—once privately owned by the producers themselves—into capital.

Capitalism values most highly the capitalist's self-interest—not loyalty to community, society, or kin. Capitalists compete with other capitalists, and the one who buys commodities at the cheapest cost and sells them at the highest price will be the most successful. The growth of capitalism is facilitated in the sixteenth century when John Calvin founds the Calvinist religious sect. In his classic book, *The Protestant Ethic and the Spirit of Capitalism*, Max Weber argued that Calvinist religious doctrine and practices created conditions that contributed to the rise of capitalism as an economic system. Calvinists believe that work is a "calling" done in the service of God, and that living in luxury is a sin. They also believe that whether people will go to heaven or to hell is decided at the moment of birth. Understandably, this creates a lot of anxiety since those who are to go to heaven do not know it and those who are condemned to hell can do nothing about it. In the face of this, it makes sense that people look for some sign of their eventual fate, something that indicates that they are among the select few who will go to heaven.

Given their beliefs about work and the importance of setting aside their wealth, it also makes sense that they interpret financial success as just such a sign. In the seventeenth century, Calvinism takes root in England and Scotland, and the accumulation of wealth becomes not only respectable, but almost a moral imperative. Members of the aristocracy, of course, were wealthy long before the seventeenth century, but Calvinism encourages them to accumulate wealth rather than use it to live luxuriously. Since capital is relatively expensive, a religious doctrine that encourages the accumulation of wealth was, Weber argued, an important cultural ingredient in the emergence of capitalism.

The rise of capitalism and the form it eventually acquires depends on far more than values and beliefs about work and wealth. In the 300 years after Calvin, technological revolutions and structural change will affect the relations of production and produce modern capitalism (see Kriedte 1984; Lachmann 1989). This brings us back to the basic problem of merchants and capitalists: how to control the cost of goods in order to maximize surplus value.

The Transformation of Labor

As goods increasingly are valued for exchange, landowners begin to use land in ways that radically alter social relationships. In feudal societies the ownership of land is the basis of power for the aristocracy: peasants grow food on land owned by the nobility and give a share of what they produce to the lord in exchange for protection. Beginning in the sixteenth century, however, the demand for wool grows so large that landowners realize that they can do far better if they become capitalists and use their wealth to buy and use land to support sheep rather than to grow crops. Over a period of some 200 years, a great deal of agricultural land in England is enclosed and used entirely for sheepraising, and thousands of peasants become landless (Lazonick 1974).

During the same period the cultural value placed on the right to own private property and do as one pleases with it reaches new heights. The centuries-old relationship between serfs and the nobility begins to fall apart, producing thousands of landless peasants who, lacking a viable alternative, sell their labor power to capitalists in exchange for wages. It is here that capitalists try to solve their problem of competing with one another by minimizing the cost of producing goods.

Landless peasants no longer control their own labor and are forced to sell their labor power to capitalists for whatever price capitalists are willing to pay. In England, the percentage of peasants who work for wages rises dramatically—from 12 to 40 percent—between 1567 and 1640 (Lachmann 1987). Labor power emerges as a major new commodity: capitalists purchase it, put it to work in factories, and then sell what is produced. Unlike previous economic arrangements, this system allows people who sell their labor power to receive in return only a portion of the value of what they produce. When I sell chairs that I have made, I receive in return their full value, a value that is determined by the labor that went into them. If I sell my labor *power* to someone else, however, I receive less, because capitalists keep some of the value of what I produce—the surplus value—for themselves.

Capitalists increase their profits in four basic ways. First, they try to control the cost of production, which is facilitated by a growing class of landless peasants who have no choice but to work for someone since they no longer own or control any means of production. Capitalists are therefore in a position to exploit the landless peasants by paying them just enough to maintain and reproduce themselves. Costs of production can also be minimized by introducing new ways of using labor power—assembly lines, for instance—or by replacing people with machines. In both cases, costs are reduced by increasing efficiency of production, which has become one of capitalism's most important values.

Second, capitalists can try to increase sales—through advertising, for example, or finding new markets. Once they maximize the surplus value of each object they produce, they can then increase overall profits by selling as many of them as possible.

Third, capitalists can introduce new products that create new markets. Home video games and personal computers were virtually unheard of just fifteen years ago, for example, but opened up vast new markets for existing manufacturers and spawned a large number of new companies. To sell new products, however, capitalists must convince potential buyers to purchase them (something they failed at with home computers). As we will see later, advertising plays an important role in this by "manufacturing desire."

Fourth, they can increase profits by maximizing the price at which they sell finished goods, and one way to do this is to have a **monopoly**—in other words, to be the sole provider of a particular product. If everyone likes to drink tea, and I am the only one who imports tea from abroad, then you will either pay the price I ask or go without tea. This is, in fact, how some early English capitalists became rich—the king sold them monopolies over the tea trade.

Few sixteenth- and seventeenth-century English capitalists are able to buy monopolies from the king, and this means that the best way to increase profits is to exploit workers, and the control of labor power becomes one of the most important goals of capitalists. To compete with one another, capitalists must continually expand by making more and more profit and by acquiring still greater productive power. To expand, however, they must increase the surplus value of what their workers produce, and this means that they must give workers a shrinking share of what they make. Whereas expansion is the basic economic process through which capitalism develops, exploitation is the basic social process.

We are now up to the nineteenth century, and the Industrial Revolution is in full swing. Before looking at modern capitalist societies as well as some alternative economic arrangements, go through Table 19-1 carefully, for it summarizes the major changes we have just described. Notice how values and the social structures through which goods are produced and exchanged have changed. Values have shifted from use to exchange to surplus value. Social obligation, cooperation, and the importance of meeting social needs are giving way to rational self-interest, control over labor power, the ideal of free competi-

TABLE 19-1 Summary of Economic Transformations: From Communalism to Capitalism

CHARACTERISTIC	COMMUNAL ECONOMIES	FEUDAL ECONOMIES	CAPITALIST ECONOMIES
Dominant Economic Values	Obligation to kin Use value of goods Cooperation Tradition Community control Social needs	Obligation to nobility and kin Exchange value of goods Regulated competition Tradition Control over labor Maintaining nobility	Rational self-interest Surplus value (profit) Free competition (capitalists) Innovation Control over labor power Efficiency
Types of Exchange	Sharing	Commodity-commodity (early) Commodity-money-commodity (early) Money-commodity-money (later)	Money-commodity-money (capitalists) Commodity-money-commodity (workers)
What Is Exchanged?	Labor	Labor, goods, and money	Labor, labor power, goods, and money
Who Owns the Means of Production?	Collective	Individual producers	Capitalists
Who Controls How Goods Are Disposed Of?	Collective	Individual producers Nobles	Capitalists
Division of Labor	Simple ————————————→		Complex
Technology	Simple ————————————→		Sophisticated
Social Organization	Gemeinschaft Primary group ——————→		Gesellschaft Bureaucracy

tion, and efficiency in the name of greater profit and capitalist expansion. Although the types of exchange are similar in feudal and capitalist societies, *what* was exchanged changed dramatically when labor power became a commodity.

All of these changes were accompanied by rapid population growth, increasingly complex divisions of labor, and a shift in social organization from gemeinschaft to gesellschaft and from primary work groups to bureaucracies. Bureaucracy reinforces the separation of workers from the means of production, for it rests on such narrowly defined tasks and limited areas of responsibility that control over production is impossible for most workers; and in modern industrial societies, if people want to work, most must sooner or later find a place in formal organizations.

Before we examine twentieth-century advanced capitalist societies in some detail, it is important to raise some warning flags. The Industrial Revolution and the rise of capitalism were closely connected to each other. Like all social systems, capitalism has both desirable and undesirable consequences, but it is difficult to know whether these are due to capi-

talism or to industrialization. Some of the negative aspects of capitalist societies—such as the alienation of workers—may occur in any industrial society whether it is capitalist or not.

As you read about capitalist societies you may also be tempted to conclude that their problems are not shared by noncapitalist societies such as the Soviet Union and China; but this is far from the truth. As ideal types capitalism and socialism differ sharply from each other. In practice, however, countries that are called capitalist and those that are called socialist have many of the same problems; and although socialist societies have claimed to have corrected many of the negative aspects of capitalism, in many areas of social life the conditions have been far worse than under capitalism. Both kinds of societies, in short, have a long way to go before resembling their ideal.

Finally, the fact that socialist and capitalist countries share many common problems does not mean that the differences between them are merely theoretical. Workers in both types of societies have very little control over the economy; but the state has most of the power in socialist countries, whereas private individuals, groups, and organizations have most of the power in capitalist societies. The difference is a profound one, even though many of the consequences for workers are similar.

ADVANCED CAPITALISM: RELATIONS OF PRODUCTION

With the exception of the Soviet Union, the capitalist model guides the leading industrial societies of the world—Japan, the United States, West Germany, Great Britain, and France. What does capitalism look like in the twentieth century? How do capitalists pursue the goals of greater profit, efficiency, and control over labor power and markets? What does the division of labor look like, and how does it affect the perpetuation of capitalism and the positions of different social classes?

Distributions of Power

The ability of capitalists to compete with one another depends on two factors: control over labor power through which goods are produced and the control over markets in which they are sold. To protect themselves, workers resist the attempts of capitalists to extract surplus value from them, and this, in turn, creates social conflict.

Controlling Labor   When wage labor was first introduced in the sixteenth century, peasants in En-

PUZZLE

WHY NO REVOLUTION?

Karl Marx predicted revolutions in advanced industrial societies such as England and the United States, revolutions in which the working class would overthrow capitalism and install socialism. Obviously Marx's prediction has not yet come true. Why not?

The answer has to do with many social changes that Marx did not foresee, including the increasing power of the modern state and divisions within the working class, matters examined later in this chapter.

PUZZLE

WHY DO WORKERS FEEL POWERLESS?

In spite of the fact that labor unions are supposed to benefit workers, more than 80 percent of workers in the U.S. do not belong to one. Why not?

While part of the answer certainly has to do with the bad reputations of many unions, most of the answer has to do with the structure of the U.S. economy and job market and the relatively powerless position of most workers within it, as this chapter explains.

gland protested the exploited position they were being forced into, and the most radical among them believed that to be forced to work for wages was to lose their birthright as free English citizens. It was a losing battle, however, for they eventually realized that they had few viable alternatives to selling their labor power. Unlike feudal serfs, workers in capitalist societies are not obliged to work for anyone, but they are obliged to sell their labor power to *someone*; and this basic structural fact about capitalism explains most of the power difference between capitalists and workers.

Although workers in the U.S. no longer protest the selling of labor power, they do make an issue of the terms on which it is sold. In the late nineteenth and early twentieth centuries, they began to organize unions because they knew that employers were powerful primarily because they could replace dissatisfied workers with others who also had no choice but to sell their labor power wherever they could find a buyer for it. If all workers refused to work under certain conditions, however, they would then have far greater power.

Capitalists—often with the active help of courts, legislatures, and government troops—retaliated against the rising power of organized labor in ways that sometimes resulted in violence (see Painter 1987). Because they were willing to work for low wages, immigrants and blacks were often used to replace strikers. Unions were attacked directly through the use of spies, disruption of meetings, and bribery of public officials. Companies also used their considerable financial resources to mount massive propaganda campaigns in which union activists were portrayed as violent anarchists (see Boswell 1986; Griffin et al. 1986).

Since the beginning of the twentieth century, relations between capitalists and workers have lost most of their violent character; but control of labor power continues to be a major means for increasing profits. How is it done? The most obvious source of control still lies in the structure of capitalist society, for so long as workers do not control the means of production, they do not control their own jobs. In his influential book, *White Collar*, C. Wright Mills wrote of the new middle class, whose insecure position in the labor market contributes to increasing feelings of anxiety and powerlessness.

A second major source of control lies in the divisions within the working class that prevent unified action on the part of workers. For example, only 17 percent of workers belong to unions (USCB 1990a). They represent an elite of the working class who often see themselves as having little in common with other workers (see Form 1985). This was not always the case. When union organizing was at its height at the turn of this century, there was relatively little distance between the least and most skilled workers, and this provided a common base of experience from which to organize. By the 1930s, however, divisions within the working class were beginning to appear as the result of specialization, job ladders, pay scales, and a routinized work process that sharply distinguishes between skilled and unskilled labor (see Griffin et al. 1986).

In her study of the steel industry in the early part of this century Stone (1974) argued that employers created mobility within the working class in order to encourage them to work harder and to control their dissatisfaction with working conditions and pay. Before the Industrial Revolution, goods were produced by skilled workers who were familiar with all aspects of production. From roughly the 1870s on, however, the factory assembly line, by splitting the production process into a series of small steps, few of which require great skill, led to a decline of skilled workers. As the range of skills in the steel industry narrowed, workers could be replaced more easily, and most found themselves stuck in dead-end jobs (see also Gordon, Edwards, and Reich 1982).

Employers responded by creating "job ladders" that took a narrow range of jobs and made fine distinctions among them by attaching slightly higher levels of pay to each. While the jobs were as dead-

During the late nineteenth and early twentieth centuries, the U.S. government openly acted against the rising tide of labor organizing. In 1912, for example, mill workers in Lawrence, Massachusetts, struck in protest over wage cuts, and the intervention of state militia troops resulted in both the end of the strike and the death of one of the strikers.

end as before, the job ladder gave workers the *feeling* of moving upward. Job ladders also encouraged workers to compete with one another for promotion, rather than unite against their employers.

The illusion of mobility is also supported by the greater cultural value placed on white-collar jobs than on blue-collar jobs. Blau and Duncan (1967) interpreted the white-collar jobs of the children of blue-collar workers as a sign of upward mobility; but the category of white-collar includes many low-level occupations; and many blue-collar jobs require more mental ability than many white-collar jobs. Is a typist's work any less manual or any more mental than a skilled tool and die marker's? Stone argued that the distinction between mental and physical labor is both unnecessary and artificial, and "only serves to maintain the power of employers over their workers" (p. 28). It does this by fostering the illusion that becoming a white-collar worker—no matter how lowly the position—is a step upward.

The best evidence of a divided working class is the decline of union membership. Why is membership so low? Part of the answer is that many workers in industrial societies (nearly a third in the U.S.) hold jobs that require relatively unsophisticated skills—clerks, assembly-line workers, farm laborers, and restaurant workers (USCB 1990a). Because there are always workers willing to take their place, most workers have a great deal to lose by making trouble, and employers generally define attempts to form unions as just that.

Union membership is also low because those who are most likely to hold low-level jobs—nonwhites, married women, college students, teenagers, and the elderly—tend to have little social power (Smith 1981). Their position in society and the labor market gives them little ability or incentive to take the risks and make the investment of time and energy that it takes to form unions and improve working conditions and pay levels. Finally, unions are weak because corporations use their considerable resources to actively limit union growth through laws that limit unions as well as sophisticated campaigns to discourage workers from forming unions (Goldfield 1987).

A third source of control lies in the segmented, bureaucratic nature of work in industrial societies. This not only makes it easier for employers to replace discontented workers, but puts most power over production in the hands of bureaucratic managers who specialize in controlling labor power. The proliferation of "management seminars" and courses in "labor relations" attests to the growing sophistication of capitalist methods for controlling workers.

One of the most important sources of control is the continuing drive for greater efficiency. In 1911 Frederick Winslow Taylor published *Principles of Scientific Management*, in which he espoused the use of scientific principles to determine the most efficient way to use workers. In time-and-motion studies, he tried to identify the single most efficient way for workers to accomplish narrowly defined physical tasks—such as screwing two pieces of wood together. The design and control of the human work process, he believed, should be no less rigorous and scientific than the design of machines (see Hounshell 1984).

In the 1920s industrial sociologists focused on how to maximize the productivity of workers (and, therefore, the surplus value that could be extracted from them). The famous Hawthorne studies (discussed in Chapters 6 and 9) were attempts to identify working conditions—such as the amount of lighting and the frequency of rest periods—that would maximize the productivity of each worker. Studying productivity from another angle, Mayo and his colleagues discovered that small primary work groups establish norms about a fair day's work that often exert more control over worker productivity than do employers (see also Jones 1990).

One of the most effective ways to increase efficiency and weaken the control of workers over productivity is to replace them with machines—a process known as **automation** (see Griffin et al. 1986; Shaiken 1986). In the eighteenth century, British textile manufacturers developed power looms with which a single worker could replace hundreds; and as industrialization has expanded over the last two centuries, increasingly sophisticated technology has rendered ever greater numbers of skills—and, in some cases, workers themselves—obsolete. Automakers in Japan and the U.S. use robots to perform many assembly-line tasks that once provided thousands of jobs. To cut costs and maintain profits, the printing industry now uses so much high technology that skills among printers have declined and the printing craft has lost its once envied position as the epitome of skilled craftwork (Wallace and Kalleberg 1982).

As these South Korean management trainees play games simulating business, one of the things they will learn is how to control workers in order to maximize productivity and profit.

The capitalist valuing of efficiency increases productivity, but workers often bear the costs. Productivity—as measured by the average value of goods produced by each worker in a day—is lower in Japan than it is in the U.S. The reason for this lies not with the characteristics of workers, the use of technology, or the organization of work; rather, it lies with the structural relationship between employers and workers.

In capitalist Japan workers generally are not laid off when sales decline; thus, during economic slumps, production is cut back while the number of workers remains the same, and productivity per worker falls. In the U.S., however, efficiency is often increased by laying workers off when sales decline; and this keeps the statistical measure of worker productivity at a higher level. Increased efficiency often benefits capitalists more than workers. Understandably, some labor unions have opposed automation and have been accused by many as being opposed to progress and efficiency. This is one of the major contradictions of capitalism, for greater efficiency often worsens the relative position of workers (Smith 1981).

In industries whose unions are strongest, workers have increased their power, in some cases by placing a representative on corporate boards of directors. It is important to note, however, that this kind of shift in the distribution of power is achieved only under intense pressure, for it works against one of capitalism's primary values: the maximization of surplus value by controlling labor power (see Vanneman and Cannon 1987).

Controlling Markets: Monopoly and Oligopoly

Adam Smith believed that the ideal capitalist economy is controlled not by individuals, groups, or formal organizations (including governments), but by the "invisible hand" of economic forces that underlie market activities. U.S. automakers, for example, lost ground to foreign competition in the 1970s because they continued to manufacture large, expensive, gas-guzzling cars long after a preference for small, inexpensive, more fuel-efficient cars appeared. From Smith's point of view, they suffered losses because they did not match consumer demand with a supply of desired goods at a price people were willing to pay.

Smith believed that in order to make a profit and compete successfully with one another, capitalists must give consumers what they want at prices they are willing to pay. Competition forces them to introduce both new products at attractive prices and more efficient ways of producing them, and in the end everyone benefits. In the ideal capitalist society, the market is controlled by competition among producers and by the balance of supply and demand—the market forces that make up the invisible hand.

In practice, capitalist economies do not come close to Adam Smith's ideal. Increased profits depend on control over both production and markets. Not only is free and open competition among capitalists anxiety-producing, but it also poses a constant threat to the ability of businesses to survive. Understandably, then, capitalists prefer an economy in which they are protected from competition (while at the same time perpetuating the belief that the market is free), and this has led to increasing control over production and marketing in the hands of a relatively few organizations—a condition known as **oligopoly**.

Many believe that small businesses are the bedrock of the U.S. economy, but the truth is that businesses owned and operated by a few individuals have a tiny share of production and income. The fact is that a small minority of corporations controls the majority of economic activity. There are almost 200,000 industrial corporations; but the largest 100 of these own 64 percent of all business assets, and the largest 200 own 76 percent. The 500 largest U.S. corporations had sales in excess of almost 2 *trillion* dollars, *an amount that exceeds the gross national product (GNP) of every country in the world, with the exception of the U.S., Japan, and the Soviet Union* (USCB 1990a).

Oligopoly describes markets for many important products and services. More than 1,800 different makes of automobiles have been manufactured in the U.S.; but there are now only 3 major U.S. automakers. A handful of companies control the entire U.S. supply of oil and natural gas, a situation that is also true for cigarettes, beer, breakfast cereals, coffee, aluminum, and personal computers. Eight huge airlines control 93 percent of U.S. domestic air traffic; two companies—Coke and Pepsi—control almost three-quarters of the entire soft drink industry; and, between the two, M&M Mars and Hershey control almost three-quarters of the entire candy bar market. Ten corporations control NBC, ABC, and CBS (both television and radio); 34 affiliated television stations; 201 cable television franchises; 59 magazines including *Newsweek* and *Time*; 20 record companies; 41 book publishers; and 58 newspapers including the *Wall Street Journal*, the *Washington*

Post, the *Los Angeles Times*, and the *New York Times* (Parenti 1985).

The importance of oligopoly lies in the ability of an organization to control prices while maintaining the appearance of a competitive marketplace. For example, we spend more than $200 billion on food each year, but less than 40 cents out of every dollar goes to farmers. Most of what we spend on food goes to middlemen—food processors—and only 50 companies control 90 percent of the food market (Hightower 1980). When Phillip Morris and Kraft merged in 1988, the resulting corporation owned companies doing business in an extraordinary array of consumer goods (see Figure 19-1). Judging from commercials on Saturday morning television, you might think that there is intense competition among the enormous number of different products such as breakfast cereals; but most of these are made by a few companies that, to a degree, compete against themselves. The extensiveness of oligopoly results in considerably less competition than there appears to be.

A few markets are monopolies. Most people, for example, buy utilities such as natural gas and electricity from companies that control the entire market in a given geographical area, and until recently, telephone service in the U.S. was controlled entirely by AT&T.

Some organizations are powerful not because they control a market, but because they own companies in many different markets. A **conglomerate** is a collection of companies in different industries that are owned by a single corporation. Conglomerates form when one company uses its profits to buy others, or when two or more companies merge to form a single organization. Phillip Morris-Kraft is a conglomerate, for example, as is the International Telephone and

FIGURE 19-1   The Combined Philip Morris and Kraft The merger of Philip Morris and Kraft will create an unequaled combination of brand names. Principle brands are listed below.

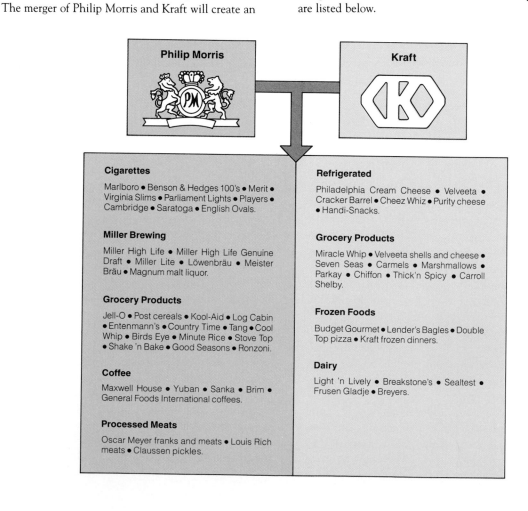

Philip Morris

Kraft

Cigarettes

Marlboro • Benson & Hedges 100's • Merit • Virginia Slims • Parliament Lights • Players • Cambridge • Saratoga • English Ovals.

Miller Brewing

Miller High Life • Miller High Life Genuine Draft • Miller Lite • Löwenbräu • Meister Bräu • Magnum malt liquor.

Grocery Products

Jell-O • Post cereals • Kool-Aid • Log Cabin • Entenmann's • Country Time • Tang • Cool Whip • Birds Eye • Minute Rice • Stove Top • Shake 'n Bake • Good Seasons • Ronzoni.

Coffee

Maxwell House • Yuban • Sanka • Brim • General Foods International coffees.

Processed Meats

Oscar Meyer franks and meats • Louis Rich meats • Claussen pickles.

Refrigerated

Philadelphia Cream Cheese • Velveeta • Cracker Barrel • Cheez Whiz • Purity cheese • Handi-Snacks.

Grocery Products

Miracle Whip • Velveeta shells and cheese • Seven Seas • Carmels • Marshmallows • Parkay • Chiffon • Thick'n Spicy • Carroll Shelby.

Frozen Foods

Budget Gourmet • Lender's Bagels • Double Top pizza • Kraft frozen dinners.

Dairy

Light 'n Lively • Breakstone's • Sealtest • Frusen Gladje • Breyers.

Bloom County / By BERKE BREATHED

© 1989, Washington Post Writers Group. Reprinted with permission.

Telegraph company which owns more than 150 different corporations that provide products and services that have nothing to do with telephones—including foods such as Wonder Bread and Hostess Twinkies.

Conglomerates have enormous power in the marketplace because their vast and diversified resources allow them to compete in ways that are beyond the resources of independent companies. As conglomerates increase their control over markets and drive smaller, independent firms out of business, oligopoly tends toward monopoly.

The Manufacture of Desire   All economies shape people's needs to fit what is produced to some degree; but the capitalist imperatives of expansion, profit, and competition make it important to control what consumers think they want and need (see Schudson 1984). In order to expand, capitalists must increase people's perceived needs and then try to meet them in a profitable way.

The manufacture of desire is an important part of capitalist economies and is often accomplished by introducing "new" products. In many cases, the products are not new at all, such as new dishwashing detergents that differ from old ones only in their packaging and smell. Production goes on as usual, but advertising campaigns foster the illusion of change (Baran and Sweezy 1966).

Desire is also manufactured by introducing products that substitute new ways of doing things for old ways that were quite sufficient. People have always managed to entertain themselves, for example—with singing, parties, games, dancing, storytelling; but

now entertainment generally involves products or services that are sold in markets—television, records, radios, cassettes, CDs, VCRs, and movies. In many cases the production process creates real needs that create new sources of profit. As Best and Connolly (1976) wrote:

> When industrial production pollutes the air, urban dwellers come to equate the need for air with a vacation, air conditioning, or a more expensive home in the suburbs. . . . When food packaging, processing, and distribution create tasteless food fortified with potentially dangerous preservatives, consumers identify the need for nutrition with expensive organic foods and natural vitamins. (pp. 57–59)

The effort to manufacture the desire to consume products that generate profits for capitalists often leads to contradictions. Full-page advertisements for cigarettes, for example, often picture people smoking after they have obviously engaged in healthy exercise, such as a handsome man sitting in a locker room or a beautiful young dancer sitting in a dance studio.

Who's in Charge?   That the economies of most advanced capitalist societies are dominated by large organizations raises the important question of who, in turn, dominates these powerful corporations? In the early stages of industrial capitalism there were no corporations, and businesses were owned and operated by no more than a few individuals who often belonged to the same family. Family control of business organizations continued well into the twentieth century and formed the basis for the fortunes of families such as the Rockefellers, Vanderbilts, Kennedys, and Hunts.

In the twentieth century, however, ownership of large businesses appeared to slip from the control of families and individuals as stock ownership spread. As business became more bureaucratic, large numbers of managers and administrators took over control of day-to-day decision making. These two developments led some to believe that ownership and control of the means of production were no longer in the same hands, and that economic power was, therefore, becoming less concentrated (Berle and Means [1932] 1968).

This view is sharply countered by a number of social scientists. Burch (1972) gathered data on the largest U.S. corporations and divided them into two groups. Corporations that were controlled by single families or groups of families who owned a controlling interest and placed some of its members in key management positions (such as chairman of the board or a top executive) were classified as owner-dominated. If controlling interest was owned by a family or group of families who did *not* also have family members in key management positions, then the corporation was classified as management-dominated. Burch concluded that owner-dominance characterized almost 60 percent of the top 300 industrial corporations, 72 percent of the top 50 merchandising corporations, and just over half of all corporations that deal in banking and transportation. In addition, the wealthiest 1 percent of U.S. families own 60 percent of all corporate stock, whereas 80 percent own no stock at all (Joint Economic Committee 1986a). It seems reasonable to conclude that although bureaucracy and its managers play increasingly important roles in production, business is still primarily controlled by a small elite.

Herman (1981) studied the 200 largest U.S. corporations and disagreed with Burch by concluding that there is no small economic elite. He agreed with Burch, however, when he noted that many high-level managers own substantial amounts of stock in their companies; and even those who do not, have the same goals and interests as those who do. In short, Herman concluded that managers and owners have essentially the same interests (see also Domhoff 1983; James and Soref 1981).

The Role of Government   To Adam Smith, government never interferes with the economy in the ideal capitalist society: laissez faire (or, "leave it alone") was his motto. Early in this century, however, U.S. officials came to believe that unrestrained

capitalist expansion threatened to damage and deplete natural resources, and that corporations were amassing so much power that monopoly and oligopoly threatened free competition and the welfare of consumers. Railroads, for example, typically charged what the market would bear, and their local monopolies over hauling freight allowed them to charge exorbitant prices.

The government played an expanding role in the regulation of business, primarily in order to ensure a stable social environment in which capitalists could pursue their interests. U.S. immigration policy played an important part in the development of capitalism by allowing millions to enter the U.S. for most of the nineteenth century when the need for cheap industrial labor was great, but then virtually excluding immigrants in the 1920s when industrial capitalism had become firmly established (see Calavita 1984). Antitrust laws forbade monopolies; and in 1983 the government won a long legal battle to end AT&T's monopoly over telephone service. During the Depression of the 1930s, Franklin Roosevelt's administration set a precedent for government action—unemployment compensation, farm subsidies, the minimum wage, social security, regulation of banking and the stock exchange, and vast government spending in the mar-

When governments act to control pollution of the environment, it often has economic consequences. Here, for example, coal miners protest U.S. clean air legislation that, they believe, will hurt the coal industry and thereby endanger miners' jobs.

ketplace—all signaled a growing economic role of government (Heilbroner 1977).

The areas in which government plays a regulatory role include work safety regulations; control of natural resources; antipollution laws; fair trade practices (such as rules that govern our rights and obligations when we sign a lease or credit agreement); regulation of nuclear power plants; product safety (such as drugs, food, and cars); and labor-management relations (such as laws that forbid employers from firing employees who promote unions). The Federal Reserve Board controls the nation's money supply and determines, among other things, how much money is available for business investment and personal loans. When the government charges tariffs on goods imported from abroad, it helps protect U.S. industries from competition. The government subsidizes the production of various agricultural products—such as tobacco—by guaranteeing a certain level of prices, and regulates the price of vital commodities such as oil, gasoline, and natural gas.

The state seems to have a great deal of power, but how and in whose interests particular administrations use that power, and how effectively they control what goes on in the marketplace, are other matters. The trend toward oligopoly strongly suggests that the government's ability (or willingness) to limit the power of corporations is itself quite limited (see Bowles and Gintis 1986; Clawson et al. 1986; Peschek 1987).

Occupational Structures and Segmented Labor Markets

As we have seen, labor power is a commodity that is bought and sold in capitalist societies. Although complexity is the most obvious characteristic of labor markets in industrial societies (the Labor Department lists over 35,000 different occupations), of more interest to sociologists is the fact that modern labor markets are divided into separate parts: they are *segmented*, and this affects the opportunities available to workers (Gordon, Edwards, and Reich 1982).

The U.S. labor market is divided into two basic segments (the characteristics of different jobs are summarized in Table 19-2). The **primary labor market** includes jobs that encourage stable work habits, involve skills that are often learned on the job, are relatively high-paying, and have job ladders. The primary segment is, itself, divided into two smaller seg-

TABLE 19-2	Segmented Labor Markets
LABOR MARKET SEGMENT	CHARACTERISTICS
Primary	Encourages stable work habits. Skills often acquired on the job. Relatively high-paying. Job ladders. Strong unions.
Subordinate primary	Routine jobs that encourage dependability, discipline, obedience to authority. EXAMPLES: Police officer, skilled blue-collar worker, bank teller, office supervisor, computer programmer, public school teacher, military officer.
Independent primary	Creative jobs that require problem solving, initiative, and decision making. EXAMPLES: Scientist, executive, college professor, public official, school principal, lawyer, newspaper editor, police chief.
Secondary	Does not require stable work habits. Relatively low-paying. High turnover. Few job ladders ("dead end jobs"). Weak unions or none at all. EXAMPLES: Laborer, clerk, day-care worker, factory assembly-line worker, restaurant worker, taxi or bus driver.

ments. **Subordinate** primary jobs involve routine tasks that encourage workers to be dependable and obedient to authority. **Independent** primary jobs, on the other hand, involve more creativity, autonomy, and power. Roughly two-thirds of workers are in the primary market, but only around 16 percent of all workers have independent jobs (compiled from USCB 1990a). The **secondary labor market** does not require stable work habits, is relatively low-paying, has few chances for advancement, and, as a result, has a high rate of turnover (people leave jobs after relatively short periods of time). Roughly a third of all workers are in this segment of the labor market.

The structure of labor markets in capitalist societies reflects the importance attached to controlling labor power, for only a small minority of all workers have jobs that bring them some measure of power, autonomy, and creativity. In their theory of **labor market segmentation**, Reich, Gordon, and Edwards (1973) argue that the goal of controlling labor power actually caused the development of segmented labor markets. During the late nineteenth century industrialization had the effect of homogenizing labor—factory work fragmented the production process and no longer required highly skilled workers who were familiar with all phases of production. This, combined with having to sell their labor power for wages, gave workers a common basis for organizing unions and opposing the power of capitalists.

Reich, Gordon, and Edwards believe that twentieth-century capitalists responded to the threat of organized labor in part by creating different jobs, making the division of labor more complex than it needed to be for efficiency. This weakened the bond of common experience that held the labor movement together. Unlike workers in the nineteenth century, in other words, twentieth-century workers had less in common with one another because some were better off. The division of labor literally divided the labor movement.

The structure of the economy also changed in ways that reinforced a segmented labor market. In the nineteenth century the economy was competitive, with large numbers of small businesses competing against one another. In the twentieth century, however, some areas of business—such as the steel, auto, and chemical industries—gradually became monopolies and oligopolies, largely because there was a steady demand for their products. Others—such as restaurants, stores, construction companies, and auto dealers—remained competitive because the demand for their goods fluctuated and they had to compete in order to stay in business.

As a result, a **dual economy** emerged—part monopolistic and part competitive—and the position of workers in them strongly affects their position in the labor market. Primary and secondary jobs exist in both sectors of the economy; but primary workers are far more likely to be found in the monopoly sector, whereas most secondary workers are in the competitive sector.

Unions are weak in the competitive sector because most of the workers are in the secondary labor market and can be replaced with relative ease. Low pay and job insecurity are, in fact, major ways in which such businesses remain competitive and control workers: when business is slow, employers simply lay them off (see Juravich 1985). Monopolistic business, however, depends on a stable demand for products and employs a larger number of highly skilled workers who cannot be replaced easily. If employees leave because they dislike working conditions, monopoly businesses stand to lose far more than competitive businesses; and, for this reason, workers have more leverage in monopoly industries, and unions are more common and more powerful.

When people think of "labor," many think of highly publicized unions such as the Teamsters or the United Auto Workers, who often use their power to exact relatively high wages from employers. It is important to remember, however, that most workers—roughly 83 percent—do not belong to unions, and only a portion of the 17 percent who are members belong to powerful unions. When the United Auto Workers gains major concessions from employers, it results in relatively few benefits for the vast majority of workers. For most, low pay and job insecurity are permanent features of their positions in a segmented job market.

Professions and Professionalization   Some occupations—both within and outside the primary labor market—are **professions**, and these have unique cultural and structural characteristics. Professional jobs are based on systematic, formal knowledge about a particular field, such as law, medicine, or engineering, and it is their monopoly over such knowledge that gives professions their power (Freidson 1986). Compared with other occupations, professionals are relatively autonomous and can determine the conditions under which they work. Professionals, however, are generally bound by codes of conduct and standards that are determined by their organizations. Physicians and lawyers, for example, are answerable primarily to other physicians and lawyers who decide what constitutes malpractice. The American Medical Association has declared that it is unethical for any physician to refuse to treat an AIDS patient. In similar ways, scientists establish norms for competent research and ethical conduct (see Chapter 18).

The boundaries of professions are tightly controlled. Scientists and professors must have advanced

BLOOM COUNTY   by Berke Breathed

© 1987, Washington Post Writers Group. Reprinted with permission.

degrees in order to practice; doctors, lawyers, nurses, and engineers must pass licensing examinations and be certified by state boards; public school teachers must be certified by the state in order to teach; and only lawyers with special training are allowed to argue cases before the Supreme Court.

Because professions provide valued services, are relatively free of outside interference, require extended training, control the size of their membership, and enjoy relatively high levels of prestige, they generally have high levels of income. The average income of U.S. physicians, for example, is $116,000; and the average starting salary for graduates with Ph.D.s in engineering, chemistry, mathematics, and physics is more than $41,000. By comparison, the average earnings of all full-time workers amount to $20,000 (USCB 1990a).

Roughly 13 percent of U.S. workers are professionals, and most of these work for someone else—in other words, they are part of the labor market. Engineers, accountants, librarians, religious workers, scientists, nurses, reporters, and teachers sell their labor power as members of what Marx considered to be the working class. Most of them are better off than other workers, and many do have authority over other workers (such as secretaries). Nonetheless, as members of the working class, they also must live with the uncertainties of a job market they do not control. An even smaller minority—just over 2 percent—are professionals who work outside the labor market—such as physicians, dentists, and lawyers in private practice. It is among these that autonomy, financial well-being, and job security reach their highest level in a capitalist economy.

Some occupations are "semiprofessions" that have only some of the characteristics of professions. A growing number of business executives have graduate degrees, for example, and often like to refer to business as a profession with its own code of ethics. In addition, professions that exist primarily as part of the labor market—such as public school teaching—have less autonomy and control over their members than do those that are largely outside the labor market.

The attractiveness of professional standing encourages many people to try to professionalize their occupation. The first step in professionalization is to form an organization whose boundaries restrict membership and create a sense of occupational identity for its members. Often, a new name for the occupation (such as "educator" for "teacher") is a part of establishing boundaries, for it helps to break the cultural association of an occupation with its previous nonprofessional standing.

The second step is to create a code of ethics to indicate to the outside world that the organization intends to regulate its own members. This is an assertion of one of the most important characteristics of a profession—autonomy from outside control. The third and final step is to gain formal public recognition—usually from political authorities—that establishes the autonomy of the organization and, in some cases, creates legal criteria for membership (such as state licensing).

Once an occupation is professionalized, its members may gain a substantial increase in collective power. The American Psychological Association, for example, limits competition by opposing the professionalization of psychotherapists who are not psychiatrists (with M.D. degrees) or clinical psychologists (with Ph.D.s). This is accomplished by having services of competing therapists made legally ineligible for health insurance policy benefits. Since people are less likely to use uninsured medical services, this limits competition. Only recently have some states included some other mental health care providers—such as psychiatric social workers—in health insurance benefits.

Postindustrial Society and Changing Occupational Structures   In preindustrial societies, most people earn a living by working directly with raw materials, such as by growing or gathering food. In industrial societies, however, most economic activity involves manufactured goods. In the early 1950s, the U.S. began a third stage in which most economic activity involved neither raw materials nor manufacturing, but *service* occupations such as sales clerk, telephone operator, travel agent, secretary, banker, real estate agent, office manager, public official, teacher, police officer, and soldier.

Bell (1973) believed that this signaled the beginning of **postindustrial society**—in which the production of goods is overshadowed by the provision of services, and relations between people and machines are gradually replaced by relationships among people. In this kind of society, he argued, social interaction becomes the most important aspect of work; disputes between workers and employers are handled through negotiation rather than angry confrontation; and most people work for small organizations rather than large corporations.

Braverman (1974) and others, however, have pointed out that although the job market is changing from factory work to office work, the relations of production—between workers and employers and between workers and their work—have not changed. The central values of capitalist societies—expansion, profit, and the exploitation of labor power—are as strong as ever. In addition, the most rapidly expanding occupations—sales and service—are in the secondary, competitive labor market, where unions are weak or nonexistent and where wages are low and profits relatively high.

Life in the Labor Force

How do different economic arrangements affect the lives of workers? Do relations of production in a postindustrial society differ substantially from those in an industrial society? Are the gaps between social classes narrower? Do people have more control over what they do?

Sophisticated technology—computers, word processors, and telecommunications equipment—is used increasingly in offices, but it is unclear whether this improves the lives of workers as much as it increases profits. Textile workers once stood for hours tending machines that turned thread into cloth; but secretaries and clerks now sit for hours in front of computer terminals. They process information—taking it from one place and putting it in another—without affecting it in any way (see Zuboff 1982, 1988).

One study of clerical workers in two New England companies found, for example, that computer operators were instructed to enter information just as they received it even when they spotted obvious errors. The work of customer representatives (who work primarily over the phone) was closely monitored by computers that allotted them a specific number of minutes to handle each customer; and if workers paid extra attention to a difficult case, they were often penalized for falling short of their work quota for the day (*Hartford Courant*, January 5, 1983). One recent study estimated that as many as seven million workers in the U.S. are already being monitored and evaluated by computers (Office of Technology Assessment 1987).

High technology in a postindustrial society certainly has the potential to make work more interesting; but the drive for greater efficiency and profit creates enormous numbers of "dumb," rigidly controlled jobs that involve "intelligent" technology. Just as early machines degraded skilled work by taking over complex manual tasks, so too does computer technology further this process by taking over increasing numbers of mental tasks. As one skilled worker put it, "You don't have to think anymore. You lose touch with what you're actually doing. . . . and . . . you yourself become a robot, because you don't get to use your mind" (in Gill 1985, p. 84; see also Zuboff 1988).

Computer technology and automation are functional for productivity and profits, but how do they and other characteristics of capitalist societies affect the lives of workers?

Going Through the Motions: Alienation in the Workplace   To Marx ([1845] 1935), **alienation** is the feeling that the world we live in is, itself, alien to us. In the workplace alienation represents a lack of connection between people and what they produce and between themselves and other people. It is the feeling that they do not know why they are doing

This engraving shows a seventeenth-century shoemaker's shop. Under the guild system, all members of the shop lived in the same house, and the design, making, and selling of shoes all occurred in the same place. Industrialization drove most such shops out of business because they could not compete with the low prices (although inferior quality) that came with mass production.

what they are doing, and yet must go on doing it anyway.

Imagine, for example, that you are a bootmaker in seventeenth-century Paris. You own a little shop, and on a typical day a man comes in and tells you he wants a pair of boots. If he is insulting, you might tell him to go to another shop and leave you alone. If not, you discuss different styles and kinds of leather, measure his feet, fix a price, and tell him when they will be ready. Your life is far from ideal. You are relatively poor, and there are months when it seems that no one needs boots. You do, however, decide when you will work, whose boots you will make, how you will make them, and for what price. Most important, you produce and sell boots by interacting both with materials that you transform into finished boots and with other people—from the purchase of leather to the final sale.

Now imagine that you work in a twentieth-century boot factory. You do not make boots; you cut out soles on a stamping machine—thousands of them every day—and you are paid a wage for each hour of work. While you work, you stand alone and tend the machine, feeding the leather in and taking the soles out. You do not control which kinds of boots are made in the factory, the leathers that are used, the style, the quality, the price for which they are sold, or to whom they are sold. Your wages are determined by your employer. You punch the time clock at 8:00 A.M., work until noon with a ten-minute break at 10:00, and then punch out at 4:00 and go home. The next day, you return to the factory and cut out thousands of soles again; and this is what you do year after year.

Stop for a moment and imagine yourself in each of these situations. Which would you prefer and why?

In comparison with the seventeenth-century worker, the twentieth-century factory worker lacks control over the process of work and the results. The process of making boots is now fragmented into many separate tasks, and what workers do has little connection to their thoughts or feelings about what they do. The shopowner could sit back occasionally and think about what he was about to do with the leather, and the unity of thought and action is what produced the boots. In the factory, however, the boots are disconnected from what the workers think or feel about them.

When we have no control over our work or what is done with the result, we tend to lose our sense that work has meaning and value; and work is one of the most important things we do. If what we do lacks meaning and value, and if our social identities are bound up in what we do, then we are in danger of feeling that *we* are meaningless.

Alienation is one of the most important concepts in the sociological analysis of work. In his classic study of alienation in U.S. car, textile, chemical, and printing industries Blauner (1964) tried to identify structural characteristics of work that affected what he believed were four key aspects of alienation: powerlessness, meaninglessness, social isolation, and a lack of personal attachment and commitment to work. Alienation was highest among auto workers, most of whom performed dull, repetitive jobs on assembly lines that isolated them from other workers and gave them no control over the work process. Alienation was lowest among printers who performed a craft with deep historical roots and controlled many aspects of production, including the pace at which they worked. Printers were able to interact with one another, and rather than perform a tiny portion of a work process, they did the whole job and had the satisfaction of seeing the final product, much like our hypothetical seventeenth-century boot-maker (see Lipset, Trow, and Coleman 1956, for a classic study of printers).

Chemical workers were only slightly more alien-ated than printers. Although they had relatively lit-tle control over production, they worked in teams of skilled workers who closely monitored production and made many decisions. In comparison with auto workers, chemical workers enjoyed far more interac-tion with one another and their decision-making powers gave them a stronger feeling of attachment to their work.

Other studies show similar patterns. A 1973 na-tional study asked workers if they would choose their present occupation again, and the results showed that as the level of skill, prestige, and control over work increases, so does satisfaction with work (U.S. Department of Health, Education, and Welfare 1973). More recent data show that those who are self-employed or who have higher prestige occupa-tions are considerably more likely to say they are very satisfied with their jobs and considerably less likely to report being dissatisfied (see Table 19-3).

Alienation seems to be closely tied to powerless-ness, meaninglessness, social isolation, and frag-mentation of work tasks (see also Kalleberg and Griffin 1980; Kohn and Schooler 1983; and Mottaz 1981). In 1990, a sample of U.S. workers was asked which aspects of occupations were most important to

them; whereas half ranked "a feeling of accomplish-ment and importance" at the top, only 20 percent placed "high income" in that position (Davis and Smith 1990).

The structure of occupational life in industrial so-cieties makes it difficult for people to care about and feel attached to their work. What, however, of those who want to work, but are unemployed? What are the social causes of unemployment, and how does it affect people's lives?

Causes and Consequences of Unemployment
Wanting a job but not having one is often a personal problem that individuals must deal with on their own. Unemployment has obvious financial conse-quences for families and individuals; when workers are the only earners in their families, the loss of a job is like firing the entire family. One study of workers who lost their jobs when a plant closed found a sharp increase in symptoms of poor physical and mental health. Reported levels of anxiety, tension, pessi-mism, depression, and insomnia increased, as did the incidence of high blood pressure and ulcers (In-stitute for Social Research 1980; see also Buss and Redburn 1983).

From a sociological perspective, unemployment is also a social problem with cultural, structural, and eco-logical causes. When unemployment rates are high, the personal desperation and despair of individuals is multiplied by thousands:

> In Detroit last month, several thousand desperate people, ranging from a 19-year-old unmarried mother to a 55-year-old unemployed automobile worker, lined up for a handful of job openings as unskilled laborers. In New York, 60 people spent the weekend in line, sleeping on the sidewalk to assure acceptance of their applications as carpenters' apprentices. Some of the out-of-work families who left the industrial mid-west for the supposedly greener pastures of Texas are being forced to live in their cars. In Austin, 2,817 appli-cants lined up for 187 jobs.

The above is not a description of the Great De-pression of the 1930s; it was written in 1982 (*New York Times*, November 3, p. C1). Between 1980 and 1982 the number of unemployed people increased by 37 percent, as did the average number of weeks that people were out of work; and in many countries—including France, Great Britain, and most of Latin America—the picture was far bleaker than it was in the U.S. (USCB 1982). Today, in addition to those who are looking for work without success, many others have become so discouraged that they have

---

TABLE 19-3   Percent Very Satisfied or Dissatisfied with Their Jobs, by Occupational Prestige and Self-Employment, U.S.

OCCUPATIONAL PRESTIGE[1]	VERY SATISFIED	DISSATISFIED
Very low	32%	19%
Low	40%	15%
Moderate	50%	11%
Upper	60%	8%
SELF-EMPLOYMENT		
Self-employed	56%	10%
Work for someone else	43%	14%

[1]Occupations rated on a scale from 1 to 100: very low = 10–19; low = 20–39; moderate = 40–59; upper = 60–89.
Source: Computed from 1990 General Social Survey data.

ONE STEP FURTHER 19-1

Who's Who in the Underside of the Labor Market

Both unemployment and under-employment are distributed quite unevenly in the United States. As you can see from the figures in Table B-19-1, although women are only slightly more likely than men to be unemployed (out of work but actively looking for a job), they are almost twice as likely as men to have given up the search for a job even though they want to work, or to be working for the minimum wage. The differences between blacks and whites are even more dramatic, with blacks more than twice as likely to be unemployed and to have given up, but only slightly more likely to be working for the minimum wage. Age differences show that all three types of experience decline sharply with age as workers get a more stable place in the job market.

TABLE B-19-1

SOCIAL CHARACTERISTICS	PERCENT WHO WANT WORK, BUT HAVE GIVEN UP LOOKING	PERCENT UNEMPLOYED	PERCENT WORKING FOR MINIMUM WAGE
Gender			
Women	5.1	7.4	10.5
Men	2.6	7.0	5.4
Race			
Black	8.3	15.1	8.7
White	3.2	6.2	7.8
Age			
16–19	10.3	18.6	28.7
20–24	4.6	11.1	10.1
25–59	2.8	5.2	4.6
60 and older	1.2	3.2	*

*not available
Source: Bureau of Labor Statistics 1987, 1988; USCB, 1986a.

given up looking altogether. Of those who have jobs, many are underemployed—which means that although they are employed, their jobs are either part-time or so poorly paid that they cannot earn enough to live on (Bureau of Labor Statistics 1986, 1987; Lichter 1988) (see One Step Further 19-1).

Most of us look upon unemployment as a fact of life. We are so accustomed to the monthly unemployment statistics that it is hard to imagine a society in which everyone who wants to work has a job. The fact that we tend to accept it as an inevitable part of economic life strongly suggests that its causes lie in the nature of the social environment that we also tend to take for granted. As Smith (1981) pointed out, once labor power becomes a commodity, then the demand for labor (and the opportunity for work) is no longer controlled by the willingness of individuals to work and the demand for the goods they produce. New factors come into play, such as the desire of capitalists to expand, to increase their profits, or to compete more successfully with one another. Most important is the fact that the historical trans-

formation of labor into a commodity has created an ongoing conflict between employers and workers.

One of the most important types of unemployment is called **structural unemployment** because it is caused by changes in the structure of occupations (see Ashton 1986). The mechanization of agriculture throws unskilled farm laborers out of work, just as automation creates unemployment by replacing factory workers with machines (Rasmussen 1982). Automated bank tellers replace human tellers; word processors enable secretaries to do work that once required several people; robots on auto assembly lines not only take over dull "dumb" jobs, but leave many assembly-line workers with no jobs at all. Since the cost of labor power is the largest single expense in many industries, automation increases profits by lowering costs; but it does so at the expense of people. The consequences are the same when corporations move operations to other regions or countries where labor costs are lower and workers easier to control. As more and more such jobs (many of them requiring low skill levels) are removed from the labor

In the Soviet Union, almost everyone has a job with a decent income, but there are chronic shortages of quality goods, causing people to wait in long lines for basic necessities. Capitalist countries, on the other hand, have solved this problem by producing huge quantities of quality goods, but also create far higher levels of poverty and unemployment, as shown in this 1983 picture of more than 1,000 people who lined up in Chester, Pennsylvania to apply for 30 job openings.

market, entire populations of workers—disproportionately poor and black—are left behind (see Willhelm 1983).

In some cases structural unemployment has demographic causes, for as populations grow and age structures change, so does the size of the labor force in relation to the number of jobs. In the 1950s, the labor force grew slowly because the low birth rates of the 1930s resulted in a relatively small number of young adults. The baby boom of the late 1940s and 1950s, however, created a huge influx of young people looking for jobs in the 1970s and 1980s. Combined with a surge of women into the job market, the labor force expanded more rapidly than the job market.

As age structures change, so does the demand for certain goods and services. The large numbers of children produced by the baby boom fostered a sharp rise in the demand for teachers; in the 1990s, however, the size of the school-age population is considerably smaller, and thousands of teachers must choose between unemployment and training for new occupations.

Sweezy (1942) also argued that the antagonistic relations between workers and employers in capitalist societies create recurring crises that inevitably raise unemployment levels. A basic tension in capitalist societies is between the desire of capitalists to expand by giving workers the smallest possible share of what they produce and the desire of workers to increase their share. When profits are high (a "boom"), workers are in a better position to demand a bigger share—in other words, an increase in wages. If their wages go up, then business profits go down, and economic growth slows (a "slump" or, in the worst cases, a "bust"). If employers are able to keep wages from rising, then workers do not have enough money to buy all of the goods being produced in a boom period, and this in turn causes business profits to fall and, with them, the expansion of the economy. When the economy goes into a slump, wages fall (as they did during the Great Depression and in the 1980s), and workers are in a weak bargaining position. This sets the stage for higher profits and renewed economic expansion, and the cycle begins again.

SOCIALISM AND COMMUNISM

In the 1800s the Industrial Revolution and the growth of capitalism went hand in hand; and, as we saw in earlier chapters, Marx wrote in response to the economic and social conditions spawned by these developments. He believed that capitalism was a stage in history that was necessary because it would bring about an enormous increase in production and technology. Because capitalism generated intense class conflict, however, Marx also believed that eventually it would be replaced by *socialism* and then by *communism*.

As an ideal type, **socialism** differs from capitalism in that under socialism the means of production are owned by the state, not by private individuals and groups. Marx believed that socialism would end class conflict by doing away with classes and by creating a workers' state. Private ownership of the means of production would not exist; satisfying social needs such as adequate housing, food, and defense would be valued more than surplus value and profit; full employment would be valued above efficiency; and cooperation would be valued more than competition.

As is true with capitalism, socialist societies have yet to get close to their ideal. Indeed, recent years have seen the virtual collapse of socialism in one society after another as democratic reforms have swept through the Soviet Union and the countries of Central Europe. Even China has begun to allow the private ownership of the means of production, although on a small scale. In spite of these recent changes—the end result of which will not be known for some time to come—it is still important to understand not only the ways in which capitalism and socialism differ from each other, but also the problems they tend to have in common, many of which stem from industrialization and the complexity of their societies.

The Structure of Socialist Economies

The distribution of power is the most important structural difference between socialist and capitalist societies. Under socialism the party and its government officials decide what wages are paid for each kind of work, which goods and services are produced and in what amount, and how goods and services are distributed (Hollander 1982; Lane 1982). Whereas capitalist societies are dominated by privately owned monopolies and oligopolies, socialist societies are dominated by state-owned monopolies and oligopolies.

Although socialist countries have been able to avoid the extremes of worker exploitation and social inequality found in many capitalist societies, they have been unable to overcome serious political and economic problems. Economically, they all began as relatively poor agricultural societies with an almost nonexistent industrial base. Because they were not able to produce an abundance of goods, for decades they struggled without success to provide both basic necessities and luxuries for their populations. In spite of considerable success at developing basic industries such as steel and raising the general standard of living, chronic shortages have been a way of life,

Thus far, wide-scale attempts to implement socialism have failed to provide material prosperity. Collective farms such as this one in the Soviet Union, for example, have increasingly given way to private farms in which farmers sell their goods in markets in order to earn a profit.

including high rates of poverty—as much as 20 percent in the Soviet Union (*New York Times*, January 29, 1989). To some degree this has also been the result of very poor management and inefficiency, attributable in part to the attempt to control large complex societies from single, centralized sources of authority.

The recent events in socialist countries in Europe and, to a lesser degree, the Soviet Union have been provoked not only by growing impatience over shortages of basic necessities, but perhaps even more so by decades of authoritarian rule and political oppression. In one country after another, workers have defied government authorities with national strikes and demanded representative government and an end to authoritarian rule, with the result that many of these societies are moving rapidly towards greater democracy and economic systems that increasingly resemble capitalism. Although these changes have been much slower to occur in the Soviet Union, significant changes are nonetheless taking place, including the passage of laws permitting the private ownership of small businesses.

In the most extreme cases—Poland and Hungary, in particular—the attempt has been made to leap immediately from socialism to capitalism. With this have come structural patterns and social problems that were previously associated primarily with capitalism, such as rapid increases in unemployment and inequalities of income and wealth. Budapest, Hungary, for example, now has emerging suburbs with expensive homes and swimming pools. Other Central European countries such as Czechoslovakia are proceeding more slowly and are less eager to embrace the benefits and the dangers of capitalist systems. Although 43 percent of Czechoslovaks favored a change in their economic system, only 3 percent said they wanted capitalism (*New York Times*, December 11, 1989).

Countries like Great Britain and France use systems known as **state capitalism**, under which the government owns and controls only the most important means of production that supply necessary goods and services. Airlines (such as British Airways), railways, and major television stations (such as the British Broadcasting Corporation or "BBC") are publicly owned; and in some countries banks, mines, and telephone systems are also publicly owned. Even in the U.S., the government owns and controls a railroad (Amtrak) and a power system (the Tennessee Valley Authority). Although it may appear that government ownership of some means of production indicates a movement toward socialism, it is important to remember that socialism is not simply a matter of government ownership. The fact that the U.S. federal government owns Amtrak, for example, does not mean that it is representing the interests of the working class. In fact, the state in capitalist societies adheres quite closely to the basic principles of capitalism (Edwards, Reich, and Weisskopf 1986).

Marx believed that once industrial capitalist societies such as the United States and France became socialist, they would eventually develop into **communist** societies, utopias in which there is no state or other form of centralized control and in which the means of production are owned communally, as they were in many preindustrial societies (see Wallerstein 1986). There are no communist industrial societies in the world today, although many people in capitalist societies mistakenly label socialist countries such as the Soviet Union and China as "communist." Since there are no existing examples of a modern communist society, it is difficult to know just how or if it could work in an industrial world. In fact, since there has not been an industrial capitalist society that has undergone a socialist revolution, it remains to be seen how such a system might work.

THE WORLD ECONOMY

As we saw earlier, before the Industrial Revolution capitalism existed primarily through trade. Seven-

---

PUZZLE

WHO PROFITS FROM A WORLD ECONOMY?

As foreign corporations invest more money in underdeveloped economies (to build factories, for example), does the relative position of the lower and working classes get better, worse, or stay the same?

The gap between social classes tends to get wider—which is to say, the position of the working class in relation to the upper class grows worse, not better. Why? World-system theory provides one answer.

teenth-century merchants might buy grain and then hold onto it until conditions—such as food shortages—in distant places increased the demand for grain and the willingness to pay high prices for it. Braudel (1983) argued that it was here that the biggest profits were to be made, and capitalism took on an international scope long before the Industrial Revolution.

While capitalism has come to dominate the economies of many societies over the past 500 years, it also dominates economic relationships among societies. There is a **world economy** (Bergesen 1980; Wallerstein 1976a, 1979, 1980) with a division of labor (Froebel Heinrichs, and Kreye 1980). Many U.S. cars, for example, contain parts manufactured in West Germany, Japan, Mexico, and Brazil, as well as the U.S.; a few countries—the U.S., the Soviet Union, and France—supply most of the world's sophisticated weapons; a few nations, including South Africa, control much of the world's supply of metals such as nickel and chromium that are in increasing demand; Middle Eastern countries such as Saudi Arabia depend primarily on the export of oil for their entire national income; and the bulk of the national income of Mexico comes from the sale of minerals and oil, tourism, and the earnings of many thousands of Mexican immigrants working in the U.S.

In a world economy no nation is self-sufficient, and this means that each must sell its goods in world markets in order to purchase everything it needs. The U.S., for example, once bought most of Nicaragua's sugar and beef production as well as almost all of its lobster and shrimp catch. When the U.S. suddenly stopped buying Nicaraguan goods in 1985 as part of its opposition to Nicaragua's socialist government, Nicaragua's economy suffered enormously. Many countries are in similarly vulnerable positions because they depend on a few goods that they sell in markets they cannot control. Colombia and Brazil, for example, depend heavily on a few cash crops such as coffee for much of their income.

Many other countries—including the U.S.—are also vulnerable because of international competition. European and Japanese steel manufacturers have for years offered their products at prices below those charged by U.S. manufacturers, and as a result the share of the steel market going to U.S. steelmakers has declined steadily. In 1983 the government imposed heavy import duties on certain kinds of steel in order to protect domestic manufacturers from foreign competition. In similar ways, car manu-

Societies that depend on a small number of agricultural products to earn cash in world markets—as Brazil and Colombia depend on coffee—are highly vulnerable to changes in demand as well as political pressure from core societies that purchase much of what they produce.

facturers have tried to limit the number of Japanese cars imported into the U.S.; and the Japanese have tried to limit the importation of beef and other products into Japan.

Although all nations are vulnerable in the world economy, the distribution of wealth and power is extremely unequal. **World-system theory** divides nations into three groups (Wallerstein 1976a, 1980). The most powerful are the **core societies** such as the United States, France, Japan, West Germany, and Great Britain. Core societies control most means of production such as factories and technology, are relatively autonomous and stable, and have great economic and military power. They have complex divisions of labor and produce a wide range of goods or services—which is to say they are diversified. Their economies are geared to manufacturing goods, not to providing raw materials.

At the other extreme of wealth and power are the **peripheral societies**, which include nonindustrial countries such as Uganda and Nicaragua. Peripheral societies own little or no means of production, are dependent on other nations, tend to be politically unstable, and are weak militarily. They have few

The interdependency of world markets was very
clear in the hectic reaction of the Japanese stock
exchange to the U.S. stock market crash of 1987.

highly skilled workers and are more likely to specialize in providing raw materials. The third group of
nations lies in between the core and peripheral societies. These **semiperipheral societies**—such as Taiwan—are generally moving toward a diversified industrial economy and provide cheap skilled labor for
core nation industries. Many electronic devices produced for U.S. firms, for example, are assembled in
Taiwan or South Korea.

The position a society occupies in the world system affects its ability to develop economically and,
therefore, the living conditions of its population. Most
core countries developed during the early stages of
the Industrial Revolution. Because industrialization
was new to the world, there was a great deal of room
for expansion, and countries that are now the world's
great industrial powers developed in an environment
that imposed few serious limitations on them. Today's semiperipheral and peripheral societies, however, face a much more limiting set of circumstances:
they must try to industrialize in a world *already* dominated by the core societies. Since core societies have
little to gain by the addition of new sources of com-

petition in world markets for manufactured goods,
their monopoly over technology and their enormous
power allow them to limit the industrialization of
most other countries.

Economic arrangements on a world scale produce
problems not only for nations, but for the world as a
whole. In order to maintain their high standards of
living, industrial nations such as the U.S., must sell
goods to other countries; but their potential buyers
are more interested in selling *their* goods than in buying from the U.S. Countries in the periphery and
semiperiphery cannot buy heavily from core countries because without an industrial base of their own,
they cannot generate enough wealth to buy what the
core societies produce (or to repay their enormous
debts to major core banks). If they *did* industrialize,
this would make things even more complicated because it would simply increase world competition.

The world system, then, is a complex interdependency plagued by the contradiction that every nation would rather sell its goods than buy from others.
Industrial nations want other nations to be prosperous enough to buy their goods but not so prosperous

as to compete with them. It is a delicate balance in which, ironically, many nations have never been more powerful nor more vulnerable. When the U.S. stock market crashed in 1987, it set off a wave of crashes in stock markets around the world, from London to Tokyo—dramatic evidence of the tight linkages that make up the world economy.

Power and Multinational Corporations

An elite of nations controls most of the world's wealth, receives most of its income, and consumes most of what is produced each year. As some sociologists and economists point out, however, the distribution of power in the world economy is shifting away from national governments to multinational corporations whose operations extend across national boundaries (see Evans 1981).

IBM, for example, is based in the U.S., but more than half of its earnings comes from its foreign operations; and almost half of the Ford Motor Company's work force is in foreign countries. U.S. and Western European firms own most of Brazil's automobile and tire plants and over half of its electrical equipment, and this is not unusual: more than a *third* of all production in the entire capitalist world is controlled by just 650 industrial firms (Smith 1981).

Whereas the economies of industrial societies are controlled by government to some degree, the world economy is independent of any government or set of governments. There is no world government, and multinationals are relatively free to shift operations to countries that offer the most profitable conditions. If labor costs rise in one country, a multinational can move to another where wages are lower (the next time you buy U.S. brand clothing, look carefully to see in what country it was made). Multinationals can also plan their operations so that they earn the highest profits in countries with the lowest income taxes.

Although multinationals play a vital part in the economic life of most societies, they often feel little loyalty to their host countries and are subject to relatively few legal restrictions. To keep multinationals from moving to other countries (and taking jobs and tax revenues with them) governments must bargain and make concessions that increase the power of multinational corporations. This is—on a larger scale—the same problem faced by communities when a business threatens to move an office or plant to another part of the country (see Chapter 10; also

Bowles and Gintis 1986). In peripheral societies, however, multinationals also often gain other concessions, such as the willingness of governments to use force to control workers and prevent strikes. As a result, the presence of multinationals has been related to tension and conflict that increase the incidence of collective political violence in peripheral societies (London and Robinson 1989).

Fatemi et al. (1982) are among those who social scientists believe that multinational corporations rival the power of most nation states. More radical writers such as Amin (1975) believe that the rising power of multinational corporations will inevitably bring about a socialist revolution as governments and citizens assert control over corporations and the means of production. These writers were responding to the phenomenal growth rates of multinationals during the 1960s, and in more recent years multinational growth rates have fallen to more moderate levels (Goodman 1980). Nevertheless, multinational corporations retain enormous amounts of economic power (Evans 1981).

THE SOCIAL CONSEQUENCES OF ECONOMIC ARRANGEMENTS

Like any social system, the cultural and structural aspects of economic institutions have both functional and dysfunctional consequences. In addition, economic arrangements play a particularly important part in social stratification, for it is through them that wealth—and to a considerable extent, power and prestige as well—is produced and distributed.

Functions and Dysfunctions

Capitalism has produced an abundance of goods and services. Marx, in fact, believed that solving the problem of production would be the most important social function of capitalism. Competition among capitalists has also produced a staggering array of inventions and innovations—from supercomputers to permanent press clothing and artificial sweeteners. There is simply no comparison between the average standard of living under capitalism and any other type of society that has ever existed.

Capitalism also produces dysfunctional consequences. As an economic system, capitalism creates recurring patterns of "boom" and "bust" and requires periods of high unemployment that are disastrous for members of the labor force (Institute for Social Research 1980; Smith 1981). We have also seen that industrialization in general and capitalism in particular contribute to alienation among workers by fragmenting the work process and denying them meaningful work over which they exercise control.

Capitalism is also dysfunctional in ways that affect every segment of society. Because profit and expansion are the primary goals of capitalism, social needs may be met only if it is profitable to do so. Drug companies resist investing in research to find cures for diseases that are relatively rare—even though they may also be highly fatal. The reason is simple: there is little profit in discovering a medicine for which the market is small. Cigarettes, however, are produced by the billions each year simply because they sell.

The high value placed on profits affects not only which needs are met, but how they are met. Hard, juiceless tomatoes were developed not to improve nutrition, but because they can be shipped with less damage; and less damage means higher profits. Chemical preservatives in foods prolong the shelf life of products—and, therefore, the chances that they will be sold—but they may threaten the health of those who eat them. Sugar-coated cereals promote tooth decay and substitute for more healthy nutrients, and yet there are now so many different kinds of such cereals that most supermarkets cannot stock them all.

Although competition among capitalists is functional for increasing efficiency and introducing new products, it also creates a great deal of waste. Building cars that last only four or five years (a practice once known as "planned obsolescence" in Detroit) increases profits by increasing sales; but it also wastes enormous amounts of raw materials, energy, and labor. Competition also generates wasteful duplication: instead of a few companies producing a product, we have several that produce essentially the same thing and compete primarily through expensive advertising. Go to a supermarket and see the number of different brands of laundry detergent—any one of which will clean your clothes. Then stop and ask yourself, "What social needs could be met with the billions of dollars spent each year on advertising?"

Like capitalism, socialism produces both functional and dysfunctional consequences. In the Soviet Union everyone has been guaranteed a job and the extreme differences between rich and poor found in the U.S. have been relatively rare. One dysfunctional consequence of full employment, however, is

that workers have known they would have jobs no matter how badly they performed. Shoddy goods and low productivity have been widespread problems in many socialist countries. On a larger scale, business and industry in socialist countries have relatively few incentives to improve productivity and efficiency, because they cannot fail in the way that capitalist enterprises can. Since they have been owned and operated by the state, they could not go bankrupt unless the state went bankrupt.

As we would expect, the cultural and structural differences between capitalism and socialism produce different consequences. Competition under capitalism produces both positive and negative consequences, just as the general absence of competition does in socialist countries. In many important respects, the two kinds of society are quite similar: both face the problems of industrialization—such as pollution and bureaucracy—and both alienate workers who control neither the physical means nor the social relations through which goods are produced (Welsh 1981).

Capitalism and socialism, however, are not simply two different and unrelated economic systems that sprang up all by themselves. Capitalism developed over a period of many centuries, and socialism emerged as a response to it. To many socialist thinkers, socialism is both a response to capitalism and an inevitable consequence of it.

Conflict, Change, and the Contradictions of Capitalism

Marx ([1884] 1961) and others have pointed out that capitalism embodies a series of contradictions that, they believe, will ultimately lead to social change through which the means of production will be taken out of private control and placed under collective control. The most fundamental contradiction is that the capitalist system itself pits workers and owners against each other—capitalists compete successfully by extracting as much surplus value from workers as they can; workers improve their position only by keeping as much of what they produce as they can. Capitalism creates class conflict, and the only real question is, who will come out ahead?

The capitalist imperatives to expand production and increase profits create a second contradiction: the more productive the work force becomes, the less able the working class is to purchase all the goods that are produced. This, in turn, creates recurring crises for capitalist societies—recessions and depressions. In this sense, capitalism creates its own crises that are more than inevitable ups and downs in business cycles. They are more than mere technical problems to be solved by fine-tuning the economic system—by increasing the number of public service jobs, changing the level of interest rates or taxes, increasing unemployment benefits, encouraging new business investment, or changing the level of government spending. Beneath the recurring crises in capitalist societies are social relationships between capitalists and workers—relationships whose effects reverberate throughout the entire society (Castells 1980). As we will see in the next chapter, many government programs are designed to temporarily correct for economic "ups and downs" while keeping the basic economic system intact.

Socialist societies also struggle with contradictions, especially in recent years. Socialist governments ideally govern in the interests of the workers and have as their major goal a communist society in which there is no state. To control a nation, however, the government gathers to itself enormous power that its officials are reluctant to share or surrender, even to the workers for whom the government supposedly exists. The irony is that in practice, socialism, which is supposed to be the path to freedom from exploitation, has had just the opposite effect in many areas of social life (Stojanovic 1981).

Socialist societies have not been in existence nearly as long as capitalist societies have, and it remains to be seen how they will change. In spite of the recent policy of *glasnost* (or "openness") in the Soviet Union, no socialist society has come close to a workers' state in which people are free of political oppression and are able to control the means of production. The most critical contradiction for socialist societies may eventually lie in its failure to deliver the material basics of human life—good food, shelter, clothing, and other necessities—to a majority of their populations.

SUMMARY

1. Economic institutions are enduring social arrangements through which goods and services are produced and distributed. They include the forces of production and the relations of production.

2. The development of capitalism depended on historical transformations through which goods took on exchange value as well as use value, and ownership of the means of production shifted from communities to individual producers and then to employers.

3. Feudal nobles protected serfs in exchange for a share of what the serfs produced. Feudalism began to break down as independent merchants bought and sold what was produced by others, often paying producers less than the cost of production and keeping the difference between that and the selling price—surplus value—for themselves as profit.

4. The key to capitalism is private ownership of the means of production. Calvinist religious beliefs supported the emergence of capitalism by making a virtue of hard work and the accumulation of wealth.

5. The development of capitalism also depended on the transformation of labor through which feudal ties between land, nobles, and serfs broke down and landless peasants were available as sources of cheap labor power to the rising urban capitalist class. Labor power became a commodity that was bought and sold in the marketplace.

6. Capitalists try to maximize profits by controlling labor power and markets. Monopoly describes a market dominated by a single organization, whereas oligopoly is a market dominated by a few. A conglomerate is a centrally owned collection of organizations that produce for different markets. Most powerful business organizations are controlled by a small elite.

7. Industrial society labor markets tend to be segmented, divided into jobs that have different requirements and prospects. The primary market is divided into subordinate and independent sectors, and the secondary market includes low-level jobs that carry with them little power, income, or chance for advancement. Professionals are relatively autonomous and well paid and determine the conditions under which they work. For this reason, people often try to professionalize their occupations.

8. The economy is also divided into two parts, noncompetitive and competitive. In general, workers in the noncompetitive economy earn higher wages and are more likely to belong to unions.

9. The United States is moving into a postindustrial era in which people are increasingly likely to provide services rather than produce goods. Although this changes the job market, it has little effect on relations between employers and workers.

10. Alienation is the feeling that we lack a connection with the work we do, and it is closely tied to work that is experienced as powerless, meaningless, socially isolating, and fragmented.

11. Unemployment has many social causes, including changing job markets, shifting age structures, and tension between workers and employers.

12. Socialism differs from capitalism in that the means of production are owned by the state. Existing socialist societies tend to be far less efficient than capitalist ones and tend to have authoritarian states. Under democratic socialism, only major industries are owned by the state. Communism is a system in which the means of production are communally owned and there is no state.

13. Regardless of its economic institutions, each society is part of a world economy in which nations are divided into the core, the periphery, and the semiperiphery. In this system multinational corporations wield enormous power, in many cases rivaling that of nations.

14. Both capitalism and socialism produce functional and dysfunctional consequences. Capitalism generates enormous wealth but also classes of the very poor. Socialist societies, however, have eliminated gross class differences, but are generally inefficient and politically repressive.

KEY TERMS

alienation   486
automation   478
capital   473
capitalism   473
commodity   471
communism   492
conglomerate   480
core society   493
dual economy   484
economic institution   470
exchange value   471
feudalism   471

forces of production   469
independent primary jobs   473
labor market
    segmentation   484
market economy   471
merchant   472
mode of production   469
monopoly   474
oligopoly   479
peripheral society   493
postindustrial society   486
primary labor market   483

profession   484
relations of production   469
secondary labor market   473
semiperipheral society   494
socialism   490
state capitalism   492
structural unemployment   489
subordinate primary jobs   473
surplus value   472
use value   470
world economy   493
world system theory   493

LOOKING ELSEWHERE

Having studied Chapter 19, you might want to look at related discussions in *Human Arrangements*, which include

■ the relationship between economic and population growth (Chapter 4, pp. 74–76, 79, 85–87)

■ colonialism and international stratification (Chapter 12, pp. 289–91)

■ occupation and racial inequality (Chapter 13, pp. 304–308, 320–21)

■ occupation and gender inequality (Chapter 14, pp. 336–40, 354–55)

■ occupation and age inequality (Chapter 15, pp. 369–70, 374–75, 379–80)

■ the relationship between schools and the economy (Chapter 17, pp. 415–16, 427–29, 429–30, 431–32)

■ the use of high technology to break strikes and control labor costs (Chapter 18, pp. 457)

■ the role of the state in supporting capitalism and socialism (Chapter 20, pp. 512, 519–21)

■ socialism as a political system (Chapter 20, pp. 510, 520–21)

■ world-systems theory and social change (Chapter 23, pp. 583–84)

■ science as a profession (Chapter 18, pp. 450–53)

■ professional socialization (Chapter 7, p. 154)

RECOMMENDED READINGS

Aronowitz, S. 1983. *Working-class hero: A new strategy for labor*. New York: Pilgrim Press. Sociologist and longtime labor activist Stanley Aronowitz provides an important history of the U.S. labor movement and a diagnosis of its current weakness.

Braverman, H. 1974. *Labor and monopoly capital: The degradation of work in the twentieth century*. New York: Monthly Review Press. An analysis of the transformation and control of labor power in capitalist societies.

Marx, K. 1964. *Selected writings in sociology and social philosophy*. Edited by T. Bottomore and M. Rubel. Baltimore, MD: Penguin Books. An excellent introduction to Marx's major ideas on stratification and alienated work.

Nelkin, D., and Brown, M. S. 1984. *Workers at risk: Voices from the workplace*. Chicago: University of Chicago Press. The authors counter the belief that workers are free to choose jobs according to how much danger they are willing to expose themselves to.

Shannon, T. R. 1989. *An introduction to the world-system perspective*. Boulder, CO: Westview Press. A concise, clearly written look at world-systems theory as well as alternative explanations of world economic relations and development.

Smith, J. 1981. *Social issues and the social order: The contradictions of capitalism*. Cambridge, MA: Winthrop. An interesting, well-written book that tries to understand the ways in which economic arrangements such as capitalism contribute to social problems.

Terkel, S. 1974. *Working*. New York: Pantheon. Studs Terkel is a journalist with a marvelous talent for getting people to talk about themselves. This collection of interviews in which people talk about "what they do all day long" is fascinating and thought-provoking.

20
POLITICAL INSTITUTIONS

 Before its recent revolution, the government of Rumania banned the ownership of typewriters by former convicts or anyone who posed "a danger to public order or state security." People could not buy a typewriter without permission from the government, and those who already owned one had to register it with the police, including a sample of the typewriter's print for identification of anything written on it. It is easier to own a gun in most of the U.S. than it was to own a typewriter in Rumania.

Politics refers to the social process through which power is distributed and used at all levels from groups to societies, and the preceding example illustrates important aspects of political structures. The Rumanian government's decision was an exercise of power that affected all members of its society, and this by itself is enough to make it political. It was also political in that it was designed to make it more difficult for opponents to publish antigovernment leaflets. The government's control of something as simple as a typewriter was an attempt to maintain its power and perpetuate a form of government.

Previous chapters explored the importance of power in social interaction (Chapter 8), groups and organizations (Chapter 9), and communities (Chapter 10). In this chapter, we are interested primarily in the distribution of power in societies. In particular, we focus on **political institutions**—the relatively permanent social systems through which authority is distributed and exercised. Who has the power to make what kinds of decisions? How evenly distributed is decision-making power? How are decisions actually made and how are they put into effect? How do political institutions affect the people who occupy different statuses? What are the functional and dysfunctional consequences of different political arrangements, and what is the relationship between political power and social change?

Since the sociological study of politics centers on the concept of power, we begin by taking a closer look at this by-now-familiar concept.

POLITICAL POWER AND THE STATE

We have defined power as the potential to have an effect on ourselves or our environment even when there is resistance. This includes not only direct control over people—such as the conditions under which they can own typewriters or guns—but also the ability to decide how the resources of a society will be used. Deciding how tax money will be spent is as much a use of political authority as the ability to force people to pay taxes in the first place.

As we now know, the most important form of social power is **authority**, a unique form of socially supported power that rests on the beliefs that those who possess it have a right to it and those who do not have a duty to obey. Weber identified three types, the first of which is **legal-rational authority**, power based on clearly stated norms. The norms that define legal-rational authority specify who holds power in relation to whom and under what circumstances. The power of professors to grade students, of people to control who enters their houses, and of bosses to hire and fire workers are all examples of legal-rational authority. In the U.S. the police may not enter someone's home without a proper warrant; but in many countries such as El Salvador, it has not been uncommon for the police literally to kidnap suspects who are never heard from again.

Unlike legal-rational authority, **charismatic authority** is based on the belief that someone possesses special abilities or characteristics. Prophets, heroes,

Sociologists are interested not simply in the amount of authority someone has, but its social basis. Gandhi had enormous charismatic authority as leader of India's successful struggle for independence from Britain, but he never held political office. Japan's emperor, in contrast, wielded absolute traditional and legal-rational authority. With Japan's defeat in World War II, however, a new constitution stripped the emperor of virtually all authority, although he continues to enjoy great prestige, as pictured here, at Emperor Akihito's 1990 coronation.

demagogues, and mass murderers—from Jesus Christ and Gandhi, to Napoleon Bonaparte and Adolph Hitler—all have had this type of authority (Willner 1984). **Traditional authority** rests on the belief that the occupants of certain statuses are legitimately powerful because "that's the way it's always been." The authority of kings, queens, and emperors and, on a smaller scale, of elderly Japanese over their adult children—does not depend solely on legal-rational rules; rather, it also flows from a commitment to traditional arrangements that confer power on the occupants of particular statuses.

It is important to emphasize that legal-rational and traditional authority are not forms of personal power, for they are attached to particular statuses under socially defined conditions. When soldiers salute each other, for example, they pay respect to a person's rank, not to the individual who holds it. When police officers go off duty, they lose much of their authority, just as former U.S. presidents no longer control the use of nuclear weapons.

A number of sociologists (see Haskell 1984) point out that in technologically sophisticated societies *expertise* in a specialized area is becoming an increasingly important source of authority in addition to Weber's three classic types. Experts in fields such as medicine, computer science, economics, business management and accounting, and nuclear weapons technology often exercise considerable authority because they command information necessary for important decisions.

In sharp contrast with authority, **coercive power** lacks social legitimacy. When one country invades another and imposes its will on the inhabitants, its control over that society is not socially supported. Rather, it is based on fear and, for this reason, tends to be relatively unstable. In the aftermath of revolutions (such as that in Nicaragua) and invasions (such as Iraq's invasion of Kuwait), guerilla warfare often becomes a fact of everyday life, and the new leaders live with continuing awareness that they might be ousted at any time. In countries such as Japan and the U.S., however, leaders know that while they may lose office with the next election, their opponents do not question their basic right to use the authority of their office so long as they occupy it.

Weber's three forms of authority are ideal types that rarely exist by themselves. A president may combine legal-rational, charismatic, and traditional authority, and the power of parents in relation to their children combines both traditional and legal-rational authority. If one source of power declines, status occupants tend to rely more heavily on others. Former national leaders have no legal-rational authority over their government but may try to use charismatic or traditional authority to influence decisions long after they leave office.

How is authority organized in societies? This question brings us to perhaps the most important concept in the study of political institutions—the *state*.

The Emergence of the State

Weber ([1921] 1958) defined the **state** as the institution that "claims the monopoly of the use of force within a given territory" (p. 78). Like other institutions, the state is defined in part by the social functions it performs. It is responsible for establishing and enforcing legal norms; it sets goals; it acts as an umpire in disputes among individuals, groups, and communities; and it establishes and maintains relationships with other societies, including trade agreements and military alliances. One function underlies all of these: the state is responsible for maintaining order and stability.

States vary in how they perform these functions, and it is these differences that are the focus for most of this chapter. In this sense, the state is not a static thing; rather, it is a set of cultural ideas and dynamic social relationships through which power is used by some individuals and groups over others. The U.S. judicial system, for example—going all the way to the Supreme Court—is, above all, a social mechanism for resolving disputes and using the authority to determine guilt and innocence and inflict punishment. The rules that regulate what happens in courts are part of the normative structure of the state and affect many aspects of social life.

The state is not the same as the *government*, just as "The U.S. Family" is not the same thing as an individual family. A **government** is the collection of people who occupy positions of authority within the framework of relationships that define the state. There are thus two answers to questions such as "What is the Soviet Politburo?" As a part of the Soviet government, it is a collection of leaders who come and go, different people at different times. As part of the Soviet state, it is a group whose members—*whoever they may be*—have particular powers in relation to the citizens of the Soviet Union and particular relationships with the leaders of other societies.

Like most gatherer-hunter societies, Inuit bands have no formal leaders. Important decisions are based on a consensus or, where specialized knowledge is needed, by those considered best qualified to decide.

The U.S. government may change considerably with each presidential election, but the state remains unchanged. The Bill of Rights (the first 10 amendments to the Constitution) is a set of norms that defines relationships between the state and its citizens, and it applies no matter which government is in power. The distinction between the state and government may be clearer if we remember that although many governments during U.S. history have violated the Bill of Rights by abusing the power of the state, such violations have had a relatively small effect on the nature of the state itself.

Historically, the state is a relatively new institution. Gatherer-hunter societies had no state; decisions generally rested on community consensus, and the kinship group was the only focus of power. Horticultural societies often had a few leaders who depended on traditional authority, but it was not until the agricultural era produced surpluses of wealth that social classes and the state emerged. Kings and emperors were at the center of the first states. Their authority was strictly traditional, and they were involved in continuous power struggles with nobles and with religious and military leaders. It was not until the last few centuries—particularly in Europe and then the United States—that the state began to acquire a monopoly over political power and the many social functions that characterize its modern form. With the emergence of the state came new cultural concepts—"nation" and "patriotism"— that have become basic organizing concepts in relations between societies. As the Industrial Revolution spawned a growing middle class of well-educated citizens who demanded a voice in the exercise of power in their societies, and as divisions of labor made social life increasingly complex, the functions of the state—and its power—expanded enormously.

Although one might argue that the emergence of powerful states was inevitable as societies industrialized and became more complex, as explained later in this chapter, the development of the state and its power has served some social classes more than others. Since the prime function of the state is to maintain order and stability in a society, and since a given social order usually favors some groups over others, the state inevitably plays an important part in the perpetuation of social inequality. This also means that the characteristics of the state inevitably mirror to some degree the society it is designed to protect and perpetuate.

CULTURE, POLITICS, AND THE STATE

The power exercised by the state represents the collective ability of a society to "mobilize its resources in the interest of goals" (Parsons 1969, p. 204). In other words, the state uses laws and policies to support selected values. How do such values and norms differ from one society to another, and how are they reflected in the state as an institution? Does the state value personal freedom more than social order and conformity, a strong military more than a healthy population free of poverty, equality more than the freedom to pursue individual gain, the rights of accused criminals more than the rights of their victims? The answers to such questions define the goals the state pursues in the name of society, and affect how particular governments use political power.

In capitalist societies, for example, the right to own and use the means of production for private gain is an important economic value. The state, in turn, is responsible for protecting private property rights and fostering social conditions in which capitalists can maximize profits (see Smith 1981). From Marx's perspective, economic arrangements form the most important institutions in any society, and a key function of a capitalist state is to support the values of the capitalist class.

Consider antitrust laws that forbid monopolies in which one organization completely dominates a product or service. Whose interests do such laws best serve? Do they protect consumers from the ability of monopolies to dictate any price they want? Apparently not, for a few large companies in an industry can maintain high prices even though no one of them has a monopoly. There are three major U.S. automobile manufacturers, for example, and yet there is little price competition. Each waits for one of the others to raise prices at the beginning of the new model year and then one by one the others raise their prices by a comparable amount (Baran and Sweezy 1966). The only serious price competition in the automobile market has come from foreign manufacturers, which has nothing to do with U.S. antitrust laws.

From Marx's perspective, antitrust laws primarily serve those who own and control capital. This appears to be a contradiction, for why would the state serve the interests of capitalists by restricting them? One answer is that antitrust laws protect capitalists from being driven out of business by other capitalists who monopolize a market. The 1983 breakup of AT&T, for example, was urged less by consumer groups than by companies that wanted a larger slice of the long distance telephone market. The long and unsuccessful antitrust suit against IBM was inspired primarily by IBM's competitors—such as Xerox—not by consumers. In both cases, the millions of dollars spent by the government to sue the companies involved were supplied by taxpayers.

The protection of private property rights is not the only function of the state in capitalist countries. Values such as privacy and the freedoms to vote, express opinions, move from one place to another, and follow religious beliefs are also legally protected. The state takes major responsibility for providing for the poor, for protecting consumers against fraud or the hazards of dangerous products, for supporting public education, and for protecting the environment.

Some of the values supported by the state in socialist countries such as the Soviet Union and China are very different from those emphasized in capitalist countries. Personal freedom is far more restricted, and people live in continuing fear that they will be reported to the authorities for doing something that might offend officials. Rock music was once banned in the Soviet Union because of its supposed subversive effects; and artists, musicians, and writers have been persecuted for undermining the state.

The announced aim of socialist societies has been to promote equality by refusing to support what is, in capitalist societies, one of the most important personal freedoms—the right to own capital. The welfare of the community, socialists argue, is of more value than the freedom of individuals to exploit the community for personal gain. Consequently, full employment has been more highly valued than efficient production.

The contrast between capitalist and socialist states might lead one to conclude that personal freedom and equality are inherently incompatible values, that it is impossible for a society to vigorously support both at the same time. It is important to remember, however, that the right to own capital is only one of many personal freedoms, and human history is full of examples—including most gatherer-hunter and horticultural societies—of societies in which people owned no capital and inequality was minimal and in which personal freedom in other areas of life was *not* tightly restricted as it is in so many societies today. Whether or not freedom and equality can be achieved simultaneously in industrial societies remains to be seen.

It is also important to remember that most socialist societies were created through violent revolutions or foreign invasions that transformed societies in which private property rights and severe inequality had existed for hundreds of years. To Lenin ([1917] 1949), the most powerful leader of the Russian Revolution, the state had to assume great powers over individual freedom in order to crush opposition to the revolution and break the control of the ruling class over the society.

Regardless of their differences, all societies where the state has developed as an institution have one value in common: the preservation of the state itself. The state is the institution that monopolizes the use of force, and when the perpetuation of the state is threatened, the governments of the U.S. or Britain are no less likely to respond with force than are those of China, Rumania, or the Soviet Union. It is a federal crime to advocate—even by merely writing a letter or making a speech—the violent overthrow of the U.S. government; but it is legal for the state to use police and soldiers to disperse a crowd of demonstrators. The state is an institution that, at best, walks a fine line between the protection of citizens and their oppression. In the name of safeguarding society, it seeks to increase its authority; but those same powers—the monopoly of violence—can then be used against those same citizens.

STRUCTURES OF POWER: BASIC TYPES OF POLITICAL INSTITUTIONS

It is in the structures of power—how it is distributed and used—that the greatest differences between societies are found. As we have seen before, power structures have two basic characteristics: the equality of distribution, and the amount of power a social system has.

Distributions of Power: Democracy, Oligarchy, and Autocracy

The word **democracy** joins the Greek words "cracy" ("rule") and "demo" ("of the people"). In pure democracies power is shared equally by all members of a society. In ancient Greece, decisions were made at meetings in which every citizen had a vote. Virtually all gatherer-hunter societies operated as democracies, and some New England towns still have town meetings in which residents voice their opinions and vote on the issues. Democracies always place some restrictions on who is defined as a citizen eligible to participate in decision making. Children cannot vote, just as slaves and women could not in ancient Greece.

Few states take the form of pure democracy, in large part because it is impractical in large complex societies. How would millions of citizens meet to thrash out national issues? If every decision required a vote by the entire population, we would spend most of our time at the polls. One common response to this problem is the **representative democracy**, in which citizens delegate authority to elected representatives—such as those who serve in legislatures. Theoretically, the elected representatives speak for the voters, who are too numerous to speak for themselves.

Democracy depends on several key characteristics of social systems. Countries with advanced economies and urban, literate, middle-class populations tend to be more democratic than societies that are underdeveloped and have largely illiterate, rural, peasant populations (Lipset 1959). Although Bollen (1983) found that economic development and democratic institutions tend to go hand in hand, he also found that democracy depends on the position of a country in the world economy (see Chapter 19). Democracy is most common in wealthy core countries such as the U.S., West Germany, and Japan and least common in peripheral countries such as Nigeria and Iran. The stability of democracies also varies with the degree social inequality: regardless of their level of economic development, societies with highly unequal distributions of wealth and income are more likely to be politically unstable than those with intermediate or low levels of inequality (Muller 1988).

Cultural characteristics of a society also play a part. Democracy depends on norms that restrict the power of the state in relation to the people—such as the U.S. Constitution and its Bill of Rights. Values and attitudes are also important, especially those that tolerate and support dissent (see McClosky and Brill 1983). In the U.S. **civil disobedience**—the deliberate and open violation of a norm for the purpose of changing it because it is perceived as being unjust—is culturally defined as legitimate behavior,

Democracy has been more successful in industrial than in agrarian societies, such as Guatemala. Here, a Guatemalan woman casts her vote in the 1990 presidential election—the first time in the country's history that one president was succeeded by another through free elections.

even though those who engage in it are punished. A special respect is reserved for those who openly defy unjust laws and willingly accept the consequences in the name of improving society.

Two important aspects of social structure also support democracies. Since citizens must be in a position to elect representatives who act in their best interests, it is important for citizens to know what their representatives are doing with their authority. This produces a continuing tension between the desire of those in authority to keep their activities secret and the need of the people to know about government decisions and activities. In some cases, secrets do protect national security. If the public had access to the military's plans for national defense, so would its enemies. In other cases, however, secrecy serves the interests of leaders who want to conceal activities that the public would oppose. Many instances of official misconduct—such as the sale of arms to Iran in return for hostages—are concealed by government officials on the grounds of national security, when in fact the only security involved is that of the government officials themselves.

Democracy also depends on diffusion of power among many different individuals, groups, and organizations, for when power is concentrated in the hands of a relative few, democracies are in danger of becoming *oligarchies* and, in the most extreme cases, *autocracies*.

Oligarchy and Autocracy   Michels (1911) argued that the mere existence of leaders in a society guarantees that democracy cannot last, because power is corrupting no matter how noble a leader's intentions may be. Michels believed that an "Iron Rule of Oligarchy" dictates that complex societies always become **oligarchies**, in which the power of the state is monopolized by an elite.

Michels based his rule on three arguments, the first of which is that most people, either because of apathy or incompetence, would rather let others make decisions for them. It is difficult for most people, for example, to actively involve themselves in debate over nuclear weapons and the economy without a thorough understanding of the complex issues involved.

Second, Michels argued that in complex societies it is impossible to pay attention to every point of view. Although there may be opinion polls, elections, and referenda on important issues, it is impossible to conduct a national debate that includes the active participation of millions of people. Decisions are therefore left to a small number of leaders. Third, leaders enjoy the privileges that come with power and, therefore, want to keep their positions. In order to keep their power, leaders seek more by trying to control their rivals, or silence their opposition by controlling criticism in the media.

From Michels' point of view, the increasing complexity of societies and their reliance on leaders results in a loss of individual power and freedom and growing opportunities for abuses that result in social oppression. As Tannenbaum (1968) pointed out, however, things are not so simple. Industrial societies are organized around bureaucracies that control complex divisions of labor. No small group can control national governments in countries such as the U.S. Every four years, a new president vows to control the vast federal bureaucracy and, inevitably, realizes that

he and his aides cannot possibly do it. As Etzioni-Halévy (1983) argued, bureaucracy is necessary for managing the affairs of a complex representative democracy, and yet its size and power coupled with its inherent rigidity threaten democratic institutions.

Socialist countries such as the Soviet Union and China are, in comparison with North America and most of Europe, far more oligarchic and bureaucratic. When Soviet jet fighters shot down a Korean airliner that strayed into Soviet airspace in 1983, for example, one fact that became clear in the aftermath was that the Soviet government had great difficulty monitoring and controlling military units far on the other side of the country. As tightly controlled as many aspects of social life are in socialist countries, gross inefficiency is one of their hallmarks, and this is due in no small part to the vastness and complexity of the bureaucracies through which a relatively small number of leaders try to govern entire societies.

The most extreme concentration of political authority is an **autocracy** in which the power of the state is wielded by one leader. Hitler in Germany, Stalin in Russia, Idi Amin in Uganda, and the Shah of Iran were all autocrats, as were most kings and queens prior to the twentieth century. Autocracy describes only a few national leaders in recent years, including the head of the royal family in Saudi Arabia, Muammar al-Qaddafi in Libya, and Saddam Hussein in Iraq.

The scale running from democracy to autocracy describes the range within which states distribute political power. A second important dimension of the state, however, is the amount of power it has.

How Much Power?
Authoritarianism and Totalitarianism

The concept of **authoritarianism** describes the degree to which the state controls the lives of its citizens. Since all states, by definition, monopolize the use of force, they are all authoritarian to some de-

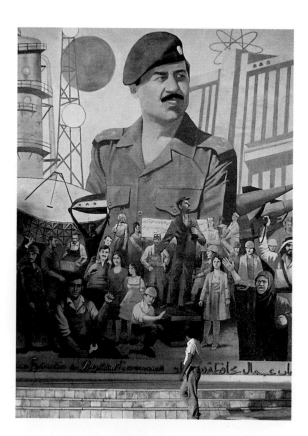

One sign of a true autocrat is a public image that is larger than life. Here Iraq's President Saddam Hussein is portrayed in dramatic and heroic fashion on an Iraqi street mural.

Perhaps no other institution so exemplifies the horrors of authoritarianism than the Soviet Union's secret police, the KGB. In 1989, 1,000 demonstrators gathered outside KGB headquarters to commemorate and protest the murder of millions of citizens by the KGB. That the demonstration was not brutally suppressed indicates how much the Soviet Union has changed in recent years.

gree; but sociologists generally reserve the term authoritarian for states that exercise high levels of control over people's lives.

In spite of movements towards greater democracy, much of the population of the world lives in authoritarian states (see Rubin 1987). Under authoritarianism, the state has the power to control the mass media, schools, and the economy. It often uses terror—inflicted by military and secret police organizations—to control its citizens. The ability of people to migrate often is restricted, and there are few restraints on the government's ability to enact and enforce laws, however unjust they may be (Friedrich and Brzezinski 1965).

The most extreme form of authoritarianism is **totalitarianism**, under which the state attempts to control not only people's behavior, but virtually all aspects of their private lives. Best described in George Orwell's 1949 classic novel, *Nineteen Eighty-four*, the totalitarian state tries to control what people think and feel as well as what they do through complete control over all social institutions, from the family and mass communications to religion. In Orwell's nightmarish vision, society is ruled by "Big Brother"; television sets are two-way, allowing authorities to monitor people's homes; history is rewritten in order to conform to the state's version of the truth; and those who refuse to conform are tortured until they think and behave "correctly."

Of all the forms that the state can take, totalitarianism is probably the least stable and is as uncommon as pure democracy (Walzer, in Howe 1983). In the twentieth century, Nazi Germany and Russia under Stalin came closest to Orwell's vision of totalitarianism, but even these extreme cases were far from monolithic states that effectively ruled the private lives of their citizens. In both cases dissent was not uncommon and there were frequent power struggles (Peukert 1987). History seems to show that the totalitarian state is unattainable (see Nee and Mozingo 1983; Schlesinger 1983).

In general, the likelihood of authoritarianism increases as a society becomes more unstable, especially during crises such as wars or internal upheaval.

When the state is used as an instrument of social oppression of minorities, its monopoly over the use of force becomes all the more important and dangerous. This picture was taken near Cape Town, South Africa, where blacks, whose shantytown was being demolished by the government, demonstrated in protest because they had no other place to live. The response from the police was a volley of tear gas. Like most minorities, black South Africans cannot begin to match the enormous military power of their government.

In 1986, for example, as antiapartheid protests increased in South Africa, the government made it illegal for anyone to criticize the government in public. In 1798, shortly after the American Revolution, Congress passed the Sedition Act, which allowed the government to prosecute anyone who wrote or published anything that was "false, scandalous, or malicious" against any branch of the federal government. In short, open criticism of the government was banned by law. In the early 1950s the fear of communism allowed Senator Joseph McCarthy to conduct his infamous Senate hearings to identify communists. Hundreds of people were subpoenaed to testify before his committee, and anyone who had ever belonged to a communist organization, or who had associated with those who had, was labeled a communist (or a communist sympathizer). McCarthy never identified a single communist in the government, but by the time he was stopped, hundreds of innocent people—from government employees to teachers, writers, artists, and actors—had lost their jobs and suffered permanent damage to their reputation.

There is no such thing as a state that cannot become more authoritarian under the control of a particular government, and the state's monopoly over the use of force creates a continuing tension between the functional importance of state institutions and the potential for abuse of authority. Nor is majority rule—a hallmark of democracy—a guarantee that the power of the state will not be used to oppress citizens. More than a century ago, Alexis de Tocqueville ([1835] 1954) visited the U.S. and warned

of the possibility of a "tyranny of the majority," in which the rights of minorities would not be protected. In a racist, sexist, anti-Semitic society conformity to prevailing norms results in the oppression of nonwhites, women, and Jews for whom the law—which is controlled by the state—is "a sword, not a shield" (Burns 1973). Without the acceptance of Nazi ideology by millions of Germans, for example, the Nazi state never would have been able to perpetrate the Holocaust in which more than 11 million people were murdered.

It is important to note that while many of today's authoritarian states are also socialist countries, there is no necessary connection between economic and political arrangements. Nazi Germany was both capitalist and antisocialist; some of the world's most oppressive military dictatorships are allies of the U.S.; and in state-capitalist countries such as Sweden and Norway, the state is not authoritarian. As the socialist countries of Eastern Europe continue to change over the coming years, it will be interesting to see to what extent they give up their socialist economic system as they build more democratic political institutions.

Who Rules? Power in U.S. Politics

Sociologists have developed several views of the distribution of political power in societies, two of which we encountered in Chapter 10. Mills (1956) and Hunter (1953) argued that power is monopolized by an elite of business, government, and the military leaders who have similar backgrounds and move easily from one sphere of power to another (see also Useem 1984). Below the power elite a variety of interest groups have some power, and at the bottom lies the mass of unorganized people who have little power to affect national decisions.

The power elite, Mills argued, is bound together by common interests. Military leaders want to expand the number and sophistication of weapons, and corporations want to build such weapons for profit. As a result, decisions about the nuclear arms race are based not only on national defense, but on the economic interests of corporations as well. The concept of a power elite identifies several consequences of concentrated political power, the most important of which are the growth of corporate power and the decline of public participation in decision making.

Riesman (1961) offered a different view, arguing that power is divided pluralistically among a variety of interest groups over which the mass of unorganized citizens has some control. Different interest groups dominate decision making in different areas, and recognize that they have limited power and depend on others in order to accomplish their goals. Riesman believed, however, that when pluralism is taken to extremes it interferes with leadership because each interest group exercises veto power over the issues that define its goals. Governing bodies such as the U.S. Congress have difficulty making decisions because they are besieged by well-organized interest groups at every turn. The result is often legislation that offends a minimal number of groups but also fails to establish clear and decisive directions for national programs and policy.

Lieberson (1971) also contended that when interest groups become so numerous and powerful that they dominate political decision making, it is difficult for a national consensus to emerge on any given issue. Each group tends to fight for its special interest and for nothing else, and this tends to fragment society and break down social cohesion.

There is little doubt that political power is concentrated in the U.S., although certainly not to the degree found in authoritarian societies. Domhoff's 1967 study and Freitag's study in 1975 both support Mills' belief in the existence of a power elite (see also Domhoff 1983). Freitag found that almost 90 percent of federal cabinet officers between 1897 and 1973 had also served as high-level officers in corporations (see One Step Further 20-1).

ONE STEP FURTHER 20-1

The Political Power of the Upper Class

Although Domhoff estimates that the U.S. upper class makes up only 0.5 percent of the population, its share of politically powerful positions is considerably larger. The data in Table B-20-1 are from two historical studies of U.S. cabinet members from 1897 to 1973 and from 1932 to 1964. In both periods, roughly two-thirds of cabinet members had upper-class family origins (percentages that, although omitted below, are only slightly higher for Republican cabinets than for Democratic). The first set of percentages shows how presidential cabinets compared with the entire U.S. adult population on a variety of class indicators. Notice how strong the elite Anglo-Saxon background of cabinet members is in comparison with a miniscule percentage of the general population.

If we add to this Mintz's finding that 90 percent of cabinet members were either from the upper class or were associated with major corporations, it becomes clear that the upper class and those who share its interests have a virtual monopoly over high level positions in the administrative branch of the federal government. Freitag (1975) finds that this pattern is not only quite stable over time, but varies little from one cabinet position to another, including secretary of labor.

Table B-20-1

1897–1973 PERCENT	CABINETS	GENERAL U.S. POPULATION
in the business elite	78%	less than 0.5%
in the social elite	66%	less than 1.0%
listed in the *Social Register*	25%	less than 0.1%
who belong to elite clubs	48%	less than 1.0%
who attended elite schools	29%	less than 0.5%
with British background	82%	19%
1932–1964 PERCENT IN THE UPPER CLASS		
Secretaries of state	63%	
Secretaries of defense	62%	
Secretaries of treasury	63%	

Source: For 1897–1973, Mintz (1975); for 1932–1964, Domhoff (1967).

This does not mean the power elite is a unified group whose members meet to agree on political decisions. It does imply that a relatively small number of people have far greater access to political power than do most citizens, and their interests tend to coincide. Middle- and lower-class people have some voice in selecting presidents and congressional representatives, but they have virtually no power in choosing cabinet members and the heads of powerful agencies such as the departments of State and Defense. Nor does the average citizen have access to these officials once they are appointed.

Members of the power elite certainly differ on various issues and may oppose one another; but when they choose to work toward common goals, they wield enormous political power. As one study of corporate campaign contributions in the 1980 elections showed, businesses as a group tend to support the same candidates (Clawsen et al. 1986); and when businesses go against the tide and support candidates or issues that are generally unpopular in the business community, there are powerful sanctions that can be used to enforce conformity (see Mintz and Schwartz 1985; Useem 1984). If the U.S. political system is pluralistic, it is what Kornhauser (1966) called an "elite pluralism," in which a select few vie with one another over control of the state (see also Knoke 1981).

The U.S. Voter   The right to vote is the most direct form of political power available. Although we rarely use it to decide specific issues, we can use it to elect nominated candidates for public office. This represents a very indirect form of power in an important respect, for once candidates are elected, their need to worry about pleasing their constituents lessens until the next election. In the 1964 presidential election, for example, Lyndon Johnson overwhelmed his opponent, Barry Goldwater, in large part because voters feared that Goldwater would be too quick to involve the U.S. in war. Within a few years after his election, however, Johnson had led the U.S. deep into the disastrous war in Vietnam. Ronald Reagan won landslide victories as a presidential candidate in part by promising to control the federal budget deficit. Under his leadership, however, it grew to record high levels. In his election campaign, George Bush promised no new taxes as a major part of his platform, and yet went back on his pledge and agreed to new taxes two years later.

U.S. voters are considerably less likely to vote in national elections than are the citizens of other in-

TABLE 20-1   Voter Participation in Selected Countries

COUNTRY	PERCENTAGE VOTING[1]
Switzerland	52
United States	59
India	60
Canada	71
Finland	74
Ireland	76
Israel	79
Great Britain	79
Norway	83
Denmark	89
West Germany	91

[1]Percentage of population of voting age that actually voted in national elections.

Source: USCB 1980b.

dustrial societies (Table 20-1). This may be due in part to the fact that responsibility for registering as voters rests entirely with the individual, whereas in Canada, Finland, Great Britain, and West Germany registration is either required or actively facilitated by the government by allowing registration by mail or automatically registering all citizens. Among U.S. registered voters, 71 percent voted in the 1988 election, which suggests that if registration were more widespread, voting might be as well (Piven and Cloward 1988; USCB 1990a).

There is also evidence, however, that Americans generally pay little attention to political issues. Only 23 percent report that they are "very interested in politics and national affairs," and more than a third say they are "only somewhat interested" or "not at all" (Davis and Smith 1987). National surveys suggest that these relatively low levels of political involvement may reflect a lack of faith in government, the belief that government is not responsive to the people, and the perception that the political process serves primarily the interests of elites (Vanneman and Cannon 1987). More than two-thirds report the belief that most public officials have little interest in the average citizen's problems, and less than 20 percent express a great deal of confidence in either the Congress or the executive branch. Voter nonparticipation is also related to the statuses people occupy. In general, those who occupy the highest positions are the most likely to vote (Table 20-2). An exception to this is that women and men are equally likely to vote, even though women as a category occupy an inferior social position.

Is the general lack of political interest and participation some kind of national personality trait? While this is a possible explanation, sociologists are more likely to consider how the structure of political institutions affects the ability and motivation of people to participate in them. For more insight into this, we turn to political parties, the first level of political organization above the "unorganized mass of people" (see Teixeira 1987).

Political Parties   A **political party** is an organization whose main goal is to acquire power by placing members in positions of authority. In authoritarian countries that allow voting, a single party dominates the state and voters must choose between voting for the official party candidates or not voting at all. In a few countries, such as Mexico, the state is

---

TABLE 20-2   Who Votes in Presidential Elections? (United States, 1988)

CHARACTERISTIC	PERCENTAGE VOTING[1]
Gender	
Male	56
Female	58
Race	
White	59
Black	52
Hispanic	29
Age	
18–20	33
21–24	38
25–34	48
35–44	61
45–64	68
65 and older	69
Education	
8 years or less	37
1–3 years high school	41
High school graduate	55
1–3 years college	64
College graduate or more	78
Employment Status	
Employed	58
Unemployed	39

[1]Percentage of adult citizen population that actually voted in the 1988 presidential election.

Sources: USCB 1990a

---

not authoritarian, but the ruling party is so firmly entrenched that opposition parties rarely win elections. Most countries have a handful of parties, and a few, such as Italy, have a dozen or so.

Since parties are the main source of candidates for public office, they are an important link between citizens and government. Through their candidates, parties define positions on issues, map solutions to problems, and transmit public opinion to those who make decisions. If voters, then, feel unmotivated to participate in political activities, part of the explanation may lie in the characteristics of parties through which most of the power of voters is felt.

The sociological importance of parties lies in two areas that distinguish parties in the U.S. from those in most other representative democracies. The first concerns the legal norms that control elections, which, in turn, define the relationship between parties and the state. The second focuses on the structural and cultural characteristics of parties themselves, both of which are tied closely to the first.

Unlike elections in most democracies, U.S. norms dictate a winner-take-all system in which a candidate must receive more votes than any other candidate. The composition of Congress is determined by the outcome in each of 50 state elections. Under this system, even if 49 percent of the voters favor candidates from party "A," it is possible that *none* of those who are elected will be from that party. In this extreme hypothetical case the interests of almost half of the adult population would have no representation in Congress.

In most other representative democracies, the composition of legislatures is proportional, which is to say it is determined by the percentage of the vote received by each party, not whether individual candidates get more votes than do their opponents. If only 10 percent of the voters favor party "A," then 10 percent of the seats in the legislature will be filled by members of that party. Such legislatures reflect the diversity of their populations in a way that is almost impossible in the U.S.

The norms that govern elections affect the composition—the structure—of governing bodies such as the Congress and state legislatures or European parliaments. If U.S. voters want to use their votes to elect candidates, their only hope is to vote for a candidate who can beat all opponents. If the candidate who seems most likely to win does not represent their views, then from a practical standpoint, their votes have no effect on the ultimate composition of the government.

The effects of the winner-take-all system extend to the social characteristics of parties themselves, and U.S. parties differ from those in other representative democracies in several ways. Suppose, for example, that you belong to the Freedom Party, whose members favor, among other things, legalization of marijuana, a position shared by only 16 percent of adults (Davis and Smith 1990). How does your party win seats in Congress? In most democracies, you could gain as many as 16 percent of the legislative seats—in other words, representation in direct proportion to the percentage of your supporters in the population. In the U.S., however, you would win no seats unless you ran candidates in congressional districts where most voters favor legalization of marijuana—an extremely unlikely possibility. If you are serious about winning—rather than merely expressing your views—one response to this problem is to do whatever you can to avoid offending potential supporters, and one obvious way to do this is not to take a clear and open stand in favor of legalizing marijuana.

In most representative democracies, when parties take a clear stand on the issues, it does not destroy their chances of gaining some political power; but in the U.S., it can be disastrous. Many analysts, for example, agreed that Ronald Reagan's 1984 landslide victory over Walter Mondale was helped considerably by Reagan's avoidance of controversial issues and his refusal to reveal his plans for a second term. Mondale announced that he would raise taxes in order to lower the federal deficit, while Reagan said he would not raise taxes but did not reveal any alternative. To avoid such defeats, parties try to attract a majority of voters by offending as few people as possible. As a consequence, party platforms—statements of positions on important issues—tend to be vague and wishy-washy, and members of the same party may hold sharply different views. Southern Democrats, for example, are often more conservative than northern Republicans.

This, in turn, makes it difficult for parties to be tightly organized on a national level. More important, it forces voters to choose between candidates whose political differences are often hard to detect and who do not represent what voters want. (The disaffection of voters was perhaps best expressed by a candidate who tried unsuccessfully to change his name to "None of the Above," figuring that he would attract a large number of voters.) As a result, U.S. voters tend to base votes more on perceptions of candidates' personalities than on their positions on issues. Early in the 1988 presidential campaign, for example, front-runner Gary Hart dropped out after reports of extramarital affairs, and Joseph Biden withdrew after it was revealed that he quoted the words of others in his speeches without giving credit and had been convicted of plagiarism in law school. By comparison, most other democracies do not share this intense focus on the personal behavior and characteristics of candidates and instead vote for the political party, not individual candidates.

The relative importance of parties and candidates affects the characteristics of parties. In France, for example, individuals can gain public office only through the success of their parties. There are no primary elections; party officials decide who will occupy the seats won in an election. This gives parties enormous power over officeholders, for those who fail to support party positions on important issues may be expelled from the party and, therefore, denied access to office. Under this system, representatives must either reflect the views of those who elected them or leave office.

In the U.S., by contrast, the focus is on the candidate, not the party, and this means that parties have little control over those they help elect. Individuals can defy their parties and maintain their power on the basis of their own resources. Since most voters do not follow politics closely, they often have no idea of what their representatives are actually doing, and when election time rolls around, personality often plays a far more important part than ability or political ideology. (See Granberg and Holmberg 1988).

It should come as no surprise that Americans are less and less likely to vote in elections and increasingly identify themselves as independents rather than as members of a political party. Since 1972 the proportion of adults who identify themselves as independents has risen from 26 to 32 percent, and only 24 percent classify themselves as strong members of a major political party (Davis and Smith 1990).

Political parties, then, are not very powerful in the U.S. Given the fact that voters are, for the most part, disorganized and not very committed to actively following political affairs, where else can we look for concentrations of political power? One answer is the interest group.

Interest Groups   Whereas the goal of political parties is to place their members in positions of authority, an **interest group** attempts to affect political

Gun control in the U.S. has spawned numerous interest groups, the most powerful being the National Rifle Association (NRA). Although 78 percent of U.S. adults favor some form of gun control (Davis and Smith 1990), the NRA has blocked most efforts by groups such as Handgun Control, whose ad appears here.

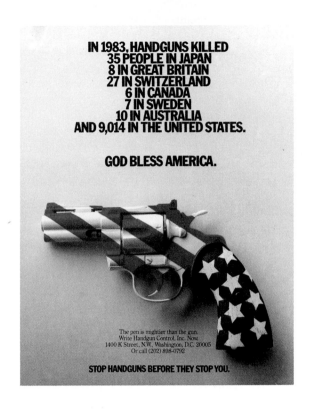

IN 1983, HANDGUNS KILLED
35 PEOPLE IN JAPAN
8 IN GREAT BRITAIN
27 IN SWITZERLAND
6 IN CANADA
7 IN SWEDEN
10 IN AUSTRALIA
AND 9,014 IN THE UNITED STATES.

GOD BLESS AMERICA.

The pen is mightier than the gun. Write Handgun Control, Inc. Now. 1400 K Street, N.W., Washington, D.C. 20005 Or call (202) 898-0792

STOP HANDGUNS BEFORE THEY STOP YOU.

decisions by supporting candidates who are sympathetic to their goals and by influencing those who are already in positions of authority. Parties generally have broad platforms that cover many issues, but interest groups usually focus on single issues such as abortion, gun control, consumer affairs, the arms race, prayer in public schools, the environment, benefit levels for retired people, the Equal Rights Amendment, or legislation that affects a particular business, industry, or occupation. As you can see, the list could go on and on, and this gives some sense of how many different interest groups focus their attention on officials.

Interest groups influence officials primarily by providing them with expert information on complex issues and by contributing money to election campaigns. When legislators consider bills that would affect nuclear power plants, for example, they must take into account a vast array of scientific information that describes, among other things, the risks of nuclear disasters. Few legislators in the U.S. Congress are scientists (most are lawyers), and they therefore depend on outsiders for the technical information needed to make decisions.

This is where interest groups often exert influence by employing **lobbyists**—representatives who meet with officials and provide expert information that tends to support the interest group's goals. Lobbyists for pronuclear power groups, then, might provide studies that indicate that nuclear power is both safe and economical, while lobbyists for anti-nuclear interest groups might provide information that underscores the dangers and high cost of nuclear power. Since legislators usually lack independent sources of expertise on complex issues, their own positions often result from the relative persuasiveness of different lobbyists.

Because some interest groups are well organized and can hire full-time lobbyists, they can exert far more influence over government than citizens who have neither the time nor the money to lobby. This is particularly true of corporations whose resources are greater than those of any other organization with the exception of the state. In 1986, lobbyists spent a total of $61 million to influence congressional legislation, an average of more than $113,000 per legislator (Associated Press 1987). It is also true of elite think tanks and foundations such as the Brookings Institute, the Trilaterial Commission, and the Heritage Foundation whose publications about national policy often reflect the views and interests of the wealthy supporters who underwrite their work (Peschek 1987).

The importance of money in politics goes beyond lobbying, for elected officials depend on contributions in order to finance their campaigns for reelection. (As the late humorist Will Rogers put it, "Politics has got so expensive that it takes a lot of money even to get beat with.") When politicians take positions that affect interest groups, they cannot ignore the fact that they might offend those whose contributions could make the difference in a campaign for reelection.

Some political writers, such as Drew (1983), argue that the connection between money and politics is unnecessary. The greatest campaign expense is television advertising, and in Great Britain television time is given to candidates free of charge, substantially reducing candidates' dependence on private contributions from interest groups. Others urge public campaign financing, where candidates receive equal amounts of money from tax revenues and are forced to rely exclusively on these funds.

Efforts to limit the dependency of officeholders on private supporters have generally been unsuccessful. The Federal Election Campaign Act severely limited the amount that each individual could contribute to a campaign, but interest groups soon found a way around the law. There is no limit on the amount that groups and organizations can contribute, and interest groups—from corporations to social movements—have formed political action committees (called "PACs") through which great amounts of money from individuals are funneled into campaigns.

Organized interest groups are a major focus of political power in many countries; but groups can multiply their power by temporarily forming coalitions with other interest groups.

Political Coalitions   Interest groups often combine in order to accomplish goals that temporarily overlap, and this can produce unexpected combinations. The American Civil Liberties Union, for example, generally opposes the activities of the Ku Klux Klan; but when the Klan has tried to conduct public demonstrations, the Civil Liberties Union has often defended the right of Klan members to assemble publicly and express their views. As Charles D. Warner ([1870] 1955) put it a century ago, "politics makes strange bedfellows."

Coalitions abound in the political life of any complex society, in part because as the number of interest groups grows, the relative power of any group declines in relation to all the rest. In the debate over abortion, organizations that favor free choice for women include the Planned Parenthood Federation, the American Civil Liberties Union, the National Organization for Women, and a variety of religious and feminist groups. While these groups form a coalition around the issue of abortion, however, they sometimes oppose one another on other issues. Some feminist groups oppose the free availability of hard-core pornography; the Civil Liberties Union, however, opposes this position on the grounds that it would interfere with constitutionally guaranteed freedoms.

Coalitions are also a part of everyday life within governments. In Congress, senators and representatives regularly form coalitions in order to muster enough votes to pass their favorite bills ("I'll vote for your bill if you'll vote for mine"). In some countries—such as Italy and Israel—there are so many political parties that it is rare for any one party to win a majority of the vote in elections; so they are forced to form a coalition government in which several parties share ruling power. The stability of such governments depends on the ability of diverse groups to maintain a consensus, and if that consensus breaks down, the government falls and new elections are called. This is in sharp contrast to the U.S. winner-take-all system in which one candidate controls the entire administration after being elected president.

While most coalitions are temporary and focus on specific issues, some appear to be permanent. In the U.S., one of the most powerful coalitions is what President Dwight D. Eisenhower (a former army general) called the **military-industrial complex**—a coalition consisting of the military and industrialists who profit by manufacturing military hardware. Both share the goal of developing expensive new armaments, but for different reasons. The military justifies its budget and its importance as an institution only by justifying the need for more and better weapons which, in turn, provide profits for industry. Both use their expertise and financial resources to lobby Congress to authorize increased military spending.

As we have seen in the preceding sections, the cultural and structural characteristics of political systems define them as institutions through which decisions about life in a society are made. Political power is also affected by ecological arrangements, for the definition of the state itself includes the physical territory within which governments exercise authority.

POLITICAL ECOLOGY

Geography and population are two of the most important factors that affect the ability of a government to exercise the authority of the state. The territory of the Soviet Union is more than twice as large as the U.S., four times as large as Europe, and slightly larger than all of Latin America. Obviously, for a central government to control a vast territory is at best an enormously difficult task, and that helps explain why the state in societies such as the Soviet Union, China, and the U.S. depends so heavily on a huge bureaucracy, military, and police force. It also helps explain why such governments are so inefficient, for it is very difficult for central planners in Moscow (or Washington) to monitor what is happening 4,000 miles away in Vladivostok (or 3,000 miles away in Los Angeles).

The government of China faces additional obstacles to controlling its population, for not only is China large (roughly the area of the U.S.) but it has a population of more than 1 billion people—four times larger than the U.S. population and amounting to a fifth of all the people in the world (PRB 1990). It is one thing for the government to institute a policy—such as limiting families to one child in order to lower birth rates—and quite another to enforce it.

In any society, regardless of its size, the state cannot effectively control its citizens without their cooperation; but this is particularly true in societies with large populations or territories. If just 20 percent of U.S. taxpayers refused to file income tax returns, the Internal Revenue Service would be faced with tracking down and prosecuting 20 *million* lawbreakers distributed over almost 4 million square miles.

The Geography of Political Power

Geography is an important aspect of the distribution of political power. In the simplest sense, geographical boundaries define legal jurisdictions—the territories that are under the authority of the governments of towns, cities, counties, states, and nations. Geography, however, often plays a more complex part in political life.

Consider the problem of adding the Equal Rights Amendment to the U.S. Constitution. The amendment was passed by both houses of Congress and sent to state legislatures, 38 of which had to ratify the amendment in order for it to become part of the Constitution. In the spring of 1982, 91 percent of adults reported that they had heard of and understood the ERA, and of these, 75 percent favored its passage (Davis and Smith 1987); yet when the deadline for passage came, the amendment had fallen 3 states short.

There are many explanations for the ERA's defeat (see McGlen and O'Connor 1983), but one aspect simply involves the social geography of political power. Regardless of the relative size of its population, each state has an equal vote in deciding the fate of constitutional amendments. A significant portion of ERA opponents are religious fundamentalists, most of whom live in rural southern and western states with small populations. The combined populations of the states whose legislatures opposed the ERA made up only 28 percent of the U.S. population, and yet because each of these sparsely settled states had an equal vote, they were able to block the amendment. The ERA failed in part because most of its supporters were concentrated in a relatively small number of states, each of which could cast only one vote for the amendment (an arrangement designed by the framers of the Constitution to ensure that large urban states could not dominate and exploit small, rural states).

Political geography has perhaps its greatest effects on relationships between societies. The vastness and harsh climate of Russia condemned to failure Napoleon's and Hitler's dreams of conquest. The flat, level terrain of Western and Central Europe makes the passage of armies so easy that this region has been a recurring battleground for centuries. Before the invention of nuclear weapons, the Atlantic and Pacific oceans virtually ensured that no invader from beyond the Americas could easily attack the U.S., just as the stormy English Channel has protected the British Isles for almost 1,000 years.

In many cases, the distribution of natural resources plays an important part in determining the power of societies in relation to one another. Were it not for their great supplies of oil, most of the countries of the Middle East would have far less influence over industrial societies than they now enjoy; nor would the U.S. be as hesitant as it has been to take action against apartheid in South Africa were it not for the important minerals that South Africa supplies to the U.S.

Many societies are influenced by the belief that a nation is powerful in direct proportion to the size of its population, and that efforts by industrial countries to encourage birth control in Third World countries is an attempt to limit their power. Although the world is now dominated by countries that contain only a small fraction of total world population, it is understandable that many poor societies see the sheer size of their populations as their only hope for influence in a world dominated by economic and technological superpowers.

THE USES OF POLITICAL POWER

Like all institutions, political arrangements have cultural, structural, and ecological characteristics. What kinds of consequences do they produce, what part do they play in social conflict, and how are they related to social change?

Functions and Dysfunctions

Like all institutions, political systems produce both functional and dysfunctional consequences. Representative democracy, for example, allows a great deal of public debate and criticism of government. Many officials—from presidents to city council members—are elected and can, therefore, be held accountable for their decisions. These characteristics of democracies are functional for restraining the power of government and encouraging authorities to weigh their decisions carefully. Compared with authoritarian states, democratic governments have much less authority to arrest, detain, and punish people without due cause, to invade privacy or use torture to extract information. Widespread opportunities for participation in the political process strengthen the social legitimacy of the state and, therefore, help to perpetuate it. People may oppose a particular government, but since representative democracy is the source of the ability to protest in the first place, it is less likely to be challenged.

These same characteristics also produce dysfunctional consequences, however. Public debate often requires a great deal of time, and it can take years for new policies to emerge and take effect. While the accountability of authorities to the public limits their power, it also tends to make officials wary of making decisions that will offend voters, especially voters of interest groups. The relative openness of democratic societies also encourages conflict as interest groups clash over the goals a government pursues and the means it uses to accomplish them. The turbulent decade of the 1960s is a perfect example of the instability that can occur when the public takes full advantage of the right to protest government policies.

Unlike democracies, authoritarian states are more insulated from public opinion and enjoy greater freedom to make decisions and act on them as they see fit. This can lead to greater efficiency. There was no public debate in the Soviet Union over the invasion of Afghanistan; the violent and nonviolent protests that took place in the U.S. over the Vietnam War never would have been tolerated in the Soviet Union. Nor has there been public debate in Russia over the Soviet position at international arms control negotiations.

The price that is commonly paid for such efficiency, however, is rigidity, stagnation, and oppression (Stojanovic 1981). Without criticism and public debate, governments can easily fall into a set of inflexible policies that discourage the introduction of new and better ideas. The Soviet state's control over the economy is a perfect example of inefficiency and backwardness that is so extreme that it has been a favorite source of sarcastic humor among Russian citizens themselves.

A primary goal of authoritarian states is to control as many aspects of social life as possible, and this produces a number of dysfunctional consequences. There is, of course, the obvious problem of abused authority through which people are arrested, tortured, and imprisoned without legal representation or due process of law. It is estimated that government agents in various countries murder tens of thousands of people each year, a pattern of abuse that sometimes includes the imprisonment and torture of children (Amnesty International 1989). There are also

In the 1970s, between 6,000 and 15,000 people in Argentina were kidnapped, tortured, and murdered by government security forces in an attempt to silence opposition to strict military rule. After a new civilian government was elected, protests spread throughout Argentina as the families of those who had disappeared demanded justice. This picture shows mothers with posters of their missing children.

less obvious effects. Authoritarian societies often appear to be very stable, for example, as if the government is in complete control and can do as it pleases. Authoritarian governments, however, stay in power by taking maximum advantage of the state's monopoly over the use of force, and this means that their stability depends heavily on coercive power. "The one means," wrote Adolph Hitler ([1924] 1948, p. 53) "that wins the easiest victory over reason: terror and force."

Leaders in all societies face the problem of knowing what people are thinking, but the problem is even more acute in authoritarian states because they forbid dissent. This necessitates enormous and complex institutions—such as secret police—whose sole function is to find out if people are thinking and doing anything that might threaten the government (Hollander 1982).

Authoritarian leaders sometimes try to increase their security by identifying themselves with the state—in other words, by removing the distinction between the state and a government. "I am the state," declared Napoleon Bonaparte to the French Senate in 1814. This statement, in effect, implied that since Napoleon was the state, the state as an institution could not be used to limit his authority. The dangers inherent in this view make clear why the separation of government from the state is an important principle in representative democracies. The principle—"no one is above the law, not even the president"—was the basis for Richard Nixon's forced resignation in 1974. His removal from office underscored the supremacy of the state over any particular government.

The State and Social Conflict

As the institution responsible for maintaining order and stability, the state inevitably plays a part in social conflict. The state, however, is rarely a neutral umpire, for by preserving a social system, it also preserves those aspects of it that create social inequality. This is most apparent in authoritarian states. In authoritarian societies the power of the state is used to maintain the wealth, power, and prestige of government and military leaders, and there is a basic conflict between the government and the people. In capitalist authoritarian societies, the state also supports the interests of capitalists, whether or not they occupy formal positions in the government. In El Salvador, for example, leaders of labor unions are regularly harassed by the police and military, and many have been kidnapped and murdered by "death squads" who support the government.

State support for those who dominate society is less visible in representative democracies, but it is important and widespread nonetheless. The U.S. is a capitalist democracy where government rarely uses its authority to hurt the interests of capitalism as an economic system. This means that most government programs support the interests of capitalists.

The French philosopher Jean-Jacques Rousseau ([1762] 1950) believed that the state came into being because the right to own property caused such chaotic competition over ownership that an institution was needed to restore order. Rousseau also believed, however, that the state did more than maintain order: It also defended the wealthy—the largest and most influential class of property owners.

Marx expanded Rousseau's analysis and concluded that democracy is an illusion, that because the masses of people do not control *economic* institutions the belief that they can still control political institutions is false. It is of course true that voters can elect anyone they want to public office, but Marx believed that the basic structure of the state supports the interests of capitalism and capitalists, not the vast majority of people who must sell their labor power in order to survive.

In the simplest sense, the state in capitalist democracies supports capitalism by refraining from doing anything that hurts the interests of capitalists as a class. Although many laws serve the interests of working people—minimum wage laws, occupational health and safety laws, and laws protecting labor unions, for example—none threatens capitalism as a system. Nor have they significantly altered the unequal distribution of wealth, power, and prestige between classes (see Chapter 12). A variety of other programs benefit capitalists in ways that are not readily apparent. Welfare and unemployment insurance obviously benefit workers and families; but they also soften the negative effects of job shortages, and this makes it easier for employers to lay off workers when it is profitable to do so. Social Security lessens the need for workers to set aside money during their working years, and this lessens the pressure for higher wages. (see Williamson et al. 1985).

In a more complex sense, the state actively supports capitalism by creating and maintaining social conditions that enable capitalists to expand and more efficiently profit from the labor power of

堅持四项基本原则　开创

Nowhere is the importance of political economy clearer than in socialist countries where the state and economic institutions are strongly identified with each other. This Chinese propaganda poster purports to depict the rise of communism and, with it, the political and economic well-being of the people.

workers. In the world economy, the U.S. State Department conducts relations with other countries in ways that foster a stable world social order, within which capitalists can invest money in other countries and be assured that their investments are safe. This often puts the U.S. in the position of supporting authoritarian states such as South Korea and Chile because U.S. corporations have huge investments in those countries.

In the U.S. many domestic government programs that are officially defined as for the benefit of workers also support capitalism, particularly those that increase the productivity of labor and help to train and educate new workers. Each year the government spends billions of dollars on research that benefits industry and also maintains railroads, highways, airports, and other utilities that directly benefit businesses. The military provides huge sources of income and profit, and policies of the Treasury Department and the Federal Reserve affect interest rates and the money supply—both of which are vital to the investment needs of capitalists.

Businesses also depend on a steady supply of trained, educated workers. Public education, subsi-dized housing, federally guaranteed mortgages, school lunch programs, and publicly funded daycare centers not only benefit families but also capitalists, by helping to prepare each generation of workers at public expense. Without such programs, individuals would have to shoulder the expense and would, therefore, be far more likely to demand much higher wages from their employers.

Perhaps the most important way in which all states—whether authoritarian or democratic, capitalist or socialist—maintain economic arrangements and the resulting inequalities is by legitimating them through identifying with them. Many people tend to think of the U.S. as both capitalist and democratic, for example, and most have a hard time imagining one without the other. They tend to believe that democracy *implies* capitalism and that capitalism implies democracy; that socialism implies authoritarianism (and, erroneously, that authoritarianism implies socialism). Because economic institutions affect so many aspects of life in a society, and because the state's prime function is to maintain order and stability, when people affirm their loyalty and affection for their country, they also tend to affirm their support for its economic system. When children learn the pledge of allegiance to the flag and develop a love for their country, they also are socialized to accept prevailing economic institutions as the right way to produce and distribute wealth.

"Capitalism," wrote French historian Fernand Braudel (1977), "only triumphs when it becomes identified with the state, when it is the state" (p. 64). In this sense, political and economic institutions are so intertwined that we need to think in terms of **political economy**—the social arrangements through which political and economic institutions support and maintain each other (see Froman 1984). We may think of them as separate, but as is true of so many social arrangements described in earlier chapters, these two institutions are integral parts of the same whole and do not operate independently of each other (Domhoff 1983).

The state cannot single-mindedly pursue the interests of one class or interest group, however, without alienating the vast majority of its citizens and threatening the legitimacy of state authority. As O'Connor (1973) put it, this produces a serious tension:

> The state must try to maintain or create conditions in which profitable capital accumulation is possible. However, the state also must try to maintain or create conditions for social harmony. A capitalist state that openly uses its coercive forces to help one class accumulate capital at the expense of other classes loses its legitimacy and hence undermines the basis of its loyalty and support. But a state that ignores the necessity of assisting the process of capital accumulation risks drying up the source of its power, the economy's surplus production capacity and the taxes drawn from this surplus. (p. 6)

This source of conflict is even more apparent in authoritarian states such as the Soviet Union. On the one hand, civilian leaders must support the interests of powerful groups such as the military, who demand a huge share of national resources. On the other hand, high levels of defense spending leave a relatively small share for consumer goods—from meat to decent housing. One of the most persistent social problems of Soviet society is the demoralization of its people, who are frustrated in their desire to improve their standard of living. As events of recent years have made clear, their frustration often supports a crisis of faith in society itself.

In most societies, then, governments use the authority of the state to maintain what is often a delicate balance between the demands of interest groups,

the needs of the population, and the pressures of maintaining the legitimacy of the state itself. When a government can no longer maintain that balance, political change may be unavoidable.

Politics and Social Change: Rebellions, Coups, and Revolutions

Political change generally takes one of three basic forms. A **rebellion** challenges the policies of a government without trying to change the cultural or structural characteristics of the state. In 1786, for example, poverty was widespread in the American colonies in the aftermath of the Revolutionary War; and poor farmers, unable to pay their debts, were stripped of their possessions—their land, animals, and equipment—by the courts. Led by Daniel Shays, mobs of farmers prevented Massachusetts courts from meeting to prosecute indebted farmers,

Revolution often pits the wealthy and powerful against the impoverished and weak; but when the state is vulnerable, as it was in Russia before the 1917 revolution, the weak can band together to bring down the powerful. This is suggested in Marc Chagall's 1919 painting, *War on the Palaces*.

and eventually there was an armed confrontation between Shays' followers and the Massachusetts militia. "Shays' Rebellion" was not an attempt to change the form of political institutions. Its goal was to change the policies of government—in other words, to change the ways in which the government used the power of the state.

Like rebellion, a **coup d'état** (pronounced "coo day ta"—whose meaning in French is "a blow concerning the state") does not try to change the character of the state; but unlike rebellion, a coup is an illegal attempt to replace one government with another, often with the use of force. In many countries—especially in Latin America and Africa—coups have been so frequent that they have been a main way for leadership to pass from one group to another. Because the military has a virtual monopoly on the instruments of force, it is often the source of coups. In the simplest case, military leaders decide that they can do a better job of governing a country than civilian leaders can. One morning the president wakes up to find that the presidential residence is surrounded by tanks and that key resources—television and radio stations, telephone exchanges, airports, and power plants—are under military control. In other cases, coups occur while the leader is out of the country. It was through a coup, for example, that General Manuel Noriega seized power in Panama in 1987 after the president tried to fire him from his post as leader of the military.

Of all the forms of political change, **revolution** is by far the most serious, both in its goals and its methods. Unlike rebellions and coups d'état, revolutions seek to install a new government *and* to change the fundamental character of the state and society (Skocpol 1979). Because revolutions seek to change the most fundamental cultural and structural characteristics of a society and its institutions, they almost always include considerable violence. In 1789 French revolutionaries toppled the autocracy of Louis XVI in what was to be the first stage of a prolonged period of violence and chaos as France searched for new political and economic institutions. In March 1917 the Russian Revolution forced Czar Nicholas II to give up his throne (he and his family were killed) and installed a new provisional government; but in October, a second revolution brought Lenin and his communist followers to power, and Russia became the Soviet Union. In the decades that followed—particularly under the rule of Stalin—millions of Russians who were suspected of opposing the new state were imprisoned, exiled, or executed.

Revolutions have been common occurrences in the twentieth century. In 1949 the Communist forces of Mao Tse-tung defeated the armies of Chiang Kai-shek and established a socialist state in mainland China. In 1954 Vietnamese revolutionaries under the leadership of Ho Chi Minh defeated a French army and ended French colonial rule in Indochina. North Vietnam became an authoritarian socialist state and South Vietnam became an authoritarian capitalist state. In 1959 revolutionaries under the leadership of Fidel Castro overthrew Batista's authoritarian capitalist state and replaced it with an authoritarian socialist state. In 1973 the socialist government of Chile's Salvador Allende was overthrown by the military and replaced with an authoritarian capitalist state. In 1979 Marxist revolutionaries overthrew the government of Nicaragua, and Islamic revolutionaries replaced the Shah of Iran with an authoritarian state based on Islamic religious law. And in 1989 a series of relatively nonviolent revolutions swept through the socialist countries of Central Europe and toppled one authoritarian government after another. At the same time the three Baltic states of Lithuania, Latvia, and Estonia began a process designed to accomplish their eventual independence from the Soviet Union.

The American Revolution actually began as a rebellion in which colonists demanded the same rights as those enjoyed by British citizens living in Britain. It became a revolution when colonists declared their independence from Great Britain and precipitated a

---

PUZZLE

WHEN ARE REVOLUTIONS MOST LIKELY TO OCCUR?

Are revolutions more likely when injustice and miserable living conditions persist for long periods of time or when there are rapid improvements in social justice and standards of living?

As surprising as it may seem, revolutions are more likely when conditions are getting better than they are when they remain steadily poor. This apparent paradox is explained here and in Chapter 23.

war that resulted in a new country with political institutions that differed sharply from those of the past. Although the new state borrowed heavily from British political institutions, the Constitution, the office of the president, and the two houses of Congress were all major departures from the British form of government.

The Causes of Revolution   Sociologists have identified several cultural and structural characteristics of political institutions and societies that are conducive to revolution (Goldstone 1982). From a cultural perspective, revolutions are based on a profound shift in beliefs and values and a sharp drop in the acceptance of norms. Belief in the legitimacy of the state tends to crumble and this is often due to a chronic inability of the state to solve routine problems of government and meet the needs of the people, coupled with a rising expectation among the people that those needs should be met. The Russian Revolution occurred in a society in which a huge peasant class had, for centuries, lived in poverty under the oppressive rule of the czars. In 1914 Germany declared war on Russia and in the three years that followed, millions of Russians died and shortages of food and other necessities became critical. Russia's continued participation in the war greatly aggravated long-standing social problems (Skocpol 1979).

Revolution is also more likely to occur when people begin to share the beliefs that inequality and injustice are widespread and that more effective political institutions are possible. Perhaps most important is the shared belief that radical change cannot be achieved peacefully, that the state can be changed only through violence because the government will not respond positively to the needs and desires of the people.

Shifts in beliefs are closely related to changing values, particularly those that affect what people expect for themselves. When expectations are rising—when people think that living conditions, freedoms, and other aspects of social life should improve—they are far more likely to question the legitimacy of a state that offers little hope of making those expectations a reality. As values change, so too does allegiance to norms that define legitimate means for achieving goals. If the norms of the state support values that the people oppose, then the norms begin to lose their power over behavior.

Cultural shifts are closely tied to important aspects of social structure. The belief that peaceful change is impossible is often based on the refusal of government authorities to communicate with the people. In January 1905, for example, 12 years before the 1917 Russian Revolution, thousands of workers peacefully marched to the czar's winter palace to protest poverty and hunger. They were met by troops who attacked the crowd, wounding and killing hundreds of unarmed people. The response to "Bloody Sunday" was a series of strikes and protests. Since even these did not bring about change, the eventual response was revolution.

As allegiance to the state erodes, and as lines of communication are blocked (or shown to be nonexistent in the first place) the state loses its authority and the government increasingly relies on coercion in order to stay in power. This further erodes the population's belief that the state and its government are legitimate, and only increases the chances for a revolution.

In the aftermath of revolution, the state is often authoritarian—sometimes more authoritarian than the state it replaced (Goldstone 1982). This occurs primarily because the new government sets as its first goal the crushing of all opposition. There were even hints of this in the years following the American Revolution, when the Sedition Act made it a crime to publish criticism of the government. The relative absence of violence in the recent Central European revolutions may allow for a more democratic outcome than would otherwise have been the case.

It should come as no surprise that revolutions are as violent or rare as they are, for no social institution regularly serves the function of deliberately turning itself into something else. What Miliband (1969) observed in capitalist societies is true in virtually all societies in which the state exists as a social institution:

> The politics of advanced capitalism have been about different conceptions of how to run the same economic and social system and not about radically different social systems. (p. 72)

In most societies, governments come and go and the balance of power between interest groups shifts one way or another; but the cultural and structural form of the state remains largely intact. As with economic arrangements, real change in political institutions is rare.

SUMMARY

1. Political institutions are enduring sets of cultural ideas and social structures through which power is distributed and used in societies.

2. Authority is the most important form of political power; it may be based on legal-rational, charismatic, or traditional grounds, or on expertise in an important field. Coercion, on the other hand, is the use of power not considered legitimate by those who are subject to it.

3. The state is the institution that has a monopoly over the use of force. A government is a collection of people who happen to occupy the positions of authority that make up the state.

4. As an institution, the state may support a variety of cultural values, such as those promoting equality or individual freedoms.

5. States differ in how power is distributed. In a democracy, power is shared equally by all citizens. In a representative democracy, citizens elect people to exercise authority in their name. Democracy is fostered by a number of social factors, including economic development, cultural homogeneity, norms that restrict the power of the state, tolerance of dissent, and access to information about government activities.

6. Unlike democracy, an oligarchy is ruled by an elite, and an autocracy is ruled by one person. According to Michels' "Iron Rule of Oligarchy," oligarchy is inevitable because of citizen apathy, the complexity of societies, and the desire of leaders to keep their power.

7. States also vary in how authoritarian—or powerful—they are in relation to their citizens. Totalitarianism is an extreme in which the state tries to control virtually all aspects of life.

8. The power structure in the U.S. is neither dominated by a unified power elite nor spread pluralistically among many different interest groups. Rather, it is an elite pluralism in which a relatively small number of interest groups struggle over control of the state.

9. U.S. citizens are less likely to vote and be involved in politics than citizens of most democracies. Generally those in the most advantaged social positions are the most likely to vote and be involved in politics.

10. Political parties are organizations whose main goal is to place members in positions of authority, and parties in the U.S. differ sharply from those in European democracies. U.S. elections are based on a winner-take-all system that encourages candidates to take ambiguous positions on issues and weakens the ability of parties to control their candidates once elected. Unlike parties, interest groups do not try to place members in positions of authority but rather try to influence elected officials.

11. A political coalition is a set of interest groups who temporarily combine in order to increase their power. This often means that groups that oppose each other on one issue work together on another.

12. Geography often plays an important part in political life. The larger a society is the more difficult it is for the state to control its citizens.

13. Like all social institutions, a given political arrangement will have both functional and dysfunctional consequences. Democracy is functional for protecting individual freedom but is dysfunctional for reaching rapid decisions in times of crisis.

14. Its monopoly over the use of force inevitably means that the state will play a role in social conflict. While it sometimes acts as an umpire between conflicting groups, it more often promotes the interests of dominant groups. This is particularly true of those who dominate economic institutions. Through political economy, political and economic institutions support each other and promote the interests of those who dominate them.

15. Political institutions change through rebellion, in which policies are changed without affecting the state, through coups d'état, in which only the government is changed by forcibly replacing old leaders with new, and through revolution, in which the state itself is changed. Revolution is most likely to occur in societies in which the state is no longer able to perform basic governmental tasks, citizens no longer view the state as a legitimate wielder of authority, and beliefs in the existence of injustice and inequality become widespread.

KEY TERMS

authoritarian   508
authority   502
autocracy   508
charismatic authority   502
civil disobedience   506
coercive power   503
coup d'état   522
democracy   506
government   503

interest group   514
legal-rational authority   502
lobbyist   515
military-industrial complex   516
oligarchy   507
political economy   521
political institution   501
political party   513

politics   501
rebellion   521
representative democracy   506
revolution   522
state   503
totalitarianism   509
traditional authority   503

LOOKING ELSEWHERE

Having studied Chapter 20, you might want to look at related discussions in *Human Arrangements*, which include

■ communication structures in authoritarian and democratic governments (Chapter 3, p. 59)

■ gerontocracy: age and political power (Chapter 15, pp. 370–71)

■ schools, propaganda, and nationalism (Chapter 17, pp. 432–33)

■ the role of government in the economy (Chapter 19, pp. 482–83)

■ socialism as a political system (Chapter 19, pp. 491–92)

■ religious support for the state (Chapter 21, pp. 531, 536, 537, 544)

■ the state as a substitute for religion (Chapter 21, pp. 548–49)

■ the origins and effects of social movements (Chapter 22, pp. 584–93)

RECOMMENDED READINGS

Edelman, M. 1988. *Constructing the political spectacle.* Chicago: University of Chicago Press. A tightly argued, highly readable analysis of how elites and the mass media shape the reality of the U.S. political system in order to enhance and support their own power. See also Herman, E. S., and Chomsky, N. 1988. *Manufacturing consent: The political economy of the mass media.* New York: Pantheon.

Elder, C. D., and Cobb, R. W. 1983. *The political use of symbols.* New York: Longman. A valuable introduction to the use of symbols in the political processes through which power is distributed, held, and used.

Froman, C. 1984. *The two American political systems: Society, economics, and politics.* Englewood Cliffs, NJ: Prentice-Hall. How does the U.S. political system *really* operate? The author provides one answer in a clear, straightforward look at political economy—the important relationship between political and economic institutions—in the United States.

Mills, C. W. 1956. *The power elite.* New York: Oxford. A sociological classic in which Mills provides a provocative answer to the question, "Who rules America?"

Orum, A. M. 1983. *Introduction to political sociology* (2nd ed.). Englewood Cliffs, NJ: Prentice-Hall. A comprehensive text on the many sociological aspects of politics, from socialization to the structures of power.

Rejai, M., and Phillips, K. 1983. *World revolutionary leaders.* New Brunswick, NJ: Rutgers University Press. A short, readable book that explores the relationship between leaders and revolutions. Do revolutions create leaders or do leaders make revolutions?

Skocpol, T. 1979. *States and social revolutions.* New York: Cambridge University Press. An important study of the causes of revolution in China, Russia, and France.

Tufte, E. R. 1978. *Political control of the economy.* Princeton, NJ: Princeton University Press. An important and highly interesting exploration of the connection between politics and economics.

21
Religious Institutions

 Have you ever taken the time to sit down and seriously ask yourself, "What will happen to me after I die?" I vividly remember the first time I thought about that question and the other questions it inevitably raised: What do I mean by "me"; what is there about me that might exist after my body does not; and what might that existence be like?

In struggling over the meaning of death, I inevitably had to think about the meaning of life. As I thought about it that first time, I imagined my life as a slender slice out of an infinity of time before my birth and an infinity of time after my death. Suddenly, I felt frightened, as if my life would be replaced by nothingness and meaninglessness. The most frightening thing was to realize that I did not know what would happen.

People have wrestled with the meaning of death and life for thousands of years. Sociologically, the most important thing about these concepts is that they deal with the known, the unknown, and meaning. Although people place great emphasis on the truth of particular beliefs, our interest here centers on the fact that people in all societies wrestle with these basic themes.

At the core of culture are symbols and ideas that we use to attach meaning to objects, events, and experiences, those that we can see and touch and smell, and those which we cannot. An important latent consequence of our ability to give meaning to life is that it creates the possibility of meaninglessness. I doubt very much that my dog contemplates the meaning of life after death, just as she never contemplates the meaning of life before death. Meaning and meaninglessness, the known and the unknown are not problems for her; but they are for us.

As with much of art, the universal, enduring mysteries of life and death, as portrayed in Gustav Klimt's famous painting, *Death and Life*, are at the core of all religious institutions.

As social animals, we tend to join together to solve such problems, and these collective solutions lie at the heart of religion and religious institutions. As we will see, all religions have certain things in common. They distinguish between what is considered sacred and what is not and are organized around groups of believers who use ritual to express religious beliefs, especially those describing their relationship to the sacred.

We begin our examination of these subjects by defining some basic concepts and then look at the variety of religious ideas and ways of structuring religious institutions. From there we explore the effects of population and ecology on religious institutions, and use the functional and conflict perspectives to better understand the relationship between religion, society, and social change.

WHAT IS RELIGION?

The substance of **religion** is a set of symbols and ideas that focus on the meaning of life and the nature of the unknown. The symbols are important because they describe visions of the ultimate nature of both the world and human experience in it, and they establish in people "powerful, pervasive, and long-lasting moods and motivations" that affect their feelings and behavior (Geertz 1973, p. 90).

Just as words do not constitute a language unless they are shared by members of a speech community, ideas about existence and the unknown constitute a religion only when they are shared among members of a community of believers. I may believe that there is a heaven and that no one who flies in an airplane or talks on a telephone can go there after they die; but, from a sociological perspective, my beliefs are not part of a religion unless a group of people shares them.

Religion, of course, is not the only source of ideas about the unknown. Scientists, for example, spend their lives trying to understand the unknown, but they do so in a fundamentally different way. In the simplest sense, science looks upon the unknown as something that is ultimately knowable through observation, experiment, and verifiable fact. Religion, however, is not a method for pursuing truth; it is the embodiment of what is already believed to be true. Christians regard their beliefs about the origins of the universe as truths to be learned and shared in the community of believers. The only confirmation of such beliefs lies within the community itself: individuals must look to the faith of others in order to confirm their own. To cosmologists, on the other hand, beliefs about the universe are scientific hypotheses waiting to be tested.

There is a more important difference between religion and science, a difference that focuses both on the aspects of the unknown to which people pay attention and on how they pay attention to them. In his classic sociological study of religion, Durkheim ([1912] 1965) noted that all religions distinguish between the *sacred* and the *profane*. To consider an object, experience, or unknown force as **sacred** is to give it meaning and value that inspire feelings of awe and place it outside of the natural human world. To Christians, the cross, the idea of God, and the life of Jesus Christ are all sacred, just as the city of Jerusalem is sacred both to Jews and Muslims, and dharma, the Ganges River, and the cow are sacred to Hindus.

The concept of the **profane** refers to what we can experience directly as ordinary aspects of the natural world. As a profane experience, death involves the cessation of biological functioning and physical and mental experience. The concept of the sacred focuses on the *meaning* of death, on its place in a cosmic order of things. In sacred terms, we are concerned not with what death consists of or how it happens, but why people die and what it means to die—and, therefore, what it means to live—in an ultimate sense.

Science and religion pay attention to fundamentally different aspects of the unknown. What causes a dying person to suffer is something that scientists can determine; but why suffering seems to be an inherent part of human experience is a question that scientists consider to be unanswerable in scientific terms and therefore irrelevant to scientific inquiry. In most religions, however, the meaning and reason for earthly suffering are major concerns.

The sacred and the profane are not two separate and disconnected cultural realms; on the contrary, the sacred is used to give a sense of ultimate understanding and meaning to the profane, and by doing so it affects it (Geertz 1973). In a religion that includes the belief that death is always a matter of divine will that is not to be interfered with, believers may refuse medical intervention and will be much more likely to die. By providing an account of what the world is like in an ultimate sense, religion can affect what the world in fact becomes.

In some cases, science and religion focus on similar problems, but from different perspectives. In the debate over the origins of human life some religions frame explanations in sacred terms, as Christianity does with the belief that a male God created man in "His" own image and then created woman from Adam's rib. As far as we know, the existence of God cannot be proved or disproved with objective evidence and, hence, the Christian explanation of the origin of human life holds little interest for scientists. By definition, science cannot draw upon supernatural explanations, for the province of science is the natural world.

Religion, then, is defined by its concentration on the sacred and supernatural. The sociology of religion is principally concerned with the place of religions and religious institutions in societies.

Religion and Society

The distinction between the sacred and the profane lies at the heart of religion, but religious institutions are sociologically significant primarily because of the consequences they produce. From a cultural point of view, religion attaches meaning and value to human life and supports major cultural ideas. All religions offer believers some form of salvation—whether it be the heaven of Christianity, the earthly peace offered by Buddhism and Taoism, Hindu reincarnation into a higher social caste, or the simple curing of an illness (Wilson 1982). Most important, religion

French artist Paul Gauguin's *We Greet Thee Mary* is more than an idealization of the Tahitian society in which he lived for much of his life. Its vision of paradise and bliss reflects a desire for salvation that is a part of most religious faiths.

For these Jewish mourners in Jerusalem, a funeral is a ceremony that brings people together and reinforces bonds by sharing in a common faith that makes sense of both their lives and the fact that they, too, will die.

helps believers explain and accept the suffering that plagues human life, by offering a coherent world view in which suffering makes sense and is, therefore, sufferable.

> The dumb senselessness of intense or inexorable pain, and the enigmatic unaccountability of gross iniquity all raise the uncomfortable suspicion that perhaps the world, and hence man's life in the world, has no genuine order at all—no empirical regularity, no emotional form, no moral coherence. And the religious response to this suspicion is in each case the same: the formulation, by means of symbols, of an image of such a genuine order of the world which will account for, and even celebrate, the perceived ambiguities, puzzles, and paradoxes in human experience. The effort is not to deny the undeniable—that there are unexplained events, that life hurts, or that rain falls upon the just—but to deny that there are inexplicable events, that life is unendurable, and that justice is a mirage. (Geertz 1973, p. 108)

Religion locates a community of believers in relation to spiritual and supernatural forces as well as the profane world (the meaning of life, the nature of the universe) and this is an important ingredient in collective definitions of who we are in the ultimate scheme of things (Mol 1976). In most religions, people are not lost bodies floating aimlessly through time and space. Life has meaning and an ultimate purpose, and people are part of something larger than themselves and their societies. Religion, then, can reduce anxiety and uncertainty in its believers by connecting the profane world with the mysteries of life, which are given sacred meaning and value. In the same way, religion can increase anxiety—by leading people to believe that they will suffer endless torture in another world after they die.

Religion is also a major source of social cohesion. The roots of the word religion lie in the Latin words "re" and "lig" which together mean to tie or bind again. Because a community of believers shares basic ideas about the known and the unknown, they can give one another comfort and support when suffering and misfortune strike their members or share in joy or ecstasy when something happens that suggests that their lives are in harmony with the sacred order of things. When people come together for a funeral, they reinforce their bonds with one another. When two people marry, religious ceremonies bind them to their cultural community as well as to each other, for it is their society and its religious institutions that legitimate and assign meaning, value, and expectations to their relationship.

Religious institutions also legitimate other social institutions. In medieval Europe, the Church supported the "divine right of kings" to rule: the coronations of kings and queens were, more than anything else, religious ceremonies in which rulers of the profane world identified with the sacred and therefore drew authority from those who represented sacred powers. In return, religious institutions often received special protection and large amounts of property and other wealth from kings and emperors.

Most modern states no longer depend on the blessing of religious institutions and their leaders to justify their power; but they often identify with religious symbols in order to reinforce their authority. U.S. coins bear the words "In God We Trust"; political leaders often refer to God as being "on our side"; the Pledge of Allegiance to the flag includes the words "one nation, under God"; the song "America the Beautiful" includes the words "God shed His grace on thee"; and both houses of Congress begin their sessions with prayer.

Gatherer-hunter and horticultural societies had no state (see Chapter 20); and in his studies of such societies Durkheim ([1912] 1965) first formulated his theory of the relationship between religion and society. In the aboriginal tribes of Australia, each clan worshiped a **totem**—an animal or plant considered sacred in that society. Each totem represented not a god, but the clan itself, and from this observation, Durkheim argued that religion is in fact a way in which people worship their own societies. A totem gives supernatural significance and power to the bonds that hold people together and through which they survive.

Durkheim was one of the first in a long line of sociologists who accepted the belief that religion and religious institutions are part of culture and are, therefore, of human and not divine origin. Is it, however, necessary to accept this belief in order to study religion from a sociological point of view?

Can a Sociologist Believe in God?

The first sociologists who studied religion—Comte, Marx, Durkheim, and Weber—were part of a revolutionary period of history during which science challenged religion as the dominant cultural framework for interpreting and explaining the world and human experience. These sociologists were in the thick of an intense conflict between supporters of religion and of science as points of view. In that social environment, they found themselves trying to explain the existence of religion—why people hold beliefs even though they may appear to be untrue—and to explain religion *away* (Wilson 1982).

Modern sociology is not antireligious, but the definition of religion as a part of culture is generally accepted in the sociological study of religion. This raises a disturbing question for those who use sociology as a perspective and who belong to a community of religious believers: Can sociologists be religious? Can a Christian, Muslim, or Jewish sociologist, for example, study religion as a set of cultural ideas and believe in the existence of a supreme being?

The answer to all these questions is yes, and the reason is quite straightforward: It is not the goal of sociology to test the truth or falsity of religious beliefs. "Does God exist?" is not a sociological question; but "Do people believe that God exists?" is. Sociologists want to understand how religious ideas and practices affect the lives of those who belong to communities of believers and influence the societies in which those people live. They want to understand how religious institutions are organized and how they affect other institutions. They want to understand the functional and dysfunctional consequences of religion and the part religion plays in social conflict and change.

None of these problems requires that we assume that particular religious beliefs are either true or false. Wherever specific religions may have come from, they affect social life in a variety of ways in different societies, and it is the job of sociology to understand those effects.

CULTURE: LINKING THE KNOWN AND THE UNKNOWN

The core of any religion is a set of cultural ideas and practices that provide a framework for interpreting the known and unknown in relation to the sacred world of the supernatural. While all four components of culture are important in religion, beliefs are what distinguish different religions most clearly from one another.

Religious Belief: Some Major Types of Religion

Religious belief systems focus on describing the ultimate nature of reality and the place of human beings in it. Most religions can be categorized as one of a few major types, each of which corresponds to a different view of the sacred, the profane, and the relationship between the two.

Theistic Religion   A theistic religion includes the belief in one or more supreme beings. Chris-

tianity, Judaism, and Islam are **monotheistic** religions because each generally recognizes the existence of only one supreme being. To Christians it is God; to Jews it is Yahweh; and to Muslims it is Allah; but what all have in common is a single supreme being who allows allegiance only to himself (note that all also envision the supreme being as male).

Hinduism is a **polytheistic** religion; it allows for the existence of five gods. The concept of god is not central in the Hindu religion, for the power of the supernatural is vested in a spiritual concept of "oneness" through which people are born into social castes and are reincarnated in succeeding lives as members of higher or lower castes, depending on how well they satisfy the duties associated with their current caste. The Hindus of India, Pakistan, and Bangladesh do not believe in a single supreme being that decides their fate but in a vision of life as a succession of lives in which the ultimate goal is a state of unity with supernatural forces.

Animistic and Totemic Religion   Many religions give little or no importance to the idea of a supreme being. Some African and native American tribes practice **animistic** religions in which spirits and ghosts are believed to inhabit sacred objects such as trees, rocks, or animals. To the Mbuti of Africa, the forest is the sacred giver of life and death (Turnbull 1965). The Shinto religion of Japan vests supernatural power—Kami—both in objects such as stones and trees and in ancestors (and, for this reason, Shintoism is also a religion involving ancestor worship). In some societies, animism takes the form of **shaminism**. A shaman is someone believed to have the power to communicate with and embody the spirits and thereby influence human life by, for example, healing the sick or foreseeing the future.

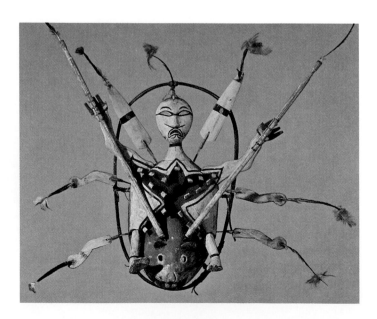

This ceremonial Inuit mask represented a shaman's vision of spirits believed to be found in animals and the forces of nature. The mask shows the spirit of the shaman riding the spirit of a beaver.

As we saw earlier, **totemic** religions in Australia and the South Pacific believe that totems—plants or animals closely related to a society's way of life or natural environment—have supernatural powers to help and protect or punish and bring misfortune to humans and their communities. Totems must be treated with great respect, if not fear and awe, for if a totem is touched, killed, or even looked upon the consequences may be disastrous.

Although both animistic and totemic religions involve supernatural forces, these spirits, ghosts, and totems do not have the standing of powerful gods considered worthy of worship. Even further removed from the worship of gods are religions based entirely on abstract ideals.

Ethicalist Religion   A large portion of the world's population—living mostly in India and East Asia—have religions that focus more on sets of abstract ideals than on supernatural powers vested in gods, objects, or animals. The largest of these **ethicalist religions** are Buddhism, Confucianism, and Taoism, and they are concerned with how people can achieve a better life on earth.

Buddhism (from "Buddha" meaning "enlightened one") was founded in the sixth-century B.C. by an Indian Hindu named Guatama who believed that human misery is caused primarily by desire for pleasure and material things, by too great an attachment to earthly existence. He believed that the physical realities of our existence are in fact illusions, and that if we could only give up those illusions, we would give up the suffering that goes with them as well. To accomplish this, Buddhists engage in meditation and other practices intended to free people's minds of all desire. The highest result of this practice is a state of bliss known as nirvana.

Confucius was a Chinese contemporary of Buddha who believed that salvation lay in a state of harmony, serenity, and self-confidence that could only be achieved through careful attention to proper social conduct in relation to other people. Confucianism emphasizes the idea of doing one's duty to family and community, of valuing social harmony above the desires of individuals.

Taoism is more abstract than Confucianism; it is based on the belief that the universe itself is held together by ethical principles that are beyond human control. The best that humans can do is not try to control events, but to follow their own spontaneous natures and live in harmony with the world as they find it. For all three of these ethicalist religions, the fundamental idea is to fit into the scheme of things in a harmonious way, however that scheme may be defined.

Ritual   Religions use a variety of practices—called **rituals**—to maintain relationships among believers and between believers and the supernatural. Ritual may be as simple as uttering a sacred word or as complex as an elaborate ceremony involving sacred objects and specialized roles. Religions that include one or more gods use ritual to reaffirm loyalty to supernatural powers and to satisfy their gods. The ancient Aztecs of Mexico performed rituals in which a priest cut the heart from a living person, in the belief that this would appease their gods (Diaz 1974). Christians, Jews, and Muslims use prayer to maintain their connection with the supernatural. Christianity is one of the few religions that emphasizes the concept of sin and uses ritual to reestablish a state of grace that will enable sinners to enter heaven when they die (Wilson 1982).

The Trobriand Islanders use magic in their efforts to control the powers of the unknown (Malinowski 1948), and the followers of the Shinto religion worship both nature and their ancestors in order to maintain a relationship with the supernatural power of the Kami. Buddhists, Taoists, and Confucians meditate in order to establish an inner sense of harmony between themselves and the ethical principles they believe tie all the parts of the universe into a single, integrated whole.

These are only some of the major differences between the belief systems of the major religions, to which must be added thousands of specific beliefs about the universe and the place of humans in it. Most religions, for example, pay little attention to life after death. It is also important to be aware that there is a great variety of beliefs not only between religions, but within them as well. Some Orthodox Jews, for example, differ sharply from other Jews in their strict adherence to the belief that the Jews may not have their own homeland until God sends a Messiah. These Jews therefore oppose the existence of the state of Israel.

There are also different beliefs among Christians, even on such central issues as the existence of God, Jesus as the Son of God, life after death, and the

TABLE 21-1   Varieties of Religious Beliefs among U.S. Christians

PERCENT WHO BELIEVE	BAPTIST	METHODIST	LUTHERAN	PRESBYTERIAN	EPISCOPALIAN	CATHOLIC
The Bible is literally true[1]	58	31	27	22	21	20
There is life after death[1]	70	73	77	67	67	73
Life after death is very much like life on earth[2]	46	27	48	31	18	36
God is a judge[1]	51	40	38	33	33	36
Women should be ordained[3]	50	80	75	77	71	55
The world is full of evil and sin	21	13	23	6	0	12
Have great confidence in leaders of organized religion[1,2]	23	29	26	26	23	23

[1]1990
[2]1989
[3]1986
Source: Computed from 1986, 1989, and 1990 General Social Survey data.

importance of religion (see Glock and Stark 1968). Sharp differences exist not only between denominations (Table 21-1) but also between societies that are predominantly Christian (Table 21-2). In societies whose people are predominantly white, for example, Christians believe that Jesus was white; but many African Christians believe he was black.

Religious Values, Norms, and Attitudes

One of the most important goals in any religion is salvation, although each religion defines it in its own way (Wilson 1982). To the Melanesian tribes of Southern Indonesia, salvation is safety on the sea when they go fishing. For many Christians, it includes going to heaven rather than hell when they die. In Judaism, salvation is the coming of the Messiah, signaling that Jews once again enjoy the favor of God. In Hinduism, salvation is reincarnation into a higher social caste in the next life, which, after an appropriate number of lives results in a complete identification with the Divine. In Buddhism, salvation is the achievement of a mystical state of "oneness" with the Divine. In Taoism and Confucianism, salvation is oriented to the present life. In Taoism, it takes the form of withdrawing from all earthly plea-

TABLE 21-2   Percentage of People Reporting Belief in God or Universal Spirit and in Life after Death (Selected Countries)

COUNTRY	PERCENTAGE WHO REPORT BELIEF IN "GOD" OR A "UNIVERSAL SPIRIT"	PERCENTAGE WHO REPORT BELIEF IN LIFE AFTER DEATH	PERCENTAGE WHO VALUE RELIGIOUS BELIEFS AS "VERY" IMPORTANT"
United States	94	69	56
Canada	89	54	36
Italy	88	46	36
Australia	80	48	25
Belgium	78	48	26
United Kingdom	76	43	23
France	72	39	22
West Germany	72	33	17
Sweden, Norway, Denmark, and Finland	65	35	17

Source: Gallup Report, September 9, 1976.

sures and ending all desire and, therefore, all feelings of deprivation and suffering; in Confucianism, it is harmonious living by the principles of a unified universe. In animistic and totemic religion, salvation often takes the form of deliverance from the misfortunes of everyday life such as disease and accidents.

Religious norms define socially approved means for achieving salvation. Orthodox Judaism requires obedience both to the Ten Commandments and to the complex set of laws contained in the Talmud, including dietary laws forbidding the eating of pork. Among Hindus, reincarnation into a higher social caste depends on performing the duties associated with their current caste, including obedience to sacred laws such as those forbidding the killing of cows.

In Buddhism, meditation is the chief means for achieving the end of desire, which is believed to lead to the salvation of a nonexistence free from earthly suffering. As in animistic religions, the Shinto of Japan appease the spirits in objects and ancestors by worshipping them and by taking care not to harm them. Followers of totemic religions carry totems to appease supernatural forces.

Ethical religions such as Taoism and Confucianism stress respect for others and goodness and love as the means for achieving harmony with the universe. Confucianism in particular stresses respect for the family and those in higher classes. Confucianism demands support for the existing social system as the means for achieving religious values.

To sociologists, the most important religious attitudes focus on relationships among people, not between believers and the sacred and supernatural. Among Hindus, religious beliefs and values underlie a caste system that includes attitudes of respect for those in higher castes and contempt for the untouchables who are outside the caste system. Confucianism stresses attitudes of respect and subservience toward family elders and those in higher classes. Christianity and Judaism tend to regard females as inferior, and Catholicism in particular—in spite of its adoration for the Virgin Mary—carries a deep tradition of negative attitudes toward women, beginning with the belief that Eve was responsible for

Adam's fall from grace in the Garden of Eden (Chernin 1987; Daly 1973; Walker 1987).

Together, beliefs, values, attitudes, and norms form the cultural core of religion, but a full sociological understanding of the importance of religion in society must also pay attention to how religious ideas are expressed through socially structured relationships.

The expulsion of Adam and Eve from the Garden of Eden and the idea that it was primarily Eve's fault are central images in Christianity that feminist scholars often associate with the inferior standing of women in Christian societies.

SOCIAL STRUCTURE: THE SOCIAL ORGANIZATION OF RELIGION

As institutions, religions are more than collections of ideas, for they also include relationships within a community of believers and between it and society. These relationships affect how religious ideas are expressed and in many cases how social life in general is carried out in a society.

Religious institutions have boundaries that define both active and potential membership, role structures that divide labor and power, and patterns of interaction through which religious ideas are expressed and perpetuated. In relatively simple societies, religious institutions are not separate from family, economic, and political institutions; but in complex industrial societies, religious institutions are more likely to stand apart and are related to other social institutions in complex ways. These structural differences can be described in terms of several major types of religious institutions: the *ecclesia*, the *church*, the *denomination*, the *sect*, and the *cult*.

The Ecclesia

The ecclesia is the most powerful of all religious institutions. Islam in Iran and Catholicism in Italy are examples of an **ecclesia**, in which all or most of the people in the society belong to the community of believers from the moment they are born.

The role structure of an ecclesia is formal and bureaucratic. It has a highly trained corps of religious leaders and workers, and one leader usually dominates the entire system. Authority is primarily traditional and legal-rational, although in some cases charismatic leaders, such as Iran's late Ayatollah Khomeini, emerge. In no ecclesia, however, is charismatic authority the main source of power.

The time structure of an ecclesia is indefinite (Islam's followers expect it to last forever), and religious practices consist primarily of rituals that include relatively little expression of emotion.

Perhaps the most important structural characteristic of the ecclesia is that unlike all other religious institutions, it is closely identified and allied with political, economic, and family institutions. In ancient Egypt, for example, the Pharaohs were, themselves, regarded as gods and thus the rulers of both the profane and sacred worlds. The ecclesia is less common today than it once was, but it still exists. In Iran, the Islamic ecclesia is virtually amalgamated with the government. Criminals are tried in religious courts under religious law, and no major governmental decision can be made without the approval of the country's highest religious leader (see Arjomand 1988). In Italy, the position of the Catholic ecclesia is not so powerful, but the pattern is similar nonetheless. The pope is a powerful figure in Italy, and while the government often makes decisions that the pope condemns—such as allowing divorce or abortion—the government cannot afford to ignore completely the views of the Catholic ecclesia.

The Church

A **church**—such as the Church of England, the Catholic Church outside of Italy, the Methodist, Episcopalian, and Lutheran churches in the U.S., and the Greek Orthodox Church—is similar to an ecclesia in several ways. Membership is usually ascribed at birth and includes people from all social classes. There is a formal bureaucracy with a highly

The Muslim religion in Iran is a powerful example of an ecclesia in which the highest religious leader—the Ayatollah—is also the leader of the government. When Khomeini died, it held great religious as well as political significance for his mourners, shown here crowding to touch the dead leader. In the frenzy, four people were trampled to death.

trained priesthood, authority is based more on tradition and legal-rational rules than on charisma, the institution is expected to last indefinitely, and religious practice is highly ritualized with relatively little display of emotion.

Two important structural characteristics distinguish churches from ecclesia, however. Membership does not include all members of a society, and the relationship between churches and other social institutions is far more loose. Churches such as the Church of England generally ally themselves with the ruling class and support the status quo; but they do not have the power of an ecclesia to influence political and economic institutions. In many authoritarian societies, churches oppose the power of the state, in some cases because the state at best only tolerates religion.

The Denomination

Denominations—such as Congregational and Unitarian Universalists—are the smallest religious institutions that still have a formal role structure with trained leaders. Like churches and ecclesiae, denominations generally draw new members from families that already belong to the community of believers, and religious rituals usually involve little expression of emotion.

Unlike churches and ecclesiae, denominations draw members from a limited range of class backgrounds. Congregationalists and Unitarians, for example, are most likely to come from the upper-middle and upper classes, while almost 70 percent of Baptists are in the working and lower classes (Chalfant, Beckley, and Palmer 1981). Mintz's (1975) study of U.S. presidential cabinet members from 1897 to 1972 found that almost half were either Presbyterians or Episcopalians, even though these denominations account for only 7 percent of the entire U.S. population.

Denominations also lack the bureaucratic structure that is the hallmark of ecclesiae and churches, and they have a much looser power structure based on traditional authority. The relationship between denominations and other social institutions is also far more distant. Rather than allying themselves with governments, denominations are more likely to coexist with them and avoid active involvement in political or economic issues.

The U.S. is one of the few religiously pluralist societies, in which no single church dominates. As we will see later, this results in a high degree of religious tolerance and freedom, but also tends to lessen the influence of religion on social life.

The Sect

Sects are religious groups that have broken off from churches and denominations, and their structures are radically different. Membership is usually through conversion rather than ascribed at birth, and new members are converted through persuasion. Their role structure is informal and leaders have little if any formal training. There are minimal divisions of power and leaders are usually chosen by the community. Religious ceremonies encourage spontaneous shows of emotion and have little of the rigid, abstract form found in the ecclesia, church, or denomination.

Sects also differ from other religious institutions in their opposition to other institutions. Members of the lower classes are more likely than others to belong to religious sects, perhaps because they have less to gain by supporting existing political and economic institutions that place them at the bottom of the social stratification system. Engels (in Feuer 1959)

The emotionalism of sects and cults is readily apparent in this San Francisco revival meeting.

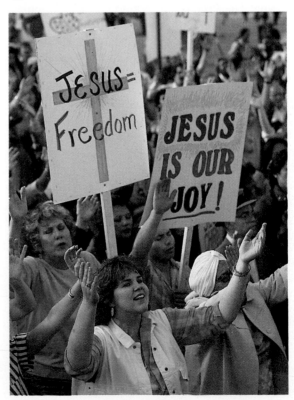

draws striking parallels between revolutionary movements and the early history of Christianity as a religious sect:

> Christianity was originally a movement of oppressed people; it first appeared as the religion of slaves and emancipated slaves, or poor people deprived of their rights, of peoples subjugated or dispersed by Rome. (p. 168)

Niebuhr (1929) argued that sects form when churches develop to a point where they no longer serve the interests of lower- and working-class members, and this helps explain why Christianity is divided into many different sects. As churches become more established, they also come to be dominated by the more prosperous middle and upper classes and reflect their needs and interests more than those of members lower in the class system. Those who are deprived often look to religion to provide comfort and reassurance that their deprivation during life will be compensated for after death. Their orientation tends to be away from the material conditions of life and towards a direct relationship with God and the supernatural.

Those who are prosperous, however, have less reason to escape or reject the material conditions of life, and will tend to shape their religion in ways that accept, if not actively support, their material well-being. The result is a more abstract, detached orientation to God and the supernatural, which does not meet the needs of those who must reconcile themselves with deprivation. Consequently, as churches become increasingly dominated by the upper classes, lower-class members are more likely to break away and establish sects that more effectively meet their religious needs. Over time, sects may succeed to the point where the cycle begins again. The Mormons, for example, began as a sect but today more closely resemble a denomination.

In the 1970s roughly 55 percent of sect members in the U.S. belonged to the working and lower classes, compared with just over 40 percent of Presbyterians and Jews and just over 30 percent of Episcopalians. Only around 14 percent of those who belong to sects are from the upper class, compared with 30 percent of Presbyterians and Jews and 40 percent of Episcopalians (Chalfant, Beckley, and Palmer 1981).

The deviant status of many sects often causes tense and hostile relationships both with the parent church and the surrounding society. In the fifth century B.C., the first Buddhists were persecuted as a sect of Hinduism. Early Christians were a sect of Jews who believed that Jesus was the Son of God, and they were persecuted by the Romans. In the seventeenth century, English Quakers were persecuted by Christians, as were Mormons in the eighteenth century; in this century, members of the Baha'i sect are persecuted in countries such as Iran; and in India, members of the Sikh sect of Hinduism have frequent violent confrontations with other Hindus.

The Cult

Cults are the least organized religious institutions (see Merton and Moore 1982). Most members join through conversion—usually in response to a personal crisis—and tend to come from the poorest social classes. Ceremonies tend to be highly emotional and spontaneous. The role structure of cults is informal, but power is concentrated in a charismatic leader.

The cult is the only religious institution in which charisma is the main form of authority. For this rea-

Defeated and forced to live on desolate reservations, the Sioux Indians were deep in despair and starvation in 1881 when they heard of a prophecy of a return to the prosperity and peace they had once known. This developed into the Ghost Dance cult, named for the dance they believed would drive whites away and realize the prophecy. The Ghost Dance included religious frenzy, and semiconscious trances and visions. The shirt they wore was believed to protect its wearer from the bullets of white soldiers.

son, the time structure of a cult tends to be no longer than the life of its leader, for once he or she is gone (or loses charismatic appeal), the central organizing force in the cult disappears. The importance of charismatic authority in cults also creates conditions in which leaders may easily abuse their power, as happened in 1978 when the Reverend Jim Jones led 900 of his followers in a mass suicide (Hall 1987).

Cults also differ from other religious institutions in their rejection of and withdrawal from the rest of society (see Flowers 1984). While sects are critical of other social institutions, cults tend to reject them entirely. This perhaps explains why cults attract so many people from the poorest social classes, people who see little to be gained by trying to participate in the existing institutions of their society.

The followers of Jim Jones were almost all poor people who saw the Jones cult as their last hope for a decent life, and who willingly left the U.S. to create their own colony in the small South American country of Guyana. Their mass suicide (in which a few unwilling participants were murdered) was based on the same kind of fear of outsiders that prompted them to move to Guyana: they believed that outsiders were coming to destroy their cult.

It is important to be aware that all major religions began as cults. Islam, Buddhism, and Christianity have enormous influence in the world today, and yet all were once regarded by the societies in which they first appeared as deviant. In this sense, the cult represents true religious innovation in a society, for although sects often form in rebellion against churches, they remain within the same religious tradition. As different as the many Christian sects are, for example, they are all, nonetheless, Christian.

We have seen that religions differ both in their ideas and the ways in which institutional arrangements are structured (Table 21-3). Not all religious

TABLE 21-3   Summary of Major Structural Types of Religious Institutions

STRUCTURAL CHARACTERISTIC	ECCLESIAE	CHURCHES	DENOMINATIONS	SECTS	CULTS
Boundaries and Membership	Ascribed; most people belong	Mostly ascribed; broad membership	Mostly ascribed; limited in social class	Mostly achieved, through persuasion; lower class	Mostly achieved, through emotional crisis; lower class
Time Structure	Indefinite	Indefinite	Indefinite	Moderately long	Usually temporary
Role Structure	Formal and bureaucratic with trained clergy	Formal and bureaucratic with trained clergy	Formal but not bureaucratic; trained clergy	Informal with relatively untrained leadership chosen by community	Infoormal, loosely organized; charismatic leadership
Authority Structure	Legal-rational and traditional	Legal-rational and traditional	Traditional	Minimal authority structure	Charismatic
Patterns of Interaction	Highly abstract ritual; relatively little emotion	Highly abstract ritual; relatively little emotion	Abstract ritual; relatively little emotion	Few formal rituals; spontaneous show of emotion	No formal rituals; highly emotional
Relation to Other Institutions	Closely identified with political and economic institutions	Often allied with ruling class and status quo	Coexist with political and economic institutions	Oppose institutions; nonconformist	Reject institutions; retreatist

institutions can be classified in terms of the major types described in the preceding sections, however, for the structures of religious institutions are connected with religious ideas. Ecclesiae and churches, for example, are more common among monotheistic religions such as Christianity, Judaism, and Islam than they are among polytheistic religions such as Hinduism and ethical religions such as Taoism and Confucianism. Religions based on belief in a single all-powerful god are more likely to develop complex structures through which religious leaders represent and administer what is believed to be the will of the supreme being. Monotheism also creates a need for institutions that have power to force followers to be religiously faithful, for monotheistic gods are generally viewed as jealous and intolerant of allegiance to any other sacred force (Wilson 1982).

Ethical religions, by comparison, do not view sacred power as flowing from a single source such as a god; rather, the sacred consists of all things—of which each believer is a part. This cultural aspect of ethical religions gives them less need for formally structured religious institutions. It is one thing to have a church leadership that represents God on earth; but it makes little sense to have church leaders who represent the entire universe.

THE SOCIAL ECOLOGY OF RELIGIOUS INSTITUTIONS

Like all cultural and structural aspects of social systems, religions and religious institutions are affected by how populations grow and distribute themselves and the ways in which societies use physical environments to meet their material needs.

The Importance of Size

The number of people who belong to a community of believers directly affects the power of religious institutions (see Tables 21-4 and 21-5); but as we saw in Chapter 9, the effect of numbers on group power depends as much on relative size as it does on absolute size (Merton 1968; Simmel [1902] 1950). As an ecclesia, for example, the Iranian Islamic religion is powerful because its membership is large and because it includes almost all of Iran's population. Under such conditions, it is difficult for other religious institutions to survive, much less compete successfully. In a religiously pluralistic society such as the U.S., however, dominance by a single religion is more difficult, in part because there are so many different communities of believers. Absolute size alone, then, does not determine social power.

TABLE 21-4   Estimated Membership in Major Religions of the World, by Region, Late 1980s

RELIGION	NORTH AMERICA	SOUTH AMERICA	EUROPE	ASIA	USSR	AFRICA	OCEANIA	WORLD
Total Christian	84.5%	90.3%	82.0%	7.0%	35.6%	46.7%	83.1%	32.9%
Roman Catholic	(34.3)	(84.0)	(52.1)	(3.3)	(1.8)	(17.5)	(29.3)	(18.7)
Protestant	(37.2)	(3.6)	(21.1)	(2.0)	(3.2)	(15.2)	(49.5)	(8.1)
Other Christian	(13.0)	(2.7)	(8.8)	(1.7)	(30.0)	(14.0)	(34.3)	(6.1)
Jewish	2.6	0.2	0.3	0.1	1.1	*	0.3	0.3
Muslim	1.9	0.3	2.5	18.3	11.6	39.5	0.4	17.8
Hindu	0.4	0.2	0.1	20.6	*	0.2	1.2	13.2
Buddhist	0.1	0.1	*	9.3	*	*	*	6.0
Other Religions[1]	2.7	4.8	0.6	19.8	2.9	13.3	1.1	8.6
Nonreligious	7.8	3.5	10.4	20.7	28.9	0.3	11.9	16.7
Atheists	0.4	0.6	3.7	4.5	19.9	*	2.0	4.5
TOTAL	100.0%	100.0%	100.0%	100.0%	100.0%	100.0%	100.0%	100.0%
(N in millions)	(273.8)	(439.1)	(496.7)	(3,051.6)	(285.8)	(628.3)	(26.1)	(5,201.4)

*less than 0.1%
[1]Other religions include Chinese folk religionists, new religionists, tribal religionists, Sikhs, shamanists, Confucians, Bahai's, Shintoists, and Jains.
Source: Encyclopedia Britannica 1990 *Book of the Year*, p. 316.

TABLE 21-5   Membership in Major Religions (United States).

RELIGION	NUMBER OF MEMBERS	PERCENTAGE OF U.S. POPULATION
Protestant	78,700,000	33
Catholic	53,300,000	23
Eastern Orthodox	4,000,000	2
Jewish	5,800,000	2
Other	290,000	0*
Nonmembers	95,000,000	40

*less than .2%
Source: USCB 1986a.

Size helps account for several social characteristics of smaller religious groups such as sects and cults. Small numbers not only lessen their power but also make it more difficult to perpetuate themselves across generations. This problem is particularly acute in the predominantly black Father Divine cult in the United States, whose norms forbid marriage and sexual relations among its members. Since reproduction is a major way to increase community size, this policy removes what is obviously a very important source of new members (Kephart and Zellner 1990).

The instability of cults reinforces members' fears of the surrounding society and their urge to isolate and protect themselves from it; but this is not restricted to sects and cults. The state of Israel, for example, attracts many Jews in part because while Jews are a tiny minority around the world, in Israel they constitute an overwhelming numerical majority, making them less vulnerable to persecution and discrimination.

Technology, Production, and Religion

Sociologists and anthropologists have long noted aspects of religion that vary between societies according to ecological differences (Table 21-6). The religions of most gatherer-hunter societies do not include belief in a supreme being who created the earth, while this belief is found in the religions of almost all herding societies. Among gatherer-hunters, animism is the most common form of religion (Turnbull 1961).

Notice in Table 21-6 that as we move toward societies that use more advanced technology, belief in a supreme creator who is active in human affairs and supports moral behavior becomes more common—with the interesting exception of herding societies, 80 percent of whose religions do include this belief. Although we do not know just why the belief in an active and caring creator is so common among herders, it is possible that they draw upon their experience as

TABLE 21-6   Percentage of Societies Whose Religion Includes Selected Beliefs, by Type of Society

RELIGIOUS BELIEF	TYPE OF SOCIETY				
	Gathering and Hunting	Herding	Simple Horticultural	Advanced Horticultural	Agrarian
No concept of a supreme creator	61%	4%	61%	21%	23%
Belief in a passive supreme creator who is unconcerned with human affairs	29	10	35	51	6
Belief in an active supreme creator who does not support human morality	8	6	2	12	5
Belief in an active supreme creator who supports human morality	2	80	2	16	66
TOTAL	100%	100%	100%	100%	100%
(Number of Societies)	(85)	(50)	(43)	(131)	(66)

Source: Lenski and Lenski 1987, Table 4-4.

The depiction of Christ as a good shepherd—in what kinds of societies is such an image most likely to be found?

herders to envision a supreme being that cares for them in the same way that they care for their animals (Lenski and Lenski 1982).

The mode of production in a society is also related to whether or not its religion includes the worship of ancestors. Ancestor worship is found in only 17 percent of gatherer-hunter societies, but in more than two-thirds of simple and advanced horticultural societies. This difference may be due to the simple fact that unlike gatherer-hunters, peoples who live by tending small gardens tend to live in one place and this keeps them near the graves of their ancestors (Shiels 1975).

Technology and modes of production are also related to the size, power, and complexity of religious institutions. As is true of political institutions, a full-time, highly trained, and powerful class of religious leaders can only be supported in a society that is able to produce a surplus of goods, and it was not until the agrarian age that ecclesiae and churches came into being. Religious institutions in industrial societies, however, are far less powerful than they were in agrarian Europe of the Middle Ages. As we saw in Chapter 20, church and state in medieval Europe were the two dominant and competing sources of power. The Protestant Reformation, however, inspired by Martin Luther in the sixteenth century challenged the absolute authority of the Catholic Church and undermined its claim to obedience and wealth. In addition, in the eighteenth and nineteenth centuries, science weakened the monopoly of religion over cultural explanations of the world; and with the Industrial Revolution the state and the emerging capitalist class claimed an increasing share of wealth. The result was a dramatic decline in the economic and political power of religious institutions.

Here it is especially important to remember that religions and religious institutions are not the same thing. Nowhere in the world, perhaps, has the power of the state caused so dramatic a decline in the power of a church as it did in Russia after the 1917 revolution that began the transformation of feudal Russia into the socialist Soviet Union. In the Soviet Union, the Russian Orthodox Church has little authority as a

So effective was the suppression of organized religion by the state in the Soviet Union that it was not until 1989 that a church procession was allowed within Moscow's Kremlin walls.

social institution; but the religious ideas and practices of Christianity still have considerable power in a large segment of the Russian population (Shipler 1983).

FUNCTION, DYSFUNCTION, AND SOCIAL CONFLICT

All religious institutions are defined in part by the functions they perform in a community of believers. As we have seen in other chapters, however, this does not mean that institutional characteristics cannot also have dysfunctional consequences, or that they never play a part in social conflict.

Some Dysfunctions of Religion and Religious Institutions

Religious ideas often have dysfunctional consequences. Because religious communities often view their beliefs and values as absolutely correct, it is only a short step to the ethnocentric view that their religion is superior to all others. The absoluteness with which many religious ideas are held also increases the chance that religion will serve as an ideology.

No war is so fierce as a holy war fought in the name of religion, and as the seventeenth-century French philosopher and mathematician Pascal wrote, "Men never do evil so completely and cheerfully as when they do it from religious conviction." As long as the religion of ancient Rome was polytheistic, for example, Christians were favorite objects of persecution; but when Christianity became the official religion of Rome in the fourth century, Jews became the new target and have remained an object of persecution based on the mistaken belief that Jews were responsible for the death of Christ. The crusades of the eleventh, twelfth, and thirteenth centuries pitted Christians against Muslims. The Spanish Inquisition at the turn of the sixteenth century sent thousands of suspected heretics to their death, focusing particularly on Jews and Christians with Moorish backgrounds. In the sixteenth century, French Catholics and Protestants fought for

more than 30 years during which massacres and other atrocities were commonplace.

Religion still plays a part in aggression and war. Catholics and Protestants in Northern Ireland have been fighting for much of this century. Muslims and Christians in Lebanon have fought with each other in religious wars that continue into the 1990s. Violence against Jews in France, the Soviet Union, the U.S., and many other countries still occurs. In India, violence between Muslims and Hindus is common, and in 1984 members of the Sikh religious sect assassinated Prime Minister Indira Gandhi in retaliation for alleged mistreatment by the government. The 1979 revolution in Iran replaced the oppressive authoritarian state of the shah with an equally or more oppressive authoritarian state based on Islamic religious law. Arrest, torture, and execution of those who oppose Islamic rule has become common in Iran, and the ensuing war with Iraq was characterized by Iranian leaders as a holy war whose ultimate goal was to bring about the supremacy of Islam as the basis for all political institutions in the Middle East.

Religion is not the sole cause of such violence; as in the case of Northern Ireland, conflict often has more to do with economic and political issues than with differences of faith. Religion, however, fuels conflict by giving each side the belief that their cause is just in an ultimate and absolute sense.

Social conflict is more likely to involve monotheistic religions such as Islam, Christianity, and Judaism than polytheistic religions such as Hinduism or ethical religions such as Buddhism, Confucianism, and Taoism. By definition, monotheism includes the belief that there is not only a god, but one god only. Any other religion that does not focus on that god is likely to be seen as a threat to believers in a monotheistic religion.

Violence is not the only dysfunctional consequence of religion. The Buddhist emphasis on people removing themselves from earthly concerns and putting an end to all feelings of desire, for example, tends to remove them from the ongoing conflict through which positive social change often occurs (Wilson 1982). The Islamic religion carries a strong sense of fatalism in the belief that everything that happens on earth is a matter of Allah's will. This interferes with economic progress that usually involves long-range planning and a belief that the future can be affected by what people do in the present.

In the simplest sense, religion can be dysfunctional when it includes false beliefs. In Europe of the Middle Ages and into the eighteenth century, the advance of science and technology was slowed by religious doctrines that argued a very different view of how things work. Scientists such as Galileo and Copernicus were persecuted by the Catholic Church for their theories about the solar system, and early medical researchers were forbidden from cutting open corpses and had to steal them from graveyards.

In general, sociologists are not very interested in the truth or falsity of particular religious beliefs, because the social power and importance of religion does not lie in the content of religious ideas; rather, it lies in the commitment of a community of believers to a set of ideas that form a sacred framework within which people interpret and explain the world and their experience in it. In general, the ideas that make up a religion are far less significant than the fact that people believe in them.

Religion, Class, and Social Conflict

The relationship between religious institutions and class systems in stratified societies is both long-standing and common in part because the rise of religious institutions was spurred by the same changes that supported the emergence of stratification systems and the state. Since religious and political institutions depend on wealth that they do not produce, it is not surprising that they have often found themselves either supporting each other or competing for a greater share of power. Religious leaders consti-

tuted one of the first elites to emerge when societies began to produce a surplus of goods that allowed the accumulation and concentration of wealth and power.

Religious beliefs and values have supported social inequality in many societies. The Hindu caste system is supported by the belief in reincarnation and the importance attached to caste boundaries. Respect for elders and others in positions of authority is an important part of Confucianism that supports inequality of wealth and power. Buddhist values and beliefs support the status quo by denying the importance of anything that occurs in the profane world and striving for a cessation of all desire for wealth, power, and prestige (Wilson 1982).

For centuries the Catholic Church was one of the most powerful social institutions in Europe, rivaled only by the nobility; and even when the state emerged as the dominant institution, the church continued to have great wealth and influence. In Mexico, the Catholic Church was so closely allied with the upper class that during the violent revolutions of the nineteenth century the church and its priesthood were targets of the anger and frustration of the peasant class. Not only did the church lose most of its wealth, but for several years priests were forbidden to wear religious clothing in public, and they are still constitutionally prohibited from voting or holding public office.

Religion does not, however, always serve the interests of dominant classes and the status quo. While the Mexican revolutionaries identified the church as an enemy, for example, the Mexican people were at the same time deeply religious. Here the distinction between religion and religious institutions is once again important, for it was the church and not religion that Mexicans rejected.

In some societies, religious institutions openly oppose the state, especially when it is oppressive and authoritarian. This is true of most religious sects and cults that draw their members largely from the lowest social classes; but it is also true of the Catholic Church in Latin American countries that are ruled by authoritarian governments. The church in such societies becomes a place for people to meet, to discuss political and social issues that affect their lives, and to make plans for change. In a few Latin American countries, such as El Salvador and Nicaragua, the priesthood serves as an active source of criticism of government policy and of awareness of the true conditions of life in the profane world. Most important, religion in these societies—and others such as socialist Poland—is a source of emotional attachment

In many Latin American countries, movements for social justice have often involved members of the clergy. In El Salvador, this included Archbishop Romero, a critic of the government and an outspoken advocate of human rights who was assassinated in 1980 by unknown gunmen while conducting services.

and power whose mere existence has threatened the dominance of the state. In 1984, for example, the Polish government ordered the enforcement of a previously passed law banning the display of crucifixes in public schools and universities, a move that prompted violent demonstrations against the government.

Religion and False Consciousness   When Karl Marx described religion as the "opium of the people," he was arguing that the focus of religion on the sacred and unknown world distracts attention from the realities of life in the profane world of inequality and injustice. As Max Weber ([1923] 1950) wrote, "It was possible for the working class to accept its lot as long as the promise of eternal happiness could be held out to it" (p. 369).

Marx's use of opium as an image is powerful because opium is a depressant drug that dulls sensation, including pain. To Marx, religion is often used to explain and justify the suffering that people experience during their lives. The key, however, is that religion explains earthly conditions not as the result of social relationships but as part of a natural, sacred order. In this way, religion contributes to false consciousness by substituting a sacred explanation of earthly conditions for a social one. The problem, argued Marx, lies not with the conditions created by

sacred or supernatural forces, but with those created by societies, and when we focus attention on the sacred as the source of all things—including poverty, oppression, and suffering—we are less likely to identify the social sources of inequality and the suffering and deprivation that result.

Slaves in the American South were told that their condition was a matter of God's will (Stampp 1956); and mill owners in North Carolina near the turn of the twentieth century supported local churches primarily in order to distract workers from the social causes of their deprivation (Pope 1942). Many Christians believe that inequality between men and women is based on the word of God as revealed in the Bible, a belief that prompted pioneer feminist Elizabeth Cady Stanton to argue that "The first step in the elevation of women under all systems of religion is to convince them that the great Spirit of the Universe is in no way responsible for any of these absurdities" (in Daly 1973, p. 13).

Harris (1974) argued that false consciousness lay at the heart of the persecution of witches throughout Europe during the Middle Ages. In those times of severe economic hardship, women accused of being witches served as scapegoats, which encouraged the poor to believe that "they were being victimized by witches and devils instead of princes and popes" (p. 237).

Christianity is not the only religion that contributes to false consciousness in this way. The Hindu religion is a perfect example, for people who are born into lower castes cannot hope to return in a higher caste unless they accept their current lot in life and meet their prescribed obligations to the castes above them.

In a deeper sense, all religion contributes to false consciousness by alienating people from the simple fact that the social world and its institutions are the products of human activity. When family roles, the roles of men and women, or the roles of kings are shrouded in religious symbolism, we tend to treat them as inevitable parts of the ultimate reality that religious ideas purport to describe.

> Just as religion mystifies and thus fortifies the illusionary autonomy of the humanly produced world, so it mystifies and fortifies its introjection in individual consciousness. The internalized roles carry with them the mysterious power ascribed to them by their religious legitimations. Socialized identity as a whole can be apprehended by the individual as something sacred, grounded in the "nature of things" as created or willed by the gods. As such, it loses its character as a product of human activity. (Berger 1967, p. 95)

The black civil rights movement depended heavily on the leadership of ministers such as Martin Luther King, Jr. Throughout the South, churches served as a focus not only of religious faith, but of political organization and action.

There is nothing about religion that necessarily means that it supports false consciousness and, therefore, existing social conditions. Some argue, for example, that Jesus Christ was one of many Jews who led the Jewish rebellion against the Roman Empire (Harris 1974). The Mexican revolution that overthrew Spanish rule early in the nineteenth century was led by a soldier and a priest, and in the 1980s and 1990s Catholic prelates have played prominent roles in opposition to authoritarian governments in many countries, including El Salvador, the Philippines, and South Africa. In the U.S., priests and ministers played active roles in the civil rights movement, and Martin Luther King, Jr.—one of the most powerful of all civil rights leaders—was himself a minister. Now many U.S. religious leaders are playing an active part in the nuclear freeze movement that opposes the spread of nuclear weapons (Castelli 1983), and the Reverend Jesse Jackson almost captured the Democratic presidential nomination in 1988.

Religion and religious institutions, therefore, have both opposed and inspired social conflict aimed at changing the social conditions in which people live. Religions and religious institutions themselves, however, are also subject to the pressures that lead to change.

RELIGION AND SOCIAL CHANGE

Like all social systems, religions change, for they exist in relation to larger social environments.

Cultural Change

In general, the ideas that constitute a religion change less easily than the structures through which a community of believers practices a religion, for these ideas form the most basic visions of what life is about, both in this world and in the unknown. Nevertheless, they do change. Norms once forbade the participation of women in religious services among Catholics, Jews, and several Protestant denominations; but under the pressure of the women's movement, those norms are breaking down. There is continuing pressure on the Catholic Church to relax norms that forbid abortion, divorce, and the use of contraceptives, as well as those that forbid priests from marrying.

In 1983 the National Council of Churches released a new translation of key passages in the Bible, designed to remove the male-oriented, sexist bias of earlier translations. The new version replaces "mankind" with "humankind," refers to God as "my Mother and Father" and to Jesus as the Child of God rather than as the Son of God. For all of the protest and praise the new version has inspired, it is important as an institutional acknowledgment of the impact of religious ideas on the most basic aspects of social life and of the pressures exerted on religion by change in the surrounding society.

Specific changes such as these are not isolated social phenomena, for they are related to a much broader and more powerful trend in industrial societies called *secularization*.

Secularization   Secularization is a social process through which "beliefs concerning the supernatural and practices associated with them are discredited and the institution of religion loses social influence" (J. Wilson 1978, p. 397). Secularization involves cultural and structural change within religions as well as changes in the relationship between religious and other institutions.

In 1990, for example, only 20 percent of U.S. Catholics said they believed that the Bible is the literal word of God as did only roughly a third or less of all Protestant denominations except Baptists. Only 23 percent of U.S. adults had "a great deal of confidence" in the leaders of organized religion (see Table 21–1). For many, religious holidays are no longer occasions of worship but opportunities to escape the demands of work and spend time with families.

The declining influence of religion is common in industrial societies, and there are several likely social causes. The most obvious is the steady rise of scientific thinking that began in the seventeenth century and undermined religion as a framework for explaining the natural world (Berger 1967). Physical science challenged the Christian view of the origins of the universe and human life, and in no industrial society is the Biblical version of creation widely used as an explanation (Wilson 1982). As we saw earlier, Weber, Marx, and Durkheim challenged religion by focusing on social rather than divine causes of social conditions. They even went so far as to argue that religion, itself, was a human creation.

The Industrial Revolution added to this an explosion of material goods and, with it, an increased social value placed on material prosperity at the expense of religion's orientation to the sacred and spiritual worlds (J. Wilson 1978). Industrialization also brought with it the need for increased mobility and migration, and with this the ties between church and community became increasingly difficult to maintain. Perhaps most important, the Industrial Revolution rationalized both thought and social relationships, and this undermined the social importance of the sacred in relation to the profane.

As a cultural system, religion has not simply changed in response to cultural changes in society, however, for as the structures of industrial societies have become more complex, religious institutions have been challenged by other institutions.

Changing Structures

Secularization affects not only the ideas that constitute religions but also the structures of religious institutions and their relationships with society. The most dramatic structural change in religious institutions has been a drastic decline in power and authority. In preindustrial societies religion is directly involved in virtually all aspects of social life, from the rituals that mark the passage from one stage of the life course to another—birth, adulthood, marriage, and death—to healing the sick, caring for the poor, administering justice, explaining the world, and educating the young.

In industrial societies, however, many of these social functions are performed by other institutions. It is now possible to marry and have children with no involvement with religious institutions; physicians heal the sick, schools educate the young, scientists in universities and business provide socially acceptable explanations of the world, and the state determines the law, administers justice, and provides for the poor.

In comparison with preindustrial societies in which religion and religious institutions are deeply embedded in all aspects of social life, religious institutions in industrial societies tend to be separate, private, and isolated (see Bellah et al. 1985). They must compete with a variety of other institutions that perform many of the former functions of religion and place demands on the attention of believers (Luckmann 1967). Religious institutions are no longer the major source of cultural ideas that they once were, a fact that is particularly apparent in the high degree of religious tolerance found in most industrial societies. As Wilson (1982) wrote:

> The very fact that religion becomes an optional matter, the fact that there is freedom of religion, tolerance, and choice, is an indication that religion is apparently of little direct consequence to the functioning of the social order, at least as that order is understood by those who have helped to build it, modify it, and maintain it. (p. 46)

There are some indicators that suggest that while the power of religions has certainly diminished in relation to society as a whole, they have held a steady appeal to their members. Among Protestants, for

TABLE 21-7   Percent Who Attended Church in the Preceding Week, by Religion, U.S., 1939–84

YEAR	PROTESTANTS	CATHOLICS	JEWS	OTHERS
1939	40%	64%	12%	**
1950	36%	63%	32%	56%
1959	39%	72%	20%	49%
1960	39%	70%	11%	57%
1969	39%	64%	8%	18%
1979	40%	53%	19%	40%
1980	43%	47%	5%	16%
1984	42%	52%	13%	46%

**No data available
Source: Hout and Greeley 1987, Table 1.

example, the percent who attend church on a weekly basis was roughly the same in 1984 as it was in 1939; and although weekly attendance among Catholics is lower now than it was (due primarily to disagreements with the pope on issues of sexual morality) the drop is not very great (Greeley 1989; Hout and Greeley 1987; see Table 21-7). Since 1950, religious membership has remained relatively constant at around 60 percent, and those who say they "believe in God or a universal spirit" have stayed very close to 95 percent (Caplow et al. 1983; see also Bilheimer 1983; National Council of Churches 1987).

Although religious institutions in general have declined in importance in most other ways in industrial societies, this has been confined largely to ecclesiae, churches, and denominations. Cults such as the Unification Church of Sun Myung Moon and the Hare Krishna movement and the various fundamentalist Christian sects involved in the new evangelicalism still constitute a very small portion of the U.S. population, but have nonetheless enjoyed large increases in membership (Hadden and Swann 1981; Lofland 1977; Robbins 1988). In comparison with larger religious institutions, cults and sects offer a mystical and absolute view of the world that may be a backlash against the secularization process that helps make the world increasingly rational, formal, impersonal, and unemotional.

Civil Religion and Other Alternatives

If involvement in religion is declining, what becomes of its most important social functions—increasing social cohesion and providing a sense of individual and group identity that rests on a set of shared ideas about the meaning of life and our relation to the unknown? Durkheim argued that religious institutions in preindustrial societies allowed people to worship their societies. The sociologist Robert Bellah (1973) contended that in industrial societies, the state itself has become a kind of religious institution. Through **civil religion**, we worship society directly rather than indirectly through religious institutions. Civil religion cuts across all lines drawn by churches, denominations, sects, and cults and helps to unite a pluralistic society (Bellah and Hammond 1980).

The evidence of civil religion is everywhere. In the U.S., God is mentioned at most important public occasions: at the opening of Congress, in courts, in the Pledge of Allegiance to the Flag, at presidential inaugurations. The words "In God We Trust" appear on money; the bald eagle and the flag are sacred symbols of national unity, purpose, and strength; the Fourth of July and Memorial Day are ritual celebrations of a common heritage and the belief that God is somehow on our side. Figures such as George Washington are made into national symbols, and monuments such as the Lincoln Memorial in Washington, D.C., resemble religious shrines (see Schwartz 1987).

Perhaps the most striking example of civil religion is the Soviet Union, which, paradoxically, officially has opposed organized religion. From its revolutionary beginnings in 1917, the Soviet state has identified religion as a negative force that does little more than contribute to false consciousness and the dominance of the ruling class. The Soviet state has tried to replace religion with the state itself and with a Marxist theory of the world based entirely on the production process. Yet in this society that officially has opposed the very idea of the sacred, Russians stand in line for hours to visit the tomb of Lenin in which the Soviet Union's first Marxist leader lies in his casket, perfectly preserved for all to view with quiet religious reverence.

In some ways, the concept and the reality of civil religion represent a contradiction in terms. Religion focuses on sacred and unknown forces that are believed to affect human life, whereas the word "civil" refers to the profane world of ordinary life in a society. Marxism is grounded in the material conditions of human existence, not in unknown forces beyond the understanding of everyday experience. This is also true of civil religion in the U.S.: people may love their country, feel awe in the presence of monuments, and feel full of emotion when they hear

The immensity and majesty of the Lincoln Memorial in Washington, D.C., inspires in many a sense of awe that has sacred overtones typical of those associated with the idea of civil religion.

"America the Beautiful"; but it remains to be seen if an attachment to a country can substitute for answers to the ultimate questions that religions try to answer.

Civil religion cannot explain why we were put on this earth; nor can it tell us what will become of us when we die. It cannot, by definition, provide a meaning of life grounded in beliefs that have a sacred source beyond everyday human experience. While it can, in short, bind us to a society, it cannot secure a place for us in the universe and the endless stretches of time that include our short earthly existence. While civil religion performs some of the functions once performed by religious institutions, it is not a true religion. Bellah (1973), in fact, believed that civil religion is little more than a "broken and empty shell" (p. 142) and that an increased reliance on science, technology, and the state to provide ultimate solutions to human dilemmas will cause a crisis of major proportions.

The rise of the state and civil religion and the declining influence of religious institutions do not necessarily mean that people are no longer concerned with understanding the unknown and attaching a cosmic meaning to life. While sociologists can measure how often people attend church, it is very difficult to measure aspects of religious faith and concern scientifically. Sixty-nine percent of U.S. adults reported a belief in life after death, and although only a minority of adults attend church on a regular basis, 56 percent oppose the Supreme Court's ban on religious observances in public schools. One out of four adults opposes allowing atheists to give speeches in their communities and 44 percent do not think atheists should be allowed to teach in colleges and universities (Davis and Smith 1990).

Again we can see the importance of the distinction between religion and religious institutions. Although attendance at church services in many industrial societies is declining, there is some evidence that people are turning to more private settings for religious behavior. Televised services have a growing—although still relatively small—audience in the United States (Hadden and Swann 1981). In 1983 the coach of a professional football team, a U.S. senator, professional athletes, and prominent businessmen all appeared on television to promote a book that, they promised, would give its readers "a personal relationship with God."

Major religious institutions appear to be losing much of their former authority as sources of the ultimate meanings and truths that make up a religion, and, at the same time, religion has become a more private matter. Rather than adopting the organized beliefs of a particular religion, individuals are now more likely to construct their own view of ultimate truth from a variety of available beliefs and values. With the decline of primary religious institutions, other institutions have taken over some of the role of spreading ideas that ultimately become part of people's religious framework. The family, schools, and the media all offer and support an assortment of ultimate truths from which individuals construct what amount to private religious systems (Luckmann 1967).

It appears that religion is becoming less visible as people turn away from major institutions as the main setting for religious expression; but a lack of visibility does not mean such feelings and beliefs no longer exist. It does suggest, however, that religion is on the decline as a social force that binds people together and forms a basis for group identity. How well other institutions can perform this important social function remains to be seen.

SUMMARY

1. Religion consists of symbols and ideas that focus on the meaning of life and the nature of the unknown. The profane is what we can experience directly as ordinary aspects of the natural world, but the sacred is outside the natural world and inspires feelings of awe.

2. Like all institutions, religion is defined in part by the functions it performs. It helps believers cope with pain and suffering and contributes to social cohesion.

3. It is not the task of sociology to prove the truth or falsity of religious beliefs; rather, sociologists try to understand how religion affects the lives of individuals, groups, and societies.

4. Religions differ primarily in their beliefs. Theistic religion includes the belief in one (monotheism) or more (polytheism) supreme beings. Animists believe that spirits inhabit objects such as trees, and totemists believe objects (totems) have supernatural power. Ancestor worshippers believe the dead can influence life among the living. Ethicalist religions such as Buddhism and Confucianism focus more on abstract ideas as guides for ethical living than on supernatural forces. Religions employ practices called rituals through which religious beliefs are acted out.

5. Salvation is one of the most important values in any religion, and many religious norms define appropriate means for achieving it. Religions also include a variety of attitudes, from adoration of sacred figures to hatred of nonbelievers.

6. Ecclesiae, churches, denominations, sects, and cults are five basic structural types of religious institutions. They differ from each other in how powerful they are and how universal their membership is in a society; in how bureaucratic they are; in the closeness of their ties to other institutions, especially the state; in the selectivity of their membership, especially in terms of social class, and in the ways in which people become members.

7. As with all institutions, religions are affected by population and ecology. The relative and absolute number of followers helps account for both the power of ecclesiae and the weakness of cults. Religious ideas are also affected by technology and the mode of production in a society. The more technologically advanced a society is, the more likely are its religions to include belief in a supreme being who takes an active interest in human affairs.

8. Like all institutions, religion has both functional and dysfunctional consequences. Belief in the absolute truth of religious ideas fosters ethnocentrism and conflict with other religions.

9. Frequently religious institutions are either allied with or actively opposed to the state and dominant social classes. Marx believed that religion often contributes to false consciousness by distracting members of oppressed groups from the true nature and causes of their oppression.

10. A major trend in religious change has been secularization, the process by which religious institutions lose influence to nonreligious institutions such as the state and schools. Compared with religious institutions in preindustrial societies, those in industrial societies have far less authority and influence over people's lives.

11. Some have pointed to the emergence of civil religion as a substitute for the declining influence of religious institutions. In civil religion, society is the focus of worship. In some ways, however, civil religion is a contradiction in terms.

KEY TERMS

animism   532
church   536
civil religion   548
cult   538
denomination   537
ecclesia   536

ethicalist religion   533
monotheism   532
polytheism   532
profane   528
religion   528
ritual   533

sacred   528
sect   537
secularization   547
shamanism   532
totem   531
totemism   533

LOOKING ELSEWHERE

Having studied Chapter 21, you might want to look at related discussions in *Human Arrangements*, which include

- the Jim Jones cult as an in-group (Chapter 9, p. 189)
- anti-Semitism (Chapter 13, pp. 300, 307–308, 313, 315)

- religion and science (Chapter 18, pp. 443–44, 450)
- the caste system and social inequality (Chapter 12, p. 283)

RECOMMENDED READINGS

Berger, P. L. 1969. *A rumor of angels: Modern society and the rediscovery of the supernatural.* New York: Doubleday. A thoughtful exploration of the place of religion in modern industrial societies.

Fowler, J. W. 1981. *Stages of faith.* New York: Harper and Row. A study of religious socialization that focuses on the ways in which people acquire religious faith.

Hunter, J. D. 1983. *American evangelicalism: Conservative religion and the quandry of modernity.* New Brunswick, NJ: Rutgers University Press. A historical study that shows how the traditional basis of evangelicalism has adapted and survived alongside modernization in most major regions of the world.

Robbins, T., and Anthony, D. (Eds.). 1980. *In gods we trust: New patterns of religious pluralism in America.* New Brunswick, NJ: Transaction Books. An important set of articles that focus on religious change in the United States, from social conflict to the rise of civil religion and new religious institutions.

Wilson, J. 1978. *Religion in American society: The effective presence.* Englewood Cliffs, NJ: Prentice-Hall. An excellent introduction to the sociology of religion in the United States. See also Wilson, B. 1982. *Religion in sociological perspective.* New York: Oxford.

Wuthnow, R. 1988. *The restructuring of American religion: Society and faith since World War II.* Princton, NJ: Princeton University Press. A richly detailed and comprehensive view of how religion in the United States has changed over the last forty-five years.

PART SIX

SOCIAL CHANGE

M ost of this book has focused on trying to describe the cultural, structural, and ecological characteristics of social systems and to explain how they operate and affect human life. We have covered a considerable distance—from the process through which children learn language and discover themselves and other people to the ways in which political and economic systems work.

Most of the chapters have ended with a section on change, and this in itself indicates an important sociological problem that extends across all of the areas we study: it is not enough to describe and explain social systems, for the systems change, and each change brings new problems to solve. It is one thing to see clearly how things are and to describe how they work; but it is quite another to understand how things got to be the way they are, and still another to have some idea of how things will be in the next year or the next decade. And given the rapid pace of change in today's societies, it is more important than ever to wrestle successfully with these kinds of questions.

In these last two chapters we look first at the phenomenon of collective behavior, which often plays an important role in bringing about social change. Then, in the last chapter, we focus on the dynamics of social change, from social movements to the influence of technology on the speed, patterns, and direction of change.

22
Collective Behavior

In the spring of 1989, more than 1,000,000 Chinese marched peacefully in Beijing to support calls for greater democracy. There was little violence associated with the march, although later the army attacked protesters in Tiananmen Square. In the months just before Christmas in 1983, however, the "Cabbage Patch" brand of dolls became wildly popular in the United States, and in Charleston, West Virginia, 5,000 shoppers started a near riot in a department store. "They knocked over tables, fighting with each other—there were people in mid-air," reported the store manager. "It got ugly." Huge crowds waited for hours—often in biting cold winds—for a chance to snatch up the dolls, and the rush often resulted in injuries, including broken bones (Associated Press 1983). In 1989, 93 fans at a British soccer game were crushed to death when crowds surged in an overcrowded stadium.

In 1983, hundreds of thousands of people gathered in cities across Western Europe to protest the deployment of nuclear missiles. In England protesters chained themselves to fences surrounding military bases; many people were arrested and police used water cannons to disperse some of the crowds. In 1987, a panic seized the New York Stock Exchange, and as the average value of stocks crashed as dramatically as they did in the crash of 1929, the panic spread around the world to stock exchanges from London to Tokyo. In 1990, 250,000 French university students demonstrated in the streets of Paris and other cities to demand greater government spending on education. While many of the marches were peaceful, in Paris confusion reigned as small gangs looted stores, attacked reporters, and fought with police.

Crowds often serve to focus human energy and emotion in dramatic ways. Here a crowd of thousands gathers at a London concert in tribute to South African black leader Nelson Mandela.

Where in the sociological framework do we find a place for people pushing and shoving over a doll, battling with police in the streets, calmly marching in huge numbers without violence? A clue lies in the concept of collective behavior, and in this chapter we examine the forms it takes and some major attempts to understand it sociologically. We begin with some basic concepts.

CROWDS, MASSES, AND COLLECTIVE BEHAVIOR

Collective behavior refers to social interaction in crowds and masses (Lofland 1981; see also McPhail and Wohlstein 1986). A **crowd** is a temporary collection of people who happen to be in the same place at the same time and close enough so that they can interact with and affect one another. A collection of people on a sidewalk, the audience at a rock concert, passengers on a bus—all are crowds, in which membership is a temporary, situational status. Standing in a telephone booth, we are not part of a crowd; but when we open the door and step out on the sidewalk, we are.

Unlike a crowd, a **mass** is a collection of people who pay attention to and react to the same thing without being in one another's presence. The 1963 assassination of President John F. Kennedy set off a wave of shock and sadness that went around the world and was shared by tens of millions of people who were thousands of miles apart. The collective reaction were examples of mass shock and grief, within which people also expressed their feelings as members of crowds such as those that lined the route of the funeral procession. One of the most telling indicators of the mass experience of Kennedy's assassination is that virtually everyone who was old enough to be aware of the event knows exactly what they were doing when they first heard about it.

The development of the mass media has greatly expanded the opportunities for such phenomena. Until relatively recently, for example, war was beyond the view of those not actually on the scene. All of this changed with the Vietnam War, which was witnessed on a daily basis by millions of people watching the television news. As with the Vietnam War, the transition of war to a mass spectacle has had a great impact on public opinion and the ability of political leaders to gain support for military action. Because television can convey the destruction and brutality of war so vividly and immediately, public opposition to war is likely to form more quickly and powerfully than in the past. When the U.S. went to war with Iraq over the invasion of Kuwait in 1991, for example, politicians and the military were careful to prevent coverage of actual fighting and casualties, for fear that images of the brutality of the war would very quickly undermine public support.

The creation of mass collective behavior by the media has had quite different effects in religious life as well. Television evangelists, for example, are increasingly popular in the United States and have, for many people, replaced group worship in churches with isolated mass worship in the privacy of people's homes. This brings religious services to those who would not otherwise attend, but it also fundamentally alters the social nature of religious ritual. The emphasis on belonging to and worshiping in the presence of a shared community of believers tends to shift toward goals such as developing a "personal relationship with God." Another difference is the heavy emphasis on fund-raising by selling souvenirs, personal advice, healing, or religious objects, a goal for which television is ideally suited.

There are four basic types of collective behavior (Blumer [1939] 1951) that can occur either in crowds or in masses (see Table 22-1). **Casual behavior**—such as people walking on a sidewalk—lacks a common purpose or goal around which people interact or focus attention. **Conventional behavior** involves a specific purpose such as watching a parade. **Expressive behavior**—as you might suppose—centers on feelings. Protest marches, riots, religious revival meetings, funerals, and the congregation of tens of thousands of people in New York City's Times Square each New Year's Eve are all examples of expressive collective behavior. Finally, **acting behavior** is oriented to specific goals—whether it be to lynch someone, block traffic, or prevent workers from crossing a picket line.

These four categories include most types of crowd behavior, but miss several kinds of collective behavior that take place in masses. **Fashion** refers to relatively temporary standards of appearance and behavior that are considered to be socially acceptable or desirable. Men's hairstyles in the U.S., for example, were generally short in the 1950s, longer in the 1960s and 1970s, and shorter again in the 1980s. **Fads** have a shorter life span than fashions and rarely become general standards for behavior or appearance; but what they lack in staying power and social acceptability they make up for in the enthusiasm of their followers. In the 1930s, for example, trying to swallow goldfish was popular among college students, just as trying to fit as many people as possible into a telephone booth was in the 1950s, or "streaking" (running naked through a public place) was in the 1970s (Aguirre et al. 1988).

Collective behavior has long been an important problem for sociologists because it so often has an impact on societies. Crowd behavior is highly visible, and when it is focused on grievances over social conditions, it openly threatens the status quo and stability of institutions and those who occupy positions of authority in them. Crowds also have the collective capacity to seriously threaten both life and property, from killing people and destroying property to overthrowing a government. Such violence may provoke equal or greater violence from authorities, resulting in a polarization of society as people take sides. It is also not uncommon, however, for authorities such as the police to violently attack a peaceful but disruptive crowd. This, in turn, often provokes a violent response from the crowd.

Most important, the behavior of people in crowds seems to be highly unpredictable, and the combination of danger and unpredictability provides a compelling reason to understand it.

Mobs

A **mob** is an emotionally aroused, acting crowd that typically has a leader and focuses on a specific goal, the achievement of which usually involves violence. In the late 1800s and early 1900s, for example, lynch mobs were common in the U.S. and resulted in the murder of more than 5,000 people, most of them blacks living in the South (Cantril 1963; Raper 1933).

Mobs often play an important part in causing or preventing social change. In the 1930s mobs of Nazis roamed German cities and established a pattern of intimidation of opponents and persecution of Jews that solidified Adolph Hitler's authority and laid the groundwork for the Holocaust. In the 1970s mobs of Japanese tried to prevent the opening of a new airport near Tokyo. In 1980 a mob of Iranians seized the U.S. embassy in Tehran, made hostages of the embassy employees, and precipitated an international crisis that—among other things—played a major part in ending President Carter's hopes for a second term.

Its potential for violence has always made the mob an object of fear. Authoritarian governments rarely allow crowds to gather unless they are tightly controlled, in part to prevent a crowd from turning into a mob. In some cases, however, authorities allow mob violence when this supports their goals. In the U.S. South early in this century, attacks on blacks served to keep blacks "in their place," and were often inflicted as punishment for "offenses" such as trying to vote or daring to use facilities

---

TABLE 22-1   Examples of Collective Behavior in Crowds and Masses

TYPE OF BEHAVIOR	IN A CROWD	IN A MASS
Casual	Waiting for bus	Watching the Superbowl
Conventional	Church service	4th of July celebrations
Expressive	Protest march	Nationwide fear over AIDS
Acting	Lynch mob Social movement	Voting Social movement

Sources: Based on Blumer ([1939] 1951) and Lofland 1981.

In Teheran, Iran, a mob burns American flags as
part of an anti-American demonstration in 1986.

reserved for whites (Raper 1933). The mobs in Nazi
Germany served Hitler's purposes in a similar way.

Riots

Unlike mob action, a **riot** lacks leadership, organization, and clear goals. Riots often allow people to express frustration and anger that have been contained
for years. Riots may involve the destruction or theft
of property or attacks on people. In 1984, thousands
of people in the Tunisian capital of Tunis rioted for
three days after the government doubled the price of
bread and other staples. Shops that sold luxury goods
were attacked, as were drivers of expensive cars, and
some 50 people were killed. The government then
restored the lower prices, and within a few hours the
streets were filled with people in a festive mood.

As a form of violent collective behavior, the riot
has played an important part in the life of most societies. In 1986, hundreds of thousands of French
college students staged violent protests against the
government's plan to allow universities to be more
selective in admitting students and granting degrees,
reforms that students believed threatened the principle of free higher education for all. The government
eventually reversed its decision. In 1987, riots by
South Korean students forced their government to
make reforms in that country's election laws.

In 1863 residents of New York City rioted in protest against military draft laws instituted to recruit
soldiers for the Civil War. In Chicago in 1919 and in
Detroit in 1943 rioting whites attacked blacks in two
of the nation's worst race riots. In the 1930s conflict
between striking workers and management resulted
in frequent riots. In the 1960s blacks rioted in U.S.
ghettos to protest poverty and racial discrimination.
In 1968 at the Democratic National Convention in
Chicago, hundreds of anti-Vietnam War demonstrators clashed with police in the streets outside the
convention hall, and although many observers defined the demonstrators as the rioters, an Illinois
commission later decided that it was the police who
had rioted by attacking nonviolent demonstrators
indiscriminately and without justification.

Riots often pose a more serious danger to social
order than mobs do precisely because they have nei-

ther leadership nor clear goals. A mob can often be stopped through its leaders or by meeting its goals without violence. Once a riot has started, however, it is difficult to stop without the use of equal or greater violence, and each use of official violence often has the effect of provoking still more violence from rioters.

Panics

As a form of collective behavior, a **panic** is a collective attempt to escape a perceived danger or respond to acute uncertainty. By definition a panic is an irrational response in that cooperation breaks down completely and this usually results in greater danger, not greater safety. When someone yells "Fire!" in a crowded theater, a panic reaction would be for everyone to try to run to the exits at once. The result would most likely be injury or death for most of the people and escape for a relative few.

Panics can also occur at the level of masses. When people hear that a bank is about to fail, for example, they may panic and rush to withdraw their money,

In 1989, during May Day demonstrations in Europe, violent riots broke out, including turning this car over and setting it afire.

an action that ensures the bank's failure. In 1984 false rumors that the Continental Illinois Bank was about to fail began to spread, and large-scale depositors withdrew billions of dollars in a matter of weeks. The bank—the eighth largest in the U.S.—was not in good financial shape when the rumors began to circulate, but it was not in immediate danger of failing. By mid-summer, however, more than $20 billion had been withdrawn and neither the government nor the bank management was able to restore public confidence. Finally, the Federal Depositor's Insurance Corporation stepped in and made an arrangement to ensure the bank's survival. Panic withdrawals were prevented in Ohio in 1985 because the governor ordered the temporary closing of the state's savings and loan institutions after one of the largest failed.

A similar phenomenon occurred in the Soviet Union in 1990 when the government announced economic reforms that would result in sharp increases in bread prices. What followed was a panic of buying not only bread, but other basic foods such as butter and flour, and within days store shelves were nearly empty. People came from such distances in their attempts to stock up in Moscow stores that the government tried to slow the panic by requiring shoppers to show identification papers proving they were Moscow residents.

Hysteria

Panic in crowds and masses is often preceded by mass **hysteria**, a state of rapidly spreading anxiety based on a danger or opportunity that is usually misperceived. In 1982, for example, people in the U.S. became aware of a new disease that appeared to be confined to a small subgroup of the population—most notably male homosexuals (Fettner and Check 1984; Shilts 1987). Anxiety over what came to be known as AIDS spread quickly. Although discrimination against homosexuals was certainly nothing new, it now took on an added dimension of open fear of any physical contact with homosexuals, a fear based on the mistaken belief that the disease could be transmitted merely by being near or touching a person with AIDS. Suddenly, homosexuals were losing jobs and being denied housing that was formerly open to them. Many health workers and ambulance personnel refused to handle possible AIDS patients; and some police officers wore rubber gloves and protective masks while arresting homosexuals.

In the hysteria that has accompanied the AIDS epidemic, police and other public workers have responded with extreme measures to protect themselves from what they erroneously believed to be a highly contagious disease.

As telephone hot lines were flooded with thousands of anxious calls from around the country, it became clear that mass hysteria had set in and that a medical emergency was compounded by widespread fear based on false beliefs. For homosexuals, the result was a double victimization—once by the disease and again by the mass hysteria that followed.

Mobs, riots, panics, and mass hysteria are forms of collective behavior that have attracted much attention from sociologists, and for more than a century they have tried to explain why and how they occur.

SOME THEORIES OF BEHAVIOR IN CROWDS

Perspectives on crowd behavior can be divided into two types. The earliest theories—and some later ones—saw behavior in crowds in largely psychological terms. Crowds were viewed as having person-alities and tendencies that explained the behavior of people in them. In fact, the earliest theories treated crowds as if they were some kind of distinct organisms with minds and lives of their own. Later theories placed more importance on the social conditions that cause collective behavior and the processes through which it occurs. In short, over the last century thinking about collective behavior has become less psychological and more sociological.

Like sociology itself, theories of crowd behavior first emerged in the nineteenth century, a period full of rapid social change that often involved violence and revolution. While this led thinkers to pay a lot of attention to the characteristics of social systems, it provided particular reasons to focus on crowds and masses, for in many cases—the most notable being the French Revolution—they played a direct and important role in bringing about dramatic change.

Those opposed to change tended to see crowds and masses as menacing forces that threatened the fabric of civilized society, whereas those in favor of change often saw them as evidence of an aroused lower class whose awareness of social conditions was, to paraphrase Marx, the engine of progress. Clearly, many early theorists were particularly affected by the times they lived in; they used unscientific data and often had a personal ax to grind. Nowhere was this more apparent than in the nevertheless pioneering work of Gustave Le Bon.

Le Bon and "Mob Psychology"

Writing at the end of the nineteenth century, Le Bon made one of the earliest serious attempts to analyze collective behavior with a psychology of crowds—**mob psychology**. Like all thinkers, his ideas reflected the social conditions and the dominant ideas of his time. France had endured a violent revolution a century before and the pace of change had, if anything, quickened since. The working class struggled for better working conditions and a greater share of political power, and the emerging capitalist middle class threatened the dominance of the upper class. The old feudal order was gone, but capitalism was too new to provide a sense of order and continuity in social life.

In short, change was rapid and often accompanied by violence, and Le Bon ([1895] 1960) feared that his society was going out of control. Without the social bonds and obligations of feudalism, he feared that society would be ruled by mobs of igno-

Part of Le Bon's concern with the power of mobs was rooted in the French Revolution, when the monarchy was overthrown in what eventually became a prolonged orgy of almost uncontrollable violence. In his famous painting, *Liberty Leading the People*, Eugène Delacroix evokes both the power of collective behavior to bring about change and its frightening potential.

rant and irresponsible lower-class people. As he put it,

> Today the claims of the masses are becoming more and more sharply defined, and amount to nothing less than a determination to utterly destroy society as it now exists, with a view to making it hark back to . . . before the dawn of civilization. (p. 16)

Le Bon believed that collective violence occurs because people who are prone to violence are drawn together by an event, what Turner (1964) called Le Bon's **convergence theory**. Crowds consist of like-minded people who assemble in one place. Collective violence depends on individuals who are already prone to violent behavior. Perhaps most important in Le Bon's theory is his reliance on leaders who con-

trol crowds through a kind of hypnotism. "A crowd," he wrote, "is a servile flock that is incapable of ever doing without a master" (p. 118). Le Bon believed that leaders exert power by flattery, strong rhetoric, presentation of only one side of an issue, repetition, and clever use of symbols. In short, they succeed by appealing to people's nonrational, emotional, and unconscious motivations. People can be controlled through such techniques, he believed, because in crowds they are "leveled"—which is to say, everyone comes to think, feel, and behave in the same way. Le Bon believed that in a crowd people no longer exist as individuals: only the crowd exists.

According to Le Bon, once a crowd forms, several things happen. Individuals lose their ability to think rationally, lose touch with abstract ideas (especially those about right and wrong), and become very suggestible and willing to do what they are told. They become shortsighted and misperceive what is going on around them. To Le Bon, then, people in crowds are suggestible, blind, and fickle.

As a process, crowd behavior in Le Bon's view is quite simple and depends on what he called **contagion**: people copy one another's behavior, and this sets off a chain reaction. Le Bon deserves credit for making an early connection between social conditions and collective behavior and for drawing attention to the importance of unconscious psychological motivations (such as those that play a role in lynch mobs). Most important, he focused serious attention on crowds as a subject of study. His ideas, however, have little credibility among sociologists, for there is no compelling evidence that contagion either describes or explains what goes on in crowds, or that social influence in crowds differs substantially from social influence in general. Nor is there any evidence that hypnotism operates in crowds.

Le Bon's most serious shortcomings are his view of the nature of crowds and his reliance on the power of leaders as an explanation of collective behavior. As we will see shortly, many studies find that people in crowds are far more rational than Le Bon thought they were; and there is a division of labor in most crowds that is ignored by his view of crowds as a group in which all members are alike. During anti-Vietnam War demonstrations in the 1960s, for example, some demonstrators specialized in acting as "medics" who took care of the injured, while others looked out for police movements and possible avenues of escape.

People do not all think, feel, and act alike in crowds (see McPhail and Wohlstein 1983). Watch a crowd at a sporting event, for example, and you will see a lot of variation in what people do and appear to feel. Some watch the game enthusiastically; some talk with friends and seem to ignore the game; some play games that compete with what is happening on the field. Le Bon barely scratched the surface of the complexity of collective behavior in even the most common social situations.

Blumer and Stampeding Cattle   In the 1930s the U.S. sociologist Herbert Blumer ([1939] 1951) used many of the same assumptions that underlay Le Bon's work. Unlike Le Bon, however, Blumer focused on interaction among crowd members rather than between leaders and followers, and this was an important shift in emphasis.

Like Le Bon, Blumer assumed that crowds are homogeneous and that individuals in crowds are irrational. Blumer also relied on a concept he called **circular reaction**, which was like the concept of contagion in viewing crowd behavior as a chain reaction, but differed in an important way: people in crowds do not simply set each other off; rather, when one person affects a second, the act of witnessing the result acts back on the first person and *amplifies* the affect. So, my excitement stimulates you, and when I see your excitement I become still more excited, and so on. In this way, Blumer believed, feelings and tendencies in crowds spread and increase rapidly. To describe this, Blumer used the image of a herd of cattle in which cows progressively become more and more excited until they stampede.

Blumer believed that crowds form around some precipitating incident. Then people mill around, talking with one another, being stimulated by and amplifying one another's moods. Someone does something, and instead of interpreting the behavior as they would normally do, people react without thinking. As collective excitement builds, it focuses on a common object, and in the final stage of excitement, people act impulsively and irrationally toward it.

Blumer's ideas have many problems in common with those of Le Bon—most notably his reliance on the idea of circular reaction and his assumptions about the homogeneity and irrationality of people in crowds. Also like Le Bon's theory, Blumer's theory of circular reaction describes more than it explains and cannot explain why not everyone in a crowd is aroused or why the mood in a crowd can change quickly.

Le Bon's and Blumer's theories have a deeper problem, however, for both view crowds as irrational, uncivilized collections of people. This means that neither fully appreciates the fact that many crowds contain people who can protest social conditions in no other way. Unlike theorists discussed later in this chapter, Le Bon and Blumer de-emphasize the importance of collective behavior as both a reflection of social problems and an important vehicle for positive social change.

Collective Behavior as Social Interaction

From a social interaction perspective, the challenge of explaining collective behavior is similar to understanding any form of social behavior. How are collective situations defined? How do people make choices within them? What do the patterns of interaction in crowds look like?

Emergent Norms   One of the paradoxes of collective behavior is that people in crowds behave in a variety of ways, but at the same time often feel a sense of shared purpose with people they have never met. Often there is no prior planning in crowd behavior, and yet clearly discernible patterns of interaction emerge, and people feel constrained by a set of informal norms. How does this happen? Where do these norms come from?

Turner and Killian (1987) offer **emergent norm theory** to explain how patterns of interaction and expectation evolve in crowds. In most situations, we rely on the definition of the situation in order to know what is expected. When shopping in a store, for example, we are bound by certain legal norms (paying for what we take) and informal folkways (waiting our turn). In a crowd, however, the definition of the situation may be unclear. Suppose that we have been waiting for eight hours outside a ticket office in order to buy tickets to an upcoming concert. People are cold, a little irritable, and anxious that there will not be enough tickets to go around. What norms apply here as the opening time nears? How do you know "what goes" and what does not?

Chances are that you would look around at what other people are doing. Are they staying in line? Are people slowly inching their way toward the door so that they will be in a better position when the office opens? In usual circumstances the norms about waiting in line would be clear; but the tension in this situation creates unusual circumstances in which no one is sure if other people will abide by the usual norms. There is, in short, a sense of anomie—or normlessness—in this situation, and people look at what others are doing in order to establish the norms. This is just the opposite of what usually happens: rather than having the patterns of interaction emerge out of an established set of norms, the norms emerge out of a pattern of interaction.

According to emergent norm theory, in crowds people look for signs of what norms will apply in that situation. This is due, in part, to earlier experiences in groups in which behavior is rewarded or punished depending on whether or not it conforms to group norms. Since we are actively looking for norms to emerge, we are unusually susceptible to suggestion

and are likely to accept emerging norms with little criticism. We tend, in short, to approach all collective situations with a certain amount of anxiety and, therefore, a desire to define the situation quickly so that we know what is going on. This, in turn, means that we tend to accept definitions of crowd situations without exercising very much independent critical judgment. The desire of crowd members to identify quickly a set of norms to guide behavior means that some visible members can have considerable power to define the situation through the example set by their behavior. In a tense, yet ambiguous crowd situation, the difference between violence and peaceful protest may hinge on whether someone yells "Get them!" or "Stay calm!"

Emergent norm theory is useful because it focuses on the ways in which social interaction in crowds establishes norms. Crowds generally contain a collection of people who have diverse motives, feelings, and beliefs about what is going on, and yet somehow through social interaction a common purpose and set of shared expectations often emerge.

Emergent norm theory also contains traces of a problem found with its predecessors: a tendency to view behavior in crowds as less rational than that in other situations. More recent theories have directly challenged that longstanding view, arguing that social interaction is no less rational or intelligent in a crowd than in any other situation.

Decision Theory   As a view of human nature and behavior, **decision theory** is about as far as one could get from Le Bon's view of uncivilized mobs. Decision theory has been applied to many aspects of behavior, and essentially rests on the idea that people usually act rationally in order to solve problems. Problem solving—whether by an individual on a desert island or members of a crowd at a football game—is a process that may be thought of as consisting of a series of steps (Luce and Raiffa 1957; Raiffa 1970). We gather and interpret information about what is happening and about what might happen; list our options and rank them according to the desirability of their probable consequences; and make choices in order to gain the best possible outcome.

Suppose, for example, that you are eating lunch in a college dining room and suddenly some people start throwing food at each other. It is the last day of the term and there is a lot of laughing as food flies through the air. What do you do? According to decision theory, the behavior of most people will depend on some weighing of the alternatives and their probable consequences: "What happens if I join in? What happens if I just sit here? If I try to stop it? If I leave?"

If you join in, you might have some fun or release some tension; you might also get covered with food, be punished by college authorities, and offend other students. If you just sit there, you run the risk of having some students think you do not like to have a good time—and you will probably end up with food on you anyway. If you try to stop it, even those students who do not participate might think you are being a "wet blanket"; and if you leave, you leave your lunch behind along with everything else.

Somewhere among those options you will decide which consequences are the most important to you, and this will be the basis of your decision. Notice that in this and many other crowd situations, people are not all behaving in the same way, even though you might later describe the incident as a "food riot." There is at least circumstantial evidence that people are making decisions about their behavior, rather than blindly copying the behavior of others.

Notice also that your decision depends on how other people react, both to your behavior and the behavior of others. This kind of situation—in which consequences for an individual depend on what other people do—has been called a *game* by some theorists.

Game Theory   According to **game theory**, people try to achieve what is called a "minimax" solution, one that minimizes costs and maximizes rewards (Luce and Raiffa 1957; Zagare 1984). In order to find such a solution in a crowd, each person has to consider what other people are likely to do, a process that is central to the game theory approach to collective behavior (Berk 1974a, 1974b).

In game theory, the decision facing people in crowds boils down to two problems: Will others support what I do, and what difference will it make? Of the two, predicting whether or not other people in the crowd will support what we do is the most difficult, and the ability to predict depends on a number of structural and ecological characteristics of crowds as social systems (Berk 1974b). The more people there are who appear to act in a particular way and the more visible their behavior is, the more likely we are to perceive support for ourselves if we join in.

From a game perspective, collective behavior is a case of collective problem solving in which individuals compromise and cooperate with one another in order to maximize their rewards through mutual support. "Each crowd member tries to make the most of the situation while constrained by the need for support from others" (Berk 1974b, p. 73). This approach is most useful in explaining why people participate in crowds that require cooperation. It is also useful, however, for understanding crowds that involve competition among members (Berk 1974b).

Suppose, for example, that you hear on the radio that a nearby nuclear power plant is about to melt down and cause a nuclear disaster. A rational response would be for everyone to leave the city in a rapid but orderly manner, for if everyone makes a mad dash for the highways and public transportation systems, the confusion and inevitable accidents might make it virtually impossible for all but a few to escape. Suppose, however, that you notice a few people driving wildly toward the highway entrance ramp, screaming out their car windows for everyone else to get out of the way and waving pistols in the air just to make sure everyone gets the point. You might conclude that those few people have panicked unnecessarily and that the best thing for everyone to do is to proceed in a quick and orderly manner and ignore the panicked few.

It is also possible, however, that the mad dashers know something that you do not—that, perhaps, the reactor has already melted down and fatal radiation is only minutes behind you. In that case, it may be impossible for everyone to get out alive, and only those who force their way through will escape unharmed. This is a very different kind of game from a peace demonstration in which people cooperate with one another in pursuit of common goals, for in this game the rational choice is to maximize the chance of survival by struggling against everyone else.

The line between cooperation and competition, then, is a thin one, and which side of it you wind up on depends on your perceptions of what is going on; and, as we have seen before, our perceptions of the world are strongly affected by the social environment. The environment provides us with *information*, a key ingredient in collective behavior; and *rumor* is an important social mechanism through which information is communicated.

Rumor   A **rumor** is an unverified belief that arises from social interaction. Most rumors arise in situations in which people need to have information that is otherwise unavailable (Rosnow and Fine 1976): when daily routines are disrupted (the buses are all running late); when the environment changes dras-

Rumor often plays a part in panic situations in which vital information is missing. This has been the case in stock market crashes such as the one that occurred first in the U.S. and then in major world markets in 1987. Like everyone else, these traders on the London exchange are trying to find out what is happening in time to protect themselves from financial loss. Often the rumors themselves spur further panic and still greater losses than would otherwise have occurred.

tically (there is an earthquake); when we must make choices but are uncertain of the outcomes (which courses to sign up for); when there is sustained tension (families of prisoners of war must wait for news); or when there is prolonged boredom without knowing the cause (people wait in a theater line that stretches halfway around the block and does not move).

That rumor spreads informally does not mean that it is a random process in which everyone is equally likely to be included. Instead, most rumors are nurtured by established social networks of people who share statuses that make the content of the rumor relevant to them (Milgram 1977). In Lillian Hellman's powerful play, *The Children's Hour*, for example, a girl in a boarding school mentions to her grandmother that she saw the two women who run the school hugging each other in their room. This simple observation soon becomes embellished into a supposed lesbian relationship, and the rumor spreads quickly among the parents of girls who attend the school—but not in the community as a whole. In similar ways, rumors about the 1987 stock market crash spread more quickly among executives than among small stockholders.

As a social process, rumor has been viewed as an example of human failing and as a normal part of social life. In early studies of rumor, Bartlett (1932) and later Allport and Postman (1947) treated rumors as accounts passed in series from one person to another, and they used experiments to explore how this occurs. They asked one person to repeat a simple statement to the next person in a chain and recorded each transmission until the last person was reached. In these and many subsequent experiments the findings were the same: as the account is transmitted down the line, it tends to become shorter, more concise, and easier to understand (an effect called *leveling*); limited to a relatively few details (*sharpening*);

and more coherent and consistent with the interests and beliefs of the participants (*assimilation*). The general conclusion from these experiments was that distortion is inevitable in rumor because of faulty perception and memory, and the inability to repeat a message verbatim.

In spite of the fact that many replications of the Allport and Postman experiments generated similar results, many researchers have challenged the results because they were obtained in an artificial laboratory setting. Caplow (1947) argued that in many situations—such as combat—the accuracy of information is so important that people are critical about what they accept and what they subsequently pass on to others. The fact that rumor usually travels through established social networks means that unreliable people tend to be discounted and eliminated from the network. The result, he believed, is that rumors may become more—not less—accurate as they go along.

Others, such as Festinger (1948) and Peterson and Gist (1951), have also pointed out that in many situations rumors become longer and more elaborate—not shorter and simpler—as they are spread through a network. This may be due in part to the fact that since rumors are beliefs they must be plausible for us to believe in them; and this encourages the development of details related to the main piece of information.

Several researchers have argued that rumor is part of a collective effort to define social situations (Shibutani 1966, 1968; Turner 1964). While something important is unexplained, there is "a distracting sense of incompleteness" and a desire "to understand the new circumstances by completing the incomplete" (Shibutani 1968, p. 579). The more important it is to us to understand a situation and the more ambiguous the available information is, the more likely it is that rumors will develop as a way for increasing understanding and defining the situation with greater clarity (Jaeger, Anthony, and Rosnow 1979). As rumors develop, they tend to become more plausible and complete. Details that do not fit are eliminated, whereas those that are consistent with the rumor are added, thereby making it more convincing.

According to Shibutani, the ways in which rumor develops depend on the social situation. When the situation is relatively unimportant to the participants, information is handled through established social networks. In situations of high excitement, however, such as during natural disasters, established networks tend to break down and new lines of communication spring up spontaneously. Under such conditions, it is harder to verify new information before it is spread further.

When people are bored, rumor can serve quite different functions: it can be a source of entertainment or a vehicle for expressing attitudes. Students may spread bad rumors about a disliked teacher because it lets them express negative feelings; and by passing it through the student network, they strengthen the bonds among them. The ultimate truth or falsity of the rumor is, in this case, irrelevant to its social functions.

Like all social phenomena, the process of spreading rumors has a structure that can involve a variety of different roles (Shibutani 1966, 1968). Transmitters simply pass on messages ("I heard that today's final exam is going to include the whole book."), while interpreters place them in context, evaluate their truth or falsity, and speculate about details that are left out ("That doesn't make any sense; I was in class when the announcement was made. Then again, worse things have happened in that course."). Skeptics play the important role of challenging new information ("That can't be true."), and agitators urge action based on the rumor ("That's totally outrageous; let's go see the dean.").

This model of the rumor process clearly reflects more recent views of collective behavior, in that it looks upon it as a rational process through which people try to achieve goals, define situations, and take action they perceive to be in their best interests. From this perspective, collective behavior is a normal consequence of the social and ecological conditions in which we live.

Smelser and Structural Strain

Smelser (1962) developed a **structural strain theory** to focus on social conditions that contribute to psychological states in people that in turn motivate them to participate in collective behavior. Smelser's theory includes a wide range of social factors from the characteristics of societies to the dynamics of crowds.

To illustrate and explain Smelser's theory, consider the recent wave of prodemocracy protests in China. Demonstrations were nothing new in China, but they took on a particular sense of urgency in the spring of 1989. Two years earlier, communist Party General Secretary Hu Yaobang showed a great deal of tolerance for student protests, for which he was driven from office. At his death thousands of students gathered to mourn him. Their demonstration was met with a violent response from police, which prompted students to begin a hunger strike to demand basic civil rights such as freedom of the press, speech, assembly, and association, as well as an end to widespread corruption in the vast government bureaucracy.

Seven weeks of protest followed, involving as many as a million people at once. Almost 30,000 people camped out in Tiananmen Square in the heart of China's capitol of Beijing, enduring harsh conditions and the fear of official violence against them rather than give up their demands. Finally, on June 5, army units sealed off the square in the middle of the night and opened fire on the unarmed demonstrators. Estimates of the number of casualties ran as high as 2,600. The student rebellion had been crushed.

Smelser's theory of collective behavior can be broken down into several parts. First, Smelser argues that the ultimate cause of collective behavior is some form of strain or contradiction in a social system that leads to widespread feelings of uncertainty, anxiety, or discontent. People participate in collective behavior as a way of dealing with such feelings. As we have seen in earlier chapters, contradiction, tension, and conflict exist to some extent in all social systems, especially if they are complex. In a general

Demonstrators in Tienanmen Square, Beijing, evacuate a student who has been injured in the government's crackdown on the pro-democracy movement.

sense, Smelser's concept of strain refers to differences between social conditions as they are and conditions as people want or expect them to be. Strain abounds in Chinese society, especially around the issues of political freedom and government corruption. The cultural ideal of Chinese society is that it is a free and democratic people's republic governed for the benefit of all. In reality, however, China is a tightly controlled communist state whose government bureaucracy is widely known for its levels of corruption.

Second, Smelser argues that people respond to such situations by trying to make sense of things as a way of relieving the strain. This results in shared beliefs that people seize upon in order to justify their actions and reduce feelings of uncertainty. Smelser contended that beliefs are often irrational because they exist not to provide a rational framework for bringing about social change, but to provide a common motivation and justification for people to take part in collective behavior in order to reduce strain.

These beliefs differ . . . from those that guide many other types of behavior. They involve a belief in the existence of extraordinary forces—threats, conspiracies, etc.—which are at work in the universe. They also involve an assessment of the extraordinary consequences which will follow if the collective attempt to reconstitute social action is successful. The beliefs on which collective behavior is based . . . are thus akin to magical beliefs (p. 8).

Perhaps the most important belief among the protestors was that they actually had a chance to force the authoritarian Chinese government to change its policies and not use the military to crush their rebellion. Related to this were other beliefs—that soldiers would not shoot their fellow citizens, for example, that the Chinese leadership was in a state of disarray and therefore unable to act decisively, and that the students would be joined by millions of citizens whose numbers would make it difficult for the government to do anything other than agree to the demonstrators' demands.

Third, Smelser argues that when there is a sufficient level of strain and shared belief among those who might act, there must then be some kind of incident that, as interpreted by those beliefs, triggers a collective response. In this case, the incident was the demonstration mourning Hu Yaobang's death and the government's response to it.

The fourth step is mobilization, in which people gather into a crowd capable of producing collective behavior. Mobilization depends on a number of social factors. Communication must be effective enough for people to know about what is happening, to share in emerging beliefs, and to be aware of opportunities for collective action. People must be available to participate and able to get together (McPhail and Miller 1973). This last factor helps explain why young people—students in particular— are so well represented at protest demonstrations. Since they are less likely to have job or family responsibilities, they are more available.

Finally, once mobilization occurs, the forces of social control are all that stand in the way of collective behavior. In China, the government delayed the use of violence for some time. In fact, during the first encounters between troops and students, the students were quite successful in persuading soldiers that it would be wrong to move against them. It was only when the government brought in seasoned combat troops from other provinces that the protest movement was finally crushed. In contrast, during similar prodemocracy demonstrations in Eastern Europe later in that same year, governments did not use military force and ultimately these movements helped bring about revolutionary change.

As you can see, the social potential and significance of collective behavior is greatest in relation to social change, especially when collective behavior is part of organized social movements. For more on this as well as an extended discussion of social change in general we turn now to the closing chapter.

SUMMARY

1. Collective behavior refers to how we think, feel, and behave as members of crowds and masses. In crowds, collective behavior includes casual, conventional, expressive, and collective action. In addition to these kinds of collective behavior, fads and fashion also occur in masses.

2. Some of the most volatile forms of collective behavior are mobs, riots, panics, and hysteria.

3. Le Bon's theory of mob psychology was one of the earliest attempts to understand collective behavior. His theory emphasizes the importance of leaders, the like-mindedness and irrationality of crowd members, and people copying one another's behavior. Blumer also viewed crowds as irrational, uncivilized collections of people.

4. From a social interaction perspective, collective behavior involves interpretations of behavior and defining the situation. Emergent norm theory argues that people observe one another's behavior in crowds in order to establish the norms that will apply in that situation. Decision theory and game theory emphasize the rational calculations that we make in deciding how to behave in crowd and mass situations.

5. Rumor is an important ingredient in collective behavior because it is a major source of information. As in all social situations, people perform different roles in the rumor process, and the patterns through which rumor develops and spreads depend on the situation.

6. Smelser's structural strain theory argues that collective behavior is based on psychological needs that arise from social conditions. Strain in social conditions, he argues, leads to uncertainty and tension among people who then seize upon beliefs to explain their condition in much the same way that people appeal to magic. Such beliefs are then used to justify collective action around a precipitating incident. The outcome of collective behavior depends both on mobilizing participants and on the ability of authorities to exercise social control.

KEY TERMS

acting behavior   557
casual behavior   557
circular reaction   562
collective behavior   556
contagion   562
conventional behavior   557
convergence theory   561
crowd   556

decision theory   563
emergent norm theory   563
expressive behavior   557
fad   558
fashion   557
game theory   564
hysteria   559

mass   556
mob   557
mob psychology   560
panic   559
riot   558
rumor   564
structural strain theory   566

LOOKING ELSEWHERE

Having read Chapter 22, you might want to look at related discussions in *Human Arrangements*, which include

■ the role of riots in advancing the civil rights movement (Chapter 13, pp. 321–22)

■ why people in crowds often do not help those in distress (Chapter 8, pp. 161–62)

■ pressures to conform (Chapter 9, pp. 186–87)

RECOMMENDED READINGS

Rosnow, R. L., and Fine, G. A. 1976. *Rumor and gossip.* New York: Elsevier. An interesting study of the forms and functions of rumor in social life.

Shibutani, T. 1966. *Improvised news: A sociological study of rumor.* Indianapolis: Bobbs-Merrill. Shibutani's fascinating account of case studies illustrating and seeking a deeper understanding of rumor as a social process.

Turner, R., and Killian, L. M. 1987. *Collective behavior* (3rd ed.). Englewood Cliffs, NJ: Prentice-Hall. An up-to-date text on the many forms of collective behavior.

Useem, B., and Kimball, P. 1989. *States of siege: U.S. prison riots, 1971–1986.* New York: Oxford. An insightful analysis of the institutional breakdowns that make prison riots more likely to occur.

Wright, S. 1978. *Crowds and riots: A study in social organization.* Beverly Hills, CA: Sage. A three-year study of crowds and riots, their causes and consequences.

23

Social Change and Social Movements

 Questions about social change are relatively easy to ask, but are among the most difficult of those that sociologists try to answer. Why did the women's movement emerge with such strength in the 1960s and what has happened to it since? Where did capitalism and socialism come from? Will the widespread use of computers make it easier for government to invade the privacy of individuals? How will AIDS affect sexual relationships? What will happen to relations between the wealthy and poor countries of the world?

Much of the relevant information about social change is historical, and it is, therefore, especially difficult to scientifically measure the factors that might account for the change. Added to this is the difficulty with most research problems that sociologists deal with: social change involves simultaneously many factors that affect one another in complex ways. New social ideas and relationships do not come about through events that can be precisely located in time or simply explained. We cannot say that the modern women's movement began on January 4, 1963, in New York City. History is not a simple sequence of events, each of which is neatly caused by previous events. It is, rather, like a river into which flow many streams that mingle and affect both one another and the river itself in countless different ways.

This concluding chapter looks at the sources of social change and theories that have been developed to explain the patterns, speed, and causes of change in societies. It includes an analysis of basic questions about social movements—why they emerge when they do, why some fail and others succeed, and the effects they have on social systems.

CULTURE, STRUCTURE, AND SOCIAL CHANGE

As we have seen in many previous chapters, the functional and conflict perspectives provide two major sociological frameworks for explaining what goes on in social systems. These perspectives have also been applied to the problem of social change. Before discussing and evaluating their usefulness, we turn first to a look at some of the ways in which culture and social structure contribute to change.

Cultural Sources of Change

As we saw in Chapter 19, Weber's classic book *The Protestant Ethic and the Spirit of Capitalism* ([1904] 1958) analyzed the impact of beliefs and values on the structure of economic systems. According to the Calvinist religion, the assignment of people to heaven or hell is determined at birth, and nothing a person can do will alter that fate. Calvinism also placed a high value on frugal living and hard work, and only through success in a calling could people lower their anxiety over what their fate would be. Prior to Calvin, the idea of a calling in Christianity applied only to religious occupations. Calvin, however, defined all occupations as callings and this injected into everyday work a new religious motivation. Weber argued that Calvinist beliefs and values helped foster the emergence of capitalism, for as an economic system capitalism depends on the accumulation of wealth, which is then available for investment.

There are countless examples of the effect of ideas on social systems. Albert Einstein's theories about the laws that govern the universe, for example, were basic to the discovery of atomic fission and the invention of nuclear weapons that have changed the nature of warfare and the structure of political power in the world. The writings of Karl Marx and Friedrich Engels became the cultural basis for revolutions that have radically affected a wide range of societies from the Soviet Union to China to Cuba and Nicaragua. In similar ways the U.S. Declaration of Independence and Constitution embody ideas that have been used as inspirations and blueprints in the transformation of many societies.

As the last two examples show, the effect of culture on social change is particularly evident when ideas take the form of ideology, for an ideology serves the function of explaining or justifying particular social arrangements. In his role as leader in the civil rights movement, for example, Martin Luther King, Jr., increased his support among whites by appealing to strongly held values placed on equality, fairness, and justice. He was able to enlist the support of whites who otherwise did not share the high value he placed on racial equality in its own right.

Culture also causes change in more direct ways, especially through norms that explicitly require it. The 1954 Supreme Court decision that outlawed racially segregated schools and the 1983 decision that banned the use of gender by insurance companies in setting rates for life insurance and annuities changed the social system, as did federal regulations requiring affirmative action in hiring and federal legislation requiring equal treatment of male and female students in schools that receive federal aid.

Structural Sources of Change: Social Interaction

Just as new ideas often bring about change in social structure, so too does structural change affect culture. One way to break down stereotypes is to increase interaction between those who hold stereotypes and those who are the object of them (see Miller and Brewer 1984). This is particularly true when the people involved must cooperate with one another in order to achieve shared goals (Allport 1954).

Laws that forbid racial segregation, for example, are aspects of culture that affect the structure of social systems. Increasing the frequency of interaction between people of different races is a structural change that can, in turn, have the effect of weakening cultural stereotypes. It has long been noted that it is almost impossible to change people's beliefs about and perceptions of others by requiring them to do so; but this example shows how changes in the structure of social systems—how often people of different races interact with one another—can affect how they perceive and think about one another.

Such effects of structure on culture are common in social life. Over the last several decades people in the U.S. have become increasingly tolerant and supportive of women working outside the home and having careers. Some of this cultural shift is probably due to the entry of massive numbers of women into the labor force as the economy shifted from industry to services and the demand for secretaries and other service workers mushroomed. As women had fewer children and growing opportunities outside the home,

Even the strongest stereotypes and prejudices may not survive situations whose structure requires people to depend on one another. In this picture, a black marine in Vietnam refuses to leave his wounded white friend.

they had new reason to question the terms on which they were living their lives and to seek alternatives. It was only a matter of time before cultural ideas about men and women began to adjust to this structural change.

It is important to keep in mind that behind the relatively small scale structural changes that we identify around us often lie major macrostructural changes that take place over many generations. As Tilly (1985) argues, in order to understand social change it is necessary to include what he calls "big structures" and "large processes" such as the development of capitalism or the emergence of powerful nation states. The macrostructures that make up economic, political, and religious systems form the basic limitations of social life from which many aspects of everyday life take shape. Changes in the roles of men and women, the organization of family life, or the importance of religion in people's lives can only be understood in the context of major institutional arrangements which, barring revolutions, change only over long periods of time.

Ecological Sources of Change

Because they represent interdependencies among living things in relation to physical environments, ecosystems constantly change through a process called **ecological succession** (see Hawley 1986). As one species thrives by consuming others, its food source declines as its population grows, and resulting starvation sends its population on a downward slide. Or, a change in the physical environment may benefit some forms of life at the expense of others: water pollution kills fish but supports bacteria and algae. Humans benefit from covering land with buildings, but most other forms of life do not (except, perhaps, rats and cockroaches).

Human populations initiate succession by changing patterns of consumption (what and how much we consume); by altering the physical environment; and by changing population size or distribution. These sources of change depend heavily, in turn, on technology. Much of the early work of sociologists such as Robert Park and Ernest Burgess focused on how urban areas develop as physical environments (Park, Burgess, and McKenzie 1925). Over the last century, for example, New York City's Harlem changed from an area of pastures to an upper-class neighborhood, then a lower-middle-class neighborhood, and finally, today, a largely black ghetto (Osofsky 1966). Succession is still commonplace in urban environments. Urban renewal, for example, typically transforms run-down neighborhoods by restoring buildings. This, however, displaces residents who can no longer afford to live there, and what was, perhaps, a working-class neighborhood becomes a middle-class neighborhood.

Population and Social Change

Perhaps the most important source of ecological succession is the size and distribution of population, for these directly affect how much people consume and how they use land. A growing population creates pressure that may lead to technological innovation—such as the invention of the plow—and this, in turn, both supports larger populations and alters their relationship with physical environments by making it

Overurbanization is often aggravated by natural disasters that make it difficult to survive in rural areas. In 1988, for example, massive floods in Bangladesh created thousands of refugees who crowded onto trains to flee to already crowded cities.

possible to overcultivate the land, exhaust the fertility of the soil, and promote soil erosion (Harris 1974).

The rapid growth of the world's population during the last two centuries has resulted primarily from increased production supported by new technology and increasingly complex divisions of labor, and from the dramatic lowering of death rates, particularly among infants and children. In many societies, however, control over many causes of death has made populations grow faster than the production of goods needed to support them.

The technology for controlling disease was first discovered in rapidly developing industrial societies in North America and Europe at a time when birth rates were falling. As death rates declined, so did birth rates; and, while populations grew because death rates fell faster than birth rates, expanding industry allowed them to support more people. Once these medical technologies were discovered, however, they were easily and cheaply applied in societies whose birth rates remained high and whose economies could barely support rapidly growing populations. This ecological change has reached crisis proportions in much of the world in which population now grows much faster than production. While world population grew slowly prior to 1800—perhaps no more than 0.1 percent per year—it now grows by more than 1.7 percent. While it once took nearly 700 years for the world population to double, at current rates it will double in only 39 years (PRB 1990; Thompson and Lewis 1965).

The resulting imbalance between population and production contributes to extreme poverty in rural areas that make up most of developing countries, whose people migrate in droves to already crowded cities, seeking opportunities that simply do not exist. Such overurbanization plagues many developing countries, such as India, Egypt, and Mexico. In New Delhi, India, thousands of urban squatters sleep in vacant lots, school playgrounds, and city streets. As we saw in Chapter 4, Mexico City is rapidly becoming the largest city in the world—inhabited primarily by unemployed peasants—and demands for water will soon outrun the supply. It is ironic that what threatens to become a major ecological and social disaster was precipitated by an undeniably positive innovation—the elimination of many diseases as causes of death.

Population processes also prompt social change by altering the age structure. As we saw in Chapter 15, for example, the job opportunities available in a society may not match the age structure, creating an imbalance that is difficult both for individuals and societies as a whole. As the U.S. population ages, the number of teenagers declines and the number of elderly increases. One result is that there are more opportunities for young people than there are young people to fill them; and there are more elderly people who would like to continue working than there are jobs for them. This is a case of structural lag in which the occupational structure has not yet caught up to changes in the age structure (Riley et al. 1988).

When we realize that humans affect ecosystems in countless ways by initiating thousands of ecological changes, we can see how difficult it is to understand where the process of ecological succession will lead. The danger of this is that ecosystems may change in ways that no longer support human life. In ecosystems, one form of life is no more valuable than another: to us, a polluted lake may be awful, but to bacteria and algae, it is an ideal environment. Although most cultures may value humanity as the most important form of life, in ecosystems, we enjoy no such privileged standing.

Cohorts   The birth cohort is an important concept in the study of social change, for as each new generation is socialized, its members continue existing traditions and modify them through their own fresh experience (Ryder 1965; Riley 1987). Each generation has a comparatively low level of commitment to a past it has not experienced, and

The shift in the portrayal of "Uncle Sam" between World War II enlistment posters and a 1972 anti-Vietnam War protest illustrated the changes that can occur between cohorts who grow up under different social conditions. How do you feel about each of these? What does that say about your cohort?

so it brings with it an openness to new ideas and so-cial relationships (Mannheim 1952). The inevitable movement of new cohorts through the stages of the life course under historical circumstances that differ for each generation makes social change inevitable.

Since 1972, for example, there has been a steady decline in reports of racial prejudice in national surveys in the United States. Some of this shift was due to changes spread across the entire population, but much of the change occurred because less prejudiced younger generations were replacing more prejudiced older generations. In other words, a shift in racial attitudes seems to have occurred in part because of a shift in the characteristics of different cohorts (Firebaugh and Davis 1988).

Each generation is both a source of new ideas and a continuing threat to the perpetuation of social systems. In the Israeli kibbutz, for example, younger members often feel a strong pull toward the comforts of city life, for they did not share in the early years of excitement and challenge when the kibbutz was first tried as a new form of community and family life (Bettelheim 1969). Many Jews also worry because the number of people who actually experienced the Holocaust grows smaller each year. There are fewer witnesses who can speak of the horror, who can perpetuate the memory of it in order to ensure that it will never happen again.

Technology

Technological change occurs in three basic ways. A **discovery** is an instance of finding out about something that already exists (such as gravity or the effects of cocaine on the brain), whereas an **invention** is something new created from things that already exist (such as the plow or the computer chip). Although discovery and invention obviously have been crucial sources of innovation in the world as a whole, the introduction of new technology in most societies has occurred through the process of **diffusion**, which is the borrowing of knowledge from other societies (see Rogers 1983). As far as we know, printing was invented in the sixth century by Chinese who used engraved wooden blocks. During the next 1,000 years printing technology spread from China through the Middle East and Europe, and a German printer named Johann Gutenberg is credited with inventing movable reusable type in the fifteenth century. Printing technology is now used around the world, and yet it was not invented anew in each society.

A major part of the ecological perspective focuses on the ways in which societies apply discoveries and inventions to physical environments. As we have seen, technology affects the niches human societies occupy in ecosystems; but it also affects the characteristics of social systems. The invention of printing and movable type made books available to a wide population for the first time. This greatly increased literacy, and the rapid spread of ideas stimulated the development of scientific, political, religious, and philosophical thought (see Eisenstein 1980). In similar ways, the computer is now revolutionizing our ability to store, retrieve, and communicate information with phenomenal speed and accuracy.

The invention of the cotton gin in the late 1700s made the production of cotton in the American South far more profitable, and this led to a dramatic increase in the slave population (Rasmussen 1982). The Industrial Revolution rested on an astonishingly rapid series of innovations in the design of machinery and the development of nonhuman sources of energy. Industrialization, in turn, virtually transformed work and affected institutions such as the family and schools.

The mechanization of agriculture in the 1930s and 1940s helped to transform the U.S. from a nation of farmers into a nation of urban workers whose entire food supply is provided by less than 3 percent of the population (Rasmussen 1982). The decline in the demand for manual farm labor also stimulated a mass migration of southern blacks from rural areas, first to southern cities, and then to the cities of the North. The urbanization of blacks led to better education and job opportunities, and these, in turn, helped to lay the groundwork for the civil rights movement of the 1960s.

Cultural Lag Technology often creates dilemmas around deeply held values, in part because technological change moves at a faster pace than changes in cultural ideas, creating what W. F. Ogburn called **cultural lag**. We develop new technologies faster than we develop new cultural ideas that regulate how we use them (Ogburn 1922, 1964). Medical technology enables doctors to artificially inseminate a woman with any man's sperm, making it possible for wives to bear children even if their husbands are sterile. It also makes it possible for married couples to have the husband's sperm used to impregnate another woman when the wife is infertile. In

PUZZLE

WHO OWNS THE EGGS?

In 1981 an Australian married couple discovered that the only way they could have children was through test tube fertilization. Several eggs were removed from the wife and fertilized with the husband's sperm. Two of the resulting embryos were frozen while the third was implanted in the wife. She miscarried 10 days later. In 1983 the couple was killed in a plane crash and left an estate valued at several million dollars.

Are the frozen embryos heirs to the estate? Does anyone own them? Can they be destroyed? If they are implanted in a woman who becomes their mother, can she claim part of the estate on their behalf?

These and other difficult questions that faced Australian legal authorities are examples of the kinds of problems that arise when technology allows us to do things faster than we create norms, beliefs, and values to deal with the consequences.

the late 1980s, several couples tried this approach. They signed legal contracts with what were called surrogate mothers who, for a fee, agreed to turn over the child after it was born. What happens, however, when the mother, who is carrying the child, decides to keep it? Who is the actual mother under the law, the woman who bore the child or the woman who paid the surrogate mother? How are the biological father's rights balanced against those of the biological mother (who is not his wife)? Where in all of this do the child's best interests lie?

Although in a major case involving "Baby M" a New Jersey court awarded custody of the child to the natural father and his wife, the issue is far from settled. Many states are considering laws that would outlaw such agreements altogether. Without the reproductive technology that allows artificial insemination the legal and moral questions raised by such cases would never arise in the first place. In this case, as with so many others like it, our cultural grasp of ethical and legal issues lags far behind technological capabilities.

Cultural lag also involves norms, for the introduction of new technology often alters human behavior and interaction patterns faster than groups and societies are able to construct new norms to regulate them. Prior to the widespread use of computers, for example, most records in business, government, and other organizations were kept in written form, and this made it relatively easy to control who had access to them. As computers have taken over the job of filing and keeping track of vast quantities of information, however, entirely new security problems are introduced (Parker 1983). Operators of personal computers—called hackers—began to figure out how to break into large computers by guessing passwords. When hospitals, banks, the military, and government agencies became alarmed at the prospect of unauthorized entry into and alteration of highly important information, they discovered that no laws existed which dealt with breaking and entering into a computer through the use of a telephone.

The rapid growth of computer technology introduces other problems as well (see Sherman 1985). Because most information held by governments in the past was in written form, it was relatively difficult to keep track of detailed information from diverse sources about millions of citizens. Computers, however, make it possible for government agencies to compile and access detailed records about citizens quickly and efficiently, and Marx and Reichman (1984) and others have argued that this gives the state an unprecedented ability to invade the privacy of individuals (see Office of Technology Assessment 1986a).

The Speed of Change   The rate at which new ideas and technologies are introduced depends on a variety of social and ecological factors (see Rogers 1983). In the simplest sense, scientific and technological knowledge is largely cumulative: the more we know, the more we are able to know. Since inventions are new combinations of existing ideas and inventions, the more we start with, the more combinations we can invent. Large populations can be conducive to innovation because the more people there are, the more likely it is that someone will come up with something new (Ogburn 1922). Population size, however, like any other factor, is not sufficient to guarantee innovation, as the examples of India and China during the last few centuries illustrate. A quarter of the world's population lives in China, and yet in terms of industrial technology China is an underdeveloped country.

A third factor affecting the rate of innovation is the stability of environments. A society that must

In no area of technology has the power of diffusion been more frightening than with nuclear weapons. Even the poorest countries—such as Pakistan and India—have managed to borrow the technology needed to manufacture them. If carried far enough, diffusion could make the use of such weapons all but inevitable.

adapt to rapidly changing physical or social conditions will tend to produce more innovations than a society that exists in stable conditions. In the 1970s, for example, oil-producing nations in the Middle East refused to sell oil to the U.S., and the ensuing shortages stimulated the development of solar energy technology. The nuclear arms race is another example of rapidly shifting environmental conditions that stimulate an equally rapid pace of technological development as each country struggles to keep up with the other.

Since most innovation occurs through diffusion, a fourth factor affecting the rate of innovation is the amount of contact between societies. Isolated societies have less opportunity to borrow from others than societies that are actively engaged in trade or other forms of exchange. In some cases, societies try to isolate themselves in order to avoid new ideas. This was true of Japan prior to the nineteenth century and until recently was also true of the Soviet Union, whose government has feared the diffusion of Western culture into their society. The importation of magazines, films, and books from the West has been tightly controlled by the government, and Soviet citizens have been discouraged from interacting with tourists from Western countries. Only recently has the Soviet policy of *glasnost* (or "openness") begun to loosen this control.

Having examined the effects of population and ecology on societies, we look now at some specific theories that draw on these and other factors in their attempts to understand patterns of social change.

THEORIES OF SOCIAL CHANGE

In addition to the functional and conflict approaches, sociologists have developed a number of models that try to account for the patterns and pace of change that characterize the historical experience of many societies, especially those that are now industrialized. Many of the earliest of these theories

The Functional Perspective

were largely descriptive, but some more recent attempts pay attention to the problem of explanation as well.

Durkheim developed the idea that a society is a complex network of interdependent parts—such as the family, government, religion, and economy—each of which either contributes to or interferes with the maintenance of the whole. Parsons (1937, 1951, 1966, 1971) built on Durkheim's work by exploring what he regarded as the most important sociological problem: What causes social systems to stay together or to fall apart?

Parsons believed that societies have built-in mechanisms that help them adapt and remain stable. Shared cultural ideas and the relationships between their various parts help a society maintain equilibrium—or balance—among its different parts. When strain develops within the system or is introduced from the outside, it stimulates responses that help to reduce it. Social change, then, is a process through which societies regain their balance as they adjust to strain that arises through their normal functioning.

Consider what happened in 1986 when police and federal agents began a major effort to stem the flow of the potent form of crack cocaine in New York City. Their efforts were so successful that the criminal justice system was soon faced with overcrowded jails and prisons, long court backlogs, and overburdened prosecutors, public defenders, and probation officers. The policing system was working just as it was supposed to, and yet enormous strains in the criminal justice system resulted from it.

Several changes are possible in this kind of situation. Crimes such as drug use might be reclassified as legal acts (as some officials urge), reducing the number of arrests and prosecutions. More prisons might be built, diverting resources from other uses, such as the relief of poverty. Or, courts might dispense with some civil rights that slow down trials—such as the right of appeal. Each of these changes is a possible response to strain that develops through the normal operation of the institutional parts that make up a society.

Although Parsons' ideas had considerable influence in the 1940s and 1950s, they came under attack during the 1960s. Because he was interested primarily in the problem of how societies maintain themselves as systems of social relationships and cultural ideas, he paid relatively little attention to social conflict and social change. Like all investigators, he was selective in his choice of research problems; but his focus on social order during a period of intense unrest and awareness of injustice in existing social conditions led many sociologists to misperceive Parsons and the entire functional perspective as inherently supportive of the status quo, including social inequality. As civil rights and antiwar protests challenged the status quo in the United States, any focus on the maintenance of social order as a theoretical problem became increasingly unpopular among sociologists.

In fact, however, leading functional theorists had recognized since the late 1940s that "strain, tension, contradiction, and discrepancy between the component parts of social structure" are inevitable in any society and that these often produce positive social change (Merton 1948). Merton and others, such as Lewis Coser (1956, 1967), incorporated important elements of social conflict into the functional perspective by highlighting the fact that social systems can produce dysfunctional as well as functional consequences.

The Conflict Perspective

While Parsons' functional theory views change as an adaptive response to disturbances in an otherwise balanced society, the conflict perspective focuses on different aspects of society and social change. Both perspectives view change as a normal process, but they differ in their view of what holds societies together. To Parsons, society is held together primarily by a consensus over values. The conflict perspective, however, views society as held together by the ability of the powerful to coerce the weak, and the resulting conflict among different groups is a continuing source of change.

Marx and Engels ([1848] 1932) believed that "All history is the history of class conflict"—which in capitalist societies means a struggle between those who own the means of production and those who do not. Class divisions inevitably lead to struggles to alter social conditions that produce and support exploitation and inequality. As Schaff (1970) summarized some of Marx's early ideas,

> To liberate the individual . . . it is necessary to effect a change in social relations and institutions, to overthrow them by overthrowing the prevalent pattern of class relations. (p. 31)

These pro-choice and anti-abortion demonstrators typify the forces that oppose each other in the continuing controversy over the rights of women and the rights of unborn children.

From a conflict perspective, oppressed groups cannot depend on their society to reach an equilibrium that includes social justice, for without conflict, social systems tend to remain stable. Consequently, Marx believed that societies inevitably change, but not necessarily for the better; rather, they often perpetuate inequality and injustice in the name of stability and the interests of powerful elites.

Social conflict arises because internal contradictions are inevitable in any complex society. We generally value equality and fairness and yet our society includes cultural ideas and social structures that discriminate against minorities such as nonwhites and women. We value both economic progress and a physical environment free of pollution; and we value the efficiency of rationally structured bureaucracies, and yet we also value the attention to individuals and their feelings that bureaucracies ignore.

The division of industrial societies into social classes based on unequal distributions of wealth, power, and prestige produces the inherent structural contradiction that each class often prospers at the expense of another. The structure of industrial society produces conflict between classes, and conflict, in turn, produces pressures for new arrangements and accommodations.

Evolutionary and Unilinear Theory

In trying to identify laws of social change, early thinkers often used biological evolution as a model.

Herbert Spencer drew on Darwin's ideas about natural evolution to develop a theory of **social evolution** through which societies naturally change toward superior forms (Spencer 1891, 1896). From this point of view, social change is **unilinear**, which means that all societies pass through predictable stages: from primitive to civilized, simple to complex, inferior to superior, from militant to peaceful, and from agricultural to industrial.

Like all ideas, Spencer's reflected his society, for England was rapidly colonizing much of the world and encountering a vast array of peoples living in relatively simple societies at comparatively low levels of economic development. The theory of social evolution supported the Europeans' belief in their own superiority by focusing on economic development as the most important indicator of a superior society.

The U.S. sociologist Thorstein Veblen also used evolutionary theory as a framework, but focused more on the effects of technology (see Lerner 1948). Like later theorists, however, Veblen did not believe that social change is unilinear, for he was aware of how easily technology can be transplanted from one society to another. China, for example, is still a largely agricultural society, and yet trade with industrial countries will bring computer and nuclear power technology to what is otherwise a technology-poor society. Despite their poverty, both India and Pakistan now have the ability to manufacture nuclear weapons.

Cyclical Theory

Early in this century, the German philosopher Oswald Spengler (1926) produced a variation on evolutionary theory by suggesting that societies change in predictable cycles, in the same way that people progress from birth toward maturity, old age, and death. Like Spencer, Spengler's ideas about **cyclical change** reflected his environment, for the chaos and mass destruction of World War I shook Europeans' belief that societies naturally progress toward better forms. Obviously, change did not necessarily imply an improvement in social life, for in the midst of the greatest economic progress ever known, millions of people were systematically slaughtering one another.

The U.S. sociologist Pitirim Sorokin also believed in cyclical change. According to his principle of **immanent change**, cultures have material and nonmaterial characteristics that cause societies to develop in certain directions. Eventually these are taken to their logical extreme, after which they go too far and "become less and less capable of serving as an instrument of adaptation, as an experience for real satisfaction of the needs of its bearers, and as foundation for their social and cultural life" (Sorokin 1937–41).

The unprecedented carnage of World War I shattered the illusion that civilizations inevitably progress towards higher and better forms. So fierce was the slaughter in some battles that within periods of only a few days hundreds of thousands of soldiers were killed or wounded by rifle and artillery fire. This picture was taken after the battle of the Somme in 1916.

Sorokin argued that as a society develops the ability to produce goods, for example, it will tend to go too far, and as people focus on owning more and more possessions, life begins to lose its sense of meaning and they will turn away from the material aspects of their culture to nonmaterial aspects such as religious belief. During the two decades that followed World War II, the U.S. enjoyed a period of great economic prosperity. In the 1960s there was a strong movement away from materialism and toward various forms of spiritualism, especially in the form of Eastern religions such as Zen Buddhism. This movement was strongest among college students, many of whom came from prosperous families. In the 1970s, 1980s, and 1990s there also has been a strong growth in fundamentalist religion and religious cults.

In spite of the insights that the early evolutionary and cyclical theories of change provide, they have a number of drawbacks that make them of relatively little interest to today's sociologists (Zeitlin 1981). Their most obvious shortcoming is that they often do not fit the facts: as Veblen noted, societies often skip stages of development, especially when technology is introduced from the outside. It took the Industrial Revolution to ultimately produce the telephone, television, computer, nuclear reactor, and such deadly weapons as hydrogen bombs, yet these technologies have spread rapidly to societies that have yet to industrialize. These theories also do not appreciate the enormous complexity of social change and the phenomenal variation found among societies.

Multilinear Theories

More recent evolutionary theories show greater appreciation for the complexity of social change (see Johnson and Earle 1987). **Multilinear change** theories in particular identify certain changes that appear to be universal—from small, simple, rural, and low technology to large, complex, urban, and high technology—and yet acknowledge that such changes take place in a variety of ways and do not necessarily result in progress (Smelser 1973; Steward 1955).

Perhaps the best developed of the recent multilinear theories is Lenski's theory of social evolution (Lenski and Lenski 1987). There are important similarities between the biological evolution of living species and the social evolution of human societies. Both depend on the transmission of information—via DNA molecules in genes in the case of biological evolution and via cultural symbol systems in social

ARRIVALS

PESTILENCE	4:02
FAMINE	4:15
MARTIAL LAW	4:21
TRIPLE LOCKS	5:00
UNEMPLOYMENT	5:20
INFLATION	5:32
SHORTER SUMMERS	5:43
LONGER ZIP CODES	5:46
PLASTIC SILVERWARE	6:01

DEPARTURES

GOOD TASTE	3:32
SLEIGH RIDES	3:49
ALL-BEEF BURGERS	4:15
HAPPINESS	5:11
SECURITY	5:15
FRIENDLY LOAN COMPANIES	5:58
WARM BLANKETS	6:10
HARDWOOD FLOORS	6:15
HOMEMADE ICE CREAM	6:31

Drawing by Ziegler © 1979, The New Yorker Magazine, Inc.

evolution. Both forms of evolution arise from the interaction of populations with their environments, and in each case the evolutionary trend involves an increase in the amount and complexity of information. In comparison with the simplest virus, for example, human genes hold a million times more information (Curtis and Barnes 1981). In similar ways, industrial societies are far more complex than gatherer-hunter societies.

Biological and social evolution differ in important ways, however. The genetic information that controls biological evolution can be transmitted only through reproduction, and two different species cannot mate—that is, they cannot exchange genetic information. Since different species of life cannot share the same genetic information, biological evolution tends to produce greater diversity as each species develops in its own way. Human societies, however, can share information quite easily, and in this way they tend to become more similar. Less than a century ago, basic technologies such as electricity and telecommunications were found in only a few countries, but now exist in almost every society. Other aspects of culture, from fast food restaurants and computers to jeans and rock music, have also spread rapidly.

Like some earlier theorists, Lenski regards information as the key to social change. It was new technology that enabled populations and societies to grow. The expanding resources of larger societies spawned new cultural and structural developments:

systems of written language, new vocabularies, more complex divisions of labor, and greater production of goods. According to modern evolutionary theory, in short, information is the engine of social change. Social change, in turn, creates pressures for new information and further change. One consequence of industrial technology, for example, has been damage to the physical environment, and, therefore, to the well-being of populations. This, in turn, has created pressures for new technology (such as pollution control devices) and for change in political arrangements (such as greater government regulation of industry).

Modernization Theory

The concept of **modernization** refers to a process through which the social and ecological characteristics of societies change in predictable ways (Parsons 1951; Rostow 1960). In its earliest form, which was most popular during the 1950s and 1960s, modernization theory was actually a form of evolutionary theory that tried to describe how the process of industrialization takes place. For two decades the idea of modernization dominated thinking about economic and social change in underdeveloped countries, and it held out the expectation that the economic prosperity and democratic political institutions found in the countries of North America and Western Europe would spread throughout the world.

According to modernization theory, development depends on both complex technology and a variety of structural, cultural, and ecological changes. Cultures become more heterogeneous and subcultures flourish. People become more oriented to the future and open to change, and the rights of the individual increase in value. Social relationships shift from informal and primary to formal, bureaucratic, and secondary, and populations become more urban. Social inequality increases during the early stages of modernization as an elite profits from exploiting an unsophisticated, unskilled labor force; but as a society industrializes, social mobility increases and rigid stratification systems based on ascribed statuses such as race, caste, and gender tend to break down. Traditional sources of authority—such as respect for the elderly—also tend to weaken as social institutions such as schools and the state take on increasing responsibility and authority.

At the heart of modernization is technological innovation that makes industrialization possible, and scientific research and technological innovation are highly valued in modern societies. With industrialization comes a specialized division of labor, a more skilled and educated work force, and greater alienation in the workplace. Contact with modern working conditions, in turn, tends to make workers more modern in their values and beliefs, more supportive of democratic institutions, and more committed to the rights of individuals (Inkeles and Smith 1974). As we saw in Chapter 19, some theorists believe that the most advanced stage of modernization is *post-industrial* society, in which sophisticated technology replaces much of human labor and most people work as service providers (such as nurses and computer programmers) rather than as producers of goods (Daniel Bell 1973).

There is little doubt that most societies are committed to economic development, for the lure of higher standards of living is a strong one. What is not clear, however, is how useful the theory of modernization is for predicting patterns of change in underdeveloped societies. As we saw in Chapter 12, the gap between rich and poor nations has been growing, not shrinking. Is economic prosperity an attainable goal for all countries of the world as modernization theory seems to suggest? Supporters of world-system theory believe the answer is no.

World-System Theory

World-system (or **dependency**) **theory** was developed in the 1970s as a direct challenge to modernization theory, most notably by Immanuel Wallerstein (1976, 1979, 1980). As we saw in Chapter 19, Wallerstein divides societies into three categories. Core societies such as Britain, the U.S., and Japan occupy dominant positions in the world economy by con-

trolling the development and flow of new technology as well as the wealth necessary for the creation of new capital. Countries in the periphery—such as most of Africa and much of Asia—are poor and underdeveloped and supply core societies with raw materials, food, and other products that can be produced without sophisticated technology or an educated work force. Semiperiphery countries such as Brazil and Taiwan stand between the core and the periphery and often provide cheap but well-trained industrial labor when labor costs in core countries go up.

A world-system perspective has important implications for social change, for it is based on the view that economic development depends not simply on a society's characteristics, but also on its position in the world system. It argues that even the leading socialist country in the world—the Soviet Union—cannot be completely socialist so long as it must deal with a largely capitalist world economy (Wallerstein 1979), a fact that underlies much of that nation's recent moves towards capitalism. It also argues that backward conditions found in many peripheral societies arise not only from their internal conditions, but also from their relationship with societies at the

From a world systems perspective, a key to Taiwan's rapid economic development has been massive assistance and investment from the United States.

core or in the semiperiphery of the world system. We cannot understand the phenomenal economic growth in Taiwan over the past 30 years, for example, without taking into account Taiwan's close relationship with the U.S.

An important aspect of world-system theory focuses on the ways in which core and peripheral societies change due to their positions in the system. When Great Britain was an empire, it systematically destroyed the textile industry in India—one of its colonies—and forced Indians to purchase cloth made in Britain by not allowing them to produce any themselves. This eliminated competition and provided a captive market for British goods. One result of this policy was increased revenues for Britain, which contributed to the industrial revolution that was the basis for modern core societies (Baran 1957).

The economic problems of many countries are also tied to dependency relationships in the world system. Mexico is an urban, industrial, rich country compared to most underdeveloped nations, and yet in spite of its wealth of natural resources it has widespread poverty and an enormous gap between rich and poor. Gonzalez Casanova (1980) argued that this is due in part to the relationship between Mexico and corporations in core countries, the U.S. in particular. So much of Mexico's industry is owned by foreigners, and so much of its foreign sales depend on a few customers, that Mexican leaders lack the flexibility they need to make the domestic investments that lead to improved living conditions.

Like all theories, world-system theory has its shortcomings. Few social scientists would deny that a world system exists or that there are dependent relations between societies. What is unclear, however, are the reasons that some societies are at the core and others are in the periphery or semiperiphery. Brenner (1976) showed that economic "backwardness" in eastern Europe arose less from economic dependence than on a lack of technology that preceded the development of its dependent position in the world system (see also Chirot 1980, 1985; Chirot and Hall 1982; and Lenski 1976b).

For all their shortcomings, theories of social change have come a long way from the relatively simplistic notions of unilinear evolution. Multilinear, world-system, and dependency theory in particular show a development toward more comprehensive theories that appreciate the complexity of social change. All of these, however, pay attention to social change on a macrolevel that does not ac-

count very well for the effects of human action on social systems. As the interactionist perspective makes clear, people continually create and recreate social systems through their behavior, and in doing so have enormous potential for bringing about change. This is especially true when behavior is organized into social movements.

SOCIAL MOVEMENTS

Social movements are organized attempts to cause or prevent social change. In addition to being organized, they are social in that they attempt to change cultural or structural aspects of society; but they are social in another perhaps more important respect as well. So long as people do not identify the social causes of their life circumstances, they have no other explanation than luck or personal characteristics. Once they focus on social systems, however, they can see the social problems of which their personal troubles are a part. It is only when people go beyond psychological and biological frameworks that social movements become possible.

Social movements usually focus on reform, revolution, or resistance to change. **Reform** movements try to improve existing arrangements by altering specific aspects of them. Various civil rights movements, for example, do not seek to dismantle and change an entire society; rather, they demand that members of disadvantaged social categories have the right to participate fully in political and economic life and receive a fair share of wealth, power, and prestige. In similar ways, movements to save the physical environment often focus on specific ecological choices (such as between solar or nuclear technology) rather than society as a whole.

Unlike reform movements, **revolutions** attempt to replace an existing social or ecological arrangement (Goldstone 1982; Skocpol 1979). The French Revolution attempted to replace a monarchy with a more democratic government; and the American Revolution—which began as a reform movement to guarantee colonists the same rights as other British subjects—rapidly turned into a revolution that completely separated the colonies from the British Empire. In early 1917 the Czar of Russia was overthrown and replaced by a government that began to introduce a kind of Western democracy. Later in that same year, the Bolsheviks under the leadership of Lenin carried out yet a second revolution that led to the socialist state that rules the Soviet Union to-

The anti-nuclear power movement is a powerful example of a resistance movement that has had considerable success. In 1983, these marchers protested the Shoreham nuclear power plant on Long Island, New York on the grounds that it would be impossible to evacuate residents in the event of an accident. After years of protest, the power company was ordered in 1988 to dismantle the completed plant before it was put into operation.

day—although it now finds itself under intense pressure to change towards greater democracy.

More recently, religious fundamentalists in Iran joined with other dissatisfied groups to overthrow the shah's monarchy and replace it with a government strictly guided by religious principles. In Nicaragua a revolutionary movement in the early 1980s installed a socialist government which was then opposed by a *counter*revolutionary movement; and in neighboring El Salvador a socialist revolutionary movement is trying to depose a capitalist government with strong ties to the U.S. Most recently the countries of Central Europe have undergone revolutionary changes from state socialism to various forms of democracy and capitalism, including the reunification of Germany.

Although social movements often cause change, their purpose is sometimes just the opposite—to oppose or undo change (Lo 1982)—in which case they are called **resistance** movements. In 1982, for example, organized opposition defeated the Equal Rights Amendment in spite of the fact that a clear majority of adults supported it. In 1983, a nuclear weapons freeze movement grew rapidly, and opposed the introduction of newer, more deadly weapons. Other movements support a return to prayer in public schools, the dismantling of school busing programs, and the reversal of Supreme Court decisions that support abortion rights.

Social movements have attracted increasing attention from sociologists during the past 40 years and have been a topic of intense debate since the mid-1970s. Why do they emerge when they do? What determines their success or failure? In the following sections, we look at some attempts to answer such questions.

Classical Social Movement Theory

Like early theories of behavior in crowds, early social movement theories often relied heavily on psychological explanations for what is essentially a social phenomenon. What McAdam (1982) called **classical social movement theory** actually includes several

FIGURE 23-1   Classical Theories of Social Movements

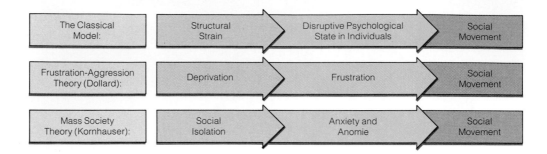

Classical theories of social movements are psychological in that they argue that social movements are a way for people to relieve uncomfortable and disruptive feelings that are caused by social conditions. They tend to ignore the social factors that determine whether a social movement will emerge or succeed.
Source: McAdam 1982.

specific approaches, all based on the same general model: some kind of strain or disturbance (such as an economic depression) creates disruptive psychological states in individuals (such as anxiety) and individuals then channel their energy into social movements in order to relieve their emotional difficulties (Figure 23-1). In the sections that follow we will take a critical look at each of these approaches.

Frustration, Deprivation, and Aggression
Dollard and colleagues (1939) were the first to outline the **frustration-aggression theory** of social movements, according to which social strain in the form of frustration is an underlying motive for aggressive behavior, including the formation of social movements. A frustration-aggression explanation of lynch mobs in the South during the late nineteenth and early twentieth centuries, for example, might go like this: Cotton is the main crop in southern states and most poor whites make a living from it. When the cotton market is good and prices are high, everyone does reasonably well. When the market is bad, poor whites suffer and in their frustration seek a relatively safe target on which to vent their feelings. The obvious choice was blacks. (Blacks also suffered from poor economic conditions, but lacked a safe target.) (Dollard et al. 1939).

In trying to explain violent social movements, Gurr (1970) argued that frustration most often arises from people's anger over **relative deprivation**—not getting what they think they deserve in comparison with others who they think should not be any better off than they are. If I have enough food to guarantee good nutrition, I may feel physically fit and therefore not suffer any **absolute deprivation**. If my reference groups (such as friends and co-workers) can afford fancy wines and lots of meals in restaurants, however, I am more likely to experience relative deprivation.

The distinction between absolute and relative deprivation is important, for the use of one concept rather than the other generates quite different predictions. If we think in terms of absolute deprivation, we would predict that societies with the highest incidence of poverty will be the ones to experience the highest levels of violent behavior, and that the most violent society will be one in which everyone is poor. If, however, we use the concept of relative deprivation, we would predict that the highest levels of collective violence will occur in societies in which the *gap* between the richest and the poorest is perceived to be the widest and the most out of line with people's expectations, even though no one might be poor in an absolute sense. This can result in a paradoxical situation, for an improvement in absolute conditions may stimulate people's expectations to rise even faster, and as this widens the gap between what people have and what they think they should have, the chances for violence should increase.

This is how some sociologists explained the increase in urban riots and other collective violence in the U.S. during the 1960s (Graham and Gurr 1979; Gurr 1970). In 1954 the Supreme Court banned racial segregation in schools, and segregation in other public facilities—such as restaurants, buses, and restrooms—was outlawed shortly thereafter. The economy boomed during the 1960s, President Johnson declared a war on poverty, and civil rights legislation outlawed racial discrimination and strengthened blacks' voting rights.

In an absolute sense, then, conditions were improving for many blacks, but for many others conditions remained largely the same. What were changing dramatically, however, were black people's perceptions of what they ought to have relative to everyone else. Severe inequality continued while the social acceptability of poverty and inequality declined and the promise of an end to poverty was offered by the federal government. It is likely that one result of this was a widespread feeling among poor urban blacks that the promise was an empty one, that economic prosperity was passing them by, and that in a relative sense, they were worse off than ever before.

In addition to relative deprivation, frustration-aggression theorists focus on two other sources of frustration. In the above account, for example, federal antipoverty programs may have created the hope and the expectation among blacks that things would improve rapidly for them. Such rising expectations, argue some sociologists, form the basis for frustration and then social movements when they fail to materialize. Davies (1962) argued that social movements are more likely if a period of rapid improvement is followed by a sharp downturn. According to his **J-curve** theory of black rebellion in the 1960s, a period of rising expectations and actual improvements in living conditions was followed by a rapid worsening of the relative position of blacks, a sudden reversal they found intolerable.

Theories that rely on frustration, relative deprivation, rising expectations, and sudden reversals to explain social movements have been criticized on a number of grounds (see McAdam 1982; Morris 1984). First, most studies that use this framework have not measured the existence of these key psychological states over time. Since the theories argue that it is an *increase* in such disruptive feelings that prompts social movements, the failure to link movements with changes in levels of frustration is a crucial one.

Second, studies do not compare the levels of frustration in those who participate in social movements with those who do not. When Orum (1972) did this in his study of black student participation in civil rights protests, he found that those who participated were no more likely to have experienced rising expectations than those who did not (see also Olzak 1989.)

Third, the indicators that are typically used to measure the presence of strain do not correlate with the level of social movement activity. McAdam (1982) compared economic indicators—such as the ratio of black incomes to white incomes—with the annual number of black civil rights movement events for the period between 1948 and 1976. He found no significant relationship between them.

Fourth, as Shorter and Tilly (1974) and Tilly (1978a) argued, emotional arousal—however intense—is not enough to create a social movement. As they wrote in their study of strikes in France,

In 1983, hundreds of thousands of people gathered in Washington, D.C. to mark the 20th anniversary of Martin Luther King, Jr.'s "I Have a Dream" speech. The level of organization and resources needed for this kind of collective action raises serious questions about the theory that social movements can result simply from psychological states such as frustration.

individuals are not magically mobilized for participation in some group enterprise, regardless of how angry, sullen, hostile, or frustrated they may feel. Their aggression may be channeled to collective ends only through the coordinating, directing functions of an organization, be it formal or informal" (p. 38).

In short, a collection of angry people is not a social movement. To be a social movement, the anger and energy must be organized, and frustration-aggression, relative deprivation, rising expectations, and J-curve theories ignore this vital *social* aspect of social movements.

Kornhauser, Mass Society, and Social Isolation

In the aftermath of World War II Kornhauser (1959) focused on how conditions in societies as a whole promoted or inhibited collective violence that seemed—to many living in the cold-war atmosphere

These Germans protesting the arms race in 1983 carry a banner portraying the U.S. and the Soviet Union as vultures perched on eggs (bombs) in a weapons nest. In Germany the vulture is often a symbol of old, worn out ideas, and the people shown between the two world powers are obviously taking things into their own hands.

of the 1950s—to lead to authoritarian governments. Kornhauser believed that movements are most likely when people feel a lack of connection between themselves and their communities. This happens when there are no groups through which people can affect political decisions or feel like they belong in their communities. Kornhauser called this condition of widespread social isolation **mass society**, and the social isolation it reflects is similar to Durkheim's concept of anomie that we discussed in Chapter 11 as a cause of deviant behavior.

To Kornhauser, large numbers of unattached and alienated people are the raw material of social movements. When people feel submerged in a mass, they feel disconnected from meaningful involvements and relationships, and this leads them to experience strong feelings of anxiety. In order to escape these feelings, people engage in extreme behavior, including social movements (see Figure 23-1).

Kornhauser argued that social movements are ultimately caused by social systems; but it is important to see that he did not see social movements as attempts to *change* those conditions. Rather, he explained them as mechanisms through which individuals try to reduce unpleasant psychological conditions such as strain and anxiety. Violent behavior may discharge tension, and participation in a movement may provide feelings of belonging and connection with other human beings. "Mass movements," he wrote, "appeal to the unemployed on psychological . . . grounds, as ways of overcoming feelings of anxiety and futility, of finding new solidarity and forms of activity" (p. 167). This is similar to Smelser's theory of structural strain described in more detail in Chapter 22. Smelser argued that strain and contradiction in social systems give rise to feelings of uncertainty, anxiety, and discontent, and that people then engage in collective behavior (including social movements) as a way of relieving those feelings.

Some Problems with Mass Society and Structural Strain Theories

Kornhauser's and Smelser's theories are sociologically important because they explicitly include social conditions in their explanations of social movements. They have been criticized, however, on several grounds, the most important being their heavy reliance on psychological explanations. Structural strain and social isolation are always present in complex societies, but social movements are relatively rare occurrences. When a movement occurs, one can always note the existence of strain or isolation. What this ignores is the fact that there are often *no* social movements in *spite* of the existence of strain or mass society conditions. It may be that social movements will not occur without strain in a society, critics argue, but strain by itself is not enough to bring them about.

In addition, as Tilly (1978a) and others argued in relation to theories of frustration and aggression, any attempt to explain social movements as an expression of individual psychological need ignores the importance of social organization. Classical theories underestimate the importance of social movements as organized political attempts to bring about change. As McAdam (1982) put it,

> If movement participants are motivated only by the desire to . . . manage "feelings of anxiety and futility," then we would hardly expect social movements to be effective. . . . In fact, however, movements are, and always have been, an important impetus to sociopolitical change. The American colonists defeated the British on the strength of an organized insurgent movement. Mao, Lenin, Khomeini, and Castro all came to power as a result of similar movements. An incumbent American president, Lyndon Johnson, was forced from office and this country's policy on Vietnam altered as a result of the antiwar movement. And through the collective protest efforts of blacks, the South's elaborate system of Jim Crow racism was dismantled in a matter of a decade. Are we to conclude that such significant historical processes were simply the unintended byproducts of a collective attempt at tension management? The argument is neither theoretically nor empirically convincing. (p. 18)

Oberschall (1973), McAdam (1982), and others argue that classical social movement theory falls short because it rests on a false view of the societies in which movements occur. Specifically, classical theories assume a pluralistic distribution of power in which no group dominates decision making and everyone has some access to major institutions. In such a world, it makes sense to view social movements as aberrations resulting from the personal troubles of individuals. Why else, after all, would great numbers of people take to the streets and protest when legitimate avenues were available to them to make grievances known and to effect change?

One answer is that the distribution of power is not pluralistic. From a conflict point of view, legitimate means for changing a society are controlled by an elite, and the only way to bring about change is through some organized action. To go against dominant groups, however, requires *resources* as well as motivation, and this brings us to more recent—and more sociological—theories of social movements.

Resource Mobilization Theory

Inequality, discontent, frustration, anxiety, and social isolation are nothing new to complex societies, and the relative rarity of social movements underscores the fact that such conditions, even when shared by many people, are not in themselves sufficient to bring about collective action (Jenkins and Perrow 1977; Oberschall 1973). In response to this inadequacy of classical social movement theories, **resource mobilization theory** argues that people with common interests form social movements only when they have access to resources—time, people, skills, money, and organization—that give them some hope of achieving their goals in spite of opposition from the powerful groups that dominate society (Jenkins 1983; Lofland 1985).

It takes time, energy, and money to change the world, and most people can spare little of any of these, especially if they are poor. This simple fact helps explain why so many social movements—even those that act in the interests of poor people—tend to draw heavily on the time and energy of middle- and upper-class, relatively well-educated people. The Cuban Revolution that brought Fidel Castro to power was founded by young professionals and well-educated intellectuals (Draper 1962). Over two-thirds of the founders of the Chinese Communists Party came from upper-class—not peasant—backgrounds (Lee 1968). A large percentage of the activists in the civil rights, anti-Vietnam War, women's, and nuclear freeze movements have been young college students, middle-class professionals such as physicians and lawyers, and the elderly—all of whom have relatively high levels of free time and autonomy (Snow, Zurcher, and Eckland-Olson 1980).

The fact that disadvantaged groups are the least likely to command the resources necessary to sustain a social movement has led several theorists to argue that such movements succeed only with support from the outside. In the U.S. civil rights movement, for example, blacks had to attract the support of elite outsiders—in this case the federal government, upper-middle- and upper-class Northern whites, and young college students (McCarthy and Zald 1973; Oberschall 1973). Similarly, the farm workers movement relied on strong support from liberal churches and powerful labor unions (Jenkins 1981b, 1983). As Jenkins and Perrow (1977) wrote, "collective action is rarely a viable option because of a lack of resources and the threat of repression. . . . When deprived groups do mobilize, it is due to the interjection of external resources" (p. 251). As McAdam (1982) pointed out, this view suggests that most groups are powerless and that initiation of social movements lies with groups that control crucial resources. It is they, and not deprived groups, who are ultimately responsible for social movements and, therefore, for social change.

Evaluating the Theory   Resource mobilization theory is a substantial improvement over classical theories in several respects (see McAdam 1982). First, it explicitly defines social movements as organized social behavior rather than characterizing them as little more than manifestations of shared feelings of tension, anxiety, and discontent. In short, it puts the "social" back into social movements. Second, by taking social movements out of the realm of the psychological problems of individuals, mobilization theory makes them more understandable as political actions that are as rationally motivated as any other political behavior including that of those who control social institutions.

Third, mobilization theory includes the influence of groups outside social movements in order to explain the emergence and development of social movements, whereas classical theories focused primarily on the characteristics of movements and their participants. Finally, mobilization theory underscores the importance of organization to the success of social movements. Movements do not depend only on the motivation of their participants; rather, like all social systems, they require a steady supply of resources that include everything from money to administrative skills.

Although mobilization theory has stimulated a great deal of interest in what was considered by many to be a dying field in sociology, it has several weaknesses. In general, it is more effective at explaining the success or failure of movements initiated by those who already have some power in society, as is the case with environmental and consumer groups (McCarthy and Zald 1973). It is less successful, however, at explaining movements among minorites who are generally excluded from legitimate means for bringing about change (Piven and Cloward 1979).

It is important to note that the involvement of elites in social movements by powerless groups can have negative as well as positive effects (Jenkins 1981b; Jenkins and Eckert 1986). If a movement becomes dependent on outside support, it may take fewer risks for fear of alienating its sponsors. Since members of the elite have an interest in preserving the social systems that support their elite status, they may support some movements in order to ultimately gain control over them and limit their effectiveness.

A more serious problem with resource mobilization theory is that by focusing on the importance of outside support, it underestimates the resources of minorities and their ability to bring about change on their own. McAdam's (1982) analysis of the black civil rights movement during the late 1950s suggests that it was not a sudden infusion of outside support that led to an increase of black civil rights activity. It was the other way around: increased militancy led to increased levels of outside support (see also Haines 1988). In their analysis of strikes in France, Shorter and Tilly (1974) emphasized the importance of preexisting organization among workers and "the availability of a structure which identifies, accumulates, and communicates grievances on the one hand, and facilitates collective action on the other" (p. 284). As Morris (1984) shows, this was particularly important in the U.S. civil rights movement which was planned, organized, and led primarily on the local level using community resources and networks of urban churches and their ministers (see also Jenkins 1985; Jenkins and Eckert 1986; Morrison 1987).

An additional problem with mobilization theory is that it has yet to include a clear definition of resources. Since the concept can include anything from organizational skills to money, it is usually possible to find an increase of some kind of resource that precedes the emergence, rise, or decline of a social movement. It is also possible, therefore, to find many instances in which resources increased without leading to a social movement. As theorists define resources more narrowly, it will be possible to test the theory more conclusively.

Political Process Theory

As we have seen, whereas classical movement theory focuses on the intensity of feeling among participants, resource mobilization theory focuses on the importance of support from outside the movement. Skocpol (1979), Tilly (1978a), McAdam (1982), and others concentrate on an important additional aspect of the problem: what goes on inside and outside social movements. At the heart of **political process theory** is the idea that social movements "develop in response to an ongoing process of interaction between movement groups and the larger sociopolitical environment they seek to change" (McAdam 1982, p. 40).

The emergence of a political protest movement depends on a combination of factors. First, there must be an opportunity to bring about change, which means that the more vulnerable dominant groups and institutions are, the more likely open opposition to them will be. When the general political situation in a country is unstable, protest movements are more likely to occur, because the forces that might oppose them are weaker and less well organized. In their analysis of strikes in France, Shorter and Tilly (1974) found that strike activity in France was most common during times of intense struggle over who would rule the country.

As Skocpol (1979) argued in her analysis of the French, Chinese, and Russian revolutions, this is particularly true in the case of revolutions through which entire social systems may undergo radical change. In each of these cases the state was in crisis, and its inability to perform the basic tasks that defined its role as a social institution prompted opposition from deprived groups such as the peasantry and aggravated old conflicts among dominant groups as well. The 1917 Russian Revolution took place while the Russian state was in turmoil over repeated defeats in World War I. More recently, the Solidarity labor movement in Poland and other recent upheavals throughout Eastern Europe began amid general social unrest over poor economic conditions.

Second, the emergence and success of movements depends on the level of organization that exists among opposing groups. The black civil rights movement owed much of its success to the existing organizational network of black churches (Morris 1984). Widespread church membership among southern blacks provided a source of social movement members, facilitated communication, gave members a sense of belonging that encouraged them to stay with the movement, and generated leaders such as Martin Luther King. Tilly's (1978a) studies of social movements in Europe show a steady change over the past 400 years from temporary disorganized movements to more organized efforts with lasting influence (see also Shorter and Tilly 1974; Tilly and Tilly 1981; and Tilly, Tilly, and Tilly 1975).

Third, even when dominant groups and instituions are vulnerable to pressure and subordinate groups have the potential to organize a social movement, collective action depends on how potential participants *think* about their situation. Movements tend to emerge only when people begin to (1) question the legitimacy of authorities, (2), assert what they want as rights, and (3) believe that they are not helpless and that they have the potential to bring about change (Piven and Cloward 1979). In addition, when oppressed groups come to believe that peaceful protest is ineffective, they are also more likely to engage in violence (see White 1989).

As McAdam (1982) summarized this part of political process theory, the emergence of social movements depends on expanding political opportunities, the organizational strength of subordinate groups, and "cognitive liberation," or new ways of thinking about their situation and prospects for change (see Figure 23-2). Both the availability of political

FIGURE 23-2   Political Process and the Emergence of Social Movements

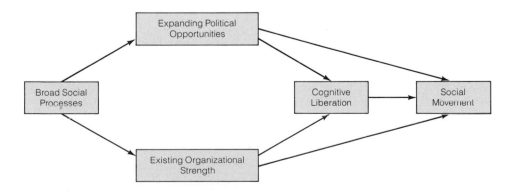

Political process theory tries to take into account a variety of factors that affect the emergence and success of social movements, from the people who are involved to the strength of organizations and institutions that oppose or support the movement's goals.

Source: McAdam, 1982.

ONE STEP FURTHER 23-1

The Civil Rights Movement, White Opposition, and the Government: Political Process Theory in Action

The civil rights movement provides a vivid illustration of political process theory, for as McAdam (1982) shows, blacks used political protest to provoke responses from their white supremacist opponents which were so extreme that

the federal government intervened on behalf of blacks.

Figure B-23-1 covers the period from 1961 into 1965 and shows the timing of actions by civil rights groups, white supremacists, and the government. What is most striking is that the peaks in civil rights activity (blue line) almost always occur *before* peaks in white supremacist activity

(red line) which, in turn, are often followed by peaks in government action (green line). In other words, the data support the idea that civil rights activities provoked white supremacist reactions which in turn forced the government to act. As a result, the movement elicited federal involvement in the defense of their rights and the promotion of their cause.

FIGURE B-23-1
Source: McAdam 1982, Figure 7-5.

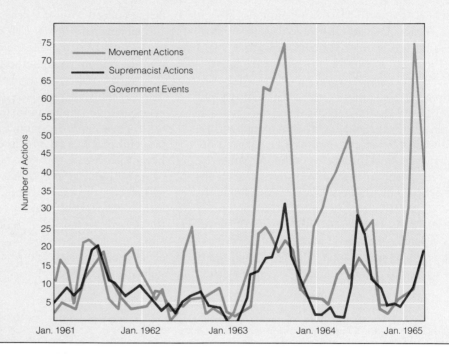

opportunities and organizational potential are the result of long-term social changes, and cognitive liberation results both from the perceived vulnerability of dominant groups and institutions by the subordinate group and from the organizational strength of the subordinate group itself.

Once a movement emerges, its success depends on a variety of factors that involve dynamics within the movement, its opposition, and the relationship between the two (see One Step Further 23-1). Protest movements may encounter violent opposition from governing institutions. This, in turn, may provoke outraged responses that strengthen the move-

ment's organization by increasing membership and outside support. It may also produce a response that is so violent and repressive that even the most well organized movement cannot sustain itself, as happened in the recent pro-democracy movement in China. To a lesser degree, this also has been true of the U.S. labor union movement which, especially in the early part of this century, had to struggle against the powerful and often overwhelming opposition of the capitalist class whose resources included not only great wealth and control over capital, but influence over government officials, legislatures, and the courts (see Griffin et al. 1986).

A political process approach offers some advantages over its predecessors. Its most important feature may be its inclusiveness, for it tries to cover the entire range between the characteristics of participants and groups and the society in which they and the forces they oppose exist. It fills an enormous gap between classical and resource mobilization theory and goes significantly beyond them.

SUMMARY

1. Social change refers to the ways in which social and ecological arrangements change.

2. Cultural ideas often promote change. New beliefs alter ways of perceiving the world; shifting values affect goals; and changing norms alter expectations in social relationships.

3. The structure of social relationships also causes change. Prejudice may be reduced by changing patterns of interaction between members of different groups.

4. Succession is the process through which ecosystems change, and it often causes social change. The shift from gatherer-hunter to horticultural and then agricultural societies laid a foundation for the emergence of social stratification and complex divisions of labor.

5. Rapid population growth and the changing characteristics of populations promote social change in a variety of ways. The pressure of an expanding population stimulates the development of new technology; overpopulation contributes to poverty, urban congestion, and pollution; the movement of cohorts through the life course under social conditions that differ for each generation makes change inevitable.

6. New technology acquired through discovery, invention, or diffusion is one of the most important sources of change. Cultural lag occurs when technology changes faster than other aspects of culture, as when medical technology raises moral questions that have yet to be resolved.

7. The rate of innovation in a society depends on existing knowledge, population size, the stability of social and physical environments, and the extent of contact with other societies.

8. A functional perspective views social change as an adaptive response to the strains that arise through normal activity in a society. When mothers enter the labor force in increasing numbers, for example, subsequent changes in beliefs, values, attitudes, and norms that apply to working mothers affect social cohesion and order.

9. The conflict perspective focuses on social change as the result of struggles between groups. This perspective would focus on protest as a source of changing beliefs, values, attitudes, and norms that apply to working mothers.

10. Early evolutionary theory drew on Darwin's theory of evolution and argued that societies progress toward superior forms. Some theorists believed that change is unilinear, always taking place in the same stages.

11. According to Spengler's cyclical theory, societies have periods that correspond to youth, middle- and old-age in humans. Sorokin believed that societies tend to overdevelop dominant cultural characteristics and then go into a period of decline.

12. More recent multilinear evolutionary theories show greater appreciation for the complexity of change. Lenski's theory suggests that social and biological evolution have much in common, especially their reliance on the accumulation and transmission of information.

13. Modernization theory attempts to describe the process through which societies change from traditional to modern, rural to urban, nonindustrial to industrial, simple to complex, and from primary, informal relationships to those that are predominantly secondary, formal and bureaucratic.

14. World-system theory argues that modernization is not a universal phenomenon but rather depends on the position a society occupies—core, semiperiphery, or periphery—in the world economic system. Dependent relationships between periphery and core societies, for example, often make it difficult if not impossible for periphery societies to modernize.

15. Social movements are organized, collective attempts to change or preserve some aspects of a social environment.

16. Classical theories have in common a reliance on the view that movements develop in order to

relieve psychological strain brought about by strain in the social environment. Frustration-aggression theory argues that relative deprivation leads to frustration, which in turn leads to social movements. Rising expectations as well as rapid improvement followed by sharp declines (the J-curve) have also been suggested as causes of frustration and social action.

17. According to Kornhauser, the existence of mass society in which people feel socially isolated produces feelings of anxiety, and people engage in collective behavior and social movements in order to relieve such feelings and restore a feeling of connection with others. This is similar to Smelser's theory of structural strain and collective behavior.

18. Classical theories have been criticized on many grounds, including their reliance on psychology to explain social phenomena; their failure to link changes in psychological states such as frustration and relative deprivation with the occurrence of collective behavior; and their failure to see the importance of social change as a major goal of social movements.

19. Resource mobilization theory focuses on social organization by explaining the development of social movements in terms of available resources.

20. Political process theory goes beyond resource mobilization and classical theory by looking at what goes on both within social movements and in their relationship to major social institutions. In this model, movements depend on opportunities, existing organizational resources, and a shared perception that collective behavior is legitimate and has some chance of success.

KEY TERMS

absolute deprivation   586
classical social movement
    theory   585
cultural lag   576
cyclical change   580
diffusion   576
discovery   576
ecological succession   573
frustration-aggression
    theory   586

immanent change   581
invention   576
J-curve   587
mass society theory   588
modernization   582
multilinear change   581
political process theory   590
reform   584
relative deprivation   586
resistance   585

resource mobilization
    theory   589
revolution   584
social evolution   580
social movement   584
unilinear change   580
world-system (dependency)
    theory   583

LOOKING ELSEWHERE

Having studied Chapter 23, you might want to look at related discussions in *Human Arrangements*, which include change and

- the importance of groups (Chapter 9, pp. 204–206)
- communities (Chapter 10, pp. 226–31)
- the class system (Chapter 12, pp. 292–93)
- race relations (Chapter 13, pp. 317–23)
- the civil rights movement (Chapter 13, pp. 317–22; 322–23)
- gender inequality (Chapter 14, pp. 351–58)
- the women's movement (Chapter 14, pp. 351–58)
- age inequality (Chapter 15, pp. 377–80)
- the family (Chapter 16, pp. 406–411)

- schools (Chapter 17, pp. 436–40)
- science and technology (Chapter 4, pp. 82–85; Chapter 18, pp. 443, 445–46, 452–54)
- scientific revolutions (Chapter 18, pp. 445–47)
- capitalism (Chapter 19, pp. 496–97)
- world-system theory and international inequality (Chapter 12, pp. 287–91; Chapter 19, pp. 492–95)
- the labor movement (Chapter 19, pp. 476–80, 482–84)
- political revolution (Chapter 20, pp. 521–23)
- revolution and political change (Chapter 20, pp. 521–23)
- religion (Chapter 21, pp. 546–49)

RECOMMENDED READINGS

Adam, B.D. 1987. *The rise of the gay and lesbian movement.* Boston: Twayne. A comprehensive study of the emergence and growth of the worldwide movement for gay and lesbian civil rights.

Chirot, D. 1977. *Social change in the twentieth century.* New York: Harcourt Brace Jovanovich. An interesting look at social change from a world-system perspective. See also his more recent book (1986). *Social change in the modern era* which changes many of his earlier views.

Freeman, J. (Ed.). 1983. *Social movements of the sixties and seventies.* New York: Longman. A penetrating look at the factors that affected the emergence and progress of 18 social movements of the 1960s and 1970s.

Gamson, W. A., Fireman, B., and Rytina, S. 1982. *Encounters with unjust authority.* Homewood, IL: Dorsey Press. An intriguing experimental study of what it takes for small groups to rebel against the unjust demands of those in authority.

Liebman, R. C., and Wuthnow, R. 1983. *The new Christian right.* New York: Aldine. A collection of essays that tries to explain why many conservative evangelicals have joined social movements to bring about political change in the U.S., and the significance of this political activism for both religion and politics.

Marsh, J. C., Geist, A., and Caplan, N. 1982. *Rape and the limits of law reform.* Boston: Auburn House. A case study that examines the effect of a radical rewriting of Michigan's sexual assault laws on the ways in which subsequent cases were handled. It illustrates the difficulty of bringing about change through legal reform in an area of entrenched beliefs and values such as those that surround gender and violence.

Nyden, P. W. 1984. *Steelworkers rank-and-file: The political economy of a union reform movement.* New York: Praeger. Based on interviews with dozens of union workers in a midwest steel plant, this excellent study shows how rank-and-file union members rebelled against authorities in an attempt to gain a voice in the affairs of their own union.

Price, J. 1982. *The antinuclear movement.* Boston: Twayne. A richly drawn portrait of the antinuclear movement, starting with its beginnings in the 1950s.

Robertson, C. C. 1984. *Sharing the same bowl: A socioeconomic history of women and class in Accra.* Bloomington: Indiana University Press. A book that adds an important piece to dependency and world-system theory by looking at the ways in which colonialism, capitalism, and peripheral status in the world system have changed the status of women in urban Africa.

Weller, R. P., and Guggenheim, S. E. (Eds.). 1982. *Power and protest in the countryside: Studies of rural unrest in Asia, Europe, and Latin America.* Durham, NC: Duke University Press Policy Studies. A collection of articles that explores protest and rebellion in the rural areas of a variety of societies.

APPENDIX A
A STUDENT RESEARCH GUIDE

At some point during your study of sociology, you may have to write a research paper, and this appendix will help you (see Figure A-1). You have probably never done original research; and even if you are an old hand at using libraries, sociology has its own resources, of which you should be aware before you start.

DECIDING WHAT YOU WANT TO KNOW

Whether you do your own research or use the results of someone else's in order to write a paper, you cannot get very far without a clear idea of what it is you want to know. Without a doubt, this is the most difficult part of research for most people, amateurs and professionals alike. Notice that saying, "I want to write a paper on the family" is not a statement of what you want to know; rather, it defines a general area within which lie hundreds of different topics.

One of the best ways to define a topic is to put it in the form of questions to which you can imagine clear answers. For example: How common is family violence in the U.S.? What kinds of families are the most prone to violence? How is the likelihood of violence affected by such things as the age of spouses and children, the employment status and relative earnings of wives and husbands, whether or not both parents are living at home, whether or not parents were victims of abuse as children? Is family violence more common in some societies than in others? Why? With each of these questions, you can have a clear idea of what you are looking for—an idea you cannot have with something like "I want to write a paper on the family."

Once you have made up clear, specific questions, you will probably still have to narrow your topic even further since you are working at a disadvantage that you do not share with most other researchers: College terms rarely last more than 12 or 13 weeks, and you may have less than a month to complete your work. Any one of the questions in the preceding paragraph could lead to a substantial term paper.

DESIGNING YOUR RESEARCH

Once you have decided what you want to know, the next thing to do is to plan how you are going to go after it. You may decide to use only published sources or you may supplement this by gathering new information. You might be interested in finding out just how prevalent family violence is in the U.S. As part of your research, you would use the library to review what is known about family violence. You might want to supplement this, however, by doing a survey of students in your college in order to find out how many of them come from families in which violence has taken place during the past year.

FIGURE A-1   Steps in the Research Process

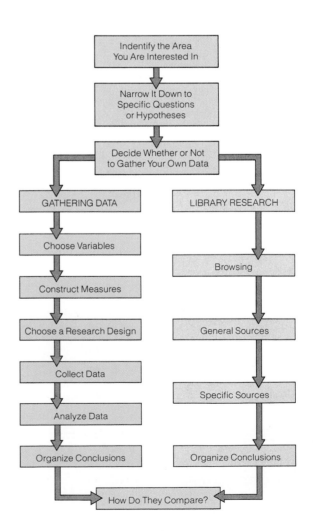

If you decide to supplement library research with your own fieldwork, I suggest that you assume that it will take you at least twice as long to do your fieldwork as you think it will. This is not meant to discourage you from gathering your own data—far from it. There are few things as exciting in academic work as doing your own research. It is meant to help you to be realistic about the time constraints you are probably working under. Writing questionnaires and having them duplicated, distributed, returned, tabulated, and analyzed takes a lot of time. One excellent way to deal with this problem—if your professor allows it—is to work in teams of two or three students so that you can divide the labor.

HOW TO USE A LIBRARY

Many people go through their entire educational career without realizing what extraordinary resources libraries and their staffs are. To use a library well, however, you will first have to get to know your way around it.

The first thing you have to know is how a library is laid out. In writing this book, I have spent a great deal of time just wandering through the stacks of my library, getting a sense of what is located where. You will find that most sociology books are shelved in the same general area, and you can get an excellent feel for any discipline by spending an hour or so just browsing. You can benefit from this both in getting to know the field as a whole and in becoming familiar with specific areas within it, such as demography, the sociology of gender, stratification, urban studies, or the family. How do you find out what is where? Ask a librarian. Most librarians are justifiably proud of their libraries and are more than happy to show people how to use them.

Some subjects will be catalogued in several locations. You will find sources that discuss family violence under sociology as well as anthropology, psychology, and government studies that treat family violence as a problem in law enforcement.

Whether or not you decide to gather data of your own, at some point you should make yourself aware of what others have found and had to say about the topic you are investigating. Out of the millions of books and articles contained in many libraries, you need ways of locating just the ones that are most likely to help you understand the relatively narrow subject you have selected.

General Sources

The most obvious place for you to begin is with the references in *Human Arrangements*, provided that this book discusses the topic you are interested in. The section in Chapter 16 on family violence indicates several recent sources. Rather than spend hours finding them on your own, take advantage of the fact that I have already done some of your work for you—just as other authors did some of my work for me.

Another place to look is a general source such as an encyclopedia. In addition to widely known ones such as *Britannica*, there is the *International Encyclopedia of the Social Sciences*, which contains hundreds of articles written by specialists. Although it is a bit dated for some purposes (it was published in 1977, with biographical update volumes), for general background discussions of major concepts and areas of the social sciences it is an excellent resource.

You might also look at recent issues of *Annual Review of Sociology*, a hardbound book containing reviews of entire areas of sociological inquiry. If you are lucky enough to find a recent review of your area of interest, it can save you a great deal of time.

Specific Sources in Sociology

Sociological articles appear in a number of journals (see Table A-1), and you should familiarize yourself with them. An hour or so spent browsing through the tables of contents for the previous year can give you a good idea of the kinds of subjects found in each.

Tracking Down Sources

There are several ways to find scholarly writings. Card catalogues usually consist of two sections. One lists books by author and title and the other lists them by subject. If you are doing a project on family violence, for example, you might look under "family," "violence," "domestic violence," or "child abuse." In general, it is best to go after the most recent titles, since they are likely to include summaries of previously published research.

In addition to the card catalogue, there are books in the reference department that you can use to locate books and articles about a particular subject. The multivolume annual *Books in Print* lists all currently published books by subject, author, and title, and it can be a useful guide to books that your library does not own but which may be obtained through

TABLE A-1   Useful Journals in Sociological Research
MAJOR SOCIOLOGICAL JOURNALS
American Sociological Review *American Journal of Sociology* *Social Forces*
MORE SPECIALIZED JOURNALS IN SOCIOLOGY
Contemporary Sociology (book reviews) *Journal of Marriage and the Family* *Journal of Health and Social Behavior* *Public Opinion Quarterly* *Social Problems* *Sociology of Education* *Demography* *Population Studies*
JOURNALS IN SOCIAL PSYCHOLOGY
Social Psychology Quarterly *Journal of Experimental Social Psychology* *Journal of Applied Social Psychology* *Journal of Abnormal and Social Psychology* *Personality and Social Psychology*

interlibrary loan systems. The *Social Science Index* and *Sociological Abstracts* are published each year and contain brief descriptions of every article and book of interest to sociologists. There are similar volumes for other areas, such as education, psychology, and crime. As before, begin with the most recent year and work backward. Most reference departments also have a variety of annotated bibliographies: books that describe articles and books that focus on a particular subject, such as blacks or women. These can be enormously useful.

For some topics, none of these sources will provide you with information, and this often happens when you are interested in a subject that focuses on recent events. If you cannot find what you need in scholarly sources, turn to the *Reader's Guide to Periodical Literature*, which is published each year and gives listings by subject of articles that appear in magazines such as *Newsweek*. In addition, newspapers of record, such as the *New York Times* and the London *Times*, publish annual indexes that list every person, event, or subject that has appeared in their newspapers. Be careful when using popular sources such as those found in the *Reader's Guide*, however, for they are not generally bound by the same rigorous scientific standards that sociologists try to follow.

Finding Statistical Information

Perhaps the best source of statistical information about the U.S. is the federal government. Some libraries are Government Document Depositories which contain most major documents published by the federal government (and usually have a documents librarian to help you find them). The Census Bureau publishes not only the results of the census but also the periodic *Current Population Reports*, whose surveys cover such important areas as race, income and poverty, marital status and living arrangements, divorce and marriage, and migration.

The National Center for Health Statistics publishes detailed information on births, deaths, marriages, and divorces each year, often broken down by race, gender, and age. The Department of Labor publishes highly detailed reports on work and earnings, and the Justice Department reports on crime and law enforcement.

If you do not have access to a depository library, the best source is the annual *Statistical Abstract of the United States*, which presents highlights of all federal statistics, with supplements from other sources as well. In addition, the federal government publishes other excellent statistical source books, including *Historical Statistics of the United States from Colonial Times to 1970* and *Social Indicators*, the latter being a series of volumes that periodically report on selected social conditions and trends with some comparative data from other countries.

Many libraries also own annual volumes of the Gallup Opinion Poll Index (usually found in the reference section), which lists each question asked along with the responses, which are often broken down by characteristics such as age, gender, race, religion, education, or income.

For statistical information about countries in addition to the U.S., the best source is the United Nations, especially its *Demographic Yearbook*, which contains the most complete and accurate information available on the social, political, and economic conditions of all countries belonging to the United Nations. For more recent information on issues related to population, a good source is the Population Reference Bureau, whose current, inexpensive publications are available at Box 35012, Washington, DC 20013.

APPENDIX B
USING SAMPLES: A PRIMER ON STATISTICAL INFERENCE

Researchers often try to describe very large populations, such as the adult population of the United States, with the results of surveys that involve only a relatively small sample, such as 1,300 to 1,500 people. If you have ever followed a national election, you know that such polls can predict results with astonishing accuracy. How is this possible? The procedure is called **statistical inference**. It involves some sophisticated mathematics that we will not go into here; but you can get some idea of the reasoning behind it by considering the following example.

Suppose you shoot dice with Fred (using his dice) and he rolls a total of "7" three times in a row. "Lucky throws," you think. Then he rolls three more 7s, for a total of six straight. "*Very* lucky," you think. "Maybe *too* lucky." As Fred keeps rolling 7s, you begin to doubt the "fairness" of the dice, and at some point you will conclude that something is fishy with the dice, and perhaps with Fred.

Without knowing it, you are performing some sophisticated statistical reasoning. You start with a **null hypothesis**, a testable assumption that both dice are "fair," which means that on each throw, all numbers have an equal chance to come up. You then watch the dice, and after a sample of three rolls, you note the result: "all 7s." At this point, there are two possibilities: (1) the dice are fair (the null hypothesis is correct) and Fred is lucky, or (2) a fair pair of dice would hardly ever give a total of "7" three times in a row, and the null hypothesis is wrong. After only three rolls, you would most likely choose the first possibility.

With a sample of ten rolls of all 7s, however, the second possibility looks more likely: A fair pair of dice would almost never give you ten 7s in a row. Therefore, the dice are *almost certainly* loaded.

"But," protests Fred, "ten 7s in a row isn't *impossible* with fair dice."

"True," you reply, "but if I call the dice loaded, *the chances are mighty slim that I'm wrong.*"

This last statement is an example of statistical inference, and it is the key to the use of samples to draw conclusions about populations. Theoretically the population of all possible throws of a pair of dice is not just very large, it is *infinitely* large (we could keep throwing dice forever); but instead we use a sample of only ten throws to draw a conclusion about the population that consists of "all possible throws of a pair of dice."

Scientists in many disciplines use samples to test ideas. Physicians testing a new drug begin with the assumption that the drug is useless. They administer it to a sample of people and find, perhaps, that it is effective half the time. They then must choose between two possibilities: (1) the drug is in fact useless and its effectiveness in half the cases was a fluke or (2) a useless drug is very unlikely to be effective half the time; therefore, it must be a useful drug. The key here is the phrase "very unlikely" (and this is where the sophisticated mathematics comes in): *if the sample is properly selected, it is possible to mathematically calculate the chances that a useless drug would be effective half the time simply by chance.*

This is essentially how pollsters predict election winners long before all the votes are in. If they draw a sample that shows candidate Mary Jones the winner, they start with the assumption that, at best, the election will end in a tie when all votes are counted. They then ask, "How likely is it that Jones would win in a sample we drew from a population in which she actually has no more votes than her opponent? (the same reasoning as "How likely are ten 7s with a pair of fair dice?"). If this possibility is very *un*likely, they reject the assumption that at best Jones will tie, and predict her victory.

There are four important points to be made here. First, when scientists draw conclusions from samples, there is always a possibility that they are wrong (just as ten 7s in a row is possible, however improbable it is). The mathematics of statistical inference, however, allows researchers to know just how likely such a mistake is. When election predictors say, "It's too close to call," they are in effect saying that if they predict a winner, the chances of being wrong are unacceptably high.

Second, they can make such statements only if they can *calculate* the chance of making an error, and this can only be done with samples selected so that every member of the population has an equal chance of being included. With "haphazard" samples there is no way to draw a conclusion and calculate the chances of making a mistake. They might be right; they might be wrong. More than that, they cannot say.

In the 1936 U.S. presidential election, the *Literary Digest* selected a sample of adults from telephone directories and found overwhelming support for Republican Alfred Landon among its two million replies. The magazine predicted an easy victory over his Democratic opponent, Franklin Roosevelt. George Gallup, however, used a far smaller sample and correctly predicted Roosevelt's victory. What happened?

The *Literary Digest* violated the most important principle of scientific sampling when it used telephone directories to select its sample. During the Depression, only middle- and upper-class people could afford telephones, and such people tended to vote Republican. Less affluent people, on the other hand, heavily favored Roosevelt and were never considered for the *Digest* sample. By using scientific techniques to draw his sample, Gallup accurately predicted the outcome with a far smaller sample.

Third, note that the conclusion, "Jones will win the election" rests on the *rejection of other possible outcomes*. This illustrates a basic aspect of scientific research. We cannot explain something merely by finding an explanation that "fits the facts," because there may be many competing explanations that also might "fit the facts." The only way to prove a theory, then, is to systematically eliminate every alternative theory. To test the theory that employers discriminate against women by paying them less than men for doing the same work, we must first eliminate alternative explanations—men are more competent, have more experience or higher educations. Only if we eliminate all possible alternative causes of pay differences, can we attribute any differences in earnings to discrimination.

Fourth, statistical inferences must be carefully interpreted. When a drug company tests its toothpaste against competing brands, it selects samples of children. One group uses "Brand A" and the other uses "Brand B," and after several years, the two groups are compared. The null hypothesis in this case is: "There is no difference between the two Brands." Suppose the Brand A group has fewer cavities than the Brand B group. Does this mean Brand A is better?

The problem is that it is possible to have two equally effective products produce differences *by chance* in a sample of users (just as it is possible to get six 7s in a row with a fair pair of dice). Researchers then use the mathematics of statistical inference to answer the question: "Could the difference between the two groups have occurred simply by chance?" Suppose they conclude the following: "It's *very* unlikely that two samples using equally effective toothpastes would differ this much simply by chance.

Therefore, the two brands must *not* be equally effective: Brand A is better."

Such conclusions are frequently presented as "Children using Brand A had *significantly* fewer cavities." This is where caution is needed, for to most people, "significant" means "important" or "substantial"; but scientific "significance" has a much narrower meaning. To say that two groups are "significantly different" means *only* that we are very certain they are not exactly the same. By itself, it does *not* mean that the difference is either large or important.

Many studies show that when punishment is swift and certain, crime rates tend to fall. The swiftness and certainty of punishment have "significant effects" on crime rates. While this is an important finding, it is also important to ask, "How much of an effect?" The answer, disappointingly, is, "Not very much" (Tittle 1975). Whenever you read a scientific report that refers to "significant differences," be sure to search for statements that indicate the actual magnitude of the difference.

Used correctly, samples and statistical inference are very efficient research tools, for they enable us to study populations that would otherwise be too large to study at all.

GLOSSARY

Aberrant behavior (aberrance)   Behavior that violates norms in secret and for personal gain. **239**

Absolute deprivation   A lack of basic necessities relative to a fixed standard such as the amount of food necessary for survival. **586**

Achieved status   A status entered after birth and usually due at least in part to individual behavior. **48**

Acquired status   (See **Achieved status**.) **48**

Acting collective behavior   Crowd or mass behavior oriented to specific goals. **557**

Ageism   Prejudice based on age. **363**

Age structure   The relative number of people of each age in a population. **78**

Aggregate   A collection of people who happen to be in the same place at the same time. **86** (See also **Situational status**.)

Agrarian society   A society in which agriculture is the primary means of subsistence. **83**

Alienation   The psychological condition in which individuals feel detached from work, social relationships, and the results of their own behavior. **293, 486**

Aligning action   An action that signals an actor's acceptance of a new definition of the situation. **174**

Amalgamation   The combination of several cultures in a society to produce a new culture. **302**

Ancestor worship   The religious worship of ancestors based on the belief that they possess supernatural power. **548**

Androcracy   A social system organized around the principle of male dominance. **341**

Androgyny   The combining of masculine and feminine personality traits in a single individual. **352**

Animism   A religion based on the belief that spirits and ghosts inhabit sacred objects such as trees and rocks. **532**

Anomalies   Scientifc findings that either contradict or cannot be explained by a paradigm. **445**

Anomie   A social condition in which members of groups, communities, or societies no longer feel allegiance to norms. **251**

Anthropology   The study of culture in small, preindustrial societies.

Anticipatory socialization   The process of learning how to perform a role attached to a status we do not yet occupy. **148**

Apartheid   South Africa's policy of racial discrimination and segregation. **289**

Ascribed status   A status assigned at birth. **48**

Assimilation   The conformity of members of ethnic groups to the culture of the dominant group. **302**

Attitudes   Positive or negative evaluations of people, objects, or situations that often predispose people to feel and behave positively or negatively toward them. **39**

Audience segregation   In the dramaturgical approach to interaction, the effort by social actors to keep their "frontstage" and "backstage" selves separate. **174**

Authoritarian power structure   A power structure in which power is concentrated in the hands of a relative few. **190**

Authoritarianism   The degree to which the state controls the lives of its citizens. **508**

Authority   Power assigned according to norms and generally accepted as legitimate by those over whom it is exercised. **57, 502**

Autocracy   A state ruled by a single person. **508**

Automation   The replacement of human labor with machines. **478**

Backstage   In the dramaturgical approach, the place where players are freed from the requirements of a particular role. **174**

Balance theory   A theoretical perspective on social interaction that suggests that people organize their perceptions of people and objects into units and strive for some consistency in the positive and negative feelings among them. **178**

Behavioral approach (to learning)   A theoretical approach to learning and behavior that focuses on the importance of reward, punishment, and conditioning. **138**

Beliefs   Statements about what is real. **30**

Bias   The tendency of research results to be in error in one respect more than in any other. **117**

Bilateral descent   Kinship arrangements in which descent is traced through both the mother's and father's blood relatives. **388**

Bilocal marriage   A kinship system in which married couples must live near or in the household of the wife's mother or the husband's father. **391**

Biological determinism   The belief that individual differences are biologically caused and, therefore, unchangeable.

Birth cohort   People who share the same period of birth. **79**

Birth rate   The number of children born each year for every thousand members of a population. **67**

Blue-collar   Referring to occupations that primarily involve manual work. **271**

Boundary   The specification of who may occupy a particular status. The clarity of boundaries describes how easily people can tell who occupies a status. The openness of boundaries refers to how easy it is for individuals to occupy a particular status. **53**

Bourgeoisie   (See **Capitalist**.)

Bureaucracy   A complex set of formal, secondary relationships in which (1) entry into statuses is controlled by rigid norms; (2) people specialize in narrowly-defined tasks; (3) roles are rigidly defined by rules; (4) power is distributed in a clear hierarchy; (5) managers specialize in making sure everything works according to the rules; and (6) decisions are based on rational considerations of the organization's best interests rather than on personal feelings of individuals. **193**

Capital   Means of production such as machinery that is owned by those who hire others to produce wealth in exchange for wages. **473**

Capitalism   An economic system in which the means of production are privately owned and in which workers produce goods in exchange for wages. **473**

Capitalist   A person who owns or controls capital. **268**

Case study   A research design that focuses on a single example rather than a representative sample. **118**

Caste   A social category in a stratification system in which membership depends on ascribed statuses and cannot be changed after birth. **283**

Casual collective behavior   Crowd or mass behavior that involves no common goal or purpose around which people interact. **557**

Census   A gathering of information on all members of a population. **117**

Charismatic authority   Authority based on the belief that a particular individual possesses special abilities or characteristics. **502**

Church   The second most powerful religious institution, with a broad membership that includes a majority of the members of a society, a formally trained and bureaucratic clergy, governed by legal-rational and traditional authority, focusing on highly abstract unemotional ritual, and often although not always allied with the ruling class. **536**

Circular reaction   In Blumer's theory of collective behavior, the belief that people copy one another and amplify their emotional state in the process. **562**

Civil disobedience   The deliberate and open violation of a norm for the purpose of changing it. **506**

Civil law   A norm that regulates social relationships in order to prevent or undo the negative effects of particular acts.

Civil religion   A set of cultural ideas, symbols, and practices oriented to the direct worship of a society by its members. **548**

Class consciousness   An awareness among members of a social class of the true extent and social causes of inequality in a society. **292**

Classical social movement theory   A theory (including several specific approaches) based on the following general model: some kind of strain or disturbance in the social environment (such as an economic depression) creates disruptive psychological states in individuals (such as anxiety) and individuals then channel their energy into social movements in order to relieve their emotional difficulties. **585**

Coalition   A subgroup whose members join forces in order to increase their control over group process. **171**

Coercive power   Power that lacks the social legitimacy of authority and is based on fear and the use of force. **503**

Cognitive development perspective   A theoretical perspective on socialization that focuses on the growth of mental abilities to make increasingly complex judgments about ourselves as well as our physical and social environments. **139**

Cohort   (See **Birth cohort**.) **79**

Cohort effect   Effects on people's lives that arise from the characteristics of the historical periods during which they experienced stages of life such as childhood or middle age. **373**

Collective behavior   The relatively unstructured behavior of people in crowds and masses. **556**

Collective conscience   Durkheim's term for the moral consensus that is violated by deviant acts. **237**

Collectivity   A set of people who share a culture and think of themselves as a unit, but generally do not interact with one another. **196**

Colonialism   The relationship between countries in which one dominates the other and exploits its natural and human resources. **290**

Commodity   A good or service produced primarily for its exchange value, not for direct consumption by the producer. **471**

Communal economy   An economy based on collective ownership of means of production, primary ties, and sharing.

Communication structure   The pattern of frequency and duration of interaction among participants in a social system. **58**

Communism   An economic system in which the means of production are communally owned and there is no state. **492**

Communism, norm of   A norm that requires scientists to share their findings with one another. **448**

Community   A social system, usually identified with a particular geographic territory, in which a population lives and carries out the major activities of their lives. **209**

Compound family   A nuclear family in which children are directly related to only one of the parents. **393**

Compound status   A status consisting of one or more statuses joined together as one—as "policeman" joins occupation with gender.

Concentric-zone theory   A theory of urban land use according to which cities develop in rings around a core of business activity; outer rings are higher in class than inner rings. **225**

Conflict perspective A theoretical perspective that focuses on the struggle among different social groups over scarce rewards. **100**

Conformity Behavior or appearance consistent with norms. **235**

Conglomerate A collection of companies in different industries that are owned by a single corporation. **480**

Conspicuous consumption Consumption intended to affirm or enhance an individual's prestige. **281**

Constant A behavior or characteristic that does not vary from one observation to another.

Contagion In Le Bon's theory of collective behavior, the process through which people uncritically copy one another's behavior, setting off a chain reaction. **562**

Content analysis Analysis of words and images contained in written, spoken, and visual media. **123**

Control group A group of people in an experiment who are not exposed to the experimental stimulus under study. **120**

Control variable A variable introduced into a statistical analysis to see if a statistical relationship holds among people who are alike on a particular characteristic. **126**

Conventional collective behavior Crowd or mass behavior that involves a specific common purpose such as watching a parade. **557**

Convergence theory Le Bon's belief that crowds consist of like-minded people who assemble in one place. **561**

Core society In world-system theory, a society that is in an economically dominant position. **493**

Correlation A measure of association that indicates the strength of the relationship between two variables. **128**

Coup d'état An attempt to illegally replace one government with another, often through the use of force. **522**

Crime Acts that violate laws regarded as relatively serious. **241**

Crime rate The number of crimes per year per thousand people in a population.

Criminal justice system A set of institutions including police, courts, and prisons. **247**

Criminal law A law that links specific acts with punishments.

Cross-cultural method Research that tries to identify the origins of cultural ideas, social structures, or ecological arrangements by comparing different societies. **124**

Crowd A relatively temporary collection of people who happen to be in the same place at the same time in close enough proximity to one another so that they can interact with and be affected by one another. **556**

Crude birth rate (See **Birth rate**.) **67**

Crude death rate (See **Death rate**.) **69**

Cult A relatively temporary religious group whose members are generally recruited among poor people in a state of emotional crisis, which has an informal, loosely

organized structure governed by charismatic leadership, involves no formal rituals, relies on emotional displays during ceremonies, and actively rejects major social institutions. **538**

Cultural determinism The belief that individual differences are caused by socialization and are, therefore, changeable.

Cultural relativism A concept that refers to the fact that the importance of a particular cultural idea varies from one society or subgroup to another. **40**

Cultural universal An element of culture—such as dance—found in all societies. **40**

Culture The accumulated sum of symbols, ideas, and material products associated with life in a social system. **25**

Culture lag An instance in which technological change occurs before cultural norms and values can be introduced to govern its use. **576**

Cyclical theory of social change The theory that the development of societies occurs in cycles (rather than a straight line) that parallel the lives of individuals. Societies are born, mature, age, and die. **580**

Death rate The number of people who die in a given year for every thousand people in a population. **69**

Decision theory A theoretical perspective that views collective behavior—and human behavior in general—as the result of rational attempts to solve problems. **563**

De facto segregation Segregation that is an unintended consequence of social or ecological arrangements. **312**

Definition of the situation The determination of which statuses and roles are relevant in a social situation. **104, 165**

Degradation ceremony An important part of the socialization process in total institutions, in which inmates are subjected to humiliation and labeled as inferior. **250**

De jure segregation Segregation that is required by law. **312**

Democracy A social system in which power is evenly distributed. **190, 506**

Democratic structure see **Democracy**. **190**

Democratic socialism see **State capitalism.**

Demographic transition A theory describing the pattern of falling death and birth rates that has characterized the recent history of industrialized countries. **74**

Demography The study of the size, composition, growth, and distribution of human populations. **66**

Denomination The third most powerful type of religious institution, with a membership generally dominated by a single social class, a formal but not bureaucratic role structure, a trained clergy, traditional authority, abstract relatively unemotional ritual, and a condition of coexistence between it and dominant political and economic institutions. **537**

Dependency theory (See **World-system theory**.)

Dependent variable A variable affected by another variable. **126**

Deviance   Any behavior or appearance that violates a norm. **235**

Differential association (theory)   A theory of deviance that argues that in the socialization process people vary in the norms and values they feel allegiance to because they are not equally exposed to the same norms and values. **254**

Diffusion   The process through which elements of culture spread from one society to another. **576**

Discovery   An instance of finding out about something that already exists. **576**

Discrimination   Positive or negative behavior based on stereotyped beliefs about the occupants of a status. **316**

Disinterestedness, norm of   A norm that requires scientists to not allow personal or other nonscientific interests to influence their work. **448**

Division of labor   The allocation of different roles among positions in a social system.

Divorced family   A family structure in which the parents are divorced and yet are still part of an ongoing family system. **393**

Dramaturgy (dramaturgical approach)   The study of social interaction as theater in which actors play roles before audiences. **104, 174**

Dual economy   An economy that is part monopolistic and part competitive. **484**

Dyad   A pair of social actors. **171**

Dysfunction   The interference of an aspect of a social system with the maintenance or adaptation of that system or its values. **98**

Ecclesia   The most powerful of religious institutions, including most members of a society, dominated by a formal and bureaucratic clergy, governed by legal-rational and traditional authority, focusing on highly abstract ritual, and closely identified with dominant political and economic institutions. **536**

Ecological succession   The process through which ecosystems change. **573**

Ecology   The study of the relationship between populations and physical environments, including the ability to use natural resources and technology. **66**

Economic institutions   Enduring arrangements of cultural ideas and social relationships through which goods and services are produced and distributed in societies. **470**

Ecosystem   All forms of life that live in relation to one another and a shared physical environment. **81**

Education   The systematic formal transmission of skills, knowledge, beliefs, values, attitudes, and norms. **416**

Egalitarian family (marriage)   A family in which authority is evenly divided between husbands and wives. **395**

Emergent norm theory   A theory of collective behavior that tries to explain how patterns of expectation and interaction emerge in crowds that involve no prior planning. **563**

Emigrant   Someone who moves out of a territory. **76**

Endemic disease   A disease normally found in a population. **71**

Endogamy   The practice of requiring people to marry someone belonging to their own social group or community. **391**

Epidemic disease   A disease not normally found in a population, which spreads rapidly. **71**

Epidemiology   The study of where diseases come from, how they are distributed geographically and socially, and how they are transmitted from one place or person to another. **71**

Ethicalist religion   A religion that focuses more on sets of abstract ideals than on supernatural powers vested in gods, objects, or animals. **533**

Ethnic group   A set of people who identify with a common cultural heritage.

Ethnicism   Prejudice based on ethnicity. **300**

Ethnicity   A concept that refers to statuses based on a shared cultural heritage. **298**

Ethnocentrism   The tendency of people to assume that ideas and practices of other cultures are incorrect, if not inferior. **40**

Ethnomethodology   The study of the unspoken rules and meanings through which people define and sustain a social situation. **106**

Evolutionary theories of social change   Theories that argue that all societies develop along predetermined paths that take them from inferior to superior forms, from simple to complex, and from "primitive" to "civilized."

Exchange theory   An approach to social interaction that focuses on how people exchange one thing for another in social relationships. **176**

Exchange value   The attribution of value to goods or services based upon how much can be gotten for them in exchange for other goods and services. **471**

Exogamy   The practice of requiring people to marry someone outside their own social group or community. **391**

Experiment   A research design in which similar groups of subjects are exposed to conditions that differ in only one respect (the independent variable) in order to establish cause-and-effect relationships. **120**

Expressive collective behavior   Crowd or mass behavior that focuses on the expression of feelings toward some common object or event. **557**

Expressive leader   A leader who focuses on maintaining harmony among members. **190**

Expulsion   A form of social oppression in which minorities are forced to leave their communities or societies. **313**

Extended family   A family that includes a nuclear family plus additional relatives such as grandparents, aunts, or cousins. **393**

External causes   In social attribution, aspects of people's social situations that are used to explain their behavior. **166**

Extrapolation An estimate of future conditions based on the assumption that "current trends will continue."

Extrinsic reward A reward given to someone by someone else.

Fad A short-lived standard of appearance or behavior marked by great enthusiasm among its followers. **558**

False consciousness A state of unawareness of, or misperception of, social conditions and their causes, especially when applied to social stratification. **276**

Family A primary group organized around kinship ties and designed to regulate sexual behavior and reproduce, nurture, protect, and socialize the young. **386**

Family disorganization The result of unoccupied statuses or inadequately performed roles within a family.

Fashion A temporary standard of appearance or behavior considered to be socially acceptable or desirable. **557**

Femininity A set of beliefs describing the ideal female. **331**

Feminism A theoretical and ideological framework that directly opposes sexism by supporting gender equality. **352** (See **Liberal feminism**; **Socialist feminism**; **Radical feminism**.)

Feudalism The social system that characterized medieval Europe and other preindustrial societies, based upon mutual obligation between nobility and serfs. **471**

Field experiment A non-laboratory experiment. **121**

Folkways The set of manners and customary acts that characterize everyday life in a social system. **34**

Forces of production The combination of raw materials, means of production, technology, energy, knowledge, skill, and labor that go into the production of goods and services. **469**

Formal organization A social system that exists for a specific purpose and is dominated by social relationships governed by clearly stated, rigidly enforced norms. **193**

Formal relationship A relationship governed by norms that rigidly control interactions among status occupants.

Formal sanction A clearly defined reward or punishment with specific people authorized to deliver it. **37**

Front In the dramaturgical approach, a person's physical appearance and behavior, that helps define the situation. **174**

Frontstage In the dramaturgical approach, the place where roles are performed before an audience. **174**

Frustration-aggression theory A theory that argues that collective behavior is an aggressive response to feelings of frustration. **586**

Function A contribution of a characteristic of a social system and the maintenance and adaptation of that system and its values. **98**

Functional perspective A theoretical perspective that focuses on the ways in which cultural ideas and social structures contribute to or interfere with the maintenance or adaptation of a social system. **98**

Game theory A theoretical perspective that views collective behavior—and human behavior in general—as an attempt by people to maximize rewards while minimizing costs. **564**

Gatherer-hunter society A society in which subsistence needs are met primarily by gathering existing vegetation and hunting wild game.

Gemeinschaft A concept that describes communities in which social cohesion is based on primary relationships, shared culture, and similarity of life experience. **220** (Referred to by Durkheim as **Mechanical solidarity**.)

Gender Social statuses to which males and females are assigned in a society. **328**

Gender role A role that applies to people of different genders. **329**

Generalized belief In Smelser's theory of collective behavior, an irrational belief seized upon as a way of justifying behavior and reducing uncertainty and feelings of anxiety.

Generalized other Our perception of the role expectations that generally apply to people in a particular social situation. **143**

Genocide The systematic attempt to kill all occupants of a particular status, especially ethnic, religious, racial, or national. **313**

Gentrification A process of community change through which housing in old neighborhoods is restored, often resulting in higher rents and the displacement of previous tenants who can no longer afford to live there. **230**

Gerontocracy A society ruled by an elderly elite. **370**

Gesellschaft A concept that describes communities in which social cohesion is based on secondary relationships and interdependencies created by complex divisions of labor. **220** (Referred to by Durkheim as **Organic solidarity**.)

Gesture An action that has symbolic meaning. **26**

Government The collection of people who happen to occupy positions of authority within the framework of social relationships that define the state. **503**

Group Two or more people who interact with each other in patterned ways and are identified as members. **8**

Group effectiveness The extent to which a group accomplishes the goals it sets for itself. **198**

Group process What group members actually do, regardless of role expectations. **197**

Groupthink An example of group process in which a shared desire for consensus outweighs members' better judgment. **199**

Hawthorne effect A distortion of research results caused by the response of subjects to the special attention they receive from researchers. **186**

Hidden curriculum In schools, knowledge, values, attitudes, norms, and beliefs that people acquire because of the educational process that is used to learn something else. **421**

Historical (analysis) research The use of historical

Historical (analysis) research (*continued*) documents to analyze the development and change of social systems. **123**

Horticultural society A society in which subsistence needs are met primarily through cultivation of small gardens without the use of the plow. **83**

Hospice An organization designed to care for the terminally ill. **377**

Hunter-gatherer society (See **Gatherer-hunter society**). **83**

Hypothesis A statement that predicts a relationship between variables. **126**

Hysteria A state of rapidly spreading anxiety that affects people in crowds and masses. **559**

I Mead's concept that refers to that part of us that directly experiences ourselves and others. **143**

Ideal self Our image of ourselves as we believe we ought to be. **147**

Ideal type A concept that describes a "pure" analytical type that does not actually exist. **220**

Ideology A set of interrelated beliefs, values, attitudes, and norms that are used to explain and/or justify change or preservation of the status quo. **276**

Immanent change Sorokin's principle that cultures have material and nonmaterial characteristics that cause societies to develop in certain directions. **581**

Immigrant Someone who moves into a territory. **76**

Incest taboo A norm that forbids sexual contact between people who are culturally defined as kin.

Income Money that people receive each year. **280**

Independence The condition in which one variable has no effect on another. **125**

Independent primary (labor market) jobs In the primary labor market, jobs that involve relatively high levels of creativity, autonomy, and power. **473**

Independent variable A variable considered to cause variation in a second variable. **125**

In-depth interview A survey method designed to collect extensive information from each respondent. **118**

Infant mortality rate The number of infants under the age of one who die in a given year for every 1,000 births that occur during that year. **67**

Informal relationship A relationship governed by flexible, implicit norms.

Informal sanction A loosely defined reward or punishment with no specific people authorized to impose it. **37**

In-group A group in which members share a sense of "we-ness" that often excludes and devalues outsiders. **189**

Innovation A form of deviance in which a person accepts values but uses deviant ways to achieve them. **239**

Institution An enduring set of cultural ideas and social relationships that are designed to accomplish one or more goals. **60**

Instrumental leader A leader who focusses on achieving goals in a social system. **190**

Insulation The practice of managing our role performances so that role partners cannot observe our behavior in two or more conflicting roles. **52**

Integration The degree to which members of groups in a community are distributed according to their relative numbers. **322**

Interaction (See **Social interaction**.) **161**

Interactionist perspective A theoretical perspective that focuses on the causes and consequences of social behavior, based on the importance of assigning symbolic meaning to appearance, behavior, and experience. **103**

Interest group An organization that attempts to affect political decisions by supporting candidates sympathetic to their interests and by influencing those already in positions of authority. **514**

Intergenerational mobility When the class position of children differs from that of their parents.

Internal causes In social attribution, personal motives, abilities, and emotional states used to explain behavior. **166**

Internal migration Migration within a social system.

International migration Migration between social systems.

International stratification Systematic patterns of inequality among societies.

Interview A method of gathering data through which people are asked a series of questions. **118**

Intrinsic reward A reward that people give to themselves.

Invention Something created from things that already exist. **576**

Iron rule of oligarchy Michels' theory that all states inevitably become oligarchies.

Isolation The degree to which groups do not live in the same communities. **322**

J-curve theory A theory of social movements that argues that movements are most likely to occur when a period of rising expectations is followed by sharp and rapidly worsening conditions for members of deprived groups. **587**

Juvenile delinquency Criminal acts committed by minors.

Kin People bound together by ties of ancestry, adoption, or marriage.

Kinship Social relationships based on common ancestry, adoption, or marriage. **387**

Labor The production of goods or services that can either be used directly or exchanged. **268**

Labor market segmentation The division of job markets into distinct parts to which access is unequally distributed among workers. **484**

Labor power The potential to produce goods—usually measured in terms of time—which workers sell to employers in return for wages. **269**

Language A collection of symbols (words) and rules for their usage (syntax and grammar). **27**

Latent consequence An unintended effect of a characteristic of a social system on the maintenance or adaptation of that system and its values. **98**

Latent status A status not included in the definition of a situation, but which nonetheless may affect the expectations of the participants. **51**

Law A norm with formal sanctions. **37**

Leadership The exercise of authority. **190**

Legal-rational authority Power based on culturally defined rules that regulate social interaction. **502**

Liberal feminism A branch of feminism that argues that gender equality can be achieved without challenging men as a group or changing basic economic and political arrangements such as capitalism. Equality is primarily a matter of gaining equal legal rights and equal access to higher level statuses. **352**

Life course The culturally defined "normal" set of passages from one age category to another. **362**

Life expectancy The average number of remaining years people can expect to live if current death rates remain unchanged throughout their lifetime. **69**

Lifetime mobility The degree to which individuals change class position within their lifetimes.

Lobbyist A representative of an interest group who meets with government officials and tries to influence decisions by providing information and arguments that tend to support the goals of the group. **515**

Longitudinal (study) survey A research design in which information is gathered from the same sample of people at specified intervals of time. **119**

Looking-glass self Our perception of how other people perceive and evaluate us. **145**

Macrosociology (macrolevel) A branch (level) of sociology that focuses on the cultural and structural characteristics of major social systems. **17, 61**

Manifest consequence An intended effect of a characteristic of a social system on that system and its values. **98**

Manifest status A status included in the definition of a situation. **51**

Market economy An economy based primarily upon competition and exchange of goods and services rather than cooperation and sharing. **471**

Marriage A socially supported union between individuals in what is intended to be a stable, enduring relationship that involves sexual interaction as a key element. **386**

Marriage rules Norms that regulate whom people may marry, when, and under what circumstances. **390**

Masculinity A set of beliefs describing the ideal male. **331**

Mass A collection of people who pay attention to and react to the same thing without being in one another's presence. **556**

Mass society theory Kornhauser's theory that collective behavior is caused by a social condition in which people feel isolated from one another and from their communities. **588**

Master status A status regarded as the most important status in a status set. **50**

Material culture Objects made by people as they interact with one another and the physical world. **41**

Matriarchy A society or family system organized around dominance by females, especially mothers. **340, 395**

Matrilineal descent A kinship system in which descent is traced through mothers and their blood relatives. **387**

Matrilocal marriage A kinship system in which married couples live in or near the household of the wife's mother. **391**

Me Mead's concept that refers to the part of the self that looks upon and thinks about the self as an object. **143**

Mean A statistical measure used to describe the average score in a sample or population. It is computed by adding all the scores together and dividing by the number of scores. **125**

Means of production The physical means through which goods and services are produced in a society. **268**

Measurement instrument A procedure that classifies observations according to a behavior or characteristic. **114**

Measure of association A number varying between $+1.0$ and -1.0 that indicates how accurately an independent variable can be used to predict a dependent variable.

Mechanical solidarity (See **Gemeinschaft**.) **214**

Median A statistical measure used to describe the typical score in a sample or population. It is equal to the score that divides a sample or population so that half the scores are above the median and half are below. **125**

Medicalization The process through which medical perspectives and treatment become increasingly influential and common in a society. **462**

Medicine The social institution responsible for maintaining health, healing injury, and curing disease. **458**

Merchants In a market economy, those who do not produce, but make a living by buying and selling what others produce. **472**

Metropolitan area A city with at least 50,000 inhabitants, *or* an urbanized area that is socially and economically integrated with surrounding communities that bring the total population to 100,000 or more. **210**

Microecology The study of how the number of people involved in a social situation and their physical arrangement in relation to one another affect social interaction. **170**

Microsociology (microlevel) A branch (level) of sociology that focuses on social relationships among individuals. **17**

Migration The movement of people from one place to another, either between societies or within them. **76**

Military-industrial complex A coalition consisting of

Military-industrial complex (*continued*) the military and industrialists who profit by manufacturing arms and selling them to the government. **516**

Mind   The ability to use symbols in order to understand other people's thoughts, feelings, and expectations. **143**

Minority   A collection of people who, because of physical or cultural characteristics, are singled out from others for differential and unequal treatment. **299**

Misanthropy   Hatred of all people.

Misogyny   Hatred of females. **330**

Mob   An emotionally aroused, acting crowd that typically has a leader and focuses on a specific goal, the achievement of which usually involves some form of force or violence. **557**

Mobilization   In Smelser's theory of collective behavior, the phase in which people gather into a crowd.

Mob psychology   A theoretical approach that tries to explain collective behavior solely on the basis of the psychological states of people who participate. **560**

Mode   A statistical measure used to describe groups, equal to the most frequent score in a sample or population. **125**

Model   A person whose behavior or appearance we use as an example of what to imitate or what to avoid. **138**

Mode of production   The way in which a society goes about producing goods and services, consisting of the forces and relations of production. **469**

Modern community   A community with a relatively complex division of labor, whose inhabitants tend to welcome change, use sophisticated technology, have well-developed mass media, and rely more on formal, secondary relationships than on primary or informal relationships. **211**

Modernization   A concept describing a process through which societies are believed to change from less to more developed forms through the introduction of new technology and other social change. **582**

Monogamy   Marriage to only one spouse at a time. **391**

Monopoly   A condition in a market economy in which a particular good or service has only one provider who thereby controls the market. **474**

Monotheism   Religious belief in a single supreme being. **532**

Morbidity   Any condition that causes illness. **69**

Mores   The set of deeply held cultural ideas about how people ought to appear or behave. **35**

Multilinear (change) theory   Theories of change that identify some change as universal, but also acknowledge that change takes place in ways that do not necessarily result in "progress." **581**

Multinational corporation   A large business organization whose operations extend across international boundaries.

Multiple-nuclei theory (model)   A theory of urban land use according to which cities develop many different "cores" of activity. **226**

Multistage sample   A sample selected in stages, beginning with the most unspecific level (such as regions) and ending with the most specific (such as houses on selected city blocks).

Negative relationship   A relationship in which high scores on one variable are related to low scores on another. **128**

Neighborhood   Collections of people who live close to one another within a community.

Neolocal family   A kinship arrangement in which married couples start new households. **391**

Niche   The position a species of life occupies in an ecosystem. **81**

Nonconformist behavior (nonconformity)   Behavior that openly violates norms in order to bring about social change. **239**

Nonmaterial culture   The products of collective human activity that have no physical reality, including symbols, language, music, beliefs, values, norms, and attitudes. **25**

Norm   A rule that attaches sanctions to the behavior or appearance of status occupants. **34**

Nuclear family   A family consisting of parents and their natural or adopted children. **393**

Null hypothesis   A testable assumption about a population. (See Appendix B.)

Oligarchy   A state ruled by a privileged elite. **507**

Oligopoly   A condition in a market economy in which production of a good or service is controlled by a few organizations. **479**

Opportunity structure   The distribution of opportunities to achieve goals in a social system. **258**

Organic solidarity   (See **Gesellschaft**.) **214**

Organization   A social system consisting of two or more social systems related to each other through shared expectations and goals.

Organized skepticism, norm of   A norm that requires scientists to scrutinize all findings carefully before accepting them as true. **448**

Outer city   A form of community emerging as suburbs become more densely settled and dominated by business and manufacturing that have moved from central cities, and which in some cases compete successfully with major cities as centers of economic life. **227**

Out-group   A group toward which hostile attitudes are directed by members of another group. **189**

Overpopulation   An ecological condition in which a society is unable to support all its members with available technology and natural resources. **85**

Pandemic disease   An epidemic that spreads across several different populations, even to include the entire world. **71**

Panic   A form of collective behavior in which people try to escape from a perceived danger in an uncooperative, often irrational way. **559**

Paradigm   A framework of guiding assumptions, theories, and methods that define a particular approach to scientific problems. **445**

Participant observation   A research method in which researchers observe behavior in real-life settings in which they are participants. **121**

Party   Weber's term for people who share similar levels of social power, usually in relation to groups and organizations. **270**

Patriarchy   A society or family system organized around dominance by males, especially fathers. **340, 395**

Patrilineal descent   A kinship system in which descent is traced through fathers and their blood relatives. **388**

Patrilocal family   A kinship system in which married couples live near or in the household of the husband's father. **391**

Pattern of communication   (See **Communication structure**.)

Peer group   People who share a level of social standing, especially in terms of age. **152**

Percentage   The number of people in a sample or population who have a particular characteristic, divided by the size of the population or group, and multiplied by 100. **115**

Performative language   A meaningful utterance that alters people's positions in social relationships. **29**

Peripheral society   In world-system theory, a society in an economically subordinate position. **493**

Personality   The complex patterns of thought, feeling, and behavior that make each individual unique.

Personal power   Power based not on status occupancy, but on personal attributes such as physical strength or persuasiveness. **57**

Pluralism (ethnic)   The coexistence of diverse ethnic groups in the same society. **302**

Pluralism (political)   The distribution of power among a variety of interest groups.

Pluralistic power structure   A system in which the right to make decisions is divided among different specialists. **190**

Pluralist theory   The theory that holds that power in social systems is distributed among a wide variety of groups and individuals. **219**

Political economy   The social arrangements through which political and economic institutions support each other. **521**

Political institution   The relatively permanent social system through which power is distributed and exercised in societies. **501**

Political party   An organization whose main goal is to acquire power by placing members in positions of authority in political institutions. **513**

Political process theory   An approach to social movements that concentrates both on what goes on within movements and on the relationship between movements and institutions in the surrounding society. **590**

Politics   The social process through which power is distributed among and used by social systems. **501**

Polyandry   Marriage between a woman and more than one man. **391**

Polygamy   Marriage to more than one spouse at a time. **391**

Polygyny   Marriage between a man and more than one woman at a time. **391**

Polytheism   In religion, the belief in more than one god. **532**

Population   A collection of people who share a geographic territory. In research, any precisely defined set of objects, people, groups, or societies. **117**

Population density   The number of people per unit of area (e.g., per square mile). **80**

Population distribution   A concept that refers to (1) the density of populations, (2) how people of different social statuses are distributed spatially, and (3) the physical arrangement of individuals as they interact with each other.

Population growth rate   The net result of births, deaths, in-migration, and out-migration in a population.

Positive relationship   A statistical relationship in which high scores on one variable are related to high scores on another variable. **128**

Postindustrial society   A society in which the production of goods is overshadowed by the provision of services, and in which relations between people and machines are gradually replaced by relationships between people. **486**

Power   The potential to have an effect on ourselves, others, or our environment in spite of opposition. **56**

Power elite   A group of people who dominate decision making in all important areas of life in a community or society.

Power-elite theory   The theory that argues that power in communities is concentrated in the hands of a relatively small group. **219**

Power structure   The distribution of power in social systems. **56**

Precipitating incident   In Smelser's theory of collective behavior, an event that triggers a collective response.

Prejudice   A positive or negative attitude directed toward people simply because they occupy a particular status. **300**

Prestige   Respect or deference accorded to people because of the social statuses they occupy. **58**

Primary deviance   Deviant acts committed without the actor having been labelled. **256**

Primary group   A group valued for its own sake which endures through time, and involves people in many aspects of one another's lives. **192**

Primary labor market   The portion of the segmented labor market that includes jobs that require stable work habits, involve skills that are often learned on the job, are relatively high-paying, and have job ladders. **483**

Prisoner's dilemma   An experiment in which actors must choose between the risks of cooperation and competition.

Profane   In religion, the designation of an object, experience, idea, symbol, or person as part of the natural world. **528**

Profession   An occupation based on systematic, formal knowledge about a particular field (such as law) and involves high levels of autonomy and codes of conduct formulated and administered by other members of the occupation. **484**

Professionalization   The social process through which an occupation acquires the cultural and structural characteristics of a profession.

Proletariat   In Marx's framework, the working class, which neither owns nor controls any means of production, but instead works for wages. **268**

Pull factor   In migration, a positive social or ecological condition in one area that motivates people living in another area to move there. **76**

Push factor   In migration, a negative social or ecological condition in people's home areas that motivates them to leave. **76**

Questionnaire   A method of gathering information in which respondents complete a written form. **118**

Race (biological)   A collection of people with distinct physical characteristics that are passed on through reproduction. **298**

Race (social)   A social status defined in terms of cultural beliefs about biological race. **298**

Racism   Prejudice based on perceived racial differences. **300**

Radical feminism   A branch of feminism that argues that patriarchy centers on a fundamental difference in interests between men and women, and that equality for women cannot be achieved unless men collectively give up the power, wealth, and privilege that patriarchy grants them. **352**

Random sample   A sample drawn so that all members of the population have an equal chance of being included. **117**

Rate of natural increase   The difference between birth and death rates in a population. **73**

Realigning action   An action through which an actor tries to introduce a new definition of the situation. **176**

Rebellion   A form of deviance in which a person challenges values and norms that define legitimate means for achieving them. In politics, a rebellion challenges the policies of a government without trying to change the characteristics of the state as a social system. **239, 521**

Reference group   A group used as a standard of desirable or undesirable appearance or behavior. **148**

Reference individual   An individual used as a standard of desirable or undesirable appearance or behavior. **148**

Reform movement   A social movement that seeks to improve a social system without changing its basic characteristics. **584**

Relations of production   The social relationships through which goods or services are produced. **469**

Relative deprivation   The perception that one's position in a stratification system is worse than the position of others with whom one compares oneself. **586**

Reliability   The degree to which a measurement instrument gives the same results with repeated measurements (assuming that whatever is being measured does not change). **114**

Religion   A set of cultural ideas, symbols, and practices that focus on the meaning of life and the nature of the unknown. **528**

Replication   The scientific practice of repeating research studies in order to confirm the original findings. **121**

Representative democracy   A state in which citizens delegate authority to elected representatives. **506**

Research design   The set of procedures that guide the gathering of research data. (See Appendix A.)

Resistance movement   A social movement intended to stop social change. **585**

Resource mobilization theory   An approach to social movements that tries to explain their emergence, success, or failure in terms of access to resources such as time, money, people, and leadership and organizational skills. **589**

Retreatism   A form of deviance in which a person withdraws from social life by rejecting values and norms without offering alternatives. **239**

Revolution   A social movement seeking to change the fundamental character of one or more social institutions in a society. **522, 584**

Riot   A leaderless, unorganized crowd whose members often focus on destruction and the expression of frustration and anger. **558**

Rising expectations   The hope or expectation of a deprived group that social conditions will improve in the near future—thought by some sociologists to be a cause of social movements.

Rite of passage   A ceremony marking the transition of individuals from one social status to another. **149**

Ritual   A religious practice intended to maintain the relationship between believers and the supernatural and among one another. **533**

Ritualism   Outward conformity to norms without a commitment to values they support. **260**

Role   A set of beliefs, values, norms, and attitudes shared by status occupants in their relationships with the occupants of other statuses. **50**

Role conflict   The tension that results when we have difficulty performing a role or satisfying the conflicting demands of two or more roles. **51**

Role distance   The disassociation or "distancing" of people from a role they are performing in order to distract themselves and others from negative aspects of the role performance. **52**

Role partner   The occupant of a status in relation to whom we perform roles. **50**

Role performance   The actual behavior of people who occupy a status. **50**

Role segregation   The practice of avoiding occupying statuses for which specific individuals are role partners for more than one of our roles. **52**

Role set   A set of roles attached to a status. **50**

Role structure   The set of roles performed by members of a group. **55**

Rumor   An unverified belief that arises from informal social interaction. **564**

Rural community   A small, homogeneous, and sparsely settled community. **210**

Sacred   In religion, the designation of an object, person, idea, symbol, or experience as having meaning and value that inspire feelings of awe and place it outside of the natural human world. **528**

Sample   A subgroup of a population. **117**

Sanction   A social punishment or reward associated with obeying or violating a norm. **34**

School   A formal organization whose primary function is education. **415**

Science   A social institution responsible for seeking verifiable knowledge about the natural world. **443**

Scientific method   A method of posing and answering questions that relies on clear, objective guidelines for gathering and interpreting observable evidence. **111**

Scientific revolution   The replacement of one scientific paradigm with another. **445**

Secondary analysis   The use of information already gathered by others, such as government agencies and universities. **122**

Secondary deviance   Deviant acts committed partly in response to being labeled "deviant." **256**

Secondary group   A group valued only insofar as it allows members to accomplish specific goals. **192**

Secondary labor market   That segment of the labor market that includes jobs that do not require stable work habits, are relatively low-paying, have few chances for advancement, and have a high turnover. **473**

Sect   A religious group that draws most members by persuasion from the lower class, that has an informal structure and an untrained clergy, is governed with minimal authority, has few formal rituals, involves spontaneous displays of emotion, and generally opposes the dominant institutions of its society. **537**

Sector theory (model)   A theory of urban land use according to which cities grow in "pie-shaped" segments going out of a central business core. **226**

Secularization   The social change process through which religious beliefs and practices lose influence in a society. **547**

Segregation   The practice of physically separating the occupants of some social statuses from the occupants of others. **311**

Self-concept   The sum total of our thoughts and feelings about ourselves. **145**

Self-esteem   The positive and negative feelings people feel toward themselves. **148**

Self-fulfilling prophecy   A belief that becomes true because people think and act as if it were true. **163**

Semiperipheral society   In world-system theory, a society that is in the process of industrializing. **494**

Serfs   In a feudal economy, those who give a share of what they produce to the nobility in exchange for protection and use of the land controlled by the nobility.

Sex   Biological differences that define male and female.

Sexism   Prejudice based on gender. **334**

Sex role   (See **Gender role**.)

Shamanism   A form of animism in which a shaman is believed to have the power to communicate with spirits and thereby influence human life. **532**

Significant other   A particular individual whose beliefs, evaluations, attitudes, and expectations affect our appearance or behavior.

Single-parent family   A nuclear family with one parent. **393**

Situational status   A status occupied only in a particular social situation. **49**

Social attribution   The process through which we interpret and explain other people's appearance and behavior. **166**

Social boundary   The protection from various kinds of social contact, offered by the roles attached to social statuses.

Social category   Two or more people who have a social status in common. **8**

Social change   The ways in which the characteristics of social systems change.

Social class (Marx)   A category of people who occupy a similar position in relation to the means through which goods and services are produced in a society. **268**

Social class (Weber)   A set of people who have similar levels of access to markets and the goods and services they distribute. **269**

Social cohesion   The degree to which participants in social systems feel committed to the system and the well-being of other participants. **202**

Social Darwinism   A late nineteenth-century theory (used to explain and justify social inequality) that held that the most capable people will and should gain more in the struggle for survival than the less capable. **277**

Social evolution   Spencer's theory (adapted from Darwin's ideas about natural evolution) that all societies naturally change toward superior forms. **580**

Social identity   Who we think we are based on the statuses we occupy. **146**

Social institution   (See **Institution**.)

Social interaction   The process through which individuals act in relation to one another. **161**

Socialism   An economic arrangement in which the means of production are owned and controlled by the state, not by private individuals or groups. **490**

Socialist feminism   A branch of feminism that argues that patriarchy is closely connected with capitalism,

Socialist feminism (*continued*)
and that equality for women cannot be achieved without also making major political/economic changes in capitalism as a system. **352**

Socialization   The process through which people learn to think, feel, evaluate, and behave as individuals in relation to others and social systems. **135**

Social labeling perspective   A perspective that holds that societies often reinforce their boundaries by labeling people as well as their acts as deviant. **256**

Social learning theory (perspective)   A theory of socialization that focuses on learning through the imitation of models. **138**

Social mobility   The process through which people move from one position in a stratification system to another. **283**

Social movement   A collective effort aimed at either changing or preserving some aspect of social systems. **584**

Social oppression   The systematic, socially supported mistreatment and exploitation of a group or category of people by another. **299**

Social promotion   A practice in which students who have not mastered the skills of a particular grade or level are nevertheless sent on to the next higher grade.

Social psychology   The study of the effects of social environments on the psychological functioning of individuals.

Social script   In the dramaturgical approach to interaction, the role we perform in relation to a particular audience. **174**

Social status   A position in a social relationship, a characteristic that locates individuals in relation to other people and sets of role expectations. (See also **status** for additional meaning.) **48**

Social stratification   The systematic, uneven distribution of valued products of social life such as wealth, power, and prestige among the occupants of different social statuses. **267**

Social structure   The arrangement of people and social systems in relation to one another and the patterns of expectation associated with them. Also the distribution of people among various social positions, and the distribution of social rewards. **48**

Social system   Any interdependent arrangement of cultural and structural elements that can be thought of as a whole. **6**

Society   A relatively autonomous population whose members share a cultural identity and way of life, interact in patterned ways, and occupy common geographic territory. **8**

Sociobiology   A perspective that views social patterns among humans and other species as the result of genetics.

Socioeconomic status   An overall rank based on characteristics such as education and occupation, used to describe people's positions in stratification systems. **271**

Sociogram   A method of "mapping" patterns of personal loyalty and affection among group members. **56**

Sociology   The systematic study of social life and behavior, especially in relation to social systems. **6**

Sociometry   The study of patterns of affection and loyalty that bind some group members more closely than others. **56**

Special language   A language developed by a subgroup in order to set themselves apart from others. **29**

Speech community   A set of people who share a language. **28**

Spurious relationship   When two variables that have no causal connection are, nonetheless, statistically related to each other.

State   The social institution that claims the monopoly of the use of force within a given territory. **503**

State capitalism   An economic system in which the state owns some means of production but operates them according to capitalist principles. **492**

Statistical independence   A condition in which scores on one variable do *not* differ according to scores on another. **128**

Statistical inference   A mathematical procedure used to test null hypotheses by comparing sample information with an assumption about a population. (See Appendix B.)

Statistical relationship   A condition in which scores on one variable differ according to scores on another. **128**

Statistics   A collection of numerical data; also, the branch of mathematics dealing with the collection and analysis of numerical data. **124** (See also Appendix B.)

Status   Weber's term for the amount of prestige people receive. **270** (See also **Social status** for additional meaning.)

Status inconsistency   The occupancy of statuses whose levels of various rewards are inconsistent with one another. **271**

Status segregation   (See **Role segregation**.) **52**

Status set   The entire collection of social statuses occupied by an individual. **50**

Stereotype   A rigid, oversimplified belief that is applied to all members of a group or social category. **164**

Stigma   Personal characteristics that others treat as deviant. **240**

Structural lag   A condition that occurs when a structural aspect of a society changes more slowly than other related aspects of society and is therefore out of balance with them. **372**

Structural mobility   Mobility resulting from a change in the distribution of occupations, expanding opportunities in some and decreasing them in others. **285**

Structural strain   In Smelser's theory of collective behavior, the result when people perceive a contradiction between the reality of social life and what their values say it ought to be. **566**

Structural unemployment   Unemployment caused by

changes in the structure of occupational opportunities, such as when a steel factory closes and the number of steelworker jobs declines. **489**

Structuralist theory   A theory of community power according to which cities are dominated by fairly stable coalitions of a variety of different interest groups. **219**

Subculture   A distinctive set of cultural ideas that sets a group of people apart from the culture of a surrounding community or society. **40**

Subfamily   A family that shares a household with another family. **410**

Subgroup   A group that is part of a larger group.

Subordinate primary (labor market) jobs   In the primary labor market, jobs that involve routine tasks and encourage workers to be obedient to authority. **473**

Suburb   A community lying close to a city. **210**

Succession   (See **Ecological succession.**)

Surplus value   The value of goods and services that is kept by employers as profit after paying workers whatever is needed to buy their labor power and reproduce themselves. **472**

Survey   A method of gathering data through which people are asked a series of questions either by an interviewer or in questionnaire form. **118**

Symbols   Objects, characteristics of objects, gestures, or words that represent more than themselves. **26**

Symbolic interaction   The use of symbols by people to present themselves to others and interpret one another's behavior. **103**

Syndicated crime   Crime perpetrated by formal organizations with rigid authority structures and complex divisions of labor. **246**

Systematic sample   A sample drawn by selecting a random starting point in a list of a population and skipping through the list at regular intervals.

Technocracy   A society dominated by experts, especially those in the sciences. **456**

Technology   A society's accumulated knowledge of how to use the natural environment. **19, 82**

Temporary status   A situational or transitional status. **49**

Theocracy   A state dominated by religious leaders and religious institutions.

Theoretical perspective   A non-explanatory, general framework that defines a point of view within a discipline, including basic assumptions that draw attention to particular aspects of a phenomenon and, therefore, generate particular kinds of questions about it. **96**

Theory   A set of interrelated propositions designed to explain a phenomenon. **94**

Time structure   The ways in which relationships in social systems are defined, conditioned, and regulated according to time. **54**

Token   People who have a social characteristic that is unusual in a particular social system.

Total institution   An organization such as a prison in which all aspects of people's daily lives are controlled by authorities. **250**

Totalitarianism   The political condition in which the state attempts to control not only people's behavior, but virtually all aspects of their private lives as well. **509**

Totem   In totemist religions, a sacred object believed to possess supernatural power. **531**

Totemism   A religion based on the belief that sacred objects (totems) possess supernatural power. **533**

Tracking   An educational practice in which students are divided into groups on the basis of such factors as ability measured by test scores. **435**

Traditional authority   Authority based on the belief that occupants of certain statuses are legitimately powerful because "that's the way it's always been." **503**

Traditional community   A community with a relatively simple division of labor, whose inhabitants tend to resist change, use unsophisticated technology, have less developed mass media, and rely more on informal relationships than on secondary, formal relationships. **211**

Transitional status   A status occupied solely as a stepping stone toward the occupancy of another status. **49**

Triad   A group with three members. **171**

Unilinear (change) theory   A theory of social change according to which all societies follow the same path of development. **580**

Universalism, norm of   A norm that requires scientists to evaluate scientific findings using the same criteria regardless of the source of the findings. **448**

Urban community   A large, heterogeneous, and densely settled community. **210**

Urbanized area   A city and the densely settled territory around it that, together, contain 50,000 or more people. **210**

Use value   The attribution of value to goods and services based upon their usefulness to those who consume them. **470**

Validity   The degree to which a measurement instrument measures what it is intended to measure. **114**

Value   An idea about what is socially defined as good or desirable. **31**

Variable   In sociology, a behavior or characteristic that varies from one observation to another. **113**

Victimless crime   Acts that violate legal norms but do not involve individuals as victims. **247**

Wealth   Valued possessions not needed for immediate consumption. **280**

White-collar   Referring to occupations that primarily involve mental work. **271**

White-collar crime   Crimes that people are able to commit because of the power and opportunities afforded by social statuses—usually occupations—they occupy. **244**

Worker   (See **Proletariat.**)

World economy (system)   The economic arrangement

World economy (system) (*continued*)
among all nations, in which there is a division of labor and varying degrees of dependency, dominance, and inequality. **493**

World-system (dependency) theory   A theory that divides nations into three groups (based on the worldwide distribution of wealth and power) and argues that the economic development of societies depends on their position in the world system. **493, 583**

Xenocentrism   The tendency to assume that aspects of other cultures are superior to one's own. **41**

Xenophobia   The fear of strangers and outsiders. **215**

Zero-sum game   A game in which the success of one player requires the failure of another.

REFERENCES*

AACJC (American Association of Community and Junior Colleges). May 1977. *Students in two-year colleges.*

AAMC (American Association of Medical Colleges). 1987. Reported in the *New York Times*, June 29.

AARP (American Association of Retired Persons). 1989a. Reported in the *New York Times*, July 19, p. 1.

_____. 1989b. Reported in the *New York Times*, January 26, p. B8.

ABFP (American Board of Family Practice). 1990. *Perspectives on middle age: The vintage years.* Jefferson Valley, NY: American Board of Family Practice.

Abadinsky, H. 1983. *The criminal elite: Professional and organized crime.* Westport, CT: Greenwood Press.

Abbey, A. 1987. Misperceptions of friendly behavior as sexual interest. *Psychology of Women Quarterly* 11(2):173–94.

Abel, E. K. 1984. *Terminal degrees: The job crisis in higher education.* New York: Praeger.

Aboulafia, M. 1986. *The mediating self: Mead, Sartre, and self-determination.* New Haven, CT: Yale University Press.

Abrahamson, M. 1980. *Urban sociology* (2nd ed.). Englewood Cliffs, NJ: Prentice-Hall.

Abrahamson, M., and Carter, V. J. 1986. Tolerance, urbanism, and region. *American Sociological Review* 51(2):287–94.

Adas, M. 1989. *Machines as the measure of men.* Ithaca, NY: Cornell University Press.

Adler, P. A. 1985. *Wheeling and dealing: An ethnography of an upper-level drug dealing and smuggling community.* New York: Columbia University Press.

Adler, P. A., Adler, P., and Fontana, A. 1987. Everyday life sociology. *Annual Review of Sociology* 13:217–35.

Adorno, R. W., Frenkel-Brunswik, E., Levinson, D. J., and Sanford, R. N. 1950. *The authoritarian personality.* New York: Harper and Row.

Ageton, S. S. 1983. *Sexual assault among adolescents.* Lexington, MA: Lexington Books.

Aguirre, B. E., Quarantelli, E. L., and Mendoza, J. L. 1988. The collective behavior of fads: The characteristics, effects, and careers of streaking. *American Sociological Review* 53(4):569–84.

Alba, R. D., and Chamlin, M. B. 1983. A preliminary examination of ethnic identification among whites. *American Sociological Review*, 48 (April):240–47.

Alba, R. D., and Golden, R. 1986. Patterns of ethnic marriage in the United States. *Social Forces*, 1:202–23.

Alba, R. D., and Moore, G. 1982. Ethnicity in the American elite. *American Sociological Review*, 47 (June):373–83.

Alessio, J. C. 1990. A synthesis and formalization of Heiderian balance and social exchange theory. *Social Forces* 68(4):1267–85.

Alexander, K. L., and Reilly, T. W. 1981. Estimating the effects of marriage timing on educational attainment. *American Journal of Sociology* 87:143–56.

Alexander, N. C., and Wiley, M. G. 1981. Situated activity and identity formation. In M. Rosenberg and R. Turner (Eds.), *Social psychology: Sociological perspectives.* New York: Basic Books.

Allan, L. J. 1978. Child abuse: A critical review of the research and the theory. In J. P. Martin (Ed.), *Violence and the family.* New York: Wiley.

Allen, I. L. 1983. *The language of ethnic conflict.* New York: Columbia University Press.

Allen, M. P., and Broyles, P. 1989. Class hegemony and political finance: Presidential campaign contributions of wealthy capitalist families. *American Sociological Review* 54(2):275–87.

Allport, F. H. 1920. The influence of the group upon association and thought. *Journal of Experimental Psychology* 3:159–82.

Allport, G. W. 1935. Attitudes. In C. Murchison (Ed.), *A handbook of social psychology.* Worcester, MA: Clark University Press.

_____. 1954. *The nature of prejudice.* Garden City, NY: Doubleday Anchor Books.

Allport, G. W., and Postman, L. 1947. *The psychology of rumor.* New York: Holt.

Alreck, P. L., and Settle, R. B. 1985. *The survey research handbook.* Homewood, IL: Richard D. Irwin, Inc.

Altman, D. 1986. *AIDS in the mind of America: The social, political, and psychological impact of a new epidemic.* Garden City, NY: Anchor.

Altman, I., Taylor, D. A., and Wheeler, L. 1971. Ecological aspects of group behavior in social isolation. *Journal of Applied Social Psychology* 1:76–100.

AMA (American Medical Association). 1990. Reported in the *New York Times*, February 19, p. 1.

Ambron, S. R. 1978. *Child development* (2nd ed.). New York: Holt, Rinehart, and Winston.

Amin, S. 1975. Toward a structural crisis of world capitalism. *Socialist Review*, 5 (April):9–44.

---

*Where two years are given, as in Durkheim ([1893] 1933), the first year is the year in which the work was first published.

Amnesty International. 1989. Reported in the *New York Times*, March 1, p. A14, and October 25, p. A8.

Anderson, A. G. 1979. *The business of organized crime.* Stanford, CA: Hoover Institution Press.

Anderson, B. A., Silver, B. D., and Abramson, P. R. 1987. The effects of race of the interviewer on race-related attitudes of black respondents in SRC/CPS national election studies. Population Studies Center Research Report 86-113. Ann Arbor, MI: Population Studies Center, University of Michigan.

Anderson, B. S., and Zinsser, J. P. 1988. *A history of their own: Women in Europe from prehistory to the present. Vol. 1.* New York: Harper and Row.

Anderson, M. J. 1988. *The American census: A social history.* New Haven, CT: Yale University Press.

Apple, M. W. 1986. *Teachers and texts: A political economy of class and gender relations in education.* New York: Routledge and Kegan Paul.

Applewhite, S. R. (Ed.). 1988. *Hispanic elderly in transition: Theory, research, policy, and practice.* Westport, CT: Greenwood Press.

Archer, D., and Gartner, R. 1984. *A comparative perspective on the legitimation of homicide.* New Haven, CT: Yale University Press.

Arens, W. 1986. *The original sin: Incest and its meaning.* New York: Oxford University Press.

Argyris, C. 1957. The individual and the organization: Some problems of mutual adjustment. *Administrative Science Quarterly* 1:1–24.

Ariès, P. 1962. *Centuries of childhood: A social history of family life.* New York: Knopf.

Arjomand, S. A. 1988. *The turban for the crown: The Islamic revolution in Iran.* New York: Oxford University Press.

Aronowitz, S. 1973. *False promises.* New York: McGraw-Hill.

Asch, S. E. 1952. *Social psychology.* Englewood Cliffs, NJ: Prentice-Hall.

Ash, D. 1967. *Automobile almanac.* New York: Essandess/Simon and Schuster.

Ash, T. G. 1984. *The Polish revolution: Solidarity.* New York: Charles Scribner's Sons.

Ashton, D. N. 1986. *Unemployment under capitalism: The sociology of British and American labor.* Westport, CT: Greenwood Press.

ASPRS (American Society of Plastic and Reconstructive Surgeons). 1985. In *Newsweek*, May 27, pp. 66–67.

Association of American Medical Colleges. 1987. Reported in Women as surgeons: Fighting for success. *New York Times*, June 29.

Atchley, R. C. 1982. Retirement as a social institution. *Annual Review of Sociology*, 8:263–87.

Auden, W. H. 1965. Prologue: The birth of architecture. In *About the house.* New York: Random House.

Aukett, R., Ritchie, J., and Mill, K. 1988. Gender differences in friendship patterns. *Sex Roles* 19(1/2):57–66.

Avorn, J. 1988. Reported in the *New York Times*, March 13, p.1.

Axelrod, R. 1984. *The evolution of cooperation.* New York: Basic Books.

Babst, D. V., et al. 1976. Assessing length of institutionalization in relation to parole outcome. *Criminology*, 14 (May):41–54.

Back, K. W. 1981. Small groups. In M. Rosenberg and R. H. Turner (Eds.), *Social psychology: Sociological perspectives*, pp. 320–43. New York: Basic Books.

Baldassare, M. 1983. Residential crowding and social behavior. In J. S. Pipkin, M. LaGory, and J. R. Blau (Eds.), *Remaking the city*, pp. 148–62. Albany, NY: State University of New York Press.

Baldridge, J. V., and Deal, T. 1983. *The dynamics of organizational change in education.* Berkeley, CA: McCutchan.

Baldus, D. 1987. Research on the death penalty reported in the *New York Times*, March 23. See also *New York Times*, April 23, p. A1.

Bales, R. F. 1950. *Interaction process analysis: A method for the study of small groups.* Cambridge, MA: Addison-Wesley.

_____. 1968. Interaction process. In D. L. Sills (Ed.), *The international encyclopedia of the social sciences.* Vol. 7. New York: Macmillan/Free Press.

Bales, R. F., and Borgatta, E. F. 1955. A study of group size: Size of group as a factor in the interaction profile. In A. P. Hare, E. F. Borgatta, and R. F. Bales. *Small groups.* New York: Knopf.

Bamberger, J. 1974. The myth of matriarchy: Why men rule in primitive society. In M. Z. Rosaldo and L. Lamphere (Eds.), *Women culture, and society*, pp. 263–80. Stanford, CA: Stanford University Press.

Bandura, A. 1977. *Social learning theory.* Englewood Cliffs, NJ: Prentice-Hall.

Bane, M. J. 1976. *Here to stay: American families in the twentieth century.* New York: Basic Books.

Bane, M. J., and Jencks, C. 1972. The schools and equal opportunity. *Saturday Review of Education*, September 16:37–42.

Banfield, E. C. 1965. *Political influence.* New York: Free Press.

Bannister, R. C. 1987. *Sociology and scientism: The American quest for objectivity.* Chapel Hill: University of North Carolina Press.

Baran, P. A. 1957. *The political economy of growth.* New York: Monthly Review Press.

Baran, P. A., and Sweezy, P. M. 1966. *Monopoly capital.* New York: Modern Reader Paperbacks.

Bardwell, J. R., Cochran, S. W., and Walker, S. 1986. Relationship of parental education, race, and gender to sex-role stereotyping in five-year-old kindergartners. *Sex Roles* 15:275–81.

Barlow, W. B. 1989. *"Looking up at down": The emergence of blues culture.* Philadelphia: Temple University Press.

Barnes, B. 1985. *About science.* New York: Basil Blackwell.

Barnet, R. J., and Muller, R. J. 1974. *Global reach*. New York: Simon and Schuster.

Barnett, R. C., and Baruch, G. K. 1983. *Women's involvement in multiple roles, role strain, and psychological stress.* (Working Paper 107). Wellesley, MA: Wellesley College Center for Research on Women.

Baron, J. N., and Newman, A. E. 1989. Pay the man: Effects of demographic composition on wage rates in the California civil service. In R. T. Michael and H. I. Hartmann (Eds.), *Pay equity: Empirical inquiries.* Washington, D.C.: National Academy Press.

Barry, H., and Paxson, L. M. 1989. Cited in Konner, M., Where should baby sleep? *The New York Times Magazine*, January 8, pp. 39–40.

Barry, T. 1987. *Roots of rebellion: Land and hunger in Central America.* Boston: South End Press.

Barsh, R. L., and Henderson, J. Y. 1980. *The road: Indian tribes and political liberty.* Berkeley and Los Angeles, CA: University of California Press.

Bart, P. B. 1971. Depression in middle-aged women. In V. Gornick and B. Moran (Eds.), *Woman in sexist society*, pp. 163–86. New York: Signet.

Barth, H. 1976. *Truth and ideology.* Berkeley, CA: University of California Press.

Barth, R. J., and Kinder, B. N. 1988. A theoretical analysis of sex differences in same-sex friendship. *Sex Roles* 19(5/6):349–63.

Barthel, D. 1988. *Putting on appearances: Gender and advertising.* Philadelphia: Temple University Press.

Bartlett, F. C. 1932. *Remembering.* Cambridge, England: Cambridge University Press.

Barton, A. 1985. Determinants of economics attitudes in the American business elite. *American Journal of Sociology*, 91:54–87.

Barton, E. M., Baltes, M. M., and Orzech, M. J. 1980. Etiology of dependence in older nursing home residents during morning care. *Journal of Personality and Social Psychology* 38:423–31.

Bates, F. L., and Peacock, W. G. 1989. Conceptualizing social structure: The misuse of classification in structural modeling. *American Sociological Review* 54(4):565–77.

Bavelas, A. 1950. Communication patterns in task-oriented groups. *Journal of the Acoustical Society of America*, 22:725–30.

Baxandall, R., Gordon, L., and Reverby, S. 1976. *America's working women.* New York: Vintage.

Beale, H. K. 1975. The education of Negroes before the Civil War. In J. Barnard and D. Burner (Eds.), *American experience in education*, pp. 88–90. New York: Watts.

Bean, F. D., and Tienda, M. 1988. *The hispanic population of the United States.* New York: Russell Sage Foundation.

Beauvais, K. 1986. Workshops to combat sexual harassment: A case study of changing attitudes. *Signs: Journal of Women in Culture and Society* 12(1):130–45.

Beauvoir, S. de. 1952. An androgynous world. In B. Roszak and T. Roszak (Eds.), *Masculine/feminine*, pp. 148–57. New York: Harper and Row.

Becker, H. S. 1953. Becoming a marijuana user. *American Journal of Sociology* 59 (November):235–42.

———. (Ed.). 1964. *The other side.* New York: Free Press.

———. 1973. *Outsiders: Studies in the sociology of deviance* (rev. ed.). New York: Free Press.

———. 1982. *Art worlds.* Berkeley: University of California Press.

Becker, H. S., and Geer, B. 1958. The fate of idealism in medical school. *American Sociological Review*, 23:50–56.

Beeghley, L. 1983. *Living poorly in America.* New York: Praeger.

Bell, D. 1973. *The coming of postindustrial society.* New York: Basic Books.

———. 1987. *And we are not saved: The elusive quest for racial justice.* New York: Basic Books.

Bell, W. 1969. Urban neighborhoods and individual behavior. In P. Meadows and E. H. Mizburchi (Eds.), *Urbanism, urbanization, and change.* Reading, MA: Addison-Wesley.

Bellah, R. N. 1970. *Beyond belief.* New York: Harper and Row.

———. 1973. *The broken covenant.* New York: Seabury Press.

Bellah, R. N., and Hammond, P. E. 1980. *Varieties of civil religion.* New York: Harper and Row.

Bellah, R. N., Madsen, R., Sullivan, W. M., Swidler, A., and Tipton, S. M. 1985. *Habits of the heart: Individualism and commitment in American life.* Berkeley, CA: University of California Press.

Bem, S., and Bem, D. 1976. Training the woman to know her place: The power of nonconscious ideology. In S. Cox (Ed.), *Female psychology: The emerging self.* Chicago: St. Martin's Press.

Benderly, B. L. 1987. *The myth of two minds: What gender means and doesn't mean.* Garden City, NY: Doubleday.

Bendix, R., and Lipset, S. M. (Eds.). 1966. *Class, status, and power.* New York: Free Press.

Benedict, R. 1934. *Patterns of culture.* New York: New American Library.

———. 1946. *The chrysanthemum and the sword.* Boston: Houghton Mifflin.

Bennett, D. H. 1989. *The party of fear: From nativist movements to the new right in American history.* Chapel Hill, NC: University of North Carolina Press.

Benoliel, J. Q. 1973. *The nurse and the dying patient.* New York: Macmillan.

Bensman, J., and Rosenberg, B. 1979. The peer group. In P. I. Rose (Ed.), *Socialization and the life cycle.* New York: St. Martin's Press.

Ben-Yehuda, N. 1980. The European witch craze of the

Ben-Yehuda, N. (*continued*)
14th and 17th centuries: A sociologist's perspective. *American Journal of Sociology*, 86(1):1–31.

Berger, B. M. 1960. *Working class suburb: A study of autoworkers in suburbia.* Berkeley, CA: University of California Press.

Berger, P. L. 1963. *Invitation to sociology: A humanistic perspective.* New York: Anchor Books.

———. 1967. *The sacred canopy.* New York: Doubleday.

———. 1970. *A rumor of angels.* Garden City, NY: Doubleday.

Berger, P. L., and Kellner, H. 1964. Marriage and the construction of reality. *Diogenes* 45:1–25.

Berger, P. L., and Luckman, T. 1967. *The social construction of reality.* Garden City, NY: Doubleday.

Bergesen, A. (Ed.). 1980. *Studies of the modern world system.* New York: Academic Press.

Bergmann, B. R. 1986. *The economic emergence of women.* New York: Basic Books.

Berk, R. A. 1974a. A gaming approach to crowd behavior. *American Journal of Sociology*, 79 (June):355–73.

———. 1974b. *Collective behavior.* Dubuque, IA: William C. Brown.

Berk, R. A., and Berk, S. F. 1983. Supply-side sociology of the family. *Annual Review of Sociology*, 9, pp. 375–95.

Berk, R. A., and Newton, P. J. 1985. Arrest and wife battery. *American Sociological Review*, 50(2):253–62.

Berk, S. F., and Loseke, D. R. 1981. Handling family violence: Situational determinants of police arrest in domestic disturbances. *Law and Society Review*, 15:315–46.

Berkowitz, L. 1978. Decreased helpfulness with increased group size through lessening the effects of the needy individual's dependency. *Journal of Personality*, 46:299–310.

Berle, A. A., Jr., and Means, G. C. [1932] 1968. *The modern corporation and private property* (rev. ed.). New York: Harcourt Brace Jovanovich.

Berman, P. W., and Smith, V. L. 1984. Gender and situational differences in children's smiles, touch, and proxemics. *Sex Roles* 10:347–56.

Bernard, J. 1972. *The future of marriage.* New York: Bantam.

Berry, B. J., and Kasarda, J. D. 1977. The congruence of social and spatial structure: Neighborhood status and white resistance to residential integration as an example. In *Contemporary urban ecology* (Chapter 2). New York: Macmillan.

Besser, J. D. 1979. Gentrifying the ghetto. *The Progressive* January:30–32.

Best, M. H., and Connolly, W. E. 1976. *The politicized economy.* Lexington, MA: D. C. Heath.

Best, R. 1983. *We've all got scars: What boys and girls learn in elementary school.* Bloomington, IN: Indiana University Press.

Bettelheim, B. 1969. *Children of the dream.* New York: Macmillan.

Bettelheim, B., and Janowitz, M. 1950. *Dynamics of prejudice: A psychological and sociological study of veterans.* New York: Harper and Row.

Beuf, A. H. 1990. *Beauty is the beast.* Philadelphia: University of Pennsylvania Press.

Biddle, B. 1979. *Role theory: Expectations, identities, and behaviors.* New York: Academic Press.

Bielby, W. T., and Bielby, D. D. 1989. Family ties: Balancing commitments to work and family in dual earner households. *American Sociological Review* 54(5):776–89.

Bierhoff, H.-W. 1989. *Person perception and attribution.* New York: Springer-Verlag.

Bilheimer, R. S. (Ed). 1983. *Faith and ferment: An interdisciplinary study of Christian beliefs and practices.* Minneapolis: Augsburg.

Binford, H. C. 1985. *The first suburbs: Residential communities on the Boston periphery, 1815–1860.* Chicago: University of Chicago Press.

Birren, J. E. 1968. Psychological aspects of aging and intellectual functioning. *The Gerontologist* 8(1, Part II):19.

BJS (Bureau of Justice Statistics). 1987a. *Recidivism of young parolees.* Washington, D.C.: U.S. Government Printing Office.

———. 1987b. *Violent crime by strangers and nonstrangers.* Washington, D.C.: U.S. Government Printing Office.

———. 1989a. *Recidivism of prisoners released in 1983.* Washington, D.C.: U.S. Government Printing Office.

———. 1991. Reported in the *New York Times*, January 15, p. A5.

Blackburn, M. L. and Bloom, D. E. 1985. What is happening to the middle class? *American Demographics* 7:18–25.

Blake, J. 1982. Demographic revolution and family evolution: Some implications for American women. In P. W. Berman and E. R. Ramey (Eds.), *Women: A developmental perspective*, pp. 299–312. (NIH Publication No. 82–2298). Washington, D.C.: U.S. Department of Health and Human Services.

———. 1985. Number of siblings and educational mobility. *American Sociological Review* 50(1):84–93.

Blalock, H. M. 1964. *Causal inferences in nonexperimental research.* Chapel Hill: University of North Carolina Press.

———. **(Ed.).** 1985. *Causal models in experimental and panel designs.* Chicago: Aldine.

Blau, P. M. 1964. *Exchange and power in social life.* New York: Wiley.

———. 1973. *The dynamics of bureaucracy* (2nd rev. ed.). Chicago: University of Chicago Press.

———. **(Ed.).** 1975. *Approaches to the study of social structure.* New York: Free Press.

Blau, P. M., Blum, T. C., and Schwartz, J. E. 1982. Heterogeneity and intermarriage. *American Sociological Review* 47(1):45–62.

Blau, P. M., and Duncan, O. D. D. 1967. *The American occupational structure.* New York: Wiley.

Blau, Z. S. 1982. *Old age in a changing society* (2nd ed.). New York: Watts.

Blauner, R. 1964. *Alienation and freedom.* Chicago: University of Chicago Press.

————. 1972. Racism as the negation of culture. In *Racial oppression in America.* New York: Harper and Row.

————. 1989. *Black lives, white lives: Three decades of race relations in America.* Berkeley: University of California Press.

Bleier, R. 1984. *Science and gender: A critique of biology and its theories on women.* New York: Pergamon Press.

Bloch, M. 1961. *Feudal society.* Chicago: University of Chicago Press.

Block, A. A., and Chambliss, W. J. 1981. *Organizing crime.* New York: Elsevier North Holland.

Block, N. J., and Dworkin, G. (Eds.). 1976. *The IQ controversy.* New York: Pantheon.

Blood, R. O., and Wolfe, D. M. 1960. *Husbands and wives.* New York: Free Press.

Bloom, D. E. 1982. What's happening to the age at first birth in the United States? A study of recent cohorts. *Demography* 19(3):351–70.

BLS (Bureau of Labor Statistics). 1986. Findings reported in the *New York Times,* November 30, Business Section, p. 1.

————. 1987. Findings reported in the *New York Times,* September 27, Business Section, p. 1.

————. 1988. Findings reported in the *New York Times,* January 24.

————. 1990. Findings reported in the *New York Times,* June 2, p. 13.

Bluestone, B., and Harrison, B. 1982. *The deindustrialization of America: Plant closings, community abandonment, and the dismantling of basic industry.* New York: Basic Books.

Blumin, S. M. 1989. *The emergence of the middle class: Social experience in the American City, 1760–1900.* Cambridge: Cambridge University Press.

Blumenthal, M. D., Kahn, R. L., Andrews, F. M., and Head, K. B. 1972. *Justifying violence: Attitudes of American men.* Ann Arbor, MI: Institute for Social Research.

Blumer, H. [1939] 1951. Collective behavior. In A. M. Lee (Ed.), *New outline of the principles of sociology.* New York: Barnes and Noble.

————. 1969. *Symbolic interactionism: Perspective and method.* Englewood Cliffs, NJ: Prentice-Hall.

Blumer, M. 1984. *The Chicago school of sociology: Institutionalization, diversity, and the rise of sociological research.* Chicago: University of Chicago Press.

Bogard, W. 1989. *The Bhopal tragedy: Language, logic, and politics in the production of a hazard.* Boulder: Westview Press.

Bok, S. 1979. *Lying: Moral choice in public and private life.* New York: Vintage.

Bollen, K. 1983. World system position, dependency, and democracy. *American Sociological Review* 48 (August):468–79.

Bollen, K., and Jackman, R. W. 1985. Political democracy. *American Sociological Review* 50(4): 438–57.

Booth, A., and Edwards, J. N. 1985. Age at marriage and marital instability. *Journal of Marriage and the Family* 47:67–75.

Bose, C. E. 1985. *Jobs and gender: A study of occupational prestige.* New York: Praeger.

Bosrup, E. 1981. *Population and technological change.* Chicago: University of Chicago Press.

Boss, P. G. 1980. Normative family stress: Family boundary changes across the life span. *Family Relations* 29:445–50.

Boswell, T. E. 1986. Discrimination and Chinese immigration. *American Sociological Review* 51(3):352–71.

Bottles, S. L. 1987. *Los Angeles and the automobile: The making of the modern city.* Berkeley and Los Angeles: University of California Press.

Bottomore, T. (Ed.). 1963. *Karl Marx: Early writings.* London: Watts.

————. 1975. Structure and history. In P. M. Blau (Ed.), *Approaches to the study of social structure.* New York: Free Press.

————. **(Ed.).** 1983. *A Dictionary of Marxist Thought.* New York: Basil Blackwell.

Bottomore, T., and Brym, R. J. (Eds.). 1989. *The capitalist class: An international study.* New York: New York University Press.

Bottomore, T., and Nisbet, R. (Eds.). 1978. *A history of sociological analysis.* New York: Basic Books.

Bottomore, T., and Rubel, M. (Eds.). 1965. *Karl Marx: Selected writings in sociology and social philosophy.* New York: McGraw-Hill.

Bouvier, L. F., and Gardner, R. W. 1986. Immigration to the U.S.: The unfinished story. *Population Bulletin* 41(1, November). Washington, D.C.: Population Reference Bureau.

Bouvier, L. F., Shyrock, H. S., and Hendersen, H. W. 1977. International migration: Yesterday, today, and tomorrow. *Population Bulletin* 30: 3–24.

Bowen, H. R., and Schuster, J. H. 1986. *American professors: A national resource imperiled.* New York: Oxford University Press.

Bowen, W. G., and Sosa, J. A. 1989. *Prospects for faculty in the arts and sciences.* Princeton, NJ: Princeton University Press.

Bowles, S. 1968. Toward equality of educational opportunity? *Harvard Educational Review* 38:89–99.

Bowles, S., and Gintis, H. 1976. *Schooling in capitalist America: Educational reform and the contradictions of economic life.* New York: Basic Books.

————. 1986. *Democracy and capitalism.* New York: Basic Books.

Bowles, S., and Nelson, V. 1974. The 'inheritance of IQ' and the intergenerational reproduction of economic inequality. *Review of Economics and Statistics* 56(1).

Boyd, R., and Richersen, P. J. 1985. *Culture and the evolutionary process.* Chicago: University of Chicago Press.

Bradbury, K., Downs, A., and Small, K. A. 1982. *Urban decline and the future of American cities.* Washington, D.C.: Brookings Institution.

Bradshaw, Y. W. 1985. Dependent development in black Africa. *American Sociological Review* 50(2):195–206.

————. 1987. Urbanization and underdevelopment: A global study of modernization, urban bias, and economic dependency. *American Sociological Review* 52(2):224–39.

Braithwaite, J. 1981. The myth of social class and criminology reconsidered. *American Sociological Review* 46 (February):36–57.

Braudel, F. 1977. *Afterthoughts on material civilization and capitalism.* Baltimore: Johns Hopkins University Press.

————. 1981. *The structures of everyday life: Civilization and capitalism, 15th-18th century, volume one.* New York: Harper & Row.

————. 1983. *The wheels of commerce: Civilization and capitalism, 15th-18th century, volume one.* New York: Harper and Row.

————. 1984. *The perspective of the world: Civilization and capitalism, 15th-18th century, volume three.* New York: Harper & Row.

Braverman, H. 1974. *Labor and monopoly capital.* New York: Monthly Review Press.

Breault, K. D. 1986. Suicide in America: A test of Durkheim's theory of religious and family integration. *American Journal of Sociology* 92(3):628–56.

Brenner, R. 1976. Agrarian class structure and economic development in preindustrial Europe. *Past and Present,* 70:30–75.

Bretl, D. J., and Cantor, J. 1988. The portrayal of men and women in U.S. television commercials. *Sex Roles* 18(9/10):595–609.

Brim, O. G., Jr. 1966. Socialization after childhood. In O. G. Brim, Jr., S. Wheeler, *Socialization after childhood: Two essays.* New York: Wiley.

Brint, S., and Karabel, J. 1989. *The diverted dream: Community colleges and the promise of education.* New York: Oxford University Press.

Brissett, D., and Edgley, C. (Eds.). 1990. *Life as theater: A dramaturgical sourcebook* (2nd ed.). Hawthorne, NY: Aldine de Gruyter. Broad, W. J. 1988. Science can't keep up with flood of new journals. *New York Times* February 14:C1.

Broad, W., and Wade, N. 1983. *Betrayers of the truth: Fraud and deceit in the halls of science.* New York: Simon and Schuster/Touchstone.

Brody, J. A. 1983. Life expectancy and the health of older people. *American Journal of Geriatric Sociology.*

Bronfenbrenner, U. 1970. *Two worlds of childhood.* New York: Russell Sage Foundation.

Broverman, I. K., Broverman, D., Clarkson, F., Rosenkrantz, P., and Vogel, S. 1970. Sex-role stereotypes and clinical judgements of mental health. *Journal of Consulting and Clinical Psychology* 34:1–7.

Brown, A. S. 1990. *The social processes of aging and old age.* Englewood Cliffs, NJ: Prentice-Hall.

Brown, D. L., and Wardwell, J. M. (Eds.). 1980. *New directions in urban-rural migration: The population turnaround in rural America.* New York: Academic Press.

Brown, R. 1965. *Social psychology.* New York: Free Press.

Brownmiller, S. 1975. *Against our will: Men, women, and rape.* New York: Simon and Schuster.

Brumberg, J. J. 1988. *Fasting girls: The emergence of anorexia nervosa as a modern disease.* Cambridge, MA: Harvard University Press.

Bumpass, L. L., and Sweet, J. A. 1989. National estimates of cohabitation. *Demography* 26(4):615–25.

Bumpass, L. L., Sweet, J. A., and Martin, T. C. 1990. Changing patterns of remarriage. *Journal of Marriage and the Family* 52(3):747–56.

Burawoy, M., and Lukacs, J. 1985. Capitalist and socialist work. *American Sociological Review* 50(6):723–37.

Burch, P. H., Jr. 1972. *The managerial revolution reassessed.* Lexington, MA: D. C. Heath.

Burke, K. 1935. *Permanence and change.* New York: Republic.

————. 1945. *A grammar of motives.* Englewood Cliffs, NJ: Prentice-Hall.

Burke, P. J., and Reitzes, D. C. 1981. The link between identity and role performance. *Social Psychology Quarterly* 44:83–92.

Burns, H. 1973. Black people and the tyranny of American law. *The Annals* 407 (May):156–66.

Burnside, I. M. 1975. Sexuality and the older adult: Implications for nursing. In I. M. Burnside (Ed.), *Sexuality and aging.* Los Angeles: Ethel Percy Andrus Gerontology Center.

Bush, D. M., and Simmons, R. G. 1981. Socialization processes over the life course. In M. Rosenberg and R. H. Turner (Eds.), *Social psychology: Sociological perspectives,* pp. 133–64. New York: Basic Books.

Buss, T. F., and Redburn, F. S. 1983. *Shutdown at Youngstown: Public policy for mass unemployment.* Albany, NY: State University of New York Press.

Bussey, K., and Bandura, A. 1984. Influence of gender constancy and social power on sex-linked modeling. *Journal of Personality and Social Psychology* 47:1292-1302.

Buttel, F. H. 1987. New directions in environmental sociology. *Annual Review of Sociology* 13:465–88.

Calavita, K. 1984. *U.S. immigration law and the control of labor: 1820–1924.* Orlando, FL: Academic Press.

Calhoun, J. B. 1962. Population density and social pathology. *The Scientific American* CCVI:139–48.

Callahan, R. E. 1962. *Education and the cult of efficiency.* Chicago: University of Chicago Press.

Campbell, A. A. 1947. Factors associated with attitudes towards Jews. In T. Newcomb and E. Hartley (Eds.), *Readings in social psychology.* New York: Holt, Rinehart, and Winston.

————. 1971. *White attitudes toward black people.* Ann

Arbor, MI: University of Michigan Institute for Social Research.

Campbell, A. A., and Schuman, H. 1968. Racial attitudes in fifteen American cities. In *Supplementary studies for the national advisory commission on civil disorders* (see Kerner Commission). Washington, D.C.: U.S. Government Printing Office.

Cantor, M. G., and Pingree, S. 1983. *The soap opera.* Beverly Hills, CA: Sage Publications.

Cantril, H. 1963. *The psychology of social movements.* New York: Wiley.

Caplow, T. 1947. Rumors in war. *Social Forces* 25: 298–302.

————. 1956. A theory of coalitions in the triad. *American Sociological Review* 21:489–93.

————. 1968. *Two against one: Coalitions in triads.* Englewood Cliffs, NJ: Prentice-Hall.

————. 1982. Christmas gifts and kin networks. *American Sociological Review* 47 (June):383–92.

Caplow, T., et al. 1983. *All faithful people.* Minneapolis: University of Minnesota Press.

Carnegie (Council on Policy Studies in Higher Education). 1979. Giving youth a better change: Options for education, work, and service. *The Chronicle of Higher Education* (December 3):11–13.

Carnegie (Foundation for the Advancement of Teaching). 1988. *An imperiled generation: Saving urban schools.* New York: Carnegie Foundation.

————. 1990. *Campus: In research of community.* Princeton, NJ: Princeton University Press.

Carnoy, M., and Levin, H. 1985. *Schooling and work in the democratic state.* Stanford, CA: Stanford University Press.

Case, C. E., Greeley, A. M., and Fuchs, S. 1989. Social determinants of racial prejudice. *Sociological Perspectives* 32(4):469–83.

Castelli, J. 1983. *The bishops and the bomb: Waging peace in a nuclear age.* New York: Image.

Castells, M. 1977. *The urban question: A Marxist approach.* (A. Sheridan, Trans.). Cambridge, MA: The MIT Press.

————. 1980. *The economic crisis of American society.* Princeton, NJ: Princeton University Press.

Cath, S. H., Gurwitt, A. R., and Ross, J. M. (Eds.). 1982. *Father and child: Developmental and clinical perspectives.* Boston: Little Brown.

CAWP (Center for the American Woman and Politics). 1991. Reported in the *New York Times*, February 25, p. A6.

CBO (Congressional Budget Office). 1987. Findings reported in the *New York Times*, November 12, p. A26.

————. 1988. Reported in the *New York Times*, February 2, p. 1.

Chackerian, R., and Abcarian, G. 1984. *Bureaucratic power in society.* Chicago: Nelson-Hall.

Chafetz, J. S. 1984. *Sex and advantage: A comparative,*

macro-structural theory of sex stratification. Totowa, NJ: Rowman and Allanheld.

Chafetz, J. S., and Dworkin, A. G. 1986. *Female revolt: Women's movements in world and historical perspective.* Totowa, NJ: Rowman & Allanheld.

Chalfant, H. P., Beckley, R. E., and Palmer, L. E. 1981. *Religion in contemporary society.* Palo Alto, CA: Mayfield.

Chambliss, W. J. 1969. *Crime and legal process.* New York: McGraw-Hill.

————. 1973. The Saints and the Roughnecks. *Society* 11:24–31.

————. 1978. Toward a political economy of crime. In C. E. Reasons and R. M. Rich (Eds.), *The sociology of law: A conflict perspective.* Toronto: Butterworths.

Chapman, J. I. 1976. An economic model of crime and police: Some empirical results. *Journal of Research in Crime and Delinquency* 13 (January):48–63.

Cheng, L., and Bonacich, E. 1984. *Labor immigration under capitalism: Asian workers in the United States before World War II.* Berkeley, CA: University of California Press.

Cherlin, A. 1981. *Marriage, divorce, remarriage.* Cambridge, MA: Harvard University Press.

————. 1983. Changing family and household: Contemporary lessons from historical research. *Annual Review of Sociology* 9:51–66.

Cherlin, A., and Furstenberg, F. F. 1983. The American family in the year 2000. *The Futurist* June:7–14.

Cherlin, A., and McCarthy, J. 1985. Remarried households: Data from the June 1980 Current Population Survey. *Journal of Marriage and the Family* 47(1):23–30.

Cherlin, A. J. (Ed.). 1988. *The changing American family and public policy.* Washington, D.C.: Urban Institute Press.

Chernin, K. 1981. *The obsession: Reflections on the tyranny of slenderness.* New York: Harper and Row.

————. 1987. *Reinventing Eve.* New York: Times Books.

Cherry, K. 1988. *Womansword: What Japanese words say about women.* New York: Kodansha International.

Chirot, D. 1977. *Social change in the twentieth century.* New York: Harcourt Brace Jovanovich.

————. 1980. Changing fashions in the study of the social causes of economic and social change. In J. F. Short (Ed.), *The state of sociology*, pp. 259–82. Beverly Hills, CA: Sage Publications.

————. 1985. The rise of the west. *American Sociological Review* 50(2):181–94.

————. 1986. *Social change in the modern era.* San Diego, CA: Harcourt Brace Jovanovich.

Chirot, D., and Hall, T. D. 1982, World-system theory. *Annual Review of Sociology* 8:81–106.

Chomsky, N. 1957. *Syntactic structures.* The Hague: Mouton.

————. 1966. *Cartesian linguistics.* New York: Harper and Row.

Christ, C. P. 1983. Heretics and outsiders: The struggle

Christ, C. P. (continued)
over female power in western religion, in L. Richardson and V. Taylor (Eds.), *Feminist Frontiers*, pp. 87–94. Reading, MA: Addison-Wesley.

Clark, B. R. 1960. The cooling-out function in higher education. *American Journal of Sociology* 65 (May).

Clark, B. R., and Trow, M. 1966. The organizational context. In B. R. Clark and M. Trow (Eds.), *College peer groups*. Chicago: Aldine.

Clark, C. 1987. Sympathy biography and sympathy margin. *American Journal of Sociology* 93(2):290–300.

Clark, G. K. 1962. *The making of Victorian England*. Cambridge, MA: Harvard University Press.

Clark, K. B. 1965. *Dark ghetto*. New York: Harper and Row.

Clausen, J. A. 1976. Drug use. In R. K. Merton and R. Nisbet (Eds.), *Contemporary social problems* (4th ed.). New York: Harcourt Brace Jovanovich.

————. 1986. *The life course: A sociological perspective*. Englewood Cliffs, NJ: Prentice-Hall.

Clawson, D., Neustadtl, A., and Bearden, J. 1986. The logic of business unity. *American Sociological Review* 51(6):797–811.

Clinard, M. B. 1983. *Corporate ethics and crime: The role of middle management*. Beverly Hills, CA: Sage Publications.

Clinard, M. B., and Yeager, P. C. 1980. *Corporate crime*. New York: The Free Press.

Cloward, R. A., and Ohlin, L. E. 1960. *Delinquency and opportunity: A theory of delinquent gangs*. New York: Free Press.

Coale, A. J. 1964. How a population ages or grows younger. In R. Freedman (Ed.), *Population: The vital revolution*. New York: Anchor Books.

Cockerham, W. C. 1986. *Medical sociology* (3rd ed.). Englewood Cliffs, NJ: Prentice-Hall.

————. 1991. *This aging society*. Englewood Cliffs, NJ: Prentice-Hall.

Cohen, A. K. 1955. *Delinquent boys: The culture of the gang*. New York: Free Press.

Cohen, A. M. 1990. The case for community colleges. *American Journal of Education* 98 (August).

Cohen, S. 1985. *Visions of social control*. Cambridge: Polity Press.

Cohen, L. E., and Land, K. C. 1987. Age structure and crime: Symmetry versus asymmetry and the projection of crime rates. *American Sociological Review* 52(2):170–83.

Cohen, L. E., and Machalek, R. 1988. A general theory of expropriative crime: An evolutionary ecological approach. *American Journal of Sociology* 94(3):465–501.

Cole, S. G., and Cole, M. W. 1954. *Minorities and the American promise*. New York: Harper and Row.

Coleman, J. S. 1961. *The adolescent society*. New York: Free Press.

Coleman, J. S., et al. 1966. *Equality of educational opportunity*. Washington, D.C. U.S. Government Printing Office.

————. 1974. *Youth: Transition to adult*. Chicago: University of Chicago Press.

Coleman, J. S., Kelly, S. D., and Moore, J. A. 1975. *Trends in school segregation, 1968–1973*. Washington, D.C.: The Urban Institute.

Coleman, R. P., Rainwater, L. (with McClelland, K. A.). 1978. *Social standing in America*. New York: Basic Books.

Coleman, J. W. 1987. Toward an integrated theory of white-collar crime. *American Journal of Sociology* 93 (September):406–39.

Coles, R. 1968. *Children in crisis*. New York: Dell.

Collins, R. 1975. *Conflict sociology: Toward an explanatory science*. New York: Academic Press.

————. 1982. *Sociological insight: An introduction to nonobvious sociology*. New York: Oxford University Press.

————. 1989. Sociology: Proscience or antiscience? *American Sociological Review* 54(1):124–39.

Coltrane, S. 1988. Father-child relationships and the status of women: A cross-cultural study. *American Journal of Sociology* 93(5):1060–1095.

Commission on Minority Participation. 1988. *One-third of a nation*. Washington, D.C.: American Council on Education.

Comte, A. [1854] 1898. *The course of positivist philosophy* (H. Martineau, trans.) London: Bell & Sons.

Conklin, N. F., and Lourie, M. A. 1983. *A host of tongues: Language communities in the United States*. New York: Free Press.

Connor, W. P. 1979. *Socialism, politics, and equality*. New York: Columbia University Press.

Cook, R. C. 1957. World migration: 1945–1955. *Population Bulletin* 13:77–94.

Cookson, P. W., and Persell, C. H. 1985. *Preparing for power: America's elite boarding schools*. New York: Basic Books.

————. 1986. The price of privilege. *Psychology Today* (March):30–35.

Cooley, C. H. [1902] 1964. *Human nature and the social order*. New York: Schocken.

————. [1909] 1962. *Social organization*. New York: Schocken Books.

————. 1927. *Life and the student*. New York: Knopf.

Cooper, H. M., and Good, T. L. 1983. *Pygmalion grows up*. New York: Longman.

Cordes, C. 1984. Easing toward perfection at Twin Oaks: Walden Two model now 17. *APA Monitor* (November):1. Washington, D.C.: American Psychological Association.

Corea, G., Klein, R. D., Hanmer, J., Holmes, H. B., Hoskins, B., Kishwar, M., Raymond, J., Rowland, R., and Steinbacker, R. (Eds.). 1987. *Man-made women: How reproductive technologies affect women*. Bloomington, IN: Indiana University Press.

Coser, L. A. 1964. *The functions of social conflict*. Glencoe, IL: The Free Press.

————. 1967. *Continuities in the study of social conflict.* New York: Free Press.

————. (Ed.). 1975a. *The idea of social structure: Papers in honor of Robert K. Merton.* New York: Harcourt Brace Jovanovich.

————. 1975b. Structure and conflict. In P. M. Blau (Ed.), *Approaches to the study of social structure.* New York: Free Press.

————. 1977. *Masters of sociological thought* (2nd ed.). New York: Harcourt Brace Jovanovich.

Coser, R. L. 1966. Role distance, sociological ambivalence, and transitional status systems. *American Journal of Sociology* 77(2):173–87.

Cott, N. F. 1987. *The grounding of modern feminism.* New Haven: Yale University Press.

Coulton, G. G. 1926. *The medieval village.* London: Cambridge University Press.

Courtney, A. E., and Whipple, T. W. 1983. *Sex stereotyping in advertising.* Lexington, MA: Lexington Books.

Coverman, S. 1983. Gender, domestic labor time, and wage inequality. *American Sociological Review* 48: 623–37.

Cox, H. G. 1990. *Later life: The realities of aging* (2nd ed.). Englewood Cliffs, NJ: Prentice-Hall.

Crain, R. L. 1975. School integration and occupational achievement of Negroes. In Pettigrew (1975), pp. 206–24.

Crowne, D. P., and Marlowe, D. 1980. *The approval motive.* Westport, CT: Greenwood Press.

CSAWF (Commission on the Skills of the American Workforce). 1990. Reported in the *New York Times,* June 18, p. A1.

Csikszentmihalyi, M., and Rochberg-Halton, E. 1981. *The meaning of things: Symbols in the development of the self.* Cambridge, England: Cambridge University Press.

Curtin, P. D. 1969. *The Atlantic slave trade.* Madison, WI: University of Wisconsin Press.

Curtis, H., and Barnes, N. S. 1981. *Invitation to biology* (3rd ed.). New York: Worth.

Dadrian, W. N. 1971. Factors of anger and aggression in genocide. *Journal of Human Relations* 19:394–417.

Dahl, R. A. 1961. *Who governs? Democracy and power in an American city.* New Haven: Yale University Press.

Dahrendorf, R. 1958. Out of utopia: Toward a reorientation of sociological analysis. *American Journal of Sociology* 63:115–27.

————. 1959. *Class and class conflict in industrial society.* Stanford, CA: Stanford University Press.

————. 1973. Toward a theory of social conflict. In A. Etzioni and E. Etzioni-Halvey (Eds.), *Social change: Sources, patterns, and consequences.* New York: Basic Books.

Daly, M. 1973. *Beyond God the Father.* Boston: Beacon Press.

Dantin, H. M., and Carver, C. S. 1982. Induced competences and the bystander effect. *Journal of Applied Social Psychology* 12(2):100–111.

Dar, Y., and Resh, N. 1986. *Classroom composition and pupil achievement: A study of the effect of ability-based classed.* New York: Gordon and Breach.

Darwin, C. [1859] 1962. *On the origin of species.* New York: Macmillan.

Das, M. S., and Bardis, P. D. (Eds.). 1978. *The family in Asia.* Flushing, NY: Asia Book Corporation.

Davies, J. C. 1962. Toward a theory of revolution. *American Sociological Review* 27:5–18.

Davis, J. A., and Smith, T. W. 1977. *General social surveys, 1972–1977: Cumulative codebook.* Chicago: National Opinion Research Center.

————. 1987. *General social surveys, 1972–1987: Cumulative codebook.* Chicago: National Opinion Research Center.

————. 1989. *General social surveys, 1972–1989: Cumulative codebook.* Chicago: National Opinion Research Center.

————. 1990. *General social surveys, 1972–1990: Cumulative codebook.* Chicago: National Opinion Research Center.

Davis, K. 1940. Extreme social isolation of a child. *American Journal of Sociology* 45:554–64.

————. 1947. Final note on a case of extreme isolation. *American Journal of Sociology,* 50, pp. 432–37.

————. 1953. Reply to Tumin. *American Sociological Review,* 18 (August), pp. 394–97.

————. 1974. The migrations of human populations. *Scientific American* 231:92–105.

Davis, K., Bernstam, M., and Ricardo-Campbell, R. 1987. *Below-replacement fertility in industrial societies: Causes, consequences, policies.* Cambridge, England: Cambridge University Press.

Davis, K., and Blake, J. 1956. Social structure and fertility: An analytic framework. *Economic Development and Cultural Change* 4:211–35.

Davis, K., and Moore, W. E. 1945. Some principles of stratification. *American Sociological Review* 10:242–49.

Davis, M. H., and Stephan, W. G. 1980. Attributions for exam performance. *Journal of Applied Social Psychology* 10(3):235–48.

Davis, N., and Robinson, R. V. 1991. Men's and women's consciousness of gender inequality: Austria, West Germany, Great Britain, and the United States. *American Sociological Review* 56(1):72–84.

Davis-Friedmann, D. 1983. *Long lives: Elderly and the communist revolution.* Cambridge, MA: Harvard University Press.

Dawidowicz, L. S. 1975. *The war against the Jews: 1933–1945.* New York: Holt, Rinehart and Winston.

Deane, P., and Cole, W. A. 1962. *British economic growth 1688–1959: Trends and structure.* London: Cambridge University Press.

Deaux, K. 1972. To err is humanizing. But sex makes a

Deaux, K. *(continued)*
difference. *Representative Research in Social Psychology* 3:20–28.

Deci, E. L. 1975. *Intrinsic motivation.* New York: Plenum.

Degler, C. N. 1980. *At odds: Women and the family in America from the revolution to the present.* New York: Oxford University Press.

D'Emilio, J., and Freedman, E. B. 1988. *Intimate matters: A history of sexuality in America.* New York: Harper and Row.

Demos, J. 1970. *A little commonwealth: Family life in Plymouth Colony.* New York: Oxford University Press.

———. 1986. *Past, present, and personal: The family and the life course in American history.* New York: Basic Books.

Denton, N. A., and Massey, D. S. 1988. Residential segregation of blacks, hispanics, and asians by socioeconomic status and generation. *Social Science Quarterly* 69 (December):797–817.

———. 1989. Racial identity among caribbean hispanics: The effect of double minority status on residential segregation. *American Sociological Review* 54(5):790–808.

Deutsch, M., and Gerard, H. B. 1955. A study of normative and informational social influences upon individual judgement. *Journal of Abnormal and Social Psychology* 51:629–36.

Devine, J. A. 1983. Class inequality and state policy. *American Sociological Review* 48 (October):606–22.

DHHS (Department of Health and Human Services). 1990. *Report of the United States Advisory Board on Child Abuse and Neglect.* Washington, D.C.: U.S. Government Printing Office.

Diaz, B. 1974. *The conquest of New Spain* (J. M. Cohen, Trans.). London: The Folio Society.

Dijkstra, B. 1987. *Idols of perversity: Fantasies of feminine evil.* New York: Oxford University Press.

Dobash, R. E., and Dobash, R. 1979. *Violence against wives.* New York: Free Press.

Dobbs, J. 1972. *Sex, setting, and reactions of crowding on sidewalks.* Paper presented at the American Psychological Association meeting, Honolulu.

Dohrenwend, B. P., and Dohrenwend, B. S. 1976. Sex differences in psychiatric disorders. *American Journal of Sociology* 81:1447–54.

Dollard, J., et al. 1939. *Frustration and aggression.* New Haven: Yale University Press.

Domhoff, G. W. 1967. *Who rules America?* Englewood Cliffs, NJ: Prentice-Hall.

———. 1971. *The higher circles.* New York: Random House.

———. 1983. *Who rules America now?* Englewood Cliffs, NJ: Prentice-Hall.

Domhoff, G. W., and Zweigenhaft, R. L. 1983. Jews in the corporate establishment. *New York Times,* April 24.

Dornbusch, S. M. 1989. The sociology of adolescence. *Annual Review of Sociology* 15:233–59.

Douglas, J. D., and Waksler, F. C. 1982. *The sociology of deviance: An introduction.* Boston: Little Brown.

Douvan, E., and Adelson, J. 1966. *The adolescent experience.* New York: Wiley.

Dovidio, J., and Gaertner, S. (Eds.). 1986. *Prejudice, discrimination, and racism.* Orlando: Academic Press.

Draper, T. 1962. *Castro's revolution: Myths and realities.* New York: Praeger.

Drew, E. 1983. *Politics and money.* New York: Macmillan.

Dubnos, P. 1985. Attitudes toward women executives: A longitudinal approach. *Academy of Management Journal* 28(1):235–39.

Dudley, J. R. 1983. *Living with stigma: The plight of people we label mentally retarded.* Springfield, IL: Charles C. Thomas.

Duleep, H. O. 1988. *The economic status of Americans of Asian descent.* Washington, D.C.: U.S. Commission on Civil Rights.

Duncan, G. J., Coe, R. D., Corcoran, M. E., Hill, M. S., Hoffman, S. D., and Morgan, J. N. 1984. *Years of poverty, years of plenty: The changing economic fortunes of American workers and families.* Ann Arbor, MI: Institute for Social Research, University of Michigan.

Duncan, G. J., and Smith, K. R. 1989. The rising affluence of the elderly: How far, how fair, and how frail? *Annual Review of Sociology* 15:261–89.

Duncan, O. D. 1961. From social system to ecosystem. *Sociological Inquiry* 31:140–49.

———. 1969. Inheritance of poverty or inheritance of race? In D. P. Moynihan (Ed.), *On understanding poverty* 85–110. New York: Basic Books.

Duncan, O. D., and Duncan, B. 1955. Residential distribution and occupational stratification. *American Journal of Sociology* 60(5):493–503.

Duncan, O. D., and Schnore, L. F. 1959. Cultural, behavioral, and ecological perspectives in the study of social organization. *American Journal of Sociology* 65.

Dunn, J., and Kendrick, C. 1982. *Siblings: Love, envy, and understanding.* Cambridge, MA: Harvard University Press.

Durden-Smith, J., and DiSimone, D. 1983. *Sex and the brain.* New York: Arbor House.

Durkheim, E. [1893] 1933. *The division of labor in society.* New York: Free Press.

———. [1895] 1938. *The rules of the sociological method.* New York: Free Press.

———. [1897] 1951. *Suicide.* New York: Free Press.

———. [1912] 1965. *The elementary forms of religious life.* New York: Free Press.

———. [1924] 1974. *Sociology and philosophy.* New York: The Free Press.

Duverger, M. 1959. *Political parties* (B. North and R. North, Trans.). London: Methuen.

Dworkin, A. 1974. *Woman hating.* New York: E. P. Dutton.

Dziech, B. W., and Weiner, L. 1984. *The lecherous professor: Portrait of an artist.* Boston: Beacon Press.

Eagly, A. H. 1987. *Sex differences in social behavior*. Hillsdale, NJ: Laurence Erlbaum Associates.

Eckert, P. 1989. *Jocks and burnouts: Social categories and identity in high school*. New York: Teachers College Press.

Edelman, M. W., et al. 1985. *Barriers to excellence: Our children at risk*. Boston: National Coalition of Advocates for Students.

Edgerton, R. B. 1985. *Rules, exceptions, and social order*. Berkeley, CA: University of California Press.

Edwards, J. 1984. Language, diversity, and identity. In Edwards, J. (Ed.), *Linguistic minorities: Policies and pluralism*, pp. 277–310. New York: Academic Press.

Edwards, J. R., and Williams, J. E. 1980. Sex-trait stereotypes among young children and young adults: Canadian findings and cross-national comparisons. *Canadian Journal of Behavioral Science* 12:210–20.

Edwards, R. C., Reich, M., and Weisskopf, T. E. 1986. The capitalist economy: Structure and change. In Edwards, Reich, and Weisskopf (Eds.), *The capitalist system* (3rd ed.), pp. 4–15. Englewood Cliffs, NJ: Prentice-Hall.

Ehrenreich, B., and English, D. 1979. *For her own good: 150 years of the experts' advice to women*. Garden City, NY: Anchor.

Eisenstadt, S. N. 1956. *From generation to generation*. New York: Free Press.

Eisenstein, E. 1980. *The printing press as an agent of change*. Cambridge, England: Cambridge University Press.

Eisler, R. 1987. *The chalice and the blade*. New York: Harper and Row.

Elder, G. H. 1974. *Children of the Great Depression*. Chicago: University of Chicago Press.

Eldridge, H. T. 1968. Population policies. In D. L. Sills (Ed.), *The international encyclopedia of the social sciences* (Vol.12). New York: Macmillan/Free Press.

Elliot, D. S., and Ageton, S. S. 1980. Reconciling race and class differences in self-reported and official estimates of delinquency. *American Sociological Review* 45 (February):95–110.

Ellis, G., Lee, G., and Peterson, L. 1978. Supervision and conformity: A cross-cultural analysis of parental socialization values. *American Journal of Sociology* 84:386–403.

Ellison, R. 1968. *The invisible man*. New York: Random House.

Ellwood, D. T. 1988. *Poor support: Poverty in the American family*. New York: Basic Books.

Emerson, R. M. 1981a. Social exchange theory. In M. Rosenberg and R. H. Turner (Eds.), *Social psychology: Sociological perspectives*. New York: Basic Books.

————. 1981b. Observational field work. *Annual Review of Sociology* 7:315–78.

Empey, L. 1982. *American delinquency: Its meaning and construction*. Homewood, IL: Dorsey.

Engels, F. [1845] 1962. *Conditions of the working class in England in 1844*. Moscow: Foreign Languages Publishing House.

————. [1891] 1972. *The origin of the family, private property, and the state*. New York: Pathfinder Press.

England, P., and Dunn, D. 1988. Evaluating work and comparable worth. *Annual Review of Sociology* 14:227–48.

England, P., Farkas, G., Kilbourne, B. S., and Dou, T. 1988. Explaining occupational sex segregation and wages: Findings from a model with fixed effects. *American Sociological Review* 53(4):544–58.

Epstein, A. L. 1967. Urbanization and social change in Africa. *Current Anthropology* 8:275–95.

Epstein, C. F. 1983. *Women in law*. New York: Doubleday/Anchor.

————. 1989. *Deceptive distinctions: Sex, gender, and the social order*. New Haven, CT: Yale University Press.

Epstein, C. F., and Coser, R. L. (Eds.). 1981. *Access to power: Cross-national studies of women and elites*. London: Allen Unwin.

Erikson, E. H. 1963. *Childhood and society* (2nd ed.). New York: Norton.

————. 1968. *Identity, youth, and crisis*. New York: Norton.

Erikson, K. T. 1966. *Wayward Puritans: A study in the sociology of deviance*. New York: Wiley.

————. 1986. Work and alienation. *American Sociological Review* 51(1):1–8.

Erkut, S. 1984. Exploring sex differences in expectancy, attribution, and academic achievement. *Sex Roles* 9:217–31.

Espenshade, T. J. 1984. *Investing in children: New estimates of parental expenditures*. Washington, D.C.: Urban Institute Press.

Etaugh, C., and Kasley, H. C. 1981. Evaluating competence: Effects of sex, marital status, and parental status. *Psychology of Women Quarterly* 6(2):196–203.

Etienne, M., and Leacock, E. (Eds.). 1980. *Women and colonization: Anthropological perspectives*. New York: Praeger.

Etzioni-Halevy, E. 1983. *Bureaucracy and democracy: A political dilemma*. Boston: Routledge and Kegan Paul.

Eurich, N. P. 1981. *Systems of higher education in twelve countries*. New York: Praeger.

Evans, P. B. 1979. *Dependent development: The alliance of multinational, state, and local capital in Brazil*. Princeton, NJ: Princeton University Press.

————. 1981. Recent research on multinational corporations. *Annual Review of Sociology* 7:199–223.

Evans, P. B., and Timberlake, M. 1980. Dependence, inequality, and the growth of the tertiary: A comparative analysis of less developed countries. *American Sociological Review* 45(4):531–52.

Evans, S. M., and Nelson, B. J. 1989. *Wage justice: Comparable worth and the paradox of technocratic reform*. Chicago: University of Chicago Press.

Fagot, B., Hagan, R., Leinbach, M., and Kronsberg, S. 1985. Differential reactions to assertive and communicative acts of toddler boys and girls. *Child Development* 56:1499–1505.

Farb, P. 1973. *Word play: What happens when people talk.* New York: Alfred A. Knopf. (1975 refers to the Bantam paperback edition).

Farb, P., and Armelagos, G. 1980. *Consuming passions: The anthropology of eating.* Boston: Houghton Mifflin.

Farley, R. 1980. The long road back: Blacks and whites in America. *American Demographics* 2(2):11–17.

————. 1984. *Blacks and whites.* Cambridge, MA: Harvard University Press.

Farley, R., and Allen, W. R. 1987. *The color line and the quality of life in America.* New York: Russell Sage Foundation.

Farley, R., Bianchi, S., and Colasanto, D. 1979. Barriers to the racial integration of neighborhoods: The Detroit case. *Annals of the American Academy of Political and Social Science,* 441 (January):97–113.

Farley, R., and Neidert, L. J. 1984. *How effective was the melting pot? An analysis of current ethnic differences in the United States* (Population Studies Center Research Report 84–68). Ann Arbor, MI: University of Michigan.

Farley, R., Richards, T., and Wurdock, C. 1980. School desegregation and white flight: An investigation of competing models and their discrepant findings. *Sociology of Education* 53(3):123–39.

Farley, R., Schuman, H., Bianchi, S., Colasanto, D., and Hatchett, S. 1978. "Chocolate city, vanilla suburbs:" Will the trend toward racially separate communities continue? *Social Science Research* 7(4):319–44.

Farnworth, M., and Leiber, M. 1989. Strain theory revisited: Economic goals, educational means, and delinquency. *American Sociological Review* 54(2):263–74.

Fatemi, N. S., Williams, G. W., and de Saint-Phalle, T. L. T. 1982. *Multinational corporations* (2nd rev. ed.). San Diego, CA: A. S. Barnes.

Fausto-Sterling, A. 1985. *Myths of gender: Biological theories about women and men.* New York: Basic Books.

Feagin, J. R. 1991. The continuing significance of race: Antiblack discrimination in public places. *American Sociological Review* 56(1):101–16.

Featherman, D. L. 1983. Life-span perspectives in social science research. In P. B. Baltes and O. G. Brim (Eds.), *Life-span development and behavior* (Vol. 5, pp. 1–59). New York: Academic Press.

Featherman, D., and Hauser, R. 1978. *Opportunity and change.* New York: Academic Press.

Featherman, D. L., and Lerner, R. M. 1985. Ontogenesis and sociogenesis. *American Sociological Review* 50(5):659–76.

Feldman, A. S., and Tilly, C. 1960. The interaction of social and physical space. *American Sociological Review* 25:877–84.

Feldman, D. A., and Johnson, T. M. 1986. *The social dimensions of AIDS: Method and theory.* New York: Praeger.

Feldman, W., Feldman, E., and Goodman, J. T. 1988. Children's attitudes towards thinness and fatness. *Pediatrics* 81 (2, February):190–94.

Feldman-Summers, S., and Kiesler, J. 1974. Those who

are number two try harder: The effects of sex on attributions of causality. *Journal of Personality and Social Psychology* 30:846–55.

Ferree, M. M., and Hess, B. B. 1985. *Controversy and coalition: The new feminist movement.* Boston: Twayne.

Festinger, L. 1948. A study of rumor: Its origin and spread. *Human Relations* 1:464–85.

Festinger, L., Riecken, H. W., and Schacter, S. 1956. *When prophecy fails.* New York: Harper and Row.

Fettner, A. G., and Check, W. A. 1984. *The truth about AIDS.* New York: Holt, Rinehart and Winston.

Feuer, L. (Ed.). 1959. *Marx and Engels: Basic writings on politics and philosophy.* Garden City, NY: Doubleday.

FHA (Farmers Home Administration). 1987. Reported in the *Hartford Courant,* February 20. See also *American Demographics,* January-February, 1987.

Fidell, L. 1970. Empirical investigation of sex discrimination in hiring practices in psychology. *American Psychologist* 25:1094–97.

Fiedler, F. E., Chemers, M. M., and Mahan, L. 1976. *Improving leadership effectiveness.* New York: Wiley.

Fingerhut, L. A., and Kleinman, J. C. 1990. International and interstate comparisons of homicide among young males. *Journal of the American Medical Association* 263(24):3292–95.

Finkelhor, D., Gelles, R. J., Hotaling, G. T., and Straus, M. A. (Eds.). 1983. *The dark side of families: Current family violence research.* Beverly Hills, CA: Sage.

Finkelhor, D., and Yllo, K. 1985. *License to rape: Sexual abuse of wives.* New York: Holt, Rinehart, and Winston.

Firebaugh, G., and Davis, K. E. 1988. Trends in antiblack prejudice, 1972–1984: Region and cohort effects. *American Journal of Sociology* 94(2):251–72.

Firestone, S. 1970. *The dialectic of sex: The case for feminist revolution.* New York: William Morrow.

Fischer, C. S. 1975. Toward a subcultural theory of urbanism. *American Journal of Sociology* 80 (May):1319–41.

————. 1982. *To dwell among friends: Personal networks in town and city.* San Diego, CA: Harcourt Brace Jovanovich.

————. 1984. *The urban experience* (2nd ed.). San Diego, CA: Harcourt Brace Jovanovich.

Fischer, H. W., and Lazerson, A. 1984. *Human development.* New York: W. H. Freeman.

Fisher, E. 1980. *Woman's creation: Sexual evolution and the shaping of society.* New York: McGraw-Hill.

Fisher, H. T., and Fisher, M. H. (Eds.). 1966. *Life in Mexico: The letters of Fanny Calderon de la Barca.* Garden City, NY: Doubleday.

Fisher, J. D., Nadler, A., and DePaulo, B. M. (Eds.). 1983. *New directions in helping: Recipient reactions to aid,* (Vol. 1). New York: Academic Press.

Fisher, R. 1984. *Let the people decide: Neighborhood organizing in America.* Boston: Twayne Publishers.

Flitcraft, A. 1987. Violence among intimates: An epidemiological review. In V. N. Hasselt et al. (Eds.), *Handbook of family violence* 293–318. New York: Plenum.

Flowers, R. B. 1984. *Religion in strange times: The 1960s and 1970s.* Macon, GA: Mercer University Press.

Foner, N. 1984. *Ages in conflict: A cross-cultural perspective on inequalities between young and old.* New York: Columbia University Press.

Forer, L. G. 1984. *Money and justice.* New York: Norton.

Form, W. 1985. *Divided we stand: Working class stratification in America.* Champaign, IL; University of Illinois Press.

Fortes, M., Steel, R. W., and Ady, P. 1947. Ashanti survey, 1945–1946: An experiment in social research. *Geographical Journal* 110:149–79.

Fox, M., Gibbs, M., and Auerbach, D. 1985. Age and gender dimensions of friendship. *Psychology of Women Quarterly* 9:489–502.

Fox, T., and Miller, S. M. 1965. Intra-country variations: Occupational stratification and mobility. *Studies in Comparative International Development* 1:3–10.

Frank, E. J. 1988. Business students' perception of women in management. *Sex Roles* 19(1/2):107–18.

Franklin, B. 1751. *Observations concerning the increase of mankind.*

Franks, V., and Rothblum, E. D. (Eds.). 1983. *The stereotyping of women: Its effects on mental health.* New York: Springer.

Frederickson, G. M. 1981. *White supremacy: A comparative study in American and South African history.* New York: Oxford University Press.

Freedman, J. L. 1984. Effects of television violence on aggression. *Psychological Bulletin* 96:227–46.

———. 1986. Television violence and aggression: A rejoinder. *Psychological Bulletin* 100:372–78.

Freeman, D. 1983. *Margaret Mead and Samoa: The making and the unmaking of an anthropological myth.* Cambridge, MA: Harvard University Press.

Freeman, R. B. 1975. Changes in job market discrimination and black economic well-being. Paper delivered at Notre Dame Civil Rights Conference (April), South Bend, Indiana.

———. 1976. *The overeducated American.* New York: Academic Press.

Freidson, E. 1986. *Professional powers: A study in the institutionalization of formal knowledge.* Chicago: University of Chicago Press.

Freire, P. 1972. *Pedagogy of the oppressed.* New York: Herder and Herder.

———. 1985. *The politics of education: Culture, power, and liberation.* South Hadley, MA: Bergin & Garvey.

Freitag, P. 1975. The Cabinet and big business: A study of interlocks. *Social Problems* 2 (December):137–52.

Freud, S., and Dann, S. 1951. An experiment in group upbringing. *Psychoanalytic study of the child.* New York: International Universities Press.

Freudenburg, W. R. 1986. The density of acquaintanceship: An overlooked variable in community research? *American Journal of Sociology* 92(1):27–63.

Frey, W. H. 1983. *Lifecourse migration of metropolitan whites and blacks and the structure of demographic change in large central cities* (Research Report No. 83–47). Ann Arbor, Michigan: University of Michigan Population Studies Center.

Frey, W. H., and Kobrin, F. 1982. Changing families and changing mobility: Their impact on the central city. *Demography* 19:261–77.

Frey, W. H., and Speare, A. 1988. *Regional and metropolitan growth and decline in the United States.* New York: Russell Sage Foundation.

Friedan, B. 1963. *The feminine mystique.* New York: Dell.

Friedl, E. 1962. *Vasilika: A village in modern Greece.* New York: Holt, Rinehart and Winston.

———. 1975. *Men and women: An anthropologist's view.* New York: Holt, Rinehart and Winston.

Friedman, H. S., Riggio, R. E., and Segall, D. O. 1980. Personality development and the enactment of emotion. *Journal of Nonverbal Behavior* 5:35–48.

Friedman, J. 1974. Marxism, structuralism, and vulgar materialism. *Man* 9:444–69.

Friedrich, C. J., and Brzezinski. 1965. *Totalitarian dictatorship and autocracy* (Vol. 2). Cambridge, MA: Harvard University Press.

Friedrich-Cofer, L., and Huston, A. C. 1986. Television violence and aggression: The debate continues. *Psychological Bulletin* 100:364–71.

Froebel, F., Heinrichs, J., and Kreye, O. 1980. *The new international division of labor.* New York: Cambridge University Press.

Froissart, J. 1961. *The chronicles of England, France, and Spain.* New York: Dutton.

Froman, C. 1984. *The two American political systems: Society, economics, and politics.* Englewood Cliffs, NJ: Prentice-Hall.

Furstenberg, F. F., Jr., Morgan, S. P., and Allison, P. D. 1987. Paternal participation and children's well-being after marital dissolution. *American Sociological Review* 52(5):695–701.

Furstenberg, F. F., Jr., and Spanier, G. B. 1984. *Recycling the family: Remarriage after divorce.* Beverly Hills, CA: Sage Publications.

Gaertner, S. 1989. Reported in the *New York Times*, (September 5), p. C1.

Gagliani, G. 1981. How many working classes? *American Journal of Sociology* 87(2):259–73.

Gallup Poll. 1991. Reported in *The New York Times* (January 1), p. A35.

Gamson, W. A. 1961. An experimental test of a theory of coalition formation. *American Sociological Review* 26:565–73.

———. 1964. Experimental studies in coalition formation. In L. Berkowitz (Ed.), *Advances in experimental social psychology* (Vol. 1). New York: Academic Press.

———. 1968a. A theory of coalition formation. *American Sociological Review* 22:373–79.

———. 1968b. *Power and discontent.* Homewood, IL: Dorsey Press.

———. 1974. Violence and political power: The meek don't make it. *Psychology Today* (July) 8(2):35–41.

Gamson, W. A. (*continued*)

———. 1975. *The strategy of social protest.* Homewood, IL: Dorsey Press.

Gans, H. J. 1962. Urbanism and suburbanism as ways of life: A re-evaluation of definitions. In A. Rose (Ed.), *Human behavior and social processes.* Boston: Houghton-Mifflin and Routledge & Kegan Paul.

———. 1971. The uses of poverty: The poor pay all. *Social Policy* (July/August).

———. 1973. *More equality.* New York: Pantheon.

———. 1980. *Deciding what's news.* New York: Vintage.

———. 1982. *The urban villagers* (2nd ed.). New York: The Free Press.

———. 1987. Author's postscript. In Henslin, J. M., *Down to earth sociology* (5th ed.), p. 277. New York: Free Press.

Garfinkel, H. 1956. Conditions of successful degradation ceremonies. *American Journal of Sociology* 61:420–24.

———. 1967. *Studies in ethnomethodology.* Englewood Cliffs, NJ: Prentice-Hall.

Gartner, A., Greer, C., and Riessman, F. (Eds.). 1973. *After deschooling, what?* New York: Harper and Row.

Gartner, R. 1990. The victims of homicide: A temporal and cross-national comparison. *American Sociological Review* 55(1):92–106.

Gecas, V. 1981. Contexts of socialization. In M. Rosenberg and R. Turner (Eds.), *Social psychology: Sociological perspectives.* New York: Basic Books.

———. 1982. The self-concept. *Annual Review of Sociology* 8:1–33.

Geertz, C. 1973. *The interpretation of cultures.* New York: Basic Books.

Gelb, J. 1989. *Feminism and politics: A comparative perspective.* Berkeley, CA: University of California Press.

Geller, D. M., Goldstein, L. S. M., and Sternberg, W. C. 1974. On being ignored: The effects of violation of implicit rules of social interaction. *Sociometry* 37:541–56.

Gelles, R. J. 1972. *The violent home: A study of physical aggression between husbands and wives.* Beverly Hills, CA: Russell Sage Foundation.

Gelles, R. J., and Cornell, C. P. 1985. *Intimate violence in families.* Beverly Hills, CA: Sage.

Genicut, L. 1966. Crisis from the Middle Ages to modern times. In M. M. Postan (Ed.), *The agrarian life of the Middle Ages* (Vol. 1 of *The Cambridge economic history of Europe*). Cambridge, England: The University Press.

George, A. L. 1971. Primary groups, organization, and military performance. In R. W. Little (Ed.), *Handbook of military institutions*, pp. 293–318. New York: Russell Sage Foundation.

Gergen, M. M. 1980. The effects of age and type of residence on forms of social explanation. Unpublished doctoral dissertation. Temple University, Philadelphia. Cited in Gergen, K. J. and Gergen, M. M. 1981. *Social Psychology*, p. 331. New York: Harcourt Brace Jovanovich.

Gerstel, N., and Gross, H. 1984. *Commuter marriage: A study of work and family.* New York: Guilford Press.

Gevitz, N. (Ed.). 1988. *Other healers: Unorthodox medicine in America.* Baltimore, MD: Johns Hopkins University Press.

Giddens, A. 1973. *The class structure of advanced societies.* New York: Harper and Row.

———. 1983. *A contemporary critique of historical materialism.* Berkeley and Los Angeles: University of California Press.

———. 1984. *The constitution of society: Outline of a theory of structuration.* Berkeley and Los Angeles: University of California Press.

Gieryn, T. F., Bevins, G. M., and Zehr, S. C. 1985. The professionalization of American scientists. *American Sociological Review* 50(3):392–408.

Gilbert, M. 1986. *The holocaust: A history of the jews in Europe during the second world war.* New York: Holt, Rinehart, and Winston.

Gill, C. 1985. *Work, unemployment, and the new technology.* Cambridge, England: Polity Press (Basil Blackwell).

Gilligan, C. 1982. *In a different voice.* Cambridge, MA: Harvard University Press.

Giniger, H. 1981. Quebec meets defiance in enforcing language law. *New York Times* October 5:2.

Glaser, B. G., and Strauss, A. 1965. *Awareness of dying.* Chicago: Aldine.

Glass, J., Bengston, V. L., and Dunham, C. C. 1986. Attitude similarity in three-generation families: Socialization, status inheritance, or reciprocal influence? *American Sociological Review* 51(5):685–98.

Gleick, J. 1987. *Chaos: Making a new science.* New York: Viking.

Glenn, C. L. 1988. *The myth of the common school.* Amherst: University of Massachusetts Press.

Glenn, N., and McLanahan, S. 1983. Children and marital happiness: A further specification of the relationship. *Journal of Marriage and the Family* 44:63–72.

Glick, P. C., and Lin, S. 1986a. More young adults are living with their parents: Who are they? *Journal of Marriage and the Family* 48(1):107–12.

———. 1986b. Recent changes in divorce and remarriage. *Journal of Marriage and the Family* 48(1):737–47.

Glick, P. C., and Norton, A. J. 1979. Marrying, divorcing, and living together in the U.S. today. *Population Bulletin* 32(5). Washington, D.C.: Population Reference Bureau.

Glock, C. Y., and Stark, R. 1968. *American piety: The nature of religious commitment.* Berkeley, CA: University of California Press.

Goffman, E. 1956–57. Embarrassment and social organization. *American Journal of Sociology* 62:264–71.

———. 1959. *The presentation of self in everyday life.* New York: Doubleday and Company.

———. 1961a. *Asylums.* New York: Anchor Books.

———. 1961b. *Encounters.* Indianapolis: Bobbs-Merrill.

———. 1963a. *Behavior in public places.* New York: Free Press.

————. 1963b. *Stigma: Notes on the management of a spoiled identity*. Englewood Cliffs, NJ: Prentice-Hall.

————. 1967. *Interaction ritual*. New York: Anchor Books.

————. 1976. *Gender advertisements*. New York: Harper Colophon.

————. 1981. *Forms of talk*. Philadelphia, PA: University of Pennsylvania Press.

Goldberg, S. 1973. *The inevitability of patriarchy*. New York: William Morrow.

Goldfield, M. 1987. *The decline of organized labor in the United States*. Chicago: University of Chicago Press.

Golding, J. M. 1990. Division of household labor, strain, and depressive symptoms among Mexican American and non-Hispanic whites. *Psychology of Women Quarterly* 14(1):103–17.

Goldscheider, F., and Lebourdais, C. 1986. The falling age at leaving home, 1920–1979. *Sociology and Social Research* 70:99–102.

Goldscheider, F. K., and Waite, L. J. 1986. Sex differences in the entry into marriage. *American Journal of Sociology* 92(1):91–109.

Goldstein, M. C. 1987. Polyandry: When brothers take a wife. In J. P. Spradley and D. W. McCurdy (Eds.), *Conformity and conflict: Readings in cultural anthropology* (7th ed.):190–97. Glenview, IL: Scott, Foresman.

Goldstein, S., and Sly, D. F. 1977. Recent and projected trends in world urbanization. In S. Goldstein and D. F. Sly (Eds.), *Patterns of urbanization: Comparative country studies*. Bolhain: Ordina Editions.

Goldstone, J. A. 1982. The comparative and historical study of revolutions. *Annual Review of Sociology* 8:187–207.

Gonzalez Casanova, P. 1980. The economic development of Mexico. *Scientific American* 243:192–204.

Goode, W. J. 1959. The theoretical importance of love. *American Sociological Review* 24:38–47.

————. 1963. *World revolution and family patterns*. New York: Free Press.

————. 1976. Family disorganization. In R. K. Merton and R. Nisbet (Eds.), *Contemporary social problems* (4th ed.). New York, Harcourt Brace Jovanvich.

Goodman, L. W. 1980. Horizons for research on international business in developing nations. *Latin American Research Review* 15:225–40.

Goodsell, C. T. 1983. *The case for bureaucracy: A public administration polemic*. Chatham, NJ: Chatham House.

Goody, J. 1976. *Production and reproduction*. New York: Cambridge University Press.

Goolrich, W., and Tanner, O. 1980. *The Battle of the Bulge*. New York: Time-Life Books.

Gora, J. D. 1982. *The new female criminal: Empirical reality or social myth?* New York: Praeger.

Gordon, C. 1976. Development of evaluated role identities. *Annual Review of Sociology* 2:405–33.

Gordon, D. M., Edwards, R., and Reich, M. 1982. *Segmented work, divided labor*. Cambridge, England: Cambridge University Press.

Gordon, M. 1978 *Final payments*. New York: Ballantine.

Gordon, M. T., and Riger, S. 1989. *The female fear*. New York: Free Press.

Gordon, S. L. 1981. The sociology of sentiments and emotion. In M. Rosenberg and R. H. Turner (Eds.), *Social psychology: Sociological Perspectives*. New York: Basic Books.

Goring, C. 1913. *The English convict*. London: His Majesty's Stationery Office.

Gornick, V. 1979. Introduction. In E. Goffman, *Gender advertisements*. New York: Harper Colophon.

Gottdiener, M. 1985. *The social production of urban space*. Austin: University of Texas Press.

Gottfredson, M. R., and Hindelang, M. J. 1981. Sociological aspects of criminal victimization. *Annual Review of Sociology* 7:107–28.

Gottfried, R. S. 1983. *The black death: Natural and human disaster in medieval Europe*. New York: Free Press.

Gottfried, A. E., and Gottfried, A. W. 1988. *Maternal employment and children's development: Longitudinal research*. New York: Plenum.

Gough, E. K. 1974. Nayar: Central Kerala. In D. Schneider and E. K. Gough (Eds.), *Matrilineal kinship*. Berkeley, CA: University of California Press.

Gouldner, A. W. 1960. A norm of reciprocity: A preliminary statement. *American Sociological Review* 25:161–78.

————. 1970. *The coming crisis of western sociology*. New York: Avon.

Gove, E., and Tudor, J. 1973. Adult sex roles and mental illness. *American Journal of Sociology* 78:812–35.

Gove, W. R. 1980. Labeling and mental illness: A critique. In Gove, W. (Ed.), *Labeling deviant behavior*, 53–109. Beverly Hills, CA: Sage Publications.

————. 1982. The current status of the labeling theory of mental illness. In Gove, W. R. (Ed.), *Deviance and mental illness*. Beverly Hills, CA: Sage Publications.

Gove, W. R., and Carpenter, G. R. 1982. *The fundamental connection between nature and nurture*. Lexington, MA: Lexington Books.

Gover, W. R., Ortega, S. T., and Style, C. B. 1989. The maturational and role perspectives on aging and self through the adult years. *American Journal of Sociology* 94(5):1117–45.

Grabill, W. H., Kiser, C. V., and Whelpton, P. K. 1959. *The fertility of American women*. New York: Wiley.

Gracey, H. L. 1972. *The civil structure and ideology of an elementary school*. Chicago: University of Chicago Press.

Grady, W. R. 1980. Remarriages of women 15–44 years of age whose first marriage ended in divorce: The United States, 1976. *Advancedata* 58 (February):1–12.

Graebner, I, and Britt, S. H. (Eds.). 1942. *Jews in a gentile world*. New York: Macmillan.

Graham, H. D., and Gurr, T. R. (Eds.). 1979. *The history of violence in America*. National Commission on the Causes and Prevention of Violence. New York: Bantam.

Graham, L. 1981. *Between science and values.* New York: Columbia University Press.

Granberg, D., and Holberg, S. 1988. *The political system matters: Social psychology and voting behavior in Sweden and the United States.* Cambridge, England: Cambridge University Press.

Greeley, A. M. 1989. *Religious change in America.* Cambridge, MA: Harvard University Press.

Greenberg, D. F. 1989. *The construction of homosexuality.* Chicago: University of Chicago Press.

Greenfeld, L. 1988. Soviet sociology and sociology in the Soviet Union. *Annual Review of Sociology* 14:99–123.

Greenfield, S., Blanco, D. M., Elashoff, R. M., and Ganz, P. A. 1987. Patterns of care related to age of breast cancer patients. *Journal of the American Medical Association* 257(20):2766–70.

Greif, G. L. 1985. Single fathers rearing children. *Journal of Marriage and the Family* 47(1):185–91.

Griffin, L. J., Wallace, M. E., and Rubin, B. A. 1986. Capitalism and labor organization. *American Sociological Review* 51(2):147–67.

Griffin, S. 1978. *Woman and nature.* New York: Harper and Row.

Griffith, J. 1973. Social pressure on family size intentions. *Family Planning Perspectives* 5(4):237–42.

Grindle, M. S. 1988. *Searching for rural development: Labor migration and employment in rural Mexico.* Ithica, NY: Cornell University Press.

Grossholtz, J. 1984. *Forging capitalist patriarchy: The economic and social transformation of feudal Sri Lanka and its impact on women.* Durham, N.C.: Duke University Press.

GSS (General Social Survey). Various years. Results computed by the author from General Social Survey data supplied by the National Opinion Research Center, University of Chicago, Chicago, Illinois. Analysis performed with MicroCase software (Cognitive Development, Inc., Seattle Washington).

Gulick, J. 1989. *The humanity of cities: An introduction to urban society.* Granby, MA: Bergin and Garvey.

Gulliver, P. H. 1968. Age differentiation. In D. L. Sills (Ed.), *The International Encyclopedia of the Social Sciences* (Vol. 1). New York: Macmillan/Free Press.

Gurr, T. R. 1970. *Why men rebel.* Princeton, NJ: Princeton University Press.

Gutek, B. A. 1985. *Sex and the workplace: The impact of sexual behavior and harassment on women, men, and organizations.* San Francisco: Jossey-Bass.

Guttmacher Institute. 1987. *Teenage pregnancy in industrialized countries.* New York: Alan Guttmacher Institute.

Guzzardi, W. 1976. The uncertain passage from college to job. *Fortune Magazine* (January).

Haas, V. B., and Perucci, C. C. (Eds.). 1984. *Women in scientific and engineering professions.* Ann Arbor, MI: University of Michigan Press.

Haavio-Mannila, E. 1985. *Unfinished democracy: Women in nordic politics.* Oxford: Pergamon Press.

Haber, C. 1983. *Beyond sixty-five.* Cambridge, England: Cambridge University Press.

Habermas, J. 1971. *Toward a rational society.* London: Heinemann.

Hacker, H. 1951. Women as a minority group. *Social Forces* 30:60–69.

Hadden, J. K., and Swann, C. E. 1981. *Prime time preachers: The rising power of Televangelism.* Reading, MA: Addison-Wesley.

Hadley, J. 1991. Research reported in the *New York Times,* (January 16), p. A20.

Hagan, J. 1989. *Structural criminology.* New Brunswick, NJ: Rutgers University Press.

————. 1990. The gender stratification of income inequality among lawyers. *Social Forces* 68(3):835–55.

Hagan, J., and Abonnetti, C. 1982. Race, class, and the perception of criminal injustice in America. *American Journal of Sociology* 88(2):329–55.

Hagan, J., and Bumiller, K. 1983. Making sense of sentencing: A review and critique of sentencing research. In A. Blumstein, J. Cohen, S. Martin, and M. Tonry (Eds.), *Research on sentencing: The search for reform* (Vol. 2). Washington, D.C.: National Academy Press.

Hagan, J., Gillis, A. R., and Simpson, J. 1985. The class structure of gender and delinquency: Toward a power-control theory of common delinquent behavior. *American Journal of Sociology* 90(6):1151–78.

Hagan, J., and Palloni, A. 1986. Structural criminology. *Annual Review of Sociology* 12:431–49.

Hagan, J., and Parker, P. 1985. White-collar crime and punishment. *American Sociological Review* 50(3): 302–16.

Hagan, J., Simpson, J., and Gillis, A. R. 1987. Class in the household: A power-control theory of gender and delinquency. *American Journal of Sociology* 92(4):788–816.

Hagen, R., and Kahn, A. 1975. Discrimination against competent women. *Applied Social Psychology* 5:362–76.

Hagestad, G. O. 1984. The continuous bond: A dynamic multigenerational perspective on parent-child relations between adults. In M. Perlmutter (Ed.), *Minnesota symposium on child psychology,* pp. 129–58.

Haines, H. H. 1988. *Black radicals and the civil rights mainstream, 1954–1970.* Knoxville, Tenn: University of Tennessee Press.

Halberstadt, A. G., Hayes, C. W., and Pike, K. M. 1988. Gender and gender role differences in smiling and communication consistency. *Sex Roles* 19(9/10):589–604.

Halberstam, D. 1972. *The best and the brightest.* New York: Random House.

Hale, M. 1847. A husband cannot be guilty. In *History of the pleas of the crown* (Vol. 1, p. 628). Philadelphia: R. H. Small.

Hale-Benson, J. 1987. *Black children: Their roots, culture, and learning styles.* Baltimore: Johns Hopkins University Press.

Hall, E. T. 1959. *The silent language.* Greenwich, CT: Fawcett.

————. 1969. *The hidden dimension.* Garden City, NY: Anchor.

————. 1983. *The dance of life.* Garden City, NY: Doubleday.

Hall, J., and Watson, W. H. 1970. The effects of normative intervention on group decision-making performance. *Human Relations* 23:299–317.

Hall, J. R. 1987. *Gone from the promised land: Jonestown in American cultural history.* New Brunswick, NJ: Transaction Books. See pp. 52–61.

Hallinan, M. T. 1988. Equality of educational opportunity. *Annual Review of Sociology* 14:249–68.

Hallinan, M. T., and Sørensen, A. B. 1987. Ability grouping and sex differences in mathematics achievement. *Sociology of Education* 60(2):63–72.

Hallinan, M. T., and Williams, R. 1989. Interracial friendship choices in secondary schools. *American Sociological Review* 53(4):67–78.

Hallman, H. W. 1984. *Neighborhoods: Their place in urban life.* Beverly Hills, CA: Sage Publications.

Hamilton, M. C. 1988. Using masculine generics: Does generic "he" increase male bias in the user's imagery? *Sex Roles* 19(11/12):785–99.

Hammer, H. and Gartrell, J. W. 1986. Canada and mature dependency. *American Sociological Review* 51(2):201–13.

Hammer, M., and McFerran, J. 1988. Preference for sex of child: A research update. *Individual Psychology* (December):486–92.

Haney, C., Banks, C., and Zimbardo, P. G. 1973. Interpersonal dynamics in a simulated prison. *International Journal of Criminology and Penology* 1:69–97.

Hansberry, L. 1950. *A raisin in the sun.* New York: Random House.

Hansen, C. H., and Hansen, R. D. 1988. How rock music videos can change what is seen when boy meets girl. *Sex Roles* 19(5/6):287–316.

Haritos-Fatouros, M. 1988. The official torturer: A learning model for obedience to the authority of violence. *Journal of Applied Social Psychology* 18(13):1107–20.

Harkins, S. G. 1981. *Effects of task difficulty and task responsibility on social loafing.* Presentation to the First International Conference on Social Processes in Small Groups, Kill Devil Hills, NC.

Harkins, S. G., Latané, B., and Williams, K. 1980. Social loafing: Allocating effort or taking it easy? *Journal of Experimental Social Psychology* 16:457–65.

Harlow, H. F. 1958. The nature of love. *The American Psychologist,* 69 (December): 685.

Harlow, H. F., and Harlow, M. K. 1969. Effects of various mother-infant relationships on rhesus monkey behaviors. In B. M. Foss (Ed.), *Determinants of infant behavior* (Vol. 4). London: Methuen.

Harriman, A. 1985. *Women/men management.* New York: Praeger.

Harrington, M. 1963. *The other America: Poverty in the United States.* Baltimore, MD: Penguin Books.

Harris, C. D., and Ullman, E. L. 1945. The nature of cities. *The Annals of the American Academy of Political and Social Science* 242:7–17.

Harris, M. 1974. *Cows, pigs, wars, and witches.* New York: Random House.

————. 1977. *Cannibals and kings: The origins of cultures.* New York: Random House.

————. 1979. *Cultural materialism.* New York: Random House.

————. 1985. *Good things to eat: Riddles of food and culture.* New York: Simon and Schuster.

Harris, M., and Ross, E. B. 1987. *Death, sex, and fertility: Population regulation in preindustrial and developing societies.* New York: Columbia University Press.

Hart, C. W. M., and Pilling, A. R. 1960. *The Tiwi of North Australia.* New York: Holt, Rinehart and Winston.

Hart, H. H. 1970. *Summerhill: For and against.* New York: Hart.

Harter, C. L. 1977. *The 'good times' cohort of the 1930s* (PRB Report 3, April). Washington, D.C.: Population Reference Bureau.

Hartley, E. L. 1946. *Problems in prejudice.* New York: Columbia University Press/King's Crown Press.

Hartmann, H. I. (Ed.). 1985. *Comparable worth: New directions for research.* Washington, D.C.: National Academy Press.

Hartshorn, T. A., and Muller, P. O. 1987. *Suburban business centers: Employment implications.* U.S. Department of Commerce. Washington, D.C.: U.S. Government Printing Office.

Haskell, T. L. (Ed.). 1984. *The authority of experts.* Bloomington, IN: Indiana University Press.

Hastorf, A. H. 1965. The 'reinforcement' of individual actions in a group situation. In L. Krasner and L. P. Ullmann (Eds.), *Research in behavior modification: New developments and implications.* New York: Holt, Rinehart and Winston.

Haug, M., and Lavin, B. 1983. *Consumerism in medicine: Challenging physician authority.* Beverly Hills, CA: Sage.

Haviland, J. J., and Malatesta, C. Z. 1981. The development of sex differences in nonverbal signals: Fallacies, facts, and fantasies. In C. Mayo and N. M. Henley (Eds.), *Gender and nonverbal behavior,* pp. 184–1208. New York: Springer-Verlag.

Hawke, D. F. 1988. *Everyday life in early America.* New York: Harper and Row.

Hawley, A. H. 1968. Human ecology. In D. L. Sills (ed.), *The international encyclopedia of the social sciences* (Vol. 4, pp. 328–37). New York: Macmillan Company/Free Press.

————. 1981. *Urban society: An ecological approach* (2nd ed.). New York: Wiley.

————. 1984. Human ecological and Marxian theories. *American Journal of Sociology* 89:904–17.

————. 1986. *Human ecology: A theoretical essay.* Chicago: University of Chicago Press.

Hawthorne, N. 1979. *The scarlet letter.* New York: Dodd.

Hayes, C. D., and Kamerman, S. B. 1983. *Children of working parents: Experiences and outcomes.* Washington, D.C.: National Academy Press.

Hazarika, S. 1983. 600 reported dead after Hindu raids on Indian villages. *New York Times*, February 21, p. 1.

Heaton, T. B. 1990. Marital stability throughout the child-rearing years. *Demography* 27(1):55–63.

Heider, R. 1946. Attitudes and cognitive organization. *Journal of Personality* 21:107–12.

Heider, K. G. 1972. *The Dani of West Irian.* Andover, MD: Warner Modular.

Heilbroner, R. L. 1977. *The economic transformation of America.* New York: Harcourt Brace Jovanovich.

Heiss, J. 1981. Social roles. In M. Rosenberg and R. H. Turner (Eds.), *Social psychology: Sociological perspectives.* New York: Basic Books.

Heller, J. 1961. *Catch-22.* New York: Dell.

Hellman, L. [1934] 1979. *The children's hour.* In *Six plays by Lillian Hellman.* New York: Vintage.

Helsing, K. J., and Szklo, M. 1981. Mortality after bereavement. *American Journal of Epidemiology* 114: 41–52.

Henley, N. M. 1973. Status and sex: Some touching observations. *Bulletin of the Psychonomic Society* 2:91–93.

————. 1977. *Body politics: Power, sex, and nonverbal communication.* Englewood Cliffs, NJ: Prentice-Hall.

Henley, N., Hamilton, M., and Thorne, B. 1985. Womanspeak and manspeak: Sex differences and sexism in communication. In A. G. Sargent (Ed.), *Beyond sex roles*, pp. 168–85. New York: West.

Henry, J. 1963. *Culture against man.* New York: Random House.

Herdt, G. H. (Ed.). 1984. *Ritualized homosexuality in Melanesia.* Berkeley and Los Angeles: University of California Press.

Heritage, J. 1984. *Garfinkel and ethnomethodology.* New York: Basil Blackwell.

Herman, E. S. 1975. The income counter-revolution. *Commonweal* (January 3).

Herman, E. S. 1981. *Corporate control, corporate power.* New York: Cambridge University Press.

Hernandez, D. J. 1985. Fertility reduction policies and poverty in third world countries: Ethical issues. *Studies in Family Planning* 16(2):76–87.

Hersch, S. M. 1970. *My Lai 4: A report on the massacre and its aftermath.* New York: Vintage.

Herzig, A. C., and Mali, J. L. 1980. *Oh Boy! Babies!* Boston: Little Brown.

Hess, R. D. 1970. Social class and ethnic influences upon socialization. In P. H. Mussen (Ed.), *Carmichael's manual of child psychology* (Vol. 2). New York: Wiley.

Hesse-Biber, S. 1989. Eating patterns and disorders in a college population. *Sex Roles* 20(1/2):71–89.

Heyl, B. S. 1977. The madam as teacher: The training of house prostitutes. *Social Problems*:24(5).

Hightower, J. 1980. Food monopoly. In M. Green and R.

Massie (Eds.), *The big business reader*, pp. 9–18. New York: Pilgrim.

Hilbert, R. A. 1990. Ethnomethodology and the micro-macro order. *American Sociological Review* 55(6):794–808.

Hill, G. W. 1982. Group versus individual performance: Are n + 1 heads better than one? *Psychological Bulletin* 91:517–39.

Hill, R. J. 1981. Attitudes and behavior. In M. Rosenberg and R. H. Turner (Eds.), *Social Psychology: Sociological perspectives.*

Hillman, A. L. 1987. Financial incentives for physicians in HMOs: Is there a conflict of interest? *New England Journal of Medicine* 317(27):1743–48.

Hills, S. L. 1987. *Corporate violence: Injury and death for profit.* Totowa, NJ: Rowman and Littlefield.

Hindelang, M. J. 1978. Race and involvement in common law personal crimes. *American Sociological Review* 43:93–109.

Hirschi, T. 1969. *Causes of delinquency.* Berkeley, CA: University of California Press.

Hirschi, T., and Gottfredson, M. 1983. Age and the explanation of crime. *American Journal of Sociology*, 89: 552–84.

————. 1985. Age and crime: Logic and scholarship. *American Journal of Sociology* 90(5):1330–33.

Hitler, A. [1924] 1948. *Mein kampf* (R. Mannheim, Trans.). Boston: Houghton Mifflin.

Hobsbawm, E. 1971. *Bandits.* New York: Dell.

Hochschild, A. 1979. Emotion work, feeling rules, and social structure. *American Journal of Sociology* 85: 551–75.

————. 1989. *The second shift.* New York: Viking Press.

Hodge, R. W., Siegel, P. M., and Rossi, P. H. 1964. Occupational prestige in the United States, 1925–1963. *American Journal of Sociology* 70:286–302.

Hodge, R. W., and Treiman, D. J. 1968. Class identification in the United States. *American Journal of Sociology* 73:535–47.

Hodge, R. W., Treiman, D. J., and Rossi, P. H. 1966. A comparative study of occupational prestige. In R. Bendix and S. M. Lipset (Eds.), *Class, status, and power: Social stratification in comparative perspective* (2nd ed.). New York: Free Press.

Hofferth, S. L. 1985. Updating children's life course. *Journal of Marriage and the Family* 47(1):93–115.

Hofstadter, R. 1955. *Social Darwinism in American thought.* Boston: Beacon.

Holland, B. (Ed.). 1985. *Soviet sisterhood.* Bloomington, IN: University of Indiana Press.

Hollander, E. P. 1960. Competence and conformity in the acceptance of influence. *Journal of Abnormal and Social Psychology* 51:365–69.

Hollander, P. 1982. Research on Marxist societies: The relationship between theory and practice. *Annual Review of Sociology* 8:319–51.

Holmes, L. D. 1986. *Quest for the real Samoa: The Mead/Freeman controversy and beyond*. South Hadley, MA: Bergin and Garvey.

Holmstrom, L. L., and Burgess, A. W. 1983. *The victim of rape*. New Brunswick, NJ: Transaction Books.

Holt, J. 1972. The little red prison. *Harper's* 244 (June):80–82.

Homans, G. C. 1950. *The human group*. New York: Harcourt Brace Jovanovich.

————. 1974. *Social behavior: Its elementary forms* (rev. ed.). New York: Harcourt Brace Jovanovich.

Hood, J. C. 1983. *Becoming a two-job family*. New York: Praeger.

Horowitz, I. L. 1965. *The rise and fall of Project Camelot*. Cambridge, MA: MIT Press.

Hounshell, D. A. 1984. *From the American system to mass production 1900–1932: The development of manufacturing technology in the United States*. Baltimore, MD: Johns Hopkins University Press.

House Select Committee on Aging. 1990. Reported in the *Hartford Courant*, May 1, p. A3.

Hout, M. 1984. Occupational mobility of black men: 1962–1973. *American Sociological Review* 49 (June):308–22.

————. 1986. Opportunity and the middle class. *American Sociological Review* 51(2):214–23.

Hout, M., and Greeley, A. M. 1987. The center doesn't hold: Church attendance in the United States, 1940–1984. *American Sociological Review* 52(3):325–45.

Howe, I. (Ed.). 1983. *1984 revisited: Totalitarianism in our century*. New York: Harper and Row.

Hoyt, H. 1939. *The structure and growth of residential neighborhoods in American cities*. Washington, D.C.: Federal Housing Authority.

Huber, J. 1989. A theory of gender stratification. In L. Richardson and V. Taylor (Eds.), *Feminist frontiers II*, pp. 110–119.

————. 1990. Macro-micro links in gender stratification. *American Sociological Review* 55(1):1–10.

Huber, J., and Spitze, G. 1983. *Sex stratification: Children, housework, and jobs*. New York: Academic Press.

Huber, R. M. 1971. *The American idea of success*. New York: McGraw-Hill.

Hughes, M., and Demo, D. H. 1989. Self-perceptions of black Americans: Self-esteem and personal efficacy. *American Journal of Sociology* 95(1):132–59.

Hughes, M., and Hertel, B. R. 1990. The significance of color remains: A study of life chances, mate selection, and ethnic consciousness among black Americans. *Social Forces* 68(4):1105–20.

Humphreys, L. 1970. *Tearoom trade: Impersonal sex in public places*. Chicago: Aldine.

————. 1975. *Tearoom trade: Impersonal sex in public places* (2nd ed.). Chicago: Aldine.

Hunter, R. 1953. *Community power structure: A study of decision makers*. Chapel Hill, NC: University of North Carolina Press.

————. 1980. *Community power succession*. Chapel Hill, NC: University of North Carolina Press.

Hyde, J. S. 1979. *Understanding human sexuality*. New York: McGraw-Hill.

Hyman, H. H. 1972. *Secondary analysis of sample surveys*. New York: Wiley.

————. 1983. *Of time and widowhood*. Durham, NC: Duke University Press.

Hyman, H. H., and Singer, E. (Eds.). 1968. *Readings in reference group theory and research*. New York: Free Press.

Ianni, F. A. J. 1972. *A family business: Kinship and social control in organized crime*. New York: Russell Sage Foundation.

Ihinger-Tallman, M. 1988. Research on stepfamilies. *Annual Review of Sociology* 14:25–48.

Illich, I. 1971. *Deschooling society*. New York: Harper and Row.

Inkeles, A., and Smith, D. H. 1974. The fate of personal adjustment in the process of modernization. *International Journal of Comparative Sociology* 11 (June):101–3.

INS (Immigration and Naturalization Service). 1989. Reported in the *New York Times*, October 11.

Institute for Social Research. 1980. Faltering economy takes its toll on Americans' mental health. *Institute for Social Research Newsletter*, (August):3.

Intons-Peterson, M. J. 1988. *Gender concepts of Swedish and American youth*. Hillsdale, NJ: Lawrence Erlbaum Associates.

Irons, P. 1983. *Justice at war*. New York: Oxford University Press.

IRS (Internal Revenue Service). 1990. *Statistics of Income Bulletin* (August). Washington, D.C.: U. S. Government Printing Office.

Ishii-Kuntz, M., and Lee, G. R. 1987. Status of the elderly: An extension of the theory. *Journal of Marriage and the Family* 49(3):413–20.

Itard, J.-M.-G. [1801] 1962. *The wild boy of Aveyron* (G. and M. Humphrey, Trans.). Englewood Cliffs, NJ: Prentice-Hall.

Jack, R., and Jack, D. C. 1990. *Moral vision and professional decisions: The changing values of women and men lawyers*. New York: Cambridge University Press.

Jackson, K. T. 1986. *The suburbanization of the United States*. New York: Oxford University Press.

Jackson, P. 1968. *Life in classrooms*. New York: Holt, Rinehart and Winston.

Jackson, E. F., and Crockett, H. J., Jr. 1964. Occupational mobility in the United States. *American Sociological Review* 24:5–15.

Jacobs, D. 1981. Inequality and economic crime. *Sociology and Social Research* 66(1):12–28.

Jacobs, J. A. 1989. Long-term trends in occupational

Jacobs, J. A. *(continued)*
segregation by sex. *American Journal of Sociology* 95(1):160–73.

Jacobson, P. H. 1959. *American marriage and divorce.* New York: Rinehart.

Jacoby, R. 1987. *The last intellectuals.* New York: Basic Books.

Jaeger, M. L., Anthony, S., and Rosnow, R. L. 1979. Some determining factors in the transmission of a rumor. Unpublished study, London School of Economics, London, and Temple University, Philadelphia. Cited and discussed in K. J. Gergen and M. M. Gergen. 1981. *Social psychology* (p.366). New York: Harcourt Brace Jovanovich.

Jain, U. 1989. *The psychological consequences of crowding.* New Delhi and Newbury Park, CA: Sage.

JAMA (Journal of the American Medical Association). 1990. "Medical news and perspectives." Vol. 264, No. 8, p. 939.

James, D., and Soref, M. 1981. Profit constraints on managerial autonomy: Managerial theory and the unmaking of the corporation president. *American Sociological Review* 46:1–18.

Janeway, E. 1971. *Man's world, woman's place.* New York: Dell.

──────. 1987. *Improper behavior: When and how misconduct can be healthy for society.* New York: William Morrow.

Janis, I. L. 1951. *Air war and emotional stress: Psychological studies of bombing and civilian defense.* New York: McGraw-Hill.

──────. 1968. Group identification under conditions of extreme danger. In D. Cartwright and A. Zander (Eds.), *Group dynamics: Research and theory.* New York: Harper and Row.

──────. 1982. *Victims of groupthink.* Boston: Houghton-Mifflin.

Jaret, C. 1983. Recent neo-Marxist urban analysis. *Annual Review of Sociology* 9:499–525.

Jaynes, G. 1982. Suit on race recalls lines drawn under slavery. *New York Times* September 30:B16.

JEC (Joint Economic Committee). 1986a. The concentration of wealth in the United States. Washington, D.C.: Joint Economic Committee of the U.S. Congress.

──────. 1986b. The great American job machine: The proliferation of low wage employment in the U.S. economy. Washington, D.C.: Joint Economic Committee of the U.S. Congress.

Jencks, C. 1983a. Discrimination and Thomas Sowell. *New York Review of Books* March 3:33ff.

──────. 1983b. Special treatment for blacks? *New York Review of Books* March 17:12ff.

Jencks, C., and Reisman, D. 1968. *The academic revolution.* New York: Doubleday.

Jencks, C., Smith, M., Acland, H., Bane, M. J., Cohen, D., Gintis, H., Heyns, B., and Michelson, S. 1972. *Inequality: A reassessment of the effect of family and schooling in America.* New York: Basic Books.

Jencks, C., Bartlett, S., Corcoran, M., Crouse, J., Eaglesfield, D., Jackson, G., McClelland, K., Mueser, P., Olneck, M., Schwartz, J., Ward, S., and Williams, J. 1979. *Who gets ahead? The determinants of economic success in America.* New York: Basic Books.

Jenkins, J. C. 1981a. On the neofunctionalist theory of inequality. *American Journal of Sociology* 87(1):177–79.

──────. 1981b. Sociopolitical movements. In S. Long (Ed.), *Handbook of political science,* pp. 81–153. New York: Plenum Press.

──────. 1983. Resource mobilization theory and the study of social movements. *Annual Review of Sociology* 9:527–53.

──────. 1985. *The politics of insurgency: The farm worker movement in the 1960s.* New York: Columbia University Press.

Jenkins, J. C., and Eckert, C. M. 1986. Channeling black insurgency: Elite patronage and professional social movement organizations in the development of the black movement. *American Sociological Review* 51(6):812–29.

Jenkins, J. C., and Perrow, C. 1977. Insurgency of the powerless: Farm workers movements (1946–72). *American Sociological Review* 42 (April):249–68.

Jensen, A. R. 1969. How much can we boost IQ and scholastic achievement? *Harvard Educational Review* 39 (Winter):1–123.

Johnson, A. G. 1980. On the prevalence of rape in the United States. *Signs: Journal of Women in Culture and Society* 6(1):136–46.

──────. 1988. *Statistics.* San Diego, CA: Harcourt Brace Jovanovich.

Johnson, A. W., and Earle, T. 1987. *The evolution of human societies: From foraging groups to agrarian state.* Stanford, CA: Stanford University Press.

Johnson, D. G., and Lee, R. D. 1986. *Population growth and economic development.* Washington, D.C.: National Academy of Sciences.

Johnson, L. D. 1988. Cited in the *New York Times,* April 12, p. A1.

Johnson, K. A. 1983. *Women, the family, and peasant revolution in China.* Chicago: University of Chicago Press.

Johnson, M. M. 1988. *Strong mothers, weak wives: The search for gender equality.* Berkeley, CA: University of California Press.

Johnson, P. 1987. *A history of the jews.* New York: Harper and Row.

Johnson, P., Conrad, C., and Thomson, D. (Eds.). 1989. *Workers versus pensioners: Intergenerational justice in an aging world.* Manchester and New York: Manchester University Press.

Johnson, R. 1990. *Death work: A study of the modern execution process.* Pacific Grove, CA: Brooks/Cole.

Johnson, R. E. 1980. Social class and delinquent behavior: A new test. *Criminology* 18:86–93.

Johnston, L. D., O'Malley, P. M., and Bachman, J. G. 1986. *Use of licit and illicit drugs by American high school seniors, college students, and other young adults.* Ann Arbor, MI: Institute for Social Research.

Jones, E. E., and Nisbett, R. E. 1971. *The actor and the observer: Divergent perceptions of the cause of behavior.* Morristown, NJ: Silver Burdett/General Learning Press.

Jones, G. 1980. *Social Darwinism and English thought: The interaction of biological and social theory.* Atlantic Highlands, NJ: Humanities Press.

Jones, R. 1977. *The other generation: The new power of older Americans.* Englewood Cliffs, NJ: Prentice-Hall.

Jones, S. R. 1990. Worker interdependence and output: The Hawthorne studies reevaluated. *American Sociological Review* 55(2):176–90.

Jorgensen, D. L. 1989. *Participant observation: A methodology for human studies.* Newbury Park, CA: Sage.

Josephy, A. M., Jr. 1973. Freedom for the American Indian. *The Critic.* Chicago: Thomas More Associates.

Juravich, T. 1985. *Chaos on the shop floor: A worker's view of quality, productivity, and management.* Philadelphia, PA: Temple University Press.

Juster, S. M., and Vinovskis, M. A. 1987. Changing perspectives on the American family in the past. *Annual Review of Sociology* 13:193-216.

Kagan, J., and Havemann, E. 1980. *Psychology: An introduction* (4th ed.). New York: Harcourt Brace Jovanovich.

Kahl, J. A. 1961. *The American class structure* (2nd ed.). New York: Holt Rinehart and Winston.

Kahn-Hut, R., Daniels, A. K., and Clovard, R. (Eds.). 1982. Unresolved questions: Three feminist perspectives in *Women and work: Problems and perspectives.* New York: Oxford University Press.

Kalleberg, A., and Griffin, L. 1980. Class, occupation, and inequality in job rewards. *American Journal of Sociology* 85:731–68.

Kalton, G. 1984. *Introduction to survey sampling.* Beverly Hills, CA: Sage Publications.

Kalven, H., Jr., and Zeisel, H. 1966. *The American jury.* Boston: Little Brown.

Kamenetsky, C. 1984. *Children's literature in Nazi Germany.* Athens, OH: Ohio University Press.

Kamin, L. J. 1974. *Science and the politics of IQ.* Hillsdale, NJ: Erlbaum.

————. 1986. Is crime in the genes? The answer may depend on who chooses what evidence. *Scientific American* (February):22–27.

Kammeyer, K. C., and Ginn, H. 1986. *An introduction to population.* Chicago: The Dorsey Press.

Kanter, R. M. 1972. *Commitment and community: Communes and utopias in sociological perspective.* Cambridge, MA: Harvard University Press.

————. 1976. When bosses turn bitchy. *Psychology Today* 9 (May):56–59.

————. 1977a. *Men and women of the corporation.* New York: Basic Books.

————. 1977b. Some effects of proportions on group life: Skewed sex rations and responses to token women. *American Journal of Sociology* 82:965–90.

Karnow, S. 1983. *Vietnam: A history.* New York: Viking Press.

Karp, D. 1989. Cited in the *New York Times* (February 7), p. C1.

Karp, D. A., and Yoels, W. C. 1979. The college classroom: Some observations on the meanings of student participation. In H. Robboy, S. L. Greenblatt, and C. Clark (Eds.), *Social interaction.* New York: St. Martin's Press.

Kasarda, J. D. 1986. Reported in the *New York Times*, October 22, p. A1.

Kasarda, J. D., and Janowitz, M. 1974. Community attachment in mass society. *American Sociological Review* 39:328–39.

Katz, D., and Braly, K. W. 1933. Racial stereotypes of 100 college students. *Journal of Abnormal and Social Psychology* 28:280–90.

Katz, P. A., and Taylor, D. A. (Eds.). 1988. *Eliminating racism: Profiles in controversy.* New York: Plenum.

Kauffman, K. 1988. *Prison officers and their world.* Cambridge, MA: Harvard University Press.

Keller, E. F. 1985. *Reflections on gender and science.* New Haven, CT: Yale University Press.

Kelley, A., and Williamson, J. 1984. *What drives third world city growth? A dynamic general equilibrium approach.* Princeton, NJ: Princeton University Press.

Kelley, H. H. 1950. The warm-cold variable in first impressions of people. *Journal of Personality* 18:431–39.

Kelman, H. C., and Hamilton, V. L. 1989. *Crimes of obedience: Toward a social psychology of authority and responsibility.* New Haven, CT: Yale University Press.

Kemper, S. 1984. When to speak like a lady. *Sex Roles* 10:435–43.

Kemper, T. D. 1987. How many emotions are there? *American Journal of Sociology* 93(2):263–89.

Kendall, P. M. 1962. *The Yorkist age.* Garden City, NY: Doubleday.

Kephart, W. M., and Zellner, W. W. 1990. *Extraordinary groups: An examination of unconventional life-styles* (4th ed.). New York: St. Martin's Press.

Kerbo, H. R. 1983. *Social stratification and inequality: Class conflict in the United States.* New York: McGraw-Hill.

————. 1991. *Social stratification and inequality: Class conflict in historical and comparative perspective* (2nd ed.). New York: McGraw-Hill.

Kerner Commission (National Advisory Commission on Civil Disorders). 1968. *Report of the National Advisory Commission on Civil Disorders.* New York: Bantam.

Kessler, R. C., and McRae, J. A., Jr. 1982. The effects of wives' employment on the mental health of married

Kessler, R. C., and McRae, J. A., Jr. *(continued)* men and women. *American Sociological Review* 47 (April):216–27.

Kessler, S. 1975. Psychiatric genetics. In D. A. Hamburg and K. Brodie (Eds.), *American handbook of psychiatry* (Vol. 6). New York: Basic Books.

Kessler-Harris, A. 1982. *Out to work: A history of wage-earning women in the United States.* London: Oxford University Press.

Kiecolt, K. J. 1988. Recent developments in attitudes and social structure. *Annual Review of Sociology* 14: 381–403.

Kiecolt, K. J., and Acock, A. C. 1988. The long-term effects of family structure on gender-role attitudes. *Journal of Marriage and the Family* 50(3):709–17.

Kingston, P. W., and Nock, S. L. 1987. Time together among dual-earner couples. *American Sociological Review* 52(3):391–400.

Kipnis, D. 1972. Does power corrupt? *Journal of Personality and Social Psychology* 24:33–41.

Kirschenbaum, H., et al. 1971. *Wad-ja-get?* New York: A & W.

Klein, D. 1982. The dark side of marriage: Battered wives and the domination of women. In N. H. Rafter and E. A. Stanko (Eds.), *Judge, lawyer, victim, thief: Women, gender roles, and criminal justice.* Boston, MA: Northeastern University Press.

Kluegel, J. R., and Smith, E. R. 1982. Whites' beliefs and blacks' opportunity. *American Sociological Review* 47 (August):518–32.

———. 1986. *Beliefs about inequality: American's views of what is and what ought to be.* New York: Aldine.

Knoke, D. 1981. Power structures. In S. Long (Ed.), *Handbook of political behavior.* New York: Plenum.

Knottnerus, J. D. 1987. Status attainment research and its image of society. *American Sociological Review* 52(1):113–21.

Knox, R. E., and Safford, R. K. 1976. Group caution at the racetrack. *Journal of Experimental Social Psychology* 12:317–24.

Kohlberg, L. 1963. The development of children's orientations toward a moral order: I. Sequence in the development of moral thought. Vita hum., Basel.

Kohn, M. L. 1977. *Class and conformity.* Chicago: University of Chicago Press.

Kohn, M. L., and Schooler, C. 1983. *Work and personality: An inquiry into the impact of social stratification.* Norwood, NJ: Ablex.

Kohn, M. L., Atsushi, N., Schoenbach, C., Schooler, C., and Slomczynski, K. M. 1990. Position in the class structure and psychological functioning in the United States, Japan, and Poland. *American Journal of Sociology* 95(4):964–1008.

Kollock, P., Blumstein, P., and Schwartz, P. 1985. Sex and power in interaction. *American Sociological Review* 50(1):34–46.

Kolson, A. 1979. Sexual harassment on the job. *Detroit Free Press*, February 4:1C.

Konner, M. 1989. Where should baby sleep? *The New York Times Magazine* January 8:39–40.

Korbin, J. E. (Ed.). 1983. *Child abuse and neglect: Cross-cultural perspectives.* Berkeley, CA: University of California Press.

Kornhauser, W. 1959. *The politics of mass society.* New York: The Free Press.

———. 1966. 'Power elite' or 'veto groups'? In R. Bendix and S. M. Lipser (eds.). *Class, status, and power.* New York: Free Press.

Korman, A. K. 1988. *The outsiders: Jews and corporate America.* Lexington, MA: Lexington Books.

Koss, M. P., Gidycz, C. A., and Wisniewski, N. 1987. The scope of rape. *Journal of Consulting and Clinical Psychology* 52(2):162–70.

Kramer, L., and Freed, A. F. 1991. Gender and language. In L. Kramer (Ed.), *The Sociology of Gender*, pp. 23–29. New York: St. Martin's Press.

Kranichfeld, M. L. 1987. Rethinking family power. *Journal of Family Issues* 8:42–56.

Kriedte, P. 1984. *Peasants, landlords, and the merchant capitalists: Europe and the world economy, 1500–1800.* Cambridge, England: Cambridge University Press.

Kristof, N. D. 1990. More in China willingly rear just one child. *New York Times* (May 9):1.

Kübler-Ross, E. 1969. *On death and dying.* New York: Macmillan.

———. 1975. *Death, the final stage of growth.* Englewood Cliffs, NJ: Prentice-Hall.

Kuhn, M. H. 1964. Major trends in symbolic interaction theory in the past twenty-five years. *Sociological Quarterly* 5 (Winter):61–84.

Kuhn, M. H., and McPartland, T. 1954. An empirical investigation of self attitudes. *American Sociological Review* 19:68–76.

Kuhn, T. S. 1970. *The structure of scientific revolutions* (2nd enlarged ed.). Chicago: University of Chicago Press.

Kuper, H. 1963. *The Swazi: A South African kingdom.* New York: Holt, Rinehart and Winston.

Kuper, L. 1977. *The pity of it all: Polarization of racial and ethnic relations.* Minneapolis, MN: University of Minnesota Press.

———. 1982. *Genocide: Its political use in the twentieth century.* New Haven, CT: Yale University Press.

———. 1985. *The prevention of genocide.* New Haven, CT: Yale University Press.

———. 1989. *The roots of evil: The origins of genocide and other group violence.* Cambridge, England: Cambridge University Press.

Kurtz, R. A., and Chalfant, H. P. 1984. *Sociology of medicine and illness.* Boston: Allyn and Bacon.

Kurz, K., and Muller, W. 1987. Class mobility in the industrial world. *Annual Review of Sociology* 13:417–42.

Kuttner, R. 1984. *The economic illusion.* Boston: Houghton Mifflin.

Lachmann, R. 1987. *From manor to market: Structural*

change in England 1536–1640. Madison, WI: University of Wisconsin Press.

_____. 1989. Origins of capitalism in Western Europe: Economic and political aspects. *Annual Review of Sociology* 15:47–72.

LaFrance, M., and Mayo, C. 1978. *Moving bodies: Nonverbal communication in social relationships.* Monterey, CA: Brooks/Cole.

LaFree, G. D. 1980. The effect of sexual stratification by race on official reactions to rape. *American Sociological Review* 45 (October):842–54.

_____. 1989. *Rape and criminal justice.* Belmont, CA: Wadsworth.

Lakoff, R. T. 1975. *Language and woman's place.* New York: Harper and Row.

Lakoff, R. T., and Scherr, R. L. 1984. *Face value: The politics of beauty.* Boston: Routledge & Kegan Paul.

Lamb, M. E., and Goldberg, W. A. 1982. The father-child relationship: A synthesis of biological, evolutionary, and social perspectives. In L. W. Hoffman, R. Gandelman, and H. R. Schiffman (Eds.), *Parenting: Its causes and consequences,* pp. 55–73. Hillsdale, NJ: Lawrence-Erlbaum.

Landes, J. B. 1977–1978. Women, labor, and family life. *Science and Society* 41 (Winter):386–409.

Landry, B. 1987. *The new black middle class.* Berkeley and Los Angeles: University of California Press.

Lane, D. 1982. *The end of social inequality? Class, status, and power under state socialism.* London: Allen Unwin.

Langer, S. K. 1962. The growing center of knowledge. In *Philosophical sketches.* Baltimore, MD: Johns Hopkins Press.

Lapidus, G. 1983. *Women in Soviet society.* Magnolia, MA: Peter Smith.

LaPonce, J. A. 1987. *Languages and their territories.* Toronto: University of Toronto Press.

Larkin, Jack. 1988. *The reshaping of everyday life: 1790–1840.* New York: Harper and Row.

Lasch, C. 1977. *Haven in a heartless world: The family besieged.* New York: Basic Books.

Laska, S. B., Seaman, J. M., and McSeveney, D. R. 1982. Inner-city reinvestment: Neighborhood characteristics and spatial patterns over time. *Urban Studies* 19:155–65.

Laslett, B., and Brenner, J. 1989. Gender and social reproduction: Historical perspectives. *Annual Review of Sociology* 15:381–404.

Latané, B., and Darley, J. M. 1970. *The unresponsive bystander: Why doesn't he help?* New York: Appleton-Century-Crofts.

Latané, B., and Nida, S. 1981. Ten years of research on group size and helping. *Psychological Bulletin* 89:308–24.

Latour, B. 1987. *Science in action: How to follow scientists and engineers through society.* Cambridge, MA: Harvard University Press.

Lauer, R. H. 1981. *Temporal man: The meaning and uses of social time.* New York: Praeger.

Laughlin, P. R. 1980. Social combination processes of cooperative problem solving groups on verbal intellective tasks. In M. Fishbein (ed.), *Progress in social psychology.* Hillsdale, NJ: Lawrence Erlbaum.

Lazonick, W. 1974. Karl Marx and enclosures in England. *The Review of Radical Economics* 6(2, Summer):1–32.

Leacock, E. 1969. *Teaching and learning in city schools.* New York: Basic Books.

Leavitt, H. J. 1951. Some effects of certain communication patterns on group performance. *Journal of Abnormal and Social Psychology* 46:38–50.

Leavitt, R. 1971. Women in other cultures. In V. Gornick and B. K. Moran (Eds.), *Woman in sexist society,* pp. 393–427. New York: Basic Books.

Le Bon, G. [1895] 1960. *The crowd: A study of the popular mind.* New York: Viking Press.

Lederer, L. (Ed.). 1980. *Take back the night: Women on pornography.* New York: William Morrow.

Lee, M. T. 1968. The founders of the Chinese Communist party. *Civilizations* 18.

LeMasters, E. E. 1975. *Blue-collar aristocrats.* Madison, WI: University of Wisconsin Press.

Lemert, E. M. 1951. *Human deviance, social problems, and social control.* New York: McGraw-Hill.

Lenin, V. I. [1917] 1949. *The state and revolution.* Moscow: Progress Publishers.

Lenski, G. E. 1966. *Power and privilege.* New York: McGraw-Hill.

_____. 1975. Social structure in evolutionary perspective. In P. M. Blau (Ed.), *Approaches to the study of social structure.* New York: Free Press.

_____. 1976a. History and social change. *American Journal of Sociology* 82 (3, November):548–64.

_____. 1976b. Immanuel Wallerstein. The modern world system. *Social Forces* 54:701–702.

Lenski, G. E., and Lenski, J. 1982. *Human societies* (4th ed.). New York: Oxford University Press.

_____. 1987. *Human societies* (5th ed.). New York: Oxford University Press.

Lepper, M. R., Greene, D., and Nisbett, R. E. 1973. Undermining children's intrinsic interest with extrinsic reward: A test of the 'overjustification' hypothesis. *Journal of Personality and Social Psychology* 28:129–37.

Lerner, G. 1986. *The creation of patriarchy.* New York: Oxford University Press.

Lerner, M. (Ed.). 1948. *The portable Veblen.* New York: Viking Press.

Leslie, G. R. 1989. *The family in social context* (7th ed.). New York: Oxford University Press.

Leslie, G. R., and Korman, S. K. 1988. *The family in social context* (7th ed.). New York: Oxford University Press.

Lesser-Blumberg, R. 1983. Kibbutz women: From the fields of revolution to the laundries of discontent. In M. Palgi, J. R. Blasi, M. Rosner, and M. Safir (Eds.),

Lesser-Blumberg, R. (*continued*)
Sexual equality: The Israeli kibbutz tests the theories (pp. 130–150). Norwood, PA: Norwood Editions.

Lester, D. 1983. *Why people kill themselves.* Springfield, IL: Charles C. Thomas.

Levant, R. F., Slattery, S. C., and Loiselle, J. E. 1987. Fathers' involvement in housework and child care with school aged daughters. *Family Relations* 36:152–57.

Lever, H. 1981. Sociology of South Africa: Supplementary comments. *Annual Review of Sociology* 7:249–62.

Lévi-Strauss, C. 1956. The family. In H. L. Shapiro (ed.), *Man, culture, and society.* New York: Oxford University Press.

Levy, F. 1988. *The changing American income distribution.* New York: Russell Sage Foundation/Basic Books.

Lewis, L. A. 1990. *Gender politics and mtv.* Philadelphia, PA: Temple University Press.

Lewis, N. 1983. *Life in Egypt under Roman rule.* Oxford: Clarendon Press.

Lewontin, R., Rose, S., and Kamin, L. J. 1984. *Not in our genes: Biology, ideology, and human nature.* New York: Pantheon.

Lichter, D. T. 1988. Racial differences in underemployment in American cities. *American Journal of Sociology* 93(4):771–97.

———. 1989. Race, employment hardship, and inequality in the American nonmetropolitan south. *American Sociological Review* 54(3):436–46.

Lieberman, S. 1956. The effects of changes in roles on the attitudes of role occupants. *Human Relations* 9: 385–402.

Lieberson, S. 1971. An empirical study of military-industrial linkages. *American Journal of Sociology* 76 (January):562–83.

———. 1980. *A piece of the pie.* Berkeley, CA: University of California Press.

———. 1982. Stereotypes: Their consequences for race and ethnic interaction. In R. M. Hauser, D. Mechanic, A. O. Haller, and T. S. Hauser (Eds.), *Social structure and behavior,* pp. 47–68. New York: Academic Press.

———. 1985. *Making it count: The improvement of social research and theory.* Berkeley, CA: University of California Press.

Lieberson, S., and Waters, M. C. 1988. *From many strands: Ethnic and racial groups in contemporary America.* New York: Russell Sage Foundation.

Liebert, R. M., Sprafkin, J. N., and Davidson, E. S. 1982. *The early window: Effects of television on children and youth* (2nd ed.). New York: Pergamon.

Liebman, R. C., Sutton, J. R., and Wuthnow, R. 1988. Exploring the social sources of denominationalism: Schisms in American protestant denominations. *American Sociological Review* 53(3):343–52.

Lifton, R. J. 1986. *The Nazi doctors: Medical killing and the psychology of genocide.* New York: Basic Books.

Limerick, P. N. 1987. *The legacy of conquest: The Unbroken past of the American west.* New York: W. W. Norton & Company.

Lin, N., and Xie, W. 1988. Occupational prestige in urban China. *American Journal of Sociology* 93(4):793–832.

Link, B. G. 1987. Understanding labeling effects in the area of mental disorders: An assessment of expectations of rejection. *American Sociological Review* 52(1): 96–112.

Link, B. G., Cullen, F. T., Frank, J., and Wozniak, J. F. 1987. The social rejection of former mental patients: Understanding why labels matter. *American Journal of Sociology,* 92(6):1461–1500.

Link, B. G., Cullen, F. T., Struening, E., and Shrout, P. E. 1989. A modified labeling theory approach to mental disorders: An empirical assessment. *American Sociological Review* 54(3):400–423.

Linton, R. 1936. *The study of man.* New York: Appleton-Century-Crofts.

Lipset, S. M. 1959. Democracy and working-class authoritarianism. *American Sociological Review* 24:482–501.

———. 1963. *Political man.* New York: Anchor Books.

Lipset, S. M., and Bendix, R. 1959. *Social mobility in industrial society.* Berkeley, CA: University of California Press.

Lipset, S. M., Trow, M., and Coleman, J. S. 1956. *Union democracy.* Glencoe, IL: Free Press.

Lipton, D., Martinson, R., and Wilks, J. 1975. *The effectiveness of correctional treatment.* New York: Praeger.

Lipton, M. 1984. Urban bias revisited. *Journal of Development Studies* 20(3):139–66.

Liska, A. E., and Reed, M. D. 1985. Institutions and delinquency. *American Sociological Review* 50(4):547–60.

Litwak, E., and Messeri, P. 1989. Organizational theory, social supports, and mortality rates. *American Sociological Review* 54(1):49–66.

Livingston, E. 1987. *Making sense of ethnomethodology.* London: Routledge & Kegan Paul.

Lo, C. Y. H. 1982. Countermovements and conservative movements in the contemporary U.S. *Annual Review of Sociology* 8:107–34.

Lofland, J. 1977. *Doomsday cult* (enlarged ed.). New York: Irvington.

———. 1981. Collective behavior: Elementary forms and processes. In M. Rosenberg and R. Turner (Eds.), *Social psychology: Sociological Perspectives.* New York: Basic Books.

———. 1985. *Protest: Studies in collective behavior and social movements.* Brunswick, NJ: Transaction Books.

Lombroso, C. 1911. *Crime: Its causes and remedies.* Boston: Little Brown.

London, B. 1987. Structural determinants of third world urban change: An ecological and political economic analysis. *American Sociological Review* 52(1):28–43.

London, B., and Robinson, T. D. 1989. The effect of international dependence on income inequality and political violence. *American Sociological Review* 54(2):305–8.

London, B., and Smith, D. A. 1988. Urban bias, dependence, and economic stagnation in noncore nations. *American Sociological Review* 53(3):454–63.

Long, J. E. 1981. Population deconcentration in the United States. (Special Demographic Analysis COS-81–5). Washington, D.C.: U.S. Government Printing Office.

Long, L. H., and Boertlein, C. 1976. *The geographic mobility of Americans.* (Current Population Reports, Series P-23, No. 64). Washington, D.C.: U.S. Government Printing Office.

Long, L. H., and De Are, D. 1981. The suburbanization of blacks. *American Demographics* (September).

Lopata, H. Z., Miller, C. A., and Barnewolt, D. 1984. *City women: Work, jobs, occupations, careers, Volume 1: America.* New York: Praeger.

Lopata, H. Z., Barnewolt, D., and Miller, C. A. 1985. *City women: Work jobs, occupations, careers, Volume 2: Chicago.* New York: Praeger.

Lott, B. 1981. A feminist critique of androgyny: Toward the elimination of gender attributions for learned behavior. In C. Mayo and N. M. Henley (Eds.), *Gender and nonverbal behavior,* pp. 171–180. New York: Springer-Verlag.

Lovdal, L. 1989. Sex role messages in television commercials: An update. *Sex Roles* 21 (11/12):715–27.

Luce, R. D., and Raiffa, H. 1957. *Games and decisions.* New York: Wiley.

Luckmann, T. 1967. *The invisible religion.* New York: Macmillan.

Luebke, B. F. 1989. Out of focus: Images of women and men in newspaper photographs. *Sex Roles* 20(3/4): 121–29.

Luker, K. 1984. *Abortion and the politics of motherhood.* Berkeley, CA: University of California Press.

Lukes, S., and Scull, A. (Eds.). 1983. *Durkheim and the law.* New York: St. Martin's Press.

Lyman, S. M., and Vidich, A. J. 1988. *Social Order and Public Philosophy: An Analysis and Interpretation of the Work of Herbert Blumer.* Fayetteville and London: University of Arkansas Press.

Lynd, R. S. 1939. *Knowledge for what?* Princeton, NJ: Princeton University Press.

Lynd, R. S., and Lynd, H. M. 1929. *Middletown: A study in American culture.* New York: Harcourt Brace.

Lynd, R. S., and Lynd, H. M. 1937. *Middletown in transition: A study in cultural conflicts.* New York: Harcourt Brace.

Maccoby, E. E., and Jacklin, C. N. 1974. *The psychology of sex differences.* Stanford, CA: Stanford University Press.

Maccoby, E. E., and Martin, J. A. 1983. Socialization in the context of the family: Parent-child interaction. In P. H. Mussen (ed.), *Handbook of child psychology* (4th ed.), Volume 4: E. M. Hetherington (Ed.), *Socialization, personality, and social behavior.* New York: Wiley.

MacDermid, S. M., Huston, T. L., and McHale, S. M. 1990. Changes in marriage associated with the transition to parenthood. *Journal of Marriage and the Family* 52(2):475–86.

MacDonald, J. F. 1985. *Television and the red menace: The video road to Vietnam.* New York: Praeger.

Mach, B., and Wesolowski, W. 1986. *Social mobility and social structure.* London and New York: Routledge & Kegan Paul.

Maciak, B. J. 1987. Reported in the *New York Times,* October 20.

MacKenzie, M. 1980. *The politics of body size: Fear of fat.* Los Angeles, CA: Pacifica Tape Library.

MacKinnon, C. A. 1987. *Feminism unmodified.* Cambridge, MA: Harvard University Press.

Maines, D. R. 1987. The significance of temporality for the development of social theory. *Sociological Quarterly* 28(3):303–11.

Major, B., Schmidlin, A. M., and Williams, L. 1990. Gender patterns in social touch. *Journal of Personality and Social Psychology* 58(4):634–43.

Malamuth, N. M., and Donnerstein, E. (Eds.). 1984. *Pornography and sexual aggression.* Orlando, FL: Academic Press.

Malandro, L. A., and Barker, L. L. 1983. *Nonverbal communication.* Reading, MA: Addison-Wesley.

Malbix/Ricks Music, BMI. 1976. *Chocolate city.* (Available on Casablanca Records, NBLP 7014).

Malinowski, B. 1922. *Argonauts of the Western Pacific.* New York: Dutton.

———. 1929. *The sexual life of savages.* New York: Harcourt Brace and World.

———. 1948. *Magic, science, and religion.* New York: Free Press.

Malthus, T. [1798] 1960. *Essay on the principle of population.* New York: Modern Library.

Mamdani, M. 1981. The ideology of population control. In K. L. Michaelson (ed.), *And the poor get children.* New York: Monthly Review Press.

Mandel, E. 1968. *Marxist economic theory.* New York: Monthly Review Press.

Mandel, R. B. 1987. Findings reported in the *New York Times,* May 26.

Manley, J. 1983. Neo-pluralism: A class analysis of pluralism I and pluralism II. *American Political Science Review* 77:368–83.

Mann, H. 1842. *Fifth annual report to the secretary of the board.* Boston: Dutton and Wentworth, State Printers, 1842.

Mann, K. 1985. *Defending white-collar crime: A portrait of attorneys at work.* New Haven, CT: Yale University Press.

Mann, T. [1924] 1956. *The magic mountain.* New York: Alfred A. Knopf.

Mannheim, K. 1952. *Essays on the sociology of knowledge.* London: Routledge and Kegan Paul.

Marcus, G. E. 1983. One man's Mead. *New York Times Book Review*, March 27:3.

Margolin, L., and White, L. 1987. The continuing role of physical attractiveness in marriage. *Journal of Marriage and the Family* 49(1):21–27.

Marini, M. M. 1980. Sex differences in the process of occupational attainment. *Social Science Research* 9: 307–61.

————. 1989. Sex differences in earnings in the United States. *Annual Review of Sociology* 15:343–80.

Marini, M. M., and Brinton, M. 1984. Sex typing in occupational socialization. In B. F. Reskin (Ed.) *Sex segregation in the workplace*, pp. 192–232. Washington, D.C.: National Academy Press.

Markham, J. M. 1982. In barren Iceland, culture blossoms. *The New York Times* April 4.

Markides, K. C., and Cohen, S. F. 1982. External conflict/internal cohesion: A reevaluation of an Old Theory. *American Sociological Review* 47 (February):88–98.

Markovsky, B., Smith, L. F., and Berger, J. 1984. Do status interventions persist? *American Sociological Review* 49 (June):373–82.

Marks, C. 1989. *Farewell–We're good and gone: The great black migration.* Bloomington, IN: University of Indiana Press.

Markson, S. 1990. Personal communication.

Mars, G. 1983. *Cheats at Work: An Anthropology of Workplace Crime.* Winchester, MA: Allen and Unwin.

Martin, P. Y., and Hummer, R. A. 1989. Fraternity rapes on campus. *Gender and Society* 3(4):457–73.

Martin, T. C., and Bumpass, L. 1989. Recent trends in marital disruption. *Demography* 26:37–51.

Martinson, R. 1974. What works? Questions and answers about prison reform. *The Public Interest* 35 (Spring):22–54.

Martyna, W. 1980. Beyond the "he/man" approach: The case for nonsexist language. *Signs* 5:482–93.

Marx, G. T., and Reichman, N. 1984. Routinizing the discovery of secrets: Computers as informants. *American Behavioral Scientist* 27:4(March-April), 423–52.

Marx, K. [1843] 1967. Critiques of Hegel's philosophy of rights. In L. D. Easton and K. Guddat (trans. and eds.). *Writings of the young Marx on philosophy and society.* New York: Doubleday.

————. [1845] 1935. Theses on Feuerbach, in F. Engels, *Ludwig Feuerbach and the outcome of classical German philosophy.* New York: International Publishers.

————. [1859] 1970. *A contribution of the critique of political economy.* New York: International Publishers.

————. [1867] 1975. *Capital: A critique of political economy.* New York: International Publishers.

————. 1961. *Economic and philosophical manuscripts of 1884.* (T. B. Bottomore, Trans.). In E. Fromm, *Marx's concept of man.* New York: Ungar.

Marx, K., and Engels, F. [1846] 1976. The German ideology, in *Collected works of Marx and Engels*, Vol. 5. New York: International Publishers.

————. [1848] 1932. *Manifesto of the Communist party.* New York: International Publishers.

Mason, K. O. 1982. Norms relating to the desire for children. In R. A. Bulatao and R. D. Lee (eds.), *Determinants of fertility in developing countries: A summary of knowledge.* (Panel on Fertility Determinants, Report No.3). Washington, D.C.: National Academy Press.

————. 1988a. A feminist perspective on fertility decline. Research Report No. 88–119. Ann Arbor, MI: University of Michigan Population Studies Center.

————. 1988b. The impact of women's position on demographic change during the course of development: What do we know? Research Report No. 88–123. Ann Arbor, MI: University of Michigan Population Studies Center.

Massey, D. S. 1981a. Dimensions of the new immigration to the United States and prospects for assimilation. *Annual Review of Sociology* 7:57–85.

————. 1981b. Hispanic residential segregation: A comparison of Mexicans, Cubans, and Puerto Ricans. *Sociology and Social Research* 65.

————. 1990. American apartheid: Segregation and the making of the underclass. *American Sociological Review* 92(2):329–57.

Massey, D. S., Alarcon, R., Durand, J., and Gonzalez, H. 1987. *Return to Aztlan: The social process of international migration from Western Mexico.* Berkeley, CA: University of California Press.

Massey, D. S., and Denton, N. A. 1985. Spatial assimilation as a socioeconomic outcome. *American Sociological Review* 50(1):94–105.

————. 1987. Trends in the residential segregation of blacks, hispanics, and asians: 1970–1980. *American Sociological Review* 52(6):802–25.

————. 1988. Suburbanization and segregation in U.S. metropolitan areas. *American Journal of Sociology* 94(3):592-626.

————. 1989. Hypersegregation in U. S. metropolitan areas. *Demography* 26(3):373–91.

Massey, D. S., and Eggers, M. L. 1990. The ecology of inequality: Minorities and the concentration of poverty, 1970–1980. *American Journal of Sociology* 95(5):1153–88.

Mathais, P. 1983. *The first industrial revolution: An economic history of Britain 1700–1914* (2nd edition). London and New York: Methuen.

Matsueda, R. L. 1982. Testing control theory and differential association. *American Sociological Review* 47 (August):489–504.

Matthiessen, P. 1984. *Indian country.* New York: Viking Press.

Mayo, C., and Henley, N. M. (Eds.). 1981. *Gender and nonverbal behavior.* New York: Springer-Verlag.

McAdam, D. 1982. *Political process and the development of black insurgency 1930–1970.* Chicago: University of Chicago Press.

McArthur, L. Z. 1982. Television and sex role stereotyping. *The Brandeis Quarterly* 2 (January):12–13.

McCarthy, J. D., and Zald, M. N. 1973. *The trend of social movements in America: Professionalization and resource mobilization.* Morristown, NJ: General Learning Press.

McClelland, D. C. 1973. Testing for competence rather than for "intelligence." *American Psychologist* 29 (January).

————. 1986. Some reflections on the two psychologies of love. *Journal of Personality* (July):334–53.

McClosky, H., and Brill, A. 1983. *Dimensions of tolerance: What Americans believe about civil liberties.* New York: Russell Sage Foundation.

McCrea, F. B., and Markle, G. E. 1989. *Minutes to midnight: Nuclear weapons protest in America.* Newbury Park, CA: Sage.

McDougall, W. [1908] 1950. *An introduction to social psychology* (30th edition). London: Methuen.

McGlen, N., and O'Connor, K. 1983. *Women's rights: The struggle for equality in the 19th and 20th centuries.* New York: Praeger.

McGuire, W.J., McGuire, C.V., Child, P., and Fujioka, T. 1978. Salience of ethnicity in the spontaneous self-concept as a function of one's ethnic distinctiveness in the social environment. *Journal of Personality and Social Psychology* 36:511–20.

McHugh, P. 1968. *Defining the situation.* Indianapolis: Bobbs-Merrill.

McIntosh, J. L., and Osgood, N. J. 1989. Suicide and the elderly. Cited in *The New York Times*, July 19, p. 1.

McLanahan, S. 1985. Family structure and the reproduction of poverty. *American Journal of Sociology* 90(4):873–901.

McLanahan, S., and Adams, J. 1987. Parenthood and psychological well-being. *Annual Review of Sociology* 13:237–57.

McPhail, C., and Miller, D. 1973. The assembling process: A theoretical and empirical examination. *American Sociological Review* (December).

McPhail, C., and Wohlstein, R. T. 1983. Individual and collective behaviors within gatherings, demonstrations, and riots. *Annual Review of Sociology* 9:579–600.

————. 1986. Collective locomotion as collective behavior. *American Sociological Review* 51(4):447–63.

McPherson, J. M. 1988. *Battle cry of freedom: The civil war era.* New York: Oxford University Press.

McRae, K. D. 1984. *Conflict and compromise in multilingual societies, Vol 1: Switzerland.* Waterloo, Ontario: Wilfrid Laurier University Press.

————. 1986. *Conflict and compromise in multilingual societies, Vol 2: Belgium.* Waterloo, Ontario: Wilfrid Laurier University Press.

Mead, G. H. 1934. *Mind, self, and society.* Chicago: University of Chicago Press.

Mead, M. [1928] 1953. *Coming of age in Samoa.* New York: Modern Library.

————. [1935] 1963. *Sex and temperament in three primitive societies.* New York: William Morrow.

————. 1968. Incest. In David L. Sills (Ed.), *The inter-national encyclopedia of the social sciences,* Vol. 7, pp. 115–122. New York: Macmillan/Free Press.

Medea, A., and Thompson, K. 1974. *Against Rape.* New York: Farrar, Straus, and Giroux.

Mehrabian, A. 1972. *Nonverbal communication.* Chicago: Aldine-Atherton.

Meier, R. F., and Short, J. F., Jr. 1982. The consequences of white-collar crime. In H. Edelhertz and T. D. Overcast (Eds.), *White-collar crime: An agenda for research,* pp. 23–50. Lexington, MA: Lexington Press.

Melbin, M. 1978. Night as frontier. *American Sociological Review* 43 (February):3–22

Meltzer, B. N., and Petras, J. W. 1970. The Chicago and Iowa Schools of Symbolic Interactionism. In T. Shibutani (Ed.), *Human Nature and Collective Behavior.* Englewood Cliffs, NJ: Prentice-Hall.

Memmi, A. 1964. *Dominated man.* New York: Orion Press.

Merit Systems Protection Board. 1988. Reported in the *Hartford Courant,* June 30, p. A2.

Merrick, T. W. 1986. World population in transition. *Population Bulletin* 41(2, April). Washington, D.C.: Population Reference Bureau.

Merton, J. G., and Moore, R. L. 1982. *The cult experience: Responding to the new religious pluralism.* New York: Pilgrim Press.

Merton, R. K. 1936. The unanticipated consequences of purposive social action. *American Sociological Review* 1:894–904.

————. 1938. Social structure and anomie. *American Sociological Review* 3:672–82.

————. 1948. Discrimination and the American creed. In R. M. MacIver (Ed.), *Discrimination and National Welfare.* New York: Harper and Brothers, pp. 99–126.

————. 1957a. *Social theory and social structure.* New York: Free Press.

————. 1957b. Priorities in scientific discovery: A chapter in the sociology of science. *American Sociological Review* 22(6):635–59.

————. 1968. *Social theory and social structure* (enlarged ed.). New York: Free Press.

————. 1973. *The sociology of science: Theoretical and empirical investigations.* Chicago: University of Chicago Press.

————. 1975. Structural analysis in sociology. In P. Blau (Ed.), *Approaches to the study of social structure,* pp. 21–52. New York: Free Press.

————. 1976a. The sociology of social problems. In R. K. Merton and R. Nisbet (Eds.), *Contemporary Social Problems* (4th ed.). New York: Harcourt Brace Jovanovich.

————. 1976b. *Sociological ambivalence and other essays.* New York: Free Press.

————. [1938] 1978. *Science, technology, and society in seventeenth-century England.* Atlantic Highlands, NJ: Humanities.

————. 1984a. Scientific fraud and the first to be first. *Times Literary Supplement* November 2.

Merton, R. K. (*continued*)

_____. 1984b. Social expected durations I: A caste study of concept formation in sociology. In W. W. Powell and R. Robbins (Eds.), *Conflict and consensus*, pp. 262–83. New York: Free Press.

_____. 1987. Three fragments from a sociologist's notebooks: Establishing the phenomenon, specified ignorance, and strategic research materials. *Annual Review of Sociology* 13:1–28. Palo Alto, CA: Annual Reviews.

Merton, R. K., and Rossi, A. S. 1968. Contributions to the theory of reference group behavior. In Merton (1968), pp. 279–334.

Meyer, J., and Sobieszek, B. 1972. Effect of a child's sex on adult interpretations of its behavior. *Developmental Psychology* 6:42–48.

Michels, R. 1911/1967. *Political parties*. New York: Free Press.

Michelson, W. 1985. *From sun to sun: Daily obligations and community structure in the lives of employed women and their families*. Totowa, NJ: Rowman & Allanheld.

Micklin, M., and Choldin, H. M. (Eds.). 1984. *Sociological human ecology: Contemporary issues and applications*. Boulder, CO: Westview Press.

Milgram, S. 1965. Some conditions of obedience and disobedience to authority. *Human Relations* 18:57–76.

_____. 1974. *Obedience to authority*. New York: Harper and Row.

_____. 1977. *The individual in a social world*. Reading, MA: Addison-Wesley.

Miliband, R. 1969. *The state in capitalist society*. New York: Basic Books.

Milkman, R. 1987. *Gender and work: The dynamics of job segregation by sex during World War II*. Chicago: University of Chicago Press.

Miller, J. D. 1989. Quoted in *Chemical and Engineering News*, January 30, p. 24.

Miller, N., and Brewer, M. B. (Eds.). 1984. *Groups in contact: The psychology of desegregation*. New York: Academic Press.

Miller, W. B. 1958. Lower-class culture as a generating milieu of gang delinquency. *Journal of Sociological Issues* 14 (Summer):5–19.

Millett, K. 1971. *Sexual politics*. Garden City, NY: Doubleday.

Mills, C. W. 1951. *White collar*. New York: Oxford University Press.

_____. 1956. *The power elite*. New York: Oxford University Press.

_____. 1959. *The sociological imagination*. New York: Oxford University Press.

Miner, H. M. 1968. Community-society continnua. In D. L. Sills (Ed.), *The international encyclopedia of the social sciences* (vol. 3, pp. 174–80). New York: Macmillan/Free Press.

Mintz, B. 1975. The President's cabinet, 1897–1972: A contribution to the power structure debate. *Insurgent Sociologist* 5:131–48.

Mintz, B., and Schwartz, M. 1985. *The power structure of American business*. Chicago: University of Chicago Press.

Mirowsky, J. 1985. Depression and marital power: An equity model. *American Journal of Sociology* 91(3):557–92.

Mirowsky, J., and Ross, C. E. 1987. Belief in innate sex roles: Sex stratification versus interpersonal influence in marriage. *Journal of Marriage and the Family* 49(3):527–40.

_____. 1989. *Social causes of psychological distress*. New York: Aldine de Gruyter.

Mishler, E. G. 1986. *Research interviewing: Context and narrative*. Cambridge, MA: Harvard University Press.

Mitchell, J. 1966. The longest revolution. *New Left Review* (November/December):11–37.

Mitroff, I. I., Mason, R. O., and Barabba, V. P. 1983. *The 1980 census*: Policymaking amid turbulence. Lexington, MA: Lexington Books.

Mizrahi, T. 1986. *Getting rid of patients: Contradictions in the socialization of physicians*. New Brunswick, NJ: Rutgers University Press.

Moede, W. 1927. Die Richtlinien der Leitungspsychologie. Industrielle Psychotechnik 4, 193–209. Cited and Discussed in Raven (1968).

Moen, P. 1989. *Working parents: Transformations in gender roles and public policies in Sweden*. Madison, WI: University of Wisconsin Press.

Mol, H. 1976. *Identity and the sacred: A sketch for a new social-scientific theory of religion*. Oxford: Blackwell.

Mollenkopf, J. 1989. Who (or what) runs cities, and how? *Sociological Forum* 4(1):119–37.

Molotch, H. L., and Boden, D. 1985. Talking social structure. *American Sociological Review* 50(3):273–87.

Money, J., and Ehrhardt, A. 1972. *Man and woman, boy and girl*. Baltimore, MD: Johns Hopkins University Press.

Monk-Turner, E. 1990. The occupational achievements of community college entrants. *American Sociological Review* 55(5):719–25.

Monson, T. C., and Hesley, J. W. 1982. Causal attributions for behaviors consistent or inconsistent with an actor's personality traits: Differences between those offered by actors and observers. *Journal of Experimental Social Psychology* 18(5):416–32.

Montagu, A. M. F. 1971. *Touching: The human significance of the skin*. New York: Columbia University Press.

Mor, V. 1987. *Hospice care systems: Structure, process, costs, and outcomes*. New York: Springer.

Morello, K. B. 1986. *The invisible bar: The woman lawyer in America*. New York: Random House.

Moreno, J. L. 1943. Sociometry and the cultural order. *Sociometry* 6:299–344.

Morgan, S. P., and Hirosima, K. 1983. The persistence of extended family residence in Japan. *American Sociological Review* 48 (April):269–81.

Morgenstern, O. 1968. Game theory: Theoretical aspects.

In D. L. Sills (Ed.) *The international encyclopedia of the social sciences*, Vol. 6. New York: Macmillan/Free Press.

Morison, S. E. 1965. *The Oxford history of the American people.* New York: Oxford University Press.

Morris, A. 1984. *The origins of the civil rights movement: Black communities organizing for change.* New York: Free Press.

Morrison, K. C. 1987. *Black political mobilization: Leadership, power, and mass behavior.* Albany, NY: SUNY Press.

Mortimer, J. T., Finch, M. D., and Kumka, D. 1981. Persistence and change in human development: The multidimensional self-concept. In P. B. Bates, and O. G. Brim, Jr. (Eds.), *Life-span development and behavior* Volume 4. New York: Academic Press.

Mosher, W. D. 1988. Fertility and family planning in the U.S. *Family Planning Perspectives* 20(5):207–17.

Mosher, W. D., and Hendershot, G. E. 1984. Religion and fertility: A replication. *Demography* 21(2):185–92.

Moskos, C. 1969. Why men fight: American combat soldiers in Vietnam. *Transaction*, 7(1).

———. 1990. Army women. *The Atlantic Monthly* (August):70–78.

Mottaz, Clifford J. 1981. Some Determinants of Work Alienation. *The Sociological Quarterly* 22 (Autumn):515–29.

Mullen, B. 1983. Operationalizing the effect of the group on the individual: A self-attention perspective. *Journal of Experimental Social Psychology* 19(4):295–322.

Muller, E. N. 1988. Democracy, economic development, and income inequality. *American Sociological Review* 53(1):50–68.

Muller, P. O. 1981. *Contemporary suburban America.* Englewood Cliffs, NJ: Prentice-Hall.

Mulligan, M. A. 1978. *An investigation of factors associated with violent modes of conflict resolution in the family.* Unpublished Masters Thesis, University of Rhode Island. Cited in Gelles (1978), p. 173.

Mumford, L. 1961. *The city in history.* New York: Harcourt Brace Jovanovich.

Munley, A. 1983. *The hospice alternative: A new context for death and dying.* New York: Basic Books.

Munsinger, H. 1975. The adopted child's IQ: A critical review. *Psychological Bulletin* 82:623–59.

Murdock, G. P. 1943. The common denominator of cultures. In R. Linton (Ed.), *The science of man in the world crisis.* New York: Columbia University Press.

———. 1949. *Social structure.* New York: Macmillan.

———. 1967. *Ethnographic atlas.* Pittsburgh, PA: Pittsburgh University Press.

Murray, C. 1984. *Losing ground: American social policy 1950–1980.* New York: Basic Books.

Myrdal, G. 1945. *An American dilemma.* New York: Harper and Row.

Nag, M. 1962. *Factors affecting human fertility in nonindustrial societies: A cross-cultural study.* New Haven, CT: Yale University Press.

———. 1967. Family type and fertility. *Proceedings of the world population conference, Volume II*:160–63. New York: United Nations.

Nakell, B., and Hardy, K. A. 1987. *The arbitrariness of the death penalty.* Philadelphia, PA: Temple University Press.

Namboodiri, K. 1988. Ecological demography: Its place in sociology. *American Sociological Review* 5(4):619–33.

Nasaw, D. 1979. *Schooled to order.* New York: Oxford University Press.

National Commission on Excellence in Education. 1983. *A nation at risk: The imperative for educational reform.* Washington, D.C.: U.S. Government Printing Office.

National Council of Churches. 1987. *Yearbook of American and Canadian Churches: 1987.* Nashville, Tenn: Abingdon Press.

National Council on Aging. 1975. *The myth and reality of aging in America.* America (Mimeograph). Washington, D.C.. Cited and quoted in Riley and Waring (1976), p. 398.

National Law Journal. 1989. Reported in the *New York Times*, December 4, p. A21.

National Law Review. 1984 (May 21).

National Office of Health Statistics. 1956. *Death rates by age, race, and sex, United States, 1900–1953: Suicide.* (Vital Statistics-Special Reports, 43,30. Washington, D.C.: U.S. Government Printing Office.

National Research Council. 1989. *A common destiny: Blacks and American society.* Washington, D.C.: National Academy Press.

National Women's Studies Association. 1989. Reported in the *New York Times*, May 17, p. B6.

NCHS (National Center for Health Statistics). 1985. *Advance report of final marriage statistics, 1981.* Monthly Vital Statistics Report 32, 11, Feburary 29.

———. 1986. Findings reported in the *New York Times*, May 25, p. 32.

———. 1987. *Vital statistics of the United States, 1983, Vol. II, Mortality, Part A.* Washington, D.C.: U.S. Government Printing Office.

———. 1988. *Health United States 1987.* Washington, D.C.: U.S. Government Printing Office.

———. 1990a. *Health: United States 1989.* Washington, D.C.: U.S. Government Printing Office.

———. 1990b. Reported in the *New York Times*, August 17, p. A14.

———. 1991. Reported in the *Hartford Courant*, March 14, p. A4.

NCPE (National Committee on Pay Equity). 1987. Ford Foundation study reported in the *Hartford Courant*, March 1.

NDHN (National Displaced Homemakers Network). 1990. Reported in the *New York Times*, June 2, p. 13.

Nee, V., and Mozingo, D. 1983. *State and society in contemporary China.* Ithica, NY: Cornell University Press.

Neidert, L. J. and Farley, R. 1985. Assimilation in the

Neidert, L. J. and Farley, R. *(continued)* United States. *American Sociological Review* 50(6): 840–49.

Neill, A. S. 1961. *Summerhill*. New York: Hart.

Nemeth, R. J., and Smith, D. A. 1985. The political economy of contrasting urban hierarchies in South Korea and the Philippines. In Timberlake, M. (Ed.), *Urbanization in the world economy*, pp. 183–206. New York: Academic Press.

Neugarten, B. L., et al. 1965. Age norms, age constraints, and adult socialization. *American Journal of Sociology* 70:710–17.

Neustadt, R. E. and May, E. R. 1986. *Thinking in time*. New York: Free Press.

Newcomb, T. M. 1956. The prediction of interpersonal attraction. *American Psychologist* 1:575–86.

————. 1961. *The acquaintance process*. New York: Holt, Rinehart and Winston.

Newman, K. S. 1988. *Falling from grace: The experience of downward mobility in the American middle class*. New York: Free Press. *New York Times*. 1988. September 27, p. C9.

NIAPV (National Institute Against Prejudice and Violence). 1990. Reported in the *New York Times*, May 9, p. 1.

Nichols, E. K. 1986. *Mobilizing against AIDS*. Cambridge, MA: Harvard University Press.

NIDA (National Institute of Drug Abuse). 1991. Reported in *The New York Times* (January 1), p. A35.

Niebuhr, R. 1929. *The social sources of denominationalism*. New York: Holt.

Noelle-Neumann, E. 1984. *The spiral of silence: Public opinion and our social skin*. Chicago: University of Chicago Press.

North, C. C., and P. K. Hatt. 1947. Jobs and occupations: A popular evaluation. *Opinion News* 9:3–13.

Norton, A. J., and Moorman, J. E. 1987. Current trends in marriage and divorce among American women. *Journal of Marriage and the Family* 49(1):3–14.

Oakes, J. 1985. *Keeping track: How schools structure inequality*. New Haven, CT: Yale University Press.

Oakley, A. 1974. *Woman's work: The housewife, past and present*. New York: Pantheon.

Oberschall, A. 1973. *Social conflict and social movements*. Englewood Cliffs, NJ: Prentice-Hall.

Obaler, R. S. 1985. *Women, power, and economic change: The Nandi of Kenya*. Stanford, CA: Stanford University Press.

O'Brien, R. M. 1987. The interracial nature of violent crimes: A reexamination. *American Journal of Sociology* 92(4):817–35.

O'Connor, J. 1973. *The fiscal crisis of the state*. New York: St. Martin's Press.

OECD (Office for Economic Cooperation and Development). 1987. Reported in the *New York Times*, November 15.

Office of Technology Assessment. 1986a. Electronic record systems and individual privacy. Washington, D.C.: U.S. Government Printing Office.

————. 1986b. Reported in the *New York Times*, March 18.

————. 1987. The electronic supervisor: New technology, new tensions. Reported in the *New York Times*, September 28.

Ogburn, W. F. 1922. *Social Change*. New York: Viking Press.

————. 1964. Cultural lag as theory. In William F. Ogburn (Ed.), *On culture and social change*, pp. 86–95. Chicago: University of Chicago Press.

Older Women's League. 1989. Cited and quoted in the *New York Times*, May 14, p. 26.

Olzak, S. 1989. Analysis of events in the study of collective action. *Annual Review of Sociology* 15:119–41.

Orfield, G., and Montford, F. 1988. *Racial change and desegregation in large school districts*. Washington, D.C.: National School Boards Association.

Orum, A. M. 1972. *Black students in protest*. Washington, D.C.: The American Sociological Association.

Orwell, G. [1949] 1971. *Nineteen eighty-four*. New York: Signet.

Osborne, J. J., Jr. 1979. *The paper chase*. New York: Popular Library.

Osofsky, G. 1966. *Harlem: The making of a ghetto*. Irvington.

Page, B. I. 1983. *Who gets what from government*. Berkeley, CA: University of California Press.

Pagelow, M. D. 1984. *Family violence*. New York: Praeger.

Painter, N. I. 1987. *Standing at armageddon: The United States, 1877–1919*. New York: W.W. Norton and Company.

Paludi, M. A. 1990. *Ivory power: Sexual harassment on campus*. Albany, NY: State University of New York Press.

Paludi, M. A., and Strayer, L. A. 1985. What's in an author's name? *Sex Roles* 12 (3/4):353–62.

Pankratz, D. B., and Morris, V. (Eds.). 1990. *The future of the arts: Public policy and arts research*. New York: Praeger.

Parenti, M. 1985. *Inventing reality*. New York: St. Martin's Press.

Park, R. E. [1925] 1967. The city: Suggestions for the investigation of human behavior in the urban environment in Park, R. E. and Burgess, E. W. (Eds.). *The city*. Chicago: University of Chicago Press.

————. 1926. The urban community as a spatial pattern and moral order. In E. W. Burgess (Ed.), *The urban community*. Chicago: University of Chicago Press.

————. [1939] 1950. The nature of race relations. In Park, R. E., *Race and culture*, pp. 81–116. Glencoe, IL: Free Press.

Park, R. E., and Burgess, E. (Eds.). 1921. *An introduction to the science of sociology*. Chicago: University of Chicago Press.

Park, R. E., Burgess, E., and McKenzie, R. D. (Eds.). 1925. *The city*. Chicago: University of Chicago Press.

Parker, D. P. 1983. *Fighting computer crime.* New York: Charles Scribners and Sons.

Parsons, H. M. 1982. More on the Hawthorne effect. *American Psychologist* 37, 7 (July):856–57.

Parsons, T. 1937. *The structure of social action.* New York: McGraw-Hill Book Company.

————. 1951. *The social system.* Glencoe, IL: Free Press.

————. 1964. A revised approach to the theory of social stratification. In Parsons, T., *Essays in sociological theory,* pp. 386–439. New York: Free Press.

————. 1966. *Societies: Evolutionary and comparative perspectives.* Englewood Cliffs, NJ: Prentice-Hall.

————. 1969. *Politics and social structure.* New York: Free Press.

————. 1971. *The system of modern societies.* Englewood Cliffs, NJ: Prentice-Hall.

Parsons, T., and Bales, R. F. 1953. *Family, socialization, and interaction process.* Glencoe, IL: Free Press.

Pascal, B. *Pensees,* Section XIV, No.894.

Pastner, C. 1974. Accommodations to Purdah: The female perspective. *Journal of Marriage and the Family* 36 (May):408–14.

Patterson, M. L. 1983. *Nonverbal behavior.* New York: Springer-Verlag.

Patzer, G. L. 1985. *The physical attractiveness phenomena.* New York: Plenum Press.

Paulus, P. B. 1983. *Basic group processes.* New York: Springer-Verlag.

Payer, L. 1988. *Medicine and culture: Varieties of treatment in the United States, England, West Germany, and France.* New York: Henry Holt and Company.

Pear, R. 1982. How poor are the elderly? *New York Times,* December 19.

Peattie, L., and Aldrete-Haas, J. A. 1981. 'Marginal' settlements in developing countries. *Annual Review of Sociology* 7:157–75.

Pechman, J. A. 1984. *Who paid the taxes?* Washington, D.C.: Brookings Institution.

Perrin, S., and Spencer, C. 1980. The Asch effect—A child of its time? *Bulletin of the British Psychology Society* 32:405–6.

Perrow, C. 1984. *Normal accidents: Living with high-risk technologies.* New York: Basic Books.

Peschek, J. 1987. *Policy-planning organizations: Elite agendas and America's rightward turn.* Philadelphia, PA: Temple University Press.

Pescosolido, B. A., and Georgianna, S. 1989. Durkheim, suicide, and religion: Toward a network theory of suicide. *American Sociological Review* 54(1):33–48.

Pessen, E. 1984. *The log cabin myth: The social backgrounds of the presidents.* New Haven, CT: Yale University Press.

Peter, L. J., and Hull, R. 1969. *The Peter Principle.* New York: William Morrow.

Petersen, A. C. 1980. Biopsychosocial processes in the development of sex-related differences. In Parsons (1980), pp. 31–56.

Peterson, R. A. (Ed.). 1990. Symposium: The many facets of culture. *Contemporary Sociology* 19(4):498–523.

Peterson, W., and Gist, N. P. 1951. Rumor and public opinion. *American Journal of Sociology* 57:159–67.

Pettigrew, T. F. 1968. Race relations: Social and psychological aspects. In D. Sills (Ed.), *The international encyclopedia of the social sciences* (Vol.13, pp. 277–82). New York: Macmillan/Free Press.

Peukert, D. J. K. 1987. *Inside nazi Germany: Conformity, opposition and, racism in everyday life* (translated by R. Deveson). New Haven, CT: Yale University Press.

Pfeffer, J. 1981. *Power in organizations.* Marshfield, MA: Pitman.

Pfeiffer, E., Verwoedt, A., and Davis, G. 1972. Sexual behavior in middle life. *American Journal of Psychiatry* 128(10):82.

Piaget, J. 1965. *The moral judgement of the child.* Glencoe: IL: Free Press.

Piaget, J., and Inhelder, B. 1969. *The psychology of the child.* New York: Basic Books.

Piliavin, I., Gartner, R., Thornton, C., and Matsueda, R. L. 1986. Crime, deterrence, and choice. *American Sociological Review* 51(1):101–19.

Piven, F. F., and Cloward, R. A. 1979. *Poor people's movements.* New York: Vintage Books.

————. 1988. *Why Americans don't vote.* New York: Pantheon.

Pleck, E. 1987. *Domestic tyranny: The making of American social policy against family violence from colonial times to the present.* New York: Oxford University Press.

Pleck, J. H. 1977. The work-family role system. *Social Problems* 24:417–27.

————. 1985. *Working wives/Working husbands.* Beverly Hills, CA: Sage Publications.

Polatnick, M. 1973. Why men don't rear children: A power analysis. *Berkeley Journal of Sociology* 18:45–86.

Polednak, A. P. 1989. *Racial and ethnic differences in disease.* New York: Oxford University Press.

Polit, D. F., and Falbo, T. 1987. Only children and personality development: A quantitative review. *Journal of Marriage and the Family* 49(2):309–25.

Pollock, L. A. 1984. *Forgotten children: Parent-child relations from 1500 to 1900.* Cambridge, England: Cambridge University Press.

Pomer, M. I. 1986. Labor market structure, intragenerational mobility, and discrimination: Black male advancement out of low-paying occupations. *American Sociological Review* 51(5):650–59.

Pomerance, B. 1979. *The elephant man.* New York: Grove Press.

Pomeroy, S. 1975. *Goddesses, whores, wives, and slaves.* New York: Schocken.

Pope, L. 1942. *Millhands and preachers.* New Haven, CT: Yale University Press.

Popenoe, D. 1985. *Private pleasure, public plight: American metropolitan community life in comparative perspective.* New Brunswick, NJ: Transaction Books.

Popenoe, D. (continued)

————. 1987. Beyond the nuclear family: A statistical portrait of the changing family in Sweden. *Journal of Marriage and the Family* 49(1):173–83.

Popper, F. J. et al. 1987. Reported in the *New York Times*, December 12, p. 13.

Porter, J. N. (Ed.). 1982. *Genocide and human rights: A global anthology*. Lanham, MD: University Press of America.

Portes, A., and Truelove, C. 1987. Making sense of diversity: Recent research on Hispanic minorities in the United States. *Annual Review of Sociology* 13:359–85.

Posner, G. L. 1988. *Warlords of crime; Chinese secret societies*. New York: McGraw-Hill.

Powell, B., and Steelman, L. C. 1989. The liability of having brothers: Paying for college and the sex composition of the family. *Sociology of Education* 62(2):134–47.

Powell, W. 1985. *Getting into print*. Chicago: University of Chicago Press.

Powers, M. G. (Ed.). 1982. *Measures of socioeconomic status*. Boulder, CO: Westview Press.

PRB (Population Reference Bureau). 1980. *World's women data sheet*. Washington, D.C.: Population Reference Bureau.

————. 1984. *World population data sheet: 1984*. Washington, D.C.: Population Reference Bureau.

————. 1987. *1987 world population data sheet*. Washington, D.C.: Population Reference Bureau.

————. 1990. *World population: Fundamentals of growth* (2nd ed.). Washington, D.C.: Population Reference Bureau.

Price, D. J. 1986. *Little science: Big science*. New York: Columbia University Press.

Price, T. D., and Brown, J. A. 1985. *Prehistoric hunter-gatherers: The emergence of cultural complexity*. New York: Academic Press.

Projector, D., and Weiss, G. 1966. Survey of financial characteristics of consumers. (Federal Reserve Technical Paper, p. 148) Washington, D.C.: U.S. Government Printing Office.

Proctor, R. N. 1988. *Racial hygiene: Medicine under the Nazis*. Cambridge, MA: Harvard University Press.

Przeworski, A. 1985. *Capitalism and social democracy*. Cambridge, England: Cambridge University Press.

Purcell, P., and Stewart, L. 1990. Dick and Jane in 1989. *Sex Roles* 22(3,4):177–85.

Quadagno, J. S. 1976. Occupational sex-typing and internal labor market distributions: An assessment of medical specialties. *Social Problems* 23(4):442–53.

Quinney, R. 1970. *The social reality of crime*. Boston: Little, Brown.

————. 1972. The ideology of law: Notes for a radical alternative to legal oppression. *Issues in Criminology* 7(1):1–35.

Radcliffe-Brown, A. R. 1948. *The Andaman Islanders*. Glencoe, IL: Free Press.

Radecki, C., and Walstedt, J. J. 1980. Sex as a status position in work settings: Female and male reports of dominance behavior. *Journal of Applied Social Psychology* 10(1):71–85.

Raiffa, H. 1970. *Decision analysis*. Reading, MA: Addison Wesley.

Raines, J. C., Berson, L. E., and Gracie, D. 1982. *Community and capital in conflict*. Philadelphia, PA: Temple University Press.

Rand Corporation. 1990. Reported in the *New York Times* September 20, 1990, p. A14.

Rands, M., and Levinger, G. 1979. Implicit theories of relationship: An intergenerational study. *Journal of Personality and Social Psychology* 37:645–61.

Ransford, H. E., and Miller, J. 1983. Race, sex and feminist outlooks. *American Sociological Review* 48(1):46–59.

Raper, A. 1933. *The tragedy of lynching*. Chapel Hill, NC: University of North Carolina Press.

Raphael, R. 1989. *The men from the boys: Rites of passage in male America*. Lincoln, NE: University of Nebraska Press.

Rappoport, D. C., and Alexander, Y. (Eds.). 1982. *The morality of terrorism: Religious and secular justifications*. New York: Pergamon Press.

Raskin, P. A., and Israel, A. C. 1981. Sex-role imitation in children: Effects of sex of child, sex of model, and sex-role appropriateness of modeled behavior. *Sex Roles* 7:1067–77.

Rasmussen, W. D. 1982. The mechanization of agriculture. In *Scientific American. The mechanization of work*, pp. 15–30. San Francisco: W. H. Freeman and Company.

Ravitch, D. 1983. *The troubled crusade: American education, 1945–1980*. New York: Basic Books.

Reckless, W. C. 1973. *The crime problem*. Englewood Cliffs, NJ: Prentice-Hall.

Redfield, R. 1947. The folk society. *American Journal of Sociology* 52:293–308.

Reed, J. 1960. *Ten days·that shook the world*. New York: Random House.

Reeder, G. D., and Spores, J. M. 1983. The attribution of morality. *Journal of Personality and Social Psychology* 44(4):736–45.

Reich, M. 1981. *Racial inequality: A political-economic analysis*. Princeton, NJ: Princeton University Press.

————. 1986. The political-economic effects of racism. In Edwards, R. C., Reich, M., and Weisskopf, T. E. (Eds.). *The capitalist system* (3rd ed.). Englewood Cliffs, NJ: Prentice-Hall.

Reich, M., Gordon, D. M., and Edwards, R. C. 1973. A theory of labor market segmentation. *American Economic Review* LXIII, 2(May).

Reilly, M. E., Lott, B., and Gallogly, S. M. 1986. Sexual harassment of university students. *Sex Roles* 15:333–58.

Reiss, A. J., and Biderman, A. D. 1980. *Data sources on* *white-collar law-breaking.* Washington, D.C.: Bureau of Social Research.

Remick, H. (Ed.). 1984. *Comparable worth and wage discrimination: Technical possibilities and political realities.* Philadelphia, PA: Temple University Press.

Renzetti, C. M., and Curran, D. J. 1989. *Women, men, and society.* Boston: Allyn and Bacon.

Reskin, B., and Hartmann, H. I. 1986. *Women's work, men's work: Sex segregation on the job.* Washington, D.C.: National Academy Press.

Reynolds, P. D. 1971. Comment on 'The distribution of participation in group discussions' as related to group size. *American Sociological Review* 36:704–6.

————. 1982. *Ethics and social science research.* Englewood Cliffs, NJ: Prentice-Hall.

Reynolds, V. 1980. *The biology of human action.* San Francisco: W. H. Freeman and Company.

Rich, A. 1976. *Of woman born: Motherhood as experience and institution.* New York: W. W. Norton & Company.

Richardson, L. W. 1977. *The dynamics of sex and gender.* Boston: Houghton Mifflin.

————. 1981. *The dynamics of sex and gender* (2nd ed.). Boston: Houghton Mifflin.

Ridgeway, C. L. 1981. Nonconformity, competence, and influence in groups. *American Sociological Review* 46 (June):333–47.

Ridgeway, C. L., and Berger, J. 1986. Expectations, legitimation, and dominance behavior in task groups. *American Sociological Review* 51(5):603–17.

Ridgeway, C. L., Berger, J., and Smith, L. 1985. Nonverbal cues and status: An expectation states approach. *American Journal of Sociology* 90(5):955–78.

Riding, Alan. 1983. Problems of Mexico City: Warning to the third world. *The New York Times* May 15:p. 1.

Riesman, D. 1961. *The lonely crowd.* New Haven, CT: Yale University Press.

Rifkin, J. 1987. *Time wars.* New York: Holt and Company.

Riley, J. W., Jr. 1983. Dying and the meanings of death: Sociological inquiries. *Annual Review of Sociology* 9:191–216. Palo Alto, CA: Annual Reviews.

Riley, M. W. 1974. The perspective of age stratification. *School Review* 82(1).

————. 1976. Age strata in social systems. In J. E. Birren (Ed.), *Handbook of aging and the social sciences.* New York: Van Nostrand Reinhold.

————. 1983. The family in an aging society: A matrix of latent relationships. *Journal of Family Issues* (September).

————. 1987. On the significance of age in sociology. *American Sociological Review* 52(1):1–14.

Riley, M. W. et al. 1970. *Aging and society* (Volume 2). New York: Russell Sage Foundation.

Riley, M. W., and Foner, A. 1968. *Aging and society* (Volume 1). New York: Russell Sage Foundation.

————. 1972. *Aging and society* (Volume 3). New York: Russell Sage Foundation.

Riley, M. W., Foner, A., and Waring, J. 1988. A sociology of age. In Smelser, N. J. and Burt, R. (Eds.), *Handbook of sociology.* New York: Russell Sage Foundation.

Riley, M. W., and Riley, J. W., Jr. 1986. Longevity and social structure: The added years. *Daedalus,* 115:51–75.

Riley, M. W., and Waring, J. 1976. Age and Aging. In R. K. Merton and R. Nisbet (Eds.), *Contemporary social problems* (4th ed.). New York: Harcourt, Brace, Jovanovich.

Rindfuss, R., Bumpass, L., and St. John, C. 1980. Education and fertility: Implications for the roles women occupy. *American Sociological Review* 45:431–47.

Risman, B. J. 1987. Intimate relationships from a microstructuralist perspective: Men who mother. *Gender and Society* 1(1):6–32.

Ritzer, G., and Walczak, D. 1988. Rationalization and the deprofessionalization of physicians. *Social Forces* 67(1):1–22.

Robbins, T. 1988. *Cults, converts, and charisma: The sociology of new religious movements.* Newbury Park, CA: Sage.

Robinson, J. C. 1984. Racial inequality and the probability of occupation related injury or illness. *Milbank Memorial Fund Quarterly* 62(4):567–90.

Robinson, J. G. 1980. Estimating the approximate size of the illegal alien population in the United States by the comparative trend analysis of age specific death rates. *Demography* 17:159–76.

Robinson, P. 1969. Poor black women. In B. Roszak and T. Roszak (Eds.), *Masculine/feminine,* pp. 208–13. New York: Harper and Row.

Robinson, R. V. 1984. Reproducing class relations in industrial capitalism. *American Sociological Review* 49 (June):182–96.

Rodin, J. 1986. Reported in the *New York Times,* October 7, p. C1.

Rodin, J., and Langer, E. 1977. Long-term effects of a control-relevant intervention with the institutionalized aged. *Journal of Personality and Social Psychology* 35:897–902.

Roethlisberger, F. J., and Dickson, W. 1939. *Management and the worker.* Cambridge, MA: Harvard University Press.

Rogers, E. M. 1983. *Diffusion of innovations* (3rd ed.). New York: Free Press.

Rogers, W. 1931, June 28. Syndicated newspaper column. In *Bartlett's Quotations* 13th ed., p. 904. Boston: Little Brown, 1955.

Rose, P. I. 1981. *They and we: Racial and ethnic relations in the United States.* New York: Random House.

Rosenberg, C. E. 1987. *The care of strangers: The rise of America's hospital system.* New York: Basic Books.

Rosenberg, M. 1979. *Conceiving the self.* New York: Basic Books.

————. 1981. The self-concept: Social product and social force. In M. Rosenberg and R. H. Turner (Eds.),

Rosenberg, M. (continued)

Social psychology: Sociological perspectives, pp. 593–624. New York: Basic Books.

Rosenberg, M., and Kaplan, H. B. (Eds.). 1982. Social psychology of the Self-Concept. Arlington Heights, IL: Harlan Davidson.

Rosenhan, D. L. 1973. On being sane in insane places. Science 179, 4070 (January 19):1–9.

Rosenthal, A. M. 1987. The 39th witness. New York Times (February 12).

Rosenthal, C. J. 1985. Kinkeeping in the familial division of labor. Journal of Marriage and the Family 47(4): 965–74.

Rosenthal, K. M., and Keshet, H. F. 1978. Childcare responsibilities of part-time and single fathers. Alternative Lifestyles 1,4 (November):465–91.

Rosenthal, R., and Jacobson, L. 1968. Pygmalion in the classroom: Teacher expectation and pupils' intellectual development. New York: Holt, Rinehart and Winston.

Rosnow, R. L., and Fine, G. A. 1976. Rumor and gossip. New York: Elsevier.

Ross, H. L. 1984. Social control through deterrence: Drinking-and-driving laws. Annual Review of Sociology 10:21–35.

Rossi, A. S. 1969. Sex equality: The beginning of ideology. In B. Roszak and T. Roszak (Eds.), Masculine/feminine. New York: Harper and Row.

———. 1982. Feminists in politics: A panel analysis of the first national women's conference. New York: Academic Press.

———. 1984. Gender and parenthood. American Sociological Review 49(1):1–19.

Rossi, P. H. 1989. Down and out in America: The origins of homelessness. Chicago: University of Chicago Press.

Rossides, D. W. 1990. Social stratification: The American class system in comparative perspective. Englewood Cliffs, NJ: Prentice-Hall.

Rostow, W. W. 1960. The stages of economic growth: A noncommunist manifesto. Cambridge, England: Cambridge University Press.

Roszak, B., and Roszak, T. (Eds.). 1969. Masculine/feminine. New York: Harper and Row.

Rousseau, J. J. [1762] 1950. New York: E. P. Dutton.

Rowbotham, S. 1973. Woman's consciousness, man's world. New York: Penguin Books.

Ruback, R. 1987. Deserted (and nondeserted) aisles: Territorial intrusion can produce persistence, not flight. Social Psychology Quarterly 50:270–76.

Rubin, B. 1987. Third world coup makers, strongmen, and populist tyrants. New York: McGraw-Hill.

Rubin, L. B. 1976. Worlds of pain. New York: Basic Books.

Rubin, N. 1982. Learning how children learn from the first moments of life. The New York Times, January 10 (Education Supplement).

Rubin, R., and Byerly, G. 1983. Incest: The last taboo (An Annotated bibliography). New York: Garland.

Ruffini, J. L. (Ed.). 1983. Advances in medical social science. New York: Gordon and Breach.

Russell, D. E. H. 1982. Rape in marriage. New York: Macmillan.

———. 1984. Sexual exploitation: Rape, child sexual abuse, and workplace harassment. Beverly Hills, CA: Sage Publications.

Russell, D. E. H., and Howell, N. 1983. The prevalence of rape in the United States revisited. Signs 8(4):688–95.

Russell, J. C. 1972. Medieval regions and the cities. Bloomington, IN: Indiana University Press.

Russman, L. 1989. Survey of news magazines shows little news coverage of women. Media Report to Women 17(6):p. 1.

Ryder, N. B. 1965. The cohort as a concept in the study of social change. American Sociological Review 30:843–61.

Ryder, N. B., and Westoff, Charles F. 1971. Reproduction in the United States, 1965. Princeton, NJ: Princeton University Press.

Rytina, J. H., Form, W. H., and Pease, J. 1970. Income and stratification ideology: Beliefs about the American opportunity structure. American Journal of Sociology 75 (January):703–16.

Sabini, J., and Silver, M. 1982. Moralities of everyday life. New York: Oxford University Press.

Sachs, C. E. 1983. The invisible farmers: Women in agricultural production. Totowa, NJ: Rowman and Allanheld.

Sacks, K. 1974. Engels revisited: Women, the organization of production, and private property. In M. Z. Rosaldo and L. Lamphere (Eds.), Woman, culture, and society, pp. 207–22. Stanford, CA: Stanford University Press.

Sadker, M., and Sadker, D. 1985. Sexism in the schoolroom of the '80s. Psychology Today (March):54–57.

Sagatun, I. J., and Knudsen, J. H. 1982. Attributional self presentation for actors and observers in success and failure situations. Scandinavian Journal of Psychology 23:243–52. Cited in Annual Review of Sociology 9(1983), p. 441.

Sahlins, M. D. 1976. The use and abuse of biology: An anthropological Critique of sociobiology. Ann Arbor, Michigan: University of Michigan Press.

Sahlins, M. D., and Service, E. R. (Eds.). 1960. Evolution and Culture. Ann Arbor, Michigan: University of Michigan Press.

St. Peter, S. 1979. Jack went up the hill. . . but where was Jill? Psychology of Women Quarterly 4:256–60.

Sale, K. 1980. Human scale. New York: Coward, McCann, and Geoghegan.

Sampson, A. 1983. The changing anatomy of Britain. New York: Random House.

Sampson, R. J. 1986. Effects of socioeconomic context on official reaction to juvenile delinquency. American Sociological Review 51(6):876–85.

Sanday, P. R. 1981. Female power and male dominance. Cambridge, England: Cambridge University Press.

Sandler, B. R., and Hall, R. M. 1986. The campus climate revisited: Chilly for women faculty, administrators, and graduate students. Washington, D.C.: Project on the Status and Education of Women.

Schaff, A. 1970. *Marxism and the human individual.* New York: McGraw-Hill.

Schaffer, K. F. 1981. *Sex roles and human behavior.* Cambridge, MA: Winthrop.

Scheff, T. J. 1968. Negotiating reality: Notes on power in the assessment of responsibility. *Social Problems* 16 (Summer):3–17.

_____. 1975. *Labeling madness.* Englewood Cliffs, NJ: Prentice-Hall.

_____. 1984. *Becoming mentally ill: A sociological theory* (2nd ed.). Chicago: Aldine.

_____. 1987. Shame and conformity: The deference-emotion system. *American Sociological Review* 53(3):395–406.

Scheider, J., and Hacker, S. 1973. Sex role imagery in the use of the generic 'man' in introductory texts: A case in the sociology of sociology. *American Sociologist* 8: 12–18.

Schlesinger, A. 1983. Familiar barbarities (Review of Howe, 1983). The *New York Times Book Review* September 25:1.

Schrecker, E. W. 1986. *No ivory tower: McCarthyism and the Universities.* New York: Oxford University Press.

Schroeder, R. C. 1974. Policies on population around the world. *Population Bulletin* 29. Washington, D.C.: Population Reference Bureau.

Schudson, M. 1984. *Advertising, the uneasy persuasion: Its dubious impact on American society.* New York: Basic Books.

Schulz, R. 1976. Control, predictability, and the institutionalized aged. *Journal of Personality and Social Psychology* 33:563–73.

Schulz, R., and Hanusa, B. H. 1980. Experimental social gerontology: A social psychological perspective. *Journal of Social Issues* 36(2):30–46.

Schuman, H., and Bob, L. 1988. Survey-based experiments on white racial attitudes toward residential integration. *American Journal of Sociology* 94(2):273–99.

Schuman, H., and Presser, S. 1981. *Questions and answers in attitude surveys.* New York: Academic Press.

Schuman, H., and Scott, J. 1989. Generations and collective memories. *American Sociological Review* 54(3):359–81.

Schuman, H., Steeh, C., and Bob, L. 1985. *Racial attitudes in America: Trends and interpretations.* Cambridge, MA: Harvard University Press.

Schur, E. M. 1965. *Crimes without victims.* Englewood Cliffs, NJ: Prentice-Hall.

_____. 1971. *Labeling deviant behavior.* New York: Harper and Row.

_____. 1984. *Labeling women deviant: Gender, stigma, and social control.* New York: Random House.

Schwartz, B. 1987. *George Washington: The making of an American symbol.* New York: Free Press.

Schwendinger, J. R., and Schwendinger, H. 1983. *Rape and inequality.* Beverly Hills: Sage Publications.

Seeman, M. 1959. On the meaning of alienation. *American Sociological Review* 24:783–89.

_____. 1975. Alienation studies. In *Annual Review of Sociology,* 1, pp. 91–123.

_____. 1981. Intergroup relations. In M. Rosenberg and R. H. Turner (Eds.), *Social psychology: Sociological perspectives,* pp. 378–410. New York: Basic Books.

_____. 1983. Alienation motifs in contemporary theorizing: The hidden continuity of the classic themes. *Social Psychology Quarterly,* 46, pp. 171–84.

Selnow, G. W. 1985. Sex differences in uses and perceptions of profanity. *Sex Roles* 12:303–12.

Selznick, G. J., and Steinberg, S. 1969. *The tenacity of prejudice.* New York: Harper and Row.

Sennett, R. 1981. *Authority.* New York: Vintage.

Sennett, R., and Cobb, J. 1973. *The hidden injuries of class.* New York: Vintage Books.

Service, E. 1962. *Primitive social organization: An evolutionary perspective.* New York: Random House.

Sewell, W. H., Hauser, R. M., and Wolf, W. C. 1980. Sex, schooling, and occupational status. *American Journal of Sociology* 8:551–83.

Seymour, W. N. 1973. Social and ethical considerations in assessing white-collar crime. *American Criminal Law Review* 11:821–34.

Shapiro, S. P. 1990. Collaring the crime, not the criminal: Reconsidering the concept of white-collar crime. *American Sociological Review* 55(3):346–65.

Shaiken, H. 1986. *Work transformed: Automation and labor in the computer age.* Lexington, MA: Lexington.

Shaw, G. B. 1904. *Plays pleasant and unpleasant* (Volume II, Preface). Chicago: H. S. Stone.

Shaw, M. E. 1954. Some effects of problem complexity upon problem solution efficiency in various communication nets. *Journal of Experimental Psychology* 48: 211–17.

Sheldon, W. R. 1949. *Varieties of delinquent behavior.* New York: Harper.

Shelton, B. A., and Firestone, J. 1989. Household labor time and the gender gap in earnings. *Gender and Society* 3(1):105–12.

Sherif, M. 1936. Formation of social norms: The experimental paradigm. In Sherif, M. *The psychology of social norms.* New York: Harper and Row. Reprinted in H. Proshansky and B. Seidenberg (Eds.). 1966. *Basic studies in social psychology.* New York: Holt, Rinehart and Winston.

Sherman, B. 1985. *The new revolution: The impact of computers on society.* New York: John Wiley and Sons.

Sherman, L. W., and Berk, R. A. 1984. The specific deterrent effects of arrest for domestic assault. *American Sociological Review,* 49 (June):261–72.

Shibamoto, J. S. 1985. *Japanese women's language.* New York: Academic Press.

Shibutani, T. 1966. *Improvised news: A sociological study of rumor.* Indianapolis, IN: Bobbs Merrill.

————. 1968. Rumor. In D. L. Sills (Ed.), *The international encyclopedia of the social sciences* (Vol. 13, pp. 576–80). New York: Macmillan/Free Press.

Shiels, D. 1975. Toward a unified theory of ancestor worship. *Social Forces* 54 (December): appendix, part B.

Shils, E. A., and Janowitz, M. 1948. Cohesion and disintegration in the Wehrmacht in World War II. *Public Opinion Quarterly* 12 (Summer):280–315.

Shilts, R. 1987. *While the band played on: Politics, people, and the AIDS epidemic.* New York: St. Martin's Press.

Shipler, D. K. 1983. Russia: A people without heroes. *New York Times Magazine* October 16:29.

Shlapentokh, V. 1987. *The politics of sociology in the Soviet Union.* Boulder, CO: Westview Press.

Shor, I. 1986. *Culture wars: School and society in the conservative restoration 1969–1984.* Boston: Routledge and Kegan Paul.

Shorter, E., and Tilly, C. 1974. *Strikes in France: 1830–1968.* London: Cambridge University Press.

Showalter, E. 1985. *The female malady: Women, madness, and English culture, 1830–1980.* New York: Pantheon.

Shrauger, J. S., and Schoeneman, T. J. 1979. Symbolic interactionist view of self-concept: Through the looking glass darkly. *Psychological Bulletin* 86:549–73.

Shupe, A., Stacey, W. A., and Hazlewood, L. R. 1987. *Violent men, violent couples: The dynamics of domestic violence.* Lexington, MA: Lexington Books.

Silberman, C. 1971. *Crisis in the classroom.* New York: Random.

Silk, L. 1983. Andropov's economic dilemma. *New York Times Magazine,* October 9.

Silverman, M. 1976. Toward a theory of criminal deterrence. *American Sociological Review* 41:442–61.

Simmel, G. [1902] 1950. *The sociology of Georg Simmel* (K. H. Wolff, Ed. and Trans.). New York: Free Press.

————. [1907] 1978. *The philosophy of money.* (trans. T. Bottomore and D. Frisby). Boston: Routledge & Kegan Paul.

————. [1908a] 1956. *Conflict and the web of group affiliation* (K. H. Wolff, trans.). Glencoe, IL: Free Press.

————. [1908b] 1965. The poor (C. Jacobson, Trans.). *Social Problems* 13:118–40.

Simmons, R. G., and Blyth, D. A. 1986. *Moving into adolescence: The impact of pubertal change and school context.* New York: Aldine de Gruyter.

Singer, C., Holmyard, E. J., and Hall, A. R. 1954. A history of technology (4 volumes). New York: Oxford University Press.

Singer, E. 1981. Reference groups and social evaluations. In M. Rosenberg and R. H. Turner (Eds.), *Social psychology: Sociological perspectives,* pp. 66–93. New York: Basic Books.

Skinner, B. F. 1938. *The behavior of organisms.* New York: Appleton-Century-Crofts.

————. 1948. *Walden two.* New York: Macmillan.

————. 1971. *Beyond freedom and dignity.* New York: Alfred A. Knopf.

————. 1981. Selection by consequences. *Science* 213:501–4.

Skocpol, T. 1979. *States and social revolutions.* New York: Cambridge University Press.

Skolnick, A. 1975. The family revisited. *Journal of Interdisciplinary History* 5(4):715.

Slambrouck, P. V. 1983. South Africa: The limits of dissent. *Christian Science Monitor* May 27:1.

Slater, P. E. 1958. Contrasting correlates of group size. *Sociometry* 21:129–39.

————. 1976. *The pursuit of loneliness* (rev. ed.). Boston: Beacon.

Slomczynski, K. M., Miller, J., and Kohn, M. L. 1981. Stratification, work, and values. *American Sociological Review* 46:720–44.

Smelser, N. J. 1959. *Social change in the industrial revolution.* Chicago: University of Chicago Press.

————. 1962. *Theory of collective behavior.* New York: Free Press.

————. 1973. Toward a theory of modernization. In A. Etzioni and E. Etzioni-Halevy (Eds.), *Social change: Sources, patterns, and consequences.* New York: Basic Books.

————. 1981. *Sociology.* Englewood Cliffs, NJ: Prentice-Hall.

Smith, A. [1776] 1982. *The wealth of nations.* New York: Penguin.

Smith, D. 1987. The neighborhood context of police behavior. In A. J. Reiss and M. Tonry (Eds.), *Communities and cities.* Chicago: University of Chicago Press.

Smith, D. A., and Visher, C. A. 1980. Sex and involvement in deviance/crime. *American Sociological Review* 45 (August):691–701.

Smith, J. 1981. *Social issues and the social order: The contradictions of capitalism.* Cambridge, MA: Winthrop.

Smith, J. O. 1987. *The politics of racial inequality: A systematic comparative macro-analysis from the colonial period to 1970.* Westport, CT: Greenwood Press.

Smith, P. M. 1985. *Language, society, and the sexes.* New York: Basil Blackwell.

Smith-Lovin, L., and Brody, C. 1989. Interruptions in group discussions: The effect of gender and group composition. *American Sociological Review* 51(3):424–35.

Snipp, C. M. 1989. *The first of this land.* New York: Russell Sage Foundation.

Snow, D. A., and Anderson, L. 1987. Identity work among the homeless: The verbal construction and avowal of personal identities. *American Journal of Sociology* 92(6):1336–71.

Snow, D. A., Zurcher, L. A., and Eckland-Olson, S. 1980. Social networks and social movements. *American Sociological Review* 45:787–801.

Sobel, R. 1989. *The white-collar working class: From structure to politics*. New York: Praeger.

Social Security Administration. 1988. Reported in the *New York Times*, November 27, p. E5.

Sommer, R. 1969. *Personal space: The behavioral analysis of design*. Englewood Cliffs, NJ: Prentice-Hall.

Sorokin, P. A. 1937–1941. *Social and cultural dynamics* (Vol. 4). New York: American Book Company.

Sorokin, P. A., and Merton, R. K. 1937. Social time: A methodological and functional analysis. *American Journal of Sociology* 42:615–29.

South, S. J. 1985. Economic conditions and the divorce rate. *Journal of Marriage and the Family* 47(1):31–41.

South, S. J., and Messner, S. F. 1986. Structural determinants of intergroup association: Interracial marriage and crime. *American Journal of Sociology* 91(6): 1409–30.

South, S. J., and Spitze, G. 1986. Determinants of divorce over the marital life course. *American Sociological Review* 51(4):583–90.

Spaeth, J. L. 1985. Job power and earnings. *American Sociological Review* 50(5):603–17.

Speizer, J. J. 1981. Role models, mentors, and sponsors: The elusive concepts. *Signs: Journal of Women in Culture and Society* 6:692–712.

Spencer, H. 1891. *The study of sociology*. New York: Appleton.

————. 1896. *The principles of sociology*. New York: Appleton.

Spengler, O. 1926. *The decline of the west*. New York: Alfred A. Knopf.

Spenner, K. I., Otto, L. B., and Call, V. R. A. 1982. *Career lines and careers*. Lexington, MA: Lexington Books.

Spiro, M. E. 1956. *Kibbutz: Venture in utopia*. Cambridge, MA: Harvard University Press.

Stacey, J. 1983. *Patriarchy and socialist revolution in China*. Berkeley, CA: University of California Press.

Stack, C. 1974. *All our kin: Strategies for survival in a black community*. New York: Harper and Row.

Stack, S. 1987. Celebrities and suicide: A Taxonomy and analysis. *American Sociological Review* 52(3):401–12.

Stahura, J. M. 1983. Determinants of change in the distribution of blacks across suburbs. *Sociological Quarterly* 24:423–33.

————. 1986. Black suburbanization. *American Sociological Review* 51(1):131–44.

Stampp, K. 1956. *The peculiar institution*. New York: Alfred A. Knopf.

Staples, R. 1976. *Introduction to black sociology*. New York: McGraw-Hill.

————. 1981. *The world of black singles*. Westport, CT: Greenwood Press.

Starr, P. 1982. *The social transformation of American medicine*. New York: Basic Books.

Steenland, S. 1989. *The unequal picture: Black, hispanic, asian, and native American characters on television*. Reported in the *Hartford Courant*, August 26, p. B2.

Steffensmeier, D. J. 1986. *The fence: In the shadow of two worlds*. Totowa, NJ: Rowman and Littlefield.

Steffensmeier, D. J., Allan, E. A., Harer, M. D., and Streifel, C. 1989. Age and the distribution of crime. *American Journal of Sociology* 94(4):803–31.

Stein, D. 1978. Women to burn. *Signs*, 4:253–68.

Stein, D. D., Hardyck, J. A., and Smith, M. B. 1965. Race and belief: An open and shut case. *Journal of Personality and Social Psychology* 1(4):281–89.

Stein, P. J. (Ed.). 1981. *Single life*. New York: St. Martins.

Steinbeck, J. [1939] 1969. *The grapes of wrath*. New York: Bantam Books.

Steinmetz, G., and Wright, E. O. 1989. The fall and rise of the petty bourgeoisie: Changing patterns of self-employment in the postwar United States. *American Journal of Sociology* 94(5):973–1018.

Stephan, C. W., and Corder, J. 1985. The effects of dual-career families on adolescents' sex-role attitudes, work and family plans, and choices of important others. *Journal of Marriage and the Family* 47(4):921–29.

Stephan, G. E., and McMullin, D. R. 1982. Tolerance of sexual nonconformity: City size as a situational and early learning determinant. *American Sociological Review* 47 (June):411–15.

Stephens, W. N. 1963. *The family in cross-cultural perspective*. New York: Holt, Rinehart and Winston.

Stern, M., and Karraker, K. H. 1989. Sex stereotyping of infants. *Sex Roles* 20(9/10):501–22.

Stevens, G. 1985. Nativity, intermarriage, and mother-tongue shift. *American Sociological Review* 50(1):74–83.

Stevens, G., and Swicegood, G. 1987. The linguistic context of ethnic endogamy. *American Sociological Review* 52(1):73–82.

Steward, J. H. 1955. *Theory of culture change: The methodology of multilinear Evolution*. Urbana, Ill: University of Illinois Press.

————. 1956. Cultural evolution. *Scientific American* 194:70–80.

Stilgoe, J. R. 1989. *Borderland: Origins of the American suburb*. New Haven, CT: Yale University Press.

Stojanovic, S. 1981. *In search of democracy in socialism*. Buffalo, NY: Prometheus Books.

Stone, K. 1974. The origins of job structures in the steel industry. In R. C. Edwards, M. Reich, and D. M. Gordon (Eds.), *Labor market segmentation*, pp. 27–84. Lexington, MA: DC Heath Company.

Stoner, J. A. F. 1961. A Comparison of Individuals and Group Decisions Involving Risk. Unpublished Master's Thesis, Massachusetts Institute of Technology, Cambridge, MA.

Stouffer, S. A., et al. 1949. *The American soldier*. Princeton, NJ: Princeton University Press.

Stover, E., and Nightingale, E. O. 1985. *The breaking of bodies and minds: Torture, psychiatric abuse, and the health professions*. New York: St. Martin's Press.

Straus, M. A., and Gelles, R. J. 1986. Societal change and change in family violence from 1975 to 1985 as revealed by two national surveys. *Journal of Marriage and the Family* 48(3):465–79.

Straus, M. A., Gelles, R. J., and Steinmetz, S. K. 1980. *Behind closed doors.* New York: Anchor.

Strauss, A. L. 1959. *Mirrors and masks.* New York: Free Press.

Strober, M. M., and Arnold, C. L. 1987. The dynamics of occupational segregation among bank tellers. In C. Brown and J. A. Pechman (Eds.), *Gender in the workplace*, pp. 107–48. Washington, D.C.: Brookings Institution.

Strodtbeck, F. L., James, R. M. and Hawkins, C. 1957. Social status in jury deliberations. *American Sociological Review* 22:713–19.

Strong, D. S. 1941. *Organized anti-Semitism in the United States.* American Council on Public Affairs.

Stryker, S. 1981. Symbolic interactionism: Themes and variations. In M. Rosenberg and R. H. Turner (Eds.), *Social psychology: Sociological perspectives*, pp. 3–29. New York: Basic Books.

Sudnow, D. 1967. *Passing on: The social organization of dying.* Englewood Cliffs, NJ: Prentice-Hall.

Sullivan, D. A., and Weitz, R. 1988. *Labor pains: Modern midwives and home birth.* New Haven, CT: Yale University Press.

Sumner, W. G. 1883. *What social classes owe to each other.* New York: Harper.

_____. 1906. *Folkways.* Boston: Ginn & Company.

Sussman, N. M., and Rosenfeld, H. M. 1982. Influence of culture, language, and sex on conversational distance. *Journal of Personality and Social Psychology* 42:66–74.

Sutherland, E. H. 1983. *White collar crime: The uncut version.* New Haven, CT: Yale University Press.

Sutherland, E. H., and Cressey, D. R. 1978. *Criminology* (10th ed.). Philadelphia, PA: Lippincott.

Suttles, G. D. 1972. *The social construction of communities.* Chicago: University of Chicago Press.

Sutton, H. E. 1988. *Genetics.* San Diego, CA: Harcourt Brace Jovanovich.

Sutton, J. R. 1983. Social structures, institutions, and the legal status of children. *American Journal of Sociology* 88(5):915–47.

Suzuki, D. T., Griffiths, A. J. F., and Lewontin, R. C. 1981. *An introduction to genetic analysis* (2nd ed.). San Francisco: W. F. Freeman and Company.

Swanson, Guy E. 1960. *The birth of the gods: The origin of primitive beliefs.* Ann Arbor, MI: University of Michigan Press.

Sweet, J. A., and Bumpass, L. L. 1987. *American families and households.* New York: Russell Sage Foundation.

Sweezy, Paul M. 1942. *The theory of capitalist development: Principles of Marxian political economy.* New York: Modern Reader Paperbacks.

Swidler, A. 1986. Culture in action. *American Sociological Review* 51(2):273–86.

Sykes, G. 1958. *The society of captives: A study of a maximum security prison.* Princeton, NJ: Princeton University Press.

Szaz, T. 1987. *Insanity: The idea and its consequences.* New York: Wiley.

Szelenyi, I. 1983. *Urban inequalities under state socialism.* New York: Oxford University Press.

Tanfer, K. 1987. Patterns of premarital cohabitation among never-married women in the United States. *Journal of Marriage and the Family* 49(3):483–97.

Tannen, D. 1984. *Conversational style: Analyzing talk among friends.* Norwood, NJ: Ablex.

Tannenbaum, A. S. 1968. Leadership: Sociological aspects. In D. L. Sills (Ed.), *The international encyclopedia of the social sciences* (Vol. 9). New York: Macmillan/Free Press.

Tarrow, S. 1988. National politics and collective action: Recent theory and research in Western Europe and the United States. *Annual Review of Sociology* 14:421–40.

_____. 1989. *Struggle, politics, and reform: Collective action, social movements, and cycles of protest.* Ithaca, NY: Cornell University Press.

Task Force on Women and Depression. 1990. Reported in the *New York Times* (December 6), p. B18.

Tavris, C., and C. Wade. 1984. *The longest war: Sex differences in perspective* (2nd ed.). New York: Harcourt, Brace Jovanovich.

Taylor, F. W. 1911. *The principles of scientific management.* New York: Harper and Row.

Teachman, J. D., and Polonko, K. A. 1988. Marriage, parenthood, and the college enrollment of men and women. *Social Forces* 67(2):512–24.

Tedeschi, J. T., and Riess, M. 1981. Identities, the phenomenal self, and laboratory research. In J. Tedeschi (Ed.), *Impression management theory and social psychological research*, pp. 3–22. New York: Academic Press.

Teitelbaum, M. S., and Winter, J. M. 1985. *The fear of population decline.* Orlando, FL: Academic Press.

Teixeira, R. A. 1987. *Why Americans don't vote.* Westport, CT: Greenwood Press.

Terkel, S. 1974. *Working.* New York: Pantheon.

Tetlock, P. E. 1981. The influence of self-presentation goals on attributional reports. *Social Psychology Quarterly* 44:300–11.

Thoits, P. A. 1985. Self-labeling processes in mental illness: The role of emotional deviance. *American Journal of Sociology* 91(2):221–49.

_____. 1989. The sociology of emotions. *Annual Review of Sociology* 15:317–42.

Thomas, M., and Hughes, M. 1986. The continuing significance of race: A study of race, class, and quality of life in America, 1972–1985. *American Sociological Review* 51(6):830–41.

Thomas, R. K. 1966–1967. Powerless politics. *New University Thought* 4 (Winter).

Thomas, W. I. 1931. *The unadjusted girl.* Boston: Little Brown and Co.

Thomas, W. I., and Thomas, D. S. 1928. *The child in America.* New York: Alfred A. Knopf.

Thompson, S. K. 1975. Gender labels and early sex-role development. *Child Development* 46:339–47.

Thompson, S. K., and Bentler, P. M. 1971. The priority of cues in sex discrimination by children and adults. *Developmental Psychology* 5:181–85.

Thompson, W., and Lewis, D. 1965. *Population problems* (5th ed.). New York: McGraw-Hill.

Thompson, W., and Whelpton, P. K. 1933. *Population trends in the United States.* New York: McGraw-Hill.

Thornberry, T. P. 1973. Race, socioeconomic status, and sentencing in the juvenile justice system. *Journal of Criminal Law and Criminology* 64:90–98.

Thornton, A. 1985. Changing attitudes toward separation and divorce: Causes and consequences. *American Journal of Sociology* 90(4):856–72.

Thornton, A., Alwin, D. F., and Camburn, D. 1983. Causes and consequences of sex-role attitudes and attitude change. *American Sociological Review* 48 (April):211–27.

Thornton, A., and Freedman, D. 1982. Changing attitudes toward marriage and single life. *Family Planning Perspectives* 14(6, November/December):297–303.

————. 1983. The Changing American Family. *Population Bulletin* 38(4). Washington, D.C.: Population Reference Bureau.

Thornton, A., and Rodgers, W. L. 1983. *Changing patterns of marriage and divorce in the United States.* Final Report Prepared for the National Institute for Child Health and Human Development, Ann Arbor, Michigan.

Thornton, R. 1987. *American Indian holocaust and survival: A population history since 1492.* Norman, OK: University of Oklahoma Press, 1987.

Thurow, L. C. 1975. *Generating inequality.* New York: Basic Books.

————. 1980. *The zero-sum society: Distributions and the possibilities for economic change.* New York: Basic Books.

————. 1983. *Dangerous currents: The state of economics.* New York: Random House.

Tilly, C. 1978a. *From mobilization to revolution.* Reading, MA: Addison-Wesley.

————. 1978b. *Historical studies of changing fertility.* Princeton, NJ: Princeton University Press.

————. 1985. *Big structures, large processes, huge comparisons.* New York: Russell Sage Foundation.

Tilly, C., Tilly, L., and Tilly, R. 1975. *The rebellious century.* Cambridge, MA: Harvard University Press.

Tilly, L. A., and Scott, J. W. 1978. *Women, work, and the family.* New York: Holt, Rinehart, and Winston.

Tilly, L. A., and Tilly, C. (Eds.). 1981. *Collective action and class conflict.* Beverly Hills, CA: Sage Publications.

Timko, C., and Moos, R. H. 1989. Choice, control, and adaptation among elderly residents of sheltered care settings. *Journal of Applied Social Psychology* 19(8):636–55.

Tissue, T. 1979. Downward mobility in old age. In P. I. Rose (Ed.), *Socialization and the life cycle*, pp. 355–67. New York: St. Martin's Press.

Tittle, C. R. 1975. Deterrence or labelling? *Social Forces* 53 (March):399–419.

Tittle, C. R., and Villemez, W. J. 1977. Social class and criminality. *Social Forces* 56(2):474–502.

Tittle, C. R., Villemez, W. J., and Smith, D. A. 1978. The myth of social class and criminality: An empirical assessment of empirical evidence. *American Sociological Review* 43:643–56.

Tocqueville, A. de. [1835] 1954. *Democracy in America.* New York: Random House.

Tönnies, F. [1887] 1963. *Community and society.* New York: Harper.

Toynbee, A. 1956. *The industrial revolution.* Boston: Beacon Press.

Treiman, D. J. 1977. *Occupational prestige in comparative perspective.* New York: Academic Press.

Treiman, D. J., and Hartmann, H. I. (Eds.). 1981. *Women, work, and wages: Equal pay for jobs of equal value.* Washington, D.C.: National Academy Press.

Treiman, D. J., and Roos, P. A. 1983. Sex and earnings in industrial society. *American Journal of Sociology* 89(3):612–50.

Trimberger, E. K. 1971. The ideological function of grading in American education. Paper read at the Annual Meeting of the American Sociological Association.

Tuchman, B. W. 1978. *A distant mirror.* New York: Alfred A. Knopf.

Tuddenham, R. D., and McBride, P. 1959. The yielding experiment from the subject's point of view. *Journal of Personality* 27:259–71.

Tulkin, S. R. 1989. Cited in Konner, M., Where should baby sleep? The *New York Times Magazine*, January 8, pp. 39–40.

Tumin, M. M. 1953. Some principles of stratification: A critical analysis. *American Sociological Review* 18:378–94.

————. 1964. Business as a social system. *Behavioral Science* 9(2):120–30.

Turk, A. 1979. Law as a weapon in social conflict. *Social Problems* 23(3):276–91.

Turnbull, C. 1961. *The forest people.* New York: Simon and Schuster.

————. 1965. The Mbuti Pygmies of the Congo. In J. L. Gibbs, Jr. (Ed.), *People of Africa.* New York: Holt, Rinehart and Winston.

Turner, B. S. 1986. *Equality.* New York: Tavistock.

————. 1987. *Medical power and social knowledge.* Beverly Hills, CA: Sage Publications.

Turner, J. H. 1987. Toward a sociological theory of motivation. *American Sociological Review* 52(1):15–27.

Turner, R. H. 1964. Collective behavior. In R. E. L. Faris (Ed.), *Handbook of modern sociology.* Chicago: Rand McNally.

Turner, R. H., and Killian, L. 1987. *Collective behavior* (3rd ed.). Englewood Cliffs, NJ: Prentice-Hall.

Uhlenberg, P. 1980. Death and the family. *Journal of Family History* 5:313–20.

Uhlenberg, P. *(continued)*

———. 1988. Does population aging produce increasing gerontocracy? *Sociological Forum* 3(3):454–63.

UN (United Nations). 1973. *The determinants and consequences of population trends: New summary of findings on interaction of demographic, economic, and social factors.* I. Population Studies 50. New York: United Nations Department of Economic and Social Affairs, 1973.

———. 1974. *Demographic yearbook 1971:* Table 1. New York: United Nations.

———. 1985. *Demographic yearbook: 1985.* New York: United Nations.

———. 1987. *The state of the world's population.* New York: United Nations.

———. 1990. *The state of the world population 1990.* New York: United Nations.

Unger, A. 1983. TV is offering fairer image, but mainly for certain groups. *Christian Science Monitor* May 10:12.

UNICEF. 1988. *The state of the world's children 1989.* New York: The United Nations.

———. 1990. *The lesser child: The girl in India.* Cited and reported in the *New York Times,* October 5, 1990, p. A5.

United Nations Fund for Population Activities. 1987. *Population Images* (2nd ed.). New York: United Nations.

USCB (U.S. Census Bureau). 1918. *Negro population: 1790–1915.* Washington, D.C.: Government Printing Office.

———. 1975. *Historical statistics of the United States: Colonial times to 1970.* Washington, D.C.: U.S. Government Printing Office.

———. 1979. *Fertility of American women: June 1978.* Current Population Reports, Series P-20, No. 341. Washington, D.C.: U.S. Government Printing Office.

———. 1980b. *Social indicators III.* Washington, D.C.: U.S. Government Printing Office.

———. 1981. *Statistical abstract of the United States, 1981.* Washington, D.C.: U.S. Government Printing Office.

———. 1982. *Statistical abstract of the United States, 1982.* Washington, D.C.: U.S. Government Printing Office.

———. 1983a. *Households, families, marital status, and living arrangements: March, 1983.* Washington, D.C.: U.S. Government Printing Office.

———. 1983b. *Money income and poverty status of families and persons in the United States, 1982.* Current Population Reports, Series P-60, No.140. Washington, D.C.: U.S. Government Printing Office.

———. 1983c. *Statistical abstract of the United States: 1984.* Washington, D.C.: U.S. Government Printing Office.

———. 1986a. *Statistical abstract of the United States: 1987.* Washington, D.C.: U.S. Government Printing Office.

———. 1986b. Reported in the Hartford *Courant,* November 21.

———. 1986c. Advance report on geographical mobility reported in the *New York Times,* April 13, p. 1.

———. 1986d. *Household wealth and asset ownership.* Washington, D.C.: U.S. Government Printing Office.

———. 1986e. Statistics reported in the Hartford *Courant,* May 7, p. A5.

———. 1986f. Findings reported in the *New York Times.*

———. 1987a. *Money income of households, families, and persons in the United States: 1985.* Current Population Reports Series P-60, No. 156. Washington, D.C.: U.S. Government Printing Office.

———. 1987b. Household after-tax income: 1985. *Current Population Reports* Series P-23, No. 151. Washington, D.C.: U.S. Government Printing Office.

———. 1987c. *Male-female differences in work experience, occupation, and earnings: 1984.* Current Population Reports Series P-70, No. 10. Washington, D.C.: U.S. Government Printing Office.

———. 1987d. Poverty figure for 1986 reported in the *New York Times,* July 3, p. A12.

———. 1987e. Reported in the *New York Times,* October 1.

———. 1987f. *What's it worth? Educational background and economic status: Spring 1984.* Washington, D.C.: U.S. Government Printing Office.

———. 1987g. *Money income and poverty status of families and persons in the United States: 1986.* Current Population Reports Series P-60, No. 157. Washington, D.C.: U.S. Government Printing Office.

———. 1987h. *Households, families, marital status, and living arrangements: March* (Advance Report). Current Population Reports Series P-20, No. 417. Washington, D.C.: U.S. Government Printing Office.

———. 1987i. *America's centenarians.* Current Population Reports Series P-23, No. 153. Washington, D.C.: U.S. Government Printing Office.

———. 1988a. *Household after-tax income: 1986.* Current population reports, Series P-23, No. 157. Washington, D.C.: U.S. Government Printing Office.

———. 1989a. Reported in the *New York Times,* February 1, p.1.

———. 1989b. Reported in the *New York Times,* September 16, p.9.

———. 1989c. *Studies in marriage and the family.* Washington, D.C.: U.S. Government Printing Office.

———. 1989d. *Money income and poverty status in the United States: 1988.* Current Population Reports Series P-60, No. 166. Washington, D.C.: U.S. Government Printing Office.

———. 1989e. *Money income of persons, households, and families in the United States: 1987.* Current Population Reports Series P-60, No. 162. Washington, D.C.: U.S. Government Printing Office.

———. 1989f. *Fertility of American women.* Current Population Reports Series P-20, No. 436. Washington, D.C.: U. S. Government Printing Office.

———. 1989g. Household and family characteristics.

Current Population Reports Series P-20 No. 437. Washington, D.C.: U.S. Government Printing Office.

————. 1990a. *Statistical Abstract of the United States 1990*. Washington, D.C.: U. S. Government Printing Office.

————. 1990b. School enrollment — Social and economic characteristics of students. Current Population Reports P-20, No. 443. Washington, D.C.: U. S. Government Printing Office.

————. 1991. Reported in the *New York Times*, January 11, p.1.

————. 1991a. Reported in the *New York Times*, March 11, p.1

U.S. Commission on Civil Rights. 1967. *Racial isolation in the public schools* (Vol.1). Washington, D.C.: U.S. Government Printing Office.

USDD (U.S. Department of Defense). 1990. Reported in the *New York Times*, September 12, p. A22.

U.S. Department of Health, Education, and Welfare. 1973. *Work in America*. Washington, D.C.: U.S. Government Printing Office.

U.S. Department of Housing and Urban Development. 1981. *Residential displacement: An update*. Washington, D.C.: U.S. Government Printing Office.

USDJ (U.S. Department of Justice). 1980. *Criminal victimization in the United States: A comparison of 1977 and 1978 findings*. Washington, D.C.: U.S. Government Printing Office.

————. 1989. *Criminal victimization in the United States: 1988*. Washington, D.C.: U. S. Government Printing Office.

————. 1990. *Crime in the United States 1989*. Washington, D.C.: U. S. Government Printing Office.

————. 1990a. *Jail inmates 1989*. Washington, D.C.: Bureau of Justice Statistics.

————. 1990b. Crime and the Nation's Households, 1989. Washington, D.C.: Bureau of Justice Statistics.

USDL (U.S. Department of Labor). 1990. *Employment and earnings, January*. Washington, D.C.: U.S. Government Printing Office.

Useem, M. 1984. *The inner circle: Large corporations and the rise of business political activity in the U.S. and U.K.* New York: Oxford University Press.

Useem, M., and Karabel, J. 1986. Pathways to top corporate management. *American Sociological Review* 51(2):184–200.

Uyeki, E. S. 1964. Residential distribution and stratification. *American Journal of Sociology* 69(5):491–98.

Vacon, R. 1990. Rethinking the war on drugs. The *Hartford Courant*, May 27:1.

Van Creveld, M. 1982. *Fighting power: German and U.S. army performance, 1939–1945*. Westport, CT: Greenwood Press.

Van de Kaa, D. J. 1987. *Europe's second demographic transition*. Population Bulletin, 42(1). Washington, D.C.: Population Reference Bureau.

Vandenberg, S. G., Singer, S. M., and Pauls, D. L. 1986.

The heredity of behavior disorders in adults and children. New York: Plenum.

Van Dijk. 1987. *Communicating racism: Ethnic prejudice in thought and talk*. Newbury Park, CA: Sage.

Van Gennep, A. [1909] 1960. *The rites of passage*. Chicago: University of Chicago Press.

Vanneman, R., and Cannon, L. W. 1987. *The American perception of class*. Philadelphia, PA: Temple University Press.

Van Til, J. 1980. Citizen participation in neighborhood transformation: A social movements approach. *Urban Affairs Quarterly* 15:439–52.

Vaupel, J. W., and Gowan, A. E. 1986. Passage to Methuselah. *American Journal of Public Health* (April).

Veblen, T. 1934. *The theory of the leisure class*. New York: Modern Library.

Verbrugge, L., and Wingard, D. L. 1987. Sex differentials in health and mortality. *Women and Health* 12(2).

Von Neumann, J., and Morgenstern, O. 1964. *Theory of games and economic behavior* (3rd ed.). New York: Wiley.

Vos, S. de. 1984. *The old-age economic security value of children in the Philippines and Taiwan*. Papers of the East-West Population Institute, No. 60-G. Honolulu: East-West Population Institute.

Wade, N. 1976. IQ and heredity: Suspicion of fraud beclouds classic experiment. *Science* 194 (November 26):916–19.

Waite, L. J., Goldscheider, F. K., and Witsberger, C. 1986. Nonfamily living and the erosion of traditional family orientations among young adults. *American Sociological Review* 51(4):541–54.

Walker, B. G. 1983. *The women's encyclopedia of myths and secrets*. New York: Harper and Row.

————. 1987. *The skeptical feminist*. New York: Harper and Row.

Wallace, M., and Kalleberg, A. L. 1982. Industrial transformation and the decline of craft: The decomposition of skill in the printing industry, 1931–1978. *American Sociological Review* 47 (June):307–24.

Wallerstein, I. 1974. Dependence in an interdependent world: The limited possibilities of transformation within the capitalist world-economy. *African Studies Review* 17:1–26.

————. 1976a. *The modern world system*. New York: Academic Press.

————. 1976b. Semi-peripheral countries and the contemporary world crisis. *Theory and Society* 3:461–83.

————. 1979. *The capitalist world-economy*. Cambridge: Cambridge University Press.

————. 1980. *The modern world system II: Mercantilism and the consolidation of the European world economy, 1600–1750*. New York: Academic Press.

————. 1986. Marxisms as utopias: Evolving ideologies. *American Journal of Sociology* 91(6):1295–1308.

————. 1989. *The modern world-system III: The second era of great expansion of the capitalist world-economy, 1730–1840*. New York: Academic Press.

Walum, L. R. 1974. The changing door ceremony: Notes on the operation of sex roles. *Urban Life and Culture* 2:506–15.

Warner, C. D. [1870] 1955. My *summer in a garden.* Quoted in Bartlett, J., *Familiar Quotations* (13th ed.), p. 645.

Warner, R. L., Lee, G. R., and Lee, J. 1986. Social organization, spousal resources, and marital power: A cross-cultural study. *Journal of Marriage and the Family* 48(1):121–28.

Warnick, D. H., and Sanders, G. 1980. The effects of group discussion on eyewitness accuracy. *Journal of Applied Social Psychology* 10(3):249–59.

Watson, J. B. 1928. *Psychological care of infant and child.* New York: W. W. Norton.

Watson, J. B., and Rayner, R. 1920. Conditioned emotional reactions. *Journal of Experimental Psychology* 3:1–14.

Watzlawick, P. 1976. *How real is real? Confusion, disinformation, communication.* New York: Random House.

Weary, G., Stanley, M. A., and Harvey, J. H. 1989. *Attribution.* New York: Springer-Verlag.

Weber, M. [1904] 1958. *The Protestant ethic and the spirit of capitalism.* New York: Charles Scribner's and Sons.

――――. [1921] 1958. Politics as a vocation. In H. H. Gerth and C. W. Mills (Eds. and Trans.), *From Max Weber: Essays in sociology.* New York: Oxford University Press.

――――. [1922] 1954. In M. Rheinstein (Ed.), *Max Weber on law in economy and society.* Cambridge, MA: Harvard University Press.

――――. [1922] 1958. Bureaucracy. In H. H. Gerth and C. W. Mills (Eds. and Trans.), *From Max Weber: Essays in sociology.* New York: Oxford University Press.

――――. [1923] 1950. *General economic history.* New York: The Free Press.

――――. [1925] 1947. *The theory of social and economic organization.* New York: Oxford University Press.

――――. 1946. *From Max Weber: Essays in sociology* (H. H. Gerth and C. W. Mills, Eds. and Trans.). New York: Oxford University Press.

――――. 1949. *The methodology of the social sciences.* New York: Free Press.

――――. 1968. *Economy and society.* New York: Bedminster Press.

Weede, E. 1980. Beyond misspecification in sociological analysis of income inequality. *American Sociological Review* 45:497–501.

Weinstein, J. A. 1976. *Demographic transition and social change.* Morristown, NJ: General Learning Press.

Weiss, C. S. 1981. The development of professional role commitment among graduate students. *Human Relations* 34:13–31.

Weissberg, R. 1981. *Understanding American government* (Alternate ed.). New York: Holt, Rinehart and Winston.

Weitzman, L. J. 1981. *The marriage contract.* New York: Free Press.

――――. 1985. *The divorce revolution: The unexpected social and economic consequences for women and children in America.* New York: Free Press.

Weller, R. H. 1977. Demographic Correlates of Women's Participation in Economic activities. *International population conference: Mexico 1977*, pp. 497–516. Liege, Belgium: International Union for the Scientific Study of Population.

Weller, R. H., and Bouvier, L. F. 1981. *Population: Demography and policy.* New York: St. Martin's Press.

Weller, R. P., and Guggenheim, S. E. (Eds.). 1982. *Power and protest in the countryside: Studies of rural unrest in Asia, Europe, and Latin America.* Durham, N.C.: Duke University Press.

Welsh, W. A. (Ed.). 1981. *Survey research and public attitudes in Eastern Europe and the Soviet Union.* New York: Pergamon Press.

West, C. 1982. Why can't a woman be more like a man? *Sociology of Work and Occupations* 9:5–29.

West, S. G., Gunn, S. P., and Chernicky, P. 1975. Ubiquitous Watergate: An attributional analysis. *Journal of Personality and Social Psychology* 32:55–65.

Westing, A. 1981. Cited in the *New York Times*, October 6.

Westoff, C. F. 1978a. Some speculations on the future of marriage and fertility. *Family Planning Perspectives* 10:79–83.

――――. 1983. Fertility decline in the West: Causes and prospects. *Population and Development Review* 9:99–105.

Westoff, C. F., and Jones, E. F. 1979. The end of 'Catholic' fertility. *Demography* 16 (May):209–17.

Whitaker, J. S. 1989. *How can Africa survive?* New York: Harper and Row.

White, L., and Edwards, J. N. 1990. Empting the nest and parental well-being: An analysis of national panel data. *American Sociological Review* 55(2):235–42.

White, L., and Keith, B. 1990. The effect of shift work on the quality and stability of marital relations. *Journal of Marriage and the Family* 52(2):453–62.

White, L. K., and Brinkerhoff, D. B. 1981. The sexual division of labor: Evidence from childhood. *Social Forces* 60:170–81.

White, L. K., and Booth, A. 1985. Stepchildren in remarriages. *American Sociological Review* 50(5):689–98.

White, R. W. 1989. From peaceful protest to guerrilla war: Micromobilization of the Provisional Irish Republican Army. *American Journal of Sociology* 94(6):1277–1302.

Whiting, B. (Ed.). 1963. *Six cultures—Studies in child rearing.* New York: Wiley.

WHO (World Health Organization). 1987. Reported in the Hartford *Courant*, December 22, p. A6.

――――. 1990. Reported in the *New York Times*, May 2, p. A21.

Whorf, B. L. 1956. *Language, thought and reality.* Cambridge, MA: M.I.T. Press.

Whyte, W. F. 1950. The social structure of the restaurant. *American Journal of Sociology* 54:302–10.

Whyte, W. F. 1981. *Street corner society* (3rd ed.). Chicago: University of Chicago Press.

Whyte, W. H. 1956. *The organization man*. New York: Simon and Schuster.

Wiatrowski, M. D., Griswold, D. B., and Roberts, M. K. 1981. Social control theory and delinquency. *American Sociological Review*, 46 (October):525–41.

Wice, P. B. 1973. *Bail and its reform: A national survey*. Washington, D.C.: U.S. Government Printing Office.

WIFP (Women's Institute for Freedom of the Press). 1986. 1955–1985: Women in prime time tv still traditional. *Media Report to Women* (July-August):7.

Wilentz, S. 1984. *Chants democratic: New York City and the rise of the American working class*. New York: Oxford University Press.

Wilkes, M. S., and Shuchman, M. 1989. What is too old? *New York Times Magazine* June 4:58.

Willhelm, S. 1983. *Black in a white America*. Cambridge, MA: Schenkman.

Williams, D. G. 1985. Gender, masculinity-femininity, and emotional intimacy in same-sex friendship. *Sex Roles* 12(5/6):587–600.

Williams, D. R. 1990. Socioeconomic differentials in health. *Social Psychology Quarterly* 53(2):81–99.

Williams, J. 1987. *Psychology of women* (3rd ed.). New York: Norton.

Williams, J. E., and Best, D. L. 1982. *Measuring sex stereotypes: A thirty nation study*. Beverly Hills, CA: Sage Publications.

Williams, R. B. 1988. *Religions of immigrants from India and Pakistan: New trends in the American tapestry*. Cambridge: Cambridge University Press.

Williams, R. M., Jr. 1970. *American society: A sociological interpretation* (3rd edition). New York: Alfred A. Knopf.

———. 1975. Relative deprivation. In L. A. Coser (Ed.). *The idea of social structure*, pp. 355–378. New York: Harcourt Brace Jovanovich.

Williams, T. 1989. *The cocaine kids: The inside story of a teenage drug ring*. Reading, MA: Addison-Wesley.

Williams, V. J. 1989. *From a caste to a minority: Changing attitudes of American sociologists toward Afro-Americans, 1896–1945*. Westport, CT: Greenwood Press.

Williamson, J. 1984. *The crucible of race*. New York: Oxford University Press.

Williamson, N. 1976. Sex preferences, sex control, and the status of women. *Signs: Journal of Women in Culture and Society* 1:847–62.

Williamson, J. B., Shindul, J. A., and Evans, L. 1985. *Aging and public policy: Social control or social justice?* Springfield, IL: Charles C. Thomas.

Willie, C. V. 1978. The inclining significance of race. *Society* 15(10):12–15.

———. 1979. *The caste and class controversy*. Bayside, NY: General Hall, Inc.

Willner, A. R. 1984. *The spellbinders: Charismatic political leadership*. New Haven, CT: Yale University Press.

Wilson, B. 1982. *Religion in sociological perspective*. New York: Oxford University Press.

Wilson, E. O. 1975. *Sociobiology*. Cambridge, MA: Belknap.

———. 1977. Biology and the social sciences. *Daedalus*, 106 (Fall):127–40.

Wilson, J. 1978. *Religion in American society: The effective presence*. Englewood Cliffs, NJ: Prentice-Hall.

Wilson, J. G. 1988. Reported in the *New York Times*, March 2.

Wilson, J. Q. 1983. *Thinking about crime* (rev. ed.). New York: Basic Books.

Wilson, J. Q., and Herrnstein, R. J. 1985. *Crime and human nature*. New York: Simon and Schuster.

Wilson, R. S., and Harpring, E. B. 1972. Mental and motor development in infant twins. *Developmental Psychology* 7:277–87.

Wilson, T. C. 1985. Urbanism and tolerance. *American Sociological Review* 50(1):117–23.

———. 1986. Community population size and social heterogeneity: An empirical test. *American Journal of Sociology* 91(5):1154–69.

———. 1991. Urbanism, migration, and tolerance: A reassessment. *American Sociological Review* 56(1): 117–23.

Wilson, W. J. 1973. *Power, racism, and privilege*. New York: Macmillan.

———. 1978. *The declining significance of race*. Chicago: University of Chicago Press.

———. 1987. *The truly disadvantaged: The inner city, the underclass, and public policy*. Chicago: University of Chicago Press.

Wirth, L. 1938. Urbanism as a way of life. *American Journal of Sociology* 44:1–24.

———. 1945. The problem of minority groups. In R. Linton (Ed.), *The science of man in the world crisis*. New York: Columbia University Press.

Wissler, C. 1911. The social life of the Blackfoot Indians. *Anthropological Papers of the American Museum of Natural History*, 7(1). New York: American Museum of Natural History.

Withey, S. B., and Abeles, R. P. (Eds.). 1980. *Television and social behavior*. Hillsdale, NJ: Erlbaum.

Wohl, A. S. 1983. *Endangered lives: Public health in Victorian England*. Cambridge, MA: Harvard University Press.

Wolfe, S. J., Struckman-Johnson, C., and Flanagin, J. 1986. "Generic man": Grammatical distribution and perception. Paper presented at the annual conference of the Speech Communication Association, Chicago, IL.

Wolfgang, M. E., Figlio, R. M., and Sellin, T. 1972. *Delinquency in a birth cohort*. Chicago: University of Chicago Press.

Women on Words and Images. 1975a. *Dick and Jane as victims: Sex stereotyping in children's readers* (Enlarged Ed.). Princeton, NJ: Women on Words and Images.

————. 1975b. *Channeling children: Sex stereotyping on prime TV*. Princeton, NJ: Women on Words and Images.

Woolf, V. 1929. *A room of one's own*. New York: Harcourt, Brace and World.

World Resources Institute. 1990. *World resources 1990–91*. Washington, D.C.: World Resources Institute.

Worldwatch Institute. 1987. *State of the world in 1987*. Washington, D.C.: Worldwatch Institute.

Wright, E. O. 1985. *Classes*. New York: Schocken Books.

Wright, E. O., Hacken, D., Costello, C., and Sprague, J. 1982. The American class structure. *American Sociological Review* 47 (December):709–26.

Wright, E. O., and Martin, B. 1987. The transformation of the American class structure, 1960–1980. *American Journal of Sociology* 93(1):1–29.

Wright, J. D. 1989. *Address unknown: The homeless in America*. New York: Walter de Gruyter, Aldine.

Wright, J. D., Rossi, P. H., and Daly, K. 1983. *Under the gun: Weapons, crime, and violence in America*. Chicago: Aldine.

Wright, J. D., and Wright, S. R. 1976. Social class and parental values for children: A partial replication and extension of the Kohn thesis. *American Sociological Review* 41 (June):527–48.

Writers Guild of America. 1987. Findings reported in the *New York Times*, June 24.

Wrong, D. H. 1961. The oversocialized conception of man in modern sociology. *American Sociological Review*, 26, pp. 183–93.

————. 1980. *Power: Its forms, bases, and uses*. New York: Harper and Row.

Wurdock, C. 1979. Public school resegregation after desegregation: Some preliminary findings. *Sociological Focus* 12(4):263–74.

Wurdock, C., and R. Farley. 1979. School integration and enrollments in the nation's largest cities: An analysis of recent trends. *Proceedings of the American Statistical Association (Social Statistics Section)*, pp. 359–63.

Wuthnow, R. 1987. *Meaning and moral order: Explorations in cultural analysis*. Berkeley, CA: University of California Press.

————. 1988. *The restructuring of American religion: Society and faith since World War II*. Princeton, NJ: Princeton University Press.

Wuthnow, R., and Witten, M. 1988. New directions in the study of culture. *Annual Review of Sociology* 14:49–67.

Wyman, D. S. 1984. *The abandonment of the Jews: America and the holocaust*. New York: Pantheon.

Wyszomirski, M. J. 1988. *Congress and the arts: A precarious alliance?* New York: American Council for the Arts.

Yarrow, L. J., Rubenstein, J. L., and Pedersen, F. A. 1975. *Infant and environment: Early cognitive and emotional development*. Washington, D.C.: Hemisphere Publishing Company (Distributed by Wiley).

Young, M. 1988. *The metronomic society: Natural rhythms and human timetables*. Cambridge, MA: Harvard University Press.

Zablocki, B. 1980. *The joyful community*. Chicago: University of Chicago Press.

Zagare, F. C. 1984. *Game theory: Concepts and applications*. Beverly Hills, CA: Sage Publications.

Zald, M. N., and McCarthy, J. D. (Eds.). 1979. *The dynamics of social movements*. Cambridge, MA: Winthrop.

Zangwill, I. [1909] 1933. *The melting pot*. New York: Macmillan.

Zborowski, M. 1953. Cultural components in responses to pain. *Journal of Social Issues* 8:16–31.

Zeisel, H. 1977. The Deterrent effect of the death penalty: Facts v. faith. In P. B. Kurland (Ed.), *The Supreme Court Review*. Chicago: University of Chicago Press.

————. 1981. Race bias in the administration of the death penalty. *Harvard Law Review* 95(2):456–68.

Zeitlin, I. M. 1981. Karl Marx: Aspects of his social thought and their contemporary relevance. In B. Rhea (Ed.), *The future of the sociological classics*, pp. 1–15. London: George Allen & Unwin.

Zelditch, M., and Walker, H. A. 1984. Legitimacy and the stability of authority. In E. Lawler (Ed.), *Advances in group process: Theory and research* (Vol. 1, pp. 1–27). Greenwich, CT: JAI Press.

Zelizer, V. A. 1985. *Pricing the priceless child: The changing social value of children*. New York: Basic Books.

Zelnick, M., and Kanter, J. F. 1976. Sexual and contraceptive experience of young unmarried women in the United States, 1976 and 1971. *Family Planning Perspectives* 9 (March-April):55–71.

————. 1978. First pregnancies to women aged 15–19: 1976 and 1971. *Family Planning Perspectives* 10 (January-February):11–20.

Zerubavel, E. 1981. *Hidden rhythms: Schedules and calendars in social life*. Chicago: University of Chicago Press.

————. 1985. *The seven-day week: The history and meaning of the week*. New York: Free Press.

Zimbardo, P. G. 1971. *The psychological power and pathology of imprisonment*. Cited and quoted in D. G. Myers. 1983. *Social psychology* (pp. 179–180). New York: McGraw-Hill.

Zimmer, L. E. 1988. Tokenism and women in the workplace. *Social Problems* 35:64–77.

Zolberg, V. L. 1990. *Constructing a sociology of the arts*. Cambridge: Cambridge University Press.

Zopf, P. E. 1989. *American women in poverty*. Westport, CT: Greenwood Press.

Zorbaugh, H. W. 1929. *The Gold Coast and the slum: A sociological study of Chicago's Near North Side*. Chicago: University of Chicago Press.

Zuboff, S. 1982. New worlds of computer-mediated work. *Harvard Business Review* (September/October).

————. 1988. *In the age of the smart machine*. New York: Basic Books.

Zucker, L. 1983. Organizations as institutions. In S. B. Bacharach (Ed.), *Research in the sociology of organizations* (Volume 2). Greenwich, CT: JAI Press.

Zuckerman, H. 1977. Deviant behavior and social control in science. In Sagarin, E. (Ed.), *Deviance and social change*, pp. 87–138. Beverly Hills, CA: Sage Publications.

————. 1988. The sociology of science: A selective review. In Smelser, N. (Ed.). 1988. *Handbook of sociology*. Beverly Hills: Sage Publications.

Zukin, S. 1987. Gentrification: Culture and capital in the urban core. *Annual Review of Sociology* 13, pp. 129–47.

Zuriff, G. E. 1985. *Behaviorism: A conceptual reconstruction*. New York: Columbia University Press.

ILLUSTRATION CREDITS

Photos

Part opening woodcuts and chapter opening details by David Diaz.

CHAPTER 1: **Pages 4–5**: © Fotex/Zephyr Pictures; **7**: © Susan McCartney/Photo Researchers, Inc.; **9**: (left) © Jerry Schad; (right) © Susan Holtz; **10**: Photofest; **11**: Mary Cassatt, American, 1844–1926, *The Bath*, oil on canvas, 1891/92, 39½" × 26", Robert A. Waller Fund, 1910.2, photograph © 1990, The Art Institute of Chicago. All rights reserved; **12**: © Carmine Gallasco/*The Record*, Hackensack, NJ; **17**: Hieronymus Bosch, *Hell*, 1505–1510, detail of right panel from *The Garden of the Delights* triptych, Museo del Prado, Madrid. Photo by ARXIUMAS; **18**: (left) © Jack Fields/Photo Researchers, Inc.; (right) © Paul Conklin/Monkmeyer Press Photos. **20**: © 1991 M.C. Escher heirs/ Cordon Art, Baarn, Holland.

CHAPTER 2: **Pages 24–25**: © John de Nisser/Black Star; **26**: © Rob Nelson/Black Star; **29**: © Camerapix; **30**: © Lennart Nilsson, *A Child is Born*, Dell Publishing Company; **31**: Anonymous, *The Quilting Party*, western Virginia, c. 1854. Oil on wood, 13¼" × 25¼". Abby Aldrich Rockefeller Folk Art Collection, Williamsburg, VA. Photo courtesy of the Colonial Williamsburg Foundation; **35**: © R. Bossu/Sygma; **37**: AP/Wide World Photos; **38**: (top) © Eric Roth/The Picture Cube; (bottom) © Owen Franken/Stock, Boston; **39**: © Stanley Forman; **41**: © 1970 R. Malloch/Magnum Photos.

CHAPTER 3: **Pages 46–47**: © Richard Nesdale; **48**: © Stanley Tretick; **49**: Museum of Modern Art/Film Stills Archive; **52**: HBJ Photo; **54**: © Sara Krulwich/New York Times Pictures; **55**: © Owen Franken/Stock, Boston; **57**: © Charles Kennard/Stock, Boston.

CHAPTER 4: **Pages 64–65**: © Ray Moore/PhotoEdit; **66**: © Peter Menzel/Stock, Boston; **68**: © Owen Franken/Stock, Boston; **72**: © George Goodwin/Monkmeyer Press Photos; **76**: © The Christian Science Monitor/Peter Main; **81**: © Alain Nogues/ Sygma; **84**: (top) Courtesy of the City of Memphis, John Abbott, photographer; (bottom) © John Ross/Robert Harding Picture Library.

CHAPTER 5: **Pages 92–93**: © Dan McCoy/Rainbow; **94**: The Bettmann Archive; **95**: Hans Holbein the Younger, *The French Ambassadors*, 1533. Oil and tempera on wood, approx. 6'8" × 6'9 ½ ". Reproduced by courtesy of the Trustees of the National Gallery, London. Photo from Art Resource, NY; **96**: Bettmann/ Hulton; **99**: © Christopher Morris/Black Star; **101**: © Chip Hires/Gamma-Liaison; **102**: George Tooker, *Government Bureau*, 1956. The Metropolitan Museum of Art, George A. Hearn Fund, 1956 (56.78); **103**: AP/Wide World Photos; **105**: Turtle Mask, Oceanic-Melanesia, Torres Strait, Mabuiag Island, shellwork, 18th century. The Metropolitan Museum of Art, The Michael C. Rockefeller Memorial Collection, Purchase, Nelson A. Rockefeller Gift, 1967 (1978.412.1510), photograph by Schecter Lee.

CHAPTER 6: **Pages 110–11**: Michael Heron/Woodfin Camp & Associates; **112**: Michelangelo, *The Temptation and Expulsion of Adam and Eve*, ceiling of the Sistine Chapel, 1508–1512, The Vatican, Rome. Photo Scala/Art Resource, NY; **116**: © 1987, Anglo-Australian Telescope Board; **119**: © William Hubbell 1981/Woodfin Camp & Associates; **122**: Winslow Homer, *The Morning Bell*, ca. 1866. Yale University Art Gallery, Bequest of Stephen Carlton Clark, B.A. 1903; **129**: © Michael D. Sullivan/TexaStock.

CHAPTER 7: **Pages 134–35**: © Zephyr Pictures; **136**: © Douglas Faulkner/S. Faulkner Collection; **137**: © Ellis Herwig/ The Picture Cube; **139**: Reuters/Bettmann Newsphotos; **142**: Ruth Silverman/Stock, Boston; **144**: (left) © Alan Carey/The Image Works; (right) © Carol Palmer/The Picture Cube; **146**: (left) © Ted Speigel/Black Star; (center) © Nik Wheeler/Black Star; (right) © Y. Arthus-Bertrand/Peter Arnold, Inc.; **148**: Photofest/© Twentieth Century Fox Film Corporation; **153**: © Bob Daemerich/Stock, Boston; **157**: The Bettmann Archive.

CHAPTER 8: **Pages 160–61**: © Nancy Ploeger/Monkmeyer Press Photos; **163**: Edward Hopper, *Automat*, 1927. Oil on canvas, 28" × 36", Des Moines Art Center, James D. Edmundson Fund; **164**: Joe Overstreet, *The New Jemima*, 1964. Construction, 102½" × 61" × 17", Courtesy of The Menil Collection, Houston, Texas; **166**: © Robert Rathe/Stock, Boston; **167**: © M. Bertinetti/Photo Researchers, Inc.; **169**: © Danny Lyon/Magnum Photos; **173**: (left) © Stacy Pick/Stock, Boston; (right) © Jorgensen/Rex Features, London.

CHAPTER 9: **Pages 184–85**: © Bettye Lane/Photo Researchers, Inc.; **189**: © D. Copaken/Gamma-Liaison; **194**: © Sullivan/ TexaStock; **199**: (left) © Philip J. Griffiths/Magnum Photos; (right) AP/Wide World Photos; **202**: US Signal Corps; **203**: UPI Bettmann Newsphotos.

CHAPTER 10: **Pages 208–9**: © Richard Nesdale; **210**: © MacDonald Photography/EKM-Nepenthe; (right) © Richard Nesdale; **211**: © Joel Gordon; **213**: Jane Evershed, *News of Freedom Reaches the Valley of a Thousand Hills*, from Dream Series. Photo courtesy of the artist; **215**: © Alexandra Avakian/Woodfin Camp & Associates; **216**: (left) © Tom McHugh/Photo Researchers, Inc.; (right) © Michael Weisbrot/Stock, Boston; **221**: George Benjamin Luks, *Hester Street*, 1905. Oil on canvas, 66.3 × 91.8 cm (26⅛" × 36⅛"). The Brooklyn Museum, 56.22. Gift of the Borough of Brooklyn; **227**: © Alan S. Weiner/New York Times Pictures; **229**: Diego Rivera, *The Liberation of the Peon*, 1931. Fresco, 74" × 95". Philadelphia Museum of Art, Gift of Mr. and Mrs. Herbert C. Morris.

CHAPTER 11: **Pages 234–35**: © Joe McNally/Sygma; **236**: © Ellis Herwig, Stock, Boston; **237**: © Al Freni/*Time* Magazine; **238**: © John Campbell/EKM-Nepenthe; **241**: Los Angeles Times photo by Gary Friedman; **246**: © 1988 Donna Ferrato/Black Star; **250**: © Richard Nesdale; **251**: Jasper Johns, *Target with Four Faces*, 1955. Assemblage: encaustic and collage on canvas with objects, 26" × 26" (66 × 66 cm), surmounted by four tinted plaster faces in wood box with hinged front. Box closed, 3¾" × 26" × 3½" (9.5 × 66 × 8.9 cm). Overall dimensions with box open, 33⅝" × 26" × 3" (85.3 × 66 × 7.6 cm). Collection, The Museum of Modern Art, New York. Gift of Mr. and Mrs. Robert C. Scull; **252**: (left) Evans/The White House; (right) © J. P.

CHAPTER 11, *(continued)*
Laffont/Sygma; **254**: © Clifford Graves/Wheeler Pictures; **257**: Museum of Modern Art/Film Stills Archive; **259**: © J. R. MacMillan/Union-Tribune Publishing Company.

CHAPTER 12: **Pages 266–67**: © Joel Gordon 1983; **268**: Boris Maluev, *Construction Workers*, 1975, approx. 5′2″ × 6′6″, Union of Artists of the USSR; **273**: (left) © George W. Gardner/The Image Works; (right) © Tom Tracy/Photophile; **275**: From *Britons* by Neal Slavin, photo courtesy Andre Deutsch, Ltd., London; **278**: © 1988 Lynn Johnson/Black Star; **281**: © Freda Leinwand/Monkmeyer Press Photos; **283**: © 1988 Tom Sobolik/Black Star; **284**: (left) © Marilyn Silverstone/Magnum Photos; (right) © J. P. Laffont/Sygma; **288**: © Rameshwar Das/Monkmeyer Press Photos; **289**: © 1984 Anthony Suau/Black Star; **290**: © Jeff Shane/Black Star; **293**: Jose Clemente Orozco, *The Epic of American Civilization*, 1932–34, detail of panel 16, "Hispano–America," Fresco, P. 934.13.16. Courtesy of the Trustees of Dartmouth College, Hanover, New Hampshire.

CHAPTER 13: **Pages 296–97**: © Myrleen Ferguson/PhotoEdit; **298**: © 1990 Martha Swope; **299**: © William Campbell/Sygma; **300**: Jacob Lawrence, *Ironers*, 1943. Gouache on paper, 21½″ × 29½″. Private Collection. Photo courtesy Terry Dintenfass Gallery, New York; **303**: © J. R. Holland/Stock, Boston; **306**: © George Gardner; **307**: The Bettmann Archive; **309**: © Jim Heemstra/The Picture Group; **313**: Robert Lindneux, *The Trail of Tears*, 20th century. Oil on canvas. Woolaroc Museum, Bartlesville, Oklahoma; **315**: © Randy Taylor/Gamma-Liaison; **317**: © James H. Karales/Peter Arnold, Inc.; **321**: AP/Wide World Photos.

CHAPTER 14: **Pages 326–27**: © Allen Horne/Columbus-Enquirer Newspaper; **328**: © Terry Eiler/Stock, Boston; **333**: California Museum of Photography, Keystone-Mast Collection University of California, Riverside; **335**: © David Woo/Stock, Boston; **342**: © Paul Conklin; **344**: Photo by Sacha Van Dorsen; **346**: © David Schaefer/Monkmeyer Press Photos; **348**: (left) Library of Congress; (right) Margaret Bourke-White, *Life* Magazine, © 1943 Time, Inc.; **350**: © Ingeborg Lippmann/New York Times Pictures; **351**: © Bill Swersey/New York Times Pictures; **356**: © The Christian Science Monitor/R. Norman Matheny; **370**: Allsport.

CHAPTER 15: **Pages 360–61**: © Michael McAndrews/The Hartford Courant; **362**: © Erika Stone; **363**: © Milton Feinberg/The Picture Cube; **364**: Diego Velasquez, *Las Meninas*, 1656. Oil on canvas, approx. 10′5″ × 9′. Copyright Museo del Prado, Madrid. Photo ARXIUMAS; **366**: © Arthur Tress/Magnum Photos; **376**: Mark Jury Communications; **368**: International Museum of Photography at George Eastman House; **371**: © Sullivan/TexaStock; **378**: © 1981 Dennis Brack/Black Star.

CHAPTER 16: **Pages 384–85**: © Paul Conklin/Monkmeyer Press Photos; **387**: (left) © Ellis Herwig/The Picture Cube; (center) © Robert Fried/Stock, Boston; (right) © J. R. Holland/Stock, Boston; **388**: © Burton Pasternak; **389**: © William Mares/Monkmeyer Press Photos; **390**: © Robert Isaacs/Photo Researchers, Inc.; **391**: © Tony Howarth/Woodfin Camp & Associates, **392**: © Bruno Maso/PhotoEdit; **394**: © Patrick Ward/Stock, Boston; **398**: International Museum of Photography at George Eastman House; **399**: Courtesy of La Federation des Cooperatives du Quebec, Montreal; **403**: Larry Burrows, *Life* Magazine, © Time Warner, Inc.; **408**: © Terrance McCarthy/New York Times Photos.

CHAPTER 17: **Pages 414–15**: © David Turnley/Black Star; **416**: Anonymous, *A Scholar Composes a Poem While Sitting Under the*

Shade of a Willow-tree, Sung Dynasty (960–1279). Collection of the National Palace Museum, Taiwan, Republic of China; **421**: © Mary Kute Denny/PhotoEdit; **422**: AP/Wide World Photos; **424**: Winslow Homer, *The Country School*, 1871. Oil on canvas, 54.3 × 97.5 cm. The Saint Louis Art Museum, Museum Purchase; **425**: © Peter Silva/The Picture Group; **429**: © Diane Lowe/Stock, Boston; **432**: © 1983 James Balog/Black Star; **434**: (left) © Smiley/TexaStock; (right) © J. D. Sloan/The Picture Cube; **438**: AP/Wide World.

CHAPTER 18: **Pages 442–43**: © Peter Menzell/Stock, Boston; **444**: (left) © Hiroji Kubota/Magnum Photos; (right) Albert Edelfeld, *Pasteur dans son laboratoire*, 1885. Musée de Orsay, Paris. Photo © Reunion des Musées Nationaux; **446**: "Angels Turning Planets," Harley Manuscript 4940, Folio 28. Reproduced by permission of The British Library; **497**: Courtesy of *New Scientist*, London; **449**: AP/Wide World Photos; **450**: Flemish School, *Cognoscenti in a Room Hung with Pictures*, 17th century. Reproduced by courtesy of the Trustees of the National Gallery, London; **451**: © J. R. Holland/Stock, Boston; **453**: © Jan Halaska/Photo Researchers, Inc.; **454**: © D. Gutekunst/Gamma-Liaison; **455**: © Baldev/Sygma; **459**: Thomas Eakins, *The Agnew Clinic*, 1889. Oil on canvas, 331.5 × 179.1 cm. University of Pennsylvania, School of Medicine; **461**: (left) © Christopher Brown/Stock, Boston; (right) © L. Zilberman/Sygma; **462**: The Bettmann Archive.

CHAPTER 19: **Pages 468–69**: © Richard Nesdale; **470**: © Owen Franken/Stock, Boston; **472**: Hans Holbein the Younger, *George Gisze*, 1532. Gemäldgaleria Staatliche Museen Preussicher Kulturbesitz, Berlin. Foto Jörg P. Anders; **477**: Library of Congress; **478**: © Nathan Benn/Stock, Boston; **482**: © Paul Conklin/PhotoEdit; **487**: Culver Pictures; **490**: © Brad Bower/The Picture Group; **491**: © Wojtek Laski/SIPA; **493**: © Alain Keler/Sygma; **494**: AP/Wide World Photos.

CHAPTER 20: **Pages 500–1**: AP/Wide World Photos; **502**: (left) Hulton/Bettmann Newsphotos; (right) Reuters/Bettmann Newsphotos; **504**: Neg. No. 2A-3766, Courtesy Department of Library Services, American Museum of Natural History; **507**: AP/Wide World Photos; **508**: © 1987 Anthony Suau/Black Star; **509**: AP/Wide World Photos; **510**: Courtesy, *The Argus*, Cape Town; **515**: Courtesy of Handgun Control, Inc.; **518**: AP/Wide World Photos; **520**: © Richard Nesdale; **521**: Courtesy Soviet Life.

CHAPTER 21: **Pages 526–27**: © Richard Nesdale; **528**: Gustav Klimt, *Death and Life*, 1908 and 1911. 5′10″ × 6′6″. Collection of Maria Preleuthner, Salzburg. Photo courtesy Galerie Welz (reproduced from a collotype print); **529**: Paul Gaugin, *Ira Orana Maria*, 1891. Oil on canvas, 44¾″ × 34½″ (113.7 × 87.7 cm). The Metropolitan Museum of Art, Bequest of Sam A. Lewisohn, 1951 (51.112.2); **530**: FPG International; **532**: Hamburgisches Museum for Völkerkunde; **535**: Masaccio, *The Expulsion from Eden*, fresco, c. 1425. Brancacci Chapel, Santa Maria del Carmine, Florence. Photo Scala/Art Resource, NY; **536**: AP/Wide World Photos; **537**: © Rick Browne/Stock, Boston; **538**: Ghost Dance Shirt, buckskin, painted decoration, 36″ x 53″, Arapaho. National Museum of the American Indian, Smithsonian Institution; **542**: *Christ as the Good Shepherd*, mosaic from the entrance wall of the mausoleum of Galla Placidia, Ravenna, A.D. 425–450. Photo from Scala/Art Resource, NY; **543**: © Wojtek Laski/SIPA; **545**: © P. Chauvel/Sygma; **546**: © Danny Lyon/Magnum Photos; **549**: © D. E. Cox/TSW-Click, Chicago, Ltd.

CHAPTER 22: **Pages 554–55**: © Rogers/Monkmeyer Press Photos; **556**: © D. Aubert/Sygma; **558**: © Moshe Shandiz/Sygma; **559**: AP/Wide World Photos, **560**: © Owen Franken/Stock, Boston; **561**: Eugène Delacroix, *Liberty Leading the People*, 1830. Approximately 10'8" × 8'6". Louvre, Paris. Photo © Reunion des Musées Nationaux; **565**: © P. Habans/Sygma; **567**: © J. Langevin/Sygma.

CHAPTER 23: **Pages 570–71**: © Paul Conklin/Monkmeyer Press Photos; **573**: Larry Burrows, *Life* Magazine, © Time Warner, Inc.; **574**: AP/Wide World Photos; **575**: (left) Library of Congress; (right) HBJ Photo; **578**: HBJ Photo; **580**: © Paul Conklin/Monkmeyer Press Photos; **581**: Imperial War Museum, London; **583**: © John Lei/Stock, Boston; **585**: © Tannenbaum/Sygma; **587**: © Bruce Hoertel; **588**: © Regis Bossu/Sygma.

Figures

4–1: Copyright © 1989 by The New York Times Company. Reprinted by permission. **B–4–1**: From Thomas W. Merrick, with PRB Staff, "World population in transition," *Population Bulletin*, Vol. 41, No. 2 (April 1986). Adapted by permission of the Population Reference Bureau, Inc. **4–2**: From Leon F. Bouvier and Robert W. Gardner, "Immigration to the US: The unfinished story," *Population Bulletin*, Vol. 41, No. 4 (November 1986). Adapted by permission of the Population Reference Bureau, Inc. **4–4**: United Nations Fund for Population Activities, *Population Images*, 2ed., 1987. Adapted courtesy of UNFPA. **7–1**: Copyright © 1989 by The New York Times Company. Reprinted by permission. **9–1**: Adapted from S. E. Asch, 1952, *Social Psychology*, Englewood Cliffs, NJ: Prentice-Hall, Inc., with permission of the author. **9–3**: Adapted from *The Business of Organized Crime: A Costa Nostra Family* by Annelise Graebner, with permission of the

publisher, Hoover Institution Press. © 1979 by the Board of Trustees of the Leland Stanford Jr. University. **10–2**: Reprinted from "The Nature of Cities" by Chauncy D. Harris and Edward L. Ullman in volume no. 242 of the *Annals of the American Academy of Political and Social Science*. **11–1**: Adapted from L. A. Fingerhut and J. C. Kleinman, 1990, "International and interstate comparisons of homicides among young males," *Journal of the American Medical Association*, 263 (24), pp. 3292–95, Figure 1. **12–1**: Adapted from E. O. Wright, D. Hacken, C. Costello, and J. Sprague, 1982, "The American class structure," *American Sociological Review*, 47 (December), pp. 709–726. **12–2**: Copyright © 1989 by The New York Times Company. Reprinted by permission. **B–13–2**: Copyright © 1988 by The New York Times Company. Reprinted by permission. **14–1**: Adapted from J. A. Davis and T. W. Smith, 1987, *General Social Surveys, 1972–1987: Cummulative Codebook*, Chicago: National Opinion Research Center. **15–2**: Copyright © 1988 by The New York Times Company. Reprinted by permission. **16–2**: Copyright © 1989 by The New York Times Company. Reprinted by permission. **B–16–1**: Adapted from M. A. Straus, R. J. Gelles, and S. K. Steinmetz, 1980, *Behind Closed Doors*, New York, Anchor, by permission. **B–17–1**: Copyright © 1988 by The New York Times Company. Reprinted by permission. **17–2**: Copyright © 1989 by The New York Times Company. Reprinted by permission. **18–1**: Copyright © 1988 by The New York Times Company. Reprinted by permission. **19–1**: Copyright © 1988 by The New York Times Company. Reprinted by permission. **23–1, 23–2, B–23–1**: Adapted from Doug McAdam, 1982, *Political Process and the Development of Black Insurgence: 1930–1970*, Chicago, University of Chicago Press, pp. 7, 9, 51.

COPYRIGHTS AND ACKNOWLEDGMENTS

NAME INDEX

The following are authors whose works are cited in the text. Names of people who are discussed as subjects will be found in the Subject Index which follows this index.

Miller, J. D., 456
Miller, N., 320, 572
Miller, W. B., 253
Mills, C. W., 20, 23, 103, 280, 293, 446, 510
Miner, H. M., 220
Mintz, B., 219, 511, 512, 537
Mirowsky, J., 179, 346, 395, 401, 402
Mishler, E. G., 116
Mitchell, J., 348
Mitroff, I. I., 117
Mizrahi, T., 154
Moede, W., 199
Moen, P., 340
Mol, H., 530
Mollenkopf, J., 219
Molotch, H. L., 170
Monson, T. C., 166
Montagu, A. M. F., 137, 389, 399
Montford, F., 322
Moore, G., 308
Moore, J. A., 323
Moore, R. L., 538
Moore, W. E., 272, 292, 346
Moorman, J. E., 410
Moos, R. H., 170, 371
Mor, V., 377
Morello, K. B., 350
Moreno, J. L., 56
Morgan, S. P., 354, 400
Morgenstern, O., 178, 420
Morris, A., 587, 590, 591
Morris, V., 43
Morrison, K. C., 590
Mortimer, J. T., 181
Mosher, W. D., 67, 68
Moskos, C., 188, 327, 354
Mottaz, C. J., 488
Mozingo, D., 509
Mullen, B., 201
Muller, E. N., 506
Muller, P. O., 212, 215, 227
Muller, R. J., 290
Muller, W., 284
Munley, A., 377
Munsinger, H., 136
Murdock, G. P., 40, 83, 195, 388, 389, 391
Myrdal, G., 317

Nadler, A., 36, 165
Nag, M., 397
Nakell, B., 248
Nasaw, D., 428, 431
Nee, V., 509
Neidert, L. J., 307, 310
Neill, A. S., 439
Nelson, V., 286
Neustadt, R. E., 204
Neustadtl, A., 483, 512
Newcomb, T. M., 179
Newman, A. E., 340
Newman, K. S., 285
Newton, P. J., 406
Nichols, E. K., 71
Nida, S., 162
Niebuhr, R., 538
Nightingale, E. O., 465

Nisbett, R. E., 166, 420
Nock, S. L., 404
Noelle-Neumann, E., 187
North, C. C., 282
Norton, A. J., 397, 410

Oakes, J., 435
Oakley, A., 342
Obaler, R. S., 391
Oberschall, A., 589
O'Brien, R. M., 246
O'Connor, J., 375, 521
O'Connor, K., 517
Ogburn, W. F., 576, 577
Ohlin, L. E., 258
Olzak, S., 577
Orfield, G., 322
Ortega, S. T., 156
Orum, A. M., 587
Orwell, G., 509
Orzech, M. J., 371
Osborne, J. J., Jr., 154
Osgood, N. J., 465
Osofsky, G., 573
Otto, L. B., 127, 340

Page, B. I., 292
Pagelow, M. D., 405, 406
Painter, N. I., 476
Palloni, A., 244
Palmer, L. E., 537, 538
Paludi, M. A., 120, 332, 350
Pankratz, D. B., 43
Parenti, M., 275, 480
Park, R. E., 80, 181, 221, 225, 573
Parker, D. P., 577
Parker, R., 249
Parsons, H. M., 120
Parsons, T., 98, 271, 274, 281, 345, 446, 460, 579, 582
Pascal, B., 543
Pastner, C., 389
Patterson, M. L., 26
Patzer, G. L., 163
Pauls, D. L., 136
Paxson, L. M., 402
Payer, L., 459
Peacock, W. G., 48
Pease, J., 277
Peattie, L., 228
Pechman, J. A., 276
Pedersen, F. A., 137
Perrin, S., 187
Perrow, C., 454, 455, 589
Persell, C. H., 150, 152, 280, 416, 434
Perucci, C. C., 339
Peschek, J., 275, 277, 281, 483, 515
Pescosolido, B. A., 113
Pessen, E., 280
Peter, L. J., 201
Peterson, L., 150
Peterson, R. A., 43
Peterson, W., 565
Petras, J. W., 104

Peukert, D. J. K., 157, 509
Pfeffer, J., 190
Piaget, J., 139
Pike, K. M., 349
Piliavin, I., 250
Pilling, A. R., 388
Pingree, S., 123
Piven, F. F., 512, 590, 591
Pleck, E., 406
Pleck, J. H., 354
Polatnick, M., 342, 348, 356
Polednak, A. P., 71
Polit, D. F., 68
Pollock, L. A., 364
Polonko, K. A., 336
Pomer, M. I., 310
Pomerance, B., 240
Pomeroy, S., 333
Pope, L., 545
Popenoe, D., 223, 389, 409
Popper, F. J., 245
Portes, A., 303
Posner, G. L., 246
Postman, L., 565
Powell, W., 43
Powers, M. G., 271
Presser, S., 114, 118
Price, D. J., 451
Price, T. D., 83
Proctor, R. N., 465
Projector, D., 276
Purcell, P., 123, 343

Quadagno, J. S., 118
Quarantelli, E. L., 557
Quinney, R., 238

Radcliffe-Brown, A. R., 365
Radecki, C., 170
Raiffa, H., 177, 563, 564
Raines, J. C., 219
Rainwater, L., 291
Rands, M., 350
Raper, A., 557
Raphael, R., 367
Rappoport, D. C., 240
Raskin, P. A., 343
Rasmussen, W. D., 489, 576
Ravitch, D., 418, 423, 433
Reckless, W. C., 244
Redburn, F. S., 219, 488
Redfield, R., 221
Reed, M. D., 252
Reeder, G. D., 166
Reich, M., 108, 314, 469, 477, 483, 484, 492
Reichman, N., 577
Reilly, M. E., 350
Reilly, T. W., 336
Reiss, A. J., 244
Reitzes, D. C., 181
Remick, H., 340
Renzetti, C. M., 329
Resh, N., 435
Reverby, S., 124, 337
Reynolds, P. D., 129, 190
Reynolds, V., 136

Ricardo-Campbell, R., 74
Rich, A., 345
Richards, T., 323
Richardson, L. W., 329, 349
Richersen, P. J., 329
Ridgeway, C. L., 57, 170, 191
Riding, A., 65
Riecken, H. W., 121
Riesman, D., 281, 511
Riess, M., 174
Riessman, F., 439
Rifkin, J., 27
Riger, S., 261
Riggio, R. E., 349
Riley, J. W., Jr., 377
Riley, M. W., 79, 154, 364, 365, 367, 369, 370, 372, 373, 379, 399, 465, 575
Rindfuss, R., 75
Risman, B. J., 346
Ritchie, J., 350
Ritzer, G., 463
Robbins, T., 548
Roberts, M. K., 252
Robinson, J. C., 71
Robinson, R. V., 151
Robinson, T. D., 495
Rochberg-Halton, E., 147
Rodgers, W. L., 390
Rodin, J., 170, 371
Roethlisberger, F. J., 120, 186
Rogers, E. M., 576, 577
Rogers, W., 515
Roos, P. A., 346
Rose, P. I., 306
Rosenberg, C. E., 461
Rosenberg, M., 145, 146, 148, 181
Rosenfeld, H. M., 350
Rosenhan, D. L., 256
Rosenthal, A. M., 161
Rosenthal, K. M., 155
Rosenthal, R., 427, 434
Rosnow, R. L., 564, 566
Ross, C. E., 179, 346, 401, 402
Ross, E. B., 74, 75
Ross, H. L., 250
Ross, J. M., 354
Rossi, A. S., 148, 329, 338, 345, 355, 394
Rossi, P. H., 230, 242, 272, 273, 274, 282
Rossides, D. W., 284
Rostow, W. W., 582
Roszak, B., 353
Roszak, T., 353
Rothblum, E. D., 346
Rousseau, J. J., 519
Rowbotham, S., 400
Ruback, R., 167
Rubel, M., 258
Rubenstein, J. L., 137
Rubin, B., 509
Rubin, L. B., 118, 401
Rubin, N., 140
Rubin, R., 390
Russell, D. E. H., 168, 254, 350, 351
Russell, J. C., 223
Russman, L., 344
Ryder, N. B., 79, 373, 390, 575
Rytina, J. H., 277

SUBJECT INDEX

Aberrant behavior, 239–40
Abortion
  beliefs and, 30
  political coalition and, 516
  women and, 356
Absolute deprivation, 586
Academic subculture, 421
Achieved status, 48
Acquired status, 48
Acting collective behavior, 557
Acton, Lord, 170
Adolescence
  crime and, 367, 371–72
  nonconformity during, 252
  patterns of interaction during,
    376
  power and prestige during,
    371–72
  socialization of, in industrial
    societies, 152
Adultery
  as deviant behavior, 237
  values about, 89, 408
Advertising, 474, 481
  capitalism and, 481
  gender and, 344
  socialization and, 153
Affection, structures of, 56. See
  also Friendship; Sociometry
Affirmative action, 321
Afghanistan
  birth rates in, 73
  death rates in, 70
  divorce in, 403
  infant mortality rates in, 70
  literacy rate in, 429
  population increase in, 73
Africa
  birth rate in, 67
  literacy in, 429
Age. See also Children; Elderly
  criminal behavior and, 243, 260
  culture and, 362–66
  division of labor and, 368–69
  income and, 369–70
  marriage and, 392
  population distribution by,
    59–60, 78–79
  role sets and, 376
  social change and, 377–80, 575
  social conflict and, 374–75
  social structure and, 366–72
  as a status, 361–62
  suicide and, 14–15
  victimization and, 245
Age cohorts, 367–68, 575–76
Age Discrimination Act, 369
Age groups, 362
  boundaries, 366–67
  defined by culture, 363
Ageism, 363, 376

Age stratification, 361–81
  ecology and, 372–74
  explanations for, 374–77
  minorities and, 362, 376
  population and, 372–74
  social change and, 377–80
  social conflict and, 374–75
  social consequences of, 374
Age structures, 59–60, 78–79
  birth rate affected by, 69
  crude death rate and, 70
  industrialization and, 79
  role structures and, 372–73
  social change and, 378
  social security and, 375
  unemployment and, 490
Aging
  culture and, 362–66
  families and, 407
  socialization and, 156
Agrarian societies, 83
  family in, 395
  religion in, 541
Agriculture
  mechanization and, 489, 576
  technology and, 226
AIDS, 71–73
  effects on social life, 72–73
  hysteria and, 559–60
  origins of, 71–72
  as scientific problem, 447, 451,
    455
  spread of, 71–72, 458
  as stigma, 240
Alcoholism, definition as medical
    problem, 459, 463
Alienation, 205, 293
  religion and, 545
  social stratification and, 293
  from work, 486–88
Aligning action, 174
Allen, Woody, 165
Allende, Salvador, 538
Amalgamation, cultural, 302
American Association for Retired
    Persons (AARP), 377
American Civil Liberties Union
    (ACLU), 196, 439, 516
American Dilemma, An, 317
American Jury, The, 248
American Medical Association
    (AMA), 461–62, 484
American Psychiatric Association,
    459
American Psychological
    Association, 485
American Revolution, 510, 522,
    584
Amish, 142, 211
Ancestor worship, 387, 542
Androcracy, 341

Androgyny, 352
Animistic religion, 532, 541
Anomalies, scientific, 445
Anomie
  deviance and, 251, 260, 261
Anthropology, 121–22
Anticipatory socialization, 148–49
Antinuclear protests, 555
Antitrust laws, 482, 505
Apartheid, 288–89
Argentina
  birth rate in, 67
  political violence in, 465
Arrest, 247–48
Art, 43
Ascribed status, 48
  family as source of, 386
  prestige and, 282
Ashanti, 391–92
Asian-Americans, 319
Assimilation, cultural, 302–3, 318
Assumptions, theoretical, 95
As You Like It, 104
Attendance, church, 547–48
Attitudes, cultural, 39–40
  age and, 365
  families and, 390
  gender and, 332–33
  marriage and, 390
  religion and, 535
  schools and, 420–21
  socialization and, 141
Attribution, social, 166
Audience, 174, 176
Australia
  aborigines in, 389
  homicide in, 242
  religion in, 531, 534
Austria
  homicide in, 242
Authenticity, in role performance,
    180–81
Authoritarian groups, power in, 59
Authoritarianism, 509–10
  and collective behavior, 557
  conflict view of, 519–21
  functional view of, 518–19
Authoritarian leaders, 190
Authority, 57, 502–3
  charismatic, 502–3, 538–39
  in cults, 538–39
  expertise and, 503
  legal-rational, 502
  in medicine, 461–62
  traditional, 503
Autocracy, 508
Automation, 285, 478
Automobile, as material culture,
    42
Ayatollah Khomeini, 536
Aztecs, 533

Baby boom
  and age structure, 79, 80
  and cohort effects, 79–80,
    373–74
  and school enrollment, 428
  and unemployment, 490
Baby M, 577
Backstage, in social interaction,
    174, 175
Balance theory, 178–80
Bales' categories, 198
Bangladesh
  birth rates in, 73
  death rates in, 70, 73
  infant mortality rates in, 70
  population increase in, 73
  population size, 80
  religion in, 532
Bank failures, 559
Bart, Pauline, 367
Behaviorism, 138
Belgium
  religion in, 534
Beliefs, 30–31
  age and, 363–64
  families and, 387–88
  gender and, 331, 353
  marriage and, 387–88
  religious, 532–34, 541
  revolution and, 523
  schools and, 417–18
  science and, 445–47
  socialization and, 141
  stereotypes and, 164
Bhopal, 455
Biden, Joseph, 514
Big science, 451
Bilateral descent, 388
Bill of Rights, 504, 506
Bilocal marriage, 391
Biology
  and age, 363–64
  and gender differences, 328–29
  and human nature, 136
  as a perspective, 93
  and race, 298
Birth cohort. See Cohorts
Birth rate, 67
  family life and, 67, 396–98
  industrialization and, 67, 74,
    574
  marriage and, 67, 396–97
  school enrollment and, 428
  teenage, 397
Blackfeet Indians
  bilocal family among, 391
  marriage among, 388
Blacks
  civil disobedience and, 239
  crime rates among, 243–44
  cultural destruction of, 303